A-Z MANCHESTER

CONT[ENTS]

Key to Map Pages	2-3
Large Scale City Centre	4-11
Map Pages	12-167
Postcode Map	168-169

...[...] Connections Back Cover

REFERENCE

Motorway	**M60**	Map Continuation / Large Scale City Centre	**86** / **8**
Under Construction		Car Park (Selected)	**P**
Proposed		Church or Chapel	†
A Road	**A57**	Fire Station	■
Under Construction		Hospital	**H**
Proposed		House Numbers — 'A' and 'B' Roads only	13 / 8
B Road	**B5228**	Information Centre	**i**
Dual Carriageway		National Grid Reference	³95
One-way Street — Traffic flow on A Roads is also indicated by a heavy line on the driver's left.	➡	Police Station	▲
Restricted Access		Post Office	★
Pedestrianized Road		Toilet — with facilities for the Disabled	▽ / ♿
Track / Footpath		Educational Establishment	
Railway — Level Crossing / Station / Tunnel		Hospital or Hospice	
East Lancashire Railway		Industrial Building	
Metrolink (LRT) — The boarding of Metrolink trains at stops may be limited to a single direction, indicated by the arrow.		Leisure or Recreational Facility	
Built-up Area	MILL ST.	Place of Interest	
Local Authority Boundary	—··—··—	Public Building	
Posttown Boundary	————	Shopping Centre or Market	
Postcode Boundary — Within Posttowns	————	Other Selected Buildings	

SCALE

Map Pages 12-167 — 1:18,103 (3½ inches to 1 mile)	Map Pages 4-11 — 1:9,051 (7 inches to 1 mile)
0 — ¼ — ½ Mile	0 — ⅛ — ¼ Mile
0 — 250 — 500 — 750 Metres	0 — 100 — 200 — 300 Metres

Head Office :
Fairfield Road, Borough Green, Sevenoaks, Kent TN15 8PP
Tel: 01732 781000 (General Enquiries & Trade Sales)

Showrooms :
44 Gray's Inn Road, London WC1X 8HX
Tel: 020 7440 9500 (Retail Sales)
www.a-zmaps.co.uk

Ordnance Survey®

This product includes mapping data licensed from Ordnance Survey® with the permission of the Controller of Her Majesty's Stationery Office.

© Crown Copyright 2002. Licence number 100017302
EDITION 10 2002
Copyright © Geographers' A-Z Map Co. Ltd. 2002

CHORLEY

Darwen

Edenfield

Knowl Moor

Belmont Resr.

Wayoh Resr.

Ramsbottom

12 13

Nuttall

Coppull

Reservoirs

Egerton 18 19 Eagley

Greenmount 20 21 Tottington

Summerseat 22 23 Walmersley

Norden 24 25 Birtle

Adlington

Rivington Moor

BOLTON WEST

Standish

Horwich 30 31

Barrow Bridge

32 33 BOLTON

Ainsworth 34 35

BURY 36 37 Fishpool

Hooley Bridge 38 39 Heywood

Aspull

Lostock 44 45

46 47

Radcliffe 48 49 Little Lever

Hollins 50 51

BIRCH 52 53 Langley

Westhoughton

Hindley

WIGAN

Ince-in-Makerfield

Atherton

Farnworth 62 63 Walkden

Kearsley 64 65

Whitefield 66 67 Prestwich

Rhodes 68 69 Crumpsall

Tyldesley

LEIGH

4 5 6 7 LARGE SCALE CITY CENTRE 8 9 10 11

Worsley 76 77 Boothstown

Swinton 78 79

Pendlebury 80 81

Cheetham Hill 82 83

Ashton-in-Makerfield

Golborne

Eccles 90 91

MANCHESTER 92 93 94 95 SALFORD

Moss Side 108 109

Newton-le-Willows

Burtonwood

Culcheth

102 103 Irlam

104 105 Urmston

Stretford 106 107

Old Trafford

BURTONWOOD

Risley

118 119 120 121 Partington

Flixton

Sale 122 123

124 125 Fallowfield

WARRINGTON

Warburton

Woodhouses 132 133 Broadheath

Brooklands 134 135

136 137 Didsbury Gatley

Lymm

Bowdon 144 145 Hale

ALTRINCHAM 146 147

148 149 Heald Green

Appleton Thorn

Daresbury

Bucklow Hill

Manchester Airport 156 157 158 159 Morley Handforth

WILMSLOW 166 167

Preston on the Hill

Pick Mere

KNUTSFORD

Mobberley

Knutsford

Alderley Edge

Inset Page 167

River Weaver

Budworth Mere

Tabley Mere

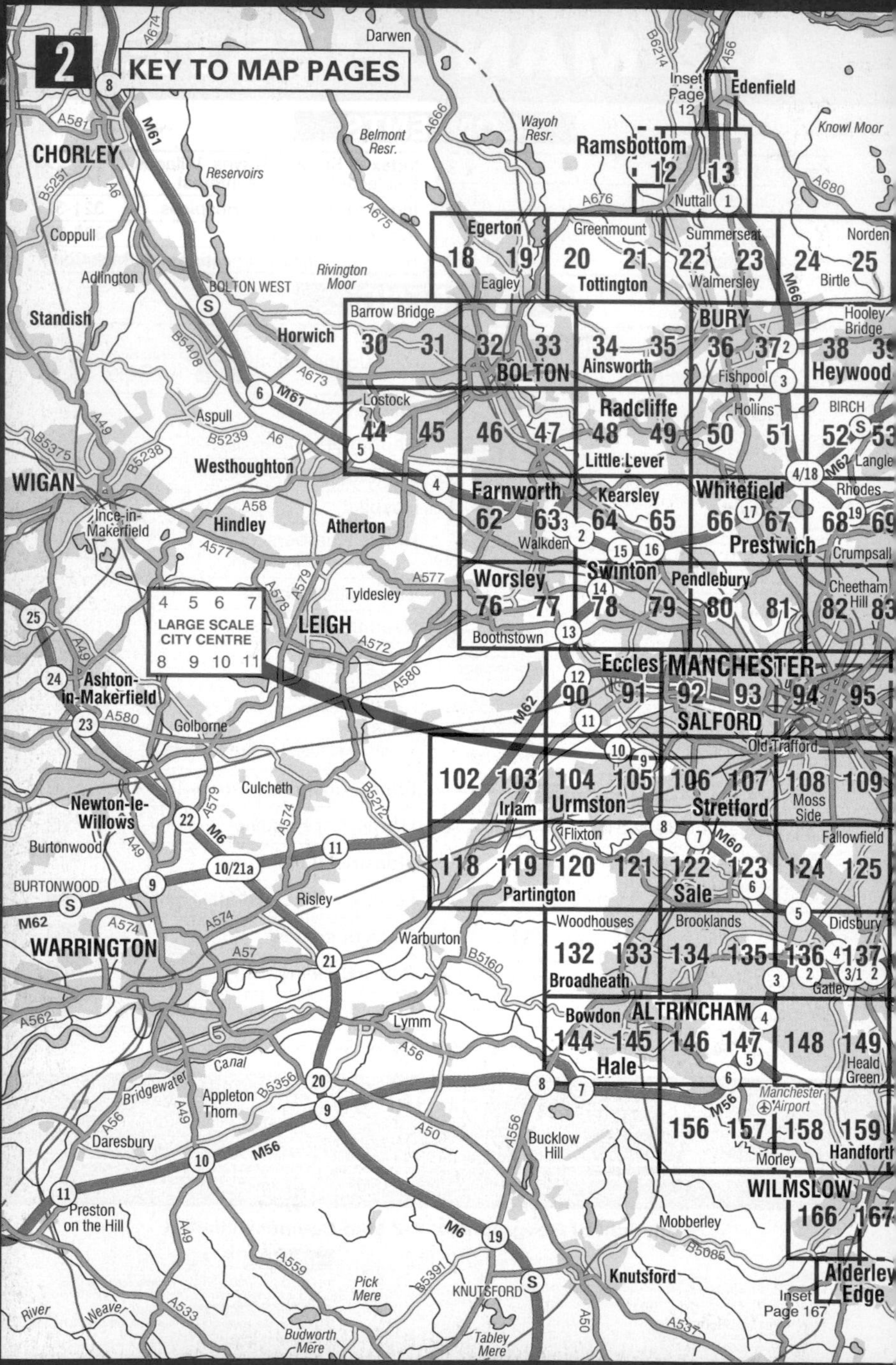

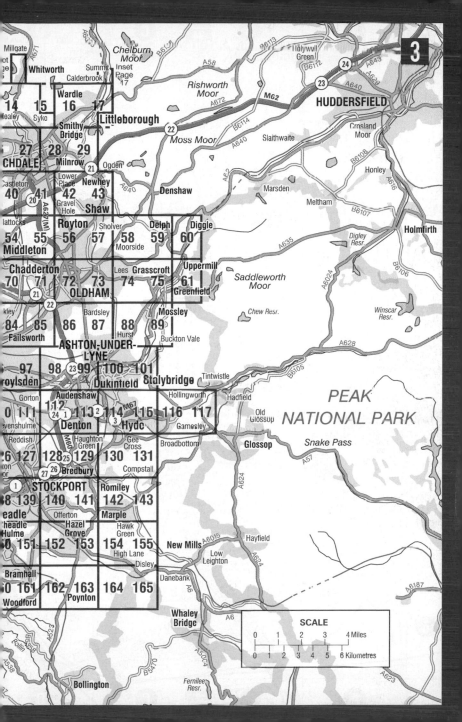

3

Millgate

Whitworth

Chelburn Moor

Summit
Calderbrook

Inset Page 17

Hollywell Green

B6113

A58

Rishworth Moor

A672

M62

HUDDERSFIELD

B6112

24

23

A643

A640

A629

Wardle

14 15 16 17

Littleborough

Healey Syke

Smithy Bridge

22

Moss Moor

B6114

A640

Slaithwaite

Crosland Moor

27 28 29

RCHDALE Milnrow

21

Ogden

Denshaw

A62

Marsden

Meltham

B6107

Honley

A616

B6108

Castleton

40 41

20

A627(M)

Lower Place

Newhey

42 43

A640

Gravel Hole

Shaw

lattocks

Royton Sholver

54 55 56 57

Middleton

Moorside

58

Delph

59

Diggle

60

A635

Digley Resr.

Holmfirth

B6106

Chadderton

70 71 72 73

21

OLDHAM

22

Lees Grasscroft

74 75

Uppermill

61

Greenfield

Saddleworth Moor

A6024

Winscar Resr.

kley

84 85

Failsworth

Bardsley

86 87

88

Hurst

Mossley

89

Chew Resr.

A628

Buckton Vale

ASHTON-UNDER-LYNE

97 98 23 99 100 101

roylsden Dukinfield Stalybridge Tintwistle

Gorton

112

24 1

111

113

2

114

M67

115 116 117

Hollingworth

Hadfield

B6105

PEAK
NATIONAL PARK

Audenshaw

Denton

3

Hyde

Gamesley

Old Glossop

evenshulme

Reddish

Haughton Green

M60

Gee Cross

Broadbottom

Glossop

Snake Pass

6 127 128 25 129 130 131

Compstall

A57

A624

27 26 Bredbury

1

STOCKPORT Romiley

8 139 140 141 142 143

eadle Offerton Marple

headle Hazel Grove Hawk Green

Hulme

0 151 152 153 154 155

High Lane

New Mills A6015

Hayfield

A624

Disley

Low Leighton

Bramhall

0 161 162 163 164 165

Woodford Poynton

Danebank

A6

A6187

Whaley Bridge

A6

SCALE

0 1 2 3 4 Miles

0 1 2 3 4 5 6 Kilometres

A523

A538

A5004

B5470

A623

Bollington

Fernilee Resr.

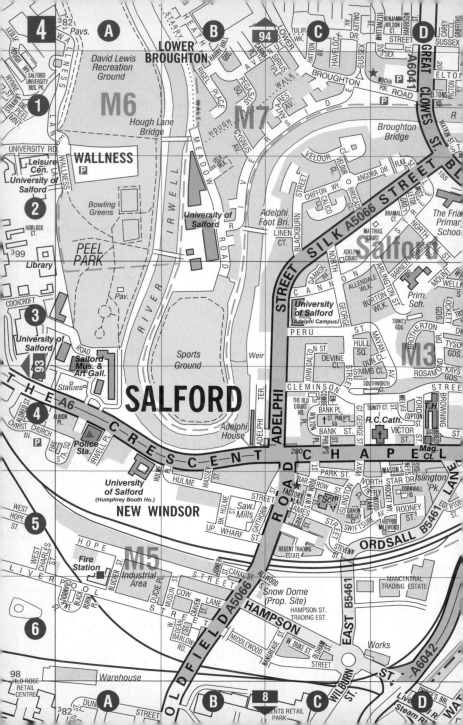

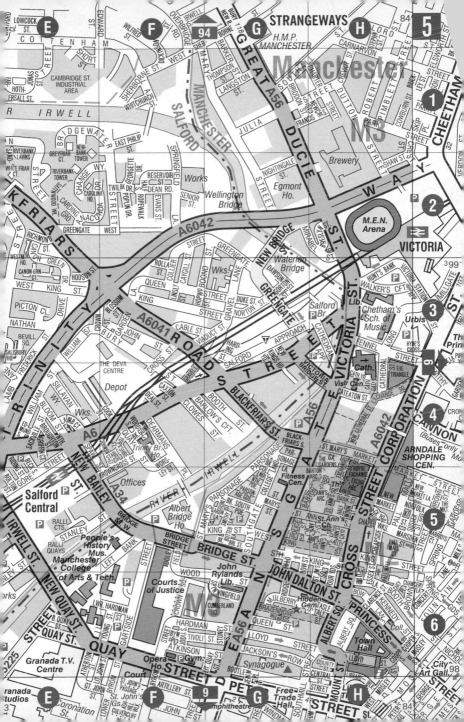

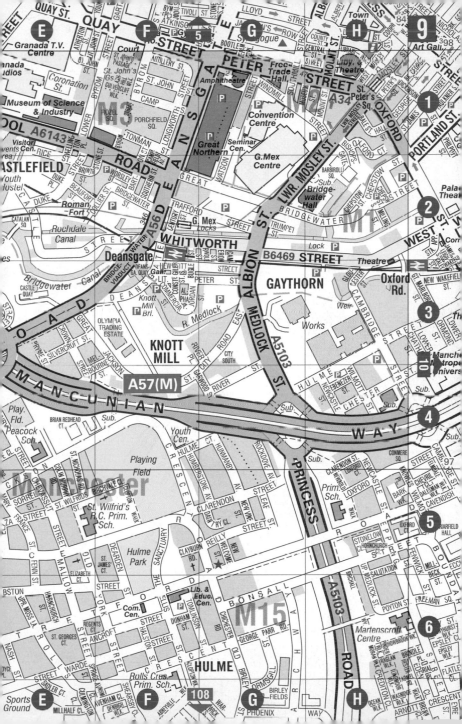

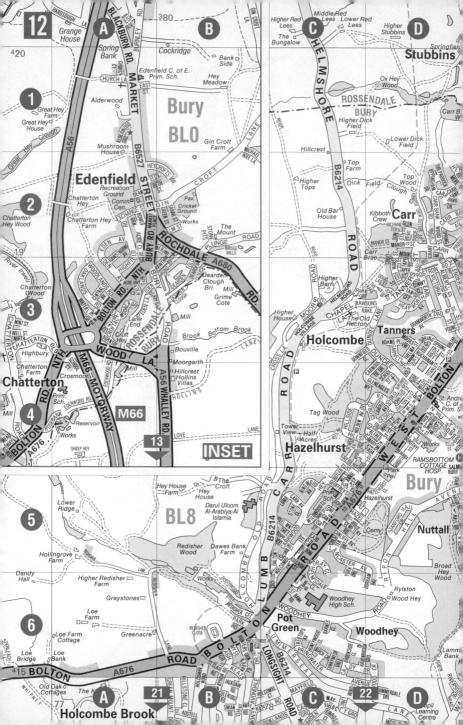

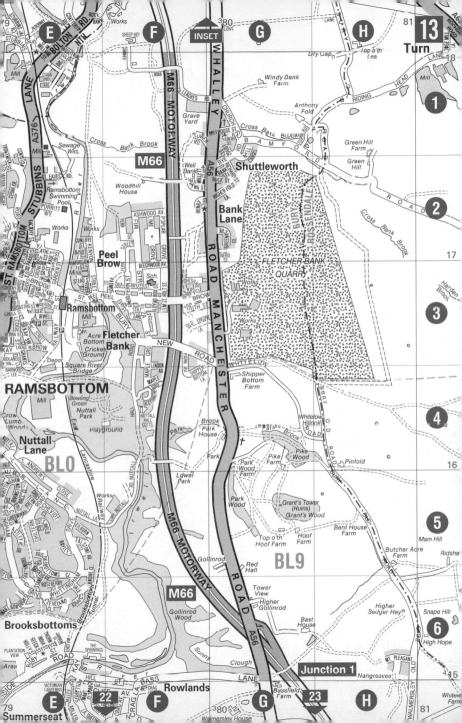

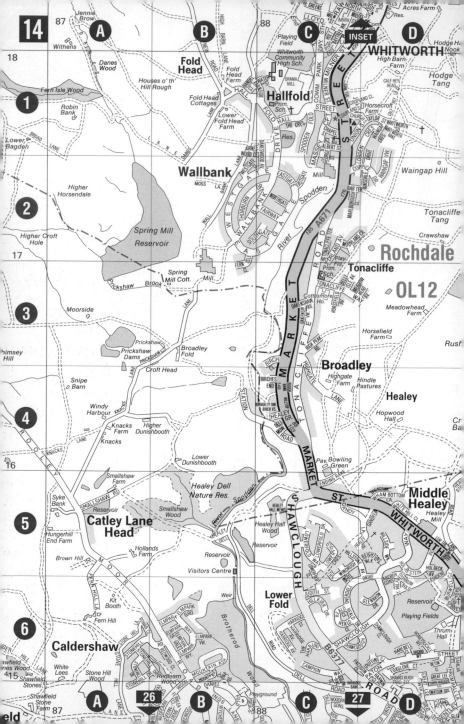

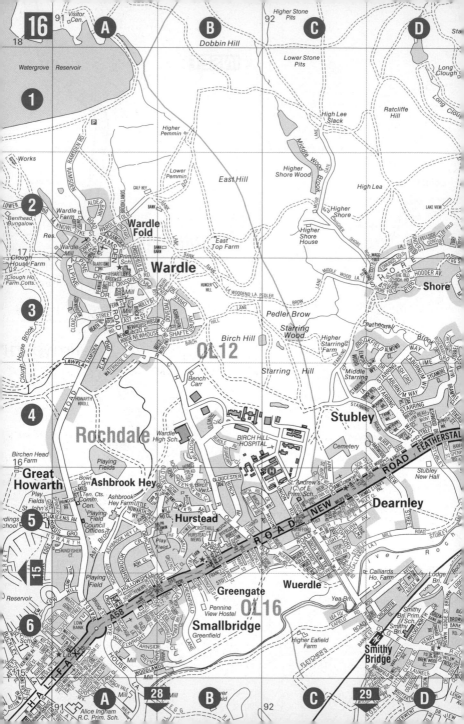

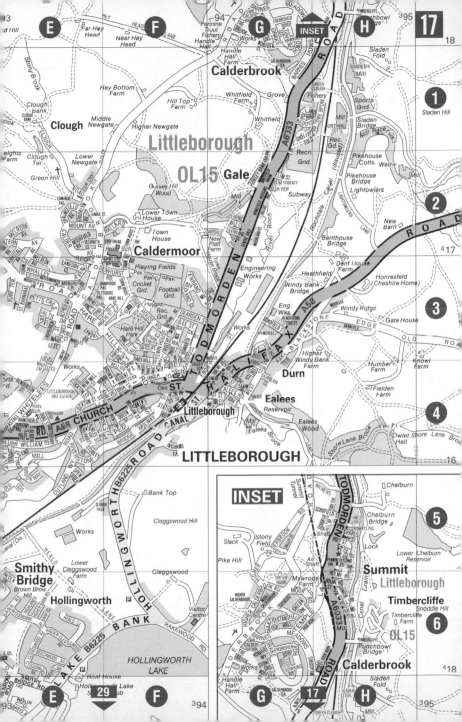

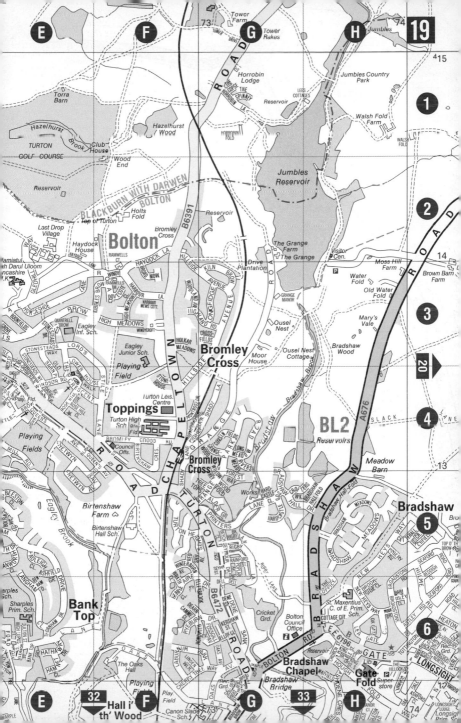

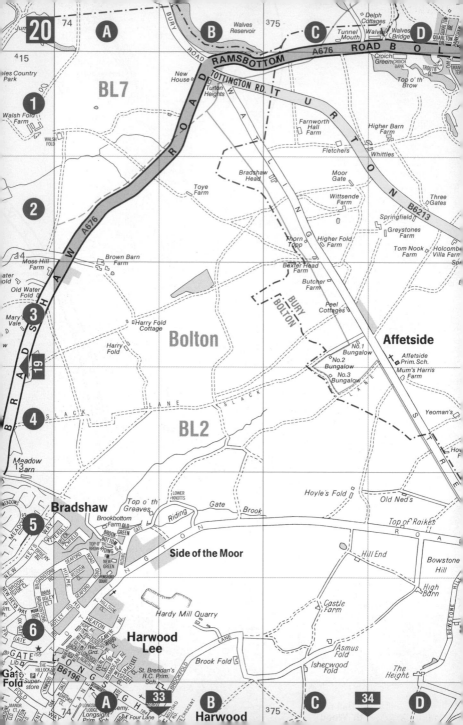

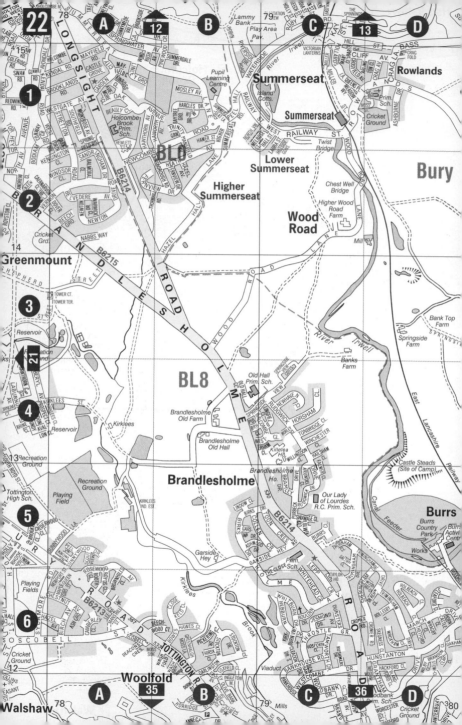

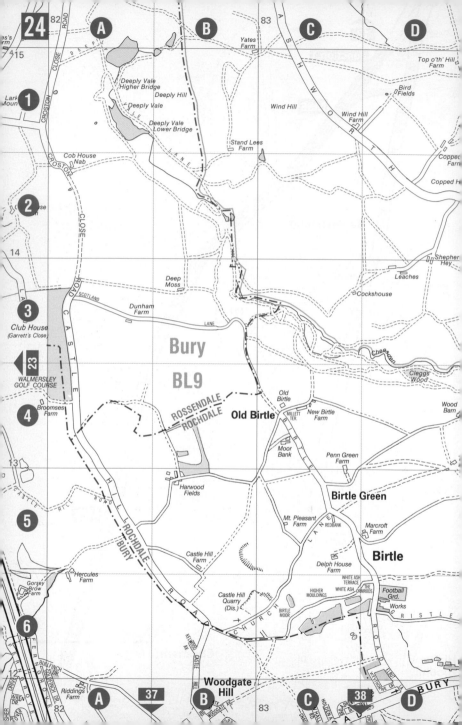

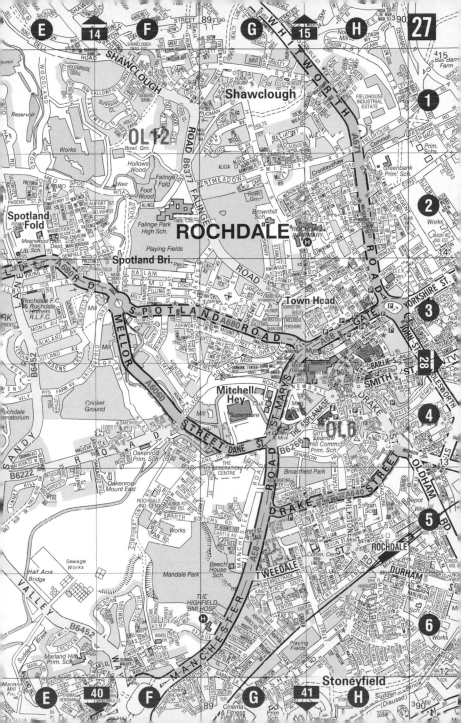

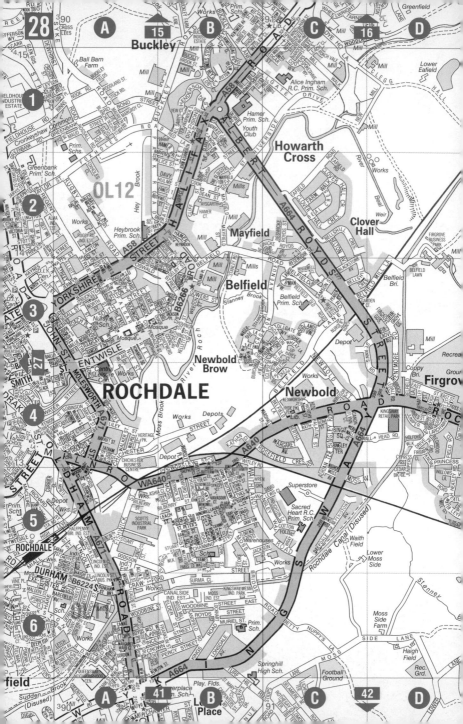

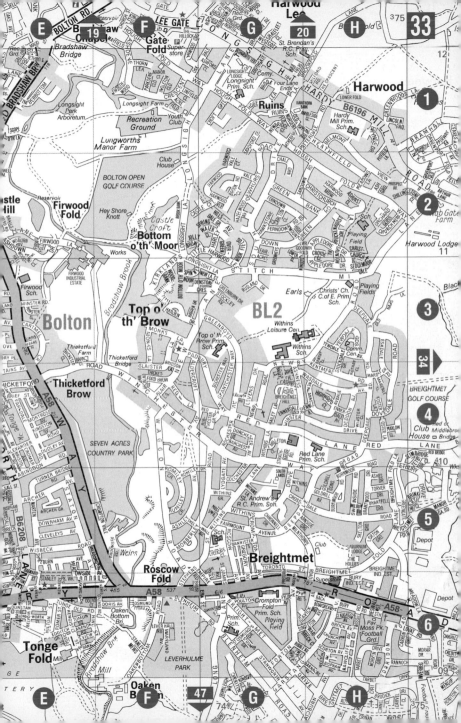

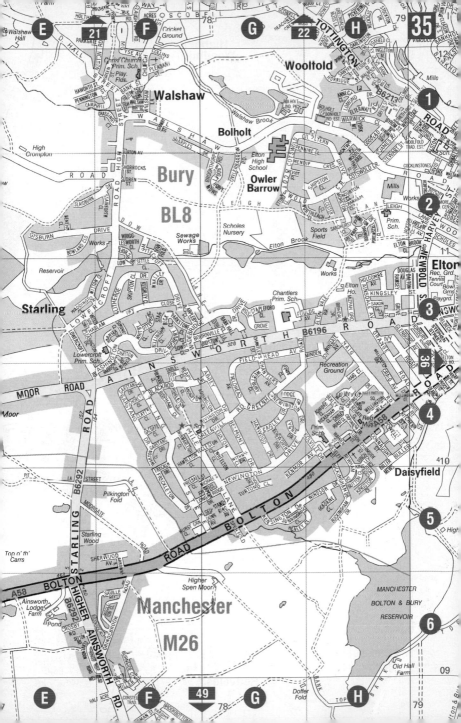

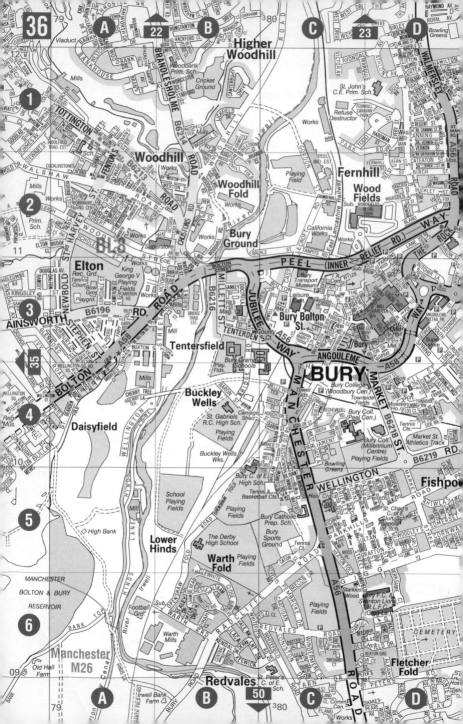

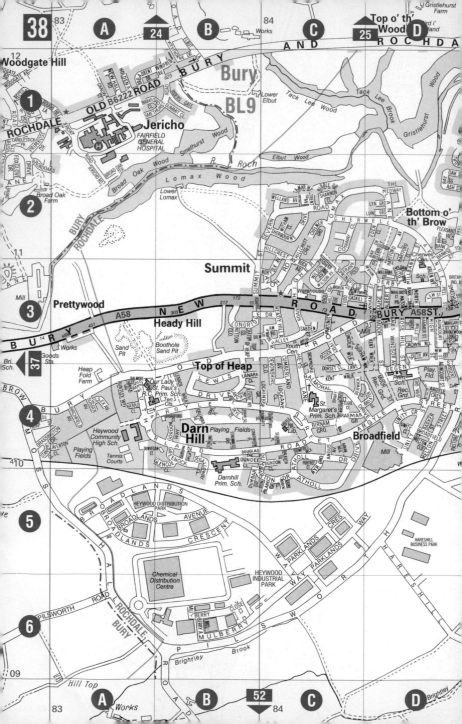

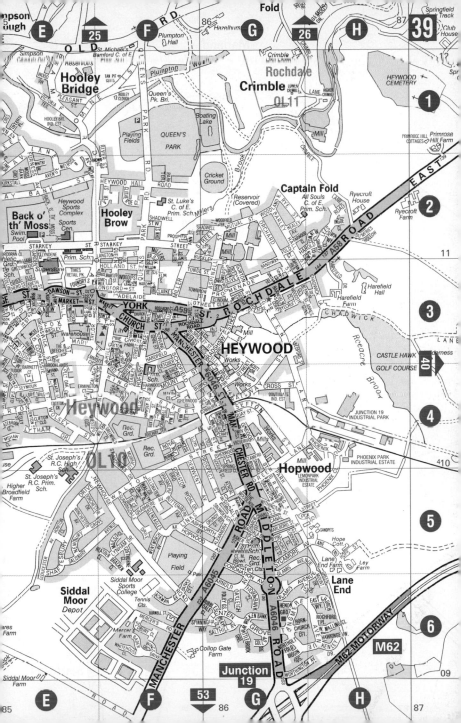

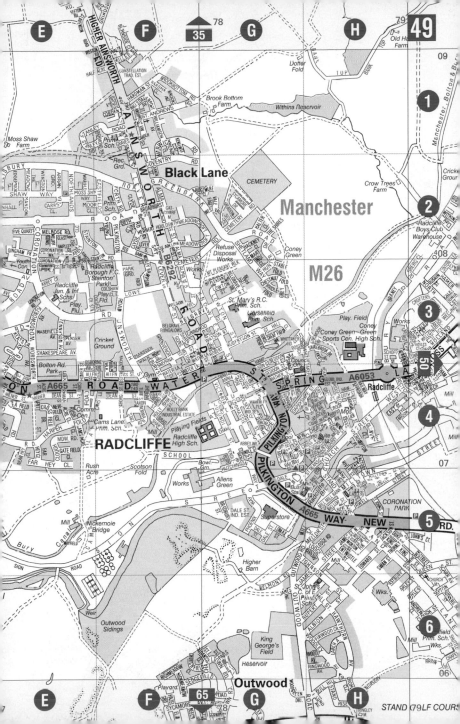

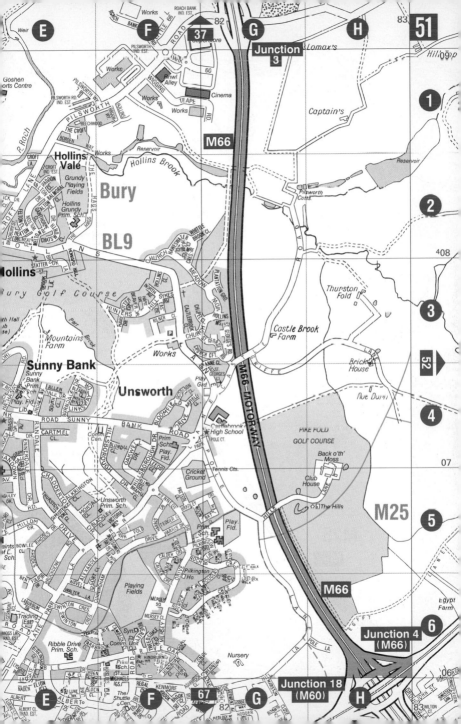

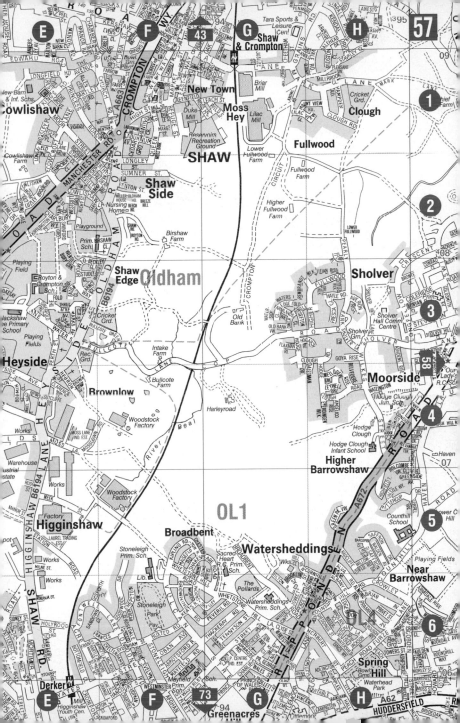

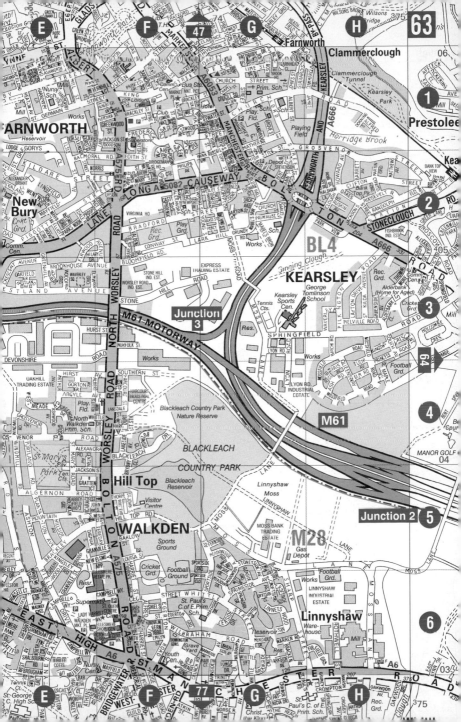

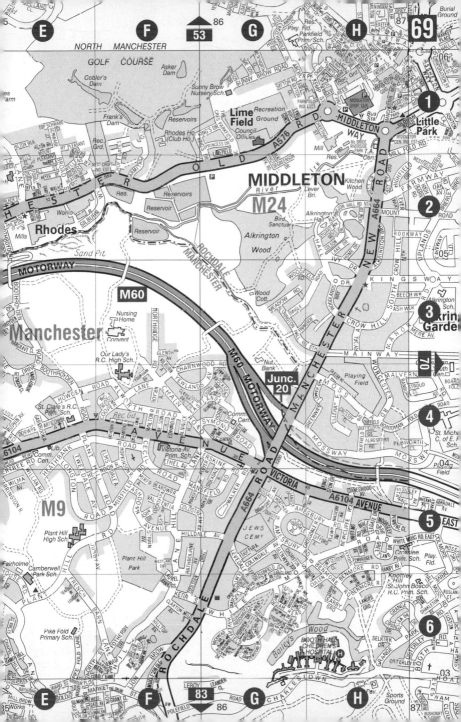

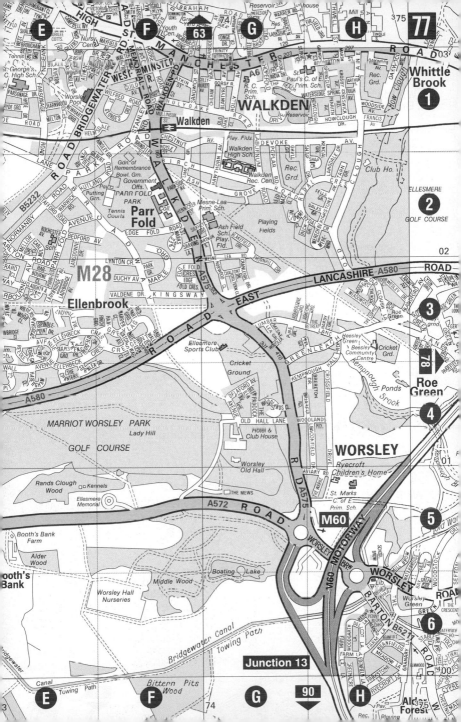

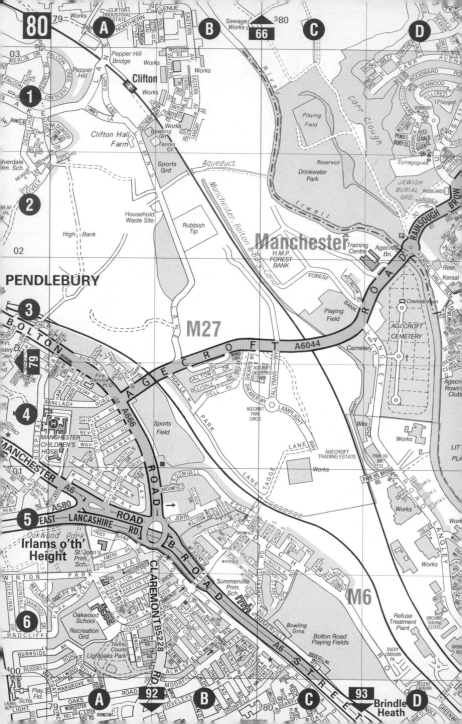

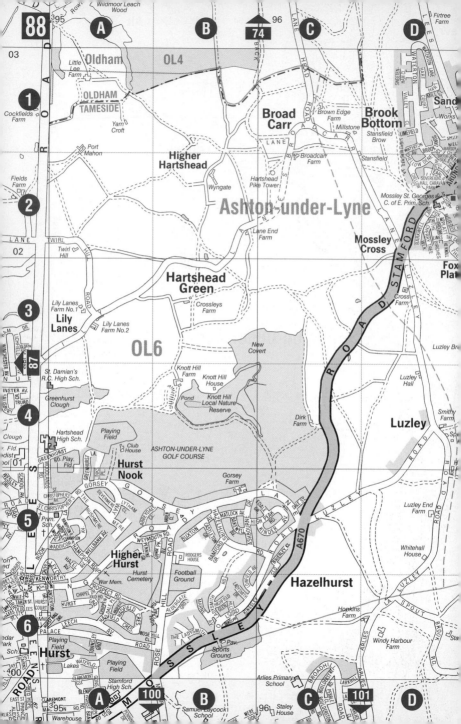

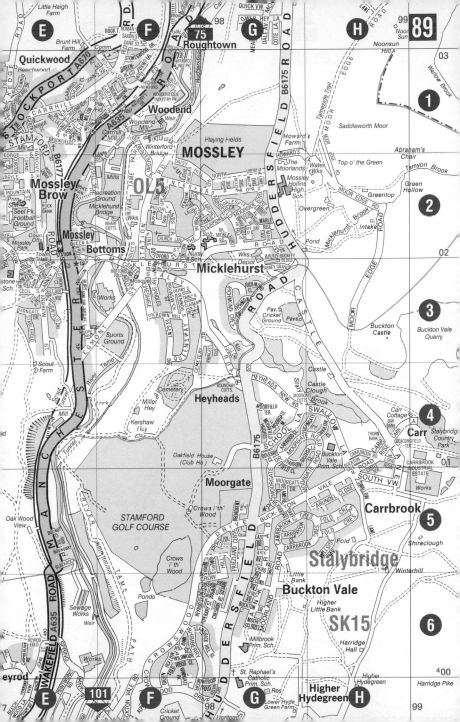

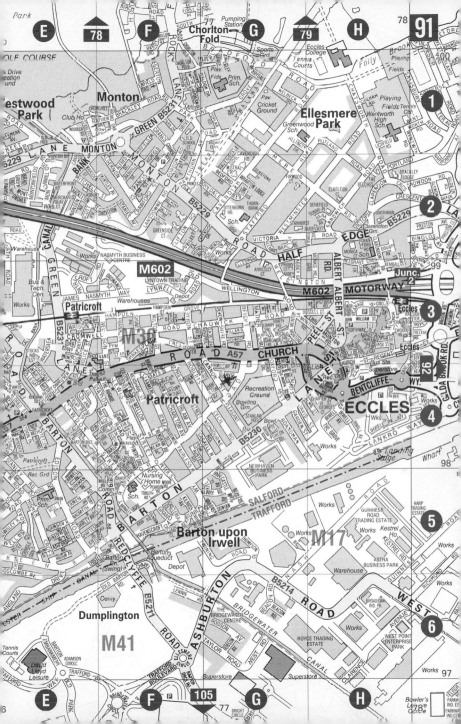

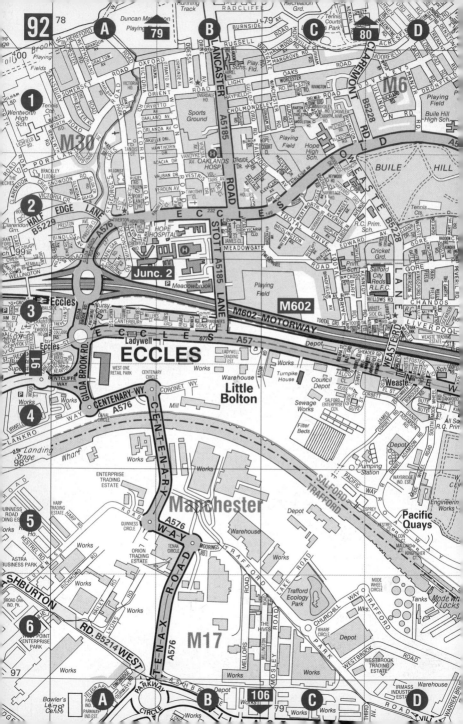

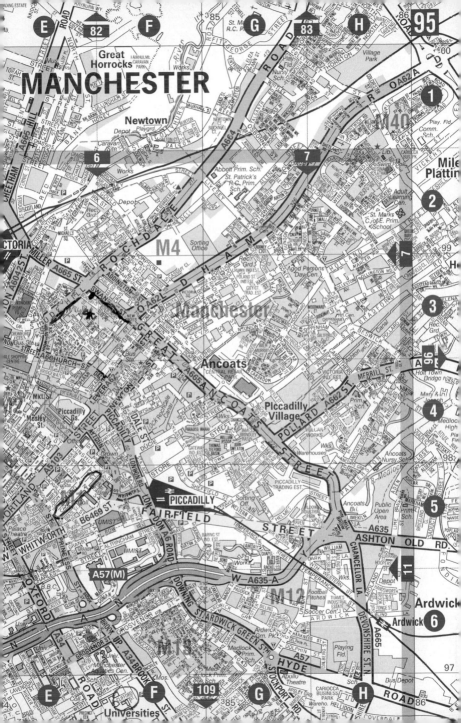

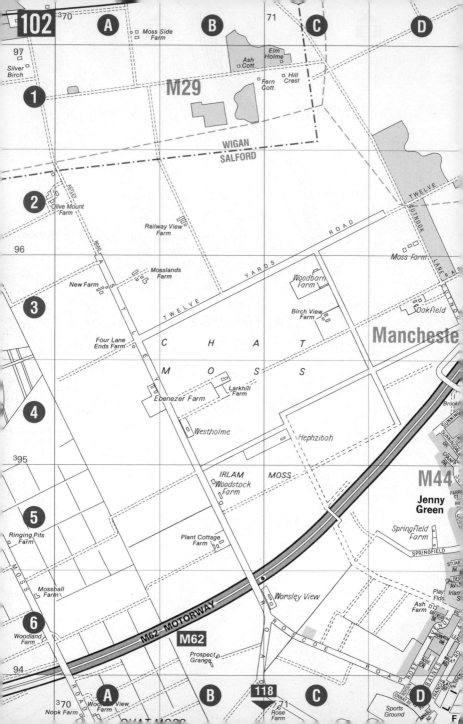

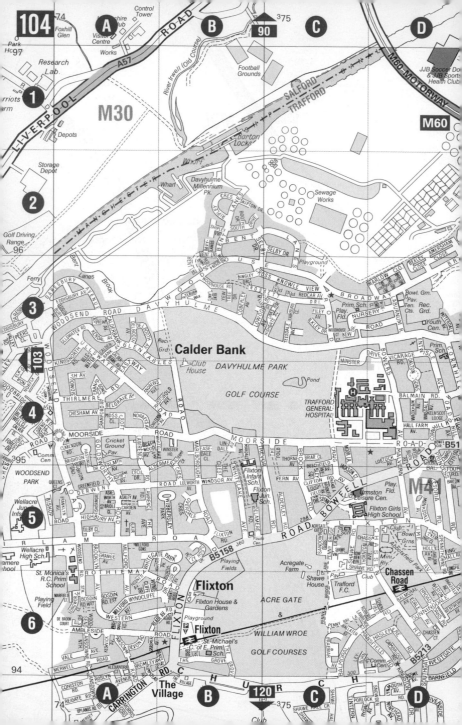

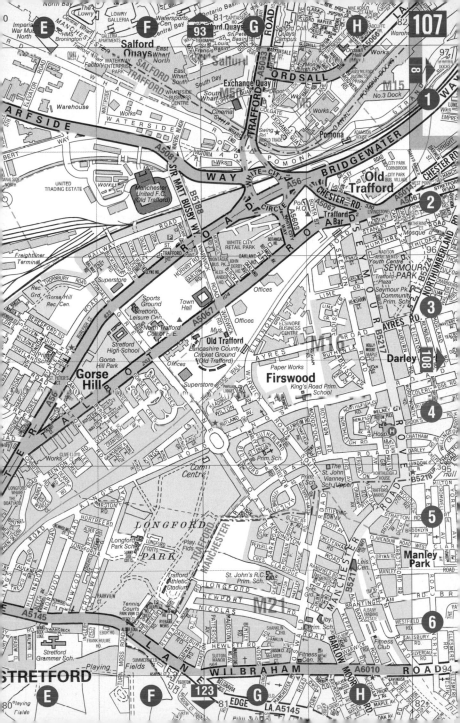

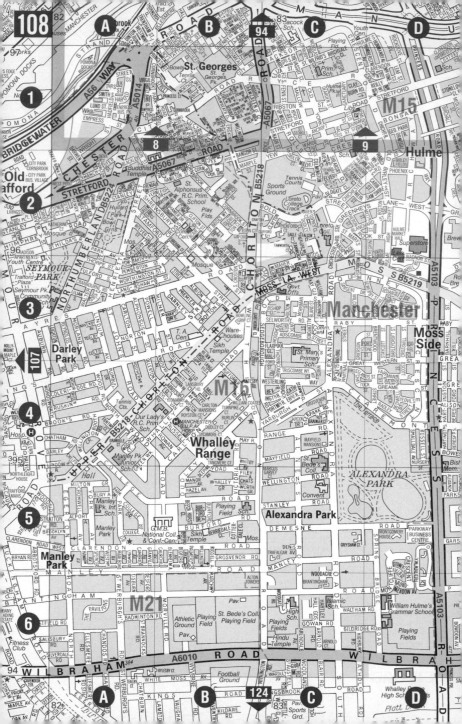

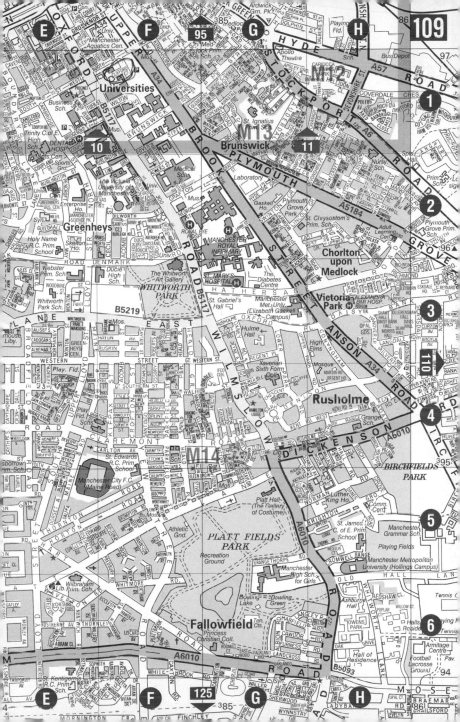

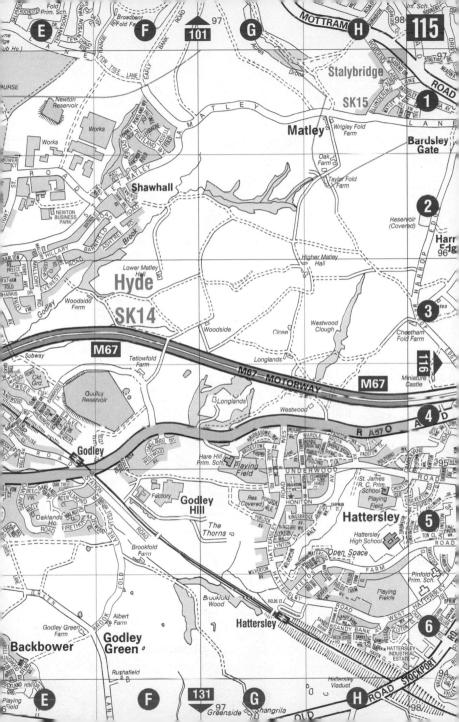

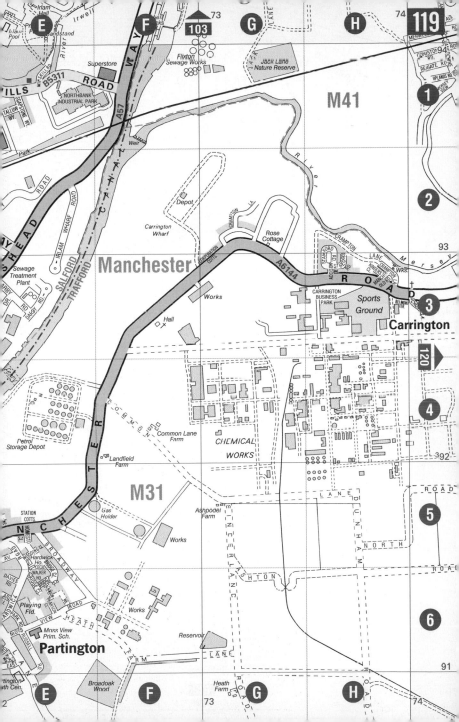

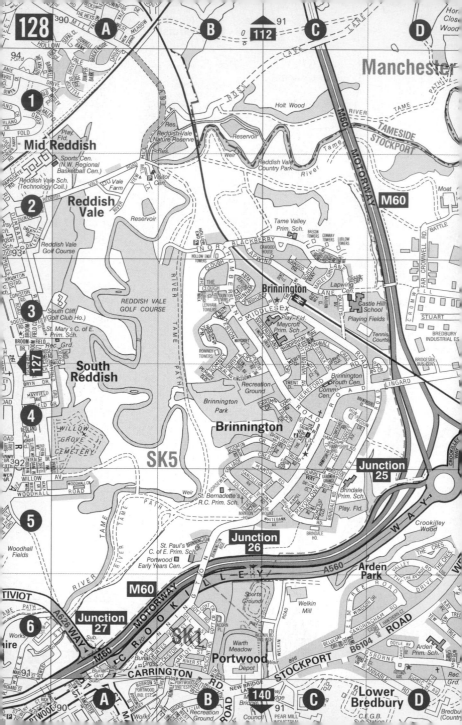

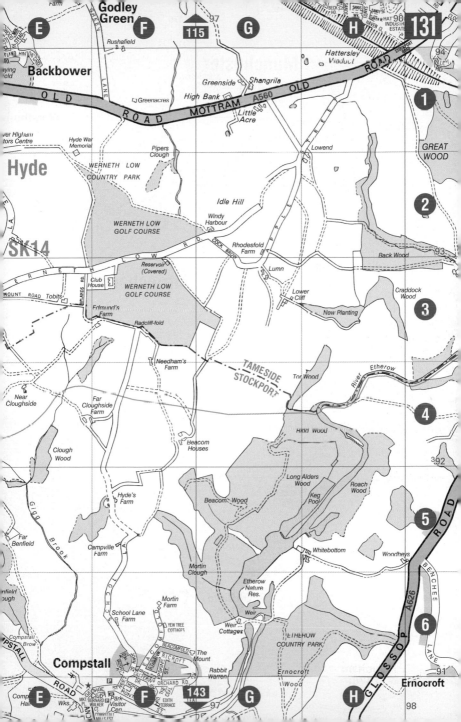

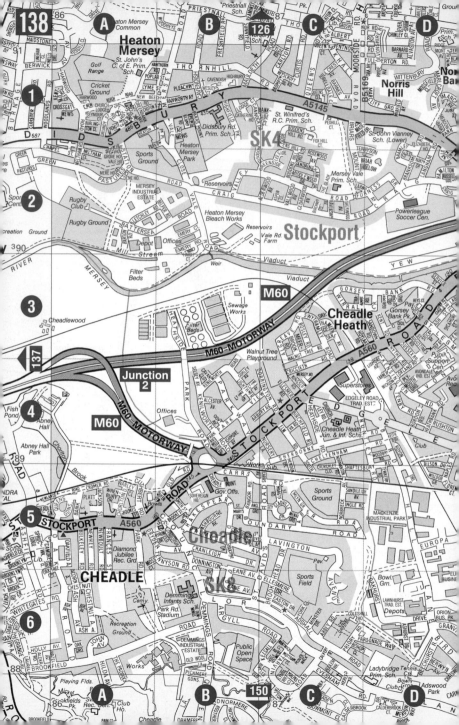

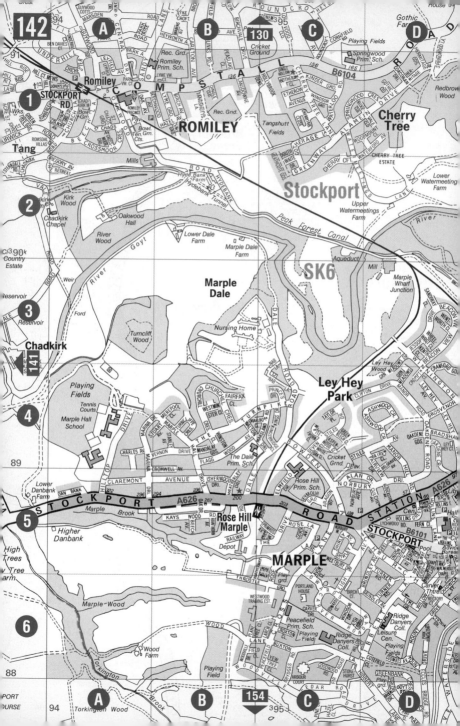

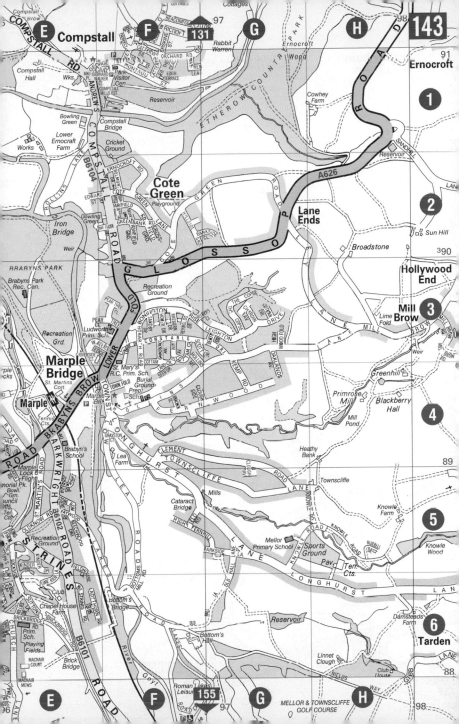

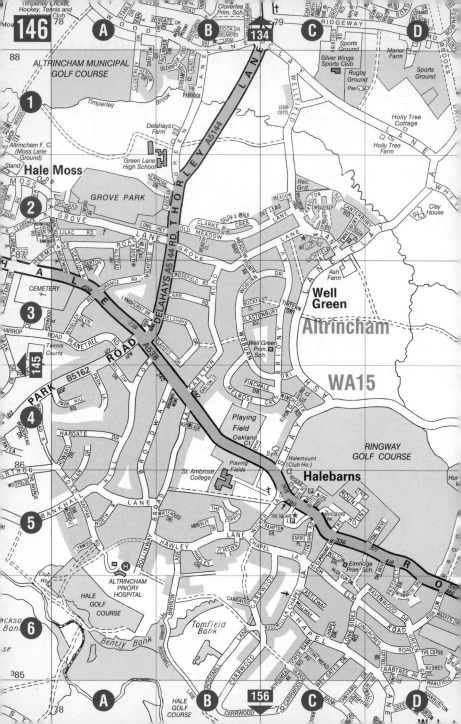

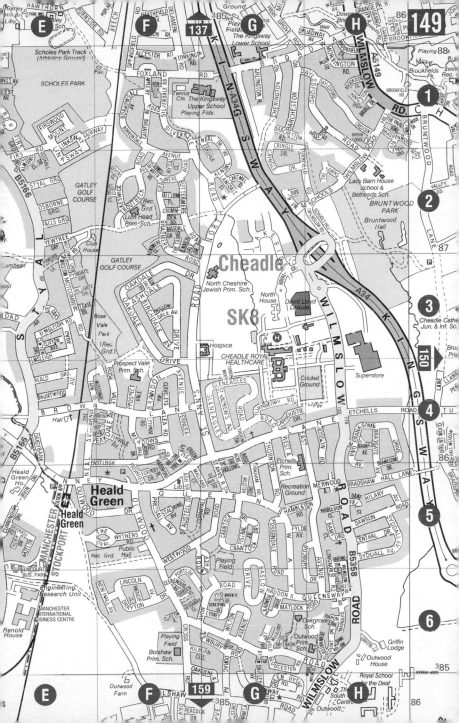

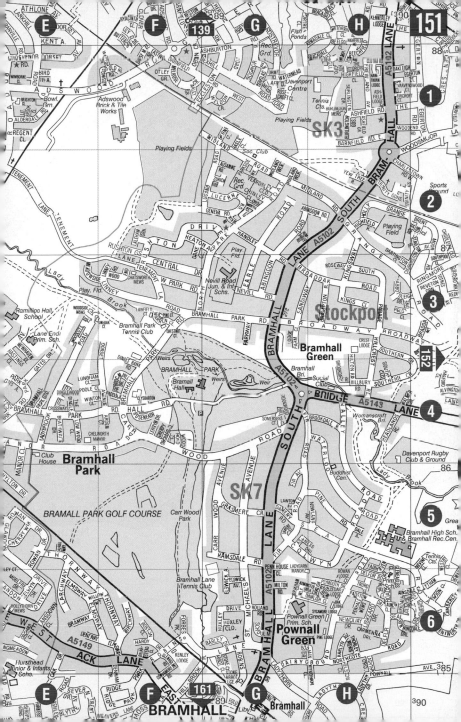

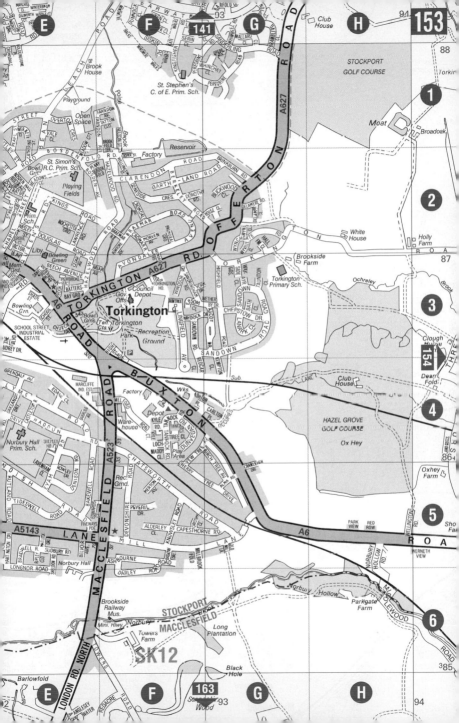

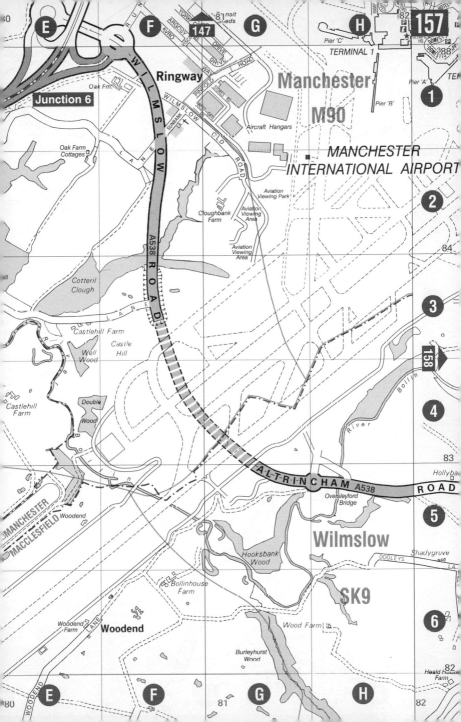

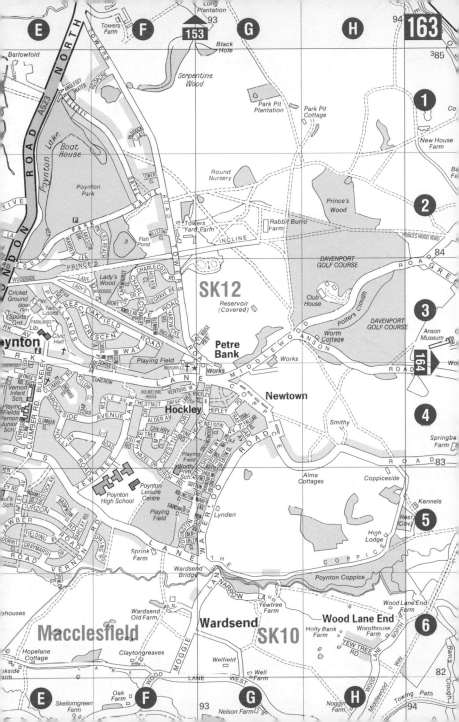

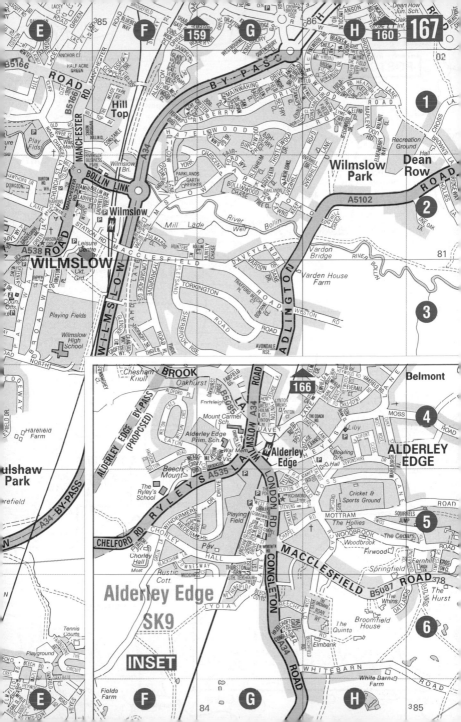

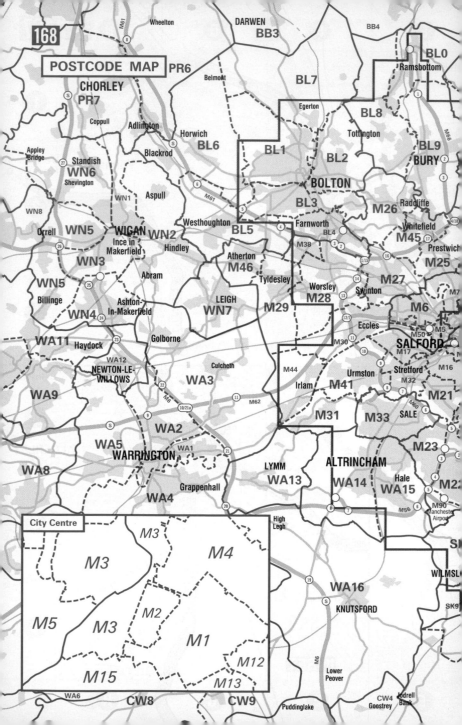

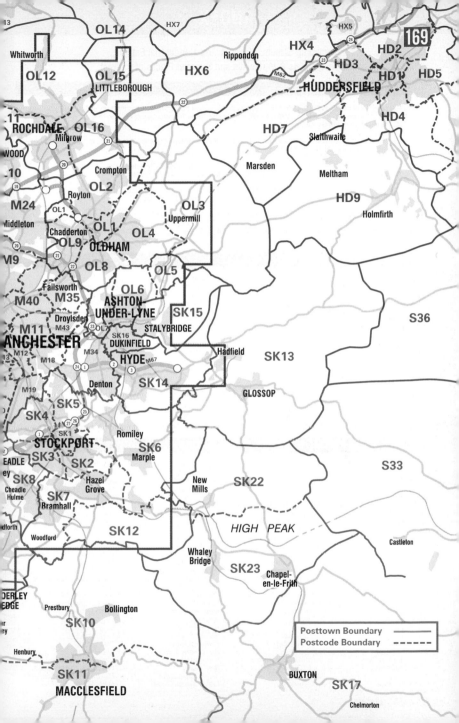

INDEX

Including Streets, Places & Areas, Industrial Estates,
Selected Flats & Walkways and Selected Places of Interest.

HOW TO USE THIS INDEX

1. Each street name is followed by its Postal District (or, if outside the Manchester Postal District, by its Posttown or Postal Locality), and then by its map reference; e.g. Abberton Rd. *M20* ....3E **125** is in the Manchester 20 Postal District and is to be found in square 3E on page **125**. The page number being shown in bold type.

2. A strict alphabetical order is followed in which Av., Rd., St., etc. (though abbreviated) are read in full and as part of the street name; e.g. Acres Ct. appears after Acresbrook Wlk. but before Acresdale.

3. Streets and a selection of flats and walkways too small to be shown on the maps, appear in the index in *Italics* with the thoroughfare to which it is connected shown in brackets; e.g. *Abbeydale. Roch ....3G 27 (off Spotland Rd.)*

4. Places and areas are shown in the index in **blue type** and the map reference is to the actual map square in which the town centre or area is located and not to the place name shown on the map; e.g. **Adswood 5F 139**

5. An example of a selected place of interest is **Abbotsfield Pk. Miniature Railway 5D 104**

6. Map references shown in brackets; e.g. *Abbeyville Wlk. M15 ....2C* **108** (6F 9) refer to entries that also appear on the large scale pages **4-11**.

GENERAL ABBREVIATIONS

All : Alley	Ct : Court	Lit : Little	Rd : Road
App : Approach	Cres : Crescent	Lwr : Lower	Shop : Shopping
Arc : Arcade	Cft : Croft	Mc : Mac	S : South
Av : Avenue	Dri : Drive	Mnr : Manor	Sq : Square
Bk : Back	E : East	Mans : Mansions	Sta : Station
Boulevd : Boulevard	Embkmt : Embankment	Mkt : Market	St. : Street
Bri : Bridge	Est : Estate	Mdw : Meadow	Ter : Terrace
B'way : Broadway	Fld : Field	M : Mews	Trad : Trading
Bldgs : Buildings	Gdns : Gardens	Mt : Mount	Up : Upper
Bus : Business	Gth : Garth	Mus : Museum	Va : Vale
Cvn : Caravan	Ga : Gate	N : North	Vw : View
Cen : Centre	Gt : Great	Pal : Palace	Vs : Villas
Chu : Church	Grn : Green	Pde : Parade	Vis : Visitors
Chyd : Churchyard	Gro : Grove	Pk : Park	Wlk : Walk
Circ : Circle	Ho : House	Pas : Passage	W : West
Cir : Circus	Ind : Industrial	Pl : Place	Yd : Yard
Clo : Close	Info : Information	Quad : Quadrant	
Comn : Common	Junct : Junction	Res : Residential	
Cotts : Cottages	La : Lane	Ri : Rise	

POSTTOWN AND POSTAL LOCALITY ABBREVIATIONS

Abb H : Abbey Hey	*Bury* : Bury	*Elton* : Elton	*Heat M* : Heaton Mersey
A'ton : Adlington	*Cad* : Cadishead	*Fail* : Failsworth	*H'rod* : Heyrod
Aff : Affetside	*Carr* : Carrbrook	*Fall* : Fallowfield	*Heyw* : Heywood
A'wth : Ainsworth	*C'ton* : Carrington	*Farn* : Farnworth	*Hey D* : Heywood Distribution Pk.
Ald E : Alderley Edge	*Chad* : Chadderton	*Fir* : Firgrove	*Higg* : Higginshaw
Alt : Altrincham	*Charl* : Charlesworth	*Firs* : Firswood	*H Lane* : High Lane
Ard : Ardwick	*Chea* : Cheadle	*Gam* : Gamesley	*Holc* : Holcombe
Ash : Ashley	*Chea H* : Cheadle Hulme	*Gat* : Gatley	*Holl* : Hollingworth
Ash L : Ashton-under-Lyne	*Chis* : Chisworth	*G'brk* : Glazebrook	*Hor* : Horwich
A'wrth : Ashworth	*Chor H* : Chorlton cum Hardy	*Glos* : Glossop	*Hulme* : Hulme
Aud : Audenshaw	*Clay* : Clayton	*Gort* : Gorton	*Hurs* : Hurstead
Aus : Austerlands	*Col* : Collyhurst	*Grass* : Grasscroft	*Hyde* : Hyde
Bag : Baguley	*Comp* : Compstall	*G'fld* : Greenfield	*Irlam* : Irlam
Bar : Bardsley	*Crum* : Crumpsall	*G'mnt* : Greenmount	*Kear* : Kearsley
Boll : Bollington	*Del* : Delph	*G'ton* : Grotton	*Kno V* : Knolls Green Village
Bolt : Bolton	*Dem I* : Demmings Ind. Est.	*Had* : Hadfield	*Lees* : Lees
Bow : Bowdon	*Dens* : Denshaw	*Hale* : Hale	*Lev* : Levenshulme
Brad F : Bradley Fold	*Dent* : Denton	*Haleb* : Halebarns	*L'boro* : Littleborough
Brad : Bradshaw	*Did* : Didsbury	*Hand* : Handforth	*L Hul* : Little Hulton
Bram : Bramhall	*Dig* : Diggle	*Harp* : Harpurhey	*L Lev* : Little Lever
Bred : Bredbury	*Dis* : Disley	*Har* : Harwood	*Long* : Longsight
Brei : Breightmet	*Dob* : Dobcross	*Has* : Haslingden	*Los* : Lostock
B'btm : Broadbottom	*Droy* : Droylsden	*Hawk* : Hawkshaw	*Lyd* : Lydgate
B'hth : Broadheath	*Duk* : Dukinfield	*Haz G* : Hazel Grove	*Lymm* : Lymm
Brom X : Bromley Cross	*Dun M* : Dunham Massey	*H Grn* : Heald Green	*Mac* : Macclesfield
Brook : Brooklands	*Dun T* : Dunham Town	*Heal* : Healey	*Man A* : Manchester Airport
Burn : Burnage	*Eccl* : Eccles	*Heap B* : Heap Bridge	*Man S* : Manchester Science Pk.
B'edge : Burnedge	*Eger* : Egerton	*Heat C* : Heaton Chapel	*Marp* : Marple

Marp B : Marple Bridge
Mat : Matley
Mell : Mellor
Mere : Mere
Midd : Middleton
Mile P : Miles Platting
Mill : Millbrook
Miln : Milnsbridge
Mobb : Mobberley
Moss : Mossley
Moss S : Moss Side
Most : Moston
Mot : Mottram
Neth A : Nether Alderley
N Mills : New Mills
New M : New Moston
Newt H : Newton Heath
N'den : Northenden
Oldh : Oldham
Old T : Old Trafford

Open : Openshaw
Part : Partington
Platt B : Platt Bridge
Poy : Poynton
P'wich : Prestwich
Rad : Radcliffe
Rams : Ramsbottom
Redd : Reddish
Ring : Ringway
Rix : Rixton
Roch : Rochdale
Rom : Romiley
Rost : Rostherne
Round I : Roundthorn Ind. Est.
Rytn : Royton
Rush : Rusholme
Sale : Sale
Salf : Salford
Scout : Scouthead
Shar I : Sharston Ind. Area

Shaw : Shaw
Shire : Shore
Smal : Smallbridge
S'bri : Smithybridge
Sower B : Sowerby Bridge
S'head : Springhead
Stal : Stalybridge
Stoc : Stockport
Stret : Stretford
Strin : Strines
S'dale : Strinesdale
Styal : Styal
S'seat : Summerseat
Summ : Summit
Swin : Swinton
Timp : Timperley
Tin : Tintwistle
T'ton : Tottington
Traf P : Trafford Park
Tur : Turton

Tyl : Tyldesley
Uns : Unsworth
Upperm : Uppermill
Urm : Urmston
Walm : Walmersley
Wals : Walsden
Ward : Wardle
W'head : Waterhead
W'houg : Westhoughton
W Timp : West Timperley
Whal R : Whalley Range
W'fld : Whitefield
Whitw : Whitworth
Wilm : Wilmslow
Wthtn : Withington
Woodf : Woodford
Wood I : Woodley
Wors : Worsley
Wyth : Wythenshawe

A

Abberley Dri. M40 .....1D 84
Abberton Rd. M20 ...3E 125
Abbey Clo. Bow 4C 144
Abbey Clo. Rad 2E 49
Abbey Clo. Stret 4H 105
Abbey Ct. M18 ....1G 111
Abbey Ct. Eccl 3G 91
Abbey Ct. Rad 3E 49
Abbey Ct. Stoc 3B 140
Abbey Cres. Heyw 1D 38
Abbeydale. Roch 3G 27
(off Spotland Rd.)
Abbeydale Clo. Ash L ..5A 88
Abbeydale Gdns. Wors ..6E 63
Abbey Dri. Bury 4C 35
Abbey Dri. L'boro 6D 16
Abbey Dri. Swin 2E 79
Abbeyfield Ho. Wors ...5F 63
Abbeyfield Sq. Open ...5D 96
(off Herne St.)
Abbey Gdns. Mot   4R 116
Abbey Gro. Chad 5G 71
Abbey Gro. Eccl 3G 91
Abbey Gro. Mot 4B 116
Abbey Gro. Stoc 3B 140
Abbey Hey. 1H 111
Abbey Hey La. Abb H ..2G 111
Abbey Hey La.
Open & M18 .....6G 97
Abbey Hills Rd. Oldh 4F 73
Abbey Lawn M16 ......4H 107
Abbey Rd. Chea 6C 138
Abbey Rd. Del 2G 59
Abbey Rd. Droy 2H 97
Abbey Rd. Fall 3H 85
Abbey Rd. Midd 3H 53
Abbey Rd. Sale 3A 122
Abbeyville Wlk.
M15 ......2C 108 (6F 9)
Abbey Way. Rad 4G 49
Abbeywood Av. M18 ...3G 111
(in two parts)
Abbotsbury Clo. M12 ...1C 110
Abbotsbury Clo. Poy ...2D 162
Abbots Clo. Sale 4D 122
Abbots Clo. Sale 4D 122
Abbotsfield Clo. Urm ...4H 103
Abbotsfield Pk. Miniature
Railway. 5D 104
Abbot's Fold Rd. Wors , ,4D 76
Abbotsford. Whitw 3H 15
(off Millfold)
Abbotsford Dri. Midd ...3F 53

Abbotsford Gro. Timp ...3G 133
Abbotsford Rd. M21 ....5H 107
Abbotsford Rd. Bolt 4E 31
Abbotsford Rd. Chad ...1E 71
Abbotsford Rd. Oldh ...6F 57
Abbotside Clo. M16 ...4B 108
Abbotsleigh Dri.
Bram 3H 151
Abbott St. Bolt 2A 46
Abbott St. Roch 2B 40
Abden St. Rad 4G 49
Abels La. Upperm 1G 61
Aber Av. Stoc 1C 152
Abercarn Clo. M8 .....4C 82
Abercorn Rd. Bolt 2F 31
Abercorn St. Oldh 3H 73
Abercrombie Ct. Sale ...4D 122
Aberdare Wlk. M9 .....4G 69
(off Brockford Dri.)
Aberdaron Wlk.
M13 ......6F 95 (4D 10)
Aberdeen. Eccl 3G 91
(off Monton La.)
Aberdeen Cres. Stoc ...3F 139
Aberdeen Gdns. Roch ...5D 14
Aberdeen Gro. Stoc 3F 139
Aberdeen Ho. M15 .....2F 109
Aberdeen St. M15 .....2F 109
Aberford Rd. M23 .....6G 135
Abergele Rd. M14 .....1A 126
Abergele St. Stoc 6A 140
Aberley Fold. L'boro ...2D 16
Abernant Clo. M11 ....4B 96
Aber Rd. Chea 5C 138
Abersoch Av. M14 .....1A 126
Abingdon Av. W'fld 5D 50
Abingdon Clo. Chad ...5H 71
Abingdon Clo. Roch ...6G 27
Abingdon Clo. W'fld ...5D 50
Abingdon Rd. Bolt 5E 33
Abingdon Rd. Bram ...3G 151
Abingdon Rd. Stoc 2H 127
Abingdon Rd. Urm 4G 105
Abingdon St.
M1 ....5E 96 (1A 10)
Abinger Wlk. M40 .....1F 97
Abington Rd. Sale 6B 122
Abney Grange. Moss ...3G 89
Abney Rd. Moss 3E 89
Abney Rd. Stoc 4E 127
Abney Steps. Moss 3E 89
(off Apsley Side)
Aboukir St. Roch 3B 28
Abraham Moss Leisure Cen.
............3C 82
Abram Clo. M14 ......6E 109

Abram St. Salf 5D 80
Absalom Dri. M8 .....3B 82
Abson St. Chad 6A 56
Acacia Av. Chea H 3C 150
Acacia Av. Dent 4G 113
Acacia Av. Hale 2H 145
Acacia Av. Swin 5E 79
Acacia Av. Wilm 4C 166
Acacia Dri. Hale 2H 145
Acacia Gro. Stoc 5H 127
Acacia Rd. Oldh 2B 86
Acaclas. Urm 5G 105
Acadomy Wlk. M15 ....2C 108
Ace Mill. Chad 5F 71
Acer Clo. Hyde 5E 115
Acer Clo. Roch 2H 25
Acer Gro. Salf 4H 81
Acheson St. M18 ......2F 111
Ackers La. C'ton 3A 120
(in two parts)
Ackersley Ct. Chea H ..6D 150
Ackers St.
M13 ......2F 109 (6D 10)
Acker St. Roch 3H 27
Ack La. E. Bram 6E 151
Ack La. W. Chea H 6D 150
Ackroyd Av. M18 .....1H 111
Ackroyd St. M11 .....6G 97
(in two parts)
Ackworth Dri. M23 ....5G 135
Ackworth Rd. Swin 2E 79
Acme Dri. Swin 3H 79
Acomb St. M14 ....4F 109
Acomb St. M15 ....2F 109
Acorn Av. Chea 6A 138
Acorn Av. Hyde 1C 130
(in three parts)
Acorn Bus. Pk. Stoc ...2F 139
Acorn Cen., The. Oldh ...1F 73
Acorn Clo. M19 ......1B 126
Acorn Clo. W'fld 3D 66
Acorn Pl. Stoc 6B 128
Acorn St. Lees 3A 74
Acorn Way. Oldh 2C 72
Acre. 1F 73
Acre Barn. Shaw 5C 42
Acre Clo. Rams 2A 12
Acre Fld. Bolt 1F 33
Acrefield. Sale 6A 122
Acrefield Av. Stoc 5C 126
Acrefield Av. Urm 6H 105
Acregate. Urm 5G 104
Acregate Cotts. Urm ...5G 104
Acre La. Chea H 2D 160
Acre La. Oldh 6E 57
Acres. 5E 55

Acresbrook. Stal 6G 101
Acresbrook Av. T'ton ..6H 21
Acresbrook Wlk. T'ton ..2A 62
Acres Ct. M22 ....1B 148
Acresdale. Los 6A 30
Acresfield Av. Aud 4C 98
Acresfield Clo. Swin ...5G 79
Acresfield Rd. Hyde ...2D 114
Acresfield Rd. L Hul ...5D 62
Acresfield Rd. Midd ...4D 54
Acresfield Rd. Salf 6B 80
Acresfield Rd. Timp ...3A 134
Acres La. Stal 4F 101
Acres Pass. M21 ......1G 123
Acres Rd. M21 ....1G 123
Acres Rd. Gat 6E 137
Acres St. T'ton 6H 21
Acre St. Chad 1H 85
Acre St. Dent 4E 113
Acre St. Rad 4E 49
Acre St. Rom 1H 141
Acre St. Whitw 4H 15
Acre Top Rd. M9 .....4D 68
Acre Vw. Rams 3A 12
Acre Wood. Los 4A 44
Acton Av. M40 ....1D 96
Acton Sq. Salf 3H 93 (4A 4)
Acton St. Oldh 1E 73
Acton St. Roch 2A 28
Adair St. M1 .....5G 95 (1E 11)
Adair St. Roch 3B 40
Adam Clo. Chea H 1D 150
Adams Av. M21 ....3H 123
Adams Clo. Poy 5E 163
Adamson Circ. Urm 6E 91
Adamson Gdns. M20 ...6D 124
Adamson Ho. M16 .....1H 107
Adamson Ind. Est.
Hyde 5A 114
Adamson Rd. Eccl 5E 91
Adamson St. Duk 1A 114
Adamson Wlk. M14 ....4G 109
Adam St. Ash L 2A 100
Adam St. Bolt 2B 46
Adam St. Oldh 1D 86
Ada St. M9 ....2F 83
Ada St. Oldh 3E 73
Ada St. Rams 4D 12
Ada St. Roch 1A 28
Adcroft St. Stoc 4H 139
Addenbrook Rd. M8 ...6A 82
Adderley Pl. Glos 6H 117
Adderley Rd. Glos 6H 117
Addingham St. M9 ....4D 68
Addington Rd. Bolt 4D 44
Addington St.
M4 ....3F 95 (3C 6)

Addison Av. *Ash L* 2B **100**
Addison Clo.
  M13 . . . . . .1G **109** (6E **11**)
Addison Cres. *M16* 3H **107**
Addison Dri. *Midd* 5C **54**
Addison Grange. *Sale* . . .6C **122**
Addison Rd. *Hale* 3G **145**
Addison Rd. *Irlam* 3G **103**
Addison Rd. *Part* 3H **119**
Addison Rd. *Stret* 4B **106**
Addison Rd. *Urm* 6F **105**
Addison Ter. *M14* 3H **109**
Adelaide Rd. *Bram* 1H **161**
Adelaide Rd. *Stoc* 3E **139**
Adelaide St. *M8* 6B **82**
Adelaide St. *Bolt* 3H **45**
Adelaide St. *Eccl* 4F **91**
Adelaide St. *Heyw* 3F **39**
Adelaide St. *Midd* 1A **70**
Adelaide St. *Rams* 5C **12**
Adelaide St. *Swin* 4D **78**
Adelaide St. E. *Heyw* 3G **39**
Adelphi Ct. *Salf* . . .2B **94** (2C **4**)
Adelphi Dri. *L Hul* 4D **62**
Adelphi Gro. *L Hul* 4D **62**
Adelphi St. *Rad* 2F **49**
Adelphi St. *Salf* . . .3B **94** (4C **4**)
Adelphi Ter. *Salf* . . .3A **94** (4B **4**)
Aden Clo.
  M12 . . . . . .5H **95** (1H **11**)
Aden St. *Oldh* 4H **73**
Aden St. *Roch* 2A **28**
Adisham Dri. *Bolt* 4B **32**
Adlington Clo. *Bury* 4G **35**
Adlington Clo. *Poy* 5F **163**
Adlington Clo. *Timp* 5D **134**
Adlington Dri. *Stret* 3F **107**
Adlington Ind. Est.
  A'ton 5C **162**
Adlington Pk. *Mac* 6C **162**
Adlington Rd. *Wilm* 3G **167**
Adlington St.
  M12 . . . . . .5H **95** (2G **11**)
Adlington St. *Bolt* 4H **45**
Adlington St. *Oldh* 6H **57**
Adlington Wlk. *Stoc* 2G **139**
Adlington Way. *Dent* 6G **113**
Admel Sq.
  M15 . . . . . .2E **109** (6H **9**)
Adrian Rd. *Bolt* 3G **31**
Adrian St. *M40* 4A **84**
Adrian Ter. *Roch* 5C **28**
Adria Rd. *M20* 6G **125**
Adscombe St. *M16* 3C **108**
Adshall Rd. *Chea* 6C **138**
Adshead Clo. *M22* 2H **147**
Adstock Wlk.
  M40 . . . . . . .2G **95** (2F **7**)
Adstone Clo.
  M4 . . . . .4H **95** (5H **7**)
Adswood. 5F **139**
Adswood Clo. *Oldh* 6H **57**
Adswood Gro. *Stoc* 5F **139**
Adswood Ind. Est.
  Stoc 5F **139**
Adswood La. E. *Stoc* 5H **139**
Adswood La. W. *Stoc* 5H **139**
Adswood Old Hall Rd.
  Chea H 1F **151**
Adswood Old Rd.
  Stoc 5G **139**
Adswood Rd.
  Chea H & Stoc 1E **151**
Adswood Rd. *Stoc* 5G **139**
Adswood St. *M40* 3A **96**
Adswood Ter. *Stoc* 5G **139**
Aegean Gdns. *Salf* 6G **81**
Aegean Rd. *B'hth* 5C **132**
Affetside. 3D **20**
Affetside Dri. *Bury* 3E **35**
Affleck Av. *Rad* 1A **64**
Afghan St. *Oldh* 1F **73**

Age Cft. *Oldh* 6G **73**
Agecroft Crematorium. *Salf*3D **80**
Agecroft Enterprise Pk. *Swin* 4B **80**
Agecroft Pk. Circ. *Swin* . .4B **80**
Agecroft Rd. *Rom* 2G **141**
Agecroft Rd. *Swin* 4A **80**
Agecroft Rd. E. *P'wich* . . .1E **81**
Agecroft Rd. W. *P'wich* . . .1D **80**
Agecroft Trad. Est.
  Swin 4C **80**
Agincourt St. *Heyw* 3D **38**
  (in two parts)
Agnes Clo. *Oldh* 5A **72**
Agnes St. *M14* 2G **125**
Agnes St. *M19* 5C **110**
Agnes St. *Chad* 4H **71**
Agnes St. *Roch* 6A **28**
Agnes St. *Salf* 4B **82**
Agnew Pl. *Salf* 1G **93**
Agnew Rd. *M18* 2E **111**
Aigburth Gro. *Stoc* 5G **111**
Ailsa Clo. *M40* 6F **83**
Ailsa Ct. *Salf* 4F **93**
  (off Milford St.)
Aimson Pl. *Timp* 4C **134**
Aimson Rd. E. *Timp* 5C **134**
Aimson Rd. W. *Timp* 4C **134**
Aines St. *M12* 6C **96**
Ainley Rd. *M22* 2B **148**
Ainley Wood. *Del* 2G **59**
Ainley Wood. *Duk* 6B **100**
Ainsbrook Av. *Del* 3H **59**
Ainsbrook Ter. *Dig* 2D **60**
  (off Harrop Ct. Rd.)
Ainsdale Av. *Bury* 3H **35**
Ainsdale Av. *Salf* 2H **81**
Ainsdale Clo. *Bram* 6H **151**
Ainsdale Clo. *Oldh* 5B **72**
Ainsdale Ct. *Bolt* 4B **46**
Ainsdale Cres. *Rytn* 5C **56**
Ainsdale Dri. *H Grn* 4F **149**
Ainsdale Dri. *Sale* 1G **133**
Ainsdale Dri. *Whitw* 2D **14**
Ainsdale Gro. *Stoc* 1H **127**
Ainsdale Rd. *Bolt* 5A **46**
  (in two parts)
Ainsdale St. *M12* 1B **110**
Ainsford Rd. *M20* 4H **125**
Ainsley Gro. *Wors* 1F **77**
Ainsley St. *M40* 6C **84**
Ainslie Rd. *Bolt* 4E **31**
Ainsty Rd. *M14* 3E **109**
Ainsworth. 4C **34**
Ainsworth Clo. *Dent* 4B **112**
Ainsworth Ct. *Bolt* 6E **33**
Ainsworth Hall Rd.
  Bolt & L'a. 6B **34**
Ainsworth La. *Bolt* 4D **32**
Ainsworth Rd. *Bury* 4F **35**
Ainsworth Rd. *L Lev* 3A **48**
Ainsworth Rd. *Rad* 1F **49**
Ainsworth Sq. *Bolt* 2H **31**
  (off Ainsworth St.)
Ainsworth St. *Bolt* 3G **31**
Ainsworth St. *Roch* 5A **28**
Ainthorpe Wlk. *M40* 6D **84**
Aintree Av. *Sale* 6E **121**
Aintree Clo. *Haz G* 3F **153**
Aintree Dri. *Roch* 3A **26**
Aintree Gro. *Stoc* 5G **139**
Aintree Rd. *L Lev* 5A **48**
Aintree St. *M11* 4D **96**
Aintree Wlk. *Chad* 2A **72**
Airedale Clo. *Chea* 5G **137**
Airedale Ct. *Alt* 6G **133**
Aire Dri. *Bolt* 6F **19**
Air Hill Ter. *Roch* 2E **27**
Airton Clo. *M40* 2G **95** (1F **7**)
Aitken Clo. *Rams* 4D **12**
Aitken St. *M19* 6E **111**
Ajax Dri. *Bury* 4D **50**

Ajax St. *Rams* 4D **12**
Ajax St. *Roch* 2B **40**
Aked Clo.
  M12 . . . . . .1H **109** (6H **11**)
Akesmoor Dri. *Stoc* 5C **140**
Alamein Dri. *Rom* 1C **142**
Alan Av. *Fail* 6F **85**
Alanbrooke Wlk. *M15* . . .2C **108**
Alandale Av. *Aud* 6E **99**
Alandale Dri. *Rytn* 2A **56**
Alandale Rd. *Stoc* 4D **138**
Alan Dri. *Hale* 5A **146**
Alan Dri. *Marp* 5C **142**
Alan Rd. *M20* 3G **125**
Alan Rd. *Stoc* 6C **126**
Alan St. *Rams* 2H **31**
Alan Turing Way. *M11* . . .2B **96**
Alasdair Clo. *Chad* 1F **71**
Alba Clo. *Eccl* 4E **91**
Alban St. *Salf* 6H **81**
Albany Av. *M11* 6H **97**
Albany Clo. *L Hul* 3D **62**
Albany St. *M20* 3E **125**
Albany Ct. *Urm* 4D **104**
Albany Dri. *Bury* 6D **36**
Albany Rd. *M21* 6H **107**
Albany Rd. *Bram* 3G **161**
Albany Rd. *Eccl* 2D **90**
Albany Rd. *Wilm* 4C **166**
Albany St. *Midd* 2B **70**
Albany St. *Oldh* 6H **57**
Albany St. *Roch* 6A **28**
Albany Trad. Est.
  M21 . . . . .6H **107**
Albany Way. *Hyde* 5A **116**
Albany Way. *Salf* 2G **93**
Alba St. *Holc* 3C **12**
Alba Way. *Stret* 2A **106**
Albemarle Av. *M20* 3E **125**
Albemarle Rd. *M21* 1G **123**
Albemarle Rd. *Swin* 4E **79**
Albemarle St. *M14* 3E **109**
Albemarle Ter. *Ash L* 2A **100**
Alberbury Av. *Timp* 4D **134**
Albermarle St. *Ash L* 2A **100**
Alberta St. *Bolt* 2G **45**
Alberta St. *Stoc* 3H **139**
Albert Av. *M18* 3H **111**
Albert Av. *Duk* 1A **114**
Albert Av. *P'wich* 2G **81**
Albert Av. *Shaw* 2E **57**
Albert Av. *Urm* 5G **105**
Albert Av. *Wors* 4E **63**
Albert Clo. *Chea H* 3C **150**
Albert Clo. *W'fld* 1E **67**
Albert Clo. Trad. Est.
  W'fld 1E **67**
Albert Ct. *Alt* 1F **145**
Albert Gdns. *M40* 6D **84**
Albert Gro. *M12* 3C **110**
  (in two parts)
Albert Gro. *Farn* 1F **63**
Albert Halls. 6B **32**
  (Bolton Town Hall)
Albert Hill St. *M20* 6F **125**
Albert Mt. *Oldh* 6E **57**
Albert Park. 4E **125**
Albert Pk. Rd. *Salf* 6G **81**
Albert Pl. *M13* 4B **110**
Albert Pl. *Alt* 6F **133**
Albert Pl. *Lees* 3A **74**
Albert Pl. *W'fld* 6F **51**
Albert Rd. *M19* 6B **110**
Albert Rd. *Bolt* 5F **31**
Albert Rd. *Chea H* 3C **150**
Albert Rd. *Eccl* 2H **91**
Albert Rd. *Farn* 1E **63**
Albert Rd. *Hale* 2G **145**
Albert Rd. *Hyde* 5B **114**
Albert Rd. *Sale* 5C **122**
Albert Rd. *Stoc* 6C **126**

Albert Rd. *W'fld* 1E **67**
Albert Rd. *Wilm* 3D **166**
Albert Rd. E. *Hale* 2G **145**
Albert Rd. W. *Bolt* 4D **30**
Albert Royds St. *Roch* 1B **28**
Albert Sq. *M2* 4D **94** (6H **5**)
  (in two parts)
Albert Sq. *Bow* 2E **145**
Albert Sq. *Stal* 4D **100**
Albert St. *M11* 4B **96**
Albert St. *Bury* 3E **37**
Albert St. *Cad* 3C **118**
Albert St. *Chad* 6H **71**
Albert St. *Dent* 4F **113**
Albert St. *Droy* 4B **98**
Albert St. *Eccl* 3H **91**
Albert St. *Farn* 2F **63**
Albert St. *Had* 2H **117**
Albert St. *Haz G* 2D **152**
Albert St. *Heyw* 3D **38**
Albert St. *Hyde* 4D **114**
Albert St. *Kear* 1G **63**
Albert St. *Lees* 4A **74**
Albert St. *L'boro* 3E **17**
Albert St. *L Lev* 4B **48**
Albert St. *Midd* 1A **70**
Albert St. *Miln* 6G **29**
Albert St. *Oldh* 2E **73**
Albert St. *P'wich* 5G **67**
Albert St. *Rad* 4H **49**
Albert St. *Rams* 3D **12**
Albert St. *Rytn* 3B **56**
Albert St. *Shaw* 6E **43**
Albert St. *Stoc* 2F **139**
Albert St. *Whitw* 1C **14**
Albert St. W. *Fail* 5D **84**
Albert St. Works. *Droy* 4B **98**
Albert Ter. *Stoc* 2H **139**
Albert Wlk. *Ash L* 4G **99**
Albine St. *M40* 3H **83**
Albinson Wlk. *Part* 6E **119**
Albion Clo. *Stoc* 6G **127**
Albion Ct. *Bury* 3B **36**
Albion Dri. *Droy* 3A **98**
Albion Fold. *Droy* 3A **98**
Albion Gdns. *Stal* 3F **101**
Albion Gdns. Clo. *Rytn* . . .3D **56**
Albion Gro. *Sale* 5A **122**
Albion Pl. *Haz G* 2D **152**
Albion Pl. *P'wich* 5E **67**
Albion Pl.
  Salf (M5) . . .3A **94** (4A **4**)
Albion Pl. *Salf* (M7) 6G **81**
Albion Rd. *M14* 6G **109**
Albion Rd. *Roch* 5F **27**
Albion Rd. Ind. Est. *Roch* .5F **27**
Albion St. *M1* 6D **94** (3G **9**)
Albion St. *Ash L* 2A **100**
  (in two parts)
Albion St. *Bolt* 2B **46**
Albion St. *Bury* 3B **36**
Albion St. *Chad* 2G **71**
Albion St. *Fail* 4E **85**
Albion St. *Kear* 2A **64**
Albion St. *L'boro* 4E **17**
Albion St. *Oldh* 2D **72**
  (in two parts)
Albion St. *Old T* 3B **108**
Albion St. *Rad* 6H **49**
Albion St. *Roch* 4C **40**
Albion St. *Sale* 5B **122**
Albion St. *Stal* 3F **101**
Albion St. *Swin* 3G **79**
Albion Ter. *Bolt* 2F **31**
Albion Towers. *Salf* 3H **93**
Albion Trad. Est.
  Ash L 2B **100**
Albion Trad. Est. *Salf* 1G **93**
Albion Way. *Salf* 4H **93**
Albury Dri. *M19* 1H **137**
Albury Dri. *Roch* 1B **26**
Albyns Av. *M8* 4C **82**

Alcester Av.—Almond Tree Rd.

Alcester Av. *Stoc* 4B **138**
Alcester Clo. *Bury* 2H **35**
Alcester Clo. *Midd* 3B **70**
Alcester Rd. *Gat* 1F **149**
Alcester Rd. *Sale* 1B **134**
Alcester St. *Chad* 6G **71**
Alcester Wlk. *M9* 4E **69**
Alconbury Ct. Droy 5B ***98***
(off Williamson La.)
Alconbury Wlk. *M9* 3D **68**
Aldborough Clo. *M20* 3F **125**
Aldbourne Clo. *M40* 6F **83**
Aldbury Ter. *Bolt* 4H **31**
Aldcroft St. *M18* 1H **111**
Alden Clo. *W'fld* 1E **67**
Alden Wlk. *Stoc* 2F **127**
Alder Av. *Bury* 2G **37**
Alder Av. *Poy* 4F **163**
Alderbank. *Ward* 2A **16**
Alderbank Clo. *Kear* 3H **63**
Alderbrook Rd. *L Hul* 6B **62**
Alder Clo. *Ash L* 4F **87**
Alder Clo. *Bury* 3A **36**
Alder Clo. *Duk* 6E **101**
Alder Ct. *M8* 2B **82**
Aldercroft Av. *M22* 3A **148**
Aldercroft Av. *Bolt* 4F **33**
Alderdale Clo. *Stoc* 4C **126**
Alderdale Dri. *Droy* 3G **97**
Alderdale Dri. *H Lane* 6C **154**
Alderdale Dri. *Stoc* 4C **126**
Alderdale Gro. *Wilm* 4B **166**
Alderdale Rd. *Chea H* 1E **151**
Alder Dri. *Stal* 2G **101**
Alder Dri. *Swin* 2C **78**
Alder Dri. *Timp* 6D **134**
Alder Edge. *M21* 6F **107**
Alderfield Ho. *M21* 6F **107**
Alderfield Rd. *M21* 6F **107**
Alderford Pde. *M8* 5B **82**
(in two parts)
Alder Forest. **1C 90**
Alder Forest Av. *Eccl* 1C **90**
Aldergate Ct. *Swin* 4C **78**
Aldergate Gro. *Ash L* 6B **88**
Alderglen Rd. *M8* 5B **82**
Alder Gro. *Brom X* 5G **19**
Alder Gro. *Dent* 4G **113**
Alder Gro. *Stoc* 3E **139**
Alder Gro. *Stret* 5E **107**
Alder La. *Oldh* 1B **86**
Alderley Av. *Bolt* 6C **18**
Alderley Clo. *Haz G* 5F **153**
Alderley Clo. *Poy* 5F **163**
Alderley Dri. *Bred* 6E **129**
Alderley Edge. **4G 167**
Alderley Lodge. *Wilm* 4D **166**
Alderley Rd. *Sale* 1E **135**
Alderley Rd. *Stoc* 4H **127**
Alderley Rd. *Urm* 5C **104**
Alderley Rd. *Wilm* 5D **166**
Alderley St. *Ash L* 6H **87**
Alderley Ter. *Duk* 4H **99**
Alderman Foley Dri.
Roch 1C **26**
Alderman Sq.
M12 5A **96** (1H **11**)
Aldermary Rd. *M21* 4B **124**
Aldermaston Gro. *M9* 3D **68**
Alder Mdw. Clo. *Roch* 2C **26**
Aldermere Cres. *Urm* 5A **104**
Alderminster Av. *L Hul* 4C **62**
Aldermoor Clo. *M11* 5E **97**
Alder Rd. *Chea* 6H **137**
Alder Rd. *Fail* 6F **85**
Alder Rd. *Midd* 5C **54**
Alder Rd. *Roch* 3D **40**
Alder Root. **3H 71**
Alders Av. *M22* 6A **136**
Alders Ct. *Oldh* 3E **87**
Aldersgate Rd.
Chea H 2E **161**
Aldersgate Rd. *Stoc* 5B **140**
Aldersgreen Av.
H Lane 6D **154**
Aldershot Wlk. *M11* 4B **96**
Alderside Rd. *M9* 3F **83**
Aldersley Av. *M9* 4D **68**
Alderson St. *Oldh* 2C **72**
Alderson St. *Salf* 1G **93**
Alders Rd. *M22* 6A **136**
Alders Rd. *Dis* 6E **155**
Alder St. *Bolt* 4B **46**
Alder St. *Eccl* 1C **90**
Alder St. *Salf* 3F **93**
Aldersyde St. *Bolt* 4H **45**
Alderue Av. *M22* 5B **136**
Alderway. *Rams* 1E **13**
Alderwood Av. *Stoc* 2C **138**
Alderwood Fold. *Lees* 4B **74**
Alderwood Gro. *Rams* 1A **12**
Alderwood Wlk. M8 5B ***82***
(off Dalmain Clo.)
Aldfield Rd. *M23* 2F **135**
Aldford Clo. *M20* 6G **125**
Aldford Gro. *Brad F* 2B **48**
Aldford Pl. *Ald E* 4F **167**
Aldham Av. *M40* 1E **97**
Aldow Ind. Pk.
M12 5G **95** (1F **11**)
Aldred Clo. *M8* 5D **82**
Aldred St. *Bolt* 4F **45**
Aldred St. *Eccl* 4E **91**
Aldred St. *Fail* 4E **85**
Aldred St. *Salf* 3H **93** (4A **4**)
Aldridge Wlk. *M11* 5B **96**
Aldsworth Dri. *M40* 5G **83**
Aldsworth Dri. *Bolt* 3A **46**
Aldwick Av. *M20* 6G **125**
Aldwinians Clo. *Aud* 2E **113**
Aldworth Gro. *Sale* 6F **121**
Aldwych. *Roch* 2F **41**
Aldwych Av. *M14* 4F **109**
Aldwyn Clo. *Aud* 2E **113**
Aldwyn Cres. *Haz G* 3C **152**
Aldwyn Pk. Rd. *Aud* 5C **98**
Alexander Av. *Fail* 3G **85**
Alexander Briant Ct.
Farn 2E **63**
Alexander Dri. *Bury* 6E **51**
Alexander Dri. *Miln* 5E **29**
Alexander Dri. *Timp* 5A **134**
Alexander Gdns. *Salf* 1B **94**
Alexander Ho. *M16* 3G **107**
Alexander Rd. *Bolt* 4E **33**
Alexander St. *Roch* 3B **40**
Alexander St. *Salf* 3E **93**
Alexandra Av. *M14* 5D **108**
Alexandra Av. *Hyde* 5A **114**
Alexandra Av. *W'fld* 1E **67**
Alexandra Cen. Retail Pk.
Oldh 3D **72**
Alexandra Clo. *Stoc* 5E **139**
Alexandra Ct. Salf 5G ***93***
(off Rowland St.)
Alexandra Ct. *Urm* 6A **104**
Alexandra Cres. *Oldh* 1F **73**
Alexandra Dri. *M19* 2B **126**
Alexandra Gro. *Irlam* 1D **118**
Alexandra Ho. Eccl 4E ***91***
(off Liverpool Rd.)
Alexandra Ho. *Oldh* 1F **73**
Alexandra Ind. Est.
Dent 3G **113**
Alexandra M. *Oldh* 4E **73**
Alexandra Park. **5C 108**
Alexandra Park Vis. Cen.
4D 72
Alexandra Rd. *M16* 4C **108**
Alexandra Rd. *Ash L* 2H **99**
Alexandra Rd. *Dent* 3G **113**
Alexandra Rd. *Eccl* 4D **90**
Alexandra Rd. *Kear* 2A **64**
Alexandra Rd. *Oldh* 5E **73**
Alexandra Rd. *Rad* 1A **64**
Alexandra Rd. *Sale* 5C **122**
Alexandra Rd. *Stoc* 6E **127**
Alexandra Rd. *Wors* 4E **63**
Alexandra Rd. S. *M16* 4C **108**
Alexandra St. *Ash L* 1B **100**
Alexandra St. *Farn* 2F **63**
Alexandra St. *Heyw* 5G **39**
Alexandra St. *Hyde* 6A **114**
Alexandra St. *Oldh* 4E **73**
Alexandra St.
Salf 2B **94** (1D **4**)
Alexandra Ter. *M19* 6C **110**
Alexandra Ter. *Oldh* 4H **57**
Alexandra Ter. *Sale* 3A **122**
Alexandra, The. *M14* 1H **125**
Alford Av. *M20* 1E **125**
Alford Clo. *Bolt* 1H **47**
Alford Rd. *Stoc* 3D **126**
Alford St. *Oldh* 1H **85**
Alfred Av. *Wors* 4A **78**
Alfred James Clo. *M40* 2G **95**
(2G **7**)
Alfred St. *M9* 3F **83**
Alfred St. *Ash L* 1B **100**
Alfred St. *Bolt* 3D **46**
Alfred St. *Bury* 5E **37**
Alfred St. *Cad* 3C **118**
Alfred St. *Eccl* 2F **91**
Alfred St. *Eger* 1B **18**
Alfred St. *Fail* 3F **85**
Alfred St. *Farn* 1H **63**
Alfred St. *Hyde* 4A **114**
Alfred St. *Kear* 5F **47**
Alfred St. *L'boro* 3E **17**
Alfred St. *Oldh* 3A **72**
(in two parts)
Alfred St. *Rams* 4D **12**
Alfred St. *Shaw* 6E **43**
Alfred St. *Whitw* 3H **15**
Alfred St. *Wors* 6F **63**
Alfreton Av. *Dent* 1G **129**
Alfreton Rd. *Stoc* 5D **140**
Alfreton Wlk. M40 5A ***84***
(off Thorpebrook Rd.)
Alfriston Dri. *M23* 1G **135**
Alger M. *Ash L* 1B **100**
Algernon Rd. *Wors* 5E **63**
Algernon St. *Ash L* 4B **100**
Algernon St. *Eccl* 2F **91**
Algernon St. *Farn* 5F **47**
Algernon St. *Swin* 3D **78**
Alger St. *Ash L* 1B **100**
(in two parts)
Algreave Rd. *Stoc* 3C **138**
Alice Ingham Ct. *Roch* 2D **26**
Alice St. *Bolt* 2G **45**
Alice St. *Hyde* 2C **130**
Alice St. *Roch* 2B **28**
Alice St. *Sale* 5D **122**
Alice St. *Swin* 3H **79**
Alicia Ct. *Roch* 2G **27**
Alicia Dri. *Roch* 2G **27**
Alison Ct. *Stoc* 5D **126**
Alison Kelly Clo. *M9* 3H **83**
Alison St. *M14* 4D **108**
Alison St. *Shaw* 5E **43**
Alker Rd. *M40* 2H **95** (2H **7**)
Alkrington Clo. *Bury* 5E **51**
Alkrington Ct. *Midd* 4B **70**
Alkrington Garden
Village. **3A 70**
Alkrington Grn. *Midd* 3H **69**
Alkrington Hall Rd. N.
Midd 2H **69**
Alkrington Hall Rd. S.
Midd 3G **69**
Alkrington Pk. Rd.
Midd 2G **69**
Allamaiqbal Rd. *Oldh* 4G **73**
Allams St. *M11* 3A **96**
Allan Ct. *M21* 2G **123**
Allandale. *Alt* 1D **144**
Allandale Ct. *Salf* 2A **82**
Allandale Rd. *M19* 6B **110**
Allan Roberts Clo. *M9* 2F **83**
Allanson Rd. *M22* 2C **136**
Alldis Clo. *M12* 2A **110**
Alldis St. *Stoc* 6B **140**
Allen Av. *Hyde* 1D **130**
Allenby Rd. *Cad* 5D **118**
Allenby Rd. *Swin* 5C **78**
Allenby St. *Shaw* 6E **43**
Allenby Wlk. *M40* 6E **83**
Allen Clo. *Shaw* 1E **57**
Allendale Dri. *Bury* 4E **51**
Allendale Gdns. *Bolt* 3A **32**
Allendale Wlk.
Salf 3B **94** (3C **4**)
Allen Rd. *Urm* 5H **105**
Allen St. *Bury* 2A **36**
Allen St. *L Lev* 4A **48**
Allen St. *Oldh* 3B **72**
Allen St. *Rad* 4E **49**
(in two parts)
Allen St. *Roch* 5A **28**
Allerdean Wlk. *Stoc* 6A **126**
Allerford St. *M16* 3C **108**
Allerton Ct. Bolt 5A ***32***
(off School Hill)
Allerton Wlk.
M13 1F **109** (6D **10**)
Allesley Dri. *Salf* 6A **82**
Allgreave Clo. *Sale* 2D **134**
Alligin Clo. *Chad* 1G **71**
Allingham St. *M13* 3A **110**
Allington. *Roch* 5G **27**
Allington Dri. *Eccl* 1G **91**
Alliott Wlk. *M15* 2C **108**
Allison Gro. *Eccl* 4D **90**
Allison St. *M8* 6B **82**
Allonby Wlk. *Midd* 5E **53**
Allotment Rd. *Cad* 3B **118**
Alloway Wlk. *M40* 5A **84**
All Saint's Clo. *Rytn* 2B **56**
All Saints Ct. *Stret* 5B **106**
All Saints' Rd. *Stoc* 5F **127**
All Saints St. *M40* 6C **84**
All Saints St. *Bolt* 5B **32**
All Saints Ter. *Roch* 1B **28**
Allsopp St. *Bolt* 1B **46**
Allwood St. *Salf* 4A **94** (5B **4**)
Alma Ct. *M15* 3C **108**
Alma Ind. Est. *Roch* 2H **27**
Alma La. *Wilm* 3D **166**
Alma Park. **1C 126**
Alma Rd. *M19* 1C **126**
Alma Rd. *Haz G* 5G **153**
Alma Rd. *Sale* 1G **133**
Alma Rd. *Stoc* 4D **126**
Alma St. *Bolt* 3G **45**
Alma St. *Eccl* 4H **91**
Alma St. *Hyde* 4A **114**
Alma St. *Kear* 4B **64**
Alma St. *L Lev* 4B **48**
Alma St. *Rad* 2F **49**
Alma St. *Roch* 2H **27**
Alma St. *Stal* 3F **101**
Alminstone Clo.
M40 1F **97**
Almond Av. *Bury* 2G **37**
Almond Clo. *Fail* 5F **85**
Almond Clo. *L'boro* 3D **16**
Almond Clo. *Salf* 2G **93**
Almond Clo. *Stoc* 3E **139**
Almond Ct. *Duk* 4A **100**
Almond Dri. *Sale* 3H **121**
Almond Gro. *Bolt* 2B **32**
Almond Rd. *Oldh* 6H **57**
Almond St. *M40* 1F **95**
Almond St. *Bolt* 1B **32**
Almond St. *Farn* 1E **63**
Almond Tree Rd.
Chea H 4C **150**

Almond Wlk. *Part* 6B **118**
Almond Way. *Hyde* 5E **115**
Alms Hill Rd. *M8* 5C **82**
Almshouses. *Sale* 5E **123**
Alness Rd. *M16* 4C **108**
Alnwick Dri. *Bury* 2E **51**
Alnwick Rd. *M9* 4F **69**
Alperton Wlk. *M40* 1F **97**
Alphabet Zoo. 4H **99**
Alpha Ct. *Aud* 4C **112**
Alpha Ct. Ind. Est.
  Dent 4C **112**
Alphagate Dri. *Dent* 4C **112**
Alpha Pl. *M15* 6C **94** (3F **9**)
Alpha Rd. *Stret* 6C **106**
Alpha St. *Open* 6G **97**
Alpha St. *Rad* 3F **49**
Alpha St. *Salf* 2F **93**
Alpha St. W. *Salf* 2E **93**
Alphin Clo. *G'fld* 4F **61**
Alphin Clo. *Moss* 6G **75**
Alphingate Clo. *Stal* 1H **101**
Alphin Sq. *Moss* 2F **89**
Alphonsus St. *M16* 3A **108**
Alpine Dri. *Miln* 4G **29**
Alpine Dri. *Rytn* 4A **56**
Alpine Dri. *Ward* 3A **16**
Alpine Rd. *Stoc* 1A **140**
  (in two parts)
Alpine St. *M11* 3D **96**
Alpine Ter. *Farn* 1G **63**
Alpington Wlk. *M40* 1C **84**
Alport Av. *M16* 5A **108**
Alport Gro. Glos 5G **117**
  (off Brailsford M)
Alport Lea. Glos 5G **117**
  (off Brailsford M.)
Alport Way. Glos 5G **117**
  (off Melandra Castle Rd.)
Alresford Rd. *Midd* 4H **69**
Alresford Rd. *Salf* 6B **80**
Alric Wlk. *M22* 5C **148**
Alsager Clo. *M21* 3H **123**
Alsham Wlk. *M8* 5C **82**
Alsop Av. *Salf* 4F **81**
Alstead Av. *Hale* 2A **146**
Alston Av. *Sale* 6H **121**
Alston Av. *Shaw* 5F **43**
Alston Av. *Stret* 4B **106**
Alston Clo. *Haz G* 4A **152**
Alstone Dri. *Alt* 5C **132**
Alstone Rd. *Stoc* 3E **127**
Alston Gdns. *M19* 4B **126**
Alston Rd. *M18* 2G **111**
Alston St. *Bolt* 4A **46**
Alston St. *Bury* 1A **36**
Alston Wlk. *Midd* 5E **53**
Alt. 6H **73**
Altair Av. *M22* 4B **148**
Altair Pl. *Salf* 1A **94**
Altcar Gro. *Stoc* 5G **111**
Altcar Wlk. *M22* 3A **148**
  (in two parts)
Alt Fold Dri. *Oldh* 6H **73**
Alt Gro. *Ash L* 5F **87**
Altham Clo. *Bury* 6B **36**
Altham Wlk. M40 . . . . . .5A **84**
  (off Craiglands Av.)
Alt Hill. 3G **87**
Alt Hill La. *Ash L* 3F **87**
Alt Hill Rd. *Ash L* 2G **87**
Althorn Wlk. *M23* 6G **135**
Althorpe Wlk. *M40* 1F **97**
Alt La. *Oldh* 1G **87**
Alton Av. *Urm* 4H **103**
Alton Clo. *Ash L* 4G **87**
Alton Clo. *Bury* 2E **51**
Alton Rd. *Wilm* 1C **166**
Alton Sq. *Open* 6G **97**
Alton St. *Oldh* 6D **72**
Alton Towers. *M16* 6B **108**
Altrincham. 1F **145**

Altrincham Crematorium.
  Alt 3A **132**
Altrincham Football Club.
  . . . . .1H **145**
Altrincham Ice Rink. . . .5F **133**
Altrincham Leisure Cen.
  . . . . .1G **145**
Altrincham Retail Pk.
  B'hth 4E **133**
Altrincham Rd.
  M22 & Gat 4A **136**
  (in two parts)
Altrincham Rd. *M23* 4D **134**
Altrincham Rd. *Styal* 3B **158**
Altrincham Rd. *Wilm* 5G **157**
Altrincham St.
  M1 . . . . .5F **95** (2C **10**)
  (in two parts)
Altrincham Tourist Info. Cen.
  . . . . .1F **145**
Alt Rd. *Ash L* 5F **87**
Alt Wlk. *W'fld* 5G **51**
Alum Cres. *Bury* 4E **51**
Alvanley Clo. *Sale* 2B **134**
Alvanley Cres. *Stoc* 5E **139**
Alvanley Ind. Est.
  Bred 5F **129**
Alvanley St. *Bred* 5G **129**
Alvan Sq. *M11* 6G **97**
Alva Rd. *Oldh* 5H **57**
Alvaston Av. *Stoc* 1D **138**
Alvaston Rd. *M18* 3G **111**
Alveley Av. *M20* 4G **125**
Alverstone Rd. *M20* 5G **125**
Alveston Dri. *Wilm* 1F **167**
Alvington Gro. *Haz G* 4A **152**
Alvon Ct. *Hyde* 5E **115**
Alwin Rd. *Shaw* 5E **43**
Alwinton Av. *Stoc* 6A **126**
Alworth Rd. *M9* 4F **69**
Alwyn Dri. *M13* 3A **110**
Ambassador Pl. *Alt* 6G **133**
Amber Gdns. *Duk* 5H **99**
Amberhill Way. *Wors* 6B **76**
  (in two parts)
Amberley Clo. *Bolt* 2D **44**
Amberley Dri. *M23* 1G **147**
Amberley Dri. *Haleb* 5B **146**
Amberley Dri. *Irlam* 6E **102**
Amberley Rd. *Sale* 4G **121**
Amberley Wlk. *Chad* 2A **72**
Amber St. *M4* 3E **95** (3B **6**)
Amberwood. *Chad* 1E **71**
Amberwood Dri. *M23* 5D **134**
Amblecote Dri. E.
  L Hul 3C **62**
Amblecote Dri. W.
  L Hul 3C **62**
Ambleside. *Stal* 3G **101**
Ambleside Av. *Ash L* 1F **99**
Ambleside Av. *Timp* 6C **133**
Ambleside Clo. *Bolt* 1H **33**
Ambleside Clo. *Midd* 6G **53**
Ambleside Clo. *Chea* 6G **137**
Ambleside Ct. *Stal* 2E **101**
Ambleside Rd. *Stoc* 3H **127**
Ambleside Rd. *Urm* 6A **104**
Ambleside Wlk. *M9* 1A **84**
Amblethorn Dri. *Bolt* 6B **18**
Ambrose Ct. *M22* 2B **136**
  (off Kenworthy La.)
Ambrose Cres. *Dig* 4B **60**
Ambrose Dri. *M20* 5B **124**
Ambrose Gdns. *M20* 5C **124**
Ambrose St. *M12* 6C **96**
Ambrose St. *Hyde* 2C **130**
Ambrose St. *Roch* 6H **27**
Ambush St. *M11* 6H **97**
Amelia St. *Hyde* 5C **114**
Amelia St. W. *Dent* 3F **113**
Amersham Clo. *Urm* 2D **104**
Amersham Pl. *M19* 3C **126**

Amersham St. *Salf* 4F **93**
Amesbury Gro. *Stoc* 4H **127**
Amesbury Rd. *M9* 5G **69**
Amherst Rd.
  M20 & M14 . . . . . .2G **125**
Amlwch Av. *Stoc* 5D **140**
Ammon's Way. *Del* 2H **59**
Ammon Wrigley Clo.
  Oldh 2D **72**
Amory St.
  M12 . . . . . . .5G **95** (2E **11**)
Amos Av. *M40* 1E **97**
Amos St. *M9* 4H **83**
Amos St. *Salf* 3E **93**
Ampleforth Gdns. *Rad* . . .2E **49**
Ampney Clo. *Eccl* 4D **90**
Amport Wlk. *M40* 1C **84**
Amwell St. *M8* 4D **82**
Amy St. *Midd* 6B **54**
Amy St. *Roch* 2D **26**
Anaconda Dri.
  Salf 2C **94** (2E **5**)
Ancaster Wlk. *M40* 1C **84**
Anchorage Quay. *Salf* 5G **93**
Anchorage Rd. *Urm* 6A **106**
Anchorage Wlk. *M18* 1E **111**
Anchor Clo. *M19* 6E **111**
Anchor Ct. *M8* 2B **82**
Anchor Ct. *Wilm* 1E **167**
Anchor La.
  Farn & M38 . . . . .1B **62**
Anchorside Clo. *M21* 2H **123**
Ancroft St. *Oldh* 1D **72**
Ancoats. 3G **95** (5E **7**)
Ancoats Gro.
  M4 . . . . .4H **95** (6G **7**)
Ancoats Gro. N.
  M4 . . . . .4H **95** (6G **7**)
Ancoats St. *Lees* 3A **74**
Ancroft Gdns. *Bolt* 4G **45**
Ancroft St.
  M15 . . . . . .1C **108** (6F **9**)
Anderton Clo. *Bury* 4F **35**
Anderton Gro. *Ash L* 6A **88**
Anderton Way. *Hand* 4H **159**
Andoc Av. *Eccl* 4A **92**
Andover Av. *Midd* 4B **70**
Andover St. *Eccl* 4E **91**
Andover Wlk. *M8* 2C **82**
Andre St. *M11* 3E **97**
Andrew Clo. *G'mnt* 2H **21**
Andrew Clo. *Rad* 6A **50**
Andrew Ct. *M20* 3F **125**
Andrew Gro. *Duk* 5B **100**
Andrew La. *Bolt* 5D **18**
Andrew La. *H Lane* 4C **154**
Andrew Rd. *M9* 2F **83**
Andrews Av. *Urm* 4A **104**
Andrew's Brow. *M40* 1F **97**
Andrews Bldgs. Ash L . . .2A **100**
  (off Glebe St.)
Andrews Bldgs. Moss 2G **89**
  (off Bk. Micklehurst Rd.)
Andrews Clo. *Dent* 6H **113**
Andrew St. *Ash L* 6H **87**
Andrew St. *Bury* 3E **37**
Andrew St. *Chad* 1H **71**
Andrew St. *Comp* 1E **143**
Andrew St. *Droy* 1C **98**
Andrew St. *Fail* 3E **85**
Andrew St. *Hyde* 4D **114**
Andrew St. *Midd* 2C **70**
Andrew St. *Moss* 3E **89**
Andrew St. *Stoc* 1F **139**
Andy Nicholson Wlk.
  M9 . . . . .3H **83**
Anerley Rd. *M20* 5F **125**
Anfield Clo. *Bury* 4F **51**
Anfield M. *Chea H* 2B **150**
Anfield Rd. *M40* 2D **84**
Anfield Rd. *Bolt* 4A **46**
Anfield Rd. *Chea H* 3B **150**

Anfield Rd. *Sale* 4C **122**
Angela Av. *Rytn* 5C **56**
Angela St. *M15* 6B **94** (4D **8**)
Angel Clo. *Duk* 6H **99**
Angelico Ri. *Oldh* 4H **57**
Angelo St. *Rams* 3H **31**
  (in two parts)
Angel St. *M4* 2E **95** (2B **6**)
Angel St. *Dent* 3G **113**
Angel St. *Haz G* 2D **152**
Angel Trad. Est. *M4* 2B **6**
Angier Gro. *Dent* 4F **113**
Anglers Rest. *Cad* 4C **118**
Anglesea Av. *Stoc* 5H **139**
Anglesey Clo. *Ash L* 5E **87**
Anglesey Dri. *Poy* 1E **163**
Anglesey Gro. *Chea* 5B **138**
Anglesey Rd. *Ash L* 5D **86**
Anglesey Water. *Poy* 1E **163**
Angleside Av. *M19* 5A **126**
Angle St. *Bolt* 4D **32**
Anglia Gro. *Bolt* 3G **45**
Angora Dri. *Salf* . . .2B **94** (2C **4**)
Angouleme Retail Pk.
  Bury 3D **36**
Angouleme Way. *Bury* . . .3C **36**
Angus Av. *Heyw* 4C **38**
Aniline St. *M11* 4D **96**
Animal World. 2E **31**
Anita St. *M4* 3F **95** (3D **6**)
Annable Rd. *M18* 1G **111**
Annable Rd. *Bred* 6D **128**
Annable Rd. *Droy* 4B **98**
Annable Rd. *Irlam* 1D **118**
Annald Sq. *Droy* 5A **98**
Annan St. *Dent* 3F **113**
Annecy Clo. *Bury* 1H **35**
Anne Line Clo. *Roch* 6A **28**
  (off Wellfield St.)
Anne Nuttall Rd.
  M15 . . . . . . .6B **94** (4D **8**)
Annersley Av. *Shaw* 6E **43**
Annersley Ct. *Eccl* 3G **91**
Annesley Gdns. *M18* 1F **111**
Annesley Rd. *M40* 2E **85**
Anne St. *Duk* 5B **100**
Anne Darby Ct. *M9* 4F **83**
Annie St. *Rams* 5C **12**
Annie St. *Salf* 3E **93**
Annis Clo. *Ald E* 4H **167**
Annisdale Clo. *Eccl* 3D **90**
Annisfield Av. *G'fld* 4F **61**
Annis Rd. *Ald E* 4H **167**
Annis Rd. *Bolt* 3F **45**
Annis St. *M9* 3G **83**
Ann Sq. *Oldh* 1H **73**
Ann St. *Ash L* 5F **99**
Ann St. *Dent* 4E **113**
Ann St. *Heyw* 2F **39**
Ann St. *Hyde* 4A **114**
Ann St. *Kear* 2G **63**
Ann St. *Roch* 5H **27**
  (in two parts)
Ann St. *Stoc* 5G **127**
Anscombe Clo.
  M40 . . . . .2H **95** (2H **7**)
Anscombe Wlk.
  M40 . . . . .2H **95** (2G **7**)
Ansdell Av. *M21* 1H **123**
Ansdell Dri. *Droy* 3G **97**
Ansdell Rd. *Roch* 1H **41**
Ansdell Rd. *Stoc* 6A **112**
Ansdell St. *M8* 4C **82**
Ansell Clo. *M18* 1F **111**
Anselms Ct. *Oldh* 5A **72**
Ansford Wlk. *M9* 5E **83**
  (off Hendham Va.)
Ansleigh Av. *M8* 2C **82**
Ansley Gro. *Stoc* 6D **126**
Anslow Clo. *M40* 6F **83**
Anson Av. *Swin* 5E **79**
Anson Clo. *Bram* 2H **161**

Anson Mus. 3A 164
Anson Rd. *M14* 3H **109**
Anson Rd. *Dent* 5A 112
Anson Rd. *Poy* 3H 163
Anson Rd. *Swin* 5E 79
Anson Rd. *Wilm* 6A 160
Anson St. *Bolt* 2B 32
Anson St. *Eccl* 2D 90
Anson Vw. *M14* 4H 109
Answell Av. *M8* 1C 42
Antares Av. *Salf* . .2B 94 (1C 4)
Anthistle Ct. *Salf* 4D 92
Anthony Clo. *M12* 6A 96
Anthony St. *Bolt* 4B 46
Anthony St. *Moss* 2D 88
Antilles Clo. *M12* 3C 110
Anton Wlk. *M9* 4F 83
Antrim Clo. *M19* 1H 137
Anvil Way. *Oldh* 2C 72
Apethorn La. *Hyde* 2B 130
Apfel La. *Chad* 2H 71
Apollo Av. *Bury* 4D 50
Apollo Theatre.
. . . . .1G 109 (5F 11)
Apollo Wlk. *M12* 1C 110
Apperley Grange. *Eccl* . .1G 91
Appian Way.
Salf & M8 . . . . . .5A 82
Appleby Av. *M12* 4D 110
Appleby Av. *Hyde* 2A 114
Appleby Av. *Timp* 6C 134
Appleby Clo. *Bury* 3F 35
Appleby Clo. *Stoc* 6F 139
Appleby Gdns. *Bolt* 4C 32
Appleby Gdns. *Bury* 4D 50
Appleby Lodge. *M14* 5H 109
Appleby Rd. *Gat* 1F 149
Appleby Wlk. *Rytn* 3C 56
Apple Clo. *Oldh* 6G 73
Applecross Wlk. *Open* . . .5E 97
Appledore Dri. *M23* 4D 134
Appledore Dri. *Bolt* 2H 33
Appledore Wlk. *Chad* . . .3H 71
Appleford Av. *M23* 1G 147
Appleford Dri. *M9* 5D 82
Apple St. *Hyde* 2G 131
Appleton Ct. *Sale* 5B 122
Appleton Gro. *Sale* 1G 133
Appleton Rd. *Hale* 1C 146
Appleton Rd. *Stoc* 3F 127
Appleton Wlk. *Wilm* 6A 160
Apple Tree Ct. *Salf* 3G 93
Apple Tree Wlk. *Sale* 4E 121
Apple Way. *Midd* 3B 70
Applewood. *Chad* 2E 71
Apprentice Ct. *M9* 3G 83
Apprentice La. *Wilm* 4D 158
(in two parts)
April Clo. *Oldh* 5G 73
Apsley Clo. *Bow* 4D 144
Apsley Gro.
M12 . . . . . .1G 109 (5F 11)
Apsley Gro. *Bow* 4D 144
Apsley Pl. *Ash L* 3G 99
Apsley Rd. *Dent* 3F 113
Apsley Side. *Moss* 3E 89
Apsley St. *Stoc* 2H 139
Aquarius La. *Salf* 1A 94
Aquarius St. *M15* 2E 109
Aqueduct Rd. *Bolt* 2E 47
Aragon Dri. *Heyw* 3E 39
Aragon Way. *Marp* 5C 142
Arbor Av. *M19* 2B 126
Arbor Dri. *M19* 2B 126
Arbor Gro. *Droy* 2A 98
Arbory Av. *M40* 3B 84
Arbour Clo. *Bury* 5E 23
Arbour Clo. *Salf* 2G 93
Arbour St. *Marp* 6C 142
Arbour Rd. *Oldh* 5A 74
Arbroath St. *M11* 4F 97

Arbury Av. *Roch* 6G 27
Arbury Av. *Stoc* 4B 138
Arcades, The. *Ash L* 2H 99
Arcade, The. *Stal* 5D 100
Arcade, The. *Stoc* 4C 128
Arcadia Av. *Sale* 2A 134
Arcadia Sports Cen. . .6C 110
Archer Av. *Bolt* 5E 33
Archer Gro. *Bolt* 5E 33
Archer Pk. *Midd* 1G 69
Archer Pl. *Urm* 4H 105
Archer St. *M11* 3C 96
Archer St. *Moss* 1E 89
Archer St. *Stoc* 6C 140
Archer St. *Wors* 4A 76
Archie St. *Salf* 6G 93
Arch St. *Bolt* 4C 32
Arclid Clo. *Wilm* 6A 160
Arcon Clo. *Roch* 5E 29
Arcon Dri. *M16* 4C 108
Arcon Pl. *Alt* 5C 132
Ardale Av. *M40* 1C 84
Ardcombe Av. *M9* 4E 69
Ardeen Wlk.
M13 . . . . . . .1G 109 (5E 11)
Arden Av. *Midd* 4B 70
Arden Clo. *Ash L* 5B 88
Arden Clo. *Bury* 5C 36
Arden Ct. *M21* 2H 123
Arden Ct. *Bram* 4F 151
Ardenfield. *Dent* 2G 129
Ardenfield Dri. *M22* 2C 148
Arden Gro. *M40* 2C 84
Arden Ho. *Rytn* 3C 56
Arden Lodge Rd. *M23* . . .4E 135
Arden Park. 6D 128
Arden Rd. *Bred* 2E 129
Ardens Clo. *Swin* 1D 78
Arden St. *Chad* 6G 71
Ardent Way. *P'wich* 2F 81
Arden Wlk. *Sale* 4E 121
Arderne Pl. *Ald E* 5G 167
Arderne Rd. *Timp* 3A 134
Ardern Fld. Ct. *Stoc* 4H 139
Ardern Gro. *Stoc* 3H 139
Ardern Rd. *M8* 1B 82
Ardern Wlk. *Stoc* 2G 139
Ardingly Wlk. *M23* 3D 134
Ardmore Wlk. *M22* 3C 148
Ardwick. 6H 95 (4E 11)
Ardwick Grn. N.
M12 . . . . . . .6G 95 (3E 11)
Ardwick Grn. S.
M13 . . . . . . .6G 95 (3E 11)
Ardwick Sports Hall.
. . . . .2A 110 (6H 11)
Argo St. *Bolt* 3H 45
Argosy Dri. *Eccl* 6B 90
Argosy Dri. *Timp* 6F 147
Argus St. *Oldh* 1A 86
Argyle Av. *M14* 3A 110
Argyle Av. *W'fld* 1E 67
Argyle Av. *Wors* 4E 63
Argyle Cres. *Heyw* 4D 38
Argyle Pde. *Heyw* 4C 38
Argyle St. *M18* 1F 111
Argyle St. *Bury* 1D 36
Argyle St. *Droy* 4A 98
Argyle St. *Haz G* 3E 153
Argyle St. *Heyw* 4B 38
Argyle St. *Moss* 2E 89
Argyle St. *Oldh* 1F 73
Argyle St. *Roch* 1G 41
Argyle St. *Swin* 4E 79
Argyll Av. *Stret* 5B 106
Argyll Clo. *Fail* 4H 85
Argyll Pk. Rd. *Fail* 4H 85
Argyll Rd. *Chad* 6F 71
Argyll Rd. *Chea* 6B 138
Argyll St. *Ash L* 2C 100
Arkendale Clo. *Fail* 4A 86

Arkholme. *Wors* 3C 76
Arkholme Wlk. *M40* 4B 84
Arkle Av. *Hand* 3A 160
Arkle Dri. *Chad* 1F 71
Arkley Wlk.
M13 . . . . . .1F 109 (5D 10)
Ark St. *M19* 5C 110
Arkwright Clo. *Bolt* 4G 31
Arkwright Dri. *Marp* 5E 143
Arkwright Rd. *Marp* 4E 143
Arkwright St. *Oldh* 3A 72
Arkwright Way.
M4 . . . . . . .3E **95** (4A **6**)
(off Arndale Shop. Cen.)
Arkwright Way. *Roch* 3G 41
Arlen Ct. *Bolt* 2D 46
Arlen Rd. *Bolt* 2D 46
Arlen Way. *Heyw* 3D 38
Arley Av. *M20* 4D 124
Arley Av. *Bury* 5E 23
Arley Clo. *Duk* 1B 114
Arley Clo. *W Timp* 3F 133
Arley Dri. *Shaw* 5G 43
Arley Dri. *Sale* 1A 134
Arley Gro. *Stoc* 1F 151
Arley Ho. *M23* 1G 147
Arley Ho. *Salf* 4H 81
Arleymere Clo.
Chea 2B 150
Arley Moss Wlk.
M13 . . . . . . .6F **95** (4D **10**)
Arley St. *Hyde* 4A 114
Arley St. *Rad* 6H 49
Arley Way. *Dent* 6G 113
Arlies Clo. *Stal* 1E 101
Arlies La. *Stal* 6D 88
Arlies St. *Ash L* 1B 100
Arlington Av. *Dent* 5G 113
Arlington Av. *P'wich* 1G 81
Arlington Av. *Swin* 5D 78
Arlington Clo. *Bury* 1C 22
Arlington Clo. *Rytn* 5C 56
Arlington Cres. *Wilm* 4D 166
Arlington Dri. *Poy* 4D 162
Arlington Dri. *Stoc* 2A 152
Arlington Rd. *Chea* 1G 149
Arlington Rd. *Stret* 5B 106
Arlington St. *M8* 3B 82
Arlington St. *Ash L* 2A 100
Arlington St. *Bolt* 4B 46
Arlington St. *Salf* . .3B 94 (3D 4)
Arlington Way. *Wilm* 4B 166
Arliss Av. *M19* 1C 126
Armadale Av. *M9* 5A 70
Armadale Clo. *Stoc* 6H 139
Armadale Ct. *Bolt* 2C 44
Armadale Rd. *Bolt* 1C 44
Armadale Rd. *Duk* 5A 100
Armdale Ri. *Oldh* 6A 58
Armentieres Sq. *Stal* 4E 101
Armentieres Way. Stal . .4E **101**
(off Melbourne St.)
Armitage Cen. 6A 110
Armitage Clo. *Hyde* 1C 130
Armitage Clo. *Midd* 2F 69
Armitage Clo. *Oldh* 6A 72
Armitage Gro. *L Hul* 5B 62
Armitage Ho. *Salf* 2C 92
Armitage Owen Wlk.
M40 . . . . .4A 84
Armitage Rd. *Alt* 2F 145
Armitage St. *Eccl* 4E 91
Armit Rd. *G'fld* 5G 75
Armour Pl. *M9* 1E 83
Armoury St. *Stoc* 3G 139
Arm Rd. *L'boro* 4C 16
Armstrong Hurst Clo.
Roch 6H 15
Arncliffe Clo. *Farn* 6F 47
Arncliffe Dri. *M23* 2G 147
Arncliffe Ri. *Oldh* 3B 58

Arncot Rd. *Rams* 6D 18
Arncott Clo. *Rytn* 3E 57
Arndale Shop. Cen.
M4 . . . . . .3E **95** (4A **6**)
Arndale Shop. Cen.
Stret 6C 106
Arne Clo. *Stoc* 6G 141
Arnesby Av. *Sale* 4E 123
Arnesby Gro. *Bolt* 5D 32
Arne St. *Chad* 4G 71
Arnfield Dri. *Wors* 5D 76
Arnfield Rd. *M20* 3F 125
Arnfield Rd. *Stoc* 6F 139
Arnold Av. *Heyw* 6G 39
Arnold Av. *Hyde* 2D 130
Arnold Clo. *Duk* 6E 101
Arnold Ct. *M16* 6C 108
Arnold Dri. *Droy* 4A 98
Arnold Dri. *Midd* 4C 54
Arnold Rd. *M16* 6C 108
Arnold Rd. *Eger* 3D 18
Arnold Rd. *Hyde* 2D 130
Arnold St. *Ash L* 1A 100
Arnold St. *Bolt* 3G 31
Arnold St. *Oldh* 1E 73
Arnold St. *Stoc* 4G 139
Arnolds Yd. *Alt* 6F 133
Arnold Wlk. *Dent* 2G 129
Arnott Cres.
M15 . . . . . .2D 108 (6H **9**)
Arnside Av. *Chad* 3G 71
Arnside Av. *Haz G* 3C 152
Arnside Av. *Stoc* 3F 127
Arnside Clo. *Gat* 1F 149
Arnside Clo. *H Lane* 5C 154
Arnside Clo. *Shaw* 6H 43
Arnside Dri. *Hyde* 3A 114
Arnside Dri. *Roch* 6A 26
Arnside Gro. *Bolt* 5G 33
Arnside Gro. *Sale* 3B 122
Arnside St. *M14* 4F 109
Arosa Ct. *M20* 2G 125
Arran Av. *Oldh* 6D 72
Arran Av. *Sale* 6C 122
Arran Av. *Stret* 5A 106
Arran Clo. *Bolt* 1C 44
Arran Ct. *Chea H* 3C 150
Arrandale Ct. *Urm* 4F 105
Arran Gdns. *Urm* 2E 105
(in three parts)
Arran Gro. *Rad* 2E 49
Arran Rd. *Duk* 6A 100
Arran St. *M40* 3H 83
Arran St. *Salf* 5H 81
Arran Wlk. *Heyw* 4C 38
Arras Gro. *Dent* 4H 111
Arreton Sq. *M14* 4H 109
Arrivals Way. *Man A* 6H 147
Arrowfield Rd. *M21* 2B 124
Arrowhill Rd. *Rad* 5F 35
Arrowscroft Way. *Holl* . . .2F 117
Arrowsmith Wlk. *M11* . . .4B **96**
(off Redfield Clo.)
Arrow St. *Rams* 5A 32
Arrow St. *Salf* 6H 81
Arrow Trad. Est. *Aud* 2D 112
Arthington St. *Roch* 3B 28
Arthog Dri. *Hale* 5H 145
Arthog Rd. *M20* 6G 125
Arthog Rd. *Hale* 5H 145
Arthur Av. *Wors* 4E 63
Arthur La. *Bolt & A'wth* . .2A 34
Arthur Millwood Ct.
Salf 4B **94** (5D **4**)
Arthur Pits. *Roch* 4B 26
Arthur Rd. *M16* 4A 108
Arthur St. *Bury* 3A 36
Arthur St. *Eccl* 4E 91
Arthur St. *Farn* 1F 63
Arthur St. *Heyw* 3F 39
Arthur St. *Hyde* 6A 114

Arthur St.—Ashover Av.

Arthur St. *L Lev* 4B **48**
Arthur St. *P'wich* 5D **66**
Arthur St. *Roch* 3F **27**
Arthur St. *Shaw* 6E **43**
Arthur St. *Stoc* 2G **127** (Houldsworth St.)
Arthur St. *Stoc* 2G **127** (Margaret St.)
Arthur St. *Swin* 4D **78** (in two parts)
Arthur St. *Wors* 1H **77** (Old Clough La.)
Arthur St. *Wors* 2G **77** (Walkden Rd.)
Arthur Ter. *Stoc* 2G **127**
Artillery Pl. *M22* 1D **148**
Artillery St. *M3* 5C **94** (1F **9**)
Artillery St. *Bolt* 2B **46**
Arundale Av. *M16* 6C **108**
Arundale Clo. *Mot* 4B **116**
*Arundale Ct. M16 6C **108** (off Arundale Av.)*
Arundale Gro. *Mot* 4B **116**
Arundel Av. *Haz G* 5D **152**
Arundel Av. *Roch* 1E **41**
Arundel Av. *Urm* 6G **103**
Arundel Av. *W'fld* 2F **67**
Arundel Clo. *Bury* 5C **22**
Arundel Clo. *Carr* 5H **89**
Arundel Clo. *Hale* 4C **146**
Arundel Ct. *M9* 4C **68**
Arundel Gro. *Stoc* 1B **152**
Arundel Rd. *Chea H* 1C **160**
Arundel St. *M15* 6B **94** (3D **8**)
Arundel St. *Ash L* 3C **100**
Arundel St. *Bolt* 6C **18**
Arundel St. *Moss* 2D **88**
Arundel St. *Oldh* 2G **73**
Arundel St. *Roch* 1E **41**
Arundel St. *Swin* 2C **78**
Arundel Wlk. *Chad* 3G **71**
Asbury Ct. *Eccl* 2E **91**
Asby Clo. *Midd* 5F **53**
Ascension Rd. *Salf* 1B **94**
Ascot Av. *Sale* 6E **121**
Ascot Av. *Stret* 4F **107**
Ascot Clo. *Chad* 2A **72**
Ascot Clo. *Roch* 3A **26**
Ascot Ct. *Sale* 6F **121**
Ascot Dri. *Haz G* 3G **153**
Ascot Dri. *Urm* 5G **103**
Ascot Ho. *Sale* 6E **121**
Ascot Mdw. *Bury* 5C **36**
Ascot M. *Salf* 5H **81**
Ascot Pde. *M19* 3B **126**
Ascot Rd. *M40* 1D **96**
Ascot Rd. *L Lev* 4H **47**
Ascot Wlk. *Salf* 6E **81**
Ascroft Ct. *Oldh* 3D **72**
Ascroft St. *Oldh* 3D **72**
Asgard Dri. *Salf* 5A **94** (2B **8**)
Asgard Gro. *Salf* 5A **94** (2B **8**)
Ash Av. *Alt* 6C **132**
Ash Av. *Cad* 4B **118**
Ash Av. *Chea* 6A **138**
Ashawe Clo. *L Hul* 6A **62**
Ashawe Gro. *L Hul* 6A **62**
Ashawe Ter. *L Hul* 6A **62**
Ashbank Av. *Bolt* 1C **44**
Ashbee St. *Bolt* 2A **32**
Ashberry Clo. *Wilm* 1G **167**
Ashborne Dri. *Bury* 1D **22**
Ashbourne Av. *Bolt* 1D **46**
Ashbourne Av. *Chea* 5B **138**
Ashbourne Av. *Midd* 4C **54**
Ashbourne Av. *Urm* 5A **104**
Ashbourne Clo. *Ward* 3B **16**
Ashbourne Cres. *Sale* 1D **134**
Ashbourne Dri. *Ash L* 5B **88**
Ashbourne Dri. *H Lane* 1C **164**
Ashbourne Gro. *Salf* 4A **82**
Ashbourne Gro. *W'fld* 6B **50**
Ashbourne Gro. *Wors* 3G **77**
Ashbourne Rd. *Dent* 5E **113**
Ashbourne Rd. *Eccl* 4G **91**
Ashbourne Rd. *Haz G* 5F **153**
Ashbourne Rd. *Salf* 6A **80**
Ashbourne Rd. *Stret* 3A **106**
Ashbourne Sq. *Oldh* 4C **72**
Ashbourne St. *Roch* 2A **26**
Ashbridge. *Traf P* 1B **106** (in two parts)
Ashbridge Rd. *Fail* 5H **85**
Ashbrook Av. *Dent* 4B **112**
Ashbrook Clo. *Dent* 4B **112**
Ashbrook Clo. *H Grn* 4F **149**
Ashbrook Clo. *W'fld* 1F **67**
Ashbrook Cres. *Roch* 6A **16**
Ashbrook Farm Clo. *Stoc* 5H **111**
Ashbrook Hey. 5A 16
Ashbrook Hey La. *Roch* 5A **16**
Ashbrook La. *Stoc* 5H **111**
Ashbrook Rd. *S'head* 4B **74**
Ashbrook St. *Open* 6A **98**
Ashburn Av. *M19* 4B **126**
*Ashburne Ho. M14 3H **109** (off Conyngham Rd.)*
Ashburner St. *Bolt* 1A **46** (in two parts)
*Ashburn Flats. Heyw 3E **39** (off School St.)*
Ashburn Gro. *Stoc* 6E **127**
Ashburn Rd. *Stoc* 6E **127**
Ashburton Clo. *Hyde* 5A **116**
Ashburton Rd. *Stoc* 1G **151**
Ashburton Rd. W. *Urm & Traf P* 6F **91**
Ashbury Clo. *Bolt* 2A **46**
Ashbury Pl. *M40* 1A **96**
Ashby Av. *M19* 5A **126**
Ashby Clo. *Farn* 5E **47**
Ashby Gro. *W'fld* 2F **67**
Ash Clo. *Ash L* 6H **87**
Ash Clo. *Mot* 3C **116**
Ash Clo. *Roch* 5A **16**
Ash Clo. *Stoc* 6C **140**
Ashcombe Dri. *Bolt* 1A **48**
Ashcombe Dri. *Rad* 2D **48**
*Ashcombe Wlk. M11 4B **96** (off Aldershot Wlk.)*
Ashcott Av. *M22* 1B **148**
Ashcott Clo. *Los* 2C **44**
Ash Ct. *Stoc* 6D **126**
Ash Ct. *Woodl* 4G **129**
Ashcroft. *Roch* 5B **16**
Ashcroft Av. *Salf* 1E **93**
Ashcroft Clo. *Wilm* 4C **166**
Ashcroft St. *Chad* 4G **71**
Ashdale Av. *Bolt* 2C **44**
Ashdale Clo. *Stoc* 4H **127**
Ashdale Cres. *Droy* 4H **97**
Ashdale Dri. *M20* 4H **125**
Ashdale Dri. *H Grn* 3F **149**
Ashdene. *Ash L* 3B **100**
Ashdene. *Roch* 6D **14**
Ashdene Clo. *Chad* 6A **56**
Ashdene Clo. *S'head* 2B **74**
Ashdene Cres. *Bolt* 6H **19**
Ashdene Ri. *Oldh* 3H **57**
Ashdene Rd. *M20* 3H **125**
Ashdene Rd. *Stoc* 1H **137**
Ashdene Rd. *Wilm* 4C **166**
Ashdown Av. *M9* 5F **69**
Ashdown Av. *Woodl* 4A **130**
Ashdown Dri. *Bolt* 2E **33**
Ashdown Dri. *Swin* 5G **79**
Ashdown Dri. *Wors* 4C **76**
Ashdowne Lawns. *Stal* 2H **101**
Ashdown Gro. *M9* 5F **69**
Ashdown Rd. *Stoc* 6E **127**
Ashdown Ter. *M9* 5F **69**
Ashdown Way. *Shaw* 5C **42**
Ash Dri. *Swin* 1C **78**
Ashenhurst Ct. *M9* 6C **68**
Asher St. *Bolt* 5G **45**
Ashes Clo. *Stal* 5G **101**
Ashes Dri. *Bolt* 5H **33**
Ashes La. *Miln* 4E **29**
Ashes La. *S'head* 3B **74**
Ashes La. *Stal* 5G **101**
Ashfell Ct. *M32* 6F **107**
Ash Fld. *Dent* 2G **113**
Ashfield Av. *Roch* 6H **27**
Ashfield Clo. *Salf* 2E **93**
Ashfield Cres. *Chea* 5H **137**
Ashfield Cres. *S'head* 3B **74**
Ashfield Dri. *M40* 1F **97**
Ashfield Gro. *M18* 3H **111**
Ashfield Gro. *Bolt* 5E **19**
Ashfield Gro. *Irlam* 3C **118**
Ashfield Gro. *Marp B* 2F **143**
Ashfield Gro. *Stoc* 1H **151**
Ashfield Ho. *Roch* 6H **27**
Ashfield La. *Miln* 1D **42**
Ashfield Lodge. *M20* 1D **136**
Ashfield Lodge. *Stoc* 1H **151**
Ashfield Rd. *M13* 4A **110**
Ashfield Rd. *Alt* 2G **145**
Ashfield Rd. *Chea* 5H **137**
Ashfield Rd. *Had* 4H **117**
Ashfield Rd. *Roch* 1E **41**
Ashfield Rd. *Sale* 4B **122**
Ashfield Rd. *Stoc* 1H **151**
Ashfield Rd. *Urm* 5F **105**
Ashfield Sq. *Droy* 4H **97**
Ashfield St. *Oldh* 6A **72**
Ashford. *Sale* 5E **121**
Ashford Av. *Eccl* 5E **91**
Ashford Av. *Stoc* 5H **111**
Ashford Av. *Swin* 5C **78**
Ashford Av. *Wors* 5B **76**
Ashford Clo. *Bolt* 1G **33**
Ashford Clo. *Bury* 4H **35**
Ashford Clo. *Hand* 3G **159**
Ashford Ct. *Oldh* 6H **57**
*Ashford Grn. Glos 6G **117** (off Ashford M.)*
Ashford Gro. *Wors* 3H **77**
Ashford M. *Glos* 6G **117**
Ashford Rd. *M20* 2E **125**
Ashford Rd. *Stoc* 3F **127**
Ashford Rd. *Wilm* 5D **166**
Ashford St. *Heyw* 3B **38**
Ashford Wlk. *Bolt* 4A **32**
Ashford Wlk. *Chad* 3H **71**
Ashgate Av. *M22* 1C **148**
*Ashgill Wlk. M9 4G **83** (off Fernclough Rd.)*
Ash Gro. *M14* 3A **110**
Ash Gro. *Bolt* 5F **31**
Ash Gro. *Bow* 4E **145**
Ash Gro. *Droy* 5A **98**
Ash Gro. *Hand* 4G **159**
Ash Gro. *Har* 2H **33**
Ash Gro. *H Grn* 5F **149**
Ash Gro. *L'boro* 4D **16**
Ash Gro. *Marp* 6C **142**
Ash Gro. *Miln* 2E **43**
Ash Gro. *P'wich* 3E **67**
Ash Gro. *Rams* 6B **12**
Ash Gro. *Roch* 4H **41**
Ash Gro. *Rytn* 1B **56**
Ash Gro. *S'head* 2C **74** (in two parts)
Ash Gro. *Stal* 2D **100**
Ash Gro. *Stoc* 4F **127**
Ash Gro. *Stret* 1C **122**
Ash Gro. *Swin* 6D **78**
Ash Gro. *Timp* 4H **133**
Ash Gro. *T'ton* 6A **22**
Ash Gro. *Wors* 2F **77**
Ash Hill Dri. *Moss* 3G **89**
Ashia Clo. *Roch* 5A **28**
Ashill Wlk. *M3* 5C **94** (1F **9**)
Ashington Clo. *Bolt* 2F **31**
Ashington Dri. *Bury* 4F **35**
Ashkirk St. *M18* 2F **111**
Ashlands. *Sale* 4A **122**
Ashlands Av. *M40* 2C **84**
Ashlands Av. *Swin* 5C **78**
Ashlands Av. *Wors* 4C **76**
*Ashlands Clo. Rams 3A **12** (off Water La.)*
Ashlands Dri. *Aud* 1E **113**
Ashlands Rd. *Timp* 2A **134**
Ash La. *Hale* 4C **146**
Ashlar Dri. *M12* 5H **95** (1H **11**)
Ash Lawns. *Bolt* 6F **31**
Ashlea Gro. *G'ton* 3D **74**
Ashleigh Clo. *Rytn* 5C **56**
Ashleigh Dri. *Bolt* 5C **30**
*Ashleigh Gdns. M9 2E **83** (off Slack Rd.)*
Ashleigh Rd. *Timp* 3B **134**
Ashley Av. *M16* 3B **108**
Ashley Av. *Bolt* 5F **33**
Ashley Av. *Swin* 5D **78**
Ashley Av. *Urm* 5A **104**
Ashley Clo. *Roch* 1C **40**
Ashley Ct. *M40* 2F **85**
Ashley Ct. *Hale* 4G **145**
Ashley Ct. *Stoc* 5D **126**
Ashley Ct. *Swin* 1F **79**
Ashley Ct. *Whitw* 3H **15**
Ashley Ct. Dri. *M40* 2F **85**
Ashley Cres. *Swin* 4D **78**
Ashley Dri. *Bram* 1E **161**
Ashley Dri. *Sale* 1G **133**
Ashley Dri. *Swin* 4D **78**
Ashley Gdns. *H Lane* 5B **154**
Ashley Gdns. *Hyde* 6C **114**
Ashley Gro. *Farn* 1E **63**
Ashley Heath. 4F 145
Ashley La. *M9* 3H **83**
Ashley M. *Hyde* 6C **114** (in two parts)
Ashley M. *W'fld* 2F **67**
Ashley Mill La. *Ash* 5F **145**
Ashley Mill La. N. *Hale* 5F **145**
Ashley Rd. *Alt & Hale* 2F **145**
Ashley Rd. *Droy* 3G **97**
Ashley Rd. *Hale & Ash* 6G **145**
Ashley Rd. *Stoc* 3C **140**
Ashley Rd. *Wilm* 6F **159**
Ashleys, The. *Stoc* 6D **126**
Ashley St. *M4* 2F **95** (2C **6**)
Ashley St. *Hyde* 3C **114**
Ashley St. *Oldh* 1A **72**
Ashley St. *Salf* 3E **93**
Ash Lodge. *Poy* 3D **162**
Ashlor St. *Bury* 4C **36**
Ashlyn Gro. *M14* 1H **125**
Ashlynne. *Ash L* 2A **100**
Ashmeade. *Haleb* 4B **146**
Ashmill Wlk. *M9* 5E **83**
Ashmond. *S'head* 3B **74**
Ashmond Rd. *S'head* 3B **74**
Ashmoor Rd. *M22* 4C **148**
Ashmoor Wlk. *M22* 4C **148**
Ashmore Av. *Stoc* 4B **138**
Ashmount Dri. *Roch* 1H **27**
Ashness Dri. *Bolt* 4G **33**
Ashness Dri. *Bram* 5G **151**
Ashness Dri. *Midd* 4F **53**
Ashness Gro. *Bolt* 4G **33**
Ashness Pl. *Bolt* 4G **33**
Ashover Av. *M12* 1B **110**

Ashover Clo. *Bolt* 5D **18**
Ashover St. *Stret* 4E **107**
Ashridge Clo. *Lus* 1A **44**
Ashridge Dri. *Duk* 6H **99**
Ashridge Dri. *Eccl* 5E **91**
Ash Rd. *Dent* 4H **111**
Ash Rd. *Droy* 3H **97**
Ash Rd. *Kear* 4H **63**
Ash Rd. *Part* 6B **118**
Ash Rd. *Poy* 4F **163**
Ash Sq. *Oldh* 1H **73**
Ashstead Rd. *Sale* 2C **134**
Ash Ct. *Aud* . . . . .GD **90**
Ash St. *Bolt* 1C **46**
Ash St. *Bury* 3E **37**
Ash St. *Fail* 3E **85**
Ash St. *Harp* 4F **83**
Ash St. *Haz G* 2D **152**
Ash St. *Heyw* 2D **38**
Ash St. *Midd* 6C **54**
Ash St. *Oldh* 3F **73**
Ash St. *Roch* 3C **40**
Ash St. *Salf* 3F **93**
Ash St. *Stoc* 3D **138**
Ashton Av. *Alt* 5G **133**
Ashton Ct. *Aud* 1F **113**
Ashton Ct. *Sale* 5G **121**
Ashton Cres. *Chad* 6G **71**
Ashton Fld. Dri. *Wors* . . .5E **63**
Ashton Gdns. *Roch* 6G **27**
Ashton Hill La. *Droy* 5A **98**
Ashton La. *Midd* 1A **70**
Ashton La. *Sale* 4H **121**
Ashton New Rd.
    M11 . . . . . .4A **9G** (5ll **7**)
Ashton Old Rd. *M12* &
    M11 . . . . . .5H **95** (2H **11**)
Ashton on Mersey Health &
    Fitness Cen. . . . . .GG **121**
Ashton Pl. *Haz G* 4F **153**
Ashton Rd. *M9* 4F **69**
Ashton Rd. *Bred* 4E **129**
Ashton Rd. *Dent* 2F **113**
Ashton Rd. *Droy* 4B **98**
Ashton Rd. *Fail* 5A **86**
Ashton Rd. *Hyde* 1B **114**
Ashton Rd. *Oldh* 4C **72**
Ashton Rd.
    Part & Sale 6G **119**
Ashton Rd. E. *Fail* 3F **85**
Ashton Rd W *Fail* 4F **85**
Ashton St. *M9* 3H **83**
Ashton St. *Bolt* 3F **45**
Ashton St. *Chad* 6G **71**
Ashton St. *Duk* 1G **113**
Ashton St. *Heyw* 3E **39**
Ashton St. *L Lev* 4B **48**
Ashton St. *Roch* 6G **27**
Ashton St. *Woodl* 3A **130**
Ashton Swimming Pool.
    . . . . .2H **99**
Ashton-under-Lyne. 2H **99**
Ashton-under-Lyne.
    St Michael's & All Angels
    Church. 3A **100**
Ashton-under-Lyne Tourist
    Info. Cen. 2A **100**
Ashton Upon Mersey.
    . . . . .5G **121**
Ash Tree Av. *Droy* 3H **97**
Ash Tree Dri. *Duk* 6D **100**
Ash Tree Gro. *Droy* 2H **97**
Ash Tree Rd. *M8* 2C **82**
Ashtree Rd. *Hyde* 2F **115**
Ashurst Av. *M11* 3D **96**
Ashurst Clo. *Bolt* 2A **44**
Ashurst Clo. *Hyde* 6E **115**
Ashurst Dri. *Stoc* 6D **138**
Ashurst Gdns. *Ash L* 6F **87**
Ashurst Rd. *M22* 1D **148**
Ash Vw. *Ash L* 1A **100**
Ashville Ter. *M40* 2H **83**

Ash Wlk. *Chad* 1H **71**
Ash Wlk. *Midd* 3H **69**
Ash Wlk. *Sale* 4F **121**
Ashwater Wlk. M9 . . . . .4G **69**
    (off Brockford Dri.)
Ashway. *Ash L* 2G **99**
Ashway Clough N.
    Stoc 6D **140**
Ashway Clough S.
    Stoc 6E **141**
Ashwell M. *Bolt* 2E **33**
Ashwell Rd. *M23* 4H **135**
Ashwell Ct. Dolt 2D **32**
Ashwin Wlk. M8 . . . . . .5B **82**
    (off Dalmain Clo.)
Ashwood. *Bow* 4D **144**
Ashwood. *Chad* 2E **71**
Ashwood. *Rad* 2B **64**
Ashwood Av. *M20* 5C **124**
Ashwood Av. *Dent* 4A **112**
Ashwood Av. *Rams* 2F **13**
Ashwood Av. *Sale* 6G **121**
Ashwood Av. *Wors* 4E **63**
Ashwood Cres. *Marp* 4D **142**
Ashwood Dri. *Bury* 5B **22**
Ashwood Dri. *L'boro* 4D **16**
Ashwood Dri. *Rytn* 2A **56**
Ashwood Rd. *Dis* 1H **165**
Ashworth Av. *Aud* 6E **99**
Ashworth Av. *L Lev* 4C **48**
Ashworth Av. *Urm* 5A **104**
Ashworth Clo. *Bow* 4D **144**
Ashworth Clo. *Chad* 5H **71**
Ashworth Clo. *L'boro* 2E **17**
Ashworth Clo. *Rytn* 3D **56**
Ashworth Ct. *Rad* 3A **50**
Ashworth Ct. *Shaw* 1F **57**
    (off Ashworth St.)
Ashworth Gdns. *G'fld* 4F **61**
Ashworth La. *Bolt* 6D **18**
Ashworth La. *Mot* 5B **116**
Ashworth Rd.
    Roch & Heyw 1C **24**
Ashworth St. *Bury* 2A **36**
    (in two parts)
Ashworth St. *Dent* 3E **113**
Ashworth St. *Fail* 5D **84**
Ashworth St. *Farn* 1E **63**
Ashworth St. *Heyw* 5F **39**
Ashworth St. *Oldh* 3D **72**
Ashworth St. *Rad* 3B **50**
Ashworth St. *Roch* 3F **27**
Ashworth St. *Shaw* 1F **57**
Ashworth Ter. *Bolt* 1G **33**
Ashworth Vw. Salf 6H **93**
    (off Ordsall Dri.)
Ashworth Way. *Mot* 4B **116**
Asia St. *Bolt* 4C **46**
Askern Av. *M22* 2B **148**
Askett Clo. M4U 5D **84**
Askrigg Wlk. *M13* 3B **110**
Aspell Clo. *Midd* 6H **53**
Aspen Clo. *Stoc* 2C **138**
Aspen Clo. *Timp* 6E **135**
Aspen Gdns. *Roch* 2C **26**
Aspen Grn. *Dent* 5G **113**
Aspens, The. *Gat* 5E **137**
Aspen Way. *H Lane* 6E **155**
Aspen Wood. *Hyde* 4D **114**
Aspenwood Clo.
    Marp 4C **142**
Aspenwood Dri. *Chad* . . .2E **71**
Aspenwood Dri. *Sale* 5E **121**
Aspinall Clo. *Wors* 6B **62**
Aspinall Cres. *Wors* 6B **62**
Aspinall Gro. Wors 6B **62**
Aspinall St. *Heyw* 3G **39**
Aspinall St. *Midd* 2C **70**
Aspinal St. *M14* 4G **109**
Aspin La. *M4* 2E **95** (2A **6**)
Aspland Rd. *Hyde* 1D **130**
Aspull St. *Oldh* 4G **73**

Aspull Wlk.
    M13 . . . . .1G **109** (6F **11**)
Asquith Av. *Duk* 1A **114**
Asquith Rd. *M19* 3B **126**
Asquith St. *Stoc* 6H **111**
Assheton Av. *Aud* 4C **98**
Assheton Clo. *Ash L* 2H **99**
Assheton Cres. *M40* 1F **97**
Assheton Ho. *Ash L* 2H **99**
Assheton Rd. *M40* 1F **97**
Assheton Rd. *Shaw* 6D **42**
Assheton St. *Midd* 6A **54**
    (Clarke Brow)
Assheton St. *Midd* 5A **54**
    (King St.)
Assheton Way. *Midd* 1A **70**
Assisi Gdns. *M12* 1D **110**
Assumption Rd. *Midd* 4F **53**
Astan Av. *Droy* 2F **97**
Astbury Av. *M21* 5A **124**
Astbury Av. *Aud* 4D **98**
Astbury Clo. *Alt* 5G **133**
Astbury Clo. *S'head* 3B **74**
Astbury Cres. *Stoc* 5F **139**
Astbury St. *Rad* 6H **49**
Astbury Wlk. *Chea* 6C **138**
Aster Av. *Farn* 6C **46**
Aster Ho. *Oldh* 6C **56**
Aster St. *Oldh* 6C **56**
Aster Wlk. *Part* 6D **118**
Astley Bridge. 1A **32**
Astley Cheetham Art Gallery.
    . . . . .3E **101**
Astley Clo. *Shaw* 6D **42**
Astley Gdns. *Duk* 5H **99**
Astley Gro. *Stal* 2D **100**
Astley Hill Dri. *Rams* 5E **13**
Astley La. *Rams* 2A **32**
Astley Rd. *Bolt* 6A **32**
Astley Rd. *Irlam* 2A **102**
    (in two parts)
Astley Rd. *Stal* 3D **100**
Astley St. *M11* 4E **97**
    (in two parts)
Astley St. *Bolt* 3A **32**
Astley St. *Duk* 6G **99**
Astley St. *Hyde* 3A **114**
Astley St. *Stal* 5E **101**
Astley St. *Stoc* 2G **139**
Astley Ter. *Duk* 4A **100**
Aston Av. *M14* 5D **108**
Aston Clo. *Stoc* 5E **139**
Aston Ct. *Oldh* 1C **72**
Aston Gdns. *Farn* 6F **47**
Aston Ho. *Bolt* 6G **31**
Aston Way. *Hand* 2H **159**
Astor Rd. *M19* 2A **126**
Astor Rd. *Salf* 4B **92**
Astra Bus. Pk. Trat P 5H **91**
Astra Cen., The. *Roch* 2C **40**
Astral M. *M14* 4H **109**
Atcham Gro. *M9* 3D **68**
Athenian Gdns. *Salf* 6G **81**
Athens Dri. *Wors* 1E **77**
Athens St. *Stoc* 2A **140**
Athens Way. *Lees* 3A **74**
Atherfield. Bolt 1G **33**
Atherfield Clo. *M18* 1H **111**
    M40 & Chad 1F **85**
Atherstone. Roch 3H **27**
    (off Redcross St.)
Atherstone Av. M8 . . . . . .1C **82**
Atherstone Clo. *Bury* 1A **36**
Atherton Av. *Mot* 3C **116**
Atherton Clo. *Fail* 6H **85**
Atherton Gro. *Mot* 3C **116**
Atherton La. *Cad* 4C **118**
Atherton St. *M3* . . .4C **94** (6E **5**)
Atherton St. *Eccl* 4D **90**
Atherton St. *Lees* 4A **74**

Atherton St. *S'head* 3B **74**
    (in two parts)
Atherton St. *Stoc* 3F **139**
Atherton Way. *Eccl* 4D **90**
Athlone Av. *M40* 3A **84**
Athlone Av. *Bolt* 6A **18**
Athlone Av. *Bury* 1D **36**
Athlone Av. *Chea H* 6E **139**
Athole St. *Salf* 4F **93**
Atholl Av. *Stret* 5A **106**
Atholl Clo. *Bolt* 1D **44**
Atholl Dri. *Heyw* 4C **38**
Athol Rd. M1G . . . . .GC **100**
Athol Rd. *Bram* 2F **161**
Athol St. *M18* 4G **111**
Athol St. *Ash L* 2A **100**
Athol St. *Eccl* 4D **90**
Athol St. *Rams* 2E **13**
Athol St. *Roch* 2B **28**
Athol St. *Stoc* 6F **127**
Athos Wlk. *M40* 1C **84**
Atkinson Av. *Bolt* 4D **46**
Atkinson Ho. *Sale* 4B **122**
Atkinson Rd. *Sale* 3A **122**
Atkinson Rd. *Urm* 5F **105**
Atkinson St.
    M3 . . . .4C **94** (6F **5**)
Atkinson St. *Oldh* 1B **72**
Atkinson St. *Roch* 3C **40**
Atkinson St. *Stoc* 4A **140**
Atkin St. *Wors* 1F **77**
Atlanta Av. *Man A* 5G **147**
Atlantic Bus. Cen.
    B'hth 4E **133**
Atlantic St.
    Alt & B'hth 5C **132**
Atlantic Wlk. M11 . . . . . .4B **96**
    (off Seabright Wlk.)
Atlas Bus. Pk. *M22* 4D **148**
Atlas Ho. *Rams* 5B **32**
Atlas St. *Ash L* 1G **99**
Atlas St. *Duk* 5B **100**
Atlas Trad. Est. *Stoc* 2H **127**
Atlow Dri. *M23* 6H **135**
Attenburys La. *Timp* 3G **133**
Attenbury's Pk. Est.
    Timp 3G **133**
Attercliffe Rd. *M21* 2G **123**
Attewell St. *Open* 5C **96**
Attingham Wlk. *Dent* 6E **113**
Attleboro Rd. *M40* 4A **84**
Attlee Way. *M12* 4A **96**
Attwood Rd. *Timp* 6B **134**
Attwood St. *M12* 4C **110**
Attwood Rd. *M20* 6G **125**
Atwood St. *M1* . . .5E **95** (2A **10**)
Auberge Ho. *Stoc* 5A **140**
Auberson Rd. *Bolt* 4H **45**
Aubrey Rd. *M14* 2A **126**
Aubrey St. *Roch* 6H **27**
Aubrey St. *Salf* 6G **93**
Auburn Av. *Bred* 5F **129**
Auburn Av. *Hyde* 6C **114**
Auburn Dri. *Urm* 6G **105**
Auburn Rd. *Dent* 5D **112**
Auburn St. *M1* 4F **95** (6C **6**)
Auburn St. *Bolt* 3H **45**
Auckland Dri. *Salf* 6E **81**
Auckland Rd. *M19* 1B **126**
Audax Wlk. *M40* 1D **96**
Auden Clo. *M11* 4F **97**
Auden Ct. *M11* 4F **97**
    (off Auden Clo.)
Audenshaw. 2E **113**
Audenshaw Hall Gro.
    Aud 6B **98**
Audenshaw Rd. *Aud* 6B **98**
    (in two parts)
Audlem Clo.
    M40 . . . . . .3H **95** (3H **7**)
Audlem Wlk. *Chea* 6C **138**

Audley Av. Stret 3H 105
Audley Rd. M19 .....5D 110
Audley St. Ash L 3C 100
Audley St. Moss 2F 89
(in two parts)
Audlum Ct. Bury 3E 37
Audrey Av. M18 .....2G 111
Audrey St. M9 .....4H 83
Augusta Clo. Roch 1G 27
(in two parts)
Augusta St. Roch 2G 27
Augustine Webster Clo.
M9 .....3G 83
Augustus St.
M3 .....1E 95 (1A 6)
Augustus St. Bolt 3C 46
Augustus Way. M15 ....3B 108
Austell Rd. M22 .....5B 148
Austen Av. Bury 1D 50
Austen Rd. Eccl 4F 91
Austen Wlk. Oldh 3A 58
Auster Clo. M14 .....1E 125
Austerlands. 1C 74
Austin Ct. M20 .....5G 125
(off Austin Dri.)
Austin Dri. M20 .....5G 125
Austin Gro. M19 .....1B 126
Austin St. Bury 6E 23
Avallon Clo. T'ton 4H 21
Avalon Dri. M20 .....3G 137
Avebury Clo. Salf 5B 82
Avebury Rd. M23 .....6G 135
Avenham Clo.
M15 .....2C 108 (6F 9)
Avening Wlk. M22 .....3A 148
Avens Rd. Part 6D 118
Avenue St. Bolt 5H 31
Avenue St. Stoc 1H 139
Avenue, The. Ald E 5G 167
Avenue, The. Bolt 6D 32
Avenue, The. Bred 6D 128
Avenue, The. Bury 6F 23
Avenue, The. Eccl 4F 91
Avenue, The. Had 3H 117
Avenue, The. Hale 5H 145
Avenue, The. H Grn 4E 149
Avenue, The. Sale 6F 121
Avenue, The. Salf 6G 81
Avenue, The. Shaw 1E 57
Avenue, The. Urm 5A 104
Avenue, The. Wors 4G 77
Averhill. Wors 3D 76
Averill St. M40 .....6D 84
Averon Ri. Oldh 3H 57
Aveson Av. M21 .....3H 123
Avian Clo. Eccl 6B 90
Avian Dri. M14 .....1F 125
Aviary Rd. Wors 5H 77
Aviator Way. M22 .....5A 148
Aviemore Clo. Rams 1A 22
Aviemore Wlk. M11 .....5E 97
Avis St. Shaw 6F 43
Avocet Dri. B'hth 3D 132
Avocet Dri. Irlam 3E 103
Avon Bank. Bred 6F 129
Avonbrook Dri. M40 .....1F 85
Avoncliff Clo. Bolt 2H 31
Avon Clo. Marp 5C 142
Avon Clo. Miln 5G 29
Avon Clo. Wors 1C 76
Avon Cotts. P'wich 4C 66
Avon Ct. M15 .....1B 108 (6C 8)
Avoncourt Dri. M20 .....6E 125
Avondale. Swin 1G 79
Avondale Av. Bury 1C 36
Avondale Av. Haz G 3F 153
Avondale Ct. Roch 6D 40
Avondale Cres. Urm 4E 105
Avondale Dri. Rams 1H 21
Avondale Dri. Salf 6H 79
Avondale Ind. Est.
Stoc 4D 138

Avondale Lodge. Sale 6B 122
Avondale Recreation Cen.
.....4D 138
Avondale Ri. Wilm 3G 167
Avondale Rd. Farn 1B 62
Avondale Rd. Haz G 2F 153
Avondale Rd. Stoc 4D 138
Avondale Rd. Stret 3E 107
Avondale St. M8 .....4C 82
Avondale St. Bolt 4G 31
Avon Dri. Bury 3F 23
Avon Flats. Heyw 3E 39
(off Kay St.)
Avon Gdns. M19 .....3C 126
Avonlea Dri. M19 .....3A 126
Avonlea Rd. Droy 3G 97
Avonlea Rd. Sale 2F 133
Avonleigh Gdns. Oldh 6G 57
(off Clyde St.)
Avon Rd. M19 .....3B 126
Avon Rd. Chad 1F 71
Avon Rd. Hale 5G 145
Avon Rd. H Grn 6G 149
Avon Rd. Heyw 3C 38
Avon Rd. Kear 4B 64
Avon Rd. Shaw 5F 43
Avon St. Oldh 5D 72
Avon St. Rams 4F 31
Avon St. Stoc 4G 139
Avril Clo. Stoc 1H 127
Avro Clo. M14 .....6F 109
Avro Ct. Midd 1D 70
Avroe Rd. Eccl 6B 90
Avro Way. Timp 6F 147
Awburn Rd. Hyde 6A 116
Axbridge Wlk.
M40 .....3H 95 (3H 7)
Axford Clo. Salf 5B 82
Axminster Wlk. Bram ...6G 151
Axon Sq. M16 .....3D 108
Aycliffe Av. Chor H 4B 124
Aycliffe Gro. Long 4A 110
Aylesbury Av. Dent 6F 113
Aylesbury Av. Urm 3G 105
Aylesbury Clo. Salf 4G 93
Aylesbury Gro. Midd 5C 54
Aylesby Av. M18 .....3D 110
Aylesby Ct. M21 .....6B 108
Aylesford Rd. M14 .....4H 109
Aylestone Wlk. Bolt 4A 32
Aylestone Wlk. M40 .....4A 84
Aylsham Clo. Bred 4F 129
Aylsham M. Swin 6D 78
Aylwin Dri. Sale 6C 122
Ayr Av. Oldh 6D 72
Ayr Clo. Haz G 3G 153
Ayres Rd. M16 .....3G 107
Ayr Gro. Heyw 4C 38
Ayrshire Rd. Salf 5F 81
Ayr St. Bolt 1E 33
Ayrton Gro. L Hul 3C 62
Aysgarth. Roch 2B 28
Aysgarth Av. M18 .....2G 111
Aysgarth Av. Chea 5G 137
Aysgarth Av. Rom 5B 130
Aysgarth Clo. Sale 6F 121
Aysgarth Clo. Alt 5D 132
Ayton Ct. M16 .....3B 108
Ayton Gro. M14 .....3A 110
Aytoun St. M1 .....4E 95 (6B 6)
Azalea Av. M18 .....1F 111

B

Babbacombe Gro. M9 ...4D 68
Babbacombe Rd.
Stoc 5C 140
Baber Wlk. Bolt 1A 32
Bk. Acton St.
M1 .....5F 95 (1C 10)

Bk. Ainscow St. Bolt 5A 32
Bk. Ainsworth Rd.
Bury 3A 36
(off Stephen St.)
Bk. Ainsworth Rd. N.
Bury 3H 35
(off Ainsworth Rd., in two parts)
Bk. Ainsworth Rd. N.
Bury 3A 36
(off Cameron St.)
Bk. Albany St. Roch 6A 28
Bk. Albert St. Bury 3E 37
(off Albert St.)
Bk. Albion Pl. Bury 1D 36
Bk. Alfred St. Rams 4D 12
(off Mary St.)
Bk. America Row. Bolt 2G 31
(off Elliott St.)
Bk. Anson St. Bolt 2B 32
(off Anson St.)
Bk. Apple Ter Bolt 3H 31
Bk. Argyle St. Bury 6F 23
Bk. Ashley St.
M4 .....2F 95 (2C 6)
(off Ash St.)
Bk. Ash St. Bury 3F 37
(off Ash St.)
Bk. Ashworth St. Bury 2A 36
Bk. Astley St. Rams 3A 32
Bk. Augustus St. Bolt 3C 46
Pk. Augustus St. W. Bolt .3B 46
Bk. Avondale St. Rams 4G 31
B c. Baldwin St. N. Bolt 2A 46
Bk. Balloon St. M4 .3E 95 (3A 6)
Bk. Bank St. M8 .....1E 95
Bk. Belbeck St. Bury 3A 36
(off Belbeck St.)
Bk. Belfast St. Rams 3A 32
Bk. Bennett's La. Rams ..3G 31
(in two parts)
Bk. Birch St. Bury 2D 36
(in two parts)
Bk. Blackburn Rd. Bolt 4B 32
Bk. Blackburn Rd. W.
Bolt 1A 32
(off Blackburn Rd.)
Bk. Blackburn Rd. W.
Eger 3C 18
(off Nicola St.)
Bk. Blackburn Rd. W.
Eger 1B 18
(Blackburn Rd.)
Bk. Bolton Rd. S. Bury ...3A 36
Bk. Bolton St. Bolt 3B 32
Bk. Bolton St. S. Bury ...3C 36
(off Bolton St.)
Backbower. 6D 114
Bk. Bower La. Hyde 1D 130
Bk. Bowness Rd. Bolt 3H 45
Bk. Bradford St. W.
Bolt 6C 32
(off Bradford St.)
Bk. Bradshaw Brow E.
Bolt 1E 33
(off Bradshaw Brow)
Bk. Bradshaw Brow W.
Bolt 1E 33
(off Bradshaw Brow)
Bk. Bradshaw Rd. E.
Bolt 6H 19
(off Bradshaw Rd.)
Bk. Bridge St.
M3 .....4D 94 (5G 5)
Bk. Bridge St. Rams 3E 13
Bk. Brierley St. Bury 5C 36
Bk. Broad St. Bury 3C 36
(off Broad St.)
Bk. Brook St. N. Bury 1E 37
(in two parts)
Bk. Broom St. Bolt 6C 32
Bk. Burnley Rd. Bury 3E 23
Bk. Bury Rd. S. Bolt 6G 33
(in two parts)

Bk. Byrom St. Bury 1H 35
(off Byrom St.)
Bk. Byrom St. S. Bury ...1H 35
Bk. Cambridge St.
Ash L 4F 99
Bk. Cambridge St.
Rams 4A 32
Bk. Camp St. Salf 6H 81
Bk. Canning St. Bury 1D 36
Bk. Cateaton St. Bury ...2D 36
Bk. Chapel St. M19 .....6C 110
Bk. Chapel St. Eccl 3H 91
Bk. Chapel St. Haz G ...2E 153
Bk. Chapel St. T'ton 4H 21
Bk. Chapel St. Ward 2A 16
Bk. Cheapside. Bolt 6B 32
Bk. Chesham Rd. S.
Bury 1E 37
(off Chesham Rd.)
Bk. Chesham Rd. S.
Bury 1E 37
(off Greenbrook St.)
Bk. Chester St. Bury 1E 37
(off Chester St.)
Bk. China La.
M1 .....4F 95 (6C 6)
Bk. Chorley Old Rd.
Bolt 4D 30
Bk. Chorley Old Rd. S.
Rams 4E 31
Bk. Church Rd. N.
Rams 3F 31
Bk. Church St. Bolt 5A 32
(off Wickliffe St.)
Bk. Clay St. E. Brom X ...4E 19
Bk. Clifton St. Bury 1D 36
Bk. College Land. Salf 4G 5
Bk. Cowm La. Whitw 2G 15
(in two parts)
Bk. Cox Grn. Rd. N.
Eger 3D 18
Bk. Cox Grn. Rd. S.
Eger 3D 18
Bk. Crostons Rd. Bury ...2B 36
Bk. Cyril St. Bolt 2C 46
(off Cyril St.)
Bk. Dale St. Miln 6F 29
Bk. Darwen Rd. N.
Brom X 3D 18
(off Hardman's La.)
Bk. Darwen Rd. N.
Brom X 3D 18
(off Hospital Rd.)
Bk. Darwen Rd. N.
Brom X 3E 19
(off Blair St.)
Bk. Darwen Rd. N.
Brom X 3E 19
(Darwen Rd.)
Bk. Darwen Rd. N.
Eger 3D 18
(off Smith La.)
Bk. Darwen Rd. N.
Eger 3D 18
(Arnold Rd.)
Bk. Darwen Rd. N.
Eger 2C 18
(Darwen Rd.)
Bk. Darwen Rd. N. Tur ...4F 19
(off Bromley Cross Rd.)
Bk. Darwen Rd. S.
Brom X 4E 19
(off Hough La.)
Bk. Darwin St. Bolt 3H 31
(off Darwin St.)
Bk. Dashwood Rd.
P'wich 5B 80
Bk. Deacon's Dri. Salf ...5B 80
Bk. Deal St. Bury 3F 37
(off Deal St.)
Bk. Deane Chu. La. Bolt ..3F 45
(in two parts)

Bk. Delamere St. S.
   Bury 6G **23**
      (off Delamere St.)
Bk. Denton St. *Bury* 1D **36**
Bk. Derby St. Bury 3D **36**
      (off Derby St.)
Bk. Devonshire Rd.
   Rams 4F **31**
Bk. Devon St. N. Bury . . .5C **36**
Bk. Devon St. S. Bury . . .5D **36**
Bk. Deyne Av. P'wich 5F **67**
Bk. Drake St. Roch 5H **27**
Bk. Dumers La. Rad 2C **50**
Bk. Duncan St. Salf 4G **81**
Bk. East St. Bury 4D **36**
      (off East St., in two parts)
Bk. Eden St. Rams 2A **32**
Bk. Eldon St. Bury 1D **36**
Bk. Elm St. Bury 3F **37**
      (off Elm St.)
Bk. Elsworth St.
   M3 . . . . .2E **95** (1A **6**)
Bk. Everton St. N.
   Rams 3B **32**
Bk. Fairhaven Rd.
   Rams 2B **32**
Bk. Federation St.
   P'wich 4D **66**
Bk. Fern St. E. Bolt 1G **45**
Bk. Fletcher St. Rad 1B **64**
Backford Wlk. M20 . . . . .2E **125**
Bk. Frank St. Bury 4D **36**
      (off Frank St.)
Bk. Garden St.
   Salf 3C **94** (4F **5**)
Bk. Garston St. Bury 1E **37**
      (off Garston St.)
Bk. George St.
   M1 . . . . . . .5E **95** (1A **10**)
      (in two parts)
Bk. George St. Bolt 3B **46**
Bk. Georgiana St. Bury . . .3C **36**
      (off Kay Garden Shop. Cen.)
Bk. Georgiana St. W.
   Bury 1D **36**
      (off Georgiana St.)
Bk. Gigg La. Bury 5D **36**
Bk. Gladstone St. Oldh . . .3F **73**
Bk. Glenboro Av. Bury . . .3A **36**
      (off Glenboro Av.)
Bk. Goodlad St. Bury 1H **35**
      (off Goodlad St.)
Bk. Gorton St. Bolt 1C **46**
      (off Gorton St.)
Bk. Grafton St. Alt 1F **145**
Bk. Grantham Clo.
   Rams 4A **32**
Bk. Grasmere St. Bolt 3B **32**
      (off Blackburn Rd.)
Bk. Grosvenor St. Bury . . .5D **36**
Bk. Grosvenor St. Stal 4E **101**
Bk. Halliwell Rd. S.
   Bolt 3H **31**
      (off Nut St.)
Bk. Hamel St. Hyde 2D **114**
Bk. Hamilton St. Salf 4H **81**
Bk. Hampson St. M40 . . .1H **95**
Bk. Hanson St. Bury 1D **36**
Bk. Harvey St. Bury 2A **36**
Bk. Harvey St. Rams 2H **31**
      (off Harvey St.)
Bk. Haslam St. Bury 1E **37**
Bk. Hatfield Rd. Rams 4G **31**
Bk. Haymarket St. Bury . . .3C **36**
      (off Haymarket St.)
Bk. Heywood St. Bury 4E **37**
Bk. Higher Shady La. W.
   Brom X 4F **19**
Bk. Higher Swan La. W.
   Bolt 4H **45**
Bk. High St. Bolt 3H **45**
      (off High St.)

Bk. High St. Heyw 3D **38**
      (off High St.)
Bk. Hilton St. Bury 1D **36**
Bk. Hilton St. Salf 4H **81**
Bk. Holland St. Rams 1B **32**
Bk. Holly St. Bury 3E **37**
      (off Holly St., in two parts)
Bk. Holly St. S. Bury 3E **37**
      (off Holly St.)
Bk. Hope St. Oldh 2F **73**
Bk. Hope St. Salf 4H **81**
Bk. Horbury St. Bury 3A **36**
      (off Horbury Dri.)
Bk. Hornby St. Bury 6F **23**
Bk. Hornby St. W. Bury . . .2D **36**
      (off Hornby St.)
Bk. Horne St. N. Bury 5C **36**
Bk. Horne St. S. Bury 5C **36**
Bk. Hotel St. Rams 6B **32**
Bk. Hough La. E.
   Brom X 4E **19**
      (off Wilfred St.)
Bk. Howe St. Salf 4G **81**
Bk. Hulme St. Bury 2B **36**
      (off Hulme St.)
Bk. Hulme St.
   Salf 4A **94** (5B **4**)
Bk. Hulton La. Bolt 4E **45**
Bk. Hulton La. S. Bolt 5E **45**
Bk. Huntley Mt. Rd.
   Bury 1F **37**
Bk. Ingham St. Bury 4E **37**
Bk. Ingham St. E. Bury . . .4F **37**
      (off Ingham St.)
Bk. Ivanhoe St. Bolt 5E **47**
Bk. Ivy Bank Rd. Rams . . .6C **18**
Bk. Ivy Rd. Rams 3G **31**
Bk. James St. L Lev 4B **48**
Bk. John St. Bolt 1A **46**
Bk. Kingholm Gdns.
   Rams 4H **31**
Bk. King St. Oldh 3C **72**
Bk. King St. N. Eger 3D **18**
      (off Hardman's La.)
Bk. King St. S. Bolt 6H **10**
Bk. Knight St. Bury 3A **36**
      (off Knight St.)
Bk. Knowl St. Stal 3F **101**
Bk. Knowsley St. Bury . . .3C **36**
      (off Angouleme Way)
Bk. Knowsley St. Bury . . .4C **36**
      (off Knowsley St.)
Back La. Ash 2A **156**
Back La. Ash L 6C **86**
      (in two parts)
Back La. Bolt 5A **32**
Back La. Dun T 1A **144**
Back La. Mot 4C **116**
Back La. Oldh & Moss 6C **74**
Back La. Roch 1B **26**
Back La. Scout 6E **59**
Back La. Whitw 2G **15**
Bk. Leachfield St.
   Bolt 2H **31**
Bk. Lee St. Upperm 1F **61**
Bk. Lever St. Bolt 3A **46**
Bk. Lightburne Av.
   Rams 6F **31**
Bk. Linton Av. Bury 6F **23**
      (off Linton Av.)
Bk. Longsight N. Bolt 6A **20**
Bk. Longsight S. Bolt 6A **20**
      (off Longsight)
Bk. Longworth Rd.
   Eger 1B **18**
Bk. Lonsdale Rd. Bury 3A **36**
      (off Lonsdale St.)
Bk. Louise St. Roch 6H **15**
Bk. Lucas St. Bury 2E **37**
Bk. Luton St. Bolt 3C **46**
      (off Luton St.)
Bk. Lydia St. Bolt 6C **32**

Bk. Malvern Av. Bury 6F **23**
      (off Malvern Av.)
Bk. Manchester Old Rd.
   Bury 4C **36**
Bk. Manchester Rd.
   Bury 3C **36**
      (off Manchester Rd.)
Bk. Manchester Rd. E.
   Bury 5C **36**
      (off Manchester Rd.)
Bk. Manchester Rd. W.
   Bury 2D **50**
      (Manchester Rd.)
Bk. Manchester Rd. W.
   Bury 5C **36**
      (Olivant St.)
Bk. Manchester St.
   Heyw 4G **39**
      (off Hall St.)
Bk. Manor St. Bury 3E **37**
Bk. Market St. Rad 2B **64**
Bk. Market St. W. Bury 3C **36**
      (off Market St.)
Bk. Markland Hill La. Rams4D **30**
Bk. Markland Hill La. E. Bolt
   . . . . .4D **30**
      (off Whitecroft Rd.)
Bk. Markland Hill La. W.
   Rams 4D **30**
Bk. Massie St. Chea 5H **137**
Bk. Mawdsley St. Bolt 6B **32**
Bk. Maxwell St. Bolt 1A **32**
Bk. Melbourne St.
   Stal 3E **101**
Bk. Mere Gdns. Rams 5A **32**
Bk. Merton St. Bury 2B **36**
Bk. Micklehurst Rd.
   Moss 2G **89**
Bk. Millett St. Bury 3B **36**
      (off Millett St.)
Bk. Mill La. Moss 1E **89**
Backmill St. M4 . . . . .4G **95** (6F **7**)
Bk. Mill St. N. Eger 3D **18**
      (off Mill St.)
Bk. Milner Av. Bury 6F **23**
      (off Milner Av.)
Bk. Mirey La. Los 3A **44**
Bk. Monmouth St. Bury . . .6F **23**
Bk. Moorgate. Bury 2E **37**
      (off Moorgate)
Bk. Morris Grn. La. Bolt . .4G **45**
      (off Morris Grn. La.)
Bk. Moss Ter. Bolt 5B **32**
      (off All Saints St.)
Bk. Mostyn Av. Bury 6F **23**
      (off Mostyn Av.)
Bk. Myrtle St. S. Bury 3F **37**
      (off Myrtle St.)
Bk. Nelson St. N. Bury 5D **36**
Bk. Nelson St. S. Bury 5D **36**
Bk. Newbold St. Bury 3A **36**
      (off Newbold St.)
Bk. New George St.
   Bury 2A **36**
Bk. Newton St. Rams 3A **32**
Bk. Nook Ter. Roch 6F **15**
Bk. Oak St. Rad 6A **50**
      (off Oak St.)
Bk. Oldham Rd. Roch 5A **28**
Bk. Olga St. Bolt 3H **31**
Bk. Olive Bank. Bury 1H **35**
      (off Olive Bank)
Bk. Oram St. Bury 1E **37**
      (off Oram St.)
Back o' th' Bank. 3B **32**
Back o' th' Hill. 4B **130**
Back o' th' Low Rd.
   Oldh 1B **74**
Back o' th' Moss. 2E **39**
Bk. o' th' Moss La.
   Heyw 2E **39**
      (Clay Bank St.)

Back o' th' Moss La.
   Heyw 2E **39**
      (Lime Gro.)
Bk. Parkfield Vw. Roch . . .3H **41**
Bk. Parkhills Rd. Bury 4E **37**
Bk. Parkhills Rd. N.
   Bury 5D **36**
Bk. Parkhills Rd. S.
   Bury 5C **36**
Bk. Park Vw. Bolt 5D **18**
Bk. Parsons La. Bury 2D **36**
      (off Parsons La.)
Bk. Patience St. Roch 2E **27**
Bk. Peers St. Bury 3A **36**
      (off Peers St.)
Bk. Peter St. Bury 2E **37**
      (off Peter St.)
Bk. Phoenix St. Bury 3C **36**
      (off Phoenix St.)
Back Piccadilly.
   M4 & M1 . . . . .4E **95** (5B **6**)
Bk. Pine St. Miln 1F **43**
      (off Newhey Rd.)
Bk. Pool Fold.
   M2 . . . . .4D **94** (5H **5**)
Bk. Porter St. Bury 1D **36**
Bk. Portland St. Ash L 3G **99**
Bk. Prestbury Clo.
   Bury 4E **37**
Bk. Quay St. M3 . . .4C **94** (6E **5**)
Bk. Queen St. Bolt 6A **32**
      (off Queen St.)
Bk. Rake St. Bury 1D **36**
Bk. Ramsden Rd. Roch . . .2A **16**
Bk. Raven St. Bury 1D **36**
      (off Raven St.)
Bk. Rawson Rd. Bolt 4G **31**
      (off Oxford Gro.)
Bk. Raymond Av. Bury 6F **23**
      (off Raymond Av.)
Bk. Red Bank.
   M4 . . . . .2E **95** (1B **6**)
Bk. Regent St. Bury 1D **36**
      (off Regent St.)
Bk. Rigby La. N. Bolt 5G **19**
      (off Rigby La.)
Bk. Rigby La. S. Bolt 5G **19**
      (off Rigby La.)
Bk. Rigby La. W. Bolt 5G **19**
      (off Rigby La.)
Bk. Rochdale Old Rd. N.
   Bury 1H **37**
      (off Rectory La.)
Bk. Rochdale Old Rd. N.
   Bury 2G **37**
      (off Coppice St.)
Bk. Rochdale Old Rd. S.
   Bury 2G **37**
      (off Rochdale Old Rd.)
Bk. Rochdale Old Rd. S.
   Bury 2G **37**
      (off Topping Fold Rd.)
Bk. Rochdale Old Rd. S.
   Bury 2G **37**
      (Cuckoo La.)
Bk. Rochdale Rd. Bury 3E **37**
      (off Rochdale Rd.)
Bk. Rochdale Rd. Bury 3F **37**
      (off Deal St.)
Bk. Roman Rd. Salf 5A **82**
Bk. Rooley Moor Rd.
   Roch 2E **27**
Bk. Rowena St. Bolt 5E **47**
Bk. Royal Av. Bury 6F **23**
      (off Royal Av.)
Bk. Royds St. Roch 6A **28**
Bk. Rutland Gro. Bolt 4G **31**
      (off Oxford Gro.)
Bk. St Anne's St. Bury 1D **36**
Bk. St Georges Rd.
   M4 . . . . .2F **95** (2D **6**)
Bk. St George's Rd.
   Rams 5A **32**

Bk. St James St. *Oldh* 2F **73**
Bk. St Mary's Pl. *Bury* 3C **36**
   (off St Mary's Pl.)
Bk. Salford St. *Bury* 1E **37**
   (off Salford St.)
Bk. Sankey St. *Bury* 3B **36**
   (off Sankey St.)
Bk. Sapling Rd. S.
   Bolt 5F **45**
Bk. Scott St. *Oldh* 4D **72**
   (off Scott St.)
Bk. Settle St. N. *Bolt* 4H **45**
Bk. Seymour Rd. *Bolt* 2B **32**
Bk. Shepard St. *Bury* 3D **36**
Bk. Shipton St. *Rams* 4F **31**
Bk. Silver St. *Bury* 3C **36**
   (off Silver St.)
Bk. Somerset Rd. W.
   Rams 5F **31**
Bk. South Pde. *M3* 4D **94** (5G **5**)
Bk. Spear St. *M1* . .3F **95** (4C **6**)
Bk. Spring St. E. *Bury* 4D **36**
   (off Spring St.)
Bk. Spring St. W. *Bury* . . .4D **36**
Bk. Square St. *Rams* 3E **13**
Bk. Stanley St. *Rams* 4D **12**
   (off Buchanan St.)
Bk. Stephen St. *Bury* 3A **36**
   (off Stephen St.)
Back St. *P'wich* 4D **66**
Bk. Teak St. *Bury* 3F **37**
Bk. Tenterden St. *Bury* . . .3B **36**
   (off Tenterden St.)
Bk. Tenterden St. *Bury* . . .3C **36**
   (off St Mary's Pl.)
Bk. Thomasson Clo.
   Rams 4A **32**
Bk. Thomas St.
   M4 . . . . . .3E **95** (4B **6**)
Bk. Thorns Rd. *Rams* 2A **32**
Bk. Tonge Moor Rd.
   Bolt 2D **32**
   (off Colmore St.)
Bk. Tonge Moor Rd.
   Bolt 2D **32**
   (off Tonge Moor Rd.)
Bk. Tonge Moor Rd. E.
   Bolt 2D **32**
Backton Pl. *M40* 1H **95**
Bk. Tootal Rd. *Salf* 3D **92**
Bk. Tottington Rd.
   Bury 1H **35**
   (off Tottington Rd.)
Bk. Tottington Rd. E.
   Bolt 6A **20**
   (off Tottington Rd.)
Bk. Tottington Rd. N.
   Bury 1A **36**
Bk. Tottington Rd. S.
   Bury 1A **36**
Bk. Turner St.
   M4 . . . . . .3E **95** (4B **6**)
Bk. Turton Rd. E. *Bolt* 5G **19**
   (off Turton Rd.)
Bk. Turton Rd. W. *Bolt* . . .6G **19**
   (off Ellerbeck Clo.)
Bk. Turton Rd. W. *Bolt* . . .6G **19**
   (off Turton Rd.)
Bk. Turton Rd. W. *Bolt* . . .1E **33**
   (off Maud St.)
Bk. Union Rd. *Roch* 5C **16**
Bk. Vernon St. *Bury* 1D **36**
Bk. Vernon St. *Rams* 5A **32**
Bk. Victoria Gro. *Bolt* 4G **31**
   (off Oxford Gro.)
Bk. Viola St. *Bolt* 2A **32**
Bk. Walmersley Rd. E.
   Bury 6F **23**
   (off Mostyn Av.)
Bk. Walmersley Rd. E.
   Bury 1D **36**
   (Chesham Rd.)

Bk. Walmersley Rd. E.
   Bury 5F **23**
   (Walmersley Rd.)
Bk. Walmersley Rd. W.
   Bury 4F **23**
   (Limefield Brow)
Bk. Walmersley Rd. W.
   Bury 1D **36**
   (Russell St.)
Bk. Walshaw Rd. N.
   Bury 2A **36**
Bk. Walshaw Rd. S.
   Bury 2A **36**
Bk. Wash La. S. *Bury* 3F **37**
   (off Wash La.)
Bk. Water St. *Eger* 1B **18**
   (off Water St.)
Bk. Water St. *Stoc* 1H **139**
Bk. Wellington Rd. S.
   Bury 5C **36**
   (off Wellington Rd.)
Bk. Wells St. *Bury* 4C **36**
   (off Wells St.)
Bk. Weston St. N. *Bolt* 3C **46**
   (off Weston St.)
Back Whitegate. *L'boro* . . .5C **16**
Bk. Wigan Rd. N. *Bolt* 3E **45**
   (Dealey St.)
Bk. Wigan Rd. N. *Bolt* 2F **45**
   (Grange Rd.)
Bk. Willows La. *Bolt* 3G **45**
Bk. Woking Gdns.
   Rams 4A **32**
Bk. Young St. *Farn* 2G **63**
Bacon Av. *Dent* 2G **129**
Bacup St. *M40* 3A **84**
Badby Clo. *M4* 4H **95** (5H **7**)
Baddeley Clo. *Stoc* 6F **139**
Badder St. *Rams* 5B **32**
Baden St. *M11* 5A **96**
Bader Dri. *Heyw* 6F **39**
Badger Clo. *Roch* 2H **41**
Badger Edge La.
   Oldh 4E **59**
Badger La. *Roch* 3H **41**
   (in three parts)
Badger St. *Bury* 2D **36**
Badgers Wlk. *M22* 4C **148**
Badminton Rd. *M21* 6A **108**
Bagnall Clo. *Roch* 1B **26**
Bagnall Clo. *Upperm* 6C **60**
Bagnall Ct. *M22* 3C **136**
Bagnall Wlk. *M22* 3C **136**
Bagot St. *M11* 3E **97**
Bagot St. *Swin* 2C **78**
Bagshaw St. *Hyde* 2C **114**
Bagslate Moor. 3B **26**
Bagslate Moor La.
   Roch 3B **26**
Bagslate Moor Rd.
   Roch 4A **26**
Bagstock Av. *Poy* 5E **163**
Baguley. 4G **135**
Baguley Cres. *Midd* 2C **68**
Baguley Cres. *Stoc* 5F **139**
Baguley Dri. *Bury* 5E **51**
Baguley La. *Sale* 6E **123**
   (in three parts)
Baguley Rd. *Sale* 5E **123**
Baguley St. *Droy* 4B **98**
Baildon Rd. *Roch* 2D **26**
Baildon St. *M40* 2A **84**
Bailey La. *Bolt* 4G **33**
   (in two parts)
Bailey La. *Man A* 4H **147**
Bailey La. *Part* 5D **118**
Bailey Rd. *Traf P* 6A **92**
Bailey St. *M11* 4F **97**
Bailey St. *Oldh* 2E **73**
Bailey St. *P'wich* 4G **67**
Bailey Wlk. *Bow* 5E **145**
Baillie St. *Rad* 2C **50**

Baillie St. *Roch* 4H **27**
   (in three parts)
Baillie St. E. *Roch* 3A **28**
Bails, The. *Salf* 5G **81**
Bainbridge Clo.
   M12 . . . . .1H **109** (6H **11**)
Bainbridge Rd. *Oldh* 6H **57**
Bainburgh Clough.
   Oldh 5G **73**
Baines Av. *Irlam* 1D **118**
Baines St. *Rams* 5F **31**
Bain St. *Swin* 4F **79**
Bainton Wlk. *M9* 4E **69**
Baird St. *M1* 5F **95** (1D **10**)
Baitings Clo. *Roch* 1G **25**
Baitings Row. *Roch* 1G **25**
Baker Ho. *Rytn* 3C **56**
   (off Royton Hall Wlk.)
Baker St. *Ash L* 5E **87**
Baker St. *Heyw* 5G **39**
Baker St. *Kear* 3B **64**
Baker St. *Midd* 1B **70**
Baker St. *Rams* 4D **12**
Baker St. *Stal* 4F **101**
Baker St. *Stoc* 6G **127**
Baker St. *Timp* 4C **134**
Bakewell Av. *Ash L* 5B **88**
Bakewell Av. *Dent* 1G **129**
Bakewell Bank. *Glos* 6F **117**
   (off Bakewell Gro.)
Bakewell Clo. *Glos* 6F **117**
   (off Bakewell M.)
Bakewell Fold. *Glos* 6F **117**
   (off Bakewell M.)
Bakewell Gdns. *Glos* 6F **117**
   (off Bakewell M.)
Bakewell Grn. *Glos* 6F **117**
   (off Bakewell M.)
Bakewell Gro. *Glos* 6F **117**
   (off Bakewell M.)
Bakewell Lea. *Glos* 6F **117**
   (off Bakewell M.)
Bakewell M. *Glos* 6F **117**
Bakewell Rd. *Droy* 3G **97**
Bakewell Rd. *Eccl* 5E **91**
Bakewell Rd. *Haz G* 5E **153**
Bakewell Rd. *Stret* 4A **106**
Bakewell St. *M18* 3E **111**
Bakewell St. *Stoc* 3F **139**
Bakewell Wlk. *Glos* 6F **117**
   (off Bakewell Gro.)
Bala Clo. *Salf* 3G **93**
Balcary Gro. *Bolt* 5F **31**
Balcombe Clo. *Bury* 4C **22**
Balderstone. 2H **41**
Balderstone Rd. *Roch* 3F **41**
Baldingstone. 2F **23**
Baldock Rd. *M20* 6H **125**
Baldwin Rd. *M19* 3B **126**
Baldwin St. *Bolt* 2H **45**
   (in two parts)
Bale St. *M2* 5D **94** (1H **9**)
Balfour Gro. *Stoc* 6H **111**
Balfour Rd. *Alt* 4F **133**
Balfour Rd. *Roch* 2E **27**
Balfour Rd. *Urm* 5D **104**
Balfour St. *M8* 3C **82**
Balfour St. *Bolt* 1H **45**
Balfour St. *Oldh* 2G **73**
Balfour St. *Salf* 5E **81**
Balfour St. *Shaw* 6F **43**
Balham Wlk. *M12* 1B **110**
Ballantine St. *M40* 1E **97**
Ballard Clo. *L'boro* 2F **17**
Ballard Way. *Shaw* 5G **43**
Ballater Av. *Urm* 6C **104**
Ballater Clo. *Heyw* 4D **38**
Ballater Wlk. *M8* 4B **82**
Ballbrook Av. *M20* 4E **125**
Ballbrook Ct. *M20* 5F **125**
Balleratt St. *M19* 6C **110**
Balliol Clo. *Woodl* 5A **130**
Balliol St. *Cale* 4F **121**
Balliol St. *M8* 3C **82**

Balliol St. *Swin* 3E **79**
Balloon La. *M4* 3A **6**
Balloon St. *M4* 3E **95** (3A **6**)
Ball St. *Roch* 3A **28**
Ball Wlk. *Hyde* 6B **116**
Ballygreen. *Roch* 2C **40**
Balmain Av. *M18* 4E **111**
Balmain Rd. *Urm* 4D **104**
Balmer Dri. *M23* 1H **147**
Balmfield St. *M8* 6C **82**
Balmforth St.
   M15 . . . . .6B **94** (3D **8**)
Balmoral Av. *Aud* 6D **98**
Balmoral Av. *Chea H* 3C **150**
Balmoral Av. *Hyde* 1C **130**
Balmoral Av. *L Lev* 4A **48**
Balmoral Av. *Roch* 3D **26**
Balmoral Av. *Rytn* 3D **56**
Balmoral Av. *Stret* 4D **106**
Balmoral Av. *Urm* 6D **104**
Balmoral Av. *W'fld* 2E **67**
Balmoral Clo. *Bury* 2E **51**
Balmoral Clo. *G'mnt* 2A **22**
Balmoral Clo. *Miln* 5G **29**
Balmoral Ct. *M8* 4B **68**
Balmoral Dri. *Dent* 3A **112**
Balmoral Dri. *Heyw* 4C **38**
Balmoral Dri. *H Lane* 6C **154**
Balmoral Dri. *Poy* 4D **162**
Balmoral Dri. *Stal* 2E **101**
Balmoral Dri. *Timp* 3H **133**
Balmoral Grange.
   P'wich 6A **68**
Balmoral Gro. *Haz G* 2F **153**
Balmoral Ho. *Eccl* 3E **91**
   (off Queen Victoria St.)
Balmoral Rd. *M14* 1H **125**
Balmoral Rd. *Alt* 1G **145**
Balmoral Rd. *Farn* 2E **63**
Balmoral Rd. *Stoc* 6C **126**
Balmoral Rd. *Swin* 1G **79**
Balmoral Rd. *Urm* 6C **104**
Balmoral St. *M18* 3E **111**
Balmoral Way. *Wilm* 3D **166**
Balmore Clo. *Bolt* 4E **45**
Balmore Ct. *Heyw* 4A **38**
Balm St. *Rams* 5C **12**
   (in two parts)
Balsam Clo.
   M13 . . . . . .6G **95** (4E **11**)
Balshaw Av. *Irlam* 5D **102**
Balshaw Clo. *Bolt* 2G **45**
Balshaw Ct. *Irlam* 5E **103**
Baltic Rd. *B'hth* 5C **132**
Baltic St. *Salf* 3E **93**
Baltimore St. *M40* 6H **83**
Bamber Av. *Sale* 6E **123**
Bamber Wlk. *Bolt* 2H **45**
Bamburgh Clo. *Rad* 2C **48**
Bamburgh Dri. *Ash L* 6C **86**
Bambury St. *Bury* 2D **36**
Bamford. 5A **26**
Bamford Av. *Dent* 1F **129**
Bamford Av. *Midd* 5A **54**
Bamford Clo. *Bury* 1A **38**
Bamford Clo. *H Grn* 5F **149**
Bamford Ct. *Roch* 5D **26**
   (off Half Acre M.)
Bamford Fold. *Glos* 6G **117**
   (off Castleton Cres.)
Bamford Gdns. *Timp* 5D **134**
Bamford Grn. *Glos* 6G **117**
   (off Castleton Cres.)
Bamford Gro. *M20* 6E **125**
Bamford Gro. *Ash L* 5B **88**
Bamford La. *Glos* 6G **117**
Bamford M. *Glos* 6G **117**
Bamford Pl. *Roch* 2G **27**
Bamford Rd. *M9* 4F **69**
Bamford Rd. *M20* 6E **125**
Bamford Rd. *Heyw* 1E **39**

Bamford Rd.—Barmhouse M.

Bamford Rd. Rams 1G 13
Bamford Shop. Cen.
Roch 4A 26
Bamfords Pas. L'boro 3F 17
Bamford St. M11 . . . . . . .3D 96
Bamford St. Chad 1A 72
Bamford St. L'boro 4D 16
(Featherstall Rd.)
Bamford St. L'boro 3C 16
(Shore Rd.)
Bamford St. Rytn 4C 56
Bamford St. Stoc 3H 139
Bamford Way. Roch 5A 26
Bampton Clo. Stoc 4B 140
Bampton Rd. M22 . . . . .4B 148
Bampton Wlk. Midd 5G 53
Banbury Dri. Timp 3G 133
Banbury M. Swin 2D 78
Banbury Rd. M23 . . . . . .6F 135
Banbury Rd. Fail 1G 97
Banbury Rd. Midd 4H 69
Banbury St. Bolt 4E 33
Banbury St. Stoc 2H 139
Bancroft Av. Chea H 4C 150
Bancroft Clo. Bred 6E 129
Bancroft Ct. Hale 2H 145
Bancroft Fold. Hyde 2F 115
Bancroft Rd. Hale 2A 146
Bancroft Rd. Swin 2E 79
Banff Gro. Heyw 4C 38
Banff Rd. M14 . . . . . . .3G 109
Bangor Rd. Chea 5B 138
Bangor St.
M15 . . . . .2B 108 (6D 8)
Bangor St. Ash L 3C 100
Bangor St. Bolt 5A 32
Bangor St. Roch 5B 28
Bangor St. Stoc 5H 127
Bank. Roch 2A 16
Bank Barn. Ward 2B 16
Bank Barn La. Ward 2B 16
Bankbottom. Had 2H 117
Bank Bri. Rd. M11 . . . . . .2D 96
Bank Clo. L'boro 6E 17
Banker St. Bolt 2E 47
Bankfield. Bolt 5C 34
Bankfield. Hyde 2B 114
Bankfield Av. M13 . . . . . .4A 110
Bankfield Av. Cad 4B 118
Bankfield Av. Droy 3A 98
Bankfield Av. Stoc 1E 139
Bankfield Clo. A'wth 4C 34
Bankfield Cotts. Dob 5H 59
Bankfield Cotts.
Woodl 4G 129
Bankfield Dri. Oldh 1F 87
Bankfield Dri. Wors 4D 76
Bankfield Ho. Woodl 4H 129
Bankfield La. Roch 3A 26
Bankfield M. Bury 6C 36
Bankfield Rd. Chea H . . .4B 150
Bankfield Rd. Sale 3G 121
Bankfield Rd. Tyl 3A 76
Bankfield Rd. Woodl 4H 129
Bankfield St. Bolt 3G 45
(Anglia Gro.)
Bankfield St. Bolt 2G 45
(Deane Rd.)
Bank Fld. St. Rad 2D 64
Bankfield St. Stoc 5G 127
Bankfield Trad. Est.
Stoc 5G 127
Bankfoot Wlk. M8 . . . . . . .6C 82
(off Alderglen Rd.)
Bankgate. B'btm 6C 116
Bank Gro. L Hul 3B 62
Bank Hall Clo. Bury 3G 35
Bankhall La. Hale 5G 145
Bankhall Rd. Stoc 6C 126
Bankhall Wlk. M9 . . . . . . .4G 83
(off Broadwell Dri.)
Bank Hill St. Oldh 2G 73
Bankhirst Clo. Crum 2C 82
Bank Ho. Tyl 2A 76
Bank Ho. Rd. M9 . . . . . . .5D 68
Bankhouse Rd. Bury 6C 22
Banklands Clo. Cad 4B 118
Bank Lane. 2G 13
Bank La. G'fld 5H 61
Bank La. L Hul 3B 62
Bank La. Swin & Salf 6B 80
Bank La. Tin 1H 117
Bank La. Ward 2B 16
Bankley St. M19 . . . . . . .6C 110
Bankmill Clo.
M13 . . . . . . .6F 95 (4D 10)
Bank Pl. Bury 2A 36
Bank Pl. Salf 3B 94 (4C 4)
Bank Rd. M8 . . . . .1C 82
Bank Rd. Bolt 6C 18
Bank Rd. Bred 6G 129
Bank Rd. Carr 6G 89
Banks Ct. Timp 6D 134
Banks Cft. Heyw 6F 39
Bankside. Haleb 1D 156
Bankside. Hyde 6H 115
Bank Side. Moss 3E 89
Bankside Av. Rad 3B 50
Bankside Av. Upperm 2G 61
Bankside Clo. Marp B . . .2F 143
Bankside Clo. Oldh 3B 72
Bankside Clo. Wilm 5H 159
Bankside Ct. M12 . . . . . .3D 110
Bankside Ct. Stoc 1C 138
Bankside Rd. M20 . . . . . .4F 137
Bankside Wlk. Hyde 5H 115
Banks La. Stoc 3B 140
Bank Sq. Wilm 2E 167
Banks, The. 2H 155
Bank St. M7 . . . . .3B 82
Bank St. M11 . . . . .2C 96
(in two parts)
Bank St. Ash L 3H 99
Bank St. Aud 1F 113
Bank St. Bolt 6B 32
Bank St. B'btm 6C 116
Bank St. Bury 3C 36
Bank St. Chea 5A 138
Bank St. Dent 1G 129
Bank St. Droy 5H 97
Bank St. Farn 1F 63
Bank St. G'brk 4A 118
Bank St. Had 2H 117
Bank St. Heyw 3D 38
(in two parts)
Bank St. Hyde 4B 114
Bank St. Oldh 3H 73
Bank St. Rad 5H 49
Bank St. Rams 2G 13
Bank St. Roch 1G 41
Bank St. Sale 4C 122
Bank St. Salf 3B 94 (4C 4)
Bank St. Shaw 6E 43
Bank St. Wals 1F 35
Bank St. W'fld 6C 50
Bank St. Woodl 4H 129
Bankswood Clo. Had . . .3H 117
Bank Ter. Whitw 1C 14
Bank, The. Roch 4H 27
Bank Top. 6E 19
(Bolton)
Bank Top. 3H 73
(Greenacres)
Bank Top. 3C 72
(Oldham)
Bank Top. Ash L 3A 100
Bank Top. Bury 2F 23
Bank Top. Rad 1H 49
Bank Top Gro. Bolt 6E 19
Bank Top Pk. Oldh 3H 73
Bank Top St. Heyw 2D 38
Bank Top Vw. Kear 2A 64
Bank Vw. Farn 2G 63
Bank Wood. Bolt 6D 30
Banky La. Sale 3E 121
Bannach Dri. Chad 6G 55
Bannatyne Clo. M40 . . . . .2E 85
Bannerdale Clo. M13 . . .3B 110
Bannerman Av. P'wich . . .6F 67
Bannerman Rd. Droy 4B 98
Bannerman St. Salf 4A 82
Banner Wlk. M11 . . . . . . .4B 96
Bannister Dri. Chea H . . .3B 150
Bannister St. Bolt 5G 33
Bannister St. Stoc 4H 139
Bann St. Stoc 3G 139
Banstead Av. M22 . . . . .4B 136
Bantry Dri. M9 . . . . .6D 68
Bantry St. Bolt 2A 46
Bantry St. Roch 1A 28
Baptist St. M4 . . . .2F 95 (2C 6)
Barathea Clo. Roch 2A 40
Barbara Rd. Bolt 5E 45
Barbara St. Bolt 3H 45
Barbeck Clo.
M40 . . . . . . .2A 96 (2H 7)
Barberry Bank. Eger 1B 18
Barberry Clo. B'hth 4D 132
Barberry Wlk. Part 6D 118
Barbican St. M20 . . . . . .2F 125
(in two parts)
Barbirolli Mall.
M4 . . . . .3E 95 (4A 6)
(off Arndale Shop. Cen.)
Barbirolli Sq.
M2 . . . . .5D 94 (2H 9)
(off Lwr. Mosley St.)
Barbon Wlk. M4 . . .3G 95 (4E 7)
Barchester Av. Bolt 4G 33
Barcheston Rd. Chea . . .1G 149
Barcicroft Rd.
M19 & Stoc 5A 126
Barcicroft Wlk. M19 . . . .5A 126
Barclay Dri. Eccl 2G 91
Barclay Rd. Poy 5E 163
Barclays Av. Salf 5B 80
Barcliffe Av. M40 . . . . . . .1C 84
Barclyde St. Roch 6G 27
Barcombe Clo. Oldh 5H 57
Barcombe Clo. Urm 4H 105
Barcombe Wlk. M9 . . . . . .4F 83
(in two parts)
Barcroft Rd. Bolt 3F 31
Barcroft St. Bury 2D 36
Bardell Cres. Poy 5D 162
Bardon Clo. Bolt 4H 31
Bardon Rd. M23 . . . . . . .5F 135
Bardsea Av. M22 . . . . . .4B 148
Bardsley. 3E 87
Bardsley Av. Fail 4F 85
Bardsley Clo. Bolt 6H 19
Bardsley Clo. Hyde 5A 116
Bardsley Gate. 1A 116
Bardsley Ga. Av. Stal 1A 116
Bardsley St. M40 . . . . . . .6D 84
Bardsley St. Chad 6F 71
Bardsley St. Lees 4A 74
Bardsley St. Midd 6A 54
Bardsley St. Oldh 1A 74
Bardsley St. Stoc 6F 127
Bardsley Va. Av. Oldh 3E 87
Barehill St. L'boro 3F 17
Bare St. Rams 5C 32
Barff Rd. Salf 3C 92
Barfold Clo. Stoc 6G 141
Barford Dri. Wilm 6G 159
Barford Wlk. M23 . . . . . .1H 147
Bar Gap Rd. Oldh 1D 72
Baric Clo. Eccl 4H 91
Baring St. M1 . . . .5F 95 (2D 10)
Baring St. Ind. Est.
M1 . . . . .5G 95 (2E 11)
Barkan Way. Swin 3H 79
Barker Rd. Bred 1F 141
Barkers La. Sale 4H 121
Barker St. M3 . . . .2D 94 (1G 5)
Barker St. Bury 4C 36
Barker St. Heyw 4D 38
Barker St. Oldh 2C 72
Barke St. L'boro 6C 16
Barking St. M40 . . . . .2A 96
Bark St. Bolt 6A 32
(in two parts)
Bark St. E. Bolt 5B 32
Bark Wlk. M15 . . .1D 108 (5H 9)
Barkway Rd. Stret 5A 106
Barkwell La. Moss 2D 88
Barkworth Wlk. M40 . . . . .5B 84
Bar La. Bolt 6C 18
Barlby Wlk. M40 . . . . .5B 84
Barlea Av. M40 . . . . .2D 84
Barley Brook Mdw.
Bolt 5D 18
Barleycorn Clo. Sale 6F 123
Barley Cft. Chea H 5B 150
Barleycroft. Had 3H 117
Barley Cft. Rd. Hyde 1C 114
Barleycroft St. M16 . . . .3D 108
Barley Dri. Bram 6G 151
Barleyfield Wlk. Midd 6H 53
Barley Hall St. Heyw 2G 39
Barleywood Wlk. Stal . . .5H 101
Barlow Ct. Wors 6G 63
Barlow Cres. Marp 1D 154
Barlow Fold. 2D 50
(Bury)
Barlowfold. 6B 130
(Stockport)
Barlow Fold. Bury 2D 50
Barlow Fold. Rom 6B 130
Barlow Fold Clo. Bury 2D 50
Barlow Fold Rd. Rom . . .6B 130
Barlow Fold Rd. Stoc . . .1H 127
Barlow Hall Rd. M21 . . . .4A 124
Barlow Ho. Bolt 3F 31
Barlow Ho. Oldh 4D 72
Barlow La. Eccl 3E 91
Barlow La. N. Stoc 1H 127
Barlow Moor. 4A 124
Barlow Moor Clo.
Roch 1A 26
Barlow Moor Ct. M20 . . .6D 124
Barlow Moor Rd.
M21 & M20 . . . . . .6H 107
Barlow Pk. Av. Bolt 6B 18
Barlow Pl.
M13 . . . . . . .6G 95 (4E 11)
Barlow Rd. B'hth 3D 132
Barlow Rd. Duk 5B 100
Barlow Rd. Lev 6C 110
Barlow Rd. Salf 4A 94 (6B 4)
Barlow Rd. Stret 3F 107
Barlow Rd. Wilm 6F 159
Barlow's Cft.
Salf 3C 94 (4F 5)
Barlow's La. S. Haz G . . .2C 152
Barlow St. Bury 2D 36
Barlow St. Eccl 4F 91
Barlow St. Heyw 5G 39
Barlow St. Oldh 3E 73
Barlow St. Rad 4H 49
Barlow St. Roch 4A 28
Barlow St. Wors 5F 63
Barlow Ter.
M13 . . . . . .6G 95 (4D 10)
(off Wadeson Rd.)
Barlow Ter. M21 . . . . . . .4A 124
(off Barlow Hall Rd.)
Barlow Wlk. Stoc 1H 127
Barlow Wood Dri.
Marp 2F 155
Barmeadow. Dob 5H 59
Barmhouse Clo. Hyde . . .4E 115
Barmhouse La. Hyde . . .4E 115
(Rowanswood Dri.)
Barmhouse La. Hyde 4E 115
(Sheffield Rd.)
Barmhouse M. Hyde 4E 115

A-Z Manchester 181

Barmouth St. *M11* 5B **96**
Barmouth Wlk. *Oldh* 1H **85**
Barnaby Rd. *Poy* 5D **162**
Barnacre Av. *M23* 2F **147**
Barnacre Av. *Bolt* 6H **33**
Barnard Av. *Stoc* 1D **138**
Barnard Av. *W'fld* 2F **67**
Barnard Clo. *Ash L* 6D **86**
Barnard Rd. *M18* 4D **110**
Barnard St. *Bolt* 5E **33**
Barnbrook St. *Bury* 2E **37**
Barnby St. *M12* 4C **110**
Barn Clo. *Urm* 5G **103**
Barnclose Rd. *M22* 4B **148**
Barn Ct. *Bolt* 3E **33**
Barncroft Gdns. *M22* . . .6A **136**
Barncroft Rd. *Farn* 1F **63**
Barnes Av. *Stoc* 1C **138**
Barnes Clo. *Farn* 1G **63**
Barnes Clo. *Rams* 6C **12**
Barnes Green 2F **83**
Barnes Ho. Farn 1F *63*
  (off Hesketh Wlk.)
Barnes Meadows.
  L'boro 6G **17**
Barnes St. *Farn* 1D **62**
Barnes Ter. *Kear* 2A **64**
Barnet Rd. *Rams* 3G **31**
Barnett Ct. *Heyw* 4E **38**
Barnett Dri. *Salf* . . .3B **94** (3D **4**)
Barnfield. *L'boro* 3H **17**
Barnfield. *Urm* 6D **104**
Barnfield Av. *Rom* 6B **130**
Barnfield Clo. *Eger* 1C **18**
Barnfield Clo. *Rad* 4E **49**
Barnfield Clo. *Salf* 4F **93**
Barnfield Cres. *Sale* 3H **121**
Barnfield Dri. *Wors* 5D **76**
Barnfield Ri. *Shaw* 4E **43**
Barnfield Rd. *M19* 5A **126**
Barnfield Rd. *Hyde* 2E **115**
Barnfield Rd. *Swin* 1D **78**
Barnfield Rd. E. *Stoc* . . .1H **151**
Barnfield Rd. W. *Stoc* . . .1F **151**
Barnfield St. *Dent* 3D **112**
Barnfield St. *Heyw* 3G **39**
Barnfield St. *Roch* 1H **27**
Barnfield Wlk. *Timp* 6C **134**
  (in two parts)
Barn Fold. *Lees* 4A **74**
Barnford Bus. Pk.
  Stoc 4G **127**
Barngate Dri. *Moss* 3E **89**
Barngate Rd. *Gat* 5E **137**
Barn Gro. *Aud* 6E **99**
Barnham Wlk. *M23* 3E **135**
Barnhill Av. *P'wich* 1F **81**
Barnhill Dri. *P'wich* 1F **81**
Barnhill Rd. *P'wich* 6D **66**
Barnhill St. *M14* 3D **108**
Barnley Clo. *Irlam* 4F **103**
Barnsdale Clo. *A'wth* 5C **34**
Barnsdale Dri. *M8* 5C **82**
Barnsfold Av. *M14* 1G **125**
Barnsfold Rd. *Marp* 2D **154**
Barnside. *Whitw* 1C **14**
Barnside Av. *Wors* 6G **63**
Barnside Clo. *Bury* 3E **23**
Barnside Way. *Fail* 5A **86**
Barnsley St. *Stoc* 3B **140**
Barns Pl. *Haleb* 5C **146**
Barnstaple Dri. *M40* 5E **83**
Barnstead Av. *M20* 4H **125**
Barnston Av. *M14* 5F **109**
Barnston Clo. *Bolt* 1B **32**
Barn St. *Oldh* 3C **72**
Barn St. *Rad* 3A **50**
Barn St. *Rams* 6A **32**
Barn St. *W'fld* 2D **66**
Barnswell St. *M40* 6C **84**
Barnview Dri. *Irlam* 6D **102**

Barn Wlk. *Open* 6G **97**
Barnway Wlk. *M40* 1C **84**
Barnwell Clo. *Aud* 2E **113**
Barnwood Clo. Bolt 4A *32*
  (off Barnwood Dri.)
Barnwood Dri. *Rams* 4A **32**
Barnwood Rd. *M23* . . .3G **147**
Barnwood Ter. Bolt 4A *32*
  (off Barnwood Dri.)
Baroness Gro. *Salf* 1A **94**
Baron Fold. *L Hul* 4C **62**
Baron Fold Cres. *L Hul* . . .4B **62**
Baron Fold Gro. *L Hul* . . .4B **62**
Baron Fold Rd. *L Hul* 4B **62**
Baron Grn. *H Grn* 6H **149**
Baron Rd. *Hyde* 2D **130**
Barons Ct. *Fail* 5D **84**
Barons Ct. *Wilm* 2E **167**
Baron St. *Bury* 4B **36**
  (in three parts)
Baron St. *Oldh* 4F **73**
Baron St. *Roch* 4H **27**
Baron Wlk. *L Lev* 4C **48**
Barrack Hill. 6G **129**
Barrack Hill. *Rom* 1G **141**
Barrack Hill Clo. *Bred* . . .6G **129**
Barracks La. *Sale* 3F **121**
Barrack St. *M15* . . .6B **94** (4C **8**)
Barra Dri. *Urm* 2F **105**
Barrass St. *M11* 6F **97**
Barratt Gdns. *Midd* 3F **53**
Barrett Av. *Kear* 2H **63**
Barrett Ct. *Bury* 3E **37**
Barrett St. *Oldh* 4F **73**
Barrfield Rd. *Salf* 1E **93**
Barr Hill Av. *Salf* 6C **80**
Barrhill Clo.
  M15 . . . . . .1C **108** (5E **9**)
Barrie Way. *Bolt* 1D **32**
Barrington Av. *Chea H* . . .4C **150**
Barrington Av. *Droy* 4H **97**
Barrington Clo. *Alt* 5F **133**
Barrington Rd. *Alt* 5F **133**
Barrington St. *M11* 3E **97**
Barrisdale Clo. *Bolt* 2D **44**
Barrow Bridge. 1D **30**
Barrow Bri. Rd. *Bolt* 1D **30**
Barrowdene Ho. *Bolt* 2D **30**
Barrowfield Rd. *M22* 3G **147**
Barrowfields. *Midd* 5A **54**
Barrowfield Wlk. *Midd* . . .6A **54**
Barrow Hill Rd. *M8* 6B **82**
Barrow La. *Hale* 6B **146**
  (in two parts)
Barrow Mdw. *Chea H* . . .5A **150**
Barrows Ct. *Rams* 1B **46**
Barrowshaw Clo. *Wors* . . .1E **77**
Barrow St. *Salf* . . .4B **94** (5C **4**)
Barr St. *Kear* 4B **64**
Barrule Av. *Haz G* 4E **153**
Barry Ct. *M20* 3F **125**
Barry Cres. *Wors* 6C **62**
Barry Lawson Clo.
  M8 . . . . .4B **82**
Barry Ri. *Bow* 3C **144**
Barry Rd. *M23* 1H **135**
Barry Rd. *Stoc* 4H **127**
Barry St. *Oldh* 1F **73**
Barsham Dri. *Bolt* 2H **45**
Bar Ter. *Whitw* 2C **14**
Bartlam Pl. *Oldh* 2D **72**
Bartlemore St. *Oldh* 6E **57**
Bartlett Rd. *Shaw* 1E **57**
Bartlett St. *M11* 6D **96**
Bartley Rd. *M22* 3A **136**
Barton Aerodrome Vis. Cen.
  . . . . .6A **90**
Barton Arc. M2 . . .4D **94** (5H *5*)
  (off Deansgate)
Barton Av. *Urm* 5D **104**
Barton Bus. Pk. *Eccl* 4E **91**
Barton Clo. *Wilm* 5H **159**

Barton Dock Rd.
  Urm & Stret 1G **105**
Barton Embkmt. *Urm* 6E **91**
Barton Fold. *Hyde* 6B **114**
Barton Hall Av. *Eccl* 4C **90**
Barton Ho. *Salf* 1C **92**
Barton La. *Eccl* 5H **91**
Barton Moss Rd. *Eccl* . . .1H **103**
Barton Rd. *Duk* 1A **114**
Barton Rd. *Eccl* 4E **91**
Barton Rd. *Farn* 2D **62**
Barton Rd. *Midd* 1H **69**
Barton Rd. *Stoc* 2A **138**
Barton Rd. *Stret* 3H **105**
Barton Rd. *Swin* 4G **79**
Barton Rd. *Urm* 3E **105**
Barton Rd. *Wors* 6H **77**
Barton Sq. *M2* . . .4D **94** (5F **5**)
Barton St. *M3* . . .5C **94** (2F **9**)
  (in two parts)
Barton St. *Kear* 2G **63**
Barton St. *Oldh* 1B **72**
Barton St. *Swin* 1F **79**
Barton Ter. *Irlam* 4G **103**
Barton Upon Irwell. 5F **91**
Barton Wlk. *Farn* 2D **62**
Barway Rd. *M21* 6F **107**
Barwell Clo. *Stoc* 1H **127**
Barwell Rd. *Sale* 4G **121**
Barwell Sq. *Farn* 1D **62**
Barwick Pl. *Sale* 5A **122**
Barwood Lee. *Rams* 4E **13**
Basechurch Wlk. M12 . . .1B *110*
  (off Skarratt Clo.)
Basford Rd. *M16* 4H **107**
Bashall St. *Bolt* 5G **31**
Basil Ct. *Roch* 5B **28**
Basildon Clo. *M13* 2H **109**
Basil St. *M14* 4G **109**
Basil St. *Bolt* 2A **46**
Basil St. *Roch* 5B **28**
Basil St. *Stoc* 6G **127**
Basle Clo. *Bram* 1G **151**
Baslow Av. *M19* 5D **110**
Baslow Clo. Glos 6G *117*
  (off Baslow M.)
Baslow Dri. *Haz G* 5F **153**
Baslow Dri. *H Grn* 6G **149**
Baslow Fold. Glos 6G *117*
  (off Baslow M.)
Baslow Grn. Glos 6G *117*
  (off Baslow M.)
Baslow Gro. *Stoc* 4H **127**
Baslow M. *Glos* 6G **117**
Baslow Rd. *Dent* 1F **129**
Baslow Rd. *Droy* 2G **97**
Baslow Rd. *Stret* 4A **106**
Baslow St. *M11* 4A **96**
Baslow Way. Glos 6G *117*
  (off Baslow M.)
Basset Av. *Salf* 6G **81**
Bassett Clo. *Roch* 6E **15**
Bassett Gdns. *Roch* 6E **15**
Bassett Way. *Roch* 1G **27**
Bass La. *Bury* 6H **13**
Bass St. *Bolt* 6E **33**
Bass St. *Duk* 5H **99**
Basten Dri. *Salf* 5A **82**
Batchelor Clo. *M21* 2C **124**
Bates Clo. *Roch* 4D **40**
Bateson Dri. *S'head* 3B **74**
Bateson St. *Stoc* 1A **140**
Bateson Way. *Oldh* 4D **72**
Bates St. *M13* 3B **110**
Bates St. *Duk* 5A **100**
Bath Clo. *Haz G* 3G **153**
Bath Cres. *M16* 2A **108**
Bath Cres. *Chea H* 1D **160**
Bath Pl. *Hale* 3F **145**
Bath St. *Alt* 3F **145**
Bath St. *Bolt* 5B **32**
Bath St. *Chad* 2H **71**

Bath St. *Oldh* 4A **72**
Bath St. *Roch* 2A **28**
Batley St. *M9* 3G **83**
Batley St. *Moss* 2D **88**
Batsmans Dri. *Swin* 5E **65**
Battenberg Rd. *Bolt* 5G **31**
Battersbay Gro. *Haz G* . . .3E **153**
Battersby Ct. *Stoc* 5E **141**
Battersby St. *M11* 6G **97**
Battersby St. *Bury* 2H **37**
Battersby St. *Roch* 5D **26**
Battersea Rd. *Stoc* 2A **138**
Battle La. *Stoc* 2D **128**
Batty St. *M8* 6E **83**
Baum, The. *Roch* 3H **27**
Baxendale St. *Bolt* 1A **32**
Baxter Gdns. *M23* 4G **135**
Baxter Rd. *Sale* 5B **122**
Baxter St. *Oldh* 1H **85**
Baybutt St. *Rad* 4A **50**
Baycliffe Wlk. *M8* 5B **82**
Baycroft Gro. *M23* 2G **135**
Baydon Av. *Salf* 5B **82**
Bayfield Gro. *M40* 2A **84**
Bayley Clo. *Hyde* 2C **114**
Bayley Ct. *Bolt* 5H **31**
Bayley Ind. Est. *Stal* 4D **100**
Bayley St. *Rams* 5H **31**
Bayley St. *Stal* 3C **100**
Baynard Wlk. *M9* 5D **68**
Baysdale Av. *Bolt* 3D **44**
Baysdale Dri. *Rytn* 2A **56**
Baysdale Wlk. *M11* 4B **96**
Bayston Wlk. M12 . . . . .1B *110*
  (off Wenlock Way)
Bay St. *Heyw* 2D **38**
Bay St. *Oldh* 2B **72**
Bay St. *Roch* 2A **28**
Bayswater Av. *M40* 1D **96**
Bayswater St. *Bolt* 5G **45**
Baythorpe St. *Bolt* 2B **32**
Baytree Av. *Chad* 1E **71**
Baytree Av. *Dent* 3G **113**
Bay Tree Av. *Wors* 6A **78**
Baytree Dri. *Bred* 5F **129**
Baytree Gro. *Rams* 1B **22**
Baytree La. *Midd* 1D **70**
Baytree Wlk. *Whitw* 4G **15**
Baywood St. *M9* 3F **83**
Bazaar St. *Salf* 1G **93**
Bazley Rd. *M22* 2B **136**
Bazley St. *Bolt* 1D **30**
Beacomfold. *Rom* 6F **131**
Beacon Dri. *M23* 3G **147**
Beaconfield Av. *Hyde* . . .5C **114**
Beacon Gro. *Oldh* 5G **73**
Beacon Rd. *Rom* 2F **141**
Beacon Rd. *Traf P* 6G **91**
Beaconsfield. *M14* 2G **125**
Beaconsfield Rd. *Alt* 4F **133**
Beaconsfield St. *Bolt* 1H **45**
Beaconsfield Ter. *Stal* . . .4H **89**
Beacon Vw. *Marp* 3D **142**
Beadham Dri. *M9* 4C **68**
Beadle Av. *Roch* 4B **16**
Beagle Wlk. *M22* 5C **148**
Bealbank Clo. *Miln* 2E **43**
Beal Clo. *Stoc* 6H **125**
Beal Cres. *Roch* 2C **28**
  (in two parts)
Bealcroft Clo. *Miln* 4E **29**
Bealcroft Wlk. *Miln* 4E **29**
Beale Gro. *M21* 1H **123**
Bealey Av. *Rad* 2C **50**
Bealey Clo. *M18* 2D **110**
Bealey Clo. *Rad* 3B **50**
Bealey Dri. *Bury* 6B **36**
Bealey Ind. Est. *Rad* 2B **50**
Bealey Row. *Rad* 3A **50**
Beal La. *Shaw* 1F **57**
Beal Ter. *Miln* 5F **29**
Beal Vw. *Shaw* 6H **43**

Beal Wlk. *W'fld* 1G **67**
Beaminster Av. *Stoc* . . .6B **126**
Beaminster Clo. *Stoc* 6B **126**
Beaminster Ct. *Stoc* 6C *126*
    (off Beaminster Clo.)
Beaminster Rd. *Stoc* . . .6B **126**
Beaminster Wlk.
   M13 . . . . . .2G **109** (6F **11**)
Beamish Clo.
   M13 . . . . . .1G **109** (5E **11**)
Beamsley Dri. *M22* 3H **147**
Beanfields. *Wors* 6H **77**
Boanfiold Tor. *Wors* 6H **77**
Bean Leach Av. *Stoc* 5F **141**
Bean Leach Dri. *Stoc* 5F **141**
Bean Leach Rd.
   Haz G & Stoc 1E **153**
Beard Rd. *M18* 3E **111**
Beard St. *Droy* 4H **97**
Beard St. *Rytn* 4C **56**
Beardwood Rd. *M9* 5F **69**
Bearswood Clo. *Hyde* . . .6D **114**
Beathwaite Dri. *Bram* 4E **151**
Beatrice Av. *M18* 3H **111**
Beatrice Av. *Chea H* 3B **150**
Beatrice Rd. *Bolt* 5G **31**
Beatrice Rd. *Wors* 4B **78**
Beatrice St. *Dent* 4E **113**
Beatrice St. *Farn* 1E **63**
Beatrice St. *Roch* 4F **27**
Beatrice St. *Swin* 2D **78**
Beatrice Wignall St.
   Droy 5A **98**
Beatrix Dri. *Had* 4G **117**
Beattock Clo.
   M15 . . . . .6B **94** (4D **8**)
Beauchamp St. *Ash L* . . .1A **100**
Beaufort Dri. *Oldh* 4G **73**
Beaufort Av. *M20* 4E **125**
Beaufort Av. *Sale* 6C **122**
Beaufort Av. *Swin* 4D **78**
Beaufort Chase. *Wilm* . . .6B **160**
Beaufort Clo. *Hyde* 6A **116**
Beaufort Rd. *Ash L* 2B **100**
Beaufort Rd. *Hyde* 5A **116**
Beaufort Rd. *Sale* 6C **122**
Beaufort Rd. *Stoc* 1D **152**
Beaufort St. *M3* . . .5C **94** (2E **9**)
Beaufort St. *Eccl* 2D **90**
Beaufort St. *P'wich* 5G **67**
Beaufort St. *Roch* 2E **27**
Beaufort Wlk. *Hyde* 6A **116**
   (in two parts)
Beaulieu. *Hale* 3H **145**
Beauly Clo. *Rams* 1A **22**
Beaumaris Clo. *M12* 1B **110**
Beaumaris Cres.
   Haz G 5C **152**
Beaumonds Way. *Roch* . . .5C **28**
Beaumont Chase. *Bolt* 4D **44**
Beaumont Clo. *L'boro* 4D **16**
Beaumont Ct. *Bolt* 5B **30**
Beaumont Dri. *Hand* 2G **159**
Beaumont Dri. *Bolt* 2C **44**
Beaumont Rd. *M21* 2H **123**
Beaumont Rd.
   Bolt & Los 6B **30**
Beaumont St. *Ash L* 2A **100**
Beauvale Av. *Stoc* 4C **140**
Beaver Dri. *Bury* 3F **51**
Beaver Ho. *Stoc* 3B **140**
Beaver Rd. *M20* 6F **125**
Beaver St. *M1* . . .5E **95** (2A **10**)
Beaver Wlk. *Hyde* 6H **115**
Bebbington Clo. *Sale* 6F **123**
Bebbington St. *M11* 4E **97**
Beccles Rd. *Sale* 2B **134**
Beckenham Clo. *Bury* 4H **35**
Beckenham Rd. *M8* 4C **82**
Becket Av. *Salf* 5A **82**
Becket Meadows. *Oldh* . . .3F **73**

Becket Mdw. St. *Oldh* 3F **73**
Beckett St. *M18* 3E **111**
Beckett St. *Lees* 2A **74**
Beckfield Rd. *M23* 6G **135**
Beckfoot Dri. *M13* 4A **110**
Beckford Dri. *M40* 6G **83**
Beck Gro. *Shaw* 5H **43**
Beck Gro. *Wors* 2G **77**
Beckhampton Clo.
   M13 . . . . . .2G **109** (6F **11**)
Beck Ho. *Hyde* 6H **115**
Beckley Av. *P'wich* 1E **81**
Bookloy Clo. *Rytn* 3E **57**
Beckside. *Stoc* 6A **112**
Beck St. *M11* 6G **97**
Beck St. *Salf* 3C **94** (4E **5**)
Beckton Gdns. *M22* 2A **148**
Becontree Av. *Dent* 3G **113**
Becontree Dri. *M23* 4F **135**
Bedells La. *Wilm* 3D **166**
Bede St. *Rams* 3G **31**
Bedfont Wlk. *M9* 2G *83*
   (off Polworth Rd.)
Bedford Av. *M16* 5B **108**
Bedford Av. *Hyde* 4C **114**
Bedford Av. *Sale* 1D **134**
Bedford Av. *Shaw* 6D **42**
Bedford Av. *Swin* 4E **79**
Bedford Av. *Wors* 2E **77**
Bedford Ct. *Salf* 2H **81**
Bedford Ct. *Timp* 5C **134**
Bedford Dri. *Timp* 4C **134**
Bedford Gro. *Cad* 3A **118**
Bedford Rd. *M16* 4G **107**
Bedford Rd. *Eccl* 2G **91**
Bedford Rd. *Urm* 3F **105**
Bedford St. *Ash L* 3A **100**
Bedford St. *Bolt* 5H **31**
Bedford St. *Bury* 1E **37**
Bedford St. *Eger* 1B **18**
Bedford St. *Heyw* 3G **39**
Bedford St. *P'wich* 4G **67**
Bedford St. *Stoc* 1G **127**
   (in two parts)
Bedford Wlk. *Dent* 6F **113**
Bedlam Grn. *Bury* 3D *36*
   (off Butcher La.)
Bedlington Clo. *M23* 5D **134**
Bednal Av. *M40* 1A **96**
Bedwell St. *M16* 4D **108**
Bedworth Clo. *Bolt* 2D **46**
Beechacre. *Rams* 4F **13**
Beech Av. *M22* 3B **136**
Beech Av. *Chad* 5G **55**
Beech Av. *Dent* 3D **112**
Beech Av. *Droy* 4H **97**
Beech Av. *Farn* 1C **62**
Beech Av. *Gat* 6F **137**
Beech Av. *Glos* 6H **117**
Beech Av. *G'fld* 3F **61**
Beech Av. *Haz G* 3E **153**
Beech Av. *Irlam* 4G **103**
Beech Av. *Kear* 4B **64**
Beech Av. *L Lev* 5B **48**
Beech Av. *Marp* 5B **142**
Beech Av. *Oldh* 1H **73**
Beech Av. *Rad* 1F **65**
Beech Av. *Salf* 1E **93**
Beech Av. *Stoc* 5H **139**
Beech Av. *Strot* 6E **107**
Beech Av. *Timp* 3D **134**
Beech Av. *Urm* 5E **105**
Beech Av. *W'fld* 2D **66**
Beech Av. *Wors* 5C **76**
Beech Clo. *Ald E* 6E **167**
Beech Clo. *Bolt* 5G **19**
Beech Clo. *Part* 6D **118**
Beech Clo. *P'wich* 6G **67**
Beech Clo. *Whitw* 4G **15**
Beech Cotts. *Ald E* 6G **167**
Beech Ct. *M8* 2B **82**
Beech Ct. *M14* 1G **125**

Beech Ct. *M32* 6F **107**
Beech Ct. *Sale* 5H **121**
Beech Ct. *Salf* 2G **93**
Beech Ct. *Wilm* 3G **167**
Beech Cres. *Poy* 3E **163**
Beechcroft. *P'wich* 6G **67**
Beechcroft Av. *Bolt* 1G **47**
Beechcroft Clo.
   M40 . . . . .2H **95** (2G **7**)
Beechcroft Gro. *Bolt* 1G **47**
Beechdale Clo. *M40* 3C **84**
Beecher Wlk. *M9* 5F *83*
   (off Kelvington Dri.)
Beeches M., The.
   M20 . . . . .5D **124**
Beeches, The. *Stoc* 5D **124**
Beeches, The. *Ash L* 3B *100*
   (off Crawford St.)
Beeches, The. *Bolt* 5B **18**
Beeches, The. *Bow* 3E **145**
Beeches, The. *Chea H* . . .4D **150**
Beeches, The. *Eccl* 2H **91**
Beeches, The. *Heyw* 3E **39**
Beeches, The. *Moss* 2G **89**
Beeches, The. *Whitw* 4G **15**
Beechey Sq. *Oldh* 2E **73**
Beechfield. *Bow* 2E **145**
Beechfield. *Grass* 3A **124**
Beechfield. *Roch* 5A **26**
Beechfield Av. *L Hul* 4C **62**
Beechfield Av. *Rad* 6A **50**
Beechfield Av. *Urm* 4C **104**
Beechfield Av. *Wilm* 4B **166**
Beechfield Clo. *Roch* 5A **26**
Beechfield Clo. *Sale* 1H **133**
Beechfield Ct. *Bury* 6C **36**
Beechfield Dri. *Bury* 6C **36**
Beechfield M. *Hyde* 4E **115**
Beechfield Rd. *Ald E* 6G **167**
Beechfield Rd. *Bolt* 3F **31**
Beechfield Rd.
   Chea H 5D **150**
Beechfield Rd. *Had* 4G **117**
Beechfield Rd. *Miln* 6E **29**
Beechfield Rd. *Stoc* 1H **151**
Beechfield Rd. *Swin* 6D **78**
Beechfield St. *M8* 5C **82**
Beech Gro. *M14* 2H **125**
Beech Gro. *Ash L* 4F **99**
Beech Gro. *G'mnt* 2A **22**
Beech Gro. *L Hul* 4A **62**
Beech Gro. *Sale* 5H **121**
Beech Gro. *Salf* 1E **93**
Beech Gro. *Stal* 5D **100**
Beech Gro. *Wilm* 3D **166**
Beech Gro. Clo. *Bury* 1F **37**
Beech Hill Rd. *Grass* 3F **75**
Beech Holme Gro.
   Stoc 3C **140**
Beech Ho. *Eccl* 4D **90**
Beech Ho. *Shaw* 2F **57**
Beech Ho. Gdns.
   Timp 3A **134**
Beech Hurst Clo. *M16* . . .5B **108**
Beech La. *Grass* 4F **75**
Beech La. *Rom* 1A **142**
Beech La. *Wilm* 3D **166**
Beech Lawn. *Alt* 1E **145**
Beech M. *M21* 1H **123**
Beech M. *Stoc* 6A **140**
Beech Mt. *M9* 3E **83**
Beech Mt. *Ash L* 5E **87**
Beechpark Av. *M22* 4A **136**
Beech Range. *M19* 6C **110**
Beech Rd. *M21* 1G **123**
Beech Rd. *Ald E* 6E **167**
Beech Rd. *Chea H* 4D **150**
Beech Rd. *Hale* 2G **145**
Beech Rd. *H Lane* 6D **154**
Beech Rd. *Sale* 5D **122**
Beech Rd. *Stoc* 5G **139**

Beech St. *Bolt* 3B **32**
Beech St. *Bury* 3F **37**
Beech St. *Chad* 6H **71**
Beech St. *Eccl* 4D **90**
Beech St. *Fall* 3E **85**
Beech St. *Hyde* 4B **114**
Beech St. *Midd* 1H **69**
Beech St. *Miln* 1E **43**
Beech St. *Oldh* 2E **73**
Beech St. *Rad* 6A **50**
Beech St. *Roch* 5F **27**
   (in two parts)
Beech St. *S'boat* 6E **13**
Beech St. *Swin* 4F **79**
Beech Tree Bank.
   P'wich 5E **67**
Beechurst Rd.
   Chea H 6D **138**
Beech Vw. *Hyde* 5F **115**
Beech Vs. *Sale* 5D **122**
Beech Wlk. *Midd* 3H **69**
Beech Wlk. *Stret* 6C **106**
Beechway. *H Lane* 6D **154**
Beechway. *Wilm* 4D **166**
Beechwood. *Bow* 4D **144**
Beechwood. *Bury* 1E **51**
Beechwood. *Shaw* 5H **43**
Beechwood Av. *M21* 2A **124**
Beechwood Av. *L'boro* 6E **17**
Beechwood Av. *Rams* 3F **13**
Beechwood Av. *Rom* 1A **142**
Beechwood Av. *Stal* 1G **101**
Beechwood Av. *Urm* 4A **104**
Beechwood Ct. *P'wich* 6H **67**
Beechwood Ct. *T'ton* 6B **22**
Beechwood Dri. *Hyde* 6D **114**
Beechwood Dri. *Marp* 5E **143**
Beechwood Dri. *Moss* 1E **89**
Beechwood Dri. *Rytn* 1A **56**
Beechwood Dri. *Sale* 5E **121**
Beechwood Dri. *Wilm* . . .1H **167**
Beechwood Dri. *Wors* 5B **78**
Beechwood Gro. *M9* 4G **83**
Beechwood Gro.
   Chea H 5C **150**
Beechwood La. *Stal* 1G **101**
Beechwood Rd. *Oldh* 1D **86**
Beechwood Rd. *P'wich* . . .6H **67**
Beechwood St. *Bolt* 4B **46**
Beede St. *Open* 5D **96**
Beedon Av. *L Lev* 3A **48**
Beehive Grn. *W'houg* 6A **44**
Beehive St. *Oldh* 6D **72**
Beeley St. *Hyde* 5C **114**
Beeley St. *Salf* 6F **81**
Beenham Clo. *Sale* 6E **121**
Beeston Av. *Salf* 5F **81**
Beeston Av. *Timp* 5H **133**
Beeston Clo. *Bolt* 5E **19**
Beeston Gro. *Stoc* 6G **139**
Beeston Gro. *W'fld* 2F **67**
Beeston Rd. *Hand* 2H **159**
Beeston Rd. *Sale* 5H **121**
Beeston St. *M9* 3G **83**
Beeth St. *M11* 6F **97**
Beeton Gro. *M13* 3A **110**
Beetoon Wlk. *M4* 5E **7**
Beever St. *M16* 2A **108**
Beever St. *Oldh* 2E **73**
Begley Clo. *Rom* 2F **141**
Begonia Av. *Farn* 6D **46**
Begonia Wlk. *M12* 1B **110**
Beightons Wlk. *Roch* 5D **14**
Belayse Clo. *Bolt* 3F **31**
Belbeck St. *Bury* 3A **36**
Belcroft Clo. *M22* 3C **136**
Belcroft Dri. *L Hul* 3A **62**
Belcroft Gro. *L Hul* 4A **62**
Belding Av. *M40* 2F **85**
Beldon Rd. *M9* 5D **68**
Belfairs Clo. *Ash L* 4F **87**

Belfield. 3C 28
Belfield Clo. Roch 3C 28
Belfield Ho. Bow 3E 145
Belfield La. Roch 4C 28
  (Milnrow Rd.)
Belfield La. Roch 4D 28
  (Rochdale Rd.)
Belfield Lawn. Roch 3D 28
Belfield Mill La. Roch . . .3C 28
Belfield Old Rd. Roch . . .3C 28
Belfield Rd. M20 . . . . . .5F 125
Belfield Rd. P'wich 6A 68
Belfield Rd. Roch 3B 28
Belfield Rd. Stoc 4H 111
Belford Av. Dent 4A 112
Belford Dri. Bolt 3A 46
  (in two parts)
Belford Rd. Stret 4D 106
Belford Wlk. M23 . . . . . .5G 135
Belfort Dri. Salf 5H 93 (2A 8)
Belfry Clo. Wilm 1G 167
Belgate Clo. M12 . . . . . .3C 110
Belgian Ter. Rytn 3D 56
Belgium St. Roch 4A 26
Belgrave Av. M14 . . . . . .4A 110
Belgrave Av. Fail 3H 85
Belgrave Av. Marp 4D 142
Belgrave Av. Oldh 5E 73
Belgrave Av. Urm 4A 104
Belgrave Bungalows.
  Rad 3F 49
Belgrave Clo. Rad 3G 49
Belgrave Ct. Aud 3D 112
Belgrave Ct. Oldh 4D 72
Belgrave Cres. Eccl 3H 91
Belgrave Cres. Stoc 1B 152
Belgrave Dri. Rad 3G 49
Belgrave Gdns. Bolt 3A 32
Belgrave Rd. M40 . . . . . .2E 85
Belgrave Rd. Bow 2E 145
Belgrave Rd. Cad 4B 118
Belgrave Rd. Oldh 5D 72
Belgrave Rd. Sale 5A 122
Belgrave St. Dent 3D 112
Belgrave St. Heyw 4E 39
  (in two parts)
Belgrave St. Rad 3F 49
Belgrave St. Rams 3A 32
  (in two parts)
Belgrave St. Roch 2F 27
Belgrave St. S. Bolt 4A 32
Belgrave Ter. M40 . . . . . .5G 83
Belgravia Gdns. M21 . . . .1G 123
Belgravia Gdns. Hale . . .5G 145
Belgravia M. Shaw 6G 43
Belhaven M. M8 . . . . . . .1B 82
Belhill Gdns. Salf 2F 93
Bellairs St. Bolt 4G 45
Bellamy Ct. M18 . . . . . . .1G 111
  (in two parts)
Bella St. Bolt 3G 45
Bell Clough Rd. Droy 2B 98
Bell Cres. M11 . . . . .5A 96
Belldale Clo. Stoc 1C 138
Belle Isle Av. Roch 3C 14
Bellerby Clo. W'fld 1C 66
Belleville Av. M22 . . . . . .5C 148
Belle Vue. 2D 110
Belle Vue Av. M12 . . . . . .2B 110
Belle Vue Greyhound
  Race Track. 2D 110
Belle Vue Leisure Cen.
  . . . . .3C 110
Belle Vue Speedway Track.
  . . . . .2D 110
Belle Vue St. M12 . . . . . .1C 110
Belle Vue Ter. Bury 4C 36
Bellew St. M11 . . . . .5A 96
Bellfield Av. Chea H 4D 150
Bellfield Av. Oldh 1D 86

Bellis Clo. M12 . . . . .4A 96
Bell La. Bury 2E 37
Bell La. Miln 4H 29
Bell Mdw. Dri. Roch 6B 26
Bellott St. M8 . . . . .5C 82
Bellott Wlk. Oldh 1C 72
Bellpit Clo. Wors 4E 77
Bellscroft Av. M40 . . . . . .4B 84
Bellshill Cres. Roch 2C 28
  (in two parts)
Bell St. Droy 3B 98
Bell St. Oldh 2E 73
Bell St. Roch 3H 27
Bell Ter. Eccl 5E 91
Belmont Av. Dent 3D 112
Belmont Av. Salf 3A 92
Belmont Av. S'head 2B 74
Belmont Av. Swin 4D 64
Belmont Clo. Stoc 6G 127
Belmont Ct. Stoc 6G 127
Belmont Dri. Bury 4G 35
Belmont Dri. Marp B 2F 143
Belmont Rd. Bolt 3A 18
Belmont Rd. Bram 2G 161
Belmont Rd. Hale 3G 145
Belmont Rd. Rad 6G 49
Belmont Rd. Sale 3A 122
Belmont Shop. Cen.
  Stoc 1G 139
Belmont St. M16 . . . . . . .2B 108
Belmont St. Eccl 2F 91
Belmont St. Lees 4A 74
Belmont St. Oldh 1C 72
Belmont St. Salf 4D 92
Belmont St. Stoc 6F 127
Belmont Ter. Part 3H 119
Belmont Vw. Bolt 1H 33
Belmont Wlk.
  M13 . . . . . . .1G 109 (5E 11)
Belmont Way. Chad 1A 72
Belmont Way. Roch 1G 27
Belmont Way. Stoc 1F 139
Belmore Av. M8 . . . . .2B 82
Belper Rd. Eccl 5D 90
Belper Rd. Stoc 2B 138
Belper St. Ash L 1H 99
Belper Wlk. M18 . . . . . . .1E 111
Belper Way. Dent 1G 129
  (in two parts)
Belroy Ct. P'wich 6F 67
Belsay Clo. Ash L 6D 86
Belsay Dri. M23 . . . . .1G 147
Belstone Av. M23 . . . . . .2G 147
  (in two parts)
Belstone Clo. Bram 3H 151
Belsyde Wlk. M9 . . . . . . .4G 83
  (off Craigend Dri.)
Belthorne Av. M9 . . . . . . .1A 84
Belton Av. Roch 2C 28
Beltone Clo. Stret 6B 106
Belton Wlk. M8 . . . . .5C 82
Belton Wlk. Oldh 3B 72
Belvedere Av. G'mnt 2A 22
Belvedere Av. Stoc 5H 111
Belvedere Ct. P'wich 6E 67
Belvedere Dri. Bred 6C 128
Belvedere Dri. Duk 5C 100
Belvedere Ri. Oldh 4H 57
Belvedere Rd. M14 . . . . .1A 126
Belvedere Rd. Salf 2G 93
Belvedere Sq. M22 . . . . . .2D 148
Belvedere St. Salf 2H 93
Belvoir Av. M19 . . . . .5C 110
Belvoir Av. Haz G 5E 153
Belvoir Meadows.
  Roch 5C 16
Belvoir St. Bolt 6E 33
Belvoir St. Roch 2F 27
Belvor Av. Aud 6E 99
Belwood Rd. M21 . . . . . .2H 123
Bembridge Clo. M14 . . . .4G 109

Bembridge Dri. Bolt 2F 47
Bembridge Rd. Dent 1H 129
Bempton Clo. Stoc 6G 141
Bemrose Av. B'hth 5E 133
Bemsley Pl. Salf 5G 93
Benbecula Way. Urm 2E 105
Benbow Av. M12 . . . . . . .2B 110
Benbow St. Sale 4B 122
Ben Brierley Way. Oldh . . .2D 72
Benbrook Gro. Wilm 5A 160
Bench Carr. Roch 2G 27
Benches La. Marp B 6H 131
Benchill. 1C 148
Benchill Av. M22 . . . . . . .6B 136
Benchill Ct. M22 . . . . . . .1C 148
Benchill Ct. Rd. M22 . . . .1C 148
Benchill Cres. M22 . . . . . .6A 136
Benchill Dri. M22 . . . . . . .6A 136
Benchill Rd. M22 . . . . . . .5A 136
Bendall St. Open 5G 97
Ben Davies Ct. Rom 6A 130
Bendemeer. Urm 4E 105
Bendix St. M4 . . . . . .3F 95 (3C 6)
  (in two parts)
Benedict Clo. Salf 6G 81
Benedict Dri. Duk 1B 114
Benfield Av. M40 . . . . . . .1C 84
Benfield St. Heyw 3F 39
Benfleet Clo. M12 . . . . . . .1C 110
Bengain. Salf 5H 81
  (off Murray St.)
Bengal La. Ash L 1A 100
  (in three parts)
Bengal Sq. Ash L 1A 100
Bengal St. M4 . . . . . .3F 95 (3D 6)
Bengal St. Stoc 3G 139
Benhale Wlk. M8 . . . . . . .5C 82
  (off Tamerton Dri.)
Benham Clo. M20 . . . . . . .6G 125
Benin Wlk. M40 . . . . .6C 84
Benja Fold. Bram 1G 161
Benjamin St. Ash L 4G 99
  (in two parts)
Benjamin Wilson Ct.
  Salf 1B 94 (1D 4)
  (off Fitzwilliam St.)
Benmore Clo. Heyw 3C 38
Benmore Rd. M9 . . . . . . .5H 69
Bennett Clo. Stoc 3E 139
Bennett Dri. Salf 5A 82
Bennett M. Hyde 2B 114
  (off Glenwood Av.)
Bennett Rd. M8 . . . . .2B 82
Bennett St. M12 . . . . .1A 110
Bennett St. Ash L 4F 99
Bennett St. Hyde 2A 114
Bennett St. Rad 3D 48
Bennett St. Roch 6A 28
Bennett St. Stal 4E 101
Bennett St. Stoc 3E 139
Bennett St. Stret 6C 106
Bennon Clo. Salf 5A 82
Benny La. Droy 2C 98
Benson Clo. Salf 6A 82
Benson St. Bury 4E 37
Benson Wlk. Wilm 5H 159
Ben St. M11 . . . . .3D 96
Bentcliffe Way. Eccl 4H 91
Bentfield Cres. Miln 1E 43
Bentfield Ind. Units.
  Chad 3H 71
Bentfold Dri. Bury 6E 51
Bentham Clo. Bury 2E 35
Bentham Clo. Farn 6F 47
Bent Hill S. Bolt 3E 45
Bentinck Clo. Alt 1E 145

Bentinck Ho. Ash L 3G 99
Bentinck Ind. Est. M15 . . . .4C 8
Bentinck Rd. Alt 1E 145
Bentinck St.
  M15 . . . . . . .6B 94 (4C 8)
Bentinck St. Ash L 2G 99
  (in two parts)
Bentinck St. Bolt 4F 31
Bentinck St. Farn 6E 47
Bentinck St. Oldh 5D 72
Bentinck St. Roch 2E 27
Bentinck Ter. Ash L 3G 99
Bent La. M8 . . . . .4B 82
Bent La. P'wich 5G 67
Bent Lanes. Urm 2B 104
  (in two parts)
Bentley Av. Midd 2D 54
Bentley Clo. Rad 3B 50
Bentley Ct. Farn 6F 47
Bentley Ct. Salf 3A 82
Bentley Hall Rd. Bury 1C 34
Bentley La. Bury 2F 23
Bentley M. Roch 1G 27
Bentley Rd. M21 . . . . .6G 107
Bentley Rd. Dent 4F 113
Bentley Rd. Salf 3A 82
Bentleys, The. Stoc 6H 127
Bentley St. Bolt 2E 47
Bentley St. Chad 2H 71
Bentley St. Farn 6F 47
Bentley St. Oldh 1F 73
Bentley St. Roch 1F 27
Bentmeadows. Roch 2G 27
Benton Dri. Marp B 3G 143
Benton St. M9 . . . . .4H 83
Bents Av. Bred 6F 129
Bents Av. Urm 6B 104
Bents Farm Clo.
  L'boro 4D 16
Bentside Rd. Dis 2H 165
Bent Spur Rd. Kear 4A 64
Bent St. M8 . . . . .1E 95
Bent St. Kear 2G 63
Bent Ter. Urm 3E 105
Bentworth Wlk. M9 . . . . . .4G 83
Benville Wlk. M40 . . . . . . .5B 84
  (off Troydale Dri.)
Benwick Ter. Bolt 3A 32
Benyon St. Lees 3A 74
Berberis Wlk. Sale 3E 121
Beresford Av. Bolt 2G 45
Beresford Ct. M20 . . . . . .5E 125
Beresford Cres. Oldh 1H 73
Beresford Cres. Stoc 4G 111
Beresford Rd. M13 . . . . . .4B 110
Beresford Rd. Stret 3E 107
Beresford Rd. M14 . . . . . .4D 108
Beresford St. Fail 4E 85
Beresford St. Miln 1F 43
Beresford St. Oldh 1H 73
Berger St. M40 . . . . .6D 84
Bergman Wlk. M40 . . . . . .5B 84
  (off Harmer Clo.)
Berigan Clo. M12 . . . . . . .2A 110
Berisford Clo. Timp 4G 133
Berkeley Av. M14 . . . . . . .3A 110
Berkeley Av. Stret 3A 106
Berkeley Av. Chad 6F 71
Berkeley Clo. Hyde 6B 114
Berkeley Clo. Stoc 3C 140
Berkeley Ct. M8 . . . . .2A 82
Berkeley Ct. M20 . . . . . . .6D 124
Berkeley Cres. Hyde 6B 114
Berkeley Cres. Rad 2C 48
Berkeley Dri. Roch 1H 41
Berkeley Dri. Rytn 5B 56
Berkeley Ho. Bolt 6G 31
Berkeley Rd. Bolt 1A 32
Berkeley Rd. Haz G 2F 153
Berkeley St. Ash L 2G 99
Berkeley St. Rytn 2B 56
Berkley Av. M19 . . . . .6C 110

Berkley Wlk.—Birch Tree Dri.

Berkley Wlk. L'boro 4D 16
Berkshire Clo. Chad 4H 71
Berkshire Ct. Bury 6D 36
Berkshire Dri. Cad 4A 118
Berkshire Pl. Oldh 4A 72
Berkshire Rd. M40 . . . . . . .2H 95 (1H 7)
Berlin Rd. Stoc 5F 139
Berlin St. Bolt 1G 45
Bermondsay St. Salf 5H 93
Bernard Gro. Bolt 3G 31
Bernard St. M9 . . . . .3F 83
Bernard St. Roch 6E 15
Bernard Walker Ct. Comp 1F 143
Berne Clo. Bram 1G 151
Berne Clo. Chad 3A 72
Bernice Av. Chad 3H 71
Bernice St. Bolt 3G 31
Berriedale Clo. M16 . . . .5B 108
Berrie Gro. M19 . . . . . . .1D 126
Berrington Wlk. Bolt 4C 32
Berry Brow. M40 . . . . . . .1F 97 (in two parts)
Berry Clo. Wilm 4D 166
Berrycroft La. Rom 6G 129
Berry St. M1 . . . .5F 95 (2D 10)
Berry St. Eccl 5D 90
Berry St. G'fld 4F 61
Berry St. Stal 5G 101
Berry St. Swin 1F 79
Bertha Rd. Roch 4C 28
Bertha St. M11 . . . . .6D 96
Bertha St. Bolt 3H 31
Bertha St. Shaw 2F 57
Bertie St. Roch 1D 40
Bertram St. M12 . . . . . . .1C 110
Bertram St. Sale 5E 123
Bertrand Rd. Bolt 6G 31
Bert St. Bolt 4F 45
Berwick Av. Stoc 6H 125
Berwick Av. Urm 5A 106
Berwick Av. W'fld 2E 67
Berwick Clo. Heyw 4C 38
Berwick Clo. Wors 4B 76
Berwick St. Roch 5B 28
Berwyn Av. M9 . . . . .4D 68
Berwyn Av. Chea H 6D 138
Berwyn Av. Midd 1C 70
Berwyn Clo. Oldh 6C 72
Beryl Av. T'ton 4H 21
Beryl St. Rams 2B 32
Besom Hill. 2B 58
Besom La. Mill 2H 101
Bessemer Rd. Irlam 3D 118
Bessemer St. M11 . . . . . .6E 97
Bessemer Way. Oldh 2C 72
Besses o' th' Barn. 2E 67
Bessybrook Clo. Los 1A 44
Besthill Cotts. Charl 6D 116
Beswick. 5C 96
Beswick Dri. Fail 5G 85
Beswicke Royds St. Roch 2B 28
Beswicke St. L'boro 4G 17
Beswicke St. Roch 3G 27
Beswick Row. M4 . . . . .2E 95 (2A 6)
Beswicks La. Ald E 6A 166
Beswick St. M4 . . . . . . .3H 95 (4G 7)
Beswick St. Droy 4B 98
Beswick St. Rytn 5C 56
Beta Av. Stret 6C 106
Beta St. Rams 5A 32
Bethany La. Miln 1G 43
Bethel Av. Fail 4E 85
Bethel Grn. L'boro . . . . . .6G 17 (off Calderbrook Rd.)
Bethel St. Heyw 3E 39
Bethesda Ho. M7 . . . . . . .3A 82
Bethesda St. Oldh 5D 72
Bethnall Dri. M14 . . . . . .6E 109
Betjeman Pl. Shaw 5H 43
Betleymore Rd. Chea H 1B 150
Betley Rd. Stoc 6H 111
Betley St. M1 . . . .5G 95 (1E 11)
Betley St. Heyw 4E 39
Betley St. Rad 3A 50
Betnor Av. Stoc 2B 140
Betony Clo. Roch 6D 14
Bettwood Dri. M8 . . . . . . .1B 82
Betty Nuppy's La. Roch 6C 28
Betty's Fitness Cen. . . .6G 107
Betula Gro. Salf 4H 81
Betula M. Roch 2H 25
Beulah St. M11 . . . . .6E 97
Bevan Clo. M12 . . .4A 96 (6H 7) (in two parts)
Bevendon Sq. Salf 5A 82
Beverdale Clo. M11 . . . . .5C 96
Beveridge St. M14 . . . . .4E 109
Beverley Av. Dent 5G 113
Beverley Av. Urm 3G 105
Beverley Clo. Ash L 5F 87
Beverley Clo. W'fld 6F 51
Beverley Flats. Heyw . . . . .3E 39 (off Wilton St.)
Beverley Pl. Roch 3A 28
Beverley Rd. Bolt 5F 31
Beverley Rd. L Lev 4H 47
Beverley Rd. Stoc 3C 140
Beverley Rd. Swin 4A 80
Beverley St. M9 . . . . .2G 83
Beverley Wlk. Oldh 4C 72
Beverley Wlk. Rom 2G 141
Beverly Rd. M14 . . . . . . .2H 125
Beverston. Roch 5G 27
Beverston Dri. Salf 5A 82
Bevill Sq. Salf 3C 94 (3E 5)
Bevis Green. 3E 23
Bevis Grn. Bury 3F 23
Bewick St. Bolt 2D 32
Bewley St. Oldh 1B 86
Bewley Wlk. M40 . . . . . . .5A 84
Bexhill Av. Timp 5H 133
Bexhill Clo. L Lev 4C 48
Bexhill Dri. M13 . . . . . . .4A 110
Bexhill Rd. Stoc 1G 151
Bexhill Wlk. Chad 3H 71
Bexington Rd. M16 . . . . .4C 108
Bexley Clo. Urm 3D 104
Bexley Dri. Bury 4H 35
Bexley Dri. L Hul 5E 63
Bexley Ho. Bolt 4A 32
Bexley Sq. Salf . . .3B 94 (4D 4)
Bexley St. Oldh 4A 72
Bexley Wlk. M40 . . . . . . .5B 84 (off John Foran Clo.)
Beyer Clo. M18 . . . . .2E 111
Bibby La. M19 . . . . .3B 126 (in two parts)
Bibby St. Bury 2D 50
Bibby St. Hyde 2B 114
Bibury Av. M22 . . . . .2H 147
Bickerdike Av. M12 . . . . .4D 110
Bickerdyke Ct. M12 . . . . .4D 110
Bickershaw Dri. Wors . . . .1E 77 (in two parts)
Bickerstaffe Clo. Shaw . . .1E 57
Bickerton Ct. Chad 6A 72
Bickerton Dri. Haz G 4A 152
Bickerton Rd. Alt 6D 132
Biddall Dri. M23 . . . . . .5H 135
Biddisham Wlk. M40 . . . . .6F 83 (in two parts)
Biddulph Av. Stoc 6C 140
Bideford Dri. M23 . . . . . .3F 135
Bideford Dri. Bolt 1A 48
Bideford Rd. Roch 2B 40
Bideford Rd. Stoc 2C 140
Bidston Av. M14 . . . . . . .5F 109
Bidston Clo. Bury 3G 35
Bidston Clo. Shaw 1H 57
Bidston Dri. H'land 6A 160
Bidworth La. Glos 6F 117
Biggin Gdns. Heyw 6G 39
Bigginwood Wlk. M40 . . . . .4A 84 (off Halliford Rd.)
Bignor St. M8 . . . . .5C 82
Bilbao St. Bolt 5G 31
Bilberry St. Roch . . . . . . .5A 28 (in two parts)
Billbrook St. M4 . . .2F 95 (1C 6)
Billberry Clo. W'fld 1F 67
Billinge Clo. Bolt 5B 32
Billing St. M12 . . .6G 95 (3F 11)
Billington Rd. Swin 3C 80
Bill La. W'fld 1D 66
Bill Williams Clo. M11 . . . .5E 97
Billy La. Swin 1F 79
Billy Meredith Clo. M14 . . . . .4E 109
Billy's La. Chea H 4C 150
Billy Whelan Wlk. M40 . . . . .6B 84
Bilsland Wlk. M40 . . . . . .6C 84
Bilson Dri. Stoc 4D 138
Bilson Sq. Miln 6G 29
Bilton Wlk. M8 . . . . .3E 83
Binbrook Wlk. Bolt 3B 46
Bincombe Wlk. M13 . . . .2G 109
Bindloss Av. Eccl 2A 92
Bindon Wlk. M9 . . . . .4F 83 (off Carisbrook St.)
Bingham Dri. M23 . . . . . .5F 135
Bingham St. Swin 3F 79
Bingley Clo. M11 . . . . . . .5B 96
Bingley Dri. Urm 3B 104
Bingley Rd. Roch 4C 28
Bingley Sq. Roch 4C 28
Bingley Ter. Roch 4C 28
Bingley Wlk. Salf 3D 80
Binns Nook Rd. Roch 1A 28
Binns Pl. M4 . . . . .4F 95 (5D 6)
Binns St. Stal 4G 100
Binn's Ter. L'boro . . . . . . .3F 17 (off Lodge St.)
Binsley Clo. Irlam 6E 103
Binstead Clo. M14 . . . . .4A 110
Birbeck St. Stal 4D 100
Birch. 3E 53
Birchacre Gro. M14 . . . .2H 125
Birchall Clo. Duk 1B 114
Birchall Grn. Woodl 4F 129
Birchall Way. M15 . . . . .1D 108 (6H 9)
Birch Av. M16 . . . . .3G 107
Birch Av. Cad 4B 118
Birch Av. Chad 5G 55
Birch Av. Fail 5F 85
Birch Av. Midd 2A 70
Birch Av. Oldh 1B 86
Birch Av. Roch 5B 16
Birch Av. Rom 1B 142
Birch Av. Sale 6B 122
Birch Av. Salf 6C 80
Birch Av. Stoc 5D 126
Birch Av. T'ton 6A 22
Birch Av. W'fld 3D 66
Birch Av. Wilm 3D 166
Birch Clo. Whitw 3C 14
Birch Ct. M13 . . . . .4A 110
Birch Ct. Duk 5B 100
Birch Ct. Heyw . . . . .4G 39 (off Twin St.)
Birch Ct. Marp 6C 142
Birch Cres. Miln 2E 43
Birchdale. Bow 3E 145
Birchdale Av. H Grn 3F 149
Birch Dri. Haz G 3C 152
Birch Dri. Lees 4B 74
Birch Dri. Swin 3H 79
Birchenall St. M40 . . . . . .3H 83
Birchen Bower Dri. T'ton 6H 21
Birchen Bower Wlk. T'ton 6H 21
Birchenlea St. Chad 6G 71
Birches End. Whitw 4C 14
Birches, The. Moss 2D 88
Birches, The. Sale 4G 121
Birchfield. Bolt 5A 20
Birchfield Av. Bury 4A 38
Birchfield Dri. Roch 6E 27
Birchfield Dri. Wors 4C 76
Birchfield Gro. Bolt 3C 44
Birchfield M. Hyde 5B 114
Birchfield Rd. Stoc 4C 138
Birchfields. Ash L 5F 99
Birchfields. Hale 4H 145
Birchfields Av. M13 . . . . .4A 110
Birchfields Rd. M13 & M14 . . . . . .4A 110
Birchfold. L Hul 5D 62
Birchfold Clo. L Hul 5D 62
Birchgate Wlk. Bolt 2A 46
Birch Gro. M14 . . . . .4H 109
Birch Gro. Aud 1F 113
Birch Gro. Dent 4E 113
Birch Gro. P'wich 3E 67
Birch Gro. Rams 6C 12
Birch Gro. Timp 6E 135
Birchgrove Clo. Bolt 5E 45
Birch Hall Clo. Oldh 5A 74
Birch Hall La. M13 . . . . .5A 110
Birch Hey Clo. Roch 5A 16
Birch Hill Cres. Roch 5B 16
Birch Hill La. Ward 3B 16
Birch Hill Wlk. L'boro 4D 16
Birch Ho. Bram 2G 161
Birch Ind. Est. Heyw 2C 52
Birchington Rd. M14 . . . .1E 125
Birchin La. M4 . . . .4E 95 (5B 6)
Birchinlee Av. Rytn 4H 55
Birchinley Manor Equestrian Cen. . . .3F 29
Birchin Pl. M4 . . . .4F 95 (5B 6) (off Birchin La.)
Birch La. M13 . . . . .4A 110
Birch La. Duk . . . . .5B 100 (in two parts)
Birchlea. Alt 1H 145
Birch Lea Clo. Bury 6D 36
Birchleaf Gro. Salf 3C 92
Birch Mt. Roch 5B 16
Birch Polygon. M14 . . . .4H 109
Birch Rd. M8 . . . . .2D 82
Birch Rd. C'ton & B'hth 5B 120
Birch Rd. Gat 6E 137
Birch Rd. Kear 3H 63
Birch Rd. Midd 5C 54
Birch Rd. Part 6B 118
Birch Rd. Poy 5F 163
Birch Rd. Swin 6D 78
Birch Rd. Uppermill 2G 61
Birch Rd. Ward & Roch 3A 16
Birch Rd. Wors 2F 77
Birch St. M12 . . . . .1C 110
Birch St. Ash L 4E 99
Birch St. Bolt 1C 46
Birch St. Bury 1D 36
Birch St. Droy 4B 98
Birch St. Heyw 4F 39
Birch St. Rad 2C 50
Birch St. Stal 1G 101
Birch St. Ward 3A 16
Birch Ter. Hyde . . . . . . .3B 114 (off Spring Gdns.)
Birch Tree Av. Haz G 4G 153
Birch Tree Clo. Bow 4E 145
Birch Tree Ct. M22 . . . . .2B 148
Birch Tree Dri. M22 . . . .2B 148

Birchvale Clo.—Bloomsbury La.

Birchvale Clo. *M15* 1C **108** (5F **9**)
Birchvale Dri. *Rom* 6B **130**
Birch Vs. *Whitw* 4C **14**
Birchway. *Bram* 6F **151**
Birchway. *H Lane* 6D **154**
Birchwood. *Chad* 2E **71**
Birchwood. *Droy* 2B **98**
Birchwood Clo. *Stoc* 2C **138**
Birchwood Dri. *Wilm* 1G **167**
Birchwood Rd. *Midd* 1C **70**
Birchwood Way. *Duk* 1B **114**
Bird Hall Av. *Chea H* 1E **151**
Birdhall Gro. *M19* 1C **126**
Bird Hall La. *Stoc* 4D **138**
Bird Hall Rd. *Chea H* 6D **138**
Birdlip Dri. *M23* 2G **147**
Birkby Dri. *Midd* 5G **53**
Birkdale Av. *Rytn* 5C **56**
Birkdale Av. *W'fld* 3B **66**
Birkdale Clo. *Bram* 6H **151**
Birkdale Clo. *Heyw* 5F **39**
Birkdale Clo. *Hyde* 2C **114**
Birkdale Dri. *Bury* 3H **35**
Birkdale Dri. *Sale* 1G **133**
Birkdale Gdns. *Bolt* 2H **45**
Birkdale Gro. *Eccl* 3H **91**
Birkdale Gro. *Stoc* 4H **127**
Birkdale Pl. *Sale* 3H **121**
Birkdale Rd. *Roch* 1A **42**
Birkdale Rd. *Stoc* 4G **127**
Birkdale St. *M8* 4C **82**
Birkenhills Dri. *Bolt* 2C **44**
Birkett Clo. *Bolt* 5B **18**
Birkett Dri. *Bolt* 5B **18**
Birkinbrook Clo. *W'fld* 6E **51**
Birkleigh Wlk. *Bolt* 1G **47**
Birks. 1B 74
Birks Av. *Lees* 1B **74**
Birks Dri. *Bury* 5B **22**
Birkworth Ct. *Stoc* 5D **140**
Birley Clo. *Timp* 4H **133**
Birley Ct. *Salf* 3G **93**
Birley Fields. *M15* 2D **108** (6G **9**)
Birley Pk. *M20* 6D **124**
Birley St. *Bolt* 1A **32**
Birley St. *Bury* 6F **23**
Birley St. *Roch* 2A **28**
Birling Dri. *M23* 1H **147**
Birnam Gro. *Heyw* 4C **38**
Birshaw Clo. *Shaw* 2F **57**
Birstall Wlk. *M23* 5G **135**
Birtenshaw Cres. *Brom X* 4F **19**
Birtle. 5D 24
Birtle Green. 5C 24
Birtle Moor. *Bury* 6C **24**
Birtle Rd. *Bury* 4C **24**
Birtles Av. *Stoc* 4H **111**
Birtles Clo. *Chea* 6C **138**
Birtles Clo. *Duk* 1B **114**
Birtlespool Rd. *Chea H* 1B **150**
Birtles, The. *Wyth* 3B **148**
Birtles Way. *Hand* 1H **159**
Birtley Wlk. *M40* 2G **95** (2F **7**)
Birt St. *M40* 1H **95** (1G **7**)
Birwood Rd. *M8* 1D **82**
Biscay Clo. *M11* 4B **96**
Bishop Clo. *M16* 3C **108**
Bishop Clo. *Ash L* 6E **87**
Bishopdale Clo. *Rytn* 2B **56**
Bishop Marshall Clo. *M40* 6F **83**
Bishop Marshall Way. *Midd* 3F **53**
Bishop Rd. *Salf* 1B **92**
Bishop Rd. *Urm* 5H **103**
Bishopsbridge Clo. *Bolt* 3B **46**
Bishop's Clo. *Bolt* 5C **46**
Bishops Clo. *Bow* 4D **144**
Bishops Clo. *Chea* 6C **138**
Bishopscourt. *Salf* 3G **81**
Bishopsgate. *M2* 5D **94** (1H **9**)
Bishops Ga. St. *Chad* 3G **71**
Bishopsgate Wlk. *Roch* 1A **42**
Bishops Mdw. *Midd* 4F **53**
Bishops M. *Sale* 3G **121**
Bishop's Rd. *Bolt* 5C **46**
Bishops Rd. *P'wich* 6G **67**
Bishops St. *Stoc* 2A **140**
Bishop St. *Midd* 2D **70**
Bishop St. *Roch* 2B **28**
Bishops Wlk. *Ash L* 4G **99**
Bishopton Clo. *M19* 6E **111**
Bisley Av. *M23* 5F **135**
Bisley St. *Oldh* 3B **72**
Bismark St. *Oldh* 4E **73**
Bispham Av. *Bolt* 6H **33**
Bispham Av. *Stoc* 5H **111**
Bispham Clo. *Bury* 4F **35**
Bispham Gro. *Salf* 4A **82**
Bispham St. *Bolt* 5E **33**
Bittern Clo. *Poy* 4A **162**
Bittern Clo. *Roch* 4B **26**
Bittern Dri. *Droy* 2C **98**
Blackbank St. *Bolt* 3B **32**
Blackberry Clo. *B'hth* 3D **132**
Blackberry La. *Stoc* 2B **128**
Black Brook Rd. *Stoc* 2F **127**
Blackburn Gdns. *M20* 5E **125**
Blackburn Pl. *Salf* 4A **94** (6A **4**)
Blackburn Rd. *Bolt* 1A **32**
Blackburn Rd. *Has & Rams* 1A **12**
Blackburn Rd. *Tur & Eger* 1B **18**
Blackburn St. *M16* 2A **108**
Blackburn St. *P'wich* 5G **67**
Blackburn St. *Rad* 4G **49**
Blackburn St. *Salf* 2B **94** (2C **4**)
Blackcap Clo. *Wors* 4D **76**
Blackcarr Rd. *M23* 5H **135**
Blackchapel Dri. *Roch* 2H **41**
Blackcroft Clo. *Swin* 3E **79**
Black Dad La. *Roch* 3E **25**
Blackden Wlk. *Wilm* 6H **159**
Blackdown Gro. *Oldh* 6C **72**
Blackett St. *M12* 5H **95** (2G **11**)
Blackfield La. *Salf* 3G **81** (in two parts)
Blackfields. *Salf* 3G **81**
Blackford Av. *Bury* 3D **50**
Blackford Bridge. 3D 50
Blackford Rd. *Stoc* 2D **126**
Blackford Wlk. *M40* 2H **95** (1G **7**)
Black Friar Ct. *Salf* 1D **4**
Blackfriars Rd. *Salf* 2C **94** (2D **4**)
Blackfriars St. *Salf* 3D **94** (4G **5**)
Blackhill Clo. *M13* 6F **95** (4D **10**)
Black Horse St. *Bolt* 6A **32**
Black Horse St. *Farn* 2G **63**
Black Lane. 1F 49
Black Leach. *S'head* 2C **74**
Blackleach Country Pk. 4F 63
Blackleach Country Pk. Nature Reserve. 4F 63
Blackleach Country Pk. Vis. Cen. 5F 63
Blackleach Dri. *Wors* 4F **63**
Blackledge St. *Bolt* 3G **45**
Blackley. 2G 83
Blackley Clo. *Bury* 5F **51**
Blackley Ct. *M9* 6C **68**
Blackley Crematorium. *M9* 5C **68**
Blackley New Rd. *M9* 6B **68**
Blackley Pk. Rd. *M9* 2F **83**
Blackley St. *M16* 2A **108** (6B **8**)
Blackley St. *Midd* 2D **68**
Blacklock St. *M8* 1D **94**
Black Moor. *Mot* 3C **116**
Black Moss Clo. *Rad* 4D **48**
Black Moss Rd. *Dun M* 4A **132**
Blackpits Rd. *Roch* 2H **25**
Blackpool St. *M11* 3F **97** (Powell St.)
Blackpool St. *M11* 3E **97** (Walsden St.)
Blackrock. *Moss* 5E **89**
Blackrock St. *M11* 4B **96**
Blackrod Dri. *Bury* 4F **35**
Black Sail Wlk. *Oldh* 6E **57**
Blackshaw Ho. *Bolt* 1G **45**
Blackshaw La. *Ald E* 5F **167**
Blackshaw La. *Bolt* 1G **45**
Blackshaw La. *Rytn* 3D **56**
Blackshaw Row. *Bolt* 2G **45**
Blackshaw St. *Stoc* 3G **139**
Blacksmith La. *Roch* 1B **40**
Blackstock St. *M13* 3G **109**
Blackstone Av. *Roch* 3C **28**
Blackstone Edge Ct. *L'boro* 3G **17**
Blackstone Edge Old Rd. *L'boro* 3G **17**
Blackstone Ho. *Stoc* 6D **140**
Blackstone Rd. *Stoc* 6D **140**
Blackstone Wlk. *M9* 5F **83**
Blackthorn Av. *M19* 2C **126**
Blackthorn Clo. *Roch* 1G **27**
Blackthorne Clo. *Bolt* 4E **31**
Blackthorne Dri. *Sale* 1F **133**
Blackthorne Rd. *Hyde* 3C **130**
Blackthorn M. *Roch* 1G **27**
Blackthorn Rd. *Oldh* 3B **86**
Blackthorn Wlk. *Part* 6C **118**
Blackwell Wlk. *M4* 4F **7**
Blackwin St. *M12* 1C **110**
Blackwood Dri. *M23* 3D **134**
Blackwood St. *Bolt* 3C **46**
Bladen Clo. *Chea H* 1C **150**
Blair Av. *L Hul* 5D **62**
Blair Av. *Urm* 5A **104**
Blair Clo. *Haz G* 5C **152**
Blair Clo. *Sale* 2E **133**
Blair Clo. *Shaw* 6F **43**
Blairhall Av. *M40* 4A **84**
Blair La. *Bolt* 4F **33**
Blairmore Dri. *Bolt* 2C **44**
Blair Rd. *M16* 6C **108**
Blair St. *M16* 2B **108**
Blair St. *Brom X* 3D **18**
Blair St. *Kear* 3B **64**
Blair St. *Roch* 2F **27**
Blakedown Wlk. M12 2A 110 (off Cochrane Av.)
Blake Dri. *Stoc* 4E **141**
Blakefield Dri. *Wors* 2G **77**
Blake Gdns. *Bolt* 3H **31**
Blakelock St. *Shaw* 6F **43**
Blakemere Av. *Sale* 6E **123**
Blakemore Wlk. *M12* 4A **96**
Blake St. *Brom X* 4E **19**
Blake St. *Rams* 3H **31**
Blake St. *Roch* 3A **28**
Blakeswell Clo. *Urm* 4H **103**
Blakey Clo. *Bolt* 3D **44**
Blakey St. *M12* 3C **110**
Blanchard St. *M15* 2C **108**
Blanche St. *Roch* 1A **28**
Blanche Wlk. *Oldh* 1E **73**
Bland Clo. *Fail* 4E **85**
Blandford Av. *Wors* 3H **77**
Blandford Clo. *Bury* 6D **22**
Blandford Ct. *Stal* 3E **101**
Blandford Dri. *M40* 1D **84**
Blandford Rd. *Eccl* 3D **90**
Blandford Rd. *Salf* 6F **81**
Blandford Rd. *Stoc* 1D **138**
Blandford St. *Ash L* 2G **99**
Blandford St. *Stal* 3E **101**
Bland Rd. *P'wich* 1F **81**
Bland St. *M16* 3C **108**
Bland St. *Bury* 2D **36**
Blanefield Clo. *M21* 2C **124**
Blantyre Av. *Wors* 1G **77**
Blantyre Rd. *Swin* 5H **79**
Blantyre St. *M15* 6B **94** (3D **8**)
Blantyre St. *Eccl* 2C **90**
Blantyre St. *Swin* 3D **78**
Blanwood Dri. *M8* 4D **82**
Blaven Clo. *Stoc* 6H **139**
Blaydon St. *M1* 5F **95** (1C **10**)
Blazemoss Bank. *Stoc* 6D **140**
Bleackley St. *Bury* 1A **36**
Bleak Hey Rd. *M22* 3D **148**
Bleakley St. *W'fld* 6C **50**
Bleaklow Gdns. Glos 6G 117 (off Castleton Cres.)
Bleaklow La. *Glos* 6G **117**
Bleaklow Wlk. Glos 6G 117 (off Castleton Cres.)
Bleak St. *Bolt* 3D **32**
Bleasby St. *Oldh* 2G **73**
Bleasdale Clo. *Bury* 4E **51**
Bleasdale Rd. *M22* 3G **147**
Bleasdale Rd. *Bolt* 3D **30**
Bleasdale St. *Rytn* 2B **56**
Bleasefell Chase. *Wors* 6C **76**
Bleatarn Rd. *Stoc* 4B **140**
Bledlow Clo. *Eccl* 2G **91**
Blencarn Wlk. *M9* 5F **83**
Blendworth Clo. *M8* 4B **82**
Blenheim Av. *M16* 5B **108**
Blenheim Av. *Oldh* 4H **57**
Blenheim Clo. *Bow* 4F **145**
Blenheim Clo. *Bury* 2E **51**
Blenheim Clo. *Heyw* 3G **39**
Blenheim Clo. *Poy* 3F **163**
Blenheim Clo. *Wilm* 2G **167**
Blenheim Ct. M9 4C 68 (off Deanswood Dri.)
Blenheim Rd. *Bolt* 6F **33**
Blenheim Rd. *Chea H* 3D **150**
Blenheim Rd. *Old T* 4G **107**
Blenheim Rd. Est. *Bolt* 1H **47**
Blenheim St. *Roch* 2E **27**
Blenheim Way. *Ash L* 1C **100**
Blenmar Clo. *Rad* 2A **50**
Bleriot St. *Bolt* 4H **45**
Bletchley Clo. *M13* 2H **109**
Bletchley Rd. *Stoc* 2A **138**
Blethyn Clo. *Bolt* 5F **45**
Blinco Rd. *Urm* 6H **105**
Blind La. *M12* 6H **95** (3H **11**)
Blindsill Rd. *Farn* 2D **62**
Blisworth Av. *Eccl* 5G **91**
Blisworth Clo. *M4* 4H **95** (6H **7**)
Blithfield Wlk. *Dent* 5E **113**
Block La. *Chad* 4H **71**
Blocksage St. *Duk* 6B **100**
Blodwell St. *Salf* 3F **93**
Blofield Ct. *Farn* 2F **63**
Blomley St. *Roch* 3C **40**
Bloomfield Dri. *Bury* 4F **51**
Bloomfield Dri. *Wors* 4C **76**
Bloomfield Rd. *Farn* 3F **63**
Bloomfield St. *Bolt* 2A **32**
Bloomsbury Gro. *Timp* 5A **134**
Bloomsbury La. *Timp* 5A **134**

186 A-Z Manchester

Bloom St.—Borrowdale Av.

Bloom St. M1 5E 95 (2A 10) (in two parts)
Bloom St. Oldh 3C 72
Bloom St. Rams 5C 12
Bloom St. Salf 3C 94 (4E 6)
Bloom St. Stoc 3E 139
Blossom Pl. Roch 3H 27
Blossom Rd. Part 6C 118
Blossoms Hey. Chea H 4A 150
Blossoms Hey Wlk. Chea H 4A 150
Blossoms La. Woodf 5C 160
Blossoms St. Stoc 5H 139
Blossom St. M4 3F 95 (4D 6)
Blossom St. Salf 3C 94 (3F 5)
Bloxham Wlk. M9 6H 69
Blucher St. M12 1A 110 (5H 11)
Blucher St. Ash L 5E 87
Blucher St. Salf 4A 94 (6A 4)
Blue Bell Av. M40 2A 84
Blue Bell Clo. Hyde 2D 114
Bluebell Dri. Marp B 5H 143
Bluebell Dri. Roch 2B 40
Bluebell Gro. Chea 1H 149
Bluebell Way. Wilm 6G 159
Blueberry Dri. Shaw 6H 43
Blueberry Rd. Bow 3C 144
Blue Chip Bus. Pk. B'hth 4E 133
Bluefields. Shaw 5H 43
Blue Ribbon Wlk. Swin 2G 79
Bluestone Dri. Stoc 6A 126
Bluestone Rd. M40 3A 84
Bluestone Rd. Dent 5A 112
Bluestone Ter. Dent 5A 112
Blundell Clo. Bury 4F 51
Blundell St. Rams 6A 32
Blundering La. Stal 1H 115
Blunn St. Oldh 5D 72
Blyborough Clo. Salf 1E 93
Blyth Av. M23 1A 136
Blyth Av. L'boro 6D 16
Blyth Clo. Timp 4D 134
Blythe Av. Bram 1E 101
Blyton St. M15 2F 109
Blyton Way. Dent 1F 129
Boad St. M1 5F 95 (1D 10)
Boardale Dri. Midd 6G 53
Boardman Clo. Rams 3A 32
Boardman Clo. Stoc 5H 127
Boardman Fold Clo. Midd 4A 70
Boardman Fold Rd. Midd 4H 69
Boardman La. Midd 1D 68
Boardman Rd. M8 1B 82
Boardman St. Eccl 4G 91
Boardman St. Hyde 5B 114
Boardman St. Rams 3A 32
Board St. Ash L 1B 100
Boar Grn. Clo. M40 4C 84
Boarshaw Clough. Midd 5B 54
Boarshaw Clough Way. Midd 5B 54
Boarshaw Crematorium. Midd 5C 54
Boarshaw Cres. Midd 5C 54
Boarshaw Ind. Est. Midd 5B 54
Boarshaw La. Midd 4D 54
Boarshaw Rd. Midd 6A 54
Boarshurst. 4G 61
Boarshurst Bus. Pk. G'fld 4F 61
Boarshurst La. G'fld 4F 61
Boat La. M22 2C 136
Boat La. Dig 2D 60
Boat La. Irlam 5F 103
Boat La. Ct. M22 2C 136
Boatyard, The. Stret 5E 107
Bobbin Wlk. M4 5F 7
Bobbin Wlk. Oldh 3E 73
Bob Massey Clo. Open 4E 97
Bob's La. Cad 5B 118
Boddens Hill Rd. Stoc 1C 138
Boddington Rd. Eccl 4C 90
Bodlam Rd. G'mnt 2H 21
Bodley St. M11 3E 97
Bodmin Clo. Rytn 4E 57
Bodmin Cres. Stoc 4B 128
Bodmin Dri. Bram 6G 151
Bodmin Rd. Sale 4F 121
Bodmin Wlk. M23 6G 135
Bodney Wlk. M9 6D 68
Bodyline Health & Fitness Cen. 4A 122
Bodyshapers Fitness Club. 6H 107
Body Work Gymnasium. 4F 49
Bogart Ct. Salf 1E 93
Bognor Rd. Stoc 1G 151
Bolam Clo. M23 2F 135
Boland Dri. M14 1G 125
Bolderrod Pl. Oldh 1E 73
Bolderstone Pl. Stoc 1E 153
Bold Row. Swin 4F 79
Bold St. Alt 2F 145
Bold St. Bolt 6B 32
Bold St. Bury 2E 37
Bold St. Hulme 2C 108
Bold St. Moss S 3C 108
Bold St. Swin 1F 79
Bolesworth Clo. M21 1F 123
Boleyn Ct. Heyw 4E 39
Bolholt. 1G 35
Bolholt Ind. Pk. Bury 1G 35
Bolholt Ter. Bury 1H 35
Bolivia St. Salf 3C 92
Bolleyn Wood Ct. Wilm 6F 159
Bollin Av. Bow 5D 144
Bollin Clo. M15 1B 108 (6C 8)
Bollin Clo. Kear 3A 64
Bollin Clo. Wilm 1F 167
Bollin Ct. M15 1B 108 (6C 8)
Bollin Ct. Bow 4D 144
Bollin Ct. Wilm 2F 167
Bollin Dri. Sale 1B 134
Bollin Dri. Timp 3G 133
Bollings Yd. Bolt 1B 46
Bollington Rd. M40 3H 95 (3G 7)
Bollington Rd. Stoc 4F 127
Bollington St. Ash L 4G 99
Bollin Hill. Wilm 1D 166
Bollin Ho. Salf 6G 81 (off Lwr. Broughton Rd.)
Bollin Link. Wilm 2F 167
Bollin Sq. Bow 4D 144
Bollin Wlk. Stoc 4H 127
Bollin Wlk. W'fld 5G 51
Bollin Wlk. Wilm 2F 167
Bollinway. Hale 5A 146
Bollin Way. W'fld 5G 51
Bollinwood Chase. Wilm 2G 167
Bolney Wlk. M40 1H 95
Bolshaw Farm La. H Grn 1G 159
Bolshaw Rd. H Grn 1F 159
Boltmeadow. G'fld 5E 61
Bolton. 6B 32
Bolton Av. M19 1H 137
Bolton Av. Chea H 1D 160
Bolton Clo. Poy 3D 162
Bolton Clo. P'wich 1D 80
Bolton Excel Leisure Cen. 1C 46
Bolton Ga. Retail Pk. Bolt 4B 32
Bolton Mus. & Art Gallery. 6B 32 (Library)
Bolton Rd. Brad 6G 19
Bolton Rd. Bury 5G 35
Bolton Rd. Farn 5F 47
Bolton Rd. Hawk 1D 20
Bolton Rd. Kear 2G 63
Bolton Rd. Rad 3D 48
Bolton Rd. Roch 1A 40
Bolton Rd. Salf 5B 80
Bolton Rd. Swin 1F 79
Bolton Rd. Wors 5F 63
Bolton Rd. N. Rams 4A 12
Bolton Rd. W. Rams 6B 12
Bolton Steam Mus. 5G 31
Bolton St. Bury 3B 36
Bolton St. Oldh 3F 73 (in two parts)
Bolton St. Rad 4F 49
Bolton St. Rams 4D 12
Bolton St. Salf 4C 94 (5E 5)
Bolton St. Stoc 2G 127
Boltons Yd. Upperm 1F 61
Bolton Technology Exchange. Bolt 6H 31
Bolton Tourist Info. Cen. 6B 32
Bolton Wholesale Pk. Bolt 4B 32
Bombay Rd. Stoc 4E 139
Bombay Sq. M1 5E 95 (2B 10) (off Bombay St.)
Bombay St. M1 5E 95 (2B 10)
Bombay St. Ash L 1B 100
Bonar Clo. Stoc 3E 139
Bonar Rd. Stoc 3E 139
Boncarn Dri. M23 1G 147
Bonchurch Wlk. M18 1D 110
Bondmark Rd. M18 1E 111
Bond Sq. Salf 5A 82
Bond St. M12 5G 95 (2E 11)
Bond St. Bury 3E 37
Bond St. Dent 4F 113
Bond St. Rams 3B 12
Bond St. Roch 1A 28
Bond St. Stal 2E 101
Bongs Rd. Stoc 5F 141 (in two parts)
Bonhill Wlk. M11 3D 96
Bonholt Ind. Est. Bury 1H 35
Bonington Ri. Marp B 3F 143
Bonis Cres. Stoc 1C 152
Bonny Brow St. Midd 2D 68
Bonnyfields. Rom 1H 141
Bonsall Bank. Glos 5G 117 (off Rowsley Clo.)
Bonsall Clo. Glos 5G 117 (off Rowsley Clo.)
Bonsall Fold. Glos 5G 117 (off Rowsley Clo.)
Bonsall St. M15 1D 108 (6G 9)
Bonscale Cres. Midd 4G 53
Bonthe St. Irlam 2D 118
Bonville Chase. Alt 1C 144
Bonville Rd. Alt 6C 132
Boodle St. Ash L 2H 99
Bookham Wlk. M9 3G 83
Boond St. M4 4H 95 (5G 7)
Boond St. Salf 3C 94 (3F 5)
Boonfields. Brom X 3E 19
Booth Av. M14 2H 125
Booth Bri. Clo. Midd 2E 69
Boothby Ct. Swin 2D 78
Boothby Rd. Swin 2E 79
Boothby St. Stoc 1C 152
Booth Clibborn Ct. Salf 3H 81
Booth Clo. Stal 4D 100
Booth Clo. T'ton 6A 22
Boothcote. Aud 1D 112
Booth Ct. Farn 1F 63
Booth Dri. Urm 2B 104
Boothfield. Eccl 2C 90
Boothfield Av. M22 5B 136
Boothfield Dri. M22 5B 136
Boothfield Rd. M22 5A 136
Boothfields. Bury 2A 36
Booth Hall Dri. T'ton 6H 21
Booth Hall Rd. M9 6A 70
Booth Hill La. Oldh & Rytn 6C 56
Booth Ho. Trad. Est. Oldh 3A 72
Booth La. M9 5C 68
Boothman Ct. Eccl 2H 91
Booth Rd. M16 4A 108
Booth Rd. Alt 1E 145
Booth Rd. Aud 6A 98
Booth Rd. L Lev 5B 48
Booth Rd. Sale 3B 122
Booth Rd. Wilm 6E 159
Boothroyden Clo. Midd 2D 68 (in two parts)
Boothroyden Rd. M9 3E 69
Boothroyden Rd. Midd 2E 69 (in two parts)
Boothroyden Ter. M9 3E 69
Booth's Bank. 5D 76
Boothsbank Av. Wors 5D 76
Booth's Hall Gro. Wors 5D 76
Booths Hall Paddock. Wors 6D 76
Booth's Hall Rd. Wors 5D 76
Boothshall Way. Wors 6C 76
Boothstown. 5C 76
Boothstown Dri. Wors 6C 76
Booth St. M2 4D 94 (6H 5)
Booth St. Ash L 3H 99
Booth St. Bolt 2G 31
Booth St. Dent 2F 113
Booth St. Fail 4E 85
Booth St. Holl 2E 117
Booth St. Hyde 6C 114
Booth St. Lees 3A 74
Booth St. Midd 3D 70
Booth St. Oldh 3C 72
Booth St. Salf 3D 94 (4G 5)
Booth St. Stal 5C 100
Booth St. Stoc 4G 139
Booth St. T'ton 5H 21
Booth St. E. M13 1F 109 (5B 10)
Booth St. W. M15 1E 109 (6A 10)
Boothway. Eccl 3H 91
Booth Way. T'ton 6G 21
Boothwood Stile. Holc 6D 12
Boot La. Bolt 4B 30
Bootle St. M2 4D 94 (6G 5)
Bordale Av. M9 4H 83
Bordan St. M11 5B 96
Borden Way. Bury 1E 51
Border Brook La. Wors 4C 76
Bordesley Av. L Hul 3C 62
Bordley Wlk. M23 2E 135
Bordon Rd. Stoc 4D 138
Boringdon Clo. M40 5B 84
Borland Av. M40 2D 84
Bornmore Ind. Cen. Bury 2A 36
Borough Arc. Hyde 4B 114
Borough Av. Rad 2B 50
Borough Av. Swin 2G 79
Borough Rd. Alt 1G 145
Borough Rd. Salf 4D 92
Borough St. Stal 4E 101
Borrans, The. Wors 6B 76
Borron St. Stoc 1A 140
Borrowdale Av. Bolt 5E 31

Borrowdale Av.—Brackenwood Clo.

Borrowdale Av. Gat 1F 149
Borrowdale Clo. Rytn 1B 56
Borrowdale Cres. M20 . . . . .5C 124
Borrowdale Cres. Ash L 6D 86
Borrowdale Dri. Bury 4E 51
Borrowdale Dri. Roch 1B 40
Borrowdale Rd. Midd 5F 53
Borrowdale Rd. Stoc 4B 140
Borrowdale Ter. Stal 1E 101
Borsden St. Swin 1D 78
Borth Av. Stoc 4C 140
Borth Wlk. M23 . . . . . . .5F 135
Borwell St. M18 . . . . . . .1F 111
Boscobel Rd. Bolt 5D 46
Boscombe Av. Eccl 5E 91
Boscombe Dri. Haz G . . .3C 152
Boscombe St. M14 . . . . .5F 109
Boscombe St. Stoc 5H 111
Boscow Rd. L Lev 5A 48
Bosden Av. Haz G 2E 153
Bosden Clo. Hand 2H 159
Bosden Clo. Stoc . . . . . .3H 139 (off Bosden Fold)
Bosden Fold. Stoc 3H 139
Bosdenfold Rd. Haz G . . .2E 153
Bosden Hall Rd. Haz G 2E 153
Bosdin Rd. E. Urm 6A 104
Bosdin Rd. W. Urm 6A 104
Boslam Wlk. M4 . . .3G 95 (4F 7) (off Saltford Av.)
Bosley Av. M20 . . . . .1E 125
Bosley Clo. Wilm 5H 159
Bosley Dri. Poy 4G 163
Bosley Rd. Stoc 3C 138
Bossall Av. M9 . . . . .5G 69
Bossington Clo. Stoc . . .3C 140
Bostock Wlk. M13 . . . . . . .6F 95 (4D 10)
Boston Clo. Bram 6F 151
Boston Clo. Fail 2F 85
Boston Ct. Salf 5E 93
Boston St. M15 . . . . . . .2D 108
Boston St. Bolt 3A 32
Boston St. Hyde 5C 114
Boston St. Oldh 5D 72
Boston Wlk. Dent 6G 113
Boswell Av. Aud 4D 98
Boswell Way. Midd 3E 55
Bosworth Clo. W'fld 1G 67
Bosworth Sq. Roch 1D 40
Bosworth St. M11 . . . . . .5C 96
Bosworth St. Roch 1D 40
Botanical Av. M16 . . . . .2G 107
Botanical Ho. M16 . . . . .2G 107
Botany Clo. Heyw 2D 38
Botany La. Ash L 1A 100
Botany Rd. Eccl 1C 90
Botany Rd. Woodl 3G 129
Botesworth Grn. Miln 6G 29
Botha Clo. M11 . . . . .6F 97
Botham Clo. M15 . . . . . .2D 108
Botham Ct. Eccl 2D 90
Bothwell Rd. M40 . . . . .2G 95 (2E 7)
Bottesford Av. M20 . . . . .4D 124
Bottomfield Clo. Oldh 6E 57
Bottomley Side. M9 . . . . .1E 83
Bottom of Woodhouses. 6G 85
Bottom o' th' Brow. 2D 38
Bottom o' th' Moor. 2F 33
Bottom o' th' Moor. A'wth 4B 34
Bottom o' th' Moor. Brad 3F 33
Bottom o' th' Moor. Oldh 2F 73
Bottoms. 3F 89
Bottoms Fold. Moss 3F 89
Bottoms Mill Rd. Marp 6F 143
Bottom St. Hyde 4D 114
Boulden Dri. Bury 6C 22
Boulder Dri. M23 . . . . . .3G 147
Boulderstone Rd. Stal . . .1E 101
Boulevard, The. Haz G . . .3E 153
Boulevard, The. Holl 2F 117
Bouley Wlk. M12 . . . . . .1C 110
Boundary Clo. Moss . . . . .5E 89 (in two parts)
Boundary Clo. Woodl . . .4A 130
Boundary Cotts. Carr 4G 89
Boundary Ct. Chea 6G 137
Boundary Dri. Brad F 2A 48
Boundary Gdns. Bolt 3H 31
Boundary Gdns. Oldh 6C 56
Boundary Grn. Dent 2E 113
Boundary Gro. Sale 6F 123
Boundary Ind. Est. Bolt 6A 34
Boundary La. M15 . . . . . .1E 109 (5A 10)
Boundary Pk. Rd. Oldh 6A 56
Boundary Rd. Chea 5B 138
Boundary Rd. Irlam 4F 103
Boundary Rd. Swin 2F 79
Boundary St. M12 . . . . .2C 110
Boundary St. Bolt 3H 31
Boundary St. Roch 5G 27
Boundary St. E. M13 . . . . . . .6E 95 (4B 10)
Boundary St. W. M15 . . . . . .1E 109 (5A 10) (in two parts)
Boundary, The. Swin 5D 64
Boundary Trad. Est. Irlam 4G 103
Boundary Wlk. Roch 6G 27
Bourdon St. M40 . . . . . . .2H 95 (2H 7)
Bourget St. M8 . . . . .3B 82
Bournbrook Av. L Hul 3C 62
Bourne Av. Swin 4F 79
Bourne Dri. M40 . . . . .2B 84
Bourne Ho. Salf 3F 93
Bournelea Av. M19 . . . . .3B 126
Bourne Rd. Shaw 5E 43
Bourne St. Chad 1H 85
Bourne St. Stoc 5G 127
Bourne St. Wilm 3C 166
Bourne Wlk. Bolt 4B 32
Bournville Av. Stoc 5G 127
Bournville Dri. Bury 3G 35
Bournville Gro. M19 . . . .6D 110
Bourton Clo. Bury 2H 35
Bourton Dri. M18 . . . . . .3D 110
Bowden Clo. Hyde 6A 116
Bowden Clo. Roch 5D 40
Bowden Cricket Club 4F 145
Bowden La. Marp 4C 142
Bowden Rd. Swin 4G 79
Bowden St. Dent 4E 113
Bowden St. Haz G 2E 153
Bowden Vw. Urm 5C 104
Bowdon. 3E 145
Bowdon Av. M14 . . . . . .6D 108
Bowdon Ho. Stoc 3G 139
Bowdon Ri. Bow 3F 145
Bowdon Rd. Alt 2E 145
Bowdon St. Stoc . . . . . .3G 139 (in two parts)
Bowen Clo. Bram 2H 161
Bowen St. Bolt 4F 31
Bower Av. Haz G 4D 152
Bower Av. Roch 5B 16
Bower Av. Stoc 6E 127
Bower Ct. Hyde 2E 115
Bowercup Fold. Carr . . . . .6G 89 & 1H 101
Bowerfield Av. Haz G . . .5D 152
Bowerfield Cres. Haz G 5D 152
Bower Fold. 5G 101
Bowerfold La. Stoc . . . . .1E 139 (in three parts)
Bower Gdns. Stal 5H 101
Bower Gro. Stal 3G 101
Bower La. Chad 1G 85
Bower Rd. Hale 4G 145
Bowers Av. Urm 3D 104
Bower St. Bury 2G 37
Bower St. Newt H 6H 83
Bower St. Oldh 2F 73
Bower St. Salf 4A 82
Bower St. Stoc 5H 111
Bower Ter. Droy 2C 98
Bowery Av. Chea H 1B 160
Bowes Clo. Bury 6B 22
Bowes St. M14 . . . . .4D 108
Bowfell Circ. Urm 4D 104
Bowfell Dri. H Lane 5C 154
Bowfell Gro. M9 . . . . .5D 68
Bowfell Rd. Urm 5C 104
Bowfield Wlk. M40 . . . . . .6C 84
Bowgreave Av. Bolt 6H 33
Bowgreen. 4E 145
Bow Grn. M. Bow 3D 144
Bow Grn. Rd. Bow 4B 144
Bowgreen Wlk. M15 . . . . . .1B 108 (6D 8)
Bowker Av. Dent 1H 129
Bowker Bank Av. M8 . . . . .1B 82
Bowker Bank Ind. Est. M8 . . . . .6C 68
Bowker Clo. Roch 2A 26
Bowker Ct. Salf 5H 81
Bowkers Row. Bolt 6B 32
Bowker St. Hyde 4C 114
Bowker St. Rad 4G 49
Bowker St. Salf 5H 81
Bowker St. Wors 6D 62
Bowker Va. Gdns. M9 . . . .6B 68
Bowlacre Rd. Hyde 3B 130
Bowland Av. M18 . . . . . .3A 112
Bowland Clo. Ash L 4G 87
Bowland Clo. Bury 2E 35
Bowland Clo. Shaw 6C 42
Bowland Clo. Stoc 6E 141
Bowland Ct. Sale 5B 122
Bowland Dri. Bolt 3C 30
Bowland Gro. Miln 1D 42
Bowland Rd. M23 . . . . . .5F 135
Bowland Rd. Dent 4B 112
Bowland Rd. Woodl 4H 129
Bow La. M2 . . . . .4D 94 (6H 5)
Bow La. Bow 5C 144
Bow La. Heyw 3F 39
Bowlee. 6D 52
Bowlee Clo. Bury 5E 51
Bowler's Leisure Cen. . .1A 106
Bowler St. Lev 1D 126
Bowler St. Shaw 6F 43
Bowlers Wlk. Roch 1H 27
Bowley Av. M22 . . . . . . .3G 147
Bowling Ct. Bolt 6C 18
Bowling Grn. Rams 2A 12
Bowling Grn. Ct. M16 . . .3B 108
Bowling Grn. St. Heyw . . .3F 39
Bowling Grn. St. Hyde 5B 114
Bowling Grn. Way. Roch 4B 26
Bowling Rd. M18 . . . . . .4G 111
Bowling St. Chad 1H 85
Bowman Cres. Ash L . . .2B 100
Bowmeadow Grange. M12 . . . . .3B 110
Bowmead Wlk. M8 . . . . . .5B 82 (off Ermington Dri.)
Bowmont Clo. Chea H . . .1C 150
Bowness Av. Cad 5B 118
Bowness Av. Chea H 4D 150
Bowness Av. Roch 2E 27
Bowness Av. Stoc 3G 127
Bowness Ct. Midd 5F 53
Bowness Dri. Sale 4H 121
Bowness Rd. Ash L 1F 99
Bowness Rd. Bolt 3H 45
Bowness Rd. L Lev 3H 47
Bowness Rd. Midd 6E 53
Bowness Rd. Timp 6D 134
Bowness St. M11 . . . . . . .6H 97
Bowness St. Stret 4D 106
Bowness Wlk. Rytn . . . . .3C 56 (off Shaw St.)
Bowscale Clo. M13 . . . . .3B 110
Bowstone Hill Rd. Bolt 6D 20
Bow St. M2 . . . . . .4D 94 (5G 5)
Bow St. Ash L . . . . .2H 99 (Warrington St.)
Bow St. Ash L . . . . .3A 100 (Whitelands Ter.)
Bow St. Bolt 6B 32
Bow St. Oldh 2D 72
Bow St. Roch 2D 40
Bow St. Stoc 3E 139
Bow Vs. Bow 3D 144
Bowyers St. M14 . . . . . .2A 126
Boxgrove Rd. Sale 4H 121
Boxgrove Wlk. M8 . . . . . .5C 82
Boxhill Dri. M23 . . . . . . .2G 135
Box St. L'boro 4E 17
Box St. Rams 3F 13
Boxtree Av. M18 . . . . . . .3F 111
Box Wlk. Part 6C 118
Box Works, The. M15 . . . . . . .6B 94 (3D 8)
Boyd St. M12 . . . . .6C 96
Boyd's Wlk. Duk 6A 100
Boyer St. M16 . . . . .2H 107
Boyle St. M8 . . . . .5D 82
Boyle St. Rams 4E 31
Boysnope Cres. Eccl 3G 103
Boysnope Wharf. Eccl 3H 103
Brabant Rd. Chea H 3D 150
Brabham Clo. M21 . . . . .1H 123
Brabham M. Swin 4C 78
Brabyns Av. Rom 6B 130
Brabyns Brow. Marp & Marp B 4E 143
Brabyns Park Recreation Cen. 3E 143
Brabyns Rd. Hyde 2C 130
Bracadale Dri. Stoc 6G 139
Bracewell Clo. M12 . . . . .2C 110
Bracken Av. Wors 6G 63
Brackenbury Wlk. M15 . . . . .2E 109
Bracken Clo. Bolt 5B 18
Bracken Clo. Droy 3C 98
Bracken Clo. Heyw 5F 39
Bracken Clo. Holl 1F 117
Bracken Clo. Marp B 4F 143
Bracken Clo. Sale 4E 121
Bracken Clo. S'head 3B 74
Bracken Dri. M23 . . . . . .6H 135
Brackenfield Wlk. Timp 5D 134
Brackenhall Ct. Heyw . . . .3C 38 (off Todd St.)
Brackenhill Ter. Dent . . . .2G 129 (off Wordsworth Rd.)
Brackenhurst Av. Moss 2G 89
Brackenlea Fold. Roch 1D 26
Brackenlea Pl. Stoc 6F 139
Bracken Lodge. Rytn 6C 56
Brackenside. Stoc 1A 128
Brackenwood Clo. Rytn 5A 56

Brackenwood Dri.
  Chea 1H 149
Brackenwood M.
  Wilm 1H 167
Brackley Av.
  M15 . . . . . . .6B 94 (4C 8)
Brackley Av. Cad 3B 118
Brackley Ct. M22 . . . . .3B 136
Drackley Dri. Midd 4A 70
Brackley Lodge. Eccl . . .2H 91
Brackley Rd. Bolt 6E 45
Brackley Rd. Eccl 1F 91
Bràckley Rd. Stoc 5F 127
Brackley Sq. Oldh 1E 73
Brackley St. Farn 1F 63
        (in two parts)
Brackley St. Oldh 1E 73
Brackley St. Wors 5E 63
Bracknell Dri. M9 . . . . .6C 68
Bracondale Av. Bolt 3F 31
Bradburn Av. Eccl 4F 91
Bradburn Cio. Eccl 3F 91
Bradburn Gro. Eccl 4F 91
Bradburn Dri. Irlam 2C 118
Bradburn St. Eccl 4F 91
Bradburn Wlk. M8 . . . . .5D 82
        (off Moordown Clo.)
Bradbury Av. Alt 6C 132
Bradbury's La. G'fld 5G 61
Bradbury St. Ash L 1G 99
Bradbury St. Bury 2E 51
Bradbury St. Hyde 6C 114
Bradbury St. Rad 5G 49
Bradbury Wlk. Hytn 3C 56
        (off Shaw St.)
Bradda Mt. Bram 3A 152
Braddan Av. Sale 6C 122
Braddocks Clo. Roch . . .5B 16
Braddon Av. Urm 5F 105
Braddon Rd. Woodl 4G 129
Braddon St. M11 . . . . . .4E 97
Brade Clo. M11 . . . . . . .5E 97
Bradfield Av. Salf 3C 92
Bradfield Clo. Stoc 5G 111
Bradfield Rd.
  Urm & Stret 5H 105
Bradfield St. M4 . . . 4G 95 (6F 7)
Bradford. 3B 96
Bradford Av. Bolt 4D 46
Bradford Ct. M40 . . . . . .2C 84
Bradford Cres. Bolt 3C 46
Bradford Pk. Dri.
  Bolt 1D 46
Bradford Rd.
  M40 . . . . . . .3H 95 (4G 7)
Bradford Rd. Eccl 6E 79
Bradford Rd.
  Farn & Bolt 6C 46
Bradford St. Bolt 1C 46
Bradford St. Farn 2F 63
        (in two parts)
Bradford St. Oldh 1C 72
Bradford Ter. Bury 4B 36
Bradgate Av. H Grn 4H 149
Bradgate Rd. M22 . . . . .3C 136
Bradgate Rd. Alt 6C 132
Bradgate Rd. Sale 1B 134
Bradgate St. Ash L 3G 99
        (Park St.)
Bradgate St. Ash L 3G 99
        (Victoria St.)
Bradgreen Rd. Eccl 2E 91
Brading Wlk. M22 . . . . .5C 148
Bradley Av. Salf 4F 81
Bradley Clo. Aud 6E 99
Bradley Clo. Timp 4G 133
Bradley Dri. Bury 5F 51
Bradley Fold. Stal 3F 101
Bradley Fold Cotts.
  Bolt 1B 48

Bradley Fold Rd.
  A'wth & Bolt 5C 34
Bradley Fold Trad. Est.
  Brad F 1C 48
Bradley Grn. Rd.
  Hyde 1D 114
Bradley Ho. Oldh 4D 72
Bradley La. Bolt 2B 48
Bradley La. Miln 1F 43
Bradley La. Stret 2A 122
Bradley's Ct. M1 . . .4F 95 (5C 6)
Bradley Smithy Clo.
  Roch 1G 27
Bradley St. M1 . . . . .4C 6
Bradley St. Miln 1F 43
Bradney Clo. M9 . . . . . .5D 68
Bradnor Rd. Shar I 4B 136
Bradshaw. 5H 19
Bradshaw Av. M20 . . . .2F 125
Bradshaw Av. Fail 6E 85
Bradshaw Av. W'fld 5C 50
Bradshaw Brow. Bolt . . .1E 33
Bradshaw Chapel. 6G 19
Bradshaw Cres. Marp . . .4E 143
Bradshaw Fold Av.
  M40 . . . . .6D 70
Bradshawgate. Bolt 6B 32
Bradshaw Hall Dri.
  Bolt 5G 19
Bradshaw Hall Fold.
  Bolt 5H 19
Bradshaw Hall La.
  H Grn 5H 149
        (in two parts)
Bradshaw La. Stret 6D 106
Bradshaw Meadows.
  Bolt 5H 19
Bradshaw Rd.
  Bolt & Tur 6H 19
Bradshaw Rd. Marp 4D 142
Bradshaw Rd. T'ton 5E 21
Bradshaw St.
  M4 . . . . . . .3E 95 (3A 6)
Bradshaw St. Farn 2F 63
Bradshaw St. Heyw 3G 39
        (in two parts)
Bradshaw St. Midd 2C 70
Bradshaw St. Oldh 2D 72
Bradshaw St. Rad 4F 49
Bradshaw St. Roch 3A 28
Bradshaw St. N. Salf . . .4H 81
Bradshaw Trad. Est.
  Midd 3C 70
Bradstock Rd. M16 . . . .4C 108
Bradstone Rd. M8 . . . . .6B 82
Bradwell Av. M20 . . . . .3D 124
Bradwell Av. Stret 4A 106
Bradwell Dri. H Grn 6G 149
Bradwell Fold. Glos 6G 117
        (off Riber Bank)
Bradwell Lea. Glos 6G 117
        (off Duxton M.)
Bradwell Pl. Bolt 4D 32
Bradwell Rd. Haz G 5E 153
Bradwell Ter. Glos 6G 117
        (off Buxton M.)
Bradwell Wlk. Urm 4H 103
Bradwen Av. M8 . . . . . .2C 82
Bradwen Clo. Dent 6G 113
Braemar Av. Stret 5A 106
Braemar Av. Urm 6C 104
Braemar Ct. M9 . . . . . . .4C 68
Braemar Dri. Bury 3H 37
Braemar Dri. Sale 1E 133
Braemar Gdns. Bolt 2C 44
Braemar Gro. Heyw 4C 38
Braemar La. Wors 5D 76
Braemar Rd. M14 . . . . .1A 126
        (in two parts)
Braemar Rd. Haz G 2F 153
Braemar Wlk. Bolt 2C 44

Braemore Clo. Shaw 5C 42
Braemore Dri. B'btm 6B 116
Brae Side. Oldh 1C 86
Braeside. Stret 6A 106
Braeside Clo. Stoc 5F 141
Braeside Gro. Bolt 2C 44
Braewood Clo. Bury 2G 37
Bragenham St. M18 . . . .2E 111
Drailsford Av. Glos 5G 117
Brailsford Clo. Glos 5G 117
        (off Brailsford Av.)
Brailsford Gdns. Glos 5G 117
        (off Brailsford Av.)
Brailsford Grn. Glos 5G 117
        (off Brailsford Av.)
Brailsford M. Glos 5G 117
Brailsford Rd. M14 . . . .1A 126
        (in two parts)
Brailsford Rd. Bolt 2E 33
Braintree Rd. M22 . . . . .5C 148
Braithwaite Rd. Midd 3F 53
Brakehouse Clo. Miln . . .5E 29
Brakenhurst Dri. Salf . . .5B 82
Brakesmere Gro. Wors . .5B 62
Braley St. M12 . . .6F 95 (3D 10)
Bramah Edge Ct. Tin . . .1H 117
Bramall Av. Bury 5F 51
Bramall Ct. Salf . . .2B 94 (2D 4)
Bramall Hall. 4F 151
Bramber Way. Chad 3H 71
Bramble Av. Oldh 6H 57
Bramble Av.
  Salf 6A 94 (3A 8)
Bramble Clo. L'boro 4D 16
Bramble Wlk. M22 . . . . .3A 148
Bramble Wlk. Sale 4E 121
Bramblewood. Chad 1E 71
Brambling Clo. Aud 3C 98
Brambling Clo. Stoc 6G 141
Bramcote Av. M23 . . . . .5H 135
Bramcote Av. Bolt 2D 46
Bramcote Av. Bolt 6A 20
Dramfield Wlk.
  M15 . . . . . .6B 94 (4D 8)
Bramhall. 1G 161
Bramhall Av. Bolt 1A 34
Bramhall Cen., The.
  Bram 1G 161
Bramhall Clo. Duk 1R 114
Bramhall Clo. Miln 5E 29
Bramhall Clo. Sale 6C 123
Bramhall Clo. Timp 5D 134
Bramhall Green. 3H 151
Bramhall La. Bram 3G 151
Bramhall La.
  Stoc (SK2) 5H 139
Bramhall La.
  Stoc (SK3) 2H 151
Bramhall La. S. Bram . . .1G 161
Bramhall Moor Ind. Est.
  Haz G 3B 152
Bramhall Moor La.
  Haz G 4A 152
Bramhall Mt. Stoc 6H 139
Bramhall Park. 4E 151
Bramhall Pk. Gro.
  Bram 4E 151
Bramhall Pk. Rd.
  Bram (SK7) 4F 151
Bramhall Pk. Rd.
  Bram (SK8) 4E 151
Bramhall St. M18 . . . . . .2G 111
Bramhall St. Bolt 4D 46
Bramhall St. Hyde 3B 114
Bramhall Wlk. Dent 5E 113
Bramham Rd. Marp 1E 155
Bramhope Wlk. M9 . . . .4F 83
Bramley Av. M19 . . . . . .1C 126
Bramley Av. Stret 5B 106
Bramley Clo. Bram 1G 161
Bramley Clo. Swin 5C 78
Bramley Clo. Wilm 5A 166

Bramley Cres. Stoc 2D 138
Bramley Dri. Bram 1G 161
Bramley Dri. Bury 5C 22
Bramley Meade. Salf . . .4H 81
Bramley Rd. Bolt 5D 18
Bramley Rd. Bram 1G 161
Bramley Rd. Roch 3A 26
Bramley St. Salf 1C 94
Brammay Dri. T'ton 5G 21
Brampton Rd. Bolt 4F 45
Brampton Rd. Bram 3H 151
Brampton Wlk. M40 . . . .5B 84
Bramway. Bram 6E 151
Bramway. H Lane 6D 154
Bramwell Dri.
  M13 . . . . . .1G 109 (5E 11)
Bramwell St. Stoc 3B 140
Bramwood Ct. Bram 1G 161
Bramworth Av. Rams . . .3D 12
Brancaster Rd.
  M1 . . . . . . .6E 95 (3B 10)
Branch Clo. Bury 2B 36
Branch Rd. L'boro 1E 29
Branckar St. W'houg 6A 44
Brandish Clo. M13 . . . . .2H 109
Brandle Av. Bury 1A 36
Brandlehow Dri. Midd . . .5E 53
Brandlesholme. 5C 22
Brandlesholme Rd.
  G'mnt & Bury 2H 21
Brandon Av. M22 . . . . .3A 136
Brandon Av. Dent 4H 111
Brandon Av. Eccl 6G 79
Brandon Av. H Grn 4F 149
Brandon Brow. Oldh 1C 72
Brandon Clo. Bury 6D 22
Brandon Clo. Wilm 5H 159
Brandon Cres. Shaw 5E 43
Brandon Rd. Salf 1B 92
Brandon St. Bolt 3H 45
Brandon St. Miln 5E 29
        (off Nail St.)
Drandram Rd. P'wich . . .5G 67
Brandsby Gdns. Salf . . .5G 93
Brandwood. Chad 6E 55
Brandwood Av. M21 . . . .5R 124
Brandwood Clo. Wors . . .3C 76
Brandwood St. Bolt 3G 45
        (in two parts)
Branfield Av. H Grn 4H 149
Drankgate Ct. M20 . . . . .4C 125
Branksome Av. P'wich . .5E 67
Branksome Dri. M9 . . . .4D 68
Branksome Dri.
  H Grn 4H 149
Branksome Dri. Salf 6G 79
Branksome Rd. Stoc . . .2D 138
Bransby Av. M9 . . . . . . .5G 69
Branscombe Dri. Sale . . .4E 121
Branscombe Gdns.
  Bolt 2F 47
Bransdale Av. Rytn 3A 56
Bransdale Clo. Bolt 3D 44
Bransford Rd. M11 . . . .5G 97
Bransford Rd. Urm 3E 105
Branson St.
  M40 . . . . . . .3H 95 (4H 7)
Branson Wlk. Timp 5D 134
Branston Rd. M40 . . . . .1D 84
Brantfell Gro. Bolt 5H 5
Brantingham Ct. M16 . . .6C 108
Brantingham Rd.
  M21 & Whal R 6H 107
Brantwood Clo. Rytn . . .2A 56
Brantwood Ct. Salf 3H 81
Brantwood Dri. Bolt 5H 33
Brantwood Rd.
  Chea H 4B 150
Brantwood Rd. Salf 3H 81
Brantwood Rd. Stoc 5E 127
Brantwood Ter. M9 . . . .4H 83
Brassey St. Ash L 1H 99

Brassey St. *Midd* 6A **54**
Brassica Clo. *Eccl* 1C **90**
Brassington Av. *M21* . . .2H **123**
Brassington Av. *Salf* . . .5H **93**
Brassington Cres.
 Glos 5F **117**
Brassington Rd. *Stoc* . .5A **126**
Brathay Clo. *Bolt* 3H **33**
Bratton Wlk.
 M13 . . . . .1H **109** (6G **11**)
Brattray Dri. *Midd* 4G **53**
Braunston Clo. *Eccl* . . .5G **91**
Braxton Wlk. *M9* 3G **83**
Bray Av. *Eccl* 2D **90**
Braybrook Dri. *Bolt* . . .6B **30**
Bray Clo. *Chea H* 3A **150**
Brayford Rd. *M22* 4B **148**
Brayshaw Clo. *Heyw* . . .4E **39**
Brayside Rd.
 M20 & M19 . . . . .5H **125**
Braystan Gdns. *Gat* . . .5F **137**
Brayton Av. *M20* 1G **137**
Brayton Av. *Sale* 3F **121**
Brazennose St.
 M2 . . . . . .4D **94** (6G **5**)
Brazil Pl. *M1* . . .5E **95** (2B **10**)
Brazil St. *M1* . . .5E **95** (1B **10**)
Brazley Av. *Bolt* 4C **46**
Breach Ho. La. *Mobb* . .5A **156**
Bread St. *M18* 1G **111**
Brean Wlk. *M22* 4A **148**
Brechin Wlk. *Open* 4E **97**
Brechin Way. *Heyw* 4C **38**
Breckland Dri. *Stal* 3H **101**
Breckland Dri. *Bolt* . . .5B **30**
Breckles Pl. *Bolt* 2H **45**
 (off Kershaw St.)
Breck Rd. *Eccl* 3D **90**
Brecon Av. *M19* 2B **126**
Brecon Av. *Chea H* 4A **150**
Brecon Av. *Dent* 6F **113**
Brecon Av. *Urm* 4H **103**
Brecon Clo. *Poy* 3F **163**
Brecon Cres. *Ash L* 5F **87**
Brecon Dri. *Bury* 6C **36**
Brecon Towers. *Stoc* . . .2C **128**
Brecon Wlk. *Oldh* 1H **85**
Bredbury. 6F **129**
Bredbury Dri. *Farn* 1G **63**
Bredbury Green. 1G **141**
Bredbury Grn. *Rom* . . .1G **141**
Bredbury Ind. Est.
 Bred 3D **128**
Bredbury Ind. Est.
 Rom 3E **129**
Bredbury Pk. Ind. Est.
 Bred 4E **129**
Bredbury Pk. Way.
 Bred 3E **129**
Bredbury Rd. *M14* 5F **109**
Bredbury St. *Chad* 3H **71**
Bredbury St. *Hyde* 2B **114**
Brede Wlk. *M23* 2D **134**
Bredon Way. *Oldh* 6C **72**
Breeze Hill. *Shaw* 2F **57**
Breeze Hill Rd. *Oldh* . . .4H **73**
Breeze Mt. *P'wich* 1F **81**
Breightmet. 6H **33**
Breightmet Dri. *Bolt* . . .6G **33**
Breightmet Fold. *Bolt* . .5H **33**
Breightmet Fold La.
 Bolt 5H **33**
Breightmet Hill. *Bolt* . . .4G **33**
Breightmet Ind. Est.
 Bolt 5H **33**
Breightmet St. *Bolt* . . .1B **46**
Brellafield Dri. *Shaw* . . .4D **42**
Brenbar Cres. *Whitw* . . .4G **15**
Brenchley Dri. *M23* . . .1G **135**
Brencon Av. *M23* 2C **134**
Brendall Clo. *Stoc* 6G **141**

Brendon Av. *M40* 4A **84**
Brendon Av. *Stoc* 3H **127**
Brendon Dri. *Aud* 4D **98**
Brendon Hills. *Rytn* 4B **56**
Brenley Wlk. *M9* 3F **83**
 (off Maybrook Wlk.)
Brennan Clo.
 M15 . . . . . .2E **109** (6A **10**)
Brennan Ct. *Oldh* 1A **86**
Brennock Clo. *M11* 5B **96**
Brentbridge Rd. *M14* . . .1F **125**
Brent Clo. *Brad F* 2B **48**
Brent Clo. *Poy* 3B **162**
Brentfield Av. *M8* 5B **82**
Brentford Av. *Bolt* 3F **31**
Brentford Rd. *Stoc* 3H **127**
Brentford St. *M9* 4G **83**
Brent Ho. *Bolt* 4A **32**
 (off Enfield Clo.)
Brent Moor Rd. *Bram* . . .2A **152**
Brentnall St. *Stoc* 4H **139**
Brenton Av. *Sale* 5A **122**
Brent Rd. *M23* 1G **135**
Brent Rd. *Stoc* 2E **139**
Brentwood. *Sale* 5A **122**
Brentwood. *Salf* 2E **93**
Brentwood. *Urm* 6B **104**
Brentwood Av. *Cad* 3B **118**
Brentwood Av. *Timp* . . .4G **133**
Brentwood Av. *Urm* 5F **105**
Brentwood Av. *Wors* . . .5B **78**
Brentwood Clo.
 L'boro 6D **16**
Brentwood Clo. *Stal* 3G **101**
Brentwood Clo. *Stoc* . . .4C **128**
Brentwood Ct. *P'wich* . .6D **66**
Brentwood Cres. *Alt* . . .5G **133**
Brentwood Dri. *Eccl* 1F **91**
Brentwood Dri. *Farn* 5E **47**
Brentwood Dri. *Gat* 6F **137**
Brentwood Rd. *Swin* . . .5D **78**
Brentwood St. *M16* 3D **108**
Brereton Clo. *Bow* 4E **145**
Brereton Ct. *Chea H* . . .4A **150**
Brereton Dri. *Wors* 4H **77**
Brereton Gro. *Cad* 3C **118**
Brereton Rd. *Eccl* 4B **90**
Brereton Rd. *Hand* 4A **160**
Breslyn St. *M3* . . .2D **94** (2H **5**)
Brethren's St. *Droy* 5A **98**
Bretland Gdns. *Hyde* . . .6A **116**
Bretland Wlk. *M22* 2D **148**
Brettargh St. *Salf* 1G **93**
Bretton Wlk. *M22* 5B **148**
Brett Rd. *Wors* 5C **76**
Brett St. *M22* 2C **136**
 (in two parts)
Brewers Grn. *Haz G* . . .2D **152**
Brewer St. *M1* . . .4F **95** (5C **6**)
Brewerton Rd. *Oldh* 4G **73**
Brewery St. *Alt* 1F **145**
Brewery St. *Stoc* 1H **139**
 (in two parts)
Brewster St. *M9* 3F **83**
Brewster St. *Midd* 5A **54**
Brian Av. *Droy* 2C **98**
Brian Farrell Dri. *Duk* . . .1C **114**
Brian Redhead Ct.
 M15 . . . . . .6C **94** (4E **9**)
Brian Rd. *Farn* 6C **46**
Brian St. *Roch* 3B **40**
Briar Av. *Haz G* 3E **153**
Briar Av. *Oldh* 6H **57**
Briar Clo. *Roch* 2C **26**
Briar Clo. *Sale* 5E **121**
Briar Clo. *Urm* 4C **104**
Briar Cres. *M22* 6C **136**
Briardene. *Dent* 2G **113**
Briardene Gdns. *M22* . . .1C **148**
Briarfield. *Eger* 1B **18**
Briarfield Hall. *M15* 5A **10**

Briarfield Rd.
 M20 & M19 . . . . .3H **125**
Briarfield Rd. *Chea H* . . .2D **150**
Briarfield Rd. *Dob* 5A **60**
Briarfield Rd. *Farn* 6C **46**
Briarfield Rd. *Stoc* 3G **127**
Briarfield Rd. *Timp* 6C **134**
Briarfield Rd. *Wors* 4G **77**
Briar Gro. *Chad* 6H **55**
Briar Gro. *Woodl* 4G **129**
Briar Hill Av. *L Hul* 5A **62**
Briar Hill Clo. *L Hul* 5A **62**
Briar Hill Ct. *Salf* 2G **93**
 (off Briar Hill Way)
Briar Hill Gro. *L Hul* 5A **62**
Briar Hill Way. *Salf* 2G **93**
Briar Hollow. *Stoc* 2D **138**
Briarlands Av. *Sale* 1H **133**
Briarlands Clo. *Bram* 1F **161**
Briar Lea Clo. *Bolt* 3A **46**
Briarlea Gdns. *M19* 4A **126**
Briarley Gdns. *Woodl* . . .3A **130**
Briarmere Wlk. *Chad* . . .2A **72**
Briars Mt. *Stoc* 1C **138**
Briarstead Clo. *Bram* . . .6F **151**
Briar St. *Bolt* 6F **33**
Briar St. *Roch* 5F **27**
Briarthorn Clo. *Marp* . . .2D **154**
Briarwood. *Wilm* 2F **167**
Briarwood Av. *M23* 3E **135**
Briarwood Av. *Droy* 2G **97**
Briarwood Chase.
 Chea H 4D **150**
Briarwood Cres. *Marp* . . .2E **155**
Brice St. *Duk* 5H **99**
Brickbridge Rd. *Marp* . . .6E **143**
 (in two parts)
Brickfield St. *Roch* 1B **28**
Brick Ground. *Roch* 1G **25**
Brickhill La. *Ash* 3B **156**
Brickkiln Row. *Bow* 4E **145**
Brickley St. *M3* . . .2E **95** (1H **5**)
Brick St. *Bury* 2E **37**
Bricram St. *M8* 6C **82**
Briddon St. *M3* . . .2D **94** (1G **5**)
 (in two parts)
Brideoak St. *M8* 4C **82**
Brideoak St. *Oldh* 1A **74**
Bridestowe Av. *Hyde* . . .4G **115**
Bridestowe Wlk.
 Hyde 4G **115**
 (in two parts)
Bride St. *Bolt* 3A **32**
Bridge Av. *Woodl* 4G **129**
 (in two parts)
Bridge Clo. *Part* 6E **119**
Bridge Clo. *Rad* 5H **49**
Bridgecrest Ct.
 Chea H 3D **150**
Bridge Dri. *Chea* 1H **149**
Bridge Dri. *Hand* 4H **159**
Bridge End. *Del* 3H **59**
Bridgefield Av. *Wilm* . . .6G **159**
Bridgefield Clo.
 H Lane 6C **154**
Bridgefield Cres.
 S'head 3B **74**
Bridgefield Dri. *Bury* 3G **37**
Bridgefield St. *Rad* 4H **49**
Bridgefield St. *Roch* 4F **27**
Bridgefield St. *Stoc* 2G **139**
Bridgefield Wlk. *Rad* 4H **49**
Bridgefold Rd. *Roch* 4E **27**
Bridgefoot Clo. *Wors* . . .6C **76**
Bridgeford Ct.
 M15 . . . . . .1E **109** (6B **10**)
Bridge Gro. *Timp* 4H **133**
Bri. Hall Dri. *Bury* 2G **37**
 (in two parts)

Bri. Hall Fold. *Bury* 3G **37**
Bri. Hall Ind. Est.
 Heap B 3G **37**
Bri. Hall La. *Bury* 3G **37**
Bridgelea Rd. *M20* 3F **125**
Bridgeman Ho. *Farn* 2F **63**
Bridgeman Pl. *Bolt* 1C **46**
Bridgeman St. *Bolt* 3H **45**
Bridgeman St. *Farn* 6F **47**
Bridgemere Clo. *Rad* 2F **49**
Bridge Mills. *Rams* 2B **12**
Bri. Mills Bus. Pk. *Salf* . . .6D **80**
Bridgend Clo. *M12* 1C **110**
Bridgend Clo. *Chea H* . . .1D **150**
Bridgenorth Av. *Urm* 5H **105**
Bridgenorth Dri. *L'boro* . . .6D **16**
Bridge Rd. *M23* 4C **134**
Bridge Rd. *Bury* 4B **36**
Bridges Av. *Bury* 1D **50**
Bridges Ct. *Bolt* 1B **46**
 (off Soho St.)
Bridgeside Bus. Cen.
 Bred 3D **128**
Bridge St. *Aud* 6F **99**
Bridge St. *Bolt* 6A **32**
Bridge St. *Bury* 1E **37**
Bridge St. *Droy* 5G **97**
Bridge St. *Duk* 1G **113**
Bridge St. *Farn* 6G **47**
Bridge St. *Heyw* 3E **39**
Bridge St. *Midd* 1A **70**
Bridge St. *Miln* 5F **29**
Bridge St. *Oldh* 3E **73**
Bridge St. *Rad* 1B **64**
Bridge St. *Rams* 3E **13**
Bridge St.
 Roch (OL11) 4C **40**
Bridge St.
 Roch (OL12) 6A **16**
Bridge St. *Salf* . .4C **94** (5F **5**)
Bridge St. *Shaw* 5G **43**
Bridge St. *S'head* 3B **74**
Bridge St. *Stal* 4D **100**
Bridge St. *Stoc* 1H **139**
Bridge St. *Swin* 3G **79**
Bridge St. *Upperm* 2F **61**
Bridge St. *Whitw* 4G **15**
Bridge St. Brow. *Stoc* . . .1H **139**
Bridge St. W.
 Salf 4C **94** (5F **5**)
Bridges Way. *Dent* 2F **129**
Bridge Ter. *Bury* 3G **37**
Bridge Trad. Est. *Bury* . . .3B **36**
Bridgewater Cen., The.
 Urm 6G **91**
Bridgewater Circ.
 Urm 1F **105**
Bridgewater Clo.
 H Grn 6H **149**
Bridgewater Clo. *W'fld* . . .1E **67**
Bridgewater Hall. 2H **9**
Bridgewater Hall.
 M1 . . . . . . .5D **94** (2G **9**)
 (off Gt. Bridgewater St.)
Bridgewater Pl.
 M4 . . . . . . .4E **95** (5A **6**)
Bridgewater Rd. *Alt* 4F **133**
Bridgewater Rd. *Swin* . . .4H **79**
Bridgewater Rd. *Wors* . . .4B **76**
 (Mosley Common)
Bridgewater Rd. *Wors* . . .1E **77**
 (Walkden)
Bridgewater St.
 M3 . . . . . . .5C **94** (2E **9**)
 (in two parts)
Bridgewater St. *Bolt* 1H **45**
Bridgewater St. *Eccl* 3D **90**
Bridgewater St. *Farn* 1G **63**
Bridgewater St. *L Hul* . . .5G **62**
Bridgewater St. *Oldh* 1E **73**
Bridgewater St. *Sale* 4B **122**

Bridgewater St.—Broad St.

Bridgewater St. *Salf* 2C 94 (1E 5)
Bridgewater St. *Stret* 5F 107
Bridgewater Viaduct. *M15* 6C 94 (3F 9)
Bridgewater Wlk. Wors 6F 63 *(off Victoria Sq.)*
Bridgewater Way. *M16* 2H 107 (6A 8)
Bridgeway. *Marp* 5C 142
Bridgewood Lodge. *Heyw* 3D 38
Bridgnorth Rd. *M9* 6C 68
Bridle Clo. *Droy* 2C 98
Bridle Clo. *Urm* 5A 104
Bridle Ct. *Woodf* 5H 161
Bridle Fold. *Rad* 3G 49
Bridle Rd. *P'wich* 2H 67
Bridle Rd. *Woodf* 4H 161
Bridle Way. *Woodf* 5H 161
Bridlington Av. *Salf* 2C 92
Bridlington Clo. *M40* 5C 84
Bridlington Sq. *Roch* 5H 27
Bridport Av. *M40* 3D 84
Bridson La. *Bolt* 4F 33
Bridson St. *Oldh* 2G 73
Bridson St. *Salf* 4E 93
Brief St. *Bolt* 4E 33
Brien Av. *Alt* 4F 133
Briercliffe Clo. *M18* 1F 111
Briercliffe Rd. *Bolt* 2G 45
Brierfield Dri. *Bury* 3E 23
Brierfields. Fail 4G 85 *(off Brierley Av.)*
Brierholme Av. *Eger* 2C 18
Brierley Av. *Fail* 4F 85
Brierley Av. *W'fld* 5C 50
Brierley Clo. *Ash L* 5C 88
Brierley Clo. *Dent* 6E 113
Brierley Dri. *Midd* 2A 70
Brierley Rd. E. *Swin* 2E 79
Brierley Rd. W. *Swin* 2E 79
Brierleys Pl. *L'boro* 3E 17
Brierley St. *Bury* 5C 36
Brierley St. *Chad* 1A 72
Brierley St. *Duk* 4B 100
Brierley St. *Heyw* 3F 39
Brierley St. *Oldh* 6D 72
Brierley St. *Stal* 4F 101
Brierley Wlk. *Chad* 1A 72
Brierton Dri. *M22* 4H 147
Brierwood Clo. *Oldh* 6C 56
Briery Av. *Bolt* 5H 19
Brigade Dri. *Stret* 4C 106
Brigade St. *Bolt* 6G 31
Brigadier Clo. *M20* 3F 125
Brigantine Clo. *Salf* 5G 93
Briggs Clo. *Sale* 2E 133
Briggs Fold. *Eger* 1C 18
Briggs Fold Clo. *Eger* 1C 18
Briggs Fold Rd. *Eger* 1C 18
Briggs Rd. *Stret* 3F 107
Briggs St. *Salf* 2B 94 (2D 4)
Brigham St. *M11* 5E 97
Bright Circ. *Urm* 1G 105
Brightman St. *M18* 1F 111
Brighton Av. *M19* 2B 126
Brighton Av. *Bolt* 4E 31
Brighton Av. *Salf* 5A 82
Brighton Av. *Stoc* 5H 111
Brighton Av. *Urm* 4A 104
Brighton Clo. *Chea H* 1E 151
Brighton Ct. *Salf* 6H 93
Brighton Gro. *M14* 5H 109
Brighton Gro. *Hyde* 6C 114
Brighton Gro. *Sale* 4A 122
Brighton Gro. *Urm* 5A 104
Brighton Pl. *M13* 1F 109 (6C 10)
Brighton Range. *M18* 3H 111
Brighton Rd. *Scout* 1C 74
Brighton Rd. *Stoc* 2E 139
Brighton Rd. Ind. Est. *Stoc* 2E 139
Brighton St. *M4* 2E 95 (1B 6)
Brighton St. *Bury* 2F 37
Bright Rd. *Eccl* 3G 91
Brightstone Wlk. *M13* 3A 110
Bright St. *Ash L* 3B 100
Bright St. *Aud* 3E 113
Bright St. *Bury* 2E 37
Bright St. *Chad* 5G 71
Bright St. *Droy* 4B 98
Bright St. *Eger* 1B 18
Bright St. *Oldh* 4B 72
Bright St. *Rad* 3A 50
Bright St. *Roch* 6A 28
Brightwell Wlk. M4 3F 95 (4C 6) *(off Foundry La.)*
Brigsteer Wlk. M40 6F 83 *(off Thornton St. N.)*
Brigstock Av. *M18* 2E 111
Briksdal Way. *Los* 6A 30
Brimelow St. *Bred* 6C 128
Brimfield Wlk. *M40* 5C 84
Brimpton Wlk. M8 5B 82 *(off Kenford Wlk.)*
Brimrod La. *Roch* 6F 27
Brimscombe Av. *M22* 3A 148
Brindale Ho. *Stoc* 5C 128
Brindale Rd. *Stoc* 5C 128
Brindle Clo. *Salf* 1F 93
Brindle Heath. 1F 93
Brindle Heath Ind. Est. *Salf* 1G 93
Brindle Heath Rd. *Salf* 1F 93
Brindle Pl. *M15* 1E 109 (6A 10)
Brindle Way. *Shaw* 6H 43
Brindley Av. *M9* 4D 68
Brindley Av. *Marp* 6D 142
Brindley Av. *Sale* 3C 122
Brindley Clo. *Eccl* 5F 91
Brindley Clo. *Farn* 1D 62
Brindley Dri. *Wors* 5C 76
Brindley Gro. *Wilm* 5A 160
Brindley Lodge. *Swin* 5E 79
Brindley Rd. *M16* 2H 107
Brindley St. *Bolt* 1B 32
Brindley St. *Eccl* 2D 90
Brindley St. *Swin* 1F 79 (in two parts)
Brindley St. *Wors* 5B 76 (Chaddock La.)
Brindley St. *Wors* 1F 77 (Park Rd.)
Brinell Dri. *Irlam* 3C 118
Brinkburn Rd. *Haz G* 2G 153
Brinklow Clo. *M11* 6G 97
Brinkshaw Av. *M22* 3C 148
Brinks La. *Bolt* 1A 48
Brinksway. *Bolt* 6A 30
Brinksway. *Stoc* 3E 139
Brinksway Trad. Est. *Stoc* 3E 139
Brinksworth Clo. *Bolt* 5A 34
Brinnington. 4C 128
Brinnington Cres. *Stoc* 5D 128
Brinnington Ri. *Stoc* 5D 128
Brinnington Rd. *Stoc* 6A 128
Brinsop Sq. *M12* 1D 110
Brinston Wlk. *M40* 4A 84
Brinsworth Dri. *M8* 5C 82
Briony Av. *Hale* 3C 146
Briony Clo. *Rytn* 5C 56
Brisbane Clo. *Bram* 2H 161
Brisbane Rd. *Bram* 2H 161
Brisbane St. *M15* 2F 109
Briscoe La. *M40* 2B 96
Briscoe M. *Bolt* 3C 46
Briscoe St. *Oldh* 1D 72
Briscoe Wlk. *Midd* 5E 53
Bristol Av. *M19* 1D 126
Bristol Av. *Ash L* 4F 87
Bristol Av. *Bolt* 4E 33
Bristol Clo. *H Grn* 6G 149
Bristol Ct. *Salf* 2A 82
Bristol St. *Salf* 4A 82
Bristowe St. *M11* 2F 97
Britain St. *Bury* 1C 50
Britannia Av. *Shaw* 1G 57
Britannia Clo. *Rad* 4G 49
Britannia Ind. Est. *Heyw* 3D 38
Britannia Rd. *Sale* 4B 122
Britannia St. *Ash L* 5F 99
Britannia St. *Heyw* 3D 38
Britannia St. *Oldh* 2E 73
Britannia St. *Salf* 5E 81
Britannia Way. *Bolt* 3C 32
Britnall Av. *M12* 2A 110
Briton St. *Roch* 3A 28
Briton St. *Rytn* 5C 56
Britton St. *Oldh* 2A 72
Britwell Wlk. M8 3E 83 *(off Mawdsley Dri.)*
Brixham Av. *Chea H* 6B 150
Brixham Dri. *Sale* 3F 121
Brixham Rd. *M16* 3H 107
Brixham Wlk. *M13* 2G 109 (6F 11)
Brixham Wlk. *Bram* 6G 151
Brixton Av. *M20* 3E 125
Brixworth Wlk. M9 6G 69 *(off Greendale Dri.)*
Broach St. *Bolt* 3A 46
Broad Acre. *Roch* 1A 26
Broadacre. *Stal* 1A 116
Broadacre Rd. *M18* 4G 111
Broadbent. 5F 57
Broadbent Av. *Ash L* 5G 87
Broadbent Av. *Duk* 5B 100
Broadbent Clo. *Rytn* 2E 57
Broadbent Clo. *Stal* 5G 89
Broadbent Dri. *Bury* 1A 38
Broadbent Gro. *Hyde* 6A 116
Broadbent Rd. *Oldh* 5G 57
Broadbent St. *Hyde* 3B 114
Broadbent St. *Swin* 4D 78
Broadbottom Rd. *Mot* 6B 116
Broad Carr. 1C 88
Broadcarr La. *Moss* 1C 88
Broad Ees Dole Nature Reserve. 2D 122
Broadfield. 4C 38
Broadfield Clo. *Dent* 5G 113
Broadfield Dri. *L'boro* 6D 16
Broadfield Gro. *Stoc* 4G 111
Broadfield Rd. *M14* 3E 109
Broadfield Rd. *Stoc* 4G 111
Broadfield Stile. *Roch* 5G 27
Broadfield St. *Heyw* 4D 38
Broadfield St. *Roch* 5H 27
Broadford Ct. *Heyw* 4B 38
Broadford Rd. *Bolt* 2D 44
Broadgate. *Bolt* 2D 44
Broadgate. *Chad* 6E 71
Broadgate. *Dob* 6G 59
Broadgate. *Midd & Chad* 3D 70
Broadgate Ho. *Bolt* 2D 44
Broadgate Mdw. *Swin* 4F 79
Broadgate Wlk. M9 3G 83 *(off Roundham Wlk.)*
Broadgreen Gdns. *Farn* 5F 47
Broadhalgh. 4C 26
Broadhalgh Av. *Roch* 4C 26
Broadhalgh Rd. *Roch* 5C 26
Broadhaven Rd. *M40* 1H 96 (1H 7)
Broadhead Wlk. *W'fld* 6F 51
Broadheath. 4F 133
Broad Hey. *Rom* 6B 130
Broadhill Clo. *Bram* 3A 152
Broadhill Rd. *M19* 3A 126
Broadhill Rd. *Stal* 6C 88
Broadhurst. *Dent* 2G 113
Broadhurst Av. *Oldh* 6H 55
Broadhurst Av. *Swin* 6F 65
Broadhurst Ct. *Bolt* 3H 45
Broadhurst Gro. *Ash L* 5G 87
Broadhurst St. *Bolt* 3H 45
Broadhurst St. *Rad* 2F 49
Broadhurst St. *Stoc* 4G 139
Broad Ing. *Roch* 2E 27
Broadlands Av. *Hey D* 5A 38
Broadlands Cres. *Hey D* 5A 38
Broadlands Rd. *Wors* 5C 78
Broadlands Wlk. *M40* 5A 84
Broadlands Way. *Hey D* 5A 38
Broad La. *Del* 1G 59
Broad La. *Hale* 5A 146
Broad La. *Roch* 2H 41
Broad La. *Whitw* 1A 14
Broadlea. *Urm* 4E 105
Broadlea Gro. *Roch* 1E 27
Broadlea Rd. *M19* 4A 126
Broadley. 3C 14
Broadley Av. *M22* 1B 148
Broadley Vw. *Whitw* 4C 14
Broad Link. *Midd* 3D 70
Broad Mdw. *Brom X* 3F 19
Broadmeadow Av. *M16* 6D 108
Broadmoss Dri. *M9* 6A 70
Broadmount Ter. Oldh 5H 71 *(off Devon St.)*
Broad Oak. 5B 78
Broadoak Av. *M22* 6A 136
Broadoak Av. *Wors* 4B 76
Broadoak Ct. *M8* 5D 82
Broadoak Cres. *Ash L* 6F 87
Broadoak Cres. *Oldh* 1E 87
Broadoak Dri. *M22* 6B 136
Broad Oak Ind. Pk. *Traf P* 6H 91
Broad Oak La. *M20* 3G 137 (Morningside Dri.)
Broad Oak La. *M20* 3F 137 (Parrs Wood Rd., in two parts)
Broad Oak La. *Bury* 2G 37
Broadoak Park. 6C 78
Broad Oak Pk. *Eccl* 1F 91
Broadoak Rd. *M22* 1A 148
Broadoak Rd. *Ash L* 6F 87
Broadoak Rd. *Bolt* 5C 46
Broadoak Rd. *Bram* 3G 151
Broadoak Rd. *Roch* 5A 26
Broad Oak Rd. *Wors* 5B 78
Broadoaks. *Bury* 2H 37
Broadoak Sports Cen. 5H 87
Broadoaks Rd. *Sale* 5A 122
Broadoaks Rd. *Urm* 6D 104
Broad Oak Ter. *Bury* 2A 38
Broad o' th' La. *Bolt* 1A 32 (in two parts)
Broad Rd. *Sale* 4C 122
Broad Shaw La. *Miln* 3B 42 (in two parts)
Broadstone Av. *Oldh* 3B 58
Broadstone Clo. *P'wich* 6E 67
Broadstone Clo. *Roch* 2C 26
Broadstone Hall Rd. N. *Stoc* 3F 127
Broadstone Hall Rd. S. *Stoc* 3F 127
Broadstone Rd. *Bolt* 6H 19
Broadstone Rd. *Stoc* 3F 127
Broad St. *Bolt* 1H 45 (in two parts)
Broad St. *Bury* 3C 36

Broad St. *Midd* 2E **69**
Broad St. *Swin & Salf* 5B **80**
     (in two parts)
Broad Wlk. *Salf* 2G **93**
Broad Wlk. *Wilm* 1C **166**
Broadway.
  M40 & Chad 2D **84**
Broadway. *Bram* 3G **151**
Broadway. *Chad* 4G **71**
Broadway. *Chea* 1G **149**
Broadway. *Droy* 6A **98**
Broadway.
  Duk & Hyde 1H **113**
Broadway. *Fail* 4D **84**
Broadway. *Farn* 6C **46**
Broadway. *Hale* 4A **146**
Broadway. *Irlam* 6E **103**
Broadway. *Part* 5E **119**
Broadway. *Rytn* 5A **56**
Broadway. *Sale* 4A **122**
Broadway. *Salf* 5D **92**
Broadway. *Stoc* 4C **140**
Broadway. *Urm* 3C **104**
Broadway. *Wilm* 3E **167**
Broadway. *Wors* 2E **77**
Broadway Av. *Chea* 6H **137**
Broadway Clo. *Urm* 2E **105**
Broadway Ind. Est
  Hyde 1H **113**
Broadway Ind. Est.
  Salf 5G **93**
Broadway M. *Hale* 4B **146**
Broadway N. *Droy* 5A **98**
Broadway St. *Oldh* 5D **72**
Broadway Swimming Pool.
  . . . . .1E **85**
Broadway, The. *Bred* 5E **129**
Broadwell Dri. *M9* 4G **83**
Broadwood. *Los* 6A **30**
Broadwood Clo. *Dis* 6D **84**
Brocade Clo.
  Salf 2B **94** (2C **4**)
Broche Clo. *Roch* 2B **40**
Brock Av. *Bolt* 6H **33**
Brock Clo. *M11* 6F **97**
Brock Dri. *Chea H* 5D **150**
Brockenhurst Dri. *Bolt* . . .2H **33**
Brockford Dri. *M9* 4G **69**
Brocklebank Rd. *M14* . . .1G **125**
Brockledale Rd. *Roch* 4D **28**
Brocklehurst Av. *Bury* . . .4D **36**
Brocklehurst St. *M9* 3A **84**
Brockley Av. *M14* 5F **109**
Brock St. *M1* 4F **95** (6D **6**)
Brockton Wlk. *M8* 3C **82**
Brockway. *Roch* 2A **42**
Brocton Ct. *Salf* 2H **81**
Brodick Dri. *Bolt* 1H **47**
Brodick St. *M40* 3H **83**
Brodie Clo. *Eccl* 3D **90**
Brogan St. *M18* 2F **111**
Brogden Dri. *Gat* 6F **137**
Brogden Gro. *Sale* 6A **122**
Brogden Ter. *Sale* 6A **122**
Bromborough Av.
  M20 . . . . .1E **125**
Bromfield. Roch 3H **27**
  (off Redcross St.)
Bromfield Av. *M9* 2F **83**
Bromleigh Av. *Gat* 5F **137**
Bromley Av. *Rytn* 1A **56**
Bromley Av. *Urm* 4A **104**
Bromley Cres. *Ash L* 5F **87**
Bromley Cross. 3F **19**
Bromley Cross Rd.
  Brom X 4F **19**
Bromley Rd. *Sale* 4C **122**
Bromley St. *M4* . . .2F **95** (1C **6**)
Bromley St. *Chad* 6G **71**
Bromley St. *Dent* 4F **113**
Bromlow St. *M11* 4E **97**
Brompton Av. *Fail* 3H **85**

Brompton Rd. *M14* 5F **109**
Brompton Rd. *Stoc* 1C **138**
Brompton Rd. *Stret* 4H **105**
Brompton St. *Oldh* 4E **73**
Brompton Ter. Duk 4H **99**
  (off Queen St.)
Brompton Way. *Hand* . . .2G **159**
Bromsgrove Av. *Eccl* 3E **91**
Bromshill Dri. *Salf* 5A **82**
Bromwich Dri. *M9* 4F **83**
Bromwich St. *Bolt* 1C **46**
Bronington Clo. *M22* 4C **136**
Bronte Av. *Bury* 1D **50**
Bronte Clo. *Bolt* 4H **31**
Bronte Clo. *Oldh* 3H **57**
Bronte Clo. *Roch* 2C **26**
Bronte St. *M15* 2E **109**
Bronville Clo. *Chad* 6A **56**
Brookash Rd. *M22* 5E **149**
Brook Av. *M19* 5D **110**
Brook Av. *Droy* 4H **97**
Brook Av. *Shaw* 5F **43**
Brook Av. *Stoc* 4F **127**
Brook Av. *Swin* 4F **79**
Brook Av. *Timp* 5G **133**
Brook Av. *Upperm* 1G **61**
Brook Bank. *Bolt* 2F **33**
Brookbank Clo. *Midd* 2B **70**
Brook Bottom. 1D **88**
Brookbottom. *Bolt* 5A **20**
Brookbottom Rd. *Rad* 1F **49**
Brookburn Rd. *M21* 2G **123**
Brook Clo. *Timp* 5G **133**
Brook Clo. *W'fld* 1F **67**
Brookcot Rd. *M23* 4F **135**
Brook Ct. *Salf* 2G **81**
Brookcroft Av. *M22* 5B **136**
Brookcroft Rd. *M22* 6B **136**
Brookdale. *Roch* 6E **15**
Brookdale Av. *M40* 6D **84**
Brookdale Av. *Aud* 6D **98**
Brookdale Av. *Marp* 1E **155**
Brookdale Clo. *Bolt* 3B **32**
Brookdale Clo. *Bred* 6F **129**
Brookdale Cotts. *Stoc* . . .4F **141**
Brookdale Ct. *Sale* 2C **134**
Brookdale Pk. Cvn. Site.
  L Hul 3D **62**
Brookdale Ri. *Bram* 4H **151**
Brookdale Rd. *Bram* 4H **151**
Brookdale Rd. *Gat* 6D **136**
Brookdale St. *Fail* 4E **85**
Brookdean Clo. *Bolt* 2G **31**
Brookdene Rd. *M19* 3A **126**
Brookdene Rd. *Bury* 6E **51**
Brook Dri. *Marp* 1D **154**
Brook Dri. *W'fld* 1F **67**
Brooke Av. *Hand* 3H **159**
Brooke Dri. *Hand* 3H **159**
Brookes St. *Midd* 5B **54**
Brooke Way. *Hand* 3H **159**
Brookfield. 4G **117**
Brookfield. *Glos* 4G **117**
Brookfield. *P'wich* 5F **67**
Brookfield. *Shaw* 4E **43**
Brookfield Av. *M21* 2A **124**
Brookfield Av. *Bolt* 4C **34**
  (in two parts)
Brookfield Av. *Bred* 5G **129**
Brookfield Av. *Poy* 4C **162**
Brook Fld. Av. *Rytn* 4B **56**
Brookfield Av. *Salf* 2C **92**
Brookfield Av. *Stoc* 4A **140**
Brookfield Av. *Timp* 3H **133**
Brookfield Av. *Urm* 5C **104**
Brookfield Clo. *P'wich* 5F **67**
Brookfield Clo. *Stoc* 4A **140**
Brookfield Ct. *M18* 3F **111**
Brookfield Ct. *M19* 1B **126**
Brookfield Cres. *Chea* . . .1H **149**
Brookfield Dri. *L'boro* 3C **16**

Brookfield Dri. *Swin* 2E **79**
Brookfield Dri. *Timp* 4A **134**
Brookfield Dri. *Wors* 5B **76**
Brookfield Gdns. *M22* . . .5A **136**
  (in three parts)
Brookfield Gro. *M18* 3F **111**
Brookfield Gro. *Ash L* . . .3B **100**
Brookfield Ho. *Chea* 1H **149**
Brookfield Ind. Est.
  Glos 4G **117**
Brookfield Rd. *M8* 2C **82**
Brookfield Rd. *Bury* 3E **23**
Brookfield Rd. *Chea* 6H **137**
Brookfield Rd. *Eccl* 1D **90**
Brookfields. *Moss* 1E **89**
Brookfield St. *Oldh* 6D **32**
Brookfield St. *Oldh* 4D **72**
Brookfield Ter. *Haz G* 1F **153**
Brookfold. *Fail* 3E **85**
Brookfold La. *Bolt* 1H **33**
Brook Fold La. *Hyde* 5F **115**
  (in two parts)
Brookfold Rd. *Stoc* 3F **127**
Brook Gdns. *Bolt* 1G **33**
Brook Gdns. *Heyw* 3E **39**
Brook Green. 3G **111**
Brook Grn. La. *M18* 4H **111**
Brook Gro. *Irlam* 5E **103**
Brookhead Av. *M20* 2D **124**
Brookhead Dri. *Chea* 6C **138**
Brookhey Av. *Bolt* 4B **46**
Brook Hey Clo. *Roch* 5B **16**
Brookheys Rd. *Part* 5A **120**
Brookhill Clo. *Dig* 2C **60**
Brookhill St. *M40* 2A **96**
Brook Ho. Timp 4C **134**
  (off Bridge Rd.)
Brookhouse Av. *Eccl* 4C **90**
Brookhouse Av. *Sale* 3E **63**
Brook Ho. Clo. *Bolt* 2G **33**
Brook Ho. Clo. *G'mnt* 3G **21**
Brookhouse Mill La.
  G'mnt 3H **21**
Brookhurst La. *L Hul* 3A **62**
Brookhurst Rd. *M18* 3F **111**
Brookland Av. *Farn* 2E **63**
Brookland Clo. *Irlam* 5D **102**
Brookland Gro. *Bolt* 3E **31**
Brooklands. 1D **134**
Brooklands. *Roch* 2A **16**
Brooklands Av. *M20* 3E **125**
Brooklands Av. *Chad* 4H **71**
Brooklands Av. *Dent* 5D **112**
Brooklands Clo. *Dent* 3D **112**
Brooklands Clo. *Moss* . . .1D **88**
Brooklands Clo. *Stoc* 4F **127**
Brooklands Ct. *M8* 1B **82**
Brooklands Ct. *Roch* 5E **27**
Brooklands Ct. *Sale* 1B **134**
Brooklands Cres. *Sale* . . .6B **122**
Brooklands Dri. *Droy* 2C **98**
Brooklands Dri. *G'ton* 3D **74**
Brooklands Pde. *G'ton* . . .3D **74**
Brooklands Pl. *Sale* 6A **122**
Brooklands Rd. *Haz G* . . .4E **153**
Brooklands Rd.
  P'wich & Sale 1A **82**
Brooklands Rd. *Rams* 1A **22**
Brooklands Rd.
  Sale & M23 . . . . . . .1B **134**
Brooklands Rd. *Stoc* 5G **111**
Brooklands Rd. *Swin* 5D **78**
Brooklands Sports Club.
  . . . . .1C **134**
Brooklands Sta. App.
  Sale 6A **122**
Brooklands St. *Midd* 6A **54**
Brooklands St. *Rytn* 2B **56**
Brooklands, The.
  Heyw 3E **39**
Brookland St. *Roch* 2H **41**

Brook La. *Ald E* 6B **166**
Brook La. *Bury* 3E **51**
  (in two parts)
Brook La. *Dob* 5H **59**
Brook La. *Lees* 3A **74**
Brook La. *Oldh* 5E **73**
  (in five parts)
Brook La. *Roch* 2H **41**
Brook La. *Timp* 5G **133**
Brooklawn Dri. *M20* 5F **125**
Brooklawn Dri. *P'wich* 3G **67**
Brookleigh Rd. *M20* 3H **125**
Brooklet Clo. *S'head* 4B **74**
Brook Lodge. *Chea* 1H **149**
Brooklyn Av. *M16* 5A **108**
Brooklyn Av. *L'boro* 2E **17**
Brooklyn Av. *Roch* 5B **16**
Brooklyn Av. *Urm* 5A **104**
Brooklyn Ct. *M20* 2G **125**
Brooklyn Cres. *Chea* 6H **137**
Brooklyn Pl. *Chea* 5H **137**
Brooklyn Rd. *Chea* 6H **137**
Brooklyn Rd. *Stoc* 5C **140**
Brooklyn St. *Bolt* 4A **32**
Brooklyn St. *Oldh* 6G **57**
Brook M. *M14* 1H **125**
Brook Rd. *M14* 2G **125**
Brook Rd. *Chea* 5H **137**
Brook Rd. *Stoc* 4E **127**
  (in two parts)
Brook Rd. *Urm* 4C **104**
Brooks Av. *Haz G* 2D **152**
Brooks Av. *Hyde* 6C **114**
Brooks Av. *Rad* 1F **49**
Brooksbottoms. 6E **13**
Brooksbottoms Clo.
  Rams 5E **13**
Brooks Dri. *Fail* 5E **85**
Brooks Dri. *Hale* 5D **146**
  (in two parts)
Brooks Dri.
  Timp & Hale 4D **134**
  (in six parts)
Brooks End. *Roch* 2A **26**
Brookshaw St. *M11* 4C **96**
Brookshaw St. *Bury* 1D **36**
  (in two parts)
Brookside. *M20* 1D **136**
Brookside. *Ald E* 4G **167**
Brook Side. *Lees* 3H **73**
Brookside. *Moss* 2D **88**
Brookside Av. *Droy* 2C **98**
Brookside Av. *Farn* 2E **63**
Brookside Av. *G'ton* 3D **74**
Brookside Av. *Poy* 4E **163**
Brookside Av. *Stoc* 5E **141**
Brookside Bus. Pk.
  Midd 3D **70**
Brookside Clo. *Bolt* 6H **19**
Brookside Clo. *Chea* 1H **149**
Brookside Clo. *Had* 3H **117**
Brookside Clo. *Hyde* 4E **115**
Brookside Clo. *Rams* 6C **12**
Brookside Ct. *M19* 5C **110**
Brookside Cres. *G'mnt* . . .2G **21**
Brookside Cres. *Midd* 3C **70**
Brookside Cres. *Wors* 6G **63**
Brookside Dri. *Hyde* 4E **115**
Brookside Dri. *Salf* 2H **81**
Brookside La. *H Lane* 6C **154**
Brookside Miniature Railway.
  . . . . .6F **153**
Brookside Railway Mus.
  . . . . .6F **153**
Brookside Rd. *M40* 2A **84**
Brookside Rd. *Bolt* 5F **33**
Brookside Rd. *Gat* 5E **137**
Brookside Rd. *Sale* 1A **134**
Brookside Ter. *Ald E* 6B **166**
Brookside Ter. *Del* 3G **59**
  (off High St.)
Brookside Vs. *Gat* 5E **137**

Brookside Wlk.—Buckingham Rd. W.

Brookside Wlk. Rad 6E 35
Brooksmouth. Bury 3B 36
Brook's Pl. Oldh 5C 72
Brook's Pl. Roch 3G 27
Brook's Rd. M16 . . . . . . .4A 108
Brookstone Clo.
M21 . . . . .3B 124
Brook St. M1 . . . .6E 95 (3B 10)
Brook St. Bolt 6B 32
Brook St. Bury 1E 37
Brook St. Chad 1H 71
Brook St. Chea 5B 138
Brook St. Fail 5C 84
Brook St. Farn 6G 47
Brook St. Haz G 3E 153
Brook St. Hyde 4C 114
Brook St. Kear 2A 64
Brook St. L'boro 4G 17
Brook St. Oldh 2E 73
Brook St. Rad 4H 49
Brook St. Rytn 4B 56
Brook St. Sale 4C 122
Brook St. Salf 1H 93
Brook St. Stoc 4H 139
Brook St. Swin 3D 78
Brook St. Ward 3A 16
Brook St. E. Ash L 3G 99
Brook St. W. Ash L 3G 99
Brook Ter. M12 . . . . .4B 110
Brook Ter. Miln 1G 43
Brook Ter. Urm 3E 105
Brook, The. L'boro 6G 17
Brookthorn Clo. Stoc 6F 141
Brookthorpe Av. M19 . . .3A 126
Brookthorpe Meadows.
Wals 2G 35
Brookthorpe Rd. Wals . . .2G 35
Brook Vw. Ald E 6D 166
Brook Vs. M9 . . . . .4G 83
Brookville Flats. Whitw . . .4G 15
(off Rawstron St.)
Brook Wlk. Dent 1F 129
Brookwater Clo. T'ton 5H 21
Brookway. Grass 3G 75
Brookway. Lees 4A 74
Brookway. L'boro 5E 17
Brookway. Timp 4H 133
Brookway Clo. M19 . . . .5A 126
Brookway Ct. M23 . . . . .4F 135
Brookway Retail Pk.
M23 . . . . .3E 135
Brookwood Av. M8 . . . . . .3E 83
Brookwood Av. Sale 6G 121
Brookwood Clo. Dent . . .2G 129
Broom Av. M19 . . . . . . .1D 126
Broom Av. Salf 3A 82
Broom Av. Stoc 3H 127
Broom Cres. Salf 2C 92
Broomedge. Salf 3H 81
Broome Gro. Fail 5F 85
Broomehouse Av.
Irlam 1C 118
Broome St. Oldh 3B 72
Broomfield. Salf 5B 80
Broomfield. Swin 5B 80
Broomfield Clo. A'wth 5C 34
Broomfield Clo. Stoc . . .3H 127
Broomfield Clo. Wilm . . .1H 167
Broomfield Ct. M20 . . . .5D 124
Broomfield Ct. Hale 2G 145
Broomfield Cres. Midd . . .6F 53
Broomfield Cres. Stoc . . .1A 152
Broomfield Dri. M8 . . . . . .4B 82
Broomfield Dri. Stoc 3H 127
Broomfield La. Hale 3G 145
Broomfield Rd. Bolt 3G 45
Broomfield Rd. Stoc 5E 127
Broomfields. Dent 2G 113
Broomfield Sq. Roch 6H 27
Broomfield Ter. Miln 1F 43
Broomgrove La. Aud . . .3G 113
Broomhall Rd. M9 . . . . . .4C 68
Broomhall Rd. Swin 5B 80
Broomhill Dri. Bram 4F 151
Broomhill Ho. Dent 4B 112
(off Thompson Ct.)
Broomhill Ho. Moss 1E 89
(off Manor St.)
Broomhurst Av. Oldh 5B 72
Broom La. M19 . . . . . . .1D 126
Broom La. Salf 3H 81
Broom Rd. Hale 2G 145
Broom Rd. Part 6D 118
Broomstair Rd. Aud 1F 113
Broom St. Bolt 6C 32
Broom St. Bury 3B 36
Broom St. Miln 1F 43
Broom St. Swin 4F 79
Broomville Av. Sale 5B 122
Broomwood Gdns.
Timp 6C 134
Broomwood Rd. Timp . . .6C 134
Broomwood Wlk.
M15 . . . . . .1E 109 (5A 10)
(off Chevril Clo.)
Broseley Av. M20 . . . . . .6H 125
Broseley Rd. M16 . . . . . .5G 107
Brosscroft. Had 1H 117
Brotherdale Clo. Rytn 2B 56
Brotherod Hall Rd.
Roch 1E 27
Brotherton Clo.
M15 . . . . . . .1B 108 (4C 8)
Brotherton Dri.
Salf 3B 94 (3D 4)
Brougham St. Wors 6E 63
Brough St. M11 . . . . .6G 97
Broughton Av. L Hul 5C 62
Broughton Clo. Midd 5F 53
Broughton La.
Salf & M8 . . . . .6H 81
(in two parts)
Broughton M. Sale 6C 122
Broughton Park. 2H 81
Broughton Recreation Cen.
. . . . .6H 81
Broughton Rd. Salf 1G 93
Broughton Rd. Stoc 5H 127
Broughton Rd. E. Salf 1H 93
Broughton St. M8 . . . . . . .6B 82
Broughton St. Bolt 3H 31
Broughton Swimming Pool.
. . . . .5H 81
Broughton Trade Cen.
Salf 1B 94
Broughton Vw. Salf 2H 93
Broughville Dri. M20 . . .3G 137
Brow Av. Midd 3B 70
Browbeck. Oldh 2C 72
Browfield Av. Salf 6H 93
Browfield Way. Oldh 6C 56
Browmere Dri. M20 . . . .5D 124
Brownacre St. M20 . . . . .3F 125
Brown Bank Rd. L'boro . . .6D 16
Brownbank Wlk. M15 . . .2D 108
(off Greenthorn Wlk.)
Brown Ct. M4 . . . . .3E 95 (4A 6)
(off Arndale Shop. Cen.)
Browncross St.
Salf 4C 94 (5F 5)
Brown Edge Rd. Oldh 5A 74
Brownhill Countryside Cen.
. . . . .6A 60
Brownhill Dri. Aus 2C 74
Brownhill La. Upperm 6B 60
Brownhills Clo. T'ton 6A 22
Browning Av. Droy 4A 98
Browning Clo. Bolt 4H 31
Browning Rd. Midd 5B 54
Browning Rd. Oldh 6F 57
Browning Rd. Stoc 6F 111
Browning Rd. Swin 3E 79
Browning St.
M15 . . . . . .1B 108 (6D 8)
Browning St.
Salf 3B 94 (4D 4)
Brown La. H Grn 4E 149
Brownlea Av. Duk 6A 100
Brownley Ct. M22 . . . . . .6C 136
Brownley Ct. Rd. M22 . . .6B 136
Brownley Rd. M22 . . . . .5B 136
Brown Lodge Dri.
L'boro 6D 16
Brown Lodge St.
L'boro 6D 16
Brownlow. 4F 57
Brownlow Av. Rytn 4E 57
Brownlow Cen. Bolt 4A 32
Brownlow Clo. Poy 5E 163
Brownlow Fold. 3G 31
Brownlow Way. Bolt 4A 32
Brown's La. Wilm 6A 160
(in two parts)
Brownslow Wlk.
M13 . . . . . . .6F 95 (4D 10)
Brownson Wlk. M9 . . . . . .3G 83
Browns Rd. Brad F 1B 48
Brown St. M2 . . . .4E 95 (6H 5)
Brown St. Ald E 5G 167
Brown St. Alt 2F 145
Brown St. Aud 2E 113
(off Barnwell Clo.)
Brown St. Bolt 6B 32
Brown St. Chad 1G 71
Brown St. Fail 4E 85
Brown St. Heyw 2F 39
Brown St. L'boro 4F 17
Brown St. Midd 5A 54
Brown St. Oldh 2E 73
Brown St. Rad 1F 49
Brown St. Rams 4D 12
Brown St. Salf 4F 93
Brown St. Stoc 1G 139
Brownsville Ct. Stoc 4E 127
Brownsville Rd. Stoc . . .4D 126
Brownville Gro. Duk 6C 100
Brownwood Av. Stoc . . .2B 140
Brownwood Clo. Sale . . .2C 134
Brows Av. M23 . . . . . . .1G 135
Browsholme Ho. Bolt 6G 31
Browside Clo. Roch 6A 16
Brow St. Roch 1G 41
Brow, The. M9 . . . . .1F 83
Brow Wlk. M9 . . . . .6F 69
Broxton Av. Bolt 4F 45
Broxton St. M40 . . . . . . .2B 96
Broxwood Clo. M18 . . . .2F 111
Bruce St. Roch 1C 40
Bruce Wlk. M11 . . . . .6F 97
Brundage Rd. M22 . . . . .3B 148
Brundrett Pl. Sale 5H 121
Brundrett's Rd. M21 . . . .1H 123
Brundrett St. Stoc 3A 140
Brunel Av. Salf 4H 93
Brunel Clo. Stret 5E 107
Brunel St. Bolt 2H 31
Brunet Wlk. M12 . . . . . .1B 110
(off Skarratt Clo.)
Bruno St. M9 . . . . .5D 68
Brunstead Clo. M23 . . . .5D 134
Brunswick. 1G 109
Brunswick Ct. Bolt 5A 32
Brunswick Rd. M20 . . . .3G 125
Brunswick Rd. Alt 4F 133
Brunswick St.
M13 . . . . . .1F 109 (6C 10)
Brunswick St. Bury 2D 36
Brunswick St. Duk 4A 100
Brunswick St. Heyw 3E 39
(in two parts)
Brunswick St. Moss 3F 89
Brunswick St. Oldh 3C 72
Brunswick St. Roch 3A 28
Brunswick St. Shaw 6F 43
Brunswick St. Stret 1D 122
Brunton Rd. Stoc 3H 127
Brunt St. M14 . . . . .4F 109
Bruntwood Av. H Grn . . .4E 149
Bruntwood La. Chea 1A 150
Bruntwood La.
Chea H 4A 150
Brushes. 2H 101
Brushes Av. Stal 2H 101
Brushes Rd. Stal 2H 101
(in two parts)
Brussels Rd. Stoc 5F 139
Bruton Av. Stret 6B 106
Brutus Wlk. Salf 5A 82
Bryan Rd. M21 . . . . .5H 107
Bryan St. Oldh 6G 57
Bryant Clo.
M13 . . . . .1G 109 (6F 11)
Bryant's Acre. Bolt 6B 30
Bryantsfield. Bolt 1A 44
Bryceland Clo.
M12 . . . . .5A 96 (2H 11)
Bryce St. Bolt 2A 46
Bryce St. Hyde 3B 114
Brydges Rd. Marp 6C 142
Brydon Av.
M12 . . . . . .6G 95 (3F 11)
Brydon Clo. Salf 3G 93
Bryndale Gro. Sale 2H 133
Brynden Av. M20 . . . . . .4G 125
Bryn Dri. Stoc 4H 127
Brynford Av. M9 . . . . .4C 68
Bryngs Dri. Bolt 1H 33
Brynhall Clo. Rad 2E 49
Brynheys Clo. L Hul 4C 62
Bryn Lea Ter. Bolt 1E 31
Brynorme Rd. M8 . . . . . . .1C 82
Brynton Rd. M13 . . . . . .4A 110
Bryn Wlk. Bolt 5B 32
Bryone Dri. Stoc 6B 140
Bryony Clo. M22 . . . . . .4A 148
Bryony Clo. Wors 4F 63
Bryson Wlk. M18 . . . . . .2E 111
Buccleuch Lodge.
M20 . . . . .4D 124
Buchanan St. Rams 3D 12
Buchanan St. Swin 2F 79
Buchan St. M11 . . . . .3D 96
Buckden Rd. Stoc 2F 127
Buckden Wlk. M23 . . . . .1F 135
Buckfast Clo. M21 . . . . .6H 107
Buckfast Clo. Chea H . . .1D 160
Buckfast Clo. Hale 3B 146
Buckfast Clo. Poy 2D 162
Buckfast Rd. Midd 4H 53
Buckfast Rd. Sale 3F 121
Buckfast Wlk. Salf 5A 82
Buckfield Av. Salf 6H 93
Buckfield Dri. Salf 6H 93
Buckhurst Rd. M19 . . . .6C 110
Buckingham Av. Dent . . .5H 113
Buckingham Av. Salf 3D 92
Buckingham Av. W'fld 2E 67
Buckingham Dri. Bury . . .5H 35
Buckingham Dri. Duk . . .6D 100
Buckingham Gro.
Timp 2H 133
Buckingham Rd. M21 . . .5H 107
Buckingham Rd. Cad . . .3A 118
Buckingham Rd.
Chea H 3B 150
Buckingham Rd. Droy . . .4G 97
Buckingham Rd. Poy . . .4D 162
Buckingham Rd.
P'wich 1F 81
Buckingham Rd. Stal . . .2E 101
Buckingham Rd. Stoc . . .4D 126
(in two parts)
Buckingham Rd. Stret . . .2F 107
Buckingham Rd. Swin . . .1G 79
Buckingham Rd.
Wilm 3C 166
Buckingham Rd. W.
Stoc 5C 126

Buckinghamshire Pk. Clo.
Shaw 5F 43
Buckingham St. Roch . . .3A 28
Buckingham St. Salf 4F 93
Buckingham St. Stoc . . .5A 140
Buckingham Way.
Stoc 5A 140
(off Windsor St.)
Buckingham Way.
Timp 4A 134
Buckland Av. M9 . . . . .6C 68
Buckland Gro. Hyde . . .1E 131
Buckland Rd. Salf 1D 92
Buckland St.
M4 . . . . . . .4H 95 (6G 7)
Buck La. Sale 3G 121
Buckle Ho. Eccl 3G 91
Buckle St. Rad 4G 49
Buckley. 6H 15
Buckley Av. M18 . . . . .3E 111
Buckley Barn Ct. Roch . .4C 40
(off Heape St.)
Buckley Brook St.
Roch 1B 28
Buckley Bldgs. Moss . .2G 89
Buckley Chase. Miln . . .6E 29
Buckley Clo. Hyde 2C 130
Buckley Dri. Rom 2G 141
Buckley Farm La. Roch . .6H 15
Buckley Fields. Roch . . .1A 28
Buckley Hall Ind. Est.
Roch 6H 15
Buckley Hill La. Miln . . .6E 29
Buckley La. Farn 3D 62
Buckley La. Roch 6H 15
Buckley La. W'fld 6C 66
Buckley Rd. M18 . . . .3D 110
Buckley Rd. Oldh 1H 73
Buckley Rd. Roch 1B 28
Buckley Sq. Farn 3E 63
Buckley St. Aud 6D 98
Buckley St. Bury 2D 36
Buckley St. Chad 2G 71
Buckley St. Droy 4A 98
Buckley St. Heyw 2F 39
Buckley St. Lees 4A 74
Buckley St. Open 5F 97
Buckley St. Roch 3A 28
Buckley St. Shaw 6G 43
Buckley St. Stal 5D 100
Buckley St. Stoc 5G 111
Buckley St. Upperm 1F 61
Buckley Ter. Roch 6H 15
Buckley Vw. Roch 6H 15
Buckley Wells. 4B 36
Buckley Wood. 4G 55
Bucklow Av. M14 . . . .6F 109
Bucklow Av. Part 6D 118
Bucklow Clo. Mot 6B 116
Bucklow Clo. Oldh 3A 58
Bucklow Dri. M22 . . . .3C 136
Bucklow Vw. Bow 2C 144
Bucknell Ct.
M40 . . . . . . .1G 95 (1E 7)
Buckstones Rd. Shaw &
Oldh . . . . .4G 43 & 1A 58
Buckthorn Clo. M21 . . .2B 124
Buckthorn Clo. Timp . . .6E 135
Buckthorn La. Eccl 4B 90
Buckton Clo. Dig 2C 60
Buckton Dri. Stal 6G 89
Buckton Vale. 5G 89
Buckton Va. M. Carr . . .4H 89
Buckton Va. Rd. Carr . . .5G 89
Buckton Va. Rd. Mill . . .1H 101
Buckwood Clo. Haz G . .2G 153
Buddleia Gro. Salf 5H 81
(off Bk. Hilton St.)
Bude Av. Stoc 4B 128
Bude Av. Urm 1D 120
Bude Clo. Bram 6H 151
Bude Ter. Duk 4H 99

Bude Wlk. M23 . . . . . .6H 135
Budsworth Av. M20 . . .2F 125
Budworth Gdns. Droy . .4B 98
Budworth Rd. Sale 6E 123
Budworth Wlk. Wilm . . .6A 160
Buersil. 3H 41
Buersil Av. Roch 1H 41
Buersil Gro. Roch 2H 41
(in two parts)
Buersil Head. 4H 41
Buersil St. Roch 2H 41
Buerton Av. M9 . . . . . .4C 68
Buffalo Ct. Salf 5E 93
Buffoline Trad. Est.
Lev 6D 110
Bugle St.
M15 & M1 . . .6C 94 (3F 9)
Buile Dri. M9 . . . . . . .5H 69
Buile Hill Av. L Hul 5D 62
Buile Hill Dri. Salf 2D 92
Buile Hill Gro. L Hul . . .4D 62
Buile Ho. Salf 2E 93
Buile St. Salf 4A 82
Bulford Av. M22 . . . . .3H 147
Bulkeley Rd. Chea 5A 138
Bulkeley Rd. Hand 4G 159
Bulkeley Rd. Poy 4E 163
Bulkeley St. Stoc 3F 139
Bullcote Grn. Rytn 3E 57
Bullcote La. Oldh 3E 57
Buller M. Bury 4H 35
Buller Rd. M13 . . . . . .5B 110
Buller St. Bolt 5E 47
Buller St. Bury 4H 35
Buller St. Droy 5B 98
Buller St. Oldh 1H 73
Bullfinch Dri. Bury 6H 23
Bullfinch Wlk. M21 . . . .2B 124
Bull Hill Cres. Rad 1H 65
Bullock St. Stoc 4H 139
Bullows Rd. L Hul 3B 62
Bulrush Clo. Wors 4F 63
Bulteel St. Bolt 5G 45
Bulteel St. Eccl 2D 90
Bulteel St. Wors 5A 76
Bulwer St. Roch 3A 28
Bunkers Hill. 3G 141
Bunkers Hill. W'fld 5B 66
Bunkers Hill Rd. Hyde . .5A 116
Bunkers Hill Rd. Rom . .2H 141
Bunsen St. M1 . . .4F 95 (5C 6)
Bunting M. Wors 3D 76
Bunyan Clo. Oldh 3A 58
Bunyan St. Roch 2H 27
Bunyard St. M8 . . . . . .5D 82
Burbage Bank. Glos . . .6H 75
(off Edale Cres.)
Burbage Gro. Glos 5G 117
(off Edale Cres.)
Burbage Rd. M23 . . . . .3G 147
Burbage Way. Glos 5G 117
(off Edale Cres., in two parts)
Burbridge Clo. M11 . . . .5A 96
Burchall Fld. Roch 4B 28
Burcot Wlk. M8 . . . . . .1C 94
Burdale Dri. Salf 1B 92
Burdale Wlk. M23 . . . . .2F 135
Burder St. Oldh 1A 86
Burdett Av. Roch 2B 26
Burdett Way. M12 . . . . .2A 110
Burdith Av. M14 . . . . . .5E 109
Burdon Av. M22 . . . . .2C 148
Burford Av. M16 . . . . .5B 108
Burford Av. Bram 2E 161
Burford Av. Urm 3G 105
Burford Clo. Wilm 4B 166
Burford Cres. Wilm 4B 166
Burford Dri. M16 . . . . .5B 108
Burford Dri. Bolt 2A 46
Burford Dri. Swin 1E 79
Burford Gro. Sale 2G 133
Burford Rd. M16 . . . . .5B 108

Burford Wlk. M16 . . . . .5B 108
Burgess Av. Ash L 6G 87
Burgess Dri. Fail 4F 85
Burghley Av. Oldh 3H 73
Burghley Clo. Rad 2B 48
Burghley Clo. Stal 3E 101
Burghley Dri. Rad 2B 48
Burgin Wlk. M40 . . . . . .6E 83
Burgundy Dri. T'ton 4H 21
Burke St. Bolt 3H 31
Burkitt St. Hyde 5C 114
Burland Clo. Salf 6A 82
Burleigh Clo. Haz G 4A 152
Burleigh Ct. Stret 3E 107
Burleigh Ho. M15 . . . . .2F 109
Burleigh M. M21 . . . . .3H 123
Burleigh Rd. Stret 4E 107
Burleigh St. M15 . . . . .2F 109
Burlescombe Clo. Alt . . .5D 132
Burley Ct. Stoc 1E 139
Burlin Ct. M16 . . . . . .4B 108
Burlington Av. Oldh 5C 72
Burlington Clo. Stoc 1A 138
Burlington Ct. Alt 6F 133
Burlington Dri. Stoc 1H 151
Burlington Gdns.
Stoc 1H 151
Burlington Ho. Ash L . . .2G 99
(off North St.)
Burlington M. Stoc 1H 151
Burlington Pl. M15 . . . .2E 109
(off Burlington St.)
Burlington Rd. M20 . . . .2G 125
Burlington Rd. Alt 6F 133
Burlington Rd. Eccl 1G 91
Burlington St.
M15 . . . . . .2E 109 (6B 10)
Burlington St. Ash L 3F 99
Burlington St. Roch 1G 41
Burlington St. E.
M15 . . . . . .2F 109 (6B 10)
Burman St.
M11 & Droy 6H 97
Burnaby St. Bolt 2H 45
Burnaby St. Oldh 4A 72
Burnaby St. Roch 1C 40
Burnage. 4A 126
Burnage Av. M19 . . . . .1B 126
Burnage Hall Rd.
M19 . . . . .2A 126
Burnage La. M19 . . . . .1H 137
Burnage Range. M19 . . .6C 110
Burn Bank. G'fld 4G 75
Burnbray Av. M19 . . . . .3A 126
Burnby Wlk. M23 . . . . .2F 135
Burndale Dri. Bury 4E 51
Burnden. 3D 46
Burnden Ind. Est. Bolt . .3D 46
Burnden Rd. Bolt 2D 46
Burnedge. 4B 42
Burnedge Clo. Whitw . . .3H 15
Burnedge Fold Rd.
Grass 3F 75
Burnedge La.
Grass & Dob 3E 75
Burnedge M. Grass 3F 75
Burnell Clo.
M40 . . . . . . .2H 95 (2G 7)
Burnell Ct. Heyw 6F 39
Burnet Clo. Roch 1A 42
Burnett Av. Salf 5H 93
Burnett Clo. M40 . . . . .6F 83
Burnfield Rd. M18 . . . .4F 111
Burnfield Rd. Stoc 4G 111
Burnham Av. Bolt 4E 31
Burnham Av. Stoc 6H 111
Burnham Clo. Chea H . .3B 150
Burnham Dri. M19 . . . .1B 126
Burnham Dri. Urm 4E 105
Burnham Wlk. Farn 6F 47
Burnleigh Ct. Bolt 6D 44
Burnley Brow. 1B 72

Burnley La. Chad 5G 55
(in two parts)
Burnley Rd. Bury 3E 23
(in two parts)
Burnley Rd. Rams 1A 12
Burnley St. Chad 2H 71
Burnley St. Fail 3G 85
Burnmoor Rd. Bolt 5H 33
Burnsall Av. W'fld 1C 66
Burnsall Gro. Rytn 3B 56
Burnsall Wlk. M22 . . . .3G 147
Burns Av. Bury 1D 50
Burns Av. Chea 5B 138
Burns Av. Swin 2D 78
Burns Clo. M11 . . . . . .4B 96
Burns Clo. Oldh 2A 58
Burns Cres. Stoc 4E 141
Burns Fold. Duk 6E 101
Burns Gdns. P'wich 6D 66
Burns Gro. Droy 3A 98
Burnside. Had 3H 117
Burnside. Haleb 6D 146
Burnside. Rams 3A 12
Burnside. Shaw 5H 43
Burnside. Stal 6H 101
Burnside Av. Salf 6H 79
Burnside Av. Stoc 3G 127
Burnside Clo. Bred 6F 129
Burnside Clo. Heyw 4F 39
Burnside Clo. Rad 6F 35
Burnside Clo. Stal 6H 101
Burnside Clo. Wilm 3F 167
Burnside Cres. Midd . . .4G 53
Burnside Dri. M19 . . . .2A 126
Burnside Rd. Bolt 3F 31
Burnside Rd. Gat 6E 137
Burnside Rd. Roch 5C 28
Burns Rd. Dent 2G 129
Burns Rd. L Hul 4D 62
Burns St. Bolt 1B 46
Burns St. Heyw 4F 39
Burnthorpe Av. M9 . . . .6D 68
Burnthorpe Clo. Roch . . .5A 26
Burntwood Wlk. M9 . . . .3G 83
(off Naunton Wlk.)
Burran Rd. M22 . . . . . .5B 148
Burrows Av. M21 . . . . .3H 123
Burrs. 5D 22
Burrs Activity Cen. 5D 22
Burrs Clo. Bury 5C 22
Burrs Country Pk. 5D 22
Burrs Lea Clo. Bury 5E 23
Burrswood Av. Bury 5E 23
Burrwood Dri. Stoc 6F 139
Burslem Av. M20 . . . . .1E 125
Burstead St. M18 . . . . .6G 97
Burstock St. M4 . . .2F 95 (1C 6)
Burston St. M18 . . . . .1E 111
Burtinshaw St. M18 . . . .2F 111
Burton Av. M20 . . . . . .3E 125
Burton Av. Timp 2A 134
Burton Av. Wals 1F 35
Burton Dri. Poy 3D 162
Burton Gro. Wors 3C 78
Burton Ho. Wilm 2E 167
Burton M. M20 . . . . . .4D 124
Burton Rd. M20 . . . . . .5D 124
Burton St. M40 . . . . . .1F 95
Burton St. Lees 4A 74
Burton St. Midd 1H 69
(in two parts)
Burton St. Stoc 6G 127
Burton Wlk. Salf . . .3B 94 (3C 4)
Burton Wlk. Stoc 6G 127
(off Heskith St.)
Burtonwood Ct.
Midd 6H 53
Burtree St. M12 . . . . . .1C 110
Burwell Clo. Bolt 3H 45
Burwell Clo. Roch 6D 14
Burwell Gro. M23 . . . . .4F 135
Bury. 3D 36

Bury and Bolton Rd.
  Rad 6C **34**
Bury & Rochdale Old Rd.
  Bury & Heyw 1B **38**
Bury Art Gallery & Mus.
  . . . . .3C **36**
Bury Av. M16 . . . . . . .5A **108**
Bury Bus. Cen. Bury 2E **37**
Bury Football Club. . . .6D **36**
  (Gigg La.)
Bury Ground. 2B **36**
Bury Ind. Est. Bolt 6H **33**
Bury New Rd. Bolt 5C **32**
Bury New Rd. Brei 6A **34**
Bury New Rd.
  Bury & Heyw 3G **37**
Bury New Rd. Rams 3F **13**
Bury New Rd.
  Salf 3G **81** (1G **5**)
Bury New Rd.
  W'fld & P'wich 6C **50**
Bury Old Rd. A'wth 4A **34**
Bury Old Rd. Bolt 6C **32**
  (in two parts)
Bury Old Rd.
  Bury & Heyw 4H **37**
Bury Old Rd.
  P'wich & Salf 6H **67**
Bury Old Rd. Rams 1H **13**
Bury Old Rd. Walm 4H **13**
  (in two parts)
Bury Old Rd.
  W'fld & P'wich 2D **66**
Bury Pl. M11 . . . . .3E **97**
Bury Rd. Bolt 6D **32**
Bury Rd. Rad 3H **49**
Bury Rd. Rams 2A **12**
Bury Rd. T'ton 5H **21**
Bury Rd. Tur 1B **20**
Bury St. Heyw 3D **38**
Bury St. Moss 3E **89**
Bury St. Rad 3A **50**
Bury St. Rams 6C **32**
Bury St. Salf 3C **94** (3F **5**)
Bury St. Stoc 6H **127**
Bury Tourist Info. Cen.
  . . . . .3C **36**
Bury Transport Mus. . . .3C **36**
Bushell St. Bolt 3F **45**
Bushey Dri. M23 . . . . . .6G **135**
Busheyfield Clo. Hyde . .2B **114**
Bushfield St. Bury 4E **135**
Bushgrove Wlk. M9 . . . .4F **69**
  (off Claygate Dri.)
Bushmoor Wlk. M13 . . .2H **109**
Bushnell Wlk. M9 . . . . . .4F **69**
  (off Eastlands Rd.)
Bush St. M40 . . . . .6G **83**
Bushton Wlk. M40 . . . . .6E **83**
Bushway Wlk. M8 . . . . . .5D **82**
  (off Moordown Clo.)
Busk. 1A **72**
Busk Rd. Chad 1A **72**
  (in two parts)
Busk Wlk. Chad 1A **72**
Butcher La. M23 . . . . . .4D **134**
  (in two parts)
Butcher La. Bury 3D **36**
Butcher La. Rytn 2A **56**
Bute Av. Oldh 6D **72**
Bute St. M40 . . . . .3H **83**
Bute St. Bolt 4F **31**
Bute St. Salf 4D **92**
Butler Ct. M40 . . . .2G **95** (2F **7**)
Butler Ct. Stret 6D **106**
Butler Green. 5G **71**
Butler Grn. Chad 5G **71**
Butler La. M4 . . . . .2G **95** (2F **7**)
Butler St. M4 . . . . .2G **95** (2F **7**)
Butler St. Rams 5C **12**
Butley St. Haz G 1E **153**
Butman St. M18 . . . . . .1H **111**

Buttercup Av. Wors 6B **62**
Buttercup Dri. Oldh 5H **57**
Buttercup Dri. Roch 2B **40**
Buttercup Dri. Stoc 6F **139**
Butterfield Clo.
  Chea H 4D **150**
Butterhouse La. Dob 5C **60**
Butter La. M3 . . . .4D **94** (5G **5**)
Butterley Clo. Duk 6D **100**
Buttermere Av. M22 . . . .3H **147**
Buttermere Av. Heyw 5F **39**
Buttermere Av. Swin 5F **79**
Buttermere Clo. L Lev . . .3H **47**
Buttermere Clo. Stret 4C **106**
Buttermere Dri. Haleb . . .1D **156**
Buttermere Dri. Midd 5G **53**
Buttermere Dri. Rams 2D **12**
Buttermere Gro. Rytn 6B **42**
Buttermere Rd. Ash L . . .1G **99**
Buttermere Rd. Farn 1A **62**
Buttermere Rd. Gat 2F **149**
Buttermere Rd. Oldh 1H **73**
Buttermere Rd. Part 6C **118**
Buttermere Ter. Stal 2E **101**
Buttermill Clo. Irlam 4F **103**
Butterstile Av. P'wich 1D **80**
Butterstile Clo. P'wich 2D **80**
Butterstile La. P'wich 1D **80**
Butterwick Clo. M12 . . . .4D **110**
Butterworth Hall. 6G **29**
Butterworth Hall. Miln . . .6G **29**
Butterworth La. Chad 6E **71**
Butterworth Pl. Shire 3E **17**
Butterworth St. M11 . . . .5C **96**
Butterworth St. Chad 2H **71**
Butterworth St. L'boro 4E **17**
Butterworth St. Midd 2C **70**
Butterworth St. Oldh 2G **73**
Butterworth St. Rad 3H **49**
Butterworth Way. G'fld . . .4F **61**
Buttery Ho. La. Hale 3E **147**
Butt Hill Av. P'wich 6F **67**
Butt Hill Ct. P'wich 6F **67**
Butt Hill Dri. P'wich 6F **67**
Butt Hill Rd. P'wich 6F **67**
Butt La. Moss 5D **74**
Button Hole. Shaw 6H **43**
Button La. M23 . . . . . . .1G **135**
Buttress St. M18 . . . . . .1E **111**
Butts Av, The. Roch 4H **27**
  (off Butts, The)
Butts La. Del 3E **59**
Butts, The. Roch 4H **27**
Buxted Rd. Oldh 6F **57**
Buxton Av. M20 . . . . . . .3D **124**
Buxton Av. Ash L 5B **88**
Buxton Clo. Glos 5G **117**
  (off Buxton M.)
Buxton Cres. Roch 1H **41**
Buxton Cres. Sale 2D **134**
Buxton La. Droy 5G **97**
Buxton La. Marp 6C **142**
Buxton M. Glos 5G **117**
Buxton Old Rd. Dis 1H **165**
Buxton Pl. Oldh 4C **72**
Buxton Rd. Dis 1H **165**
Buxton Rd. Haz G 4F **153**
Buxton Rd.
  H Lane & Dis 5B **154**
Buxton Rd. Stoc 5A **140**
Buxton Rd. Stret 4A **106**
Buxton Rd. W. Dis 1E **165**
Buxton St. M1 . . .5F **95** (2D **10**)
Buxton St. Bury 3A **36**
Buxton St. Gat 6E **137**
Buxton St. Haz G 2D **152**
Buxton St. Heyw 4F **39**
Buxton St. Whitw 2H **15**
Buxton Ter. Holl 1F **117**
Buxton Wlk. Glos 6G **117**
  (off Buxton M.)
Buxton Way. Dent 1F **129**

Bycroft Wlk. M40 . . . . . .1F **97**
Bye Rd. Rams 2G **13**
Bye St. Aud 6F **99**
Byfield Rd. M22 . . . . . . .1A **148**
Byland Av. Chea H 1D **160**
Byland Av. Oldh 5H **73**
Byland Clo. Bolt 3A **32**
Byland Gdns. Rad 3E **49**
Bylands Clo. Poy 3D **162**
Bylands Fold. Duk 1B **114**
Byland Wlk. M22 . . . . . .4B **148**
Byng Av. Cad 5A **118**
Byng St. Farn 1F **63**
Byng St. Heyw 5G **39**
Byrcot Clo. Sale 6G **123**
Byroe Ct. Alt 5F **133**
Byrom Av. M19 . . . . . . .6E **111**
Byrom Ct. Droy 4H **97**
Byrom Pde. M19 . . . . . . .6E **111**
Byrom Pl. M3 . . . .4C **94** (6F **5**)
Byrom St. M3 . . . .5C **94** (1F **9**)
  (in two parts)
Byrom St. Alt 2F **145**
Byrom St. Bury 1H **35**
Byrom St. Old T 3B **108**
Byrom St. Salf 5G **93**
Byrom St. Stal 4D **100**
Byron Av. Droy 3A **98**
Byron Av. P'wich 6D **66**
Byron Av. Rad 3D **48**
Byron Av. Swin 3E **79**
Byron Dri. Chea 5B **138**
Byron Gro. Stoc 6G **111**
Byron Rd. Dent 1F **129**
Byron Rd. G'mnt 1H **21**
Byron Rd. Midd 5B **54**
Byron Rd. Stret 4F **107**
Byrons Dri. Timp 5A **134**
Byron St. Eccl 3F **91**
Byron St. Oldh 1H **85**
Byron St. Rytn 3C **56**
Byron Wlk. Farn 3D **62**
Byron Wlk. Rytn 3C **56**
  (off Shaw St.)
Byrth Rd. Oldh 3D **86**
Bywell Wlk. M8 . . . . .4B **82**
  (off Levenhurst Rd.)
Bywood Wlk. M8 . . . . . .6A **82**

C

Cabin La. Oldh 4B **58**
Cablestead Wlk. M11 . . . .5B **96**
  (off Ranworth Clo.)
Cable St. M4 . . . .3F **95** (3C **6**)
Cable St. Bolt 5B **32**
Cable St. Salf 3C **94** (3F **5**)
Cabot Pl. Stoc 5H **127**
Cabot St.
  M13 . . . .1F **109** (5D **10**)
Caddington Rd. M21 . . . .1A **124**
Cadishead. 4C **118**
Cadishead Recreation Cen.
  . . . . .4B **118**
Cadishead Way. Irlam . . .3D **118**
Cadleigh Wlk. M40 . . . . .4A **84**
Cadmium Wlk. M18 . . . .3E **111**
Cadnam Dri. M22 . . . . . .2D **148**
Cadogan Pl. Salt 2A **82**
Cadogan St. M14 . . . . . .3E **109**
Cadum Wlk.
  M13 . . . .1G **109** (5E **11**)
Caen Av. M40 . . . . .6C **70**
Caernarvon Clo. G'mnt . .2H **21**
Caernarvon Dri.
  Haz G 4C **152**
Caernarvon Way. Dent . . .6F **113**
Caesar St. Roch 3G **41**
Cairn Dri. Roch 5A **26**
Cairn Dri. Salf 6G **81**
Cairngorm Dri. Bolt 2C **44**

Cairns Pl. Ash L 6H **87**
Cairn Wlk. M11 . . . . . . .4B **96**
Carnwell Rd. Chad 1F **71**
Caister Av. W'fld 2E **67**
Caister Clo. Urm 6G **103**
Caistor Clo. M16 . . . . . .1C **124**
Caistor St. Stoc 6B **128**
Caistor Wlk. Oldh 2D **72**
Caithness Clo. M23 . . . . .1G **147**
Caithness Dri. Bolt 1C **44**
Caithness Rd. Roch 6A **26**
Cajetan Ho. Midd 4H **69**
Cakebread St.
  M12 . . . . . .6G **95** (3E **11**)
Calbourne Cres. M12 . . .4D **110**
Calcot Wlk. M23 . . . . . . .5F **135**
Calcutta Rd. Stoc 4E **139**
Caldbeck Av. Bolt 4D **30**
Caldbeck Av. Sale 4E **123**
Caldbeck Dri. Farn 2A **62**
Caldbeck Dri. Midd 6G **53**
Caldecott Rd. M9 . . . . . .4C **68**
Calder Av. M22 . . . . .3B **136**
Calder Av. Irlam 6D **102**
Calder Av. L'boro 2E **17**
Calder Bank. 3A **104**
Calderbank Av. Urm 3A **104**
Calderbeck Way. M22 . . .5C **136**
Calderbrook. 6G **17**
Calderbrook Ct.
  Chea H 1D **150**
Calderbrook Dri.
  Chea H 1C **150**
Calderbrook Rd. L'boro . .3E **17**
Calderbrook Ter. L'boro . .1G **17**
Calderbrook Wlk. M9 . . . .4F **83**
Calderbrook Way. Oldh . .4F **73**
Calder Clo. Bury 3G **23**
Calder Clo. Poy 5D **162**
Calder Clo. Stoc 4H **127**
Caldercourt. Urm 3A **104**
Calder Cres. W'fld 5F **51**
Calder Dri. Kear 4D **64**
Calder Dri. Swin 2E **79**
Calder Dri. Wors 1C **76**
Calder Flats. Heyw 3F **39**
  (off Wilton St.)
Calder Gro. Shaw 5E **43**
Calder Ho. Salf 6G **81**
Caldermoor. 3E **17**
Calder Rd. Bolt 4A **46**
Caldershaw. 1D **26**
Caldershaw Cen., The.
  Roch 1D **26**
Caldershaw La. Roch 1C **26**
Caldershaw Rd. Roch 2C **26**
Calder St. Roch 1B **28**
Calder St. Salf 5B **94** (2C **8**)
Caldervale Av. M21 . . . . .3A **124**
Calder Wlk. Midd 5E **53**
Calder Wlk. W'fld 5F **51**
Calder Way. W'fld 5F **51**
Calderwood Clo. T'ton . . .5H **21**
Caldey Rd. Round I 6E **135**
Caldon Clo. Eccl 5F **91**
Caldwell St. Stoc 6H **111**
Caldy Dri. Rams 6C **12**
Caldy Rd. Hand 4H **159**
Caldy Rd. Salf 1D **92**
Caledon Av. M40 . . . . . .3A **84**
Caledonia Dri. Eccl 5G **91**
Caledonia St. Bolt 2G **45**
Caledonia St. Rad 3A **50**
  (in two parts)
Caledonia Way. Stret 2A **106**
Cale Green. 5H **139**
Cale Grn. Stoc 5H **139**
Cale Grn. Ct. Stoc 5H **139**
Cale St. Stoc 4H **139**
Caley St. M1 . . . . .6C **95** (3A **10**)
Caley St. Bolt 3D **30**
Calf Hey. L'boro 3D **16**

Calf Hey—Cardwell Gdns.

Calf Hey. Roch .2A 16
Calf Hey Clo. Rad .4D 48
Calf Hey Head. Whitw .1D 14
Calf Hey La. Whitw .1D 14
Calf Hey N. Roch .1G 41
Calf Hey Rd. Shaw .5H 43
Calf Hey S. Roch .1G 41
Calgarth Dri. Midd .4F 53
Calgary St. M18 .2E 111
Calico Clo. Salf .2B 94 (2C 4)
California Fitness Cen. .5B 6
Callaghan Wlk. Heyw .4E 39
Calland Av. Hyde .4D 114
Callander Sq. Heyw .4B 38
Callender St. Rams .3D 12
Calliards La. L'boro .5C 16
Calliard's Rd. Roch .5C 16
Callingdon Rd. M21 .4B 124
Callington Clo. Hyde .5A 116
Callington Dri. Hyde .5A 116
(in two parts)
Callington Wlk. Hyde .5A 116
Callis Rd. Bolt .1G 45
Callum Wlk. M13 .1G 109 (6E 11)
Calluna M. M20 .5E 125
Calne Wlk. M23 .6G 135
Calow Clo. Glos .5G 117
Calow Grn. Glos .6G 117
Caltha St. Rams .3D 12
Calthorpe Av. M9 .4E 83
Calton Av. Salf .4E 81
Calve Cft. Rd. M22 .3C 148
Calver Av. Eccl .5E 91
Calver Bank. Glos .5G 117
(off Eyam La., in two parts)
Calver Clo. Glos .5G 117
Calver Clo. Urm .4H 103
Calver Fold. Glos .5F 117
(off Calver M.)
Calver Hey Clo. W'houg .5A 44
Calverleigh Clo. Bolt .5E 45
Calverley Av. M19 .2B 126
Calverley Clo. Wilm .1F 167
Calverley Rd. Chea .6C 138
Calverley Way. Roch .5E 15
Calver M. Glos .5F 117
Calver Pl. Glos .5F 117
Calverton Dri. M40 .4C 84
Calvert Rd. Bolt .4A 46
(in three parts)
Calvert St. Salf .3D 92
Calver Wlk. M40 .2G 95 (2F 7)
Calver Wlk. Chea H .4A 150
Calver Wlk. Dent .1G 129
Calvine Wlk. M40 .2G 95 (2F 7)
Calvin St. Bolt .4B 32
Cambeck Clo. W'fld .6F 51
Cambeck Wlk. W'fld .6E 51
Cambell Rd. Eccl .3D 90
Camberley Clo. Bram .6A 152
Camberley Clo. T'ton .6A 22
Camberley Dri. Roch .5B 26
Cambert La. M18 .2E 111
(Garratt Way)
Cambert La. M18 .2F 111
(Wellington St.)
Camberwell Dri. Ash L .5E 87
Camberwell St. M8 .1E 95
Camberwell St. Oldh .5C 72
Camberwell Way. Rytn .3A 56
Camborne St. M14 .4F 109
Cambourne Dri. Bolt .2E 45
Cambourne Rd. Hyde .4A 116
Cambo Wlk. Stoc .6A 126
Cambrai Cres. Eccl .1C 90
Cambrian Dri. Miln .5G 29
Cambrian Dri. Rytn .4A 56
Cambrian Rd. Stoc .3E 139
Cambrian St. M40 & M11 .3A 96 (3H 7)
Cambria Sq. Bolt .2G 45
(off Cambria St.)
Cambria St. Bolt .2G 45
Cambria St. Oldh .2H 73
Cambridge Av. M16 .5A 108
Cambridge Av. Roch .5C 26
Cambridge Av. Wilm .2C 166
Cambridge Clo. Farn .6B 46
Cambridge Clo. Sale .6F 121
Cambridge Dri. Dent .4A 112
Cambridge Dri. L Lev .3B 48
Cambridge Dri. Woodl .4A 130
Cambridge Gro. Eccl .3H 91
Cambridge Gro. W'fld .1E 67
Cambridge Ind. Area. Salf .1B 94
(in two parts)
Cambridge Rd. M9 .2F 83
Cambridge Rd. Droy .2H 97
Cambridge Rd. Fail .6F 85
Cambridge Rd. Gat .5F 137
Cambridge Rd. Hale .3G 145
Cambridge Rd. Stoc .4E 127
Cambridge Rd. Urm .6D 104
Cambridge St. M1 & M15 .6D 94 (3H 9)
(in two parts)
Cambridge St. Ash L .4F 99
Cambridge St. Duk .4A 100
Cambridge St. Oldh .4H 71
Cambridge St. Salf .1C 94
Cambridge St. Stal .3E 101
Cambridge St. Stoc .5A 140
Cambridge St. Ind. Area. Salf .1C 94
(Cambridge St.)
Cambridge St. Ind. Area. Salf .2C 94 (1E 5)
(Short St.)
Cambridge Ter. Mill .1H 101
Cambridge Ter. Stoc .5A 140
(off Russell St.)
Camdale Wlk. M8 .5B 82
(off Ermington Dri.)
Camden Av. M40 .1E 97
Camden Clo. A'wth .4C 34
Camden Ho. Bolt .4A 32
Camden St. Moss .6F 75
Camelford Clo. M15 .1E 109 (6A 10)
Camelia Rd. M9 .4E 83
Camellia Clo. Bolt .6F 31
Cameron Ct. Rytn .1B 56
Cameron Ho. Bury .3A 36
Cameron St. M1 .5D 94 (2G 9)
Cameron St. Bolt .6B 18
Cameron St. Bury .3A 36
Camley Wlk. M8 .5D 82
(off Appleford Dri.)
Camomile Wlk. Part .6D 118
Campania St. Rytn .5C 56
Campanula Wlk. M8 .5C 82
(off Magnolia Dri.)
Campbell Clo. Wals .1E 35
Campbell Ct. Farn .5E 47
Campbell Ho. Farn .6D 46
Campbell Rd. M13 .5B 110
Campbell Rd. Bolt .5E 45
Campbell Rd. Sale .6H 121
Campbell Rd. Swin .5E 79
Campbell St. Farn .5D 46
Campbell St. Roch .1G 27
Campbell St. Stoc .6H 111
Campbell Wlk. Farn .5E 47
Campbell Way. Wors .6E 63
(in two parts)
Campden Way. Hand .3H 159
Campfield Av. M3 .2F 9
Campion Wlk. M11 .5B 96
Campion Way. Dent .1G 129
Campion Way. Roch .6C 14
Camponia Gdns. Salf .6H 81
Camp St. M3 .5C 94 (1F 9)
Camp St. Ash L .2H 99
Camp St. Bury .2A 36
Camp St. Salf .6G 81
Camrose Wlk. M13 .2H 109
Cams Acre Clo. Rad .4E 49
Cams La. Rad .5E 49
(in two parts)
Canada St. M40 .1A 96
Canada St. Bolt .3G 31
Canada St. Stoc .5A 140
Canal Bank. Eccl .2E 91
(in two parts)
Canal Circ. Eccl .4A 92
Canal Rd. Timp .4G 133
Canal Side. Bolt .6A 48
Canal Side. Eccl .2E 91
Canalside Ind. Est. Roch .6B 28
Canalside N. Traf P .2E 107
Canal St. M1 .5E 95 (1B 10)
Canal St. Chad .6H 71
Canal St. Droy .5A 98
Canal St. Heyw .5G 39
Canal St. Hyde .4A 114
Canal St. L'boro .4F 17
Canal St. Marp .5E 143
Canal St. Roch .6A 28
Canal St. Salf .4A 94 (5B 4)
Canal St. Stal .4E 101
Canal St. Stoc .2H 139
Canal Wharf. Stoc .6G 127
Canberra Rd. Bram .2G 161
Canberra St. M11 .3E 97
Candahar St. Bolt .4C 46
Candleford Pl. Stoc .1E 153
Candleford Rd. M20 .3F 125
Candlestick Pk. Bury .1H 37
Candy La. A'ton .6C 162
Canisp Clo. Chad .6F 55
Canley Clo. Stoc .3H 139
Canmore Clo. Bolt .4E 45
Cannel Fold. Wors .4D 76
Canning Dri. Bolt .3A 32
Canning St. Bolt .3A 32
Canning St. Bury .1D 36
Canning St. Stoc .1G 139
Cannock Dri. Stoc .1B 138
Cannon Ct. Salf .3D 94 (4H 5)
(off Cateaton St.)
Cannon Gro. Bolt .1H 45
Cannon St. M4 .3E 95 (4A 6)
Cannon St. Bolt .2H 45
Cannon St. Bury .1E 37
Cannon St. Eccl .4G 91
Cannon St. Holl .2E 117
Cannon St. Oldh .2C 72
Cannon St. Rad .2F 49
Cannon St. Rams .5C 12
Cannon St. Salf .3B 94 (3C 4)
Cannon St. N. Bolt .1H 45
Cannon Wlk. Dent .5E 113
Cann St. T'ton .3F 21
Canon Dri. Bow .4D 144
Canon Flynn Ct. Roch .4C 28
Canon Grn. Ct. Salf .3C 94 (3E 5)
Canon Grn. Dri. Salf .2C 94 (2E 5)
Canon Hussey Ct. Salf .5C 4
Canons Clo. Bolt .3F 31
Canons Gro. M40 .6G 83
Canonsleigh Clo. M8 .6A 82
Canon St. Roch .1B 28
Canonsway. Swin .3E 79
Canon Tighe Ct. Chad .2G 71
Canterbury Clo. Duk .1B 114
Canterbury Clo. Roch .4C 26
Canterbury Cres. Midd .5D 54
Canterbury Dri. Bury .1B 36
Canterbury Dri. P'wich .1G 81
Canterbury Gdns. Salf .3A 92
Canterbury Gro. Bolt .4H 45
Canterbury Pk. M20 .6D 124
Canterbury Rd. Hale .2C 146
Canterbury Rd. Stoc .2B 140
Canterbury Rd. Urm .4E 105
Canterbury St. Ash L .1A 100
Canterfield Clo. Droy .3D 98
Cantrell St. M11 .4D 96
Canute Ct. Stret .4E 107
Canute Rd. Stret .4E 107
Canute St. Bolt .4E 33
Canute St. Rad .4E 49
Canute St. Salf .3H 93
Capella Wlk. Salf .1A 94
Capenhurst Clo. M23 .1F 147
Capenhurst Clo. Poy .3F 163
Capesthorne Clo. Haz G .5F 153
Capesthorne Dri. Shaw .6D 42
Capesthorne Rd. Duk .1B 114
Capesthorne Rd. Haz G .5F 153
Capesthorne Rd. H Lane .6C 154
Capesthorne Rd. Timp .5D 134
Capesthorne Rd. Wilm .4B 166
Capesthorne Wlk. Dent .5E 113
Cape St. M20 .2G 125
Capital Ho. Salf .6G 93
Capital Quay. Salf .6G 93
Capital Rd. M11 .6H 97
Capitol Clo. Bolt .2E 31
Capricorn Way. Salf .1A 94
Capstan St. M9 .3G 83
Captain Clarke Rd. Hyde .2H 113
Captain Fold. .2G 39
Captain Fold. Heyw .3G 39
Captain Fold Rd. L Hul .4A 62
Captain's Clough Rd. Bolt .3E 31
Captain Wlk. Salf .5H 93
(off Robert Hall St.)
Capton Clo. Bram .3A 152
Caradoc Av. M8 .5D 82
Carberry Rd. M18 .2F 111
Carbis Wlk. M8 .6A 82
Cardale Wlk. M9 .4F 83
(off Conran St.)
Carden Av. Swin .4D 78
Carden Av. Urm .5A 104
Cardenbrook Gro. Wilm .5H 159
Carder Clo. Swin .4E 79
Carders Ct. Roch .2B 40
Cardew Av. M22 .1C 148
Cardiff Clo. Oldh .1H 85
Cardiff St. Salf .4A 82
Cardiff Wlk. Dent .6F 113
Cardigan Dri. Bury .6C 36
Cardigan Rd. Oldh .1H 85
Cardigan St. Rad .1F 49
Cardigan St. Roch .6E 15
Cardigan St. Rytn .3C 56
Cardigan St. Salf .3E 93
Cardigan Ter. M14 .3D 108
Cardinal M. Midd .5F 53
Cardinal St. M8 .5D 82
Cardinal St. Oldh .2E 73
Carding Gro. Salf .2C 94 (2E 5)
Cardroom Rd. M4 .3G 95 (4E 7)
Cardus St. M19 .6C 110
Cardwell Gdns. Bolt .3A 32

Cardwell Rd. *Eccl* 4C **90**
Cardwell St. *Oldh* 6D **72**
Carey Clo. *Salf* . . .1B **94** (1D **4**)
Carey Wlk. *M15* 2D **108**
(off Arnott Cres.)
Carfax Fold. *Roch* 1D **26**
Carfax St. *M18* 2F **111**
Carforth Av. *Chad* 3G **71**
Cargate Wlk. *M8* 5B **82**
Carib St. *M15* 2D **108**
Carill Av. *M40* 2A **84**
Carill Dri. *M14* 1H **125**
Corina Pl. *Salf* 1A **94** (1B **4**)
Cariocca Bus. Pk.
M12 . . . .1H **109** (5G **11**)
Cariocca Bus. Pk.
Mile P 2H **95** (1H **7**)
Carisbrook Av. *Urm* 5E **105**
Carisbrook Av *W'fld* 3F **67**
Carisbrook Dri. *Swin* 5G **79**
Carisbrooke Av.
Haz G 4D **152**
Carisbrooke Dri. *Bolt* 2B **32**
Carisbrook St. *M9* 4F **83**
Carlburn St. *M11* 3F **97**
Carleton Rd. *Poy* 3A **164**
Carley Gro. *M9* 5D **68**
Carlford Gro. *P'wich* 6D **66**
Carlin Ga. *Timp* 5A **134**
Carling Dri. *M22* 3C **148**
Carlingford Clo. *Stoc* 6G **139**
Carlisle Clo. *L Lev* 5A **48**
Carlisle Clo. *Rom* 2G **141**
Carlisle Clo. *W'fld* 2F **67**
Carlisle Cres. *Ash L* 4C **87**
Carlisle Dri. *Irlam* 5E **103**
Carlisle Dri. *Timp* 3G **133**
Carlisle St. *Ald E* 5G **167**
Carlisle St. *Brom X* 3E **19**
Carlisle St. *Oldh* 5A **72**
(in two parts)
Carlisle St. *Roch* 1H **27**
Carlisle St. *Stoc* 3G **139**
Carlisle St. *Swin* 1F **79**
Carlisle Way. *Dent* 6F **113**
Carloon Rd. *M23* 2H **135**
Carlow Dri. *M22* 3C **148**
Carl St. *Bolt* 3H **31**
Carlton Av. *Bolt* 3E **45**
Carlton Av. *Bram* 2F **161**
Carlton Av. *Chea H* 2B **150**
Carlton Av. *Fall* 4F **109**
Carlton Av. *Firs* 3H **107**
Carlton Av. *Oldh* 6H **57**
Carlton Av. *Rom* 6B **130**
Carlton Av. *W'fld* 6B **50**
Carlton Av. *Wilm* 5G **159**
Carlton Clo. *Bolt* 2G **33**
Carlton Clo. *Wors* 2E **77**
Carlton Ct. *Hale* 4B **146**
Carlton Ct. *P'wich* 2E **81**
Carlton Cres. *Stoc* 1A **140**
Carlton Cres. *Urm* 6F **105**
Carlton Dri. *Gat* 5E **137**
Carlton Dri. *P'wich* 1A **82**
Carlton Flats. *Heyw* 3E **39**
(off Brunswick St.)
Carlton Gdns. *Farn* 6F **47**
Carlton Mans. *M16* 4B **108**
Carlton Pl. *Farn* 6F **47**
Carlton Pl. *Haz G* 4G **153**
Carlton Range. *M18* 3H **111**
Carlton Rd. *M16* 4B **108**
Carlton Rd. *Ash L* 6G **87**
Carlton Rd. *Bolt* 5E **31**
Carlton Rd. *Hale* 4B **146**
Carlton Rd. *Hyde* 4E **115**
Carlton Rd. *Sale* 3A **122**
Carlton Rd. *Salf* 1E **93**
Carlton Rd. *Stoc* 1C **138**
Carlton Rd. *Urm* 6F **105**

Carlton Rd. *Wors* 2E **77**
Carlton St. *M16* 3A **108**
Carlton St. *Bolt* 1B **46**
Carlton St. *Bury* 5D **36**
Carlton St. *Eccl* 2F **91**
Carlton St. *Farn* 6F **47**
Carlton Way. *G'brk* 4A **118**
Carlton Way. *Rytn* 5B **56**
Carlyle Clo. *M8* 5C **82**
Carlyle St. *Bury* 2B **36**
Carlyn St. *Sale* 5D **122**
Carmel Av. *Salf* . . .5A **94** (2A **8**)
Carmol Clo. *Salf* . .5A **94** (2A **8**)
Carmel Ct. *M8* 1B **82**
Carmel Ct. *M9* 2G **83**
Carmenna Dri. *Bram* 6H **151**
Carmichael Clo. *Part* 6C **118**
Carmichael St. *Stoc* 3F **139**
Carmine Fold *Midd* 5H **53**
Carmona Dri. *P'wich* 5E **67**
Carmona Gdns. *Salf* 2G **81**
Carmoor Rd. *M13* 2G **109**
Carnaby St. *M9* 2H **83**
Carna Rd. *Stoc* 5G **111**
Carnarvon St.
M3 . . . . .1D **94** (1H **5**)
Carnarvon St. *Oldh* 1H **85**
Carnarvon St. *Salf* 4A **82**
Carnarvon St. *Stoc* 2A **140**
Carnation Rd. *Farn* 6C **46**
Carnation Rd. *Oldh* 5A **74**
Carnegie Av. *M19* 6D **110**
Carnegie Clo. *Sale* 6F **121**
Carnforth Av. *Roch* 6D **40**
Carnforth Dri. *G'mnt* 1A **22**
Carnforth Dri. *Sale* 6A **122**
Carnforth Rd. *Chea H* . . .1D **150**
Carnforth Rd. *Stoc* 3F **127**
Carnforth Sq. *Roch* 6D **40**
Carnforth St. *M14* 4F **109**
Carnoustie. *Bolt* 4E **45**
Carnoustie. *M40* 4C **84**
Carnoustie Clo. *Wilm* 1G **167**
Carnoustie Dri. *H Grn* . . .4G **149**
Carnoustie Dri. *Rams* 4D **12**
Carnwood Clo. *M40* 1F **97**
Carolina Ho.
Salf 2C **94** (2E **5**)
Caroline Dri. *M4* . .4G **95** (5E **7**)
Caroline St. *Ash L* 2A **100**
Caroline St. *Bolt* 3H **45**
Caroline St. *Salf* 1C **94**
Caroline St. *Irlam* 1D **118**
Caroline St. *Stal* 4E **101**
Caroline St. *Stoc* 4F **139**
(in two parts)
Caronet Way. *Salf* 4B **92**
Carpenters La.
M4 . . . . .3E **95** (4B **6**)
Carpenters Wlk. *Droy* 4H **97**
Carpenters Way. *Roch* 1H **41**
Carr. 2D **12**
(Bury)
Carr. 2C **60**
(Oldham)
Carr. 4H **89**
(Stalybridge)
Carradale Dri. *Sale* 4E **121**
Carradale Wlk. *M40* 5A **84**
Carr Av. *P'wich* 1D **80**
Carr Bank. 3F **23**
Carr Bank *Rams* 2D **12**
Carr Bank Av. *M9* 6B **68**
Carr Bank Av. *Rams* 2D **12**
Carr Bank Dri. *Rams* 2D **12**
Carr Bank Rd. *Rams* 2D **12**
Carrbrook. 5G **89**
Carrbrook Clo. *Carr* 5G **89**
Carrbrook Cres. *Carr* 5G **89**
Carrbrook Dri. *Rytn* 6C **56**
Carrbrook Ind. Est.
Carr 4H **89**

Carrbrook Rd. *Carr* 4H **89**
(in two parts)
Carrbrook Ter. *Rad* 3H **49**
Carr Brow. *H Lane* 6E **155**
Carr Clo. *Stoc* 3B **140**
Carrfield Av. *L Hul* 5A **62**
Carrfield Av. *Stoc* 1A **152**
Carrfield Av. *Timp* 6D **134**
Carrfield Clo. *L Hul* 5A **62**
Carrfield Gro. *L Hul* 5A **62**
Carr Fold. *Rams* 2D **12**
Carrgate Rd. *Dent* 6H **113**
Carrgroon Clo. *M10* 4B **126**
Carr Gro. *Miln* 5G **29**
Carr Head. *Dig* 1C **60**
Carrhill Quarry Clo.
Moss 1E **89**
Carrhill Rd. *Moss* 1E **89**
Carrhouse La. *Holl* 3F **117**
Carr Ho. Rd. *S'head* 2B **74**
Carriage Dri. *Mot* 6F **83**
Carriage Dri. *L'boro* 2G **17**
Carriage Dri., The.
Had 3H **117**
Carriages, The. *Alt* 1E **145**
Carriage Sq. *M16* 2B **108**
Carrick Gdns. *M22* 1B **148**
Carrick Gdns. *Midd* 3H **53**
Carrie St. *Rams* 5F **31**
Carrigart. *P'wich* 6F **67**
Carrill Gro. *M19* 6C **110**
Carrill Gro. E. *M19* 6C **110**
Carrington. 3A **120**
Carrington Bus. Pk.
C'ton 3H **119**
Carrington Clo. *Roch* 6B **16**
Carrington Dri. *Bolt* 2B **46**
Carrington Fld. St.
Stoc 4H **139**
Carrington Ho. *Salf* 1C **92**
Carrington La.
C'ton & Sale 2B **120**
Carrington Rd. *M14* 1G **125**
Carrington Rd. *Stoc* 6A **128**
Carrington Rd. *Urm* 1A **120**
Carrington Spur.
Sale & Urm 3E **121**
Carrington St. *Chad* 6H **71**
Carrington St. *Swin* 2H **79**
Carrington Ter. *Swin* 2G **79**
(off Carrington St.)
Carr La. *Ald E* 6A **166**
Carr La. *Carr* 4H **89**
Carr La. *Dig* 2C **60**
Carr La. *G'fld* 3F **61**
Carr La. *Miln* 5H **29**
Carrmel Ct. *Del* 4H **59**
Carr Mill M. *Wilm* 5F **159**
Carrock Wlk. *Midd* 6D **52**
Carron Av. *M9* 2H **83**
Carron Gro. *Bolt* 6H **33**
Carroway St. *M40* 6G **83**
Carr Ri. *Carr* 4H **89**
Carr Rd. *Hale* 3B **146**
Carr Rd. *Irlam* 5F **103**
Carrs Av. *Chea* 5C **138**
Carrsfield Rd. *M22* 5C **136**
Carrslea Clo. *Rad* 2E **49**
Carrs Rd. *Chea* 5B **138**
Carr St. *Ash L* 6H **87**
Carr St. *Rams* 2D **12**
Carr St. *Swin* 4D **78**
Carrsvale Av. *Urm* 4D **104**
Carrswood Rd. *M23* 3C **134**
Carruthers Clo. *Heyw* 2H **39**
Carruthers St.
M4 . . . . .3H **95** (4G **7**)
Carr Wood. 4G **25**
Carrwood. *Haleb* 6B **146**
Carr Wood Av. *Bram* 5G **151**
Carrwood Hey. *Rams* 5C **12**
Carr Wood Rd. *Bram* 4F **151**

Carrwood Rd. *Wilm* 6D **158**
Carsdale Rd. *M22* 5C **148**
Carslake Av. *Bolt* 5G **31**
Carslake Rd. *M40* 6F **83**
Carson Rd. *M19* 1C **126**
Carstairs Av. *Stoc* 1A **152**
Carstairs Clo. *M8* 4B **82**
Car St. *Oldh* 2E **73**
Carter Clo. *Dent* 5F **113**
Carter Pl. *Hyde* 2B **114**
Carter St. *Bolt* 3C **46**
Carter St. *Hyde* 2B **114**
Cartor St. *Koar* 2G **63**
Carter St. *Moss* 3E **89**
Carter St. *Salf* 6H **81**
Carter St. *Stal* 3E **101**
Carthage St. *Oldh* 5D **72**
Carthorpe Arch. *Salf* 4F **93**
Cartleach Gro. *Wors* 1C **76**
Cartleach La. *Wors* 1B **76**
Cartmel. *Roch* 3H **27**
(off Redcross St.)
Cartmel Av. *Miln* 1D **42**
Cartmel Av. *Stoc* 3G **127**
Cartmel Clo. *Bolt* 5B **44**
Cartmel Clo. *Bury* 4E **51**
Cartmel Clo. *Gat* 2G **149**
Cartmel Clo. *Haz G* 2C **152**
Cartmel Clo. *Oldh* 6B **72**
Cartmel Cres. *Bolt* 3E **33**
Cartmel Cres. *Chad* 1F **85**
Cartmel Dri. *Timp* 5D **134**
Cartmel Gro. *Wors* 4B **78**
Cartmel Wlk. *M9* 4F **83**
(in two parts)
Cartmel Wlk. *Midd* 5G **53**
Cartridge Clo. *M22* 2D **148**
Cartridgo St. *Heyw* 3E **39**
Cartwright Rd. *M21* 1F **123**
Cartwright St. *Aud* 1F **113**
Cartwright St. *Hyde* 2E **115**
Carver Av. *P'wich* 4G **67**
Carver Clo. *M16* 2H **107**
Carver Dri. *Marp* 6C **142**
Carver Rd. *Hale* 3G **145**
Carver Rd. *Marp* 6C **142**
Carver St. *M16* 2H **107**
Carver Theatre. 6D **142**
Carver Wlk. *M15* 2D **108**
(off Arnott Cres.)
Carville Rd. *M9* 6B **70**
Cascade Dri. *Salf* 6A **82**
Cash Ga. Ct. *Oldh* 6B **72**
Cashmere Rd. *Stoc* 4E **139**
Cashmoor Wlk. *M12* 1A **110**
(6H **11**)
Caspian Rd. *B'hth* 5C **132**
Cassandra Ct.
Salf 5A **94** (2B **8**)
Cass Av. *Salf* 5G **93**
Cassidy Clo.
M4 . . . . .3F **95** (3D **6**)
Cassidy Ct. *Salf* 5E **93**
Cassidy Gdns. *Midd* 3F **53**
Casson Ga. *Roch* 2G **27**
Casson St. *Fail* 4F **85**
Casterton Way. *Wors* 6C **76**
Castle Av. *Dent* 5E **113**
Castle Av. *Roch* 5G **27**
Castlebrook Clo. *Bury* 3F **51**
Castle Clo. *Droy* 3B **98**
Castle Ct. *Ash L* 4F **87**
Castle Courts. *Salf* 4H **93**
Castle Cft. *Bolt* 2F **33**
Castlecroft Rd. *Bury* 3C **36**
Castledene Av. *Salf* 2E **93**
Castle Farm Dri. *Stoc* 6B **140**
Castle Farm La. *Stoc* 5B **140**
(in three parts)
Castlefield. 5C **94** (2E **9**)
Castlefield Av. *Salf* 3A **82**

Castlefield Gallery. 3F 9
Castlefield Vis. Cen.
. . . . .5C 94 (1E 9)
Castleford Clo. Bolt 5H 31
Castleford St. Chad 6A 56
Castleford Wlk. M21 . . . .2B 124
Castle Gro. Rams 1A 22
Castle Hall. 5F 101
Castle Hall Clo. Stal 4E 101
Castle Hall Ct. Stal 4E 101
Castle Hall Vw. Stal 4E 101
Castle Hill. 2D 32
(Bolton)
Castle Hill. 2E 129
(Stockport)
Castle Hill. Bred 2E 129
Castle Hill. Roch 5G 27
Castle Hill Cres. Roch . . .5G 27
Castle Hill Mobile Home Pk.
Woodl 3F 129
Castle Hill Pk. Woodl . . .3F 129
Castle Hill Rd. Bury 3A 24
(in two parts)
Castle Hill Rd. P'wich . . .1H 81
Castle Hills. 5B 144
Castle Hill St. Bolt 3D 32
(in two parts)
Castle Irwell Student Village.
Salf 6F 81
Castle La. Carr 3G 89
Castle Leisure Cen. 3C 36
Castlemere Dri. Shaw . . .5H 43
Castlemere Rd. M9 . . . . .6E 69
Castlemere St. Roch 5G 27
Castlemere Ter. Roch . . .5H 27
Castle M. Farn 2F 63
(off Castle St.)
Castle Mill La. Ash 1A 156
Castle Mill St. Oldh 2F 73
Castlemoor Av. Salf 3F 81
Castle Pk. Ind. Est.
Oldh 1F 73
Castle Quay.
M15 . . . . .6C 94 (3E 9)
Castlerea Clo. Eccl 5F 91
Castlerigg Clo. Heat C . .2F 127
Castlerigg Dri. Midd 5E 53
Castlerigg Dri. Rytn 1A 56
Castle Rd. Bury 4G 51
Castleshaw Rd. Stoc . . .6D 140
Castle St. M3 . . . .5C 94 (2E 9)
Castle St. Bolt 6C 32
Castle St. Bury 3C 36
Castle St. Eccl 3H 91
Castle St. Farn 2F 63
Castle St. Had 3H 117
Castle St. Hyde 4D 114
Castle St. Midd 2D 70
Castle St. Stal 4E 101
Castle St. Stoc 4F 139
Castle St. S'seat 1D 22
Castle Ter. Carr 5H 89
Castleton. 3C 40
Castleton Av. Stret 3B 106
Castleton Bank. Glos . . .6G 117
(off Castleton Cres.)
Castleton Ct. Dent 1G 129
Castleton Cres. Glos . . .6G 117
Castleton Dri. H Lane . . .1D 164
Castleton Grn. Glos 6G 117
(off Castleton Cres.)
Castleton Gro. Ash L 5B 88
Castleton Gro. Glos 6G 117
(off Castleton Cres.)
Castleton Rd. Haz G 4E 153
Castleton Rd. Rytn 5A 42
Castleton Rd. Salf 2A 82
Castleton Rd. S.
Roch 2D 40
Castleton St. Alt 4E 133
Castleton St. Bolt 3D 32
Castleton St. Oldh 3A 72

Castleton Swimming Pool.
. . . . .3B 40
Castleton Ter. Glos 6G 117
Castleton Wlk. M11 . . . . .4B 96
Castleton Way. Dent 1G 129
Castle Wlk. Ash L 4F 87
Castle Wlk. Stal 4E 101
Castleway. Haleb 6C 146
Castleway. Roch 4B 40
Castleway. Salf 1E 93
Castle Way. Swin 1G 79
Castlewood Gdns.
Stoc 6C 140
Castlewood Rd. Salf 3E 81
Castlewood Sq. Bolt 4E 33
Castle Yd. Stoc 1H 139
Catalan Sq. M3 . . . .5C 94 (2E 9)
Catchdale Clo. M9 . . . . . .4E 69
Catches Clo. Roch 3D 26
Catches La. Roch 3D 26
Cateaton St. M3 . . .3D 94 (4H 5)
Cateaton St. Bury 2D 36
Caterham Av. Bolt 5E 45
Caterham St.
M4 . . . . . .4H 95 (6H 7)
Catesby Rd. M16 . . . . . .4B 108
Catfield Wlk.
M15 . . . . . .6B 94 (4D 8)
Catford Rd. Round I 6E 135
Cathedral App.
Salf 3D 94 (3H 5)
Cathedral Clo. Duk 1B 114
Cathedral Gates.
M3 . . . . .3D 94 (4H 5)
Cathedral Rd. Chad 6F 55
Cathedral St.
M4 . . . . . .3D 94 (4H 5)
Cathedral Yd.
Salf 3D 94 (4H 5)
Catherine Ho. Stoc 1B 138
Catherine Rd. M8 . . . . . .2A 82
Catherine Rd. Bow 2E 145
Catherine Rd. Rom 2F 141
Catherine Rd. Swin 4C 78
Catherine St. M11 . . . . . .6G 97
Catherine St. Bolt 5F 45
Catherine St. Bury 1C 50
Catherine St. Eccl 2C 90
Catherine St. Haz G 2E 153
Catherine St. Hyde 4B 114
Catherine St. Lees 3A 74
Catherston Rd. M16 . . . .4C 108
Cathrine St. E. Aud 4D 112
Cathrine St. W. Aud 4D 112
Catley Lane Head. 5A 14
Catlow La. M4 . . .3E 95 (4B 6)
Catlow St. Salf 1C 94
Caton Clo. Bury 5C 36
Caton St. Roch 5H 27
Cato St. Rams 5C 12
Catterall Cres. Bolt 5H 19
Catterick Av. M20 . . . . . .6G 125
Catterick Av. Sale 1E 133
Catterick Dri. L Lev 4A 48
Catterick Rd. M20 . . . . . .6G 125
Catterwood Dri. Comp . . .6F 131
Catterwood Rd.
Marp B 1F 143
Cattlin Way. Oldh 1A 86
Causeway, The. Alt 1F 145
Causeway, The. Chad 4E 71
Causewood Clo. Oldh . . .3A 58
Causey Dri. Midd 4F 53
Cavalier St.
M40 . . . . . . .3H 95 (4H 7)
Cavanagh Clo.
M13 . . . . . .1H 109 (6G 11)
Cavan Clo. Stoc 4B 138
Cavannah Ct. Oldh 4A 58
Cavell St. M1 . . . .4F 95 (5C 6)
(off Newton St.)
Cavell Way. Salf & M6 . . .4G 93

Cavendish Av. M20 . . . . .3D 124
Cavendish Av. Swin 6A 66
Cavendish Ct. M9 . . . . . .4C 68
(off Deanswood Dri.)
Cavendish Ct. Salf 2H 81
Cavendish Ct. Stoc 1B 138
Cavendish Ct. Stret 3E 107
Cavendish Ct. Urm 5G 105
(off Cavendish Rd.)
Cavendish Gdns.
M20 . . . . .3D 124
Cavendish Gdns. Bolt 4G 45
Cavendish Gro. Eccl 2G 91
Cavendish Ho. Eccl 1G 91
Cavendish Ind. Est.
Ash L 2G 99
Cavendish M. Wilm 3D 166
Cavendish Mill. Ash L 3H 99
Cavendish Pl. M11 . . . . . .3C 96
Cavendish Pl. Swin 3G 79
Cavendish Rd. M20 . . . .3D 124
Cavendish Rd. Bow 2E 145
Cavendish Rd. Eccl 2G 91
Cavendish Rd. Haz G 4D 152
Cavendish Rd. Roch 2E 41
Cavendish Rd. Salf 2G 81
Cavendish Rd. Stoc 1B 138
Cavendish Rd. Stret 3E 107
Cavendish Rd. Urm 5G 105
(in two parts)
Cavendish Rd. Wors 5B 78
Cavendish St.
M15 . . . . . .1E 109 (5A 10)
(in two parts)
Cavendish St. Ash L 2G 99
Cavendish St. Oldh 3C 72
Cavendish Ter. M21 . . . .1H 123
Cavendish Way. Rytn 5A 56
Cavenham Gro. Bolt 5G 31
Cavenham Wlk. M9 . . . . .4E 83
(off Hendham Va.)
Caversham Dri. M9 . . . . .3G 83
Cawdor Av. Farn 5D 46
Cawdor Ct. Farn 5E 47
Cawdor Ho. Eccl 5F 91
(off Enfield Clo.)
Cawdor Pl. Timp 5C 134
Cawdor Rd. M14 . . . . . .6G 109
Cawdor St. M15 . . .6B 94 (4C 8)
Cawdor St. Eccl 4E 91
Cawdor St. Farn 5D 46
Cawdor St. Swin 3D 78
Cawdor St. Wors 1G 77
Cawdor Wlk. Farn 5E 47
Cawley Av. P'wich 1D 80
Cawley Ter. M9 . . . . .4C 68
Cawood Ho. Rom 2C 128
Cawood Sq. Stoc 3C 128
Cawston Wlk. M8 . . . . . .5C 82
Cawthorne Ct. Swin 2D 78
Caxton Rd. M14 . . . . . . .6F 109
Caxton St. Heyw 3F 39
Caxton St. Roch 3C 40
Caxton St. Salf 4F 5
Caygill St. Salf . . .3C 94 (3F 5)
Cayley St. Roch 4B 28
Caythorpe St. M14 . . . . . .4E 109
Cayton St. M12 . . . . .4C 110
Ceal, The. Comp 1F 143
Cecil Av. Sale 6G 121
Cecil Ct. Hale 3G 145
Cecil Ct. Stoc 3D 138
Cecil Dri. Urm 5A 104
Cecil Gro. M18 . . . . .2F 111
Cecilia Ct. N. Bolt 3C 46
Cecilia Ct. S. Bolt 3C 46
Cecil Rd. M9 . . . . .4F 69
Cecil Rd. Eccl 4G 91
Cecil Rd. Hale 3G 145
Cecil Rd. Stret 6C 106
Cecil St. M15 . . . . .2F 109

Cecil St. Ash L 4F 99
Cecil St. Bolt 6C 32
Cecil St. Bury 4D 36
Cecil St. Duk 5H 99
Cecil St. L'boro 4D 16
Cecil St. Moss 3E 89
Cecil St. Oldh 4C 72
Cecil St. Roch 6H 27
Cecil St. Rytn 4A 56
Cecil St. Stal 4F 101
Cecil St. Stoc 4G 139
Cecil St. Wors 6F 63
Cecil Wlk. Ash L 4F 99
Cecil Walker Ho. Part 5E 119
Cedar Av. Alt 1E 145
Cedar Av. Ash L 6H 87
Cedar Av. Haz G 3E 153
Cedar Av. Heyw 2E 39
Cedar Av. L Lev 5B 48
Cedar Av. Stal 2G 101
Cedar Av. W'fld 3D 66
Cedar Bank Clo. Fir 5D 28
Cedar Clo. Poy 4E 163
Cedar Ct. M14 . . . . .6G 109
Cedar Ct. Chea H 3C 150
Cedar Ct. Timp 6B 134
Cedar Cres. Chad 1H 71
Cedar Cres. Rams 2E 13
Cedar Dri. Droy 3C 98
Cedar Dri. Swin 5D 64
Cedar Dri. Urm 6E 105
Cedar Gro. M14 . . . . . . .1H 125
Cedar Gro. Dent 4E 113
Cedar Gro. Duk 5D 100
Cedar Gro. Farn 1D 62
Cedar Gro. P'wich 3E 67
Cedar Gro. Rytn 1B 56
Cedar Gro. Shaw 1F 57
Cedar Gro. Stoc 4E 127
Cedar La. Grass 3F 75
Cedar La. Miln 2E 43
Cedar Lodge. Bram 6H 151
Cedar M. Ash L 6F 87
Cedar Pl. Salf 1A 94
Cedar Rd. Fail 5F 85
Cedar Rd. Gat 6E 137
Cedar Rd. Hale 2G 145
Cedar Rd. Marp 1C 154
Cedar Rd. Midd 1C 70
Cedar Rd. Part 6C 118
Cedar Rd. Sale 3F 121
Cedar Rd. Stoc 1B 152
Cedars Rd. M22 . . . . . . .2B 148
Cedars, The. Bolt 5D 18
Cedar St. Ash L 1B 100
Cedar St. Bury 2E 37
(in two parts)
Cedar St. Hyde 2C 114
Cedar St. Oldh 2G 73
(in two parts)
Cedar St. Roch 2H 27
Cedar Technology Cen.
B'hth 4D 132
Cedarway. Wilm 5C 166
Cedarwood. Poy 4E 163
Cedarwood Av. Stoc 2C 138
Cedar Wood Ct. Bolt 6E 31
Cedric Rd. M8 . . . . .1A 82
Cedric Rd. Oldh 2G 73
Cedric St. Salf 3D 92
Celandine Clo. L'boro 3D 16
Celia St. M8 . . . . .3E 83
Cellini Sq. Bolt 4H 31
Celtic St. Stoc 3A 140
Cemetery La. Bury 5D 36
Cemetery Rd. Aud 1F 113
Cemetery Rd. Bolt 6D 32
Cemetery Rd. Dent 6F 113
Cemetery Rd. Droy 4H 97
Cemetery Rd. Fail 5F 85
Cemetery Rd. Farn 6H 47
Cemetery Rd. Moss 4F 89

Cemetery Rd.—Chapel Wlk.

Cemetery Rd. *Rad* . . . . . . .3F **49** (in two parts)
Cemetery Rd. *Rams* 6C **12**
Cemetery Rd. *Rytn* 2A **56**
Cemetery Rd. *Salf* 4E **93**
Cemetery Rd. N. *Swin* 1E **79**
Cemetery Rd. S. *Swin* 2E **79**
Cemetery St. *Midd* 6A **54**
Cennick Clo. *Oldh* 3H **73**
Ceno St. *Oldh* 6E **57**
Centaur Clo. *Swin* 1F **79**
Centaur Way. *M8* 4B **82**
Centenary Circ. *Salf* 4A **92**
Centenary Ct. *Bolt* 3B **46**
Centenary Way. *Salf* 4A **92**
Central Art Gallery. . . . .3H **99** (Library)
Central Av. *M19* 5C **110**
Central Av. *Bury* 6B **36**
Central Av. *Farn* 1C **62**
Central Av. *G'fld* 4F **61**
Central Av. *L'boro* 3F **17**
Central Av. *Rams* 3A **12**
Central Av. *Sale* 2F **133**
Central Av. *Salf* 5C **80**
Central Av. *Swin* 1B **80**
Central Av. *Wors* 4E **63**
Central Dri. *M8* 2D **82**
Central Dri. *Bram* 3F **151**
Central Dri. *Bury* 3F **23**
Central Dri. *H Grn* 5H **149**
Central Dri. *Rom* 6A **130**
Central Dri. *Stoc* 4H **127**
Central Dri. *Swin* 4H **79**
Central Dri. *Urm* 5F **105**
Central Ho. *M9* 4G **69**
Central Library. 5D **94** (1H **9**)
Central Pk. Est. *Traf P* 1B **106**
Central Retail Pk. *M4* 4G **95** (5E **7**)
Central Rd. *M20* 4E **125**
Central Rd. *Part* 6D **118**
Central St. *M2* 4D **94** (6H **5**)
Central St. *Bolt* 6A **32**
Central St. *Rams* 3D **12**
Central Way. *Alt* 1F **145**
Centre Gdns. *Bolt* 4H **31**
Centre Pk. Rd. *Bolt* 4H **31**
Centrepoint. *Traf P* 2A **106**
Centre Va. *L'boro* 2G **17**
Centre Va. Clo. *L'boro* 2G **17**
Centurion Gro. *Salf* 5A **82**
Century Gdns. *Roch* 3H **27**
Century Lodge. *Farn* 1E **63**
Century Mill Ind. Est. *Farn* 2D **62**
Century Pk. Ind. Est. *B'hth* 5C **132**
Century St. *M3* 5C **94** (2F **9**)
Cestrian St. *Bolt* 4B **46**
Ceylon St. *M40* 5A **84**
Ceylon St. *Oldh* 4H **73**
Chadbury Clo. *Los* 4A **44**
Chadderton. 2F **71**
Chadderton Dri. *Bury* 5E **51**
Chadderton Fold. 5F **55**
Chadderton Fold. *Chad* . . . . .5F **55** (in two parts)
Chadderton Hall Rd. *Chad* 6F **55**
Chadderton Heights. *Chad* 4F **55**
Chadderton Ind. Est. *Midd* 4C **70**
Chadderton Park. 6E **55**
Chadderton Pk. Rd. *Chad* 1F **71**
Chadderton Precinct. *Chad* 1H **71**
Chadderton Sports Cen. 2H **71**
Chadderton St. *M4* 3F **95** (3C **6**)
Chadderton Way. *Oldh & Chad* 5H **55**
Chaddesley Wlk. *M11* 5B **96**
Chaddock La. *Tyl & Wors* 5A **76**
Chaddock Level, The. *Wors* 6C **76**
Chadkirk. 3H **141**
Chadkirk Chapel. 2H **141**
Chadkirk Ind. Est. *Rom* 3H **141**
Chadkirk M. *Rom* 1A **142**
Chadkirk Rd. *Rom* 2H **141**
Chadvil Rd. *Chea* 6G **137**
Chadwell Rd. *Stoc* 4E **141**
Chadwick Clo. *M14* 4F **109**
Chadwick Clo. *Miln* 6G **29**
Chadwick Clo. *Wilm* 6G **159**
Chadwick Fold. *Bury* 3F **23**
Chadwick Fold. Heyw . . . .*3H 39* (*off Chadwick La.*)
Chadwick Hall Rd. *Roch* 5D **26**
Chadwick La. *Heyw & Roch* . . . . . .3H **39** (in three parts)
Chadwick La. *Roch* 3A **42**
Chadwick Rd. *Eccl* 3G **91**
Chadwick Rd. *Urm* 5H **105**
Chadwick St. *Ash L* 3C **100**
Chadwick St. *Bolt* 1C **46**
Chadwick St. *Bury* 1A **38**
Chadwick St. *L Lev* 4B **48**
Chadwick St. *Marp* 6D **142**
Chadwick St. *Roch* (OL11) 4F **27**
Chadwick St. *Roch* (OL16) 4D **28**
Chadwick St. *Stoc* 3H **139**
Chadwick St. *Swin* 3F **79**
Chadwick Ter. *Roch* 5D **14**
Chaffinch Clo. *M22* 6D **136**
Chaffinch Clo. *Droy* 2C **98**
Chaffinch Clo. *Oldh* 5H **73**
Chaffinch Dri. *Bury* 1G **37**
Chain Bar. 6C **70**
Chain Bar La. *Mot* 5B **116**
Chain Bar Way. *Mot* 5B **116**
Chainhurst Wlk. M13 . . . . . .*1G 109* (*5E 11*) (*off Weald Clo.*)
Chain Rd. *M9* 4F **69**
Chain St. *M1* 4E **95** (6A **6**)
Chain Wlk. *M9* 4G **69**
Chalcombe Grange. *M12* 3B **110**
Chale Clo. *M40* . . .2H **95** (2G **7**)
Chale Dri. *Midd* 3C **70**
Chale Grn. *Bolt* 2G **33**
Chalfont Av. *Urm* 5G **105**
Chalfont Clo. *Oldh* 5F **73**
Chalfont Dri. *M8* 4C **82**
Chalfont Dri. *Wors* 3G **77**
Chalfont Ho. *Salf* 3F **93**
Chalfont St. *Bolt* . . . . .3B **32** (in two parts)
Chalford Rd. *M23* 2G **147**
Challenor Sq. *M12* 1C **110**
Challinor St. *Rams* 5F **31**
Challum Dri. *Chad* 1G **71**
Chamber Hall Clo. *Oldh* 5B **72**
Chamberhill St. *Bury* 2C **36**
Chamber Ho. Dri. *Roch* . . .1B **40**
Chamberhouse Urban Farm. 1A **40**
Chamberlain Ho. *M22* . . .1C **148**
Chamberlain Rd. *H'rod* . . .6E **89**
Chamberlain St. *Bolt* 1H **45**
Chamber Rd. *Oldh* 6A **72**
Chamber Rd. *Shaw* 6F **43**
Chambers Ct. *Mot* 4C **116**
Chambersfield Ct. *Salf* 4F **93**
Champagnole Ct. Duk . . . .*4H 99* (*off Hill St.*)
Champness Hall. *Roch* . . .4H **27**
Champneys Wlk. *M9* 5F **83**
Chancel Av. *Salf* . . .5A **94** (2A **8**)
Chancel Clo. *Duk* 1A **114**
Chancel La. *Wilm* 1E **167**
Chancellor La. *M12* 5H **95** (2G **11**)
Chancel M. *Stoc* 2A **140**
Chancel Pl. *M1* 4G **95** (6E **7**)
Chancel Pl. *Roch* 4H **27**
Chancery La. *M2* 4D **94** (6H **5**)
Chancery La. *Bolt* 6B **32**
Chancery La. *Dob* 5A **60**
Chancery La. *Shaw* 6G **43**
Chancery Pl. *M2* 4D **94** (6H **5**)
Chancery St. *Chad* 1A **72**
Chancery St. *Oldh* 3G **73**
Chancery Wlk. *Chad* 1A **72**
Chandlers Point. *Salf* 5F **93**
Chandlers Row. *Wors* 6A **78**
Chandley Ct. Stoc . . . . . .*4A 140* (*off Ward St.*)
Chandley St. *Chea* 5H **137**
Chandos Gro. *Salf* 3D **92**
Chandos Rd. *M21* 6A **108**
Chandos Rd. *P'wich* 1F **81**
Chandos Rd. *Stoc* 3D **126**
Chandos Rd. S. *M21* 1A **124**
Chandos St. *Shaw* 6G **43**
Change Way. *Salf* . .2C **94** (2E **5**)
Channing Ct. *Roch* 5B **28**
Channing Sq. *Roch* 5B **28**
Channing St. *Roch* 5B **28**
Chanters, The. *Wors* 4E **77**
Chantler's Av. *Bury* 4G **35**
Chantler's St. *Bury* 3G **35**
Chantry Clo. *Dis* 2H **165**
Chantry Clo. *Stoc* 2G **127**
Chantry Fold. *Dis* 1H **165**
Chantry Rd. *Dis* 1H **165**
Chantry Wlk. *M8* 4B **82**
Chapel All. Rams . . . .*6B 32* (*off Deansgate*)
Chapel Clo. *Duk* 5A **100**
Chapel Clo. *Uns* 3F **51**
Chapel Cotts. *Wilm* 6A **158**
Chapel Ct. *M9* 2F **83**
Chapel Ct. *Alt* 1F **145**
Chapel Ct. *Hyde* 6A **114**
Chapel Ct. *Marp* 5D **142**
Chapel Ct. *Sale* 3G **121**
Chapel Ct. *Wilm* 3D **166**
Chapel Cft. *Rytn* 3B **56**
Chapel Dri. *Ash L* 6A **88**
Chapel Dri. *Haleb* 6C **146**
Chapel Field. 6A **50**
Chapel Fld. *Rad* 6A **50**
Chapelfield Clo. *Mill* 1H **101**
Chapelfield Dri. *Wors* 6D **62**
Chapelfield Rd. *M12* 5G **95** (2F **11**)
Chapelfield Rd. *Dent* 4F **113**
Chapel Fields. Marp . . . . .*6D 142* (*off Church La.*)
Chapelfield St. *Bolt* 2A **32**
Chapel Gdns. Aud . . . . . .*1F 113* (*off Guide La.*)
Chapel Gdns. *G'mnt* 2F **21**
Chapel Ga. *Miln* 5F **29**
Chapel Grn. *Dent* 4F **113**
Chapel Gro. *Rad* 1G **65**
Chapel Gro. *Urm* 5G **105**
Chapel Hill. *Duk* 5A **100**
Chapel Hill. *L'boro* 4F **17**
Chapelhill Dri. *M9* 6E **69**
Chapel Ho. *Stoc* 1G **127**
Chapel Houses. *Haz G* 1C **152**
Chapel Houses. *Marp* . . .6E **143**
Chapel Houses. Whitw . . .*1H 15* (*off Oak Clo.*)
Chapel La. *M9* 5D **68**
Chapel La. *Had* 2H **117**
Chapel La. *Haleb* 5B **146**
Chapel La. *Holc* 3C **12**
Chapel La. *Part* 6D **118**
Chapel La. *Roch* 3F **25**
Chapel La. *Rytn* 3B **56**
Chapel La. *Stret* 6C **106**
Chapel La. *Wilm* 3C **166**
Chapel Mdw. *Wors* 4D **76**
Chapel Pl. *Bolt* 2E **47**
Chapel Pl. *Urm* 5F **91**
Chapel Rd. *M22* 3B **136**
Chapel Rd. *Ald E* 5G **167**
Chapel Rd. *G'fld* 3E **61**
Chapel Rd. *Irlam* 5E **103**
Chapel Rd. *Oldh* 6A **72**
Chapel Rd. *P'wich* 2D **80**
Chapel Rd. *Sale* 4B **122**
Chapel Rd. *Swin* 4C **78**
Chapel St. *Ald E* 5G **167**
Chapel St. *Ash L* 2A **100**
Chapel St. *Aud* 1F **113**
Chapel St. *Bolt* 5C **32**
Chapel St. *Bury* 3D **36**
Chapel St. *Chea* 6H **137**
Chapel St. *Droy* 4D **90**
Chapel St. *Duk* 5H **99**
Chapel St. *Eccl* 4E **91**
Chapel St. *Eger* 1B **18**
Chapel St. *Farn* 1G **63**
Chapel St. *Haz G* 2E **153**
Chapel St. *Heyw* . . . . .3F **39** (in two parts)
Chapel St. *Hyde* 6B **114**
Chapel St. *Lees* 3A **74**
Chapel St. *Lev* 6C **110**
Chapel St. *L'boro* 5H **17**
Chapel St. *L Lev* 4B **48**
Chapel St. *Midd* . . . . .2E **69** (Manchester Old Rd.)
Chapel St. *Midd* . . . . .1H **69** (Sadler St., in two parts)
Chapel St. *Moss* 2E **89**
Chapel St. *P'wich* 5E **67**
Chapel St. *Rad* 2B **64**
Chapel St. *Roch* 1G **41**
Chapel St. *Rytn* 3B **56**
Chapel St. *Salf* 3B **94** (4C **4**)
Chapel St. *Shaw* 6F **43**
Chapel St. *Stal* 3E **101**
Chapel St. *Stoc* 1H **137**
Chapel St. *Swin* 2G **79**
Chapel St. *T'ton* 4G **21**
Chapel St. *Upperm* . . . . . .1F **61** (in two parts)
Chapel St. *Ward* 2A **16**
Chapel St. *Whitw* 1C **14**
Chapel St. *Woodl* 4H **129**
Chapel St. *Wors* 5B **76**
Chapel Ter. *M20* 2F **125**
Chapeltown Rd. *Brom X* 4F **19**
Chapeltown Rd. *Rad* 6G **49**
Chapeltown Rd. *Tur* 1G **19**
Chapeltown St. *M1* 5F **95** (1D **10**)
Chapel Vw. *Duk* 5A **100**
Chapel Wlk. *Eccl* 3H **91**
Chapel Wlk. *Had* 2H **117**
Chapel Wlk. *Marp* 5D **142**
Chapel Wlk. *Midd* 2F **69**
Chapel Wlk. *P'wich* 3E **81**
Chapel Wlk. *Stal* 4F **101**

A-Z Manchester 199

Chapel Wlk. *W'fld* 6F **51**
Chapel Walks.
   M2 . . . . .4D **94** (5H **5**)
Chapel Walks. *Chea H* . .1D **160**
Chapel Walks. *Sale* 4B **122**
Chapelway Gdns. *Rytn* . . .1B **56**
Chaplin Clo. *Salf* 1E **93**
Chapman Ct. *Hyde* 5H **115**
Chapman M. *M18* 2F **111**
   (in two parts)
Chapman Rd. *Hyde* 6A **116**
Chapman St. *M18* 1F **111**
Chapman St. *Bolt* 4F **31**
Chappell Rd. *Droy* 3A **98**
Chapter St. *M40* 1B **96**
Charcoal Rd. *Bow* 1A **144**
Charcoal Woods.
   Bow 2C **144**
Charcon Wlk. *Rytn* 3C **56**
Chard Dri. *M22* 4B **148**
Chardin Av. *Marp B* . . .3G **143**
Chard St. *Rad* 4G **49**
Charges St. *Ash L* 4F **99**
Chariot St. *Open* 5F **97**
Charlbury Av. *P'wich* 6A **68**
Charlbury Av. *Stoc* 2H **127**
Charlbury Way. *Rytn* 2E **57**
Charlecote Rd. *Poy* 3F **163**
Charles Av. *Aud* 6A **98**
Charles Av. *Marp* 4A **142**
Charles Ct. *Bolt* 5B **32**
Charles Ct. *Timp* 5B **134**
   (in two parts)
Charles Halle Rd. *M15* . .2E **109**
Charles Holden St. *Bolt* . .1H **45**
Charles La. *Miln* 6G **29**
Charles M. *Miln* 6G **29**
Charles Morris Clo.
   Fail 3H **85**
Charles Morris Ho. Fail . . .4G **85**
   (off Gildenhall)
Charles Rupert St.
   Rams 3B **32**
Charles Shaw Clo.
   Oldh 6H **57**
   (off Adswood Clo.)
Charles St. *M1* . . .6E **95** (3A **10**)
Charles St. *Ash L* 3H **99**
Charles St. *Bolt* 5B **32**
Charles St. *Bury* 2D **36**
Charles St. *Cad* 3C **118**
Charles St. *Dent* 2F **113**
Charles St. *Droy* 4G **97**
Charles St. *Duk* 5H **99**
Charles St. *Eger* 1B **18**
Charles St. *Farn* 6G **47**
Charles St. *Haz G* 2D **152**
Charles St. *Heyw* 5G **39**
Charles St. *Kear* 2G **63**
Charles St. *L'boro* 4E **17**
Charles St. *Oldh* 3A **72**
Charles St. *Rytn* 3B **56**
Charles St. *Salf* 1F **93**
   (in two parts)
Charles St. *Stoc* 4H **139**
   (in two parts)
Charles St. *Swin* 2D **78**
Charles St. *W'fld* 2D **66**
Charleston Clo. *Sale* 1F **133**
Charleston Sq. *Urm* 4D **104**
Charleston St. *Oldh* 5D **72**
Charlestown. 6A **70**
   (Manchester)
Charlestown. 6F **81**
   (Salford)
Charlestown Ct. *Ash L* . . .1H **99**
Charlestown Ind. Est.
   Ash L 1H **99**
Charlestown Rd. *M9* 1F **83**
Charlestown Rd. E.
   Stoc 2A **152**

Charlestown Rd. W.
   Stoc 2H **151**
Charles Wlk. *W'fld* 2D **66**
Charles Whittaker St.
   Roch 2B **26**
Charlesworth Av. *Bolt* . . .4D **46**
Charlesworth Av. *Dent* . .1F **129**
Charlesworth St. *M11* . . .5B **96**
Charlesworth St. *Stoc* . .4H **139**
Charley Av. *Salf* 1B **94**
Charlock Sq. *B'hth* 3D **132**
Charlock Wlk. *Part* 6D **118**
Charlotte La. *Grass* 4G **75**
Charlotte St. *M1* . . .4E **95** (6A **6**)
Charlotte St. *Bolt* 3A **32**
Charlotte St. *Chea* 6H **137**
Charlotte St. *Rams* 4D **12**
Charlotte St. *Stoc* 6B **128**
Charlton Av. *Eccl* 4F **91**
Charlton Av. *Hyde* 2E **115**
Charlton Av. *P'wich* 6F **67**
Charlton Ct. *P'wich* 6F **67**
Charlton Dri. *Sale* 5C **122**
Charlton Dri. *Swin* 1D **78**
Charlton Pl.
   Ard 6F **95** (3D **10**)
Charlton Rd. *M19* 5D **110**
Charminster Dri. *M8* 3D **82**
Charminster M. *Swin* 5F **79**
Charmouth Wlk. *M22* . . .1D **148**
Charnley Clo.
   M40 . . . . .2A **96** (2H **7**)
Charnley St. *W'fld* 1D **66**
Charnley Wlk. *M40* 2A **96**
Charnock Dri. *Bolt* 4A **32**
Charnville Rd. *Gat* 6D **136**
Charnwood Av. *Dent* 4B **112**
Charnwood Clo. *Ash L* . . .4G **87**
Charnwood Clo. *Shaw* . . .5C **42**
Charnwood Clo. *Wors* . . .1E **77**
Charnwood Cres.
   Haz G 5D **152**
Charnwood Rd. *M9* 4F **69**
Charnwood Rd.
   Woodl 4A **130**
Charter Av. *Rad* 5A **50**
Charter Clo. *Sale* 6F **121**
Charter Ho. *Eccl* 4H **91**
Charter St. *Alt* 1G **145**
Charter St. *M3* 2D **94** (1H **5**)
Charter St. *Oldh* 1E **73**
Charter St. *Roch* 1G **41**
Chartist Ho. Hyde 5C **114**
   (off Union St.)
Chartwell Clo. *Salf* 3F **93**
Chartwell Dri. *M23* 4D **134**
Chasefield. *Bow* 3C **144**
Chaseley Rd. *Roch* 3G **27**
Chaseley Rd. *Salf* 1E **93**
Chase, The. *M4* 2E **95** (1B **6**)
Chase, The. *Bolt* 6E **31**
Chase, The. *Wors* 6A **78**
Chasetown Clo. *M23* 5D **134**
Chassen Av. *Urm* 5C **104**
Chassen Ct. *Urm* 6D **104**
Chassen Rd. *Bolt* 6F **31**
Chassen Rd. *Urm* 5D **104**
Chataway Rd. *M8* 3E **83**
Chatburn Av. *Roch* 6D **40**
Chatburn Ct. *Shaw* 5F **43**
Chatburn Gdns. *Heyw* 3B **38**
Chatburn Rd. *M21* 1A **124**
Chatburn Rd. *Bolt* 2D **30**
Chatburn Sq. *Roch* 5D **40**
Chatcombe Rd. *M22* 3G **147**
Chatfield Rd. *M21* 1H **123**
Chatford Clo.
   Salf 1C **94** (1E **5**)
Chatham Ct. *M20* 3E **125**
Chatham Gdns. *Bolt* 2H **45**
Chatham Gro. *M20* 3E **125**

Chatham Ho. *Stoc* 3G **139**
Chatham Pl. *Bolt* 2H **45**
Chatham Rd. *Gort* 4G **111**
Chatham Rd. *Old T* 4A **108**
Chatham St. *M1* . . .4F **95** (6C **6**)
Chatham St. *Hyde* 2C **130**
Chatham St. *Stoc* 4E **139**
Chatley Rd. *Eccl* 4B **90**
Chatley St. *M3* 1D **94** (1A **6**)
Chatswood Av. *Stoc* 5H **139**
Chatsworth Av. *P'wich* 5F **67**
Chatsworth Clo. *Bury* 2E **51**
Chatsworth Clo. *Droy* 2F **97**
Chatsworth Clo. *Shaw* 5H **43**
Chatsworth Clo. *Timp* 6C **134**
Chatsworth Clo. *Urm* 5G **105**
Chatsworth Ct. *M9* 4C **68**
   (off Deanswood Dri.)
Chatsworth Ct. *Stoc* 6A **140**
Chatsworth Cres.
   Stret 4H **105**
Chatsworth Gro. *M16* 5B **108**
Chatsworth Gro. *L Lev* . . .3A **48**
Chatsworth M. *Bram* 3F **151**
Chatsworth Rd. *M18* 2E **111**
Chatsworth Rd.
   Chea H 1D **160**
Chatsworth Rd. *Droy* 3G **97**
Chatsworth Rd. *Eccl* 1H **91**
Chatsworth Rd. *Haz G* . . .4F **153**
Chatsworth Rd. *H Lane* . .1D **164**
Chatsworth Rd. *Rad* 2D **48**
Chatsworth Rd. *Stret* 4A **106**
Chatsworth Rd. *Wilm* 5B **166**
Chatsworth Rd. *Wors* 5B **78**
Chatsworth St. *Oldh* 4G **73**
Chatsworth St. *Roch* 6E **15**
Chatterton. *Rams* 3A **12**
   (off Well St. N.)
Chatterton Clo. *M20* 3G **125**
Chatterton Old La.
   Rams 3A **12**
Chatterton Rd. *Rams* 3A **12**
Chattock St. *M16* 4C **108**
Chatton Clo. *Bury* 3F **35**
Chatwell Ct. *Miln* 1G **43**
Chatwood Rd. *M40* 1D **84**
Chaucer Av. *Dent* 2G **129**
Chaucer Av. *Droy* 4A **98**
Chaucer Av. *Rad* 3E **49**
Chaucer Av. *Stoc* 6F **111**
Chaucer Ho. *Stoc* 1G **127**
Chaucer M. *Stoc* 2B **140**
Chaucer Ri. *Duk* 6E **101**
Chaucer Rd. *Midd* 5B **54**
Chaucer St. *Bolt* 4H **31**
Chaucer St. *Oldh* 3C **72**
Chaucer St. *Roch* 3C **40**
Chaucer St. *Rytn* 2C **56**
Chaucer Wlk.
   M13 . . . . . . .1G **109** (6F **11**)
Chaumont Way.
   Ash L 2H **99**
Chauncy Rd. *M40* 3E **85**
Chaytor Av. *M40* 4A **84**
Cheadle. 5H **137**
Cheadle Av. *Salf* 4E **81**
Cheadle Ct. *Chea H* 4A **150**
Cheadle Grn. *Chea* 5H **137**
Cheadle Heath. 4C **138**
Cheadle Hulme. 3C **150**
Cheadle Hulme Recreation
   Cen. 6D **150**
Cheadle Old Rd. *Stoc* 4D **138**
Cheadle Point. *Chea* 5B **138**
Cheadle Rd.
   Chea & Chea H 1A **150**
Cheadle Sq. *Rams* 6A **32**
Cheadle St. *M11* 5F **97**
Cheadle Swimming &
   Recreation Cen.
   . . . . .1A **150**

Cheadle Wood.
   Chea H 5A **150**
Cheam Clo. *M11* 6D **96**
Cheam Rd. *Timp* 3H **133**
Cheapside. *M2* 4D **94** (5H **5**)
Cheapside. *Hyde* 4C **114**
Cheap Side. *Midd* 5A **54**
Cheapside. *Oldh* 2C **72**
Cheapside Sq. *Bolt* 6B **32**
Cheddar St. *M18* 2F **111**
Chedlee Dri. *Chea H* 4A **150**
Chedlin Dri. *M23* 1G **147**
Chedworth Cres. *L Hul* . . .3C **62**
Chedworth Dri. *M23* 5H **135**
Chedworth Gro. Bolt 2A **46**
   (off Parrot St.)
Cheeryble St.
   Droy & M11 . . . . . . .5H **97**
   (in two parts)
Cheesden Wlk. *W'fld* 6G **51**
Cheetham. 5B **82**
Cheetham Av. *Midd* 6B **54**
Cheetham Fold Rd.
   Hyde 1B **130**
Cheetham Hill. 4C **82**
Cheetham Gdns. *Stal* 4F **101**
Cheetham Hill. *Shaw* 1F **57**
Cheetham Hill. *Whitw* . . .2H **15**
Cheetham Hill Rd. *M4, M3 &*
   M8 . . . . .2E **95** (1A **6**)
Cheetham Hill Rd. *M8* . . .3B **82**
Cheetham Hill Rd.
   Duk & Stal 1B **114**
Cheetham Pde. *M8* 3B **82**
Cheetham Pk. Cen. *M8* . . .6B **82**
Cheetham Pl. *Bred* 5F **129**
Cheetham Rd. *Swin* 4G **79**
Cheetham Cres. *Rytn* 3E **57**
Cheetham St. *M40* 6G **83**
Cheetham St. *Fail* 3G **85**
   (in two parts)
Cheetham St. *Midd* 1H **69**
Cheetham St. *Oldh* 2F **73**
Cheetham St. *Rad* 4A **50**
Cheetham St. *Roch* 3H **27**
Cheetham St. *Shaw* 1G **57**
Cheetham Wlk. *Hyde* . . .4C **114**
Cheetwood Rd. *M8* 1D **94**
Cheetwood St. *M8* 1C **94**
Chelbourne Dri. *Oldh* . . .1H **85**
Chelburn Clo. *Stoc* 6D **140**
Chelburn Gro. *Bolt* 4H **45**
Chelburn Vw. *L'boro* 6G **17**
Cheldon Wlk. *M40* 5C **84**
Chelford Av. *Bolt* 6C **18**
Chelford Clo. *M13* 2H **109**
Chelford Clo. *Alt* 5G **133**
Chelford Clo. *Midd* 5C **54**
Chelford Ct. *Hand* 2A **160**
Chelford Dri. *Swin* 1E **79**
Chelford Gro. *Stoc* 6E **139**
Chelford Rd. *M16* 4A **108**
Chelford Rd. *Hand* 2H **159**
Chelford Rd. *Sale* 1E **135**
Chellow Ct. *Moss* 2D **88**
Chellow Dene. *Moss* 2D **88**
Chell St. *M12* 3B **110**
Chelmer Gro. *Heyw* 2C **38**
Chelmsford Av. *M40* 1D **96**
Chelmsford Rd. *Stoc* 3E **139**
Chelmsford St. *Oldh* 4C **72**
Chelmsford Wlk.
   Dent 6G **113**
Chelsea Av. *Rad* 3D **48**
Chelsea Clo. *Shaw* 6F **43**
Chelsea Rd. *M40* 6B **84**
Chelsea Rd. *Bolt* 4H **45**
Chelsea Rd. *Urm* 6G **103**
Chelsea St. *Bury* 2D **50**
Chelsea St. *Roch* 6F **27**
Chelsfield Gro. *M21* 1B **124**
Chelston Av. *M40* 1D **84**
Chelston Dri. *H Grn* 1G **159**

Cheltenham Cres. *Salf* . . .3A **82**
Cheltenham Dri. *Sale* 5C **122**
Cheltenham Grn. *Midd* . . .3A **70**
Cheltenham Rd. *M21* . . .5H **107**
Cheltenham Rd. *Midd* 3A **70**
Cheltenham Rd. *Stoc* 4C **138**
Cheltenham St. *Oldh* 6F **57**
Cheltenham St. *Roch* . . .1D **40**
Cheltenham St. *Salf* 1G **93**
Chelt Wlk. *M22* 3H **147**
Chelwood Clo. *Bolt* 4B **18**
Chelwood Dri. *Droy* 3H **97**
Cliclworth Mill. *Bram* 4E **151**
Chemist St. *Rams* 4B **32**
Chendre Clo. *Swin* 1F **79**
Chendre Rd. *M9* 6B **70**
Cheney Clo. *M11* 6F **97**
Chepstow Av. *Sale* 6E **121**
Chepstow Clo. *Roch* 3B **26**
Chepstow Dri. *Haz G* . .3G **153**
Chepstow Dri. *Oldh* 6F **57**
Chepstow Rd. *M21* 6G **107**
Chepstow Rd. *Swin* 1G **79**
Chepstow St.
   M1 . . . . . . .5D **94** (2H **9**)
Chepstow St. S.
   M1 . . . . . . .5D **94** (2H **9**)
Chequerbent 6A **44**
Chequers Rd. *M21* 1H **123**
Cherington Clo. *M23* . . .1H **135**
Cherington Clo. *Hand* . .4B **160**
Cherington Rd. *Chea* . .1G **149**
Cheriton Av. *Sale* 4C **122**
Cheriton Clo. *Hyde* 5H **115**
Cheriton Dri. *Bolt* 1G **47**
Cheriton Ri. *Stoc* 5G **141**
Cheriton Rd. *Urm* 4H **103**
Cherrington Dri. *Roch* . . .5D **40**
Cherry Av. *Ash L* 5F **87**
Cherry Av. *Bury* 2G **37**
Cherry Av. *Oldh* 6G **73**
Cherry Clo. *Bury* 6E **37**
Cherry Clo. *Stoc* 4F **141**
Cherry Ct. *Sale* 5A **122**
Cherry Ct. *Timp* 4C **134**
Cherry Cft. *Rom* 2C **142**
   (in two parts)
Cherry Dri. *Swin* 3G **79**
Cherry Gro. *Roch* 3C **26**
Cherry Gro. *Rytn* 1A **56**
Cherry Gro. *Stal* 5F **101**
Cherry Hall Dri. *Shaw* . . .6C **42**
Cherry Hinton. *Oldh* 1B **72**
Cherry Holt Av. *Stoc* . . .5B **126**
Cherry La. *Sale* 1E **133**
Cherry Orchard Clo.
   Bram 4F **151**
Cherry St. *P'wich* 4G **67**
Cherryton Wlk. *M13* . . .1G **109**
   (6E **11**)
Cherry Tree. 1C **142**
Cherry Tree Av. *Farn* . . .1B **62**
Cherry Tree Av. *Poy* 4F **163**
Cherrytree Clo. *Timp* . .6B **134**
Cherry Tree Clo. *Wilm* . .1H **167**
Cherry Tree Ct. *Salf* 3G **93**
Cherry Tree Ct. *Stoc* . . .1C **152**
Cherry Tree Dri. *Haz G* . .5F **153**
Cherry Tree Est. *Rom* . . .1D **142**
Cherry Tree La. *Bury* . . .4A **36**
Cherry Tree La. *Rom* . . .1C **142**
Cherry Tree La. *Rost* . . .6A **144**
Cherry Tree La. *Stoc* . . .6C **140**
Cherrytree Rd. *M23* . . .2F **135**
Cherry Tree Rd.
   Chea H 4B **150**
Cherry Tree Wlk.
   Moss 2D **88**
Cherry Tree Wlk. *Stret* . .6C **106**
Cherry Tree Way. *Bolt* . . .1D **32**
Cherry Wlk. *Chea H* 5E **151**

Cherry Wlk. *Part* 6B **118**
   (in two parts)
Cherrywood. *Chad* 2D **70**
Cherrywood Clo. *Wors* . . .3D **76**
Chertsey Clo. *M18* 2G **111**
Chertsey Clo. *Shaw* 5F **43**
Cherwell Av. *Heyw* 2C **38**
Cherwell Clo. *Chea H* . .6C **150**
Cherwell Clo. *Oldh* 2A **86**
Cherwell Clo. *W'fld* 1E **67**
Cherwell Ct. *Heyw* 2D **38**
   (off Peel La.)
Chesham. 6G **23**
Chesham Av. *M22* 1A **148**
Chesham Av. *Bolt* 3A **32**
Chesham Av. *Roch* 6D **40**
Chesham Av. *Urm* 4A **104**
Chesham Clo. *Wilm* 5C **166**
Chesham Cres. *Bury* 2F **37**
Chesham Fold Rd.
   Bury 2F **37**
   (in two parts)
Chesham Ho. *Salf* 4F **93**
Chesham Ind. Est.
   Bury 1E **37**
Chesham Pl. *Bow* 3E **145**
Chesham Rd. *Bury* 1D **36**
Chesham Rd. *Oldh* 3G **73**
Chesham Rd. *Wilm* 5C **166**
Chesham Rd. N. *Bury* . . .1E **37**
   (off Chesham Rd.)
Chesham St. *Bolt* 5F **45**
Cheshill Ct. *Salf* 5B **82**
Cheshire Clo. *Strct* 6B **106**
Cheshire Ct. *Rams* 3F **13**
Cheshire Gdns. *M14* . . .6E **109**
Cheshire Rd. *Carr* 6G **89**
Cheshire Rd. *Part* 6B **118**
Cheshire Sq. *Carr* 6G **89**
Cheshires, The. *Moss* . . .2F **89**
Cheshire St. *Moss* 3F **89**
Chesney Av. *Chad* 1E **85**
Chesshyre Av.
   M4 . . . . . . .4H **95** (5H **7**)
Chessington Ri. *Swin* . . .6G **65**
Chester Av. *Duk* 6C **100**
Chester Av. *Hale* 3H **145**
Chester Av. *L Lev* 3B **48**
Chester Av. *Sale* 2D **132**
Chester Av. *Urm* 4G **105**
Chester Av. *W'fld* 2E **67**
Chester Clo. *Cad* 4B **118**
Chester Clo. *L Lev* 3B **48**
Chester Dri. *Rams* 5C **12**
Chesterfield Gro.
   Ash L 2B **100**
Chesterfield St. *Oldh* . . .3F **73**
Chesterfield Way.
   Dent 1F **129**
Chestergate. *Stoc* 2F **139**
   (in two parts)
Chester Pl. *Rytn* 3B **56**
Chester Rd. *M16 & M15*
   . . . . .2H **107** (6A **8**)
Chester Rd. *Haz G* 6D **152**
Chester Rd.
   Mere & Rost 6A **144**
Chester Rd.
   Stret & M16 . . . . .2C **122**
Chester Rd. *Tyl* 3A **76**
Chester Rd.
   Woodf & Poy 6F **151**
Chester's Cft. Pk. Home Est.
   Chea H 2C **160**
Chester Sq. *Ash L* 3G **99**
Chester St.
   M15 & M1 . .6D **94** (4H **9**)
Chester St. *Bury* 1E **37**

Chester St. *Dent* 5F **113**
Chester St. *Oldh* 4A **72**
Chester St. *P'wich* 4E **67**
Chester St. *Rams* 4B **32**
Chester St. *Roch* 5A **28**
Chester St. *Stoc* 2F **139**
Chester St. *Swin* 4E **79**
Chesterton Dri. *Bolt* 2C **44**
Chesterton Gro. *Droy* . . .3A **98**
Chesterton Rd. *M23* . . .3D **134**
Chesterton Rd. *Oldh* 5F **57**
Chesterton Wlk. *M23* . . .4E **135**
Choctor Wlk. Bolt 3A **32**
   (off Boardman St.)
Chester Walks. *Rom* . . .2G **141**
   (in two parts)
Chestnut Av. *M21* 1H **123**
Chestnut Av. *Bury* 3F **37**
Chestnut Av. *Cad* 4B **118**
Chestnut Av. *Chea* 6A **138**
Chestnut Av. *Droy* 2G **97**
Chestnut Av. *T'ton* 6A **22**
Chestnut Av. *W'fld* 2D **66**
Chestnut Av. *Wors* 1F **77**
Chestnut Clo. *Bolt* 3F **45**
Chestnut Clo. *Oldh* 1H **73**
Chestnut Clo. *Stal* 5E **101**
Chestnut Clo. *Wilm* 6A **160**
Chestnut Ct. *Bram* 3F **151**
Chestnut Ct. *Bury* 5F **23**
Chestnut Cres. *Oldh* 1E **87**
Chestnut Dri. *Bury* 4F **23**
Chestnut Dri. *Poy* 4F **163**
Chestnut Dri. *Sale* 2F **133**
Chestnut Gdns. *Dent* . . .5E **113**
Chestnut Gdns. *Heyw* . . .4E **39**
Chestnut Gro. *Fail* 5F **85**
Chestnut Gro. *Rad* 1G **65**
Chestnut Pl. *Roch* 3B **28**
Chestnut Rd. *Eccl* 1C **90**
Chestnut St. *Chad* 6F **71**
Chestnut Vs. *Stoc* 1E **139**
Chestnut Wlk. *Part* 6B **118**
Chestnut Way. *L'boro* . . .3D **16**
Chesworth Clo. *Stoc* . . .3H **139**
Chesworth Ct. *Droy* 4H **97**
Chesworth Fold. *Stoc* . .3H **139**
Chesworth Wlk.
   M15 . . . . . . .1C **108** (5E **9**)
   (off Jackson St.)
Chetham Clo. *Salf* 6H **93**
Chetham's Library. 3H **5**
Chetwyn Av. *Brom X* 4E **19**
Chetwyn Av. *Rytn* 3A **56**
Chetwynd Av. *Urm* 6E **105**
Chetwynd Clo. *Sale* . . .3G **121**
Chevassut St.
   M15 . . . . . . .1C **108** (5E **9**)
Chevin Gdns. *Bram* 6A **152**
Chevington Dri. *M9* 5F **83**
Chevington Dri. *Stoc* . . .6H **125**
Chevington Gdns. *Bolt* . .2A **32**
Cheviot Av. *Chea H* 3B **150**
Cheviot Av. *Oldh* 6C **72**
Cheviot Av. *Rytn* 4A **56**
Cheviot Clo. *Bolt* 6B **18**
Cheviot Clo. *Bury* 2G **35**
Cheviot Clo. *Chad* 4G **71**
Cheviot Clo. *Midd* 1D **70**
Cheviot Clo. *Miln* 5G **29**
Cheviot Clo. *Rams* 5E **13**
Cheviot Clo. *Salf* 2E **93**
Cheviot Clo. *Stoc* 6F **127**
Cheviot Clo. *Oldh* 6C **72**
Cheviot Rd. *Haz G* 4B **152**
Cheviots, The. *Shaw* 5E **43**
Cheviot St. *M3* 2D **94** (1H **5**)
Chevithorne Clo. *Alt* 5D **132**
Chevril Clo.
   M15 . . . . . .1E **109** (5A **10**)
Chevron Clo. *Roch* 2B **40**

Chevron Clo. *Salf* 3H **93**
Chevron Pl. *Alt* 4F **133**
Chew Moor. 3A **44**
Chew Va. *Duk* 6D **100**
Chew Va. *G'fld* 4F **61**
Chew Valley Rd. *G'fld* . . .3E **61**
Chicago Av. *Man A* 6H **147**
Chichester Bus. Cen.
   Roch 4A **28**
Chichester Clo. *L'boro* . . .6E **17**
Chichester Clo. *Sale* . . .6F **121**
Chichester Cres. *Chad* . . .6G **55**
Chichester Rd. *M15* . . .2C **108**
   (Bold St.)
Chichester Rd.
   M15 . . . . . .1D **108** (6G **9**)
   (Old Birley St.)
Chichester Rd. *Rom* 1A **142**
Chichester Rd. S.
   M15 . . . . .3C **108**
Chichester St. *Roch* 4A **28**
Chichester Way. *Dent* . .6G **113**
Chidlow Av. *M20* 2E **125**
Chidwall Rd. *M22* 3H **147**
Chief St. *Oldh* 3E **73**
Chiffon Way.
   Salf 2B **94** (2C **4**)
Chigwell Clo. *M22* 6B **136**
Chilcombe Wlk. M9 . . . .4G **69**
   (off Brockford Dri.)
Chilcote Av. *Sale* 5G **121**
Childwall Clo. *Bolt* 5A **46**
Chilham Rd. *Eccl* 1H **91**
Chilham Rd. *Wors* 1G **77**
Chilham St. *Bolt* 4F **45**
Chilham St. *Swin* 5E **79**
Chillington Wlk. *Dent* . .6E **113**
Chilmark Dri. *M23* 5G **135**
Chiltern Av. *Chea H* 3B **150**
Chiltern Av. *Urm* 4A **104**
Chiltern Clo. *Haz G* 4B **152**
Chiltern Clo. *Rams* 5E **13**
Chiltern Clo. *Shaw* 5D **42**
Chiltern Clo. *Wors* 3G **77**
Chiltern Dri. *Bolt* 0E **33**
Chiltern Dri. *Bury* 1H **35**
Chiltern Dri. *Hale* 3H **145**
Chiltern Dri. *Rytn* 3A **56**
Chiltern Dri. *Stoc* 1A **152**
Chiltern Dri. *Swin* 5F **79**
Chiltern Gdns. *Sale* 3C **134**
Chiltern Rd. *Rams* 5E **13**
Chilton Av. *Chad* 3G **71**
Chilton Dri. *Midd* 2C **70**
Chilworth St. *M14* 5F **109**
Chime Bank. *M8* 4D **82**
China La. *M1* 4F **95** (6C **6**)
China La. *Bolt* 5B **32**
Chinese Arts Cen. 4B **6**
Chingford Wlk. *M13* 3B **110**
   (off Bates St.)
Chinley Av. *M40* 3A **84**
Chinley Av. *Stret* 3A **106**
Chinley Clo. *Bram* 2G **151**
Chinley Clo. *Sale* 6D **122**
Chinley Clo. *Stoc* 6D **126**
Chinley St. *Salf* 6F **81**
Chinwell Vw. *M19* 6C **110**
Chip Hill Rd. *Bolt* 3D **44**
Chippendale Pl. *Ash L* . . .6A **88**
Chippenham Av. *Stoc* . .4D **140**
Chippenham Ct.
   M4 . . . . . . .3H **95** (4G **7**)
Chippenham Rd.
   M1 . . . . .3G **95** (4F **7**)
Chipping Fold. *Miln* 6F **29**
Chipping Rd. *Bolt* 3D **30**
Chipping Sq. *M12* 3B **110**
Chipstead Av. *M12* 2A **110**
Chirmside St. *Bury* 4H **35**
Chirton Wlk. *M40* 4A **84**

Chiseldon Av. *M22* 3C **148**
Chiselhurst St. *M8* 3C **82**
Chisholm Ct. *Midd* 6H **53**
Chisholme Clo. *G'mnt* 1G **21**
Chisholm St. *Open* 6F **97**
Chisledon Av. *Salf* 5B **82**
Chiseldon Clo. Bolt 2A **46**
(off Bantry St.)
Chislehurst Av. *Urm* 4E **105**
Chislehurst Clo. *Bury* 4H **35**
Chiswick Dri. *Bolt* 2B **48**
Chiswick Rd. *M20* 6G **125**
Chisworth Clo. *Bram* 2G **151**
Chisworth St. *Bolt* 2D **32**
Chisworth Wlk. *Dent* 1G **129**
Choir St. *Salf* 1C **94**
Chokeberry Clo. *B'hth* . . .3D **132**
Cholmondeley Av. *Timp* .2G **133**
Cholmondeley Rd. *Salf* . . .1B **92**
Chomlea. *Alt* 1D **144**
Chomlea Mnr. *Salf* 1C **92**
Choral Gro. *Salf* 6A **82**
Chorley Clo. *Bury* 4F **35**
Chorley Hall Clo.
  Ald E 5F **167**
Chorley Hall La. *Ald E* . . .5F **167**
Chorley New Rd. *Bolt* . . .6A **30**
Chorley Old Rd. *Bolt* 2A **30**
Chorley Rd. *Sale* 1E **135**
Chorley Rd. *Swin* 2E **79**
Chorley St. *Bolt* 5A **32**
Chorley St. *Stret* 3F **107**
Chorley Wood Av.
  M19 . . . . .3B **126**
Chorlton Brook Ho.
  Chea 5A **138**
  (off Stockport Rd.)
Chorlton-cum-Hardy.
  . . . . .2G **107**
Chorlton Dri. *Chea* 5A **138**
Chorlton Ees Nature Reserve.
  . . . . .2F **123**
Chorlton Fold. 1F **91**
Chorlton Fold. *Eccl* 6D **78**
  (in two parts)
Chorlton Fold. *Woodl* . . .4A **130**
Chorlton Grn. *M21* 1G **123**
Chorlton Gro. *Stoc* 4B **140**
Chorlton Leisure Cen.
  . . . . .6H **107**
Chorlton Pl. *Chor H* 6H **107**
Chorlton Rd. *M16 & M15*
  . . . . .3B **108** (4D **8**)
Chorlton St.
  M1 . . . . . . .5E **95** (1B **10**)
Chorlton St.
  M16 . . . . . .2A **108** (6A **8**)
Chorlton upon Medlock.
  . . . . .2H **109**
Chorltonville. 3H **123**
Chorlton Water Pk. 5H **123**
Chretien Rd. *M22* 1B **136**
Christ Chu. Av.
  Salf 3H **93** (4A **4**)
Christchurch Clo. *Bolt* . . .2H **33**
Christchurch La. *Bolt* 2H **33**
Christchurch Rd. *Sale* . . .4E **121**
Christie Fields Office Pk.
  M21 . . . . .4B **124**
Christie Rd. *Stret* 4E **107**
Christie St. *Stoc* 4A **140**
Christine St. *Shaw* 6F **43**
  (in two parts)
Christleton Av. *Stoc* 4F **127**
Christleton Way.
  Hand 2H **159**
Christopher Acre.
  Roch 2A **26**
Christopher St. *M40* 1F **97**
Christopher St. *Salf* 4H **93**
Chronnell Dri. *Bolt* 5G **33**
Chudleigh Clo. *Alt* 5D **132**

Chudleigh Clo. *Bram* 2A **152**
Chudleigh Rd. *M8* 1C **82**
Chulsey St. *Bolt* 3F **45**
Church Av. *M40* 6C **84**
Church Av. *Bolt* 3G **45**
Church Av. *Dent* 1G **129**
Church Av. *Hyde* 1D **130**
Church Av. *Midd* 1D **54**
Church Av. *Salf* 3D **92**
Church Av. *Styal* 5E **159**
Church Bank. *Bolt* 6C **32**
Church Bank. *Bow* 3D **144**
Churchbank. Stal 3H **101**
Church Brow. *Bow* 3D **144**
Church Brow. *Hyde* 6B **114**
Church Brow. *Midd* 6A **54**
Church Brow. *Mot* 4C **116**
Church Clo. *Aud* 6F **99**
Church Clo. *Hand* 4H **159**
Church Clo. *Rad* 1B **64**
Church Clo. *Rams* 4D **12**
Church Ct. *Bury* 2E **37**
Church Ct. *Chad* 4A **72**
Church Ct. *Duk* 4H **99**
Church Ct. *Hale* 4G **145**
Church Ct. *Rams* 1A **12**
Church Cft. *Bury* 3F **51**
Churchdale Rd. *M9* 5D **68**
Church Dri. *P'wich* 5E **67**
Churchfield. *M21* 1G **123**
Churchfield Clo. *Rad* 6F **49**
Churchfield Rd. *Salf* 6B **80**
Churchfields. *Aud* 6E **99**
Churchfields. *Bow* 4D **144**
Churchfields. *Dob* 5A **60**
Churchfields. *Sale* 3F **121**
Churchfield Wlk. M11 . . . .5C **96**
  (off Outrington Dri.)
Churchgate. *Bolt* 6B **32**
Churchgate. *Stoc* 2H **139**
Churchgate. *Urm* 6G **105**
Church Gate Bldgs.
  M1 . . . . . . .5G **95** (1E **11**)
Church Grn. *Rad* 3B **50**
Church Grn. *Salf* 2F **93**
Church Gro. *Eccl* 4G **91**
Church Gro. *Haz G* 3E **153**
Churchill Av. *M16* 5B **108**
Churchill Av. *A'wth* 4D **34**
Churchill Clo. *Heyw* 5G **39**
Churchill Ct. *Salf* 3F **93**
Churchill Cres. *Marp* 4B **142**
Churchill Cres. *Stoc* 6G **111**
Churchill Dri. *L Lev* 4C **48**
Churchill Pl. *Eccl* 1E **91**
Churchill Rd. *Alt* 4F **133**
Churchill St. *Bolt* 6E **33**
Churchill St. *Oldh* 3E **73**
Churchill St. *Roch* 2E **27**
  (in two parts)
Churchill St. *Stoc* 6F **127**
Churchill St. E. *Oldh* 3E **73**
Churchill Way. *Salf* 3G **93**
Churchill Way. *Traf P* 6C **92**
Church La. *M9* 4G **83**
  (Kingscliffe St.)
Church La. *M9* 3F **83**
  (Water St.)
Church La. *Ald E* 4G **167**
Church La. *Burn* 3B **126**
Church La. *Bury* 6B **24**
Church La. *Marp* 5D **142**
Church La. *Moss* 2F **89**
Church La. *Oldh* 2D **72**
Church La. *P'wich* 5E **67**
Church La. *Rams* 1A **12**
Church La. *Roch* 4H **27**
Church La. *Rom* 1A **142**
Church La. *Sale* 3G **121**
Church La. *Salf* 2G **81**
Church La. *Upperm* 6D **60**
Church La. *W'fld* 1C **66**

Church La. *Woodf* 5E **161**
Churchley Clo. *Stoc* 5C **138**
Churchley Rd. *Stoc* 4C **138**
Church Lodge. *Stoc* 1A **138**
Church Mnr. *Stoc* 5D **126**
Church Mdw. *G'fld* 4G **75**
Church Mdw. *Hyde* 4A **114**
Church Mdw. *Uns* 2F **51**
Church Mdw. Gdns.
  Hyde 4A **114**
Church Meadows.
  Bolt 2H **33**
Church M. *Dent* 4E **113**
Church M. *Rad* 6A **50**
Church Pl. *Heyw* 3F **39**
Church Pl. *Oldh* 2D **72**
Church Rd. *M22* 2B **136**
Church Rd. *Bolt* 3E **31**
Church Rd. *Chea H* 5D **150**
Church Rd. *Eccl* 3H **91**
Church Rd.
  Farn & Kear 1G **63**
Church Rd. *Gat* 6E **137**
Church Rd. *G'fld* 4G **75**
Church Rd. *Hand* 3H **159**
Church Rd. *Holl* 3F **117**
Church Rd. *Midd* 2D **70**
Church Rd. *Rad* 1A **64**
Church Rd. *Rams* 1G **13**
Church Rd. *Roch* 5B **28**
Church Rd. *Sale* 5D **122**
Church Rd. *Shaw* 1F **57**
Church Rd. *Stoc* 1F **139**
Church Rd. *Upperm* 1F **61**
Church Rd. *Urm* 1B **120**
Church Rd. *Wilm* 5B **166**
Church Rd. *Wors* 6F **63**
Church Rd. E. *Sale* 5D **122**
Church Rd. W. *Sale* 5C **122**
Churchside. *Farn* 2D **62**
Churchside Clo. *M9* 1F **83**
Church Stile. *Roch* 4H **27**
Churchstoke Wlk.
  M23 . . . . .4E **135**
Churchston Av. *Bram* . . .3H **151**
Church St. *M4* . . .3E **95** (4B **6**)
Church St. *A'wth* 4C **34**
Church St. *Alt* 6F **133**
Church St. *Ash L* 3H **99**
Church St. *Aud* 6E **99**
Church St. *Bolt* 6H **19**
Church St. *Bred* 4G **129**
Church St. *Bury* 2E **37**
Church St. *Chea* 5H **137**
Church St. *Del* 3G **59**
Church St. *Droy* 4B **98**
Church St. *Duk* 4H **99**
Church St. *Eccl* 3G **91**
  (in three parts)
Church St. *Fail* 3F **85**
Church St. *Farn* 1G **63**
Church St. *Had* 3H **117**
Church St. *Heyw* 3F **39**
Church St. *Hyde* 6B **114**
Church St. *Kear* 2G **63**
Church St. *Lees* 4A **74**
Church St. *L'boro* 4E **17**
Church St. *L Lev* 4H **47**
Church St. *Marp* 5D **142**
Church St. *Midd* 5A **54**
Church St. *Miln* 1F **43**
Church St. *Oldh* 2D **72**
Church St. *Rams* 3E **13**
Church St.
  Roch (OL11) 5G **27**
Church St.
  Roch (OL16) 6B **16**
Church St. *Rytn* 3B **56**
Church St. *Salf* 2F **93**
Church St. *Stal* 3E **101**
Church St. *Stoc* 6F **127**
  (in two parts)

Church St. *Stret* 6C **106**
Church St. *Swin* 3H **79**
  (Bolton Rd.)
Church St. *Swin* 3E **79**
  (Chorley Rd.)
Church St. *Wals* 1F **35**
Church St. *Whitw* 1C **14**
Church St. *Wilm* 2E **167**
Church St. E. *Oldh* 1A **74**
Church St. E. *Rad* 4A **50**
  (in two parts)
Church St. Ind. Est.
  Midd 5A **54**
Church St. W. *Rad* 4H **49**
Church Ter. *Hand* 3H **159**
Church Ter. *Miln* 6G **29**
Church Ter. *Oldh* 2D **72**
Church Ter. *Sale* 3A **122**
Church Ter. *Stoc* 1F **139**
Church Ter. *Ward* 2A **16**
Churchtown Av. *Bolt* 6H **33**
Church Vw. *Bow* 4D **144**
Church Vw. *Droy* 4B **98**
Church Vw. *Fail* 3F **85**
Church Vw. *Hyde* 6B **114**
Church Vw. *Irlam* 5E **103**
Church Vw. *Mot* 4C **116**
Church Vw. *Roch* 1A **26**
Church Vw. *Styal* 5E **159**
Church Wlk. *Alt* 6F **133**
Church Wlk. *Farn* 1E **63**
Church Wlk. *G'mnt* 2F **21**
Church Wlk. *Rytn* 3B **56**
Church Wlk. *Stal* 3E **101**
  (in two parts)
Church Wlk. *Swin* 6F **65**
Church Wlk. *Wilm* 3C **166**
Churchwood Rd. *M20* . . .6F **125**
Churnet St. *M40* 6F **83**
Churning Ter. *Irlam* 4F **103**
Churston Av. *M9* 5G **69**
Churton Av. *M14* 5F **109**
Churton Av. *Sale* 6H **121**
Churton Rd. *M18* 4E **111**
Churwell Av. *Stoc* 5B **126**
Cicero St. *M9* 3H **83**
Cicero St. *Oldh* 6E **57**
Cilder's Villa. *Oldh* 5D **74**
Cinder Hill La. *Chad* 3G **55**
Cinder La. *Bolt* 2D **30**
Cinder St. *M4* 3G **95** (3E **7**)
Cinnabar Dri. *Midd* 6H **53**
Cinnamon Clo. *Roch* 3F **27**
Cinnamon St. *Roch* 3F **27**
Cipher St. *M4* 2G **95** (2E **7**)
Circle Ct. *Stret* 3H **105**
Circle S. *Traf P* 1E **107**
Circle, The. *Stret* 3H **105**
Circuit, The. *M20* 4F **125**
Circuit, The. *Ald E* 6E **167**
Circuit, The. *Chea H* 6C **150**
Circuit, The. *Stoc* 5D **138**
Circuit, The. *Wilm* 4A **166**
Circular Rd. *M20* 4F **125**
Circular Rd. *Dent* 5E **113**
Circular Rd. *P'wich* 1F **81**
Cirencester Clo. *L Hul* . . .3C **62**
Ciss La. *Urm* 5G **105**
Citrus Way. *Salf* 3G **93**
City Av. *Dent* 5E **113**
City Course Trad. Est.
  Open 6C **96**
City Ct. Trad. Est.
  M4 . . . . .3G **95** (3E **7**)
City Gdns. *Dent* 5D **112**
City of Manchester Stadium.
  . . . . .3B **96**
City Pk. Bus. Village.
  M16 . . . . .2H **107**
City Point. *M32* 2F **107**
City Rd. *M15* 1A **108** (6B **8**)
City Rd. *Wors* 3C **76**

City Rd. E. *M15* . . .6D **94** (3G **9**)
City S. *M15* 6D **94** (3G **9**)
City, The. 5D **112**
City Wlk. *Swin* 3H **79**
Civic Wlk. *Heyw* 4F **39**
Clacton Wlk.
  M13 . . . . . .1G **109** (5E **11**)
       (off Kirkstall Sq.)
Clague St. *M11* 3H **95**
Claife Av. *M40* 1B **84**
Clammerclough. 1H **63**
Clammerclough Rd.
  Kear 1ll **63**
Clandon Av. *Eccl* 3D **90**
Clapgate. *Rom* 2F **141**
Clapgate Rd. *Roch* 2A **26**
Clapham St. *M40* 3C **84**
Clara Gorton Ct. *Roch* . .5B **28**
Clara St. *Oldh* 3A **72**
Clara St. *Roch* 6H **27**
Clare Av. *Hand* 4G **159**
Clarebank. *Bolt* 6D **30**
Clare Clo. *Bury* 6D **22**
Clare Ct. *Farn* 6B **46**
Claremont Av. *M20* 4E **125**
Claremont Av. *Marp* . . .5A **142**
Claremont Av. *Stoc* 4E **127**
Claremont Av.
  W Timp 3F **133**
Claremont Dri.
  W Timp 3F **133**
Claremont Gdns. *Ash L* . .6A **88**
Claremont Gro. *M20* 6C **125**
Claremont Gro. *Hale* . . .2G **145**
Claremont Range.
  M18 . . . . .3H **111**
Claremont Rd.
  M16 & M14 . . . . .4C **108**
Claremont Rd.
  Chea H 5C **150**
Claremont Rd. *Miln* 6F **29**
Claremont Rd. *Roch* 4E **27**
Claremont Rd. *Sale* 4B **122**
Claremont Rd. *Salf* 5B **80**
Claremont Rd. *Stoc* 6B **140**
Claremont St. *Ash L* . . .1C **100**
       (in two parts)
Claremont St. *Chad* 6A **56**
Claremont St. *Fail* 3F **85**
Claremont St. *Oldh* 1D **86**
Clarence Arc. *Ash L* 3H **99**
Clarence Av. *Oldh* 5B **72**
Clarence Av. *Traf P* 6H **91**
Clarence Av. *W'fld* 2E **67**
Clarence Ct. *Bolt* 5A **32**
Clarence Ct. *Wilm* 3D **166**
Clarence Ho. *Stal* 5C **100**
Clarence Rd. *M13* 4A **110**
Clarence Rd. *Ash L* 1A **100**
Clarence Rd. *Hale* 2H **145**
Clarence Rd. *Stoc* 4D **126**
Clarence Rd. *Swin* 4C **78**
Clarence St. *M2* . . .4D **94** (6H **5**)
Clarence St. *Bolt* 5B **32**
       (in two parts)
Clarence St. *Farn* 6G **47**
Clarence St. *Hyde* 3C **114**
Clarence St. *Roch* 1F **27**
Clarence St. *Rytn* 4E **57**
Clarence St. *Salf* 1B **94**
Clarence St. *Stal* 4C **100**
Clarendon Av. *Alt* 6G **133**
Clarendon Av. *Stoc* 6D **126**
Clarendon Cres. *Eccl* . . .2H **91**
Clarendon Cres. *Sale* . . .4D **122**
Clarendon Gro. *Bolt* 1D **46**
Clarendon Ind. Est.
  Hyde 4C **114**
Clarendon Pl. *Hyde* 5C **114**

Clarendon Recreation Cen.
  . . . . .3G **93**
Clarendon Rd. *M16* 5A **108**
Clarendon Rd. *Aud* 6A **98**
Clarendon Rd. *Bolt* 6E **33**
Clarendon Rd. *Dent* 5H **113**
Clarendon Rd. *Eccl* 2H **91**
Clarendon Rd. *Haz G* . . .2F **153**
Clarendon Rd. *Hyde* . . .4B **114**
Clarendon Rd. *Irlam* 2D **118**
Clarendon Rd. *Sale* 5D **122**
Clarendon Rd. *Swin* 3F **79**
Clarendon Rd. *Urm* 4A **104**
Clarendon Rd. W.
  M21 . . . . .5H **107**
Clarendon St.
  M15 . . . . . . .1D **108** (5G **9**)
       (in two parts)
Clarendon St. *Bolt* 3A **46**
Clarendon St. *Bury* 1E **37**
Clarendon St. *Duk* 5B **100**
       (in two parts)
Clarendon St. *Hyde* 4B **114**
       (Clarke Way)
Clarendon St. *Hyde* 5B **114**
       (Market St.)
Clarendon St. *Moss* 3F **89**
Clarendon St. *Roch* 1H **41**
Clarendon St. *Stoc* 6H **127**
Clarendon St. *W'fld* 1D **66**
Clarendon Wlk. *Salf* 3G **93**
Clare Rd. *M19* 1C **126**
Clare Rd. *Stoc* 5H **127**
Clare St. *M1* 6F **95** (3D **10**)
Clare St. *Dent* 3E **113**
Claribel St. *M11* 5A **96**
Claridge Rd. *M21* 5G **107**
Clarion St. *M4* 2G **95** (2E **7**)
Clark Av. *M18* 2G **111**
Clarke Av. *Salf* 6H **93**
Clarke Brow. *Midd* 6A **54**
Clarke Cres. *Hale* 2B **146**
Clarke Cres. *L Hul* 3A **62**
Clarke Ind. Est. *Stret* . . .2H **105**
Clarkes Cft. *Bury* 2G **37**
Clarke's Hill. *W'fld* 2H **65**
Clarke's La. *Roch* 3F **27**
Clarke St. *Ash L* 5F **99**
Clarke St. *Bolt* 5G **31**
Clarke St. *B'hth* 4F **133**
Clarke St. *Farn* 2G **63**
Clarke St. *Heyw* 3F **39**
Clarke St. *Roch* 1B **28**
Clarkethorn Ter. *Stoc* . . .6G **127**
Clarksfield Rd. *Oldh* 3G **73**
Clarksfield St. *Oldh* 3G **73**
Clark's Hill. *P'wich* 5E **67**
Clarkson Clo. *Dent* 5D **112**
Clarkson Clo. *Midd* 2E **69**
Clark Way. *Hyde* 4B **114**
Clarkwell Clo. *Oldh* 1C **72**
Clatford Wlk. M9 . . . . . .4F **83**
       (off Fernclough Rd.)
Claude Av. *Swin* 3D **78**
Claude Rd. *M21* 2G **123**
Claude St. *M8* 2C **82**
Claude St. *Eccl* 2D **90**
Claude St. *Swin* 3D **78**
Claudia Sq. *Carr* 6G **89**
Claughton Av. *Bolt* 6H **33**
Claughton Av. *Wors* 3E **77**
Claughton Rd. *Wals* 6H **21**
Clavendon Rd. *Rad* 6F **35**
Claverham Wlk. *M23* . .4E **135**
Claverton Rd.
  Round I 1E **147**
Claxton Av. *M9* 6F **69**
Clay Bank. *Droy* 4H **97**
Claybank Dri. *T'ton* 4F **21**
Clay Bank St. *Heyw* 2E **39**
Claybank Ter. *Moss* 5G **75**

Claybrook Wlk. *M11* 4C **96**
Clayburn Rd.
  M15 . . . . . . .1C **108** (5F **9**)
Claycourt Av. *Eccl* 1D **90**
Clay Cft. Ter. *L'boro* 2E **17**
Claydon Dri. *Rad* 2D **48**
Clayfield Dri. *Roch* 3B **26**
Claygate Dri. *M9* 4F **69**
Clayhill Wlk. *M9* 2G **83**
Clayland Clo. *Holl* 3F **117**
Clay La. *M23* 1F **147**
Clay La. *Hand* 3F **159**
       (in two parts)
Clay La. *Roch* 3H **25**
Clay La. *Timp & Hale* . . .1C **146**
Clay La. *Wilm* 5A **166**
Claymere Av. *Roch* 3A **26**
Claymore St. *M18* 1G **111**
Claymore St. *Bolt* 4B **46**
Clay St. *Brom X* 4E **19**
Clay St. *L'boro* 4D **16**
Clay St. *Oldh* 5C **72**
Claythorpe Wlk. *M8* 1A **82**
Clayton. 3E **97**
Clayton Av. *M20* 5F **125**
Clayton Av. *Bolt* 2E **47**
Clayton Bridge. 1G **97**
Claytonbrook Rd. *M11* . .4E **97**
Clayton Clo. *M15* 2C **108**
Clayton Community Farm.
  . . . . .4E **97**
       (off Turner St.)
Clayton Hall Rd. *M11* . . .3E **97**
Clayton Ind. Ect. *M11* . . .4F **97**
Clayton La. *M11* 5D **96**
Clayton La. S. *M11* 6C **96**
Clayton's Clo. *S'head* . . .2B **74**
Clayton St. *M11* 2D **96**
       (in two parts)
Clayton St. *Bolt* 2E **47**
Clayton St. *Chad* 6G **71**
Clayton St. *Dent* 5F **113**
Clayton St. *Duk* 5B **100**
Clayton St. *Fail* 4F **85**
Clayton St. *Roch* 1B **28**
Cleabarrow Drl. *Wors* . . .6C **76**
Cleadon Av. *M18* 3E **111**
Cleadon Dri. S. *Bury* 6C **22**
Cleavley St. *Eccl* 3D **90**
Clee Av. *M13* 5B **110**
Cleethorpes Av. *M9* 6D **68**
Cleeve Rd. *M23* 1G **135**
Cleeve Rd. *Oldh* 3G **73**
Cleeve Way. *Chea H* . . .1D **160**
Clegg Hall. 2E **29**
Clegg Hall Rd.
  Roch & L'boro 1D **28**
       (in two parts)
Clegg's Av. Whitw 3G **15**
       (off Clegg St.)
Clegg's Bldgs. *Bolt* 6A **32**
Clegg's La. *L Hul* 4C **62**
Cleggs La. Ind. Site.
  L Hul 3D **62**
Clegg St. *Bolt* 6E **33**
Clegg St. *Bred* 6F **129**
Clegg St. *Droy* 4H **97**
Clegg St. *L'boro* 2D **16**
Clegg St. *Miln* 6G **29**
Clegg St. *Oldh* 3D **72**
       (in two parts)
Clegg St. *S'head* 3C **74**
Clegg St. *W'fld* 2D **66**
Clegg St. *Whitw* 3G **15**
Cleggswood Av. *L'boro* . .6E **17**
Clelland St. *Farn* 2G **63**
Clematis Wlk. *Swin* 1E **79**
Clement Ct. *M11* 6H **97**
       (off Toxteth St.)
Clement Ct. *Roch* 5B **28**

Clementina St. *Roch* 2H **27**
       (in two parts)
Clementine Clo. *Salf* 3H **93**
Clement Pl. *L'boro* 4G **17**
Clement Rd. *Roch* 3G **27**
Clement Rd. *Marp B* 4F **143**
Clement Royds St.
  Roch 3G **27**
Clements St. *M11* 6G **97**
Clement Stott Clo. *M9* . . .5H **69**
Clement St. *Chad* 6H **71**
Clement St. *Stoc* 6G **127**
Cleminson St.
  Salf 3B **94** (4C **4**)
Clemshaw Clo. *Heyw* . . .4E **39**
Clerewood Av. *H Grn* . . .6F **149**
Clerke St. *Bury* 3D **36**
Clerk's Ct. *Salf* 3B **92**
Clevedon Av. *Urm* 5A **106**
Clevedon Rd. *Chad* 6G **55**
Clevedon St. *M9* 4G **83**
Cleveland Av. *M19* 5D **110**
Cleveland Av. *Hyde* 5A **114**
Cleveland Av. *Salf* 2C **92**
Cleveland Clo. *Rams* 6E **13**
Cleveland Clo. *Swin* 1G **79**
Cleveland Dri. *Miln* 5G **29**
Cleveland Gdns. *Bolt* 3F **45**
Cleveland Gro. *Rytn* 4A **56**
Cleveland Rd. *M8* 2D **82**
Cleveland Rd. *Hale* 2H **145**
Cleveland Rd. *Stoc* 5C **126**
Clevelands Clo. *Shaw* . . .5E **43**
Cleveland St. *Bolt* 3F **45**
Cleveleys Av. *M21* 1A **124**
Cleveleys Av. *Bolt* 5E **33**
Cleveleys Av. *Bury* 5C **36**
Cleveleys Av. *H Grn* 4F **149**
Cleveleys Av. *Roch* 2H **41**
Cleveleys Gro. *Salf* 4A **82**
Cleves Ct. *Heyw* 4E **39**
Cleworth Rd. *Midd* 5H **53**
Cleworth St.
  M15 . . . . . . .6B **94** (4C **8**)
Cleworth Wlk.
  M15 . . . . . . .6B **94** (4C **8**)
Cliban St. *M8* 5D **82**
Clifden Dri. *M22* 3C **148**
Cliff Av. *Bury* 1C **22**
Cliff Av. *Salf* 5G **81**
Cliffbrook Gro. *Wilm* . . .5H **159**
Cliff Cres. *Salf* 4H **81**
Cliff Dale. *Stal* 5D **100**
Cliffdale Dri. *M8* 2C **82**
Cliffe St. *L'boro* 5H **17**
Cliff Grange. *Salf* 4H **81**
Cliff Gro. *Stoc* 5D **126**
Cliff Hill. *Shaw* 4G **43**
Cliff Hill Rd. *Shaw* 4H **43**
Cliffmere Clo. *Chea II* . . .2D **150**
Cliff Mt. *Rams* 2D **12**
Clifford Av. *Dent* 2E **113**
Clifford Av. *Timp* 5B **134**
Clifford Ct. *M15* 2C **108**
Clifford Ct. *Stoc* 6B **140**
Clifford Rd. *Bolt* 5E **45**
Clifford Rd. *Poy* 3C **162**
Clifford Rd. *Wilm* 3C **166**
Clifford St.
  M13 . . . . . .1F **109** (5C **10**)
Clifford St. *Eccl* 5D **90**
Clifford St. *Roch* 6H **27**
Clifford St. *Swin* 3H **79**
Cliff Rd. *Bury* 2D **50**
Cliff Side. *Wilm* 1E **167**
Cliff St. *Roch* 2B **28**
Cliff, The. 4G **81**
Clifton. 6F **65**
Clifton Av. *M14* 1H **125**
Clifton Av. *Alt* 6G **133**
Clifton Av. *Eccl* 2F **91**

Clifton Av. *H Grn* 3E **149**
Clifton Av. *Oldh* 4F **73**
Clifton Clo. *M16* 2B **108**
Clifton Clo. *Heyw* 4E **39**
Clifton Clo. *Oldh* 4F **73**
Clifton Country Pk. 4E **65**
Clifton Ct. *Farn* 5D **46**
Clifton Ct. *Stoc* 5C **126**
Clifton Ct. *Swin* 5E **65**
Clifton Dri. *Gat* 5D **136**
Clifton Dri. *H Grn* 3E **149**
Clifton Dri. *Marp* 4C **142**
Clifton Dri. *Swin* 2D **78**
  (Manchester Rd.)
Clifton Dri. *Swin* 1A **80**
  (Western Av.)
Clifton Dri. *Wilm* 5B **166**
Clifton Green. 6H **65**
Clifton Gro. *Old T* 2B **108**
Clifton Gro. *Swin* 1D **78**
Clifton Holm. *Del* 2G **59**
Clifton House Arboretum.
. . . . .4D **64**
Clifton Ho. Rd. *Swin* 4D **64**
Clifton Ind. Est. *Swin* 6A **66**
Clifton Lodge. *Stoc* 6A **140**
Clifton Pk. Rd. *Stoc* 6A **140**
Clifton Pl. *P'wich* 4E **67**
Clifton Rd. *M21* 1A **124**
Clifton Rd. *Eccl* 2F **91**
Clifton Rd. *Midd* 1D **54**
Clifton Rd. *Sale* 6B **122**
Clifton Rd. *Stoc* 6C **126**
Clifton Rd. *Urm* 5C **104**
Clifton Rd.
  W'fld & P'wich 5C **66**
Clifton St. *Ald E* 5G **167**
Clifton St. *Ash L* 2G **99**
Clifton St. *Bury* 1D **36**
Clifton St. *Fail* 2G **85**
Clifton St. *Farn* 5D **46**
Clifton St. *G'fld* 4F **61**
Clifton St. *Kear* 2H **63**
Clifton St. *Mile P* 2B **96**
Clifton St. *Miln* 5F **29**
Clifton St. *Old T* 2B **108**
Clifton St. *Rams* 5A **32**
Clifton St. *Tyl* 3A **76**
Clifton Vw. *Swin* 5E **65**
Clifton Vs. *Fail* 2G **85**
Cliftonville Dri.
  Swin & Salf 5G **79**
Cliftonville Rd. *Roch* 5A **42**
Clifton Wlk. *Midd* 4F **53**
Clinton Av. *M14* 5D **108**
Clinton Gdns. *M14* 5E **109**
Clinton Ho. *Salf* 4F **93**
Clinton St. *Ash L* 1B **100**
Clinton Wlk. *Oldh* 3E **73**
Clippers Quay. *Salf* 1G **107**
Clipsley Cres. *Oldh* 3B **58**
Cliston Wlk. *Haz G* 3A **152**
Clitheroe Clo. *Heyw* 2F **39**
Clitheroe Dri. *Bury* 3F **35**
Clitheroe Rd. *M13* 4B **110**
Clito St. *M9* 3H **83**
Clive Av. *W'fld* 6C **50**
Clivedale Pl. *Bolt* 6B **32**
Cliveley Wlk. *Swin* 1F **79**
Clive Lloyd Ct. *Stret* 4E **107**
Clively Av. *Swin* 1H **79**
Clive Rd. *Fail* 4E **85**
Clive St. *M4* 2F **95** (2C **6**)
Clive St. *Ash L* 6E **87**
Clive St. *Bolt* 6B **32**
Clive St. *Oldh* 1B **86**
  (in two parts)
Clivewood Wlk. *M12* 1A **110**
Clivia Gro. *Salf* 5H **81**
Cloak St. *M1* 6E **95** (3B **10**)
Clock Ho. Av. *Droy* 2G **97**
Clockhouse M. *Droy* 2G **97**

Clifton Av. *H Grn* 3E **149**
Clock St. *Chad* 1H **85**
Clock Tower Clo.
  Hyde 6C **114**
Clock Tower Clo. *Wors* . . .6B **62**
Cloister Clo. *Duk* 1A **114**
Cloister Rd. *Stoc* 1H **137**
Cloisters, The. *Chea* 6C **138**
Cloisters, The. *Roch* 2B **28**
Cloisters, The. *Sale* 5D **122**
Cloister St. *M9* 3H **83**
Cloister St. *Bolt* 3G **31**
Clondberry Clo. *Tyl* 2A **76**
Clopton Wlk.
  M15 . . . . . . .1C **108** (5F **9**)
  (Birchvale Clo.)
Clopton Wlk.
  M15 . . . . . . .1C **108** (6F **9**)
  (Rolls Cres.)
Closes Farm. *Bolt* 5F **45**
Close, The. *Alt* 6E **133**
Close, The. *Bolt* 2D **32**
Close, The. *Bury* 6C **22**
Close, The. *Dent* 3D **112**
Close, The. *Marp B* 2F **143**
Close, The. *Midd* 4B **54**
Close, The. *Stal* 1D **100**
  (in two parts)
Clothorn Rd. *M20* 5F **125**
Cloudberry Wlk. *Part* 6D **118**
Cloudstock Gro. *L Hul* 4A **62**
Clough. 1E **17**
  (Littleborough)
Clough. 1H **57**
  (Oldham)
Clough. *Shaw* 1H **57**
Clough Av. *Marp B* 4G **143**
Clough Av. *Sale* 2F **133**
Clough Av. *Wilm* 5F **159**
Clough Bank. *M9* 1F **83**
Clough Bank. *L'boro* 1E **17**
Cloughbank. *Rad* 2C **64**
Clough Clo. *Oldh* 3G **75**
Clough Ct. *Midd* 5B **54**
Clough Dri. *P'wich* 5D **66**
Clough End Rd. *Hyde* 6A **116**
Clough Fld. *L'boro* 5E **17**
Cloughfield Av.
  Salf 5H **93** (2A **8**)
Clough Flats. *Heyw* 3E **39**
  (off Brunswick St.)
Clough Fold. *Rad* 2B **64**
Clough Fold Av. *Hyde* 6B **114**
Clough Fold Rd. *Hyde* 6A **114**
Clough Ga. *Hyde* 1C **130**
Clough Ga. *Oldh* 1B **86**
Clough Gro. *W'fld* 5B **50**
Clough Head. *L'boro* 5G **17**
  (off Higher Calderbrook Rd.)
Clough La. *Grass* 3F **75**
Clough La. *Heyw* 1E **39**
Clough La. *P'wich* 5D **66**
Clough Mdw. *Bolt* 1B **44**
Clough Mdw. *Woodl* 4A **130**
Clough Mdw. Rd. *Rad* 4E **49**
Clough Pk. Av. *Grass* 3G **75**
Clough Rd. *M9* 3H **83**
Clough Rd. *Droy* 3A **98**
Clough Rd. *Fail* 4G **85**
Clough Rd. *L'boro* 1E **17**
Clough Rd. *Midd* 5A **54**
Clough Rd. *Shaw* 1H **57**
Cloughs Av. *Chad* 1D **70**
Clough Side. *M9* 2H **83**
Clough Side. *Marp B* 4F **143**
Clough St. *M40* 1E **97**
Clough St. *Kear* 2H **63**
Clough St. *Midd* 5B **54**
Clough St. *Rad* 6A **50**
Clough St. *Ward* 3A **16**
Clough, The. *Bolt* 5C **30**
Clough, The. *Stoc* 3B **128**
Cloughton Wlk. *M40* 6D **84**

Clough Top Rd. *M9* 1A **84**
Clough Wlk. *P'wich* 5D **66**
Clough Wlk. *Stoc* 3B **128**
Clovelly Av. *Oldh* 1A **86**
Clovelly Rd. *M21* 1A **124**
Clovelly Rd. *Stoc* 3C **140**
Clovelly Rd. *Swin* 4C **78**
Clovelly St. *M40* 6D **84**
Clovelly St. *Roch* 2B **40**
Clover Av. *Stoc* 6F **139**
Cloverbank Av. *M19* 5H **125**
Clover Cres. *Oldh* 6H **73**
Clover Cft. *Sale* 2D **134**
Cloverdale Sq. *Bolt* 4E **31**
Cloverfield Wlk. *Wors* 6F **63**
  (off Bolton Rd.)
Clover Hall. 2C **28**
Clover Hall Cres. *Roch* 2C **28**
Cloverley. *Sale* 1B **134**
Cloverley Dri. *Timp* 1A **146**
Clover Rd. *Rom* 6B **130**
Clover Rd. *Timp* 6A **134**
Clover St. *Roch* 3G **27**
Clover Vw. *Roch* 3C **28**
Clowes St. *M12* 1B **110**
  (in two parts)
Clowes St. *Chad* 1H **85**
Clowes St. *Salf* . . .3C **94** (4F **5**)
Club St. *M11* 6H **97**
Clumber Clo. *Poy* 4E **163**
Clumber Rd. *M18* 3H **111**
Clumber Rd. *Poy* 4E **163**
Clunton Av. *Bolt* 2F **45**
Clutha Rd. *Stoc* 1H **151**
Clwyd Av. *Stoc* 4F **139**
Clyde Av. *W'fld* 3D **66**
Clyde Ct. *Roch* 5B **28**
Clyde Rd. *M20* 5D **124**
Clyde Rd. *Rad* 2F **49**
Clyde Rd. *Stoc* 4E **139**
Clydesdale Gdns. *M11* 4C **96**
Clydesdale Ri. *Dig* 2D **60**
Clydesdale St. *Oldh* 5C **72**
Clyde St. *Ash L* 5F **99**
Clyde St. *Bolt* 3A **32**
Clyde St. *Oldh* 6G **57**
Clyde Ter. *Rad* 2F **49**
Clyne Ho. *Stret* 3F **107**
Clyne St. *Stret* 3F **107**
Clysbarton Ct. *Bram* 4F **151**
Coach Ho., The. *Ald E* . . .4H **167**
Coach La. *Roch* 6A **26**
Coach Rd. *Holl* 2C **116**
  (in two parts)
Coach St. *Bolt* 2C **46**
Coalbrook Wlk. *M12* 5A **96**
  (1H **11**)
  (off Aden Clo.)
Coalburn St. *M12* 1C **110**
Coal Pit La. *Oldh* 4A **86**
Coalshaw Grn. Rd.
  Chad 6G **71**
Coatbridge St. *M11* 3E **97**
Cobalt Av. *Urm* 1H **105**
Cobb Clo. *M8* 6A **68**
Cobbett's Way. *Wilm* 5C **166**
Cobble Bank. *M9* 2G **83**
Cobblers Yd. *Ald E* 5G **167**
Cobblestones. *Del* 4H **59**
Cobden Cen., The. *Salf* . . .4F **93**
Cobden Lodge. *Roch* 3C **40**
  (off Tudor Hall St.)
Cobden Mill Ind. Est.
  Farn 6E **47**
Cobden St. *M9* 3G **83**
Cobden St. *Ash L* 3B **100**
Cobden St. *Bolt* 2H **31**
Cobden St. *Bury* 2E **37**
Cobden St. *Chad* 2H **71**
Cobden St. *Eger* 1B **18**
Cobden St. *Heyw* 4F **39**
Cobden St. *Oldh* 6H **57**

Cobden St. *Rad* 1F **49**
Cobden St. *Salf* 1G **93**
Coberley Av. *Urm* 3B **104**
Cob Hall Rd. *Stret* 6C **106**
Cobham Av. *M40* 1C **84**
Cobham Av. *Bolt* 4H **45**
Coblers Hill. *Del* 2H **59**
Cobourg St.
  M1 . . . . . . .5F **95** (1C **10**)
Coburg Av. *Salf* 1B **94**
Cochrane Av. *M12* 2A **110**
Cochrane St. *Bolt* 2B **46**
Cockbrook. 3B **100**
Cock Brow. *Hyde* 2G **131**
Cock Clod St. *Rad* 4A **50**
Cockcroft Rd.
  Salf 3H **93** (3A **4**)
Cockcroft St. *M9* 2F **83**
Cockerell Springs. *Bolt* 1C **46**
  (off Glebe St.)
Cocker Hill. 3E **101**
Cocker Hill. *Stal* 3E **101**
Cocker Mill La. *Shaw* 2D **56**
Cockers La. *Stal* 5H **101**
Cocker St. *L Hul* 5C **62**
Cockey Moor Rd.
  A'wth & Bury 4D **34**
Cockhall La. *Whitw* 4G **15**
Cock Hollow. *Bury* 1E **37**
Cocklinstones. *Bury* 2A **36**
Coconut Gro. *Salf* 3H **93**
Codale Dri. *Bolt* 4H **33**
Coddington Av. *Open* 5G **97**
Cody Ct. *Salf* 5E **93**
Coe St. *Bolt* 2B **46**
Coghlan Clo. *M11* 3D **96**
Coke St. *Salf* 3B **82**
Colborne Av. *Eccl* 3D **90**
Colborne Av. *Rom* 1A **142**
Colborne Av. *Stoc* 4H **111**
Colbourne Av. *M8* 2B **82**
Colbourne Gro. *Hyde* 4A **116**
Colbourne Way. *Hyde* 4A **116**
Colby Wlk. *M40* 4A **84**
Colchester Av. *Bolt* 5G **33**
Colchester Av. *P'wich* 1G **81**
Colchester Clo. *M23* 2E **135**
Colchester Dri. *Farn* 6B **46**
Colchester Pl. *Stoc* 6D **126**
Colchester St. *M40* 1H **95**
Colchester Wlk. *Oldh* 2D **72**
Colclough Clo. *M40* 5B **84**
Coldfield Dri. *Round I* 5F **135**
Cold Greave Clo. *Miln* 1G **43**
Cold Hurst. 1C **72**
Coldhurst Hollow Est.
  Oldh 6C **56**
Coldhurst St. *Oldh* 1C **72**
Coldstream Av. *M9* 5F **69**
Coldwall St. *Roch* 3F **27**
Colebrook Dri. *M40* 5A **84**
Colebrook Rd. *Timp* 5A **134**
Coleby Av. *Old T* 3A **108**
Coleby Av. *Wyth* 4D **148**
Coledale Dri. *Midd* 5E **53**
Coleford Gro. *Bolt* 1A **46**
Colemore Av. *M20* 6H **125**
Colenso Ct. *Bolt* 6E **33**
Colenso Gro. *Stoc* 6D **126**
Colenso Rd. *Bolt* 6F **33**
Colenso St. *Oldh* 6B **72**
Coleport Clo. *Chea H* 4C **150**
Coleridge Av. *Midd* 4C **54**
Coleridge Av. *Rad* 4E **49**
Coleridge Clo. *Stoc* 6G **111**
Coleridge Dri. *L'boro* 1F **29**
Coleridge Rd. *M16* 4A **108**
Coleridge Rd. *G'mnt* 1H **21**
Coleridge Rd. *Oldh* 3H **57**
Coleridge Rd. *Stoc* 6G **111**
Coleridge Rd. *M40* 1E **97**
Coleridge Way. *Stoc* 6G **111**

Colesbourne Clo. *L Hul* . . .3C **62**
Coleshill St.
  M40 . . . . .2A **90** (1H **7**)
Colesmere Wlk. *M40* 2D **84**
Cole St. *M40* 3H **83**
Colgate Cres. *M14* 1F **125**
Colgate La. *Salf* 1G **107**
Colgrove Av. *M40* 1C **84**
Colina Dri. *Salf* 6A **82**
Colindale Av. *M9* 5G **69**
Colindale Clo. *Bolt* 2G **45**
Colin Murphy Rd.
  M15 . . . . . .1C **108** (5E **9**)
Colin Rd. *Stoc* 5F **127**
Colinton Clo. *Bolt* 4H **31**
Colinwood Clo. *Bury* 4D **50**
Coll Dri. *Urm* 2F **105**
College Av. *Droy* 5H **97**
College Av. *Oldh* 6D **72**
College Clo. *Bolt* 1A **46**
College Clo. *Stoc* 5A **140**
College Clo. *Wilm* 1C **166**
College Dri. *M16* 5A **108**
College Ho. *Stoc* 5D **126**
College Land.
  M3 . . . . .4D **94** (5G **5**)
College Rd. *M16* 5A **108**
College Rd. *Eccl* 3A **92**
College Rd. *Oldh* 5B **72**
College Rd. *Roch* 4F **27**
College Way. *Bolt* 1H **45**
Collen Cres. *Bury* 5B **22**
Collett St. *Oldh* 1G **73**
Colley St. *Roch* 2A **28**
Colley St. *Stret* 2F **107**
Collie Av. *Salf* 6G **81**
Collier Av. *Miln* 4F **29**
Collier Clo. *Hyde* 6A **116**
Collier Hill. *Oldh* 6B **72**
Collier Hill Av. *Oldh* 6A **72**
Collier's Ct. *Roch* 4H **41**
Collier St. *Rad* 4H **49**
Collier St. *Salf* 5C **94** (2F **9**)
  (Bridgewater St.)
Collier St. *Salf* 5D **80**
  (Langley Rd. S.)
Collier St. *Salf* 3C **94** (3F **5**)
  (Rolla St.)
Collier St. *Swin* 4E **79**
Collier Wlk. *Hyde* 6A **116**
Colliery St. *M11* 4C **96**
  (in two parts)
Collin Av. *M18* 3E **111**
Collingburn Av. *Salf* 6H **93**
Collingburn Ct. *Salf* 6H **93**
Colling Clo. *Irlam* 6E **103**
Collinge Av. *Midd* 1C **70**
Collinge St. *Bury* 1H **35**
Collinge St. *Heyw* 3E **39**
Collinge St. *Midd* 2D **70**
Collinge St. *Shaw* 6F **43**
Collingham St. *M8* 1F **96**
Colling St. *Rams* 4D **12**
Collington Clo. *M12* 2C **110**
Collingwood Av. *Droy* . . .2G **97**
Collingwood Clo. *Poy* . .4G **163**
Collingwood Dri. *Swin* . . .4H **79**
Collingwood Rd. *M19* . . .6B **110**
Collingwood St. *Roch* . . .5C **40**
Collingwood Way. *Uldh* . .1D **72**
Collins St. *Wals* 1F **35**
Collop Dri. *Heyw* 6G **39**
Coll's La. *Del* 3F **59**
Collyhurst. 6F **83**
Collyhurst Av. *Wors* 1G **77**
Collyhurst Rd.
  M40 . . . . . . .1F **95** (1D **6**)
Collyhurst St. *M40* 1G **95**
Colman Gdns. *Salf* 6H **93**
Colmore Dri. *M9* 5A **70**
Colmore Gro. *Bolt* 1D **32**

Colmore St. *Bolt* 2D **32**
Colne St. *Roch* 4D **40**
Colonial Rd. *Dtoc* 5A **140**
Colshaw Clo. E. *Rad* 3F **49**
Colshaw Clo. S. *Rad* 3F **49**
Colshaw Dri. *Wilm* 6H **159**
Colshaw Rd. *M23* 6G **135**
Colshaw Wlk. *Wilm* 6H **159**
Colson Dri. *Midd* 2H **69**
Colsterdale Clo. *Rytn* 2C **56**
Colt Hill La. *Upperm* 1H **75**
Coltishall Ho. *Chea* 6C **138**
Coltness Wlk. *M40* 6C **84**
Coltsfoot Dri. *B'hth* 3D **132**
Columbia Av. *M18* 3H **111**
Columbia Rd. *Bolt* 5G **31**
Columbia St. *Oldh* 5D **72**
Columbine Clo. *Roch* 6C **14**
Columbine St. *Open* 6F **97**
Columbine Wlk. *Part* 6D **118**
Colville Dri. *Bury* 4H **35**
Colville Gro. *Sale* 2G **133**
Colville Gro. *Timp* 5A **134**
Colville Rd. *Oldh* 6B **56**
Colwell Av. *Stret* 6B **106**
Colwell Wlk. *M9* 4D **68**
Colwick Av. *Alt* 5G **133**
Colwith Av. *Bolt* 4G **33**
Colwood Wlk. *M8* 5B **82**
  (off Elizabeth St.)
Colwyn Av. *M14* 1A **126**
Colwyn Av. *Midd* 3A **70**
Colwyn Cres. *Stoc* 4H **127**
Colwyn Gro. *Bolt* 4H **31**
Colwyn Rd. *Bram* 5G **151**
Colwyn Rd. *Chea H* 4A **150**
Colwyn Rd. *Swin* 4C **78**
Colwyn St. *Ash L* 5E **87**
Colwyn St. *Oldh* 2B **72**
Colwyn St. *Roch* 3B **40**
Colwyn St. *Salf* 2F **93**
Colwyn Ter. *Ash L* 5E **87**
Colyton Wlk. *M22* 2D **148**
Combe Clo. *M11* 2D **96**
Combermere Av. *M20* . . .2F **125**
Combermere Clo.
  Chea H 1B **150**
Combermere St. *Duk* . . .4A **100**
Combs Bank. Glos 6F **117**
  (off Melandra Castle Rd.)
Combs Fold. Glos 5F **117**
  (off Combs Way)
Combs Gdns. Glos 6F **117**
  (off Brassington Cres.)
Combs Gro. Glos 5F **117**
  (off Combs M.)
Combs Lea. Glos 6F **117**
Combs M. Glos 6F **117**
  (off Brassington Cres.)
Combs Ter. Glos 5F **117**
  (off Combs Way)
Combs Way. Glos 5F **117**
Comer Ter. *Sale* 5A **122**
Comet St. *M1* 4G **95** (6E **7**)
Commercial Av.
  Chea H 2A **160**
Commercial Brow.
  Hyde 3C **114**
Commercial Rd.
  Haz G 2D **152**
Commercial Rd.
  Oldh 3D **72**
Commercial St.
  M15 . . . . . .6C **94** (3F **9**)
Commercial St. *Hyde* . . .4C **114**
Commercial St. *Oldh* 3A **72**
Common La. *C'ton* 4F **119**
Comn. Side Rd. *Wors* . . .4B **76**
Como St. *Bolt* 3G **45**
Como Wlk. *M18* 1D **110**
Compass St. *Open* 6E **97**
Compstall. 1E **143**

Compstall Av. *M14* 5F **109**
Compstall Gro. *M18* 1G **111**
Compstall Mills Est.
  Comp 1F **143**
Compstall Rd. *Marp B* . .1E **143**
Compstall Rd. *Rom* 1A **142**
  (in two parts)
Compton Clo. *Urm* 6G **103**
Compton Dri. *M23* 3G **147**
Compton Fold. *Shaw* 5G **43**
Compton St. *Stal* 4F **101**
Compton Way. *Midd* 2C **70**
Comus St. *Salf* 5A **94** (1A **8**)
Concastrian Ind. Est.
  M9 . . . . .4E **83**
Concert La. *M2* 4E **95** (6A **6**)
Concil St.
  M15 . . . . . .1E **109** (5A **10**)
Concord Bus. Pk.
  M22 . . . . .4C **148**
Concord Pl. *Salf* 6E **81**
Concord Way. *Duk* 5A **100**
  (in two parts)
Condor Clo. *Droy* 2C **98**
Condor Pl. *Salf* 6E **81**
Condor Wlk.
  M13 . . . . .1G **109** (6D **10**)
  (off Cumbrian Clo.)
Conduit St. *Ash L* 3A **100**
Conduit St. *Oldh* 4H **57**
Conduit St. *Tin* 1H **117**
Conewood Wlk.
  M13 . . . . .1G **109** (6F **11**)
Coney Green Sports Cen.
  . . . . .3H **49**
Coney Gro. *M23* 4G **135**
Coneymead. *Stal* 1E **101**
Congham Rd. *Stoc* 3E **139**
Congleton Av. *M14* 5E **109**
Congleton Clo. *Ald E* . . .6G **167**
Congleton Rd.
  Ald E & Neth A . . .5G **167**
Congou St.
  M1 . . . . . . .5G **95** (1F **11**)
Congreave St. *Oldh* 1C **72**
Conifer Wlk. *Part* 6C **118**
Coningsby Dri. *M9* 3F **83**
Conisber Clo. *Eger* 2C **18**
Conisborough. *Roch* 5G **27**
Conisborough Pl. *W'fld* . . .2F **67**
Coniston Av. *M9* 3F **83**
Coniston Av. *Farn* 2A **62**
Coniston Av. *Hyde* 3A **114**
Coniston Av. *L Hul* 4C **62**
Coniston Av. *Oldh* 6B **72**
Coniston Av. *Sale* 1C **134**
Coniston Av. *W'fld* 1D **66**
Coniston Clo. *Chad* 2G **71**
Coniston Clo. *Dent* 5B **112**
Coniston Clo. *L Lev* 3A **48**
Coniston Clo. *Rams* 1E **13**
Coniston Dri. *Bury* 6C **36**
Coniston Dri. *Hand* 3G **159**
Coniston Dri. *Midd* 5G **53**
Coniston Dri. *Stal* 2E **101**
Coniston Gro. *Ash L* 1G **99**
Coniston Gro. *Heyw* 5F **39**
Coniston Gro. *L Hul* 5C **62**
Coniston Gro. *Rytn* 1B **56**
Coniston Rd. *Gat* 5F **137**
Coniston Rd. *H Lane* 5B **154**
Coniston Rd. *Part* 5C **118**
Coniston Rd. *Stoc* 3H **127**
Coniston Rd. *Stret* 4C **106**
Coniston Rd. *Swin* 5F **79**
Coniston Rd. *Urm* 1A **120**
Coniston St. *M40* 6C **84**
Coniston St. *Bolt* 2B **32**
Coniston St. *Salf* 1H **93**
Coniston Wlk. *Timp* 6D **134**
Conival Way. *Chad* 6G **55**

Conmere Sq.
  M15 . . . . . .6D **94** (4H **9**)
Connaught Av. *M19* 2B **126**
Connaught Av. *Roch* 2H **41**
Connaught Av. *W'fld* 2E **67**
Connaught Clo. *Wilm* . . .1F **167**
Connaught Sq. *Bolt* 3D **32**
Connaught St. *Bury* 4H **35**
Connaught St. *Oldh* 3C **72**
Connel Clo. *Bolt* 1H **47**
Connell Rd. *M23* 5G **135**
Connell Way. *Heyw* 2H **39**
Connery Cres. *Ash L* 5H **87**
Connie St. *M11* 5E **97**
Conningsby Clo.
  Brom X 3D **18**
Connington Av. *M9* 2F **83**
Connington Clo. *Rytn* 3A **56**
Connor Way. *Gat* 1D **148**
Conquest Clo. *M12* 1B **110**
Conrad Clo. *Oldh* 3A **58**
Conran St. *M9* 4F **83**
Consett Av. *M23* 5G **135**
Consort Av. *Rytn* 1A **56**
Consort Clo. *Duk* 1A **114**
Consort Pl. *Bow* 3D **144**
Constable Clo. *Bolt* 4H **31**
Constable Dri. *Marp B* . . .3F **143**
Constable Dri. *Wilm* 1H **167**
Constable St. *M18* 1G **111**
Constable Wlk. *Dent* 2G **129**
Constable Wlk. Oldh 4H **57**
  (off Hodge Clough Rd.)
Constance Gdns. *Salf* 4F **93**
Constance Rd. *Bolt* 3G **45**
Constance Rd. *Part* 6D **118**
Constance St.
  M15 . . . . . .6C **94** (3F **9**)
Constantine Rd. *Roch* . . .4H **27**
Constantine St. *Oldh* 3H **73**
Constellation Trad. Est.
  Rad 1F **49**
Consul St. *M22* 2C **136**
Contact Theatre. 2F **109**
Convamore Rd. *Bram* . . .1F **161**
Convent Gro. *Roch* 6F **27**
Convent St. *Oldh* 5G **73**
Conway Av. *Bolt* 4E **31**
Conway Av. *Irlam* 1D **118**
Conway Av. *Swin* 6H **65**
Conway Av. *W'fld* 2D **66**
Conway Clo. *M16* 4G **107**
Conway Clo. *Heyw* 2C **38**
Conway Clo. *Midd* 2A **70**
Conway Clo. *Rams* 3D **12**
Conway Cres. *G'mnt* 1H **21**
Conway Dri. *Bury* 3H **37**
Conway Dri. *Haz G* 4C **152**
Conway Dri. *Stal* 2E **101**
Conway Dri. *Timp* 5C **134**
Conway Gro. *Chad* 6F **55**
Conway Rd. *Chea H* 3A **150**
Conway Rd. *Sale* 6D **122**
Conway Rd. *Urm* 3F **105**
Conway St. *Farn* 2F **63**
Conway St. *Stoc* 5G **127**
Conway Towers. *Stoc* . . .2C **128**
Conyngham Rd. *M14* . . .3H **109**
Cookcroft. 2B **74**
Cooke St. *Dent* 4E **113**
Cooke St. *Fail* 3F **85**
Cooke St. *Farn* 2G **63**
Cooke St. *Haz G* 2D **152**
Cooke St. *Hyde* 2D **114**
Cook St. *Aud* 1F **113**
Cook St. *Bury* 3E **37**
Cook St. *Eccl* 3E **91**
Cook St. *Oldh* 2G **73**
Cook St. *Roch* 2B **28**
Cook St. *Salf* 3C **94** (4F **5**)
Cook St. *Stoc* 2G **139**

Cook Ter. Duk 4H 99
           (off Hill St.)
Cook Ter. Roch 2B 28
Coomassie St. Heyw 3E 39
Coomassie St. Rad 4G 49
Coomassie St. Salf 2F 93
Coombes Av. Hyde 6D 114
Coombes Av. Marp 6D 142
Coombes St. Stoc 6B 140
Cooperas La. Droy 5G 97
        (in three parts)
Co-operation St. Fail 2F 85
Co-operative St. Dis 1H 165
Co-operative St.
   Haz G 2E 153
Co-operative St. L Hul . . .4A 62
Co-operative St. Rad 3G 49
Co-operative St. Salf 3F 93
Co-operative St. Shaw . . .6F 43
Co-operative St.
   S'head 3B 74
Co-operative St.
   Upperm 1F 61
Cooper Fold. Midd 3A 54
Cooper Ho.
   M15 . . . . . .1E 109 (6A 10)
Cooper La. M9 . . . . .4F 69
Cooper La. Midd 4H 53
Cooper's Fold.
   Chea H 1B 160
Coopers Row. Rams 6B 32
Cooper St. M2 . . . .4D 94 (6H 5)
      (in two parts)
Cooper St. Bury 3C 36
Cooper St. Duk 4A 100
Cooper St. Haz G 2F 153
Cooper St. Rams 4B 32
Cooper St. Roch 5B 16
Cooper St. S'head 2C 74
Cooper St. Stoc 4H 139
Cooper St. Stret 6D 106
Coopers Wlk. Roch 1C 28
Cooper Ter. Roch 3B 28
Coop St. M4 . . . .3F 95 (3C 6)
Coop St. Bolt 1A 32
Coop Ter. Roch 4D 28
Copage Dri. Bred 5G 129
Cope Bank. 4F 31
Cope Bank. Bolt 3G 31
Cope Bank E. Bolt 4G 31
Cope Bank W. Bolt 3F 31
Cope Clo. M11 . . . . .6G 97
Copeland Av. Swin 2A 80
Copeland Clo. Midd 6E 53
Copeland M. Bolt 6E 31
Copeland St. Hyde 2B 114
Copeman Clo.
   M13 . . . . .1G 109 (6E 11)
Copenhagen Sq. Roch . . .3A 28
Copenhagen St. Roch 3A 28
      (in two parts)
Cope St. Rams 4G 31
Copgrove Rd. M21 . . . . .2H 123
Copgrove Wlk. M22 . . . . .6C 148
Copley. 3G 101
Copley Av. Stal 3G 101
Copley Leisure Cen. 3G 101
Copley Pk. M. Stal 3G 101
Copley Rd. M21 . . . . . .5G 107
Copley St. Shaw 5G 43
Copperas St.
   M4 . . . . . . .3E 95 (4B 6)
Copperbeech Clo.
   M22 . . . . .2C 136
Copper Beech Dri.
   Glos 6G 117
Copper Beech Dri.
   Stal 2H 101
Copper Beech Mnr.
   Glos 6G 117
    (off Copper Beech Dri.)
Copperfield Ct. Alt 2E 145

Copperfield Rd.
   Chea H 2D 160
Copperfield Rd. Poy 5D 162
Copperfields. Los 3A 44
Copperfields. Wilm 1F 167
Copper La. P'wich 3G 65
Copperways. M20 . . . . .4E 125
Coppice. 5C 72
Coppice Av. Dis 1E 165
Coppice Av. Sale 1F 133
Coppice Clo. Dis 1E 165
Coppice Clo. Woodl 4H 129
Coppice Dri. M22 . . . . . .2B 136
Coppice Dri. Whitw 2C 14
Coppice Ind. Est. Oldh . . .4B 72
Coppice La. Dis 1E 165
Coppice Rd. Poy 4G 163
Coppice St. Bury 2G 37
Coppice St. Oldh 4B 72
      (in two parts)
Coppice, The. M9 . . . . . .1A 84
Coppice, The. Bolt 6H 19
Coppice, The. Bram 1G 161
Coppice, The. Haleb 5B 146
Coppice, The. Midd 3B 70
Coppice, The. Poy 5G 163
Coppice, The. P'wich 5E 67
Coppice, The. Rams 5C 12
Coppice, The. Swin 6C 78
Coppice, The. Wors 3H 77
Coppice Wlk. Dent 5D 112
Coppice Way. Hand 3A 160
Coppingford Clo. Roch . . .1C 26
Copping St. M12 . . . . . .1B 110
Coppins, The. Wilm 5B 166
Coppleridge Dri. M8 . . . . .2C 82
Copplestone Ct. Wors 2C 78
Copplestone Dri. Sale . . .4E 121
Cop Rd. Oldh 3G 57
Copse Av. M22 . . . . . . .2C 148
Copse Dri. Bury 5F 23
Copse, The. Haleb 6D 146
Copse, The. Marp B 3G 143
Copse, The. Tur 1G 19
Copse Wlk. L'boro 4D 16
Copson St. M20 . . . . . .2F 125
Copster Av. Oldh 6C 72
Copster Hill. 6C 72
Copster Hill Rd. Oldh 6C 72
Copster Pl. Oldh 6C 72
Copthall La. M8 . . . . .3B 82
Copthorne Clo. Heyw 5F 39
Copthorne Cres. M13 . . .5A 110
Copthorne Dri. Bolt 1G 47
Copthorne Wlk. T'ton 6H 21
Coptrod Head Clo.
   Roch 5E 15
Coptrod Rd. Roch 3F 27
Coral Av. Chea H 4C 150
Coral M. Rytn 4C 56
Coral Rd. Chea H 4C 150
Coral St. M13 . . . .6G 95 (4E 11)
Coram St. M18 . . . . . . .1H 111
Corbar Rd. Stoc 6A 140
Corbett St. M11 . . . . . . .4C 96
      (in two parts)
Corbett St. Roch 3B 28
Corbridge Wlk. M8 . . . . .5D 82
Corbrook Rd. Chad 6E 55
Corby St. M12 . . . . .1C 110
Corcoran Clo. Heyw 2E 39
Corcoran Dri. Rom 1D 142
Corda Av. M22 . . . . .3B 136
Corday La. P'wich 1H 67
Cordingley Av. Droy 5H 97
Cordova Av. Dent 4H 111
Corelli St. M40 . . . . .1B 96
Corfe Clo. Urm 6G 103
Corfe Cres. Haz G 4C 152

Corinthian Av. Salf 6G 81
Corinth Wlk. Wors 1F 77
Corkland Clo. Ash L 3B 100
Corkland Rd. M21 . . . . . .1H 123
Corkland St. Ash L 3C 100
Corks La. Dis 2H 165
Cork St. M12 . . . .5H 95 (1H 11)
Cork St. Ash L 2A 100
Cork St. Bury 3E 37
Corley Av. Stoc 4B 138
Corley Wlk. M11 . . . . . . .4B 96
Cormallen Gro. Fail 4G 85
Cormorant Clo. Wors 6E 63
Cormorant Wlk. M12 . . . .1C 110
Cornall St. Bury 2A 36
Cornbrook. 6B 94 (4C 8)
Cornbrook Arches.
   M15 . . . . . . .6A 94 (4B 8)
Cornbrook Clo. Ward 3A 16
Cornbrook Ct.
   M15 . . . . . .1B 108 (6C 8)
Cornbrook Gro.
   M16 . . . . . .2B 108 (6C 8)
Cornbrook Pk. Rd.
   M15 . . . . . .1A 108 (5B 8)
Cornbrook Rd.
   M15 . . . . . . .6A 94 (5A 8)
Cornbrook St. M16 . . . . .2B 108
      (in two parts)
Cornbrook Way. M16 . . . .2B 108
Corn Clo. M13 . . . . .2G 109
Cornell St. M4 . . . .3F 95 (3D 6)
Corner Cft. Wilm 5D 166
Cornerhouse. 2A 10
        (Art Gallery)
Corner St. Ash L 3A 100
Cornerways. Had 2H 117
      (off Albert St.)
Cornet St. Salf 5H 81
Cornfield Clo. Bury 4F 23
Cornfield Clo. Sale 6F 123
Cornfield Dri. M22 . . . . . .2A 148
Cornfield Rd. Rom 6C 130
Cornfield St. Miln 6G 29
Cornford Av. M18 . . . . . .4D 110
Cornhey Rd. Sale 1E 133
Cornhill Av. Urm 4D 104
Corn Hill La. Aud 2A 112
Cornhill Rd. Urm 3D 104
Cornhill St. Oldh 5H 57
Cornish Clo. M22 . . . . . . .5B 148
Cornishway. M22 . . . . . . .4A 148
Cornish Way. Rytn 4D 56
Cornishway Ind. Est.
   M22 . . . . .5B 148
Cornlea Dri. Wors 4E 77
Corn Mill Clo. Roch 5A 16
Corn Mill La. Stal 4F 101
Corn St. Fail 5C 84
Corn St. Oldh 2E 73
Cornwall Av. M19 . . . . . .1D 126
Cornwall Clo. Bury 5E 37
Cornwall Clo. H Lane 6C 154
Cornwall Ct. M18 . . . . . .1F 111
      (off Keary Clo.)
Cornwall Cres. Dig 3B 60
Cornwall Cres. Stoc 3C 128
Cornwall Dri. Bury 5D 36
Cornwall Ho. Salf 5D 4
Cornwall Rd. Cad 4B 118
Cornwall Rd. Droy 2A 98
Cornwall Rd. H Grn 5F 149
Cornwall St. M11 . . . . . . .6F 97
Cornwall St. Eccl 4E 91
Cornwall St. Oldh 4H 71
Cornwell Clo. Wilm 1G 167
Cornwood Clo. M8 . . . . . .4B 82
Corona Av. Hyde 4C 114
Corona Av. Oldh 6B 72
Coronation Av. Duk 1D 114
Coronation Av. Heyw 5G 39
Coronation Av. Hyde 6C 114

Coronation Bldgs.
   M4 . . . . .1F 95 (1C 6)
Coronation Gdns. Rad 3E 49
      (in two parts)
Coronation Rd. Ash L 5G 87
Coronation Rd. Droy 2H 97
Coronation Rd. Fail 5E 85
Coronation Rd. Rad 2E 49
Coronation Sq.
   M12 . . . . . . .5G 95 (2F 11)
Coronation Sq. Aud 6D 98
Coronation Sq. L Lev 4B 48
Coronation St. M11 . . . . . .5E 97
Coronation St. Dent 4C 112
Coronation St. Rams 1B 46
     (off Gt. Moor St.)
Coronation St.
   Salf 5H 93 (1A 8)
Coronation St. Stoc 5G 127
Coronation St. Swin 2G 79
Coronation Vs. Whitw 3H 15
Coronation Wlk. Rad 2E 49
Corporation Cotts.
   Part 3G 119
Corporation Rd. Aud 2D 112
Corporation Rd. Eccl 3G 91
Corporation Rd. Roch 5F 27
      (in two parts)
Corporation St.
   M4 . . . . .3D 94 (4H 5)
Corporation St. Bolt 6B 32
Corporation St. Hyde 5B 114
Corporation St. Midd 1A 70
Corporation St. Stal 4E 101
Corporation St. Stoc 1H 139
Corporation Yd. Redd . . .1H 127
Corran Clo. Eccl 3D 90
Corrie Clo. Dent 6F 113
Corrie Cres. Kear 4D 64
Corrie Dri. Kear 5D 64
Corrie Rd. Swin 6G 65
Corrie St. L Hul 5C 62
Corrie Way. Bred 4E 129
Corrigan St. M18 . . . . . .1G 111
Corringham Rd. M19 . . . . .2E 127
Corring Way. Bolt 1D 32
Corrin Rd. Bolt 2D 46
Corris Av. M9 . . . . .4C 68
Corry St. Heyw 3G 39
Corson Fylde. Bolt 5F 47
Corston Wlk. M40 . . . . . .5B 84
Corwen Clo. Oldh 1H 85
Corwen St. M9 . . . . .3G 83
Cosgrove Cres. Fail 6E 85
Cosgrove Rd. Fail 6E 85
Cosham Rd. M22 . . . . . .2D 148
Costabeck Wlk. M40 . . . . .1F 97
Costobadie Clo. Mot 4B 116
Costobadie Way. Mot 5B 116
Coston Park. 5C 110
Cotaline Clo. Roch 2B 40
Cotall Wlk. M8 . . . . .1C 94
Cotefield Av. Bolt 4B 46
Cotefield Clo. Marp 6D 142
Cotefield Rd. M22 . . . . . .3H 147
Cote Green.. . . . . .2F 143
Cote Grn. La. Marp B 2F 143
Cote Grn. Rd. Marp B 2F 143
Cote La. L'boro 3D 16
Cote La. Moss 6G 75
Cotford Rd. Rams 6D 18
Cotham St. M3 . . .1D 94 (1G 5)
Cotman Dri. Marp B 3G 143
Cotswold Av. Chad 4G 71
Cotswold Av. Haz G 4B 152
Cotswold Av. Shaw 5D 42
Cotswold Av. Urm 4B 104
Cotswold Clo. P'wich 4G 67
Cotswold Clo. Rams 5E 13
Cotswold Cres. Bury 2G 35
Cotswold Cres. Miln 4G 29
Cotswold Dri. Rytn 4H 55

Cotswold Dri. Salf 2F 93
Cotswold Rd. Stoc 6F 127
Cottage Cft. Bolt 6H 19
Cottage Gdns. Bred . . . 6D 128
Cottage Gro. Wilm 4B 166
Cottage Lawns. Ald E . . .4H 167
Cottage Lawns. Glos 6G 117
Cottages, The. S'head . . . 6D 58
Cottage Wlk. Droy 2H 97
Cottage Wlk. Roch 5C 14
Cottam Cres. Marp B . . .3F 143
Cottam Gro. Swin 4G 79
Cottam St. Bury 2A 36
Cottam St. Oldh 1B 72
Cottenham La.
    Salf 1C 94 (1E 5)
Cottenham St.
    M13 . . . . . .1F 109 (5D 10)
Cotterdale Clo. M16 . . . .5B 108
Cotteridge Wlk. M11 . . . .5B 96
Cotterill Clo. M23 . . . . . .2C 134
Cottesmore Dri. M8 . . . .3E 83
Cottesmore Gdns.
    Haleb 5C 146
Cottingham Dri.
    Ash L 1A 100
Cottingham Rd.
    M12 . . . . .1A 110 (6H 11)
Cottingley Clo. Bolt 6B 18
Cottonfield Rd. M20 . . . .3G 125
Cottonfields. Brom X . . .4D 18
Cotton Fold. Roch 5C 28
Cotton Hill. M20 . . . . . .4G 125
Cotton La. M20 . . . . . . .3G 125
Cotton La. Roch 1C 40
    (in two parts)
Cotton Mill Cres. Oldh . . .5H 71
Cotton St. Bolt 3H 31
Cotton St. Hyde 4C 114
Cotton St. E. Ash L 3G 99
Cotton St. W. Ash L 3G 99
Cotton Tree Clo. Oldh . . .1H 73
Cotton Tree St. Stoc 2G 139
Cottonwood Dri. Sale 4E 121
Cottrell Rd. Haleb 6D 146
Cottrill St. Salf 3H 93
Coucill Sq. Farn 1G 63
Coulsden Dri. M9 . . . . . . .6F 69
Coulthart St. Ash L 2H 99
Coulthurst St. Rams 3D 12
Coulton Clo. Oldh 1E 73
Coulton Wlk. Salf 3F 93
Councillor La.
    Chea & Chea H 5B 138
Councillor St. M12 . . . . . .4A 96
Countess Av. Chea H . . .2A 160
Countess Gro. Salf 6H 81
Countess La. Rad 2D 48
Countess Pl. P'wich 5D 67
Countess Rd. M20 . . . . .6F 125
Countess St. Ash L 3B 100
Countess St. Stoc 6A 140
Counthill Dri. M8 . . . . . . .1A 82
Counthill Rd. Oldh 6H 57
    (in two parts)
Counting Ho. Rd. Dis . . .2H 165
Count St. Roch 6A 28
County Av. Ash L 1C 100
County End. 4B 74
County End Bus. Cen.
    S'head 3B 74
County Rd. Wors 5C 62
County St. M2 . . . 4D 94 (6H 5)
County St. Oldh 1A 86
Coupland Clo. Oldh 3B 58
Coupland Clo. Whitw 1C 14
Coupland St.
    M15 . . . . . .2E 109 (6A 10)

Coupland St. Whitw 1C 14
Coupland St. E.
    M15 . . . . .1E 100 (6D 10)
Courier St. M18 . . . . . . .1G 111
Course Vw. Oldh 6A 74
Court Dri. M40 . . . . .1G 97
Courteney Pl. Bow 4C 144
Courtfield Av. M9 . . . . . .5F 69
Courthill St. Stoc 3A 140
    (in two parts)
Court Ho. Way. Heyw 3F 39
    (off Longford St.)
Court St. Bolt 6C 32
Court St. Upperm 1F 61
Courts Vw. Sale 4C 122
Court, The. P'wich 6F 67
Courtyard Dri. Wors 6C 62
Courtyard, The. Bolt 4B 32
Courtyard, The. Holl 2F 117
Courtyard, The. Salf 3G 81
Cousin Fields. Brom X . .4G 19
Covall Wlk. M8 . . . . .5D 82
Covell Rd. Poy 2E 163
Covent Garden. Stoc . . .2H 139
Coventry Av. Stoc 4B 138
Coventry Gro. Chad 6G 55
Coventry Rd. Rad 2F 49
Coventry St. Roch 5H 27
Coverdale Av. Bolt 5E 31
Coverdale Av. Rytn 2A 56
Coverdale Clo. Heyw 4E 39
Coverdale Cres.
    M12 . . . . . .1H 109 (5H 11)
Coverham Av. Oldh 5H 73
Coverhill Rd. G'ton 4D 74
Covert Rd. M22 . . . . . . .6C 136
Covert Rd. Oldh 6H 73
Cove, The. Hale 2H 145
Covington Pl. Wilm 3E 167
Cowan St. M40 . . . .3H 95 (4H 7)
Cowburn St.
    M3 . . . . .2D 94 (1H 5)
Cowburn St. Heyw 4G 39
Cowdals Rd. Los 3A 44
Cowesby St. M14 . . . . . .4E 109
Cowhill. 3H 71
Cowhill La. Ash L 2A 100
Cowhill Trad. Est.
    Ash L 1A 100
Cowie St. Shaw 5F 43
Cow La. Alt 6A 132
Cow La. Bolt 5F 45
Cow La. Fail 4E 85
Cow La. Haz G 1D 152
    (in two parts)
Cow La. Oldh 2G 73
Cow La. Sale 3E 123
Cow La. Salf 4A 94 (6B 4)
Cow La. Wilm 2F 167
Cowley Gro. Mot 4B 116
Cowley St. M40 . . . . .5C 84
Cowling St. Oldh 5D 72
Cowling St. Swin 3D 80
Cowlishaw. 1E 57
Cowlishaw. Shaw 2E 57
Cowlishaw La. Shaw 2E 57
Cowlishaw Rd.
    Hyde & Rom 4D 130
Cowm Pk. Way N.
    Whitw 3G 15
Cowm Pk. Way S.
    Whitw 1C 14
Cowm St. Whitw 1H 15
Cowm Top La. Roch 2E 41
    (in two parts)
Cowper St. Ash L 2A 100
Cowper St. Midd 2D 70
Cowper Wlk. M11 . . . . . .4B 96
Cox Green. 2D 18
Cox Grn. Rd. Eger 1C 18

Coxton Rd. M22 . . . . . . .4C 148
Coxwold Gro. Bolt 4G 45
Crabbe Ct. M1 . . . 2E 95 (1D 6)
Crab La. M9 . . . . .5D 68
Crabtree Av. Dis 2H 165
Crabtree Av. Haleb 6D 146
Crabtree Ct. Dis 1H 165
Crabtree La. M11 . . . . . . .5F 97
    (in two parts)
Crabtree Rd. Oldh 1F 73
Craddock Rd. Sale 1C 134
Craddock St. Moss 2D 88
Cradley Av. M11 . . . . . . .5F 97
Crag Av. Bury 1D 22
Crag Fold. Bury 1D 22
Cragg Pl. L'boro 4F 17
Cragg Rd. Chad 5F 55
    (in two parts)
Crag La. Bury 1D 22
Cragside Way. Wilm 3F 167
Craig Av. Bury 4H 35
Craig Av. Urm 4C 104
Craig Clo. Stoc 2D 138
Craigend Dri. M9 . . . . . . .4G 83
Craig Hall. Irlam 2D 118
Craighall Av. M19 . . . . . .1B 126
Craighall Rd. Bolt 5C 18
Craigie St. M8 . . . . .6B 82
Craiglands. Roch 3H 41
Craiglands Av. M40 . . . . .5A 84
Craignair Av. M20 . . . . . .5B 124
Craignair Ct. Swin 4A 80
Craig Rd. M18 . . . . .3E 111
Craig Rd. Stoc 2B 138
Craig Wlk. Oldh 4C 72
Craigweil Av. M20 . . . . . .6G 125
Craigwell Rd. P'wich 1A 82
Craigwell Wlk.
    M13 . . . . . .6F 95 (4C 10)
Crail Pl. Heyw 4B 38
Cramer St. M40 . . . . .6H 83
Crammond Clo. M40 . . . .5D 84
Cramond Clo. Bolt 4H 31
Cramond Wlk. Bolt 4H 31
Crampton Dri. Haleb 5C 146
Crampton La. C'ton 2G 119
    (in three parts)
Cranage Av. Hand 2H 159
Cranage Rd. M19 . . . . . .1D 126
Cranark Clo. Bolt 6E 31
Cranberry Clo. B'hth 3D 132
Cranberry Dri. Bolt 3D 44
Cranberry Rd. Part 6D 118
Cranberry St. Oldh 3F 73
Cranbourne Av.
    Chea H 3D 150
Cranbourne Clo. Ash L . .1G 99
Cranbourne Clo. Timp . . .5A 134
Cranbourne Ct. Stoc 5D 126
Cranbourne Rd. Ash L . .1G 99
Cranbourne Rd.
    Chor H 1H 123
Cranbourne Rd. Old T . . .3A 108
Cranbourne Rd. Roch . . .5A 26
Cranbourne Rd. Stoc . . .5D 126
Cranbourne St.
    Salf 4A 94 (6A 4)
Cranbourne Ter. Ash L . . .6F 87
Cranbrook Clo. Bolt 4B 32
    (off Lindfield St.)
Cranbrook Dri. P'wich . . .1G 81
Cranbrook Gdns.
    Ash L 1H 99
Cranbrook Pl. Oldh 3G 73
Cranbrook Rd. M18 . . . . .4G 111
Cranbrook Rd. Eccl 1C 90
Cranbrook Rd. Ash L 1G 99
Cranbrook Rd. Oldh 3F 73
Cranbrook St. Rad 2A 50
Cranbrook Wlk. Chad 3G 71
Cranby Village. M1 . . . . .2B 10
Crandon Ct. Swin 1G 79

Crandon Dri. M20 . . . . . .3G 137
Cranes Bill Clo. M22 . . . .4A 148
Crane Ct. M12 . . . 6C 96 (2F 11)
Crane St. Bolt 4F 45
Cranfield Clo.
    M40 . . . . .3H 95 (3H 7)
Cranford Av. M20 . . . . . .5H 125
Cranford Av. Sale 3C 122
Cranford Av. Stret 4F 107
Cranford Av. W'fld 5C 50
Cranford Clo. Swin 5H 79
Cranford Clo. W'fld 5C 50
Cranford Dri. Irlam 4D 102
Cranford Gdns. Marp 3D 142
Cranford Gdns. Urm 4A 104
Cranford Ho. Eccl 2H 91
Cranford Rd. Urm 4A 104
Cranford Rd. Wilm 6E 159
Cranford St. Bolt 5G 45
Cranleigh Av. Stoc 5B 126
Cranleigh Clo. Oldh 6A 58
Cranleigh Dri. Brook 2C 134
Cranleigh Dri. Chea 5B 138
Cranleigh Dri. Haz G 5G 153
Cranleigh Dri. Sale 4A 122
Cranleigh Dri. Wors 3G 77
Cranlington Dri. M8 . . . . .5B 82
Cranmer Ct. Heyw 4E 39
Cranmere Av. M19 . . . . . .5E 111
Cranmere Dri. Sale 1F 133
Cranmer Rd. M20 . . . . . .5F 125
Cranston Dri. M20 . . . . . .3F 137
Cranston Dri. Sale 6E 123
Cranston Gro. Gat 6D 136
Cranswick St. M14 . . . . . .4F 109
Crantock Dri. H Grn 5G 149
Crantock Dri. Stal 2H 101
Crantock St. M12 . . . . . .4D 110
Cranwell Ct. Droy 5B 98
    (off Williamson La.)
Cranwell Dri. M19 . . . . . .5A 126
Cranworth St. Stal 4F 101
Craston Rd. M13 . . . . . . .5A 110
Crathie Ct. Bolt 4F 31
Craunton Ho. Eccl 3H 91
Craven Av. Salf 5H 93
Craven Dri. B'hth 3E 133
Craven Dri. Salf 1G 107
Craven Gdns. Roch 6G 27
Cravenhurst Av. M40 . . . .1D 96
Craven Pl. M11 . . . . .3E 97
Craven Pl. Bolt 3C 30
Craven Rd. B'hth 4E 133
    (in two parts)
Craven Rd. Stoc 3H 127
Craven St. Ash L 5H 87
Craven St. Bury 2F 37
Craven St. Droy 4A 98
Craven St. Oldh 6C 56
Craven St.
    Salf (M5) . . .4A 94 (6B 4)
Craven St. Salf (M6) 5D 80
Craven Ter. Sale 5C 122
Cravenwood Rd. M8 . . . . .3C 82
Crawford Av. Bolt 1D 46
Crawford Av. Wors 3H 77
Crawford M. Ash L 3B 100
Crawford Sq. Heyw 4C 38
Crawford St. M40 . . . . . . .6C 84
Crawford St. Ash L 3B 100
Crawford St. Bolt 1D 46
Crawford St. Eccl 2F 91
Crawford St. Roch 6A 28
Crawley Av. M22 . . . . . . .2B 148
Crawley Av. Eccl 2A 92
Crawley Gro. Stoc 5B 140
Crawley Way. Chad 3G 71
Craydon St. Open 5D 96
Crayfield Rd. M19 . . . . . .1D 126

Crayford Rd. *M40* 1D 96
Cray, The. *Miln* 5E 29
(in two parts)
Cray Wlk. *M13* . . .6F 95 (4C 10)
Creaton Way. *Midd* 3E 53
Creden Av. *M22* 2C 146
Crediton Clo.
　M15 . . . . . .2D 108 (6H 9)
Crediton Clo. *Alt* 5D 132
Crediton Dri. *Bolt* 6A 34
Crediton Ho. Salf 2A 92
　(off Devon Clo.)
Creel Clo. *M9* 5D 68
Cremer Ho. Eccl 3A 92
　(off Trevelyan St.)
Cresbury St.
　M12 . . . . .5H 95 (3G 11)
Crescent Av. *M8* 3C 82
Crescent Av. *Bolt* 5H 31
Crescent Av. *Farn* 3E 63
Crescent Av. *P'wich* 1F 81
Crescent Av. *Swin* 3A 80
Crescent Clo. *Duk* 4A 100
Crescent Clo. *Stoc* 6A 140
Crescent Ct. *M21* 6F 107
Crescent Ct. *Sale* 6B 122
Crescent Dri. *L Hul* 4D 62
Crescent Gro. *M19* 6C 110
Crescent Gro. *Chea* 5G 137
Crescent Gro. *P'wich* 1F 81
Crescent Pk. *Stoc* 1D 138
Crescent Range. *M14* . . .4G 109
Crescent Rd. *M8* 3B 82
Crescent Rd. *Ald E* 4H 167
　(in two parts)
Crescent Rd. *Alt* 5C 132
Crescent Rd. *Bolt* 3C 46
Crescent Rd. *Chad* 1E 85
Crescent Rd. *Chea* 5G 137
Crescent Rd. *Duk* 4A 100
Crescent Rd. *Hale* 3G 145
Crescent Rd. *Kear* 3H 63
Crescent Rd. *Roch* 1B 40
Crescent Rd. *Stoc* 6B 128
Crescent St. *M8* 3E 83
Crescent, The. *M19* 6C 110
Crescent, The. *Alt* 6C 132
Crescent, The. *Bolt* 1H 33
Crescent, The. *Bred* 5D 128
Crescent, The. *Brom X* . . .4E 19
Crescent, The. *Chea* 5G 137
Crescent, The. *Droy* 4H 97
Crescent, The. *Irlam* 4F 103
Crescent, The. *L Lev* 5B 48
Crescent, The. *Midd* 1G 69
Crescent, The. *Moss* 2D 88
Crescent, The. *P'wich* 5F 67
Crescent, The. *Rad* 2D 48
Crescent, The.
　Salf 3H 93 (4A 4)
Crescent, The. *Shaw* 1E 57
Crescent, The. *Stal* 1H 115
Crescent, The. *Stoc* 6H 139
Crescent, The. *Timp* 4H 133
Crescent, The. *Urm* 5B 104
Crescent, The. *Whitw* 1C 14
Crescent, The. *Wors* 6A 78
Crescent Vw. Duk 4A 100
　(off Peel St.)
Crescent Way. *Stoc* 6A 140
Cresgarth Ho. *Stoc* 1A 152
Cressfield Way. *M21* . . .2B 124
Cressingham Rd. *Bolt* 3E 45
Cressingham Rd.
　Stret 5B 106
Cressington Clo. *Salf* 3E 93
Cresswell Gro. *M20* 4E 125
Crestfold. *L Hul* 5C 62
Crest Lodge. *Bram* 3H 151
Crest St. *M3* 2E 95 (1H 5)
Crest, The. *Droy* 6A 98
Crestwood Wlk. *M40* 5E 83

Crete St. *Oldh* 5D 72
Crewe Rd. *M23* 3E 135
Crib Fold. *Dob* 5A 60
Crib La. *Dob* 5A 60
Criccieth Rd. *Stoc* 4C 138
Criccieth St. *M16* 3D 108
Cricketfield La. *Wors* 6E 63
Cricket Gro., The.
　M21 . . . . .3H 123
Crickets La. *Ash L* 2A 100
　(in two parts)
Crickets La. N. *Ash L* 2A 100
Cricket St. *Bolt* 2H 45
Cricket St. *Dent* 3G 113
Cricket Vw. *Miln* 6F 29
Cricklewood Rd. *M22* 3A 148
Crimble. 1G 39
Crimble La. *Roch* 6A 26
　(in two parts)
Crimbles St. *Oldh* 1A 74
　(in two parts)
Crimble St. *Roch* 3F 27
Crime La. *Fail & Oldh* 4B 86
Crime Vw. Cotts. *Fail* 4B 86
Crimsworth Av. *M16* 5H 107
Crinan Sq. *Heyw* 4B 38
Crinan Wlk.
　M40 . . . . .2H 95 (1G 7)
Cringlebarrow Clo.
　Wors 6B 76
Cringle Clo. *Bolt* 3C 44
Cringle Dri. *Chea* 1G 149
Cringleford Clo. *M12* 2B 110
Cringle Hall Rd. *M19* 1B 126
Cringle Rd. *M19* 2D 126
Cripple Ga. La. *Roch* 4E 41
Crispin Rd. *M22* 5C 148
Critchley Clo. *Hyde* 6D 114
Criterion St. *Stoc* 5H 111
Croal St. *Rams* 1H 45
Croal Wlk. *W'fld* 6F 51
Croasdale Dri. *Rytn* 2C 56
Croasdale St. *Bolt* 4B 32
　(in two parts)
Crocker Wlk. *M9* 4G 83
Crocus Dri. *Rytn* 2E 57
Crocus St. *Bolt* 1B 32
Crocus Wlk. *Salf* 5H 81
　(off Hilton St. N.)
Croftacres. *Rams* 3A 12
Croft Av. *P'wich* 1B 68
Croft Bank. *M18* 2G 111
Croft Bank. *Mill* 1H 101
Croft Bank. *Salf* 6G 81
Croft Bank. *Whitw* 3H 15
Croft Brow. *Oldh* 1C 86
Croft Clo. *Haleb* 1C 156
Croft Dell. *Bolt* 2E 31
Croft Dri. *T'ton* 5G 21
Croft Edge. *G'fld* 4E 61
Crofters Brook. *Rad* 3A 50
Crofters Grn. *Wilm* 3B 166
Crofters Hall Wlk. M40 . . .4B 84
　(off Kenyon La.)
Crofters, The. *Sale* 6F 123
Crofters Wlk. *Bolt* 5G 19
Croft Ga. *Bolt* 1G 33
Cft. Gates Rd. *Midd* 2F 69
Croft Gro. *L Hul* 4B 62
Crofthead. *L'boro* 2F 17
Cft. Head Dri. *Miln* 4F 29
Crofthill Ct. *M40* 5B 16
Cft. Hill Rd. *M40* 2A 84
Croft Ind. Est. *Bury* 2E 51
Croftlands. *Rams* 6C 12
Croftlands Rd. *M22* 1C 148
Croft La. *Bolt* 2D 46
Croft La. *Bury* 2E 51
Croft La. *Rad* 3A 50
Croftleigh Clo. *W'fld* 5C 50
Crofton Av. *Timp* 2A 134

Crofton St. *M14* 4F 109
Crofton St. *Oldh* 6C 72
　(in two parts)
Crofton St. *Old T* 3B 108
Croft Rd. *Chea H* 3D 150
Croft Rd. *Sale* 1D 134
Croft Rd. *Wilm* 5B 166
Crofts Bank. 3E 105
Crofts Bank Rd. *Urm* 3E 105
Croft Side. *Bolt* 2G 47
Croftside Av. *Wors* 6G 63
Croftside Clo. *Wors* 6G 63
Croftside Gro. *Wors* 6G 63
Croftside Way. *Wilm* 3F 167
Croft Sq. *Roch* 6A 16
Croft St. *M11* 4D 96
Croft St. *Bolt* 3D 46
Croft St. *Bury* 3E 37
Croft St. *Fail* 2G 85
Croft St. *Hyde* 5A 114
Croft St. *L Hul* 4B 62
Croft St. *Roch* 6A 16
Croft St. *Salf* 6G 81
Croft St. *Stal* 3F 101
Croft, The. *Bolt* 5B 32
Croft, The. *Bury* 1E 51
Croft, The. *Had* 1H 117
Croft, The. *Oldh* 1C 86
Croft, The. *Stoc* 5B 140
Croich Bank. *Hawk* 1D 20
Cromar Rd. *Haz G* 2F 153
Cromarty Av. *Chad* 6F 71
Cromarty Sq. *Heyw* 4C 38
Cromarty Wlk. *M11* 4B 96
Crombie Av. *M22* 4B 136
Crombouke Fold. *Wors* . . .4D 76
Cromdale Av. *Bolt* 5F 31
Cromdale Av. *Haz G* 2F 153
Cromer Av. *M20* 3F 125
Cromer Av. *Bolt* 4E 33
Cromer Av. *Dent* 4A 112
Cromer Ind. Est. *Midd* 6B 54
Cromer Rd. *Bury* 6C 22
　(in two parts)
Cromer Rd. *Chea* 5A 138
Cromer Rd. *Sale* 6C 122
Cromer St. *M11* 4F 97
Cromer St. *Midd* 6B 54
Cromer St. *Roch* 3G 27
Cromer St. *Shaw* 6F 43
Cromer St. *Stoc* 1B 140
Cromford Av. *Stret* 4B 106
Cromford Bank. Glos 5F 117
　(off Cromford Lea)
Cromford Bus. Cen.
　Oldh 1F 73
Cromford Clo. *Bolt* 4A 32
Cromford Clo. Glos 5F 117
　(off Cromford Lea)
Cromford Ct.
　M4 . . . . . . .3E 95 (4A 6)
　(off Arndale Shop. Cen.)
Cromford Courts.
　M4 . . . . . . .3E 95 (4A 6)
Cromford Fold. Glos 5F 117
　(off Cromford Lea)
Cromford Gdns. Bolt 3B 32
Cromford Grn. Glos 5F 117
　(off Cromford Lea)
Cromford Gro. Glos 5F 117
　(off Cromford Way)
Cromford Lea. *Glos* 5F 117
Cromford Pl. Glos 5F 117
　(off Cromford Lea)
Cromford St. *Oldh* 1E 73
Cromford Way. *Glos* 5F 117
Cromhall Wlk. *M8* 5C 82
Cromhurst St. *M8* 2C 82
Cromley Dri. *H Lane* 1C 164
Cromley Rd. *H Lane* 6C 154
Cromley Rd. *Stoc* 2A 152
Crompton Av. *Bolt* 5G 33

Crompton Av. *Roch* 2H 41
Crompton Circuit.
　Oldh & Dens 1B 58
　(Grains Bar)
Crompton Circuit.
　Oldh & Shaw 3G 57
　(Sholver)
Crompton Fold.
　Oldh 5H 43
Crompton Ho. *Swin* 3E 79
Crompton Clo. *Bolt* 1C 32
Crompton Clo. *Marp* 4D 142
Crompton Clo. *Rad* 1H 65
Crompton Ct. *L Lev* 4C 48
Crompton Fold. 5H 43
Crompton Ho. *Swin* 3E 79
Crompton Pl. *Bolt* 6B 32
Crompton Pl. *Rad* 4H 49
Crompton Rd. *M19* 2C 126
Crompton Rd. *Rad* 1A 64
Crompton St. *Ash L* 1C 100
Crompton St. *Bury* 3C 36
Crompton St. *Chad* 2A 72
　(in two parts)
Crompton St. *Farn* 2G 63
Crompton St. *L Hul* 4A 62
Crompton St. *Oldh* 1C 72
Crompton St. *Rams* 5C 32
Crompton St. *Rytn* 4C 56
Crompton St. *Shaw* 6F 43
Crompton St. *Swin* 3E 79
Crompton St. *Wors* 1H 77
Crompton Va. *Bolt* 5F 33
Crompton Way. *Bolt* 1B 32
Crompton Way. *Shaw* 1F 57
Cromwell Av. *M16* 5A 108
Cromwell Av. *Gat* 5E 137
Cromwell Av. *Marp* 4B 142
Cromwell Ct. *Irlam* 2C 118
Cromwell Ct. Oldh 3D 72
　(off Cromwell St.)
Cromwell Ct. *Salf* 1H 93
Cromwell Gro. *M19* 6C 110
Cromwell Gro. *Salf* 6G 81
Cromwell Range.
　M14 . . . . .5H 109
Cromwell Rd. *Bram* 1F 161
Cromwell Rd. *Bred* 3D 128
Cromwell Rd. *Eccl* 3E 91
Cromwell Rd. *Irlam* 2C 118
Cromwell Rd. *P'wich* 5G 67
Cromwell Rd. *Rytn* 1A 56
Cromwell Rd. *Salf* 1G 93
Cromwell Rd. *Stret* 6E 107
Cromwell Rd. *Swin* 2E 79
Cromwell Rd. *W'fld* 4F 39
Cromwell St. *Heyw* 4F 39
Cromwell St. *Oldh* 3D 72
Cromwell St. *Rams* 6A 32
Cromwell St. *Stoc* 6F 127
Crondale Wlk.
　M13 . . . . . .1G 109 (6E 11)
　(off Watkin Clo.)
Crondall St. *M14* 4E 109
Cronkeyshaw Rd.
　Roch 2G 27
Cronshaw Ind. Est.
　Roch 5A 28
　(off Durham St.)
Cronshaw St. *M19* 1D 126
Crookhill Dri. *M8* 4B 82
Crookilley Way.
　Stoc & Bred 6A 128
Crook St. *Bolt* 1B 46
Crook St. *Hyde* 5B 114
Crook St. *Rad* 4H 49
Crook St. *Roch* 3A 28
Croom Wlk.
　M40 . . . . . .3H 95 (3G 7)
Crosby Av. *Wors* 1H 77
Crosby Rd. *M40* 6C 84
Crosby Rd. *Bolt* 5F 31

Crosby Rd. *Rad* 6E **35**
Crosby Rd. *Salf* 6B **80**
Crosby St. *Roch* 1H 27
Crosby St. *Stoc* 4H **139**
Crosfield Av. *S'seat* 1C **22**
Crosfield Gro. *M18* 2F **111**
Crosland Ind. Est.
　　Bred 5E **129**
Crossacres Rd. *M22* . . .2B **148**
Cross Av. *P'wich* 3E **67**
Cross Bank. **2B 74**
Crossbank Av. *Looc* 2B **74**
Crossbank Clo. *M13* . . .2H **109**
Crossbank St. *Oldh* 3C **72**
　　　(in two parts)
Crossbank Way. *Midd* 6H **53**
Cross Bri. Rd. *Hyde* 5E **115**
Crossby Clo. *Midd* 4H **69**
Crossefield Rd.
　　Chea H 2C **150**
Crossen St. *Bolt* 2E **47**
Crossfell Av. *M9* 4D **68**
Crossfield Clo. *Dent* . . .5G **113**
Crossfield Clo. *Shaw* 4G **43**
Crossfield Clo. *Stal* 4E **101**
Crossfield Clo. *Ward* 2A **16**
Cross Fld. Dri. *Rad* 4E **49**
Crossfield Dri. *Swin* 2E **79**
Crossfield Dri. *Wors* 4H **77**
Crossfield Gro.
　　Marp B 2F **143**
Crossfield Gro. *Stoc* . . .1B **152**
Crossfield Pl. *Roch* 6A **28**
Crossfield Rd. *Eccl* 3G **103**
Crossfield Rd. *Hale* 3B **146**
Crossfield Rd. *Hand* . . .3H **159**
Crossfield Rd. *Ward* 3A **16**
Crossfields. *Brom X* 3G **19**
Crossfield St. *Bury* 3D **50**
Crossford Ct. *Sale* 3C **122**
Crossford Dri. *Bolt* 2C **44**
Crossford St. *Stret* 6D **106**
Crossgate Av. *M22* 5B **136**
Crossgate M. *Stoc* 1A **138**
Crossgates Rd. *Miln* 4F **29**
Cross Glebe St. *Ash L* . . .2A **100**
Crosshill St. *M16* 3D **108**
Cross Hill Wlk. *Bolt* 2C **44**
Cross Hope St. *Ash L* . . .1B **100**
Cross Keys St.
　　M4 . . . . .3F **95** (3C **6**)
Cross Knowle Vw.
　　Urm 3B **104**
Crossland Rd. *M21* 1G **123**
Crossland Rd. *Droy* 3B **98**
Crosslands. *P'wich* 6E **67**
Crosslands Rd. *Wors* 5B **76**
Cross La. *M18* 2F **111**
Cross La. *Droy* 1D **98**
Cross La. *Holc* 4C **12**
Cross La. *Marp* 6C **142**
Cross La. *Rad* 3A **50**
Cross La. *Salf* 4G **93**
Cross La. *Wilm* 1H **167**
Cross La. E. *Part* 6D **118**
Cross La. W. *Part* 6D **118**
Cross Lees. *Roch* 6G **15**
Crossley Ct. M4 . . .4H **95** (5H **7**)
　　　(off Merrill St.)
Crossley Cres. *Ash L* 5H **87**
Crossley Est. *Chad* 3H **71**
Crossley Rd.
　　M19 & Stoc 2B **126**
Crossley Rd. *Sale* 3A **122**
Crossley St. *M18* 1D **110**
Crossley St. *Duk* 4B **100**
Crossley St. *L Lev* 3A **48**

Crossley St. *Miln* 5E **29**
Crossley St. *Rytn* 5C **56**
Crossley St. *Shaw* 6G **43**
Crossley St. *Stal* 3D **100**
Crossmead Dri. *M9* 4G **69**
Crossmeadow Clo.
　　Roch 3C **26**
Crossmoor Cres.
　　Rom 1A **142**
Crossmoor Dri. *Bolt* 5D **32**
Crossmoor Gro. *Rom* . . .1A **142**
Cross Ormrod St. *Bolt* . . .1H **45**
Cross Rd. *H Grn* 6F **149**
Cross St. *M2* 4D **94** (6H **5**)
Cross St. *Alt* 1F **145**
Cross St. *Ash L* 3G **99**
Cross St. *Bolt* 5B **32**
Cross St. *Brom X* 4D **18**
Cross St. *Bury* 3D **36**
Cross St. *Dent* 2E **113**
Cross St. *Farn* 6F **47**
Cross St. *Fir* 4D **28**
Cross St. *Had* 2H **117**
Cross St. *Heyw* 4G **39**
Cross St. *Holl* 3F **117**
Cross St. *Hyde* 5B **114**
Cross St. *Kear* 4B **64**
Cross St. *Lees* 3A **74**
Cross St. *L Lev* 4B **48**
Cross St. *Midd* 6H **53**
　　　(Kemp St.)
Cross St. *Midd* 6H **53**
　　　(Whittaker St.)
Cross St. *Mill* 1H **101**
Cross St. *Moss* 1E **89**
Cross St. *Oldh* 2F **73**
Cross St. *Old T* 2B **108**
Cross St. *Rad* 4H **49**
Cross St. *Rams* 3E **13**
Cross St. *Roch* 3D **40**
Cross St. *Sale* 4B **122**
Cross St. *Salf* 3C **94** (4F **5**)
Cross St. *S'head* 3C **74**
Cross St. *Stret* 5D **106**
Cross St. *Swin* 1B **80**
Cross St. *Urm* 6E **105**
Cross St. *W'fld* 6C **50**
Cross St. *Wors* 4C **78**
Cross, The. *Had* 2H **117**
Crosswaite Rd. *Stoc* . . .5D **140**
Crossway. *M20* 6F **125**
Crossway. *Bram* 2G **161**
Crossway. *Droy* 6A **98**
Crossway. *Stoc* 1A **152**
Crossway Rd. *Sale* 2H **133**
Crossways. *Bram* 4E **151**
Cross Ways. *Oldh* 2E **87**
Croston Clo. *Alt E* 5H **107**
Croston Clo. Rd.
　　Bury & Rams 1A **24**
　　　(in two parts)
Crostons Rd. *Bury* 2B **36**
Croston St. *Bolt* 3G **45**
　　　(in two parts)
Croston Wlk. *M11* 4A **96**
Croton St. *Stoc* 1A **138**
Croughton Clo. *M11* 6F **97**
Crowbank Wlk. *M40* 6A **84**
Crowborough Wlk.
　　M15 . . . . .2D **108**
　　　(off Botham Clo.)
Crowbrook Gro. *Wilm* . .6H **159**
Crowcroft Park. **4C 110**
Crowcroft Rd.
　　M13 & M12 . . . . . . .4C **110**
Crowden Rd. *M40* 1B **84**
Crowhill. **1F 99**
Crow Hill. *Carr* 6G **89**
Crowhill Cotts. *Ash L* . . .1G **99**
Crow Hill N. *Midd* 3H **69**
Crowhill Rd. *Ash L* 1F **99**

Crow Hill S. *Midd* 3H **69**
Crow Hill Vw. *Oldh* 5B **74**
Crowhurst Wlk. M23 . . . .4E **135**
　　　(off Claverham Wlk.)
Crowland Gdns.
　　Chea H 1D **160**
Crowland Rd. *M23* 2F **147**
Crowland Rd. *Bolt* 3E **33**
Crow La. *Rams* 3E **13**
Crowley La. *Oldh* 6H **57**
Crowley Rd. *M9* 3H **83**
Crowley Rd. *Timp* 5B **134**
Crown Bus. Cen. *Fail* 3F **85**
Crown Ct. *Haz G* 2D **152**
Crowneast St. *Roch* 4E **27**
Crown Gdns. *Roch* 6A **28**
Crowngreen Rd. *Eccl* 4G **91**
Crown Hill. *Moss* 3F **89**
Crownhill Ct. Droy 3A **98**
　　　(off Chappell Rd.)
Crownhill Dri. *Droy* 3A **98**
Crown Ind. Est.
　　M4 . . . . . . .3G **95** (3E **7**)
Crown Ind. Est. *Timp* . . .4G **133**
Crown La. *M4* 2E **95** (2B **6**)
Crown M. *Stoc* 1C **152**
Crown Pas. *Hale* 3G **145**
Crown Point Av. *M40* 6C **84**
Crown Point (Junct.).
　　Dent 4F **113**
　　　(off Hyde Rd.)
Crown Rd. *Heyw* 3D **38**
Crown Royal Ind. Pk.
　　Stoc 3H **130**
Crown Sq. *M3* 4C **94** (6F **5**)
Crown St. *M15* 6C **94** (3E **9**)
Crown St. *M40* 6C **84**
Crown St. *Ash L* 3H **99**
Crown St. *Bolt* 6B **32**
Crown St. *Bred* 5F **129**
Crown St. *Dent* 3E **113**
Crown St. *Fail* 3F **85**
Crown St. *Marp* 2D **154**
Crown St. *Roch* 6A **28**
Crown St. *Salf* 3C **94** (3E **5**)
Crown St. *Shaw* 6F **43**
Crowsdale Pl. *Stoc* 1E **153**
Crowshaw Dri. *Roch* 6E **15**
Crows Nest. *Bolt* 2H **47**
Crowswood Dri. *Carr* 6F **89**
Crowther Av. *Salf* 5G **93**
Crowther Ct. *L'boro* 5C **16**
Crowther St. *M18* 2F **111**
Crowther St. *L'boro* 5C **16**
Crowther St. *Roch* 1H **41**
Crowther St. *Stoc* 2H **139**
Crowthorn Dri. *M23* 3G **147**
Crowthorne Rd. *Ash L* . . .4F **99**
Crowthorn Rd. Stoc 2F **127**
Crowton Av. *Sale* 1F **133**
Croxdale Clo. *Ash L* 6C **86**
Croxdale Wlk. M9 . . . . . .4F **69**
　　　(off Claygate Dri.)
Croxton Av. *Roch* 3B **28**
Croxton Clo. *Marp* 6C **142**
Croxton Clo. *Sale* 6F **121**
Croxton Wlk.
　　M13 . . . .1G **109** (5E **11**)
Croydon Av. *Roch* 3B **28**
Croydon Av. *Rytn* 1A **56**
Croydon Clo. *Salf* 5H **93**
Croydon Dri. *M40* 1D **96**
Croydon Ho. Bolt 4A **32**
　　　(off Kenton Clo.)
Croydon Sq. *Roch* 5D **40**
Crummock Clo. *L Lev* 4H **47**
Crummock Dri. *Midd* 4G **53**
Crummock Gro. *Farn* 2A **62**
Crummock Rd. *Gat* 2F **149**
Crumpsall. **2B 82**

Crumpsall Cres. *M8* 3C **82**
Crumpsall Green. **1C 82**
Crumpsall La. *M8* 2B **82**
Crumpsall St. *Bolt* 3A **32**
Crumpsall Va. *M9* 1E **83**
Crumpsall Way. *M8* 2D **82**
Crundale Rd. *Bolt* 5E **19**
Cruttenden Rd. *Stoc* . . .1C **152**
Cryer St. *Droy* 1C **98**
Cuba Ind. Est. *Rams* 1E **13**
Cuba St. *Midd* 1C **70**
Cubo Gallery. **1A 10**
Cubley Rd. *Salf* 3A **82**
Cuckoo Gro. *P'wich* 3F **67**
Cuckoo La. *Bury* 3G **37**
　　　(Bri. Hall La., in two parts)
Cuckoo La. *Bury* 2G **37**
　　　(Rochdale Old Rd.)
Cuckoo La.
　　W'fld & P'wich 3F **67**
Cuckoo Nest. *P'wich* 2F **67**
Cuddington Av. *M20* 1E **125**
Cuddington Cres.
　　Stoc 5F **139**
Cuddington Way.
　　Hand 2H **159**
Cudworth Rd. *M9* 4C **68**
Cuerdon Wlk. *M22* 3C **136**
Culand St. *M12* 1A **110**
Culbert Av. *M20* 6G **125**
Culcheth. **6C 84**
Culcheth Av. *Marp* 5D **142**
Culcheth La. *M40* 6C **84**
Culcheth Rd. *Alt* 2F **145**
Culcombe Wlk. *M13* 2G **109**
Culford Clo. *M12* 2A **110**
Culgaith Wlk. *M9* 4F **83**
Culham Clo. *Bolt* 3H **31**
Cullen Gro. *M9* 5H **69**
　　　(in two parts)
Cullercoats Wlk. *M12* . . .4D **110**
Culmere Rd. *M22* 4B **148**
Culmington Clo.
　　M15 . . . . . .2C **108** (6E **9**)
Culross Av. *M40* 2E **85**
Culross Av. *Bolt* 1C **44**
Culvercliff Wlk.
　　M3 . . . . . . .5C **94** (1F **9**)
Culverden Av. *Salf* 5D **80**
Culverden Wlk. *Salf* 5D **80**
Culver Rd. *Stoc* 6F **139**
Culvert St. *Oldh* 1A **74**
Culvert St. *Roch* 3H **41**
Culverwell Dri. *Salf* 3H **93**
Cumber Clo. *Wilm* 5A **166**
Cumber Dri. *Wilm* 5A **166**
Cumberland Av. *Cad* 5A **118**
Cumberland Av. *Duk* 5C **100**
Cumberland Av. *Heyw* . . .3C **38**
Cumberland Av. *Stoc* . . .5C **128**
Cumberland Av. *Swin* 1F **79**
Cumberland Av. *Bow* . . .5C **144**
Cumberland Dri.
　　Oldh & Rytn 6B **56**
Cumberland Gro. *Ash L* . .1H **99**
Cumberland Ho. *M34C* **94** (6G **5**)
Cumberland Rd. *M9* 2F **83**
Cumberland Rd. *Roch* . . .3F **41**
Cumberland Rd. *Sale* . . .1C **134**
Cumberland Rd. *Urm* . . .6E **105**
Cumberland St. *Salf* 1B **94**
Cumberland St. *Stal* 3D **100**
Cumberland Wlk. *Bury* . . .1C **50**
Cumber La. *Wilm* 4A **166**
Cumbrae Gdns. *Salf* 4D **92**
Cumbrae Rd. *M19* 6E **111**
Cumbria Ct. *P'wich* 2E **81**
Cumbrian Clo.
　　M13 . . . . .1G **109** (5D **10**)
Cumbrian Clo. *Shaw* 5D **42**
Cumbria Wlk. *Salf* 1H **93**
Cummings St. *Oldh* 1A **86**

Cunard Clo.
　M13 . . . . . .1G **109** (5E **11**)
Cundall Wlk. *M23* 2F **135**
Cundall Way. *Mot* 5B **116**
Cundey St. *Bolt* 4G **31**
Cundiff Ct. *M19* 6E **111**
Cundiff Rd. *M21* 3H **123**
Cundy St. *Hyde* 3C **114**
Cunliffe Av. *Rams* 5C **12**
Cunliffe Brow. *Bolt* 3F **31**
Cunliffe Dri. *Sale* 6C **122**
Cunliffe Dri. *Shaw* 6G **43**
Cunliffe St. *Hyde* 3A **114**
Cunliffe St. *Rad* 4A **50**
Cunliffe St. *Rams* 2E **13**
Cunliffe St. *Stoc* 3E **139**
Cunningham Dri. *M22* . . .5E **149**
Cunningham Dri. *Bury* . . .6E **51**
Cunningham Way.
　Oldh 1D **72**
Curate Ct. *Stoc* 2A **140**
　　　　　　(off Curate Clo.)
Curate St. *Stoc* 2A **140**
Curlew Clo. *Roch* 4B **26**
Curlew Dri. *Irlam* 3E **103**
Curlew Rd. *Oldh* 5A **74**
Curlew Wlk. *M12* 2A **110**
Curlew Way. *Glos* 6H **117**
Currier La. *Ash L* 3A **100**
Curtels Clo. *Wors* 4C **78**
Curtis Gro. *Had* 2H **117**
Curtis Rd. *Stoc* 1C **138**
Curtis St. *M19* 6E **111**
Curtis St. *Bolt* 5G **45**
Curzon Av. *M14* 3A **110**
Curzon Clo. *Roch* 3F **41**
Curzon Dri. *Timp* 5B **134**
Curzon Grn. *Stoc* 3D **140**
Curzon M. *Wilm* 3D **166**
Curzon Rd. *Ash L* 1B **100**
Curzon Rd. *Bolt* 6G **31**
Curzon Rd. *H Grn* 6F **149**
Curzon Rd. *Poy* 5E **163**
Curzon Rd. *Roch* 3F **41**
Curzon Rd. *Sale* 4B **122**
Curzon Rd. *Salf* 4H **81**
Curzon Rd. *Stoc* 4D **140**
Curzon Rd. *Stret* 4A **106**
Curzon St. *Moss* 2E **89**
Curzon St. *Oldh* 2D **72**
Cutgate. 3C **26**
Cutgate Clo. *M23* 2F **135**
Cutgate Rd. *Roch* 2D **26**
Cutgate Shop. Precinct.
　Roch 3D **26**
Cuthbert Av. *M19* 5D **110**
Cuthbert Bus. Cen.
　M11 . . . . .6E **97**
　　　　　(off Ashton Old Rd.)
Cuthbert Mayne Ct.
　Roch 5G **27**
Cuthbert Rd. *Chea* 5A **138**
Cuthbert St. *Bolt* 5F **45**
Cuthill Wlk. *M40* 1F **97**
Cutland St. *M40* 5A **84**
Cutland Way. *L'boro* 5E **17**
Cut La. *Roch* 2B **26**
Cutler Hill. 4A **86**
Cutler Hill Rd. *Fail* 4H **85**
Cutler St. *Chad* 2A **72**
Cutnook La. *Irlam* 2D **102**
Cutter Clo. *Salf* 5G **93**
Cycle St. *M11* 5D **96**
Cyclone St. *M11* 5B **96**
Cygnus Av.
　Salf 2A **94** (1B **4**)
Cymbal Ct. *Stoc* 6H **127**
Cynthia Dri. *Marp* 6D **142**
Cypress Av. *Chad* 1H **71**
Cypress Clo. *Stoc* 3E **139**
Cypress Gdns. *Fir* 4D **28**
Cypress Gro. *Dent* 4G **113**

Cypress Gro. *Kear* 2H **63**
Cypress Oaks. *Stal* 2H **101**
Cypress Rd. *Droy* 2A **98**
Cypress Rd. *Eccl* 1C **90**
Cypress Rd. *Oldh* 1H **73**
Cypress St. *M9* 4F **83**
Cypress St. *Midd* 2C **70**
Cypress Wlk. *Sale* 3E **121**
Cypress Way. *H Lane* . . .6E **155**
Cyprus Clo. *Oldh* 4H **73**
Cyprus Clo. *Salf* 4F **93**
Cyril St. *M14* 4F **109**
Cyril St. *Bolt* 2C **46**
Cyril St. *Shaw* 6F **43**
Cyrus St. *M40* 3H **95** (4H **7**)

D

Daccamill Dri. *Swin* 4F **79**
Dacre Av. *M16* 5H **107**
Dacre Clo. *Midd* 6D **52**
Dacre Rd. *Roch* 1F **41**
Dacres. 5H **75**
Dacres Av. *G'fld* 5H **75**
Dacres Dri. *G'fld* 5H **75**
Dacres Rd. *G'fld* 5H **75**
Daffodil Clo. *Roch* 6E **15**
Daffodil Rd. *Farn* 6C **46**
Daffodil St. *Rams* 6D **18**
Dagenham Rd. *M14* . . .3G **109**
Dagenham Rd. Ind. Est.
　M14 . . . . .4G **109**
　　　　　　(off Denison St.)
Dagmar St. *Wors* 5E **63**
Dagnall Av. *M21* 3H **123**
Dahlia Clo. *Roch* 6D **14**
Daimler St. *M8* 5C **82**
Dain Clo. *Duk* 5C **100**
Daine Av. *M23* 2H **135**
Dainton St.
　M12 . . . . . .6H **95** (3H **11**)
Daintry Clo.
　M15 . . . . . .1D **108** (5G **9**)
Daintry Rd. *Oldh* 2A **72**
Dairybrook Gro. *Wilm* . .6A **160**
Dairydale Clo. *Irlam* 4F **103**
Dairyground Rd.
　Bram 6G **151**
Dairyhouse La. *B'hth* . . .5C **132**
Dairy Ho. La. *Woodf* 4C **160**
　　　　　　(in two parts)
Dairy Ho. Rd. *Woodf* . . .3D **160**
Dairy St. *Chad* 2H **71**
Daisy Hill Ct. *Oldh* 1A **74**
Daisy Av. *M13* 3A **110**
Daisy Av. *Farn* 6C **46**
Daisy Bank. *M40* 6C **84**
Daisy Bank. *Hyde* 1A **130**
Daisy Bank Av.
　Swin & Salf 5A **80**
Daisybank La. *H Grn* . . .4E **149**
Daisy Bank Rd. *M14* . . .3H **109**
Daisyfield. 4H **35**
Daisyfield Clo. *M22* 4A **148**
Daisyfield Ct. *Bury* 4A **36**
Daisyfield Wlk. *Wors* 6F **63**
Daisy Hill Clo. *Sale* 5E **123**
Daisy Hill Rd. *Moss* 2F **89**
Daisy M. *Stoc* 1F **151**
Daisy Nook. 5B **86**
Daisy Nook Country Pk.
　　　　　. . . . . .5C **86**
Daisy Row. *L'boro* 6D **16**
Daisy St. *Bolt* 3G **45**
Daisy St. *Bury* 3A **36**
Daisy St. *Chad* 1G **71**
Daisy St. *Oldh* 2B **72**
Daisy St. *Roch* 3G **27**
Daisy St. *Stoc* 4H **139**

Daisy Way. *H Lane* 6D **154**
Dakerwood Clo. *M40* . . .6C **84**
Dakota Av. *Salf* 5E **93**
Dakota S. *Salf* 5E **93**
Dalbeattie St. *M9* 2G **83**
Dalberg St.
　M12 . . . . . .6H **95** (4G **11**)
Dalbury Dri. *M40* 6E **83**
Dalby Av. *Swin* 4E **79**
Dalby Gro. *Stoc* 2A **140**
Dale. 2H **59**
Dale Av. *Bram* 5H **151**
Dale Av. *Eccl* 2E **91**
Dale Av. *Moss* 6G **75**
Dale Bank M. *Swin* 4D **64**
Dalebeck Clo. *W'fld* 1G **67**
Dalebeck Wlk. *W'fld* 1G **67**
Dalebrook Av. *Duk* 1B **114**
Dalebrook Clo. *L Lev* . . .3A **48**
Dalebrook Ct. *Stoc* 2E **139**
Dalebrook Rd. *Sale* 2C **134**
Dale Ct. *Dent* 5F **113**
Dale End. *Oldh* 1E **87**
Dalefields. *Del* 3H **59**
Daleford Sq.
　M13 . . . . . . .6F **95** (4E **11**)
Dalegarth Av. *Bolt* 6A **30**
Dale Gro. *Ash L* 6E **87**
Dale Gro. *Cad* 3C **118**
Dale Gro. *Timp* 4H **133**
Dalehead Clo. *M18* 1H **111**
Dalehead Dri. *Shaw* 6H **43**
Dale Ho. *Midd* 6B **54**
Dale Ho. *Shaw* 1F **57**
Dale Ho. Fold. *Poy* 3G **163**
Dale La. *Del* 2H **59**
Dale Rd. *Marp* 3C **142**
Dale Rd. *Midd* 5B **54**
Dales Av. *M8* 1B **82**
Dales Av. *W'fld* 6B **50**
Dales Brow. 5D **78**
Dales Brow. *Bolt* 5D **18**
Dales Brow. *Swin* 5D **78**
Dales Brow Av. *Ash L* . . .6F **87**
Dalesfield Cres. *Moss* . . .2G **89**
Dales Gro. *Wors* 2H **77**
Dales La. *W'fld* 6C **50**
Dalesman Clo. *M9* 3H **83**
Dalesman Dri. *Oldh* 4H **57**
Dales Pk. Dri. *Swin* 5D **78**
Dale Sq. *Rytn* 3D **56**
Dale St. *M1* 4E **95** (5E **6**)
　　　　　　(in two parts)
Dale St. *Ash L* 5C **88**
Dale St. *B'hth* 4F **133**
Dale St. *Bury* 1A **36**
Dale St. *Kear* 6G **47**
Dale St. *Midd* 2B **70**
Dale St. *Miln* 5F **29**
Dale St. *Rad* 5G **49**
　　　　　　(Phoenix Way)
Dale St. *Rad* 5G **49**
　　　　　　(Pilkington Way)
Dale St. *Rams* 1E **13**
Dale St. *Roch* 4C **28**
Dale St. *Shaw* 1F **57**
Dale St. *Stal* 4D **100**
Dale St. *Stoc* 5F **139**
Dale St. *Swin* 5E **79**
Dale St. *W'fld* 6C **50**
Dale St. E. *Ash L* 3G **99**
Dale St. Ind. Est. *Rad* . . .5G **49**
Dale St. W. *Ash L* 3G **99**
Daleswood Av. *W'fld* 6B **50**
Dale Vw. *Dent* 2G **129**
Dale Vw. *Hyde* 1B **130**
Dale Vw. *L'boro* 1F **29**
Dalkeith Av. *Stoc* 2H **127**
Dalkeith Gro. *Bolt* 2D **44**
Dalkeith Rd. *Stoc* 2H **127**
Dalkeith Sq. *Heyw* 4C **38**

Dalkeith St. *M18* 1D **110**
Dallas Ct. *Salf* 5E **93**
Dalley Av. *Salf* 1B **94** (1C **4**)
Dallimore Rd.
　Round I 5E **135**
Dalmahoy Clo. *M40* 3C **84**
Dalmain Clo. *M8* 5B **82**
Dalmain Wlk. M8 . . . . . .5B **82**
　　　　　　(off Dalmain Clo.)
Dalmeny Ter. *Roch* 1F **41**
Dalmorton Rd. *M21* 1B **124**
Dalny St. *M19* 6D **110**
Dalry Wlk. *M23* 5G **135**
Dalston Av. *Fail* 3H **85**
Dalston Dri. *M20* 1F **137**
Dalston Dri. *Bram* 2E **161**
Dalston Gdns. Bolt 3A **32**
　　　　　　(off Gladstone St.)
Dalton Av. *M14* 5E **109**
Dalton Av. *Roch* 4D **28**
Dalton Av. *Stret* 3H **105**
Dalton Av. *Swin* 6A **66**
Dalton Av. *W'fld* 2E **67**
Dalton Clo. *Rams* 5C **12**
Dalton Clo. *Roch* 4D **28**
Dalton Ct. *M4* 1F **95** (1D **6**)
Dalton Ct. *Stoc* 5E **127**
Dalton Dri. *Swin* 4B **80**
Dalton Gdns. *Urm* 4D **104**
Dalton Gro. *Stoc* 5E **127**
Dalton Rd. *M9* 4F **69**
Dalton Rd. *Midd* 2D **68**
Dalton St.
　M4 & M40 . . .1F **95** (1D **6**)
Dalton St. *Bury* 3H **35**
　　　　　　(in two parts)
Dalton St. *Chad* 2H **71**
Dalton St. *Eccl* 2F **91**
Dalton St. *Fail* 3E **85**
Dalton St. *Oldh* 2F **73**
Dalton St. *Sale* 3C **122**
Daltrey St. *Oldh* 1E **73**
Dalveen Av. *Urm* 3E **105**
Dalveen Dri. *Timp* 4H **133**
Dalymount Clo. *Bolt* 3D **32**
Damask Av. *Salf* . . .3B **94** (3C **4**)
Dame Hollow. *H Grn* 6H **149**
Dameral Clo. *M8* 5C **82**
Damery Ct. *Bram* 5G **151**
Damery Rd. *Bram* 5G **151**
Dam Head Dri. *M9* 6G **69**
Damien St. *M12* 5C **110**
Damside. *Had* 1H **117**
Damson Grn. *Midd* 1D **70**
Damson Wlk. *Part* 6B **118**
Dan Bank. *Marp* 5A **142**
Danbury Wlk. *M23* 3D **134**
Danby Clo. *Hyde* 3D **114**
Danby Ct. *Oldh* 1C **72**
Danby Pl. *Hyde* 3D **114**
Danby Rd. *Bolt* 4A **46**
Danby Rd. *Hyde* 3D **114**
Danby Wlk. M9 . . . . .2G **83**
　　　　　　(off Polworth Rd.)
Dancehouse Theatre. . . .3A **10**
Dane Av. *Part* 5D **118**
Dane Av. *Stoc* 3C **138**
Dane Bank. 5B **112**
Dane Bank. *Midd* 1B **70**
Dane Bank Dri. *Dis* 1H **165**
Danebank M. *Dent* 5B **112**
Danebank Wlk.
　M13 . . . . . .6F **95** (4D **10**)
Danebridge Clo. *Farn* . . .1G **63**
　　　　　　(Darley St.)
Danebridge Clo. *Farn* . . .1G **63**
　　　　　　(Peel St.)
Dane Clo. *Bram* 2F **151**
Danecroft Clo.
　M13 . . . . .2H **109** (6G **11**)
Dane Dri. *Wilm* 3G **167**
Danefield Ct. *H Grn* 5H **149**

Danefield Rd. Sale 3C 122
Dane Hill Clo. Dis 2H 165
Danoholmo Rd. M10 . . . .1A 126
Dane M. Sale 3B 122
Dane Rd. Dent 5A 112
Dane Rd. Sale 3C 122
Dane Rd. Ind. Est.
　　　　Sale 3C 122
Danesbury Ri. Chea 6H 137
Danesbury Rd. Bolt 1D 32
Daneshill. P'wich 3F 67
Danes La. Whitw 1A 14
Danesmoor Dri. Bury 1E 37
Danesmoor Rd. M20 . . . .4E 125
Danes Rd. M14 . . . . . . .5H 109
Danes, The. M8 . . . . . . .2B 82
Dane St. M11 . . . . .6G 97
Dane St. Bolt 3G 45
Dane St. Moss 6F 76
Dane St. Oldh 2G 73
Dane St. Roch 4G 27
Danesway. P'wich 1H 81
Danesway. Swin 4A 80
Danesway Ct. Bolt 3H 31
Daneswood Av. M9 . . . . .5H 69
Daneswood Av. Whitw . . .1C 14
Daneswood Clo.
　　　　Whitw 1B 14
Danett Clo. M12 . . . . . .1D 110
Dane Wlk. Stoc 4H 127
Danforth Gro. M19 . . . . .1D 126
Daniel Adamson Av.
　　　　Part 6B 118
Daniel Adamson Rd.
　　　　Salf 4D 92
Daniel Ct. Part 5D 118
Daniel Fold. Roch 1D 28
Daniel's La. Stoc 1H 139
Daniel St. Haz G 3E 153
Daniel St. Heyw 3D 38
Daniel St. Oldh 1F 73
Daniel St. Rytn 4E 57
Daniel St. Whitw 3H 15
Danisher La. Oldh 3D 86
Dannywood Clo.
　　　　Hyde 1A 130
Danson St. M40 . . . . . . .2A 96
Dantall Av. M9 . . . . .6A 70
Dante Clo. Eccl 1A 92
Danty St. Duk 4H 99
Dantzic St. M4 . . . .3E 95 (4A 6)
Danwood Clo. Dent 5H 113
Dapple Gro. M11 . . . . . . .5C 96
Darbishire St. Bolt 4C 32
Darby Rd. Irlam 3E 119
Darbyshire Clo. Bolt 5G 31
Darbyshire Ho. Timp 4C 134
Darbyshire St. Rad 4G 49
Darbyshire Wlk. Rad 4H 49
Darcy Lever. 2F 47
Darcy Wlk. M14 . . . . . . .3E 109
Darden Clo. Stoc 6A 126
Daresbury Av. Alt 6G 133
Daresbury Av. Urm 3H 103
Daresbury Clo. Sale 3C 122
Daresbury Clo. Stoc 6F 139
Daresbury Clo. Wilm 1F 167
Daresbury Rd. M21 . . . . .6F 107
Daresbury St. M8 . . . . . .3C 82
Darfield Wlk.
　　　　M40 . . . . . . .2H 95 (2G 7)
Dargai St. M11 . . . . .4F 97
Dargle Rd. Sale 3B 122
Darian Av. M22 . . . . . . .5B 148
Dark La. M12 . . .5H 95 (2G 11)
Dark La. Alt 1A 132
Dark La. Bred 6D 128
Dark La. Del 1G 59
Dark La. Moss 5F 77
　　　　　　　(in two parts)
Dark La. Nature Reserve.
　　　　 . . . . .1A 132

Darlbeck Wlk. M21 . . . . .4A 124
Darley Av.
　　　M21 & M20 . . . .6H 125
　　　　　　　(in two parts)
Darley Av. Eccl 5E 91
Darley Av. Farn 6G 47
Darley Av. Gat 6F 137
Darley Ct. Rams 3G 31
Darley Park. 3A 108
Darley Rd. M16 . . . . . . .4A 108
Darley Rd. Haz G 6F 153
Darley Rd. Roch 1F 41
Darley St. M11 . . . . .4B 96
Darley St. Bolt 4H 31
Darley St. Farn 1G 63
Darley St. Sale 5B 122
Darley St. Stoc 6E 127
Darley St. Strot 3D 106
Darley Ter. Bolt 4A 32
Darlington Clo. Bury 6B 22
Darlington Rd. M20 . . . . .3E 125
Darlington Rd. Roch 2F 41
Darliston Av. M9 . . . . . . .4C 68
Darlton Wlk. M9 . . . . . . .3G 83
Darnall Av. M20 . . . . . . .1E 125
Darnbrook Dri. M22 . . . .4H 147
Darncombe Clo. M16 . . .3D 108
Darn Hill. 4B 38
Darnley Av. Wors 2E 77
Darnley St. M16 . . . . . . .3B 108
Darnton Rd.
　　　Ash L & Stal 1C 100
Darnton Rd.
　　　Ash L & Stal 1C 100
Darras Rd. M18 . . . . . . .4E 111
Darrell Wlk. M8 . . . . .5D 82
Dart Clo. Chad 1F 71
Dartford Av. Eccl 3D 90
Dartford Av. Stoc 4B 128
Dartford Clo.
　　　M12 . . . . .1H 109 (6H 11)
Dartford Rd. Urm 6E 105
Dartington Clo. M23 . . . .5D 134
Dartington Clo. Bram . . .2H 151
Dartmouth Clo. Oldh 5D 72
Dartmouth Cres. Stoc . . .4C 128
Dartmouth Rd. M21 . . . .1A 124
Dartmouth Rd. W'fld 2E 67
Dartnall Clo. Dis 1E 165
Darton Av. M40 . . .2H 95 (2H 7)
Darvel Clo. Bolt 1H 47
Darwell Av. Eccl 5E 91
Darwen Rd.
　　　Eger & Brom X 2C 18
Darwen St.
　　　M16 . . . . . .2A 108 (6A 8)
Darwin Gro. Bram 1G 161
Darwin St. Ash L 3G 99
Darwin St. Bolt 3H 31
Darwin St. Hyde 2E 115
Darwin St. Oldh 4G 73
Dashwood Rd. P'wich 4E 67
Dashwood Wlk. M12 . . . .1C 110
Datchet Ter. Roch 1F 41
Daubhill. 4G 45
Dauntesy Av. Swin 4B 80
Davehall Av. Wilm 2D 166
Davenfield Gro. M20 . . . .6F 125
Davenfield Rd. M20 . . . . .6F 125
Davenham Rd. Hand 3H 159
Davenham Rd. Sale 3G 121
Davenham Rd. Stoc 5H 111
Davenhill Rd. M19 . . . . .1C 126
Davenport. 6H 139
Davenport Av. M20 . . . . .2F 125
Davenport Av. Rad 1F 49
Davenport Av. Wilm 5B 166
Davenport Dri. Woodl . . .3H 129
Davenport Fold. Bolt 2A 34
Davenport Fold Rd.
　　　Bolt 1A 34
Davenport Gdns. Bolt 5A 32

Davenport Green. 4E 147
　　　　　　　(Altrincham)
Davenport Green. 5D 166
　　　　　　　(Wilmslow)
Davenport La. B'hth 4E 133
Davenport Lodge.
　　　Stoc 6H 139
Davenport Park. 6A 140
Davenport Pk. Rd.
　　　Stoc 6A 140
Davenport Rd.
　　　Haz G 2D 152
Davenport St. Aud 5E 99
Davenport St. Bolt 5A 32
Davenport St. Droy 4G 97
Davenport Ter. M9 . . . . . .3G 83
Daventry Rd. M21 . . . . . .1B 124
Daventry Rd. Roch 1F 41
Daventry Way. Roch 2F 41
Daveylands. Wilm 2G 167
Davey La. Ald E 4G 167
David Brow. Bolt 5E 45
David Lewis Clo. Roch . . .5C 28
David Lloyd Leisure Cen.
　　　 . . . . .6H 31
　　　　　　　(Bolton)
David Lloyd Leisure Cen.
　　　 . . . . .3G 149
　　　　　　　(Cheadle)
David Lloyd Leisure Cen.
　　　 . . . . .6E 91
　　　　　　　(Trafford Cen.)
David M. M14 . . . . .2G 125
David Pegg Wlk. M40 . . . .5B 84
David's Farm Clo. Midd . . .2C 70
David's La. S'head 2B 74
Davidson Dri. Midd 3B 70
David St. Bury 2A 36
　　　　　　　(in two parts)
David St. Dent 6G 113
David St. Oldh 3C 72
David St. Roch 2H 27
David St. Stoc 1G 127
David St. N. Roch 2H 27
Davies Av. H Grn 1F 159
Davies Ct. Stret 6D 106
Davies Rd. Bred 6D 128
Davies Rd. Part 6E 119
Davies Sq. M14 . . . . . . .3E 109
Davies St. Ash L 4F 99
Davies St. Kear 2A 64
Davies St. Oldh 1B 72
Davis Hall. M14 . . . . . . .3H 109
Davis St. Eccl 4G 91
Davis St. Swin 1B 80
Davyhulme. 4F 105
Davyhulme Circ. Urm 3E 105
Davyhulme Rd. Stret 4C 106
Davyhulme Rd. Urm 3A 104
Davyhulme Rd. E.
　　　Stret 4D 106
Davyhulme St. Roch 2B 28
Davylands. Urm 2B 104
Davy St. M40 . . . .1F 95 (1D 6)
Daw Bank. Stoc 2G 139
Dawes St. Bolt 1B 46
Dawley Clo. Bolt 1G 45
Dawley Flats. Heyw 3E 39
　　　　(off Brunswick St.)
Dawlish Av. Chad 6F 55
Dawlish Av. Chea H 5B 150
Dawlish Av. Droy 3G 97
Dawlish Av. Stoc 4C 128
Dawlish Clo. Bram 6H 151
Dawlish Clo. Hyde 4A 116
Dawlish Rd. M21 . . . . . . .1A 124
Dawlish Rd. Sale 4G 121
Dawnay St. M11 . . . . . . .5D 96
Dawn St. Shaw 1F 57
Dawson La. Bolt 6A 32
Dawson Rd. B'hth 4F 133

Dawson Rd. H Grn 5H 149
Dawson St. M3 . . . .5B 94 (2C 8)
Dawson St. Bury 1L 07
　　　　　　　(in two parts)
Dawson St. Heyw 3E 39
Dawson St. Hyde 6C 114
　　　　　　　(in two parts)
Dawson St. Lees 4A 74
Dawson St. Oldh 3H 73
Dawson St. Roch 3H 27
Dawson St. Salf . . .3D 94 (3G 5)
Dawson St. Stoc 6B 128
Dawson St. Swin 3G 79
Day Dri. Fail 5F 85
Day Gro. Mot 4C 116
Daylesford Clo. Chea . . .1H 149
Daylesford Cres.
　　　Chea 1H 149
Daylesford Rd. Chea . . .1H 149
Deacon Av. Swin 2E 79
Deacon Clo. Bow 4D 144
Deacons Clo. Stoc 2A 140
Deacons Cres. T'ton 6A 22
Deacon's Dri. Salf 5B 80
Deacon St. Roch 1B 28
Deakins Bus. Pk. Eger 2B 18
Deal Av. Stoc 4B 128
Deal Clo. M40 . . . . .6D 84
Dealey Rd. Bolt 3E 45
Deal Sq. Hyde 5C 114
　　　　　　　(off Deal St.)
Deal St. Bolt 4B 46
Deal St. Hyde 5C 114
Deal St. M11 . . . . .3C 94 (4F 5)
Deal St. N. Bury 2F 37
Deal St. S. Bury 3F 37
　　　　　　　(in two parts)
Deal Wlk. Chad 3G 71
Dean Av. Newt H 5B 84
Dean Av. Old T 4H 107
Deanbank Av. M19 . . . . .1B 126
Dean Bank Dri. Roch 4H 41
Doan Brook Clo.
　　　M40 . . . . .6B 84
Dean Clo. M15 . . . .1B 108 (6C 8)
Dean Clo. Farn 1B 62
Dean Clo. Part 5D 118
Dean Clo. Rams 2A 12
Dean Clo. Wilm 6G 159
Dean Ct. M15 . . . .1B 108 (6C 8)
Dean Ct. Bolt 5B 32
Dean Ct. Duk 4A 100
Deancourt. Roch 1F 41
Dean Dri. Bow 4D 144
Dean Dri. Wilm 6G 159
Deane. 2E 45
Deane Av. Bolt 2F 45
Deane Av. Chea 6B 138
Deane Av. Timp 6A 134
Deane Chu. Clough.
　　　Bolt 2E 45
Deane Chu. La. Bolt 3F 45
Deanc Clo. W'fld 2B 66
Deane Rd. Bolt 2G 45
Deanery Gdns. Salf 3H 81
Deanery Way. Stoc 1G 139
Deane Wlk. Bolt 1A 46
　　　　　　　(in two parts)
Dean Hall. M14 . . . . . . .3H 109
Dean Ho. Rams 5B 32
Dean La. M40 . . . . .5B 84
Dean La. Haz G 5D 152
Dean Moor Rd. Haz G . .3A 152
Dean Rd. M18 . . . . .3G 111
Dean Rd. Cad 3C 118
Dean Rd. Hand 4A 160
Dean Rd. Salf 2C 94 (2F 5)
Dean Row. 6A 160
Dean Row Rd. Wilm 6G 159
Deans. 4E 79
Deanscourt Av. Swin 4E 79

Deansgate.
   M15 & M3 . . .6C 94 (3F 9)
   (in two parts)
Deansgate. Bolt 6A 32
Deansgate. Rad 4H 49
Deansgate La. Timp 4G 133
Deansgate Quay. M3 . . . .3F 9
Deansgate, The. M14 . . .1G 125
Deanshut Rd. Oldh 1E 87
Deans Rd. Swin 4D 78
Deans Rd. Ind. Est.
   Swin 3E 79
Dean St. M1 . . . .4F 95 (5C 6)
Dean St. Ash L 2G 99
Dean St. Fail 4E 85
Dean St. Moss 2D 88
Dean St. Rad 4F 49
Dean St. Roch 2B 28
Dean St. Stal 4E 101
Deansway. Swin 3E 79
Deanswood Dri. M9 . . . .4C 68
Dean Ter. Ash L 1G 87
Dean Wlk. Midd 5F 53
Deanwater Clo.
   M13 . . . . . .6F 95 (4D 10)
Deanwater Ct. H Grn . . .6H 149
Deanwater Ct. Stret 1C 122
Deanway. M40 . . . . . .3A 84
Deanway. Urm 5H 103
Deanway. Wilm 6G 159
Deanway Technology Cen.
   Hand 4H 159
Dearden Av. L Hul 4C 62
Dearden Clough. Rams . .3B 12
   (in two parts)
Dearden Fold. Bury 4A 36
Dearden Fold. Rams 3B 12
Deardens St. Bury 4A 36
Dearden St. L'boro 3F 17
Dearden St. L Lev 3A 48
Dearden St. Stal 3E 101
Dearden Wlk.
   M15 . . . . . .1C 108 (5F 9)
Dearman's Pl.
   M3 . . . . . .3C 94 (4F 5)
Dearncamme Clo.
   Bolt 6F 19
Dearnley. 5C 16
Dearne Dri. Stret 5E 107
Dearnley Clo. L'boro 5C 16
Dearnley Pas. L'boro 5C 16
Debdale. 3H 111
Debdale Av. M18 . . . . .3H 111
Debdale La. M18 . . . . .3H 111
Debdale Outdoor Cen.
   . . . . .3G 111
Debenham Av. M40 . . . .1E 97
Debenham Ct. Farn 2F 63
Debenham Rd. Stret 5A 106
De Brook Ct. Urm 6A 104
Dee Av. Timp 6D 134
Deepcar St. M19 . . . . . .5C 110
Deepdale. Oldh 3H 73
Deepdale Av. M20 . . . . .1E 125
Deepdale Av. Roch 5C 28
Deepdale Av. Rytn 5A 42
Deepdale Clo. Stoc 6H 111
Deepdale Ct. M9 . . . . . .6B 70
Deepdale Dri. Swin 4B 80
Deepdale Rd. Bolt 3H 33
Deepdene St. M12 . . . . .1B 110
Deeping Av. M16 . . . . .5B 108
Deep La. L'boro 4H 29
   (in two parts)
Deeplish Cotts. Roch 6H 27
   (off Clifford St.)
Deeplish Rd. Roch 6H 27
Deeplish St. Roch 6H 27
Deeply Va. La. Bury 1A 24
Deeracre Av. Stoc 5C 140
Deerfold Clo. M18 . . . . .2F 111

Deerhurst Dri. M8 . . . . .5B 82
Deerook Clo. M18 . . . . .1D 110
   (in two parts)
Deerpark Rd. M16 . . . . .4C 108
Deer St. M1 . . . .5G 95 (1E 11)
Defence St. Bolt 1H 45
Deganwy Gro. Stoc 4H 127
Degas Clo. Salf 3F 81
Deighton Av. M20 . . . . .1E 125
Delacourt Rd. M14 . . . . .1E 125
De Lacy Dri. Bolt 4D 32
Delafield Av. M12 . . . . .5C 110
Delaford Av. Wors 4G 77
Delaford Clo. Stoc 1G 151
Delaford Wlk. M40 . . . . .1F 97
Delahays Dri. Hale 3B 146
Delahays Range. M18 . .3H 111
Delahays Rd. Hale 3B 146
Delaheyes Lodge.
   Timp 6B 134
Delaine Rd. M20 . . . . .3G 125
Delamere Av. Sale 6E 123
Delamere Av. Salf 5A 80
Delamere Av. Shaw 5H 43
Delamere Av. Stret 5D 106
   (in two parts)
Delamere Av. Swin 1H 79
Delamere Av. W'fld 3B 66
Delamere Clo. Carr 5G 89
Delamere Clo. Haz G . . .2G 153
Delamere Clo. Woodl . . .4A 130
Delamere Ct. M9 . . . . . .4C 68
Delamere Gdns. Bolt 2H 31
Delamere Lodge.
   Haz G 3D 152
   (off Chester Rd.)
Delamere Rd. M19 . . . . .6D 110
Delamere Rd. Dent 5B 112
Delamere Rd. Gat 6F 137
Delamere Rd. Hand 2A 160
Delamere Rd. Haz G . . .2G 153
Delamere Rd. Roch 1A 42
Delamere Rd. Stoc 1B 152
Delamere Rd. Urm 5B 104
Delamere St. M11 . . . . . .6H 97
Delamere St. Ash L 3H 99
Delamere St. Bury 6G 23
Delamere St. Oldh 4F 73
Delamer Rd.
   Bow & Alt 2E 145
Delaunays Rd.
   M8 & M9 . . . . . . .2C 82
Delaunays Rd. Sale 5H 121
Delaware Wlk. M9 . . . . .4F 83
Delbooth Av. Urm 3A 104
Delft Wlk. Salf 6E 81
Delfur Rd. Bram 6H 151
Delhi Rd. Irlam 1D 118
Dellar St. Roch 2E 27
Dell Av. Swin 4B 80
Dellcot Clo. P'wich 1H 81
Dellcot Clo. Salf 6H 79
Dellcot La. Wors 6H 77
Dell Gdns. Roch 1D 26
Dellhide Clo. S'head 3C 74
Dell Mdw. Whitw 4C 14
Dell Rd. Roch 6B 14
   (in two parts)
Dell Side. Bred 6E 129
Dellside Gro. Wors 6G 63
Dell Side Way. Roch 1E 27
Dell St. Bolt 6G 19
Dell, The. Bolt 6G 19
Dell, The. Hale 5G 145
Delph. 3G 59
Delph Av. Eger 1B 18
Delph Brook Way.
   Eger 1B 18
Delph Hill. 4C 30
Delph Hill. Bolt 3C 30
Delph Hill Clo. Bolt 3C 30

Delphi Av. Wors 1F 77
Delph La. Bolt 4C 34
Delph La. Del 2H 59
Delph New Rd.
   Del & Dob 4G 59
Delph St. Bolt 2H 45
Delside Av. M40 . . . . . .3A 84
Delta Bus. Pk. Aud 5E 99
Delta Clo. Rytn 5A 56
Delta Martial Arts, Gym &
   Fitness Cen. 2E 79
Delta Wlk. M40 . . . . . . .4A 84
Delvino Wlk. M14 . . . . . .3E 109
Delwood Gdns. M22 . . .2B 148
De Massey Clo.
   Woodl 3H 129
Demesne Clo. Stal 4G 101
Demesne Cres. Stal 4G 101
Demesne Dri. Stal 3G 101
Demesne Rd. M16 . . . . .5C 108
Demmings Ind. Est.
   Dem I 6B 138
Demmings Rd. Chea 6B 138
Demmings, The. Chea . .6B 138
Dempsey Dri. Bury 5F 51
Denbigh Clo. Haz G 5C 152
Denbigh Dri. Shaw 1D 56
Denbigh Pl. Salf 3G 93
   (in two parts)
Denbigh Rd. Bolt 2D 46
Denbigh Rd. Dent 6F 113
Denbigh Rd. Swin 1G 79
Denbigh St. Moss 3F 89
Denbigh St. Oldh 6D 72
Denbigh St. Stoc 6F 127
Denbigh Wlk.
   M15 . . . . . .2C 108 (6F 9)
Denbury Dri. Alt 6D 132
Denbury Grn. Haz G 4A 152
Denbury Wlk. M9 . . . . . .5E 83
   (off Westmere Dri.)
Denbydale Way. Rytn . . .3A 56
   (in two parts)
Denby La. Stoc 5F 127
Denby Rd. Duk 6A 100
Dencombe St. M13 . . . . .3B 110
Dene Bank. Bolt 6G 19
Dene Brow. Dent 1H 129
Dene Ct. Stoc 1E 139
Dene Dri. Midd 2H 69
Denefield Clo. Marp B . .2F 143
Denefield Pl. Eccl 2H 91
Deneford Rd. M20 . . . . .1E 137
Dene Hollow. Stoc 6A 112
Dene Ho. Stoc 2A 138
Denehurst Rd. Roch 3D 26
Dene Pk. M20 . . . . .6E 125
Dene Rd. M20 . . . . .6E 125
Dene Rd. W. M20 . . . . .6D 124
Deneside. M40 . . . . .5F 83
Deneside Cres. Haz G . . .2F 153
Deneside Wlk. M9 . . . . . .3G 83
   (off Dalbeattie St.)
Denes, The. Stoc 6H 111
Dene St. Bolt 6G 19
Denesway. Sale 6G 121
   (in two parts)
Deneway. Bram 6E 151
Deneway. H Lane 5D 154
Deneway. Stoc 1E 139
Deneway Clo. Stoc 1E 139
Deneway M. Stoc 1E 139
Denewell Clo.
   M13 . . . . . .1H 109 (6G 11)
Denewood Ct. Wilm 3D 166
Denham Clo. Bolt 6E 19
Denham Dri. Bram 6F 151
Denham Dri. Irlam 6E 103
Denham St. M13 . . . . . .3H 109
Denham St. Rad 1F 49

Den Hill Dri. S'head 3B 74
Denhill Rd. M15 . . . . . .3D 108
Denholme Rd. Roch 1F 41
Denholm Rd. M20 . . . . .3G 137
Denhurst Rd. L'boro 3F 17
Denis Av. M16 . . . . . . .5C 108
Denison Rd. M14 . . . . . .4G 109
Denison Rd. Haz G 5E 153
Denison St. M14 . . . . . .4G 109
Deniston Rd. Stoc 4D 126
Den La. S'head 2B 74
Den La. Upperm 6A 60
Denman Wlk. M8 . . . . . .5B 82
   (off Ermington Dri.)
Denmark Rd. M15 . . . . .3D 108
Denmark Rd. Sale 3B 122
Denmark St. Alt 1F 145
Denmark St. Chad 1A 72
Denmark St. Oldh 2G 73
Denmark St. Roch 3A 28
Denmark Way. Chad 1A 72
Denmore Rd. M40 . . . . . .6D 70
Dennington Dri. Urm 3E 105
Dennison Av. M20 . . . . .2F 125
Dennison Rd. Chea H . . .5D 150
Denshaw Av. Dent 2D 112
Denshaw Clo. M19 . . . . .6A 126
Denshaw Rd. Del 1E 59
Densmead Wlk.
   M40 . . . . . .2G 95 (2F 7)
Densmore St. Fail 4F 85
Denson Rd. Timp 3B 134
Denstone Av. Eccl 2G 91
Denstone Av. Sale 6G 121
Denstone Av. Urm 4E 105
Denstone Cres. Bolt 3G 33
Denstone Rd. Salf 6B 80
Denstone Rd. Stoc 6H 111
Denstone Wlk. M9 . . . . . .6G 69
   (off Woodmere Dri.)
Dent Clo. Stoc 3C 128
Dentdale Clo. Bolt 1B 44
Dentdale Wlk. M22 . . . . .5A 148
Denton. 3E 113
Denton Ct. Dent 2E 113
Denton Hall Farm Rd.
   Dent 5C 112
Denton La. Chad 4G 71
Denton Rd. Aud 2E 113
Denton Rd. Bolt 1B 48
Denton St Lawrence's
   Church 4F 113
Denton St. Bury 1D 36
Denton St. Heyw 4E 39
Denton St. Roch 2H 27
Denton Swimming Baths.
   . . . . .4E 113
Denver Av. M40 . . .2H 95 (1H 7)
Denver Dri. Timp 5A 134
Denver Rd. Roch 1F 41
Denville Cres. M22 . . . . .2C 148
Denyer Ter. Duk 4H 99
Denzell Gdns. 2C 144
Depleach Rd. Chea 6H 137
   (in two parts)
Deptford Av. M23 . . . . .2G 147
De Quincey Clo.
   W Timp 2F 133
De Quincey Rd.
   W Timp 2F 133
Deramore Clo. Ash L . . .2C 100
Deramore St. M14 . . . . .4F 109
Derby Av. Salf 3E 93
Derby Clo. Cad 4A 118
Derby Ct. Oldh 4A 72
Derby Ct. Sale 6C 122
Derby Gro. M19 . . . . . . .6D 110
Derby Ho. M15 . . . . . . .2F 109
Derby Range. Stoc 5D 126
Derby Rd. M14 . . . . . . .2G 125
Derby Rd. Ash L 2B 100
Derby Rd. Hyde 3C 114

Derby Rd. *Rad* 1A **64**
Derby Rd. *Sale* 3G **121**
Derby Rd. *Salf & M0* 4L **90**
Derby Rd. *Stoc* 5E **127**
Derby Rd. *Urm* 4F **105**
Derby Rd. *W'fld* 3F **67**
Derbyshire Av. *Stret* 4A **106**
Derbyshire Cres.
   Stret 4B **106**
Derbyshire Grn. *Stret* . . .5D **106**
Derbyshire Gro. *Stret* . . .4A **106**
Derbyshire La. *Stret* 5C **106**
Derbyshire La. W.
   Stret 4A **106**
Derbyshire Rd. *M40* 1F **97**
Derbyshire Rd. *Poy* 2A **164**
Derbyshire Rd. *Sale* 5C **122**
Derbyshire Rd. S.
   Salc 6C **122**
Derbyshire Row. *Rams* . .2A **32**
Derbyshire St. *M11* 6E **97**
Derby St. *M8* 6A **82**
Derby St. *Alt* 6G **133**
Derby St. *Ash L* 6E **87**
Derby St. *Bolt* 3H **45**
Derby St. *Bury* 3D **36**
Derby St. *Chad* 6H **71**
Derby St. *Dent* 4D **112**
   (in two parts)
Derby St. *Fail* 2G **85**
Derby St. *Heyw* 3D **38**
Derby St. *Marp* 5D **142**
Derby St. *Moss* 3F **89**
Derby St. *Oldh* 4A **72**
Derby St. *P'wich* 5E **67**
Derby St. *Rams* 3F **13**
Derby St. *Roch* 2A **28**
Derby St. *Stal* 2F **101**
Derby St. *Stoc* 3F **139**
Derby Ter. *Aud* 5D **113**
Derby Way. *Marp* 5D **142**
Dereham Clo. *Bury* 6D **22**
Derg St. *Salf* 3F **93**
Derker St. *Oldh* 1E **73**
Dermot Murphy Clo
   M20 . . . . .3D **124**
Dernford Av. *M19* 4B **126**
Derrick Walker Ct.
   Roch 3D **14**
Derry Av. *M22* 1C **148**
Derry St. *Oldh* 3D **72**
Derville Wlk. *M9* 3F **83**
   (off Alderside Rd.)
Derwen Rd. *Stoc* 4G **139**
Derwent Av. *M21* 4B **124**
Derwent Av. *Ash L* 1G **99**
Derwent Av. *Droy* 4G **97**
Derwent Av. *Heyw* 4F **39**
Derwent Av. *Miln* 5H **29**
Derwent Av. *Timp* 6D **134**
Derwent Av. *W'fld* 1F **67**
Derwent Clo. *Chor H* . . .4B **124**
Derwent Clo. *Dent* 5B **112**
Derwent Clo. *L Lev* 4H **47**
Derwent Clo. *Part* 5D **118**
Derwent Clo. *W'fld* 1F **67**
Derwent Clo. *Wors* 1D **76**
Derwent Dri. *Bram* 2E **161**
Derwent Dri. *Bury* 6B **36**
Derwent Dri. *Chad* 2G **71**
Derwent Dri. *Hand* 2G **159**
Derwent Dri. *Kear* 4B **64**
Derwent Dri. *L'boro* 1F **29**
Derwent Dri. *Sale* 1A **134**
Derwent Dri. *Shaw* 5E **43**
Derwent Ind. Area.
   Salf 6A **94** (2B **8**)
Derwent Rd. *Farn* 1B **62**
Derwent Rd. *H Lane* 6D **155**
Derwent Rd. *Midd* 4G **53**
Derwent Rd. *Stret* 4D **106**
Derwent Rd. *Urm* 5A **104**

Derwent St. *M8* 5E **83**
Derwent St. *Droy* 4F **97**
Derwent St. *Roch* 2H **27**
Derwent St. *Salf* 5A **94** (2B **8**)
Derwent Ter. *Stal* 1E **101**
Derwent Wlk. *Oldh* 2H **73**
Derwent Wlk. *W'fld* 1F **67**
Desford Av. *M21* 6A **108**
Design St. *Bolt* 3F **45**
Desmond Rd. *M22* 1C **148**
Destructor Rd. *Swin* 2E **79**
De Trafford Ho. *Eccl* 4F **91**
   (off Fintry Gro.)
De Traffords, The. *Irlam* .4F **103**
Dettingen St. *Salf* 5B **80**
Deva Cen., The.
   Salf 3C **94** (4F **5**)
Deva Clo. *Haz G* 4D **152**
Deva Clo. *Poy* 3B **162**
Deva Ct. *M16* 2A **108** (6A **8**)
Devaney Wlk. *Dent* 6E **113**
Deva Sq. *Oldh* 4A **72**
Devas St. *M15* 2F **109**
   (in two parts)
Deverill Av. *M18* 3H **111**
Devine Clo. *Rytn* 1B **56**
Devine Clo.
   Salf 3B **94** (3C **4**)
Devisdale Ct. *Alt* 2D **144**
Devisdale Grange.
   Alt 2D **144**
Devisdale Rd. *Alt* 1D **144**
Devoke Av. *Wors* 1G **77**
Devoke Gro. *Farn* 1A **62**
Devoke Rd. *M22* 3H **147**
Devon Av. *M19* 1B **126**
Devon Av. *W'fld* 6C **50**
Devon Clo. *L Lev* 3B **48**
Devon Clo. *Salf* 2A **92**
Devon Clo. *Shaw* 6D **42**
Devon Dri. *Bolt* 4C **34**
Devon Dri. *Dig* 3B **60**
Devon M. *W'fld* 6C **50**
Devonport Cres. *Rytn* . . .3D **56**
Devon Rd. *Cad* 4B **118**
Devon Rd. *Droy* 2A **98**
Devon Rd. *Fail* 5E **85**
Devon Rd. *Part* 6C **118**
Devon Rd. *Urm* 6A **104**
Devonshire Clo. *Urm* . . .5G **105**
Devonshire Ct. *Bolt* 6F **31**
   (off Devonshire Rd.)
Devonshire Ct. *Salf* 3H **81**
Devonshire Ct. *Stoc* 6A **140**
Devonshire Dri. *Ald E* . . .4H **167**
Devonshire Dri. *Wors* . . .5A **76**
Devonshire Pk. Rd.
   Stoc 6H **139**
Devonshire Pl. *P'wich* 4E **67**
Devonshire Rd. *M21* . . .1A **124**
Devonshire Rd. *Bolt* 4F **31**
Devonshire Rd. *B'hth* . . .5F **133**
Devonshire Rd. *Eccl* 3G **91**
Devonshire Rd. *Haz G* . .5F **153**
Devonshire Rd. *Roch* 3F **41**
Devonshire Rd. *Salf* 2A **92**
Devonshire Rd. *Stoc* 1D **138**
Devonshire Rd. *Wors* . . .3E **63**
Devonshire St.
   M12 . . . . .1H **109** (6G **11**)
Devonshire St. *Roch* 3F **41**
Devonshire St. *Salf* 5H **81**
Devonshire St. E. *Fail* . . .5D **84**
Devonshire St. N.
   M12 . . . . . .6H **95** (4H **11**)
Devonshire St. S.
   M13 . . . .2H **109** (6G **11**)
Devon St. *Bolt* 6C **32**
Devon St. *Bury* 5D **36**
Devon St. *Farn* 5F **47**

Devon St. *Oldh* 5H **71**
   (in two parts)
Devon St. *Roch* 5H **27**
Devon St. *Swin* 1F **79**
Dewar Clo. *M11* 4C **96**
Dewberry Clo. *Swin* 1E **79**
Dewberry Clo. *Tyl* 2A **76**
Dewes Av. *Swin* 1H **79**
Dewhirst Rd. *Roch* 3D **15**
   (in three parts)
Dewhirst Way. *Roch* 5F **15**
Dewhurst Clough Rd.
   Eger 1B **18**
Dewhurst Ct. *Eger* 1B **18**
Dewhurst Rd. *Bolt* 2G **33**
Dewhurst St. *M8* 1D **94**
Dewhurst St. *Heyw* 3G **39**
De Wint Av. *Marp B* 3F **143**
Dew Mdw. Clo. *Roch* 1G **27**
Dewsnap Bri. *Duk* 1A **114**
Dewsnap Clo. *Duk* 1A **114**
Dewsnap La. *Duk* 1A **114**
Dewsnap La. *Mot* 1B **116**
Dewsnap Way. *Hyde* 5A **116**
Dew Way. *Oldh* 2B **72**
Dexter Rd. *M9* 4C **68**
Deyne Av. *M14* 3G **109**
Deyne Av. *P'wich* 5F **67**
Deyne St. *Salf* 3E **93**
Dial Ct. *Farn* 6F **47**
Dial Pk. Rd. *Stoc* 1D **152**
Dial Rd. *Haleb* 5C **146**
Dial Rd. *Stoc* 6C **140**
Dialstone La. *Stoc* 4C **140**
Dialstone Recreation Cen.
    . . . . .5D **140**
Diamond Clo. *Ash L* 1B **100**
Diamond St. *Ash L* 1B **100**
Diamond St. *Stoc* 5A **140**
Diamond Ter. *Marp* 1D **154**
Dibden Wlk. *M23* 6G **135**
Dicken Grn. *Roch* 1F **41**
Dicken Grn. La. *Roch* 1F **41**
Dickens Clo. *Chea H* . . .2D **160**
Dickens Rd.
   M14 & M13 . . . .4G **109**
Dickens Rd. *Eccl* 4F **91**
Dickens St. *Oldh* 3A **58**
Dickinson Clo. *Bolt* 4A **32**
Dickinson St.
   M1 . . . . .5D **94** (1H **9**)
Dickinson St. *Bolt* 4A **32**
Dickinson St. *Oldh* 2F **73**
Dickinson St.
   Salf 1C **94** (1F **5**)
Dickinson Ter. *Bolt* 4A **32**
   (off Dickinson St.)
Dickins St. *Heyw* 3D **38**
Didcot Rd. *M22* 4A **148**
Didley Sq. *M12* 1C **110**
Didsbury. 6F **125**
Didsbury Ct. *M20* 5F **125**
Didsbury Pk. *M20* 1F **137**
Didsbury Rd. *Stoc* 1H **137**
Didsbury Sports Cen. &
Swimming Pool.
    . . . . .1F **137**
Digby Rd. *Roch* 1F **57**
Digby Wlk. *M11* 4B **96**
   (off Albert St.)
Dig Ga. La. *Miln* 2B **42**
Diggle. 3C **60**
Diggles La. *Roch* 4B **26**
   (Arthur Pits)
Diggles La. *Roch* 5A **26**
   (Dixon Fold)
Diggle St. *Shaw* 1F **57**
Diggle Wlk. *Carr* 5G **89**
   (off Friezland Clo.)
Digsby Ct. *M20* 5F **125**

Dijon St. *Bolt* 3G **45**
Dilham Ct. *Bolt* 5G **31**
Dillicar Wlk. *M9* 4F **83**
Dillmoss Wlk.
   M15 . . . . . . .1B **108** (6D **8**)
Dillon Dri. *M12* 2A **110**
Dilston Clo.
   M13 . . . . . .1G **109** (6F **11**)
Dilworth Clo. *Heyw* 3B **38**
Dilworth Ct. *Stoc* 6E **141**
Dilworth Ho. *M15* 2F **109**
Dilworth St. *M15* 2F **109**
Dingle Av. *Ald E* 6A **166**
Dingle Av. *Dent* 5H **113**
Dingle Av. *Shaw* 4G **43**
Dingle Bank Rd. *Bram* . . .3F **151**
Dinglebrook Gro.
   Wilm 6H **159**
Dingle Clo. *Rom* 1D **142**
Dingle Dri. *Droy* 2B **98**
Dingle Gro. *Gat* 5D **136**
Dingle Hollow. *Rom* 1C **142**
Dingle Rd. *Midd* 3G **69**
Dingle Ter. *Ash L* 1F **87**
Dingle, The. *Bram* 4E **151**
Dingle, The. *Hyde* 3C **130**
Dinglewood. *Bram* 4E **151**
Dinmore Ct. *Stoc* 6D **140**
Dinmor Rd. *M22* 4B **148**
Dinnington Dri. *M8* 5B **82**
Dinorwic Clo. *M8* 1C **82**
Dinsdale Clo.
   M40 . . . . . . .3H **95** (3H **7**)
Dinsdale Dri. *Bolt* 2H **45**
Dinslow Wlk. *M8* 4B **82**
Dinting Av. *M20* 2E **125**
Dinting La. *Glos* 6H **117**
Dinting La. Trad. Est.
   Glos 6H **117**
Dinting Rd. *Glos* 5H **117**
Dinting Vale. 5H **117**
Dinting Va. *Glos* 5G **117**
Dinting Va. Bus. Pk.
   Glos 5H **117**
Dinton Ho. *Salf* 4F **93**
   (off Buckingham St.)
Dinton St. *M15* 6A **94** (4B **8**)
Dipton Wlk. *M8* 5E **83**
   (off Smedley Rd.)
Dirty La. *S'dale* 6D **58**
Dirty Leech. *Whitw* 3F **15**
Disley. 1H **165**
Disley Av. *M20* 3D **124**
Disley Ho. *Stoc* 4G **139**
   (off Newton St.)
Disley St. *Roch* 1C **40**
Disley Wlk. *Dent* 6G **113**
Distaff Rd. *Poy* 3B **162**
Ditton Mead Clo.
   Roch 1B **28**
Ditton Wlk. *M23* 5F **135**
Division St. *Bolt* 3B **46**
Division St. *Roch* 1B **28**
Dixon Av. *Salf* 5A **82**
Dixon Clo. *Sale* 1D **134**
Dixon Closes. *Roch* 4B **26**
Dixon Ct. *Chea* 6H **137**
Dixon Dri. *Swin* 5E **65**
Dixon Fold. *Roch* 5A **26**
Dixon Fold. *W'fld* 6C **50**
Dixon Grn. Dri. *Farn* 6D **46**
Dixon Rd. *Dent* 6H **113**
Dixon St. *M40* 5B **84**
   (in two parts)
Dixon St. *Ash L* 1B **100**
Dixon St. *Irlam* 1D **118**
Dixon St. *Lees* 1A **74**
Dixon St. *Midd* 5A **54**
   (in two parts)
Dixon St. *Oldh* 1C **72**
Dixon St. *Roch* 1D **40**

Dixon St. *Salf* 5D **80**
Dobb Hedge Clo.
  Haleb 1C **156**
Dobbin Dri. *Roch* 2F **41**
Dobbinetts La.
  Hale & M23 . . . . . .1E **147**
Dob Brook Clo. *M40* 5C **84**
Dobcross. 5A **60**
Dobcross Clo. *M13* 5C **110**
Dobcross New Rd.
  Dob 6A **60**
Dobhill St. *Farn* 1F **63**
Dobroyd St. *M8* 3C **82**
Dobsen St. *Rams* 3H **31**
Dobson Clo.
  M13 . . . .1H **109** (6G **11**)
Dobson Ct. *M40* 1D **96**
Dobson Rd. *Bolt* 6G **31**
Dock Office. *Salf* 6G **93**
Dockray Ho. *Chea H* . . .6A **150**
Doctor Dam Cotts.
  Roch 1G **25**
Doctor Fold La. *Heyw* . . .1D **52**
Doctor La. *Scout* 6E **59**
Doctor Lane Head. 6E **59**
Doctor La. Head Cotts.
  Oldh 6E **59**
Doctors La. *Bury* 3B **36**
Dodd Cft. *Roch* 2H **41**
Doddington La. *Salf* 5G **93**
Doddington Wlk. *Dent* . . .6E **113**
Dodd St. *Salf* 3D **92**
Dodge Fold. *Stoc* 5E **141**
Dodge Hill. *Stoc* 1G **139**
Dodgson St. *Roch* 5A **28**
Doe Brow. *Swin* 4E **65**
Doefield Av. *Wors* 3E **77**
Doe Hey Gro. *Farn* 5D **46**
Doe Hey Rd. *Bolt* 5D **46**
Doffcocker. 4E **31**
  Rams 4D **30**
Doffcocker La. *Bolt* 4D **30**
Doffcocker Lodge Local
  Nature Reserve. 4C **30**
Dogford Rd. *Rytn* 2B **56**
Dolbey St. *Salf* 4E **92**
Dolefield. *M3* 4C **94** (5F **5**)
D'Oliveira Ct. *Midd* 5G **53**
Dollond St. *M9* 2G **83**
Dolman Wlk. *M8* 5B **82**
Dolphin Pl.
  M12 . . . . . .6G **95** (4F **11**)
Dolphin St.
  M12 . . . . . .6G **95** (4F **11**)
Dolwen Wlk. *M40* 6B **84**
Doman St. *Bolt* 2B **46**
Dombey Rd. *Poy* 5D **162**
Domestic App. *Man A* . . .6A **148**
Dome, The. Urm 1F **105**
  (off Trafford Cen., The)
Domett St. *M9* 1E **83**
Dominic Clo. *M23* 2E **135**
Donald Av. *Hyde* 6D **114**
Donald St. *M1* . . .5E **95** (2B **10**)
Dona St. *Stoc* 3A **140**
  (in two parts)
Don Av. *Salf* 3C **92**
Doncaster Av. *M20* 2E **125**
Doncaster Clo. *L Lev* 4H **47**
Doncaster Wlk. *Oldh* 2D **72**
Donhead Wlk.
  M13 . . . . . .1G **109** (6F **11**)
Donkey La. *Wilm* 4D **166**
Donleigh St. *M40* 5D **84**
Donnington. *Roch* 5G **27**
Donnington Av. *Chea* . . .5B **138**
Donnington Gdns.
  Wors 6A **77**
Donnington Rd. *M18* 2G **111**
Donnington Rd. *Rad* 2C **48**
Donnison St. *M12* 1B **110**

Donovan Av. *M40* 1G **95**
Don St. *Bolt* 4H **45**
Don St. *Midd* 6C **54**
Doodson Av. *Irlam* 5E **103**
Doodson Sq. *Farn* 1F **63**
Dooley La. *Marp* 4H **141**
Dooleys La. *Wilm* 5H **157**
Dorac Av. *H Grn* 6G **149**
Dora St. *Rams* 5C **12**
Dorchester Av. *Bolt* 4G **33**
Dorchester Av. *Dent* 6F **113**
Dorchester Av. *P'wich* . . .1G **81**
Dorchester Av. *Urm* 4H **105**
Dorchester Clo. *Hale* 2C **146**
Dorchester Clo. *Wilm* . . .1G **167**
Dorchester Ct.
  Chea H 4D **150**
Dorchester Ct. *Sale* 1B **134**
Dorchester Dri. *M23* 2E **135**
Dorchester Dri. *Rytn* 5B **56**
Dorchester Gro. *Heyw* . . .5E **39**
Dorchester Pde.
  Haz G 4B **152**
Dorchester Rd. *Haz G* . . .4B **152**
Dorchester Rd. *Swin* 5F **79**
Dorclyn Av. *Urm* 5F **105**
Dorfield Clo. *Bred* 6E **129**
Doric Av. *Bred* 6D **128**
Doric Clo. *M11* 4B **96**
Doris Av. *Bolt* 6F **33**
Doris Rd. *Stoc* 3E **139**
Doris St. *Midd* 5A **54**
Dorking Av. *M40* 1D **96**
Dorking Clo. *Bolt* 3B **32**
Dorking Clo. *Stoc* 4B **140**
Dorlan Av. *M18* 3H **111**
Dorland Gro. *Stoc* 4B **140**
Dorman St. *M11* 6F **97**
Dormer St. *Bolt* 2B **32**
Dorney St. *M18* 2F **111**
Dorning St. *Swin* 4G **79**
Dorning St. *Bury* 1H **35**
Dorning St. *Eccl* 4F **91**
Dorning St. *Kear* 1H **63**
Dornton Wlk. *M8* 5B **82**
  (off Waterloo Rd.)
Dorothy Rd. *Haz G* 2F **153**
Dorothy St. *M8* 4B **82**
Dorothy St. *Rams* 4D **12**
Dorrian M. *Bolt* 6D **30**
Dorrington Rd. *Sale* 5F **121**
Dorrington Rd. *Stoc* 4C **138**
Dorris St. *M19* 1D **126**
Dorris St. *Bolt* 4G **45**
Dorrit Clo. *Poy* 5E **163**
Dorset Av. *M14* 5E **109**
Dorset Av. *Aud* 5C **98**
Dorset Av. *Bram* 3F **151**
Dorset Av. *Chea H* 6E **139**
Dorset Av. *Dig* 3C **60**
Dorset Av. *Farn* 1E **63**
Dorset Av. *Shaw* 6D **42**
Dorset Av. *Stoc* 4C **128**
Dorset Clo. *Farn* 1E **63**
Dorset Clo. *Heyw* 4C **38**
Dorset Dri. *Bury* 5E **37**
Dorset Rd. *M19* 6E **111**
Dorset Rd. *Alt* 6D **132**
Dorset Rd. *Cad* 4B **118**
Dorset Rd. *Droy* 2H **97**
Dorset Rd. *Fail* 5F **85**
Dorset St. *Ash L* 3B **100**
Dorset St. *Bolt* 6C **32**
Dorset St. *Oldh* 4A **72**
Dorset St. *Roch* 5H **27**
Dorset St. *Stret* 6D **106**
Dorset St. *Swin* 1F **79**
Dorsey St. *M4* . . .3F **95** (4C **6**)
Dorstone Clo. *M40* 1E **97**
Dorwood Av. *M9* 4E **69**
Dougall Wlk. M12 . . . . . .1C **110**
  (off Bridgend Clo.)

Doughty Av. *Eccl* 2H **91**
Dougill St. *Bolt* 4F **31**
Douglas Av. *Bury* 3H **35**
Douglas Av. *Stret* 4D **106**
Douglas Clo. *W'fld* 6G **51**
Douglas Grn. *Salf* 6E **81**
Douglas Rd. *Haz G* 2E **153**
Douglas Rd. *Stoc* 1G **151**
Douglas Rd. *Wors* 4C **78**
Douglas Sq. *Heyw* 4B **38**
Douglas St. *M40* 4A **84**
Douglas St. *Ash L* 2C **100**
Douglas St. *Bolt* 6C **18**
Douglas St. *Fail* 4G **85**
Douglas St. *Hyde* 5C **114**
Douglas St. *Oldh* 1E **73**
Douglas St. *Rams* 3D **12**
Douglas St. *Salf* 5H **81**
Douglas St. *Swin* 4G **79**
Douglas Wlk. *Sale* 4E **121**
Douglas Wlk. *W'fld* 6G **51**
Douglas Way. *W'fld* 6G **51**
Doulton St. *M40* 3C **84**
Dounby Av. *Eccl* 2D **90**
Douro St. *M40* 6H **83**
Dove Bank. 3H **47**
Dove Bank Rd. *L Lev* 3A **48**
Dovebrook Clo. *Carr* 4G **89**
Dovecote. *Droy* 2D **98**
Dovecote Bus. & Technology Pk.
  Sale 5F **123**
Dovecote Clo. *Brom X* . . .3F **19**
Dovecote La. *Lees* 2B **74**
Dovecote La. *L Hul* 6A **62**
Dovecote M. *M21* 1G **123**
Dovedale Av. *M20* 2E **125**
Dovedale Av. *Droy* 3G **97**
Dovedale Av. *Eccl* 2G **91**
Dovedale Av. *P'wich* 6A **68**
Dovedale Av. *Urm* 5F **105**
Dovedale Clo. *H Lane* . . .6C **154**
Dovedale Ct. Midd 5G **53**
  (off Grisdale Dri.)
Dovedale Dri. *Ward* 3B **16**
Dovedale Rd. *Bolt* 4H **33**
Dovedale Rd. *Stoc* 4D **140**
Dovedale St. *Fail* 4E **85**
Dove Dri. *Bury* 1F **37**
Dove Dri. *Irlam* 3E **103**
Dovehouse Clo. *W'fld* . . .1C **66**
Doveleys Rd. *Salf* 1D **92**
Dover Clo. *G'mnt* 2A **22**
Dovercourt Av. *Stoc* 5B **126**
Dover Gro. *Bolt* 2H **45**
Doveridge Gdns. *Salf* 2F **93**
Dover Rd. *Urm* 3F **105**
Dover Pk. *Urm* 3F **105**
Dover Rd. *Swin* 1G **79**
Dover St.
  M13 . . . . .1F **109** (6C **10**)
Dover St. *Eccl* 3D **90**
Dover St. *Farn* 5F **47**
Dover St. *Oldh* 4A **72**
Dover St. *Roch* 1B **28**
Dover St. *Stoc* 2G **127**
Dovestone Cres. *Duk* 6D **100**
Dovestone Wlk. *M40* 2E **85**
Doveston Gro. *Sale* 3B **122**
Doveston Rd. *Sale* 3B **122**
Dove St. *Oldh* 3G **73**
Dove St. *Rams* 1A **32**
Dove St. *Roch* 4F **27**
Dove Wlk. *M8* 6D **82**
Dove Wlk. *Farn* 2B **62**
Dow Fold. *Bury* 2F **35**
Dowland Clo. *M23* 1F **135**
Dow La. *Bury* 2F **35**
  (in two parts)
Dowling St. *Roch* 5H **27**
Downes Way. *M22* 5C **136**
Downesway. *Ald E* 5F **167**

Downfield Clo. *Rams* 3C **12**
Downfields. *Stoc* 6A **112**
Downgate Wlk. *M8* 5C **82**
Down Grn. Rd. *Bolt* 2G **33**
Downhall Grn. *Bolt* 5B **32**
Downham Av. *Bolt* 5E **33**
Downham Chase.
  Timp 5B **134**
Downham Clo. *Rytn* 5A **56**
Downham Cres.
  P'wich 6H **67**
Downham Gdns.
  P'wich 6A **68**
Downham Gro. *P'wich* . . .6A **68**
Downham Rd. *Heyw* 3C **38**
Downham Rd. *Stoc* 4F **127**
Downham Wlk. *M23* 3D **134**
Downhill Clo. *Oldh* 6C **56**
Downing Clo. *Ash L* 5D **86**
Downing St.
  M1 . . . . . . .6F **95** (3D **10**)
Downing St. *Ash L* 6D **86**
Downing St. Ind. Est.
  Ard 3D **10**
Downley Clo. *Roch* 1D **26**
Downley Dri.
  M4 . . . . .3G **95** (4F **7**)
Downs Dri. *Timp* 3G **133**
Downshaw Rd. *Ash L* 5E **87**
Downs, The. *Alt* 2E **145**
Downs, The. *Chea* 2H **149**
Downs, The. *Midd* 3B **70**
  (in two parts)
Downs, The. *P'wich* 1E **81**
Dowry Pk. Estates.
  Oldh 2A **74**
Dowry Rd. *Lees* 2A **74**
Dowry St. *Oldh* 6D **72**
Dowson Rd. *Hyde* 2B **130**
Dowson St. *Bolt* 6C **32**
Dow St. *Hyde* 2B **114**
Doyle Av. *Bred* 6D **128**
Doyle Clo. *Oldh* 3A **58**
Doyle Rd. *Bolt* 4C **44**
Dragons Health Club.
  . . . . .1C **134**
Drake Av. *Cad* 3C **118**
Drake Av. *Farn* 2F **63**
Drake Clo. *Oldh* 1D **72**
Drake Ct. *Stoc* 5G **127**
Drake Rd. *B'hth* 3D **132**
Drake Rd. *L'boro* 6G **17**
Drake St. *Roch* 4H **27**
Draxford Ct. *Wilm* 3E **167**
Draycott St. *Bolt* 3A **32**
Draycott St. E. *Bolt* 3B **32**
Drayfields. *Droy* 3D **98**
Drayford Clo. *M23* 1F **135**
Drayton Clo. *Bolt* 3H **31**
Drayton Clo. *Sale* 1F **133**
Drayton Clo. *Wilm* 6H **159**
Drayton Dri. *H Grn* 6F **149**
Drayton Gro. *Timp* 1A **146**
Drayton Mnr. *M20* 3F **137**
Drayton Wlk. *M16* 2B **108**
Drefus Av. *M11* 3E **97**
Dresden St. *M40* 3C **84**
Dresser Cen., The.
  Open 6D **96**
Drewett St. *M40* 1A **96**
Driffield St. *M14* 4E **109**
Driffield St. *Eccl* 5E **91**
Drill Wlk. *M4* 5F **7**
Drinkwater Rd. *P'wich* . . .2D **80**
Driscoll St. *M13* 4B **110**
Drive, The. *M20* 6G **125**
Drive, The. *Bred* 6D **128**
Drive, The. *Bury* 6F **23**
Drive, The. *Chea H* 1D **150**
Drive, The. *Haleb* 5D **146**
Drive, The. *Marp* 5C **142**
Drive, The. *P'wich* 5F **81**

Drive, The. Rams 2A **12**
Drive, The. Sale 2G **133**
Drive, The. Salf 2G **81**
Drive, The. Stoc 5B **128**
Droilwich Rd.
M40 . . . . . . .1H **95** (1G **7**)
Dronfield Rd. M22 . . . . .3B **136**
Dronfield Rd. Salf 1D **92**
Droughts La. P'wich 1H **67**
Droylsden. 4A **98**
Droylsden Rd. M40 . . . . .5C **84**
Droylsden Rd. Aud 4B **98**
Droylsden Swimming Pool.
. . . . .4A **98**
Druids Clo. Eger 1B **18**
Drummond St. Bolt 1A **32**
Drury La. Chad 6G **71**
Drury St. M19 . . . . .6C **110**
Dryad Clo. Swin 1F **79**
Drybrook Clo. M13 . . . . 2A **110**
Dryburgh Av. Bolt 1H **31**
Dry Clough La.
Upperm 2E **61**
Dryclough Wlk. Rytn 4C **56**
Dryden Av. Chea 5A **138**
Dryden Av. Swin 4D **78**
Dryden Clo. Duk 6F **101**
Dryden Clo. Marp 1D **154**
Dryden Rd. M16 . . . . . . .4A **108**
Dryden St.
M13 . . . . . .1G **109** (6E **11**)
Dryden Way. Dent 1G **129**
Drygate Wlk. M9 . . . . . . .4G **83**
(off Bentworth Wlk.)
Dryhurst Dri. Dis 1H **165**
Dryhurst La. Dis 1H **165**
Dryhurst Wlk.
M15 . . . . . .1E **109** (6A **10**)
Drymoss. Oldh 2E **87**
Drysdale Vw. Bolt 1A **32**
Drywood Av. Wors 6A **78**
Ducal St. M4 . . . .2F **95** (1C **6**)
Duchess Pk. Clo.
Shaw 5F **43**
Duchess Rd. Crum 3D **82**
Duchess St. Shaw 5E **43**
Duchess St. Ind. Est.
Shaw 5F **43**
Duchess Wlk. Bolt 3F **45**
Duchy Av. Bolt 0E **45**
Duchy Av. Wors 3F **77**
Duchy Bank. Salf 5B **80**
Duchy Cvn. Pk. Salf 6D **80**
Duchy Rd. Salf 5C **80**
Duchy St. Salf 2C **94**
Duchy St. Stoc 4F **139**
Ducie Av. M15 . . . . .2F **109**
Ducie Av. Bolt 6G **31**
Ducie Cres. M15 . . . . . .2F **109**
Ducie Gro. M15 . . . . . . .2F **109**
(Denmark Rd.)
Ducie Gro. M15 . . . . . . .2F **109**
(Oxford Rd.)
Ducie Pl. Salf 4A **94** (6A **4**)
Ducie St. M1 . . . .4F **95** (6C **6**)
Ducie St. Oldh 1D **86**
Ducie St. Rad 2F **49**
Ducie St. Rams 2D **12**
Ducie St. W'fld 1D **66**
Duckchaw La. Farn 1F **63**
Duckworth Rd. P'wich . . .6D **66**
Duckworth St. Bolt 3G **45**
Duckworth St. Bury 1E **37**
(in two parts)
Duckworth St. Shaw 6G **43**
Duddon Av. Bolt 4H **33**
Duddon Clo. W'fld 1F **67**
(in two parts)
Duddon Wlk. Midd 5G **53**
Dudley Av. Bolt 4E **33**
Dudley Av. W'fld 1D **66**
Dudley Clo. M15 . . . . . . .2C **108**

Dudley Ct. M16 . . . . .4B **108**
Dudley Rd. M16 . . . . . . .5B **108**
Dudley Rd. Cad 5B **118**
Dudley Rd. Sale 3C **122**
Dudley Rd. Swin 2F **79**
Dudley Rd. Timp 4B **134**
Dudley St. Dent 3E **113**
Dudley St. Eccl 4E **91**
Dudley St. Oldh 3H **73**
Dudley St. Salf 4A **82**
Dudlow Wlk.
M15 . . . . . .1B **108** (6D **8**)
Dudwell Clo. Bolt 4G **31**
Duerden St. Bolt 5E **45**
Duffield Ct. M15 . . . . . . .2E **109**
Duffield Ct. Midd 4H **69**
Duffield Gdns. Midd 4H **69**
Duffield Rd. Midd 4H **69**
Duffield Rd. Salf 6B **80**
Duffins Clo. Roch 6D **14**
Dufton Wlk. M22 . . . . . .4C **148**
Dufton Wlk. Midd 5G **53**
Dugdale Av. M9 . . . . . . .5G **69**
Duke Av. Chea H 1B **160**
Duke Clo. M16 . . . . .2B **108**
Dukefield St. M22 . . . . . .3C **136**
Duke Pl. M3 . . . . .5C **94** (2E **9**)
Duke Rd. A'wth 4C **34**
Duke Rd. Hyde 2D **114**
Dukes All. Rams 6B **32**
(off Ridgeway Gates)
Duke's Av. L Lev 3A **48**
Dukes Platting. Ash L 6B **88**
Duke's Ter. Duk 4H **99**
(off Hill St.)
Duke St. M3 . . . . .5C **94** (2E **9**)
Duke St. Ald E 4H **167**
Duke St. Ash L 2H **99**
Duke St. Bolt 5A **32**
(in two parts)
Duke St. Dent 4E **113**
Duke St. Eccl 1E **91**
Duke St. Fail 3G **85**
Duke St. Heyw 3D **38**
Duke St. L'boro 4E **17**
Duke St. L Hul 4C **62**
Duke St. Moss 2G **89**
Duke St. Rad 5H **49**
Duke St. Rams 5C **12**
Duke St. Roch 2H **27**
(in two parts)
Duke St.
Salf (M3) . . .3D **94** (3G **5**)
Duke St. Salf (M7) 6H **81**
Duke St. Shaw 1G **57**
Duke St. Stal 4D **100**
Duke St. Stoc 2H **139**
Duke St. Wors 1A **78**
Duke St. N. Bolt 5A **32**
(Prince St.)
Duke St. N. Bolt 5A **32**
(School Hill)
Dukes Wlk. Hale 2H **145**
Duke's Wharf. Wors 6H **77**
Dukinfield. 5A **100**
Dukinfield Crematorium.
Duk 4B **100**
Dukinfield Hall. 6G **99**
Dukinfield Rd. Hyde 2A **114**
Dukinfield Swimming Baths.
. . . . .6B **100**
Dulford Wlk. M13 . . . . . .2G **109**
(off Plymouth Gro.)
Dulgar St. Open 5D **96**
Dulverton St. M40 . . . . . .5B **84**
Dulwich Clo. Sale 6F **121**
Dulwich St. M4 . . .2F **95** (1C **6**)
Dumbarton Clo. Stoc . . .3H **127**
Dumbarton Dri. Heyw . . .4C **38**
Dumbarton Rd. Stoc 2H **127**
Dumbell St. Swin 1F **79**
Dumber La. Sale 3H **121**

Dumers Clo. Rad 3B **50**
Dumers La.
Rad & Bury 3B **50**
Dumfries Hollow.
Heyw 2H **39**
Dumfries Wlk. Heyw 4C **38**
Dumplington. 6F **91**
Dunbar Av. M23 . . . . . . .2G **147**
Dunbar Dri. Bolt 4A **46**
Dunbar Gro. Heyw 5B **38**
Dunbar St. Oldh 1C **72**
Dunblane Av. Bolt 2C **44**
Dunblane Gro. Heyw 5C **38**
Duncan Av. Stoc 1F **139**
Duncan Edwards Ct.
M40 . . . . .6B **84**
(off Mitchell St.)
Duncan Edwards Ho.
Salf 2F **93**
(off Sutton Dwellings)
Duncan Rd. M13 . . . . . . .4B **110**
(in two parts)
Duncan St. Duk 1A **114**
Duncan St.
Salf (M5) . . .5A **94** (1A **8**)
Duncan St. Salf (M7) 5G **81**
Dunchurch Clo. Los 1B **44**
Dunchurch Rd. Sale 5G **121**
Dun Clo. Salf 3B **94** (3C **4**)
Duncombe Clo. Bram 2A **152**
Duncombe Dri. M40 . . . . .4B **84**
Duncombe Rd. Bolt 4A **46**
Duncombe St. Salf 5A **82**
Duncote Gro. Rytn 2D **56**
Dundee. Eccl 3G **91**
(off Monton La.)
Dundee Clo. Heyw 4B **38**
Dundee La. Rams 3D **12**
Dundonald Rd. M20 . . . .6G **125**
Dundonald Rd.
Chea H 6C **150**
Dundonald St. Stoc 5H **139**
Dundraw Clo. Midd 6D **52**
Dundrennan Clo. Poy 2D **162**
Dunecroft. Dent 3G **113**
Dunedin Dri. Salf 5D **80**
Dunedin Rd. G'mnt 1H **21**
Dunelm Dri. Sale 2D **134**
Dungeon Wlk. Wilm 2E **167**
Dunham Ho. Dow 2D **144**
Dunham Lawn. Alt 1D **144**
Dunham Mnt. Bow 4B **144**
Dunham New Pk. 1C **144**
Dunham Ri. Alt 1E **145**
Dunham Rd. Bow 4B **144**
Dunham Rd. Duk 1B **114**
Dunham Rd. Hand 2H **159**
Dunham Rd. Part 5H **119**
Dunham St.
M15 . . . . . .1C **108** (6F **9**)
Dunham St. Lees 1A **74**
Dunham Town. 1A **144**
Dunkeld Gdns. M23 . . . . .5F **135**
Dunkeld Rd. M23 . . . . . .5F **135**
Dunkerley Av. Fail 4F **85**
Dunkerleys Clo. M8 . . . . . .3B **82**
Dunkerley St. Ash L 6E **87**
Dunkerley St. Oldh 1G **73**
Dunkerley St. Rytn 3B **56**
Dunkery Rd. M22 . . . . . . .4B **148**
Dunkirk Clo. Dent 5A **112**
Dunkirk La. Hyde 2H **113**
Dunkirk Ri. Roch 4G **27**
Dunkirk Rd. W'fld 6D **50**
Dunkirk St. Droy 4B **98**
Dunley Clo. M12 . . . . . . .2C **110**
Dunlin Clo. Bolt 2C **46**
Dunlin Clo. Poy 3A **162**
Dunlin Clo. Roch 4B **26**
Dunlin Clo. Stoc 6G **141**
Dunlin Dri. Irlam 4E **103**
Dunlin Wlk. B'hth 3D **132**

Dunlop Av. Roch 2E **41**
Dunlop St. M3 . . . .4D **94** (5G **5**)
Dunmail Dri. Midd 4G **53**
Dunmaston Av. Timp 4D **134**
Dunmere Wlk. M9 . . . . . . .5E **83**
(off Hendham Va.)
Dunmore Rd. Gat 5F **137**
Dunmow Ct. Stoc 6E **141**
Dunmow Wlk. M23 . . . . .1G **135**
Dunnerdale Wlk. M18 . . . .2E **111**
Dunnisher Rd. M23 . . . . .6H **135**
Dunnock Clo. Stoc 6F **141**
Dunoon Clo. Heyw 4C **38**
Dunoon Dri. Bolt 6A **18**
Dunoon Rd. Stoc 2H **127**
Dunoon Wlk. M9 . . . . .4F **83**
Dunrobin Clo. Heyw 5C **38**
Dunscar. 3C **18**
Dunscar Bri. Eger 3C **18**
Dunscar Clo. W'fld 2B **66**
Dunscar Fold. Eger 3D **18**
Dunscar Ind. Est. Eger 4C **18**
Dunscar Sq. Eger 3C **18**
Dunsfold Dri. M23 . . . . . .3D **134**
Dunsford Ct. S'head 4B **74**
Dunsley Av. M40 . . . . .1D **84**
Dunsmore Clo. M16 . . . . .3B **108**
Dunsop Dri. Bolt 2D **30**
Dunstable. Roch 3H **27**
(off Redcross St.)
Dunstable St. M19 . . . . . .6D **110**
Dunstall Rd. M22 . . . . . .6C **136**
Dunstan Ct. M40 . . . . . . .3A **84**
Dunstan St. Bolt 6F **33**
Dunstan St. Aud 6E **99**
Dunster Av. M9 . . . . .5G **69**
Dunster Av. Roch 6G **27**
Dunster Av. Stoc 4C **128**
Dunster Av. Swin 1H **79**
Dunster Clo. Haz G 4C **152**
Dunster Dri. Urm 6G **103**
Dunster Pl. Wors 4B **76**
Dunster Rd. Wors 4B **76**
Dunsters Av. Bury 6C **22**
Dunsterville Ter. Roch 6B **27**
(off New Barn La.)
Dunston St. M11 . . . . .5E **97**
Dunton Grn. Stoc 3B **128**
Dunton Towers. Stoc 3B **128**
(off Dunton Grn.)
Dunvegan Ct. Heyw 4A **38**
Dunvegan Rd. Haz G 4F **153**
Dunwood Av. Shaw 5G **43**
Dunwood Pk. Courts.
Shaw 4G **43**
Dunworth St. M14 . . . . . .4F **109**
Durant St. M4 . . . .2F **95** (2C **6**)
Durban Clo. Shaw 1E **57**
Durban Rd. Rams 6C **18**
Durban St. Ash L 4E **99**
Durban St. Oldh 6A **72**
Durban St. Roch 3C **40**
Durden M. Shaw 1F **57**
Durham Av. Urm 4G **105**
Durham Clo. Duk 1B **114**
Durham Clo. L Lev 3B **48**
Durham Clo. Rom 2G **141**
Durham Clo. Swin 1F **79**
Durham Cres. Fail 5G **85**
Durham Dri. Ash L 3H **87**
Durham Dri. Bury 5E **37**
Durham Dri. Rams 6D **12**
Durham Gro. Cad 3A **118**
Durham Ho. Stoc 3G **139**
Durham Rd. Salf 1C **92**
Durham St. M9 . . . . .4G **83**
Durham St. Bolt 3B **32**
Durham St. Droy 5A **98**
Durham St. Oldh 5A **98**
(in two parts)

Durham St. *Rad* 2A **50**
Durham St. *Roch* 5H **27**
Durham St. *Stoc* 5G **111**
Durham St. Bri. *Roch* 6A **28**
Durham Wlk. *Dent* 6F **113**
Durham Wlk. *Heyw* 3C **38**
Durley Av. *M8* 4D **82**
Durley Av. *Timp* 4B **134**
Durling St.
   M12 . . . . . .6G **95** (4F **11**)
Durn. 3G **17**
Durnford Av. *Urm* 5A **106**
Durnford Clo. *Roch* 1H **25**
Durnford St. *Midd* 6H **53**
Durnford Wlk. *M22* 2H **147**
Durnlaw Clo. *L'boro* 4G **17**
Durn St. *L'boro* 3G **17**
Durrington Wlk. *M40* 6C **70**
   (off Moston La.)
Dutton St. *M3* 2D **94** (1H **5**)
Duty St. *Rams* 2A **32**
Duxbury Av. *Bolt* 6A **20**
Duxbury Av. *L Lev* 2A **48**
Duxbury Dri. *Bury* 3G **37**
Duxbury St. *Bolt* 3H **31**
Duxford Lodge. *M8* 1B **82**
Duxford Wlk. *M40* 6C **70**
Dyche St. *M4* 2F **95** (3B **6**)
Dyche St. Trad. Est.
   M4 . . . . .2C **6**
Dye Ho. La. *Roch* 6A **16**
Dye La. *Rom* 1H **141**
Dyers Ct. *L'boro* 3E **17**
Dyer St. *M11* 5C **96**
Dyer St. *Salf* 6A **94** (3B **8**)
Dymchurch Av. *Rad* 2C **64**
Dymchurch St. *M40* 1E **97**
Dysarts Clo. *Moss* 6G **75**
Dysart St. *Ash L* 2B **100**
Dysart St. *Stoc* 6B **140**
Dyserth Gro. *Stoc* 4H **127**
Dyson Clo. *Farn* 1F **63**
Dyson Gro. *Lees* 1B **74**
Dyson Ho. *Farn* 1F **63**
   (off Hesketh Wlk.)
Dyson St. *Farn* 2F **63**
Dyson St. *Moss* 1D **88**
Dyson St. *Oldh* 3D **72**
Dystelegh Rd. *Dis* 1H **165**

E

Eades St. *Salf* 2G **93**
Eadington St. *M8* 2C **82**
Eafield Av. *Miln* 4F **29**
Eafield Clo. *Miln* 4F **29**
Eafield Rd. *L'boro* 6C **16**
Eafield Rd. *Roch* 2C **28**
Eagar St. *M40* 5C **84**
Eagle Ct. *M15* 2C **108**
Eagle Ct. *Del* 2G **59**
Eagle Dri. *Salf* 6E **81**
Eagles Nest. *P'wich* 6E **67**
Eagle St. *M4* 3E **95** (3B **6**)
Eagle St. *Bolt* 6C **32**
Eagle St. *Oldh* 2C **72**
Eagle St. *Roch* 5A **28**
Eagle Technology Pk.
   Roch 1G **41**
Eagle Way. *Roch* 1G **41**
Eagley. 4D **18**
Eagley Bank. *Bolt* 5D **18**
   (Eagley Way)
Eagley Bank. *Bolt* 5D **18**
   (Old Eagley M.)
Eagley Brook Way. *Bolt* . . .2B **32**
Eagley Brow. *Rams* 5D **18**
Eagley Ct. *Brom X* 4E **19**
Eagley Dri. *Bury* 4G **35**
Eagley Ind. Est.
   Brom X 4D **18**

Eagley Way. *Bolt* 5D **18**
Ealees. 4G **17**
Ealees. *L'boro* 4G **17**
Ealees Rd. *L'boro* 4G **17**
Ealing Av. *M14* 5G **109**
Ealinger Way. *Swin* 1F **79**
Ealing Pl. *M19* 3C **126**
Ealing Rd. *Stoc* 3F **139**
Eames Av. *Rad* 1A **64**
Eamont Wlk. *M9* 4F **83**
Earby Gro. *M9* 6H **69**
Earle Rd. *Bram* 3G **151**
Earlesdon Cres. *L Hul* 3C **62**
Earlesfield Clo. *Sale* 1F **133**
Earle St. *Ash L* 4F **99**
Earl Rd. *Chea H* 2A **160**
Earl Rd. *Rams* 3D **12**
Earl Rd. *Stoc* 5E **127**
Earlscliffe Ct. *Bow* 1D **144**
Earls Lodge. *Fail* 5D **84**
Earlston Av. *Dent* 4A **112**
Earl St. *Bury* 3D **36**
Earl St. *Dent* 3A **112**
Earl St. *Heyw* 3E **39**
Earl St. *Moss* 2D **88**
Earl St. *P'wich* 5G **67**
Earl St. *Rams* 3F **13**
Earl St. *Roch* 5C **40**
Earl St. *Salf* 1B **94**
Earl St. *Stoc* 3F **139**
Earl's Way. *Fail* 5D **84**
Earlswood Wlk. *M18* 1E **111**
Earlswood Wlk. *Bolt* 3B **46**
Earl Ter. *Duk* 4H **99**
   (off Hill St.)
Earl Wlk. *M12* 2B **110**
Early Bank. *Stal* 6G **101**
Early Bank Rd.
   Stal & Duk 5F **101**
Earnshaw Av. *Roch* 6E **15**
Earnshaw Av. *Stoc* 2B **140**
Earnshaw Clo. *Ash L* 6D **86**
Earnshaw St. *Bolt* 4F **45**
Earnshaw St. *Holl* 3F **117**
Easby Clo. *Chea H* 1D **160**
Easby Clo. *Poy* 2D **162**
Easby Rd. *Midd* 4H **53**
Easdale Clo. *Urm* 4B **104**
Easedale Rd. *Bolt* 5E **31**
Easington Wlk. *M40* 5A **84**
Easingwold. *Alt* 1E **145**
   (off Regent Rd.)
East Av. *M19* 2B **126**
East Av. *H Grn* 4G **149**
East Av. *Stal* 2E **101**
   (in two parts)
East Av. *W'fld* 5C **50**
Eastbank St. *Bolt* 3B **32**
Eastbourne Gro. *Bolt* 5E **31**
Eastbourne St. *Oldh* 5F **73**
Eastbourne St. *Roch* 6H **27**
Eastbrook Av. *Rad* 3A **50**
Eastburn Av.
   M40 . . . . . . .2G **95** (1F **7**)
E. Central Dri. *Swin* 4H **79**
Eastchurch Clo. *Farn* 2F **63**
E. Church Way. *Heyw* 6H **39**
Eastcombe Av. *Salf* 4F **81**
Eastcote Av. *Open* 5G **97**
Eastcote Rd. *Stoc* 4H **127**
Eastcote Wlk. *Farn* 6G **47**
Eastcourt Wlk.
   M13 . . . . . .1G **109** (5E **11**)
East Cres. *Midd* 2H **69**
Eastdale Pl. *Alt* 4F **133**
East Didsbury. 2G **137**
E. Downs Rd. *Bow* 3E **145**
E. Downs Rd. *Chea H* 2B **150**
East Dri. *M32* 6F **107**
East Dri. *Bury* 3F **51**
East Dri. *Marp* 2D **154**
East Dri. *Salf* 6C **80**

East Dri. *Swin* 4H **79**
Easterdale. *Oldh* 3G **73**
Eastern Av. *Swin* 6B **66**
   (in two parts)
Eastern By-Pass. *M11* 5F **97**
   (Crabtree La.)
Eastern By-Pass. *M11* 3E **97**
   (Stanton St.)
Eastern Circ. *M19* 3C **126**
Eastfield. *Salf* 1E **93**
Eastfield Av.
   M40 . . . . . .2A **96** (2H **7**)
Eastfield Av. *Midd* 2A **70**
Eastfield Rd. *Bolt* 2F **49**
Eastford Sq. *M40* 1G **95**
E. Garth Wlk. *M9* 6G **69**
Eastgate. *Whitw* 2C **14**
Eastgate St. *Ash L* 4G **99**
E. Gate St. *Roch* 3H **27**
E. Grange Av. *M11* 2E **97**
East Gro. *M13* 2G **109**
Eastgrove Av. *Bolt* 5C **18**
Eastham Av. *M14* 6F **109**
Eastham Av. *Bury* 5E **23**
Eastham Way. *Hand* 2H **159**
Eastham Way. *L Hul* 4D **62**
Easthaven Av. *M11* 2E **97**
E. Hill St. *Oldh* 3E **73**
Eastholme Dri. *M19* 2D **126**
Easthope Clo. *M20* 2F **125**
East Lancashire Railway.
   . . . . .2C **36**
E. Lancashire Rd.
   Wors 5A **76**
Eastlands Rd. *M9* 4F **69**
East Lea. *Dent* 4G **113**
Eastleigh Av. *Salf* 3A **82**
Eastleigh Dri.
   M40 . . . . . .2H **95** (1G **7**)
Eastleigh Gro. *Bolt* 5A **32**
Eastleigh Rd. *H Grn* 4F **149**
Eastleigh Rd. *P'wich* 6A **68**
   (in two parts)
E. Lynn Dri. *Wors* 6A **64**
East Meade. *M21* 2H **123**
East Meade. *Bolt* 5A **46**
East Meade. *P'wich* 1H **81**
East Meade. *Swin* 5E **79**
East Moor. *Wors* 4C **76**
Eastmoor Dri. *M40* 1F **97**
Eastmoor Gro. *Bolt* 5F **45**
E. Newton St.
   M4 . . . . . . .2G **95** (2F **7**)
Eastnor Clo.
   M15 . . . . . .1B **108** (6C **8**)
Easton Clo. *Midd* 3D **70**
Easton Dri. *Chea* 6C **138**
Easton Rd. *Droy* 3G **97**
E. Ordsall La.
   Salf 4B **94** (6C **4**)
East Over. *Rom* 3G **141**
Eastpark Clo.
   M13 . . . . . .1G **109** (5F **11**)
E. Philip St.
   Salf 2C **94** (1F **5**)
East Rd. *Carr* 5G **89**
East Rd. *Gort* 4D **110**
East Rd. *Long* 4C **110**
East Rd. *Man A* 6A **148**
East Rd. *Stret* 3B **106**
Eastry Av. *Stoc* 3B **128**
East St. *Ash L* 1B **100**
East St. *Aud* 1F **113**
East St. *Bury* 4D **36**
East St. *Fir* 4D **28**
   (in two parts)
East St. *L'boro* 4G **17**
East St. *Rad* 4H **49**
East St. *Rams* 1A **12**
East St. *Roch* 3A **28**
   (in two parts)
East St. *Ward* 3A **16**

E. Union St.
   M16 . . . . . .1A **108** (6B **8**)
East Va. *Marp* 6E **143**
East Vw. *Bury* 6E **13**
East Vw. *Midd* 1H **69**
East Vw. *Rams* 1E **13**
East Vw. *Sale* 6B **122**
Eastville Gdns. *M19* 4A **126**
East Wlk. *Eger* 1B **18**
East Way. *Bolt* 2D **32**
Eastway. *Midd* 6H **53**
Eastway. *Sale* 1H **133**
Eastway. *Shaw* 1F **57**
Eastway. *Urm* 4A **104**
Eastwood. *M14* 6G **109**
Eastwood Av. *M40* 2F **85**
Eastwood Av. *Droy* 4G **97**
Eastwood Av. *Urm* 5F **105**
Eastwood Av. *Wors* 6C **62**
Eastwood Clo. *Bolt* 4E **45**
Eastwood Clo. *Bury* 3F **37**
Eastwood Ct. *Bury* 3F **37**
Eastwood Dri. *Stoc* 1F **151**
Eastwood Educational Reserve.
   . . . . .5F **101**
   (Bird Sanctuary)
Eastwood Rd. *M40* 2E **85**
Eastwood St. *Aud* 6D **98**
Eastwood St. *L'boro* 4F **17**
Eastwood Ter. *Bolt* 5D **30**
Eastwood Vw. *Stal* 4F **101**
Eaton Clo. *Chea H* 2B **150**
Eaton Clo. *Duk* 1A **114**
Eaton Clo. *Poy* 4G **163**
Eaton Clo. *Swin* 1F **79**
Eaton Ct. *Bow* 4E **145**
Eaton Dri. *Ald E* 4F **167**
Eaton Dri. *Ash L* 1F **99**
Eaton Dri. *Timp* 3A **134**
Eaton Rd. *M8* 2B **82**
Eaton Rd. *Bow* 4E **145**
Eaton Rd. *Sale* 5A **122**
Eaves La. *Chad* 4G **71**
Ebbdale Clo. *Stoc* 3H **139**
Ebberstone St. *M14* 5E **109**
Ebden St. *M1* 5F **95** (2C **10**)
Ebenezer St.
   M15 . . . . . .6D **94** (4H **9**)
Ebenezer St. *Ash L* 2A **100**
Ebnall Wlk. *M14* 2H **125**
Ebor Clo. *Shaw* 5E **43**
Ebor Ho. *Stret* 6F **107**
Ebor Rd. *M22* 1C **148**
Ebor St. *L'boro* 4F **17**
Ebsworth St. *M40* 3H **83**
Ebury St. *Rad* 3F **49**
Eccles. 3H **91**
Eccles Bri. Rd.
   Marp 6D **142**
Eccles Clo. *M11* 5E **97**
Eccles Crematorium.
   Eccl 5B **90**
Eccleshall Clo.
   M15 . . . . . .1E **109** (5A **10**)
Eccleshall St. *M11* 4E **97**
   (in three parts)
Eccles New Rd.
   Eccl & Salf 3A **92**
Eccles Recreation Cen.
   . . . . .4H **91**
Eccles Rd. *Swin* 5F **79**
Eccles St. *Rams* 3D **12**
Eccleston Av. *M14* 6F **109**
Eccleston Av. *Bolt* 4D **32**
Eccleston Av. *Swin* 4D **78**
Eccleston Clo. *Bury* 4G **35**
Eccleston Pl. *Salf* 3H **81**
Eccleston Rd. *Stoc* 1F **151**
Eccleston St. *Fail* 3G **85**
Eccleston Way.
   Hand 3H **159**

Eccups La.
Wilm . . . .6A **158** & 2A **166**
Echo St. *M1* 5F **95** (2C **10**)
Eckersley Clo. *M23* 5F **135**
Eckersley Rd. *Bolt* 2A **32**
Eckersley St. *Bolt* 3G **45**
Eckford St. *M8* 5D **82**
Eclipse Clo. *Roch* 4C **28**
Edale Av *M40* 3A **84**
Edale Av. *Aud* 6D **98**
Edale Av. *Dent* 1F **129**
Edale Av. *Stoc* 6A **112**
Edale Av. *Urm* 6D **104**
Edale Bank. *Glos* 5G **117**
Edale Clo. *Bow* 4E **145**
Edale Clo. *Glos* 5G **117**
Edale Clo. *Haz G* 4E **153**
Edale Clo. *H Grn* 6H **149**
Edale Clo. *Irlam* 6E **103**
Edale Cres. *Glos* 5G **117**
Edale Fold. Glos *5G 117*
    (off Edale Cres.)
Edale Gro. *Ash L* 5C **88**
Edale Gro. *Sale* 1G **133**
Edale Rd. *Bolt* 3E **45**
Edale Rd. *Farn* 2E **63**
Edale Rd. *Stret* 4B **106**
Edale St. *Salf* 6F **81**
Edbrook Wlk. *M13* 2H **109**
Eddie Colman Clo.
  M40 . . . . .6B **84**
Eddie Colman Ct. Salf *2G 93*
    (off Belvedere Rd.)
Eddisbury Av. *M20* 1D **124**
Eddisbury Av. *Urm* 3H **103**
Edditch Gro. *Bolt* 6E **33**
Eddystone Clo. *Salf* 4G **93**
Eden Av. *Bolt* 2A **32**
Eden Av. *H Lane* 6C **154**
Eden Av. *Rams* 2A **12**
Edenbridge Dri. *Rad* 2B **64**
Edenbridge Rd. *M40* 1D **96**
Edenbridge Rd.
  Chea H 1D **150**
Eden Clo.
  M15 . . . . .2E **109** (6A **10**)
Eden Clo. *Heyw* 2D **38**
Eden Clo. *Stoc* 3A **140**
Eden Clo. *Wilm* 4B **166**
Eden Ct. *M19* 1C **126**
Eden Ct. Rams *3A 12*
    (off N. Bury Rd.)
Edendale Dri. *M22* 4B **148**
Edenfield. **3A 12**
Edenfield Av. *M21* 5B **124**
Edenfield La. *Wors* 6H **77**
Edenfield Rd. *P'wich* 6A **68**
Edenfield Rd. *Roch* 1E **25**
Edenfield St. *Roch* 2E **27**
Eden Gro. *Bolt* 2A **32**
Edenhall Av. *M19* 1B **126**
Edenham Wlk. *M40* 1D **84**
Edenhurst Dri *Timp* 6B **134**
Edenhurst Rd. *Stoc* 5B **140**
Eden La. *Rams* 3A **12**
Eden Lodge. *Bolt* 2A **32**
Eden Pl. *Chea* 5H **137**
Eden Pl. *Sale* 4B **122**
Edensor Dri. *Hale* 2C **146**
Eden St. *Bolt* 2A **32**
Eden St. *Bury* 3D **36**
Eden St. *Oldh* 2C **72**
Eden St. *Rams* 3A **12**
Eden St. *Roch* 3F **27**
Edenvale. *Wors* 4C **76**
Eden Way. *Shaw* 5E **43**
Edenwood Rd. *Rams* 4A **12**
    (in two parts)
Edgar St. *Bolt* 1A **46**
Edgar St. *Rams* 4D **12**
Edgar St. *Roch* 1C **28**
Edgar St. W. *Rams* 4D **12**

Edgbaston Dri. *M16* 4G **107**
Edgedale Av. *M19* 4A **126**
Edge End. *Dob* 4A **60**
Edgefield Av. *M9* 5G **69**
Edge Fold. *Farn* 6G **45**
Edge Fold Cres. *Wors* 3F **77**
Edge Fold Ind. Est.
  W'houg 6G **45**
Edge Fold Rd. *Wors* 2F **77**
Edge Grn. *Wors* 3E **77**
Edge Hill. *Stal* 4F **101**
Edge Hill Av. *Rytn* 5C **56**
Edgehill Chase.
  Wilm 2H **167**
Edgehill Clo. *Salf* 3F **93**
Edgehill Ct. *Stret* 5E **107**
Edge Hill Rd. *Bolt* 4F **45**
Edge Hill Rd. *Rytn* 4C **56**
Edgehill Rd *Salf* 2C **92**
Edgehill St.
  M4 . . . . . .3E **95** (4B **6**)
Edge La. *Bolt* 1A **30**
Edge La. *Droy & M11* . . .3F **97**
Edge La. *Mot* 3A **116**
    (in two parts)
Edge La. *Stret & M21* . . .6D **106**
Edge La. Rd. *Oldh* 1D **72**
Edge La. St. *Rytn* 3C **56**
Edgeley. **4F 139**
Edgeley Fold. *Stoc* 4E **139**
Edgeley Rd. *Stoc* 4C **138**
Edgeley Rd. *Urm* 1C **120**
Edgeley Rd. Trad. Est.
  Stoc 4C **138**
Edgemoor. *Bow* 3C **144**
Edgemoor Clo. *Oldh* 6H **57**
Edgemoor Clo. *Rad* 2E **49**
Edgemoor Dri. *Roch* 6B **26**
Edge St. *M4* 3E **96** (4B **6**)
Edge, The. **1A 86**
Edge Vw. *Chad* 6E **55**
Edgeview Wlk.
  M13 . . . . . .6F **95** (4D **10**)
Edgeware Av. *P'wich* 5B **68**
Edgeware Rd. *Chad* 6E **71**
Edgeware Rd. *Eccl* 1C **90**
Edgewater. *Salf* 3D **92**
Edgeway. *Wilm* 4E **167**
Edgeworth Av. *Bolt* 4D **34**
Edgeworth Dri. *M14* 2A **126**
Edgmont Av. *Bolt* 3H **45**
Edgware Rd. *M40* 1D **96**
Edgworth Clo. *Heyw* 3C **38**
Edgworth Dri. *Bury* 4G **35**
Edilom Rd. *M8* 1A **82**
Edinburgh. *Eccl* 3G **91**
    (off Monton St.)
Edinburgh Clo. *Chea* 5B **138**
Edinburgh Clo. *Sale* 6F **121**
Edinburgh Dri. *Woodl* 4A **130**
Edinburgh Ho.
  Salf 4B **94** (5D **4**)
    (off Rocket St.)
Edinburgh Rd. *L Lev* 5A **48**
Edinburgh Sq. *M40* 1H **95**
Edinburgh Way. *Roch* 1D **40**
Edington. *Roch* 3H **27**
    (off Redcross St.)
Edison Rd. *Eccl* 4E **91**
Edison St. *M11* 6G **97**
Edith Av. *M14* 4E **109**
Edith Cavell Clo. *Open* 4E **97**
Edith Cliff Wlk. *M40* 2F **85**
Edith St. *Bolt* 1G **45**
Edith St. *Farn* 2F **63**
Edith St. *Oldh* 6D **72**
Edith St. *Rams* 1G **13**
Edith Ter. *Comp* 1F **143**
Edleston Gro. *Wilm* 6A **160**
Edlin Clo. *M12* 2A **110**
Edlingham. *Roch* 5G **27**
Edlington Wlk. *M40* 5C **84**

Edmonds St. *Midd* 6B **54**
Edmonton Ct. *Stoc* 1A **152**
Edmonton Rd. *M40* 1C **96**
Edmonton Rd. *Stoc* 1A **152**
Edmund Clo. *Stoc* 6G **127**
Edmunds Ct. *Bolt* 1H **45**
Edmunds Fold. *L'boro* 3D **16**
Edmunds Pas. *L'boro* 2E **17**
Edmund St. *Droy* 4A **98**
Edmund St. *Fail* 3F **85**
Edmund St. *Miln* 5F **29**
Edmund St. *Rad* 3A **50**
Edmund St. *Roch* 3F **27**
Edmund St.
  Salf (M3) . . .3C **94** (4E **5**)
Edmund St. *Salf* (M6) . . .2E **93**
Edmund St. *Shaw* 6G **43**
Edna St. *Hyde* 6B **114**
Edson Rd. *M8* 6B **68**
Edstone Clo. *Bolt* 3D **44**
Edward Av. *M21* 1F **123**
Edward Av. *Bred* 6E **129**
Edward Av. *L'boro* 6D **16**
Edward Av. *Salf* 2C **92**
Edward Charlton Rd.
  M16 . . . . .5G **107**
Edward Ct. *B'hth* 4D **132**
Edward Grant Ct. M9 . . .2G **83**
    (off Hemsley St. S.)
Edward M. *Oldh* 4A **72**
Edward Onyon Ct. *Salf* . . .2E **93**
Edward Rd. *M9* 4F **69**
Edward Rd. *Shaw* 1E **57**
Edwards Clo. *Marp* 6C **142**
Edwards Ct. *M22* 2B **148**
Edwards Ct. *Haz G* 5E **153**
Edwards Dri. *W'fld* 1F **67**
Edward St. *M9* 3G **83**
Edward St. *Ash L* 3C **100**
Edward St. *Aud* 6D **98**
Edward St. *Bolt* 2H **45**
Edward St. *Bury* 4D **36**
Edward St. *Chad* 2G **71**
Edward St. *Dent* 3F **113**
Edward St. *Droy* 5A **98**
Edward St. *Duk* 1A **114**
Edward St. *Farn* 5D **46**
Edward St. *Hyde* 4A **114**
    (in two parts)
Edward St. Marp B 2E **143**
Edward St. *Midd* 5A **54**
Edward St. *Oldh* 3A **72**
Edward St. *P'wich* 4E **67**
Edward St. *Rad* 1B **64**
    (Market St.)
Edward St. *Rad* 5H **49**
    (Stand La.)
Edward St. *Roch* 3A **28**
Edward St. *Sale* 5E **123**
Edward St. *Salf* . .1C **94** (1F **5**)
Edward St. *Stoc* 3H **139**
Edward St. *Ward* 5B **16**
Edward St. *Whitw* 3H **15**
Edward Sutcliffe Clo.
  M14 . . . . .5E **109**
Edwards Way. *Marp* 6C **142**
Edwin Rd. *M11* 3A **96**
Edwin St. *Bury* 3C **36**
Edwin St. *Stoc* 3B **140**
Edwin Waugh Gdns.
  Roch 1F **27**
Edzell Wlk. *Open* 4E **97**
Eeasbrook. *Urm* 6F **105**
Egbert St. *M40* 4A **84**
Egermont Clo. *W'fld* 6E **51**
Egerton. **1B 18**
Egerton Barn Cottage.
  Eger 1C **18**
Egerton Clo. *Heyw* 4F **39**
Egerton Ct. *M14* 3G **109**
    (off Up. Park Rd.)
Egerton Ct. *M21* 1F **123**

Egerton Ct. *Dent* 3G **113**
    (off Margaret Rd.)
Egerton Ct. *Stoc* 1H **151**
Egerton Ct. *Wors* 3A **78**
Egerton Cres. *M20* 2F **125**
Egerton Dri. *Hale* 3A **146**
Egerton Dri. *Sale* 4B **122**
Egerton Gro. *Wors* 6F **63**
Egerton Lodge. Dent 3G **113**
    (off Margaret Rd.)
Egerton Lodge. *Eger* 2C **18**
Egerton M. *M14* 1H **125**
Egerton M. *Droy* 5A **98**
Egerton Park. **4B 78**
Egerton Pk. *Wors* 4B **78**
Egerton Pl. *Shaw* 1E **57**
Egerton Rd. *M14* 1H **125**
Egerton Rd. *Eccl* 1F **91**
Egerton Rd. *Hale* 2A **146**
Egerton Rd. *Stoc* 6A **140**
Egerton Rd. *W'fld* 2D **66**
Egerton Rd. *Wilm* 6F **159**
Egerton Rd. *Wors* 6F **63**
Egerton Rd. N.
  M16 & M21 . . . . . .5A **108**
Egerton Rd. N. *Stoc* 4E **127**
Egerton Rd. S. *M21* 1A **124**
Egerton Rd. S. *Stoc* 4E **127**
Egerton St.
  M15 . . . . . .6B **94** (2D **8**)
Egerton St. *Ash L* 2A **100**
Egerton St. *Dent* 2D **112**
Egerton St. *Droy* 4B **98**
Egerton St. *Eccl* 3D **90**
Egerton St. *Farn* 6E **47**
Egerton St. *Heyw* 4E **39**
Egerton St. *L'boro* 4G **17**
Egerton St. *Midd* 2E **69**
Egerton St. *Moss* 1E **89**
Egerton St. *Oldh* 2D **72**
Egerton St. *P'wich* 5G **67**
Egerton St. *Salf* . .4B **94** (5D **4**)
Egerton Ter. *M14* 2H **125**
Egerton Wlk. *Wors* 6F **63**
Egglington St. *M40* 6E **83**
Egham Ct. *Bolt* 4D **32**
Egham Ho. *Bolt* 5F **45**
Egmont St. *M8* 3C **82**
Egmont St. *Moss* 3E **89**
Egmont St. *Salf* 5C **80**
Egremont Av. *M20* 2E **125**
Egremont Ct. *Salf* 3G **81**
Egremont Gro. *Stoc* 3D **138**
Egremont Rd. *Miln* 1C **42**
Egret Dri. *Irlam* 4E **103**
Egyptian St. *Bolt* 4B **32**
Egypt La. *P'wich* 6H **51**
Eight Acre. *W'fld* 2A **66**
Eighth Av. *Oldh* 2B **86**
Eighth St. *Traf P* 1D **106**
    (in two parts)
Eighth St. W. *Traf P* 1C **106**
Eileen Gro. *M14* 5G **109**
Eileen Gro. W. *M14* 5F **109**
Elaine Av. *M9* 1B **84**
Elbain Wlk. *M40* 6C **84**
Elborton Wlk. M8 . . . .*4B 82*
    (off Chantry Wlk.)
Elbe St. *M12* 5G **95** (2F **11**)
Elbow La. *Roch* 5A **28**
Elbow St. *M19* 6C **110**
Elbow St. Trad. Est.
  M19 . . . . .6D **110**
Elcho Ct. *Bow* 3D **144**
Elcho Rd. *Bow* 2D **144**
Elcot Clo. *M40* 6E **83**
Elderberry Clo. *Dig* 2C **60**
Elderberry Wlk. *Part* 6C **118**

Elderberry Way. *Wilm* 2H **167**
Elder Clo. *Stoc* 3D **140**
Eldercot Gro. *Bolt* 3E **45**
Eldercot Rd. *Bolt* 3E **45**
Eldercroft Rd. *Timp* 6C **134**
Elderfield Dri. *Bred* 5F **129**
Elder Gro. *M40* 1F **85**
Elder Mt. Rd. *M9* 1F **83**
Elder Rd. *Lees* 3A **74**
Elder St. *Roch* 6B **28**
Elder Wlk. *Sale* 3E **121**
Elderwood. *Chad* 2E **71**
Eldon Clo. *Aud* 6E **99**
Eldon Pl. *Eccl* 4A **91**
Eldon Precinct. *Oldh* 4C **72**
Eldon Rd. *Irlam* 5E **103**
Eldon Rd. *Stoc* 4E **139**
Eldon St. *Bolt* 4D **32**
Eldon St. *Bury* 1D **36**
Eldon St. *Oldh* 4D **72**
Eldridge Dri. *M40* 6A **84**
Eleanor Rd. *M21* 1F **123**
Eleanor Rd. *Rytn* 5C **56**
Eleanor St. *Bolt* 6E **19**
Eleanor St. *Oldh* 1B **72**
Electo St. *M11* 6G **97**
Elevator Rd. *Traf P* 1E **107**
Eleventh St. *Traf P* 1C **106**
Elf Mill Clo. *Stoc* 5G **139**
Elf Mill Ter. *Stoc* 5G **139**
Elford Gro. *M18* 3A **112**
Elgar St. *M12* 3C **110**
Elgin Av. *M20* 6H **125**
Elgin Dri. *Sale* 6E **123**
Elgin Rd. *Duk* 1A **114**
Elgin Rd. *Oldh* 4G **73**
Elgin St. *Ash L* 1G **99**
    (in two parts)
Elgin St. *Bolt* 3G **31**
Elgin St. *Roch* 6A **28**
Elgin St. *Stal* 4F **101**
Elgol Clo. *Stoc* 6H **139**
Elgol Ct. *Heyw* 4C **38**
Elgol Dri. *Bolt* 1C **44**
Elham Clo. *Rad* 2C **64**
Elim St. *L'boro* 2G **17**
Elim Ter. *L'boro* 2G **17**
Eliot Rd. *Eccl* 4F **91**
Eliot Wlk. *Midd* 4C **54**
Elisie St. *Rams* 5C **12**
Eli St. *Chad* 6G **71**
Elitex Ho. *Salf* 1C **94**
Eliza Ann St. *M40* 1G **95**
Eliza Ann St. *Eccl* 4E **91**
Elizabethan Way. *Miln* . . .5F **29**
Elizabeth Av. *Chad* 6G **71**
Elizabeth Av. *Dent* 2E **113**
    (in two parts)
Elizabeth Av. *Dis* 2H **165**
Elizabeth Av. *Rytn* 4A **56**
Elizabeth Av. *Stal* 3E **101**
Elizabeth Av. *Stoc* 3H **139**
Elizabeth Clo. *Stret* 5D **106**
Elizabeth Ct. *M14* 2H **125**
Elizabeth Ct.
    M15 . . . . . .1C **108** (5E **9**)
    (off Ribston St.)
Elizabeth Ct. *Stoc* 1E **139**
Elizabeth Gro. *Shaw* 6F **43**
Elizabeth Ho. *Stoc* 1D **138**
Elizabeth Rd. *Part* 5D **118**
Elizabeth Slinger Rd.
    M20 . . . . .5C **124**
Elizabeth St. *M8* 5B **82**
Elizabeth St. *Ash L* 1H **99**
Elizabeth St. *Dent* 4D **112**
Elizabeth St. *Heyw* 3E **39**
Elizabeth St. *Hyde* 4B **114**
Elizabeth St. *L'boro* 5C **16**
Elizabeth St. *P'wich* 5G **67**
Elizabeth St. *Rad* 4G **49**
Elizabeth St. *Rams* 2A **12**

Elizabeth St. *Roch* 2C **40**
Elizabeth St. *Swin* 2F **79**
Elizabeth St. *W'fld* 2D **66**
Elizabeth Yarwood Ct.
    M13 . . . . .5D **10**
Eliza St. *M15* 1C **108** (5E **9**)
Eliza St. *Rams* 3F **13**
Eliza St. *Sale* 4B **122**
Elkanagh Gdns. *Salf* 2F **93**
Elk Mill Central Retail Pk.
    Rytn 5H **55**
Elkstone Av. *L Hul* 3C **62**
Ella Dene Pk. *M21* 1A **124**
Ellanby Clo. *M14* 4F **109**
Elland Clo. *Bury* 5F **51**
Ellbourne Rd. *M9* 6C **68**
Ellenbrook. 3E **77**
Ellenbrook Clo. *M12* 1D **110**
Ellenbrook Rd. *M22* 5B **148**
Ellenbrook Rd. *Wors* 3D **76**
    (in two parts)
Ellenbrook St. *M12* 1D **110**
Ellendale Grange.
    Wors 3D **76**
Ellen Gro. *Kear* 4C **64**
Ellenhall Clo. *M9* 3F **83**
Ellenroad App. *Miln* 1E **43**
Ellenroad St. *Miln* 1E **43**
Ellenrod Dri. *Roch* 1C **26**
Ellenrod La. *Roch* 1C **26**
Ellenshaw Clo. *Roch* 1C **26**
Ellens Pl. *L'boro* 6D **16**
Ellen St. *Bolt* 3G **31**
    (in two parts)
Ellen St. *Droy* 5B **98**
Ellen St. *Oldh* 1B **72**
Ellen St. *Stoc* 6F **127**
Ellen Wilkinson Cres.
    M12 . . . . .2C **110**
Elleray Clo. *L Lev* 4C **48**
Elleray Rd. *Midd* 4H **69**
Elleray Rd. *Salf* 6B **80**
Ellerbeck Clo. *Bolt* 6G **19**
Ellerbeck Cres. *Wors* 3E **77**
Ellerbrook Clo. *Bolt* 6F **19**
Ellerby Av. *Swin* 6G **65**
Ellesmere Av. *Ash L* 4G **87**
Ellesmere Av. *Eccl* 3G **91**
Ellesmere Av. *Marp* 5D **142**
Ellesmere Av. *Wors* 6E **63**
Ellesmere Circ. *Urm* 6F **91**
Ellesmere Clo. *Duk* 6C **100**
Ellesmere Clo. *L Hul* 6D **62**
Ellesmere Dri. *Chea* 6C **138**
Ellesmere Gdns. *Bolt* 4H **45**
Ellesmere Park. 1H **91**
Ellesmere Pl.
    M15 . . . . . .1B **108** (6D **8**)
Ellesmere Retail Pk.
    Wors 6F **63**
Ellesmere Rd. *M21* 6A **108**
Ellesmere Rd. *Alt* 5F **133**
Ellesmere Rd. *Bolt* 4G **45**
Ellesmere Rd. *Eccl* 1G **91**
Ellesmere Rd. *Stoc* 4C **138**
Ellesmere Rd. N. *Stoc* . . .4E **127**
Ellesmere Rd. S. *M21* . . .1A **124**
Ellesmere Shop. Cen.
    Wors 6F **63**
Ellesmere Sports Club.
    . . . . .3G **77**
Ellesmere St.
    M15 . . . . . . .6B **94** (4C **8**)
Ellesmere St. *Bolt* 1H **45**
Ellesmere St. *Eccl* 4F **91**
    (in two parts)
Ellesmere St. *Fail* 3F **85**
Ellesmere St. *Farn* 1F **63**
Ellesmere St. *L Hul* 6D **62**
Ellesmere St. *Roch* 6H **27**

Ellesmere St. *Swin* 2G **79**
    (Bolton Rd.)
Ellesmere St. *Swin* 4D **78**
    (Moorside Rd.)
Ellesmere Ter. *M14* 2H **125**
Ellesmere Wlk. *Farn* 1F **63**
Ellingham Clo. *M11* 4B **96**
Ellingham Clo. *M11* 4B **96**
Elliot Sq. *Oldh* 1E **73**
Elliott Av. *Hyde* 2B **114**
Elliott Dri. *Sale* 5G **121**
Elliott St. *Bolt* 2G **31**
Elliott St. *Farn* 2E **63**
Elliott St. *Lees* 3A **74**
Elliott St. *Roch* 3A **28**
Ellisbank Wlk.
    M13 . . . . . . .6F **95** (4D **10**)
    (off Hanworth Clo.)
Ellis Cres. *Wors* 6D **62**
Ellis Dri. *M8* 2D **82**
Ellishaw Row. *Salf* 4F **93**
Ellisland Wlk. *M40* 5A **84**
Ellis La. *Midd* 1D **68**
Ellison Clo. *Holl* 2F **117**
Ellison Ho. *Ash L* 4G **99**
    (off Park St.)
Ellis St. *M15* 1C **108** (6F **9**)
Ellis St. *Bolt* 2H **45**
Ellis St. *Bury* 3H **35**
Ellis St. *Hyde* 5D **114**
Ellis St. *Rams* 4D **12**
Ellis St. *Salf* 1C **94**
Elliston Sq. *M12* 1C **110**
Ellonby Ri. *Los* 2A **44**
Ellor St. *Salf* 2F **93**
Ellor St. *Salf* 2F **93**
Ellor St. *Salf* 2F **93**
Ellwood Rd. *Stoc* 2B **140**
Elm Av. *Rad* 1F **65**
Embankment Rd. *M20* . . .5B **124**
Embankment Rd. *Midd* . . .1C **70**
Embankment Rd. . . . .
Embankment Rd. *Midd* . . .1C **70**
Elm Beds Rd. *Poy* 5A **164**
Elmbank Rd. *Midd* 1C **70**
Elm Clo. *Mot* 3C **116**
Elm Clo. *Part* 6D **118**
Elm Clo. *Poy* 4F **163**
Elm Ct. *Stoc* 3B **140**
Elm Cres. *Ald E* 4H **167**
Elm Cres. *Wors* 4A **78**
Elmdale Av. *H Grn* 3F **149**
Elmdale Wlk.
    M15 . . . . . .6E **95** (4A **10**)
Elm Dri. *Stret* 6B **106**
Elmfield Av. *M22* 3C **136**
Elm Gro. *Mot* 3C **116**
Elmfield Clo. *Ald E* 4H **167**
Elmfield Ct. *Stoc* 6H **139**
    (off Elmfield Rd.)
Elmfield Dri. *Marp* 5C **142**
Elmfield Ho. *Stoc* 6H **139**
    (off Plumley Clo.)
Elmfield Rd. *Ald E* 4H **167**
Elmfield Rd. *Aud* 5C **98**
Elmfield Rd. *Stoc* 6H **139**
Elmfield St. *M8* 5C **82**
Elmfield St. *Bolt* 2B **32**
    (Blackburn Rd.)
Elmfield St. *Bolt* 3B **32**
    (Fir St.)
Elmfield St. *Bolt* 3B **32**
    (Pendlebury St.)
Elmgate Gro. *M19* 6C **110**
Elm Gro. *M20* 6F **125**
Elm Gro. *Ald E* 4H **167**
Elm Gro. *Ash L* 6G **87**
Elm Gro. *Brom X* 3F **19**
Elm Gro. *Dent* 2D **112**
Elm Gro. *Droy* 3F **97**
Elm Gro. *Farn* 1D **62**
Elm Gro. *G'ton* 3D **74**
Elm Gro. *Hand* 4G **159**
Elm Gro. *Hyde* 5D **114**

Elm Gro. *Miln* 2E **43**
Elm Gro. *P'wich* 3E **67**
Elm Gro. *Roch* 6G **27**
Elm Gro. *Sale* 3B **122**
Elm Gro. *Swin* 1B **78**
Elm Gro. *Urm* 5G **105**
Elm Gro. *Ward* 4A **16**
Elmham Wlk.
    M40 . . . . . . .1G **95** (1F **7**)
Elmhurst Dri. *M19* 4B **126**
Elmlea. *Alt* 1H **145**
Elmley Clo. *Stoc* 6G **141**
Elmore Wood. *L'boro* 3C **16**
Elm Pk. Ga. *Roch* 6B **14**
Elm Pk. Gro. *Roch* 6B **14**
Elm Pk. Vw. *Roch* 6B **14**
Elm Pk. Way. *Roch* 6B **14**
Elmridge Dri. *Haleb* 5C **146**
Elm Rd. *M20* 5E **125**
Elm Rd. *Gat* 6E **137**
Elm Rd. *Hale* 2G **145**
Elm Rd. *H Lane* 6D **154**
Elm Rd. *Kear* 4H **63**
Elm Rd. *L Lev* 5B **48**
Elm Rd. *Oldh* 2B **86**
Elm Rd. S. *Stoc* 4C **138**
Elms Clo. *W'fld* 5D **50**
Elmscott Wlk. *M13* 2H **109**
Elmsdale Av. *M9* 4F **69**
Elmsfield Av. *Roch* 2A **26**
Elmsleigh Ct. *Eccl* 2H **91**
Elmsleigh Rd. *H Grn* 3E **149**
Elmsmere Rd. *M20* 6H **125**
Elms Rd. *Stal* 2H **101**
Elms Rd. *Stoc* 4D **126**
Elms Rd. *W'fld* 6D **50**
Elms Sq. *W'fld* 6C **50**
Elms St. *W'fld* 6C **50**
Elmstead Av. *M20* 3E **125**
Elmsted Clo. *Chea H* 2D **150**
Elms, The. *L'boro* 5C **16**
Elms, The. *Moss* 2D **88**
Elms, The. *Wilm* 3C **166**
Elmstone Gro. *Bolt* 4B **32**
Elm St. *Bred* 5F **129**
Elm St. *Bury* 3F **37**
Elm St. *Eccl* 4F **91**
Elm St. *Fail* 3F **85**
Elm St. *Farn* 6F **47**
Elm St. *Heyw* 3F **39**
Elm St. *L'boro* 1F **29**
Elm St. *Midd* 6C **54**
Elm St. *Rams* 3F **13**
    (Peel Brow)
Elm St. *Rams* 2B **12**
    (Rochdale Rd.)
Elm St. *Roch* 2H **27**
Elm St. *Swin* 2E **79**
Elm St. *Whitw* 3H **15**
Elmsway. *Bram* 6E **151**
Elmsway. *Haleb* 5B **146**
Elmsway. *H Lane* 1C **164**
Elmswood Av. *M14* 5D **108**
Elmswood Dri. *Hyde* 4E **115**
Elmsworth Av. *M19* 6D **110**
Elmton Rd. *M9* 6G **69**
Elm Tree Clo. *Fail* 4H **85**
Elm Tree Clo. *Stal* 5E **101**
Elm Tree Dri. *M22* 2B **148**
Elm Tree Dri. *Duk* 6D **100**
Elmtree Dri. *Stoc* 1D **138**
Elm Tree Rd. *Bred* 6C **128**
    (in two parts)
Elmwood. *Sale* 5E **121**
Elmwood. *Wors* 6A **78**
Elmwood Ct. *Stret* 1C **122**
Elmwood Dri. *Rytn* 2A **56**
Elmwood Gro. *M9* 4H **83**
Elmwood Gro. *Bolt* 5G **31**
Elmwood Gro. *Farn* 3E **63**
Elmwood Lodge. *M20* 5E **125**

Elmwood Pk. *Stal* 2H **101**
Elrick Wlk. *Open* 4D **96**
Elsa Rd. *M19* 6E **111**
Elsdon Dri. *M18* 1F **111**
Elsdon Gdns. *Bolt* 4D **32**
Elsdon Rd. *M13* 5B **110**
Elsfield Clo. *Bolt* 3H **31**
Elsham Clo. *Bolt* 6C **18**
Elsham Dri. *Wors* 6D **62**
Elsham Gdns. *M18* 3D **110**
Elsie St. *M9* 3G **83**
Elsie St. *Farn* 1E **63**
Elsinore Av. *Irlam* 6D **102**
Elsinore Bus. Cen.
    M16 . . . . .3G **107**
Elsinore Clo. *Fail* 4H **85**
Elsinore Rd. *M16* 3G **107**
Elsinore St. *Bolt* 2D **32**
Elsinor Ter. *Urm* 5H **105**
Elsma Rd. *M40* 1G **97**
Elsmore Rd. *M14* 6E **109**
Elson Ct. *Hyde* 2B **130**
Elson Dri. *Hyde* 2B **130**
Elson St. *Bury* 1H **35**
Elstead Wlk. *M9* 6C **68**
Elsted Rd. *G'fld* 4G **75**
Elstree Av. *M40* 1D **96**
Elstree Ct. *Urm* 5F **105**
Elstree Gro. *Stoc* 3F **139**
Elswick Av. *M21* 4B **124**
Elswick Av. *Bolt* 2F **45**
Elswick Av. *Bram* 6G **151**
Elsworth Dri. *Bolt* 1B **33**
Elsworth St.
    M3 . . . . . . .2E **95** (1A **6**)
Elterwater Clo. *Bury* 1H **35**
Elterwater Rd. *Farn* 2A **62**
Eltham Av. *Stoc* 6C **140**
Eltham Dri. *Urm* 3E **105**
Eltham St. *M19* 5C **110**
Elton. 3A **36**
Elton Av. *M19* 1C **126**
Elton Av. *Farn* 1B **62**
Elton Bank. Glos 6F **117**
    (off Brassington Cres.)
Elton Brook Clo. *Bury* . . .2H **35**
Elton Clo. Glos 6F **117**
    (off Brassington Cres.)
Elton Clo. *W'fld* 1E **67**
Elton Clo. *Wilm* 6A **160**
Elton Dri. *Haz G* 5D **152**
Elton Lea. Glos 6F **117**
    (off Langsett La.)
Elton Pl. Glos 6F **117**
    (off Brassington Cres.)
Elton Rd. *Sale* 1G **133**
Elton Sq. Ho. *Bury* 4A **36**
Elton St. *Bolt* 6C **32**
Elton St. *Roch* 4C **40**
Elton St. *Salf* 2B **94** (1D **4**)
Elton St. *Stret* 2F **107**
Eltons Yd. *Salf* 2B **94** (1D **4**)
Elton Va. Rd. *Bury* 3H **35**
Elvate Cres. *M8* 6B **82**
Elverdon Clo. *M15* 2C **108**
Elverston St. *M22* 2C **136**
Elverston Way. *Chad* 1A **72**
Elvey St. *M40* 6H **83**
Elvington Cres. *Wors* 3E **77**
Elvira Clo. *Fail* 4H **85**
Elwick Clo. *M16* 4D **108**
Elworth Way.
    Hand 3H **159**
Elwyn Av. *M22* 4B **136**
Ely Av. *Stret* 4H **105**
Ely Clo. *Wors* 3D **76**
Ely Cres. *Fail* 6F **85**
Ely Dri. *Bury* 1B **36**
Ely Gdns. *Urm* 5G **105**
Ely Gro. *Bolt* 4A **32**
Elysian St. *Open* 5E **97**
Ely St. *Chad* 4H **71**

Embankment Footway.
    Stoc 4F **139**
Embassy Wlk. *M18* 3F **111**
Ember St. *M11* 3F **97**
Embla Wlk. *Bolt* 3C **46**
Emblem St. *Bolt* 2H **45**
Embleton Clo. *Bolt* 4G **33**
Embleton Wlk. *M18* 1F **111**
Embsay Clo. *Bolt* 6B **18**
Emerald Rd. *M22* 6D **148**
Emerald St. *Bolt* 2B **32**
Emerald St. *Dent* 4E **113**
Emerson Av. *Eccl* 2A **92**
Emerson Dri. *Midd* 6H **53**
Emerson St. *Salf* 3D **92**
Emery Av. *M21* 3A **124**
Emery Clo. *Stoc* 5C **126**
Emery Ct. *Heat M* 2B **138**
Emery Rd. *Heat M* 2B **138**
Emily Beavan Clo. *M11* . .4D **96**
Emily Pl. *Droy* 4H **97**
Emley St. *M19* 6D **110**
Emlyn Gro. *Chea* 5C **138**
Emlyn St. *Farn* 6E **47**
Emlyn St. *Swin* 3D **78**
Emlyn St. *Wors* 6F **63**
Emmanuel Clo. Bolt 2H **45**
    (off Emblem St.)
Emmanuel Ct. *Ash L* 1H **99**
Emmanuel Pl. *Bolt* 2H **45**
Emma St. *Oldh* 6D **72**
Emma St. *Roch* 3G **27**
Emmaus Wlk. Salf 2F **93**
Emmeline Grange.
    Salf 3E **93**
Emmerson St. *Swin* 2F **79**
Emmett St. E. *M40* 6G **83**
Emmott Clo. *Heyw* 3E **39**
Emmott St. *Oldh* 3D **72**
Empire Rd. *Bolt* 6G **33**
Empire Rd. *Duk* 1A **114**
Empire St. *M3* 1D **94**
Empress Av. *Marp* 6D **142**
Empress Bus. Pk.
    M16 . . . . . .1A **108** (6B **8**)
Empress Ct.
    M15 . . . . . .1A **108** (6B **8**)
Empress Dri. *Stoc* 5F **127**
Empress St. *M8* 3B **82**
Empress St. *Bolt* 4F **31**
Empress St.
    Old T 1A **108** (6A **8**)
Emsworth Clo. *Bolt* 4D **32**
Emsworth Dri. *Sale* 2C **134**
Ena St. *Bolt* 4C **46**
Ena St. *Oldh* 6G **57**
Enbridge St. *Salf* 5G **93**
Encombe Pl.
    Salf 3B **94** (4C **4**)
Endcott Clo. *M18* 1D **110**
Enderby Rd. *M40* 2C **84**
Ending Rake. *Whitw* 5C **14**
Endon Dri. *M21* 1D **124**
Endon St. *Bolt* 4F **31**
Endsleigh Rd. *M20* 3G **125**
Endsley Av. *Wors* 2E **77**
Energy St. *M40* 2A **96**
Enfield Av. *M19* 3C **126**
Enfield Av. *Oldh* 6C **72**
Enfield Clo. *Bolt* 4A **32**
Enfield Clo. *Bury* 2D **50**
Enfield Clo. *Eccl* 5F **91**
Enfield Clo. *Roch* 3A **26**
Enfield Dri. *M11* 3E **97**
Enfield Ho. *Eccl* 5F **91**
Enfield Rd. *Eccl* 1F **91**
Enfield Rd. *Swin* 5E **79**
Enfield St. *Hyde* 2C **130**
Enfield St. *Wors* 4F **63**
Enford Av. *M22* 3G **147**

Engell Clo. *M18* 2F **111**
Engels Ho. Eccl 5F **91**
    (off Trafford Rd.)
Engine Fold. 1D **76**
Engine Fold Rd. *Wors* . . .6C **62**
Engine St. *Chad* 5H **71**
Engledene. *Bolt* 5B **18**
Englefield Gro. *M18* 3F **111**
Enid Clo. *Salf* 6A **82**
Ennerdale Av. *M21* 5B **124**
Ennerdale Av. *Bolt* 4H **33**
    (in two parts)
Ennerdale Av. Rytn 6A **42**
Ennerdale Av. *Swin* 5F **79**
Ennerdale Clo. *L Lev* 4H **47**
Ennerdale Dri. *Bury* 4E **51**
Ennerdale Dri. *Gat* 2F **149**
Ennerdale Dri. *Sale* 4G **121**
Ennerdale Dri. *Timp* 3A **134**
Ennerdale Gdns. *Bolt* 4G **33**
Ennerdale Gro. *Ash L* 6D **86**
Ennerdale Gro. *Farn* 1A **62**
Ennerdale Rd. *Midd* 5H **53**
Ennerdale Rd. *Part* 6C **118**
Ennerdale Rd. *Roch* 1B **40**
Ennerdale Rd. *Stoc* 4B **140**
Ennerdale Rd. *Stret* 4C **106**
Ennerdale Rd. *Woodl* 5H **129**
Ennerdale Ter. *Stal* 2E **101**
Ennis Clo. *Round I* 6E **135**
Ennismore Av. *Eccl* 3A **92**
Enoch St. *M40* 1A **96**
Enstone Dri. *M40* 2D **84**
Enterprise Cen. Two.
    Stoc 2F **139**
Enterprise Ho. *Salf* 6F **93**
Enterprise Trad. Est.
    Traf P 5A **92**
Enticott Rd. *Cad* 4A **118**
Entron Ho. *Shaw* 6D **42**
Entwisle Av. *Urm* 3D **104**
Entwisle Rd. *Roch* 3A **28**
Entwisle Row. *Farn* 1F **63**
Entwisle St. *Farn* 6F **47**
Entwisle St. *Miln* 5E **29**
Entwisle St. *Swin* 2D **78**
Entwistle St. *Bolt* 5D **32**
Entwistle St. *Rad* 5H **49**
Enver Rd. *M8* 3D **82**
Enville Rd. *M40* 2B **84**
Enville Rd. *Bow* 2E **145**
Enville Rd. *Salf* 5C **80**
Enville Rd. *M9* 6F **69**
Enville St. *Ash L* 2A **100**
Enville St. *Aud* 6E **99**
Enys Wlk. *Salf* 6E **81**
Epping Clo. *Ash L* 4G **87**
Epping Clo. *Chad* 1E **71**
Epping Dri. *Sale* 3E **121**
Epping Rd. *Dent* 5B **112**
Epping St.
    M15 . . . . . .1D **108** (5H **9**)
Epping Wlk. M15 . . . . . . .2E **109**
    (off Eden Clo.)
Eppleworth Ri. *Swin* 6G **65**
Epsley Clo.
    M15 . . . . . .1E **109** (6A **10**)
Epsom Av. *M19* 3B **126**
Epsom Av. *Hand* 3A **160**
Epsom Av. *Sale* 1E **133**
Epsom Clo. *Roch* 3B **26**
Epsom Clo. *Stoc* 3F **153**
Epsom M. *Salf* 5H **81**
Epsom Wlk. *Chad* 2A **72**
Epworth Ct. *Stoc* 6D **126**
Epworth Gro. *Bolt* 5G **45**
    (Lynton Rd.)
Epworth Gro. *Bolt* 4G **45**
    (Maltby Dri.)
Epworth St. *M1* 4G **95** (6F **7**)
Equitable St. *Miln* 6F **29**
Equitable St. *Oldh* 1H **73**

Equitable St. *Roch* 5A **28**
Era St. *Bolt* 6G **33**
Era St. *Sale* 5B **122**
Ercall Av. *M12* 1A **110**
Erica Av. *Oldh* 3B **58**
Erica Clo. *Stoc* 1H **127**
Erica Dri. *M19* 5A **126**
Eric Brook Clo. *M14* 4E **109**
Eric Bullows Clo.
    M22 . . . . .4A **148**
Eric St. *L'boro* 3E **17**
Eric St. *Oldh* 2G **73**
Eric St. *Salf* 4F **93**
Erindale Wlk. *M40* 5F **83**
Erin St. *M11* 6G **97**
Erith Clo. *Stoc* 3B **128**
Erith Rd. *Oldh* 3G **73**
Erlesdene. *Bow* 2D **144**
Erlesmere Av. *Dent* 3G **113**
Erlesmere Clo. *Oldh* 3B **58**
Erlesmere Rd. *Swin* 4A **80**
Erlington Av. *M16* 4H **107**
Erman Rd. *Eccl* 5E **91**
Ermen Rd. *Eccl* 5E **91**
Ermington Dri. *M8* 5B **82**
Erneley Clo. *M12* 4D **110**
Ernest St. *Bolt* 1H **45**
    (in two parts)
Ernest St. *Chea* 5G **137**
Ernest St. *P'wich* 5D **66**
Ernest St. *Stoc* 5A **140**
Ernest Ter. *Roch* 2B **28**
Ernlouen Av. *Bolt* 5E **31**
Ernocroft. 6H **131**
Ernocroft Gro. *M18* 1G **111**
Ernocroft Rd. *Marp B* . . .2F **143**
Erringdon Clo. *Stoc* 5D **140**
Errington Clo. *Bolt* 2D **44**
Errington Dri. *Salf* 1B **94**
Errol Av. *M9* 4C **68**
Errol Av. *M22* 1A **148**
Erwood Cres. *M19* 1C **126**
Erwood Pk. Works.
    Stoc 3D **128**
Erwood Rd. *M19* 4B **126**
Erskine Clo. *Bolt* 2C **44**
Erskine Rd. *M9* 4G **69**
Erskine Rd. *Part* 6D **118**
Erskine St.
    M15 . . . . . .1B **108** (6D **8**)
Erskine St. *Comp* 6F **131**
Erwin St. *M40* 5B **84**
Eryngo St. *Stoc* 2A **140**
Escott St. *M16* 4D **108**
Esher Dri. *Sale* 2C **134**
Esk Av. *Rams* 1A **12**
Esk Clo. *Urm* 3C **104**
Eskdale. *Gat* 1G **149**
Eskdale Av. *M20* 2E **125**
Eskdale Av. *Bolt* 3H **33**
Eskdale Av. *Bram* 2E **161**
Eskdale Av. *G'fld* 4F **61**
Eskdale Av. *Oldh* 5B **72**
Eskdale Av. *Roch* 2B **40**
Eskdale Av. Rytn 6B **42**
Eskdale Av. *Woodl* 4H **129**
Eskdale Clo. *Bury* 4E **51**
Eskdale Dri. *Midd* 4H **53**
Eskdale Dri. *Timp* 4C **134**
Eskdale Gro. *Farn* 1B **62**
Eskdale Ho. *M13* 3A **110**
Eskdale M. *G'fld* 4F **61**
Eskdale Ter. *Stal* 1E **101**
Eskrick St. *Bolt* 4H **31**
Eskrigge Clo. *M7* 3B **82**
Esmond Rd. *M8* 4C **82**
Esmont Dri. *Midd* 4G **53**
Esplanade, The. *Roch* 4G **27**
Esporta Health & Fitness.
     . . . . .2C **32**
Essex Av. *M20* 5F **125**
Essex Av. *Bury* 4A **38**

Essex Av. *Droy* 2A **98**
Essex Av. *Stoc* 3D **138**
Essex Clo. *Fail* 6F **85**
Essex Clo. *Shaw* 6D **42**
Essex Dri. *Bury* 5D **36**
Essex Gdns. *Cad* 5A **118**
Essex Pl. *Swin* 1F **79**
Essex Rd. *M18* 3H **111**
Essex Rd. *Stoc* 5D **128**
Essex St. *M2* 4D **94** (6H **5**)
Essex St. *Roch* 5H **27**
Essex Wlk.
   M15 . . . . . .2B **108** (6D **8**)
Essex Way.
   M15 . . . . . .2B **108** (6D **8**)
Essingdon St. *Bolt* 3H **45**
   (in two parts)
Essington Wlk. *Dent* 6E **113**
Essoldo Clo. *M18* 2E **111**
Estate St. *Oldh* 5D **72**
Estate St. S. *Oldh* 5D **72**
Est Bank Rd. *Rams* 6C **12**
   (in two parts)
Esther St. L'boro 4D **16**
   (off Featherstall Rd.)
Esther St. *Oldh* 2H **73**
Estonfield Dri. *Urm* 5H **105**
Eston St. *M13* 3H **109**
Eswick St. *M11* 4E **97**
Etchells Rd. *H Grn* 4H **149**
Etchells St. *Stoc* 2H **139**
Etchell St. *M40* 6E **83**
Ethel Av. *M9* 4F **69**
Ethel Av. *Swin* 3H **79**
Ethel Ct. *Roch* 5B **28**
Ethel St. *Bolt* 1H **45**
Ethel St. *Oldh* 6D **72**
Ethel St. *Roch* 5B **28**
Ethel St. *Whitw* 3H **15**
Ethel Ter. *M19* 6C **110**
Etherley Clo. *Irlam* 5E **103**
Etherow Av. *Rom* 1C **142**
Etherow Country Pk. . . .6G **131**
Etherow Country Pk.
  Local Nature Reserve.
     . . . . .6G **131**
Etherow Country Park
  Vis. Cen. 1F **143**
Etherow Ct. Hyde 5C **114**
   (off Riding La.)
Etherow Gro. *M40* 1F **85**
Etherow Ind. Est. *Holl* . . .3G **117**
Etherow Way. *Had* 2G **117**
Etherstone St. *M8* 3E **83**
Eton Av. *Oldh* 6C **72**
Eton Clo. *M16* 2B **108**
Eton Clo. *Roch* 5D **26**
Eton Ct. *M16* 2B **108**
Eton Hill Ind. Est. *Rad* . . .2B **50**
Eton Hill Rd. *Rad* 3A **50**
Eton Way N. *Rad* 2A **50**
Eton Way S. *Rad* 2A **50**
Etruria Clo. *M13* 2H **109**
Ettington Clo. *Bury* 2G **35**
Ettrick Clo. *Open* 6F **97**
Euclid Clo. *M11* 4A **96**
Europa Bus. Pk. *Stoc* . . .6D **138**
Europa Circ. *Traf P* 2D **106**
   (in two parts)
Europa Ga. *Traf P* 2D **106**
Europa Trad. Est. *Rad* . . .2B **64**
Europa Way. *Rad* 2A **64**
Europa Way. *Stoc* 5D **138**
Europa Way. *Traf P* 2D **106**
Eustace St. *Bolt* 4C **46**
Eustace St. *Chad* 6H **55**
Euston Av. *M9* 6A **70**
Euxton Clo. *Bury* 4G **35**
Evans Clo. *M20* 6E **125**
Evans Rd. *Eccl* 4C **90**
Evans St. *Ash L* 1B **100**
Evans St. *Midd* 1B **70**

Evans St. *Oldh* 1D **72**
Evans St. *Salf* 2C **94** (2F **5**)
Evan St. *M40* 6G **83**
Evanton Wlk. *M9* 4G **83**
   (off Nethervale Dri.)
Eva Rd. *Stoc* 4C **138**
Eva St. *M14* 4G **109**
Eva St. *Roch* 1A **28**
Evelyn St. *M14* 1H **125**
Evelyn St. *Oldh* 6F **57**
Evenholme Flats.
   Bow 3D **144**
Evening St. *Fail* 3F **85**
Evenley Clo. *M11* 1F **111**
Everard Clo. *Wors* 3E **77**
Everard St. *Salf* . .6A **94** (3B **8**)
Everbrom Rd. *Bolt* 5E **45**
Everdingen Wlk. *Oldh* . . .4H **57**
Everest Av. *Ash L* 6F **87**
Everest Clo. *Hyde* 3E **115**
Everest Rd. *Hyde* 3E **115**
Everest St. *Roch* 3G **41**
Everett Ct. *M20* 3F **125**
Everett Rd. *M20* 3E **125**
Everglade. *Oldh* 2E **87**
Evergreen Wlk. *Sale* 3E **121**
Everleigh Clo. *Bolt* 6A **20**
Everleigh Dri. *M7* 5B **82**
Eversden Ct. *Salf* 1C **94**
Eversley Ct. *Sale* 1B **134**
Eversley Rd. *M20* 6E **125**
Everton Rd. *Oldh* 5B **72**
Everton Rd. *Stoc* 5H **111**
Everton St. *Swin* 3E **79**
Every St. *M4* 4H **95** (1G **11**)
Every St. *Bury* 1D **36**
Every St. *Rams* 3F **13**
Evesham Av. *M23* 4D **134**
Evesham Av. *Stoc* 6D **126**
Evesham Clo. *Bolt* 1H **45**
Evesham Clo. *Midd* 4B **70**
Evesham Dri. *Farn* 5D **46**
Evesham Dri. *Wilm* 5G **159**
Evesham Gdns. *Midd* 4A **70**
Evesham Gro. *Ash L* 4G **87**
Evesham Gro. *Sale* 5E **123**
Evesham Rd. *M9* 1A **84**
Evesham Rd. *Chea* 6C **138**
Evesham Rd. *Midd* 4A **70**
Evesham Wlk. *Bolt* 2H **45**
Evesham Wlk. *Midd* 4B **70**
Evesham Wlk. *Oldh* 4C **72**
Eveside Clo. *Chea H* 1D **150**
Eve St. *Oldh* 1D **86**
Evington Av. *Open* 6A **98**
Ewan St. *M18* 1F **111**
Ewart Av. *Salf* 4G **93**
Ewart St. *Bolt* 3A **32**
Ewhurst Av. *Swin* 5D **78**
Ewing Clo. *M8* 2C **82**
Ewood. *Oldh* 3E **87**
Ewood Dri. *Bury* 5G **35**
Ewood Ho. *Eccl* 3H **91**
Exbourne Rd. *M22* 4A **148**
Exbridge Wlk. *M40* 1F **97**
Exbury. Roch 3G **27**
   (off Falinge Rd.)
Exbury St. *M14* 2H **125**
Excalibur Way. *Irlam* 2C **118**
Exchange Quay. *Salf* 1G **107**
Exchange Sq.
   M4 . . . . .3D **94** (4H **5**)
Exchange St.
   M2 . . . . .4D **94** (5H **5**)
Exchange St. *Bolt* 6B **32**
Exchange St. *Oldh* 2F **73**
Exchange St. *Rams* 2A **12**
Exchange St. *Stoc* 2G **139**
Exeter Av. *Bolt* 3D **32**
Exeter Av. *Dent* 6F **113**

Exeter Av. *Eccl* 1A **92**
Exeter Av. *Farn* 6B **46**
Exeter Av. *Rad* 2D **48**
Exeter Clo. *Chea H* 5B **150**
Exeter Clo. *Duk* 1A **114**
Exeter Ct. *Midd* 6H **53**
Exeter Dri. *Ash L* 4H **87**
Exeter Dri. *Irlam* 5F **103**
Exeter Gro. *Roch* 6H **27**
Exeter Rd. *Stoc* 4C **128**
Exeter Rd. *Urm* 3F **105**
Exeter St. *Roch* 6H **27**
Exeter Wlk. *Bram* 6H **151**
Exford Clo.
   M40 . . . . . .2H **95** (2G **7**)
Exford Clo. *Stoc* 3H **127**
Exford Dri. *Bolt* 1A **48**
Exford Wlk.
   M40 . . . . . .2H **95** (2G **7**)
Exhall Clo. *L Hul* 3C **62**
Exford Rd. W. *Man A* 6H **147**
Exmoor Clo. *Ash L* 4G **87**
Exmoor Wlk. *M23* 2G **147**
Exmouth Av. *Stoc* 4C **128**
Exmouth Pl. *Roch* 1G **41**
Exmouth Rd. *Sale* 4F **121**
Exmouth Sq. *Roch* 2G **41**
Exmouth St. *Roch* 2G **41**
Express Trad. Est. *Farn* . . .3G **63**
Eyam Clo. Glos 5F **117**
   (off Eyam La.)
Eyam Fold. Glos 5G **117**
   (off Eyam M.)
Eyam Gdns. Glos 5F **117**
   (off Eyam M.)
Eyam Grn. Glos 5F **117**
   (off Eyam La.)
Eyam Gro. Glos 5F **117**
   (off Eyam La.)
Eyam Gro. *Stoc* 6D **140**
Eyam La. Glos 5F **117**
Eyam Lea. Glos 5G **117**
   (off Eyam M.)
Eyam M. *Glos* 5F **117**
Eyam Rd. Haz G 5E **153**
Eyebrook Rd. *Bow* 3C **144**
Eynford Av. *Stoc* 3B **128**
Eyre St. *M15* . . .2E **109** (6A **10**)

F

Faber St. *M4* 2E **95** (1B **6**)
Facit. 3H **15**
Factory Brow. *Midd* 2E **69**
Factory La. *M9* 2E **81**
Factory La. *Salf* . . .4B **94** (5C **4**)
Factory St. *Midd* 1H **69**
Factory St. *Rad* 4H **49**
Factory St. *Rams* 2E **13**
Failsworth. 4F **85**
Failsworth Ind. Est. *Fail* . . .5C **84**
Failsworth Rd. *Fail* 4H **85**
Failsworth Shop. Precinct.
   Fail 4F **85**

Failsworth Sports Cen.
     . . . . .4G **85**
Fairacres. *Bolt* 2G **33**
Fairacres Rd. *H Lane* 5C **154**
Fairbank. *Droy* 5H **97**
Fairbank Av. *M14* 3F **109**
Fairbank Dri. *Midd* 5F **53**
Fairbottom St. *Oldh* 2D **72**
Fairbottom Wlk. *Droy* 5A **98**
Fairbourne Av. *Ald E* 6E **167**
Fairbourne Av. *Wilm* 5C **166**
Fairbourne Clo. *Wilm* 5C **166**
Fairbourne Dri. *Timp* 2B **134**
Fairbourne Dri. *Wilm* 5C **166**
Fairbourne Rd. *M19* 6E **111**
Fairbourne Rd. *Dent* 5E **113**
Fairbrook Dri. *Salf* 3E **93**

Fairbrother St.
   Salf 6A **94** (4A **8**)
Fairburn Clo. *Urm* 3C **104**
Fairclough St. *M11* 3C **96**
Fairclough St. *Bolt* 3B **46**
Fairfax Av. *M20* 5F **125**
Fairfax Av. *Timp* 5A **134**
Fairfax Clo. *Marp* 4B **142**
Fairfax Dri. *L'boro* 6D **16**
Fairfax Dri. *Wilm* 5C **166**
Fairfax Rd. *P'wich* 4E **67**
Fairfield. 2H **37**
               (Bury)
Fairfield. 5A **98**
       (Manchester)
Fairfield. *Ash L* 3F **87**
Fairfield Av. *Bred* 5G **129**
Fairfield Av. *Chea H* 3B **150**
Fairfield Av. *Droy* 5A **98**
Fairfield Ct. *M13* 3H **109**
Fairfield Dri. *Bury* 2H **37**
Fairfield Gdns. *Ald E* 4G **167**
Fairfield Ho. Droy 4A **98**
   (off Manchester Rd.)
Fairfield Rd. *M11* 6G **97**
Fairfield Rd. *Cad* 4A **118**
Fairfield Rd. *Droy* 5G **97**
Fairfield Rd. *Farn* 2E **63**
Fairfield Rd. *Midd* 6G **53**
Fairfield Rd. *Timp* 6C **134**
Fairfield Sq. *Droy* 5A **98**
   (in two parts)
Fairfield St. *M1 & M12*
     . . . . .5F **95** (1C **10**)
Fairfield St. *Salf* 6B **80**
Fairfield Vw. *Aud* 6A **98**
Fairford Clo. *Stoc* 4H **127**
Fairford Dri. *Bolt* 2A **46**
Fairford Way. *Stoc* 4H **127**
Fairford Way. *Wilm* 2G **167**
Fairham Wlk.
   M4 . . . . . . .4H **95** (6G **7**)
Fairhaven Av. *M21* 1H **123**
Fairhaven Av. *W'fld* 2B **66**
Fairhaven Cvn. Pk.
   Hyde 5A **114**
Fairhaven Clo. *Bram* 5H **151**
Fairhaven Clo. *W'fld* 2B **66**
Fairhaven Rd. *Bolt* 2B **32**
Fairhaven St. *M12* 1B **110**
Fairhills Ind. Est.
   Irlam 1D **118**
Fairhills Rd. *Irlam* 1D **118**
Fairholme Av. *Urm* 6E **105**
Fairholme Rd. *M20* 3G **125**
Fairholme Rd. *Stoc* 6E **127**
Fairhope Av. *Salf* 1B **92**
Fairhurst Dri. *Wors* 1B **76**
Fairisle Clo. *M11* 4B **96**
Fairlands Pl. *Roch* 3H **41**
Fairlands Rd. *Bury* 4F **23**
Fairlands Rd. *Sale* 1H **133**
Fairlands St. *Roch* 3H **41**
Fairlands Vw. *Roch* 3H **41**
Fairlawn. *Stoc* 6F **127**
Fairlawn Clo. *M14* 3E **109**
Fairlea. *Dent* 5G **113**
Fairlea Av. *M20* 1G **137**
Fairlee Av. *Aud* 4C **98**
Fairleigh Av. *Salf* 2C **92**
Fairless Rd. *Eccl* 4F **91**
Fairlie Av. *Bolt* 2D **44**
Fairlie Dri. *Timp* 3B **134**
Fairman St. *M16* 4D **108**
Fairmead Rd. *M23* 2A **136**
Fairmile Dri. *M20* 3G **137**
Fairmount Av. *Bolt* 5G **33**
Fairmount Rd. *Swin* 5B **78**

Fairoak Ct. Bolt 2H 45
Fair Oak Rd. M19 . . . . .4B 126
Fairstead Wlk. Open 6H 97
Fair St. M1 . . . .4G 95 (6E 7)
Fair St. Bolt 5G 45
Fair St. Swin 2G 79
Fairthorne Gro. Ash L . . .4F 99
Fair Vw. L'boro 2G 17
Fairview Av. M19 . . . . . .5D 110
Fairview Av. Dent 6A 112
Fairview Clo. Chad 1E 71
Fairview Clo. Marp 4D 142
Fairview Clo. Roch 1G 25
Fairview Dri. Marp 4D 142
Fairview Rd. Dent 5A 112
Fairview Rd. Timp 6C 134
Fairway. Bram 1F 161
Fairway. Droy 5A 98
Fairway. Gat 1E 149
Fairway. Miln 5G 29
Fairway. P'wich 1H 81
Fair Way. Roch 4B 40
Fairway. Swin 4A 80
Fairway. Whitw 2C 14
Fairway Av. Bolt 1A 34
Fairway Av. M23 . . . . . .4D 134
Fairway Ct. Dent 3B 112
Fairway Cres. Rytn 3B 56
Fairway Dri. Sale 1G 133
Fairway Rd. Bury 4E 51
Fairway Rd. Oldh 5A 74
Fairways, The. W'fld 3D 66
Fairway, The. M40 . . . . . .4C 84
Fairway, The. Stoc 4D 140
Fairwood Rd. M23 . . . . .4C 134
Fairy La. M8 . . . . .6A 82
Fairy La. Sale 5F 123
Fairy St. Bury 3A 36
Fairywell Clo. Wilm 6H 159
Fairywell Dri. Sale 2A 134
Fairywell Rd. Timp 3B 134
Faith St. Bolt 4E 31
Falcon Av. Urm 5G 105
Falcon Clo. Bury 1E 37
Falcon Clo. Roch 1H 25
Falcon Clo. Salf 4C 92
Falcon Ct. M15 . . . . . . .2C 108
Falcon Ct. Salf (M50) . . .5D 92
Falcon Ct. Salf (M7) 2H 81
Falcon Cres. Swin 1H 79
Falcon Dri. Chad 1A 72
Falcon Dri. Irlam 3F 103
Falcon Dri. L Hul 4C 62
Falcon Dri. Midd 4G 53
Falcon Enterprise Cen.
   Chad 1A 72
Falcon Ho. Bury 1E 37
Falcon St. Bolt 5B 32
Falcon St. Oldh 4C 72
Falcon's Vw. Oldh 6C 72
Falconwood Chase.
   Wors 5D 76
Falfield Dri. M8 . . . . .6D 82
Falinge Fold. Roch 2F 27
Falinge M. Roch 3G 27
Falinge Rd. Roch 2F 27
Falkirk Dri. Bolt 1H 47
Falkirk St. Oldh 2G 73
Falkirk Wlk. M23 . . . . . .3G 147
Falkland Av. M40 . . . . . .1A 96
Falkland Av. Roch 3E 27
Falkland Clo. Oldh 3A 58
Falkland Ho. M14 . . . . . .6G 109
Falkland Rd. Bolt 6A 34
Fall Bank. Stoc 3F 127
Fallons Rd. Wors 2C 78
Fallowfield. 1G 125
Fallowfield Av. Salf 5H 93
Fallowfield Dri. Roch 1F 27
Fallow Fields Dri. Stoc . . .6A 112
Fallowfield Shop. Cen.
   M14 . . . . .6A 110

Fallows, The. Chad 4G 71
Falls Gro. H Grn 2E 149
Falmer Clo. M18 . . . . . .1H 111
Falmer Clo. Bury 4C 22
Falmer Dri. M22 . . . . . . .4B 148
Falmouth Av. Sale 4F 121
Falmouth Av. Urm 4A 104
Falmouth Cres. Stoc 4C 128
Falmouth St. M40 . . . . . .1B 96
Falmouth St. Oldh 5D 72
Falmouth St. Roch 6A 28
Falsgrave Clo. M40 . . . . .6A 84
Falshaw Dri. Bury 2E 23
Falside Wlk. M40 . . . . . . .6C 84
Falstaff M. Bred 6G 129
   (off Higher Bents La.)
Falston Av. M40 . . . . . . .1D 84
Falstone Av. Rams 5E 13
Falterley Rd. M23 . . . . . .3E 135
Fancroft Rd. M22 . . . . . .6A 136
Fane Wlk. M9 . . . . .6D 68
Faraday Av. M8 . . . . .5C 82
Faraday Av. Swin 1B 80
Faraday Dri. Bolt 4A 32
Faraday Ho. Bolt 4A 32
   (off Faraday Dri.)
Faraday Ri. Roch 2D 26
Faraday St. M1 . . .3F 95 (4C 6)
Farcroft Av. Rad 1A 50
Farcroft Clo. M23 . . . . . .3F 135
Farcroft Clo. Stoc 4E 141
Far Cromwell Rd.
   Bred 3D 128
Fardale. Shaw 1F 57
Farden Dri. M23 . . . . . . .3D 134
Fareham Ct. M16 . . . . . . .2B 108
Farewell Clo. Roch 3C 40
Fargher St. M11 . . . . . . .4F 97
Far Hey Clo. Rad 4E 49
Farholme. Rytn 5A 56
Faringdon. Roch 5G 27
Faringdon Wlk. Bolt 2A 46
Farland Pl. Bolt 2D 44
Farlands Dri. M20 . . . . . .4F 137
Farlands Ri. Roch 2A 42
Far La. M18 . . . . .3F 111
Farley Av. M18 . . . . .3A 112
Farley Ct. Chea H 2B 150
Farley Rd. Sale 1C 134
Farley Way. Stoc 6G 111
Farman St. Bolt 4H 45
Farm Av. Stret 3A 106
Farm Clo. Stoc 3E 127
Farm Clo. T'ton 5H 21
Farmers Clo. Sale 6G 123
Farmer St. Stoc 6F 127
Farmfield. Sale 3G 121
Farmfold. Styal 3D 158
Farm La. Dis 1E 165
Farm La. Hyde 1B 130
Farm La. P'wich 1A 68
Farm La. Wors 6H 77
Farm Rd. Oldh 3A 86
Farmside Av. Irlam 4E 103
Farmside Pl. M19 . . . . . .6C 110
Farmstead Clo. Fail 5A 86
Farm St. Chad 6H 55
Farm St. Fail 5D 84
Farm St. Heyw 5G 39
Farm Wlk. Bow 3A 144
Farm Wlk. L'boro 4D 16
Farm Wlk. Roch 2C 28
Farmway. Midd 2A 70
Farm Yd. M19 . . . . .6C 110
Farn Av. Redd 5G 111
Farnborough Av. Oldh . . .3H 73
Farnborough Rd.
   M40 . . . . .2H 95 (1G 7)
Farnborough Rd. Bolt 5C 18
Farncombe Clo. M23 . . . .4D 134
Farndale Sq. Wors 6E 63

Farndale Wlk. M9 . . . . . .3G 83
   (off Up. Conran St.)
Farndon Av. Haz G 1F 153
Farndon Clo. Sale 6E 123
Farndon Dri. Timp 5A 134
Farndon Rd. Stoc 5G 111
Farnham Av. M9 . . . . . . .4F 69
Farnham Clo. Bolt 4A 32
Farnham Clo.
   Chea H 6C 150
Farnham Dri. Irlam 6E 103
Farnhill Wlk. M23 . . . . . .2E 135
Farnley Clo. Roch 1B 28
Farnsworth Av. Ash L 6F 87
Farnsworth Clo. Ash L 6F 87
Farnworth. 1F 63
Farnworth & Kearsley By-Pass.
   Farn 5F 47
Farnworth Dri. M14 . . . . .5G 109
Farnworth Leisure Cen.
   . . . . .1F 63
Farnworth St. Bolt 3G 45
Farnworth St. Heyw 3E 39
Farrand Rd. Oldh 1H 85
Farrant Rd. M12 . . . . . . .3C 110
Farrar Rd. Droy 5H 97
Farrell St. Salf . . .2C 94 (1E 5)
Farrer Rd. M13 . . . . .4B 110
Far Ridings. Rom 6B 130
Farrier Clo. Sale 6F 123
Farriers La. Roch 1B 40
Farringdon Dri. Rad 2E 49
Farringdon St. Salf 2E 93
Farrington Av. M20 . . . . . .2E 125
Farrowdale Av. Shaw 1F 57
Farrow St. Shaw 1F 57
   (in two parts)
Farrow St. E. Shaw 1F 57
   (off Market St.)
Farr St. Stoc 3F 139
Farwood Clo. M16 . . . . . .2A 108
Fastnet St. M11 . . . . .5C 96
Fatherford Clo. Dig 2D 60
Faulkenhurst M. Chad . . .6A 56
Faulkenhurst St. Chad . . .6A 56
Faulkner Dri. Timp 1B 146
Faulkner Rd. Stret 5E 107
Faulkner St.
   M1 . . . . . . .5E 95 (1A 10)
Faulkner St. Bolt 2A 46
Faulkner St. Roch 4H 27
Faversham Brow. Oldh . . .1C 72
Faversham St. M40 . . . . . .4B 84
Faversham St. Oldh 1C 72
Fawborough Rd. M23 . . . .2F 135
Fawcett St. Bolt 6D 32
Fawley Av. Hyde 6B 114
Fawley Gro. M22 . . . . . . .1A 148
Fawns Keep. Stal 1A 116
Fawns Keep. Wilm 2G 167
Fay Av. M9 . . . . .1B 84
Fay Gdns. Had 3G 117
Faywood Dri. Marp 5E 143
Fearney Side. I Lev 4H 47
Fearnhead Clo. Farn 1G 63
Fearnhead St. Bolt 3G 45
Fearn St. Heyw 3E 39
Featherstall Ho. Oldh 4A 72
   (off Featherstall Rd.)
Featherstall Rd. N.
   Oldh 2B 72
Featherstall Rd. S.
   Oldh 4A 72
Featherstall Sq. L'boro 4E 17
Federation St.
   M4 . . . . .3E 95 (3A 6)
Federation St. P'wich 4D 66
Feldom Rd. M23 . . . . . . .1F 135
Fellbrigg Clo. M18 . . . . . .4E 111
Fellfoot Clo. Wors 6B 76

Felling Wlk. M14 . . . . . . .4F 109
   (off Seaham Wlk.)
Fellpark Rd. M23 . . . . . . .1G 135
Fells Gro. Wors 2H 77
Fellside. Bolt 2A 34
Fellside. Oldh 2C 72
Fellside Clo. G'mnt 2H 21
Fellside Gdns. L'boro 2D 16
Fellside Grn. Stal 2E 101
Fell St. Bury 3A 36
Felltop Ct. Lyd 4E 75
Felltop Dri. Stoc 1A 128
Felsham Clo. Farn 6C 47
Felskirk Rd. M22 . . . . . . .5A 148
Felsted. Bolt 5C 30
Felt Ct. Dent 5C 112
Feltham St. M12 . . . . . . .1C 110
Felthorpe Dri. M8 . . . . . . .5B 82
Felton Av. M22 . . . . .2B 148
Felton Clo. Bury 2E 51
Felton Wlk. Bolt 3A 32
Fencegate Av. Stoc 4F 127
Fence St. Stoc 1D 152
Fenchurch Av. M40 . . . . . .1E 97
Fencot Dri. M12 . . . . .3C 110
Fenella St. M13 . . . . .3A 110
Fenham Clo. M40 . . . . . . .6E 83
Fenmore Av. M18 . . . . . . .4D 110
Fennel St. M4 . . . .3D 94 (3H 5)
Fenners Clo. Bolt 4H 45
Fenney St. Salf 6H 81
Fenney St. E. Salf 5A 82
Fenn St. M15 . . . .1C 108 (5E 9)
Fenny Hill. 5F 73
Fenside Rd. M22 . . . . . . .6C 136
Fenstock Wlk. M40 . . . . . .1F 97
Fentewan Wlk. Hyde 4A 116
Fenton Av. Haz G 1C 152
Fenton M. Roch 6G 27
Fenton St. M12 . . . . .2C 110
Fenton St. Bury 2A 36
Fenton St. Oldh 3F 73
Fenton St. Roch 6G 27
Fenton St. Shaw 2F 57
Fenwick Dri. Stoc 6A 126
Fenwick St.
   M15 . . . . . .1E 109 (5A 10)
Fenwick St. Roch 4G 27
Ferdinand St. M40 . . . . . .1H 95
Fereday St. Wors 5F 63
Ferguson Ct. M19 . . . . . . .1B 126
Ferguson Gdns. Roch 6F 15
Ferguson Way. Oldh 6H 57
Fernacre. Sale 4C 122
Fernally St. Hyde 5C 114
   (off Union St.)
Fern Av. Urm 5C 104
Fern Bank. 4G 101
Fernbank. Rad 1G 65
Fern Bank. Stal 5G 101
Fern Bank Clo. Stal 5G 101
Fern Bank Dri. M23 . . . . .3E 135
Fern Bank St. Hyde 1C 130
Fernbray Av. M19 . . . . . . .5H 125
Fernbrook Clo. M13 . . . . .2H 109
Fernbrook Wlk. M8 . . . . . .4B 82
   (off Hillbrow Wlk.)
Fern Clo. Marp 5D 142
Fern Clo. Midd 1D 70
Fern Clo. S'head 3B 74
Fern Clough. Bolt 6D 30
Fernclough Rd. M9 . . . . . .4F 83
Fern Comn. Shaw 6F 43
Fern Cottage. G'ton 4C 74
Fern Cres. Stal 5G 101
Ferndale Av. Roch 5A 42
Ferndale Av. Stoc 1B 152
Ferndale Av. W'fld 2A 66
Ferndale Clo. Oldh 5H 73
Ferndale Gdns. M19 . . . . .3A 126
Ferndale Rd. Sale 1B 134
Ferndene. Roch 1D 26

Ferndene Gdns.—Fitton St.

Ferndene Gdns. *M20* 4F **125**
Ferndene Rd. *M20* 4F **125**
Ferndene Rd. *W'fld & P'wich* 2G **67**
Ferndown Av. *Chad* 2D **70**
Ferndown Av. *Haz G* 4C **152**
Ferndown Dri. *Irlam* 4E **103**
Ferndown Rd. *M23* 3D **134**
Ferndown Rd. *Bolt* 2G **33**
Ferney Fld. Rd. *Chad* 2F **71**
Ferngate Dri. *M20* 3F **125**
Fern Grove. **1G 37**
Ferngrove. *Bury* 6H **23** (Bullfinch Dri.)
Ferngrove. *Bury* 1F **37** (Kingfisher Dri.)
Fernhill. **2D 36**
Fernhill. *Mell* 5F **143**
Fernhill. *Oldh* 5H **73**
Fernhill Av. *Bolt* 3E **45**
Fernhill Cvn. Pk. *Bury* 1C **36**
Fernhill Dri. *M18* 3D **110**
Fernhill Gate. **4E 45**
Fern Hill La. *Roch* 6A **14**
Fernhills. *Eger* 1C **18**
Fernhill St. *Bury* 2D **36**
Fernholme Ct. *Oldh* 5A **72**
Fern Ho. *M23* 1G **147**
Fernhurst Gro. *Bolt* 4A **32**
Fernhurst Rd. *M20* 4G **125**
Fernhurst St. *Chad* 6A **56**
Fernie St. *M4* 2E **95** (1A **6**)
Fern Isle Clo. *Whitw* 3B **14**
Fernlea. *Hale* 4H **145**
Fernlea. *H Grn* 4F **149**
Fernlea. *Stoc* 4E **127**
Fernlea Av. *Chad* 6A **56**
Fernlea Clo. *Had* 3G **117**
Fernlea Clo. *Roch* 1D **26**
Fernlea Cres. *Swin* 4E **79**
Fernleaf St. *M14* 3E **109**
Fern Lea Gro. *L Hul* 5B **62**
Fernlea Lodge. *Farn* 2G **63**
Fernleigh Av. *M19* 6E **111**
Fernleigh Dri. *M16* 2A **108**
Fernley Av. *Dent* 5G **113**
Fernley Rd. *Stoc* 5B **140**
Ferns Gro. *Bolt* 6F **31**
Fernside. *Rad* 2C **64**
Fernside Av. *M20* 4H **125**
Fernside Gro. *Wors* 5G **63**
Fernside Way. *Roch* 2C **26**
Fernstead. *Bolt* 1G **45**
Fern St. *M8* 1E **95** (1A **6**)
Fern St. *Bolt* 1G **45**
Fern St. *Bury* 2D **36**
Fern St. *Chad* 1G **71**
Fern St. *Farn* 6G **47**
Fern St. *Oldh* 4B **72**
Fern St. *Rams* 3F **13** (in two parts)
Fern St. *Roch* 5F **27**
Fern St. *Ward* 3A **16**
Fernthorpe Av. *Upperm* 6C **60**
Fern Vw. *Timp* 6E **135**
Fernview Dri. *Rams* 2B **22**
Fernwood. *Marp B* 4F **143**
Fernwood Av. *M18* 4F **111**
Fernwood Gro. *Wilm* 1F **167**
Ferrand Lodge. *L'boro* 2G **17**
Ferrand Rd. *L'boro* 3F **17**
Ferring Wlk. *Chad* 3H **71**
Ferris St. *M11* 5F **97**
Ferrous Way. *Irlam* 3D **118**
Ferryhill Rd. *Irlam* 5E **103**
Ferry Rd. *Irlam* 5E **103** (in two parts)
Ferry St. *M11* 5A **96**
Festival Theatre, The. **5B 114**
Festival Village. Urm *2G* ***105*** *(off Trafford Cen., The)*
Fettler Clo. *Swin* 5E **79**
Fewston Clo. *Bolt* 6C **18**
Fiddick Ct. Salf *3F* ***93*** *(off Milford St.)*
Fiddlers La. *Irlam* 4F **103**
Fld. Bank Gro. *M19* 6E **111**
Field Clo. *Bram* 3F **161**
Field Clo. *Marp* 6B **142**
Fieldcroft. *Roch* 4D **26**
Fielden Av. *M21* 6H **107**
Fielden Park. **5D 124**
Fielden Rd. *M20* 4D **124**
Fielden St. *L'boro* 1E **29**
Fielders Way. *Swin* 5E **65**
Fieldfare Av. *M40* 1D **96**
Fieldfare Way. *Ash L* 4E **87**
Fieldhead Av. *Bury* 3G **35**
Fieldhead Av. *Roch* 4D **26**
Fieldhead M. *Wilm* 1H **167**
Fieldhead Rd. *Wilm* 1H **167**
Fieldhouse Ind. Est. *Roch* 1H **27**
Fieldhouse La. *Marp* 5E **143**
Fieldhouse Rd. *Roch* 1H **27**
Fielding Av. *Poy* 5E **163**
Fielding St. *Eccl* 4E **91**
Fielding St. *Midd* 5A **54** (in two parts)
Field La. *Ash L* 6H **87**
Field Pl. *M20* 6F **125**
Field Rd. *Roch* 4D **28**
Field Rd. *Sale* 3G **121**
Fields Ct. *Hyde* 6G **115**
Fields Cres. *Holl* 1F **117**
Fieldsend Clo. *Stal* 5H **101**
Fields End Fold. *Eccl* 3G **103**
Fields Farm Clo. *Hyde* 6H **115**
Fields Farm Rd. *Hyde* 6G **115**
Fields Farm Wlk. *Hyde* 6H **115**
Fields Gro. *Holl* 2F **117**
Fields New Rd. *Chad* 5G **71**
Fields, The. *Rom* 2G **141**
Field St. *M18* 1G **111**
Field St. *Bred* 6F **129**
Field St. *Droy* 5H **97**
Field St. *Fail* 4E **85**
Field St. *Hyde* 2B **114**
Field St. *Roch* 1G **41**
Field St. *Salf* 3F **93**
Fieldsway. *Oldh* 1C **86**
Fld. Vale Dri. *Stoc* 6A **112**
Fieldvale Rd. *Sale* 2G **133**
Fld. View Wlk. *M16* 6D **108**
Field Wlk. *Hale* 2B **146**
Field Wlk. *Part* 6C **118**
Fieldway. *Roch* 2H **41**
Fife Av. *Chad* 5F **71**
Fifield Clo. *Oldh* 6E **73**
Fifth Av. *M11* 3E **97**
Fifth Av. *Bolt* 6F **31**
Fifth Av. *Bury* 1H **37**
Fifth Av. *Duk* 5G **99**
Fifth Av. *L Lev* 3H **47**
Fifth Av. *Oldh* 1A **86**
Fifth Av. *Traf P* 2C **106**
Fifth St. *Bolt* 1D **30**
Fifth St. *Traf P* 2C **106** (in two parts)
Filbert St. *Oldh* 6G **57**
Filby Wlk. *M40* 1A **96**
Fildes St. *Midd* 2D **70**
Filey Av. *M16* 5B **108**
Filey Av. *Urm* 3C **104**
Filey Dri. *Salf* 5B **80**
Filey Rd. *M14* 1H **125**
Filey Rd. *Stoc* 4C **140**
Filey St. *Roch* 6A **16**
Filleigh. *Bow* 2C **144**
Filton Av. *Bolt* 2H **45**
Filton Wlk. M9 *5E* ***83*** *(off Westmere Dri.)*
Finance St. *L'boro* 5D **16**
Finborough Clo. *M16* 3C **108**
Finchale Dri. *Hale* 4B **146**
Finch Av. *Farn* 2B **62**
Finchcroft. *Oldh* 2C **72**
Finchley Av. *M40* 1E **97**
Finchley Clo. *Bury* 4H **35**
Finchley Gro. *M40* 2A **84**
Finchley Rd. *M14* 1F **125**
Finchley Rd. *Hale* 2G **145**
Finchwood Rd. *M22* 6C **136**
Findlay Wlk. *M9* 4F **83**
Findon Rd. *M23* 5G **135**
Finger Post. *L Lev* 3A **48**
Finghall Rd. *Urm* 5D **104**
Finishing Wlk. *M4* 4G **95** (5F **7**)
Finland Rd. *Stoc* 4F **139**
Finlan Rd. *Midd* 2D **54**
Finlay St. *Farn* 1F **63**
Finney Clo. *Wilm* 5G **159**
Finney Dri. *M21* 2G **123**
Finney Dri. *Wilm* 5G **159**
Finney Green. **5G 159**
Finney La. *H Grn* 5E **149**
Finney St. *Bolt* 3B **46**
Finningley Rd. *M9* 3D **68**
Finny Bank Rd. *Sale* 3A **122**
Finsbury Av. *M40* 1E **97**
Finsbury Clo. *Oldh* 5F **73**
Finsbury Rd. *Stoc* 1G **127**
Finsbury St. *Roch* 6F **27**
Finsbury Way. *Hand* 5A **160**
Finstock Clo. *Eccl* 4D **90**
Fintry Gro. *Eccl* 4F **91**
Fir Av. *Bram* 5G **151**
Firbank. *P'wich* 5G **67**
Firbank Rd. *M23* 6G **135**
Fir Bank Rd. *Rytn* 1B **56**
Firbarn Clo. *Fir* 4D **28**
Firbeck Dri. *M4* 3H **95** (3G **7**)
Fir Clo. *Poy* 4E **163**
Fircroft Ct. *Stoc* 1H **151**
Fircroft Rd. *Oldh* 1E **87**
Firdale Av. *M40* 2E **85**
Firdale Wlk. *Chad* 2A **72**
Firdon Wlk. M9 *4G* ***83*** *(off Nethervale Dri.)*
Firecrest Clo. *Wors* 3D **76**
Firefly Clo. *Salf* 4B **94** (5C **4**)
Fire Sta. Sq. *Salf* 3H **93** (4A **4**)
Fire Sta. Yd. *Roch* 5H **27**
Firethorn Av. *M19* 3B **126**
Firethorn Dri. *Hyde* 5E **115**
Firethorn Wlk. *Sale* 4E **121** (in two parts)
Firfield Gro. *Wors* 6H **63**
Firgrove. **4D 28**
Fir Gro. *M19* 6C **110**
Fir Gro. *Chad* 1H **71**
Firgrove Av. *Roch* 3D **28**
Firgrove Bus. Pk. *Miln* 2D **28**
Firgrove Gdns. *Roch* 3D **28**
Fir La. *Rytn* 1B **56**
Fir Rd. *Bram* 4G **151**
Fir Rd. *Dent* 4G **113**
Fir Rd. *Farn* 1D **62**
Fir Rd. *Marp* 6C **142**
Fir Rd. *Swin* 5E **79**
Firs Av. *M16* 5H **107**
Firs Av. *Ash L* 6F **87**
Firs Av. *Fail* 4E **85**
Firsby Av. *Bred* 5F **129**
Firsby St. *M19* 6C **110**
Firs Clo. *Gat* 2E **149**
Firs Gro. *Gat* 1E **149**
Firs Rd. *Gat* 2E **149**
Firs Rd. *Sale* 5E **121** (in two parts)
First Av. *M11* 3F **97**
First Av. *Carr* 6G **89**
First Av. *L Lev* 3A **48**
First Av. *Oldh* 1B **86**
First Av. *Poy* 6D **162**
First Av. *Swin* 6D **78**
First Av. *T'ton* 5H **21**
First Av. *Traf P* 2D **106**
Firs, The. *Bow* 3D **144**
Firs, The. *Wilm* 4D **166**
Fir St. *M16* 3A **108**
Fir St. *M40* 1H **95** (1G **7**)
Fir St. *Bolt* 3B **32**
Fir St. *Bury* 3E **37**
Fir St. *Cad* 3A **118**
Fir St. *Eccl* 4F **91**
Fir St. *Fail* 4E **85**
Fir St. *Heyw* 4G **39**
Fir St. *Rad* 5H **49**
Fir St. *Rams* 2F **13**
Fir St. *Rytn* 1B **56**
Fir St. *Salf* 3F **93**
Fir St. *Stoc* 1G **139**
First St. *Bolt* 1D **30**
Firsway. *Sale* 5E **121**
Firswood. **4G 107**
Firswood Dri. *Hyde* 4E **115**
Firswood Dri. *Rytn* 1A **56**
Firswood Dri. *Swin* 5E **79**
Firswood Mt. *Gat* 1E **149**
Firth Clo. *Salf* 5H **81**
Firth Rd. *M20* 4G **125**
Firth St. *Oldh* 3D **72**
Fir Tree Av. *Oldh* 1D **86**
Firtree Av. *Sale* 5E **121**
Fir Tree Av. *Wors* 6D **76**
Fir Tree Clo. *Duk* 6D **100**
Fir Tree Cres. *Duk* 5D **100**
Fir Tree Dri. *Hyde* 2C **114**
Fir Tree La. *Duk* 6D **100**
Firvale Av. *H Grn* 4F **149**
Firwood Av. *Farn* 2E **63**
Firwood Av. *Urm* 5A **106** (in two parts)
Firwood Clo. *Stoc* 3B **140**
Firwood Ct. *Eccl* 2G **91**
Firwood Cres. *Rad* 6H **49**
Firwood Fold. **2E 33**
Firwood Fold. *Bolt* 2E **33**
Firwood Gro. *Bolt* 3D **32**
Firwood Ind. Est. *Bolt* 3E **33**
Firwood La. *Bolt* 2D **32** (in three parts)
Firwood Pk. *Chad* 2E **71**
Firwood Stables. Bolt *2E* ***33*** *(off Ashdown Dri.)*
Fiscall Way. *Fail* 4E **85**
Fishbourne Sq. *M14* 4G **109**
Fishbrook Ind. Est. *Kear* 2H **63**
Fisherfield. *Roch* 2B **26**
Fishermans Wharf. *Bolt* 2B **46**
Fishermore Rd. *Urm* 5A **104**
Fisher St. *Oldh* 1D **72**
Fishpool. **5D 36**
Fishwick St. *Roch* 5A **28**
Fistral Av. *H Grn* 5G **149**
Fistral Cres. *Stal* 2H **101**
Fitchfield Wlk. Wors *6F* ***63*** *(off Emlyn St.)*
Fitness First Club. **6C 70** **(Manchester)**
Fitness First Club. **1E 41** **(Rochdale)**
Fitton Av. *M21* 3H **123**
Fitton Cres. *Swin* 6F **65**
Fitton Hill. **1F 87**
Fitton Hill Rd. *Oldh* 5E **73**
Fitton Hill Shop. Precinct. *Oldh* 1E **87**
Fitton St. *Roch* 3A **28**

222 A-Z Manchester

Fitton St. *Rytn* 3D **56**
Fitton St. *Shaw* 6D **42**
Fitzgeorge St. *M40* 6E **83**
Fitzgerald Clo. *P'wich* . . .1D **80**
Fitzgerald Ct. *Dent* 1G **129**
Fitzgerald Way. *Salf* 2C **92**
Fitzhugh St. *Bolt* 6E **19**
Fitzroy St. *Ash L* 5F **99**
Fitzroy St. *Droy* 5B **98**
Fitzroy St. *Mill* 1H **101**
Fitzwarren Ct. *Salf* 3F **93**
Fitzwarren St. *Salf* 2F **93**
Fitzwilliam St.
    Salf 1B **94** (1C **4**)
Five Fold Ind. Pk. *Oldh* . .3B **72**
Five Quarters. *Rad* 2E **49**
Fiveways. *Droy* 3A **98**
Fiveways Pde. *Haz G* . . .5E **153**
Flag Cft. *Dri M23* 6H **135**
Flagg Wood Av. *Marp* . . .4B **142**
Flagship Av. *Salf* 5H **93**
Flake La. *Rytn* 2B **56**
Flamborough Wlk.
    M14 . . . . .3F **109**
Flamingo Clo. *M12* 1C **110**
Flamingo Vs. *Irlam* 4A **102**
Flamstead Av. *M23* 5E **135**
Flannel St. *Roch* 3A **28**
Flashfields. *P'wich* 2D **80**
Flash St. *M40* 5C **84**
Flatley Clo.
    M15 . . . . . .1E **109** (6A **10**)
Flavian Wlk. Open 5D **96**
    (off Herne St.)
Flaxcroft Rd. *M22* 2H **147**
Flaxfield Av. *Stal* 3H **101**
Flaxman Ri. *Oldh* 3G **57**
Flaxpool Clo. *M16* 3C **108**
    (in two parts)
Flax St. *Rams* 5C **12**
Flax St. *Salf* 2B **94** (2D **4**)
Flaxwood Wlk. *M22* 2H **147**
Fleece St. *M40* 4G **109**
Fleece St. *Oldh* 2F **73**
Fleece St. *Roch* 4H **27**
Fleeson St. *M14* 4G **109**
Fleet Ho. Bolt 4A **32**
    (off Nottingham Dri.)
Fleet St. *M18* 1H **111**
Fleet St. *Ash L* 3G **99**
    (in two parts)
Fleet St. *Hyde* 3C **114**
Fleet St. *Oldh* 2G **73**
Fleet St. *Roch* 5D **40**
Fleetwood Rd. *Wors* 6C **62**
Fleming Clo. *Roch* 4B **16**
Fleming Pl. *Oldh* 3E **72**
Fleming Rd. *M22* 3B **148**
Flemish Rd. *Dent* 5H **113**
Fletcher Av. *Swin* 6G **65**
Fletcher Bank. 3F **13**
Fletcher Clo. *Heyw* 4F **39**
Fletcher Clo. *Oldh* 3B **72**
Fletcher Dri. *Bow* 4E **145**
Fletcher Dri. *Dis* 1D **164**
Fletcher Fold. 6D **36**
Fletcher Fold Rd. *Bury* . . .1D **50**
Fletcher Moss Botanical Gdns.
    . . . . .2F **137**
Fletchers Pas. *L'boro* 3E **17**
Flotchor Sq. *M1* 4G **95** (6E **7**)
Fletcher's Rd. *L'boro* 6C **16**
Fletchers Sq. *L'boro* 3F **17**
    (off Sutcliffe St.)
Fletcher St. *M40* 6H **83**
Fletcher St. *Ash L* 2A **100**
Fletcher St. *Bolt* 2A **46**
Fletcher St. *Bury* 3E **37**
Fletcher St. *Farn* 1F **63**
Fletcher St. *L'boro* 3E **17**
Fletcher St. *L Lev* 4B **48**
Fletcher St. *Rad* 3A **50**
Fletcher St. *Roch* 6A **28**

Fletcher St. *Stoc* 2H **139**
Fletsand Rd. *Wilm* 3F **167**
Fletton Clo. *Roch* 1G **27**
Flexbury Wlk. *M40* 1F **97**
Flint Clo. *M11* 3D **96**
Flint Clo. *Haz G* 4C **152**
Flint Gro. *Cad* 3A **118**
Flint St. *Bury* 2D **36**
Flint St. *Droy* 3B **98**
Flint St. *Oldh* 1G **73**
Flint St. *Stoc* 4G **139**
Flitcroft Ct. *Bolt* 3B **46**
Flixton. 6B **104**
Flixton Ho. Gdns. 6B **104**
Flixton Rd. *Urm* 6B **104**
    (Flixton, in two parts)
Flixton Rd. *Urm* 1A **120**
    (Village, The)
Flixton Wlk.
    M13 . . . . .2H **109** (6H **11**)
Floatshall Rd. *M23* 5F **135**
Floats Rd. *Round I* 5F **135**
    (in two parts)
Flora Dri. *Salf* 1B **94**
Floral Ct. *Salf* 5H **81**
Flora St. *M9* 6E **69**
Flora St. *Bolt* 3H **45**
Florence Av. *Bolt* 1B **32**
Florence Ct. *Stoc* 5D **138**
Florence Pk. Ct. *M20* . . .5G **125**
Florence St. *Bolt* 3H **45**
Florence St. *Droy* 5B **98**
Florence St. *Eccl* 4D **90**
Florence St. *Fail* 3F **85**
Florence St. *Roch* 5B **28**
Florence St. *Sale* 3B **122**
Florence St. *Stoc* 1G **139**
Florence Way. *Holl* 2F **117**
Florida St. *Oldh* 4C **72**
Florin Gdns. *Salf* 2F **93**
Florist St. *Stoc* 4G **139**
Flowery Bank. *Oldh* 5F **73**
Flowery Field. 3B **114**
Flowery Fld. *Stoc* 1A **152**
Flowery Fld. Grn.
    Hyde 3A **114**
Flowery Fld. Ind. Pk.
    Hyde 2D **114**
Floyd Av. *M21* 3A **124**
Floyer Rd. *M9* 4G **69**
Flynn Ct. *Salf* 1E **93**
Foden La. *Woodf* 4F **161**
Foden Wlk. *Wilm* 5H **159**
Foggbrook. 5F **141**
Fogg La. *Bolt* 3F **47**
Fog La. *M19* 5H **125**
Fog La. *M20 & M19* 5F **125**
Fold Av. *Droy* 3B **98**
Fold Cres. *Carr* 5H **89**
Fold Gdns. *Roch* 6B **14**
Fold Grn. *Chad* 3G **71**
Fold Head. 1B **14**
Fold M. *Haz G* 2E **153**
Fold Rd. *Rad* 2C **64**
Folds Rd. *Bolt* 5B **32**
Fold St. *M40* 3A **84**
Fold St. *Bolt* 6B **32**
Fold St. *Bury* 3B **36**
Fold St. *Farn* 1G **63**
Fold St. *Heyw* 2G **39**
Fold, The. *M9* 6F **69**
Fold, The. *Rytn* 3E **57**
Fold, The. *Urm* 4C **104**
Fold Vw. *Eger* 2C **18**
Fold Vw. *Oldh* 1E **87**
Foleshill Av. *M9* 4F **83**
Foley Gdns. *Heyw* 6G **39**
Foley Wlk. *M22* 5C **148**
Foliage Cres. *Stoc* 4B **128**
Foliage Gdns. *Stoc* 4C **128**
Foliage Rd. *Stoc* 5B **128**

Folkestone Rd. *M11* 3F **97**
Folkestone Rd. E. *M11* . . .3F **97**
Folkestone Rd. W. *M11* . .2E **97**
Follows St. *M18* 1F **111**
Folly La. *Swin* 6D **78**
Folly Wlk. *Roch* 2H **27**
    (in three parts)
Fonthill Gro. *Sale* 2H **133**
Fontwell Clo. *M16* 4A **108**
Fontwell La. *Oldh* 6E **57**
Fontwell Rd. *L Lev* 5A **48**
Fontwell Wlk. *M40* 1D **84**
Foot Mill Cres. *Roch* 1F **27**
Forber Cres. *M18* 4F **111**
Forbes Clo. *Sale* 1D **134**
Forbes Clo. *Stoc* 3B **140**
Forbes Pk. *Bram* 6F **151**
Forbes Rd. *Stoc* 2B **140**
Forbes St. *Bred* 5F **129**
Fordbank Rd. *M20* 1E **137**
Fordel Wlk. *Salf* 1C **94**
Ford Gdns. *Roch* 5D **26**
Ford Gro. *Mot* 3C **116**
Fordham Gro. *Bolt* 5G **31**
Ford La. *M22 & M20* 2C **136**
    (in two parts)
Ford La. *Salf* 1G **93**
Ford Lodge. *M20* 1F **137**
Ford's La. *Bram* 1F **161**
Ford St. *M12* 6H **95** (4G **11**)
Ford St. *Duk* 1A **114**
Ford St. *Rad* 1A **64**
Ford St.
    Salf (M3) 3B **94** (4D **4**)
Ford St. *Salf* (M7) 2B **94**
Ford St. *Stoc* 2F **139**
Ford Way. *Mot* 3C **116**
Foreland Clo. *M40* 6F **83**
Forest Bank. *Swin* 3C **80**
Forest Clo. *Duk* 1A **114**
Forest Ct. *Urm* 4H **103**
Forest Dri. *Sale* 1G **133**
Forest Dri. *Timp* 5H **133**
Forest Dri. *Urm* 4H **103**
Forester Hill Av. *Bolt* 4C **46**
    (Newport Rd.)
Forester Hill Av. *Bolt* 4B **46**
    (Rishton Av.)
Forest Gdns. *Part* 6B **118**
Forest Range. *M19* 6C **110**
Forest Rd. *Bolt* 2F **31**
Forest St. *Ash L* 1A **100**
Forest St. *Eccl* 1C **90**
Forest St. *Oldh* 1D **86**
Forest Vw. *Roch* 1F **27**
Forest Way. *Brom X* 5G **19**
Forfar St. *Bolt* 6C **18**
Forge Ind. Est. *Oldh* 2F **73**
Forge St. *Oldh* 2F **73**
Formby Av. *M21* 2B **124**
Formby Dri. *H Grn* 5F **149**
Formby Rd. *Salf* 5C **80**
Forrester Dri. *Shaw* 5H **43**
Forrester Ho. *M12* 1C **110**
    (off Blackwin St.)
Forrester St. *Wors* 3A **78**
Forrest Rd. *Dent* 6H **113**
Forshaw Av. *M18* 1H **111**
Forshaw St. *Dent* 3D **112**
Forsyth St. *Stoc* 5D **82**
Forsythia Wlk. *Part* 6C **118**
Forsyth St. *Roch* 1A **26**
Fortescue Rd. *Stoc* 4D **140**
Forth Pl. *Rad* 2F **49**
Forth Rd. *Rad* 2F **49**
Forton Av. *Bolt* 6G **33**
Fortran Clo. *Salf* 4G **93**
Fort Rd. *P'wich* 1H **81**
Fortrose Av. *M9* 6D **68**

Fortuna Gro. *M19* 1B **126**
Fortune St. *Bolt* 2D **46**
Fortyacre Dri. *Bred* 6E **129**
Forum Gro. *Salf* 6A **82**
Fosbrook Av. *M20* 5G **125**
Foscarn Dri. *M23* 6H **135**
Fossgill Av. *Bolt* 6G **19**
Foster Ct. *Bury* 1H **37**
Foster La. *Bolt* 4H **33**
    (in two parts)
Foster St. *Dent* 4F **113**
Foster St. *Oldh* 2G **73**
Foster St. *Rad* 4F **49**
Foster St. *Salf* 3D **92**
Foster Ter. Bolt 4A **32**
    (off Barnwood Dri.)
Fotherby Dri. *M9* 6F **69**
Fothergill Grange.
    Chea H 5C **150**
Foulds Av. *Bury* 3G **35**
Foundry La. *M4* . .3F **95** (4C **6**)
Foundry St. *Bury* 3D **36**
Foundry St. *Duk* 5A **100**
    (in two parts)
Foundry St. *Heyw* 3E **39**
Foundry St. *L Lev* 4A **48**
Foundry St. *Oldh* 3C **72**
Foundry St. *Rad* 4G **49**
Fountain Av. *Hale* 3B **146**
Fountain Clo. *Poy* 3D **162**
Fountain Pl. *Poy* 3D **162**
Fountain Pl. *W'fld* 2D **66**
Fountains Av. *Bolt* 4E **33**
Fountain Sq. *Dis* 1G **165**
Fountain Sq. *Swin* 3F **79**
Fountains Rd.
    Chea H & Bram . . .1D **160**
Fountains Rd. *Stret* 4H **105**
Fountain St. *M2* . . .4E **95** (6A **6**)
Fountain St. *Ash L* 1C **100**
Fountain St. *Bury* 3E **37**
Fountain St. *Eccl* 5F **91**
Fountain St. *Elton* 3A **36**
Fountain St. *Hyde* 4D **114**
Fountain St. *Midd* 1H **69**
Fountain St. *Oldh* 2C **72**
Fountain St. N. *Bury* 3E **37**
Fountains Wlk. *Chad* 4G **71**
Fountains Wlk. *Duk* 1A **114**
Fouracres. *M23* 6G **135**
Fouracres Rd. *M23* 6F **135**
Four Lane Ends. 6F **21**
Four Lanes. *Mot* 3C **116**
Four Lanes Way. *Roch* . .2G **25**
Four Stalls End. *L'boro* . .4E **17**
Fourth Av. *M11* 1E **97**
Fourth Av. *Bolt* 6F **31**
Fourth Av. *Bury* 1H **37**
Fourth Av. *Carr* 5G **89**
Fourth Av. *Chad* 4G **71**
Fourth Av. *L Lev* 3H **47**
Fourth Av. *Oldh* 2A **86**
Fourth Av. *Swin* 6D **78**
Fourth Av. *Traf P* 2C **106**
Fourth St. *Bolt* 1D **30**
Fourways. *Traf P* 1A **106**
Fourways Wlk. *M40* 1B **84**
Fovant Cres. *Stoc* 6G **111**
Fowey Wlk. *M23* 6G **135**
Fowey Wlk. *Hyde* 4A **116**
Fowler Av. *M18* 6H **97**
Fowler St. *Oldh* 6A **72**
Fownhope Av. *Sale* 6H **121**
Fownhope Rd. *Sale* 6H **121**
Foxall Clo. *Midd* 2E **69**
Foxall St. *Midd* 2E **69**
Fox Bank Ct. *Stoc* 3F **139**
Foxbank St. *M13* 3A **110**
Fox Bench Clo. *Bram* . . .1E **161**
Foxbench Wlk. *M21* 3B **124**

Fox Clo. Timp 5H 133
Foxcroft St. L'boro 4D 16
Foxdale St. M11 . . . . . . .4E 97
Foxdenton Dri. Urm 4H 105
Foxdenton La.
    Midd & Chad 3E 71
Foxdenton Wlk. Dent 6E 113
Foxendale Wlk. Bolt 2B 46
Foxfield Clo. Bury 6B 22
Foxfield Dri. Oldh 2A 86
Foxfield Rd. M23 . . . . . .2F 147
Foxford Wlk. M22 . . . . . .3C 148
Foxglove Ct. Roch 6D 14
Foxglove Dri. Bury 2H 37
Foxglove La. Stal 2D 100
Foxglove Wlk. Part 6D 118
Foxhall Rd. Dent 3D 112
Foxhall Rd. Timp 5G 133
Foxham Wlk. Salf 5A 82
Foxhill. Alt 6C 132
Foxhill. Shaw 5C 42
Foxhill Chase. Stoc 6G 141
Fox Hill Ct. Stoc 1C 138
Foxhill Dri. Stal 5G 101
Foxhill Pk. Stal 5G 101
Foxhill Rd. Eccl 4B 90
Foxhill Rd. Roch 5D 40
Foxholes Clo. Roch 2A 28
Foxholes Rd. Hyde 1A 130
Foxholes Rd. Roch 2A 28
Foxlair Ct. M22 . . . . . . .2H 147
Foxlair Rd. M22 . . . . . . .2H 147
Foxland Rd. Gat 1F 149
Foxlea. Glos 6H 117
Foxley Clo. Droy 5G 97
Foxley Gro. Bolt 1H 45
Foxley Wlk. M12 . . . . . .2C 110
Fox Pk. Rd. Oldh 1A 86
Fox Platt. 3E 89
Fox Platt Rd. Moss 2D 88
Fox Platt Ter. Moss 3E 89
Fox St. Bury 2D 36
Fox St. Eccl 3H 91
Fox St. Heyw 3E 39
Fox St. Miln 5E 29
Fox St. Oldh 1A 86
Fox St. Roch 3B 28
Fox St. Stoc 3F 139
Foxton St. Midd 2E 69
Foxton Wlk. M23 . . . . . .3G 147
Foxwell Wlk. M8 . . . . . . .5D 82
Foxwood Dri. Moss 1F 89
Foxwood Gdns. M19 . . . .4A 126
Foynes Clo. M40 . . . . . . .6F 83
Framingham Rd.
    Sale 6A 122
Framley Rd. M21 . . . . . .2D 124
Frampton Clo. Midd 2B 70
Fram St. M9 . . . . .3H 83
Fram St. Salf 3E 93
Frances Av. Gat 5E 137
Francesca Wlk. M18 . . . . .1E 111
Frances St.
    M13 . . . . . .1F 109 (5D 10)
Frances St. Bolt 3H 31
Frances St. Chea 5A 138
Frances St. Hyde 4A 114
Frances St. Oldh 6E 57
    (in two parts)
Frances St. Roch 6B 16
Frances St. Stoc 3G 139
Frances St. W. Hyde 4A 114
Francis Av. Eccl 3G 91
Francis Av. Wors 5H 77
Francis Rd. M20 . . . . . . .4G 125
Francis Rd. Irlam 1D 118
Francis St. M3 . . .2D 94 (1G 5)
Francis St. Cad 4C 118
Francis St. Dent 1H 129
Francis St. Eccl 2F 91
Francis St. Fail 4F 85

Francis St. Farn 6F 47
Francis St. Tyl 3A 76
Francis Ter. Duk 4A 100
    (off Hill St.)
Francis Thompson Dri.
    Ash L 2H 99
Frandley Wlk.
    M13 . . . . . . .6F 95 (3D 10)
Frankby Clo. Swin 4A 80
Frank Cowin Ct. Salf 1B 94
Frank Fold. Heyw 3C 38
Frankford Av. Bolt 3G 31
Frankford Sq. Bolt 3G 31
Frank Hulme Ho.
    Stret 6E 107
Frankland Clo. M11 . . . . .3D 96
Franklin Av. Droy 4A 98
Franklin Clo. Oldh 1C 72
Franklin St. Eccl 3F 91
Franklin St. Oldh 1C 72
Franklin St. Roch 6B 28
Franklin Ter. L'boro 4E 17
    (off William St.)
Franklyn Av. Urm 5A 104
Franklyn Clo. Dent 5A 112
Franklyn Rd. M18 . . . . . .1G 111
Frank Perkins Way.
    Irlam 2D 118
Frank Price Ct. M22 . . . .2A 148
Frank St. Bolt 3H 31
Frank St. Bury 4D 36
Frank St. Fail 4E 85
Frank St. Hyde 5C 114
Frank St. Salf 1G 93
Frank Swift Wlk. M14 . . . .4E 109
Frankton Rd. W'fld 2D 66
Franton Rd. M11 . . . . . . .3D 96
Fraser Av. Sale 6E 123
Fraser Ho. Bolt 4H 31
    (off Kirk Hope Dri.)
Fraser Pl. Traf P 2D 106
Fraser Rd. Crum 2B 82
Fraser St. Ash L 2A 100
Fraser St. Roch 1H 41
Fraser St. Shaw 5E 43
Fraser St. Swin 2G 79
Fraternitas Ter. Droy 2G 97
Frecheville Ct. Bury 4C 36
Frecheville Pl. Bury 4C 36
Freckleton Av. M21 . . . . .5A 124
Freckleton Dri. Bury 5F 35
Freda Wlk. M11 . . . . .4B 96
Frederick Av. Shaw 2F 57
Frederick Ct. Farn 1G 63
Frederick Rd.
    Salf & M7 . . . . .2H 93
Frederick St. Ash L 3C 100
Frederick St. Chad 1H 71
Frederick St. Dent 2E 113
Frederick St. Farn 1F 63
Frederick St. L'boro 3E 17
Frederick St. Oldh 4A 72
Frederick St. Rams 4D 12
Frederick St.
    Salf 3C 94 (4E 5)
Fred Tilson Clo. M14 . . . .4E 109
Freehold St. Roch 6G 27
Freeland Wlk. Open 5E 97
Freeman Av. Ash L 2B 100
Freeman Rd. Duk 1A 114
Freeman Sq.
    M15 . . . . . .1E 109 (6A 10)
Freemantle St. Stoc 3E 139
Freestone Clo. Bury 1B 36
Freetown. 1E 37
Freetown Bus. Pk.
    Bury 1E 37
Freetown Clo. M14 . . . . .3E 109
Free Trade Hall. 1G 9
Freetrade St. Roch 6G 27
Fremantle Av. M18 . . . . .4F 111
French Av. Oldh 6G 57

French Av. Stal 4G 101
French Barn La. M9 . . . . .6E 69
Frenches. 3F 61
French Gro. Bolt 2F 47
French St. Ash L 1B 100
French St. Stal 4G 101
Frensham Wlk. M23 . . . . .1F 147
Fresca Rd. Oldh 3H 57
Freshfield. H Grn 5F 149
Freshfield Av. Bolt 5H 45
    (in three parts)
Freshfield Av. Hyde 6B 114
Freshfield Av. P'wich 3G 67
Freshfield Clo. Fail 5G 85
Freshfield Clo. Marp B . . .2F 143
Freshfield Gro. Bolt 5B 46
    (in two parts)
Freshfield Rd. Stoc 1B 138
Freshfields. Rad 2D 48
Freshfield Wlk. M11 . . . . .3E 97
Freshford Wlk. M22 . . . . .4H 147
Freshpool Way. M22 . . . .5C 136
Freshville St.
    M1 . . . . .4F 95 (6D 6)
    (off Leycroft St.)
Freshwater Dri. Dent 1H 129
Freshwater St. M18 . . . . .1G 111
Freshwinds Ct. Oldh 5H 73
Fresia Av. Wors 6B 62
Fresnel Clo. Hyde 1F 115
Frew Clo. M40 . . . . .1B 84
Frewland Av. Stoc 1H 151
Freya Gro. Salf 5A 94 (2A 8)
Friarmere Rd. Del 2G 59
Friars Clo. Bow 4D 144
Friars Clo. Tyl 2A 76
Friars Clo. Wilm 1B 166
Friar's Ct. Salf 3B 92
Friars Cres. Roch 3F 41
Friar's Rd. Sale 5B 122
Friendship Av. M18 . . . . .3G 111
Friendship Sq. Holl 2F 117
Frieston. Roch 3H 27
    (off Redcross St.)
Frieston Rd. Timp 3G 133
Friezland. 4E 61
Friezland Clo. Carr 5G 89
Friezland La. G'fld 6E 61
Frimley Gdns. M22 . . . . .2B 148
Frinton Av. M40 . . . . .6D 70
Frinton Clo. Sale 2H 133
Frinton Rd. Bolt 4F 45
Frobisher Clo. M13 . . . . .2H 109
Frobisher Pl. Stoc 5G 127
Frobisher Rd. L'boro 6G 17
Frodesley Wlk. M12 . . . . .1B 110
Frodsham Av. Stoc 6E 127
Frodsham Rd. Sale 1E 135
Frodsham St. M14 . . . . . .4F 109
Frodsham Way. Hand 3A 160
Frogley St. Bolt 2D 32
Frogmore Av. Hyde 2C 130
Frome Av. Stoc 6C 140
Frome Av. Urm 6D 104
Frome Dri. M8 . . . . .4D 82
Frome St. Oldh 3G 73
Frostlands St. M16 . . . . . .4C 108
Frost St. M4 . . . . .4H 95 (5H 7)
Frost St. Oldh 5C 72
Froxmer St. M18 . . . . . . .1E 111
Fuchsia Gro. Salf 5H 81
Fulbeck Wlk. M8 . . . . .6A 82
Fulbrook Dri. Chea H 1B 160
Fulford St. M16 . . . . .3A 108
Fulham Av. M40 . . . . .6B 84
Fulham St. Oldh 3G 73
Fulmar Clo. Poy 3B 163
Fulmar Dri. Sale 1E 133
Fulmar Dri. Stoc 6F 141

Fulmards Clo. Wilm 2F 167
Fulmar Gdns. Roch 4B 26
Fulmead Wlk. M8 . . . . . . .5B 82
    (off Kilmington Dri.)
Fulmer Dri. M4 . . .3G 95 (3F 7)
Fulmere Ct. Swin 5D 78
Fulneck Sq. Droy 5A 98
Fulshaw Av. Wilm 3D 166
Fulshaw Ct. Wilm 4D 166
Fulshaw Park. 4D 166
Fulshaw Pk. Wilm 5D 166
Fulshaw Pk. S. Wilm 5C 166
Fulshaw Wlk.
    M13 . . . . . . .6F 95 (4D 10)
Fulstone M. Stoc 5B 140
Fulton Ct. M15 . . . . .2E 109
Fulton's Ct. Lees 4A 74
Fulwood Av. M9 . . . . .5H 69
Fulwood Clo. Bury 4F 35
Furbarn La. Roch 3H 25
Furbarn Rd. Roch 4H 25
    (in two parts)
Fur Lane. 3G 61
Furlong Rd. M22 . . . . . . .2H 147
Furnace St. Duk 4H 99
Furnace St. Hyde 3A 114
Furness Av. Ash L 6D 86
Furness Av. Bolt 3D 32
Furness Av. Heyw 2E 39
Furness Av. L'boro 3E 17
Furness Av. Oldh 6G 73
Furness Av. W'fld 1E 67
Furness Clo. Miln 5E 29
Furness Clo. Poy 3C 162
Furness Gro. Stoc 2C 138
Furness Quay. Salf 6G 93
Furness Rd. M14 . . . . . . .6G 109
Furness Rd. Bolt 4D 32
Furness Rd. Chea H 1E 161
Furness Rd. Midd 4H 53
Furness Rd. Urm 4F 105
Furness Sq. Bolt 3D 32
Furnival Clo. Dent 5A 112
Furnival Rd. M18 . . . . . . .1E 111
Furnival St. Stoc 5H 111
Furrow Dri. Eccl 1D 90
Further Fld. Roch 2H 25
Further Heights Rd.
    Roch 1H 27
Further Hey Clo. Lees 2A 74
Further La. Hyde 4A 116
Further Pits. Roch 4E 27
Furtherwood Rd. Oldh 6A 56
Furzegate. Roch 2A 42
Furze La. Oldh 6H 57
    (in two parts)
Furze Wlk. Part 6E 119
Fyfield Wlk. M8 . . . . .5D 82
Fylde Av. Bolt 6G 33
Fylde Av. H Grn 5G 149
Fylde Ct. Stret 1C 122
Fylde Rd. Stoc 1C 138
Fylde St. Bolt 5F 47
Fylde St. E. Bolt 5F 47

G

Gable Av. Wilm 2D 166
Gable Ct. Dent 4F 113
Gable Dri. Midd 6G 53
Gables, The. Sale 6B 122
    (Framingham Rd.)
Gables, The. Sale 4C 122
    (Irlam Rd.)
Gable St. M11 . . . . .5B 96
Gable St. Bolt 6H 19
Gabriels Ter. Midd 2C 70
Gabriels, The. Shaw 6D 42
Gaddum Rd. M20 . . . . . .6G 125
Gaddum Rd. Bow 4C 144
Gadwall Clo. Wors 3F 77

Gail Av.—George Parr Rd.

Gail Av. Stoc 1F 139
Gail Clo. Ald E 4H 167
Gail Clo. Fail 6E 85
Gainford Av. Gat 1F 149
Gainford Gdns. M40 . . . . .2B 84
Gainford Rd. Stoc 6H 111
Gainford Wlk. Bolt 3A 46
(in two parts)
Gainsboro Rd. Aud 4D 98
Gainsborough Av.
M20 . . . . .4G 125
Gainsborough Av. Bolt . . .4G 45
Gainsborough Av.
Marp B 3F 143
Gainsborough Av. Oldh . . .5C 72
Gainsborough Av.
Stret 4F 107
Gainsborough Clo.
Wilm 1G 167
Gainsborough Dri.
Chea 5B 138
Gainsborough Dri.
Roch 2E 41
Gainsborough Rd.
Chad 6E 55
Gainsborough Rd.
Rams 2B 22
Gainsborough St. Salf 4A 82
Gainsborough Wlk.
Dent 6E 113
(in two parts)
Gainsborough Wlk.
Hyde 2C 114
Gairlock Av. Stret 5B 106
Gair Rd. Stoc 5H 127
Gair St. Hyde 3B 114
Gaitskell Clo. M12 . . . . . .4A 96
Galbraith Rd. M20 . . . . . .6G 125
Galbraith St.
M1 . . . . .5E 95 (2A 10)
Galbraith Way. Roch 3A 26
Gale. 2G 17
Gale Dri. Midd 5F 53
Gale Rd. P'wich 6D 66
Gales Ter. Roch 6G 27
(off New Barn La.)
Gale St. Heyw 3D 38
Gale St. Roch 6F 15
Galgate Clo.
M15 . . . . .6C 94 (4E 9)
Galgate Clo. Bury 4F 35
Galindo St. Bolt 1E 33
Galland St. Oldh 2H 73
Galleria Apartments.
Salf 6F 93
Galleria, The. Bolt 6B 32
Galloway Clo. Bolt 2C 44
Galloway Clo. Heyw 4B 38
Galloway Dri. Swin 5F 65
Galloway Rd. Swin 5D 78
Gallowsclough Rd.
Mat 1A 116
Galston St. M11 . . . . .5C 96
Galsworthy Av. M8 . . . . . .5C 82
Galvin Rd. M9 . . . . .6D 68
Galway St. Oldh 3D 72
Galway Wlk. M23 . . . . . .3F 147
Gambleside Clo. Wors . . .3D 76
Gambrel Bank Rd.
Ash L 5F 87
Gambrel Gro. Ash L 5F 87
Gamesley. 5G 117
Game St. Oldh 4G 73
Games Wlk. M22 . . . . . .4H 147
Gamma Wlk. M11 . . . . . .3D 96
Gandy La. Roch 5C 14
Gan Eden. Salf 3A 82
Gantock Wlk. M14 . . . . .4G 109
Ganton Av. W'fld 2B 66
Garbo Ct. Salf 1E 93
Garbrook Av. M9 . . . . .4E 69
Garden Av. Droy 3B 98
Garden Av. Stret 4D 106
Garden City. Rams 1A 22
Garden Clo. L'boro 6D 16
Garden Ct. Roch 3C 28
Gardenfold Ho. Droy 3B 98
(off Fold Av.)
Garden La. M3 . . . . .5G 5
Garden La. Alt 6F 133
Garden La. Roch 3A 28
Garden La. Salf . . .3C 94 (3F 5)
(in two parts)
Garden La. Wors 4C 76
Garden M. L'boro 4F 17
(off Industry St.)
Garden Row. Heyw 1D 38
Garden Row. Roch 1F 27
Gardens, The.
M2 . . . . .3D 94 (4H 5)
Gardens, The. Bolt 5D 18
Gardens, The. Eccl 1A 92
Garden St. M4 . . . .3E 95 (4A 6)
Garden St. Aud 1F 113
Garden St. Eccl 4G 91
Garden St. Heyw 2E 39
Garden St. Hyde 3C 114
Garden St. Kear 1G 63
Garden St. Miln 1F 43
Garden St. Oldh 2E 73
Garden St. Rams 3E 13
Garden St. S'head 4B 74
Garden St. Stoc 6C 140
Garden St. S'seat 6E 13
Garden St. T'ton 4H 21
Garden Ter. Rytn 6A 42
Garden Vw. Sale 3B 122
Garden Vs. H Grn 6F 149
Garden Wlk. Ash L 1A 100
Garden Wlk. Dent 4G 113
Garden Wlk. Part 6C 118
Garden Wall Clo.
Salf 5A 94 (2A 8)
Garden Way. L'boro 1F 29
Gardner Grange. Stoc . . .5C 128
Gardner Ho. Eccl 3G 91
Gardner Rd. P'wich 5D 66
Gardner St. M12 . . . . . . .1D 110
Gardner St. Salf 2G 93
Garfield Av. M19 . . . . . . .6D 110
Garfield Clo. Roch 3A 26
Garfield Gro. Bolt 2H 45
Garfield St. Bolt 4G 45
Garfield St. Salf 1G 107
Garfield St. Stoc 1A 140
Garforth Av. M4 . . .3G 95 (3F 7)
Garforth Cres. Droy 2B 98
Garforth St. Chad 2A 72
Gargrave Av. Bolt 3D 30
Gargrave St. Oldh 3F 73
Gargrave St. Salf 3D 80
Garland Rd. M22 . . . . . . .2C 148
Garlick St. M18 . . . . .2F 111
Garlick St. Hyde 4D 114
Garlick St. Oldh 3C 72
(in two parts)
Garnant Clo. M9 . . . . .3H 83
Garner Av. Timp 2A 134
Garner Clo. Bow 3F 145
Garner Dri. Eccl 2E 91
Garner Dri. Salf 2D 92
Garners La. Stoc 6F 139
Garnet St. Oldh 1F 73
Garnett Clo. Mot 4B 116
Garnett Rd. Mot 4B 116
Garnett St. Bolt 2A 32
Garnett St. Rams 3D 12
Garnett St. Stoc 2H 139
Garnett Way. Mot 4B 116
(off Garnett Clo.)
Garratt Way. M18 . . . . . .2E 111
Garrett Gro. Shaw 6G 43
Garrett Hall Rd.
Wors 4A 76
Garrett La. Tyl 3A 76
(in two parts)
Garrett Wlk. Stoc 3D 138
Garrick Playhouse. 5F 133
(Theatre)
Garrick Theatre. 2G 139
Garron Wlk. M22 . . . . . .3G 147
Garrowmore Wlk.
M9 . . . . .6G 69
Garsdale La. Bolt 6B 30
Garsden Wlk. M23 . . . . .1F 147
Garside Gro. Bolt 3G 31
Garside Hey Rd. Bury 5B 22
Garside St. Bolt 6A 32
Garside St. Dent 5F 113
Garside St. Hyde 6C 114
Garstang Av. Bolt 1G 47
Garstang Dri. Bury 4F 35
Garstang Ho. M15 . . . . . .2F 109
Garston Clo. Stoc 6E 127
Garston St. Bury 1E 37
Garswood Dri. Bury 5B 22
Garswood Rd. M14 . . . .5D 108
Garswood Rd. Bolt 5A 46
Garth Av. Timp 5G 133
Garth Heights. Wilm 2F 167
Garthland Rd. Haz G 2F 153
Garthorne Clo. M16 . . . .3B 108
Garthorp Rd. M23 . . . . . .2E 135
Garth Rd. M22 . . . . .1B 148
Garth Rd. Marp 5E 143
Garth Rd. Stoc 4C 140
Garth, The. Salf 3D 92
Garthwaite Av. Oldh 6C 72
Gartland Wlk. M8 . . . . . . .3E 83
Gartside St. M3 . . .4C 94 (6F 5)
Gartside St. Ash L 4F 99
Gartside St. Del 3G 59
Gartside St. Oldh 4F 73
Garwick Rd. Bolt 2F 31
Garwood St.
M15 . . . . . .6D 94 (4G 9)
Gascoyne St. M14 . . . . . .4F 109
Gaskell Clo. L'boro 3E 17
Gaskell Ri. Oldh 2A 58
Gaskell Rd. Alt 5F 133
Gaskell Rd. Eccl 4F 91
Gaskell St. M40 . . . . .6C 84
Gaskell St. Bolt 5H 31
Gaskell St. Duk 5H 99
Gaskell St. Swin 1F 79
Gaskell Swimming Pool.
. . . . .2E 39
Gaskill St. Heyw 3C 38
Gas St. Ash L 2H 99
Gas St. Bolt 6A 32
Gas St. Farn 1F 63
Gas St. Heyw 3F 39
Gas St. Holl 2F 117
Gas St. Roch 4G 27
Gas St. Stoc 2G 139
Gaston Wlk. M9 . . . . .4F 69
(off Eastlands Rd.)
Gatcombe M. Rad 2F 49
Gatcombe M. Wilm 3D 166
Gatcombe Sq. M14 . . . .4G 109
Gateacre Wlk. M23 . . . . .3E 135
Gate Cen., The. Rom 3E 129
Gate Fld. Clo. Rad 4E 49
Gate Fold. 6H 19
Gatehead Cft. Del 4H 59
Gatehead M. Del 4H 59
Gatehead Rd. Del 5H 59
Gatehouse Rd. Wors 5C 62
Gate Keeper Fold.
Ash L 4E 87
Gatemere Clo. Wors 3D 76
Gate Rd. Stret 3A 106
Gatesgarth Rd. Midd 5E 53
Gateshead Clo. M14 . . . .3F 109
Gateside Wlk. M9 . . . . . . .4G 69
(off Brockford Dri.)
Gates Shop. Cen., The.
Bolt 6B 32
Gate St. M11 . . . . .5E 97
Gate St. Duk 1G 113
Gate St. Roch 6H 27
Gateway Cres. Chad 4D 70
Gateway Ind. Est.
M1 . . . . .4F 95 (6D 6)
Gateway Rd. M18 . . . . . .1E 111
Gateways, The. Swin 2F 79
Gathill Clo. Chea H 4B 150
Gathurst St. M18 . . . . . .1G 111
Gatley. 6E 137
Gatley Av. M14 . . . . . . .6E 109
Gatley Brow. Oldh 1C 72
Gatley Ct. M22 . . . . .4C 136
Gatley Grn. Gat 6E 137
Gatley Rd. Gat & Chea . . .6F 137
Gatley Rd. Sale 6E 123
Gatling Av. M12 . . . . . . .5D 110
Gatwick Av. M23 . . . . . .5H 135
Gavel Wlk. Midd 6G 53
Gavin Av. Salf 4G 93
Gawsworth Av. M20 . . . .2G 137
Gawsworth Clo. Bram . . .2G 161
Gawsworth Clo. Poy 5F 163
Gawsworth Clo. Shaw 6D 42
Gawsworth Clo. Stoc 6F 139
Gawsworth Clo. Timp . . .5D 134
Gawsworth Ct. M9 . . . . . .4C 68
(off Deanswood Dri.)
Gawsworth M. Gat 6F 137
Gawsworth Pl. M22 . . . .4D 148
Gawsworth Rd. Sale 1E 135
Gawsworth Way.
Dent 6G 113
Gawsworth Way.
Hand 3A 160
Gawthorne Clo. Haz G . . .3C 152
Gawthorpe Clo. Bury 2E 51
Gaydon Rd. Sale 5F 121
Gayford Wlk. M9 . . . . . . .4G 69
(off Brockford Dri.)
Gaythorn. 6D 94 (3H 9)
Gaythorne St. Bolt 2B 32
Gaythorn St.
Salf 4A 94 (5B 4)
Gayton Wlk. M40 . . . . . . .1D 84
Gaywood Wlk. M40 . . . . . .5E 83
Gee Cross. 2C 130
Gee Cross Fold.
Hyde 2C 130
Gee La. Eccl 2D 90
Gee La. Oldh 1H 85
Gee St. Stoc 4F 139
Gelder Clough Cvn. Pk.
Heyw 6G 25
Gellfield La. Upperm 6D 60
Gemini Rd. Salf 1A 94
Gendre St. Eger 3C 18
Generation Cen., The.
Roch 4G 27
Geneva Rd. Bram 2G 151
Geneva Ter. Roch 3E 27
Geneva Wlk. M8 . . . . .5D 82
Geneva Wlk. Chad 3A 72
Genista Gro. Salf 5H 81
Geoff Bent Wlk. M40 . . . .6B 84
Geoffrey St. Bury 1E 37
Geoffrey St. Rams 5C 12
George Barton St.
Bolt 4D 32
George Ct. Duk 4H 99
(off Hill St.)
George H. Carnall
Leisure Cen. 3G 105
George La. Bred 5G 129
George Leigh St.
M4 . . . . .3F 95 (4D 6)
George Mann Clo. M22 . .4A 148
George Parr Rd.
M15 . . . . . .1D 108 (6G 9)

George Richards Way. *B'hth* 4D **132**
George Rd. *Rams* 4D **12**
George's Clo. *Poy* 4E **163**
George Sq. *Oldh* 3C **72**
George's Rd. *Sale* 6B **122**
George's Rd. E. *Poy* 4E **163**
George's Rd. W. *Poy* 4D **162**
George St. *M1* . . .5D **94** (1H **9**)
(in two parts)
George St. *Ald E* 5G **167**
George St. *Alt* 1F **145**
George St. *Ash L* 2A **100**
George St. *Bury* 3D **36**
George St. *Chad* 2G **71**
George St. *Comp* 1E **143**
George St. *Dent* 4G **113**
George St. *Eccl* 4E **91**
George St. *Fail* 3F **85**
George St. *Farn* 2D **62**
George St. *Fir* 4E **29**
George St. *Heyw* 2D **38**
George St. *Irlam* 4F **103**
George St. *L'boro* 3F **17**
George St. *Moss* 1E **89**
George St. *Oldh* 3C **72**
George St. *P'wich* 2F **81**
George St. *Rad* 4F **49**
George St. *Roch* 3A **28**
George St. *Shaw* 4G **43**
George St. *Smal* 6B **16**
George St. *Stal* 3E **101**
George St. *Stoc* 2A **140**
George St. *Urm* 5G **105**
George St. *W'fld* 6C **50**
George St. *Whitw* 2C **14**
George St. E. *Stoc* 3B **140**
George St. N. *M7* 3B **82**
George St. S. *M7* 3A **82**
George St. W. *Stoc* 3B **140**
George Ter. *Eccl* 3F **91**
George Thomas Ct. *M9* . . .3F **83**
Georgette Dri.
Salf 2C **94** (2F **5**)
Georgiana St. *Bury* 4D **36**
Georgiana St. *Farn* 5D **46**
Georgina Ct. *Bolt* 4F **45**
Georgina St. *Bolt* 5F **45**
Gerald Av. *M8* 3C **82**
Gerald Rd. *Salf* 6E **81**
Germain Clo. *M9* 4E **68**
Germans Bldgs. *Stoc* 5A **140**
Gerrard Av. *Timp* 3A **134**
Gerrards Clo. *Irlam* 5E **103**
Gerrards Gdns. *Hyde* 2C **130**
Gerrards Hollow.
Hyde 2B **130**
Gerrard St. *Kear* 1G **63**
Gerrard St. *Roch* 3G **41**
Gerrard St. *Salf* 2H **93**
Gerrard St. *Stal* 4F **101**
Gerrards Wood.
Hyde 2B **130**
Gertrude Clo. *Salf* 5G **93**
Gervis Clo. *M40* 6F **83**
Ghyll Gro. *Wors* 1G **77**
Gibb La. *Mell* 6H **143**
Gibbon Av. *M22* 3B **148**
Gibbon St. *M11* 3C **96**
Gibbon St. *Bolt* 2H **45**
Gibb Rd. *Wors* 4B **78**
Gibbs St. *Salf* 4B **94** (5C **4**)
(in two parts)
Gib La. *M23* 4H **135**
Gib La. Cotts. *M23* 4H **135**
Gibraltar La. *Dent* 1H **129**
Gibraltar St. *Bolt* 1H **45**
Gibraltar St. *Oldh* 4H **73**
Gibsmere Clo. *Timp* 5D **134**
Gibson Av. *M18* 6H **97**
Gibson Gro. *Wors* 6C **62**

Gibson La. *Wors* 6C **62**
Gibson Pl. *M3* 2E **95** (1A **6**)
Gibsons Rd. *Stoc* 5D **126**
Gibson St. *Bolt* 4E **33**
Gibson St. *Oldh* 3G **73**
Gibson St. *Roch* 3C **28**
Gibson Ter. *Ash L* 5G **99**
Gibson Way. *B'hth* 3E **133**
Gibwood Rd. *M22* 3A **136**
Gidlow St. *M18* 1G **111**
Gifford Av. *M9* 5H **69**
Gifford Wlk. *Bram* 3A **152**
Gigg. 6E **37**
Gigg La. *Bury* 6C **36**
Gilbertbank. *Bred* 5H **129**
Gilbert Rd. *Hale* 4G **145**
Gilbert St. *M15* 6C **94** (3F **9**)
Gilbert St. *Eccl* 5D **90**
Gilbert St. *Salf* 4F **93**
Gilbert St. *Wors* 2F **77**
Gilbert White Rd. *Alt* . . .1B **144**
Gilbrook Way. *Roch* 3H **41**
Gilcrest Rd. *Cad* 3C **118**
Gilda Brook Rd. *Eccl* 4A **92**
(in three parts)
Gilda Cres. Rd. *Eccl* 2A **92**
Gilda Rd. *Wors* 4A **76**
Gildenhall. *Fail* 4G **85**
Gilden Wlk. *M9* 4G **69**
Gilderdale Clo. *Shaw* 5F **43**
Gilderdale St. *Bolt* 3C **46**
Gildersdale Dri. *M9* 3D **68**
Gildridge Rd. *M16* 6C **108**
Gilesgate. *M14* 4G **109**
(off Grelley Wlk.)
Giles St. *M12* 3C **110**
Gillbent. 1B **160**
Gill Bent Rd. *Chea H* 1C **160**
Gillbrook Rd. *M20* 6F **125**
Gillemere Gro. *Shaw* 6G **43**
Gillers Grn. *Wors* 6E **63**
Gillford Av. *M9* 2F **83**
Gillingham Rd. *Eccl* 3D **90**
Gillingham Sq. *M11* 4B **96**
(off Jobling St.)
Gill St. *M9* 3H **83**
Gill St. *Stoc* 6B **128**
Gillwood Dri. *Rom* 2F **141**
Gilman Clo. *M9* 1E **83**
Gilman St. *M9* 1E **83**
Gilmerton Dri. *M40* 6C **84**
Gilmore Dri. *P'wich* 4F **67**
Gilmore St. *Stoc* 4G **139**
Gilmour St. *Midd* 1A **70**
Gilmour Ter. *M9* 2H **83**
(in two parts)
Gilnow. 1H **45**
Gilnow Gdns. *Bolt* 1G **45**
Gilnow Gro. *Bolt* 1H **45**
Gilnow La. *Bolt* 1G **45**
Gilnow Mill Ind. Est.
Bolt 1G **45**
Gilnow Park. 6F **31**
Gilnow Rd. *Bolt* 1G **45**
Gilpin Rd. *Urm* 6H **105**
Gilpin Wlk. *Midd* 6G **53**
Giltbrook Av. *M40* 1H **95**
Gilwell Dri. *M23* 1F **147**
Gilwood Gro. *Midd* 3H **53**
Gin Cft. La. *Rams* 2B **12**
Gingham Ct. *Rad* 3A **50**
(off Butterworth St.)
Gingham Pk. *Rad* 2E **49**
Gipsy La. *Roch* 2C **40**
(in two parts)
Girton St. *Bolt* 6F **33**
Girton St. *Salf* 1C **94**
Girton Wlk. *M40* 2D **84**
Girvan Av. *M40* 1D **84**
Girvan Clo. *Bolt* 4G **45**
Girvan Wlk. *Heyw* 4B **38**
Gisborne Dri. *Salf* 6E **81**

Gisburn Av. *Bolt* 3C **30**
Gisburn Dri. *Bury* 2E **35**
Gisburn Dri. *Roch* 2G **41**
Gisburne Av. *M40* 1D **84**
Gissing Wlk. *M9* 5F **83**
Givendale Dri. *M8* 1C **82**
Givvons Fold. *Oldh* 6H **57**
Glade Brow. *G'ton* 3C **74**
Gladeside Ct. *M22* 1A **148**
Gladeside Rd. *M22* 1A **148**
Glade St. *Bolt* 6G **31**
Glade, The. *Bolt* 4H **31**
Glade, The. *Stoc* 2C **138**
Gladewood Clo. *Wilm* 1F **167**
Glade Wood Dri. *Fail* 3H **85**
Gladstone Clo. *M15* 3C **108**
Gladstone Ct. *Farn* 3A **32**
Gladstone Ct. Ash L 3G **99**
(off Park St.)
Gladstone Ct. *Farn* 6E **47**
Gladstone Ct. Stoc 6D **126**
(off Gladstone Gro.)
Gladstone Cres. *Roch* 2F **41**
Gladstone Gro. *Stoc* 6C **126**
Gladstone Ho. Roch 3A **16**
Gladstone M. Stoc 6G **127**
(off Short St.)
Gladstone Pl. *Farn* 6E **47**
Gladstone Rd. *Alt* 5F **133**
Gladstone Rd. *Eccl* 3G **91**
Gladstone St. *Farn* 6E **47**
Gladstone St. *Urm* 5G **105**
Gladstone St. *Bolt* 3A **32**
Gladstone St. *Bury* 2F **37**
Gladstone St. *Oldh* 3F **73**
Gladstone St. *Stoc* 1C **152**
Gladstone St. *Swin* 3G **79**
Gladstone Ter. Rd.
G'fld 5E **61**
Gladville Dri. *Chea* 5C **138**
Gladwyn Av. *M20* 5C **124**
Gladys St. *M16* 3A **108**
Gladys St. *Bolt* 5F **47**
Glaisdale. *Oldh* 3H **73**
Glaisdale Clo. *Bolt* 3D **32**
Glaisdale St. *Bolt* 3D **32**
Glaister La. *Bolt* 4F **33**
Glamis Av. *M11* 2D **96**
Glamis Av. *Heyw* 5G **39**
Glamis Av. *Stret* 5A **106**
Glamorgan Pl. *Oldh* 4A **72**
Glandon Dri. *Chea H* 5E **151**
Glanford Av. *M9* 6C **68**
Glanton Wlk. *M40* 2D **84**
Glanvor Rd. *Stoc* 3E **139**
Glasshouse St.
M4 . . . . .2G **95** (2E **7**)
Glasson Wlk. *Chad* 3G **71**
Glass St. *Farn* 2G **63**
Glastonbury. Roch 3G **27**
(off Redcross St.)
Glastonbury Av.
Chea H 1D **160**
Glastonbury Av. *Hale* 3B **146**
Glastonbury Dri. *Poy* 3D **162**
Glastonbury Gdns. *Rad* . . .2E **49**
Glastonbury Rd. *Stret* . . .4H **105**
Glaswen Gro. *Stoc* 5H **127**
Glazebrook Clo. *Heyw* 4E **39**
Glazebrook La. *G'brk* 4A **118**
Glazebury Dri. *M23* 6H **135**
Glazedale Av. *Rytn* 3A **56**
Gleave Av. *Bolt* 1G **145**
Gleaves Av. *Bolt* 1A **34**
Gleaves Rd. *Eccl* 4G **91**
Gleave St. Bolt 5B **32**
(off Bark St. E.)
Gleave St. *Sale* 3B **122**
Glebe Ho. Midd 5A **54**
(off Rochdale Rd.)
Glebeland Rd. *Bolt* 2F **45**

Glebelands Rd. *M23* 5F **135**
Glebelands Rd. *P'wich* 4E **67**
Glebelands Rd. *Sale* 3H **121**
Glebelands Rd. E.
P'wich 4F **67**
Glebe La. *Oldh* 3A **58**
Glebe Rd. *Urm* 5F **105**
Glebe St. *Ash L* 2A **100**
Glebe St. *Aud* 3F **113**
Glebe St. *Bolt* 1C **46**
Glebe St. *Chad* 6G **71**
Glebe St. *Rad* 4H **49**
Glebe St. *Shaw* 6F **43**
Glebe St. *Stoc* 2A **140**
Gleden St. *M40* . . .3A **96** (3H **7**)
(in two parts)
Gledhall St. *Stal* 3E **101**
Gledhill Av. *Salf* 6G **93**
Gledhill Clo. *Shaw* 4E **43**
Gledhill St. *M20* 2F **125**
Gledhill Way. *Brom X* 3E **19**
Glemsford Clo. *M40* 5B **84**
Glenacre Gdns. *M18* 4G **111**
Glenarm Wlk. *M22* 3C **148**
Glenart. *Eccl* 2G **91**
Glen Av. *M9* 2G **83**
Glen Av. *Bolt* 2F **45**
Glen Av. *Kear* 3B **64**
Glen Av. *Sale* 3A **122**
Glen Av. *Swin* 3D **78**
Glen Av. *Wors* 3A **78**
Glenavon Dri. *Roch* 6D **14**
Glenavon Dri. *Shaw* 5D **42**
Glenbarry Clo.
M13 . . . . . .1F **109** (6D **10**)
Glenbarry St.
M12 . . . . . .5H **95** (2H **11**)
Glenbeck Rd. *W'fld* 6C **50**
Glenboro Av. *Bury* 3H **35**
Glen Bott St. *Bolt* 3H **31**
Glenbourne Pk. *Bram* 2F **161**
Glenbrook Gdns. *Farn* 5F **47**
Glenbrook Rd. *M9* 4C **68**
Glenburn St. *Bolt* 4H **45**
Glenby Av. *M22* 2D **148**
Glenby Est. *Chad* 3A **72**
Glencar Dri. *M40* 1D **84**
Glencastle Rd. *M18* 2E **111**
Glencoe. *Bolt* 6D **32**
Glencoe Clo. *Heyw* 4B **38**
Glencoe Dri. *Bolt* 1H **47**
Glencoe Dri. *Sale* 1E **133**
Glencoe Pl. *Roch* 4F **27**
Glencoe St. *Oldh* 1A **86**
Glen Cotts. *Bolt* 2C **30**
Glencoyne Dri. *Bolt* 5B **18**
Glencross Av. *M21* 5G **107**
Glendale. *Swin* 1H **79**
Glendale Av. *M19* 3B **126**
Glendale Av. *Bury* 4D **50**
Glendale Clo. *Heyw* 3F **39**
Glendale Clo. *Wors* 4B **76**
Glendale Ct. *Oldh* 5D **72**
Glendale Dri. *Bolt* 1D **44**
Glendale Rd. *Eccl* 2A **92**
Glendale Rd. *Wors* 4B **76**
Glendene Av. *Bram* 2F **161**
Glendene Av. *Droy* 2C **98**
Glenden Foot. *Roch* 1F **27**
Glendevon Clo. *Bolt* 2D **44**
Glendevon Pl. *W'fld* 2F **67**
Glendinning St. *Salf* 3E **93**
Glendon Ct. *Oldh* 3A **58**
Glendon Cres. *Ash L* 4F **87**
Glendore. *Salf* 3C **92**
Glendower Dri. *M40* 6E **83**
Gleneagles. *Bolt* 4D **44**
Gleneagles Av. *M11* 3E **97**
Gleneagles Av. *Heyw* 5F **39**
Gleneagles Clo. *Bram* 6H **151**
Gleneagles Clo. *Wilm* 1G **167**
Gleneagles Rd. *H Grn* 4G **149**

Gleneagles Rd. *Urm* 3A **104**
Gleneagles Way. *Rams* . .4D **12**
Glenfield. *All* 1D **144**
Glenfield Clo. *Oldh* 3H **73**
Glenfield Dri. *Poy* 4D **162**
Glenfield Rd. *Stoc* 5F **127**
Glenfield Sq. *Farn* 5D **46**
Glenfyne Rd. *Salf* 6B **80**
Glen Gdns. *Roch* 1H **27**
Glengarth. *Upperm* 2F **61**
Glengarth Dri.
   Los & Bolt 1A **44**
Glen Gro. *Midd* 2C **70**
Glen Gro. *Rytn* 2B **56**
Glenham Ct. *M15* 3C **108**
Glenhaven Av. *Urm* 5E **105**
Glenholme Rd. *Bram* . . .6F **151**
Glenhurst Rd. *M19* 4A **126**
Glenilla Av. *Wors* 4G **77**
Glenlea Dri. *M20* 3F **137**
Glenluce Wlk. *Bolt* 2C **44**
Glenmay Ct. *Stret* 5C **106**
Glen Maye. *Sale* 5C **122**
Glenmere Clo. *P'wich* . . .3D **66**
Glenmere Rd. *M20* 3G **137**
Glenmoor Rd. *Stoc* 3A **140**
Glenmore Av. *M20* 5C **124**
Glenmore Av. *Farn* 5C **46**
Glenmore Bungalows.
   Duk 6A **100**
   (off Glenmore Gro.)
Glenmore Clo. *Bolt* 2C **44**
Glenmore Clo. *Roch* 6A **26**
Glenmore Dri. *M8* 4D **82**
Glenmore Dri. *Fail* 3H **85**
Glenmore Gro. *Duk* 5A **100**
Glenmore Rd. *Rams* 1H **21**
Glenmore St. *Bury* 4C **36**
Glenolden St. *M11* 3F **97**
Glenpark Wlk. *M9* 4G **83**
   (off Craigend Dri.)
Glenridding Clo. *Oldh* . . .6E **57**
Glenridge Clo. *Bolt* 3B **32**
Glen Ri. *Timp* 6A **134**
Glen Rd. *Oldh* 3G **73**
Glen Royd. *Roch* 2E **27**
Glenroy Wlk. *M9* 4G **69**
Glensdale Dri. *M40* 2E **85**
Glenshee Dri. *Bolt* 2D **44**
Glenside Av. *M18* 4F **111**
Glenside Dri. *Bolt* 5B **46**
Glenside Dri. *Wilm* 3F **167**
Glenside Dri. *Wood'l* . . .4H **129**
Glenside Gdns. *Fail* 4G **85**
Glenside Gro. *Wors* 6G **63**
Glen St. *Rams* 2D **12**
Glen St. *Salf* 6G **93**
Glen, The. *Bolt* 6C **30**
Glen, The. *Midd* 3B **70**
Glenthorn Av. *M9* 3F **69**
Glenthorne Dri. *Ash L* . .1G **99**
Glenthorne St. *Bolt* 4A **32**
Glenthorn Gro. *Sale* 6B **122**
Glen Trad. Est. *Oldh* 3H **73**
Glentress M. *Bolt* 5E **31**
Glentrool M. *Bolt* 6E **31**
Glent Vw. *Stal* 1E **101**
Glentwood. *Hale* 4G **145**
Glenvale Clo. *Rad* 4H **49**
Glen Vw. *L'boro* 2G **17**
Glen Vw. *Hytn* 2B **56**
Glen Vw. *Whitw* 3G **15**
Glenville Ter. *Droy* 2G **97**
   (off Greenside La.)
Glonville Wlk. *Stal* 4E **101**
Glenville Way. *Dent* 5G **113**
Glenwood Av. *Hyde* 2B **114**
Glenwood Dri. *M9* 4G **83**
Glenwood Dri. *Midd* 5C **54**
Glenwood Gro. *Stoc* 2B **152**
Glenwyn Av. *M9* 5G **69**
Globe Clo. *M16* 2B **108**

Globe Ind. Est. *Rad* 4H **49**
Globe La. *Duk* 6G **99**
Globe La. *Lger* 1D **18**
Globe La. Ind. Est.
   Duk 1H **113**
Globe Sq. *Duk* 6G **99**
Glodwick. 4F **73**
Glodwick. *Oldh* 4F **73**
Glodwick Brook. 6E **73**
Glodwick Rd. *Oldh* 4F **73**
Glodwick Swimming Pool.
   . . . . .3F **73**
Glossop Rd.
   Charl & Glos 6F **117**
Glossop Rd. *Marp B* . . .3F **143**
Glossop Ter. *M40* 6D **70**
Gloster St. *Bolt* 6C **32**
Gloucester Av. *M19* 1D **126**
Gloucester Av. *Heyw* 5E **39**
Gloucester Av. *Marp* . . .5D **142**
Gloucester Av. *Roch* 5B **16**
Gloucester Av. *W'fld* 1E **67**
Gloucester Clo. *Ash L* . . .3H **87**
Gloucester Dri. *Dig* 3C **60**
Gloucester Dri. *Sale* 5F **121**
Gloucester Ho. *Salf* 5H **81**
Gloucester Pl. *Salf* 2G **93**
Gloucester Ri. *Duk* 6E **101**
Gloucester Rd. *Dent* 5A **112**
Gloucester Rd. *Droy* 2A **98**
Gloucester Rd. *H Grn* . . .6G **149**
Gloucester Rd. *Hyde* 1C **130**
Gloucester Rd. *Midd* 3A **70**
Gloucester Rd. *Poy* 3D **162**
Gloucester Rd. *Salf* 1C **92**
Gloucester Rd. *Urm* 5F **105**
Gloucester St.
   M1 . . . . .6D **94** (3H **9**)
Gloucester St.
   Salf (M5) . . .5A **94** (2A **8**)
Gloucester St.
   Salf (M6) 4F **139**
Gloucester St. *Stoc* 4F **139**
Gloucester St. N. *Oldh* . . .4A **72**
Gloucester St. S. *Oldh* . . .4A **72**
Glover Av. *M8* 5D **82**
Glover Ct. *M7* 3B **82**
Glover Dri. *Hyde* 5C **114**
Glover Fld. *Salf* 5H **81**
   (off Devonshire St.)
Glyn Av. *Hale* 3A **146**
Glyneath Clo. *M11* 5B **96**
Glynis Clo. *Stoc* 5H **139**
Glynne St. *Farn* 1E **63**
Glynn Gdns. *M20* 5B **124**
Glynrene Dri. *Swin* 2C **78**
Glynwood Pk. *Farn* 6E **47**
G-MEX Cen. . . .5D **94** (2G **9**)
Gnat Bank Fold. *Roch* . . .6B **26**
Goadsby St.
   M4 . . . . .3E **95** (3B **6**)
Goats. 5G **43**
Goats Ga. Ter. *W'fld* 5B **50**
Godbert Av. *M21* 4A **124**
Goddard La. *Had* 1H **117**
Goddard Rd. *Had* 3H **117**
Goddard St. *Oldh* 5D **72**
Godfrey Av. *Droy* 2F **97**
Godfrey Range. *M18* . . .3H **111**
Godfrey Rd. *Salf* 6A **80**
Godlee Dri. *Swin* 4E **79**
Godley. 4D **114**
Godley Clo. *Open* 5E **97**
Godley Ct. *Hyde* 5D **114**
   (off Woodbrooke Av.)
Godley Green. 6E **115**
Godley Hill. 5F **115**
Godley Hill Rd. *Hyde* . . .4F **115**
Godley St. *Hyde* 3D **114**
Godmond Hall Dri.
   Wors 6B **76**
Godson St. *Oldh* 6C **56**

Godwin St. *M18* 1G **111**
Goit Pl. *Roch* 4H **27**
Golborne Rd. *M40* 2D **124**
Golborne Dri. *Shaw* 5F **43**
Golborne Ho. *Shaw* 5F **43**
   (off Cowie St.)
Goldbrook Clo. *Heyw* . . .4G **39**
Goldcraft Clo. *Heyw* 4G **39**
Goldcrest Clo. *M22* 6D **136**
Goldcrest Clo. *Wors* 4D **76**
Goldenhill Av. *M11* 2E **97**
Golden Sq. *Eccl* 4F **91**
   (off Golden St.)
Golden St. *Eccl* 4F **91**
Golden St. *Shaw* 5H **43**
Goldfinch Dri. *Bury* 6A **24**
Goldfinch Way. *Droy* 2C **98**
Goldie Av. *M22* 3D **148**
Goldrill Av. *Bolt* 5H **33**
Goldrill Gdns. *Bolt* 5H **33**
Goldsmith Av. *Oldh* 3A **58**
Goldsmith Av. *Salf* 3D **92**
Goldsmith Rd. *Stoc* 6F **111**
Goldsmith St. *Bolt* 3H **45**
Goldsmith Way. *Dent* . . .2G **129**
Goldstein Rd. *Los* 3A **44**
Gold St. *M1* 4E **95** (6B **6**)
Goldsworthy Rd. *Urm* . .4A **104**
Goldwick Wlk. *M23* 2E **135**
Golf Rd. *Hale* 2H **145**
Golf Rd. *Sale* 5F **123**
Golfview Dri. *Eccl* 1F **91**
Gomer Wlk. *M8* 5E **83**
Goodacre. *Hyde* 1F **115**
Gooden St. *Heyw* 4G **39**
Goodier Ho. Fold.
   Hyde 3D **114**
Goodiers Dri. *Salf* 5G **93**
Goodier St. *M40* 6H **83**
Goodier St. *Sale* 5A **122**
Goodier Vw. *Hyde* 2D **114**
Good Intent. *Miln* 6G **29**
Goodison Clo. *Bury* 4F **51**
Goodlad St. *Bury* 1H **35**
Goodman St. *M9* 3G **83**
Goodrich. *Roch* 5G **27**
Goodridge Av. *M22* 4A **148**
Goodrington Rd.
   Hand 4A **160**
Goodshaw Rd. *Wors* 3E **77**
Good Shepherd Clo.
   Roch 3B **28**
Goodwill Clo. *Swin* 4F **79**
Goodwin Ct. *Chad* 5A **72**
Goodwin St. *Bolt* 5C **32**
Goodwood Av. *M23* 3D **134**
Goodwood Av. *Sale* 5E **121**
Goodwood Clo. *L Lev* . . .4H **47**
Goodwood Dri. *Salf* 5H **81**
   (off Bury New Rd.)
Goodwood Cres.
   Timp 5C **134**
Goodwood Dri. *Oldh* 6F **57**
Goodwood Dri. *Swin* 4H **79**
Goodwood Rd. *Marp* . . .6C **142**
Goodworth Wlk. *M40* . . .4A **84**
   (off Hanson Rd.)
Goole St. *M11* 5C **96**
Goose Cote Hill. *Eger* . . .1C **18**
Goose Grn. *All* 1F **145**
Goosehouse Grn.
   Rom 6B **130**
Goose La. *Roch* 3H **27**
Goosetrey Clo. *Wilm* . . .6A **160**
Goostrey Av. *M20* 1E **125**
Gordon Av. *M19* 6D **110**
Gordon Av. *Bolt* 2G **45**
Gordon Av. *Chad* 6G **71**
Gordon Av. *Haz G* 2D **152**
Gordon Av. *Oldh* 3F **73**
Gordon Av. *Sale* 3B **122**
Gordon Pl. *M20* 4F **125**

Gordon Rd. *Eccl* 2F **91**
Gordon Rd. *Swin* 5C **78**
Gordon St. *Abb M* 1G **111**
Gordon St. *Ash L* 1B **100**
Gordon St. *Bury* 2C **36**
Gordon St. *Chad* 5F **71**
Gordon St. *Hyde* 5C **114**
Gordon St. *Lees* 4A **74**
Gordon St. *Miln* 2F **43**
Gordon St. *Old T* 2B **108**
Gordon St. *Roch* 6A **28**
Gordon St. *Salf* 1B **94**
Gordon St. *Shaw* 6G **43**
   (in two parts)
Gordon St. *S'head* 3C **74**
Gordon St. *Stal* 4F **101**
Gordon St. *Stoc* 1G **139**
Gordon Ter. *M9* 3G **83**
Gordon Ter. *Stal* 3E **101**
Gordon Way. *Heyw* 4B **38**
Gore Av. *Fail* 3H **85**
Gore Av. *Salf* 3D **92**
Gorebrook Ct. *M12* 3C **110**
Gore Clo. *Heap B* 3G **37**
Gore Cres. *Salf* 2D **92**
Goredale Av. *M18* 4G **111**
Gore Dri. *Salf* 2D **92**
Gorelan Rd. *M18* 2F **111**
Gore St. *M1* 4F **95** (6C **6**)
Gore St.
   Salf (M3) . . .3C **94** (5E **5**)
Gore St. *Salf* (M6) 2G **93**
Goring Av. *M18* 1F **111**
Gorrells Clo. *Roch* 2D **40**
Gorrell St. *Roch* 6A **20**
Gorrells Way. *Roch* 2D **40**
   (in two parts)
Gorrells Way Ind. Est.
   Roch 2D **40**
Gorse Av. *Droy* 3C **98**
Gorse Av. *Marp* 5C **142**
Gorse Av. *Moss* 2G **89**
Gorse Av. *Oldh* 6G **73**
Gorse Av. *Stret* 4F **107**
Gorse Bank. *Bury* 2G **37**
Gorse Bank Rd. *Haleb* . .6C **146**
Gorse Cres. *Stret* 4F **107**
Gorse Dri. *L Hul* 3B **62**
Gorse Dri. *Stret* 4F **107**
Gorse Fld. Clo. *Rad* 3G **49**
Gorsefield Dri. *Swin* 4F **79**
Gorsefield Hey. *Wilm* . . .1H **167**
Gorse Hall Clo. *Duk* 6D **100**
Gorse Hall Dri. *Stal* 4D **100**
Gorse Hall Rd. *Duk* 6C **100**
Gorse Hill. 3E **107**
Gorselands. *Chea H* 2D **160**
Gorse La. *Stret* 4F **107**
Gorse Pit. *Bury* 2G **37**
Gorse Rd. *Miln* 5G **29**
Gorse Rd. *Swin* 5E **79**
Gorse Rd. *Wors* 1G **77**
Gorses Mt. *Bolt* 2E **47**
Gorse Sq. *Part* 6B **118**
Gorses Rd. *Bolt* 2F **47**
Gorse St. *Chad* 5F **71**
Gorse St. *Stret* 4E **107**
Gorse, The. *Bow* 5D **144**
Gorseway. *Stoc* 5B **128**
Gorsey Av. *M22* 6A **136**
Gorsey Bank. *L'boro* 2G **17**
Gorsey Bank Rd. *Stoc* . . .3C **138**
Gorsey Brow. *B'btm* 6C **116**
Gorsey Brow. *Rom* 1G **141**
Gorsey Brow. *Urm* 5H **105**
Gorsey Brow St. *Stoc* . . .2A **140**
Gorsey Clough Dri.
   T'ton 6H **21**
Gorsey Clough Wlk.
   T'ton 6H **21**
Gorsey Dri. *M22* 1A **148**
Gorseyfields. *Droy* 5A **98**

Gorsey Hill St. *Heyw* 4F **39**
Gorsey Intakes.
   B'btm 6C **116**
Gorsey La. *Alt* 6D **132**
Gorsey La. *Ash L* 5A **88**
Gorsey Mt. St. *Stoc* 2A **140**
            (Hall La.)
Gorsey Mt. St. *Stoc* 2H **139**
        (Up. Brook St.)
Gorsey Rd. *M22* 1A **148**
Gorsey Rd. *Wilm* 2C **166**
Gorsey Way. *Ash L* 5A **88**
Gorston Wlk. *M22* 5A **148**
Gort Clo. *Bury* 6E **51**
Gorton. 3F **111**
Gorton Cres. *Dent* 5C **112**
Gorton Cross Cen.
   M18 . . . . .2F **111**
Gorton Gro. *Wors* 4E **63**
Gorton Ind. Est. *M18* . . .1E **111**
Gorton La. *M12 &*
   M18 . . . . .6C **96**
Gorton Mkt. *M18* 2F **111**
Gorton Pk. *M18* 1E **111**
Gorton Rd.
   M11 & M12 . . . . .6B **96**
Gorton Rd. *Stoc* 1H **127**
Gorton St. *Ash L* 4F **99**
Gorton St. *Bolt* 1C **46**
Gorton St. *Chad* 3H **71**
Gorton St. *Eccl* 4C **90**
Gorton St. *Farn* 2D **62**
Gorton St. *Heyw* 3G **39**
Gorton St. *Salf* 3D **94** (3G **5**)
Gortonvilla Wlk. *M12* . . .1B **110**
Gosforth Clo. *Bury* 6C **22**
Gosforth Clo. *Oldh* 6E **57**
Gosforth Wlk. *M23* 2F **135**
Goshen Sports Cen. . . .1E **51**
Gosport Sq. *Salf* 6H **81**
Gosport Wlk. *M8* 5E **83**
     (off Smeaton St.)
Goss Hill St. *Oldh* 3G **73**
Gotha Wlk.
   M13 . . . . . .1G **109** (5F **11**)
Gotherage Clo. *Rom* 1C **142**
Gotherage La. *Rom* 1C **142**
Gothic Clo. *Rom* 1D **142**
Gough St. *Heyw* 3G **39**
Gough St. *Stoc* 2F **139**
Goulden Rd. *M20* 3E **125**
Goulden St. *M4* 3F **95** (3C **6**)
Goulden St. *Salf* 3E **93**
Goulder Rd. *M18* 4G **111**
Gould St. *M4* 2F **95** (1B **6**)
Gould St. *Dent* 4E **113**
Gould St. *Oldh* 1F **73**
Gourham Dri. *Chea H* . . .4B **150**
Govan St. *M22* 2C **136**
Gowan Dri. *Midd* 6F **53**
Gowanlock's St. *Bolt* 3A **32**
Gowan Rd. *M16* 6C **108**
Gower Av. *Haz G* 2C **152**
Gower Ct. *Hyde* 1C **130**
Gowerdale Rd. *Stoc* 4C **128**
Gower Rd. *Hyde* 6B **114**
Gower Rd. *Stoc* 5F **127**
Gowers St. *Roch* 3B **28**
Gower St. *Ash L* 2A **100**
Gower St. *Bolt* 5H **31**
Gower St. *Farn* 6E **47**
Gower St. *Oldh* 2E **73**
Gower St. *Swin* 2G **79**
Gowran Pk. *Oldh* 3H **73**
Gowy Clo. *Wilm* 5A **160**
Goya Ri. *Oldh* 3H **57**
Goyt Av. *Marp* 1D **154**
Goyt Cres. *Bred* 6F **129**
Goyt Cres. *Stoc* 6B **128**
Goyt Rd. *Dis* 2H **165**
Goyt Rd. *Marp* 1D **154**

Goyt Rd. *Stoc* 6B **128**
Goyt Valley. *Rom* 1E **141**
Goyt Valley Rd. *Bred* 6F **129**
Goyt Valley Wlk.
   Bred 6F **129**
Goyt Vw. *Rom* 1F **141**
Goyt Wlk. *W'fld* 5F **51**
Grace St. *Roch* 1A **28**
Grace Wlk. *M4* . . .4H **95** (6H **7**)
Gracie Av. *Oldh* 6F **57**
Gradwell St. *Stoc* 3F **139**
Grafton Av. *Eccl* 1A **92**
Grafton Ct. *M15* 2B **108**
Grafton Ct. *Roch* 5B **28**
Grafton Mall. *Alt* 1F **145**
Graftons, The. *Alt* 1F **145**
     (in two parts)
Grafton St. *M13* 2F **109**
Grafton St. *Alt* 1F **145**
     (in two parts)
Grafton St. *Ash L* 3B **100**
     (in three parts)
Grafton St. *Bolt* 5H **31**
Grafton St. *Bury* 5D **36**
Grafton St. *Fail* 3G **85**
Grafton St. *Hyde* 4B **114**
Grafton St. *Mill* 2H **101**
Grafton St. *Oldh* 3A **58**
Grafton St. *Roch* 5B **28**
Grafton St. *Stoc* 6G **127**
Graham Cres. *Cad* 5A **118**
Graham Dri. *Dis* 6G **155**
Graham Rd. *Salf* 1C **92**
Graham Rd. *Stoc* 3B **140**
Graham St. *M11* 5C **96**
Graham St. *Bolt* 5B **32**
Grainger Av. *M12* 4C **110**
Grains Bar. 1C **58**
Grains Rd. *Del* 1C **58**
Grains Rd. *Shaw* 1G **57**
Grain Vw. *Salf* 5G **93**
Gralam Clo. *Sale* 2E **135**
Grammar School Rd.
   Oldh 1H **85**
Grampian Clo. *Chad* 4G **71**
Grampian Way. *Shaw* . . .5D **42**
Granada M. *M16* 6C **108**
Granada Rd. *Dent* 4H **111**
Granary La. *Wors* 6H **77**
Granary Way. *Sale* 1H **133**
Granby Ho.
   M1 . . . . . .5E **95** (2B **10**)
Granby Rd. *Chea H* 5D **150**
Granby Rd. *Stoc* 6B **140**
Granby Rd. *Stret* 6D **106**
Granby Rd. *Swin* 4C **78**
Granby Rd. *Timp* 2B **134**
Granby Row.
   M1 . . . . . .5E **95** (2B **10**)
     (in two parts)
Granby St. *Chad* 6G **71**
Granby St. *T'ton* 1F **35**
Grandale St. *M14* 4G **109**
Grand Central Pools.
   . . . . .3G **139**
Grand Central Sq.
   Stoc 2G **139**
Grand Central Way.
   Stoc 2G **139**
Grandidge St. *Roch* 6G **27**
Grand Union Way. *Eccl* . .5F **91**
Grandville Clo. *Alt* 4F **133**
Grange. 1H **59**
Grange Av. *Chea H* 2B **150**
Grange Av. *Dent* 5H **113**
Grange Av. *Eccl* 1F **91**
Grange Av. *Hale* 3A **146**
Grange Av. *Lev* 1B **126**
Grange Av. *L Lev* 4C **48**
Grange Av. *Miln* 1D **42**
Grange Av. *Oldh* 5A **72**
Grange Av. *Stoc* 4F **127**

Grange Av. *Stret* 5D **106**
Grange Av. *Swin* 1D **78**
Grange Av. *Timp* 4B **134**
Grange Av. *Urm* 5A **104**
Grange Clo. *Hyde* 6D **114**
Grange Ct. *Bow* 4E **145**
Grange Ct. *Oldh* 5B **72**
Grange Cres. *Urm* 6E **105**
Grange Dri. *M9* 6H **69**
Grange Dri. *Eccl* 1F **91**
Grangeforth Rd. *M8* 3B **82**
Grange Gro. *W'fld* 1D **66**
Grange La. *M20* 1F **137**
Grange La. *Del* 1H **59**
Grange Mnr. *Brom X* 3G **19**
Grange Mill Wlk. *M40* . . .4B **84**
Grange Pk. Av. *Ash L* . . .5B **88**
Grange Pk. Av. *Chea* . . .6H **137**
Grange Pk. Av. *Wilm* . . .1D **166**
Grange Pk. Rd. *M9* 6H **69**
Grange Pk. Rd.
   Brom X 5G **19**
Grange Pk. Rd. *Chea* . . .6H **137**
Grange Pl. *Cad* 4B **118**
Grange Rd. *M21* 5G **107**
Grange Rd. *Bolt* 2F **45**
Grange Rd. *Bow* 4E **145**
Grange Rd. *Bram* 2H **151**
Grange Rd. *Brom X* 4G **19**
Grange Rd. *Bury* 3H **35**
Grange Rd. *Eccl* 1C **90**
Grange Rd. *Farn* 6C **46**
Grange Rd. *Midd* 1D **54**
Grange Rd. *Sale* 5H **121**
Grange Rd. *Timp* 4B **134**
Grange Rd. *Urm* 6E **105**
Grange Rd. *Whitw* 3H **15**
Grange Rd. *Wors* 4A **76**
Grange Rd. N. *Hyde* 5D **114**
Grange Rd. S. *Hyde* 6D **114**
     (in two parts)
Grange St. *Fail* 5D **84**
Grange St. *Oldh* 2C **72**
Grange St. *Roch* 1H **27**
Grange St. *Salf* 3E **93**
Grange, The. *M14* 4G **109**
Grange, The. *Hyde* 6D **114**
Grange, The. *Oldh* 1F **73**
Grangethorpe Dri. *M19* . .2A **126**
Grangethorpe Rd. *M14* . .5G **109**
Grangethorpe Rd. *Urm* . .6E **105**
Grange Wlk. *Midd* 5G **53**
Grangeway. *Hand* 3H **159**
Grangewood. *Brom X* . . .4G **19**
Grangewood Dri. *M9* 4F **83**
Granite St. *Oldh* 1F **73**
Gransden Dri. *M8* 5E **83**
Granshaw St. *M40* 2A **96**
Gransmoor Av. *M11* 6H **97**
Gransmoor Rd. *M11* 6H **97**
Grantchester Pl. *Farn* . . .6B **46**
Grantchester Way. *Bolt* . .4G **33**
Grant Clo. *M9* 1F **83**
Grantham Clo. *Bolt* 4A **32**
Grantham Dri. *Bury* 6D **22**
Grantham Rd. *Stoc* 1E **139**
Grantham St. *M14* 4E **109**
Grantham St. *Oldh* 4E **73**
Grant M. *Rams* 2D **12**
Grants Entry. *Rams* 3D **12**
     (off Young St.)
Grants La. *Rams* 3E **13**
Grant St. *Farn* 5D **46**
Grant St. *Roch* 3D **40**
Granville Av. *M16* 5A **108**
Granville Av. *Salf* 3A **82**
Granville Clo. *Chad* 2A **72**
Granville Ct. *M16* 4A **108**
Granville Ct. *Miln* 2F **43**
Granville Gdns. *M20* 1E **137**
Granville Rd. *M14* 1G **125**
Granville Rd. *Aud* 4B **98**

Granville Rd. *Bolt* 4G **45**
Granville Rd. *Chea H* . . .6D **138**
Granville Rd. *Timp* 5C **134**
Granville Rd. *Urm* 4G **105**
Granville Rd. *Wilm* 4C **166**
Granville St. *Ash L* 3B **100**
Granville St. *Chad* 1A **72**
Granville St. *Eccl* 2F **91**
Granville St. *Farn* 5F **47**
Granville St. *Oldh* 6C **56**
Granville St. *Swin* 3F **79**
Granville St. *Wors* 6E **63**
     (in three parts)
Granville Wlk. *Chad* 1A **72**
Grasdene Av. *M9* 6G **69**
Grasmere Av. *Farn* 2B **62**
Grasmere Av. *Heyw* 5F **39**
Grasmere Av. *L Lev* 3A **48**
Grasmere Av. *Stoc* 3G **127**
Grasmere Av. *Swin* 1C **78**
Grasmere Av. *Urm* 6A **104**
Grasmere Av. *W'fld* 2A **66**
Grasmere Clo. *Stal* 1E **101**
Grasmere Cres. *Bram* . . .5G **151**
Grasmere Cres. *Eccl* 2D **90**
Grasmere Cres.
   H Lane 4C **154**
Grasmere Gro. *Ash L* . . .1F **99**
Grasmere Rd. *Ald E* 5G **167**
Grasmere Rd. *Gat* 2F **149**
Grasmere Rd. *Oldh* 3G **73**
Grasmere Rd. *Part* 6C **118**
Grasmere Rd. *Rytn* 1A **56**
Grasmere Rd. *Sale* 1C **134**
Grasmere Rd. *Stret* 4D **106**
Grasmere Rd. *Swin* 5F **79**
Grasmere Rd. *Timp* 5C **134**
Grasmere St. *M12* 4D **110**
Grasmere St. *Bolt* 3B **32**
Grasmere St. *Roch* 2H **27**
Grasmere Wlk. *Midd* 5H **53**
Grason Av. *Wilm* 6G **159**
Grasscroft. 3G **75**
Grasscroft. *Stoc* 3C **128**
Grasscroft Clo. *M14* 5D **108**
Grasscroft Clough. 3G **75**
Grasscroft Rd. *Stal* 4E **101**
Grassfield Av. *Salf* 5G **81**
Grassholme Dri. *Stoc* . . .5G **141**
Grassingham Gdns.
   Salf 2F **93**
Grassington Av. *M40* 2A **84**
Grassington Ct. *Wals* 1F **35**
Grassington Dri. *Bury* . . .4H **37**
Grassington Pl. *Bolt* 4C **32**
Grassland Ri. *L Hul* 5A **62**
Grass Mead. *Dent* 1G **129**
Grassmoor Cres. *Glos* . . .5F **117**
Grathome Wlk. *Bolt* 4A **46**
Gratrix Av. *Salf* . . .6H **93** (4A **8**)
Gratrix La. *Sale* 6F **123**
Gratrix St. *M18* 3G **111**
Gratten Ct. *Wors* 5E **63**
Gravel Bank Rd.
   Woodl 3H **129**
Gravel Hole. 5A **42**
Gravel La. *Salf* 3C **94** (4F **5**)
     (in two parts)
Gravel La. *Wilm* 5B **166**
Gravel Walks. *Oldh* 2F **73**
Gravenmoor Dri. *Salf* . . .5A **82**
Graver La. *M40* 6D **84**
     (in three parts)
Graves St. *Rad* 1F **49**
Gray Clo. *Mot* 4B **116**
Graymar Rd. *L Hul* 5C **62**
Graymarsh Dri. *Poy* 5E **163**
Grayrigg Wlk. *M9* 4F **83**
Graysands Rd. *Hale* 2H **145**
Grayson Av. *W'fld* 1E **67**
Grayson Rd. *L Hul* 5D **62**
Grayson Way. *G'fld* 3F **61**

Grayston Ct. *Marp B* 4F **143**
Gray St. *Bolt* 5A **32**
Gray St. N. *Bolt* 5A **32**
Graythorpe Wlk. *Salf* 4G **93**
Graythorp Wlk. *M14* 4F **109**
Graythwaite Rd. *Dolt* 3D **30**
Grazing Dri. *Irlam* 4F **103**
Greame St.
   M16 & M14 . . . .4D **108**
Gt. Ancoats St.
   M4 . . . . .3F **95** (4C **6**)
Gt. Arbor Way. *Midd* 6H **53**
   (in two parts)
Gt. Bent Clo. *Roch* 5B **16**
Gt. Boys Clo. *Tyl* 2A **76**
Gt. Bridgewater St.
   M1 . . . . . . .5C **94** (2F **9**)
Gt. Cheetham St. E.
   Salf 5A **82**
Gt. Cheetham St. W.
   Salf 6G **81**
Gt. Clowes St.
   Salf & M3 . . .6H **81** (1D **4**)
   (Cheetham)
Gt. Clowes St. *Salf* 5G **81**
   (Higher Broughton)
Gt. Ducie St.
   M3 . . . . . . .2D **94** (1G **5**)
Gt. Eaves Rd. *Rams* 2E **13**
Gt. Egerton St. *Stoc* 2G **139**
Greater Manchester
   Police Mus. 5C **6**
Greatfield Rd. *M22* 2H **147**
Great Flatt. *Roch* 2D **26**
Gt. Gable Clo. *Oldh* 1E **73**
Gt. Gates Clo. *Roch* 1G **41**
Gt. Gates Rd. *Roch* 2G **41**
Gt. George St. *Roch* 5H **27**
   (in two parts)
Gt. George St.
   Salf 3B **94** (4C **4**)
Gt. Hall Clo. *Rad* 3G **49**
Gt. Heaton Clo. *Midd* . . .2E **69**
Great Holme. *Bolt* 3B **46**
Great Horrocks. 1F **95**
Great Howarth. 5H **15**
Great Howarth. *Roch* 5H **15**
Gt. Jackson St.
   M15 . . . . . .6C **94** (3E **9**)
Gt. John St. *M3* . .5C **94** (1E **9**)
Gt. Jones St. *M12* 1C **110**
Great Lee. *Roch* 6D **14**
Gt. Lee Wlk. *Roch* 6D **14**
   (in two parts)
Great Lever. 4B **46**
Gt. Marlborough St.
   M1 . . . . . .6E **95** (3A **10**)
Gt. Marld Clo. *Bolt* 3D **30**
Great Meadow. *Shaw* 5D **42**
Gt. Moor St. *Bolt* 1H **45**
Gt. Moor St. *Stoc* 6B **140**
Gt. Newton St. *M40* 6C **84**
Gt. Norbury St. *Hyde* . . .4A **114**
Great Northern.
   . . . . .5D **94** (1G **9**)
Great Northern. *M3* 5D **94**
Gt. Portwood St. *Stoc* . . .1H **139**
Gt. Southern St. *M14* 4F **109**
Great Stone Clo. *Rad* 4D **48**
Great Stone Rd.
   Stret & M16 . . . . . .3F **107**
Gt. Stones Clo. *Eger* 1C **18**
Great Underbank.
   Stoc 2H **139**
Gt. Western St.
   M16 & M14 . . . .4C **108**
Greave. 3D **26**
Greave. *Rom* 5B **130**
Greave Av. *Roch* 3D **26**
Greavefold. 5B **130**
Greave Fold. *Rom* 5A **130**
Greave Pk. *Upperm* 2F **61**

Greave Rd. *Stoc* 3C **140**
Greaves Av. *Fail* 5D **84**
Greaves Rd. *Wilm* 2A **166**
Greaves St. *Lees* 3B **74**
Greaves St. *Moss* 1E **89**
Greaves St. *Oldh* 2D **72**
Greaves St. *Shaw* 6G **43**
Grebe Clo. *Poy* 3B **162**
Grebe Wlk. *Stoc* 1G **153**
Grecian Cres. *Bolt* 3B **46**
Grecian Av. *Salf* 6G **81**
Grecian St. N. *Salf* 5G **81**
Grecian Tor. *Salf* 6C **81**
Gredle Clo. *Urm* 5H **105**
Greeba Rd. *Round I* 5E **135**
Greek St. *M1* . . .6F **95** (4C **10**)
Greek St. *Stoc* 3G **139**
Greenacre. *H Grn* 6G **149**
Greenacre Clo. *Rams* 2G **13**
Greenacre La. *Wors* 6H **77**
Grn. Acre Pk. *Bolt* 4B **32**
Greenacres. 2H **73**
Greenacres Ct. *Roch* 5B **16**
Greenacres Dri. *M19* 5A **126**
Greenacres Hill. 1G **73**
Greenacres Moor. 1G **73**
Greenacres Rd. *Oldh* 2F **73**
Green & Slater Homes.
   Stoc 6C **126**
Green Av. *Bolt* 4D **46**
Green Av. *L Hul* 4A **62**
Green Av. *Swin* 4F **79**
Green Bank. *Bolt* 2G **33**
Green Bank. *Farn* 6E **47**
Greenbank. *Had* 2H **117**
Green Bank. *Stoc* 2F **127**
Greenbank. *Whitw* 4C **14**
   (off Tonacliffe Rd.)
Greenbank Av. *Gat* 6E **137**
Greenbank Av. *Stoc* 1A **138**
Greenbank Av. *Swin* 5D **78**
Greenbank Av. *Upperm* . . .6C **60**
Greenbank Cres.
   Marp 6D **142**
Greenbank Dri. *L'boro* 6D **16**
Greenbank Ho. *Bow* 2F **145**
Greenbank Rd. *Bolt* 2F **45**
   (in two parts)
Greenbank Rd. *Gat* 6E **137**
Greenbank Rd. *Marp B* . .2F **143**
Greenbank Rd. *Rad* 2F **49**
Greenbank Rd. *Roch* 2H **27**
   (in two parts)
Greenbank Rd. *Sale* 4G **121**
Greenbank Rd. *Salf* 2E **93**
Greenbank Ter. *Midd* 6C **54**
Greenbank Ter. *Stoc* 1G **139**
Green Beech Clo.
   Marp 4C **142**
Greenbooth Clo. *Duk* 6D **100**
Greenbooth Rd. *Roch* . .1H **25**
Grn. Bridge Clo. *Roch* 1F **41**
Green Bri. La. *G'fld* 4E **61**

Greenbrook Bus. Pk.
   Bury 1E **37**
Greenbrook Clo. *Bury* 1E **37**
Greenbrook St. *Bury* 1E **37**
Greenbrow Pde. *M23* . . .1G **147**
Greenbrow Rd. *M23* 6G **135**
   (in two parts)
Greenburn Dri. *Bolt* 3G **33**
Green Clo. *Gat* 5E **137**
Green Clough. *L'boro* 1H **17**
Greencourt Dri. *L Hul* 5B **62**
Green Courts. *Bow* 2D **144**
Greencourts Bus. Pk.
   M22 . . . . .5E **149**
Green Cft. *Rom* 6B **130**
Greencroft. *Rom* 2D **55**
Greencroft Rd. *Eccl* 1D **90**
Greencroft Way. *Smal* . . .6B **16**
Greendale Dri. *M9* 6G **69**

Greendale Gro. *Dent* 1H **129**
Green Dri. *M19* 6B **110**
Green Dri. *Los* 6A **30**
Green Dri. *Timp* 4A **134**
Green Dri. *Wilm* 5H **159**
Green End. 4B **126**
Green End. *Dent* 1H **129**
Green End Rd. *M19* 4A **126**
Greenfield. 3E **61**
Greenfield Av. *Eccl* 5C **90**
Greenfield Av. *Urm* 5F **105**
Greenfield Clo. *Bury* 4G **35**
Greenfield Clo. *Stoc* 5G **139**
Greenfield Clo. *Timp* 5C **134**
Greenfield Ct. *Heyw* 4F **39**
Greenfield La. *Roch* 1G **41**
Greenfield La. *Shaw* 1F **57**
Greenfield La. *Smal* 6B **16**
Greenfield Rd. *L Hul* 5D **62**
Greenfield St. *Aud* 6D **98**
Greenfield St. *Had* 1H **117**
Greenfield St. *Hyde* 5B **114**
Greenfield St. *Roch* 1G **41**
Greenfield Ter. *Urm* 5A **104**
Green Fold. *M18* 1H **111**
Greenford Av. *Farn* 2D **62**
Greenford Clo. *Chea H* . . .1D **150**
Greenford Rd. *M8* 4C **82**
Grn. Gables Clo.
   H Grn 4F **149**
Green Gate. 2A **42**
   (Balderstone)
Greengate. 6B **16**
   (Smallbridge)
Greengate.
   M24 & Midd 6C **70**
Green Ga. *Hyde* 1D **156**
Green Ga. *Hyde* 1B **130**
Greongate. *Salf* . .2D **94** (2G **5**)
Greengate Clo. *Roch* 5B **16**
Greengate E. *M40* 6C **70**
Greengate Ind. Est.
   Midd 4C **70**
Greengate La. *Bolt* 5H **33**
Greengate La. *P'wich* 5E **67**
Greengate Rd. *Dent* 3G **113**
Greengate St. *Midd* 3D **70**
Greengate St. *Oldh* 3E **73**
   (in three parts)
Greengate W.
   Salf 2C **94** (2E **5**)
Greengrove Bank.
   Roch 6A **16**
Greenhalgh Moss La.
   Bury 6B **22**
Greenhalgh St. *Fail* 5C **84**
Greenhalgh St. *Stoc* 1G **139**
Greenhalgh Wlk.
   M4 . . . . . . .3G **95** (5E **7**)
   (off Jackroom Dri.)
Greenhall M. *Wilm* 3E **167**
Greenham Rd. *M23* 1F **135**
Greenhead Fold. *Rom* . . .2G **141**
Greenhead Wlk. *Bolt* 3A **46**
Greenheys. 2E **109**
   (Manchester)
Greenheys. 3A **62**
   (Walkden)
Greenheys. *Bolt* 3G **33**
Greenheys. *Droy* 3A **98**
Greenheys Bus. Cen.
   M15 . . . . .2E **109**
Greenheys Cen. *M14* 3E **109**
Greenheys Cres. *G'mnt* . .2H **21**
Greenheys La. *M15* 2D **108**
   Greenheys La. W.
   M15 . . . . .2C **108**
Greenheys Rd. *L Hul* 3A **62**
Green Hill. 2D **70**
   (Manchester)
Green Hill. 4C **42**
   (Oldham)

Green Hill. *P'wich* 5E **67**
Greenhill Av. *Bolt* 2F **45**
Greenhill Av. *Farn* 3E **63**
Greenhill Av. *Roch* 3G **27**
Greenhill Av. *Sale* 3A **122**
Greenhill La. *Bolt* 3D **44**
Grn. Hill Pl. *Stoc* 4F **139**
Greenhill Cotts. *Moss* 1F **89**
Greenhill La. *Bolt* 3D **44**
Greenhill Pas. *Oldh* 3E **73**
Grn. Hill Rd. *M8* 4C **82**
Greenhill Rd. *Bury* 4G **35**
Grn. Hill Rd. *Hyde* 4D **114**
Greenhill Rd. *Midd* 2C **70**
Grn. Hill Rd. *Timp* 5C **134**
Grn. Hill St. *Stoc* 4F **139**
Greenhill Ter. *Midd* 2C **70**
Grn. Hill Ter. *Stoc* 4F **139**
Greenhill Terraces.
   Oldh 3E **73**
Greenhill Wlk. *Dis* 1H **165**
Grn. Hollow Fold.
   Carr 1H **101**
Greenholme Clo. *M40* . . .2D **84**
Greenhow St. *Droy* 5H **97**
Greenhurst Cres. *Oldh* . . .1E **87**
Greenhurst La. *Ash L* 5A **88**
Greenhurst Rd. *Ash L* . . .4H **87**
Grn. Hythe Rd.
   H Grn 1G **159**
Greening Rd. *M19* 5D **110**
Greenland Rd.
   Bolt & Farn 4B **46**
Greenlands Clo.
   Chea H 5A **150**
Greenland St. *M8* 4B **82**
Greenland St. *Salf* 3E **93**
Green La. *M18* 1F **111**
Grcen La. *Ald E* 5F **167**
Green La. *Ash L* 6F **87**
Green La. *Bolt* (BL1) 6B **32**
Green La. *Bolt* (BL3) 4B **46**
Green La. *Cad* 4B **118**
Green La. *Del* 3G **59**
Green La. *Dis* 3H **165**
Green La. *Eccl* 3E **91**
Green La. *Fail* 1G **97**
Green La. *Had* 3H **117**
Green La. *Haz G* 2D **152**
Green La. *Heyw* 3G **39**
Green La. *Holl* 1F **117**
Green La. *Hyde* 5E **115**
   (Mottram Rd.)
Green La. *Hyde* 5E **115**
   (St Paul's Hill Rd.)
Green La. *Kear* 2A **64**
Green La. *Midd* 5B **54**
   (Hilton Fold La.)
Green La. *Midd* 2D **70**
   (Joshua La.)
Green La. *Moss* 5D **74**
Green La. *Oldh* 1B **86**
   (Middle Ga.)
Green La. *Oldh* 5B **58**
   (Waterworks Rd.)
Green La. *Poy* 3A **164**
Green La. *Roch* 3G **27**
Green La. *Rom* 2H **141**
Green La. *Sale* 3G **121**
Green La. *Stoc* 6D **126**
Green La. *Timp* 2B **148**
   (in two parts)
Green La. *W'fld* 6C **50**
Green La. *Wilm* 2E **167**
Green La. Ind. Est.
   Stoc 1E **139**
Green La. N. *Timp* 6B **134**
Greenlaw Ct. *M16* 2A **108**
Greenlea Av. *M18* 4F **111**
Greenleach La. *Wors* 3H **77**
Greenleaf Clo. *Wors* 5B **76**
Greenleas. *Los* 1A **44**

Greenlees St.—Grosvenor Ho.

Greenlees St. *Roch* 3H **27**
Greenleigh Clo. *Bolt* 6B **18**
Green Mdw. *Roch* 5B **16**
Green Meadows.
Marp 4D **142**
Green Meadows Dri.
Marp 4D **142**
Green Mdw. Wlk.
M22 . . . . .4C **148**
Greenmount. **2H 21**
Greenmount Clo.
G'mnt 1H **21**
Greenmount Ct. *Bolt* 5E **31**
Grn. Mount Dri. *G'mnt* . . .1H **21**
Greenmount Dri. *Heyw* . . .6H **39**
Greenmount Ho. *Bolt* 6E **31**
Greenmount La. *Bolt* 5E **31**
Greenmount Pk. *Kear* 2A **64**
Greenoak. *Rad* 2C **64**
Greenoak Dri. *Sale* 2C **134**
Greenoak Dri. *Wors* 4E **63**
Greenock Clo. *Bolt* 2C **44**
Greenock Dri. *Heyw* 4B **38**
Grn. Park Clo. *G'mnt* 2H **21**
Greenpark Rd. *M22* 2B **136**
Grn. Park Vw. *Oldh* 5H **57**
Green Pastures. *Stoc* . . .2H **137**
Green Rd. *Part* 6C **118**
Green Room Theatre. . . .**3H 9**
Greenroyd Av. *Bolt* 3G **33**
Greenroyde. *Roch* 6G **27**
Greenshank Clo. *Roch* . . .4B **26**
Greenside. **3H 97**
Greenside. *Bolt* 4C **34**
(in two parts)
Greenside. *Farn* 6E **47**
Greenside. *Stoc* 2C **138**
Greenside. *Wors* 6A **78**
Greenside Av. *Kear* 3H **63**
Greenside Av. *Oldh* 5H **57**
Greenside Clo. *Duk* 5E **101**
Greenside Clo. *Hawk* 1D **20**
Greenside Ct. *Eccl* 2F **91**
Greenside Cres. *Droy* 3H **97**
Greenside Dri. *G'mnt* 3G **21**
Greenside Dri. *Hale* 4G **145**
Greenside Dri. *Irlam* 6D **102**
Greenside La. *Droy* 2G **97**
Greenside Pl. *Dent* 1G **129**
Greenside St. *M11* 5D **96**
Greenside St. *Bolt* 4C **34**
Greenside Trad. Cen.
Droy 4A **98**
Greenside Way. *Midd* 4C **70**
Greenson Dri. *Midd* 2G **69**
Greenstead Av. *M8* 3C **82**
Greens, The. *Whitw* 4G **15**
Greenstone Dri. *Salf* 6D **80**
Green St. *M14* 2H **125**
Green St. *Ald E* 5G **167**
Green St. *Bury* 1H **35**
Green St. *Eccl* 5D **90**
Green St. *Farn* 6E **47**
Green St. *Hyde* 6C **114**
Green St. *Midd* 6B **54**
(in two parts)
Green St. *Oldh* 3B **72**
Green St. *Rad* 4G **49**
Green St. *Rams* 2B **12**
Green St. *Stoc* 5H **139**
Green St. *Stret* 1C **122**
Green St. *Wals* 1F **35**
Green, The. *Chea H* 5B **150**
Green, The. *G'mnt* 2H **21**
Green, The. *Hand* 4A **160**
Green, The. *Marp* 2E **155**
Green, The. *Mill* 1H **101**
Green, The. *Oldh* 6E **73**
Green, The. *Part* 5D **118**
Green, The. *Roch* 2C **40**
Green, The. *Stoc* 6E **127**
Green, The. *Swin* 1H **79**
Green, The. *Timp* 4B **134**
(in two parts)
Green, The. *Wors* 6H **77**
Greenthorne Av. *Stoc* . . .2F **127**
Greenthorn Wlk. M15 . . .2D 108
(off Botham Clo.)
Green Tree Gdns.
Rom 1H **141**
Greenvale. *Roch* 3A **26**
Greenvale Cotts.
L'boro 1H **17**
Greenvale Ct. *Chea* 5G **137**
Greenvale Dri. *Chea* 5G **137**
Greenview Dri. *M20* 3G **137**
Greenview Dri. *Roch* 3C **26**
Grn. Villa Pk. *Wilm* 5B **166**
Green Wlk. *M16* 4A **108**
Green Wlk. *Bow* 2C **144**
Green Wlk. *Gat* 5E **137**
Green Wlk. *Mot* 5B **116**
Green Wlk. *Part* 6C **118**
Green Wlk. *Stret* 5B **106**
Green Wlk. *Timp* 4H **133**
Green Walks. *P'wich* 6G **67**
Greenwatch Clo. *Eccl* 4E **91**
Greenwater Mdw. *Holl* . . .2F **117**
Greenway. *M22* 3C **136**
Greenway. *Alt* 6C **132**
Green Way. *Bolt* 2C **32**
Greenway. *Bram* 1F **161**
Greenway. *Hyde* 6B **114**
Greenway. *Midd* 4H **69**
Green Way. *Mot* 5B **116**
Green Way. *Roch* 4B **40**
Greenway. *Rom* 2C **142**
Greenway. *Shaw* 4D **42**
Greenway. *Wilm* 3E **167**
Greenway Av. *M19* 1D **126**
Grn. Way Clo. *Bolt* 1C **32**
Greenway Clo. *Bury* 2H **35**
Greenway Clo. *Sale* 6G **121**
Greenway Dri. *Moss* 1D **88**
Greenway M. *Rams* 5E **13**
Greenway Rd. *H Grn* 1G **159**
Greenway Rd. *Timp* 3H **133**
Greenways. *M40* 2D **84**
Greenways. *Ash L* 5D **86**
Greenwich Clo. *M40* 1F **97**
Greenwich Clo. *Roch* 5B **26**
Greenwood Av. *Ash L* 5G **87**
(in two parts)
Greenwood Av. *Stoc* 5C **140**
Greenwood Av. *Swin* 2H **79**
Greenwood Av. *Wors* 6E **63**
Greenwood Bus. Cen.
Salf 4G **93**
Greenwood Clo. *Timp* . . .6D **134**
Greenwood Clo. *Wors* 4A **76**
Greenwood Dri. *Wilm* . . .1G **167**
Greenwood Gdns.
Bred 6F **129**
Greenwood Pl. L'boro 4F 17
(off Hare Hill Rd.)
Greenwood Rd. *M22* . . .2H **147**
Greenwoods La. *Bolt* 1H **33**
Greenwood St. *Alt* 1F **145**
Greenwood St. *Bar* 2D **86**
Greenwood St. *Farn* 1F **63**
Greenwood St. *L'boro* 4F **17**
Greenwood St. *Oldh* 1G **73**
(in two parts)
Greenwood St. *Roch* 4H **27**
Greenwood St. *Salf* 1F **93**
Greenwood St. *S'head* . . .4B **74**
Greenwood Va. Bolt 2B 32
(off Beryl St.)
Greenwood Va. S. Bolt . . .2B 32
(off Beryl St.)
Greenwood Va. S. *Bolt* . . .2A **32**
(Blackburn Rd.)
Greer St. *Open* 5E **97**
Greetland Dri. *M9* 5H **69**
Gregge St. *Heyw* 4G **39**
(in two parts)
Gregg M. *Wilm* 5F **159**
Gregory Av. *Bolt* 5G **33**
Gregory Av. *Rom* 2A **142**
Gregory St. *M12* 1B **110**
Gregory St. *Hyde* 2C **114**
Gregory St. *Oldh* 6A **72**
Gregory Way. *Stoc* 3H **127**
Gregson Fld. *Bolt* 3A **46**
(in two parts)
Gregson Rd. *Stoc* 3G **127**
Gregson St. *Oldh* 3D **72**
Greg St. *Stoc* 4G **127**
Greg St. Ind. Est.
Stoc 4G **127**
Grelley Wlk. *M14* 4F **109**
Grendale Av. *Haz G* 4E **153**
Grendale Av. *Stoc* 2B **140**
Grendale Dri. *M16* 2A **108**
Grendon Av. *Oldh* 5C **72**
Grendon St. *Bolt* 4G **45**
Grendon Wlk. *M12* 1C **110**
Grenfell Rd. *M20* 6E **125**
Grenham Av.
M15 . . . . . . .1B **108** (5C **8**)
Grenville Rd. *Haz G* 2C **152**
Grenville St. *Duk* 5A **100**
Grenville St. *Mill* 1H **101**
Grenville St. *Stoc* 3F **139**
Grenville Ter. *Ash L* 3B **100**
Grenville Wlk. L'boro 6G 17
(off Drake Rd.)
Gresford Clo. *M21* 1G **123**
Gresham Clo. *W'fld* 2B **66**
Gresham Dri. *Oldh* 2A **72**
Gresham St. *Bolt* 2B **32**
Gresham St. *Dent* 3F **113**
Gresham Wlk. *Stoc* 6G **127**
Gresham Way. *Sale* 2A **134**
Gresty Av. *M22* 4D **148**
Greswell St. *Dent* 3E **113**
Greta Av. *H Grn* 1G **159**
Greton Clo. *M13* 3A **110**
Gretton Clo. *Rytn* 3D **56**
Greville St. *M13* 3A **110**
Grey Clo. *Bred* 5G **129**
Grey Friar Ct.
Salf 2C **94** (2E **5**)
Greyfriars Rd. *M22* 3H **147**
Greyhound Dri. *Salf* 6F **81**
Grey Knotts. *Wors* 6C **76**
Greylag Cres. *Wors* 3F **77**
Greylands Clo. *Sale* 5H **121**
Greylands Rd. *M20* 3G **137**
Grey Mare La. *M11* 4B **96**
Greymont Rd. *Bury* 5F **23**
Grey Rd. *Alt* 6D **132**
Greysham Ct. *M16* 5C **108**
Greystoke Av. *M19* 6E **111**
Greystoke Av. *Sale* 6B **122**
Greystoke Av. *Timp* 5D **134**
Greystoke Cres. *W'fld* 5C **50**
Greystoke Dri. *Ald E* 4G **167**
Greystoke Dri. *Bolt* 5B **18**
Greystoke Dri. *Midd* 5F **53**
Greystoke La. *Fail* 5D **84**
Greystoke St. *Stoc* 2A **140**
Greystone Av. *M21* 1D **124**
Greystone Wlk. *Stoc* 2F **127**
Grey St. *M12* 1A **110**
Grey St. *Ash L* 3A **100**
Grey St. *Dent* 4D **112**
Grey St. *Midd* 6H **53**
Grey St. *P'wich* 5G **67**
Grey St. *Rad* 4H **49**
(in two parts)
Grey St. *Stal* 4G **101**
Greyswood Av. *M8* 4B **82**
Greytown Clo. *Salf* 6D **80**
Greywood Av. *Bury* 3F **37**
Grierson St. *M16* 3C **108**
Grierson St. *Bolt* 2A **32**
Griffe La. *Bury* 4G **51**
Griffin Clo. *Bury* 1F **37**
Griffin Ct. *Salf* 3C **94** (4E **5**)
Griffin Gro. *M19* 1C **126**
Griffin Ho. *Bury* 1E **37**
Griffin La. *H Grn* 6H **149**
Griffin Rd. *Fail* 4D **84**
Griffin St. *Salf* 5G **81**
Griffiths Clo.
Salf 1B **94** (1D **4**)
Griffiths St. *M40* 6C **84**
Grimes Cotts. *Roch* 2B **26**
Grimes St. *Roch* 2B **26**
Grime St. *Rams* 5C **12**
Grimscott Clo. *M9* 2H **83**
Grimshaw Av. *Fail* 3G **85**
Grimshaw Clo. *Bred* 5G **129**
Grimshaw La. *M40* 6H **83**
Grimshaw La. *Midd* 1B **70**
Grimshaw St. *Fail* 3E **85**
Grimshaw St. *Stoc* 2A **140**
Grimstead Clo. *M23* 5E **135**
Grindall Av. *M40* 1B **84**
Grindleford Gdns.
Glos 5G 117
(off Edale Cres.)
Grindleford Gro. Gam . . .5G 117
(off Edale Cres.)
Grindleford Lea. Glos . . .5G 117
(off Edale Cres.)
Grindleford Wlk. *M21* . . .4B **124**
Grindleford Wlk. Glos . . .5G 117
(off Edale Cres.)
Grindle Grn. *Eccl* 5E **91**
Grindley Av. *M21* 4B **124**
Grindlow St. *M13* 2A **110**
Grindon Av. *Salf* 4E **81**
Grindrod St. *Rad* 3F **49**
(in two parts)
Grindrod St. *Roch* 2G **27**
Grindsbrook Rd. *Rad* 6F **35**
Grinton Av. *M13* 5A **110**
Grisdale Dri. *Midd* 5G **53**
Grisdale Rd. *Bolt* 2G **45**
Grisebeck Way. *Oldh* 2C **72**
Grisedale Av. *Rytn* 5A **42**
Grisedale Ct. *M9* 5A **70**
Grisedale Rd. *Roch* 1B **40**
Gristlehurst La. *Bury* 6D **24**
Gritley Wlk. *M22* 4A **148**
Grizebeck Clo. *M18* 1E **111**
Grizedale Clo. *Bolt* 3D **30**
Grizedale Clo. *Carr* 4G **89**
Grizedale Rd. *Woodl* 5H **129**
Groby Ct. *Alt* 1E **145**
Groby Pl. *Alt* 6E **133**
Groby Rd. *M21* 1H **123**
Groby Rd. *Alt* 1D **144**
Groby Rd. *Aud* 6E **99**
Groby Rd. N. *Aud* 5D **98**
Groby St. *Oldh* 6E **73**
Groby St. *Stal* 4G **101**
Groom St. *M1* . . .6F **95** (3C **10**)
Grosvenor Av. *W'fld* 1C **66**
Grosvenor Clo. *Wilm* . . .5D **166**
Grosvenor Clo. *Wors* 4E **63**
Grosvenor Ct. *M16* 4C **108**
Grosvenor Ct. *Ash L* 4G **99**
Grosvenor Ct. *Chea* 5H **137**
Grosvenor Ct. *Sale* 4H **121**
Grosvenor Ct. *Salf* 3H **81**
Grosvenor Cres.
Hyde 6A **114**
Grosvenor Dri. *Poy* 4C **162**
Grosvenor Dri. *Wors* 4E **63**
Grosvenor Gdns.
M22 . . . . .5C **136**
Grosvenor Gdns. *Salf* 1B **94**
Grosvenor Gdns. *Stal* . . .4E **101**
Grosvenor Ho. M16 . . . .6C 108
(off Arnold Rd.)

Grosvenor Ho.—Hall Av.

Grosvenor Ho. Ash L 4G **99** *(off Park St.)*
Grosvenor Ho. *Sale* 5H **121**
Grosvenor Ho. M. *Crum* 1B **82**
Grosvenor Ho. Sq. *Stal* 4E **101**
Grosvenor Ind. Est. *Ash L* 4G **99**
Grosvenor Pl. *Ash L* 4G **99**
Grosvenor Rd. *M16* 5B **108**
Grosvenor Rd. *Alt* 6G **133**
Grosvenor Rd. *Chea H* 1E **151**
Grosvenor Rd. *Eccl* 2C **90**
Grosvenor Rd. *Hyde* 6B **114**
Grosvenor Rd. *Marp* 4D **142**
Grosvenor Rd. *Sale* 4H **121**
Grosvenor Rd. *Stoc* 6C **126** (in two parts)
Grosvenor Rd. *Swin* 4H **79**
Grosvenor Rd. *Urm* 5E **105**
Grosvenor Rd. *W'fld* 6C **50**
Grosvenor Rd. *Wors* 4E **63**
Grosvenor Sq. *M15* 6E **95** (4B **10**)
Grosvenor Sq. *Sale* 5H **121**
Grosvenor Sq. *Salf* 1B **94**
Grosvenor Sq. *Stal* 4E **101**
Grosvenor St. *M13 & M1* 6E **95** (4B **10**)
Grosvenor St. *Ash L* 4F **99** (in two parts)
Grosvenor St. *Bolt* 1C **46**
Grosvenor St. *Bury* 5D **36**
Grosvenor St. *Dent* 3D **112**
Grosvenor St. *Haz G* 2D **152**
Grosvenor St. *Heyw* 4E **39**
Grosvenor St. *Kear* 1H **63**
Grosvenor St. *L Lev* 3A **48**
Grosvenor St. *P'wich* 5G **67**
Grosvenor St. *Rad* 3F **49**
Grosvenor St. *Roch* 4C **40**
Grosvenor St. *Stal* 4E **101** (in two parts)
Grosvenor St. *Stoc* 3H **139**
Grosvenor St. *Stret* 5D **106**
Grosvenor St. *Swin* 1F **79**
Grosvenor Way. *Rytn* 5B **56**
Grotton. **4D 74**
Grotton Hollow. *G'ton* 3C **74**
Grotton Meadows. *G'ton* 4D **74**
Grouse St. *Roch* 2H **27**
Grove Av. *Fail* 6E **85**
Grove Av. *Wilm* 2D **166**
Grove Clo. *M14* 4G **109**
Grove Cotts. *Dig* 1D **60**
Grove Ct. *Haz G* 2E **153**
Grove Ct. *Sale* 5D **122**
Grove Hill. *Wors* 5B **76**
Grove Ho. *M15* 2F **109**
Grove Ho. *Stoc* 2A **138**
Grovehurst. *Swin* 5B **78**
Grove La. *M20* 6E **125**
Grove La. *Chea H* 1C **160**
Grove La. *Hale* 2A **146**
Grove La. *Timp* 4H **133**
Grove M. *Wors* 6F **63**
Grove Pk. *Sale* 5H **121**
Grove Rd. *Hale* 2G **145**
Grove Rd. *Midd* 5B **54**
Grove Rd. *Mill* 1H **101**
Grove Rd. *Upperm* 2F **61**
Grove St. *Ash L* 6C **86**
Grove St. *Bolt* 3H **31**
Grove St. *Droy* 5H **97**
Grove St. *Duk* 4B **100**
Grove St. *G'fld* 4F **61**
Grove St. *Haz G* 2E **153**
Grove St. *Heyw* 3G **39**
Grove St. *Kear* 1G **63**
Grove St. *Roch* 6G **27**
Grove St. *Salf* 6A **82**
Grove St. *Wilm* 2F **167**
Grove Ter. *Oldh* 1A **74**
Grove, The. *M20* 2F **137**
Grove, The. *Alt* 6F **133**
Grove, The. *Bolt* 2D **46**
Grove, The. *Chea H* 1C **160**
Grove, The. *Dob* 6H **59**
Grove, The. *Eccl* 4H **91**
Grove, The. *Had* 3H **117**
Grove, The. *L Lev* 4B **48**
Grove, The. *Sale* 6B **122**
Grove, The. *Shaw* 1E **57**
Grove, The. *Stoc* 4G **139**
Grove, The. *Urm* 6B **104**
Grove Way. *Wilm* 2E **167**
Grovewood Clo. *Ash L* 6C **86**
Grundey St. *Haz G* 3E **153**
Grundy Av. *P'wich* 1D **80**
Grundy Clo. *Bury* 4E **37**
Grundy La. *Bury* 5E **37**
Grundy Rd. *Kear* 2G **63**
Grundy St. *Bolt* 3H **45**
Grundy St. *Heyw* 5G **39**
Grundy St. *Oldh* 2E **73**
Grundy St. *Stoc* 1A **138**
Grundy St. *Wors* 1H **77**
Guardian Clo. *Roch* 4B **16**
Guardian Ct. *Sale* 4A **122**
Guardian Lodge. *Gat* 6E **137**
Guardian M. *M23* 2C **134**
Guernsey Clo. *M19* 3C **126**
Guest Rd. *P'wich* 3E **67**
Guide Bridge. **5F 99**
Guide Bri. Trad. Est. *Ash L* 5E **99**
Guide La. *Aud* 1F **113**
Guide Post Sq. *M13* 1H **109** (6G **11**)
Guide St. *Salf* 4C **92**
Guido St. *Bolt* 3H **31**
Guido St. *Fail* 4E **85**
Guild Av. *Wors* 1F **77**
Guildford Av. *Chea H* 1C **160**
Guildford Clo. *Stoc* 4B **140**
Guildford Dri. *Ash L* 4G **87**
Guildford Gro. *Midd* 4C **54**
Guildford Rd. *M19* 5D **110**
Guildford Rd. *Bolt* 3F **31**
Guildford Rd. *Duk* 6E **101**
Guildford Rd. *Salf* 1B **92**
Guildford Rd. *Urm* 3G **105**
Guildford St. *Moss* 2F **89**
Guildford St. *Roch* 4A **28** (in two parts)
Guildhall Clo. *Man S* 2E **109**
Guild St. *Brom X* 5E **19**
Guilford Rd. *Eccl* 4D **90**
Guiness Ho. *Roch* 5D **20**
Guinness Circ. *Traf P* 5A **92**
Guinness Rd. *Traf P* 5H **91**
Guinness Rd. Trad. Est. *Traf P* 5H **91**
Guiseley Clo. *Bury* 3E **23**
Gullane Clo. *M40* 4C **84**
Gull Clo. *Poy* 4B **162**
Gulvain Pl. *Chad* 1F **71**
Gunson Ct. *M40* 2G **95** (2F **7**)
Gunson St. *M40* 2G **95** (2F **7**)
Gun St. *M4* 3F **95** (4D **6**)
Gurner Av. *Salf* 6H **93**
Gurney St. *M4* 4H **95** (5H **7**)
Gutter End. *Bury* 3D **36**
Gutter La. *Rams* 2D **12**
Guy Fawkes St. *Salf* 6H **93**
Guy St. *Salf* 4B **82**
Guywood Cotts. *Rom* 6A **130**
Guywood La. *Rom* 6A **130**
Gwelo St. *M11* 3C **96**
Gwenbury Av. *Stoc* 2B **140**
Gwendor Av. *M8* 6B **68**
Gwladys St. *Carr* 5G **89**
Gwynant Pl. *M20* 2G **125**
Gwyneth Morley Ct. *Hand* 4H **159**
Gylden Clo. *Hyde* 1F **115**
Gypsy La. *Stoc* 5C **140** (in three parts)
Gypsy Wlk. *Stoc* 5C **140**

H

Habergham Clo. *Wors* 4E **77**
Hackberry Clo. *B'hth* 3D **132**
Hacken Bri. Rd. *Bolt* 3E **47**
Hacken La. *Bolt* 3E **47**
Hackford Clo. *Bolt* 5G **31**
Hackford Clo. *Bury* 6D **22**
Hacking St. *Bury* 3E **37**
Hacking St. *P'wich* 5F **67**
Hacking St. *Salf* 5A **82**
Hackle St. *M11* 3E **97**
Hackleton Clo. *M4* 4H **95** (5H **7**)
Hackness Rd. *M21* 1F **123**
Hackney Av. *M40* 1E **97**
Hackney Clo. *Rad* 2G **49**
Hackwood Wlk. M8 4B **82** *(off Levenhurst Rd.)*
Haddington Dri. *M9* 6G **69**
Haddon Av. *M40* 2F **85**
Haddon Clo. *Ald E* 4F **167**
Haddon Clo. *Bury* 2E **51**
Haddon Clo. *H Lane* 1C **164**
Haddon Grn. *Glos* 5F **117**
Haddon Gro. *Sale* 5A **122**
Haddon Gro. *Stoc* 2G **127**
Haddon Gro. *Timp* 4H **133**
Haddon Hall Rd. *Droy* 3G **97**
Haddon Ho. *Salf* 2D **92**
Haddon Lea. Glos 5F **117** *(off Haddon Grn.)*
Haddon M. *Glos* 5F **117**
Haddon Rd. *M21* 4B **124**
Haddon Rd. *Eccl* 5D **90**
Haddon Rd. *Haz G* 4E **153**
Haddon Rd. *H Grn* 6G **149**
Haddon Rd. *Wors* 5C **78**
Haddon St. *Roch* 1E **41**
Haddon St. *Salf* 6F **81**
Haddon St. *Stret* 3D **106**
Haddon Way. *Dent* 1G **129**
Haddon Way. *Shaw* 5G **43**
Hadfield Av. *Chad* 4H **71**
Hadfield Cres. *Ash L* 6A **88**
Hadfield Ind. Est. *Had* 1H **117**
Hadfield Rd. *Had* 3G **117**
Hadfields Av. *Holl* 2F **117**
Hadfield St. *M16* 1A **100** (6D **8**)
Hadfield St. *Duk* 6G **99**
Hadfield St. *Oldh* 6C **72**
Hadfield St. *Salf* 5A **82**
Hadfield Ter. *Ash L* 6A **88**
Hadleigh Clo. *Bolt* 5E **19**
Hadley Av. *M13* 5A **110**
Hadley Clo. *Chea H* 4B **150**
Hadley St. *Salf* 6F **81**
Hadlow Grn. *Stoc* 3B **128**
Hadlow Wlk. *M40* 2A **96**
Hadwin St. *Bolt* 4B **32**
Hafton Rd. *Salf* 5F **81**
Hag End Brow. *Bolt* 2E **47**
Haggate. **4A 56**
Haggate. *Rytn* 4A **56**
Haggate Cres. *Rytn* 4A **56**
Hagg Bank La. *Dis* 6H **155**
Hagley Rd. *Salf* 1G **107**
Hags, The. *Bury* 2E **51**
Hague Ct. *M20* 4E **125**
Hague Ho. *Oldh* 4D **72**
Hague Pl. *Stal* 3D **100**
Hague Rd. *M20* 4E **125**
Hague Rd. *B'btm* 6D **116** (in two parts)
Hague St. *M40* 6H **83**
Hague St. *Ash L* 1A **100**
Hague St. *Oldh* 1A **74**
Hague, The. **5E 117**
Haig Av. *Cad* 5A **118**
Haig Ct. *Bury* 4H **35**
Haigh Av. *Stoc* 4G **127**
Haigh Ct. *Heat M* 2B **138**
Haigh Hall Clo. *Rams* 5D **12**
Haigh La. *Chad* 6E **55**
Haigh Lawn. *Alt* 2D **144**
Haigh Pk. *Stoc* 4G **127**
Haigh St. *Roch* 5A **28**
Haig Rd. *Bury* 3H **35**
Haig Rd. *Stret* 4D **106**
Haile Dri. *Wors* 5B **76**
Hailsham Clo. *Bury* 4C **22**
Hail St. *Rams* 5C **12**
Hailwood St. *Roch* 1E **41**
Halbury Wlk. Bolt 3B **32** *(off Ulleswater St.)*
Halcyon Clo. *Roch* 1D **26**
Haldene Wlk. *M8* 5B **82**
Haldon Rd. *M20* 4H **125**
Hale. **3G 145**
Hale Av. *Poy* 5D **162**
Hale Bank Av. *M20* 2D **124**
Halebarns. **5C 146**
Hale Ct. *Bow* 2F **145**
Hale Grn. Ct. *Hale* 2A **146**
Hale La. *Fail* 3E **85**
Hale Low Rd. *Hale* 2H **145**
Hale Moss. **2H 145**
Hale Rd. *Alt & Hale* 2F **145**
Hale Rd. *Hale & Haleb* 4B **146**
Hale Rd. *Stoc* 6E **127**
Hales Clo. *Droy* 2H **97**
Halesden Rd. *Stoc* 4F **127**
Halesworth Wlk. *M40* 1G **95**
Haletop. *Wyth* 3B **148**
Hale Vw. *Hale* 3F **145**
Hale Wlk. *Chea* 1C **150**
Haley Clo. *Stoc* 1H **127**
Haley St. *M8* 4C **82**
Half Acre. **3F 67**
Half Acre. *Rad* 1E **49**
Half Acre Dri. *Roch* 5E **27** (in two parts)
Half Acre Grn. *Wilm* 1E **167**
Half Acre La. *Roch* 5D **26**
Half Acre La. *W'fld* 3F **67** (in two parts)
Half Acre M. *Roch* 5D **26**
Halfacre Rd. *M22* 1A **148**
Half Acre Rd. *Roch* 5D **26**
Half Edge La. *Eccl* 2G **91**
Half Moon La. *Stoc* 5D **140**
Half Moon St. *M2* 4D **94** (5H **5**)
Halford Dri. *M40* 3B **84**
Halfpenny Bri. Ind. Est. *Roch* 5A **28**
Half St. *Midd* 6H **53**
Half St. *Salf* 2C **94** (2F **5**)
Halifax Rd. *L'boro* 4G **17**
Halifax Rd. *Oldh* 2C **58**
Halifax Rd. *Roch* 2B **28**
Halifax St. *Ash L* 1H **99**
Haliwell St. *Bolt* 3H **31**
Hallam Rd. *M40* 6B **84**
Hallams Pas. *Stoc* 5A **140**
Hallam St. *Rad* 3D **50**
Hallam St. *Stoc* 5A **140**
Hallas Gro. *M23* 2H **135**
Hall Av. *M14* 4H **109**
Hall Av. *H'rod* 6E **89**
Hall Av. *Sale* 3G **121**
Hall Av. *Timp* 4H **133**

Hall Bank. *Eccl* 3E 91
Hallbottom St. *Hyde* . . .2D 114
Hall Clo. *Mot* 2C 116
Hall Coppice, The. *Eger* . . .1B 18
Hallcroft. *Part* 5D 118
Hallcroft Gdns. *Miln* 5E 29
Hall Dri. *Midd* 2H 69
Hall Dri. *Mot* 2C 116
Halle Mall. M4 . . . .*3E 95 (4A 6)*
   (off Arndale Shop. Cen.)
Halle Sq. M4 . . . . .*3E 95 (4A 6)*
   (off Arndale Shop. Cen.)
Hallfold. 1C 14
Hall Fold. *Had* 2H 117
Hall Fold. *Whitw* 1B 14
Hall Gdns. *Roch* 1E 27
Hallgate Dri. *H Grn* 3E 149
Hallgate Rd. *Stoc* 3B 140
Hall Grn. Clo. *Duk* 4A 100
Hall Grn. Rd. *Duk* 4A 100
Hall Gro. *M14* 4H 109
Hall Gro. *Chea* 5G 137
Halliday Ct. *L'boro* 5C 16
Halliday Rd. *M40* 1D 96
Halliford Rd. *M40* 5A 84
Hallington Clo. *Bolt* 2B 46
Hall i' th' Wood. 1D 32
Hall i' th' Wood. *Bolt* 1C 32
Hall i' th' Wood La.
   Bolt 2D 32
Hall i' th' Wood (Mus.)
   . . . . .1C 32
Halliwell. 3H 31
Halliwell Av. *Oldh* 6C 72
Halliwell Ind. Est. Bolt . . .*2H 31*
   (off Rossini St.)
Halliwell La. *M8* 4B 82
Halliwell Rd. *Bolt* 2G 31
Halliwell Rd. *P'wich* 2D 80
Halliwell St. *Chad* 2G 85
Halliwell St. *Fir & Miln* . . .4E 29
   (in two parts)
Halliwell St. *L'boro* 4G 17
Halliwell St. *Roch* 3G 27
   (in two parts)
Halliwell St. W. *M8* 4B 82
Halliwell Wlk. *P'wich* 2D 80
Hallkirk Wlk. *M40* 1D 84
Hall La. *M23* 5H 135
Hall La. *Farn* 5F 47
   (in two parts)
Hall La. *Part* 5D 118
Hall La. *Woodl* 3H 129
   (in two parts)
Hall Mdw. *Chea H* 4A 150
Hall Moss La. *Bram* 2D 160
Hall Moss Rd. *M9* 6A 70
Hall Pool Dri. *Stoc* 4E 141
Hall Rd. *M14* 4H 109
Hall Rd. *Ash L* 6G 87
Hall Rd. *Bow* 4E 145
Hall Rd. *Bram* 4F 151
Hall Rd. *Hand* 4A 160
Hall Rd. *Wilm* 2D 166
Hallroyd Brow. *Oldh* 1C 72
Halls Cotts. *G'fld* 3F 61
Hall's Pl. *S'head* 3B 74
Hallstead Av. *L Hul* 5A 62
Hallstead Gro. *L Hul* 5A 62
Hall St. *M2* 5D 94 (1H 9)
Hall St. *Ash L* 3C 100
Hall St. *Bolt* 5F 47
   (in two parts)
Hall St. *Bury* 1C 22
   (Railway St. W.)
Hall St. *Bury* 1A 36
   (Tottington Rd.)
Hall St. *Chea* 5G 137
Hall St. *Fail* 5D 84
Hall St. *Farn* 5F 47

Hall St. *Heyw* 4G 39
Hall St. *Hyde* 4H 113
Hall St. *Midd* 1A 70
Hall St. *Oldh* 2F 73
Hall St. *Rad* 1F 49
Hall St. *Rytn* 3B 56
Hall St. *Stoc* 2A 140
Hall St. *Swin* 1F 79
Hall St. *Wals* 1E 35
Hall St. *Whitw* 1C 14
Hallsville Rd. *M19* 6E 111
Halls Way. *G'fld* 3F 61
Hallsworth Rd. *Eccl* 4C 90
Hallwood Av. *Salf* 6A 80
Hallwood Rd. *M23* 5G 135
Hall Wood Rd. *Hand* 5H 159
Hallworth Av. *Aud* 4B 98
Hallworth Rd. *M8* 3D 82
Halmore Rd.
   M40 . . . . . . .3H 95 (3G 7)
Halsall Clo. *Bury* 5F 23
Halsall Dri. *Bolt* 5A 46
Halsbury Clo. *M12* 1A 110
Halsey Clo. *Chad* 1E 85
Halsey Wlk. *M8* 4B 82
Halshaw La. *Kear* 2H 63
Halsmere Dri. *M9* 6G 69
Halstead Av. *M21* 2G 123
Halstead Av. *Salf* 6C 80
Halstead Dri. *Irlam* 6F 103
Halstead Gro. *Gat* 1D 148
Halstead St. *Bolt* 6C 32
Halstead St. *Bury* 6G 23
Halstead Wlk. *Bury* 6G 23
Halstock Wlk. *M40* 6F 83
   (off Carslake Rd.)
Halstone Av. *Wilm* 5B 166
Halston St.
   M15 . . . . .1C 108 (6F 9)
Halter Clo. *Rad* 2G 49
Halton Bank. *Salf* 1F 93
Halton Ho. *Salf* 4F 93
Halton Rd. *M11* 3E 97
Halton St. *Bolt* 6D 32
Halton St. *Hyde* 4D 114
Halvard Av. *Bury* 5F 23
Halvard Ct. *Bury* 5F 23
Halvis Gro. *M16* 4H 107
Hambleden Clo. *Bolt* 2D 44
Hambleton Clo. *Bury* 4F 35
Hambleton Dri. *Sale* 4F 121
Hambleton Rd. *H Grn* . . .5G 149
Hambridge Clo. *M8* 4C 82
Hamel St. *Bolt* 4H 45
Hamel St. *Hyde* 2D 114
Hamer Ct. *Roch* 2B 28
Hamer Dri. *M16* 2B 108
Hamer Hall Cres. *Roch* . . .1B 28
Hamer Hill. *M9* 6E 69
Hamer La. *Roch* 2B 28
Hamer's Bldgs. *Heyw* 3D 38
Hamer St. *Bolt* 4D 32
Hamer St. *Rad* 3A 50
Hamer St. *Rams* 1B 22
Hamer Ter. *Bury* 6E 13
   (off Ruby St.)
Hamerton Rd. *M40* 1G 95
Hamilcar Av. *Eccl* 3G 91
Hamilton Av. *Cad* 5B 118
Hamilton Av. *Eccl* 4G 91
Hamilton Av. *Rytn* 4H 55
Hamilton Clo. *Bury* 2H 35
Hamilton Clo. *P'wich* 6E 67
Hamilton Ct. *L Lev* 4B 48
Hamilton Ct. *Sale* 5B 122
Hamilton Cres. *Stoc* 2D 138
Hamilton Gro. *M16* 2B 108
Hamilton Ho. *Alt* 6F 133
Hamilton Lodge. *M14* . . .4G 109

Hamilton M. *Eccl* 2D 90
Hamilton M. *P'wich* 6E 67
Hamilton Pl. *Ash L* 4F 99
Hamilton Rd. *M13* 4B 110
Hamilton Rd. *P'wich* 6E 67
Hamilton Rd. *W'fld* 1C 66
Hamilton Sq. *Stoc* 6G 127
Hamilton St. *Ash L* 4F 99
Hamilton St. *Bolt* 6C 18
Hamilton St. *Bury* 1D 36
Hamilton St. *Chad* 2G 71
Hamilton St. *Eccl* 2D 90
Hamilton St. *Oldh* 3E 73
Hamilton St. *Old T* 2B 108
Hamilton St. *Salf* 4H 81
Hamilton St. *Stal* 3D 100
Hamilton St. *Swin* 2D 78
Hamilton Way. *Heyw* 4A 38
Hamlet Dri. *Sale* 3G 121
Hamlet, The. *Los* 5A 30
Hammerstone Rd.
   M18 . . . . .1E 111
Hammer St. *Heyw* 3D 38
Hammett Rd. *M21* 1G 123
Hammond Av. *Stoc* 4G 127
Hammond Flats. Heyw . . .*3E 39*
   (off Ashton St.)
Hamnet Clo. *Bolt* 6E 19
Hamnett St. *M11* 4F 97
Hamnett St. *Hyde* 4B 114
Hamon Rd. *Alt* 1G 145
Hampden Ct. *Eccl* 3F 91
Hampden Cres. *M18* 2E 111
Hampden Gro. *Eccl* 3F 91
Hampden Rd. *P'wich* 5F 67
Hampden Rd. *Sale* 6A 122
Hampden Rd. *Shaw* 1H 57
Hampden St. *Heyw* 4F 39
Hampden St. *Roch* 5H 27
Hampshire Clo. *Bury* 5E 37
Hampshire Clo. *Stoc* 4C 128
Hampshire Ho. *Stoc* 4C 128
Hampshire Rd. *Chad* 4H 71
Hampshire Rd. *Droy* 2A 98
Hampshire Rd. *Stoc* 4C 128
Hampshire St. *Salf* 4A 82
Hampshire Wlk. *M8* 5D 82
Hampson Av. *Heyw* 3E 39
Hampson Clo. *Eccl* 4D 90
Hampson Cres. *Hand* . . .3G 159
Hampson Fold. *Rad* 3F 49
Hampson Mill La.
   Bury 2D 50
Hampson Pl. *Ash L* 5A 88
Hampson Rd. *Ash L* 5A 88
Hampson Rd. *Stret* 5C 106
Hampson Sq. Rad *3G 49*
   (off Ainsworth Rd.)
Hampson St. *M40* 1H 95
Hampson St. *Droy* 3A 98
Hampson St. *Eccl* 4D 90
Hampson St. *Rad* 4G 49
Hampson St. *Sale* 5D 122
Hampson St.
   Salf 4A 94 (6B 4)
Hampson St. *Stoc* 3B 140
Hampson St. *Swin* 2G 79
Hampson St. Trad. Est.
   Salf 4B 94 (6C 4)
Hampstead Av. *Urm* 6A 104
Hampstead Dri. *Stoc* 6C 140
Hampstead La. *Stoc* 6B 140
Hampton Gro. *Bury* 5F 23
Hampton Gro. *Chea H* . . .3A 150
Hampton M. *Stoc* 1H 151
Hampton Rd. *M21* 6F 107
Hampton Rd. *Bolt* 4C 46
Hampton Rd. *Cad* 5B 118
Hampton Rd. *Fail* 3G 85
Hampton Rd. *Urm* 6F 105
Hampton St. *Oldh* 5B 72

Hamsell Rd.
   M13 . . . . . . .6G 95 (4E 11)
Hancock Clo. *M14* 4F 109
Hancock St. *Stret* 1D 122
Handel Av. *Urm* 5C 104
Handel M. *Sale* 5C 122
Handel St. *Bolt* 2H 31
Handel St. *Whitw* 1B 14
Handforth Ho. *Urm* 4G 105
Handforth. 4H 159
Handforth By-Pass.
   Wilm 6A 160
Handforth Gro. *M13* 5A 110
Handforth Rd. *Stoc* 4H 127
Handforth Rd. *Wilm* 5A 160
Handley Av. *M14* 6F 109
Handley Clo. *Stoc* 6E 139
Handley Rd. *Bram* 2G 151
Handley St. *Bury* 5D 36
Handley St. *Roch* 3F 27
Hands La. *Roch* 4C 26
Handsworth St.
   M12 . . . . . . .6H 95 (3H 11)
Hanging Birch. *Midd* 2D 68
Hanging Bri. M3 . . .*3D 94 (4H 5)*
   (off Cateaton St.)
Hanging Chadder. 6A 42
Hanging Chadder La.
   Rytn 6A 42
Hanging Lees Clo.
   Miln 1G 43
Hani Ct. *M8* 2B 82
Hani Wells Bus. Pk.
   M19 . . . . .2D 126
Hankinson Clo. *Part* 6D 118
Hankinson Way. *Salf* 2G 93
Hanley Clo. *Dis* 2H 165
Hanley Clo. *Midd* 4A 70
Hanlon St. *M8* 2B 82
Hannah Baldwin Clo.
   M11 . . . . .5B 96
Hannah Lodge. M20 . . . .*5E 125*
   (off Palatine Rd.)
Hannah St. *M12* 5C 110
Hannerton Rd. *Shaw* 5H 43
Hannet Rd. *M22* 3B 148
Hanover Bus. Pk.
   B'hth 4D 132
Hanover Ct. *Ash L* 4G 99
Hanover Ct. Bolt *2F 45*
   (off Greenbank Rd.)
Hanover Ct. *Salf* 4H 81
Hanover Ct. *Wors* 5B 78
Hanover Cres. *M14* 3H 109
Hanover Gdns. *Salf* 3A 82
Hanover Ho. *Bolt* 4F 45
Hanover Rd. *B'hth* 4D 132
Hanover St. *M4* . . .3E 95 (3A 6)
Hanover St. *Bolt* 6A 32
Hanover St. *L'boro* 4E 17
Hanover St. *Moss* 2E 89
Hanover St. *Roch* 3C 40
Hanover St. *Stal* 3D 100
Hanover St. N. *Aud* 5E 99
Hanover St. S. *Aud* 5E 99
Hanover Towers.
   Stoc 6H 127
Hansby Clo. *Oldh* 6C 56
Hansdon Clo. *M8* 5C 82
Hansen Wlk. *M22* 3A 148
Hanslope Wlk. M9 . . . . . .*3G 83*
   (off Swainsthorpe Dri.)
Hanson Clo. *Midd* 6A 54
Hanson Clo. Ind. Est.
   Midd 6A 54
Hanson M. *Stoc* 1B 140
Hanson Rd. *M40* 4A 84
Hanson St. *Bury* 1D 36
Hanson St. *Midd* 6A 54
   (in two parts)
Hanson St. *Oldh* 2G 73

Hanworth Clo.—Hart Av.

Hanworth Clo. *M13* 6F **95** (4D **10**)
Hapsford Wlk. *M40* 6A **84**
Hapton Av. *Stret* 6D **106**
Hapton Pl. *Stoc* 6F **127**
Hapton St. *M19* 5C **110**
Harbern Clo. *Eccl* 1F **91**
Harbord St. *Midd* 1A **70**
Harborne Wlk. *G'mnt* 2H **21**
Harboro Ct. *Sale* 6H **121**
Harboro Gro. *Sale* 5H **121**
Harboro Rd. *Sale* 4G **121**
Harboro Way. *Sale* 5H **121**
Harbour Farm Rd. *Hyde* 1C **114**
Harbour La. *Miln* 6F **29**
Harbour La. N. *Miln* 5F **29**
Harbour M. Cottage. *Brom X* 3F **19**
Harbourne Av. *Wors* 3E **77**
Harbourne Clo. *Wors* 3E **77**
Harburn Wlk. *M22* 5C **148**
Harbury Cres. *M22* 6A **136**
Harcles Dri. *Rams* 1B **22**
Harcombe Rd. *M20* 3G **125**
Harcourt Av. *Urm* 6H **105**
Harcourt Clo. *Urm* 6H **105**
Harcourt Ind. Cen. *Wors* 4F **63**
Harcourt Rd. *Alt* 5F **133**
Harcourt Rd. *Sale* 3A **122**
Harcourt St. *Farn* 5F **47**
Harcourt St. *Oldh* 1F **73**
Harcourt St. *Stoc* 1H **127**
Harcourt St. *Stret* 4E **107**
Harcourt St. *Wors* 4F **63**
Harcourt St. S. *Wors* 4F **63**
Hardberry Pl. *Stoc* 5E **141**
Hardcastle Av. *M21* 3A **124**
Hardcastle Clo. *Bolt* 5G **19**
Hardcastle Gdns. *Bolt* 5G **19**
Hardcastle Rd. *Stoc* 4F **139**
Hardcastle St. *Bolt* 3D **32**
Hardcastle St. *Oldh* 2D **72**
Harden Dri. *Bolt* 3F **33**
Harden Hills. *Shaw* 5H **43**
Harden Park. **6D 166**
Harden Pk. *Ald E* 6D **166**
Hardfield Rd. *Midd* 4A **70**
Hardfield St. *Heyw* 3F **39**
Hardicker St. *M19* 2D **126**
Hardie Av. *Farn* 2D **62**
Harding St. *M4* . . .4H **95** (6H **7**)
Harding St. *Hyde* 2B **114**
Harding St. *Salf* (M3) . . .3D **94** (3G **5**)
Harding St. *Salf* (M6) . . .1G **93**
Harding St. *Stoc* 2B **140**
Hardman Av. *Bred* 6G **129**
Hardman Av. *P'wich* 1H **81**
Hardman Clo. *Rad* 1F **49**
Hardman Fold. *Bolt* 5D **46**
Hardman La. *Fail* 3E **85**
Hardman Rd. *Stoc* 1H **127**
Hardmans. *Brom X* 4D **18**
Hardman's La. *Brom X* . . .3D **18**
Hardmans M. *W'fld* 3D **66**
Hardman's Rd. *W'fld* 3D **66**
Hardman St. *M3* . . .4C **94** (6F **5**)
Hardman St. *Bury* . . . . . .1D **36** (in two parts)
Hardman St. *Chad* 6H **71**
Hardman St. *Fail* 4D **84**
Hardman St. *Farn* . . . . . . .2G **63** (in two parts)
Hardman St. *Heyw* 3F **39**
Hardman St. *Miln* 6G **29**
Hardman St. *Rad* 1F **49**
Hardman St. *Stoc* . . . . . . .2F **139** (in two parts)
Hardon Gro. *M13* 5B **110**
Hardrush Fold. *Fail* 5G **85**
Hardshaw Clo. *M13* 1F **109** (5D **10**)
Hardsough La. *Rams* 1A **12**
Hardwick Clo. *H Lane* . . .1D **164**
Hardwick Clo. *Rad* 2B **48**
Hardwicke Rd. *Poy* 3F **163**
Hardwicke St. *Roch* 1E **41**
Hardwick Rd. *Part* 6E **119**
Hardwick St. *Ash L* 3F **99**
Hardwood Clo. *M8* 4C **82**
Hardy Av. *M21* 1G **123**
Hardy Clo. *Roch* 2F **41**
Hardy Dri. *Bram* 6F **151**
Hardy Dri. *Timp* 4H **133**
Hardy Gro. *Swin* 6D **78**
Hardy Gro. *Wors* 3H **77**
Hardy La. *M21* 3H **123**
Hardy Mill Rd. *Bolt* 1H **33**
Hardy St. *Ash L* 5A **88**
Hardy St. *Eccl* 5D **90**
Hardy St. *Oldh* 4E **73**
Hardywood Rd. *Dent* . . .2G **129**
Harebell Av. *Wors* 6B **62**
Harebell Clo. *Roch* 6D **14**
Harecastle Av. *Eccl* 5G **91**
Haredale Dri. *M8* 5D **82**
Hare Dri. *Bury* 3F **51**
Harefield Av. *Roch* 6A **28**
Harefield Dri. *M20* 1E **137**
Harefield Dri. *Heyw* 3H **39**
Harefield Dri. *Wilm* 4D **166**
Harefield Rd. *Hand* 3H **159**
Hareford Wlk. M9 . . . .*5E 83* (*off Westmere Dri.*)
Harehill Clo. *M13* 6F **95** (3D **10**)
Hare Hill Ct. *L'boro* 3F **17**
Hare Hill Rd. *Hyde* 4G **115**
Hare Hill Rd. *L'boro* 3E **17**
Hare Hill Wlk. *Hyde* 4G **115**
Hareshill Bus. Pk. *Heyw* 5D **38**
Hareshill Rd. *Heyw* 5D **38**
Hare St. *M4* 3E **95** (4B **6**)
Hare St. *Roch* . . . . .6H **27** (in two parts)
Harewood. *B'btm* 6C **116**
Harewood Av. *Roch* 1H **25**
Harewood Av. *Sale* 5F **121**
Harewood Clo. *Roch* 2H **25**
Harewood Ct. M9 . . . .*4C 68* (*off Deanswood Dri.*)
Harewood Ct. *Sale* 6C **122**
Harewood Dri. *Roch* 2G **25**
Harewood Dri. *Rytn* 2A **56**
Harewood Gro. *Stoc* 1G **127**
Harewood Rd. *Irlam* 5F **103**
Harewood Rd. *Roch* 1G **25**
Harewood Rd. *Shaw* 5G **43**
Harewood Wlk. *Dent* 6G **113**
Harewood Way. *Roch* 2G **25**
Harewood Way. *Swin* 1F **79**
Harford Clo. *Haz G* 4A **152**
Hargate Av. *Roch* 1C **26**
Hargate Clo. *Bury* 1C **22**
Hargate Dri. *Hale* 4A **146**
Hargate Dri. *Irlam* 4E **103**
Hargrave Clo. *M9* 3E **69**
Hargreaves Ho. *Bolt* 1A **46**
Hargreaves Rd. *Timp* . . .5C **134**
Hargreaves St. *M4* 2E **95** (1B **6**)
Hargreaves St. *Bolt* 3A **32**
Hargreaves St. *Oldh* . . . . .3A **72** (Arkwright St.)
Hargreaves St. *Oldh* . . . . .2D **72** (Henshaw St.)
Hargreaves St. *Roch* 1C **40**
Harkerside Clo. *M21* 1A **124**
Harkness St. *M12* 6G **95** (4F **11**)
Harland Dri. *M8* 4D **82**
Harland Way. *Roch* 1C **26**
Harlech Av. *W'fld* 3F **67**
Harlech Dri. *Haz G* 4C **152**
Harleen Gro. *Stoc* 4D **140**
Harlesden Cres. *Bolt* 2G **45**
Harley Av. *M14* 4A **110**
Harley Av. *A'wth* 4D **34**
Harley Av. *Bolt* 2G **33**
Harley Ct. *Midd* 6H **53**
Harley Rd. *Midd* 6H **53**
Harley Rd. *Sale* 4B **122**
Harley St. *M11* 5F **97**
Harley St. *Ash L* 2H **99**
Harling Rd. *Shar I* 4B **136**
Harlington Clo. *M23* 4D **134**
Harlow Dri. *M18* 4F **111**
Harlyn Av. *Bram* 6H **151**
Harmer Clo. *M40* 6A **84**
Harmol Gro. *Ash L* 5D **86**
Harmony St. *Oldh* 3E **73**
Harmsworth Dri. *Stoc* . . .4D **126**
Harmsworth St. *Salf* 3E **93**
Harold Av. *M18* 3H **111**
Harold Av. *Duk* 5B **100**
Haroldene St. *Bolt* 3D **32**
Harold Lees Rd. *Heyw* . . .2H **39**
Harold Priestnall Clo. *M40* 5B **84**
Harold St. *M16* 1A **108** (6B **8**)
Harold St. *Bolt* 3H **31**
Harold St. *Fail* 4E **85**
Harold St. *Midd* 6G **53**
Harold St. *Oldh* 2B **72**
Harold St. *P'wich* 5D **66**
Harold St. *Roch* 1C **28**
Harold St. *Stoc* 3B **140**
Harper Ct. *Stoc* 4G **139**
Harper Fold Rd. *Rad* 4D **48**
Harper Green. **6D 46**
Harper Green Leisure Cen. **6D 46**
Harper Grn. Rd. *Farn* 5D **46**
Harper Ho. M19 . . . .*6B 110* (*off Park Lodge*)
Harper Pl. *Ash L* 2A **100**
Harper Rd. *Shar I* 4C **136**
Harper's La. *Bolt* 3F **31**
Harper Sq. *Shaw* 6G **43**
Harper St. *Ash L* 2A **100**
Harper St. *Farn* 5D **46**
Harper St. *Oldh* 5C **72**
Harper St. *Roch* 6G **27**
Harper St. *Stoc* 4G **139**
Harpford Clo. *Bolt* 2A **48**
Harpford Dri. *Bolt* 2A **48**
Harp Ind. Est. *Roch* 3D **40**
Harp Rd. *Traf P* 5A **92**
Harp St. *M11* 6G **97**
Harp Trad. Est. *Traf P* 5A **92**
Harpurhey. **4G 83**
Harpurhey District Cen. *M9* 3G **83**
Harpurhey Rd. *M8 & M9* 3E **83**
Harpurhey Swimming Pools. **3G 83**
Harridge Av. *Roch* . . . . . .6C **14** (in two parts)
Harridge Av. *Stal* 3H **101**
Harridge Bank. *Roch* 1E **27**
Harridge St. *Roch* 6C **14**
Harridge, The. *Roch* 6C **14**
Harrier Clo. *Wors* 3F **77**
Harriet St. *M4* 3G **95** (3F **7**)
Harriet St. *Bolt* 5F **45**
Harriet St. *Roch* 4A **28**
Harriet St. *Wors* . . . . .5F **63** (in two parts)
Harriett St. *Cad* 4C **118**
Harringay Rd. *M40* 6B **84**
Harrington Rd. *Alt* 6D **132**
Harrington St. *M18* 2G **111**
Harris Av. *Dent* 4B **112**
Harris Av. *Urm* 2F **105**
Harris Clo. *Dent* 4B **112**
Harris Clo. *Heyw* 4A **38**
Harris Dri. *Bury* 5F **51**
Harris Dri. *Hyde* 3E **115**
Harrison Av. *M19* 5D **110**
Harrison Clo. *Roch* 2B **26**
Harrisons Dri. *Woodl* . . .4A **130**
Harrison St. *M4* . . .4H **95** (6G **7**)
Harrison St. *Eccl* 5D **90**
Harrison St. *Hyde* . . . . . .1D **130** (in two parts)
Harrison St. *L Hul* 5C **62**
Harrison St. *Oldh* 3D **72**
Harrison St. *Rams* 2E **13**
Harrison St. *Salf* 1B **94** (1D **4**)
Harrison St. *Stal* 3D **100**
Harrison St. *Stoc* 4H **139**
Harris St. *M8* 1C **94**
Harris St. *Bolt* 1A **46**
Harrogate Av. *P'wich* 1H **81**
Harrogate Clo. *Open* 6G **97**
Harrogate Dri. *Stoc* 1G **127**
Harrogate Rd. *Stoc* 1G **127**
Harrogate Sq. *Bury* 4F **35**
Harroll Ga. *Swin* 4G **79**
Harrop Ct. *Dig* 2D **60**
Harrop Ct. Rd. *Dig* 2D **60**
Harrop Dale. **1D 60**
Harrop Edge. **3A 116**
Harrop Edge La. *Del* 3A **60**
Harrop Edge Rd. *Mot* . . .3A **116**
Harrop Fold. *Oldh* 2E **87**
Harrop Green. **2D 60**
Harrop Grn. La. *Dig* 2C **60**
Harrop Ridge. **1D 60**
Harrop Rd. *Hale* 3G **145**
Harrop St. *M18* 1H **111**
Harrop St. *Bolt* 3E **45**
Harrop St. *Stal* 3E **101**
Harrop St. *Stoc* 4A **140**
Harrop St. *Wors* 6D **62**
Harrow Av. *M19* 3C **126**
Harrow Av. *Oldh* 6B **72**
Harrow Av. *Roch* 5C **26**
Harrowby Ct. *Farn* 1D **62**
Harrowby Dri. *M40* 6F **83**
Harrowby Fold. *Farn* 1E **63**
Harrowby La. *Farn* 1E **63**
Harrowby Rd. *Bolt* (BL1) 3D **30**
Harrowby Rd. *Bolt* (BL3) 4E **45**
Harrowby Rd. *Swin* 4E **79**
Harrowby St. *Farn* 1D **62**
Harrow Clo. *Bury* 2D **50**
Harrowdene Wlk. *M9* 3F **83**
Harrow Dri. *Sale* 1A **134**
Harrow M. *Shaw* 6F **43**
Harrow Rd. *Bolt* 5F **31**
Harrow Rd. *Sale* 1A **134**
Harrow St. *M8* 2D **82**
Harrow St. *Roch* 3H **41**
Harrycroft Rd. *Woodl* . . .4H **129**
Harryfields. *B'btm* 6B **116**
Harry Hall Gdns. *Salf* 1A **94** (1B **4**)
Harry Rd. *Stoc* 1H **127**
Harry Rowley Clo. *M22* 3A **148**
Harry St. *Oldh* 3A **72**
Harry St. *Roch* 2B **40**
Harry St. *Rytn* 5C **56**
Harry Thorneycroft Wlk. *M11* 5A **96**
Harrytown. *Rom* 1G **141**
Harry Whitehead Ct. *Bury* 5F **23**
Hart Av. *Droy* 4B **98**

Hart Av. Sale 5F 123
Hart Ct. Moss 1D 88
Hart Dri. Bury 3F 51
Harter St. M1 . . . .5E 95 (1A 10)
Hartfield Clo.
    M13 . . . . . .1G 109 (5E 11)
Hartfield Wlk. Bolt 5E 33
Hartford Av. Heyw 2D 38
Hartford Av. Stoc 3F 127
Hartford Av. Wilm 4C 166
Hartford Clo. Heyw 2D 38
Hartford Gdns. Timp 6D 134
Hartford Grange. Oldh 5B 72
Hartford Ind. Est. Oldh . . .3A 72
Hartford Rd. Sale 1F 133
Hartford Rd. Urm 3G 105
Hartford Sq. Oldh 3A 72
Hartford St. Dent 2E 113
Hart Hill Dri. Salf 2D 92
Harthill St. M8 . . . . .6B 82
Hartington Ct. Rytn 3C 56
Hartington Dri. M11 . . . . . .2D 96
Hartington Dri. Haz G 5E 153
Hartington Rd. M21 . . . . .1H 123
Hartington Rd. Alt 4F 133
Hartington Rd. Bolt 6G 31
Hartington Rd. Bram 1G 161
Hartington Rd. Eccl 2C 90
Hartington Rd. H Grn 5H 149
Hartington Rd.
    H Lane & Dis 1C 164
Hartington Rd. Stoc 6D 140
Hartington St. M14 . . . . . .4D 108
Hartis Av. Salf 5A 82
Hartland Av. Urm 5A 106
Hartland Clo. Poy 2D 162
Hartland Clo. Stoc 3C 140
Hartland Ct. Bolt 2A 32
    (off Blackburn Rd.)
Hartland St. Heyw 3F 39
Hartlebury. Roch 5G 27
Hartlepool Clo. M14 . . . .4F 109
Hartley Av. P'wich 6G 67
Hartley Gro. Irlam 3F 103
Hartley Hall Gdns.
    M16 . . . . .6C 108
Hartley La. Roch 2E 41
Hartley Pl. Fir 4D 28
Hartley Rd. M21 . . . . . . .6G 107
Hartley Rd. Alt 6E 133
Hartley St. Fir 4D 28
Hartley St. Heyw 3F 39
Hartley St. L'boro 4E 17
Hartley St. Mill 2H 101
Hartley St. Roch 2D 26
Hartley St. Ward 3A 16
Hartley Ter. L'boro 4E 17
    (off William St.)
Hartley Ter. Roch 2E 41
Hart Mill Clo. Moss 1D 88
Harton Av. M18 . . . . .4E 111
Harton Clo. Shaw 6E 43
Hart Rd. M14 . . . . .5E 109
Hartshead Av. Ash L 5G 87
Hartshead Av. Stal 2E 101
Hartshead Clo. M11 . . . . .6A 98
Hartshead Cres. Fail 5A 86
Hartshead Green. 3B 88
Hartshead Pike Tower.
    . . . . .2C 88
Hartshead Rd. Ash L 5G 87
Hartshead St. Lees 4B 74
Hartshead Vw. Hyde 6D 114
Hartsop Dri. Midd 5E 53
Hartspring Av. Swin 4G 79
Hart St. M1 . . . . .5E 95 (1A 10)
    (in two parts)
Hart St. Alt 6G 133
Hart St. Droy 3A 98

Hartswood Clo. Dent . . .3G 113
Hartswood Rd. M20 . . . .3H 125
Hartwell Clo. M11 . . . . . .5B 96
Hartwell Clo. Bolt 2E 33
Hartwell Gro. Stoc 1H 151
Harty Ho. Eccl 3G 91
Harvard Clo. Woodl 4A 130
Harvard St. Roch 1G 41
    (in two parts)
Harvest Clo. Sale 6G 123
Harvest Clo. Salf 6C 80
Harvest Pk. Bolt 5G 31
Harvey Clo. M11 . . . . . . .5B 96
Harvey Ct. L'boro 3G 17
Harvey St. Bolt 2H 31
Harvey St. Bury 2A 36
Harvey St. Roch 1B 28
Harvey St. Stoc 2H 139
Harvin Gro. Dent 5G 113
Harwich Clo. M19 . . . . . .6D 110
Harwich Clo. Stoc 3C 128
Harwin Clo. Roch 6D 14
Harwood. 1H 33
Harwood Ct. Salf 1H 93
Harwood Ct. Stoc 1A 138
Harwood Cres. T'ton 4G 21
Harwood Dri. Bury 4G 35
Harwood Gdns. Heyw 4F 39
Harwood Gro. Bolt 4D 32
Harwood Lee. 6A 20
Harwood Mdw. Bolt 2H 33
Harwood Pk. Heyw 4F 39
Harwood Rd. M19 . . . . . .3A 126
Harwood Rd. Stoc 1A 138
Harwood Rd. T'ton 1C 34
Harwood St. L'boro 4D 16
Harwood St. Stoc 6G 127
Harwood Va. Bolt 2G 33
Harwood Va. Ct. Bolt 2G 33
Harwood Wlk. T'ton 4G 21
Haseley Clo. Poy 2E 163
Haseley Clo. Rad 2B 48
Haselhurst Wlk. M23 . . . .1F 135
Hasguard Clo. Bolt 5D 30
Haslam Brow. Bury 5C 36
Haslam Ct. Bolt 2F 45
Haslam Ct. Salf 2H 81
Haslam Hall M. Bolt 6C 30
Haslam Hey Clo. Bury 3E 35
Haslam Rd. Stoc 5G 139
Haslam St. Bolt 2H 45
Haslam St. Bury 1E 37
Haslam St. Midd 2C 70
Haslam St. Roch 3F 27
Haslemere Av. Haleb 1C 156
Haslemere Dri.
    Chea H 4C 150
Haslemere Rd. M20 . . . . .3H 125
Haslemere Rd. Urm 6D 104
Haslington Rd. M22 . . . . .3C 148
Hasper Av. M20 . . . . .2E 125
Hassall Av. M20 . . . . .1D 124
Hassall St. Rad 2C 50
Hassall St. Stal 4F 101
Hassall Way. Hand 2A 160
Hassop Av. Salf 4E 81
Hassop Clo. M11 . . . . . . .4A 96
Hassop Rd. Stoc 6A 112
Hastings Av. M21 . . . . . .1G 123
Hastings Av. W'fld 2F 67
Hastings Clo. Chea H 3E 151
Hastings Clo. Stoc 4B 140
Hastings Clo. W'fld 2F 67
Hastings Dri. Urm 4A 104
Hastings Rd. Bolt 5F 31
Hastings Rd. Eccl 1C 90
Hastings Rd. P'wich 4G 67
Hastings St. Roch 6H 27
Haston Clo. Stoc 5H 127
Hasty La. Ring 6E 147
    (in two parts)
Hatchett Rd. M22 . . . . . . .4B 148

Hatchmere Clo.
    Chea H 1B 150
Hatchmere Clo. Timp 5D 134
    (in two parts)
Hateley Rd. M16 . . . . . . .5G 107
Hatfield Av. M19 . . . . . . .3B 126
Hatfield Rd. Bolt 4G 31
Hathaway Clo. H Grn 6F 149
Hathaway Dri. Bolt 6E 19
Hathaway Gdns. Bred 6E 129
Hathaway Rd. Bury 4E 51
Hatherleigh Wlk. Bolt 1H 47
Hatherley Rd. M20 . . . . .3H 125
Hatherlow. 1H 141
Hatherlow. Rom 1G 141
Hatherlow Heights.
    Rom 2G 141
Hatherlow La. Haz G 3D 152
Hatherop Clo. Eccl 4D 90
Hathersage Av. Salf 2D 92
Hathersage Cres.
    Glos 5G 117
Hathersage Rd. M13 . . . .3G 109
Hathersage St. Oldh 3A 72
Hathersage Way. Dent . . .1F 129
Hathershaw. 6D 72
Hathershaw La. Oldh 6D 72
Hatro Ct. Urm 6A 106
Hattersley. 5H 115
Hattersley Cen., The.
    Hyde 5A 116
    (off Hattersley Rd. E.)
Hattersley Ind. Est.
    Hyde 6H 115
Hattersley Rd. E.
    Hyde 6A 116
Hattersley Rd. W.
    Hyde 5G 115
Hattersley Wlk. Hyde 4G 115
Hatter St. M4 . . . .3F 95 (3C 6)
Hatton Av. Salf 2B 94 (1C 4)
Hattonfold. Sale 2C 134
Hatton Gro. Bolt 6E 19
Hattons Ct. Stret 4C 106
Hattons Rd. Traf P 1B 106
Hatton St. M12 . . . . .4C 110
Hatton St. Stoc 1G 139
    (in two parts)
Hatton Ter. Duk 4H 99
    (off Astley St.)
Hat Works. 2G 139
    (Mus. of Hatting, The)
Haugh. 1G 43
Haugh Fold. Miln 1G 43
Haugh Hill Rd. Oldh 4A 58
Haugh La. Miln 1G 43
Haugh Sq. Miln 1G 43
Haughton Clo.
    Woodl 3G 129
Haughton Dale. 2G 129
Haughton Dale Local Nature
    Reserve. 3H 129
Haughton Dri. M22 . . . . .1B 136
Haughton Green. 1G 129
Haughton Grn. Rd.
    Dent 1G 129
Haughton Hall Rd.
    Dent 4F 113
Haughton St. Aud 2F 113
Haughton St. Hyde 6C 114
Havana Clo. M11 . . . . . . .4B 96
    (in two parts)
Haveley Rd. M22 . . . . . . .6A 136
Havelock Dri.
    Salf 1B 94 (1C 4)
Havelock St. Oldh 4D 72
Havenbrook Gro.
    Rams 6C 12
Haven Clo. Grass 3F 75
Haven Clo. Haz G 4C 152
Haven Clo. Rad 2D 48
Haven Dri. Droy 3G 97

Haven La. Oldh 5A 58
Havenscroft Av. Eccl 5F 91
Haven St. Salf 4E 93
Haven, The. Hale 2H 145
Haven, The. L Lev 4B 48
Havercroft Pk. Bolt 5B 30
Haverfield Rd. M9 . . . . . .6G 69
Haverford St. M12 . . . . . .1B 110
Havergate Walks.
    Stoc 1F 153
Haverhill Gro. Bolt 3D 32
Haversham Rd. M8 . . . . . .1A 82
Havers Rd. M18 . . . . .2G 111
Haverton Dri. M22 . . . . . .3H 147
Havisham Clo. Los 3A 44
Hawarden Av. M16 . . . . .5A 108
Hawarden Rd. Alt 5F 133
Hawarden St. Bolt 6C 18
Haw Clough La. G'fld 3G 61
Hawdraw Grn. Stoc 5E 141
Hawes Av. M14 . . . . .2A 126
Hawes Av. Farn 1A 62
Hawes Av. Swin 4F 79
Hawes Clo. Bury 6B 22
Hawes Clo. Stoc 5A 140
Haweswater Clo. Dent . . .5A 112
Haweswater Cres. Uns . . .2F 51
Haweswater Dri. Midd 5G 53
Haweswater M. Midd 5G 53
Hawfinch Gro. Wors 3F 77
Hawick Gro. Heyw 4A 38
Hawk Clo. Bury 1F 37
Hawker Av. Bolt 4H 45
Hawkeshead Rd. M8 . . . . .5D 82
    (in two parts)
Hawke St. Stal 4G 101
Hawk Green. 2D 154
Hawk Grn. Clo. Marp 2D 154
Hawk Grn. Rd. Marp 2D 154
Hawkhurst Rd. M13 . . . . .4B 110
Hawkinge Vw. Heyw 6H 39
Hawkins St. Stoc 5G 127
Hawkins Way. L'boro 6G 17
Hawkridge Dri. M23 . . . . .1F 135
Hawk Rd. Irlam 4E 103
Hawkshaw Ct. Salf 4G 93
Hawkshaw La. Hawk 1D 20
Hawkshead Dri. Bolt 4E 45
Hawkshead Dri. Midd 6G 53
Hawkshead Dri. Rytn 1B 56
Hawkshead Rd. Shaw 5E 43
Hawksheath Clo. Eger 2D 18
Hawksley St. Oldh 6A 72
Hawksley Ind. Est.
    Oldh 6A 72
Hawksley St. Oldh 6A 72
Hawksmoor Dri. Shaw 5F 43
Hawkstone Av. Droy 2G 97
Hawkstone Av. W'fld 2B 66
Hawkstone Clo. Bolt 2G 33
Hawkswick Dri. M23 . . . . .1G 135
Hawk Yd. La. G'fld 4H 61
Hawley Dri. Haleb 5B 146
Hawley Grn. Roch 1F 27
Hawley La. Haleb 5B 146
Hawley St. M19 . . . . .1D 126
Haworth Av. Rams 1A 22
Haworth Ct. Rad 4H 49
    (off Haworth Wlk.)
Haworth Dri. Stret 4H 105
Haworth Rd. M18 . . . . . .3E 111
Haworth St. Oldh 6C 56
Haworth St. Rad 4H 49
Haworth St. Wals 1E 35
Haworth Wlk. Rad 4H 49
Hawsworth Clo. M15 . . . .2F 109
Hawthorn Av. Bury 1A 36
Hawthorn Av. Eccl 2F 91
Hawthorn Av. Marp 5B 142
Hawthorn Av. Rad 6H 49
Hawthorn Av. Rams 3B 12
    (Bury Rd.)

Hawthorn Av. Rams 1A 22
(Newcombe Rd.)
Hawthorn Av. Timp 4H 133
Hawthorn Av. Urm 6H 105
Hawthorn Av. Wilm 2D 166
Hawthorn Av. Wors 2G 77
Hawthorn Bank. Bolt 1G 33
Hawthorn Bank. Had 3H 117
Hawthorn Clo. Timp 4H 133
Hawthorn Ct. Bred 6D 128
Hawthorn Cres. Oldh 1D 86
Hawthorn Cres. Shaw . . .1F 57
Hawthorn Cres. T'ton 4H 21
Hawthorn Dri. M19 . . . . .2B 126
Hawthorn Dri. Cad 4B 118
Hawthorn Dri. Salf 1B 92
Hawthorn Dri. Stal 5D 100
Hawthorn Dri. Swin 4A 80
Hawthorne Av. Farn 1D 62
Hawthorne Dri. Wors 4A 78
Hawthorne Gro. Ash L . . .4F 99
Hawthorne Gro. Bred . . .5F 129
Hawthorne Gro. Chad . . .1H 71
Hawthorne Gro. Poy 3A 164
Hawthorne Rd. Bolt 2F 45
Hawthorne St. Bolt 2F 45
Hawthorn Grn. Wilm 2D 166
(off Hawthorn Vw.)
Hawthorn Gro. Bram 1E 161
Hawthorn Gro. Holl 1F 117
Hawthorn Gro. Hyde 6B 114
Hawthorn Gro. Stoc 6D 126
Hawthorn Gro. Wilm 2E 167
Hawthorn La. M21 . . . . . .1E 123
Hawthorn La. Miln 1E 43
Hawthorn La. Sale 3F 121
Hawthorn La. Wilm 2D 166
Hawthorn Lodge. Stoc . .1H 151
Hawthorn Pk. Wilm 2D 166
Hawthorn Rd. M40 . . . . .2E 85
Hawthorn Rd. Dent 4B 112
Hawthorn Rd. Droy 3C 98
(in two parts)
Hawthorn Rd. Gat 6E 137
Hawthorn Rd. Hale 2C 145
Hawthorn Rd. Kear 4B 64
Hawthorn Rd. Oldh 1H 85
Hawthorn Rd. Roch 5A 26
Hawthorn Rd. Sale 1D 122
Hawthorn Rd. Stoc 1B 138
Hawthorn Rd. S. Droy . . .3C 98
Hawthorns, The. Aud . . .1D 112
Hawthorn St. M18 . . . . .1F 111
Hawthorn St. Aud 1E 113
Hawthorn St. Wilm 2D 166
Hawthorn Ter. Stoc 6D 126
Hawthorn Ter. Wilm 3D 166
Hawthorn Vw. Wilm 2D 166
Hawthorn Wlk. L'boro . . .4D 16
Hawthorn Wlk. Part 6C 118
Hawthorn Wlk. Wilm . .2D 166
Hawthorpe Gro.
Upperm 1F 61
Haxby Rd. M18 . . . . . . .4F 111
Hayburn Rd. Stoc 3C 140
Haycock Clo. Stal 6D 101
Hay Cft. Chea H 5A 150
Hayden Ct. M40 . . . . . . .6F 83
(off Sedgeford Rd.)
Haydn Av. M14 . . . . . . .3F 109
Haydn St. Bolt 3H 31
Haydock Av. Sale 1D 132
Haydock Dri. Haz G 3F 153
Haydock Dri. Timp 6B 134
Haydock Dri. Wors 5D 76
Haydock La. Brom X 3F 19
(Chapeltown Rd.)
Haydock La. Brom X 2E 19
(Hospital Rd.)
Haydock M. Salf 5H 81
(off Epsom M.)

Haydock St. Bolt 5B 32
Haydock Wlk. Chad 2A 72
Haye's Rd. Cad 4C 118
Hayeswater Circ. Urm . . .4E 105
Hayeswater Rd. Urm 4F 105
Hayfield Av. Bred 5G 129
Hayfield Clo. M12 . . . . . .6A 96
Hayfield Clo. G'mnt 2H 21
Hayfield Clo. Midd 4C 54
Hayfield Clo. Oldh 3B 58
Hayfield Rd. Bred 5G 129
Hayfield Rd. Salf 1B 92
Hayfield St. Sale 4B 122
Hayfield Wlk. Dent 1G 129
Hayfield Wlk. Timp 5C 134
Haygrove Wlk. M9 . . . . . .3F 83
Hayle Rd. Oldh 3H 57
Hayley St. M13 . . . . . . .3A 110
Hayling Rd. Sale 4G 121
Haymaker Ri. Ward 3B 16
Haymans Wlk.
M13 . . . . . . .6F 95 (4D 10)
(in two parts)
Haymarket Clo.
M13 . . . . . . .2G 109 (6F 11)
Haymarket St. Bury 3C 36
Haymarket, The. Bury 3C 36
Haymill Av. L Hul 3C 62
Haymond Clo. Salf 5E 81
Haynes St. Bolt 4F 45
Haynes St. Roch 3H 27
Haysbrook Av. Wors 5B 62
Haysbrook Clo. Ash L 4E 87
Haythorp Av. M22 . . . . .2C 148
Hayward Av. L Lev 4C 48
Hayward Sports Cen. . . .5H 45
Hayward St. Bury 2A 36
Hayward Way. Mot 4B 116
(off Garnett Clo.)
Hazel Av. M16 . . . . .5B 108
Hazel Av. Ash L 5A 88
Hazel Av. Bury 3F 37
Hazel Av. Chea 6A 138
Hazel Av. L Hul 4A 62
Hazel Av. Miln 2C 43
Hazel Av. Rad 1A 64
Hazel Av. Rams 2B 22
Hazel Av. Rom 1B 142
Hazel Av. Sale 6B 122
Hazel Av. Swin 4G 79
Hazel Av. T'ton 6A 22
Hazelbadge Clo. Poy . . .3C 162
Hazelbadge Rd. Poy 3C 162
Hazelbank Av. M20 . . . . .2F 125
Hazelbottom Rd. M8 . . . .4D 82
Hazel Clo. Droy 3C 98
Hazel Clo. Marp 1C 154
Hazelcroft Gdns.
Ald E 6G 167
Hazel Dene Clo. Bury . . .6D 36
Hazeldene Rd. M40 . . . . .2E 85
Hazel Dri. M22 . . . . .5E 149
Hazel Dri. Poy 4F 163
Hazel Dri. Stoc 5D 140
Hazelfields. Wors 4B 78
Hazel Grove. 3D 152
Hazel Gro. Chad 1H 71
Hazel Gro. Farn 1D 62
Hazel Gro. Rad 1F 65
Hazel Gro. Salf 3C 92
Hazel Gro. Urm 5G 105
Hazel Grove Recreation Cen.
. . . . .5C 152
Hazel Grove Swimming Pool.
. . . . .4B 152
Hazel Hall La. Rams 2B 22
Hazelhurst. 5B 88
(Ashton-under-Lyne)
Hazelhurst. 5C 12
(Bury)
Hazelhurst. 4C 78
(Manchester)

Hazelhurst Clo. Bolt 3A 32
Hazelhurst Clo. Rams . . .5D 12
Hazelhurst Dri. Midd 3H 53
Hazelhurst Fold. Wors . . .4C 78
Hazelhurst M. Chad 6F 71
Hazelhurst Rd. Ash L 5B 88
Hazelhurst Rd. Stal 1E 101
Hazelhurst Rd. Wors 4B 78
Hazel La. Oldh 1B 86
Hazelmere Av. Eccl 1D 90
Hazel Mt. Eger 1C 18
Hazel Rd. Alt 6F 133
Hazel Rd. Chea H 4D 150
Hazel Rd. Midd 6B 54
Hazel Rd. Stal 2G 101
Hazel Rd. W'fld 1F 67
Hazel St. Aud 1E 113
Hazel St. Haz G 2E 153
Hazel St. Hams 5C 12
Hazel Ter. M9 . . . . .5F 69
Hazel Vw. Marp 2D 154
Hazel Wlk. Part 6C 118
Hazelwell. Sale 6B 122
Hazelwood. Chad 1E 71
Hazelwood Av. Bolt 2G 33
Hazelwood Clo. Hyde . . .5E 115
Hazelwood Ct. Urm 4F 105
Hazelwood Dri. Aud 1F 113
Hazelwood Dri. Bury 4F 23
Hazelwood Rd. Bolt 3F 31
Hazelwood Rd. Hale 3G 145
Hazelwood Rd. Haz G . . .2F 153
Hazelwood Rd. Stoc 1A 152
Hazelwood Rd. Wilm . . .1F 167
Hazlemere. Kear 2A 64
Headingley Dri. M16 . . . .4G 107
Headingley Rd. M14 . . . .2H 125
Headingley Way. Bolt 4H 45
Headlands Dri. P'wich . . .2E 81
Headlands Rd. Bram . . .4H 151
Headlands St. Roch 2G 27
Heady Hill. 3B 38
Heady Hill Ct. Heyw 3C 38
Heady Hill Rd. Heyw 3C 38
Heald Av. M14 . . . . . . .4F 109
Heald Clo. Bow 3E 145
Heald Clo. L'boro 6E 17
Heald Clo. Roch 6C 14
Heald Dri. Bow 3E 145
Heald Dri. Roch 6C 14
Heald Green. 5F 149
Heald Gro. M14 . . . . . . .3F 109
Heald Gro. H Grn 4E 149
Heald La. L'boro 5E 17
Heald Pl. M14 . . . . .3F 109
(in two parts)
Heald Rd. Bow 3E 145
Healds Green. 4F 55
Healds Grn. Chad 4F 55
Healdwood Rd.
Woodl 6A 130
(in two parts)
Healey. 4D 14
Healey Av. Heyw 2G 39
Healey Av. Roch 5D 14
Healey Clo. M23 . . . . . . .1F 135
Healey Clo. Salf 3G 81
Healey Dell. Roch 5B 14
Healey Dell Nature Reserve.
. . . . .5B 14
Healey Dell Vis. Cen. . . .5B 14
Healey Gro. Whitw 4C 14
Healey Hall M. Roch 5C 14
Healey La. Roch 6E 15
Healey Stones. Roch 5D 14
Healey St. Roch 5G 27
Healing St. Roch 6A 28
Heanor Av. Dent 1G 129
Heap Bridge. 4G 37
Heap Brow. Bury 4H 37
Heape St. Roch 6C 40
Heapfold. Roch 1D 26

Heaplands. G'mnt 2H 21
Heap Rd. Roch 1H 25
Heaps Farm Ct. Stal 5H 101
Heap St. Bolt 2A 46
Heap St. Bury 4H 37
Heap St. Oldh 2G 73
Heap St. Rad 4H 49
Heap St. W'fld 2D 66
Heapworth Av. Rams 3D 12
Heapy Clo. Bury 4F 35
Heath Av. Rams 2B 22
Heath Av. Salf 1A 94 (1B 4)
Heath Av. Urm 4G 105
Heathbank Rd. M9 . . . . .4E 69
Heathbank Rd.
Chea H 6B 150
Heathbank Rd. Stoc 4D 138
Heathcliffe Wlk.
M13 . . . . . . .2G 109 (6F 11)
Heath Clo. Bolt 5F 45
Heathcote Av. Stoc 6E 127
Heathcote Gdns. Rom . . .2C 142
Heathcote Rd. M18 . . . . .3E 111
Heath Cotts. Bolt 5B 18
Heath Cres. Stoc 6H 139
Heather Av. Cad 3B 118
Heather Av. Droy 3C 98
Heather Av. Shaw 5H 43
Heather Bank. T'ton 4G 21
Heather Brow. Stal 6H 101
Heather Clo. Heyw 5F 39
Heather Clo. Oldh 6A 58
Heather Ct. Bow 2D 144
Heather Ct. Stoc 4F 127
Heatherdale Dri. M8 . . . . .5C 82
Heatherfield. Bolt 6B 18
(in two parts)
Heatherfield Ct. Wilm . . .1H 167
Heather Gro. Droy 5B 98
Heather Gro. Holl 1F 117
Heatherlands. Whitw 1H 15
Heather Lea. Dent 5G 113
Heather Rd. Alt 4G 145
Heathersett Dri. M9 . . . . .4F 83
Heathercside. Stal 3H 101
Heatherside. Stoc 6A 112
Heatherside Av. Moss . . .2G 89
Heatherside Rd. Rams . . .2D 12
Heathers, The. Stoc 1B 152
Heather St. M11 . . . . . . .3D 96
Heather Wlk. Part 6B 118
Heatherway. M14 . . . . . .3F 109
Heather Way. Dig 3C 60
Heatherway. Marp 5C 142
Heatherway. Sale 4F 121
Heath Farm La. Part 6E 119
Heathfield. Farn 6G 47
Heathfield. Har 1H 33
Heathfield. Wilm 4D 166
Heathfield. Wors 6H 77
Heathfield Av. Dent 5D 112
Heathfield Av. Gat 6F 137
Heathfield Av. Stoc 4E 127
Heathfield Clo. Sale 5F 123
Heathfield Dri. Bolt 5F 45
Heathfield Dri. Swin 4G 79
Heathfield Dri. Tyl 2A 76
Heathfield Rd.
Bury & W'fld 4D 50
Heathfield Rd. Stoc 5H 139
Heathfields. 1G 61
Heathfields Rd.
Upperm 1G 61
Heathfields Sq.
Upperm 1G 61
Heathfield St. M40 . . . . . .6C 84
Heathland Rd. Salf 3F 81
Heathlands Dri. P'wich . . .2E 81
Heathland Ter. Stoc 4G 139
Heathlea Clo. Bolt 5C 18
Heath Rd. Hale 3F 145
Heath Rd. Stoc 5H 139

Heath Rd. *Timp* 3H **133**
Heath Rd. *Ward* 3A **16**
Heathside Gro. *Wors* 6G **63**
Heathside Pk. Rd.
   Stoc 3B **138**
Heathside Rd. *M20* 4G **125**
Heathside Rd. *Stoc* 4C **138**
Heath St. *M8* 4B **82**
Heath St. *Roch* 5F **27**
Heath, The. *Ash L* 4E **87**
Heath, The. *Midd* 3B **70**
Heath Vw. *Alt* 2F **145**
Heath Vw. *Salf* 2E **81**
Heathway Av. *M11* 3F **97**
Heathwood. *Upperm* 1G **61**
Heathwood Rd. *M19* 5A **126**
Heatley Clo. *Dent* 5B **112**
Heatley Rd. *Roch* 5D **28**
Heatley Way. *Hand* 3H **159**
Heaton. 5E **31**
Heaton Av. *Bolt* 4D **30**
Heaton Av. *Brad* 6A **20**
Heaton Av. *Bram* 2F **151**
Heaton Av. *Farn* 1E **63**
Heaton Av. *L Lev* 3A **48**
Heaton Chapel. 4E **127**
Heaton Clo. *Bury* 2E **51**
Heaton Clo. *Stoc* 6C **126**
Heaton Ct. *M9* 6C **68**
Heaton Ct. *Bury* 6C **36**
Heaton Ct. *P'wich* 6G **67**
Heaton Ct. *Sale* 5C **122**
Heaton Ct. *Stoc* 5D **126**
Heaton Ct. Gdns. *Bolt* . . .6C **30**
Heaton Dri. *Bury* 2E **51**
Heaton Fold. *Bury* 5C **36**
Heaton Grange. *Bolt* 6E **31**
Heaton Grange Dri.
   Bolt 6E **31**
Heaton Gro. *Bury* 6D **36**
Heaton Hall. 3A **68**
         (Museum)
Heaton La. *Stoc* 2G **139**
Heaton Mersey. 1A **138**
Heaton Moor. 6C **126**
Heaton Moor Rd.
   Stoc 6D **126**
Heaton Mt. *Bolt* 4D **30**
Heaton Norris. 1F **139**
Heaton Park. 5G **67**
Heaton Pk. 4H **67**
Heaton Pk. Bowling Pavilion.
         . . . . .3G **67**
Heaton Pk. Farm Cen.
         . . . . .4A **68**
Heaton Pk. Horticultural Cen.
         . . . . .4H **67**
Heaton Pk. Rd. *M9* 4C **68**
Heaton Pk. Rd. W. *M9* . . .4C **68**
Heaton Pk. Tramway. . . .4A **68**
Heaton Pk. Tramway Mus.
         . . . . .4B **68**
Heaton Pl. *Stoc* 1A **138**
Heaton Rd. *M20* 2G **125**
Heaton Rd. *Brad F* 2B **48**
Heaton Rd. *Los* 2A **44**
Heaton Rd. *Stoc* 6E **127**
Heaton St. *Dent* 4D **112**
Heaton St. *Midd* 2D **68**
Heaton St. *Miln* 6G **29**
Heaton St. *P'wich* 5F **67**
Heaton St. *Salf* 4A **82**
Heaton Towers. Stoc . . .1G **139**
     (off Wilkinson Rd.)
Heaviley. 5A **140**
Heaviley Gro. *Stoc* 5A **140**
Hebble Butt Clo. *Miln* . . .5E **29**
Hebble Clo. *Bolt* 6F **19**
Hebburn Dri. *Bury* 6C **22**
Hebburn Wlk. *M14* 3F **109**
Hebden Av. *Bred* 5G **129**
Hebden Av. *Salf* 2C **92**

Hebden Ct. *Bolt* 5A **32**
Hebden Wlk. M15 . . . . . .2D **108**
     (off Arnott Cres.)
Heber Pl. L'boro 4F **17**
     (off Victoria St.)
Heber St. *Rad* 4G **49**
Hebron St. *Rytn* 4E **57**
Hector Av. *Roch* 3B **28**
Hector Rd. *M13* 4B **110**
Heddon Clo. *Stoc* 6A **126**
Heddon Wlk. M8 . . . . . . .5E **83**
     (off Smedley Rd.)
Hedgehog Ho. *Salf* 5F **93**
Hedgelands Wlk. *Sale* . . .4E **121**
Hedge Rows. *Whitw* 4G **15**
Hedge Rows, The.
   Hyde 4E **115**
Hedges St. *Fail* 3G **85**
Hedley St. *Bolt* 3G **31**
Hedley Wlk. M8 . . . . .4B **82**
     (off Halliwell La.)
Heginbottom Cres.
   Ash L 6G **87**
Heights. 1G **59**
     (in three parts)
Heights Av. *Roch* 1G **27**
Heights Clo. *Roch* 1G **27**
Heights La. *Chad* 5F **55**
Heights La. *Del* 1G **59**
Heights La. *Roch* 1G **27**
Helena St. *Salf* 6A **80**
Helen St. *Eccl* 5D **90**
Helen St. *Farn* 1F **63**
Helen St. *Salf* 6G **81**
Helensville Av. *Salf* 6D **80**
Helga St. *M40* 1H **95**
Helias Clo. *Wors* 6B **62**
Hellidon Clo.
   M12 . . . . .1H **109** (5G **11**)
Helmclough Way. *Wors* . . .3E **77**
Helmet St. *M1* . . .5G **95** (2F **11**)
Helmsdale. *Wors* 1E **77**
Helmsdale Av. *Bolt* 1D **44**
Helmsdale Clo. *Rams* 5C **12**
Helmshore Av. *Oldh* 5A **58**
Helmshore Ho. Shaw 5F **43**
     (off Helmshore Way)
Helmshore Rd. *Holc* 1C **12**
Helmshore Wlk.
   M13 . . . . .6F **95** (4D **10**)
Helmshore Way. *Shaw* 5F **43**
Helrose St. *M40* 6C **84**
Helsby Clo. *S'head* 3C **74**
Helsby Gdns. *Bolt* 1B **32**
Helsby Rd. *Sale* 1F **135**
Helsby Wlk.
   M12 . . . . .5A **96** (1H **11**)
Helshaw Way. *Hand* 3H **159**
Helston Clo. *Bram* 6H **151**
Helston Clo. *Hyde* 6H **115**
Helston Clo. *Irlam* 5F **103**
Helston Dri. *Rytn* 3D **56**
Helston Gro. *H Grn* 5G **149**
Helston Wlk. *Hyde* 6H **115**
Helton Wlk. *Midd* 6E **53**
Helvellyn Dri. *Midd* 5F **53**
Helvellyn Wlk. *Oldh* 6E **57**
Hembury Av. *M19* 3B **126**
Hembury Clo. *Midd* 5B **54**
Hemlock Av. *Oldh* 6C **72**
Hemming Dri. *Eccl* 4G **91**
Hemmington Dri. *M9* 4F **83**
Hemmons Rd. *M12* 5D **110**
Hempcroft Rd. *Timp* 6C **134**
Hempshaw Bus. Cen.
   Stoc 4B **140**
Hempshaw La. *Stoc* 4H **139**
     (in two parts)
Hemsby Clo. *Bolt* 3E **45**
Hemsley St. *M9* 2G **83**
Hemsley St. S. *M9* 3G **83**
Hemswell Clo. *Salf* 1E **93**

Hemsworth Rd. *M18* 4F **111**
Hemsworth Rd. *Bolt* 5H **31**
Henbury Dri. *Woodl* 3H **129**
Henbury La. *Chea H* 1B **160**
Henbury Rd. *Hand* 3H **159**
Henbury St. *M14* 4E **109**
Henbury St. *Stoc* 1C **152**
Henderson Av. *Swin* 2F **79**
Henderson St. *M19* 1D **126**
Henderson St. *L'boro* 4E **17**
Henderson St. *Roch* 1B **28**
Henderville St. *L'boro* 3E **17**
Hendham Clo. *Haz G* 3A **152**
Hendham Dri. *Alt* 6D **132**
Hendham Va. *M9* 4E **83**
     (in two parts)
Hendham Wlk. *Haz G* . . .4A **152**
Hendon Dri. *Bury* 2D **50**
Hendon Dri. *Stoc* 4C **138**
Hendon Gro. *Heyw* 6G **39**
Hendon Rd. *M9* 5E **69**
Henfield Pl. *Roch* 2H **27**
Henfield Wlk. *M22* 2A **148**
Hengist St. *M18* 3F **111**
Hengist St. *Bolt* 6E **33**
Henley Av. *M16* 4H **107**
Henley Av. *Chea H* 3A **150**
Henley Av. *Irlam* 3C **118**
Henley Dri. *Ash L* 1F **99**
Henley Dri. *Timp* 4H **133**
Henley Grange. *Chea* 6G **137**
Henley Gro. *Bolt* 4H **45**
Henley Pl. *M19* 3C **126**
Henley St. *Chad* 6G **71**
Henley St. *Oldh* 1B **72**
Henley St. *Roch* 2G **27**
Henley Ter. *Roch* 6G **27**
Henlow Wlk. *M40* 1D **84**
Hennicker St. *Wors* 2F **77**
Henniker Rd. *Bolt* 5E **45**
Henniker St. *Swin* 5E **79**
Hennon St. *Bolt* 4H **31**
Henrietta St. *M16* 3A **108**
Henrietta St. *Ash L* 6F **87**
Henrietta St. *Bolt* 3F **45**
Henry Herman St. *Bolt* . . .4E **45**
     (in two parts)
Henry Lee St. *Bolt* 4G **45**
Henry Sq. *Ash L* 3G **99**
Henry St. *M4* 3F **95** (4C **6**)
     (in two parts)
Henry St. *Bolt* 1C **46**
Henry St. *Dent* 1H **129**
Henry St. *Droy* 4A **98**
Henry St. *Eccl* 4E **91**
Henry St. *Fail* 4F **85**
Henry St. *Hyde* 5B **114**
Henry St. *L'boro* 6D **16**
Henry St. *Midd* 1H **69**
Henry St. *Old T* 2A **108**
Henry St. *P'wich* 4G **67**
Henry St. *Rams* 2F **13**
Henry St. *Roch* 5H **27**
Henry St. *Stoc* 3B **140**
Henry St. *Ward* 2A **16**
Henshaw Ct. *M16* 3H **107**
Henshaw La. *Chad* 1F **85**
Henshaw St. *Oldh* 2C **72**
Henshaw St. *Stret* 5D **106**
Henshaw Wlk.
   M13 . . . . . . .6F **95** (4D **10**)
Henshaw Wlk. Bolt 3A **32**
     (off Madeley Gdns.)
Henson Gro. *Timp* 1A **146**
Henthorn St. *Oldh* 1E **73**
Henthorn St. *Shaw* 1F **57**
Henton Wlk. *M40* 1G **95**
Henwick Hall Av.
   Rams 5D **12**
Henwood Rd. *M20* 4G **125**
Hepburn Ct. *Salf* 1E **93**

Hepley Rd. *Poy* 4G **163**
Hepple Clo. *Stoc* 6A **126**
Heppleton Rd. *M40* 1D **84**
Hepple Wlk. *Ash L* 6C **86**
Heptonstall Wlk. *M18* . . .2E **111**
Hepton St. *Oldh* 1C **72**
Hepworth St. *Hyde* 2C **130**
Heraldic Ct. *Salf* 6E **81**
Herbert St. *M8* 6B **82**
Herbert St. *Chad* 2H **71**
Herbert St. *Dent* 3G **113**
Herbert St. *Droy* 4H **97**
Herbert St. *L Lev* 4B **48**
Herbert St. *Oldh* 6H **57**
Herbert St. *P'wich* 5D **66**
Herbert St. *Rad* 2F **49**
Herbert St. *Stoc* 4F **139**
Herbert St. *Stret* 5D **106**
Hereford Clo. *Ash L* 4H **87**
Hereford Clo. *Shaw* 6D **42**
Hereford Cres. *L Lev* 3A **48**
Hereford Dri. *Bury* 5D **36**
Hereford Dri. *Hand* 4A **160**
Hereford Dri. *P'wich* 6G **67**
Hereford Dri. *Swin* 5F **79**
Hereford Gro. *Urm* 5E **105**
Hereford Rd. *Bolt* 5F **31**
Hereford Rd. *Chea* 1C **150**
Hereford Rd. *Eccl* 6G **79**
Hereford Rd. *Stoc* 4C **128**
Hereford St. *Bolt* 3B **32**
Hereford St. *Oldh* 4H **71**
Hereford St. *Roch* 6A **28**
Hereford St. *Sale* 5B **122**
     (in two parts)
Hereford Wlk. *Dent* 6F **113**
Hereford Wlk. *Rom* 2G **141**
Hereford Way. *Midd* 6C **54**
Hereford Way. *Stal* 6H **101**
Herevale Grange.
   Wors 4D **76**
Herevale Hall Dri.
   Rams 5D **12**
Heristone Av. *Dent* 4E **113**
Heritage Gdns. *M20* 1F **137**
Heritage Pk. *Roch* 4A **28**
Heritage Wharf. *Ash L* . . .4G **99**
Herle Dri. *M22* 4A **148**
Hermitage Av. *Rom* 1D **142**
Hermitage Ct. *Hale* 2H **145**
Hermitage Gdns.
   Rom 1D **142**
Hermitage Rd. *M8* 2C **82**
Hermitage Rd. *Hale* 2H **145**
Hermon Av. *Oldh* 5C **72**
Herne St. *M11* 5C **96**
Heron Av. *Duk* 6C **100**
Heron Av. *Farn* 2B **62**
Heron Ct. *Salf* 2B **92**
Heron Ct. Stoc 4G **139**
     (off Worrall St.)
Herondale Clo. *M40* 6B **84**
Heron Dri. *Aud* 4C **98**
Heron Dri. *Irlam* 4E **103**
Heron Dri. *Poy* 4A **162**
Heron St. *M15* 2C **108**
Heron St. *Oldh* 5A **72**
Heron St. *Stoc* 3F **139**
Heron St. *Swin* 2G **79**
Heron's Way. *Bolt* 2C **46**
Herries St. *Ash L* 1B **100**
Herristone Rd. *M8* 1C **82**
Herrod Av. *Stoc* 4G **127**
Hersalls St. *Salf* . . .2C **94** (1E **5**)
Herschel St. *M40* 3A **84**
Hersey St. *Salf* 3E **93**
Hersham Wlk. M9 . . . . . .2G **83**
     (off Huncote Dri.)
Hertford Gro. *Cad* 3A **118**
Hertford Ind. Est.
   Ash L 4G **99**
Hertford Rd. *M9* 2F **83**

Hertfordshire Pk. Clo.
Shaw 5F 43
Hertford St. Ash L 4G 00
Hesford Av. M9 . . . . . .4H 83
Hesketh Av. M20 . . . . . .6E 125
Hesketh Av. Bolt 6D 18
Hesketh Av. Shaw 2E 57
Hesketh Ho. Farn 1F 63
(off Hesketh Wlk.)
Hesketh Rd. Roch 4C 28
Hesketh Rd. Sale 6H 121
Hesketh St. Stoc 5G 127
(All Saints' Rd.)
Hesketh St. Stoc 6G 127
(Belmont St.)
Hesketh St. Stoc 6G 127
(Short St.)
Hesketh Wlk. Farn 1F 63
Hesketh Wlk. Midd 5G 53
Hessel St. Salf 4D 92
Hester Wlk.
M15 . . . . . .1E 109 (6H 9)
Heston Av. M13 . . . . . .5A 110
Heston Dri. Urm 4E 105
Heswall Av. M20 . . . . . .2F 125
Heswall Dri. Wals 6G 21
Heswall Rd. Stoc 6H 111
Heswall St. Bolt 6H 33
Hetherington Wlk.
M12 . . . . . .3C 110
Hethorn St. M40 . . . . . .6C 84
Hetton Av. M13 . . . . . .5A 110
Heversham Av. Shaw 6H 43
Heversham Wlk. M18 . . .1E 111
(off Grizebeck Clo.)
Hever Wlk. M4 . . . . . .4F 7
Hewart Clo. M40 . . . . . .1G 95
Hewart Dri. Bury 2G 37
Howitt Av. Dent 4H 111
Hewitt St. M15 . . .6C 94 (3F 9)
Hewlett Ct. Rams 1A 22
Hewlett Rd. M21 . . . . . .6G 107
Hewlett St. Bolt 6C 32
Hexham Av. Bolt 4D 30
Hexham Clo. Chad 2A 72
Hexham Clo. Sale 6F 121
Hexham Clo. Stoc 6E 141
Hexham Rd. M18 . . . . . .4E 111
Hexon Clo. Salf 2E 93
Hexworth Wlk. Bram 3A 152
Hey Bottom La. Whitw . 4F 15
(in two parts)
Heybrook. Roch 2B 28
Heybrook Clo. W'fld 1G 67
Heybrook Rd. M23 . . . . . .6H 135
Heybrook St. Roch 3B 28
Heybrook Wlk. W'fld 1G 67
Heybury Clo. M11 . . . . . .5B 96
Hey Cres. Lees 2B 74
Hey Cft. W'fld 2A 66
Heycrofts Vw. Rams 2A 12
Heyden Bank. Glos 5F 117
(off Grassmoor Cres.)
Heyden Fold. Glos 5F 117
(off Grassmoor Cres.)
Heyden Ter. Glos 5F 117
Heyes Av. Timp 4B 134
Heyes Dri. Timp 4B 134
Heyes La. Timp 4D 134
Heyes Leigh. Timp 3B 134
Heyes Ter. Timp 3B 134
(off Old Heyes Rd.)
Hey Flake La. Del 1G 59
Heyford Av. M40 . . . . . .1D 84
Hey Head Cotts. Bolt 6D 20
Hey Head La. L'boro 1F 17
Heyheads. 4G 89
Heyheads New Rd.
Carr 4G 89
Hey Hill Clo. Rytn 2F 57
Heyland Rd. M23 . . . . . .5G 135

Hey La. Upperm 6C 60
Heylee. Ash L 5E 99
Heyridge Dri. M22 . . . . . .2D 10G
Heyrod. 1G 101
Heyrod Fold. H'rod 6E 89
Heyrod Hall Est.
H'rod 1G 101
Heyrod St. M1 . . .5G 95 (1E 11)
Heyrod St. Carr 6F 89
Heyrose Wlk.
M15 . . . . . .1B 108 (6D 8)
Heys Av. M23 . . . . .2G 135
Heys Av. Rom 6C 130
Heys Av. Swin 1C 78
Heysbank Rd. Dis 1H 165
Heys Clo. N. Swin 1C 78
Heys Ct. Stoc 3D 138
Heyscroft Rd. M20 . . . . . .3G 125
Heyscroft Rd. Stoc 1C 108
Heysham Av. M20 . . . . . .2D 124
Heysham Wlk. M23 . . . . . .1E 135
Heyside. 2E 73
Heyside. Rytn 4E 57
Heyside Av. Rytn 4E 57
Heyside Clo. Carr 5G 89
Heyside Way. Bury 4D 36
Heys La. Heyw 3C 38
Heys La. Rom 6C 130
Heys Rd. Ash L 2B 100
Heys Rd. P'wich 4F 67
Heys St. Bury 3B 36
Heys, The. P'wich 4F 67
Heys, The. Stoc 6A 112
Hey St. Roch 3B 28
Heys Vw. P'wich 5F 67
Hey Top. G'fld 6H 61
Heywood. 3F 39
Heywood Av. Aus 1C 74
Heywood Av. Swin 1H 79
Heywood Clo. Ald E 4H 167
Heywood Ct. Midd 2D 68
Heywood Distribution Pk.
Heyw 5A 38
Heywood Fold Rd.
S'head 2R 74
Heywood Gdns. Bolt 3A 46
Heywood Gdns. P'wich . . .5F 67
Heywood Gro. Sale 3A 122
Heywood Hall Rd.
Heyw 2F 39
Heywood Ho. Oldh 4D 72
Heywood Ho. Salf 2C 92
Heywood Ind. Pk.
Heyw 6B 38
Heywood La. Aus 2C 74
Heywood M. L Lev 4B 48
(off Heywood St.)
Heywood M. P'wich 5F 67
Heywood Old Rd.
Midd & Heyw 6C 52
Heywood Pk. Vw. Bolt . . .3A 46
Heywood Rd. Ald E 4H 167
Heywood Rd. P'wich 6F 67
Heywood Rd. Roch 3B 40
Heywood Rd. Sale 6R 122
Heywood's Hollow.
Bolt 2B 32
Heywood Sports Complex.
. . . . .2E 39
Heywood St. M8 . . . . . . .4C 82
Heywood St. Bolt 5B 32
Heywood St. Bury 4E 37
Heywood St. Fail 4D 84
Heywood St. L Lev 4B 48
Heywood St. Oldh 1A 74
Heywood St. Swin 3E 79
Heywood Way. Salf 2F 93
Heyworth Av. Rom 6B 130
Heyworth St. Salf 4E 93
Hibbert Av. Dent 2E 113
Hibbert Av. Hyde 6C 114
Hibbert Cres. Fail 4G 85

Hibbert La. Marp 6D 142
Hibbert St. M14 . . . . . .4G 109
Hibbert St. Dult 3B 32
(in two parts)
Hibbert St. Lees 2A 74
Hibbert St. Stoc 4G 127
Hibernia St. Bolt 2G 45
Hibernia Way. Stret 2A 106
Hibson Av. Roch 1A 26
Hibson Clo. Ward 3A 16
Hickenfield Rd.
Hyde 2D 114
Hicken Pl. Hyde 2D 114
Hickton Dri. Alt 5D 132
Hidden Gem, Manchester
St Marys Catholic
Church, The. 6G 5
Higginshaw. 5E 57
Higginshaw La.
Oldh & Rytn 5E 57
Higginshaw Rd. Oldh 6D 56
Higginson Rd. Stoc 2G 127
Higgs Clo. Oldh 2H 73
Higham Clo. Rytn 2E 57
Higham La. Hyde 1D 130
Higham St. Chea H 4C 150
Higham Vw. Salf 2G 93
High Ash Gro. Aud 6D 98
High Av. Bolt 5G 33
High Bank. M18 . . . . . .2G 111
High Bank. Alt 6F 133
High Bank. Brom X 4D 18
High Bank. Dent 5B 112
High Bank. Hale 3A 146
Highbank. Swin 3A 80
High Bank Av. Stal 6H 101
Highbank Clo. Cad 3B 118
Highbank Cres. Grass 4G 75
High Bank Cres.
P'wich 6G 67
Highbank Dri. M20 . . . . . .3F 137
High Bank Gro. P'wich . . .6G 67
High Bank La. Los 6A 30
Highbank Rd. Bury 4D 50
High Bank Rd. M18 . . . . . .6E 33
Highbank Trad. Est.
M11 . . . . .6F 97
High Barn Clo. Roch 6G 27
Highbarn Ho. Rytn 3C 56
High Barn La. Whitw 2G 15
(Facit)
High Barn La. Whitw 1B 14
(Fold Head)
Highbarn Rd. Midd 2A 70
High Barn Rd. Rytn 3D 56
High Barn St. Rytn 3C 56
High Beeches. Brad F 2B 48
High Bent Av. Chea H . . .1C 160
High Birch Ter. Roch 1B 40
Highbridge Clo. Bolt 1A 48
Highbrook Gro. Bolt 4B 32
High Brow. L Hul 6A 62
Highbury. Stoc 1B 138
Highbury Av. Irlam 6E 103
Highbury Av. Urm 5A 104
Highbury Ct. P'wich 4F 67
Highbury Rd. M16 . . . . . .6C 108
Highbury Rd. Stoc 3E 127
Highbury Way. Rytn 1B 56
Highclere Av. M7 . . . . . .5B 82
Highclere Rd. M8 . . . . . .1B 82
Highcliffe Rd. M9 . . . . . .6C 68
Highclove La. Wors 6B 76
(in two parts)
Highcrest Av. Gat 6D 136
Highcrest Gro. Tyl 2A 76
Highcroft. Hyde 2C 130

Highcroft Av. M20 . . . . . .5C 124
High Cft. Clo. Duk 5E 101
Highcroft Rd. Rom 6A 130
Highcroft Way. Roch 5F 15
High Crompton. 6D 42
Highdales Rd. M23 . . . . . .6H 135
High Down Wlk. M9 . . . . . .3G 83
(off Augustine Webster Clo.)
High Elm Dri. Haleb 5C 146
High Elm Rd. Haleb 5C 146
High Elms. Chea H 2D 160
Higher Ainsworth Rd.
Rad 6E 35
Higher Ardwick.
M12 . . . . . .6G 95 (4F 11)
Higher Arthurs. G'fld 3F 61
Higher Bank Rd.
L'boro 6E 17
Higher Barlow Row.
Stoc 3H 139
Higher Barn Rd. Had . . .3G 117
Higher Barrowshaw. 5H 57
Higher Bents La. Bred . . .6F 129
Higher Blackley. 5D 68
Higher Boarshaw. 5C 54
Higher Bri. St. Bolt 4B 32
Higher Broughton. 4H 81
Higher Bury St. Stoc 1F 139
Higher Calderbrook.
L'boro 6G 17
Higher Calderbrook Rd.
L'boro 6G 17
Higher Cambridge St.
M15 . . . . . .1E 109 (5A 10)
Higher Carr La. G'fld 2F 61
Higher Chatham St.
M15 . . . . . .1E 109 (5A 10)
Higher Cleggswood Av.
L'boro 6E 17
Higher Crimble. Roch 1H 39
Higher Cft. Eccl 5E 91
Higher Cft. W'fld 3A 66
Higher Crossbank.
Lees 1B 74
Higher Croce La.
Upperm 2G 61
Higher Crumpsall. 2D 82
Higher Darcy St. Bolt 2E 47
Higher Dean St. Rad . . .4E 49
Higher Disley. 2H 165
Higher Downs. Alt 2E 145
Higher Dunscar. Eger . . .2C 18
Higher Fold La. Rams . . .2G 13
Higher Fullwood. Oldh . . .3H 57
Higher Grn. Ash L 1B 100
Higher Hartshead. 2B 88
Higher Henry St.
Hyde 6B 114
Higher Hillgate. Stoc 3H 139
Higher Ho. Clo. Chad . . .5G 71
Higher Hurst. 5A 88
Higher Hydegreen. 6H 89
Higher Kinders. G'fld 3F 61
Higher La. Dis 6H 165
Higher La. W'fld 1C 66
Higher Lee St. Oldh 3B 72
Higher Lime Rd. Oldh . . .3A 86
Higher Lodge. Roch 1H 25
Higher Lomax La.
Heyw 3C 38
Higher Lydgate Pk.
Grass 3E 75
Higher Mkt. St. Farn 1G 63
(in two parts)
Higher Market St. Farn . . .2G 63
Higher Mouldings.
Bury 6C 24
Higher Newtons. Moss . . .1F 89
Higher Openshaw. 6H 97
Higher Ormond St.
M15 . . . . . .1E 109 (5B 10)
(in two parts)

Higher Oswald St.
  M4 . . . . .3E **95** (3B **6**)
         (off Goadsby St.)
Higher Pk. *Shaw* 3G **43**
Higher Pit La. *Rad* 5D **34**
Higher Poynton. **4A 164**
Higher Ridings.
  Brom X 3D **18**
       (in two parts)
Higher Ri. *Shaw* 4E **43**
Higher Rd. *Urm* 5F **105**
Higher Row. *Bury* 2F **37**
Higher Rushcroft. **5D 42**
Higher Shady La.
  Brom X 4F **19**
Higher Shore Rd.
  L'boro 2C **16**
Higher Stake Hill. **3F 55**
Higher Summerseat. . . .**2B 22**
Higher Summerseat.
  Rams 1B **22**
Higher Swan La. *Bolt* . . .3H **45**
Higher Tame St. *Stal* 3R **45**
Higher Turf La. *Scout* . . .1D **74**
Higher Turf Pk. *Rytn* 4C **56**
Higher Wharf St.
  Ash L 3H **99**
Higher Wheat La. *Roch* . .3C **28**
Higher Woodhill. **6D 22**
Higher Wood St. *Midd* . .6H **53**
Higher York St.
  M13 . . . . . .1F **109** (5C **10**)
Highfield. **1B 62**
Highfield. *M20* 1E **137**
Highfield. *Miln* 5G **29**
Highfield. *Sale* 6C **122**
Highfield Av. *Bolt* 2A **34**
Highfield Av. *Heyw* 3C **38**
Highfield Av. *Rad* 6A **50**
Highfield Av. *Rom* 1F **141**
Highfield Av. *Sale* 6C **122**
Highfield Av. *Wors* 4B **76**
Highfield Clo. *Hyde* 1D **114**
Highfield Clo. *Stoc* 1H **151**
Highfield Clo. *Stret* 1C **122**
Highfield Ct. *Farn* 2D **62**
Highfield Ct. *Hyde* 3C **116**
Highfield Ct. *P'wich* 4F **67**
Highfield Cres. *Wilm* . . .6G **159**
Highfield Dri. *Eccl* 2F **91**
Highfield Dri. *Farn* 1C **62**
Highfield Dri. *Midd* 2H **69**
Highfield Dri. *Moss* 3E **89**
Highfield Dri. *Rytn* 5C **56**
Highfield Dri. *Swin* 4A **80**
Highfield Dri. *Urm* 4E **105**
Highfield Est. *Wilm* 6G **159**
Highfield Gdns. *Holl* 2F **117**
Highfield Gdns. *Hyde* . . .4D **114**
Highfield Glen. *Ash L* . . .6B **88**
Highfield Ho. *Farn* 1B **62**
Highfield Ho. *Stoc* 6H **139**
Highfield La.
  Bury & W'fld 4C **50**
Highfield Pk. *Stoc* 1B **138**
Highfield Pk. Rd. *Bred* . .5E **129**
Highfield Parkway. *Bram* .3F **161**
Highfield Pl. *M18* 3H **111**
Highfield Pl. *P'wich* 4E **67**
Highfield Range. *M18* . .3H **111**
Highfield Rd. *M7* 4B **82**
Highfield Rd. *Bolt* 3F **31**
Highfield Rd. *Bram* 2H **151**
Highfield Rd. *Chea H* . . .4A **150**
Highfield Rd. *Eccl* 1F **91**
Highfield Rd. *Farn* 1A **62**
Highfield Rd. *Hale* 3A **146**
Highfield Rd. *Haz G* 3G **153**
Highfield Rd. *Lev* 6E **111**
Highfield Rd. *L Hul* 4B **62**
Highfield Rd. *Marp* 5D **142**
Highfield Rd. *Mell* 5F **143**

Highfield Rd. *Poy* 3A **162**
Highfield Rd. *P'wich* 3E **67**
Highfield Rd. *Rams* 3A **12**
Highfield Rd. *Roch* 2A **26**
Highfield Rd. *Salf* 2F **93**
Highfield Rd. *Stret* 1C **122**
Highfield Rd. *Timp* 6B **134**
Highfield Rd. Ind. Est.
  L Hul 3B **62**
Highfield St. *Aud* 1F **113**
Highfield St. *Bred* 6F **129**
Highfield St. *Dent* 2E **113**
Highfield St. *Duk* 4H **99**
Highfield St. *Kear* 3A **64**
Highfield St. *Midd* 1B **70**
Highfield St. *Oldh* 2C **72**
       (Kirkham St.)
Highfield St. *Oldh* 2C **72**
      (Middleton Rd.)
Highfield St. *Stoc* 3E **139**
Highfield St. W. *Duk* 4H **99**
Highgrove. *Sale* 2A **134**
Highgrove Clo. *Bolt* 1B **32**
Highgrove Ct. *M8* 4B **68**
Highgrove M. *Wilm* 3D **166**
High Gro. Rd. *Oldh* 6G **137**
High Gro. Rd.
  Grass & G'fld 4G **75**
Highgrove, The. *Bolt* 4B **30**
High Houses. *Bolt* 5B **18**
High Hurst Clo. *Midd* 1E **69**
Highland M. *Rom* 5A **130**
Highland Rd. *Brom X* 3F **19**
Highlands. *L'boro* 6E **17**
Highlands. *Rytn* 4A **56**
       (in two parts)
Highlands Dri. *Stoc* 5F **141**
Highlands Ho. *Aud* 2E **113**
     (off Barnwell Clo.)
Highlands Ho. *Moss* 2D **88**
     (off Highlands, The)
Highlands Rd. *Roch* 6H **25**
Highlands Rd. *Rytn* 4A **56**
Highlands Rd. *Shaw* 5D **42**
Highlands Rd. *Stoc* 5F **141**
Highlands, The. *Moss* 2D **88**
Highland Vw. *Moss* 1E **89**
Highland Wlk. *M40* 5D **84**
High Lane. **6C 154**
High La. *M21* 1G **123**
High La. *Woodl* 4H **129**
High Lawn. *Bow* 3E **145**
High Lea. *Ald E* 5H **167**
High Lea. *Chea* 6G **137**
High Lee Ho. *Sale* 4D **122**
High Lee La. *Oldh* 4D **58**
High Legh Rd. *M11* 5F **97**
High Level Rd. *Roch* 5H **27**
High Lupus St. *Bolt* 6E **19**
High Mdw. *Chea H* 5A **150**
Highmeadow. *Rad* 6F **49**
High Meadows.
  Brom X 3F **19**
High Meadows. *Rom* 6A **130**
Highmead St. *M18* 2F **111**
Highmead Wlk. *M16* 2B **108**
High Moor Cres. *Oldh* 6A **58**
Highmoor Vw. *Oldh* 6A **58**

Highmore Dri. *M9* 6G **69**
High Mt. *Bolt* 2G **33**
Highnam Wlk. *M22* 4G **147**
High Peak Rd. *Ash L* 5C **88**
High Peak Rd. *Whitw* 3C **14**
High Peak St. *M40* 5B **84**
High Rid La. *Los* 4A **30**
Highshore Dri. *M8* 4B **82**
High Stile La. *Dob* 5D **60**
High Stile St. *Kear* 2G **63**
Highstone Dri. *M8* 5E **83**
High St. *M4* 4E **95** (5A **6**)
High St. *Alt* 1F **145**
High St. *Bolt* 3H **45**
High St. *Chea* 5H **137**
High St. *Del* 3H **59**
High St. *Droy* 4A **98**
High St. *Haz G* 3F **153**
High St. *Heyw* 3D **38**
High St. *Hyde* 4D **114**
High St. *Lees* 3A **74**
High St. *L'boro* 4D **16**
High St. *L Lev* 4B **48**
High St. *Midd* 5A **54**
       (in two parts)
High St. *Moss* 1F **89**
High St. *Oldh* 2D **72**
       (in two parts)
High St. *Roch* 3H **27**
High St. *Rytn* 3B **56**
High St. *Shaw* 1F **57**
High St. *Stal* 5C **100**
High St. *Stoc* 2H **139**
High St. *Upperm* 6B **60**
High St. *Wals* 2F **35**
High St. *Wors* 6E **63**
Highthorne Grn. *Rytn* 5A **42**
Hightown. **5A 82**
High Vw. *P'wich* 6F **67**
Highview St. *Bolt* 5C **18**
High Vw. St. *Bolt* 3G **45**
Highview Wlk. *M9* 6G **69**
Highwood. *Roch* 2A **26**
Highwood Clo. *Bolt* 4H **33**
High Wood Fold.
  Marp B 3G **143**
Highworth Clo. *Bolt* 2A **46**
Highworth Dri. *M40* 1D **84**
Higson Av. *M21* 2H **123**
Higson Av. *Eccl* 5E **91**
Higson Av. *Rom* 1F **141**
Hilary Av. *H Grn* 5H **149**
Hilary Av. *Oldh* 3D **86**
Hilary Clo. *Stoc* 1F **139**
Hilary Gro. *Farn* 2E **63**
Hilary Rd. *M22* 4A **148**
Hilary St. *Roch* 4D **40**
Hilbre Av. *Rytn* 5B **56**
Hilbre Rd. *M19* 1B **126**
Hilbre Way. *Hand* 3H **159**
Hilbury Av. *M9* 2F **83**
Hilda Av. *Chea* 6A **138**
Hilda Av. *T'ton* 5H **21**
Hilda Gro. *Stoc* 5H **127**
Hilda Rd. *Hyde* 2B **130**
Hilda St. *Bolt* 3C **46**
Hilda St. *Heyw* 2F **39**
Hilda St. *Oldh* 2B **72**
       (in two parts)
Hilda St. *Stoc* 5H **127**
Hilden Ct. *M16* 3B **108**
Hilden St. *Bolt* 1C **46**
Hilditch Clo. *M23* 5H **135**
Hiley Rd. *Eccl* 5B **90**
Hillam Clo. *Urm* 6H **105**
Hillary Av. *Ash L* 6F **87**
Hillary Rd. *Hyde* 2E **115**
Hillbank Clo. *Bolt* 2G **31**
Hill Bank Clo. *Carr* 4B **89**
Hillbank St. *Midd* 1D **54**
Hill Barn La. *Dig* 4D **60**
Hillbrook Av. *M40* 1B **84**

Hillbrook Grange.
  Bram 1F **161**
Hillbrook Rd. *Bram* 1F **161**
Hillbrook Rd. *Stoc* 3C **140**
Hillbrow Wlk. *M8* 4B **82**
Hillbury Rd. *Bram* 4H **151**
Hill Carr M. *Alt* 1D **144**
Hill Clo. *Oldh* 4G **73**
Hillcote Wlk. *M18* 1D **110**
Hill Cot Rd. *Bolt* 6D **18**
Hill Ct. M. *Rom* 1H **141**
Hillcourt Rd. *H Lane* 6C **154**
Hillcourt Rd. *Rom* 5A **130**
Hillcourt St.
  M1 . . . . . . .6E **95** (4B **10**)
Hill Cres. *M9* 6C **68**
Hillcrest. *Hyde* 2D **130**
Hillcrest. *Midd* 4H **53**
Hillcrest. *Salf* 2A **92**
Hillcrest Av. *Heyw* 2C **38**
Hill Crest Av. *Stoc* 1C **138**
Hillcrest Cres. *Heyw* 2C **38**
Hillcrest Dri. *M19* 2E **127**
Hillcrest Dri. *Dent* 6H **113**
Hillcrest Rd. *Bram* 3H **151**
Hillcrest Rd. *P'wich* 1D **80**
Hillcrest Rd. *Roch* 3D **40**
       (in two parts)
Hillcrest Rd. *Stoc* 5C **140**
Hillcrest Rd. *Tyl* 3A **76**
Hillcroft. *Oldh* 2E **87**
Hill Cft. *Stoc* 5E **141**
Hillcroft Clo. *M8* 3C **82**
Hillcroft Rd. *Alt* 6C **132**
Hilldale Av. *M9* 5F **69**
Hill Dri. *Hand* 4A **160**
Hillel Ho. *M15* 2E **109**
Hillend. *B'btm* 6C **116**
Hillend. *Rom* 5B **130**
Hillend La. *Mot* 6B **116**
Hillend Pl. *M23* 1G **135**
Hillend Rd. *M23* 1G **135**
Hill End Rd. *Del* 2H **59**
Hill Farm Clo. *Oldh* 6E **73**
Hillfield. *Salf* 3D **92**
Hillfield Clo. *M13* 2H **109**
Hillfield Dri. *Bolt* 4D **32**
Hillfield Dri. *Wors* 4C **76**
Hillfield Wlk. *Bolt* 4D **32**
Hillfoot Wlk.
  M15 . . . . . .1B **108** (5D **8**)
Hillgate Av. *Salf* 6H **93**
Hillgate Bus. Cen.
  Stoc 3H **139**
Hillgate St. *Ash L* 1A **100**
Hillhead Wlk. M8 . . . .*5C 82*
     (off Barnsdale Dri.)
Hillhouse Ct. *Roch* 2B **40**
Hillier St. *M9* 3G **83**
Hillier St. N. *M9* 3G **83**
Hillingdon Clo. *Oldh* 3H **85**
Hillingdon Dri. *M9* 1B **84**
Hillingdon Ho. Bolt *4A 32*
     (off Enfield Clo.)
Hillingdon Rd. *Stret* 6E **107**
Hillingdon Rd. *W'fld* 2B **66**
Hillington Rd. *Sale* 5G **121**
Hillington Rd. *Stoc* 3E **139**
Hillkirk Dri. *Roch* 6C **14**
Hillkirk St. *M11* 4A **96**
Hill La. *M9* 6F **69**
Hill La. *Bolt* 5C **32**
Hillman Clo. *M40* 6F **83**
Hill Mt. *Duk* 5E **101**
Hillock, The. *Bolt* 6H **19**
Hill Ri. *Alt* 6C **132**
Hill Ri. *Rams* 5C **12**
Hill Ri. *Rom* 1H **141**
Hillsborough Dri.
  Bury 4F **51**
Hill's Ct. *Bury* 1H **35**
Hillsdale Gro. *Bolt* 2G **33**

Hill Side. *Bolt* 6D **30**
Hillside Av. *Brom X* 2F **19**
Hillside Av. *Carr* 5H **80**
Hillside Av. *Dig* 4B **60**
Hillside Av. *Farn* 2D **62**
Hillside Av. *G'ton* 4C **74**
Hillside Av. *Hyde* . . .3D **130**
Hillside Av. *Oldh* 2G **73**
Hillside Av. *Rytn* 2C **56**
Hillside Av. *Salf* 3E **81**
Hillside Av. *Shaw* 6H **43**
Hillside Av. *W'fld* 5C **50**
Hilloido Av. *Wors* 5C **63**
Hillside Clo. *M40* 2A **84**
Hillside Clo. *Bolt* 5B **44**
Hillside Clo. *Brad* 6A **20**
Hillside Clo. *Bram* 6A **152**
Hillside Clo. *Had* 4G **111**
Hillside Ct. *Bolt* 6D **30**
Hillside Ct. *P'wich* 6E **67**
Hillside Cres. *Ash L* 6B **88**
Hillside Cres. *Bury* 5F **23**
Hillside Dri. *Midd* 6B **54**
Hillside Dri. *Swin* 5B **80**
Hillside Gdns. *Bury* 1C **22**
Hillside Gro. *Marp B* . . .2F **143**
Hillside Ho. *Bolt* 6D **30**
Hillside Rd. *Hale* 2A **146**
Hillside Rd. *Rams* 4C **12**
Hillside Rd. *Stoc* 4D **140**
Hillside Rd.
  Woodl & Hyde . . .4A **130**
Hillside St. *Bolt* 2H **45**
Hilloido Vw. *Dent* 2G **129**
Hillside Vw. *Miln* 5G **29**
Hillside Wlk. *Roch* 5D **14**
Hillside Way. *Whitw* 4G **15**
Hillo La. *Bury* 5C **51**
Hillspring Rd. *S'head* 3C **74**
Hillstone Av. *Roch* 5C **14**
Hillstone Clo. *G'mnt* 1H **21**
Hill St. M20 . . . .*2F* **125**
  (off Brownacre St.)
Hill St. *Ash L* 3G **99**
Hill St. *B'hth* 3E **133**
Hill St. *Duk* 4H **99**
Hill St. *Heyw* 3E **39**
Hill St. *Hyde* 1D **130**
Hill St. *Midd* 4A **54**
Hill St. *Oldh* 2F **73**
Hill St. *Rad* 3F **49**
  (Ainsworth St.)
Hill St. *Rad* 6H **49**
  (Rupert St.)
Hill St. *Roch* 4A **28**
Hill St. *Rom* 1H **141**
Hill St. *Salf* 5H **81**
  (in two parts)
Hill St. *Shaw* 1G **57**
Hill St. *S'seat* 6E **13**
Hill St. *T'ton* 1F **35**
Hill Top. 1F 167
  (Manchester)
Hill Top. 1F 167
  (Wilmslow)
Hill Top. *Bolt* 2H **31**
Hill Top. *Chad* 5F **55**
Hill Top. *Hale* 4A **146**
Hill Top. *L Lev* 3A **48**
Hill Top. *Rom* 6H **129**
Hilltop. *Whitw* 4C **14**
Hilltop Av. *M9* 6F **69**
Hill Top Av. *Chea H* . . .4C **150**
Hill Top Av. *P'wich* 5F **67**
Hilltop Av. *W'fld* 1F **67**
Hill Top Av. *Wilm* 1E **167**
Hilltop Ct. *M8* 1B **82**
Hilltop Ct. *M14* 6H **109**
Hill Top Ct. *Chea H* . . .4D **150**
Hill Top Dri. *Hale* 4A **146**
Hill Top Dri. *Marp* 5A **142**

Hill Top Dri. *Roch* 3F **41**
Hilltop Dri. *Rytn* 5C **56**
Hilltop Dri. *T'ton* 6G **21**
Hilltop Gro. *W'fld* 1F **67**
Hill Top La. *Del* 3E **59**
Hill Top Rd. *Wors* 5F **63**
Hill Vw. *Del* 3H **59**
Hill Vw. *L'boro* 6H **17**
Hill Vw. *Stal* 1H **115**
Hill Vw. Clo. *Oldh* 5G **57**
Hillview Ct. *Bolt* 1A **32**
Hillview Rd. *Bolt* 1A **32**
Hillview Rd. *Dent* 6A **112**
Hillwood Av. *M8* 6B **68**
Hillyard St. *Bury* 2A **36**
Hilly Cft. *Brom X* 3D **18**
Hilmarton Clo. *Brad* 6A **20**
Hilrose Av. *Urm* 5H **105**
Hilson Ct. *Droy* 1A **98**
Hilton Arc. *Oldh* 2D **72**
Hilton Av. *Urm* 5F **105**
Hilton Bank. *Wors* 6D **62**
Hilton Ct. *Stoc* 3G **139**
Hilton Cres. *Ash L* 6G **87**
Hilton Cres. *P'wich* 1F **81**
Hilton Cres. *Wors* 5D **76**
Hilton Dri. *Cad* 4A **118**
Hilton Dri. *P'wich* 1F **81**
Hilton Fold La. *Midd* 6B **54**
Hilton Gro. *Poy* 3D **162**
Hilton Gro. *Wors* 6D **62**
Hilton La. *P'wich* 2D **80**
Hilton La. *Wors* 6D **62**
Hilton Lodge. *P'wich* 1F **81**
Hilton Park. 1F 81
Hilton Rd. *M22* 6C **136**
Hilton Rd. *Bram* 4H **151**
Hilton Rd. *Bury* 3D **36**
Hilton Rd. *Dis* 0F **155**
Hilton Rd. *Poy* 2A **164**
  (in two parts)
Hiltons Clo. *Oldh* 4C **72**
Hiltons Farm Clo. *Aud* . . .1E **113**
Hilton Sq. *Swin* 3G **79**
Hilton St. *M1* 4F **95** (5C **6**)
Hilton St.
  M4 & M1 . . . .3E **95** (4B **6**)
Hilton St. *Bolt* 6E **33**
Hilton St. *Bury* 1D **36**
Hilton St. *Hyde* 2D **114**
Hilton St. *L Hul* 5C **62**
Hilton St. *Midd* 5H **53**
Hilton St. *Oldh* 1G **73**
Hilton St. *Salf* 5H **81**
Hilton St. *Stoc* 3F **139**
Hilton St. N. *Salf* 5H **81**
Hilton Wlk. *Midd* 1E **69**
  (in two parts)
Himley Rd. *M11* 2E **97**
Hincaster Wlk. *M18* 2E **111**
Hinchcliffe St. *Roch* 3F **27**
Hinchcombe Clo. *L Hul* . . .3C **62**
Hinchley Rd. *M9* 6C **70**
Hinchley Way. *Swin* 1F **79**
Hinckley St. *M11* 5B **96**
Hindburn Clo. *W'fld* 6F **51**
Hindburn Dri. *Wors* 3C **76**
Hindburn Wlk. *W'fld* 6F **51**
Hinde St. *M40* 3A **84**
Hindhead Wlk. *M40* 1F **97**
Hind Hill St. *Heyw* 4F **39**
Hindle Dri. *Rytn* 4A **56**
Hindle St. *Rad* 4G **49**
Hindle Ter. *Del* 3H **59**
Hindley Av. *M22* 3H **147**
Hindley Clo. *Ash L* 4F **99**
Hindley St. *Ash L* 4F **99**
  (in two parts)
Hindley St. *Stoc* 3H **139**
Hindsford Clo. *M23* 2E **135**
Hinds La. *Bury* 6A **36**
Hind St. *Bolt* 6E **33**

Hinkler Av. *Bolt* 4A **46**
Hinstock Cres. *M18* 2F **111**
Hinton. *Roch* 3G **27**
  (off Redcross St.)
Hinton Clo. *Roch* 5A **28**
Hinton Gro. *Hyde* 1E **131**
Hinton M. *Stoc* 2B **140**
Hinton St. *M4* . . .2F **95** (2D **6**)
Hinton St. *Oldh* 4D **72**
Hipley Clo. *Bred* 5G **129**
Hirons La. *S'head* 4C **74**
Hirst Av. *Wors* 4E **63**
Hitchen Clo. *Duk* 6D **100**
Hitchen Dri. *Duk* 6D **100**
Hitchen Wlk. *M13* 2H **109**
Hives, The. *Traf P* 6C **92**
Hive St. *Oldh* 1H **85**
HMS Bronington. 6E 93
Hobart Clo. *Bram* 3H **161**
Hobart St. *M18* 2F **111**
Hobart St. *Bolt* 3H **31**
Hobbs Wlk. *M8* 1A **82**
Hob Hill. *Stal* 4D **100**
Hob Mill Ri. *Moss* 5G **75**
Hobson Ct. *Aud* 1E **113**
Hobson Cres. *Aud* 1E **113**
Hobson Moor Rd.
  Mot 1B **116**
  (in two parts)
Hobson St. *M11* 6A **98**
Hobson St. *Fail* 5C **84**
Hobson St. *Oldh* 3D **72**
Hobson St. *Stoc* 5H **111**
Hockenhull Clo. *M22* 3C **148**
Hockerley Clo. *Sale* 4F **121**
Hockley. 4F 163
Hockley Clo. *Poy* 4G **163**
Hockley Rd. *M23* 5F **135**
Hockley Rd. *Poy* 4F **163**
Hodder Av. *L'boro* 3D **16**
Hodder Bank. *Stoc* 6E **141**
Hodder Way. *W'fld* 1G **67**
  (in three parts)
Hoddesdon St. *M8* 4D **82**
Hodge Clough Rd.
  Oldh 3G **57**
Hodge La. *Salf* 4F **93**
Hodge Rd. *Oldh* 4H **57**
Hodge Rd. *Wors* 1F **77**
Hodge St. *M9* 2H **83**
Hodgson Dri. *Timp* 3A **134**
Hodgson St. *M8* 6B **82**
Hodgson St. *Ash L* 3G **99**
Hodnett Av. *Urm* 6A **104**
Hodnet Wlk. *Dent* 6E **113**
Hodson Fold. *Oldh* 2E **87**
Hodson Rd. *Swin* 1E **79**
Hodson St. *Salf* . . .3C **94** (3E **5**)
Hogarth Ri. *Oldh* 3G **57**
Hogarth Rd. *Marp B* 3F **143**
Hogarth Rd. *Roch* 2F **41**
Hogarth Wlk. *M8* 5E **83**
  (off Gomer Wlk.)
Holbeach Clo. *Bury* 6D **22**
Holbeck Av. *Roch* 5D **14**
Holbeck Gro. *M14* 3A **110**
Holbeton Clo. *M8* 6A **82**
Holbeton Clo. *Bram* 2A **152**
Holborn Av. *Fail* 4H **85**
Holborn Av. *Rad* 3D **48**
Holborn Dri. *M8* 6D **82**
Holborn Gdns. *Roch* 6F **27**
Holborn Sq. *Roch* 6F **27**
Holborn St. *Roch* 6F **27**
Holbrook Av. *L Hul* 3C **62**
Holbrook St. *M1* 2B **10**
Holcombe. 3C 12
Holcombe Av. *Bury* 3H **35**
Holcombe Brook. 1A 22
Holcombe Clo. *Alt* 5D **132**
Holcombe Clo. *Kear* 3A **64**
Holcombe Clo. *Salf* 3G **93**

Holcombe Clo. *S'head* 2C **74**
Holcombe Ct. *Rams* 1A **22**
Holcombe Cres. *Kear* 3A **04**
Holcombe Gdns. *M19* 4A **126**
Holcombe Lee. *Rams* 5C **12**
Holcombe M. *Rams* 6B **12**
Holcombe Old Rd.
  Holc 4C **12**
Holcombe Rd. *M14* 2A **126**
Holcombe Rd. *L Lev* 4H **47**
Holcombe Rd.
  T'ton & G'mnt 4H **21**
Holcombe Vw. Clo.
  Oldh 4H **57**
Holcombe Village. *Holc* . . .3C **12**
Holcombe Wlk. *Stoc* 2F **127**
Holden Av. *Bolt* 5C **18**
Holden Av. *Bury* 1A **38**
Holden Av. *Rams* 4C **12**
Holden Clough Dri.
  Ash L 4E **87**
Holden Fold. 5A 56
Holden Fold La. *Rytn* 5A **56**
  (in two parts)
Holden Gallery. 4B 10
Holden Rd. *Salf* 2H **81**
Holden St. *Ash L* 1A **100**
Holden St. *Oldh* 6D **72**
Holden St. *Roch* 1A **28**
Holder Av. *L Lev* 2B **48**
Holderness Dri. *Rytn* 5A **56**
Holdgate Clo. *M15* 2C **108**
Holdsworth St. *Swin* 4D **78**
Holebottom. *Ash L* 5G **87**
Holehouse Fold. *Hom* . . .1H **141**
Holford Av. *M14* 5F **109**
Holford Ct. *Aud* 4F **113**
Holford St. *Salf* 1A **94**
Holford Wlk. *Fir* 4D **28**
Holgate St. *Oldh* 6A **58**
Holhouse La. *G'mnt* 1H **21**
Holiday La. *Stoc* 5F **141**
Holkar Meadows.
  Brom X 3F **19**
Holker Clo. *M13* 2H **109**
  (in two parts)
Holker Clo. *Poy* 3F **163**
Holker Way. *Dent* 6G **113**
Holkham Clo.
  M4 . . . . .3G **95** (4F **7**)
Holland Av. *Stal* 3E **101**
Holland Clo. *Del* 3G **59**
Holland Ct. *M8* 1B **82**
Holland Ct. *Rad* 3A **50**
Holland Ct. *Stoc* 4A **140**
Holland Gro. *Ash L* 5F **87**
Holland Ri. *Roch* 3G **27**
Holland Rd. *M8* 1B **82**
Holland Rd. *Bram* 6G **151**
Holland Rd. *Hyde* 2D **114**
Holland St.
  M40 . . . . . . .3H **95** (3G **7**)
Holland St. *Bolt* 1B **32**
Holland St. *Dent* 3D **112**
Holland St. *Heyw* 3F **39**
  (in two parts)
Holland St. *Hurs* 5B **16**
Holland St. *Rad* 3A **50**
Holland St. *Roch* 4G **27**
Holland St. *Salf* (M5) 5G **93**
Holland St. *Salf* (M6) 6E **81**
Holland St. E. *Dent* 3D **112**
Holland St. W. *Dent* 3C **112**
Holland Wlk. *Salf* 6E **81**
Hollies Clo. *Sale* 5B **122**
Hollies Dri. *Marp* 6E **143**
Hollies La. *Wilm* 2H **167**
Hollies, The. *M20* 6D **124**
Hollies, The. *Boll* 5H **33**
Hollies, The. *Gat* 6F **137**
Hollies, The. *Oldh* 5B **72**
Hollies, The. *Salf* 2B **92**

Hollies, The. *Stoc* 6D **126**
Hollies, The. *Swin* 4H **79**
 (Manchester Rd.)
Hollies, The. *Swin* 5D **78**
 (Moorfield Clo.)
Hollin Bank. *Stoc* 2F **127**
Hollin Cres. *G'fld* 5G **75**
Hollney Rd. *M22* 4D **148**
Hollingwood Rd. *Dis* 1H **165**
Hollingworth. **2E 117**
 (Hyde)
Hollingworth. **6F 17**
 (Littleborough)
Hollingworth Av. *M40* 1F **85**
Hollingworth Clo.
 Stoc 3H **139**
 (off Mottram Fold)
Hollingworth Lake Cvn. Site.
 L'boro 2H **29**
Hollingworth Lake Country Pk.
 . . . . .1H **29**
Hollingworth Lake Country Pk.
 Vis. Cen. 6F **17**
Hollingworth Lake Nature
 Reserve. 1H **29**
Hollingworth Rd.
 Bred 5E **129**
Hollingworth Rd.
 L'boro 6F **17**
Hollingworth St. *Chad* . . .6H **71**
Hollin Hall St. *Oldh* 2G **73**
Hollin Hey Rd. *Bolt* 2C **30**
Hollinhey Ter. *Holl* 2E **117**
Hollin Ho. *Midd* 4A **54**
Hollinhurst Dri. *Los* 6A **30**
Hollinhurst Rd. *Rad* 5A **50**
Hollinlane. **2D 158**
Hollin La. *Midd* 2G **53**
Hollin La. *Roch* 5A **26**
Hollin La. *Styal* 1D **158**
Hollins. **2E 51**
 (Bury)
Hollins. **4A 54**
 (Manchester)
Hollins. **1A 86**
 (Oldham)
Hollins. *Farn* 6H **45**
Hollins Av. Glos 5F **117**
 (off Hollins M.)
Hollins Av. *Hyde* 2C **130**
Hollins Av. *Lees* 1B **74**
Hollins Bank. Glos 5F **117**
 (off Hollins M.)
Hollins Brook Clo. *Uns* . . .2F **51**
Hollins Brook Way.
 Bury 1F **51**
Hollins Brow. *Bury* 3D **50**
Hollins Clo. *Bury* 3F **51**
Hollins Clo. Glos 5F **117**
 (off Hollins M.)
Hollinsclough Clo.
 M22 . . . . .6C **136**
Hollinscroft Av. *Timp* . . .6D **134**
Hollins Dri. *Midd* 3G **53**
Hollins Fold. Glos 5F **117**
 (off Hollins M.)
Hollins Gdns. Glos 6F **117**
 (off Hollins La.)
Hollins Green. **1C 86**
Hollins Grn. *Midd* 4A **54**
Hollins Grn. Rd. *Marp* . . .5D **142**
Hollins Gro. *M12* 4C **110**
Hollins Gro. Glos 5F **117**
 (off Hollins M.)
Hollins Gro. *Sale* 5A **122**
Hollinshead. Salf 5A **82**
 (off Wilmur Av.)
Hollins La. *Bury* 2E **51**
Hollins La. *Duk* 5D **100**
Hollins La. *Glos* 5F **117**
Hollins La. *G'fld* 4H **61**
Hollins La. *Marp* 5D **142**

Hollins La. *Marp B* 4F **143**
Hollins La. *Moss* 2F **89**
Hollin's La. *Rams* 4B **12**
Hollins M. *Glos* 5F **117**
Hollins M. *Uns* 3G **51**
Hollins Mt. *Marp B* 3F **143**
Hollins Rd. *Oldh* 1H **85**
Hollins Rd. *W'head* 1B **74**
Hollins St. *Bolt* 1D **46**
Hollins St. *S'head* 3B **74**
Hollins St. *Stal* 5D **100**
Hollins Ter. *Marp* 5D **142**
Hollins, The. *Marp* 5D **142**
Hollins Vale. **2E 51**
Hollins Wlk. *M22* 3B **148**
Hollins Way. Glos 5F **117**
 (off Hollins M.)
Hollinswood Rd. *Bolt* 1D **46**
Hollinswood Rd. *Wors* . . .5D **76**
Hollinwood. **2A 86**
Hollinwood Av.
 M40 & Chad 6D **70**
Hollinwood Bus. Cen.
 Fail 2H **85**
Hollinwood La. *Marp* 3F **155**
 (in two parts)
Hollinworth Dri. *Marp* . . .2D **154**
Holloway Dri. *Wors* 2C **78**
Hollowbrook Way.
 Roch 1F **27**
Hollow End. *Stoc* 2B **128**
Hollow End Towers.
 Stoc 2B **128**
Hollow Fld. *Roch* 2H **25**
Hollowgate. *Swin* 5C **78**
Hollow Meadows. *Rad* . . .3C **64**
Hollows Av. *M21* 4A **124**
Hollows Farm Av. *Roch* . . .1F **27**
Hollowspell. *Roch* 6A **16**
Hollows, The. *H Grn* 4G **149**
Hollow Va. *Dri. Stoc* 6H **111**
Holly Av. *Chea* 6H **137**
Holly Av. *Urm* 5D **104**
Holly Av. *Wors* 1G **77**
Holly Bank. *Ash L* 3B **100**
Hollybank. *Droy* 2C **98**
Holly Bank. *Holl* 2F **117**
Holly Bank. *Rytn* 1B **56**
Holly Bank. *Sale* 6C **122**
Holly Bank Clo.
 M15 . . . . .1A **108** (5B **8**)
Holly Bank Cotts.
 Part 5D **118**
 (off Manchester Rd.)
Holly Bank Cotts.
 Woodl 4H **129**
Holly Bank Ct. *Chea H* . . .4C **150**
Holly Bank Dri. *Los* 5A **30**
Holly Bank St. *Rad* 4F **49**
Hollybrook. *Chad* 4H **55**
Hollybrook Dene.
 Rom 1C **142**
Hollybush St. *M18* 1G **111**
Holly Clo. *Timp* 5A **134**
Holly Ct. *M20* 3F **125**
Holly Ct. *Bury* 3E **37**
Holly Ct. *Hyde* 5E **115**
Holly Ct. *Irlam* 4F **103**
Hollycroft Av. *M22* 5B **136**
Hollycroft Av. *Bolt* 2G **47**
Holly Dene Dri. *Los* 6A **30**
Holly Dri. *Sale* 5A **122**
Hollyedge Dri. *P'wich* 1E **81**
Holly Fold. *W'fld* 6D **50**
Holly Grange. *Bow* 3F **145**
Holly Grange. *Bram* 2H **151**
Holly Grove. **4C 60**
Holly Gro. *Bolt* 4G **31**

Holly Gro. *Chad* 1H **71**
Holly Gro. *Dent* 4G **113**
Holly Gro. *Farn* 1C **62**
Holly Gro. *Lees* 1A **74**
Holly Gro. *Los* 6A **30**
Holly Gro. *Sale* 5D **122**
Holly Gro. *Stal* 5C **100**
Hollyhedge Av. *M22* 6B **136**
Hollyhedge Ct. Rd.
 M22 . . . . .6C **136**
Hollyhedge Rd.
 M22 & Gat 6B **136**
Hollyhedge Rd. *M23* 6G **135**
Hollyhey Dri. *M23* 1A **136**
Holly Ho. Dri. *Urm* 5B **104**
Hollyhouse Dri.
 Woodl 4G **129**
Hollyhurst. *Wors* 5B **78**
Holly La. *Oldh* 1A **86**
Holly La. *Styal* 3C **158**
Holly Mill Cres. *Bolt* 1B **32**
Hollymount. *M16* 3H **107**
Hollymount Av. *Stoc* 6C **140**
Hollymount Dri. *Oldh* 4A **58**
Hollymount Dri. *Stoc* 6C **140**
Hollymount Gdns.
 Stoc 6D **140**
Holly Mt. La. *G'mnt* 2F **21**
Hollymount Rd. *Stoc* 6C **140**
Holly Oak Gdns. *Heyw* . . .4E **39**
Holly Rd. *Bram* 2G **161**
Holly Rd. *H Lane* 6D **154**
Holly Rd. *Poy* 4E **163**
Holly Rd. *Stoc* 4E **127**
Holly Rd. *Swin* 5D **78**
Holly Rd. *Wilm* 3D **166**
Holly Rd. N. *Wilm* 3D **166**
Holly Rd. S. *Wilm* 4D **166**
Holly Royde Clo. *M20* 3E **125**
Holly St. *M11* 5A **96**
Holly St. *Bolt* 1B **32**
Holly St. *Bury* 3E **37**
Holly St. *Droy* 3F **97**
Holly St. *Roch* 3H **41**
Holly St. *Stoc* 2A **140**
Holly St. *S'seat* 6E **13**
Holly St. *T'ton* 5H **21**
Holly St. *Ward* 3A **16**
Hollythorn Av. *Chea H* . . .6E **151**
Hollythorn M. *Chea H* 6E **151**
Holly Vw. *M22* 6C **136**
Holly Wlk. *Part* 6B **118**
Holly Way. *M22* 3C **136**
Hollywood. *Bolt* 3F **31**
Hollywood. *Bow* 3F **145**
Hollywood End. **3H 143**
Hollywood Rd. *Bolt* 3F **31**
Hollywood Towers.
 Stoc 3F **139**
 (off Hardman St)
Hollywood Way. *Stoc* . . .2F **139**
Holmbrook Wlk. *M8* 6C **82**
Holm Ct. *Salf* 2G **93**
Holmcroft Rd. *M18* 4F **111**
Holmdale Av. *M19* 4A **126**
Holmdale Ct. *Sale* 5C **122**
Holme Av. *Bury* 6C **22**
Holmebrook Wlk. M8 . . . .5C **82**
 (off Tamerton Dri.)
Holme Cres. *Rytn* 5A **56**
Holmfield. *Sale* 5B **122**
Holmfield Dri.
 Chea H 5D **150**
Holme Ho. *L'boro* 5H **17**
Holme Ho. St. *L'boro* 6H **17**
Holmelyme Ho. *Poy* 4F **163**
Holmepark Gdns. *Wors* . . .6C **76**
Holme Pk. Way. *Fail* 4H **85**
Holme Rd. *M20* 6D **124**
Holmes Cotts. *Bolt* 2G **31**
Holmes Rd. *Roch* 4F **27**
Holmes St. *Bolt* 3C **46**

Holmes St. *Chea* 5A **138**
Holmes St. *Roch* 3F **27**
 (College Rd.)
Holmes St. *Roch* 6A **16**
 (Halifax Rd.)
Holmes St. *Stoc* 4G **139**
Holme St. *Hyde* 5B **114**
Holmes Way. *Dent* 2F **129**
Holmeswood Clo.
 Wilm 1F **167**
Holmeswood Rd. *Bolt* . . .5H **45**
Holme Ter. *L'boro* 6H **17**
Holmfield. *Ald E* 6G **167**
Holmfield Av. *M9* 4H **83**
Holmfield Av. *P'wich* 6G **67**
Holmfield Av. W. *M9* 4H **83**
Holmfield Clo. Stoc 6F **127**
Holmfield Grn. *Bolt* 4D **44**
Holmfirth Rd. *G'fld* 4G **61**
Holmfirth St. *M13* 3B **110**
Holmfoot Wlk. M9 . . . . . .4F **83**
 (off Carisbrook St.)
Holmlea Rd. *Droy* 3G **97**
Holmleigh Av. *M9* 2G **83**
Holmpark Rd. *Open* 6H **97**
Holmrook. *Alt* 6D **132**
Holmside Gdns. *M19* 5A **126**
Holmwood. *Bow* 2C **144**
Holmwood Ct. *M20* 5F **125**
Holmwood Rd. *M20* 4F **125**
Holroyd St. *M11* 5C **96**
Holroyd St. *Roch* 4A **28**
Holset Dri. *Alt* 6D **132**
Holset Wlk. *Haz G* 4A **152**
Holst Av. *M8* 5C **82**
Holstein Av. *Roch* 5D **14**
Holtby St. *M9* 2G **83**
Holthouse Rd. *T'ton* 6G **21**
Holt La. *Fail* 5G **85**
Holt Lane End. **4H 85**
Holt La. M. *Fail* 4H **85**
Holtown Ind. Est. *M40* . . .3A **96**
Holts. **5A 74**
Holts La. *Fail* 4H **85**
Holts La. *Oldh* 5H **73**
Holts La. *Styal* 4D **158**
 (in two parts)
Holts Pas. *L'boro* 4E **17**
Holts Ter. *Roch* 1G **27**
Holt St. *M40* 6H **83**
Holt St. *Aud* 5E **99**
Holt St. *Bolt* 2H **45**
Holt St. *B'hth* 3E **133**
Holt St. *Eccl* 5E **91**
Holt St. *L'boro* 5H **17**
Holt St. *Miln* 6G **29**
Holt St. *Oldh* 1G **73**
Holt St. *Rams* 3F **13**
Holt St. *Stoc* 3H **139**
Holt St. *Swin* 1F **79**
Holt St. *Whitw* 4G **15**
Holt St. W. *Rams* 4D **12**
Holt Town. **3A 96**
Holt Town. *M40* . . .3A **96** (4H **7**)
Holt Town Ind. Est.
 M40 . . . . . .3A **96** (4H **7**)
Holtwood Wlk. *Stoc* 2C **128**
Holway Wlk. M9 . . . . . . .4E **83**
 (off Hendham Va.)
Holwick Rd. *M23* 1F **135**
Holwood Dri. *M16* 1C **124**
Holybourne Wlk. *M23* . . .3D **134**
Holy Harbour St. *Bolt* 3G **31**
Holyhurst Wlk. *Bolt* 3A **32**
Holyoake Rd. *Wors* 1F **77**
Holyoake St. *Droy* 3C **98**
Holyoak St. *M40* 5C **84**
Holyrood Clo. *P'wich* 3G **67**
Holyrood Ct. *P'wich* 3G **67**
Holyrood Dri. *P'wich* 3G **67**
Holyrood Dri. *Swin* 4D **78**
Holyrood Gro. *P'wich* 3G **67**

Holyrood Rd. *P'wich* 4G 67
Holyrood St. *M40* 1G 97
Holyrood St. *Oldh* 6E 57
Holywood St. *M14* 4F 109
Homebeck Ho. *Gat* 6E 137
Homebury Dri. *M11* 3D 96
Home Dri. *Midd* 2H 69
Home Farm Av. *Mot* 6B 116
Home Front Mus. 4C 122
(Sale Leisure Cen.)
Homelands Clo. *Sale* . . .1H 133
Homelands Rd. *Sale* 1H 133
Homelands Wlk. *M9* 1F 83
Homelaurel Ho. *Sale* 1B 134
(off Whitehall Rd.)
Homer Dri. *Marp B* 3F 143
Homer St. *Rad* 4E 49
Homerton Rd. *M40* 1D 96
Homestead Clo. *Part* 5E 119
Homestead Cres.
M19 . . . . .6H 125
Homestead Gdns.
Roch 4D 16
Homestead Rd. *Dis* 1G 165
Homewood Av. *M22* 2B 136
Homewood Rd. *M22* 2A 136
Honduras St. *Oldh* 2F 73
Hondwith Clo. *Bolt* 6G 19
Honeycombe Cotts.
Chea 6A 138
(off Oak Rd.)
Honey Hill. *Lees* 4B 74
Honey St. *M8* 1F 95
Honeysuckle Clo.
M23 . . . . .2E 135
Honeysuckle Clo.
Woodl 4G 129
Honeysuckle Dri. *Stal* . . .3F 101
Honeysuckle Wlk.
Sale 4F 121
Honeysuckle Way.
Roch 6D 14
Honeywell La. *Oldh* 6D 72
Honeywood Clo. *Rams* . . .6C 12
Honford Rd. *M22* 1A 148
Hong Kong Av. *Man A* . .5G 147
Honister Dri. *Midd* 5G 53
Honister Rd. *M9* 4H 83
Honister Way. *Roch* 1B 40
Honiton Av. *Hyde* 5G 115
Honiton Clo. *Chad* 6E 55
Honiton Clo. *Heyw* 5E 39
Honiton Dri. *Bolt* 1A 48
Honiton Gro. *Rad* 2D 48
Honiton Ho. *Salf* 2A 92
Honiton Wlk. *Hyde* 5H 115
Honiton Way. *Alt* 5C 132
Honor St. *M13* 4B 110
Honsham Wlk. *M23* 2E 135
Hood Clo. *Tyl* 2A 76
Hood Sq. *G'ton* 4C 74
Hood St. *M4* 3F 95 (4D 6)
Hood Wlk. *Dent* 2G 129
Hoole Clo. *Chea* 6C 138
Hooley Bridge. 1E 39
Hooley Bri. Ind. Est.
Heyw 1E 39
Hooley Brow. 2F 39
Hooley Clough. *Heyw* . . .1F 39
Hooley Hill. 6F 99
Hooley Range. *Stoc* 6D 126
Hooper St.
M12 . . . . . .5H 95 (2H 11)
Hooper St. *Oldh* 3E 73
Hooper St. *Stoc* 2G 139
Hooton St. *M40* 2B 96
Hooton St. *Bolt* 4G 45
Hooton Way. *Hand* 2H 159
(off Beeston Av.)
Hopcroft Clo. *M9* 3D 68
Hope Av. *Bolt* 1D 46

Hope Av. *Brad* 6A 20
Hope Av. *Hand* 4G 159
Hope Av. *L Hul* 5E 63
Hope Av. *Stret* 4B 106
Hope Ct. *Roch* 3H 27
(off Hope St.)
Hopecourt Clo. *Salf* 1C 92
Hope Cres. *Salf* 2C 92
Hopedale Clo. *M11* 4B 96
Hopedale Rd. *Stoc* 3H 127
Hopefield St. *Bolt* 3H 45
Hopefold Dri. *Wors* 1G 77
Hope Grn. Way. *A'ton* . . .5D 162
Hope Hey La. *L Hul* 4B 62
Hope La. *A'ton* 6D 162
Hopelea St. *M20* 2F 125
Hope Pk. Clo. *P'wich* 6F 67
Hope Pk. Rd. *P'wich* 6F 67
Hope Rd. *M14* 3H 109
Hope Rd. *P'wich* 1E 81
Hope Rd. *Sale* 6B 122
Hopes Carr. *Stoc* 2H 139
Hope St. *M1* 4E 95 (6B 6)
Hope St. *Ash L* 1B 100
Hope St. *Aud* 2F 113
Hope St. *Duk* 5H 99
(in two parts)
Hope St. *Eccl* 3H 91
Hope St. *Farn* 1G 63
Hope St. *Haz G* 2D 152
Hope St. *Heyw* 5H 39
Hope St. *L Hul* 5C 62
Hope St. *Oldh* 2F 73
Hope St. *Rams* 4D 12
Hope St. *Roch* (OL11) . . .4C 40
Hope St. *Roch* (OL12) . . .3H 27
Hope St.
Salf (M6) 4A 94 (5A 4)
Hope St. *Salf* (M7) 4H 81
Hope St. *Shaw* 6F 43
Hope St. *Stoc* 2F 139
Hope St. *Swin* 4D 78
(Arthur St.)
Hope St. *Swin* 3G 79
(Bridge St.)
Hope Ter. *Duk* 5H 99
Hope Ter. *Stoc* 3G 139
Hopgarth Wlk. *M40* 6D 84
Hopkin Av. *Oldh* 1F 73
Hopkins Bldgs. *Moss* 6G 75
Hopkinson Av. *Dent* 2D 112
Hopkinson Clo.
Upperm 1F 61
Hopkinson Rd. *M9* 4F 69
Hopkins St. *M12* 4C 110
Hopkins St. *Hyde* 3C 114
Hopkin St. *Oldh* 2D 72
Hoppet La. *Droy* 3C 98
Hopton Av. *M22* 2C 148
Hopton Ct.
M15 . . . . . .1E 109 (5A 10)
Hopwell Dri. *M18* 1H 111
Horbury Av. *M18* 4F 111

Horbury Dri. *Bury* 3A 36
Horden Wlk. *Rytn* 3C 56
(off Shaw St.)
Hordern Clo. *Had* 3H 117
Horeb St. *Bolt* 2H 45
Hurley Clo. *Bury* 4C 22
Horlock Ct. *Salf* . . .2H 93 (2A 4)
Hornbeam Clo. *Sale* 4E 121
Hornbeam Clo. *Timp* 6F 135
Hornbeam Ct. *Salf* 2G 93
Hornbeam Rd. *M19* 5D 110
Hornby Av. *M9* 4G 69
Hornby Dri. *Bolt* 5D 44
Hornby Rd. *Stret* 3F 107
Hornby St. *M8* 1D 94
Hornby St. *Bury* 6F 23
Hornby St. *Heyw* 4F 39
Hornby St. *Midd* 1A 70
Hornby St. *Oldh* 4B 72
Horncastle Clo. *Bury* 6D 22
Horncastle Rd. *M40* 1B 84
Hornchurch Ct. *M15* 5H 9
Hornchurch Ho. *Stoc* 5A 140
Hornchurch St.
M15 . . . . .1C 108 (6E 9)
Horne Dri. *M4* 3G 95 (4F 7)
Horne St. *Bury* 5C 36
Hornet Clo. *Roch* 2G 41
Hornsea Clo. *Bury* 3F 35
Hornsea Clo. *Chad* 6F 55
Hornsea Rd. *Stoc* 6G 141
Hornsea Wlk. *M11* 4C 96
Horridge Fold. *Eger* 1C 18
Horridge Fold Av. *Bolt* . . .5D 44
Horridge St. *Bury* 1H 35
Horrobin Fold. *Tur* 1G 19
Horrobin La. *Tur* 1G 19
Horrocks Fold. 4D 10
Horrocks Fold. *Bolt* 4A 18
Horrocks Fold Av. *Bolt* . . .5B 18
Horrocks St. *Bolt* 2E 45
Horrocks St. *Rad* 3B 50
Horsa St. *Bolt* 4D 32
Horsedge St. *Oldh* 1D 72
Horsefield Av. *Whitw* 3C 14
Horsefield Clo. *M21* 2C 124
Horseshoe La. *Ald E* 4G 167
Horseshoe La. *Brom X* . . .3E 19
Horseshoe La. *Midd* 3F 71
Horsfield St. *Bolt* 2F 45
Horsfield Way. *Bred* 3E 129
Horsforth La. *G'fld* 5E 61
Horsham Av. *Haz G* 4C 152
Horsham Clo. *Bury* 4C 22
Horsham St. *Salf* 3E 93
Horstead Wlk. *M19* 5C 110
**Horticultural Cen. in
Wythenshaw Pk., The.**
. . . . .3G 135
Horton Av. *Bolt* 5C 18
Horton Rd. *M14* 5E 109
Horton Sq. *Shaw* 1F 57
Horton St. *Stoc* 4A 140
Hortree Rd. *Stret* 5E 107
Horwood Cres. *M20* 4H 125
Hoscar Dri. *M19* 2B 126
Hoskins Clo. *M12* 2C 110
Hospital Av. *Eccl* 3G 91
Hospital Rd. *Drom X* 3D 18
Hospital Rd. *Swin* 4H 79
Hotel Rd. *Man A* 6A 148
Hotel Rd. *Bolt* 6B 32
Hothersall Rd. *Stoc* 2H 127
Hothersall St.
Salf 2C 94 (1E 5)
Hotspur Clo. *M14* 1E 125
Hough Clo. *Oldh* 1E 87
Houghend Av. *M21* 3A 124
Hough End Cen. *M21* 2C 124
Houghend Cres. *M21* 1C 124
Hough Fold Way. *Bolt* 6H 19

Hough Hall Rd. *M40* 3H 83
Hough Hill Rd. *Stal* 4E 101
(in two parts)
Hough La. *Brom X* 4D 18
Hough La. *Hyde* 2D 114
Hough La. *Midd* 3F 55
Hough Rd. *M20* 2E 125
Hough St. *M40* 6G 83
Hough St. *Bolt* 2F 45
Houghton Av. *Oldh* 1B 86
Houghton Clo. *Roch* 5C 28
Houghton La. *Swin* 6D 78
Houghton Rd. *M8* 2C 82
Houghton St. *Bolt* 2A 46
Houghton St. *Bury* 4C 36
Houghton St. *Rytn* 5C 56
Houghton St. *Swin* 5B 80
Hough Wlk. *Salf* . . .2A 94 (1B 4)
Houldsworth Av.
Timp 4G 133
Houldsworth Mill Ind. Est.
Stoc 1G 127
Houldsworth Sq.
Stoc 2G 127
Houldsworth St.
M1 . . . . .3F 95 (4C 6)
Houldsworth St. *Rad* 2F 49
Houldsworth St. *Stoc* 2G 127
Hounslow Ho. *Bolt* 4H 31
Houseley Av. *Chad* 6G 71
Houson St. *Oldh* 4D 72
Houston Pk. *Salf* 4F 93
Hove Clo. *G'mnt* 2G 21
Hoveden St. *M8* 1D 94
Hove Dri. *M14* 2A 120
Hove St. *Bolt* 2G 45
Hove St. N. *Bolt* 2G 45
Hovey Clo. *M8* 4B 82
Hoviley. *Hyde* 4C 114
Hoviley Brow. *Hyde* 4C 114
Hovingham St. *Roch* 3B 28
Hovington Gdns. *M19* . . .3A 126
Hovis St. *M11* 5E 97
Howard Av. *Bolt* 3E 45
Howard Av. *Chea H* 4C 150
Howard Av. *Eccl* 2F 91
Howard Av. *Kear* 2H 63
Howard Av. *Stoc* 3E 127
Howard Clo. *Rom* 1G 141
Howard Ct. *Ash L* 2A 100
Howard Dri. *Hale* 4A 146
Howard Hill. *Bury* 2E 51
Howardian Clo. *Oldh* 6C 72
Howard La. *Dent* 3F 113
Howard Pl. *Hyde* 5B 114
(off Mall, The)
Howard Pl. *Hyde* 3D 114
(off Victoria St.)
Howard Pl. *Roch* 3H 27
Howard Rd. *M22* 2B 136
Howard's La. *Moss* 2G 89
Howard Spring Wlk.
M8 . . . . .3B 82
Howard St. *M8* 1D 94
Howard St. *Ash L* 1G 99
Howard St. *Aud* 1F 113
Howard St. *Bolt* 4B 32
Howard St. *Dent* 2E 113
Howard St. *Mill* 1H 101
Howard St. *Oldh* 1A 74
Howard St. *Rad* 4H 49
Howard St. *Roch* 3G 27
Howard St. *Salf* 5G 93
Howard St. *Shaw* 6E 43
Howard St. *Stoc* 1H 139
Howard St. *Stret* 5D 106
Howard Way. *L'boro* 6G 17
Howarth Av. *Wors* 4C 78
Howarth Clo. *M11* 4C 96
Howarth Clo. *Bury* 1D 50
Howarth Ct. *Stoc* 6B 140
Howarth Cross. 1B 28

Howarth Cross St.—Hyde Pk. Pl.

Howarth Cross St. Roch 1B **28**
Howarth Dri. Irlam 6D **102**
Howarth Farm Way. Roch 6A **16**
Howarth Grn. Roch 6A **16**
Howarth Knoll. Roch 4A **16**
Howarth Pl. Roch 1D **40**
Howarth Sq. Roch 3A **28**
Howarth St. M16 3A **108**
Howarth St. Farn 2F **63**
Howarth St. L'boro 3F **17**
Howbridge Clo. Wors 3E **77**
Howbro Dri. Ash L 6C **86**
Howbrook Wlk. M15 1D **108** (6H **9**)
Howclough Clo. Wors 1H **77**
Howclough Dri. Wors 1H **77**
Howcroft Clo. Bolt 5A **32**
Howcroft St. Bolt 2H **45**
Howden Clo. Stoc 5G **111** (in two parts)
Howden Rd. M9 4E **69**
Howe Dri. Rams 1B **22**
Howell Cft. N. Bolt 6B **32**
Howell Cft. S. Bolt 6B **32**
Howells Av. Sale 4B **122**
Howell's Yd. Bolt 6B **32**
Howe St. Ash L 5F **99**
Howe St. Salf 4G **81**
Howgill Cres. Oldh 6C **72**
Howgill St. M11 4F **97**
How La. Bury 5E **23**
How Lea Dri. Bury 5F **23**
Howsin Av. Bolt 1D **32**
Howton Clo. M12 3C **110**
Howty Clo. Wilm 6H **159**
Hoxton Clo. Bred 5G **129**
Hoy Dri. Urm 2F **105**
Hoylake Clo. M40 3D **84**
Hoylake Rd. Sale 6F **123**
Hoylake Rd. Stoc 3C **138**
Hoyland Clo. M12 1B **110**
Hoyle Av. Oldh 4C **72**
Hoyles Ct. Rad 3A **50**
Hoyle's Ter. Miln 5E **29**
Hoyle St. M12 5G **95** (2F **11**)
Hoyle St. Bolt 1A **32**
Hoyle St. Midd 3C **70**
Hoyle St. Rad 6A **50**
Hoyle St. Whitw 2H **15**
Hoyle St. Ind. Est. M12 3F **11**
Hoyle Wlk. M13 1G **109** (5E **11**)
Hubert Worthington Ho. Ald E 5G **167**
Hucclecote Av. M22 3A **148**
Hucklow Av. M23 3G **147**
*Hucklow Bank. Glos 5F **117** (off Grassmoor Cres.)*
*Hucklow Clo. Glos 5F **117** (off Grassmoor Cres.)*
*Hucklow Fold. Glos 5F **117** (off Grassmoor Cres.)*
*Hucklow Lanes. Glos 5F **117** (off Grassmoor Cres.)*
Hudcar La. Bury 1E **37**
Huddart Clo. Salf 5H **93** (1A **8**)
Huddersfield Rd. Aus 1C **74**
Huddersfield Rd. Carr 6G **89**
Huddersfield Rd. Del 3H **59**
Huddersfield Rd. Dob 4B **60**
Huddersfield Rd. Miln 1F **43**
Huddersfield Rd. Moss 2G **89**
Huddersfield Rd. Oldh & Aus 2F **73**
Huddersfield Rd. Stal & Mill 3F **101**
Hudson Ct. M9 6D **68**
Hudson Rd. Bolt 4F **45**
Hudson Rd. Hyde 2C **130**
Hudsons Pas. L'boro 2G **17**
Hudson St. Oldh 1G **85**
Hudson Wlk. Roch 4D **26**
Hudswell Clo. W'fld 1C **66**
Hughendon Ct. T'ton 4H **21**
Hughes Clo. Bury 2E **37**
Hughes Clo. Fail 3E **85**
Hughes St. M11 5A **96**
Hughes St. Bolt 3G **31** (Bennett's La.)
Hughes St. Bolt 3H **31** (Rushey Fold La.)
Hughes Way. Eccl 5C **90**
Hugh Fold. Lees 4A **74**
Hughley Clo. Rytn 3D **56**
Hugh Oldham Dri. Salf 5G **81**
Hugh St. Bolt 3G **45**
Hugh St. Roch 3A **28**
Hughtrede St. Roch 2H **41**
Hugo St. M40 4A **84**
Hugo St. Farn 5D **46**
Hugo St. Roch 3D **40**
Hulbert St. Bury 4A **36**
Hulbert St. Midd 6B **54**
Hull Mill La. Del 2H **59**
Hull Sq. Salf 3B **94** (3C **4**)
Hully St. Stal 3D **100**
Hulme. 1D 108
Hulme Ct. M15 6C **94** (4D **8**)
Hulme Dri. Timp 4C **134**
Hulme Hall Av. Chea H 5C **150**
Hulme Hall Cres. Chea H 5C **150**
Hulme Hall La. M40 & M11 1A **96**
Hulme Hall Rd. M15 6B **94** (3C **8**)
Hulme Hall Rd. Chea H 3C **150**
Hulme High St. M15 3D **108**
Hulme Mkt. Hall. M15 2D **108**
Hulme Pl. Salf 4A **94** (5A **4**)
Hulme Rd. Bolt 5A **20**
Hulme Rd. Dent 4B **112**
Hulme Rd. Rad 2C **64**
Hulme Rd. Sale 6D **122**
Hulme Rd. Stoc 4F **127**
Hulme's La. Dent 1E **129**
Hulmes Rd. M40 & Fail 6E **85** (in two parts)
Hulmes Ter. Bolt 5C **34**
Hulme St. M15 & M1 6D **94** (4H **9**) (Cambridge St.)
Hulme St. M15 6C **94** (4F **9**) (Jackson Cres.)
Hulme St. Ash L 1B **100**
Hulme St. Bury 2B **36**
Hulme St. Oldh 5C **72**
Hulme St. Salf 4A **94** (5B **4**)
Hulme St. Stoc 4B **140**
*Hulmeswood Ter. Dent 2G **129** (off Hardywood Rd.)*
Hulme Wlk. M15 1D **108**
Hulton Av. Wors 6C **62**
Hulton Clo. Bolt 3E **45**
Hulton District Cen. Wors 5C **62**
Hulton Dri. Bolt 4E **45**
Hulton La. Bolt 5E **45**
Hulton St. M16 3C **108**
Hulton St. Dent 3E **113**
Hulton St. Fail 4D **84**
Hulton St. Salf 6G **93**
Humber Dri. Bury 3F **23**
Humber Rd. Miln 5G **29**
Humberstone Av. M15 1D **108** (4F **9**)
Humber St. M8 4C **82**
Humber St. Salf 4D **92**
Hume St. M19 1D **126**
Hume St. Roch 5A **28**
Humphrey Booth Gdns. Salf 2E **93**
Humphrey Cres. Urm 5H **105**
Humphrey La. Urm 5A **106**
Humphrey Pk. Urm 5A **106**
Humphrey Rd. M16 2H **107**
Humphrey Rd. Bram 2G **151**
Humphrey St. M8 3B **82**
*Humphries Ct. M40 1G **95** (off Whitley Rd.)*
Huncoat Av. Stoc 4F **127**
Huncote Dri. M9 2G **83**
Hungerford Wlk. M23 4D **134**
Hunger Hill. 5B 44
Hunger Hill. Roch 3B **16**
Hunger Hill Av. Bolt 5C **44**
Hunger Hill La. Roch 1B **26** & 6A **14**
Hunmanby Av. M15 6D **94** (4G **9**)
Hunstanton Dri. Bury 6D **22**
Hunston Rd. Sale 6H **121**
Hunt Av. Ash L 6F **87**
Hunter Dri. Rad 3G **49**
Hunters Clo. Bred 6F **129**
Hunters Clo. Wilm 6B **160**
Hunters Ct. Duk 6D **100**
Hunters Ct. Stal 6H **101**
Hunters Grn. Rams 6B **12**
Hunters Hill. Bury 3F **51**
Hunters Hill La. Dig 1B **60**
Hunters La. Oldh 2D **72**
Hunters La. Roch 3H **27**
Hunters M. Sale 4A **122**
Hunters M. Wilm 2F **167**
Hunterston Av. Eccl 3A **92**
Hunters Vw. Hand 4G **159**
Hunt Fold Dri. G'mnt 1H **21**
Huntingdon Av. Chad 4H **71**
Huntingdon Cres. Stoc 4C **128**
Huntingdon Wlk. Bolt 3A **32**
Huntingdon Way. Dent 6F **113**
Huntington Av. M20 2E **125**
Hunt La. Chad 2F **71**
Huntley Mt. Rd. Bury 1F **37**
Huntley Rd. M8 1A **82**
Huntley Rd. Stoc 4C **138**
Huntley St. Bury 2F **37**
Huntley Way. Heyw 4A **38**
Huntly Chase. Wilm 2G **167**
Hunt Rd. Hyde 2E **115**
Huntroyde Av. Bolt 4E **33**
Hunt's Bank. M3 3D **94** (3H **5**)
Huntsham Clo. Alt 5D **132**
Huntsman Dri. Irlam 2D **118**
Huntsman Rd. M9 3H **83**
Hunts Rd. Salf 6B **80**
Hunt St. M9 2F **83**
Huntsworth Wlk. M13 2H **109** (6G **11**)
Hurdlow Av. Salf 4E **81**
*Hurdlow Grn. Glos 6F **117** (off Hurdlow M.)*
*Hurdlow Lea. Glos 6F **117** (off Hurdlow M.)*
Hurdlow M. Glos 6F **117**
Hurdlow Wlk. M9 4F **83**
*Hurdlow Way. Glos 6F **117** (off Brassington Cres.)*
Hurdsfield Rd. Stoc 1C **152**
Hurford Av. M18 1F **111**
Hurlbote Clo. Hand 2H **159**
Hurley Dri. Chea H 3A **150**
Hurlston Rd. Bolt 5H **45**
Hurst. 6H 87
Hurst Av. Chea H 1E **161**
Hurst Av. Sale 6E **121**
Hurstbank Av. M19 5H **125**
Hurst Bank Rd. Ash L 1C **100**
Hurstbourne Av. M11 2D **96**
Hurst Brook. 1A 100
Hurst Brook Clo. Ash L 1A **100**
Hurstbrook Dri. Urm 5H **105**
Hurst Ct. M23 1F **147**
Hurst Ct. Ash L 6H **87**
Hurst Cross. Ash L 6H **87**
Hurstead. 5B 16
Hurstead Grn. Roch 5B **16**
Hurstead M. Roch 5B **16**
Hursted Rd. Miln 5F **29**
Hurstfield Ind. Est. Stoc 3G **127**
Hurstfield Rd. Wors 3D **76**
*Hurst Fold. Irlam 4F **103** (off Fiddlers La.)*
Hurstfold Av. M19 6H **125**
Hurst Grn. Clo. Bury 5F **35**
Hurst Gro. Ash L 6A **88**
Hurst Hall Dri. Ash L 6A **88**
Hursthead Rd. Chea H 6D **150**
Hurstheads La. Rom 2H **141**
Hursthead Wlk. M13 6F **95** (4D **10**)
Hurst Hill Cres. Ash L 1B **100**
Hurst Knoll. 6G 87
Hurst Lea Ct. Ald E 4G **167**
Hurst Mdw. Roch 3H **41**
*Hurstmead Ter. M20 1F **137** (off South Rd.)*
Hurst Nook. 5A 88
Hurst St. Bolt 4G **45**
Hurst St. Bury 3E **37** (in two parts)
Hurst St. Oldh 2B **72**
Hurst St. Roch 6A **28**
Hurst St. Stoc 2G **127**
Hurst St. Wors 3E **63**
Hurstvale Av. H Grn 4F **149**
Hurstville Rd. M21 3H **123**
Hurst Wlk. M22 3G **147**
Hurstway Dri. M9 6G **69**
Hurstwood. Bolt 6B **18**
Hurstwood Clo. Oldh 5G **73**
Hurstwood Ct. Bolt 3D **46**
Hurstwood Gro. Stoc 5F **141**
Hus St. Droy 5H **97**
Husteads La. Dob 6G **59**
Hutchins La. Oldh 6H **57**
Hutchinson Rd. Roch 2H **25**
Hutchinson St. Rad 3A **50**
Hutchinson St. Roch 5D **26**
Hutchinson Way. Rad 4G **49**
Hutton Av. Ash L 3C **100**
Hutton Av. Wors 5B **76**
*Hutton Wlk. M13 1G **109** (6E **11**) (off Copeman Clo.)*
Huxley Av. M8 5C **82**
Huxley Clo. Bram 6G **151**
Huxley Dri. Bram 6G **151**
Huxley St. Bolt 3G **31**
Huxley St. B'hth 4F **133**
Huxley St. Oldh 4G **73**
Huxton Grn. Haz G 4A **152**
Hyacinth Clo. Stoc 6F **139**
Hyacinth Wlk. Part 6C **118**
Hyde. 5B 114
Hydebank. Rom 2B **142**
Hyde Dri. Wors 1E **77**
Hyde Fold Clo. M19 3B **126**
Hyde Gro. M13 2G **109**
Hyde Gro. Sale 5B **122**
Hyde Gro. Wors 1E **77**
Hyde Ho. Stoc 4E **127**
Hyde Pk. Pl. Roch 4C **28**

Hyde Pl. M13 . . . . .2G 109
Hyde Rd. M12 & M18
. . . . .1H 109 (4F 11)
Hyde Rd. Dent 3F 113
Hyde Rd. Midd 3E 71
Hyde Rd. Mot 4B 116
Hyde Rd. Woodl 4G 129
Hyde Rd. Wors 1E 77
Hydes. 4D 100
Hyde's Cross.
  M4 . . . . . . .3E 95 (3H 5)
Hyde Sq. Midd 6G 53
Hydes Ter. Stal 3F 101
  (in two parts)
Hyde St. Bolt 4G 45
Hyde St. Droy 1C 98
Hyde St. Duk 5B 100
Hyde Way. Mot 3B 116
Hydon Brook Wlk
  Roch 1C 40
Hydrangea Clo. Sale . . .4E 121
Hyldavale Av. Gat 5F 137
Hylton Dri. Ash L 6D 86
Hylton Dri. Chea H 5E 151
Hyman Goldstone Wlk.
  M8 . . . . .4B 82
Hyndman Ct. Salf 4D 92
Hypatia St. Bolt 5D 32
Hythe Clo. M14 . . . . . .4G 109
Hythe Rd. Stoc 3D 138
Hythe St. Bolt 3E 45
Hythe Wlk. Chad 3H 71

I

Ian Frazer Ct. Roch 1F 41
Ibberton Wlk. M9 . . . . . .2H 83
  (off Carnaby St.)
Ibsley. Roch 3G 27
  (off Spotland Rd.)
Ice Ho. Clo. Wors 6B 62
Iceland St. Salf 3F 93
Idonia St. Bolt 2H 31
Ifco Cen. M14 . . . . . . .4G 109
Ilex Gro. Salf 5H 81
Ilford St. M11 . . . . .3D 96
Ilfracombe Rd. Stoc 3D 140
Ilfracombe St. M40 . . . . .5D 84
Ilkeston Wlk. M40 . . . . .4A 84
  (off Halliford Rd.)
Ilkeston Wlk. Dent 1G 129
Ilkley Clo. Bolt 6E 33
Ilkley Clo. Chad 3H 71
Ilkley Cres. Stoc 1G 127
Ilkley Dri. Urm 3C 104
Ilkley St. M40 . . . . .2A 84
Ilk St. M11 . . . . .3D 96
Illingworth Av. Stal 4G 101
Illona Dri. Salf 3E 81
Ilminster. Roch 5G 27
Ilminster Wlk. M9 . . . . . .4G 69
  (off Crossmead Dri.)
Ilthorpe Wlk. M40 . . . . .5A 84
Imex Bus. Pk. M13 . . . .4B 110
Imogen Ct. Salf 5A 94 (2B 8)
Imperial Ter. Sale 3A 122
Imperial War Mus. North. 6E 93
Ina Av. Bolt 4D 30
Ince Clo. M20 . . . . . . .2F 125
Ince Clo. Stoc 6G 127
Ince St. Stoc 6G 127
Inchcape Dri. M9 . . . . . .5D 68
Inchfield Clo. Roch 3A 26
Inchfield Rd. M40 . . . . .2A 84
Inchley Rd.
  M13 . . . . . . .6F 95 (4C 10)
Inchwood M. Oldh 3A 58
Incline Rd. Oldh 1H 85
Independent St. L Lev . . .4A 48
India St. Bury 6E 13

Indigo St. Salf 6D 80
Indigo Wlk. Salf 6D 80
Indoor Tennis Cen. 3B 96
Industrial St. Rams 4A 12
Industry Rd. Roch 2H 27
Industry St. Chad 5G 71
Industry St. L'boro 4F 17
Industry St. Roch 2A 26
Industry St. Whitw 3H 15
Infant St. P'wich 5G 67
Infirmary St. Bolt 6B 32
Ingham Rd. W Timp 3F 133
Ingham St. M40 . . . . . . .1G 97
Ingham St. Bury 4E 37
Ingham St. Oldh 2E 73
Inghamwood Clo. Salf . . .4B 82
Ingleby Av. M9 . . . . . . .5G 69
Ingleby Clo. Shaw 5E 43
Ingleby Ct. Stret 6E 107
Ingleby Way. Shaw 5E 43
Ingledene Av. Salf 2A 82
Ingledene Ct. Salf 2A 82
Ingledene Gro. Bolt 3E 31
Ingle Dri. Stoc 4C 140
Inglefield. Roch 2B 26
Inglehead Clo. Dent 5G 113
Ingle Rd. Chea 5C 138
Ingles Fold. Wors 4D 76
Inglesham Clo. M23 . . . .5H 135
Ingleton Av. M8 . . . . . . .1D 82
Ingleton Clo. Bolt 1F 33
Ingleton Clo. Chea 5G 137
Ingleton Clo. Rytn 2B 56
Ingleton Gdns. Shaw 6H 43
Ingleton Rd. Stoc 3E 139
Inglewhite Clo. Bury 6B 36
Inglewood. Alt 2D 144
Inglewood Clo. Ash L . . .6D 86
Inglewood Clo. Bury 1G 37
Inglewood Clo. Part 5C 118
Inglewood Hollow.
  Stal 5G 101
Inglewood Rd. Chad 6D 54
Inglewood Wlk.
  M13 . . . . . .1G 109 (5E 11)
  (off Brunswick St.)
Inglis St. L'boro 3E 17
Ingoe Clo. Heyw 2H 39
Ingoldsby Av. M13 . . . . .3H 109
Ingram Dri. Stoc 6A 126
Ings Av. Roch 1D 26
Ings La. Roch 1D 26
Inkerman St. M40 . . . . . .5F 83
  (off Topley St.)
Inkerman St. Hyde 3B 114
Inkerman St. Roch 2H 27
Ink St. Roch 4H 27
Inman St. Bury 5C 36
Inman St. Dent 4F 113
Inner Relief Rd. Bury 3C 36
Innes St. M12 . . . . .4D 110
Innis Av. M40 . . . . .6C 84
Institute St. Bolt 6B 32
Instow Clo.
  M13 . . . . . .1H 109 (6G 11)
Instow Clo. Chad 6F 55
Intake La. G'fld 6E 61
International App.
  M90 . . . . .6A 148
Invar Rd. Swin 2D 78
Inverbeg Dri. Bolt 6A 34
Invergarry Wlk. M11 . . . .4E 97
Inverlael Av. Bolt 5F 31
Inverness Av. M9 . . . . . .5A 70
Inverness Rd. Duk 6A 100
Inver Wlk. M40 . . . . . . .1D 84
Inwood Wlk. M8 . . . . . .5E 83
Inworth Wlk. M8 . . . . . .4B 82
  (off Highshore Dri.)
Iona Pl. Bolt 3E 33

Iona Way. Urm 2F 105
Ionian Gdns. Salf 6G 81
Ipswich St. Roch 6H 27
Ipswich Wlk. M12 . . . . . .2A 110
  (off Martindale Cres.)
Ipswich Wlk. Dent 6G 113
Iqbal Clo. M12 . . . . .2C 110
Irby Wlk. Chea 1C 150
Ireby Clo. Midd 5E 53
Iredine St. M11 . . . . . . .4E 97
Irene Av. Hyde 2C 114
Iris Av. Farn 6C 46
Iris Av. Kear 4H 63
  (in two parts)
Iris Av. Open 5F 97
Iris St. Oldh 6D 72
Iris St. Rams 3D 12
Iris Wlk. Part 6D 118
Irkdale St. M8 . . . . .5F 83
Irk St. M4 . . . . . .2E 95 (1B 6)
Irk Va. Dri. Chad 6E 55
Irk Way. W'fld 5F 51
Irlam. 6E 103
Irlam Av. Eccl 4F 91
Irlam Ind. Est. Irlam 2C 118
Irlam Rd. Sale 4C 122
Irlam Rd. Urm 6F 103
Irlams o' th' Height. 5B 80
Irlam Sq. Salf 6B 80
Irlam St. M40 . . . . .6G 83
Irlam St. Bolt 2A 32
Irlam Swimming Pool.
  . . . . .6C 102
Irlam Wharf Rd. Irlam . . .2E 119
Irmaco Ind. Est.
  Traf P 1D 106
Irma St. Bolt 2B 32
Iron St. M40 . . . . .2A 96
Iron St. Dent 4F 113
Irvin Dri. M22 . . . . .5E 149
Irvine Av. Wors 5C 76
Irving Clo. Stoc 2A 152
Irving Ho. Bolt 3A 32
  (off Irving St.)
Irving St. Bolt 3A 32
Irving St. Oldh 1H 85
Irvin St. M40 . . . . .5C 84
Irwell Av. Eccl 4H 91
  (in two parts)
Irwell Av. L Hul 5D 62
Irwell Clo. Rad 5H 49
Irwell Gro. Eccl 4H 91
Irwell Pk. Way. Eccl 4H 91
Irwell Pl. Eccl 4H 91
Irwell Pl. Salf 3A 94 (4A 4)
Irwell St. M8 . . . . . .1C 94 (1F 5)
Irwell St. Bury 3C 36
Irwell St. Rad 2A 64
  (Ford St.)
Irwell St. Rad 5H 49
  (Stand La.)
Irwell St. Rams 3E 13
Irwell St.
  Salf (M3) 4C 94 (5E 5)
Irwell St. Salf (M6) 5E 81
Irwell Wlk. Oldh 6A 72
Irwin Dri. Hand 2G 159
Irwin Pl. Chea H 2B 150
Irwin Rd. B'hth 3E 133
Irwin St. Dent 4E 113
Isaac Clo. Salf 5G 93
Isaac St. Bolt 4H 31
Isabella Clo. M16 . . . . . .3A 108
Isabella St. Roch 1H 27
Isabel Wlk. Bolt 2H 45
Isaiah St. Oldh 5D 72
Isa St. Rams 5C 12
Isca St. M11 . . . . .4B 96
Isel Wlk. Midd 5F 53
Isherwood Clo. Heyw . . .4F 39
Isherwood Dri. Marp 5B 142
Isherwood Rd. C'ton 3B 120

Isherwood St. Heyw 4G 39
Isherwood St. Roch 6A 28
Isis Clo. Salf 3D 80
Islington Rd. Stoc 1C 152
Islington Way.
  Salf 4B 94 (5C 4)
Isobel Bailey Lodge.
  M16 . . . . .2B 108
Isobel Clo. M16 . . . . . . .3D 108
Isobel Clo. Eccl 4D 90
Ivanhoe Ct. Bolt 5E 47
Ivanhoe St. Bolt 5E 47
Ivanhoe St. Oldh 6G 57
Iveagh Ct. Roch 5B 28
Iver Ho. Salf 4F 93
  (off Amersham St.)
Ivor St. Roch 2B 40
Ivory St. M4 . . . . . .1F 95 (1D 6)
Ivy Bank Whitw 2H 15
Ivy Bank Clo. Bolt 6C 18
Ivy Bank Rd. Bolt 6C 18
Ivybridge Clo. M13 . . . . .2H 109
Ivybridge Ho. Bull 2G 45
Ivy Clo. Droy 2H 97
Ivy Clo. Shaw 6F 43
Ivy Cotts. Dent 2G 129
Ivy Cotts. Roch 2F 27
Ivy Ct. M21 . . . . .2H 123
Ivycroft. Had 3G 117
Ivy Dri. Midd 2H 69
Ivygreen Dri. S'head 3B 74
Ivygreen Rd. M21 . . . . . .1F 123
Ivy Gro. Farn 1D 62
Ivy Gro. Kear 2H 63
Ivy Gro. L Hul 5D 62
Ivy Leaf Sq. Salf 5A 82
Ivylea Rd. M19 . . . . .5A 126
Ivylodge Clo. Mill 1H 101
Ivy Rd. Bolt 4G 31
Ivy Rd. Bury 3H 35
Ivy Rd. Poy 4E 163
Ivy St. M40 . . . . .3A 84
Ivy St. Bolt 3G 45
Ivy St. Eccl 4F 91
Ivy St. Rams 6B 12
Ivy Ter. L'boro 5H 17
Ivy Villa. Lees 4B 74
Ivy Wlk. Part 6B 118

J

Jack Brady Clo. M23 . . .1E 147
Jackdaw Rd. G'mnt 1H 21
Jackie Brown Wlk. M40 . .6F 83
Jack La. Droy 3B 98
  (in two parts)
Jack La. Urm 1G 119
  (Flixton)
Jack La. Urm 5G 105
  (Urmston, in two parts)
Jack Lane Nature Reserve.
  . . . . .1G 119
Jackman Av. Heyw 6F 39
Jack McCann Ct. Roch . .3A 28
Jackroom Dri.
  M4 . . . . . . .4G 95 (5E 7)
Jackson Av. Duk 5B 100
Jackson Clo. Bury 2H 35
Jackson Clo. Oldh 4C 72
Jackson Ct. Urm 5C 104
Jackson Cres.
  M15 . . . . . .1C 108 (5E 9)
Jackson Gdns. Dent 5D 112
Jackson M. Oldh 6H 57
Jackson Pit. Oldh 3C 72
Jackson Pl. Roch 3B 28
Jacksons Edge Rd.
  H Lane & Dis 6E 155
Jacksons La. Haz G 4A 152

Jackson's Row.
  M2 . . . . . . .4D **94** (6G **5**)
Jackson St. *Ash L* 1H **99**
Jackson St. *Chea* 5A **138**
Jackson St. *Fail* 5D **84**
Jackson St. *Farn* 1F **63**
Jackson St. *Hyde* 5B **114**
Jackson St. *Kear* 2H **63**
Jackson St. *Midd* 6B **54**
Jackson St. *Mot* 4C **116**
Jackson St. *Oldh* 2F **73**
Jackson St. *Rad* 5H **49**
Jackson St. *Roch* 5B **28**
Jackson St. *Sale* 4D **122**
Jackson St. *S'head* 3B **74**
Jackson St. *Stret* 6C **106**
Jackson St. *Ward* 3A **16**
Jackson St. *W'fld* 2D **66**
Jackson St. *Wors* 5E **63**
Jack St. *Bolt* 4E **33**
Jack Talbot Sports Cen.
  . . . . .2E **39**
Jack Taylor Ct. Roch 2B **28**
  (off Athol St.)
Jacobite Clo. *Salf* 2G **81**
Jacobsen Av. *Hyde* 3D **114**
Jacob's Ladder. *Moss* 2E **89**
James Andrew St.
  . . . . .6B **54**
James Bentley Wlk.
  M40 . . . . .6C **84**
James Brindley Basin.
  M1 . . . . . .4G **95** (6E **7**)
James Butterworth Ct.
  Roch 5B **28**
James Butterworth St.
  Roch 5B **28**
James Clo. *Duk* 5C **100**
James Corbett Rd. *Salf* . . .4C **92**
James Dri. *Hyde* 5C **114**
James Henry Av. *Salf* . . .5H **93**
James Leech St. *Stoc* . .3G **139**
James Leigh St.
  M1 . . . . . .5E **95** (2A **10**)
James Nasmyth Way.
  Eccl 3E **91**
Jameson St. *Roch* 3B **40**
James Rd. *Shaw* 5F **43**
James St. *M40* . . .2H **95** (1H **7**)
James St. *Aud* 5E **99**
  (Audenshaw)
James St. *Aud* 4G **113**
  (Denton)
James St. *Bred* 4G **129**
James St. *Bury* 4E **37**
James St. *Droy* 3B **98**
James St. *Fail* 3G **85**
James St. *Fir* 4D **28**
James St. *Heyw* 2F **39**
James St. *Kear* 1H **63**
James St. *L'boro* 5C **16**
James St. *L Lev* 4B **48**
James St. *Oldh* 6H **57**
James St. *P'wich* 4E **67**
  (in two parts)
James St. *Rad* 6G **49**
James St. *Roch* 3A **28**
  (Regent St.)
James St. *Roch* 5A **16**
  (Wardle Rd.)
James St. *Sale* 5D **122**
James St. *Salf* . . .4B **94** (5C **4**)
James St. *Shaw* 2E **57**
James St. *Stal* 5C **100**
James St. *Stoc* 4G **139**
James St. *Whitw* 3H **15**
James St. N. *Rad* 5H **49**
James St. S. *Chad* 2G **71**
Jammy La. *Chad* 3H **53**
Jane Barter Ho. Farn 1F **63**
  (off Hesketh Wlk.)
Jane St. *Chad* 3H **71**

Jane St. *Roch* 3G **27**
Japan St. *M8* 3B **82**
Jardine Way. *Chad* 5F **71**
Jarvis St. *Oldh* 3E **73**
Jarvis St. *Roch* 2H **27**
Jasmine Av. *Droy* 3C **98**
Jasmine Clo. *M23* 2E **135**
Jasmine Ct. *Bolt* 4A **46**
Jasmine Wlk. *Part* 6D **118**
Jauncey St. *Bolt* 2G **45**
Jayton Av. *M20* 4F **137**
Jean Clo. *M19* 5C **110**
Jedburgh Av. *Bolt* 5F **31**
Jefferson Way. *Roch* 6F **15**
Jeffreys Dri. *Duk* 5B **100**
Jeffrey Wlk. *Heyw* 3C **38**
Jehlum Clo. *M8* 4D **82**
Jellicoe Av. *Cad* 3C **118**
Jenkinson St.
  M13 . . . . . .1E **109** (5B **10**)
Jenkinson St.
  M15 . . . . . .1E **109** (5B **10**)
Jenkyn Wlk. *M11* 4B **96**
Jennably Wlk. *Bolt* 3A **32**
Jennings Av. *Salf* 5G **93**
Jennings Clo. *Hyde* 2F **115**
Jennings Clo. *Salf* 5G **93**
Jennings St. *Stoc* 4F **139**
Jennison Clo. *M18* 1D **110**
Jenny Beck Gro. *Bolt* 3A **46**
Jenny Green. 5D **102**
Jenny La. *Woodf* 4G **161**
Jenny St. *Oldh* 1A **86**
Jepheys Pl. *Roch* 2H **27**
Jepheys St. *Roch* 2H **27**
Jepson St. *Stoc* 5A **140**
Jericho. 1A **38**
Jericho Rd. *Bury* 1A **38**
Jermyn St. *Roch* 3A **28**
Jerrold St. *L'boro* 4F **17**
Jersey Clo. *M19* 2B **126**
Jersey Rd. *Stoc* 5C **140**
Jersey St. *M4* 3F **95** (4D **6**)
Jersey St. *Ash L* 1H **99**
Jerusalem Pl.
  M2 . . . . . .5D **94** (1G **9**)
Jesmond Av. *P'wich* 1F **81**
Jesmond Dri. *Bury* 6C **22**
Jesmond Gro.
  Chea H 5D **150**
Jesmond Rd. *Bolt* 1F **31**
Jesmond Wlk. M9 . . . . . .4F **69**
  (off Claygate Dri.)
Jespersen St. *Oldh* 2D **72**
Jessamine Av. *Salf* 1B **94**
Jessel Clo.
  M13 . . . . . .1G **109** (5E **11**)
Jessie St. *M40* 5A **84**
Jessie St. *Bolt* 2G **45**
Jessop Dri. *Marp* 3D **142**
Jessop Forge. *L Lev* 4A **48**
Jessup St. *M18* 2F **111**
Jethro St. *Bolt* 5E **33**
Jethro St. *Brad* 1E **33**
Jetson St. *M18* 1H **111**
Jevington Wlk.
  M13 . . . . . .1G **109** (6F **11**)
  (off Dilston Clo.)
Jimmy McMullen Wlk.
  . . . . .4E **109**
Jinnah Clo. *Oldh* 4G **73**
Jinnah Clo. *Open* 5E **97**
JJB Soccer Dome. 1D **104**
JJB Sports Health Club.
  . . . . .1D **104**
J.J. Thomson M.
  M14 . . . . .2H **125**
Joan Lestor Ho. *L Hul* 6E **63**
Joan St. *M40* 4A **84**
Jobling St. *M11* 5B **96**
Jocelyn St. *M40* 5G **83**
Joddrell St. *M3* . . .4C **94** (6F **5**)

Joel La. *Hyde* 2C **130**
Johannesburg Dri.
  M23 . . . . .1F **147**
Johannesburg Gdns.
  M23 . . . . .1F **147**
John Ashworth St.
  Roch 2B **28**
John Atkinson Ct.
  Salf 3D **92**
John Av. *Chea* 6A **138**
John Beeley Av. *M11* 5F **97**
John Booth St. *S'head* . . .4B **74**
John Brown St. *Bolt* 5A **32**
John Clynes Av.
  M40 . . . . . . .2G **95** (1F **7**)
John Cross St. *Bolt* 3A **46**
John Dalton St.
  M2 . . . . . . .4D **94** (6G **5**)
John Dalton St. *Salf*3B **94** (4C **4**)
John Derby Ho. *M16* . . .3G **107**
John Foran Clo. *M40* 5B **84**
John Gilbert Way. *Traf P* .2D **106**
John Henry St. *Whitw* 1H **15**
John Heywood St. *M11* . .3D **96**
John Howarth Countryside
  Cen. 5B **86**
John Kemble Ct. *Roch* . . .1D **40**
John Kennedy Gdns.
  Mot 4C **116**
John Kennedy Rd.
  Mot 4B **116**
John Knott St. *Lees* 3B **74**
John Lee Fold. 6B **54**
John Lee Fold. *Midd* 6A **54**
John Lester Ct. Salf 2G **93**
  (off Belvedere Rd.)
John Lloyd St. *Irlam* 1D **118**
Johnny King Clo. *M40* 6F **83**
John Paine Ct. Swin 1F **79**
  (off Pott St.)
John Roberts Clo.
  Roch 6G **27**
John Robinson Wlk.
  M40 . . . . .4A **84**
John Rylands Library.
  . . . . .4D **94** (6G **5**)
Johns Clo. *M21* 1H **123**
John Shepley St.
  Hyde 5C **114**
John Smeaton Ct.
  M1 . . . . . . .4G **95** (6E **7**)
Johnson Av. *Oldh* 2A **58**
Johnsonbrook Rd.
  Hyde & Duk 2A **114**
Johnson Fold. 2D **30**
Johnson Fold Av. *Bolt* 3C **30**
Johnson Gro. *Midd* 1G **69**
Johnson's Sq. *M40* 1H **95**
Johnson St.
  M15 . . . . . .1B **108** (6C **8**)
Johnson St. *Bolt* 1B **46**
Johnson St. *Rad* 5H **49**
Johnson St. *Salf* . . .3C **94** (4F **5**)
Johnson St. *Swin* 5B **80**
Johnson Ter. *Duk* 4H **99**
  (off Astley St.)
John's Pl. *Rom* 1A **142**
Johnston. *Roch* 3G **27**
  (off Spotland Rd.)
Johnston Av. *L'boro* 6D **16**
John Stone Ct. *Stret* 4A **106**
John St. *M4* 3E **95** (4B **6**)
John St. *Alt* 1F **145**
John St. *Ash L* 5F **99**
John St. *Bred* 4G **129**
John St. *Brom X* 4E **19**
John St. *Bury* 2D **36**
John St. *Cad* 4C **118**
John St. *Comp* 6F **131**
John St. *Dent* 3F **113**
John St. *Droy* 4H **97**

John St. *Eccl* 4D **90**
John St. *Fail* 2F **85**
John St. *Farn* 1G **63**
John St. *Haz G* 2D **152**
John St. *H'rod* 6E **89**
John St. *Heyw* 3F **39**
  (Adelaide St.)
John St. *Heyw* 2F **39**
  (Starkey St.)
John St. *Hyde* 4B **114**
  (in two parts)
John St. *L'boro* 4E **17**
John St. *L Lev* 4B **48**
John St. *Marp* 6E **143**
John St. *Oldh* 3C **72**
John St. *P'wich* 1A **68**
John St. *Roch* 6A **16**
  (Halifax Rd.)
John St. *Roch* 3H **27**
  (St Mary's Ga.)
John St. *Rom* 1A **142**
John St. *Rytn* 3B **56**
John St. *Sale* 4B **122**
John St. *Salf* 1B **94**
  (Lower Broughton,
     in two parts)
John St. *Salf* 3C **94** (3F **5**)
  (Salford)
John St. *Shaw* 2E **57**
John St. *S'head* 3C **74**
John St. *Stoc* 3H **139**
  (in two parts)
John St. *Swin* 3G **79**
John St. *Whitw* 3G **15**
John St. *Wors* 5F **63**
John St. W. *Ash L* 5F **99**
John William St. *M11* 4E **97**
John William St. *Eccl* 3H **91**
Joiner St. *M4* 4E **95** (5B **6**)
Joiner St. *Salf* 4A **94** (5B **4**)
Join Rd. *Sale* 5D **122**
Jolly Brows. *Bolt* 2F **33**
Jonas St. *Salf* 2C **94** (1E **5**)
Jones Sq. *Stoc* 4A **140**
Jones St. *M9* 3G **83**
Jones St. *Bolt* 5B **32**
Jones St. *Had* 2H **117**
Jones St. *Oldh* 1E **73**
Jones St. *Rad* 3H **49**
Jones St. *Roch* 5A **28**
Jones St. *Rytn* 5C **56**
Jones St. *Salf* 2F **93**
Jonquil Dri. *Wors* 1B **76**
Jopson St. *Midd* 6B **54**
Jordan Av. *Shaw* 4G **43**
Jordan St. *M15* . . .6C **94** (3F **9**)
Joseph Dean Ct.
  M40 . . . . .4A **84**
Josephine Dri. *Swin* 4G **79**
Joseph Jennings Ct.
  Ash L 5E **87**
Joseph Johnson M.
  M22 . . . . .2C **136**
Joseph Mamlock Ho.
  M8 . . . . .2A **82**
Joseph St. *Eccl* 4D **90**
Joseph St. *Fail* 3F **85**
Joseph St. *Farn* 6F **47**
Joseph St. *L'boro* 3F **17**
Joseph St. *Marp* 5E **143**
Joseph St. *Midd* 6H **53**
Joseph St. *Rad* 5H **49**
Joseph St. *Roch* 1F **27**
Joshua La. *Midd* 2D **70**
Josslyn Rd. *Salf* 2D **92**
Jo St. *Salf* 4G **93**
Joule Clo. *Salf* 5G **93**
Joules Ct. *Stoc* 2H **139**
Joule St. *M9* 2G **83**
Jowett St. *Oldh* 6G **57**
Jowett St. *Stoc* 5H **127**
Jowett's Wlk. *Ash L* 3F **99**

Jowkin La. *Roch* 4H 25
Joyce St. *M40* 4B 84
Joynson Av. *Salf* 1B 94
Joynson St. *Sale* 4B 122
Joy Pl. *Roch* 1H 27
Joy St. *Rams* 3D 12
Joy St. *Roch* 1H 27
Jubilee. 3G 43
Jubilee. *Shaw* 3G 43
Jubilee Av. *Duk* 4B 100
Jubilee Av. *Rad* 6A 50
Jubilee Clo. *Eccl* 2F 91
Jubiloo Cotts. *Haz G* . . .3E 153
  (off Brook St.)
Jubilee Cotts. *Wors* 6E 63
Jubilee Ct. *M16* 3H 107
Jubilee Ct. *Stoc* 5H 111
Jubilee Ho. *Bolt* 1A 46
Jubilee pool. 4H 31
Jubilee Rd. *Midd* 6B 54
Jubilee St. *Bolt* 4G 45
Jubilee St. *Salf* 3F 93
Jubilee St. *Shaw* 1G 57
Jubilee Ter. *Midd* 6B 54
Jubilee Wlk. *Whitw* 2H 15
Jubilee Way. *Bury* 3B 36
Judith St. *Roch* 6C 14
Judson Av. *M21* 3A 124
Judy St. *M9* 3H 83
Julian Ho. *Oldh* 2D 72
Julia St. *M3* 2D 94 (1G 5)
Julia St. *Roch* 3G 27
Julius St. *M19* 1D 126
Jumbles Country Pk. . . .1H 19
Jumbloc Country Pk.
  Vis. Cen. 2H 19
Jumping Jacks Adventure
  Land. 4B 114
  (off Dukinfield Rd.)
Junction All. *Roch* 4H 27
Junction 19 Ind. Pk.
  Heyw 4H 39
Junction Rd. *Bolt* 2D 44
Junction Rd. *Stoc* 4H 139
Junction Rd. W. *Los* 2A 44
Junction St. *Hyde* 2A 114
Junction St. *Midd* 3D 70
Junction St. *Oldh* 5C 72
June Av. *Stoc* 1D 138
June St. *Ash L* 3G 99
Juniper Bank. *Stoc* 1A 128
Juniper Clo. *Bolt* 4A 32
Juniper Clo. *Oldh* 3B 58
Juniper Clo. *Sale* 3H 121
Juniper Cres. *Droy* 5H 97
Juniper Dri. *Fir* 4D 28
Juno St. *Oldh* 6E 57
Jupiter Wlk. *M40* 6A 84
Jura Clo. *Duk* 5B 100
Jura Dri. *Urm* 2G 105
Jura Gro. *Heyw* 4D 38
Jurby Av. *M9* 5E 69
Jury St. *M8* 1D 94
Justin Clo.
  M13 . . . . . .6F 95 (4C 10)
Jutland Av. *Roch* 3E 27
Jutland St. *M1* 4F 95 (6D 6)

K

Kale St. *M13* 6F 95 (4D 10)
Kalima Gro. *Salf* 5H 81
Kansas Av. *Salf* 5E 93
Kara St. *Salf* 3E 93
Kate St. *Rams* 3D 12
Kathan Clo. *Roch* 4B 28
Katherine Ct. *M16* 2A 108
Katherine Ho. *Ash L* 2G 99
Katherine Rd. *Stoc* 6C 140
Katherine St. *Ash L* 3F 99
Kathkin Av. *M8* 1D 82

Kathleen Gro. *M14* 5G 109
Kathleen St. *Roch* 4F 27
Kay Av. *Bred* 6D 128
Kay Brow. *Heyw* 3E 39
Kay Brow. *Rams* 3E 13
Kayes Av. *Stoc* 2B 140
Kayfields. *Bolt* 1G 33
Kay Garden Shop. Cen.
  Bury 3C 36
Kayley Ind. Est. *Ash L* . . .2F 99
Kays Gdns. *Salf* . . .3B 94 (4D 4)
Kay St. *M11* 6B 96
Kay St. *Bolt* 4D 32
  (Croasdale St.)
Kay St. *Bolt* 5B 32
  (St George's St.)
Kay St. *Bury* 2E 37
Kay St. *Heyw* 3E 39
Kay St. *L'boro* 1F 29
Kay St. *L Lev* 4A 48
Kay St. *Rams* 3A 12
Kay St. *Roch* 6G 27
Kay St. *Salf* 5D 80
Kay St. *Stal* 4E 101
Kay St. *S'seat* 6E 13
Kays Wood Rd.
  Marp 5B 142
Keadby Clo. *Eccl* 5F 91
Keal Dri. *Irlam* 3E 103
Keane St. *Ash L* 2G 99
Kean Pl. *Eccl* 4F 91
Kearsley Dri. *Bolt* 3A 64
Kearsley Dri. *Bolt* 4F 91
Kearsley. 3A 64
Kearsley Dri. *Bolt* 4F 91
Kearsley Hall Rd. *Rad* . . .2C 64
Kearsley Mt. *Kear* 3D 64
Kearsley Mt. Shop. Precinct.
  Kear 3B 64
Kearsley Rd. *M8* 1C 82
Kearsley Rd. *Rad* 1C 64
Kearsley Sports Cen. . . .3G 63
Kearsley St. *Eccl* 3D 90
Kearsley Va. *Rad* 1B 64
Kearton Dri. *Eccl* 4A 92
Keary Clo. *M18* 1F 111
Keaton Clo. *Salf* 1E 93
Keats Av. *Dent* 1G 129
Keats Av. *Droy* 3A 98
Keats Av. *Roch* 2C 26
Keats Cres. *Rad* 3E 49
Keats Fold. *Duk* 6F 101
Keats Ho. *Stoc* 1F 127
Keats M. *M23* 2C 134
Keats Rd. *Eccl* 4F 91
Keats Rd. *G'mnt* 1H 21
Keats Rd. *Oldh* 6F 57
Keats Wlk. *Bolt* 3A 32
Keb La. *Oldh* 3E 87
Keble Av. *Oldh* 6C 72
Kedington Clo. *M40* 6E 83
Kedleston Av. *M14* 3A 110
Kedleston Grn. *Stoc* 4D 140
Kedleston Wlk. *Dent* 6F 113
Keele Clo. *M40* 2G 95 (1F 7)
Keele Clo. *Stoc* 5B 140
Keeley Clo. *M40* 1E 97
Keepers Dri. *Roch* 1A 26
Keighley Av. *Droy* 2A 98
Keighley Clo. *Bury* 3F 35
Keighley St. *Bolt* 3G 31
Keilder M. *Bolt* 6C 31
Keith Dri. *Stoc* 4D 138
Keith Wlk. *M40* 2H 95 (2G 7)
Kelboro Av. *Aud* 6D 98
Kelbrook Ct. *Stoc* 6E 141
Kelbrook Rd. *M11* 5D 96
Kelby Av. *M23* 4H 135
Kelday Wlk. *M8* 5E 83
  (off Smedley Rd.)
Keld Clo. *Bury* 6B 22
Keld Wlk. *M18* 2E 111
Kelfield Av. *M23* 1G 135
Kelham Wlk. *M40* 2C 84

Kellbrook Cres. *Salf* 2F 81
  (in two parts)
Kellet's Row. *Wors* 4E 63
Kellett St. *Bolt* 5D 18
Kellett St. *Roch* 3B 28
Kellett Wlk. *M11* 3D 96
Kelling Wlk.
  M15 . . . . . .6B 94 (4D 8)
Kelmarsh Clo. *M11* 6G 97
Kelmscott Lodge.
  Urm 4D 104
  (off Cornhill Rd.)
Kelsall Dri. *Droy* 2H 97
Kelsall Dri. *Timp* 5C 134
Kelsall Rd. *Chea* 6C 138
Kelsall St. *M12* 1B 110
Kelsall St. *Bolt* 6E 33
Kelsall St. *Oldh* 3B 72
Kelsall St. *Roch* 3A 28
Kelsall St. *Sale* 5A 122
Kelsall Way. *Hand* 2H 159
Kelsey Flats. *Heyw* 3E 39
  (off Fearn St.)
Kelsey Wlk. *M9* 4D 68
Kelso Clo. *Oldh* 2D 86
Kelson Av. *Ash L* 6E 87
Kelstern Av. *M13* 4A 110
Kelstern Sq. *M13* 4A 110
Kelverlow St. *Oldh* 3G 73
Kelvin Av. *Midd* 3D 68
Kelvin Av. *Sale* 5B 122
Kelvindale Dri. *Timp* 4C 134
Kelvin Gro. *M8* 5C 82
Kelvin Gro. *Mill* 6G 09
Kelvington Dri. *M9* 5F 83
Kelvin St. *M4* 3E 95 (4B 6)
Kelvin St. *Ash L* 5F 99
Kelwood Av. *Bury* . . . . . .GD 24
Kemball. *Eccl* 3H 91
Kemble Av. *M23* 2A 136
Kemmel Av. *M22* 6C 136
Kemnay Wlk. *M11* 4F 97
Kemp Av. *Roch* 6F 27
Kempley Clo. *M12* 1B 110
Kempnough Hall Rd.
  Wors 4G 77
Kemp Rd. *Marp B* 4G 143
Kempsey Ct. *Chad* 2H 71
Kempsey St. *Chad* 2H 71
Kempsey Wlk. *M40* 2D 84
Kempsford Clo. *M23* 5H 135
Kempster St. *Salf* 1B 94
Kempston Gdns. *Bolt* 3A 32
Kemp St. *Hyde* 3C 114
Kemp St. *Midd* 1H 69
Kempton Av. *L Lev* 5A 48
Kempton Av. *Sale* 6F 121
Kempton Clo. *Droy* 3C 98
Kempton Clo. *Haz G* 4G 153
Kempton Ct. *Sale* 6E 121
Kempton Ho. *Salf* 5G 81
Kempton Rd. *M19* 1C 126
Kempton Way. *Chad* 2A 72
Kemsing Wlk. *Salf* 4G 93
Kenchester Av. *M11* 5F 97
Kendal Av. *Ash L* 1F 99
Kendal Av. *Dent* 6G 113
Kendal Av. *Hyde* 2A 114
Kendal Av. *Roch* 1A 26
Kendal Av. *Sale* 6C 122
Kendal Av. *Urm* 3A 104
Kendal Clo. *Heyw* 5G 39
Kendal Clo. *Timp* 6D 134
Kendal Ct. *Eccl* 4D 90
Kendal Dri. *Bram* 2E 161
Kendal Dri. *Bury* 6B 36
Kendal Dri. *Gat* 1G 149
Kendal Dri. *Shaw* 6H 43
Kendal Gdns. *Woodl* 5H 129
Kendal Gro. *W'fld* 1D 66
Kendal Gro. *Wors* 1H 77

Kendal Rd. *M8* 6B 68
Kendal Rd. *Bolt* 5G 31
Kendal Rd. *Rams* 1A 22
Kendal Rd. *Salf* 6A 80
Kendal Rd. *Stret* 4D 106
Kendal Rd. *Wors* 4A 76
Kendal Rd. W. *Rams* 1H 21
Kendal Ter. *Duk* 4A 100
  (off Astley St.)
Kendal Wlk. *Midd* 6G 53
Kendon Gro. *Dent* 4E 113
Kendrew Rd. *Bolt* 3E 45
Kendrew Wlk. *M9* 2G 83
Kenford Wlk. *M8* 5B 82
Kenilworth. *Roch* 5G 27
Kenilworth Av. *M20* 4D 124
Kenilworth Av. *Chad* 6E 55
Kenilworth Av.
  Chea H 2C 150
Kenilworth Av. *Hand* 4H 159
Kenilworth Av. *Swin* 6H 65
Kenilworth Av. *W'fld* 3E 67
Kenilworth Clo. *Marp* 3D 142
Kenilworth Clo. *Oldh* 4B 74
Kenilworth Clo. *Rad* 1F 49
Kenilworth Dri. *Haz G* . . .5D 152
Kenilworth Gro. *Aud* 5C 98
Kenilworth Rd. *Roch* 5A 42
Kenilworth Rd. *Sale* 5G 121
Kenilworth Rd. *Stoc* 4B 138
Kenilworth Rd. *Urm* 6G 103
Kenilworth Sq. *Bolt* 4F 31
Kenion Rd. *Stoc* 5D 26
Kenion St. *Roch* 4H 27
Kenley Dri. *Heyw* 6H 39
Kenley Lodge. *Bram* 6F 151
Kenley Wlk. *M8* 5E 83
  (off Smedley Rd.)
Kenmay Av. *Bolt* 1D 44
Kenmere Gro. *M40* 2B 84
Kenmor Av. *Bury* 5G 35
Kenmore Clo. *W'fld* 1F 67
Kenmore Dri. *Timp* 2A 146
Kenmore Gro. *Cad* 3B 118
Kenmore Rd. *M22* 4A 136
Kenmore Rd. *Sale* 2E 133
Kenmore Rd. *W'fld* 1F 67
Kenmore Way. *W'fld* 1F 67
Kennard Clo. *M9* 2H 83
Kennard Pl. *Alt* 5G 133
Kennedy Dri. *Bury* 5F 51
Kennedy Dri. *L Lev* 4C 48
Kennedy Rd. *Salf* 3C 92
Kennedy St. *M2* . .4D 94 (6H 5)
Kennedy St. *Bolt* 6E 33
Kennedy St. *Oldh* 4C 72
Kennedy Way. *Dent* 5D 112
Kennedy Way. *Stoc* 1E 139
Kennerley Ct. *Stoc* 6A 140
Kennerley Lodge.
  Stoc 6H 139
Kennerley Rd. *Stoc* 6A 140
Kennerley's La. *Wilm* 2D 166
Kennet Clo. *Wilm* 5H 159
Kennet Flats. *Heyw* 3E 39
  (off Meadow Clo.)
Kenneth Collis Ct.
  M22 . . . . .1A 148
Kenneth Sq. *Salf* 5A 82
Kenneth St. *Bolt* 6E 33
Kennett Rd. *M23* 2G 147
Kenninghall Rd. *M22* 2B 148
Kennington Av. *M40* 1D 96
Kennington Fold. *Bolt* 4H 45
Kenny Clo. *Lees* 4H 73
Kenside St. *M16* 4D 108
Kensington Av. *M14* 3H 109
Kensington Av. *Ash L* 1C 100
Kensington Av. *Chad* 1E 71
Kensington Av. *Hyde* 6C 114
Kensington Av. *Rad* 3D 48
Kensington Av. *Rytn* 1A 56
Kensington Clo. *G'mnt* . . .2H 21

Kensington Clo. *Miln* 5G 29
Kensington Ct. *Bolt* 6A 32
Kensington Ct. *Dent* 3B 112
Kensington Ct. *Hyde* 6C 114
Kensington Ct. *Salf* 3G 81
Kensington Ct. *Wilm* 3D 166
Kensington Dri. *Bury* 5G 35
Kensington Dri. *Salf* 2D 92
Kensington Gdns.
  Hale 4H 145
Kensington Gdns.
  Hyde 6D 114
Kensington Gro. *Dent* . . .3B 112
Kensington Gro. *Stal* 4E 101
Kensington Gro. *Timp* . . .3G 133
Kensington Rd. *M21* 5G 107
Kensington Rd. *Fail* 3H 85
Kensington Rd. *Oldh* 5B 72
Kensington Rd. *Stoc* 4D 138
Kensington St. *M14* 4E 109
Kensington St. *Bolt* 6A 32
Kensington St. *Hyde* 6C 114
Kensington St. *Roch* 1E 41
Kenslow Av. *M8* 1B 82
Kensworth Clo. *M23* 5D 134
Kensworth Clo. *Bolt* 4H 31
Kensworth Dri. *Bolt* 4H 31
Kent Av. *Chad* 3G 71
Kent Av. *Chea H* 6E 139
Kent Av. *Droy* 4G 97
Kent Clo. *Dig* 3C 60
Kent Clo. *Wors* 1D 76
Kent Ct. *Bolt* 5A 32
Kent Dri. *Bury* 5D 36
Kent Dri. *Kear* 3B 64
Kentford Dri. *M40* 1G 95
Kentford Gro. *Farn* 1E 63
Kentford Rd. *Bolt* 4A 32
Kent Gro. *Fail* 5E 85
Kentmere Av. *Roch* 6H 15
Kentmere Clo. *Gat* 2F 149
Kentmere Ct. *M9* 5A 70
Kentmere Gro. *Farn* 2B 62
Kentmere Rd. *Bolt* 4H 33
Kentmere Rd. *Timp* 5D 134
  (in two parts)
Kentmore Clo. *Stoc* 1A 138
Kenton Av. *M18* 3E 111
Kenton Clo. *Aud* 6D 98
Kenton Clo. *Bolt* 4H 31
Kenton Rd. *Shaw* 6E 43
Kenton St. *Oldh* 4F 73
Kent Rd. *Cad* 4A 118
Kent Rd. *Dent* 5A 112
Kent Rd. *Part* 6C 118
Kent Rd. *Stoc* 3D 138
Kent Rd. E. *M41* 4H 109
Kent Rd. W. *M14* 4G 109
  (in three parts)
Kentsford Dri. *Rad* 2B 48
Kentstone Av. *Stoc* 6H 125
Kent St. *M2* 4D **94** (5H **5**)
Kent St. *Bolt* 5A 32
Kent St. *Oldh* 5D 72
Kent St. *Roch* 5H 27
Kent St. *Salf* 1B 94
Kent St. *Swin* 1F 79
Kentucky St. *Oldh* 3G 73
Kent Wlk. *Heyw* 4C 38
Kentwell Clo. *Duk* 6H 99
Kenwick Dri. *M40* 1E 85
Kenwood Av. *M19* 3B 126
Kenwood Av. *Bram* 2F 161
Kenwood Av. *Gat* 5E 137
Kenwood Av. *Hale* 3A 150
Kenwood Clo. *Stret* 5E 107
Kenwood Dri. *Stret* 6E 107
Kenwood La. *Wors* 6H 77
Kenwood Rd. *Bolt* 2F 31
Kenwood Rd. *Oldh* 6A 56
Kenwood Rd. *Stoc* 5G 111

Kenwood Rd. *Stret* 6E 107
Kenworthy. 1H 135
Kenworthy Av. *Ash L* 6H 87
Kenworthy Gdns.
  Upperm 1F 61
Kenworthy La. *M22* . . .1B 136
Kenworthy St. *Roch* 4C 28
Kenworthy St. *Stal* 4E 101
  (in three parts)
Kenworthy Ter. *Roch* 4C 28
Kenwright St.
  M4 . . . . . .3E **95** (3B **6**)
Kenwyn St. *M40* 2A 96
Kenyon Av. *Duk* 6C 100
Kenyon Av. *Oldh* 6D 72
Kenyon Av. *Sale* 1E 135
Kenyon Bus. Pk.
  Bolt 2A 46
Kenyon Clo. *Hyde* 2D 114
Kenyon Fold. *Roch* 6A 26
Kenyon Fold. **6A 26**
Kenyon Gro. *L Hul* 5A 62
Kenyon Ho. Duk 4H **99**
  (off Highfield St. W.)
Kenyon La. *M40* 3A 84
Kenyon La. *Duk* 6C 100
Kenyon La. *Midd* 6B 54
Kenyon La. *P'wich* 5G 67
Kenyon Rd. *Brad F* 2B 48
Kenyon St. *M18* 1G 111
Kenyon St. *Ash L* 2G 99
Kenyon St. *Bury* 2E 37
Kenyon St. *Duk* 5H 99
Kenyon St. *Heyw* 3E 39
Kenyon St. *Rad* 4H 49
Kenyon St. *Rams* 2E 13
Kenyon Ter. *L Hul* 6A 62
Kenyon Way. *L Hul* 5A 62
Kenyon Way. *T'ton* 6H 21
Keppel Rd. *M21* 6H 107
Keppel St. *Ash L* 2A 100
Kepplecove Mdw.
  Wors 6B 76
Kepwick Dri. *M22* 4C 148
Kerenhappuch St.
  Rams 4D **12**
  (off Buchanan St.)
Kerfield Wlk.
  M13 . . . . .6F **95** (4D **10**)
Kerfoot Clo. *M22* 3C 136
Kermoor Av. *Bolt* 5C 18
Kerne Gro. *M23* 2G 135
Kerrera Dri. *Salf* 4D 92
Kerridge Dri. *Bred* 5F 129
Kerridge Wlk. M16 . . . . .4D **108**
  (off Chattock St.)
Kerrier Clo. *Eccl* 3A 92
Kerris Clo. *M22* 4C 148
Kerr St. *M9* 6F 69
Kerry Gro. *Bolt* 5D 32
Kerry Wlk. *M23* 2F 147
Kersal. **3E 81**
Kersal Av. *L Hul* 5D 62
Kersal Av. *Swin* 3A 80
Kersal Bank. *Salf* 3G 81
Kersal Bar. *Salf* 2G 81
Kersal Cell. *Salf* 3D 80
Kersal Clo. *P'wich* 2E 81
Kersal Clo. *Salf* 2G 81
Kersal Crag. *Salf* 2G 81
Kersal Dale. **3G 81**
Kersal Dri. *Timp* 4C 134
Kersal Gdns. *Salf* 2G 81
Kersal Hall Av. *Salf* 3E 81
Kersal Rd.
  P'wich & Salf 2E 81
Kersal Va. Ct. *Salf* 3E 81
Kersal Va. Rd. *Salf* 2D 80
Kersal Way. *Salf* 4F 81
Kerscott Rd. *M23* 2E 135
Kersh Av. *M19* 1D 126
Kershaw Av. *L Lev* 3A 48

Kershaw Av. *P'wich* 1D 80
  (in two parts)
Kershaw Av. *Sale* 1E 135
Kershaw Bus. Cen. *Bolt* . .2H 45
Kershaw Dri. *Chad* 6D 70
Kershaw Gro. *Aud* 5B 98
Kershaw La. *Aud* 5B 98
Kershaw Pas. *L'boro* 5C 16
Kershaw Rd. *Fail* 4F 85
Kershaw St. *Ash L* 5F 99
Kershaw St.
  Bolt (BL2) 6G 19
Kershaw St.
  Bolt (BL3) 2H 45
Kershaw St. *Bury* 3E 37
Kershaw St. *Droy* 4H 97
Kershaw St. *Heyw* 3D 38
Kershaw St. *Roch* 3H 27
Kershaw St. *Rytn* 2B 56
Kershaw St. *Shaw* 6F 43
  (in two parts)
Kershaw St. E. *Shaw* 6F 43
Kershaw Wlk. *M12* 1H 109
  (6H 11)
Kershope Gro. *Salf* 5G 93
Kersley St. *Oldh* 3E 73
Kerswell Wlk. *M40* 5A 84
Kerwin Wlk. *Open* 5C 96
Kerwood Dri. *Rytn* 4C 56
Kesteven Rd. *M9* 4F 83
Keston Av. *M9* 6A 70
Keston Av. *Droy* 4G 97
Keston Cres. *Stoc* 3B 128
Keston Rd. *Oldh* 6G 57
Kestor St. *Bolt* 5G 32
  (in two parts)
Kestral Ct. *Salf* 5D 92
Kestrel Av. *Aud* 4C 98
Kestrel Av. *Farn* 2B 62
Kestrel Av. *L Hul* 4C 62
Kestrel Av. *Oldh* 4G 73
Kestrel Av. *Swin* 1H 79
Kestrel Clo. *Marp* 2E 155
Kestrel Clo. *W'fld* 3E 67
Kestrel Dri. *Bury* 1F 37
Kestrel Dri. *Irlam* 4E 103
Kestrel M. *Roch* 4B 26
Kestrel Rd. *Traf P* 5H 91
Kestrel St. *Bolt* 5C 32
Kestrel Vw. *Glos* 6H 117
Kestrel Wlk. *M12* 1C 110
Keswick Av. *Ash L* 6D 86
Keswick Av. *Chad* 2G 71
Keswick Av. *Dent* 3D 112
Keswick Av. *Gat* 2F 149
Keswick Av. *Hyde* 3A 114
Keswick Av. *Oldh* 5E 73
Keswick Av. *Urm* 6A 104
Keswick Clo. *M13* 2H 109
Keswick Clo. *Midd* 5F 53
Keswick Clo. *Stal* 1E 101
Keswick Ct. *Midd* 5F 53
Keswick Dri. *Bram* 2E 161
Keswick Dri. *Bury* 6B 36
Keswick Gro. *Salf* 2F 93
Keswick Rd. *H Lane* 5C 154
Keswick Rd. *Stoc* 2F 127
Keswick Rd. *Stret* 4C 106
Keswick Rd. *Timp* 5D 134
Keswick Rd. *Wors* 1H 77
Keswick St. *Bolt* 3B 32
Keswick St. *Roch* 3B 40
Kesworthy Clo. *Hyde* 5A 116
Ketley Wlk. *M22* 2D 148
Kettering Rd. *M19* 5D 110
Kettleshulme Wlk.
  Wilm 6A 160
Kettleshulme Way.
  Poy 5F 163
Kettlewell Wlk. *M18* 2E 111
Ketton Clo. *M11* 6G 97

Keverlow La. *Oldh* 1G 87
Kevin Av. *Rytn* 5C 56
Kevin Ct. *Stoc* 1B 152
Kevin St. *M19* 1D 126
Kew Av. *Hyde* 6C 114
Kew Dri. *Chea H* 3A 150
Kew Dri. *Urm* 3C 104
Kew Gdns. *M40* 2A 84
Kew Rd. *Fail* 3G 85
Kew Rd. *Oldh* 3F 73
  (in two parts)
Kew Rd. *Roch* 2G 41
Key Ct. *Dent* 1G 129
Keyhaven Wlk. *M40* 6E 83
  (Dalbury Dri.)
Keyhaven Wlk. *M40* 5E 83
  (Reedshaw Rd.)
Keymer St. *M11* 3A 96
Keynsham Rd. *M11* 2D 96
Keystone Clo. *Salf* 1E 93
Key West Clo. *M11* 4B 96
Keyworth Wlk. *M40* 1A 96
Khartoum St. *M11* 3F 97
Khartoum St. *M16* 3B 108
Kibbles Brow. *Brom X* 3F 19
Kibboth Crew. *Rams* 2D 12
Kibworth Clo. *W'fld* 1B 66
Kibworth Wlk. M9 . . . . . .4G **69**
  (off Crossmead Dri.)
Kidacre Wlk. *M40* 4A 84
Kidderminster Way.
  Chad 6F 55
Kid St. *Midd* 6H 53
Kidwall Wlk. *M9* 2H 83
Kiel Clo. *Eccl* 5G 91
Kielder Hill. *Midd* 3H 53
Kielder Sq. *Salf* 4F 93
Kilbride Av. *Bolt* 1H 47
Kilburn Av. *M9* 3F 69
Kilburn Clo. *H Grn* 6F 149
Kilburn Rd. *Rad* 3D 48
Kilburn Rd. *Stoc* 4E 139
Kilburn St. *Oldh* 6G 57
Kildale Clo. *Bolt* 3C 44
Kildare Cres. *Roch* 3F 41
Kildare Rd. *M21* 1B 124
Kildare Rd. *Swin* 4E 79
Kildare St. *Farn* 2E 63
Kildonan Dri. *Bolt* 1D 44
Killer St. *Rams* 2E 13
Killon St. *Bury* 4E 37
Kilmaine Dri. *Bolt* 2C 44
Kilmarsh Wlk. *M8* 4B 82
Kilmington Dri. *M8* 5B 82
Kilmory Dri. *Bolt* 1H 47
Kiln Bank. *Whitw* 3G 15
  (off Tong End)
Kiln Bank La. *Whitw* 3G 15
Kilnbrook Clo. *G'ton* 5D 74
Kiln Brow. *Brom X* 3G 19
Kiln Cft. *Rom* 2F 141
Kiln Cft. La. *Hand* 3A 160
Kilner Clo. *Bury* 3F 51
Kilnerdeyne Ter. *Roch* 5G 27
Kilner Wlk. *M40* 1G 95
Kilnfield. *Brom X* 3D 18
Kiln Green. **3D 60**
Kiln Hill Clo. *Chad* 5F 55
Kiln Hill La. *Chad* 5F 55
Kilnhurst Wlk. *Bolt* 5H 31
Kiln La. *Had* 2H 117
Kiln La. *Miln* 5F 29
Kiln Mt. *Miln* 5F 29
Kilnsey Wlk. *M18* 2E 111
Kilnside Dri. *M9* 4F 83
Kiln St. *L Lev* 4A 48
Kiln St. *Rams* 4D 12
Kiln Wlk. *Roch* 1G 27
Kilnwick Clo. *M18* 4D 110
Kilrush Av. *Eccl* 5F 91
Kilsby Clo. *Farn* 5D 46
Kilsby Clo. *Los* 1B 44

Kilsby Wlk.
 M40 . . . . . .1H 95 (1H 7)
Kilton Wlk.
 M40 . . . . . . .1G 95 (1F 7)
Kilvert Dri. Sale 4H 121
Kilworth Av. Sale 6H 121
Kilworth Dri. Los 2B 44
Kilworth St. Roch 1D 40
Kimberley Av. Rom 1H 141
Kimberley Rd. Bolt 6C 18
Kimberley St. Oldh 6A 72
Kimberley St. Salf 4A 82
Kimberley St. Stoc 4G 139
Kimberley Wlk.
 M15 . . . . . .6B 94 (4D 8)
Kimble Clo. G'mnt 1H 21
Kimbolton Clo. M12 . . . .6C 96
Kinburn Rd. M19 . . . . .1H 137
Kinbury Wlk. M40 . . . . .1G 95
Kincardine Rd.
 M13 . . . . . .6F 95 (4C 10)
Kincraig Clo. M11 . . . . .4D 96
Kincraig Clo. Bolt 3C 44
Kinder Av. Ash L 5C 88
Kinder Av. Oldh 4G 73
Kinder Ct. Stoc 4G 139
Kinder Dri. Marp 5E 143
Kinder Fold. Stal 1H 115
Kinder Gro. Rom 1C 142
Kinder Ho. Salf 2D 92
Kinders Clo. Part 3H 119
Kinders Cres. G'fld 4F 61
Kinders Fold. L'boro 2D 16
Kinders La. G'fld 4F 61
Kinders M. G'fld 4F 61
Kinder St. Stal 3E 101
Kinder St. Stoc 4G 139
Kinderton Av. M20 . . . . .2F 125
Kinder Way. Midd 5H 53
Kinder Way. Mot 4B 116
Kineton Wlk.
 M13 . . . . . .1G 109 (6F 11)
 (off Lauderdale Cres.)
King Albert St. Shaw 6F 43
Kingcombe Wlk. M9 . . . .3G 83
King Edward Rd. Hyde . .2C 130
King Edward St. M19 . . .6D 110
King Edward St. Eccl 3E 91
King Edward St.
 Salf 5H 93 (2A 8)
Kingfisher Av. Aud 4C 90
Kingfisher Clo. M12 . . . .2A 110
Kingfisher Ct. Roch 5A 16
Kingfisher Ct. Salf 5D 92
Kingfisher Dri. Bury 1F 37
Kingfisher Dri. Farn 2B 62
Kingfisher M. Marp 5E 143
Kingfisher Rd. Stoc 1F 153
King George Rd.
 Hyde 6C 114
Kingham Dri.
 M4 . . . . .3G 95 (3F 7)
Kingholm Gdns. Bolt . . .4H 31
King La. Oldh 3A 58
Kingmoor Av. Rad 3H 49
Kings Acre. Bow 4C 144
Kings Av. M8 . . . . .3C 82
Kings Av. Gat 1E 149
Kings Av. W'fld 5C 50
Kingsbridge Av. Bolt 5D 34
Kingsbridge Av. Hyde . .5G 115
Kingsbridge Clo.
 Marp 4C 142
Kingsbridge Ct. M9 . . . . .4E 83
Kingsbridge Ho. Bolt . . .2G 45
Kingsbridge Rd. M9 . . . .4E 83
Kingsbridge Rd. Duk . . .6H 99
Kingsbridge Rd. Oldh . . .4F 73
Kingsbridge Wlk.
 Hyde 5G 115
Kingsbrook Rd. M16 . . . .1C 124
Kingsbury Av. Bolt 4E 31

Kingsbury Ct. Bolt 4E 31
Kingsbury Ct. Lodge.
 Bolt 4E 31
Kingsbury Dri. Wilm . . .6H 159
Kingsbury Rd. M11 . . . . .3E 97
Kingscliffe St. M9 . . . . .3G 83
Kings Clo. M18 . . . . . . .1H 111
Kings Clo. Bram 3H 151
Kings Clo. P'wich 4G 67
Kings Clo. Roch 3D 166
Kings Ct. Alt 1F 145
King's Ct. Salf 1G 93
 (off Union St.)
Kings Ct. Stoc 6H 127
King's Dri. Stoc 6C 126
Kingsdale Rd. M18 . . . . .3A 112
Kingsdown Dri. Bolt 4B 32
Kingsdown Gdns. Bolt . . .4B 32
 (off Kingsdown Dri.)
Kingsdown Rd. M22 . . . .4A 148
Kingsdown Wlk. Stoc . . .4B 128
Kings Dri. Chea H 2C 150
Kings Dri. Marp 4C 142
King's Dri. Midd 1G 69
Kings Dri. Stoc 6C 126
Kingsfield Dri. M20 . . . .6G 125
Kingsfold Av. M40 . . . . .1G 95
Kingsfold Clo. Bolt 1G 47
Kingsford St. Salf 3D 92
Kings Ga. Bolt 6A 32
Kingsheath Av. M11 . . . .2D 96
Kingshill Rd. M21 . . . . .1G 123
Kingsholme Rd.
 M22 . . . . .3A 148
Kingsland Clo.
 M40 . . . . . .2H 95 (1G 7)
Kingsland Rd. Farn 6C 46
Kingsland Rd. Roch 2B 40
Kingsland Rd. Stoc 4C 138
Kings La. Oldh 2A 58
Kings La. Stret 4F 107
Kingslea Rd. M20 . . . . .4G 125
Kingsleigh Rd. Stoc 6A 126
Kingsley Av. M9 . . . . . . .4H 83
Kingsley Av. Salf 4E 81
Kingsley Av. Stoc 5G 127
Kingsley Av. Stret 4F 107
Kingsley Av. Urm 5E 105
Kingsley Av. W'fld 2F 67
Kingsley Av. Wilm 5G 159
Kingsley Clo. Ash L 6B 88
Kingsley Clo. Dent 6D 112
Kingsley Ct. Salf 4G 93
Kingsley Dri. Chea H 2C 150
Kingsley Dri. Lees 2A 74
Kingsley Gro. Aud 5C 98
Kingsley Rd. M22 . . . . . .3B 136
Kingsley Rd. Midd 5B 54
Kingsley Rd. Oldh 3G 73
Kingsley Rd. Swin 2D 78
Kingsley Rd. Timp 4B 134
Kingsley Rd. Wors 5E 63
Kingsley St. Bolt 3H 31
Kingsley St. Bury 3H 35
Kingsley Clo. M20 . . . . .6F 125
Kingsmead M. M9 . . . . . .4E 69
Kingsmere Av. M19 . . . .6B 110
Kingsmill Av. M19 . . . . .1D 126
Kingsnorth Clo. Bolt 4B 32
Kingsnorth Rd. Urm 4A 104
Kings Pk. Traf P 3B 106
King Sq. Shop. Cen.
 Oldh 3C 72
King's Rd. Ash L 1A 100
King's Rd. Aud 2A 112
Kings Rd. Bred 6G 129
Kings Rd. Chad 6E 71

Kings Rd. Chea H 2B 150
Kings Rd. Chor H 1B 124
Kings Rd. Haz G 2E 153
Kings Rd. Irlam 3C 118
King's Rd. Oldh 4D 72
King's Rd. P'wlch 1G 81
Kings Rd. Rad 6E 35
Kings Rd. Roch 6B 28
Kings Rd. Sale 5H 121
King's Rd. Shaw 1E 57
King's Rd.
 Stret & M16 . . . . .6E 107
King's Rd. Wilm 1D 166
Kings Ter. Duk 4H 99
Kings Ter. Stret 4F 107
Kingston. 4H 113
Kingston Arc. Hyde 5A 116
Kingston Av. M20 . . . . .2F 137
Kingston Av. Bolt 4E 33
Kingston Av. Chad 5G 71
Kingston Av. Oldh 6F 57
Kingston Clo. Bury 5H 35
Kingston Clo. Hyde 5A 116
Kingston Clo. Sale 1F 133
Kingston Clo. Salf 3H 81
Kingston Clo. Shaw 5F 43
Kingston Ct. M20 . . . . . .2F 137
Kingston Dri. Rytn 1A 56
Kingston Dri. Sale 4D 122
Kingston Dri. Urm 1D 120
Kingston Gdns. Hyde 4H 113
Kingston Gro. M9 . . . . . .5H 69
Kingston Hill. Chea 1H 149
Kingston M. Fail 4H 85
Kingston Mill. Stoc 2F 139
Kingston Pl. Chea H 3A 150
Kingston Rd. M20 . . . . .2F 137
Kingston Rd. Fail 4H 85
Kingston Rd. I'land 2G 159
Kingston Rd. Rad 1A 50
Kingston St. Stoc 2F 139
King St. M2 . . . . . .4G 94 (5G 5)
 (in two parts)
King St. Aud 1F 113
King St. Bolt 6A 32
King St. Brad 6H 19
King St. B'btm 6C 116
King St. Brom X 3D 18
King St. Del 3H 59
King St. Dent 4F 113
King St. Droy 5A 98
 (in two parts)
King St. Duk 4H 99
King St. Eccl 4H 91
King St. Fail 5D 84
King St. Farn 1F 63
King St. Heyw 4F 39
King St. Holl 2F 117
King St. Hyde 4B 114
King St. Midd 6A 54
King St. Moss 2F 89
King St. Oldh 3C 72
King St. Rad 5H 49
King St. Rams 3E 13
King St. Roch 4H 27
King St.
 Salf (M3) . . .3C 94 (3F 5)
King St. Salf (M6) 6B 80
King St. Salf (M7) 4A 82
King St. Stal 3E 101
King St. Stret 8D 108
King St. Whitw 2H 15
Kingstreet. Woodf 6D 160
King St. E. Roch 6H 27
King St. E. Stoc 1H 139
King St. S. Roch 6G 27
 (in two parts)
King St. W. M3 . . . .4D 94 (5G 5)
King St. W. Stoc 2G 139
Kings Wlk Ash L 1B 100
 (off Waterloo St.)
Kings Wlk. Droy 5A 98

Kingsway.
 M20 & M19 . . . . . .3G 137
Kingsway. Alt 6F 133
Kingsway. Bram 3H 151
Kingsway. Bred 6E 129
Kingsway.
 Chea H & H Grn . . .3H 149
Kingsway. Duk 6C 100
Kingsway.
 Gat & Chea 6G 137
Kingsway. Kear 3H 63
Kingsway. Midd 3H 69
Kingsway. I'loch 6B 28
Kingsway. Stret 6C 106
Kingsway. Swin 5A 80
Kingsway. Urm 3G 105
Kingsway. Wors 3F 77
Kingsway Av. M19 . . . . .6B 110
Kingsway Bldgs. M19 . . .4A 126
Kingsway Clo. Oldh 4C 72
Kingsway Cres. M19 . . . .4A 126
Kingsway Pk. Urm 2E 105
Kingsway Retail Pk.
 Roch 4D 28
Kingsway S. Chea H 6A 150
Kingsway W. Ind. Pk.
 Roch 6B 28
Kingswear Dri. Bolt 4G 31
Kingswood Gro. Stoc . . .6H 111
Kingswood Rd. M14 . . . .1H 125
Kingswood Rd. Eccl 1D 90
Kingswood Rd. Midd 4H 53
Kingswood Rd. P'wich . . .4D 66
Kingthorpe Gdns. Bolt . . .3B 46
King William Enterprise Pk.
 Salf 5G 93
King William St. Eccl 2C 90
King William St. Salf 5G 93
Kingwood Av. Bolt 4D 30
Kinlett Wlk. M40 . . . . . . .1D 84
Kinley Clo. M12 . . . . . . .1B 110
Kinloch Dri. Bolt 6F 31
Kinloch St. M11 . . . . . . .3C 96
Kinloch St. Oldh 5E 73
Kinmel Av. Stoc 5C 128
Kinmel Wlk. M23 . . . . . .5F 135
Kinmount Wlk. M9 . . . . . .5F 83
 (off Lathbury Rd.)
Kinnaird Cres. Stoc 3B 140
Kinnaird Rd. M20 . . . . . .4G 125
Kinnerley Gro. Wors 2C 76
Kinross. Eccl 3H 91
 (off Peel St.)
Kinross Av. Stoc 2A 152
Kinross Clo. Rams 1A 22
Kinross Dri. Bolt 2D 44
Kinross Rd. M14 . . . . . . .4A 110
Kinsale Wlk. M23 . . . . . .2F 147
Kinsey Av. M23 . . . . .4F 135
Kinsley Dri. Wors 1E 77
Kintore Av. Haz G 2F 153
Kintore Wlk. M40 . . . . . .6E 83
 (off Keyhaven Wlk.)
Kintyre Av. Salf 4D 92
Kintyre Clo. M11 . . . . . . .4F 97
Kintyre Dri. Bolt 2C 44
Kinver Clo. Bolt 4G 45
Kinver Rd. M40 . . . . .1C 84
Kipling Av. Dent 2G 129
Kipling Av. Droy 2A 98
Kipling Clo. Stoc 5E 141
Kipling Rd. Oldh 5F 57
Kipling St. Salf 5H 81
Kippax St. M14 . . . . .4F 109
Kirby Av. Chad 6D 70
Kirby Av. Swin 6D 78
Kirby Wlk. M44 . . . . .3G 95 (4F 7)
Kirby Wlk. Shaw 5F 43
Kirkbank St. Oldh 2B 72
 (in two parts)
Kirkburn Vw. Bury 6C 22
Kirkby Av. M40 . . . . .6D 84

Kirkby Av. *Sale* 1C **134**
Kirkby Clo. *Bury* 6C **36**
Kirkby Dri. *Sale* 1D **134**
Kirkby Rd. *Bolt* 5F **31**
Kirkdale Av. *M40* 1D **84**
Kirkdale Dri. *Rytn* 2A **56**
Kirkebrok Rd. *Bolt* 3E **45**
Kirkfell Dri. *H Lane* 5C **154**
Kirkfell Wlk. *Oldh* 6D **56**
(in two parts)
Kirkgate Clo.
M40 . . . . .2G **95** (2F **7**)
Kirkhall La. *Bolt* 5G **31**
Kirkhall Workshops, The.
Bolt 5G **31**
Kirkham Av. *M18* 1F **111**
Kirkham Clo. *Dent* 4F **113**
Kirkham Rd. *H Grn* 5G **149**
Kirkhams. 2F **67**
Kirkham St. *Bolt* 4D **32**
Kirkham St. *L Hul* 4C **62**
Kirkham St. *Oldh* 2C **72**
Kirkham St. *Salf* 4E **93**
Kirkhaven Sq. *M40* 1A **96**
Kirkhill Wlk. *M40* 1D **84**
Kirkholt. 2F **41**
Kirkholt Wlk. *M9* 6G **69**
Kirk Hope Dri. *Bolt* 4H **31**
Kirk Hope Wlk. *Bolt* 4H **31**
Kirklands. *Bolt* 3F **33**
Kirklands. *Sale* 1A **134**
Kirklee Av. *Chad* 6G **55**
Kirklee Rd. *Roch* 3D **40**
Kirklees Clo. *T'ton* 4A **22**
Kirklees Ind. Est. *T'ton* . . .5A **22**
Kirklees St. *T'ton* 4H **21**
Kirklees Wlk. *W'fld* 6F **51**
Kirkley St. *Hyde* 6B **114**
Kirklinton Dri. *M9* 5F **83**
Kirkman Av. *Eccl* 5E **91**
Kirkman Clo. *M18* 3F **111**
Kirkmanshulme La.
M12 . . . . .3B **110**
Kirkman St. *Bury* 4D **50**
Kirk Rd. *M19* 2D **126**
Kirkstall. Roch 3G **27**
(off Falinge Rd.)
Kirkstall Av. *Heyw* 2E **39**
Kirkstall Av. *L'boro* 3E **17**
Kirkstall Clo. *Poy* 3D **162**
Kirkstall Gdns. *Rad* 2E **49**
Kirkstall Rd. *Midd* 4H **53**
Kirkstall Rd. *Urm* 4G **105**
Kirkstall Sq.
M13 . . . . . .1G **109** (6E **11**)
Kirkstead Clo. *M11* 5C **96**
Kirkstead Rd. *Chea H* 6E **151**
Kirkstile Pl. *Swin* 5E **65**
Kirkstone Av. *Wors* 2H **77**
Kirkstone Clo. *Oldh* 6D **56**
Kirkstone Dri. *Midd* 5G **53**
Kirkstone Dri. *Rytn* 1B **56**
Kirkstone Rd. *M40* 1C **84**
Kirkstone Rd. *Hyde* 2A **114**
Kirk St. *M18* 2F **111**
Kirkwood Wlk. *Open* 5E **97**
Kirkwall Dri. *Bolt* 2D **46**
Kirkway. *M9* 5A **70**
Kirkway. *Midd* 2A **70**
Kirkway. *Roch* 3F **41**
Kirkwood Dri. *M40* 1G **95**
Kirtley Av. *Eccl* 2F **91**
Kirtlington Clo. *Rytn* 2E **57**
Kirton Lodge. *P'wich* 5G **67**
(in two parts)
Kirton Wlk. *M9* 4E **69**
Kitchener Av. *Cad* 5A **118**
Kitchener St. *Bolt* 4D **46**
Kitchener St. *Bury* 4H **35**
Kitchen St. *Roch* 3A **28**
Kitepool St. *Eccl* 1C **90**
Kitter St. *Roch* 6H **15**

Kitt's Moss. 1F **161**
Kitt's Moss La. *Bram* 1F **161**
Kitty Wheeldon Gdns.
Sale 4A **122**
Kiveton Clo. *Wors* 1E **77**
Kiwi St. *Salf* 3G **93**
Knacks La. *Roch* 4A **14**
Knaresborough Clo.
Stoc 6G **111**
Knarr Barn La. *Dob* 4F **59**
Knarr La. *Del* 5G **59**
(in two parts)
Knight Cres. *Midd* 3F **53**
Knightley Wlk. *M40* 6F **83**
Knightsbridge.
M4 . . . . .3E **95** (4A **6**)
(off Arndale Shop. Cen.)
Knightsbridge. *Stoc* 1H **139**
Knightsbridge Clo. *Salf* . .3H **81**
Knightsbridge Clo.
Wilm 6H **159**
Knightsbridge M.
M20 . . . . .5F **125**
Knights Clo. *P'wich* 4F **67**
Knight's Ct. *Salf* 3A **92**
Knight St. *M20* 1F **137**
Knight St. *Ash L* 3F **99**
Knight St. *Bolt* 5B **32**
Knight St. *Bury* 3A **36**
Knight St. *Hyde* 6C **114**
Knightswood. *Bolt* 4D **44**
Kniveton Clo. *M12* 1B **110**
Kniveton Rd. *M12* 1B **110**
Kniveton St. *Hyde* 4D **114**
Knob Hall Gdns. *M23* 2F **147**
Knole Av. *Poy* 3F **163**
Knoll Hill Vw. *Heyw* 3C **38**
Knoll St. *Roch* 2B **40**
Knoll St. *Salf* 4H **81**
Knoll St. Ind. Pk. *Salf* 4H **81**
Knoll, The. *Alt* 6D **132**
Knoll, The. *Moss* 2D **88**
Knoll, The. *Shaw* 1G **57**
Knott Fold. *Hyde* 1B **130**
Knott Hill La. *Del* 4G **59**
Knott Hill Local
Nature Reserve. . . .4B **88**
Knott La. *Bolt* 3D **30**
Knott La. *Hyde* 1B **130**
Knott Lanes. 3D **86**
Knott Lanes. *Oldh* 3D **86**
Knott Mill. 6C **94** (3F **9**)
Knott St. *Salf* 4D **92**
Knowe Av. *M22* 4B **148**
Knowl Clo. *Dent* 5A **112**
Knowl Clo. *Rams* 6E **13**
Knowldale Way. *M12* 2A **110**
Knowle Av. *Ash L* 1F **99**
Knowle Dri. *P'wich* 1E **81**
Knowle Grn. *Hand* 4G **159**
Knowle Pk. *Hand* 4G **159**
Knowle Rd. *Mell* 5G **143**
Knowles Ct. *Salf* 2A **92**
Knowles Edge St. *Bolt* . . .3G **31**
Knowles Pl.
M15 . . . . . .1E **109** (5H **9**)
Knowles St. *Bolt* 4C **32**
Knowles St. *Rad* 3G **49**
Knowle Way. *Mot* 5B **116**
Knowl Hill Dri. *Roch* 1A **26**
Knowl Rd. *Roch* 4D **28**
Knowl Rd. *Shaw* 1G **57**
Knowls Lane. 4B **74**
Knowls La. *Lees* 4B **74**
Knowls, The. *Oldh* 2H **85**
Knowl St. *Oldh* 1A **86**
Knowl St. *Stal* 3F **101**
Knowl Syke St. *Ward* 2A **16**
Knowl Top La. *Upperm* . . .2H **61**
Knowl Vw. *L'boro* 1F **29**
Knowl Vw. *T'ton* 5A **22**
Knowsley. S'head 2C **74**

Knowsley Av. *Salf* 5H **93**
Knowsley Av. *S'head* 2C **74**
Knowsley Av. *Urm* 3E **105**
Knowsley Cres. *Stoc* 3B **140**
Knowsley Dri. *S'head* 2C **74**
Knowsley Dri. *Swin* 5D **78**
Knowsley Grange. *Bolt* . . .6B **30**
Knowsley Grn. Salf 5H **93**
(off Knowsley Av.)
Knowsley Grn. *S'head* 2C **74**
Knowsley Rd. *A'wth* 4C **34**
Knowsley Rd. *Bolt* 3F **31**
Knowsley Rd. *Haz G* 5F **153**
Knowsley Rd. *Stoc* 3B **140**
Knowsley Rd. *W'fld* 1D **66**
Knowsley St. *M8* 1D **94**
Knowsley St. *Bolt* 5B **32**
Knowsley St. *Bury* 4C **36**
Knowsley St. *Roch* 3G **27**
Knowsley Ter. *S'head* 2C **74**
Knowsley Ter. *Stoc* 3B **140**
Knutsford Av. *M16* 3B **108**
Knutsford Av. *Sale* 5E **123**
Knutsford Av. *Stoc* 2F **127**
Knutsford Rd. *M18* 2E **111**
Knutsford Rd.
Ald E & Wilm 6B **166**
Knutsford Rd.
Kno V & Ald E 6A **166**
Knutsford St. *Salf* 3E **93**
Knutsford Vw. *Haleb* 5C **146**
Knutshaw Bridge. 4D **44**
Knutshaw Cres. *Bolt* 5B **44**
Knypersley Av. *Stoc* 4C **140**
Krokus Sq. *Chad* 2G **71**
Kyle Ct. *Haz G* 4F **153**
Kylemore Av. *Bolt* 2F **45**
Kyle Rd. *Haz G* 4F **153**
Kynder St. *Dent* 4F **113**

L

Labrador Quay. *Salf* 6G **93**
Labtec St. *Swin* 2H **79**
Laburnham Rd. *Midd* 1C **70**
Laburnum Av. *Ash L* 5G **87**
Laburnum Av. *Aud* 4C **98**
Laburnum Av. *Chad* 6H **55**
Laburnum Av. *Eccl* 5C **90**
Laburnum Av. *Fail* 5F **85**
Laburnum Av. *Hyde* 1B **130**
Laburnum Av. *Shaw* 1F **57**
Laburnum Av. *Stal* 5D **100**
Laburnum Av. *Swin* 5E **79**
Laburnum Av. *T'ton* 4H **21**
Laburnum Av. *W'fld* 2D **66**
Laburnum Clo. *Timp* 6B **134**
Laburnum Ct. *T'ton* 4H **21**
Laburnum Dri. *Bury* 6E **51**
Laburnum Gro. *P'wich* 4E **67**
Laburnum Gro. *Tyl* 2A **76**
Laburnum Ho. *Shaw* 1F **57**
Laburnum La. *Hale* 5G **145**
Laburnum La. *Miln* 2E **43**
Laburnum Lodge. *Bolt* 5H **33**
Laburnum Pk. *Bolt* 6F **19**
Laburnum Rd. *M18* 3F **111**
Laburnum Rd. *Cad* 4B **118**
Laburnum Rd. *Dent* 4H **111**
Laburnum Rd. *Farn* 1D **62**
Laburnum Rd. *Oldh* 3A **86**
Laburnum Rd. *Urm* 3D **104**
Laburnum Rd. *Wors* 1G **77**
Laburnum St. *Bolt* 5H **31**
Laburnum St. *Salf* 3F **93**
Laburnum Ter. *Roch* 1E **41**
Laburnum Vs. *Oldh* 2E **87**
Laburnum Vs. Urm . . .5G **105**
(off Cavendish Rd.)
Laburnum Wlk. *Sale* 4E **121**
Laburnum Way. *L'boro* 3D **16**

Laburnum Way. *Stoc* 3D **138**
Lacey Av. *Wilm* 6F **159**
Lacey Clo. *Wilm* 6F **159**
Lacey Ct. *Wilm* 6F **159**
Lacey Green. 6F **159**
Lacey Grn. *Wilm* 1E **167**
Lacey Gro. *Wilm* 6G **159**
Lackford Dri.
M40 . . . . .1G **95** (1F **7**)
Lacrosse Av. *Oldh* 5A **72**
Lacy Gro. *Stret* 6D **106**
Lacy St. *Stoc* 3H **139**
Lacy St. *Stret* 6D **106**
Lacy Wlk. *M12* 5A **96** (1H **11**)
Ladbrooke Clo. *Ash L* 1A **100**
Ladbrooke Rd. *Ash L* 6F **87**
Ladcastle Rd. *G'fld* 6H **59**
Ladhill La. *G'fld* 4F **61**
Ladybarn. 2H **125**
Ladybarn Cres. *M14* 2H **125**
Ladybarn Cres. *Bram* 1H **161**
Ladybarn Ho. *M14* 1H **125**
Ladybarn La. *M14* 1H **125**
Ladybarn Mnr. *Bram* 5G **151**
Ladybarn Rd. *M14* 1H **125**
Ladybower. *Chea H* 1E **151**
Ladybridge Av. *Wors* 3E **77**
Lady Bri. Brow. *Bolt* 6D **30**
Lady Bri. La. *Bolt* 6D **30**
Ladybridge Ri.
Chea H 2E **151**
Ladybridge Rd.
Chea H 3D **150**
Ladybrook Av. *Timp* 3B **134**
Ladybrook Gro. *Wilm* 5H **159**
Ladybrook Rd. *Bram* 4E **151**
Ladyfield St. *Wilm* 2E **167**
Ladyfield Ter. *Wilm* 2F **167**
Lady Harriet Wlk. *Wors* . . .6E **63**
Ladyhill Vw. *Wors* 3E **77**
Lady House. 6E **29**
Ladyhouse Clo. *Miln* 6G **29**
Lady Ho. Fold. Miln 1D **42**
(off Ashfield La.)
Ladyhouse La. *Miln* 6F **29**
(in two parts)
Lady in Leisure Health &
Fitness Cen. 5G **5**
Lady Kelvin Rd. *Alt* 5E **133**
Ladylands Av. *M11* 3E **97**
Ladymere Dri. *Wors* 3D **76**
Lady Rd. *Lees* 3A **74**
Ladys Clo. *Poy* 3E **163**
Ladyshore Clo. *Salf* 4F **93**
Ladyshore Rd. *L Lev* 5C **48**
Lady's Incline. *Poy* 3E **163**
Ladysmith Av. *Bury* 6G **23**
Ladysmith Cen. *Ash L* 2H **99**
Ladysmith Dri. *Ash L* 6B **88**
Ladysmith Rd. *M20* 6G **125**
Ladysmith Rd. *Ash L* 6B **88**
Ladysmith Rd. *Stal* 1E **101**
Ladysmith St. *Oldh* 6A **72**
Ladysmith St. *Stoc* 4G **139**
Ladysmith, The. *Ash L* 6B **88**
Ladythorn Av. *Marp* 6E **143**
Ladythorn Cres.
Bram 1H **161**
Ladythorne Av. *P'wich* 1E **81**
Ladythorne Ct. *P'wich* 1E **81**
Ladythorne Dri. *P'wich* 1E **81**
Ladythorn Gro. *Bram* 6H **151**
Ladythorn Rd. *Bram* 6G **151**
Ladywell Av. *L Hul* 5C **62**
Ladywell Clo. *Haz G* 3A **152**
Ladywell Gro. *L Hul* 4C **62**
Ladywell Trad. Est. *Salf* . .3B **92**
Lagan Wlk. *M22* 3B **148**
Lagos Clo. *M14* 3E **109**
Laindon Rd. *M14* 3A **110**
Lainton Ct. *Stoc* 3E **139**
Lake Bank. *L'boro* 6E **17**

Lake Dri. Midd 2H 69
Lakeland Ct. Midd 5F 53
Lakeland Cres. Bury 1C 80
Lakeland Dri. Rytn 5A 42
Lakelands Dri. Bolt 2D 44
Lakenheath Dri. Bolt 5D 18
Lake Rd. Dent 3F 113
Lake Rd. Stal 1D 100
Lake Rd. Traf P 6C 92
Lakeside. Bury 2D 50
Lakeside. Chea 2G 149
Lake Side. Had 1H 117
Lake Side. L'boro 1G 29
Lakeside Av. Ash L 1F 99
Lakeside Av. Bolt 5C 46
Lakeside Av. Wors 4F 63
Lakeside Clo. M18 . . . . .1H 111
Lakeside Clo. Salf 2H 81
Lakeside Dri. Poy 2E 163
Lakeside Grn. Stoc 5C 140
Lakeside Way. Bury 4D 36
Lakes Rd. Duk 5A 100
Lakes Rd. Marp 5E 143
Lake St. Bolt 2B 46
Lake St. Roch 5H 27
Lake St. Stoc 6B 140
Lakeswood. Duk 5H 99
Lake Vw. M9 . . . . .1A 84
Lake Vw. L'boro 2D 16
Lakin St. M40 . . . . .4A 84
Laleham Grn. Bram 2F 151
Lamb Clo. M12 . . . . .2B 110
Lamb Ct. Salf 3C 94 (4E 5)
Lambert Dri. Sale 3F 121
Lamberton Dri. M23 . . . . .5E 135
Lambert St. Ash L 4F 99
Lambeth Av. Fail 3H 85
Lambeth Gro. Woodl 4G 129
Lambeth Rd. M40 . . . . . .1E 97
Lambeth Rd. Stoc 1H 127
Lambeth Ter. Roch 6F 27
Lamb La. Salf 3C 94 (4E 5)
Lambourn Clo. Bolt 2A 46
Lambourn Clo. Poy 3D 162
Lambourne Clo. M22 . . . .5B 148
Lambourne Gro. Miln 6F 29
Lambourn Rd. Urm 3H 103
Lambrook Wlk. M40 . . . . . .1F 97
Lambs Fold. Stoc 4F 127
Lambton Rd. M21 . . . . . .1B 124
Lambton Rd. Wors 5C 78
Lambton St. Bolt 5G 45
Lambton St. Eccl 1D 90
Lamburn Av. M40 . . . . . .1D 84
Lamb Wlk. Dent 2G 129
Lamerton Way.
    Wilm 5A 160
Lamorna Clo. Salf 3F 81
Lamphey Clo. Bolt 5B 30
Lamplight Way. Swin 4C 80
Lamport Clo.
    M1 . . . . . . .6F 95 (3C 10)
Lamport Ct.
    M1 . . . . . . .6F 95 (3C 10)
        (off Lamport Clo.)
Lampson St. M8 . . . . . . .1C 94
Lampton Clo. Alt 4G 133
Lamsholme Clo. M19 . . .5C 110
Lanark Av. M22 . . . . . . .3B 136
Lanark Clo. Haz G 3G 153
Lanark Clo. Heyw 4B 38
Lanbury Dri. M8 . . . . . . .4B 82
Lancashire Cotts. Moss . . .2F 89
Lancashire County Cricket
    Club Mus. 3G 107
Lancashire County Cricket
    Ground. 3G 107
Lancashire Ct. Oldh 4A 72
Lancashire Fusiliers Mus.
    . . . . .4H 35
Lancashire Hill. 6H 127
Lancashire Hill. Stoc . . .6G 127

Lancashire St. M40 . . . . . .6H 83
Lancaster. M1 . . . . .5E 95
Lancaster Av. Fail 4E 86
Lancaster Av. Farn 1B 62
Lancaster Av. Midd 2C 70
        (in two parts)
Lancaster Av. Rams 5C 12
Lancaster Av. Stal 2F 101
Lancaster Av. Urm 4G 105
Lancaster Av. W'fld 2E 67
Lancaster Clo. Bolt 6C 32
Lancaster Clo. Haz G . . .5D 152
Lancaster Clo. Rom 2G 141
Lancaster Ct. M19 . . . . .1B 126
Lancaster Ct. M40 . . . . . .1E 97
Lancaster Dri. Bury 3F 23
Lancaster Dri. L Lev 3B 48
Lancaster Dri. P'wich 1G 81
Lancaster Ho. Rytn 2B 56
Lancaster Ho. Stoc 3G 139
        (off York St.)
Lancaster Lodge. Salf 5H 79
        (off Lancaster Rd.)
Lancaster Rd. M20 . . . . .6E 125
Lancaster Rd. Cad 4A 118
Lancaster Rd. Dent 6F 113
Lancaster Rd. Droy 2H 97
Lancaster Rd. Salf 5H 79
Lancaster Rd. Wilm 6A 160
Lancaster Sq. Rytn 2B 56
Lancaster St. Chad 5G 71
Lancaster St. Moss 2D 88
Lancaster St. Rad 4E 49
Lancaster St. Stoc 1A 140
Lancaster Ter. Bult 3A 32
        (off Boardman St.)
Lancaster Ter. Roch 1H 25
Lancaster Wlk. Bolt 3A 32
Lancastrian Ho.
    P'wich 2G 81
Lancelot Rd. M22 . . . . . .3D 148
Lancelyn Dri. Wilm 1G 167
Lanchester Dri. Bolt 2H 45
Lanchester St. M40 . . . . . .2A 96
Lancing Av. M20 . . . . . .6H 125
Lancing Wlk. Chad 3G 71
Landcross Rd. M14 . . . . .6G 109
Landells Wlk. M40 . . . . . .6A 84
Lander Gro. M9 . . . . .6H 69
Landfield Dri. M8 . . . . . . .4B 82
Landkey Clo. M23 . . . . . .1F 135
Land La. Wilm 3F 167
        (in two parts)
Landmark Ct. Bolt 4E 31
        (off Bk. Markland Hill La. E.)
Landor Ct. Dent 4H 111
Landore Clo. Rad 3H 49
Landos St. M40 . . .2G 95 (2F 7)
Landos Rd.
    M40 . . . . .2G 95 (2F 7)
Landrace Dri. Wors 5D 76
Landsberg Rd. Fail 3H 85
Landsberg Ter. Fail 3H 85
Landseer Dri. Marp B 4F 143
Landseer St. Oldh 4F 73
Lands End Rd. Midd 2D 68
Landstead Dri.
    M40 . . . . .3A 96 (3H 7)
Lane Bottom. 1H 43
Lane Brow. G'ton 4D 74
Lane Dri. G'ton 4D 74
Lane End. 5H 39
Lane End. Eccl 4H 91
Lane End. Heyw 5H 39
Lane End Clo. Fail 5G 85
Lane Ends. 2G 143
        (Marple Bridge)
Lane Ends. 6B 130
        (Romiley)
Lane Ends. Horn 6B 130
Lanegate. Hyde 1B 130

Lane Head Rd.
    Oldh & Moss 5B 74
Lane Mdw. Shaw 1C 57
Lanesfield Wlk. M8 . . . . . .3E 83
        (off Crescent Rd.)
Lane Side. 6H 43
Laneside Av. Shaw 6H 43
Laneside Clo. L'boro 3E 17
Laneside Dri. Bram 4A 152
Laneside Rd. M20 . . . . .3G 137
Laneside Wlk. Miln 4F 29
Lane, The. Bolt 6B 30
Langcliffe Wlk. M18 . . . . .2E 111
Langcroft Dri. M40 . . . . . .6C 84
Langdale Av. M19 . . . . . .1D 126
Langdale Av. Oldh 5B 72
Langdale Av. Roch 5A 42
Langdale Clo. Dent 6E 113
Langdale Clo. Gat 2C 149
Langdale Clo. H Lane 5C 154
Langdale Clo. Timp 6G 133
Langdale Ct. M8 . . . . . . .5D 82
Langdale Dri. Bury 4E 51
Langdale Dri. Midd 4H 53
Langdale Dri. Wors 2H 77
Langdale Rd. M14 . . . . .3H 109
Langdale Rd. Bram 2E 161
Langdale Rd. Part 6C 118
Langdale Rd. Sale 2G 133
Langdale Rd. Stoc 3E 127
Langdale Rd. Stret 4C 106
Langdale Rd. Woodl 4H 129
Langdale St. Bolt 4A 46
Langdale St. Farn 2E 63
Langdale Ter. Stal 1E 101
Langden Clo. Shaw 5E 43
Langdon Clo. Bolt 4H 31
Langfield Av. M16 . . . . . .4B 108
Langfield Cres. Droy 3C 98
Langfield Wlk. Salf 3F 93
Langford Dri. Irlam 6E 103
Langford Gdns. Bolt 3A 46
Langford Rd. M20 . . . . . .3E 126
Langford Rd. Stoc 5E 127
Langford St. Dent 4F 113
Langham Clo. Bolt 6E 19
Langham Ct. M20 . . . . . .5D 124
Langham Ct. Stret 3A 106
Langham Gro. Timp 3B 134
Langham Rd. Bow 3D 144
Langham Rd. Oldh 5C 72
Langham Rd. Salf 3F 93
Langham Rd. Stoc 2D 138
Langham St. Ash L 6E 87
        (in two parts)
Langham St. Ind. Est.
    Ash L 6E 87
Langholm Dri. Bolt 1H 47
Langholme Clo.
    M15 . . . . . . .6B 94 (4D 8)
Langholme Pl. Eccl 3D 90
        (in two parts)
Langholme Way. Heyw 4B 38
Langland Clo. M9 . . . . . . .5G 69
Langland Clo. Lev 6F 111
Langland Dri. Eccl 6E 91
Langley. 5G 53
Langley Av. G'ton 4D 74
Langley Av. Haz G 4B 152
Langley Av. Midd 3G 53
Langley Av. P'wich 4F 67
Langley Clo. Urm 5G 105
Langley Ct. Salf 2A 82
Langley Cres. P'wich 3F 67
Langley Dri. Bolt 2G 45
Langley Dri. Hand 4A 160
Langley Dri. Wors 5B 76
Langley Gdns. P'wich 3F 67
Langley Grange. P'wich 3F 67
Langley Gro. P'wich 3F 67
Langley Hall Rd. P'wich 3F 67
Langley Ho. Midd 4A 54

Langley La.
    Heyw & Midd 3E 53
Langley Rd. M14 . . . . . .6G 109
Langley Rd. P'wich 4E 67
Langley Rd. Sale 6G 121
Langley Rd.
    Swin & Salf 3D 80
Langley Rd. S. Salf 5D 80
Langness St. M11 . . . . . . .4E 97
Langport St. M16 . . . . . .3A 108
Langport Av.
    M12 . . . . . .1A 110 (6H 11)
Langroyd Wlk. M8 . . . . . . .4B 82
        (off Highshore Dri.)
Langsett Av. Glos 6F 117
        (off Langsett La.)
Langsett Av. Salf 2C 92
Langsett Grn. Glos 6F 117
        (off Langsett La.)
Langsett Gro. Glos 6F 117
        (off Langsett La.)
Langsett La. Glos 6F 117
Langsett Lea. Glos 6F 117
        (off Langsett La.)
Langsett Ter. Glos 6F 117
Langshaw Rd. Bolt 2G 45
Langshaw St. M16 . . . . .3A 108
Langshaw St. Salf 4F 93
Langside Av. M9 . . . . . . .5G 69
Langston Grn. Dri. Bolt 3C 44
Langston Grn. Haz G 4A 152
Langston St.
    M3 . . . . .2D 94 (1G 5)
Langthorne St. M19 . . . .1D 126
Langthorne Wlk. Bolt 1H 45
Langton Clo. Fail 3H 85
Langton St. Heyw 2F 39
Langton St. Midd 1A 70
Langton St. Salf 3E 93
Langton Ter. Roch 1E 41
Langtree Clo. Wors 3A 78
Langworthy Av. L Hul 5D 62
Langworthy Rd. M40 . . . . .4A 84
Langworthy Rd. Salf 1E 93
Lanhill Dri. M8 . . . . .5F 83
Lankro Way. Eccl 4H 91
Lanreath Wlk. M8 . . . . . . .5D 82
        (off Moordown Clo.)
Lansbury Ho. M16 . . . . . .4B 108
Lansdale Gdns. M19 . . . .4A 126
Lansdale St. Eccl 5C 90
Lansdale St. Farn 1G 63
Lansdale St. Wors 4F 63
Lansdown Clo.
    Chea H 6E 151
Lansdowne Av. Aud 4C 98
Lansdowne Av. Rom 1B 142
Lansdowne Clo. Bolt 4D 32
Lansdowne Ct. Chad 3H 71
Lansdowne Dri. Wors 3E 77
Lansdowne Ho. M20 . . . . .1F 137
        (off Wilmslow Rd.)
Lansdowne Rd. M8 . . . . . .2C 82
Lansdowne Rd. Bolt 3D 32
Lansdowne Rd. B'hth 5F 133
Lansdowne Rd. Chad 3A 72
Lansdowne Rd. Eccl 2F 91
Lansdowne Rd. Sale 3A 122
Lansdowne Rd. Urm 1A 120
Lansdowne Rd. N.
    Urm 6A 104
Lansdowne St. Roch 4E 27
Lapwing Cen. 3C 128
Lapwing Clo. Roch 4A 26
Lapwing Clo. Stal 1E 101
Lapwing Ct. M20 . . . . . .4E 125
Lapwing La. M20 . . . . . .4E 125
Lapwing La. Stoc 2B 128
Larch Av. Chea H 4C 150
Larch Av. Rad 6H 49
Larch Av. Stret 6D 106

Larch Av. *Swin* 5C **78**
Larch Clo. *M23* 3C **134**
Larch Clo. *Fail* 5F **85**
Larch Clo. *Marp* 6C **142**
Larch Clo. *Poy* 4F **163**
Larches, The. *Moss* 2F **89**
Larch Gro. *Chad* 1H **71**
Larch Gro. *Lees* 1A **74**
Larch Gro. *Swin* 1B **78**
Larchlea. *Alt* 1H **145**
Larch Rd. *Dent* 4G **113**
Larch Rd. *Eccl* 1C **90**
Larch Rd. *Part* 6C **118**
Larch St. *Bury* 3F **37**
Larch St. *Oldh* 4B **72**
Larchview Rd. *Midd* 1C **70**
Larchway. *Bram* 6E **151**
Larchway. *Fir* 4D **28**
Larchway. *H Lane* 6D **154**
Larchwood. *Chad* 2E **71**
Larchwood. *Chea* 5H **137**
Larchwood Av. *M9* 4H **83**
Larchwood Clo. *Sale* 5E **121**
Larchwood Dri. *Wilm* . .1H **167**
Larchwood St. *Bolt* 3B **32**
Larden Wlk. *M8* 5B **82**
Largs Wlk. *M23* 5F **135**
Larkfield Av. *L Hul* 4B **62**
Larkfield Clo. *Ash L* 4F **87**
Larkfield Clo. *G'mnt* 1H **21**
Larkfield Gro. *Bolt* 5D **32**
Larkfield Gro. *L Hul* 4B **62**
Larkfield M. *L Hul* 4B **62**
Larkhall Ri. *M22* 6C **136**
Larkhill. **1A 70**
Lark Hill. *Farn* 2F **63**
Lark Hill. *Midd* 1A **70**
Larkhill. *Stal* 1E **101**
Lark Hill. *Stoc* 3E **139**
Larkhill Clo. *Timp* 5B **134**
Lark Hill Ct. *Midd* 1A **70**
Lark Hill La. *Dob* 3A **60**
Larkhill Pl. *Roch* 2G **27**
Larkhill Rd. *Chea H* 6E **139**
Lark Hill Rd. *Dob* 5H **59**
Lark Hill Rd. *Stoc* 3E **139**
Larkhill Wlk. *M8* 5D **82**
Larkside Av. *Wors* 6G **63**
Larks Ri. *Droy* 2D **98**
Lark St. *Bolt* 5B **32**
Lark St. *Farn* 2F **63**
Lark St. *Oldh* 4H **57**
Larkswood Dri. *Stoc* 6F **141**
Larkwood Clo. *Carr* 4G **89**
Larmuth Av. *M21* 3A **124**
Larne Av. *Stoc* 4D **138**
Larne Av. *Stret* 5C **106**
Larne St. *M11* 5C **96**
Larwood Av. *Stoc* 2C **138**
Lascar Av. *Salf* 5G **93**
Lashbrook Clo. *M40* 1H **95**
Lassell Fold. *Hyde* 1F **115**
Lassell St. *M11* 6H **97**
   (in two parts)
Lastingham St. *M40* 5C **84**
Latchford St. *Ash L* 1G **99**
Latchmere Rd. *M14* 1G **125**
Latham Clo. *Bred* 4F **129**
Latham St. *M11* 6H **97**
Latham St. *Bolt* 3B **32**
Lathbury Rd.
   M9 & M40 . . . . . . .5F **83**
Lathom Gro. *Sale* 6E **123**
Lathom Hall Av.
   S'head 2C **74**
Lathom Rd. *M20* 2H **125**
Lathom Rd. *Irlam* 1D **118**
Lathom St. *Bury* 1E **37**
Latimer St. *Oldh* 3E **73**
Latin St. *Roch* 5G **27**
Latrigg Cres. *Midd* 5E **53**
Latrobe St. *Droy* 5A **98**

Lauderdale Cres.
   M13 . . . . . .1G **109** (6F **11**)
Launceston Clo. *Bram* . .6H **151**
Launceston Clo. *Oldh* . . .5G **73**
Launceston Rd. *Rad* 2C **48**
Laundry St. *Salf* 1F **93**
Laura St. *Bury* 1C **22**
Laureate's Pl. *S'head* 2D **74**
Laureate Way. *Dent* 2G **129**
Laurel Av. *M14* 5E **109**
Laurel Av. *Chad* 1D **70**
Laurel Av. *Chea* 6H **137**
Laurel Bank. *Hyde* 1A **130**
Laurel Bank. *Stal* 5F **101**
Laurel Bank Gdns. *M9* . . .6F **69**
Laurel Ct. *Roch* 5B **28**
Laurel Ct. *Stoc* 5D **126**
Laurel Dri. *L Hul* 5C **62**
Laurel Dri. *Timp* 1B **146**
Laurel End La.
   Heat M 6C **126**
Laurel Grn. *Dent* 5G **113**
Laurel Gro. *M20* 3F **125**
Laurel Gro. *Salf* 3C **92**
Laurel Ho. *Salf* 1B **92**
Laurel Rd. *Stoc* 5D **126**
Laurels Dri. L'boro 6D **16**
Laurels, The. Bolt 5B *32*
   (off Haydock St.)
Laurels, The. *Moss* 2F **89**
Laurel St. *Bolt* 6G **31**
Laurel St. *Bury* 3F **37**
Laurel St. *Midd* 1D **70**
Laurel St. *Oldh* 3F **73**
Laurel St. *Stoc* 1G **139**
Laurel St. *T'ton* 5H **21**
Laurel Trad. Est. *Rytn* . . .5E **57**
Laurel Wlk. *Part* 6C **118**
   (in two parts)
Laurel Way. *Bram* 5E **151**
Laurence Clo. *M12* 1D **110**
Laurence Lowry Ct.
   Swin 2F **79**
Lauria Ter. *A'wth* 4D **34**
Laurie Pl. *Roch* 2H **27**
Laurieston Ct. *Chea* 6G **137**
Lausanne Rd. *M20* 2F **125**
Lausanne Rd. *Bram* 2G **151**
Lavender Clo. *M23* 2E **135**
Lavender Clo. *Sale* 4E **121**
Lavender Rd. *Farn* 6C **46**
Lavender Rd. *Oldh* 5A **74**
Lavenders Brow. *Stoc* . . .2H **139**
Lavender St. *Rad* 4D **48**
Lavender Wlk. *Part* 6C **118**
Lavenham Av. *M11* 4F **97**
Lavenham Clo. *Bury* 4D **50**
Lavenham Clo. *Haz G* . .4E **153**
Laverton Clo. *Bury* 4A **38**
Lavington Av. *Chea* 5C **138**
Lavington Gro. *M18* 3F **111**
Lavinia St. *Eccl* 3D **90**
Lavister Av. *M19* 6H **125**
Lawefield Cres. *Swin* 4D **64**
Lawers Av. *Chad* 1G **71**
Lawfield Ct. *Bram* 3F **151**
Lawflat. *Ward* 4A **16**
Lawler Av. *Salf* 1H **107**
Lawnbank Clo. *Midd* 6G **53**
Lawn Closes. *Oldh* 6G **73**
Lawn Dri. *Swin* 4E **79**
Lawn Dri. *Timp* 5G **133**
Lawnfold. *Had* 3G **117**
Lawngreen Av. *M21* 2G **123**
Lawnhurst Trad. Est.
   Stoc 6D **138**
Lawnside M. *M20* 4E **125**
Lawns, The. *Alt* 2E **145**
Lawns, The. *Wilm* 5A **166**
Lawn St. *Bolt* 4G **31**
Lawnswood. *Roch* 2C **40**
Lawnswood Dri. *Swin* . . .5G **79**

Lawnswood Pk. Rd.
   Swin 5G **79**
Lawnswood Wlk.
   M12 . . . . .2A **110**
Lawrence Clo. *Roch* 2C **26**
Lawrence Pl. *Poy* 5D **162**
Lawrence Rd. *Alt* 5E **133**
Lawrence Rd. *Haz G* . .2E **153**
Lawrence Rd. *Urm* 4A **104**
Lawrence St. *Bury* 3D **50**
Lawrence St. *Stoc* 2G **139**
Lawrie Av. *Rams* 4D **12**
Lawson Av. *Gat* 6F **137**
Lawson Clo. *Midd* 3A **54**
Lawson Clo. *Wors* 4C **78**
Lawson Dri. *Timp* 5A **134**
Lawson Gro. *Sale* 3A **122**
Lawson Rd. *Bolt* 3G **31**
Lawson St. *M9* 1E **83**
Lawson St. *Bolt* 1A **32**
Lawson Wlk. *Dent* 1G **129**
Laws Ter. *L'boro* 4D **16**
Law St. *Roch* 1C **40**
Lawton Av. *Bram* 5G **151**
Lawton Clo. *Rom* 2F **141**
Lawton Fold. *G'ton* 2D **74**
Lawton Moor Rd.
   M23 . . . . .2G **135**
Lawton Rd. *Stoc* 5E **127**
Lawton Sq. *Del* 3H **59**
Lawton St. *Del* 3H **59**
Lawton St. *Droy* 3B **98**
Lawton St. *Hyde* 3C **114**
Lawton St. *Open* 6F **97**
Lawton St. *Roch* 2A **28**
Lawton St. *Stal* 4F **101**
Laxey St. *M40* 4B **84**
Laxfield Dri. *Urm* 3D **104**
Layard St. *Ash L* 2G **99**
Laycock Av. *Bolt* 2D **32**
Laycock Av. *Mill* 1H **101**
Laycock Cres. *Fail* 4F **85**
Laycock Dri. *Duk* 6E **101**
Laycock Gro. *Fail* 4F **85**
Laycock St. *Roch* 6A **16**
Layfield Clo. *T'ton* 4F **21**
Laystall St. *M1* 4F **95** (5D **6**)
Laythe Barn Clo. *Miln* . . .5E **29**
Layton Av. *Hyde* 4A **114**
Layton Clo. *Stoc* 3A **140**
Layton Dri. *Kear* 3H **63**
Layton Dri. *Rom* 6A **130**
Layton St. *M40* . . .3H **95** (3H **7**)
Lazenby Wlk. *M13* 3B **110**
Leabank St. *M19* 5C **110**
Leabrook Dri. *M40* 3E **85**
Leaburn Dri. *M19* 5A **126**
Leach Clo. *Roch* 1C **28**
Leaches Rd. *Rams* 4A **12**
   (in two parts)
Leach M. *P'wich* 5D **66**
Leach's Pas. *L'boro* 5D **16**
Leach St. *M18* 1D **110**
Leach St. *Farn* 6G **47**
Leach St. *Miln* 6F **29**
Leach St. *Oldh* 1A **74**
Leach St. *P'wich* 5D **66**
Leach St. *Roch* 5B **28**
Leach St. *Shaw* 1G **57**
Leach Wlk. *Oldh* 1A **74**
Leaconfield Dri. *Wors* . . .4H **77**
Lea Ct. *Fail* 4E **85**
Lea Ct. *Stoc* 5D **126**
Leacroft Av. *Bolt* 2F **47**
Leacroft Rd. *M21* 4B **124**
Leadale Ri. *S'head* 3C **74**
Leader Williams Rd.
   Irlam 6D **102**
Lea Dri. *M9* 6H **69**

Leafield Av. *M20* 5H **125**
Lea Fld. Clo. *Rad* 4E **49**
Leafield Dri. *Chea H* . .1B **160**
Leafield Dri. *Wors* 5C **76**
Leafield Rd. *Dis* 1G **165**
Lea Fold. *L'boro* 6C **16**
Leaford Av. *Dent* 3D **112**
Leaford Clo. *Dent* 3D **112**
Leaf St. *Bolt* 2E **47**
Leaf St. *Hulme* . .1D **108** (5G **9**)
Leaf St. *Stoc* 2G **127**
Leaf Ter. *Roch* 5D **14**
Leagate. *Urm* 6G **105**
Lea Ga. Clo. *Bolt* 6H **19**
League St. *Roch* 6A **28**
Leaholm Clo. *M40* 6D **84**
Leak St. *L'boro* 4F **17**
Leak St. *M16* 1A **108** (5B **8**)
Leamington Av. *M20* . . .5D **124**
Leamington Av. *Bury* 3E **23**
Leamington Ct. *Stoc* . . .2G **127**
Leamington Rd. *Eccl* 2D **90**
Leamington Rd. *Stoc* . .2G **127**
   (in two parts)
Leamington Rd. *Urm* . . .4D **104**
Leamington St. *Oldh* 1H **73**
Leamington St. *Open* 6F **97**
Leamington St. *Roch* 3G **27**
Leamore Wlk. *M9* 6G *69*
   (off White Moss Rd.)
Lea Mt. Dri. *Bury* 1H **37**
Leam St. *Ash L* 1B **100**
Leander Clo. *M9* 1G **83**
Leander Dri. *Roch* 4D **40**
Lea Rd. *H Grn* 4F **149**
Lea Rd. *Stoc* 5D **126**
Leaside Av. *Chad* 5H **55**
Leaside Clo. *Roch* 1F **27**
Leaside Dri. *M20* 4H **125**
Leaside Gro. *Wors* 6G **63**
Leaside Way. *Wilm* 3F **167**
Leas, The. *Hale* 2C **146**
Leaton Av. *M23* 5G **135**
Leavale Clo. *L Hul* 5B **62**
Leavengreave Ct.
   Whitw 1H **15**
Lea Vw. *Rytn* 4A **56**
Leaway. *Ward* 3A **16**
Leaway Clo. *M13* 3H **109**
Le Bas Ho. *M20* 3D **124**
Lecester Rd. *M8* 5D **82**
Leckenby Clo. *Wors* 5C **76**
Leconfield Dri. *M9* 6G **69**
Leconfield Rd. *Eccl* 1B **90**
Lecturers Clo. *Bolt* 2B **46**
Lecturers Closes. **1A 46**
Ledbrooke Clo. *Salf* 5H **93**
Ledburn Clo.
   M15 . . . . . .1B **108** (5D **8**)
Ledburn Ct. *M15* 5D **8**
Ledbury Av. *Urm* 4E **105**
Ledbury Clo. *Midd* 3A **70**
Ledbury Rd. *Fail* 1G **97**
Ledbury Wlk. *M9* 6E **69**
Ledge Ley. *Chea H* 5A **150**
Ledsham Av. *M9* 4C **68**
Ledson Rd. *Round I* 6E **135**
Ledward La. *Bow* 3D **144**
Lee Av. *Bolt* 4H **45**
Lee Av. *B'hth* 4D **132**
Leech Av. *Ash L* 6A **88**
Leech Brook Av. *Aud* . . .1E **113**
Leech Brook Clo.
   M34 . . . . .1E **113**
Leech St. *Hyde* 4D **114**
Leech St. *Stal* 4E **101**
Lee Clo. *Irlam* 5D **102**
Lee Ct. *M22* 3C **136**
Lee Cres. *Stret* 4E **107**
Lee Cross. *Dig* 3D **60**
Lee Dale Clo. *Dent* 5G **113**
Leedale St. *M12* 5C **110**

Leeds Clo. *Bury* 4F **51**
Leefields. *Upperm* 1F **61**
Leefields Glo. *Upperm* 1F **61**
Lee Ga. *Bolt* 6H **19**
Leegate Clo. *Stoc* 5B **126**
Leegate Dri *M9* 5H **69**
Leegate Gdns. *Stoc* 5B **126**
Leegate Rd. *Stoc* 5B **126**
(in two parts)
Leegrange Rd. *M9* 2G **83**
Lee Gro. *Farn* 1B **62**
Leek St. *Rad* 4E **49**
Leemans Hill St. *T'ton* . . .6A **22**
Lee Rd. *M9* 3F **83**
Lees. 3A **74**
Lees Av. *Dent* 5E **113**
Leesbrook. 3H **73**
Leesbrook Pk. *Oldh* 3H **73**
Lees Cotts. *Tur* 1C **19**
Lee's Cl. *Stoc* 2H **139**
Leesfield. 4A **74**
(off Lees St.)
Leesfield. *Ash L* 1H **99**
Lees Gro. *Oldh* 4H **73**
Lees Hall Cres. *M14* 1H **125**
Lees Ho. *Lees* 2A **74**
Lee Side. *Dig* 4D **60**
(in two parts)
Leeside. *Stoc* 2C **138**
Lees New Rd. *Oldh* 6A **74**
Lees Pk. Av. *Droy* 3C **98**
Lees Pk. Way. *Droy* 3C **98**
Lees Rd.
  Ash L & Oldh 5H **87**
Lees Rd. *Bram* 2F **161**
Lees Rd. *Moss* 6D **74**
Lees Rd. *Oldh* 2E **73**
Lees Sq. *Ash L* 2A **100**
Lees St. *Ash L* 1H **99**
Lees St. *Droy* 3B **98**
Lees St. *Midd* 2D **70**
Lees St. *Moss* 1E **89**
Lees St. *Oldh* 3E **87**
Lees St. *Open & M18* 6F **97**
Lees St. *Shaw* 6F **43**
(in two parts)
Lees St. *Stal* 3E **101**
Lees St. *Swin* 2F **79**
Lees St. E. *Shaw* 6F **43**
(off Lees St.)
Lees St. Enterprise Trad. Est.
  Abb R 1G **111**
Leestone Rd. *Shar I* 5C **136**
Lee St. *Bury* 3F **23**
Lee St. *L'boro* 3F **17**
Lee St. *Midd* 4H **53**
Lee St. *Oldh* 3B **72**
Lee St. *Stoc* 2H **139**
Lee St. *Upperm* 1F **61**
Leesway. *Lees* 4A **74**
Leesway Dri. *Dent* 5G **113**
Leeswood Av. *M21* 3A **124**
Leewood. *Swin* 5D **64**
Leewood Ct. *Stoc* 6D **126**
Left Bank. *Salf* . . .4C **94** (5F **5**)
Le Gendre St *Bolt* 4D **32**
(in two parts)
Legh Clo. *Poy* 4E **163**
Legh Ct. *Sale* 6D **122**
Legh Dri. *Aud* 4B **98**
Legh Dri. *Woodl* 3H **129**
Leghorn Wlk. *M11* 4B **96**
(off Seabright Wlk.)
Legh Rd. *Dis* 1E **165**
Legh Rd. *Sale* 6E **123**
Legh Rd. *Salf* 3H **81**
Legh St. *Eccl* 4E **91**
Legh St. *Salf* 4H **81**
Legion Gro. *Salf* 5A **82**
Legwood Ct. *Urm* 5G **105**
Leicester Av. *Dent* 6F **113**
Leicester Av. *Droy* 2H **97**
Leicester Av. *Salf* 3B **82**

Leicester Av. *Timp* 3A **134**
Leicester Ct. *Salf* 2A **82**
Leicester Rd. *Fail* 0G **0G**
Leicester Rd. *Hale* 3G **145**
Leicester Rd. *Sale* 4B **122**
Leicester Rd. *Salf* 5A **82**
Leicester Rd. *W'fld* 6B **50**
Leicester St. *Ash L* 1H **99**
Leicester St. *Oldh* 3F **73**
Leicester St. *Roch* 6A **28**
Leicester Wlk. *Salf* 5A **82**
Leigh Av. *Marp* 6C **142**
Leigh Av. *Swin* 6D **78**
Leighbrook Rd. *M14* 1F **125**
Leigh Clo. *T'ton* 4G **21**
Leigh Cotts. *Timp* 1C **146**
Leigh Fold. *Hyde* 2C **114**
Leigh La. *Bury* 2G **35**
(in two parts)
Leigh Rd. *Hale* 3G **145**
Leigh Rd. *Wilm* 4A **166**
Leigh Rd. *Wors* 5C **76**
Leigh St. *Farn* 1F **63**
Leigh St. *Fir* 4D **28**
Leigh St. *Heyw* 3D **38**
Leigh St. *Hyde* 5C **114**
Leigh St. *Wals* 1F **35**
Leighton Av. *Bolt* 5F **31**
Leighton Av. *L'boro* 1F **29**
Leighton Dri.
  Marp B 3G **143**
Leighton Rd. *M16* 3A **108**
Leighton St. *M40* 3A **84**
Leinster Rd. *Swin* 4E **79**
Leinster St. *Farn* 1E **63**
Leith Av. *Sale* 5E **123**
Leith Pl. *Oldh* 1C **86**
Leith Rd. *Sale* 5E **123**
Le Mans Cres. *Bolt* 6B **32**
Lemnos St. *Oldh* 2E **73**
Lemonpark Ind. Est.
  Heyw 5G **39**
Lena St. *M1* 4F **95** (6C **6**)
Lena St *Bolt* 3B **32**
Len Cox Wlk.
  M4 . . . . .3F **95** (4B **6**)
Lenfield La. *Oldh* 6C **56**
Leng Rd. *M40* 6D **84**
Lenham Av. *Eccl* 3D **90**
Lenham Clo. *Stoc* 3B **128**
Lenham Gdns. *Bolt* 1G **47**
Lenham Towers.
  Stoc 3B **128**
Lenham Wlk. *M22* 5B **148**
Lennie Rd. *Urm* 6F **91**
Lennox Gdns. *Bolt* 2D **44**
Lennox St. *Ash L* 2A **100**
Lennox St. *Aud* 1E **113**
Lennox Wlk. *Heyw* 4B **38**
Lenora St. *Bolt* 3F **45**
Lenten Gro. *Heyw* 6G **39**
Lenthall Wlk. *M8* 4B **82**
(off Lanbury Dri.)
Lentmead Dri *M40* 2A **84**
Lenton Gdns. *M22* 6C **136**
Leominster Dri. *M22* 2C **148**
Leominster Rd. *Midd* 3B **70**
Leonardin Clo. *Shaw* 5D **42**
Leonard St. *Bolt* 4A **46**
Leonard St. *Roch* 4C **40**
Leonard Way. *Rytn* 4D **56**
Leopold Av. *M20* 4E **125**
Leopold Ct. *Roch* 4F **27**
Leopold St. *Roch* 4F **27**
Leopold St. *Salf* 4D **92**
Lepp Cres. *Bury* 5C **22**
Lepton Wlk. *M9* 5G **69**
Leroy Dri. *M9* 1F **83**
Lerryn Dri. *Bram* 4F **151**
Lesley Rd. *Stret* 6A **106**
Leslie Av. *Bury* 4D **50**

Leslie Av. *Chad* 6H **71**
Leslie Gro. *Timp* 5A **134**
Leslie Hough Way.
  Salf 1H **93** (1A **4**)
Leslie St. *M14* 4F **109**
Leslie St. *Bolt* 4D **32**
Lester Rd. *L Hul* 5A **62**
Lester St. *Stret* 5D **106**
Letchworth Av. *Roch* 6A **28**
Letchworth St. *M14* 4F **109**
Letham St. *Oldh* 1D **86**
Levedale Rd. *M9* 5G **69**
Leven Clo. *Kear* 4B **64**
Levenhurst Rd. *M8* 4B **82**
Levens Clo. *Gat* 2F **149**
Levens Dri. *Bolt* 4G **33**
Levenshulme. 6E **111**
Levenshulme Rd.
  M18 . . . . .3F **111**
Levenshulme Swimming Pool.
  . . . . .6D **110**
Levenshulme Ter.
  M19 . . . . .6C **110**
(off Yew Tree Av.)
Levenshulme Trad. Est.
  M19 . . . . .5E **111**
Levens Rd. *Haz G* 3C **152**
Levens St. *M40* 4A **84**
Levens St. *Salf* 6F **81**
Levens Wlk. *Chad* 4G **71**
Levens Wlk. *M23* 5G **135**
Leven Wlk. *W'fld* 1G **67**
Lever Av. *Swin* 1H **79**
Lever Bri. Pl. *Bolt* 2E **47**
Lever Chambers. *Bolt* . . .1B **46**
Lever Dri. *Bolt* 2A **46**
Lever Edge. 4A **46**
Lever Edge La. *Bolt* 5G **45**
Leverett Clo. *Alt* 6C **132**
Lever Gdns. *L Lev* 3A **48**
Lever Gro. *Bolt* 2C **46**
Lever Hall Rd. *Bolt* 6F **33**
**Leverhulme Park Athletics
  Stadium** 1F **47**
Lever St. *M1* 4E **95** (5B **6**)
Lever St. *Bolt* 3A **46**
(in three parts)
Lever St. *Haz G* 3D **152**
Lever St. *Heyw* 2F **39**
Lever St. *L Lev* 3A **48**
Lever St. *Midd* 6A **54**
Lever St. *Rad* 2F **49**
Lever St. *Rams* 3E **13**
Lever Wlk. *Midd* 2H **69**
Levington Dri. *Oldh* 3E **87**
Levi St. *Bolt* 4D **30**
Lewes Av. *Dent* 6F **113**
Lewes Wlk. *Chad* 3H **71**
Lewis Av. *M9* 2G **83**
Lewis Av. *Urm* 2F **105**
Lewis Dri. *Heyw* 4B **38**
Lewisham Av. *M40* 1D **96**
Lewisham Clo. *Rytn* 1A **56**
Lewisham Ho. *Bolt* 4H **31**
Lewis Rd. *Droy* 3G **97**
Lewis Rd. *Stoc* 6H **111**
Lewis St. *M40* 2H **95** (1H **7**)
(in two parts)
Lewis St. *Eccl* 4F **91**
Lewis St. *Heyw* 2G **39**
Lewis St. *Hyde* 4C **114**
Lewis St. *Shaw* 2F **57**
Lewtas St. *Eccl* 4G **91**
Lexton Av. *M8* 1D **82**
Leybourne Av. *M19* 5D **110**
Leybourne M. *Salf* 5A **82**
Leybourne St. *Bolt* 3A **32**
Leybrook Rd. *M22* 2A **148**
Leyburn Av. *Rytn* 3B **56**
Leyburn Av. *Stret* 4C **106**
Leyburn Av. *Urm* 6C **104**

Leyburn Clo. *W'fld* 1C **66**
Leyburne Rd. *Stoc* 5D **140**
Leyburn Gro. *Farn* 0F **47**
Leyburn Gro. *Rom* 1A **142**
Leyburn Ho. *M13* 3H **109**
Leyburn Rd. *M40* 1C **84**
Leycett Dri. *M23* 2G **135**
Leycroft St.
  M1 . . . . .4F **95** (1D **10**)
(in two parts)
Leyden Wlk. *M23* 1G **147**
Ley Dri. *Heyw* 6G **39**
Leyfield Av. *Rom* 1A **142**
Leyfield Ct. *Rom* 1A **142**
Leyfield Rd. *Miln* 5D **28**
Ley Hey Av. *Marp* 4D **142**
Ley Hey Ct. *Marp* 4D **142**
Ley Hey Park. 4D **142**
Ley Hey Rd. *Marp* 4D **142**
Leyland Av. *M20* 5H **125**
Leyland Av. *Gat* 5F **137**
Leyland Av. *Irlam* 3F **103**
Leyland St. *Bury* 3D **50**
Ley La. *Marp B* 2G **143**
Leys Rd. *Timp* 3G **133**
Leyton Av. *M40* 4B **84**
Leyton Clo. *Farn* 6C **46**
Leyton Dri. *Bury* 2D **50**
Leyton St. *Roch* 1H **27**
Leywell Dri. *Oldh* 4H **57**
Leywell Rd. *M9* 3H **83**
Library La. *Oldh* 1B **72**
Library Theatre, The.
  . . . . .5D **94** (1H **9**)
Library Wlk.
  M2 . . . . .4D **94** (6H **5**)
Libra St. *Bolt* 3H **31**
Lichens Cres. *Oldh* 6E **73**
Lichfield Av. *Ash L* 3H **87**
Lichfield Av. *Bolt* 3D **32**
Lichfield Av. *Hale* 2C **146**
Lichfield Av. *Stoc* 2G **127**
Lichfield Clo. *Farn* 1C **62**
Lichfield Clo. *Rad* 2D **48**
Lichfield Dri. *M8* 4D **82**
Lichfield Dri. *Bury* 1B **36**
Lichfield Dri. *Chad* 6G **55**
Lichfield Dri. *P'wich* 1G **81**
Lichfield Dri. *Swin* 5F **79**
Lichfield Rd. *Eccl* 1H **91**
Lichfield Rd. *Rad* 2D **48**
Lichfield Rd. *Urm* 3F **105**
Lichfield St. *Salf* 6E **81**
Lichfield Ter. *Roch* 1A **42**
Lichfield Wlk. *Rom* 2G **141**
Lidbrook Wlk. *M12* 1A **110**
Liddington Hall Dri.
  Rams 5D **12**
Lidgate Gro. *M20* 6E **125**
Lidgate Gro. *Farn* 1E **63**
Lidgett Clo. *L Hul* 4E **63**
Lidiard St. *M8* 2C **82**
Lieutenant Wlk.
  Salf 5H **93** (2A **8**)
(off Belfort Dri.)
Liffey Av. *M22* 2C **148**
Lifton Av. *M40* 1A **96**
Light Alders La. *Dis* 6E **155**
Lightbirches La. *Moss* . . .1D **88**
Lightborne Rd. *Sale* 5F **121**
Lightbounds Rd. *Bolt* 2D **30**
Lightbourne Av. *Swin* 4F **79**
Lightbourne Green. 4F **79**
Lightbowne Rd. *M40* 5A **84**
Lightburn Av. *L'boro* 5C **16**
Lightburne Av. *Bolt* 6F **31**
Lightfoot Wlk. *M11* 4B **96**
Lighthorne Av. *Stoc* 4B **138**
Lighthorne Gro. *Stoc* . . .4B **138**
Lighthorne Rd. *Stoc* 4B **138**
Lighthouse. *L'boro* 6G **17**
Light Oaks Rd. *Salf* 1B **92**

Lightowlers La. L'boro . . .2H 17
Lightwood. Wors 3D 76
Lightwood Clo. Farn 6B 47
Lignum Av. Chad 1H 71
Lilac Av. Bury 6B 36
Lilac Av. Hyde 1B 130
Lilac Av. Miln 2E 43
Lilac Av. Swin 3G 79
Lilac Ct. Salf 3G 93
Lilac Gro. M40 . . . . . . .2A 84
Lilac Gro. Chad 1H 71
Lilac Gro. P'wich 3E 67
Lilac La. Oldh 1B 86
Lilac Rd. Hale 2A 146
Lilac Rd. Roch 3F 41
Lilac St. Stoc 5H 139
Lilac Vw. Clo. Shaw 1G 57
Lila St. M9 . . . . .4H 83
Lilburn Clo. Rams 5E 13
Liley St. Roch 4A 28
Lilford Clo. M12 . . . . . .1C 110
Lilian St. M16 . . . . . . .3A 108
Lillian Gro. Stoc 1H 127
Lilly St. Bolt 5H 31
Lilly St. Hyde 1D 130
Lilmore Av. M40 . . . . . .5C 84
Lilstock Wlk. M9 . . . . . .6G 69
Lily Av. Farn 6D 46
Lily Clo. Stoc 6F 139
Lily Hill. 5C 50
Lily Hill St. W'fld 5C 50
Lily La. M9 . . . . .4H 83
Lily La. Ash L 5F 87
Lily Lanes. 3A 88
Lily Lanes. Ash L 3A 88
Lily St. Eccl 4D 90
Lily St. Midd 1C 70
Lily St. Oldh 6C 56
Lily St. Rytn 3D 56
Lily Thomas Ct. M11 . . . .6F 97
Lima St. Bury 2F 37
Lime Av. Swin 5C 78
Lime Av. Urm 5D 104
Lime Av. W'fld 2D 66
Lime Bank St.
   M12 . . . . . .5H 95 (2H 11)
Limebrook Clo.
   Open 6G 97
Lime Clo. Duk 1B 114
Lime Clo. Salf 2G 93
Lime Ct. Salf 2G 93
Lime Cres. M16 . . . . . .3H 107
Lime Ditch Rd. Fail 2G 85
Limefield. 5F 23
                    (Bury)
Lime Field. 1G 69
                 (Manchester)
Limefield. Midd 1D 88
Limefield. Moss 1D 88
Limefield Av. Farn 6F 47
Limefield Brow. Bury 4F 23
Limefield Clo. Bolt 1F 31
Limefield Ct. Salf 2H 81
Limefield Rd. Bolt 1E 31
Limefield Rd. Bury 4F 23
Limefield Rd. Rad 4D 48
Limefield Rd. Salf 2H 81
Limefield Ter. M19 . . . . .6C 110
Lime Gdns. Duk 5H 99
Lime Gdns. Midd 1G 69
Lime Gate. 2A 86
Lime Ga. Oldh 1A 86
Lime Grn. Oldh 2B 86
Lime Grn. Rd. Oldh 3A 86
Lime Gro.
   M15 . . . .2F 109 (6D 8)
Lime Gro. M16 . . . . . . .3H 107
Lime Gro. Ash L 6G 87
Lime Gro. Bury 4F 23

Lime Gro. Chea 5H 137
Lime Gro. Dent 3F 113
Lime Gro. Heyw 2E 39
Lime Gro. L'boro 3D 16
Lime Gro. P'wich 3E 67
Lime Gro. Rams 2F 13
Lime Gro. Rytn 1B 56
Lime Gro. Stal 5C 100
Lime Gro. Timp 4B 134
Lime Gro. Wors 2F 77
Limehurst. 5E 87
Limehurst Av. M20 . . . . .1D 124
Limehurst Av. Ash L 5E 87
Limehurst Ct. Oldh 2B 86
Limehurst Rd. Ash L 5E 87
Limekiln La.
   M12 . . . . .5H 95 (2G 11)
Lime Kiln La. Marp 6E 143
Lime La. Fail 4A 86
Lime La. Oidh 2A 86
               (in two parts)
Lime Pl. Duk 5H 99
Lime Rd. Stret 6D 106
Limers Ga. Whitw 4F 15
Limerston Dri. M40 . . . . .6H 83
Limesdale Clo. Brad F . . .2B 48
Lime Side. 2B 86
Limeside Rd. Oldh 1A 86
Limestead Av. M8 . . . . . .3C 82
Limes, The. Moss 2D 88
                (Birches, The)
Limes, The. Moss 2G 89
               (Winterford Rd.)
Limes, The. Stoc 4F 139
Lime St. Bred 5E 129
Lime St. Bury 5F 23
Lime St. Chad 6A 56
Lime St. Duk 5H 99
                (in two parts)
Lime St. Eccl 4F 91
Lime St. Farn 1G 63
Lime Tree Clo. Urm 6G 105
Lime Tree Gro. Fail 4H 85
Limetrees Rd. Midd 1H 69
Limetree Wlk. M11 . . . . . .4B 96
Limley Gro. M21 . . . . . . .2A 124
Linacre Av. Bolt 5A 46
Linby St. M15 . . . .6C 94 (4E 9)
Lincoln Av. M19 . . . . . . .6D 110
Lincoln Av. Cad 5A 118
Lincoln Av. Dent 6F 113
Lincoln Av. Droy 2A 98
Lincoln Av. H Grn 6F 149
Lincoln Av. L Lev 5A 48
Lincoln Av. Stret 4H 105
Lincoln Clo. Ash L 3H 87
Lincoln Clo. Roch 5A 28
Lincoln Ct. Ind. Est.
   Roch 5A 28
Lincoln Ct. M40 . . . . . . .1D 96
Lincoln Ct. Salf 2A 82
Lincoln Dri. Bury 5D 36
Lincoln Dri. L Lev 6E 17
Lincoln Dri. P'wich 1G 81
Lincoln Dri. Timp 6B 134
Lincoln Grn. Stoc 3B 128
Lincoln Gro. M13 . . . . . .2G 109
Lincoln Gro. Bolt 1H 33
Lincoln Gro. Sale 5E 123
Lincoln Leach Ct.
   Roch 6H 27
Lincoln Mill Enterprise Cen.
   Bolt 1G 45
Lincoln Minshull Clo.
   M23 . . . . .1F 135
Lincoln Ri. Stoc 2G 141
Lincoln Rd. Bolt 5F 31
Lincoln Rd. Fail 5G 85
Lincoln Rd. Midd 4C 70
Lincoln Rd. Swin 4E 79

Lincoln Rd. Wilm 6A 160
Lincoln Sq. M2 . . .4D 94 (6G 5)
               (off Brazennose St.)
Lincoln St. M13 . . . . . . .3B 110
Lincoln St. Bolt 4B 32
Lincoln St. Eccl 4E 91
Lincoln St. Oldh 4H 71
Lincoln St. Roch 5A 28
Lincoln St. Bus. Pk.
   Roch 6A 28
Lincoln Towers. Stoc 3H 139
Lincoln Wlk. Heyw 3C 38
Lincombe Rd. M22 . . . . .5A 148
Linda Dri. Haz G 3D 152
Lindale. Hyde 2A 114
Lindale Av. M40 . . . . . . .1D 84
Lindale Av. Bolt 5D 30
Lindale Av. Bury 4E 51
Lindale Av. Chad 3G 71
Lindale Av. Rytn 5A 42
Lindale Av. Urm 4B 104
Lindale Clo. Wors 4A 76
Lindale Dri. Midd 4G 53
Lindale Ri. Shaw 6H 43
Lindale Rd. Wors 4A 76
Lindbury Av. Stoc 4C 140
Linden Av. Alt 6G 133
Linden Av. Aud 6D 98
Linden Av. L Lev 2A 48
Linden Av. Oldh 1H 73
Linden Av. Rams 3F 13
Linden Av. Sale 5H 121
Linden Av. Salf 5C 80
Linden Av. Swin 4D 78
Linden Clo. Dent 4G 113
Linden Clo. Rams 3A 12
Linden Dri. Salf 5G 93
Linden Gro. M14 . . . . . .1H 125
Linden Gro. Bram 3F 161
Linden Gro. Cad 4B 118
Linden Gro. Stoc 1B 152
Linden Lea. Sale 1B 134
Linden M. Wors 5B 76
Linden Pk. M19 . . . . . . .1B 126
Linden Rd. M20 . . . . . . .5E 125
Linden Rd. Chea H 2C 150
Linden Rd. Dent 4G 113
Linden Rd. Stal 6H 101
Linden Rd. Wors 5B 76
Linden Wlk. Bolt 6F 19
Linden Way. Droy 5G 97
Linden Way. H Lane 6E 155
Lindenwood. Chad 1E 71
Lindeth Av. M18 . . . . . . .3F 111
Lindfield Dri. Bolt 4A 32
Lindfield Est. N. Wilm 3C 166
Lindfield Est. S. Wilm 3C 166
Lindinis Av. Salf 3G 93
Lindisfarne. Roch 3G 27
               (off Spotland Rd.)
Lindisfarne Clo. Sale 2B 134
Lindisfarne Dri. Poy 3D 162
Lindisfarne Pl. Bolt 3E 33
Lindisfarne Rd. Ash L 6C 86
Lindley Gro. Stoc 6F 139
Lindley St. Kear 3B 64
Lindley St. L Lev 4B 48
Lindley Wood Rd.
   M14 . . . . .1A 126
Lindon Av. Dent 5D 112
Lindop Rd. Hale 4H 145
Lindow Clo. Bury 5B 22
Lindow Common
   (Local Nature Reserve)
   . . . . .2B 166
Lindow Ct. Bred 6D 128
Lindow Ct. Sale 6F 123
Lindow Ct. Wilm 1B 166
Lindow Fold Dri.
   Wilm 5A 166
Lindow La. Wilm 2B 166

Lindow Moss. 2A 166
Lindow Pde. Wilm 3C 166
Lindow Rd. M16 . . . . . . .4A 108
Lindow St. Sale 6F 123
Lindrick Av. W'fld 3B 66
Lindrick Clo. M40 . . . . . .4C 84
Lindrick Ter. Bolt 2H 45
Lindsay Av. M19 . . . . . .6B 110
Lindsay Av. Chea H 4D 150
Lindsay Av. Swin 4E 79
Lindsay Clo. Oldh 5H 57
Lindsay Rd. M19 . . . . . .1B 126
Lindsay St. Stal 3F 101
Lindsell Rd. W Timp 3E 133
Lindsgate Dri. Timp 4B 134
Lindside Wlk. M9 . . . . . .6G 69
Lind St. M40 . . . .3A 96 (4H 7)
Lindum Av. M16 . . . . . . .3A 108
Lindum Ct. Heyw 3G 39
Lindum St. M14 . . . . . . .4F 109
Lindwall Clo. M23 . . . . . .1H 135
Lindy Av. Swin 6F 65
Linear Walkway. Eccl 2F 91
Linehan Clo. Stoc 1H 137
Lineholme. Rytn 5A 56
Linen Ct. Salf 2B 94 (2C 4)
Lines Rd. Droy 4B 98
Lines Rd. Irlam 1D 118
Linfield Clo. Bolt 1F 33
Linfield St. M11 . . . . . . .4D 96
Linford Av. M40 . . . . . . .1C 84
Lingard Clo. Aud 5C 98
Lingard La. Bred 4D 128
Lingard Rd. M22 . . . . . .2B 136
Lingard St. Stoc 1H 127
Lingard Ter. Aud 5C 98
Lingcrest Clo. M19 . . . . .2E 127
Lingdale Rd. Chea H 3B 150
Lingdale Wlk. M40 . . . . . .4A 84
Lingfield Av. Haz G 3F 153
Lingfield Av. Sale 1D 132
Lingfield Clo. Bury 4C 22
Lingfield Clo. Farn 2E 63
Lingfield Rd. M11 . . . . . .3E 97
Lingfield Wlk. Chad 2A 72
Lingholme Dri. Midd 5E 53
Lingmell Clo. Bolt 5D 30
Lingmell Clo. Midd 5F 53
Lingmell Clo. Urm 3C 104
Lingmoor Clo. Midd 5E 53
Lingmoor Rd. Bolt 4D 30
Lingmoor Wlk.
   M15 . . . .1D 108 (6H 9)
Lings Wlk. M22 . . . . . . .4C 148
Linhope Clo. Stoc 6A 126
Link Av. Urm 6A 106
Linkfield Dri. Wors 5B 76
Link La. Oldh 1C 86
Link Rd. Sale 2F 133
Link Rd. S'head 2B 74
Links Av. Fail 6F 85
Links Cres. P'wich 1A 82
Links Dri. M13 . . .6F 95 (4C 10)
Linksfield. Dent 2F 113
Linkside Av. Rytn 2B 56
Links Pl. Ash L 5A 88
Links Ri. Urm 3C 104
Links Rd. Bolt 2A 34
Links Rd. Heyw 5F 39
Links Rd. Marp 1D 154
Links Rd. Rom 6B 130
Links Rd. Wilm 6B 166
Links, The. M40 . . . . . . .4C 84
Links Vw. P'wich 2E 81
Links Vw. Roch 5D 26
Links Vw. Ct. W'fld 2B 66
Links Way. Chad 1A 72
Linksway. Gat 1E 149
Linksway. P'wich 1H 81
Linksway. Swin 5G 79
Linksway Clo. Stoc 4C 126
Linksway Dri. Bury 4E 51

Link, The. *Hand* 4H 159
Link, The. *Shaw* 5D 42
Link, The. *Stoc* 3C 128
Linkway Ind. Est. *Midd* . . .1B 70
Linley Dri. *Oldh* 5H 73
Linley Gro. *Rams* 1A 22
Linley Rd. *Chea H* 5D 150
Linley Rd. *Sale* 4B 122
Linley St. *Rad* 2C 50
Linnell Dri. *Roch* 3A 26
Linnet Clo. *Stoc* 6F 141
Linnot Dri. *Bury* 1F 37
Linnet Dri. *Irlam* 4E 103
Linnet Hill. *Roch* 5E 27
Linnets Wood M. *Wors* . . .6G 63
Linnett Clo. *M12* 3B 110
Linney La. *Shaw* 6G 43
Linney Rd. *Bram* 3F 151
Linnyshaw. **6H 63**
Linnyshaw La. *Wors* 5G 63
Linslade Gdns. *Bolt* 2A 46
Linslade Ho. *Salf* 4F *93*
(off Amersham St.)
Linslade Wlk. *M9* 4F *83*
(off Foleshill Av.)
Linsley St. *Salf* 3C 94 (3F 5)
Linstead Dri. *M8* 5B 82
Linthorpe Wlk. *Bolt* 3F 45
Linton Av. *Bury* 6F 23
Linton Av. *Dent* 4A 112
Linton Clo.
M4 . . . . . .5H 95 (1G 11)
Linton Rd. *Sale* 3C 122
Linton Va. *Rad* 1B *64*
(off Markot St.)
Linton Wlk. *Salf* 3D 80
(in two parts)
Linwood Gro. *M12* 5C 110
Linwood St. *Fail* 5C 84
Lion Brow. *M9* 1F 83
Lion Fold La. *M9* 6F 69
Lions Dri. *Swin* 4F 79
Lion St. *M9* 1F 83
Lisbon St. *Roch* 3E 27
Lisburn Av. *M21* 6A 108
Lisburn Av. *Sale* 6A 122
Lisburne Av. *Stoc* 5D 140
Lisburne Clo. *Stoc* 5D 140
Lisburne Ct. *Stoc* 5D 140
Lisburne La. *Stoc* 5C 140
Lisburn Rd. *M40* 3A 84
Liscard Av. *M14* 6F 109
Lisetta Av. *Oldh* 4F 73
Liskeard Av. *Rytn* 4D 56
Liskeard Clo. *Roch* 2C 28
Liskeard Dri. *Bram* 6H 151
Lisle St. *Roch* 3A 28
Lismore Av. *Bolt* 2D 44
Lismore Av. *Stoc* 4D 138
Lismore Rd. *Duk* 6B 100
Lismore Wlk. *M22* 5C 148
Lismore Way. *Urm* 2F 105
Lissadel Science Pk.
Salf 2H 93
Lissadel St. *Salf* 1G 93
Lisson Gro. *Hale* 3G 145
Lister Rd. *Midd* 3D 60
Lister St. *Bolt* 4F 45
Liston St. *Duk* 5D 100
Litcham Clo.
M1 . . . . . .6F 95 (3C 10)
Litchfield Ct. *Midd* 2E 09
Litchfield Gro. *Wors* 4A 78
Litherland Av. *M22* 3C 148
Litherland Rd. *Bolt* 5A 46
Litherland Rd. *Sale* 6E 123
Lit. Ancoats St.
M1 . . . . . .3F 95 (4C 6)

Lit. Bank St. *Oldh* 3F 73
Little Bolton. **3B 92**
Littleborough. **4F 17**
**Littleborough Coach House &
Heritage Cen.** **4F 17**
Littleborough Ind. Est.
L'boro 4E 17
Littlebourne Wlk. *Bolt* 5E 19
Lit. Brook Clo. *Chea H* . . .1F 151
Littlebrook Clo. *Had* 3H 117
Lit. Brook Rd. *Sale* 2E 133
Lit. Brow. *Brom X* 4E 19
Little Clegg. **1F 29**
Lit. Clegg Rd. *L'boro* 1E 29
Littledale St. *Roch* 3G 27
(in two parts)
Lit. David St.
M1 . . . . . .5E 95 (1B 10)
Lit. Ees La. *Sale* 3H 121
(in two parts)
Lit. Egerton St. *Stoc* 1G 139
Littlefields. *Mot* 3C 116
Little Flatt. *Roch* 2D 26
Little Green. **6C 54**
Littlegreen Gdns. *Salf* 2F 93
Littleham Wlk. *M18* 2E 111
Lit. Harwood Lee. *Bolt* 2F 33
Littlehaven Clo. *M12* 2A 110
Lit. Heath La. *Dun M* 6A 132
Lit. Hey St. *Rytn* 3E 57
Littlehills Clo. *Midd* 6G 53
Lit. Holme St.
M4 . . . . . .4H 95 (5H 7)
Lit. Holme Wlk. *Bolt* 3B 46
Little Howarth Way.
Roch 5A 16
Little Hulton. **5C 62**
Lit. John St. *M3* 4C 94 (1E 9)
Little La. *M0* 5D 82
Little Lever. **4B 48**
Lit. Lever St.
M1 . . . . . .4F 95 (5C 6)
(in two parts)
Little Meadow. *Eger* 4D 18
Lit. Meadow Rd. *Bow* 4D 144
Lit. Moor Clough. *Eger* . . .1C 18
Littlemoor Cotts. *Stoc* 3B 140
Littlemoor La. *Dig* 3B 60
Littlemoor La. *Oldh* 1G 73
Littlemoor Rd. *Mot* 5C 116
Littlemoss. **1C 98**
Lit. Moss La. *Swin* 1F 79
Littlemoss Rd. *Droy* 2C 98
Lit. Oak Clo. *Lees* 3A 74
Little Park. **1A 70**
Lit. Peter St.
M15 . . . . . .6C 94 (3F 9)
Lit. Pitt St. *M1* 4F 95 (5D 6)
Lit. Quay St.
M3 . . . . . .5C 94 (6G 5)
Littler Av. *M21* 4A 124
Littlers Point. *Traf P* 2D 106
Little 66. *Bury* 6F 37
Lit. Stones Rd. *Eger* 1C 18
Little St. *Stoc* 3B 140
Littleton Rd. *Salf & M6* . . .3E 81
Littletown. *Oldh* 5A 72
Lit. Underbank. *Stoc* 2H 139
Littlewood. **6F 23**
Littlewood. *Rytn* 3F 57
(off Oldham Rd.)
Littlewood Av. *Bury* 6F 23
Littlewood Rd. *M22* 1A 148
Littlewood St. *Salf* 3E 93
Litton Bank. *Glos* 6G 117
(off Litton Gdns.)
Littondale Clo. *Rytn* 2C 56
Litton Fold. *Glos* 6G 117
(off Riber Bank)
Litton Gdns. *Glos* 6G 117
Litton M. *Glos* 6G 117
Liverpool Clo. *Stoc* 2G 127

Liverpool Rd. *Eccl* 3H 103
Liverpool Rd.
M3 . . . . . .5B 94 (1D 8)
Liverpool Rd.
Cad & Irlam 6A 118
Liverpool Rd. Steam Railway.
. . . .**1D 8**
Liverpool St.
Salf & M6 (M5) 3D 92
Liverpool St. *Salf & M5* (M6)
. . . . .3F 93 (5A 4)
Liverpool St. *Stoc* 2G 127
Liverstudd Av. *Stoc* 1H 127
Liverton Ct. *M9* 4D 68
Liverton Dri. *M9* 4D 68
Livesey St. *M4* 2G 95 (1E 7)
Livesey St. *Lev* 1D 126
Livesey St. *Oldh* 1G 73
Livingstone Av. *Moss* 2D 88
Livingstone Pl. *M16* 2H 107
Livingstone St. *Lees* 4A 74
Livingstone St. *S'head* . . .3C 74
Living Well Health Club.
. . . .**6H 109**
**Living Well Premier
Manchester.** **6F 5**
(Gymnasium)
Livsey Ct. *Bolt* 4B 32
Livsey Ct. *Heyw* 3C 38
Livsey St. *Roch* 4A 28
Livsey St. *W'fld* 1D 66
Lizard St. *M1* 4F 95 (5C 6)
Lizmar Ter. *M9* 3H 83
Llanberis Rd. *Chea H* . . .4A 150
Llanfair Rd. *Stoc* 3C 139
Lloyd Av. *Gat* 5E 137
Lloyd Ct. *M12* 4F 109
(off Frodesley Wlk.)
Lloyd Rd. *M19* 2D 126
Lloyd's Ct. *Alt* 1F 145
Lloyd's Gdns. *Alt* 2F 145
Lloyd Sq. *Alt* 1F 145
Lloyd St. *M2* 4D 94 (6G 5)
(in two parts)
Lloyd St. *Alt* 1F 145
Lloyd St. *Droy* 4H 97
Lloyd St. *Heyw* 4F 39
Lloyd St. *Roch* 1D 40
Lloyd St. *Stoc* 6F 127
Lloyd St. *Whitw* 4G 15
Lloyd St. N.
M14 & M15 . . . . . .3E 109
Lloyd St. S. *M14* 6E 109
L&M Bus. Pk. *Alt* 5E 133
Lobden. **2E 15**
Lobden Cres. *Whitw* 2C 14
Lobelia Av. *Farn* 6C 46
Lobelia Wlk. *Part* 6C 118
Lobley Clo. *Roch* 1B 28
Lochawe Clo. *Heyw* 4C 38
Lochinver Gro. *Heyw* 4C 38
Lochmaddy Clo.
Haz G 4F 153
Lock Clo. *Heyw* 5G 39
Lockett Gdns.
Salf 3B 94 (3D 4)
Lockett St. *M8* 1C 94
Lockett St. *Salf* 6E 81
Lockhart Clo. *M12* 2C 110
Lockhart St. *Roch* 6D 20
Lockingate St. *Ash L* 5F 87
Locking Ga. Ri. *Oldh* 6A 58
Locklands La. *Irlam* 5E 103
Lock La. *Los & Bolt* 3A 44
Lock La. *Part* 6B 118
Lock Rd. *B'hth* 5E 133
Lockside. *Marp* 5E 143
Lockside Vw. *Moss* 6G 75
Locksley Clo. *Stoc* 1E 139
Lockton Clo.
M1 . . . . . .6F 95 (3D 10)
Lockton Clo. *Stoc* 3G 127

Lockton Ct. *M1* . . .6F 95 (3C 10)
Lockwood St. *M12* 4D 110
Luddon Wlk. *M9* 3G 83
Lodge Av. *Urm* 5G 105
Lodge Bank. *Had* 1H 117
Lodge Bank Rd. *L'boro* . . .6D 18
Lodge Brow. *Rad* 5H 49
Lodge Clo. *Duk* 6C 100
Lodge Ct. *M22* 6C 136
Lodge Ct. *Mot* 3C 116
Lodge Ct. *Stoc* 1B 138
Lodge Dri. *Bury* 4G 35
Lodge Farm Clo.
Bram 3G 151
Lodge Fold. *Droy* 3B 98
Lodge Grn. *Duk* 6C 100
Lodge La. *Del* 2G 59
(in two parts)
Lodge La. *Duk* 5B 100
Lodge M. *Hyde* 3B 114
Lodge M. *Rams* 3E 13
Lodge Mill La. *Rams* 1H 13
Ludgepole Clo. *Eccl* 5B 90
Lodge Rd. *Rad* 5H 49
Lodgeside Clo. *Droy* 3B 98
Lodges, The. *Wors* 3A 78
Lodge St. *M40* 6G 83
Lodge St. *Ash L* 4F 99
Lodge St. *Hyde* 2C 114
Lodge St. *L'boro* 3F 17
Lodge St. *Midd* 6A 54
Lodge St. *Rams* 1G 13
(Bye Rd.)
Lodge St. *Rams* 3E 13
(Kay Brow)
Lodge St. *Ward* 3A 16
Lodge, The. *Had* 1H 117
Lodge Vw. *Droy* 3B 98
Lodge Vw. Cvn. Pk. *Dolt* . .5C 32
(Mill Hill)
Lodge Vw. Cvn. Pk. *Bolt* . .5C 32
(Nicholas St.)
Loen Cres. *Bolt* 2G 31
Loganberry Av. *Salf* 2G 93
Logan St. *Bolt* 6C 18
Logwood Av. *Bury* 2B 36
Loisine Clo. *Roch* 2B 40
Lok Fu Gdns. *M8* 6A 82
Lomas Clo. *M19* 6A 126
Lomas St. *Fail* 2G 85
Lomas St. *Midd* 6B 54
Lomas St. *Stoc* 4F 139
Lomax's Bldgs. *Bolt* 1B 46
Lomax St. *M1* 4G 95 (5E 7)
Lomax St. *Bolt* 3A 32
Lomax St. *Bury* 2E 37
Lomax St. *Farn* 6E 47
Lomax St. *G'mnt* 2H 21
Lomax St. *L'boro* 2E 17
Lomax St. *Rad* 6G 49
Lomax St. *Roch* 2H 27
Lomax St. *W'fld* 5C 50
Lombard Clo. *Bred* 5F 129
Lombard Gro. *M14* 1G 125
Lombard St. *Oldh* 2C 72
Lombard St. *Roch* 3F 27
Lombardy Ct. *Salf* 2G 93
Lomond Av. *Hale* 2A 146
Lomond Av. *Stret* 4D 106
Lomond Clo. *Stoc* 2A 152
Lomond Dri. *Bury* 1H 35
Lomond Lodge. *M8* 1B 82
Lomond Pl. *Bolt* 1C 44
Lomond Rd.
M22 & H Grn 3D 148
Lomond Ter. *Roch* 1A 42
London Pl. *Stoc* 2H 139
London Rd. *M1* . . .4F 95 (6C 6)
London Rd. *A'ton* 6C 162
London Rd. *Ald E* 5G 167
London Rd. *Haz G* 2D 152
London Rd. *Oldh* 6F 57

London Rd. N. *Poy* 3E **163**
London Rd. S. *Poy* 5D **162**
London Sq. *Stoc* 2H **139**
London St. *Bolt* 3A **46**
London St. *Salf* 1H **93**
London St. *W'fld* 2D **66**
Longacres Dri. *Whitw* 3H **15**
Longacres La. *Whitw* 3H **15**
Longacres Rd. *Haleb* 6C **146**
Longacre St.
　　M1 . . . . . . .4G **95** (1E **11**)
Longbow Clo. *Salf* 6H **81**
Longbridge Rd. *Traf P* . . .1A **106**
Long Causeway. *Farn* 2F **63**
Longcliffe Wlk. *Bolt* 3B **32**
Longcrag Wlk. M15 . . . . .2E **109**
　　(off Botham Clo.)
Longcroft Dri. *Alt* 1D **144**
Longcroft Gro. *M23* 4F **135**
Longcroft Gro. *Aud* 5B **98**
Long Cft. La. *Chea H* 5A **138**
Longdale Clo. *Rytn* 3A **56**
Longdale Dri. *Mot* 4C **116**
Longdale Gdns. *Mot* 4C **116**
Longdell Wlk. M9 . . . . . . .3G **83**
　　(off Moston La.)
Longden Av. *Oldh* 4A **58**
Longden Ct. *Bram* 2G **161**
Longdendale Recreation Cen.
　　. . . . . .4B **116**
Longden Rd. *M12* 5C **110**
Longden St. *Bolt* 5G **31**
Longfellow Av. *Bolt* 4F **45**
Longfellow Cres. *Oldh* . . .3H **57**
Longfellow St. *Salf* 1H **93**
Longfellow Wlk. *Dent* 2G **129**
Longfield. *Bury* 6G **23**
Longfield. *P'wich* 4E **67**
Longfield Av. *H Grn* 6G **149**
Longfield Av. *Timp* 5C **134**
Longfield Av. *Urm* 6E **105**
Longfield Clo. *Hyde* 1C **114**
Longfield Cotts. Urm 5D **104**
　　(off Stamford Rd.)
Longfield Cres. *Oldh* 6G **57**
Longfield Dri. *Urm* 5D **104**
Longfield Gdns. *Cad* 5B **118**
Longfield Pk. *Shaw* 1E **57**
Longfield Rd. *M23* 3F **135**
Longfield Rd. *Bolt* 5E **45**
Longfield Rd. *Roch* 3E **27**
Longfield Rd. *Shaw* 1E **57**
Longfield Shop. Cen.
　　P'wich 4E **67**
Longford Av. *Bolt* 3G **31**
Longford Av. *Stret* 5E **107**
Longford Clo. *Stret* 4E **107**
Longford Cotts. *Stret* 5F **107**
Longford Ho. *M21* 6F **107**
Longford Pl. *M14* 3A **110**
Longford Rd. *M21* 6G **107**
Longford Rd. *Stoc* 6H **111**
Longford Rd. *Stret* 4D **106**
Longford Rd. W.
　　M19 & Stoc 6F **111**
Longford St. *M18* 1F **111**
Longford St. *Heyw* 3F **39**
Longford Trad. Est.
　　Stret 4D **106**
Longford Wharf. *Stret* 5E **107**
Long Grain Pl. *Stoc* 6D **140**
Longham Clo. *M11* 4A **96**
Longham Clo. *Bram* 4E **151**
Long Hey. *Hale* 2A **146**
Longhey Rd. *M22* 6B **136**
Long Hill. *Roch* 1D **40**
Longhill Wlk. *M40* 5A **84**
Longhirst Clo. *Bolt* 2F **31**
Longhope Rd. *M22* 3H **147**
Longhurst La.
　　Marp B & Mell 4F **143**
Longhurst Rd. *M9* 5D **68**

Longlands Dri. *Hyde* 4F **115**
Long La. *Bolt* 2F **47**
Long La. *Bury* 4E **23**
Long La. *Chad* 6F **71**
Long La. *Dis* 3H **165**
Long La. *Dob* 5A **60**
　　(Dobcross)
Long La. *Dob* 3H **61**
　　(Tunstead)
Long Levens Rd.
　　M22 . . . . .3A **148**
Longley Dri. *Wors* 5B **78**
Longley La.
　　M22 & Gat 3B **136**
Longley Rd. *Wors* 1F **77**
Longley St. *Oldh* 3D **72**
Longley St. *Shaw* 2F **57**
Long Marl Dri. *Hand* 3B **160**
Longmead Av. *Haz G* 3D **152**
Longmeade Gdns. *Wilm* . .3F **167**
Long Mdw. *Brom X* 4G **19**
Long Mdw. *Hyde* 1D **114**
Longmeadow Gro.
　　Dent 5E **113**
Long Mdw. Pas. *Hyde* . . .4B **114**
Longmead Rd. *Salf* 6B **80**
Longmead Way. *Midd* 6B **54**
Longmere Av. *M22* 2B **148**
Long Millgate.
　　M3 . . . . . . .3D **94** (3H **5**)
Longnor Grn. Glos 5F **117**
　　(off Longnor M.)
Longnor M. *Glos* 5F **117**
Longnor Rd. *Haz G* 5E **153**
Longnor Rd. *H Grn* 5H **149**
Longnor Way. Glos 5F **117**
　　(off Longnor M.)
Longport Av. *M20* 2D **124**
Longridge. *Brom X* 3G **19**
Longridge Av. *Stal* 1E **101**
Longridge Cres. *Bolt* 3D **30**
Longridge Dri. *Bury* 5G **35**
Longridge Dri. *Heyw* 3B **38**
Long Row. *Carr* 4H **89**
Long Row. *Poy* 4F **163**
Long Rushes. *Shaw* 5D **42**
Longshaw Av. *Swin* 2F **79**
Longshaw Dri. *Wors* 5C **62**
Longshaw Ford Rd.
　　Bolt 1D **30**
Longshut La. *Stoc* 4H **139**
Longshut La. W. *Stoc* 4H **139**
Long Sides Rd. *Haleb* 6C **146**
Longsight. **3B 110**
　　(Manchester)
Long Sight. **5C 56**
　　(Oldham)
Longsight. *Bolt* 6A **20**
Longsight Ind. Est.
　　Long 3B **110**
Longsight La. *Bolt* 2F **33**
　　(in two parts)
Longsight La. *Chea H* 2B **160**
Longsight Lodge. *Bolt* 1G **33**
Longsight Pk. Arboretum.
　　. . . . . .1E **33**
Longsight Rd. *M18* 4D **110**
Longsight Rd.
　　Rams & G'mnt 6C **12**
Longsight Shop. Cen.
　　M12 . . . . .3B **110**
Longsons, The. Stoc 6H **127**
　　(off Lancashire Rd.)
Longson St. *Bolt* 4C **32**
Long St. *M18* 1G **111**
Long St. *Midd* 1H **69**
　　(in two parts)
Long St. *Swin* 4F **79**
Longthwaite Clo. *Midd* . . .5F **53**
Longton Av. *M20* 4E **125**
Longton Rd. *M9* 4E **69**

Longton Rd. *Salf* 6A **80**
Longton St. *Bury* 3D **50**
Longtown Gdns. Bolt 3A **32**
　　(off Gladstone St.)
Longview Dri. *Swin* 2C **78**
Long Wlk. *Part* 6B **118**
Longwall Av. *Wors* 3D **76**
　　(in two parts)
Longwood Av. *Stoc* 5B **140**
Longwood Clo. *Rom* 6C **130**
Longwood Rd. *M22* 2C **148**
Long Wood Rd.
　　Traf P 1B **106**
Long Wood Rd. Est.
　　Traf P 1B **106**
Longworth Clo. *Urm* 6A **104**
Longworth Clough.
　　Eger 1B **18**
Longworth Rd. *Eger* 1A **18**
Longworth La. *Eger* 1A **18**
Longworth St.
　　M3 . . . . . . .5C **94** (1F **9**)
Longworth St. *Bolt* 6E **33**
Lonsdale Av. *Roch* 6B **28**
Lonsdale Av. *Stoc* 4H **111**
Lonsdale Av. *Swin* 6D **78**
Lonsdale Av. *Urm* 3D **104**
Lonsdale Gro. *Farn* 1E **63**
Lonsdale Rd. *M19* 5D **110**
Lonsdale Rd. *Bolt* 5F **31**
Lonsdale Rd. *Oldh* 1A **86**
Lonsdale St. *M40* 5C **84**
Lonsdale St. *Bury* 3A **36**
Loom St. *M4* 3F **95** (4D **6**)
Loonies Ct. *Stoc* 4F **139**
Lord Byron Sq. *Salf* 4F **93**
Lord Derby Rd. *Hyde* 4B **114**
　　(in two parts)
Lord Kitchener Ct.
　　Sale 3B **122**
Lord La. *Droy* 1G **97**
Lord La. *Fail* 4F **85**
Lord Napier Dri. *Salf* 6H **93**
Lord North St. *M40* 1A **96**
Lord's Av. *Salf* 3D **92**
Lordsfield Av. *Ash L* 1H **99**
Lord's Fold. *Bolt* 3D **30**
Lordship Clo. *M9* 2H **83**
Lordsmead St.
　　M15 . . . . . .1B **108** (5D **8**)
Lord's Stile La. *Brom X* . . .3E **19**
Lord St. *Cad* 3A **118**
Lord St.
　　M3 & M4 . .1D **94** (1H **5**)
Lord St. *Ash L* 1H **99**
Lord St. *Bury* 3D **36**
Lord St. *Dent* 3A **112**
Lord St. *Duk & Stal* 5D **100**
Lord St. *Heap B* 4G **37**
Lord St. *Holl* 3F **117**
Lord St. *Kear* 1G **63**
Lord St. *L'boro* 4G **17**
Lord St. *L Lev* 4B **48**
Lord St. *Midd* 6A **54**
Lord St. *Oldh* 1D **72**
　　(in three parts)
Lord St. *Rad* 4G **49**
Lord St. *Salf* 1A **94**
Lord St. *Stoc* 2H **139**
Loretto Rd. *Urm* 6H **105**
Lorgill Clo. *Stoc* 1H **151**
Loring St. *M40* 6C **84**
Lorland Rd. *Stoc* 4D **138**
Lorna Gro. *Gat* 5D **136**
Lorna Rd. *Chea H* 3D **150**
Lorne Av. *Rytn* 4H **55**
Lorne Gro. *Stoc* 5G **139**
Lorne Gro. *Urm* 5G **105**
Lorne St. *M14* 1G **125**
Lorne St. *M13* 2G **109**
Lorne St. *Bolt* 6B **32**

Lorne St. *Eccl* 5D **90**
Lorne St. *Farn* 5E **47**
Lorne St. *Heyw* 4F **39**
Lorne St. *Moss* 2E **89**
Lorne St. *Oldh* 5C **72**
Lorne St. *Roch* 6H **15**
Lorne Way. *Heyw* 4B **38**
Lorraine Clo. *Heyw* 5G **39**
Lorraine Rd. *Timp* 6A **134**
Lorton Clo. *Midd* 5E **53**
　　(in two parts)
Lorton Clo. *Wors* 5B **76**
Lorton Gro. *Bolt* 5H **33**
Lostock. **2A 44**
Lostock Av. *M19* 6D **110**
Lostock Av. *Haz G* 4B **152**
Lostock Av. *Poy* 3B **162**
Lostock Av. *Sale* 5E **123**
Lostock Av. *Urm* 4D **104**
Lostock Circ. *Urm* 3H **105**
Lostock Clo. *Heyw* 2D **38**
Lostock Ct. *Hand* 3H **159**
Lostock Ct. *Stret* 3H **105**
Lostock Dene. *Los* 5A **30**
Lostock Dri. *Bury* 5F **23**
Lostock Gro. *Stret* 4B **106**
Lostock Hall Fold. **2A 44**
Lostock Hall Rd. *Poy* 4B **162**
Lostock Junction. **2B 44**
Lostock Junct. La. *Los* . . .1A **44**
Lostock Rd. *Hand* 3H **159**
Lostock Rd. *Poy* 5D **162**
Lostock Rd. *Salf* 3E **93**
Lostock Rd. *Urm* 3E **105**
Lostock St.
　　M40 . . . . . .2H **95** (2G **7**)
Lostock Wlk. *W'fld* 6G **51**
Lothian Av. *Eccl* 2D **90**
Lottery Row. *Bolt* 6B **32**
Lottery St. *Stoc* 2F **139**
Lottie St. *Swin* 3G **79**
Loughborough Clo.
　　Sale 6F **121**
Loughfield. *Urm* 5C **104**
Loughrigg Av. *Rytn* 5A **42**
Louisa St. *M11* 5E **97**
Louisa St. *Bolt* 3A **32**
Louisa St. *Wors* 5F **63**
Louis Av. *Bury* 1D **36**
Louise Clo. *Roch* 6H **15**
Louise Gdns. *Roch* 6H **15**
Louise St. *Roch* 6H **15**
　　(in three parts)
Louvaine Av. *Bolt* 1D **30**
Louvaine Clo. *M18* 1G **111**
Lovalle St. *Bolt* 4G **31**
Lovat Rd. *Bolt* 6A **34**
Love La. *Rams* 4B **12**
Love La. *Stoc* 1G **139**
Lovell Ct. *M8* 1B **82**
Lovell Dri. *Hyde* 3D **114**
Lovers La. *Grass* 3E **75**
Lovers Wlk. *Alt* 1G **145**
Lovett Wlk. *M22* 3C **136**
Low Bank. *Roch* 6A **16**
Lowbrook La. *Oldh* 6B **58**
　　(in two parts)
Lowcock St.
　　Salf 1C **94** (1E **5**)
Lowcroft Cres. *Chad* 1F **71**
Low Crompton. **1C 56**
Low Crompton Rd.
　　Rytn 1C **56**
Lowcross Rd. *M40* 5A **84**
Lowe Grn. *Rytn* 2C **56**
Lwr. Albion St.
　　M1 . . . . . . .5F **95** (2C **10**)
Lwr. Alma St. *Duk* 4H **99**
Lower Arthurs. **3F 61**
Lwr. Bamford Clo.
　　Midd 5A **54**
Lower Bank. *Dent* 2F **113**

Lwr. Bank Clo. *Had* 4H **117**
Lwr. Bank St. *Bury* 3C **36**
Lwr. Barn Rd. *Had* 3G **117**
Lower Beechwood.
 Roch 6F **27**
Lwr. Bennett St. *Hyde* . . .3A **114**
Lwr. Bents La. *Bred* 5F **129**
Lower Birches. *Lees* 5B **74**
Lower Bredbury. 6D **128**
Lwr. Bridgeman St.
 Bolt 1C **46**
Lower Bridgeman St. *Stal* . .1A **116**
Lwr. Brooklands Pde.
 M8 . . . . .1A **82**
Lwr. Brook La. *Wors* 6A **78**
Lwr. Brook St. *M1* 1C **10**
Lower Broughton.
 . . . . .1B **94** (1D **4**)
Lwr. Broughton Rd.
 Salf 6G **81** (1C **4**)
Lwr. Bury St. *Stoc* 1F **139**
Lwr. Byrom St.
 M3 . . . . .5C **94** (1E **9**)
Lower Calderbrook.
 L'boro 6G **17**
Lwr. Carr La. *G'fld* 3F **61**
Lower Carrs. *Stoc* 2H **139**
Lwr. Chatham St.
 M1 . . . . .6E **95** (3A **10**)
Lwr. Chatham St.
 M15 . . . . .6E **95** (4A **10**)
Lower Chesham. *Bury* 2F **37**
Lower Crimble. *Roch* 1G **39**
Lower Croft. *W'fld* 3A **66**
Lowercroft Dri. *Bury* 3F **35**
Lowercroft Rd. *Bury* 3F **35**
Lower Crossbank.
 Lees 1B **74**
Lower Crumpsall. 3E **83**
Lwr. Darcy St. *Bolt* 2E **47**
Lower Dingle. *Oldh* 3G **57**
Lwr. Edge Av. *Oldh* 1C **72**
Lowerfield Dri. *Stoc* 6F **141**
Lowerfields. *Dob* 6A **60**
Lowerfields. *Oldh* 6F **73**
Lowerfields Ri. *Shaw* 5F **43**
Lower Fold. 6C **14**
Lower Fold. *Bolt* 1H **33**
Lower Fold. *Dent* 6G **113**
Lower Fold. *Marp B* 3F **143**
Lowerfold Av. *Rytn* 3F **57**
Lowerfold Clo. *Roch* 5C **14**
Lowerfold Cres. *Roch* 5C **14**
Lowerfold Dri. *Roch* 5C **14**
Lowerfold Way. *Roch* 5C **14**
Lwr. Frenches Dri.
 G'fld 4E **61**
Lwr. Fullwood. *Oldh* 2H **57**
Lwr. Goodwin Clo. *Bolt* . . .2G **33**
Lwr. Goodwin Fold.
 Bolt 2G **33**
Lwr. Grn. *Ash L* 1A **100**
Lower Grn. *Midd* 4H **69**
Lower Grn. *Roch* 2E **27**
Lower Hague. *N Mills* 5H **155**
Lwr. Hardman St.
 M3 . . . . .4C **94** (6E **5**)
Lower Healey. 6E **15**
Lwr. Healey La. *Roch* 1G **27**
Lwr. Hey La. *Moss* 6G **75**
Lower Higham Vis. Cen.
 . . . . .1E **131**
Lower Hillgate. *Stoc* 2H **139**
Lower Hinds. 5B **36**
Lwr. House Dri. *Los* 6A **30**
Lwr. House La. *Ward* 2A **16**
Lwr. House St. *Oldh* 1F **73**
Lwr. House Wlk.
 Brom X 3E **19**
Lower Irlam. 2C **110**
Lower Jowkin La. *Roch* 4H **25**
Lower Kersal. 5F **81**

Lwr. Knoll Rd. *Dig* 2C **60**
Lwr. Knotts. *Bolt* 5B **20**
Lower La. *Roch & Miln* . . .2A **42**
Lower Lea. *Dis* 1G **165**
Lwr. Lime Rd. *Oldh* 3A **86**
Lower Marlands.
 Brom X 3D **18**
Lwr. Mead. *Eger* 2D **18**
Lwr. Meadow Dri.
 Hand 3A **160**
Lwr. Moat Clo. *Stoc* 6G **127**
Lwr. Monton St. *Eccl* 3G **91**
Lower Moor. 1E **73**
Lwr. Mosley St. *M2* 5D **94** (2G **9**)
Lwr. Moss La. *M15* 6B **94** (4D **8**)
Lwr. Moss La. *W'fld* 1D **66**
Lwr. New Row. *Wors* 2C **76**
Lwr. Nuttall Rd. *Rams* 5F **13**
Lwr. Ormond St.
 M1 . . . . .6E **95** (3A **10**)
Lwr. Ormond St.
 M15 . . . . . . .6E **95** (4A **10**)
Lwr. Park Cres. *Poy* 1C **162**
Lwr. Park Rd. *M14* 3G **109**
Lwr. Park Rd. *Poy* 2B **162**
 (in three parts)
Lower Place. 1H **41**
Lower Pools. 3E **31**
Lower Pools. *Bolt* 3E **31**
Lwr. Rawson St. *Farn* 6G **47**
Lower Rd. *Rams* 1F **13**
Lower Roe Cross. 2B **116**
Lower Rushcroft. 4E **43**
Lwr. Seedley Rd. *Salf* 2E **93**
Lwr. Sheriff St. *Roch* 3G **27**
Lwr. Standrings. *Roch* 3C **26**
Lower Stones. *Del* 5G **59**
Lower St. *Farn* 2E **63**
Lower St. *Hoch* 1G **41**
Lwr. Strines Rd. *Marp* 6E **143**
Lower Summerseat. 2C **22**
Lwr. Sutherland St.
 Swin 3E **79**
Lower Tenterfield. *Roch* . . .1H **25**
Lower Tong. *Brom X* 4D **18**
Lwr. Turf La. *Scout* 2C **74**
Lwr. Tweedale St.
 Roch 5H **27**
Lwr. Vickers St.
 M40 . . . . . . .2H **95** (2G **7**)
Lwr. Victoria St. *Chad* 2H **71**
Lwr. Wharf St. *Ash L* 3H **99**
Lwr. Wheat End. *Roch* 3B **28**
Lwr. Woodhill Rd. *Bury* 2B **36**
 (in two parts)
Lwr. Wood La. *Bolt* 4D **32**
Lwr. Wrigley Grn. *Dig* 4C **60**
Lowes Rd. *Bury* 5F **23**
Lowestead Rd. *M11* 3E **97**
Lowes, The. *Bow* 4D **144**
Lowestoft St. *M14* 5F **109**
Loweswater Rd. *Farn* 2A **62**
Loweswater Rd. *Gat* 2F **149**
Loweswater Ter. *Stal* 1E **101**
Lowfell Wlk. *M18* 4F **111**
Lowfield Av. *Ash L* 6B **88**
Lowfield Av. *Droy* 2H **97**
Lowfield Gro. *Stoc* 4H **139**
Lowfield Wlk. *M9* 6G **69**
 (off Normanton Rd.)
Lowgill Wlk. *M18* 2F **111**
Low Gro. La. *G'fld* 4G **75**
Low Hill. *Roch* 6A **16**
Lowhouse Clo. *Miln* 4G **29**
Lowick Av. *Bult* 4C **46**
Lowick Clo. *Haz G* 3D **152**
Lowick Grn. *Woodl* 3F **129**
Lowland Gro. *Ash L* 5E **87**

Lowland Rd. *Stoc* 1B **152**
Lowlands Clo. *Midd* 4B **70**
Low Lea Rd. *Marp B* 4F **143**
Low Meadow. *Rytn* 1B **56**
Lowndes Clo. *Stoc* 5B **140**
Lowndes La. *Stoc* 4B **140**
Lowndes St. *Bolt* 5F **31**
Lowndes Wlk. *M13* 6E **11**
Lownorth Rd. *M22* 5C **148**
Lowood Av. *Urm* 3B **104**
Lowood Clo. *Miln* 5F **29**
Lowrey Wlk. *M9* 4G **83**
 (off Craigend Dri.)
Lowry Ct. *Hyde* 3C **116**
Lowry Ct. *W'fld* 5B **50**
Lowry Dri. *Marp B* 3F **143**
Lowry Dri. *Swin* 2F **79**
Lowry Galleria. *Salf* 6F **93**
Lowry Gro. *Mot* 4B **116**
Lowry Ho. *Eccl* 3G **91**
Lowry Lodge. *M16* 2B **108**
Lowry, The. 6E **93**
Lowry, The. *M14* 1G **125**
Lowry Wlk. *Bolt* 4H **31**
Low Side. 5G **73**
Lowside Av. *Bolt* 1A **44**
Lowside Av. *Woodl* 4A **130**
Lowside Dri. *Oldh* 4F **73**
Low's Pl. *Roch* 1A **28**
Lowstern Clo. *Eger* 1D **18**
Lows, The. *Oldh* 4F **73**
 (in two parts)
Low St. *Rams* 3E **13**
Lowther Av. *M18* 4D **110**
Lowther Av. *Rytn* 5A **42**
Lowther Av. *Timp* 5A **134**
Lowther Clo. *P'wich* 6E **67**
Lowther Cres. *Midd* 6D **66**
Lowther Gdns. *Urm* 4H **103**
Lowther Rd. *M8* 2C **82**
Lowther Rd. *P'wich* 6D **66**
Lowther Rd. *Roch* 1F **41**
Lowther St. *Bolt* 5C **46**
Lowton Av. *M9* 4H **83**
Lowton Rd. *Sale* 1F **133**
Lowton St. *Rad* 3G **49**
Low Wood Clo. *Bram* 4E **151**
Low Wood Rd. *Dent* 3A **112**
Loxford Ct.
 M15 . . . . . .1D **108** (5H **9**)
Loxford St.
 M15 . . . . . .1D **108** (5H **9**)
Loxham St. *Bolt* 5F **47**
Loxley Wlk. *M40* 1A **96**
Loynd St. *Rams* 3F **13**
Lubeck St. *M9* 3G **83**
Lucas Rd. *Farn* 1C **62**
Lucas St. *Bury* 2E **37**
Lucas St. *Oldh* 2F **73**
Lucas Wlk. *M11* 5B **96**
Lucerne Clo. *Chad* 3A **72**
Lucerne Rd. *Bram* 2G **151**
Lucien Clo. *M12* 2A **110**
Lucknow St. *Roch* 6H **27**
Lucy St. *M15* 1B **108** (6C **8**)
Lucy St. *Bolt* 4E **31**
Lucy St. *Salf* 6H **81**
Lucy St. *Stoc* 3G **139**
Ludford Gro. *Sale* 1H **133**
Ludgate Hill. *M4* . .2F **95** (2C **6**)
Ludgate Rd. *M40* 1E **97**
Ludgate Rd. *Roch* 3G **41**
Ludgate St. *M4* . .2F **95** (2B **6**)
Ludlow Av. *Swin* 1G **79**
Ludlow Av. *W'fld* 3F **67**
Ludlow Pk. *Oldh* 3H **73**
Ludlow Rd. *Stoc* 3C **140**
Ludlow Towers. *Stoc* 2C **128**
Ludwell Wlk. *M8* 5C **82**
Lugano Rd. *Bram* 2G **151**

Luke Kirby Ct. *Swin* 2F **79**
Luke Rd. *Droy* 4B **98**
Luke St. *Bolt* 2A **46**
Luke Wlk. *M8* 5D **82**
Lullington Clo. *M22* 4A **148**
Lullington Rd. *Salf* 1D **92**
Lulworth Av. *Urm* 5B **104**
Lulworth Clo. *Bury* 5C **22**
Lulworth Cres. *Fail* 3H **85**
Lulworth Gdns. *M23* 3F **135**
Lulworth Rd. *Bolt* 4E **45**
Lulworth Rd. *Eccl* 2E **91**
Lulworth Rd. *Midd* 5A **54**
Lumb Carr Av. *Rams* 5C **12**
Lumb Carr Rd. *Holc* 6C **12**
Lumb Clo. *Bram* 1G **161**
Lumber La. *Wors* 3G **77**
Lumb Ho. *Bram* 1G **161**
Lumb La. *Aud* 4C **98**
 (in two parts)
Lumb La. *Bram* 1G **161**
Lumb La. *Droy* 2C **98**
 (in three parts)
Lumley Clo. *M14* 3F **109**
Lumn Hollow. *Hyde* 5C **114**
 (in two parts)
Lumn Rd. *Hyde* 5C **114**
Lumn's La. *Swin* 1A **80**
Lumn St. *Bury* 3F **23**
Lumsden St. *Bolt* 2A **46**
Lum St. *Bolt* 5C **32**
Lumwood. *Bolt* 2F **31**
Luna St. *M4* 3F **95** (4C **6**)
Lundale Wlk. *M40* 5A **84**
Lund Av. *Rad* 1H **65**
Lund St. *M16* . . .1A **108** (6A **8**)
Lundy Av. *M21* 4A **124**
Lune Clo. *W'fld* 6E **51**
Lunedale Grn. *Stoc* 5D **140**
Lune Dri. *W'fld* 1E **67**
Lune Gro. *Heyw* 2D **38**
Lune St. *Oldh* 5C **72**
Lune Wlk. *Droy* 5B **98**
Lune Wlk. *W'fld* 1E **67**
Lune Way. *Stoc* 4H **127**
Lunn Av. *M18* 1H **111**
Lupin Av. *Farn* 8C **46**
Lupton St. *Dent* 3F **113**
Lupton St. *Salf* . . .3B **94** (4D **4**)
Lurden Wlk. *Chad* 5H **71**
Lurgan Av. *Sale* 6C **122**
Lutener Av. *B'hth* 3E **133**
Luton Dri. *M23* 1G **147**
Luton Rd. *Stoc* 1H **127**
Luton St. *Bolt* 3C **46**
Luton St. *Bury* 4H **35**
Luxhall Wlk. *M40* 1D **96**
Luxor Gro. *Dent* 4H **111**
Luxley. 4D **88**
Luxley Brook. 2E **57**
Luxley Brook Rd. *Rytn* . . .2E **57**
Luzley Rd.
 Ash L & Moss 6D **88**
Luzley Rd. *Stal* 2F **101**
Lyceum Pas. *Roch* 4H **27**
Lyceum Pl.
 M15 . . . . . . .6E **95** (4A **10**)
Lyceum Theatre, The.
 . . . . .3D **72**
Lychgate Ct. *Bolt* 5G **33**
Lychgate Ct. *Oldh* 5A **74**
Lychgate M. *Stoc* 1A **138**
Lychwood. *Marp* 5D **142**
Lydbrook Clo. *Bolt* 1A **46**
Lydden Av. *M11* 2F **97**
Lydford. *Roch* 5G **27**
Lydford Gdns. *Bolt* 2H **47**
Lydford St. *Salf* 6F **81**
Lydford Wlk
 M13 . . . . . .2G **109** (6F **11**)
 (off Torquay Clo.)
Lydgate. 4E **75**

Lydgate Av. *Bolt* 5G **33**
Lydgate Clo. *Carr* 5G **89**
Lydgate Clo. *Dent* 6H **113**
Lydgate Clo. *W'fld* 6E **51**
Lydgate Dri. *Oldh* 4G **73**
Lydgate Rd. *Droy* 2G **97**
Lydgate Rd. *Sale* 1C **134**
Lydgate Wlk. *W'fld* 6E **51**
Lydiate Clo. *Bolt* 4B **46**
Lydiat La. *Ald E* 6G **167**
Lydney Av. *H Grn* 6G **149**
Lydney Rd. *Urm* 4H **103**
Lyefield Wlk. *Roch* 5B **28**
Lyme Av. *Wilm* 6F **159**
Lyme Clough Way.
  Midd 3H **53**
Lymefield Dri. *Wors* 4C **76**
Lymefield Gro. *Stoc* 5B **140**
Lyme Gro. *Alt* 1E **145**
Lyme Gro. *Droy* 4H **97**
Lyme Gro. *Marp* 6D **142**
Lyme Gro. *Rom* 1B **142**
Lyme Gro. *Stoc* 4H **139**
Lyme Ho. *Heat M* 1A **138**
Lyme Rd. *Dis* 6E **155**
Lyme Rd. *Haz G* 4E **153**
Lyme Rd. *Poy* 4B **164**
Lymes, The. *Bow* 4E **145**
Lyme St. *Haz G* 2D **152**
Lyme St. *Stoc* 1A **138**
Lyme Ter. *Duk* 4H **99**
Lyme Vw. Ct. *Rom* 1B **142**
Lymewood Dri. *Dis* 1F **165**
Lymewood Dri. *Wilm* 1H **167**
Lymington Clo. *Midd* 4B **70**
Lymington Dri. *M23* 2D **134**
Lymm Clo. *Stoc* 5F **139**
Lymm Clo. *Wors* 6C **62**
Lymm Rd. *Lymm* 5A **144**
Lymm Wlk. *Chea* 1C **150**
Lyncombe Clo.
  Chea H 1D **160**
Lyndale Av. *Stoc* 4H **111**
Lyndale Av. *Swin* 5D **78**
Lyndale Dri. *L'boro* 3E **17**
Lyndene Av. *Wors* 3A **78**
Lyndene Ct. *Heyw* 2E **39**
Lyndene Gdns. *Gat* 5F **137**
Lyndene Rd. *M22* 6B **136**
Lyndhurst Av. *Ash L* 6F **87**
Lyndhurst Av. *Bred* 5F **129**
Lyndhurst Av. *Chad* 4F **71**
Lyndhurst Av. *Dent* 4E **113**
Lyndhurst Av. *Haz G* 4C **152**
Lyndhurst Av. *Irlam* 4F **103**
Lyndhurst Av. *P'wich* 6A **68**
Lyndhurst Av. *Roch* 5D **40**
Lyndhurst Av. *Sale* 6H **121**
Lyndhurst Av. *Urm* 3E **105**
Lyndhurst Clo. *Wilm* 4A **166**
Lyndhurst Dri. *Hale* 3A **146**
Lyndhurst Gdns. *Midd* . . .1G **69**
Lyndhurst Rd. *M20* 5E **125**
  (in two parts)
Lyndhurst Rd. *Oldh* 6B **72**
Lyndhurst Rd. *Stoc* 5G **111**
Lyndhurst Rd. *Stret* 4B **106**
Lyndhurst St. *Salf* 3E **93**
Lyndhurst Vw. *Duk* 4A **100**
Lyndon Clo. *Scout* 1D **74**
Lyndon Clo. *T'ton* 5H **21**
Lyndon Cft. *Oldh* 5A **72**
Lyndon Rd. *Irlam* 5D **102**
Lyne Edge Cres. *Duk* 6D **100**
Lyne Edge Rd. *Duk* 6E **101**
Lyne Gro. *Sale* 6C **122**
Lyneham Wlk. *M9* 4G **69**
Lyneham Wlk. *Salf* 5B **82**
Lyne Vw. *Hyde* 1D **114**
Lyngard Clo. *Wilm* 6A **160**
Lyngarth Ho. *Alt* 5G **133**
Lyngate Clo. *Stoc* 3A **140**

Lyn Gro. *Heyw* 2D **38**
Lynham Dri. *Heyw* 5F **39**
Lynmouth Av. *M20* 3E **125**
Lynmouth Av. *Oldh* 6D **72**
Lynmouth Av. *Rytn* 4A **56**
Lynmouth Av. *Stoc* 2G **127**
Lynmouth Av. *Urm* 1D **120**
Lynmouth Clo. *Chad* 6E **55**
Lynmouth Clo. *Rad* 3A **50**
Lynmouth Ct. *P'wich* 6D **66**
Lynmouth Gro. *P'wich* . . .6D **66**
Lynn Av. *Sale* 3D **122**
Lynn Dri. *Droy* 3G **97**
Lynnfield Ho. *Alt* 6F **133**
Lynn St. *Oldh* 5A **72**
Lynnwood Dri. *Roch* 3C **26**
Lynnwood Rd. *M19* 1H **137**
Lynroyle Way. *Roch* 2D **40**
Lynside Wlk. *M22* 6C **148**
Lynsted Av. *Bolt* 4C **46**
Lynthorpe Av. *Cad* 3B **118**
Lynthorpe Rd. *M40* 6D **70**
Lynton Av. *Cad* 3C **118**
Lynton Av. *Hyde* 5G **115**
Lynton Av. *Oldh* 1A **86**
Lynton Av. *Roch* 2B **40**
Lynton Av. *Rytn* 4A **56**
Lynton Av. *Swin* 2F **79**
Lynton Av. *Urm* 5G **103**
Lynton Clo. *Chad* 6F **55**
Lynton Ct. *Ald E* 4G **167**
Lynton Cres. *Wors* 3F **77**
Lynton Dri. *M19* 2B **126**
Lynton Dri. *H Lane* 5C **154**
Lynton Dri. *P'wich* 3G **67**
Lynton Gro. *Timp* 6H **133**
Lynton La. *Ald E* 4G **167**
Lynton Lea. *Rad* 3A **50**
Lynton M. *Ald E* 4G **167**
  (in two parts)
Lynton Pk. Rd.
  Chea H 5B **150**
Lynton Rd. *M21* 6G **107**
Lynton Rd. *Bolt* 5G **45**
Lynton Rd. *Gat* 6G **137**
Lynton Rd. *Stoc* 4D **126**
Lynton Rd. *Swin* 2F **79**
Lynton Rd. *Tyl* 3A **76**
Lynton St. *M14* 5F **109**
Lynton Ter. *Rad* 2B **64**
Lyntonvale Av. *Gat* 5E **137**
Lynton Wlk. *Hyde* 5G **115**
Lyn Town Trad. Est.
  Eccl 3F **91**
Lynway Dri. *M20* 4F **125**
Lynway Gro. *Midd* 5B **54**
Lynwell Rd. *Eccl* 3F **91**
Lynwood. *Hale* 5A **146**
Lynwood Av. *M16* 5A **108**
Lynwood Av. *Bolt* 5D **46**
Lynwood Av. *Eccl* 3F **91**
Lynwood Clo. *Ash L* 4E **87**
Lynwood Ct. *M8* 1B **82**
Lynwood Dri. *Oldh* 1H **73**
Lynwood Gro. *Aud* 4C **98**
Lynwood Gro. *Bolt* 1F **33**
Lynwood Gro. *Sale* 4C **122**
Lynwood Gro. *Stoc* 3E **127**
Lyon Gro. *Wors* 3A **78**
Lyon Ind. Est. *B'hth* 4D **132**
Lyon Rd. *B'hth* 5E **133**
Lyon Rd. *Kear* 3G **63**
Lyon Rd. Ind. Est. *Kear* . . .4G **63**
Lyons Dri. *Bury* 4G **35**
Lyon's Fold. *Sale* 3B **122**
Lyons Rd. *Traf P* 6A **92**
Lyon St. *Shaw* 6F **43**
Lyon St. *Swin* 4E **79**
Lyon Way. *Stoc* 3G **127**
Lysander Clo. *M14* 1F **125**
Lytham Av. *M21* 2A **124**
Lytham Clo. *Ash L* 5A **88**

Lytham Dri. *Bram* 6A **152**
Lytham Dri. *Heyw* 4E **39**
Lytham Rd.
  M14 & M19 . . . . . . .6A **110**
Lytham Rd. *H Grn* 4F **149**
Lytham Rd. *Urm* 5G **103**
Lytham St. *Roch* 6E **15**
Lytham St. *Stoc* 5H **139**
Lytherton Av. *Cad* 5B **118**
Lyth St. *M14* 2H **125**
Lytton Av. *M8* 5C **82**
Lytton Rd. *Droy* 3A **98**
Lytton St. *Bolt* 3H **31**

M

Mabel Av. *Bolt* 4C **46**
Mabel Av. *Wors* 4A **78**
Mabel Rd. *Fail* 2G **85**
Mabel's Brow. *Kear* 2G **63**
  (in two parts)
Mabel St. *M40* 6D **84**
Mabel St. *Bolt* 5G **31**
Mabel St. *Roch* 1F **27**
Mabfield Rd. *M14* 6G **109**
Mabledon Clo. *H Grn* 5H **149**
Mabs Ct. *Ash L* 3B **100**
Macaulay Way. *Dent* 1G **129**
Macauley Clo. *Duk* 6E **101**
Macauley Rd. *M16* 5H **107**
Macauley Rd. *Stoc* 6F **111**
Macauley St. *Roch* 4C **40**
Macauley St. *Rytn* 3C **56**
McBride Riverside Pk.
  Midd 1H **69**
McCall Wlk. *M11* 3D **96**
Maccles Ct. *L'boro* 3E **17**
Macclesfield Rd.
  Ald E & Neth A . . .5G **167**
Macclesfield Rd.
  Haz G 6E **153**
Macclesfield Rd.
  Wilm 2F **167**
McConnell Rd. *M40* 4A **84**
McCready Dri. *Salf* 5H **93**
Macdonald Av. *Farn* 2C **62**
Macdonald Rd. *Irlam* 2C **118**
Macdonald St. *Oldh* 5D **72**
McDonna St. *Bolt* 2G **31**
McDonough Clo. *Oldh* . . .6E **73**
McDougall Sports Cen.
 . . . . .2E **109**
McDowall Wlk. *M8* 1D **82**
Macefin Av. *M21* 5B **124**
Macfarren St. *M12* 4C **110**
McKean St. *Bolt* 3C **46**
Mackenzie Gro. *Bolt* 1H **31**
Mackenzie Ind. Pk.
  Stoc 5D **138**
Mackenzie Rd. *Salf* 5F **81**
Mackenzie St. *M12* 4C **110**
Mackenzie St. *Bolt* 6B **18**
Mackenzie Wlk. *Oldh* 2A **58**
Mackeson Dri. *Ash L* 1C **100**
Mackeson Rd. *Ash L* 1C **100**
McKie Clo. *Oldh* 6E **73**
Mackintosh Way. *Oldh* . . .2D **72**
McLaren Ct. *M21* 6G **107**
Maclaren Dri. *M8* 2A **82**
McLean Dri. *Irlam* 3E **103**
Maclure Rd. *Roch* 5H **27**
Macnair Ct. *Marp* 6E **143**
Macnair M. *Marp* 6E **143**
  (in two parts)
McNaught St. *Roch* 5B **28**
McOwen Pl. *Roch* 4A **28**
McOwen St. *Roch* 4A **28**
Madams Wood Rd.
  Wors 6B **62**
Maddison Rd. *Droy* 5H **97**
Madeira Pl. *Eccl* 3D **90**

Madeley Clo. *Hale* 5G **145**
Madeley Dri. *Chad* 3A **72**
Madeley Gdns. *Bolt* 3A **32**
Madeley Gdns. *Roch* 2F **27**
Madeley St. *Bolt* 5F **47**
Madens Sq. *L'boro* 4F **17**
Maden Wlk. *Chad* 1H **71**
Madison Apartments.
  M16 . . . . .2H **107**
Madison Av. *Aud* 5C **98**
Madison Av. *Chea H* 3C **150**
Madison Gdns. *Fail* 4E **85**
Madison St. *M18* 1G **111**
Madras Rd. *Stoc* 4E **139**
Mafeking Av. *Bury* 6G **23**
Mafeking Rd. *Bolt* 6G **33**
Mafeking St. *Oldh* 6A **72**
Magdala St. *Heyw* 5G **39**
Magdala St. *Oldh* 1C **72**
Magda Rd. *Stoc* 6C **140**
Magenta Av. *Irlam* 3C **118**
Magna Carta Ct. *Salf* 5H **79**
Magnolia Clo. *Part* 6C **118**
Magnolia Clo. *Sale* 3E **121**
Magnolia Ct. *Sale* 4E **121**
  (off Magnolia Clo.)
Magnolia Ct. *Salf* 3G **93**
Magnolia Dri. *M8* 5C **82**
Magpie Clo. *Droy* 2C **98**
Magpie La. *Oldh* 5H **73**
Magpie Wlk. *M11* 4B **96**
Maher Gdns. *M15* 3C **108**
Mahogany Wlk. *Sale* 4E **121**
Mahood St. *Stoc* 4F **139**
Maida St. *M12* 5D **110**
Maiden Clo. *Ash L* 5E **87**
Maiden M. *Swin* 4F **79**
Maidford Clo.
  M4 . . . . .4H **95** (5H **7**)
Maidford Clo. *Stret* 5E **107**
Maidstone Av. *M21* 6G **107**
Maidstone M. *M21* 6G **107**
Maidstone Rd. *Stoc* 6H **125**
Maidstone Wlk. *Dent* 6G **113**
Main Av. *M19* 2B **126**
Main Dri. *Alt* 2A **144**
Maine Rd. *M14* 3E **109**
  (in two parts)
Maine Road Football Ground.
 . . . . .5E **109**
  (Manchester City)
Mainhill Wlk. *M40* 6C **84**
Main Pde. *Swin* 3F **79**
Mainprice Clo. *Salf* 1F **93**
Main Rd. *Oldh* 2A **72**
Main Rd. *Swin* 6B **66**
Main St. *Fail* 3F **85**
Main St. *Hyde* 3B **114**
Main St. *Hyde* 1H **71**
Maizefield Clo. *Sale* 5F **123**
Major St. *M1* 5E **95** (1A **10**)
Major St. *Miln* 5F **29**
Major St. *Rams* 3D **12**
Major Wlk. *Salf* 5H **93**
  (off Robert Hall St.)
Makamts Clo. *Tyl* 3A **76**
Makant St. *Bolt* 2G **31**
Makepeace Wlk. *M8* 1A **82**
Makin Cft. *Heyw* 4F **39**
Makin St. *M1* 5E **95** (2A **10**)
Makkah Clo. *M40* 6A **84**

Malaga Av. *Man A* 6H **147**
Malakoff St. *Stal* 5C **100**
Malbern Ind. Est.
   Dent 3D **112**
Malbrook Wlk.
   M13 . . . . . .1G **109** (5E **11**)
   (off Jessel Clo.)
Malby St. *Oldh* 1D **72**
Malcolm Av. *Swin* 6G **65**
Malcolm Dri. *Swin* 1G **79**
Malcolm St. *Roch* 2D **40**
Malden Gro. *M23* 4G **135**
Maldon Clo. *L Lev* 4A **48**
Maldon Clo. *Stoc* 5G **141**
Maldon Cres. *Swin* 5F **79**
Maldon Dri. *Eccl* 5E **91**
Maldon St. *Roch* 6H **27**
Maldwyn Av. *M8* 1C **82**
Maldwyn Av. *Bolt* 5F **45**
Maleham Bourne. *Salf* . . .5A **82**
Malford Dri. *M8* 5B **82**
Malgam Dri. *M20* 3F **137**
Malham Clo. *Rytn* 3B **56**
Malham Ct. *Stoc* 5D **140**
Malham Dri. *W'fld* 1E **67**
Malham Gdns. *Bolt* 4G **45**
Malimson Bourne. *Salf* . . .5H **81**
   (off Gt. Cheetham St. W.)
Mallaig Wlk. *Open* 5E **97**
Mallard Clo. *Duk* 6C **100**
Mallard Clo. *Oldh* 1B **86**
Mallard Clo. *Stoc* 6G **141**
Mallard Ct. *H Grn* 5F **149**
Mallard Ct. *Salf* 5D **92**
Mallard Cres. *Poy* 3A **162**
Mallard Grn. *B'hth* 3D **132**
Mallards Reach.
   Rom 1H **141**
Mallard St. *M1* . . .0E **95** (3A **10**)
Mallett Cres. *Bolt* 3D **30**
Malley Wlk. *M9* 6G **69**
   (off Greendale Dri.)
Malling Rd. *M23* 1G **147**
Mallison St. *Bolt* 2B **32**
Mallory Av. *Ash L* 6F **87**
Mallory Ct. *Bow* 2E **145**
Mallory Rd. *Hyde* 2E **115**
Mallory Wlk. *M23* 3D **134**
Mallow Cft. *Roch* 1A **42**
Mallowdale. *Wors* 3D **76**
Mallowdale Clo.
   Bolt 6B **30**
Mallowdale Rd.
   Stoc 6E **141**
Mallow St.
   M15 . . . . . .1C **108** (5E **9**)
Mallow Wlk. *Part* 6D **118**
Mall, The. *Bury* 3D **36**
Mall, The. *Eccl* 3H **91**
Mall, The. *Hyde* 5B **114**
Mall, The. *Sale* 5B **122**
Mall, The. *Stal* 1A **116**
Mallus Ct. *Salf* 2G **93**
Mally Gdns. *Moss* 3F **89**
Malmesbury Clo.
   Poy 3D **162**
Malmesbury Rd.
   Chea H 1D **160**
Malpas Clo. *Chea* 1C **150**
Malpas Clo. *Wilm* 6A **160**
Malpas Dri. *Timp* 2G **133**
Malpas St. *M12* 1C **110**
Malpas St. *Oldh* 2D **72**
Malpas Wlk. *M16* 2B **108**
Malsham Rd. *M23* 1F **135**
Malta Clo. *Midd* 1D **70**
Malta St. *M4* 4H **95** (6G **7**)
Malta St. *Oldh* 3H **73**
Maltby Ct. *Lees* 4B **74**
Maltby Dri. *Bolt* 4G **45**
Maltby Rd. *M23* 5F **135**
Malton Av. *M21* 1H **123**

Malton Av. *Bolt* 3E **45**
Malton Av. *W'fld* 5D **50**
Malton Clo. *Chad* 6F **55**
Malton Clo. *W'fld* 5D **50**
Malton Dri. *Alt* 5C **132**
Malton Dri. *Haz G* 6D **152**
Malton Rd. *Stoc* 5C **126**
Malton Rd. *Wors* 4A **76**
Malton St. *Oldh* 4B **72**
Malt St. *M15* 6B **94** (4C **8**)
Malvern Av. *Ash L* 4G **87**
Malvern Av. *Bolt* 4E **31**
Malvern Av. *Bury* 0F **23**
Malvern Av. *Droy* 3C **98**
Malvern Av. *Gat* 6D **136**
Malvern Av. *Urm* 4D **104**
Malvern Clo. *Farn* 1B **62**
Malvern Clo. *Miln* 4G **29**
Malvern Clo. *P'wich* 4G **67**
Malvern Clo. *Rytn* 4A **56**
Malvern Clo. *Shaw* 5D **42**
Malvern Clo. *Stoc* 6F **127**
Malvern Clo. *Swin* 5B **80**
Malvern Dri. *Alt* 6D **132**
Malvern Dri. *Swin* 5B **80**
Malvern Gro. *M20* 3E **125**
Malvern Gro. *Salf* 2C **92**
Malvern Gro. *Wors* 6F **63**
Malvern Rd. *Midd* 4H **69**
Malvern Row.
   M15 . . . . . .1B **108** (6B **8**)
Malvern St.
   M15 . . . . . .1B **108** (6C **8**)
Malvern St. *Oldh* 4B **72**
Malvern St. E. *Roch* 4E **27**
Malvern St. W. *Roch* 4E **27**
Mamucium Roman Fort.
   . . . . .2E **9**
Manby Rd. *M10* 3D **110**
Manby Sq. *M18* 3D **110**
Mancentral Trad. Est.
   Salf 4B **94** (6D **4**)
Manchester 4F **95** (5A **6**)
Manchester Airport Aviation
   Viewing Pk. 2G **157**
Manchester Airport Eastern
   Link Rd. *Chea H & Bram*
   . . . . .1A **160**
Manchester Airport Tourist
   Info. Cen. 6H **147**
   (terminal 1)
Manchester Airport Tourist
   Info. Cen. 5G **147**
   (terminal 2)
Manchester Aquatics Cen.
   . . . . .6E **95** (5B **10**)
Manchester Bus. Pk.
   M22 . . . . .5B **148**
Manchester Cathedral.
   . . . . .3D **94** (4H **5**)
Manchester Cathedral
   Vis. Cen. . . .3D **94** (4H **5**)
Manchester City Art Gallery.
   . . . . .4E **95** (6A **6**)
Manchester City Football Club.
   . . . . .5E **109**
Manchester Crematorium.
   M21 . . . . .3A **124**
Manchester Ind. Cen.
   M3 . . . . . . .5B **94** (1D **8**)
Manchester International
   Airport. 1H **157**
Manchester International
   Bus. Cen. *SK8* 6E **149**
Manchester Jewish Mus.
   . . . . .1E **95**
Manchester Metropolitan
   University 1F **137**
   (Didsbury Campus)
Manchester Metropolitan
   University 3G **109**
   (Elizabeth Gaskell Campus)

Manchester Metropolitan
   University
   . . . . .6E **95** (4A **10**)
   (Faculty of Humanities &
   Social Science)
Manchester Metropolitan
   University
   . . . . .5F **95** (1C **10**)
   (Faculty of Management &
   Business)
Manchester Metropolitan
   University
   . . . . .6C **95** (3A **10**)
   (Faculty of Science &
   Engineering)
Manchester Metropolitan
   University 5H **109**
   (Hollings Campus)
Manchester Mus., The.
   . . . . . . .1F **109** (6C **10**)
Manchester New Rd.
   Midd 4G **69**
   (in two parts)
Manchester New Rd.
   Part 5D **118**
Manchester Old Rd.
   Bury 4C **36**
Manchester Old Rd.
   Midd 2D **68**
Manchester Old Rd.
   Part 3H **119**
Manchester Regiment, The
   Mus. of the 2H **99**
   (off Wellington Rd.)
Manchester Rd. *M21* . . .6H **107**
   (Barlow Moor Rd.)
Manchester Rd. *M21* . . .1G **123**
   (Wilbraham Rd.)
Manchester Rd.
   Alt & W Timp 5F **133**
Manchester Rd.
   Aud & Ash L 6A **98**
Manchester Rd. *Bolt* 1C **46**
Manchester Rd. *Bury* 3C **36**
Manchester Rd. *Chea* . . .3H **137**
Manchester Rd. *Dent* . . .3A **112**
Manchester Rd. *Droy* . . .4G **97**
Manchester Rd. *Farn* 1G **63**
Manchester Rd. *G'fld* 5H **75**
Manchester Rd. *Heyw* . . .1E **53**
Manchester Rd.
   Holl & Tin 1G **117**
Manchester Rd.
   Hyde 4H **113**
Manchester Rd.
   Kear & Swin 3A **64**
Manchester Rd. *Moss* . . .5E **89**
Manchester Rd.
   Oldh & Chad 1H **85**
Manchester Rd.
   Part & C'ton 5D **118**
Manchester Rd.
   Rams & Walm 3G **13**
Manchester Rd. *Rix* 6A **118**
Manchester Rd. *Roch* 2C **40**
   (in two parts)
Manchester Rd. *Shaw* . . .2E **57**
Manchester Rd. *Stoc* 4E **127**
Manchester Rd. *Swin* 4G **79**
Manchester Rd.
   W'houg & Bolt 6A **44**
Manchester Rd. *W'fld* . . .5D **50**
Manchester Rd. *Wilm* . . .2E **167**
Manchester Rd. *Wors* 1F **77**
Manchester Rd. E.
   L Hul 5C **62**
Manchester Rd. N.
   Dent 3C **112**
Manchester Rd. S.
   Aud 3C **112**
Manchester Rd. W.
   L Hul 3A **62**

Manchester Rugby Union
   Football Club. 2C **160**
Manchester St Ann's Church.
   . . . . .5H **5**
Manchester Science Pk.
   M15 . . . . .2E **109**
Manchester St.
   M16 . . . . . .2A **108** (6B **8**)
Manchester St. *Heyw* 3F **39**
Manchester St. *Oldh* 4B **72**
   (in two parts)
Manchester Town Hall.
   . . . . .4D **94** (6H **5**)
Manchester United
   Football Club. 2F **107**
   (Old Trafford)
Manchester United Mus. &
   Tour. 2F **107**
   (North Stand)
Manchester Vis. Info. Cen.
   . . . . .4D **94** (6H **5**)
Manchet St. *Roch* 4B **40**
Mancroft Av. *Bolt* 3H **45**
Mancroft Ter. *Bolt* 3H **45**
Mancroft Wlk.
   M1 . . . . . . .6F **95** (3C **10**)
Mancunian Rd. *Dent* 1G **129**
Mancunian Way. *M15 &*
   M12 . . . . . .6C **94** (4E **9**)
   (in two parts)
Mandalay Gdns. *Marp* . . .4B **142**
Mandarin Grn. *B'hth* 3D **132**
Mandarin Wlk. *Salf* 2G **93**
Mandeville St. *M19* 1D **126**
Mandeville Ter. *Hawk* 1D **20**
Mandley Av. *M40* 1D **84**
Mandley Clo. *L Lev* 2A **48**
Mandley Pk. Av. *Salf* 4A **82**
Mandon Clo. *Rad* 2C **49**
Manesty Clo. *Midd* 5E **53**
Manet Clo. *Salf* 3F **81**
Mangle St. *M1* 4F **95** (5C **6**)
Mango Pl. *Salf* 3G **93**
Manifold Dri. *H Lane* 1D **164**
Manifold St. *Salf* 6F **81**
Manilla Wlk. *M11* 4B **96**
Manipur St. *M11* 5B **96**
Manley Av. *Swin* 5E **65**
Manley Clo. *Bury* 1C **22**
Manley Gro. *Bram* 1G **161**
Manley Gro. *Mot* 4B **116**
Manley Park. 5A **108**
Manley Rd.
   M21 & M16 . . . . . . .6H **107**
Manley Rd. *Oldh* 5C **72**
Manley Rd. *Roch* 1C **40**
   (Hargreaves St.)
Manley Rd. *Roch* 2C **40**
   (Kingsland Rd.)
Manley Rd. *Sale* 2G **133**
Manley Row. *W'houg* 6A **44**
Manley St. *Salf* 5H **81**
Manley Ter. *Bolt* 1A **32**
Manley Way. *Mot* 4C **116**
Manningham Rd. *Bolt* 2F **45**
Mannington Dri. *M9* 4E **83**
Mannock St. *Oldh* 3B **72**
Manor Av. *M16* 5B **108**
Manor Av. *L Lev* 4C **48**
Manor Av. *Sale* 4F **121**
Manor Av. *Urm* 6F **105**
Manor Clo. *Chad* 1A **72**
Manor Clo. *Chea H* 5E **151**
Manor Clo. *Dent* 5H **113**
Manor Clo. *Grass* 4G **75**
Manor Clo. *Wilm* 1B **166**
Manor Cotts. Moss 1E **89**
   (off Wilds Sq.)
Manor Ct. *Bolt* 1F **33**
Manor Ct. *Sale* 4F **121**
Manor Ct. *Stret* 6B **106**
Manordale Wlk. *M40* 5E **83**

Manor Dri. *M21* 5B **124**
Manor Dri. *Rytn* 4C **56**
Mnr. Farm Clo. *Ash L* . . .5D **86**
Mnr. Farm Ri. *Oldh* 2H **73**
Manorfield Clo. *Bolt* 4E **31**
Manor Gdns. *Wilm* 2G **167**
Manor Ga. Rd. *Bolt* 5A **34**
Manor Heath. *Salf* 3G **81**
Mnr. Hill Rd. *Marp* 4D **142**
Manorial Dri. *L Hul* 4A **62**
Manor Ind. Est. *Stret* 1C **122**
Manor Lodge. *Chea H* . . .4D **150**
Manor Lodge. *Swin* 3B **80**
Mnr. Mill Clo. *Roch* 6B **16**
Manor Pk. *Urm* 6F **105**
Manor Rd. *Alt* 1G **145**
Manor Rd. *Aud* 6B **98**
Manor Rd.
  Chea H & Bram 4E **151**
Manor Rd. *Dent* 5H **113**
Manor Rd. *Droy* 4G **97**
Manor Rd. *Hyde* 2D **114**
Manor Rd. *Lev* 5D **110**
Manor Rd. *Marp* 4D **142**
Manor Rd. *Midd* 3H **69**
Manor Rd. *Oldh* 5G **73**
Manor Rd. *Sale* 4B **122**
Manor Rd. *Salf* 1D **92**
Manor Rd. *Shaw* 6E **43**
Manor Rd. *Stoc* 4B **128**
Manor Rd. *Stret* 6B **106**
Manor Rd. *Swin* 5F **79**
Manor Rd. *Wilm* 1B **166**
Manor Rd. *Woodl* 4H **129**
Manor St. *M12* . .6G **95** (3E **11**)
    (in two parts)
Manor St. *Aud* 6F **99**
Manor St. *Bolt* 6B **32**
Manor St. *Bury* 3E **37**
Manor St. *Farn* 2E **63**
Manor St. *Kear* 4B **64**
Manor St. *Midd* 5A **54**
Manor St. *Moss* 1E **89**
Manor St. *Rams* 2D **12**
    (in two parts)
Manor St. *Rytn* 5E **57**
Manor Vw. *Woodl* 4H **129**
Manor Yd. Upperm 1F **61**
    (off Wade Row)
Manse, The. *Moss* 3E **89**
Mansfield Av. *M9* 5F **69**
Mansfield Av. *Dent* 2D **112**
Mansfield Av. *Rams* 1B **22**
Mansfield Clo. *Ash L* 4F **99**
Mansfield Clo. *Dent* 2D **112**
Mansfield Cres. *Dent* . . .3D **112**
Mansfield Dri. *M9* 5G **69**
Mansfield Grange.
  Roch 5E **27**
Mansfield Gro. *Bolt* 4F **31**
Mansfield Rd. *M9* 5F **69**
Mansfield Rd. *Hyde* 6C **114**
Mansfield Rd. *Moss* 2G **89**
Mansfield Rd. *Oldh* 4F **73**
Mansfield Rd. *Roch* 4A **26**
Mansfield Rd. *Urm* 6D **104**
Mansfield St. *Ash L* 5E **99**
Mansfield Vw. *Moss* 2G **89**
Mansford Dri. *M40* 6H **83**
Manshaw Cres. *Aud* 6A **98**
Manshaw Rd. *M11* 6A **98**
Mansion Av. *W'fld* 4C **50**
Mansion Ho., The.
  B'hth 4F **133**
Manson Av.
  M15 . . . . .6B **94** (4C **8**)
Manstead Wlk.
  M40 . . . . .3A **96** (3H **7**)
Manston Dri. *Chea H* . . .3C **150**
Manswood Dri. *M8* 4C **82**
Mantell Wlk. *M40* 6A **84**

Manthorpe Av. *Wors* 4A **78**
Manton Av. *M9* 1B **84**
Manton Av. *Dent* 4A **112**
Manton Clo. *Salf* 5B **82**
Manton Ho. *Stoc* 5B **128**
Manvers St. *Stoc* 6G **127**
Manwaring St. *Fail* 3E **85**
Maple Av. *M21* 1H **123**
Maple Av. *Bolt* 4F **31**
Maple Av. *Bury* 2F **37**
Maple Av. *Chea H* 3B **150**
Maple Av. *Dent* 4B **98**
    (Droylsden Rd.)
Maple Av. *Dent* 4E **113**
    (Ruby St.)
Maple Av. *Eccl* 1C **90**
Maple Av. *Marp* 1D **154**
Maple Av. *Poy* 4F **163**
Maple Av. *Stal* 5D **100**
Maple Av. *Stret* 6D **106**
Maple Av. *W'fld* 2D **66**
Maple Bank. *Bow* 2D **144**
Maple Clo. *Chad* 6H **55**
Maple Clo. *Kear* 4H **63**
Maple Clo. *Midd* 1D **70**
Maple Clo. *Sale* 5E **121**
Maple Clo. *Salf* 2F **93**
Maple Clo. *Shaw* 5D **42**
Maple Clo. *Stoc* 5B **140**
Maple Ct. *M16* 3H **107**
Maple Ct. *Stoc* 5E **127**
Maple Cft. *Stoc* 3B **140**
Mapledon Rd. *M9* 3H **83**
Maple Dri. *Timp* 6E **135**
Maplefield Dri. *Wors* 4D **76**
Maple Gro. *M40* 1F **85**
Maple Gro. *Fail* 6E **85**
Maple Gro. *P'wich* 3E **67**
Maple Gro. *Rams* 4F **13**
Maple Gro. *T'ton* 6A **22**
Maple Gro. *Wors* 3F **77**
Maple Rd. *M23* 3C **134**
Maple Rd. *Ald E* 6E **167**
Maple Rd. *Bram* 2G **161**
Maple Rd. *Chad* 6H **55**
Maple Rd. *Farn* 1C **62**
Maple Rd. *Part* 6C **118**
Maple Rd. *Swin* 5E **79**
Maple Rd. W. *M23* 3C **134**
Maple St. *Bolt* (BL2) 6G **19**
Maple St. *Bolt* (BL3) 2H **45**
Maple St. *Oldh* 6A **72**
Maple St. *Roch* 5F **27**
Maple Wlk. *M23* 2C **134**
Maplewood Clo. *Rytn* . . .5A **56**
Maplewood Gdns. *Bolt* . . .3A **32**
Maplewood Gro. *Stal* . . .2G **101**
Maplewood Ho. *Bolt* 4A **32**
Maplewood Rd. *Wilm* . . .1H **167**
Mapley Av. *M22* 3B **136**
Maplin Clo. *M13* . .6G **95** (4E **11**)
Marble St. *M2* 4E **95** (5A **6**)
    (in two parts)
Marble St. *Oldh* 1F **73**
Marbury Av. *M14* 6F **109**
Marbury Clo. *Urm* 4H **103**
Marbury Dri. *Timp* 2G **133**
Marbury Rd. *Stoc* 3F **127**
Marbury Rd. *Wilm* 6F **159**
Marcer Rd.
  M40 . . . . . . .3H **95** (3G **7**)
March Av. *Stoc* 1D **138**
Marchbank Dri. *Chea* . . .5G **137**
March Dri. *Bury* 6D **22**
Marchers M. *Eccl* 4D **90**
Marches Clo. *Rytn* 3F **57**
Marchioness St. *M18* . . .1H **111**
Marchmont Clo.
  M13 . . . . .1H **109** (6G **11**)
March St. *Roch* 4A **28**
Marchwood Av. *M21* 6B **108**

Marcliffe Dri. *M19* 6E **111**
Marcliffe Dri. *Roch* 5D **26**
Marcliffe Ind. Est.
  Haz G 4E **153**
Marcroft Gro. *Stoc* 1D **138**
Marcroft Pl. *Roch* 1G **41**
Marcus Garvey Ct.
  M16 . . . . .5C **108**
Marcus Gro. *M14* 5G **109**
Marcus St. *Bolt* 4F **31**
Mardale Av. *M20* 4G **125**
Mardale Av. *Rytn* 5A **42**
Mardale Av. *Swin* 1C **78**
Mardale Av. *Urm* 4B **104**
Mardale Clo. *Bolt* 4H **33**
Mardale Clo. *Oldh* 1H **73**
Mardale Clo. *P'wich* 2G **67**
Mardale Clo. *Stal* 2E **101**
Mardale Dri. *Bolt* 4H **33**
Mardale Dri. *Gat* 5F **137**
Mardale Dri. *Midd* 6G **53**
Mardale Rd. *Swin* 5D **78**
Marden Rd. *M23* 6G **135**
Mardyke. *Roch* 3G **27**
Marfield Av. *Chad* 4G **71**
Marfield Ct. *Urm* 6A **104**
Marford Clo. *M22* 5B **136**
Marford Cres. *Sale* 1H **133**
Margaret Ashton Clo.
  M9 . . . . .4H **83**
Margaret Av. *Roch* 4C **28**
Margaret Ho. *Ash L* 3G **99**
Margaret Rd. *Dent* 3G **113**
Margaret Rd. *Droy* 3G **97**
Margaret St. *Ash L* 2G **99**
    (in two parts)
Margaret St. *Bury* 4D **36**
Margaret St. *Heyw* 3D **38**
Margaret St. *Oldh* 1H **85**
Margaret St. *Shaw* 1F **57**
Margaret St. *Stoc* 2G **127**
Margaret Ter. *Ash L* 3G **99**
Margaret Ward Ct.
  Roch 6A **28**
Margate Av. *M40* 6B **84**
Margate Rd. *Stoc* 2H **127**
Margrove Chase. *Los* 2A **44**
Margrove Clo. *Fail* 4A **86**
Margrove Rd. *Salf* 1C **92**
Margroy Clo. *Roch* 1A **28**
Marguerita Rd. *M40* 1F **97**
    (in two parts)
Marham Clo. *M21* 2C **124**
Maria St. *Bolt* 3A **32**
Marie Clo. *Dent* 5F **113**
    (in two parts)
Marie St. *Salf* 4A **82**
Marigold St. *Roch* 6H **27**
    (in two parts)
Marigold Ter. Midd 2D **70**
    (off Mills Hill Rd.)
Mariman Dri. *M8* 1C **82**
Marina Av. *Dent* 6G **113**
Marina Clo. *Hand* 2H **159**
Marina Cres. *M11* 2D **96**
Marina Dri. *Marp* 4A **142**
Marina Rd. *Bred* 5E **129**
Marina Rd. *Droy* 3B **98**
Marine Av. *Part* 6B **118**
Marion St. *Bolt* 5E **47**
Marion St. *Oldh* 6D **72**
Maritime Ct. *Sale* 5H **121**
Marjorie Clo. *M18* 1D **110**
Mark Av. *Salf* 1H **93**
Markendale St. *Salf* 1G **107**
Markenfield Dri. *Shaw* 6D **42**
Market Av. *Ash L* 2H **99**
    (in three parts)
Market Av. *Oldh* 2D **72**
Market Brow. *M9* 1F **83**
Market Cen., The.
  M2 . . . . .4E **95** (5A **6**)

Market Chambers.
  Rams 2E **13**
    (off Ramsbottom La.)
Market Hall. *Bolt* 6B **32**
Market Pde. *Bury* 3D **36**
Market Pl. *Bolt* 5B **32**
Market Pl. *Bury* 3C **36**
Market Pl. *Comp* 1E **143**
Market Pl. *Dent* 4E **113**
Market Pl. *Droy* 4A **98**
Market Pl. *Farn* 1F **63**
Market Pl. *Heyw* 3F **39**
Market Pl. *Hyde* 5B **114**
    (in two parts)
Market Pl. *Midd* 6A **54**
Market Pl. *Moss* 2D **88**
Market Pl. *Mot* 4C **116**
Market Pl. *Oldh* 2C **72**
Market Pl. *Rad* 5H **49**
Market Pl. *Rams* 2A **12**
    (Bury Rd.)
Market Pl. *Rams* 2D **12**
    (Carr St.)
Market Pl. *Roch* 4H **27**
Market Pl. *Rytn* 3B **56**
Market Pl. *Shaw* 1F **57**
Market Pl. *Stoc* 1H **139**
    (in two parts)
Market Pl. *Swin* 2G **79**
Market Pl. *Wyth* 2B **148**
Market Precinct. *Farn* 1F **63**
Market Sq. Alt 1F **145**
  (off Market St., in two parts)
Market Sq. *Rytn* 3B **56**
Market St. *M1* . . .3D **94** (4H **5**)
    (in three parts)
Market St. *Alt* 1F **145**
Market St. *Ash L* 2H **99**
Market St. *Bolt* 6B **32**
Market St. *Bury* 4D **36**
    (Angouleme Way)
Market St. *Bury* 3C **36**
    (Bolton St., in two parts)
Market St. *Dent* 4E **113**
    (in two parts)
Market St. *Dis* 1H **165**
Market St. *Droy* 5A **98**
Market St. *Farn* 6F **47**
Market St. *Heyw* 3E **39**
Market St. *Holl* 2E **117**
Market St. *Hyde* 4B **114**
Market St. *L Lev* 4A **48**
Market St. *Marp* 6D **142**
Market St. *Midd* 6H **53**
    (in two parts)
Market St. *Moss* 2E **89**
Market St. *Mot* 3C **116**
Market St. *Rad* 1B **64**
Market St. *Rams* 1A **12**
Market St. *Rytn* 3B **56**
Market St. *Shaw* 1F **57**
Market St. *Stal* 3E **101**
Market St. *Swin* 2G **79**
Market St. *T'ton* 4H **21**
Market St. *Whitw* 3C **14**
Market Wlk. *Sale* 4B **122**
Market Way. M4 . . .3E **95** (4A **6**)
    (off Arndale Shop. Cen.)
Market Way. *Roch* 3H **27**
Market Way. *Salf* 2F **93**
Markfield Av. *M13* 2H **109**
Markham Clo.
  M12 . . . . . .5H **95** (1H **11**)
Markham Clo. *Hyde* 1B **114**
Markham St. *Hyde* 1B **114**
Markington St. *M14* 4E **109**
Mark Jones Wlk. *M40* . . .6B **84**
Markland Hill. 5C **30**
Markland Hill. *Bolt* 5C **30**
Markland Hill Clo. *Bolt* . . .4D **30**
Markland Hill La. *Bolt* . . .4C **30**
Markland St. *Bolt* 1B **46**

Markland St. *Hyde* 6C **114**
(in two parts)
Markland St. *Rams* 3U **12**
Mark La. *M4* . . . . .3E **95** *(4A 6)*
(off Withy Gro.)
Mark La. *Shaw* 1G **57**
Marks St. *Rad* 4G **49**
Mark St. *Oldh* 2B **72**
Mark St. *Roch* 2B **28**
Mark St. *Wors* 4B **76**
Markwood. *Del* 3H **59**
Marland. 1B **40**
Marland Av. *Chea H* 3B **150**
Marland Av. *Oldh* 2E **87**
Marland Av. *Roch* 1B **40**
Marland Clo. *Roch* 6D **26**
Marland Cres. *Stoc* 1H **127**
Marland Fold. *Roch* 1B **40**
Marland Fold La. *Oldh* . . .2D **86**
Marland Grn. *Roch* 1B **40**
Marland Hill Rd. *Roch* . . .6E **27**
Marland Old Rd. *Roch* . . .1B **40**
Marland St. *Chad* 6G **71**
Marland Tops. *Roch* 1B **40**
Marlborough Av. *M16* . . .5A **108**
Marlborough Av.
  Ald E 4H **167**
Marlborough Av.
  Chea H 3D **150**
Marlborough Clo.
  Ash L 5E **99**
Marlborough Clo.
  Dent 4F **113**
Marlborough Clo.
  Marp 4B **142**
Marlborough Clo.
  Rams 6E **13**
Marlborough Clo.
  Whitw 2C **14**
Marlborough Ct. *M8* 4B **68**
Marlborough Dri.
  Fail 5E **85**
Marlborough Dri.
  Stoc 5F **127**
Marlborough Gdns.
  Farn 1C **62**
Marlborough Gro.
  Droy 3C **98**
Marlborough Rd. *Bow* . .3F **145**
Marlborough Rd. *Eccl* . . .1A **92**
Marlborough Rd.
  Hyde 1C **130**
Marlborough Rd.
  Irlam 4F **103**
Marlborough Rd. *Rytn* . . .5C **56**
Marlborough Rd. *Sale* . . .5B **122**
Marlborough Rd. *Salf* . . .5B **82**
(in two parts)
Marlborough Rd.
  Stret 4C **106**
Marlborough Rd.
  Urm 4B **104**
Marlborough St. *Ash L* . .5E **99**
(in two parts)
Marlborough St. *Bolt* . . .5G **31**
Marlborough St. *Heyw* . . .5G **39**
Marlborough St. *Oldh* . . .3E **73**
Marlborough St. *Roch* . . .2E **27**
Marlbrook Wlk. *Bolt* 3B **46**
Marlcroft Av. *Stoc* 1D **138**
Marld Cres. *Bolt* 3D **30**
Marle Av. *Moss* 2G **89**
Marle Cft. *W'fld* 3A **66**
Marle Ri. *Moss* 2G **89**
Marler Rd. *Hyde* 3C **114**
Marley Clo. *Timp* 4H **133**
Marley Dri. *Sale* 3A **122**
Marleyer Ri. *Rom* 3G **141**
Marleyer St. *M40* 4C **84**
Marley Rd. *M19* 1D **126**
Marley Rd. *Poy* 5E **163**
Marlfield Rd. *Haleb* 1D **156**

Marlfield Rd. *Shaw* 5C **42**
Marlfield St. *M9* 2G **83**
Marhill Clo. *Stoc* 6E **141**
Marhill Ct. *Stoc* 6E **141**
Marlinford Dri. *M40* 6C **84**
Marloes. *Bow* 3D **144**
Marlor Ct. *Heyw* 3D **38**
Marlor St. *Dent* 3E **113**
Marlow Clo. *Bolt* 4H **33**
Marlow Clo. *Chea H* 3B **150**
Marlow Clo. *Urm* 3D **104**
(in four parts)
Marlow Dri. *Bow* 3D **144**
Marlow Dri. *Hand* 2G **159**
Marlow Dri. *Irlam* 4E **103**
Marlow Dri. *Swin* 5E **79**
Marlowe Dri. *M20* 5F **125**
Marlowe Pl. *M11* 5A **96**
(off Bellew St.)
Marlowe Wlk. *Dent* 2G **129**
Marlowe Walks. *Bred* . . .1E **141**
Marlow Ho. *Salf* 4F **93**
(off Amersham St.)
Marlow Rd. *M9* 2H **83**
Marlton Wlk. *M9* 6G **69**
(off Leconfield Dri.)
Marlwood Rd. *Bolt* 3D **30**
Marlwood Way. *Rytn* 5A **56**
Marmion Dri. *M21* 1G **123**
Marne Av. *M22* 6C **136**
Marne Av. *Ash L* 6B **88**
Marne Cres. *Roch* 4E **27**
Marnland Gro. *Bolt* 3C **44**
Maroon Rd. *M22* 6D **148**
Marple. 5D **142**
Marple Av. *Bolt* 1C **32**
Marple Bridge. 4F **143**
Marple Clo. *Oldh* 1B **86**
Marple Ct. *Stoc* 4A **140**
Marple Dale. 2B **142**
Marple Gro. *Stret* 4C **106**
Marple Hall Dri. *Marp* . . .4B **142**
Marple Lock. 4E **143**
Marple Old Rd. *Stoc* 5G **141**
Marple Packhorse Bri.
  . . . . .2F **155**
Marple Rd. *Stoc* 4D **140**
Marple St.
  M15 . . . . . . .2B **108** *(6D 8)*
Marple Swimming Pool.
  . . . . .5D **142**
Marquis Av. *Bury* 1C **36**
Marquis Dri. *H Grn* 6H **149**
Marquis St. *M19* 6F **111**
Marrick Av. *Chea* 6G **137**
Marriott's Ct. *M2* . .4E **95** *(5A 6)*
Marriott St. *M20* 3F **125**
Marriott St. *Stoc* 3H **139**
Marryat Ct. *M12* 1B **110**
(off Gregory St.)
Mars Av. *Bolt* 4G **45**
Marsden Clo. *Ash L* 6C **86**
Marsden Clo. *Moss* 1D **88**
Marsden Clo. *Roch* 5A **42**
Marsden Ct.
  M4 . . . . .3E **95** *(4A 6)*
(off Arndale Shop. Cen.)
Marsden Dri. *Timp* 5C **134**
Marsden Rd. *Bolt* 6A **32**
Marsden Rd. *Rom* . . . . . .GA **130**
Marsden's Sq. *L'boro* 3F **17**
(off Sutcliffe St.)
Marsden St. *M2* . .4D **94** *(5H 5)*
Marsden St. *Bury* 2D **36**
Marsden St. *Eccl* 2E **91**
Marsden St. *Had* 3H **117**
Marsden St. *Midd* 2C **70**
Marsden St. *Wors* 1B **78**
(Manchester Rd.)
Marsden St. *Wors* 4B **76**
(Mosley Comn. Rd.)
Marsden Wlk. *Rad* 3F **49**

Marsden Way.
  M4 . . . . .3E **95** *(4A 6)*
(off Arndale Shop. Cen.)
Marsett Clo. *Roch* 2C **26**
Marsett Wlk. *M23* 1F **135**
Marshall Ct. *Ash L* 3B **100**
Marshall Ct. *Oldh* 1C **72**
Marshall Rd. *M19* 6C **110**
Marshall Stevens Way.
  Traf P 1B **106**
Marshall St. *M4* . . .3F **95** (3C **6**)
Marshall St.
  M12 . . . . . .1C **109** (5F **11**)
Marshall St. *Dent* 3E **113**
Marshall St. *Roch* 4C **28**
Marsham Clo. *M13* 2A **110**
Marsham Clo. *G'ton* 4D **74**
Marsham Dri. *Marp* 6E **143**
Marsham Rd. *Haz G* 4B **152**
Marshbrook Rd. *Urm* 4E **105**
Marsh Clo. *Stoc* 5F **139**
Marshdale Rd. *Bolt* 5D **30**
Marshfield Rd. *Timp* . . . . .GC **134**
Marshfield Wlk.
  M13 . . . . . .1G **109** (6F **11**)
(off Lauderdale Cres.)
Marsh Av. *Timp* 3B **134**
Marsh Hey Clo. *L Hul* . . .3B **62**
Marsh La. *Farn* 1C **62**
Marsh La. *L Lev* 3B **48**
Marsh La. *L Hul* 5D **62**
Marsh Rd. *L Lev* 3A **48**
Marsh St. *Bolt* 3A **32**
Marsh St. *Wors* 1H **77**
(in two parts)
Marsland Av. *Timp* 3B **134**
Marsland Clo. *Dent* 4B **112**
Marsland Rd. *Marp* 4C **142**
Marsland Rd. *Sale* 6A **122**
Marsland Rd. *Timp* 6B **134**
Marslands. 5B **60**
Marslands. *Dig* 4B **60**
Marsland St. *Haz G* 3D **152**
Marsland St. *Stoc* 6H **127**
(in two parts)
Marsland St. Ind. Est.
  Haz G 3E **153**
Marsland St. N. *Salf* 4B **82**
Marsland St. S. *Salf* 4B **82**
Marsland Ter. *Stoc* 3B **140**
Mars St. *Oldh* 2A **72**
Marston Clo. *Fail* 5A **86**
Marston Clo. *W'fld* 1G **67**
Marston Dri. *Irlam* 5F **103**
Marston Ho. Salf 4F **93**
(off Cypress Clo.)
Marston Rd. *Salf* 3A **82**
Marston Rd. *Stret* 5F **107**
Marsworth Dri.
  M4 . . . . .3G **95** (4F **7**)
Martens Rd. *Irlam* 4C **118**
Marthall Dri. *Sale* 1F **135**
Marthall Way. *Hand* 2A **160**
Martham Dri. *Stoc* 6G **141**
Martha's Ter. *Roch* 6A **16**
Martha St. *Bolt* 3H **45**
Martha St. *Oldh* 1B **72**
Martin Av. *Farn* 2B **62**
Martin Av. *L Lev* 4C **48**
Martin Av. *Oldh* 3G **73**
Martin Clo. *Dent* 2F **113**
Martin Clo. *Stoc* 6G **141**
Martindale Clo. *Rytn* 2C **56**
Martindale Cres. *M12* . . .1A **110**
Martindale Cres. *Midd* . . .4F **53**
Martindale Gdns. *Bolt* . . .3A **32**
Martin Dri. *Irlam* 3E **103**
Martingale Clo. *Rad* 2G **49**
Martingale Way. *Droy* . . .2D **98**
Martin Gro. *Kear* 2H **63**
Martin Ho. *M14* 4H **109**
Martin La. *Roch* 2D **26**
Martin Rd. *Swin* 1H **79**

Martinsclough. *Los* 1A **44**
Martinscroft Rd. *M23* . . .6H **135**
Martins Fld. *Roch* 2B **26**
Martin St. *Aud* 6F **99**
Martin St. *Bury* 2H **37**
Martin St. *Hyde* 5C **114**
Martin St. *Salf* 3D **92**
Martlesham Wlk.
  M4 . . . . .3E **95** (4B **6**)
Martlet Av. *Dis* 1G **165**
Martlet Clo. *M14* 6F **109**
Martlett Av. *Roch* 4A **26**
Martock Av. *M22* 2C **148**
Marton Av. *M20* 1G **137**
Marton Av. *Bolt* 5E **33**
Marton Grange. *P'wich* . . .6H **67**
Marton Grn. *Stoc* 6F **139**
Marton Gro. *Stoc* 3G **127**
Marton Pl. *Sale* 5A **122**
Marton Way. *Hand* 2A **160**
Marvic Ct. *M13* 4A **110**
Marwood Clo. *Alt* 5D **132**
Marwood Clo. *Rad* 1A **64**
Marwood Dri. *M23* 2F **147**
Mary Anne Clo. *Ash L* . . .5E **87**
Maryfield Ct. *M16* 1C **124**
Mary France St.
  M15 . . . . . .1C **108** (5E **9**)
Maryland Av. *Bolt* 6F **33**
Marylon Dri. *M22* 3C **136**
Mary St. *M3* 2D **94** (1F **5**)
Mary St. *Bury* 5F **23**
Mary St. *Chea* 5H **137**
Mary St. *Dent* 3G **113**
Mary St. *Droy* 4B **98**
Mary St. *Duk* 4H **99**
Mary St. *Farn* 2F **63**
Mary St. *Heyw* 3E **39**
Mary St. *Hyde* 4B **114**
Mary St. *Rams* 4D **12**
Mary St. *Roch* 5B **16**
Mary St. *Stoc* 1A **140**
Masboro St. *M8* 4B **82**
Masbury Clo. *Bolt* 4C **18**
Masefield Av. *P'wich* 6D **66**
Masefield Av. *Rad* 3E **49**
Masefield Clo. *Duk* 6F **101**
Masefield Cres. *Droy* 4A **98**
Masefield Dri. *Farn* 2D **62**
Masefield Dri. *Stoc* 1C **138**
Masefield Gro. *Stoc* . . . . .GG **111**
Masefield Rd. *Droy* 4A **98**
Masefield Rd. *L Lev* 3B **48**
Masefield Rd. *Oldh* 5F **57**
Mason Clough. *Bolt* 6D **18**
Mason Gdns. *Bolt* 1A **46**
Mason Row. *Eger* 1B **18**
Mason St. *M4* 3F **95** (3C **6**)
Mason St. *Ash L* 4F **99**
Mason St. *Bury* 3C **37**
Mason St. *Eger* 2C **18**
Mason St. *Heyw* 3D **38**
Mason St. *Roch* 4H **27**
Mason St. *Salf* 3B **94** (4D **4**)
Massey Av. *Ash L* 5G **87**
Massey Av. *Fail* 3H **85**
Massey Cft. *Whitw* 2C **14**
Massey Rd. *Alt* 1G **145**
Massey Rd. *Sale* 5E **123**
Massey St. *Ald E* 5G **167**
Massey St. *Bury* 2F **37**
Massey St. *Salf* 4A **94** (5B **4**)
Massey Wlk. *M22* 4D **148**
Massie St. *Chea* 5H **137**
Matchmoor La. *Hor* 1A **30**
Matham Wlk.
  M15 . . . . . .1E **109** (5A **10**)
(off Chevril Clo.)
Mather Av. *Eccl* 3G **91**
Mather Av. *P'wich* 2G **81**
Mather Av. *W'fld* 5D **50**
Mather Clo. *W'fld* 6D **50**

Mather Fold Cotts.
Eger 3C 18
Mather Fold Rd.
 Wors 2D 76
Mather Rd. Bury 4F 23
Mather Rd. Eccl 3G 91
Mather St. Bolt 1A 46
Mather St. Fail 4D 84
Mather St. Kear 1G 63
Mather St. Rad 4G 49
Mather Way. Salf 2G 93
Matisse Way. Salf 3F 81
Matley. 1H 115
Matley Clo. Hyde 2F 115
Matley Grn. Stoc 3C 128
Matley La. Hyde 2F 115
Matley Pk. La. Stal 1H 115
Matlock Av. M20 . . . . .3D 124
Matlock Av. Ash L 5B 88
Matlock Av. Dent 1G 129
Matlock Av. Salf 4E 81
Matlock Av. Urm 1D 120
Matlock Bank. Glos 6G 117
(off Riber Bank)
Matlock Clo. Farn 6G 47
Matlock Clo. Sale 5C 122
Matlock Dri. Haz G 5E 153
Matlock Gdns. Glos 6G 117
(off Riber Bank)
Matlock La. Glos 6G 117
(off Riber Bank)
Matlock M. Alt 6G 133
Matlock Pl. Glos 6G 117
(off Riber Bank)
Matlock Rd. H Grn 6G 149
Matlock Rd. Stoc 6A 112
Matlock Rd. Stret 4A 106
Matlock St. Eccl 5E 91
Matson Wlk. M22 . . . . .3G 147
Matt Busby Clo. Swin . . .4H 79
Matterdale Ter. Stal 1E 101
Matthew Clo. Oldh 5G 73
Matthew Moss La.
 Roch 1B 40
Matthews Av. Kear 2H 63
Matthews La. M19 . . . . .5C 110
Matthew's St. M12 . . . . .6B 96
Matthias Ct.
 Salf 2B 94 (2C 4)
Mattison St. M11 . . . . .6G 97
Maudsley St. Bury 4C 36
Maud St. Bolt 6G 19
Maud St. Roch 1A 28
Mauldeth Clo. Stoc 6C 126
Mauldeth Ct. Stoc 6C 126
Mauldeth Rd.
 M19 & Stoc 5B 126
Mauldeth Rd.
 M20 & M14 . . . . .2G 125
Mauldeth Rd. W.
 M21 & M20 . . . . .3A 124
Maunby Gdns. L Hul 6E 63
Maureen Av. M8 . . . . . .3C 82
Maureen St. Roch 1A 28
Maurice Clo. Duk 5C 100
Maurice Dri. Salf 1F 93
Maurice Pariser Wlk.
 M8 . . . . .4B 82
Maurice St. Salf 1F 93
Maveen Ct. Stoc 1A 152
Maveen Gro. Stoc 1A 152
Mavis Gro. Miln 5G 29
Mavis St. Roch 4C 40
Mawdsley Dri. M8 . . . . .3E 83
Mawdsley St. Bolt 6B 32
Maxton Ho. Farn 1G 63
Maxwell Av. Stoc 6C 140
Maxwell St. Bolt 1A 32
Maxwell St. Bury 2F 37
Max Woosnam Wlk.
 M14 . . . . .4E 109
Mayall St. Moss 2E 89

Mayall St. E. Oldh 2G 73
Mayan Av. Salf 3B 94 (3D 4)
May Av. Chea H 1D 160
May Av. Stoc 1D 138
Maybank St. Bolt 2H 45
Mayberth Av. M8 . . . . . .1C 82
Maybreck Clo. Bolt 2G 45
Mayburn Clo. Midd 4C 70
Maybury St. M18 . . . . . .1G 111
Maycroft. Stoc 3B 128
Maycroft Av. M20 . . . . .4G 125
May Dri. M19 . . . . .3B 126
Mayer St. Stoc 4C 140
Mayes Ct. M14 . . . . . . .2H 125
(off Sheringham Rd.)
Mayes Gdns.
 M4 . . . . .4H 95 (6G 7)
Mayes St. M4 . . . .3E 95 (3A 6)
(in two parts)
Mayfair. Salf 2G 81
Mayfair Av. Rad 3D 48
Mayfair Av. Salf 2B 92
Mayfair Av. Urm 5D 104
Mayfair Av. W'fld 2D 66
Mayfair Clo. Duk 5E 101
Mayfair Clo. Poy 2E 163
Mayfair Ct. M14 . . . . . .1G 125
Mayfair Ct. Timp 4B 134
(Park Rd.)
Mayfair Ct. Timp 5B 134
(Stockport Rd.)
Mayfair Cres. Fail 3H 85
Mayfair Dri. Irlam 5E 103
Mayfair Dri. Rytn 5B 56
Mayfair Dri. Sale 1G 133
Mayfair Gro. W'fld 2E 67
Mayfair Pk. M20 . . . . . .6D 124
Mayfair Rd. M22 . . . . . .1C 148
Mayfield. 2B 28
Mayfield. Bolt 6H 19
Mayfield. Rad 5E 49
Mayfield Av. Bolt 4D 46
Mayfield Av. Dent 2G 129
Mayfield Av. Farn 2E 63
Mayfield Av. Sale 5E 123
Mayfield Av. S'head 2C 74
Mayfield Av. Stoc 4H 127
Mayfield Av. Stret 6B 106
Mayfield Av. Swin 5C 78
Mayfield Av. Wors 6F 63
Mayfield Clo. Rams 1A 22
Mayfield Clo. Timp 5B 134
Mayfield Gro. M18 . . . . . .3H 111
Mayfield Gro. Stoc 4H 127
Mayfield Gro. Wilm 4B 166
Mayfield Ind. Est.
 Irlam 4G 103
Mayfield Mans. M16 . . . . .4C 108
Mayfield Rd. M16 . . . . . .4C 108
Mayfield Rd. Bram 3G 161
Mayfield Rd. Marp B 2F 143
Mayfield Rd. Oldh 6F 57
Mayfield Rd. Rams 1A 22
Mayfield Rd. Salf 2F 81
Mayfield Rd. Timp 5B 134
Mayfield St. Aud 2E 113
Mayfield St. Roch 2B 28
(in two parts)
Mayfield Ter. Roch 2B 28
Mayfield Ter. Sale 5A 122
Mayflower Av. Salf 5G 93
Mayford Rd. M19 . . . . . . .5C 110
Maygate. Oldh 1B 72
May Gro. M19 . . . . .1D 126
Mayhill Dri. Salf 1A 92
Mayhill Dri. Wors 3A 78
Mayhurst Av. M21 . . . . . .5B 124
Mayorlowe Av.
 Stoc 5C 128
Mayor's Rd. Alt 1G 145

Mayor St. Bolt 1H 45
(in two parts)
Mayor St. Bury 2A 36
Mayor St. Chad 2A 72
Mayo St. M12 . . .5H 95 (2G 11)
May Pl. L'boro 5C 16
May Pl. Roch 1G 41
(off Oldham Rd.)
Maypool Dri. Stoc 3H 127
May Rd. M16 . . . . .4B 108
May Rd. Chea H 1D 160
May Rd. Swin 5H 79
Maysmith M. Salf 5H 81
May St. M40 . . . . .6C 84
(in two parts)
May St. Bolt 6C 32
May St. Eccl 1E 91
May St. Heyw 5G 39
(in two parts)
May St. Oldh 5A 72
May St. Rad 4G 49
Mayton St. M11 . . . . .5C 96
Mayville Dri. M20 . . . . . . .4F 125
May Wlk. Part 6C 118
Maywood. Wilm 5B 166
Maywood Av. M20 . . . . . . .3F 137
Maze St. Bolt 2E 47
(in two parts)
Meachin Av. M21 . . . . . . .4A 124
Meade Clo. Urm 5E 105
Meade Gro. M13 . . . . .4B 110
Meade Hill Rd. P'wich 6A 68
Meade Mnr. M21 . . . . .2H 123
Meade, The. M21 . . . . .2H 123
Meade, The. Bolt 5A 46
Meadfoot Av. P'wich 6G 67
Meadfoot Rd. M18 . . . . . . .1F 111
Meadland Gro. Bolt 1B 32
Meadon Av. Swin 2H 79
Meadow Av. Hale 2B 146
Meadow Bank. M21 . . . . . . .2G 123
Meadowbank. Ash L 5E 87
Meadow Bank. Bred 6F 129
Meadow Bank. Holl 1F 117
Meadow Bank. Stoc 1D 138
Meadow Bank. Timp 4A 134
Meadowbank Clo. Fail 5G 85
Meadowbank Rd. Bolt 5F 45
Meadowbrook Clo.
 Bury 1G 37
Meadowbrook Clo. Los 4A 44
Meadowbrook Way.
 Chea H 1D 150
Meadow Brow. Ald E 4G 167
Meadowburn Nook.
 Eccl 1D 90
Meadow Clo. Dent 2G 129
Meadow Clo. Hale 2B 146
Meadow Clo. Heyw 3E 39
Meadow Clo. H Lane 5D 154
Meadow Clo. L Lev 5B 48
Meadow Clo. Moss 6G 75
Meadow Clo. Stret 6E 107
Meadow Clo. Wilm 5B 166
Meadow Clo. Woodl 4G 129
Meadow Cotts. Whitw 2H 15
Meadow Ct. M21 . . . . .1F 123
Meadow Ct. Hale 2C 146
Meadow Ct. Salf 2B 92
Meadow Cft. Haz G 2E 153
Meadowcroft. Mot 3C 116
Meadowcroft. Rad 2F 49
Meadow Cft. W'fld 3A 66
Meadowcroft La. Oldh 6F 57
Meadowcroft La. Roch 5B 26
Meadowfield. Los 6A 30
Meadowfield Clo. Had 4H 117
Meadowfield Clo. Roch 2H 41
Meadowfield Ct. Hyde 3B 114

Meadowfield Dri. Wors 5D 76
Meadow Fold. Upperm 1G 61
Meadowgate. Salf 3C 92
Meadowgate. Urm 6F 105
Meadowgate. Wors 3H 77
Meadowgate Rd. Salf 2B 92
Mdw. Head Av. Whitw 3C 14
Mdw. Head La. Roch 1E 25
Meadow Ind. Est.
 Stoc 6H 127
Meadow La. Bolt 6A 34
Meadow La. Dent 1G 129
Meadow La. Dis 1H 165
Meadow La. Duk 5B 100
Meadow La. Oldh 1C 86
Meadow La. Wors 6H 77
Meadow Ri. Shaw 4E 43
Meadow Rd. Midd 3G 69
Meadow Rd.
 Salf 2A 94 (1B 4)
Meadow Rd. Urm 6F 105
Meadows Clo. Haz G 2E 153
Meadowside. Bram 3E 151
Meadowside. Miln 2G 43
Meadowside Av. M22 . . . . .1B 148
Meadowside Av. Bolt 5E 33
(in two parts)
Meadowside Av. Irlam 5E 103
Meadowside Av. Wors 5G 63
Meadowside Clo. Rad 2G 49
Meadowside Gro.
 Wors 6G 63
Meadows La. Bolt 2H 33
Meadows Rd. Chea H 5B 150
Meadows Rd. H Grn 4F 149
Meadows Rd. Sale 3C 122
Meadows Rd. Stoc 3E 127
(in two parts)
Meadows, The. Cad 3B 118
Meadows, The. G'ton 3D 74
Meadows, The. Had 3H 117
Meadows, The. Midd 3B 70
Meadows, The. P'wich 5F 67
Meadows, The. Rad 2E 49
Meadows, The.
 Upperm 2F 61
Meadows, The. W'fld 2A 66
Meadows, The. Whitw 4G 15
Meadow St. Hyde 6C 114
Meadow St. Stoc 6C 140
Meadow, The. Bolt 6A 30
Meadow Vw. Roch 2C 26
Meadow Wlk. Bred 6F 129
Meadow Wlk. Farn 1C 62
Meadow Wlk. L'boro 4D 16
Meadow Wlk. Part 6C 118
Meadow Way. M40 . . . . . .2A 84
Meadow Way. Hale 2E 85
Meadow Way. S'seat 1C 22
Meadow Way. T'ton 5G 21
Meadow Way. Wilm 5B 166
Meadscroft Dri. Ald E 4F 167
Meads Gro. Farn 1A 62
Meads, The. Chad 3G 71
Mead, The. Salf 3D 92
Meadway. Bram 2G 161
Meadway. Bury 1D 50
Meadway. Chad 1E 85
Meadway. Dent 1F 129
Meadway. Duk 6C 100
Meadway. Farn 6H 47
Meadway. H Lane 5D 154
Meadway. Poy 2B 162
Meadway. Rams 4A 12
Meadway. Roch 1C 40
Meadway. Sale 6G 121
Meadway. Stal 1A 116
Meadway Clo. Sale 1G 133
Meadway Ct. Bram 2G 161
Meadway Rd. Chea H 2D 150
Mealhouse Brow.
 Stoc 2H 139

Mealhouse La. *Bolt* 6B **32**
Meal St. *Stoc* 6G **127**
Meanwood Brow. Roch . . .3F **27**
  (off Hooley Moor Rd.)
Meanwood Fold. *Roch* 3F **27**
Meddings Clo. *Ald E* 6F **167**
Medina Clo. *Chea H* 1D **150**
Medley St. *Roch* 2H **27**
Medlock Clo. *Farn* 1D **62**
Medlock Ct. *Oldh* 4A **72**
Medlock Dri. *Oldh* 2E **87**
Medlock Leisure Cen. . . .**3B 98**
Medlock Rd. *Fail* 1H **97**
Medlock St.
  M15 . . . . . .6D **94** (3G **9**)
Medlock St. *Droy* 3A **98**
Medlock St. *Oldh* 2E **73**
Medlock Vale. **1A 98**
Medlock Way. *Lees* 3A **74**
Medlock Way. *W'fld* 1G **67**
Medway Clo. *Oldh* 6A **72**
Medway Clo. *Salf* 2D **92**
Medway Clo. *Wilm* 5H **159**
Medway Cres. *Alt* 5E **133**
Medway Dri. *Kear* 4B **64**
Medway Rd. *Oldh* 6A **72**
Medway Rd. *Shaw* 5E **43**
Medway Rd. *Wors* 3D **76**
Medway, The. *Heyw* 2D **38**
Medway Wlk.
  M40 . . . . . .2H **95** (1G **7**)
Meech St. *M11* 5E **97**
Meek St. *Rytn* 5E **57**
Meerbrook Rd. *Stoc* 3C **138**
Mee's Sq. *Eccl* 5E **91**
Megabowl Bowling Alley.
  . . . . .1F **51**
Megna Clo. *Oldh* 2B **72**
Melandra Castle. **4F 117**
  (Roman Remains)
Melandra Castle Rd.
  Glos 6F **117**
Melandra Cres. *Hyde* 5A **116**
Melandra Rd. *Glos* 4F **117**
Melanie Dri. *Stoc* 1H **127**
Melba St. *Open* 5G **97**
Melbecks Wlk. *M23* 1F **135**
Melbourne Av. *Chad* 2G **71**
Melbourne Av. *Man A* . , .5G **147**
Melbourne Av. *Stret* 5D **106**
Melbourne Clo. *Roch* 3G **41**
Melbourne M. *Salf* 6A **82**
Melbourne Rd. *Bolt* 2F **45**
Melbourne Rd. *Bram* 1G **161**
Melbourne Rd. *Roch* 3G **41**
Melbourne St. *M9* 3G **83**
Melbourne St.
  M15 . . . . .6C **94** (3E **9**)
Melbourne St. *Chad* 2H **71**
Melbourne St. *Dent* 5E **113**
Melbourne St. *Salf* 6H **81**
Melbourne St. *Stal* 3E **101**
Melbourne St. *Stoc* 1H **127**
Melbourne St. *Swin* 3H **79**
Melbourne St. N.
  Ash L 1A **100**
Melbourne St. S.
  Ash L 2A **100**
Melbury Av. *M20* 5H **125**
Melbury Rd. *Chea H* 1D **160**
Meldon Rd. *M13* 5A **110**
Meldreth Dri. *M12* 3B **110**
Meldrum St. *Oldh* 5D **72**
Melford Av. *M40* 2E **85**
Melford Gro. *Oldh* 3H **73**
Melford Ho. Bolt 4A **32**
  (off Nottingham Dri.)
Melford Rd. *Haz G* 4F **153**
Melfort Av. *Stret* 6E **107**
Moliden Cres. *M22* 3C **148**
Meliden Cres. *Bolt* 4F **31**
Melksham Clo. *Salf* 3H **93**

Mellalieu St. *Heyw* 2E **39**
Mellalieu St. *Midd* 6G **53**
Mellalieu St. *Rytn* 5C **56**
Melland Av. *M21* 4A **124**
Melland Rd. *M18* 4E **111**
Melland Sports Cen. **4E 111**
Meller Rd. *M13* 5B **110**
Melling Av. *Chad* 6E **55**
Melling Av. *Stoc* 3G **127**
Melling Rd. *Oldh* 3G **73**
Melling St. *M12* 3C **110**
Mellington Av. *M20* 3F **137**
Mellodew Drl. *Oldh* 4H **57**
Mellor. **5H 143**
Mellor Brow. *Heyw* 3E **39**
Mellor Clo. *Ash L* 2C **100**
Mellor Ct. *Stoc* 4E **141**
Mellor Dri. *Bury* 6B **36**
Mellor Dri. *Wors* 2E **77**
Mellor Gro. *Bolt* 4F **31**
  (in two parts)
Mellor Ho. Rytn 3C **56**
  (off Westmorland Wlk.)
Mellor Rd. *Ash L* 1D **100**
  (in three parts)
Mellor Rd. *Chea H* 4D **150**
Mellors Rd. *Traf P* 6B **92**
Mellor St. *M12* 2F **11**
Mellor St. *M40* . . .2H **95** (2G **7**)
Mellor St. *Droy* 4H **97**
Mellor St. *Eccl* 4F **91**
Mellor St. *Fail* 5D **84**
Mellor St. *Lees* 3A **74**
Mellor St. *P'wich* 5D **66**
Mellor St. *Rad* 5H **49**
  (in two parts)
Mellor St. *Roch* 3F **27**
Mellor St. *Rytn* 2B **56**
Mellor St. *Stret* 3E **107**
Mellor Way. *Chad* 5H **71**
Mellowstone Dri. *M21* . . .1D **124**
Melloy Pl. *M8* 1E **95**
Molmerby Ct. *Salf* 4F **93**
Melon Pl. *Salf* 3H **93**
Melrose. Roch 3G **27**
  (off Spotland Rd.)
Melrose Apartments.
  M14 . . . . .3G **109**
  (off Hathersage Rd.)
Melrose Av. *M20* 6G **125**
Melrose Av. *Bolt* 4E **31**
Melrose Av. *Bury* 2A **36**
Melrose Av. *Eccl* 1C **90**
Melrose Av. *Heyw* 2E **39**
Melrose Av. *L'boro* 2E **17**
Melrose Av. *Sale* 5B **122**
Melrose Av. *Stoc* 4B **138**
Melrose Clo. *W'fld* 5D **50**
Melrose Ct. *Chad* 5G **71**
Melrose Cres. *Hale* 4B **146**
Melrose Cres. *Poy* 2B **164**
Melrose Cres. *Stoc* 1F **151**
  (in two parts)
Melrose Gdns. *Rad* 2E **49**
Melrose Rd. *L Lev* 4H **47**
Melrose Rd. *Rad* 2E **49**
Melrose St. *M40* 6C **84**
Melrose St. *Bury* 1B **22**
Melrose St. *Oldh* 6F **57**
Melrose St. *Roch* 4F **27**
Melsomby Rd. *M23* 1G **135**
Meltham Av. *M20* 3E **125**
Meltham Clo. *Stoc* 2A **138**
Meltham Pl. Bolt 3H **45**
  (off Bk. Willows La.)
Meltham Rd. *Stoc* 2A **138**
Melton Av. *Dent* 4A **112**
Melton Av. *Urm* 4H **103**
Melton Clo. *Heyw* 4D **38**
Melton Clo. *Wors* 1E **77**
Melton Dri. *Bury* 2E **51**
Melton Rd. *M8* 2A **82**

Melton Row. Rad 3F **49**
  (off Melton St.)
Melton St. *M9* 2H **83**
Melton St. *Heyw* 4D **38**
Melton St. *Rad* 3F **49**
Melton St. *Stoc* 5H **127**
Melton Wlk. Rad 3F **49**
  (off Melton St.)
Melton Way. Rad 3F **49**
  (off Melton St.)
Melverley Rd. *M9* 4C **68**
Melville Clo. *M11* 6G **97**
Melville Rd. *Cad* 4A **118**
Melville Rd. *Kear* 3H **63**
Melville Rd. *Stret* 4B **106**
Melville St. *Ash L* 2H **99**
Melville St. *Bolt* 4C **46**
Melville St. *Lees* 4A **74**
Melville St. *Roch* 4D **40**
Melville St. *Salf* . . .3B **94** (4D **4**)
Melvin Av. *M22* 1C **148**
Melyncourt Dri. *Hyde* 4A **116**
Memorial Rd. *Wors* 1F **77**
Menai Gro. *Chea* 5C **138**
Menai Rd. *Stoc* 5G **139**
Menai St. *Bolt* 3F **45**
M.E.N. Arena. . . .2D **94** (2H **5**)
  (Manchester Evening
    News Arena)
Mendip Av. *M22* 1D **148**
Mendip Clo. *Bolt* 6A **34**
Mendip Clo. *Chad* 4G **71**
Mendip Clo. *H Grn* 6F **149**
Mendip Clo. *Rytn* 4A **56**
Mendip Clo. *Stoc* 6G **127**
Mendip Ct. *Stoc* 6G **127**
Mendip Cres. *Bury* 2G **35**
Mendip Dri. *Bolt* 1A **48**
Mendip Dri. *Miln* 5G **29**
Mendip Rd. *Oldh* 6B **72**
Mendips Clo. *Shaw* 5D **42**
Menston Av. *M40* 2E **85**
Montmoro Rd. *Roch* 4D **28**
Mentone Cres. *M22* 1C **148**
Mentone Rd. *Stoc* 6D **126**
Mentor St. *M13* 4B **110**
Mercantile St. *M21* 6H **107**
Mercer La. *Roch* 3A **26**
Mercer Rd. *M18* 2F **111**
Mercer St. *M19* 6D **110**
Mercer St. *Droy* 3B **98**
Merchants Quay. *Salf* 1F **107**
Merchants Quay Ct.
  Eccl 2E **91**
Mercian Mall. *Ash L* 2H **99**
Mercian Way. *Stoc* 4F **139**
Mercia St. *Bolt* 2G **45**
Mercury Bus. Pk.
  Urm 1H **105**
Mercury Way. *Urm* 2H **105**
Mere Av. *Droy* 5G **97**
Mere Av. *Midd* 3A **70**
Mere Av. *Salf* 3E **93**
Mere Av. *Stoc* 6E **139**
Merebank Clo. *Roch* 3A **26**
Mere Bank Clo. *Wors* 6E **63**
Mere Clo. *Dent* 5B **112**
Mere Clo. *Sale* 6F **123**
Mere Clo. *Uns* 2E **51**
Mereclough av. *Wors* 2H **77**
Meredew Av. *Swin* 5E **79**
Meredith Ct.
  M15 . . . . . .1E **109** (6A **10**)
  (off Epsley Clo.)
Meredith St. *M14* 2H **125**
Meredith St. *Bolt* 4B **46**
Mere Dri. *M20* 5F **125**
Mere Dri. *Swin* 1G **79**
Merefield av. *Roch* 6G **27**
Merefield Rd. *Timp* 6C **134**
Merefield St. *Roch* 6G **27**

Merefield Ter. *Roch* 6G **27**
Mere Fold. *Wors* 6D **62**
Mere Gdns. *Bolt* 5A **32**
Merehall Clo. *Bolt* 5A **32**
Merehall Dri. *Bolt* 4A **32**
Merehall St. *Bolt* 4H **31**
Mere Ho. *Stoc* 2A **138**
Mereland Av. *M20* 5G **125**
Mere La. *Roch* 6H **27**
Meremanor. *Wors* 2H **77**
Merepool Clo. *Marp* 4B **142**
Mere Side. *Stal* 1D **100**
  (in four parts)
Mereside Clo. *Chea H* 1B **150**
Mereside Gro. *Wors* 6G **63**
Mereside Wlk.
  M15 . . . . . .1B **108** (6D **8**)
Mere St. *Roch* 5H **27**
  (in three parts)
Mere, The. *Ash L* 5A **88**
Mere, The. *Chea H* 1B **150**
Mere Wlk. *Bolt* 5A **32**
Merewood Av. *M22* 5B **136**
Meriden Clo. *Rad* 1F **49**
Meriden Gro. *Los* 1B **44**
Meridian Cen. *Oldh* 3C **72**
Meridian Pl. *M20* 5E **125**
Merinall Clo. *Roch* 4C **28**
Meriton Rd. *Hand* 3G **159**
Meriton Wlk. *M18* 3D **110**
Merlewood. *Rams* 2B **12**
Merlewood Av. *M19* 2E **127**
Merlewood Av. *Dent* 4B **98**
Merlewood Av. *Upperm* . . .1F **61**
Merlewood Dri. *Swin* 5C **78**
Merlin Clo. *L'boro* 1G **29**
Merlin Clo. *Oldh* 3E **87**
  (in two parts)
Merlin Clo. *Stoc* 5G **141**
Merlin Dri. *Swin* 1H **79**
Merlin Gro. *Bolt* 4F **31**
  (in two parts)
Merlin Rd. *Irlam* 3E **103**
Merlin Rd. *Miln* 5F **29**
Merlyn Av. *M20* 5G **125**
Merlyn Av. *Dent* 5E **113**
Merlyn Av. *Sale* 3C **122**
Merlyn Ct. *M20* 5G **125**
Merrick Av. *M22* 1C **148**
Merrick St. *Heyw* 4G **39**
Merridale, The. *Hale* 5A **146**
Merridge Wlk. *M8* 5B **82**
Merrill St. *M4* 4H **95** (5H **7**)
Merriman Hall. *Roch* 1B **28**
Merriman St. *M16* 3C **108**
Merrion St. *Farn* 5G **47**
Merrow Wlk.
  M1 . . . . .6F **95** (3C **10**)
  (off Grosvenor St.)
Merrybent Clo. *Stoc* 6D **140**
Merrybower Rd. *Salf* 3A **82**
Merrydale Av. *Eccl* 1G **91**
Merseybank Av. *M21* 5B **124**
Mersey Bank Lodge.
  Had 2H **117**
Mersey Bank Rd. *Had* 3H **117**
Mersey Clo. *W'fld* 6F **51**
Mersey Cres. *M20* 6B **124**
Mersey Dri. *Part* 5E **119**
Mersey Dri. *W'fld* 6F **51**
Mersey Ho. *Stoc* 4C **138**
Mersey Ind. Est. *Stoc* 2A **138**
Mersey Meadows.
  M20 . . . . .6D **124**
Mersey Rd. *M20* 6D **124**
Mersey Rd. *Sale* 3B **122**
Mersey Rd. *Stoc* 1B **138**
  (in two parts)
Mersey Rd. Ind. Est.
  Fail 2H **85**
Mersey Rd. N. *Fail* 2G **85**
Mersey Sq. *Stoc* 2G **139**

Mersey Sq. W'fld 6F 51
Mersey St. Open 5G 97
(in two parts)
Mersey St. Stoc 1A 140
Mersey Valley Vis. Cen.
..............4F 123
Mersey Valley Vis. Cen.
Nature Reserve. .3F 123
Mersey Vw. Urm 1A 120
Merseyway. Stoc ...2G 139
Merston Dri. M20 ....4G 137
Mersy Ct. Sale 4E 123
Mersy St. Stoc 2H 139
Merton Av. Bred 5G 129
Merton Av. Haz G ..5F 153
Merton Av. Oldh 6B 72
Merton Clo. Bolt 2G 45
Merton Dri. Droy 4G 97
Merton Gro. Chad ...6D 70
Merton Gro. Timp ...5B 134
Merton Rd. Poy 3B 162
Merton Rd. P'wich ..4G 67
Merton Rd. Sale 4A 123
Merton Rd. Stoc 4D 138
Merton St. Bury 2B 36
Merton Wlk. M9 .....4G 83
(off Nethervale Dri.)
Merville Av. M40 ....2H 83
Mervyn Rd. Salf 5E 81
Merwell Rd. Urm 6A 104
Merwood Av. H Grn ..5H 149
Merwood Gro. M14 ..3A 110
Meshaw Clo. M23 ...1E 135
Mesnefield Rd. Salf ..3E 81
Mesne Lea Gro. Wors ..3G 77
Mesne Lea Rd. Wors ..3G 77
Metcalfe Ct. L Hul ...5B 62
Metcalfe St. Fir 4D 28
Metcalf M. Upperm ..1F 61
Metcalf Ter. A'wth ...4D 34
Metfield Pl. Bolt 5G 31
Metfield Wlk. M40 ...1D 84
Methuen St. M12 ....4D 110
Methwold St. Bolt 3G 45
Metroplex Bus. Pk. Salf ..5E 93
Metropolitan Ho. Oldh ...3D 72
Mets Art Cen. 3C 36
(off Market St.)
Mevagissey Wlk. Oldh ...1G 73
Mews, The. M40 ....2B 96
Mews, The. Bolt 5F 31
Mews, The. Gat 6F 137
Mews, The. P'wich ..6F 67
Mews, The. Sale 6C 122
Mews, The. W'fld 1B 66
Mews, The. Wors ...5G 77
Meyer St. Stoc 5H 139
Meyrick Rd. Salf 2G 93
Miall St. Roch 5H 27
Micawber Rd. Poy ...5E 163
Michael Ct. M19 ....1H 137
Michaels Hey Pde.
M23 ....3C 134
Michael St. Midd 1H 69
Michael Wife La. Rams ..2B 12
(in two parts)
Michigan Av. Salf ...5F 93
Mickleby Wlk.
M40 ......2H 95 (2G 7)
Micklehurst. 3F 89
Micklehurst Av. M20 ..5C 124
Micklehurst Grn. Stoc ..6E 141
Micklehurst Rd. Moss ..3F 89
Midbrook Wlk. M22 ..4H 147
Middlebourne St. Salf ..3E 93
Middlebrook Dri. Los ..1A 44
Middle Calderbrook.
L'boro 6G 17
Middlefell St. Farn ...5F 47
Middlefield. Oldh 3E 87
Middle Fld. Roch 2A 26
Middlefields. Chea H ..1D 150

Middlegate. M40 ....6D 70
Middle Ga. Oldh 1C 86
Middle Grn. Ash L ...1A 100
Middleham St. M14 ..5E 109
Middle Healey. 5B 30
Middle Hill. Roch 5F 15
Middle Hillgate. Stoc ..3H 139
Middle Holly Gro. Dig ..4C 60
Middlesex Dri. Bury ..5D 36
Middlesex Rd. M9 ...1F 83
Middlesex Rd. Stoc ..3B 128
Middlesex Wlk. Oldh ..3B 72
Middlestone Dri. M9 ..4F 83
Middle St. Whitw ...4G 15
Middleton. 1H 69
Middleton Av. Fail ...4F 85
Middleton Cen. Ind. Est.
Midd 1H 69
Middleton Clo. Rad ...6F 35
Middleton Dri. Bury ..4D 50
Middleton Gdns. Midd ..1H 69
(in two parts)
Middleton Junction. ..3D 70
Middleton Leisure Cen.
..........1A 70
Middleton Old Rd. M9 ..6F 69
Middleton Rd.
M8 & Midd ...2B 82
(in two parts)
Middleton Rd.
Chad & Oldh ...6E 55
(in two parts)
Middleton Rd. Heyw ..5G 39
Middleton Rd. Rytn ..4H 55
Middleton Rd. Stoc ..5H 111
Middleton Shop. Cen.
Midd 1H 69
Middleton St Leonard's Parish
Church. 6A 54
Middleton Vw. Midd ..1B 70
Middleton Way. Midd ..1H 69
Middleway. G'ton 4D 97
Middlewich Wlk. M18 ..2E 111
Middlewood. 2A 164
Middlewood Ct. Chad ..1G 71
Middlewood Dri. Stoc ..2C 138
Middlewood Grn. Chad ..1G 71
Middle Wood La. Roch ..3C 16
Middlewood Rd.
H Lane 6B 154
Middlewood Rd. Poy ..6H 153
Middlewood St.
Salf 4A 94 (6B 4)
Middlewood Vw.
H Lane 5B 154
Middlewood Wlk. M9 ..4F 83
Midford Av. Eccl 3D 90
Midford Dri. Bolt 4C 18
Midford Wlk. M8 ....5C 82
Midge Hall Dri. Roch ..5C 26
Midgley Av. M18 ....1G 111
Midgley Cres. Ash L ..1C 100
Midgley Dri. Roch ...3A 42
Midgley St. Swin 5D 78
Midgrove. Del 3H 59
Midgrove La. Del 4H 59
Midhurst Av. M40 ...1D 96
Midhurst Clo. Bolt ...4A 32
Midhurst Clo. Chea H ..5B 150
Midhurst St. Roch ...6H 27
Midhurst Way. Chad ..3H 71
Midland Cotts. Haz G ..4A 154
Midland Rd. Bram ...1G 151
Midland Rd. Stoc ...5H 111
Midland St.
M12 ....6H 95 (3H 11)
Midland Ter. Hale ...3F 145
(off Bath Pl.)
Midland Wlk. Bram ..2G 151
(in two parts)
Midlothian St. M11 ..3D 96

Midmoor Wlk. M9 ...6G 69
(off Leconfield Dri.)
Mid Reddish. 1H 127
Midville Rd. M11 ....2E 97
Midway. 5D 162
Midway. Chea H 2D 160
Midway St. M12 ....5C 110
Midwood Hall. Salf ...2F 93
(off Sutton Dwellings)
Milan St. Salf 5A 82
Milbourne Rd. Bury ..5F 23
Milburn Av. M23 ....1H 135
Milburn Dri. Bolt 5H 33
Milbury Dri. L'boro ..1G 29
Milden Clo. M20 ....5G 125
Mildred Av. G'ton ...4D 74
Mildred Av. P'wich ..2G 81
Mildred Av. Rytn 5C 56
Mildred St. Salf 6G 81
Mile End. 5B 140
Mile End La. Stoc ...6B 140
Mile La. Bury 4F 35
Miles Platting. 2A 96
Miles Platting Swimming Pool
& Health Suite.
.........2H 95 (1H 7)
Miles St. M12 ......6C 96
Miles St. Bolt 3H 31
Miles St. Farn 1E 63
Miles St. Hyde 5D 114
Miles St. Oldh 1F 73
Milford Av. Oldh 1A 86
Milford Brow. Lees ..2A 74
Milford Cres. L'boro ..3F 17
Milford Dri. M19 ....2D 126
Milford Gro. Stoc ...4C 140
Milford Rd. Bolt 4A 46
Milford Rd. Har 1H 33
Milford St. M9 ......5D 68
Milford St. Roch 2H 27
Milford St. Salf 4E 93
Milkstone Pl. Roch ..5H 27
Milkstone Rd. Roch ..5H 27
(in two parts)
Milk St. M2 ....4E 95 (5A 6)
Milk St. Hyde 5B 114
Milk St. Oldh 2G 73
Milk St. Rams 4D 12
Milk St. Roch 5H 27
Milkwood Gro. M18 ..3F 111
Millais St. M40 .....3A 84
Millard St. Chad 2G 71
Millard Wlk. M18 ....3F 111
Mill Bank. Rad 5H 49
Millbank Ct. Heyw ...3D 38
Millbank St. M1 ..4G 95 (6E 7)
Millbank St. Heyw ...3D 38
Millbeck Ct. Midd ...5F 53
Millbeck Gro. Bolt ...3A 46
Millbeck Rd. Midd ...5F 53
Millbeck St.
M15 ....1E 109 (5A 10)
Millbrae Gdns. Shaw ..6D 42
Millbrook. 1H 101
Millbrook. Holl 1F 117
Millbrook Av. Dent ..6D 112
Millbrook Bank. Roch ..2H 25
Millbrook Clo. Shaw ..1H 57
Millbrook Fold. Haz G ..5F 153
Millbrook Gro. Wilm ..6H 159
Millbrook Ho. Farn ..1G 63
Mill Brook Ind. Est.
M23 ....5E 135
Millbrook Rd. M23 ..2G 147
Millbrook St. Stoc ..3H 139
Millbrook Towers.
Stoc 3H 139
Mill Brow. 4C 76
(Manchester)
Mill Brow. 3H 143
(Stockport)
Mill Brow. M9 .....1E 89

Mill Brow. Ash L 2G 87
Mill Brow. Chad 5G 55
Mill Brow. Marp B ...3H 143
Mill Brow. Wors 5H 77
Mill Brow Rd. Marp B ..3H 143
Millbrow Ter. Oldh ..5G 55
Mill Ct. Urm 5G 105
Millcrest Clo. Wors ..6B 76
Mill Cft. Bolt 5H 31
Millcroft. Shaw 1G 57
Mill Cft. Clo. Roch ..1G 25
Millcroft La. Del 1H 59
(in two parts)
Milldale Clo. Los 6A 30
Millennium Ct. Bolt ..4F 45
Millennium Ho. Dent ..5C 112
Millennium Ho. Shaw ..2F 57
Miller Mdw. Clo. Shaw ..5G 43
Miller Rd. Oldh 6C 72
Millers Brook Clo.
Heyw 2F 39
Millers Clo. Sale ...6G 123
Miller's Ct. Salf 3A 92
Millers St. Eccl 3E 91
Miller St. M4 ..3E 95 (3A 6)
Miller St. Ash L 1H 99
Miller St. Bolt 1A 32
Miller St. Bury 1C 22
Miller St. Heyw 3F 39
(in two parts)
Miller St. Rad 1F 49
Millers Wharf. Stal ..3F 101
Millett St. Bury 3B 36
Millett St. Rams 2F 13
Millett Ter. Bury 4C 24
Millfield Ct. Hale ...3G 145
Millfield Dri. Wors ..5D 76
Millfield Gro. Roch ..5B 28
Millfield Rd. Bolt 6A 34
Millfield Wlk. M40 ...1C 84
Millfold. Whitw 3H 15
Mill Fold Gdns. L'boro ..5D 16
Mill Fold Rd. Midd ..1H 69
Millford Av. Urm 5A 104
(in two parts)
Millford Gdns. Urm ..5A 104
Millgate. Del 3H 59
Millgate. Eger 1B 18
Mill Ga. Oldh 6B 72
Millgate. Roch 1B 28
Millgate. Stoc 1H 139
Mill Ga. Cen. Bury ..3D 36
Millgate Cen. Del ...3H 59
Millgate La. M20 ....3E 137
(Parrs Wood Rd.)
Millgate La. M20 ....2F 137
(Wilmslow Rd.)
Millgate Ter. Whitw ..1H 15
Mill Grn. St.
M12 ....5H 95 (2G 11)
Millhalf Clo.
M15 ....2C 108 (6E 9)
Millhead Av. M40 ...3A 96
Mill Hill. 5C 32
Mill Hill. L Hul 3A 62
Mill Hill Av. Poy 6D 152
Mill Hill Gro. Mot ...5B 116
Mill Hill Hollow. Poy ..6D 152
Mill Hill St. Bolt 5C 32
Mill Hill Way. Mot ..5B 116
Millhouse Av. M23 ..1G 147
Mill Ho. Clo. Roch ..5B 16
Millhouse St. Rams ..1G 13
Milliner Ct. Stoc 4D 140
Milling St. M1 ..5D 94 (2H 9)
Millington Rd. Traf P ..6C 92
Millington Wlk. M15 ..5D 8
Mill La. M22 ......2C 136
(in two parts)
Mill La. Ash 3D 156

Mill La. *Ash L* 3H 99
Mill La. *Bury* 1H 35
Mill La. *Chad* 5A 72
Mill La. *Chea* 5G 137
(in two parts)
Mill La. *Chea H* 2D 150
Mill La. *Dent & Hyde* ..6H 113
Mill La. *Dob* 6F 59
Mill La. *Fail* 4C 64
Mill La. *Haz G* 5F 153
Mill La. *Moss* 1E 89
Mill La. *Rytn* 3A 56
Mill La. *Stoc* 6H 111
Mill La. *Woodl* 4G 129
(off Hyde Rd)
Mill La. *Woodl* 4G 141
(Goyt Valley)
Mill La. *Woodl* 3G 129
(Lambeth Gro., in two parts)
Millom Av. *M23* 2H 135
Millom Clo. *Roch* 2C 28
Millom Ct. *Timp* 5D 134
Millom Dri. *Bury* 5E 51
Millom Pl. *Gat* 2F 149
Millow St. *M4* 2E 95 (2A 6)
Millpool Wlk. *M9* 3F 83
(off Alderside Rd.)
Milrise. *Oldh* 2C 72
Mill Rd. *Bury* 3F 23
Mill Rd. *Wilm* 2E 167
Mills Farm Clo. *Oldh* ...2E 87
Mills Hill. 1E 71
Mills Hill Rd. *Midd* 6D 54
Mills St. *Heyw* 3D 38
Mills St. *Whitw* 4H 15
Millstone Clo. *Poy* 2F 163
Millstone Rd. *Bolt* 4D 30
Millstream La. *M40* 1G 97
Mill St. *M11* 5C 96
(in two parts)
Mill St. *Alt* 6G 133
Mill St. *Bolt* 6C 32
Mill St. *Brom X* 3D 18
Mill St. *Fail* 4D 84
Mill St. *Farn* 1E 63
Mill St. *Haz G* 2D 152
Mill St. *Hyde* 2C 114
Mill St. *L'boro* 6D 16
Mill St. *Moss* 2F 89
Mill St. *Rad* 5G 49
(in two parts)
Mill St. *Rams* 5C 12
Mill St. *Rytn* 3B 56
Mill St. *Salf* 1G 93
Mill St. *Stal* 4G 101
Mill St. *T'ton* 4H 21
Mill St. *Upperm* 1F 61
Mill St. *Wilm* 2E 167
Mill St. *Woodl* 4G 129
(in two parts)
Mill St. *Wors* 5C 76
Mill St. Ind. Est.
Bolt 6C 32
Milltown Clo. *Rad* 5H 49
Milltown St. *Rad* 5H 49
Millview. *Dig* 3C 60
Millwall Clo. *M18* 2F 111
Millway. *Haleb* 6C 146
Millway Wlk. *M40* 6C 84
Millwood Clo. *Chea H* ..5A 150
Millwood Ct. *Bury* 1D 50
Millwood Ter. *Hyde* 5B 114
Millwood Vw. *Stal* 3F 101
Millwright St. *M40* 6B 84
Mill Yd. *Bury* 2C 36
Milne Clo. *M12* 1C 110
Milner Av. *B'hth* 4D 132
Milner Av. *Bury* 6F 23
Milner St. *M16* 3B 108
Milner St. *Rad* 4E 49
Milner St. *Swin* 3F 79
Milner St. *Whitw* 1C 14

Milne St. *Chad* 6A 56
(Burnley La.)
Milne St. *Chad* 2H 71
(Middleton Rd.)
Milne St. *Higg* 5E 57
Milne St. *Oldh* 4A 72
Milne St. *Roch* 3C 40
Milne St. *Shaw* 1F 57
Milngate Clo. *Roch* 2A 42
Milnholme. *Bolt* 2F 31
Milnrow. 6F 29
Milnrow Clo.
M13 ....6F 95 (3D 10)
Milnrow Rd. *L'boro* 1F 29
Milnrow Rd. *Roch* 4A 28
Milnrow Rd. *Shaw* 6F 43
Milnthorpe Rd. *Bolt* ...5G 33
Milnthorpe St. *Salf* ...6F 81
Milnthorpe Way.
M12 ....1A 110
Milo Ind. Pk. *Droy* 2C 98
Milo St. *M9* 6F 69
Milsom Av. *Bolt* 4G 45
Milstead Wlk. *M40* 6A 84
Milton Av. *Bolt* 4F 45
Milton Av. *Drny* 4A 98
Milton Av. *Irlam* 3C 118
Milton Av. *L Lev* 3B 48
Milton Av. *Mill* 1H 101
Milton Av. *Salf* 3D 92
Milton Clo. *Duk* 6F 101
(in two parts)
Milton Clo. *Marp* 1D 154
Milton Clo. *Stret* 4E 107
Milton Ct. *M19* 5A 126
Milton Ct. *Bram* 1G 161
Milton Ct. *Salf* 2A 82
Milton Cres. *Chea* 6G 137
Milton Cres. *Farn* 3D 62
Milton Dri. *Chad* 3G 71
Milton Dri. *Poy* 3D 162
Milton Dri. *Sale* 3B 122
Milton Dri. *Timp* 2A 134
Milton Gro. *M16* 5A 108
Milton Gro. *Sale* 3A 122
Milton Mt. *M18* 3F 111
Milton Pl. *Salf* 2H 93
Milton Rd. *Aud* 4D 98
Milton Rd. *Bram* 6G 151
Milton Rd. *P'wich* 4G 67
Milton Rd. *Rad* 3D 48
Milton Rd. *Stret* 4E 107
Milton Rd. *Swin* 2D 78
Milton St. *Dent* 3E 113
Milton St. *Eccl* 3F 91
Milton St. *Hyde* 3B 114
Milton St. *Midd* 6H 53
Milton St. *Moss* 1E 89
Milton St. *Oldh* 4E 73
Milton St. *Rams* 3D 12
Milton St. *Roch* 3H 27
Milton St. *Rytn* 2C 56
Milton St. *Salf* 1C 94
Milton Vw. *Moss* 1E 89
Milverton Av. *Hyde* 5G 115
Milverton Clo. *Los* 2B 44
Milverton Dri. *Bram* ...2D 160
Milverton Rd. *M14* 3H 109
Milverton Wlk. *Hyde* ...5G 115
Milwain Dri. *Stoc* 3E 127
Milwain Rd. *M19* 1B 126
Milwain Rd. *Stret* 6C 106
Mimosa Dri. *Swin* 1F 79
Mincing St. *M4* ..2E 95 (2B 6)
Minden Clo. *M20* 5G 125
Minden Clo. *Bury* 3H 35
Minden Pde. *Bury* 3D 36
Minden St. *Salf* 5C 80
Minehead Av. *M20* 2D 124
Minchcod Av. *Urm* 1D 120
Minerva Rd. *Ash L* 3A 100
Minerva Rd. *Farn* 6B 46

Minerva Ter. *L'boro* ...4E 17
(off William St.)
Mine St. *Heyw* 1E 39
(in two parts)
Minford Clo. *M40* 5B 84
Minister Dri. *Bow* 4C 144
Minnie St. *Bolt* 4G 45
Minnie St. *Whitw* 3H 15
Minoan Gdns. *Salf* 6G 81
Minorca Av. *M11* 3F 97
Minorca Clo. *Roch* 3A 26
Minorca St. *Bolt* 3A 46
Minor St. *Fail* 3G 85
(in two parts)
Minor St. *Roch* 4C 40
Minshull Ho.
M1 ......5F 95 (1C 10)
Minshull St. *M1* .4E 95 (6B 6)
Minshull St. S.
M1 ......5F **95** (1C **10**)
(off Fairfield St.)
Minsmere Wlk. *M8* 5B 82
(off Brentfield Av.)
Minsmere Walks.
Stoc 6F 141
Minstead Clo. *Hyde* 6E 115
Minstead Wlk. *M22* 3H 147
Minster Clo. *Bolt* 3E 33
Minster Clo. *Duk* 1B 114
Minster Dri. *Chea* 6C 138
Minster Rd. *M9* 3H 83
Minster Rd. *Bolt* 3E 33
Minster Way. *Chad* 6G 55
Minstrel Clo. *Swin* 4D 78
Minton St. *M40* 3C 84
Minto St. *Ash L* 1G 99
(in two parts)
Mintridge Clo. *Upen* ...6G 97
Mint St. *Rams* 3A 12
Mirabel St. *M3* ...2D 94 (2G 5)
Miranda Ct. *Salf* ..5A 94 (2B 8)
Mirfield Av. *M9* 5F 69
Mirfield Av. *Oldh* 5C 72
Mirfield Av. *Stoc* 1D 138
Mirfield Dri. *Eccl* 1F 91
Mirfield Dri. *Midd* 6H 53
Mirfield Dri. *Urm* 3E 105
Mirfield Rd. *M9* 5F 69
Miriam St. *Bolt* 3F 45
Miriam St. *Fail* 5D 84
Missenden Ho. *Salf* 4F 93
(off Cyprus Clo.)
Mission St. *Heyw* 3E 39
Missouri Av. *Salf* 4E 93
Misterton Wlk. *M23* 4D 134
(off Hungerford Wlk.)
Mistletoe Gro.
Salf 2B 94 (2D 4)
Mitcham Av. *M9* 6A 70
Mitchell Clo. *Gat* 5D 136
Mitchell Gdns. *M22* 6C 136
Mitchell Hey. 4G 27
Mitchell Hey. *Roch* 4G 27
Mitchell Ho. *Salf* 5D **136**
(off Lorna Gro.)
Mitchells Quay. *Fail* ..4E 85
Mitchell St. *M40* 6B 84
Mitchell St. *Bury* 1A 36
Mitchell St. *Eccl* 2E 91
Mitchell St. *Midd* 6H 53
Mitchell St. *Oldh* 1B 72
Mitchell St. *Roch* 6A 16
(John St.)
Mitchell St. *Roch* 3F 27
(Spotland Rd.)
Mitcheson Gdns. *Salf* ..2F 93
Mitford Ct. *M14* 2G 125
Mitford Rd. *M14* 2G 126
Mitford St. *Stret* 6C 106
Mitre Rd. *M13* 3B 110

Mitre St. *Bolt* 1A 32
Mitre St. *Bury* 2B 36
Mitre St. *Fail* 3F 85
Mitton Clo. *Bury* 3E 35
Mitton Clo. *Heyw* 3B 38
Mizpah Gro. *Bury* 3H 35
Mizzy Rd. *Roch* 2G 27
Moadlock. *Rom* 5A 130
Moat Av. *M22* 6A 136
Moat Gdns. *M22* 1A 148
Moat Hall Av. *Eccl* 5C 90
Moat Hall Sports Cen.
.....................5C 90
Moat Rd. *M22* 1A 148
Moat Wlk. *Stoc* 2C 128
Mobberley Clo. *M19* 5A 126
Mobberley Rd. *Bolt* 5F 33
Mobberley Rd. *Wilm* 6A 158
Mocha Pde.
Salf 2B 94 (1D 4)
Modbury Clo. *Raz G* 4A 152
Modbury Ct. *Rad* 2B 64
Modbury Wlk. *M8* 5C 82
Mode Hill La. *W'fld* ...1G 67
Mode Hill Wlk. *W'fld* ..1G 67
Mode Wheel Circ.
Traf P 6D 92
Mode Wheel Rd. *Salf* ...4D 92
Mode Wheel Rd. S.
Salf 5D 92
Modwen Rd. *Salf* 1H 107
Moelfre Dri. *Chea H* ...6E 151
Moffat Clo. *Bolt* 1H 47
Moffat Clo. *Duk* 4H 99
Moggie La. *A'ton* 6F 163
Moisant St. *Bolt* 4H 45
Mold St. *Bolt* 2A 32
Mold St. *Oldh* 1C 72
Molesworth St. *Roch* ...4A 28
Mollets Wood. *Dent* 2G 113
Mollington Rd. *M22* 5C 148
Molyneux Rd. *M19* 6E 111
Molyneux St. *Roch* 3F 27
Mona Av. *H Grn* 4H 149
Mona Av. *Stret* 4G 106
Monaco Dri. *M22* 1B 136
Monarch Clo. *Irlam* 3C 118
Monarch Clo. *Rytn* 5B 56
Monart Rd. *M9* 2G 83
Mona St. *Hyde* 5C 114
Mona St. *Salf* 1G 93
Moncrieffe St. *Bolt* ...1B 46
(in two parts)
Monde Trad. Est.
Traf P 1A 106
Mond Rd. *Irlam* 3F 103
Money Ash Rd. *Alt* 2F 145
Monfa Av. *Stoc* 1A 152
Monica Av. *M8* 6B 68
Monica Ct. *Eccl* 2H 91
Monica Gro. *M19* 1D 126
Monks Clo. *M8* 1D 82
Monks Clo. *Miln* 5E 29
Monk's Ct. *Salf* 3B 92
Monksdale Av. *Urm* 5D 104
Monks Hall Gro. *Eccl* ..2H 91
Monks La. *Bolt* 3F 33
Monkswood. *Oldh* 2C 72
Monkton Av. *M18* 3E 111
Monkwood Dri. *M9* 3G 83
Monmouth Av. *Bury* 6F 23
Monmouth Av. *Sale* 4H 121
Monmouth Rd.
Chea H 4D 150
Monmouth St. *M18* 1G 111
Monmouth St. *Midd* 1C 70
Monmouth St. *Oldh* 4A 72
Monmouth St. *Roch* 5H 27
Monroe Clo. *Salf* 1E 93
Monsal Av. *Salf* 4E 81
Monsal Av. *Stoc* 4D 140
Monsall Clo. *Bury* 5E 51

Monsall Rd. *M40* 5G **83**
Monsall St. *M40* 6F **83**
Monsall St. *Oldh* 6C **72**
Mons Av. *Roch* 3E **27**
Montague Bus. Pk.
  M16 . . . . .3G **107**
Montague Ct. *Sale* 5B **122**
Montague Ho. *Stoc* 3F **139**
  (off East St.)
Montague Rd. *M16* 2G **107**
Montague Rd. *Ash L* . . .3B **100**
Montague Rd. *Sale* 5B **122**
Montague St. *Bolt* 4F **45**
Montague Way. *Stal* 3E **101**
Montagu Rd. *Stoc* 4D **140**
Montagu Sq. *M11* 6G **97**
Montcliffe Cres. *M16* . . .6D **108**
Monteagle St. *M9* 5D **68**
Montford Enterprise Cen.
  Salf 4F **93**
Montford St. *Salf* 4F **93**
  (in two parts)
Montgomery. *Roch* 5G **27**
Montgomery Dri. *Bury* . . .5F **51**
Montgomery Ho.
  M16 . . . . .5D **108**
Montgomery Ho. *Oldh* . . .2H **85**
Montgomery Rd. *M13* . . .5B **110**
Montgomery St. *Oldh* . . .1H **85**
Montgomery St. Roch . . .1C **40**
  (off Manchester Rd.)
Montgomery Way. *Rad* . . .2C **48**
Monton. 2F **91**
Monton Av. *Eccl* 2G **91**
Monton Bri. Ct. *Eccl* 2E **91**
Montondale. *Eccl* 2E **91**
Monton Fields Rd. *Eccl* . .2E **91**
Monton Grn. *Eccl* 1E **91**
Monton La. *Eccl* 3G **91**
Montonmill Gdns. *Eccl* . . .2E **91**
Monton Rd. *Eccl* 2F **91**
  (in two parts)
Monton Rd. *Stoc* 5C **128**
Monton St. *M14* 3E **109**
  (in two parts)
Monton St. *Bolt* 4A **46**
Monton St. *Rad* 4F **49**
Montpellier M. *Salf* 2A **82**
Montpellior Rd. *M22* 3B **148**
Montreal St. *M19* 6D **110**
Montreal St. *Oldh* 5D **72**
Montrose. *Eccl* 3G **91**
  (off Monton La.)
Montrose Av. *M20* 4E **125**
Montrose Av. *Bolt* 4E **33**
Montrose Av. *Duk* 6A **100**
Montrose Av. *Rams* 1A **22**
Montrose Av. *Stoc* 2A **152**
Montrose Cres. *Stret* 5B **106**
Montrose Cres. *M19* 6C **110**
Montrose Dri. *Brom X* 4F **19**
Montrose Gdns. *Rytn* 3D **56**
Montrose St. *Roch* 4C **40**
Montserrat. 3C **30**
Montserrat Brow. *Bolt* . . .3B **30**
Montserrat Rd. *Bolt* 3C **30**
Monyash Ct. Glos 6F **117**
  (off Monyash M.)
Monyash Gro. Glos 6F **117**
  (off Monyash M.)
Monyash Lea. Glos 6F **117**
  (off Monyash M.)
Monyash M. Glos 6F **117**
Monyash Pl. Glos 6F **117**
  (off Monyash M.)
Monyash Way. Glos 6G **117**
  (off Ashford M.)
Moon Gro. *M14* 4H **109**
Moon St. *Oldh* 2A **72**
Moor Bank La. *Miln* 1B **42**
Moorby Av. *M19* 5A **126**

Moorby St. *Oldh* 1E **73**
Moorby Wlk. *Bolt* 2B **46**
Moorclose. 1C **70**
Moor Clo. *Rad* 2E **49**
Moorclose St. *Midd* 1B **70**
  (in two parts)
Moorclose Wlk. M9 . . . . . .4F **83**
  (off Conran St.)
Moorcock Av. *Swin* 3H **79**
Moorcot Ct. *M23* 3F **135**
Moor Cres. *Dig* 3C **60**
Moorcroft. *Rams* 3A **12**
Moorcroft. *Roch* 2F **41**
Moorcroft Dri. *M19* 5B **126**
Moorcroft Rd. *M23* 2F **135**
Moorcroft Sq. *Hyde* 1C **114**
Moorcroft St. *Droy* 4A **98**
Moorcroft St. *Oldh* 1A **86**
Moorcroft Wlk. *M19* 5A **126**
Moordale Av. *Oldh* 6A **58**
Moordale St. *M20* 4E **125**
Moordown Clo. *M8* 5D **82**
Moor Edge Rd.
  Moss & G'fld 1H **89**
  (in two parts)
Mooredge Ter. *Rytn* 5C **56**
Moore Ho. *Eccl* 5F **91**
Moor End. *M22* 3B **136**
Moor End Av. *Salf* 3G **81**
Moor End Ct. *Salf* 3G **81**
Moore's Ct. *Bolt* 5G **31**
Moore St. *Roch* 4H **27**
Moore Wlk. *Dent* 2G **129**
Moorfield. *Salf* 2G **81**
Moorfield. *Wors* 4B **76**
  (Crosslands Rd.)
Moorfield. *Wors* 3H **77**
  (Old Clough La.)
Moorfield Av. *M20* 2G **125**
Moorfield Av. *Dent* 6G **113**
Moorfield Av. *L'boro* 2E **17**
Moorfield Av. *Stal* 6H **101**
Moorfield Chase. *Farn* . . .2F **63**
Moorfield Clo. *Eccl* 4F **91**
Moorfield Clo. *Irlam* 4F **103**
Moorfield Clo. *Swin* 5D **78**
Moorfield Dri. *Hyde* 2C **114**
Moorfield Dri. *Wilm* 4B **166**
Moorfield Gro. *Bolt* 4D **32**
Moorfield Gro. *Sale* 6C **122**
Moorfield Gro. *Stoc* 5D **126**
Moorfield Hamlet.
  Shaw 6D **42**
Moorfield Heights.
  Carr 4G **89**
Moorfield M. *Shaw* 6F **43**
Moorfield Pde. *Irlam* 4F **103**
Moorfield Pl. *Roch* 2G **27**
Moorfield Rd. *M20* 5D **124**
Moorfield Rd. *Irlam* 4F **103**
Moorfield Rd. *Oldh* 1H **85**
Moorfield Rd. *Salf* 1D **92**
Moorfield Rd. *Swin* 5C **78**
Moorfield St. *M20* 2F **125**
  (in two parts)
Moorfield St. *Holl* 2F **117**
Moorfield Ter. *Carr* 4G **89**
Moorfield Ter. *Holl* 2F **117**
Moorfield Vw. *L'boro* 3E **17**
Moorfield Wlk. *Urm* 5F **105**
Moorgate. 5G **89**
Moor Ga. *Bolt* 6H **19**
Moorgate. *Bury* 2E **37**
Moorgate Av. *M20* 2D **124**
Moorgate Av. *Roch* 4C **26**
Moorgate Cotts. *Carr* 4G **89**
Moorgate Ct. *Bolt* 4D **32**
Moorgate Dri. *Carr* 5G **89**
Moor Ga. La. *L'boro* 2C **16**
Moorgate M. *Carr* 4G **89**
Moorgate Retail Pk.
  Bury 2E **37**

Moorgate Rd. *Carr* 4G **89**
Moorgate Rd. *Rad* 5E **35**
Moorgate St. *Upperm* 1F **61**
Moorhead St.
  M4 . . . . . .2F **95** (2D **6**)
Moorhey. 3F **73**
Moorhey Ind. Est. *Oldh* . . .3F **73**
Moorhey Rd. *L Hul* 3B **62**
Moorhey St. *Oldh* 3F **73**
Moor Hill. *Roch* 2B **26**
Moorhill Ct. *Salf* 2G **81**
Moorhouse Farm. *Miln* . . .5E **29**
Moorhouse Fold. *Miln* 5E **29**
Moorings Rd. *Traf P* 5B **92**
Moorings, The. *Dis* 1H **165**
Moorings, The. *Moss* 6G **75**
Moorings, The. *Wors* 6A **78**
Moorland Av. *M8* 1B **82**
Moorland Av. *Del* 4H **59**
Moorland Av. *Droy* 4G **97**
Moorland Av. *Miln* 5G **29**
Moorland Av. *Roch* 3B **26**
Moorland Av. *Sale* 6C **122**
Moorland Av. *Whitw* 2C **14**
Moorland Cres. *Whitw* 2C **14**
Moorland Dri. *Chea H* . . .5B **150**
Moorland Dri. *L Hul* 3C **62**
Moorland Gro. *Bolt* 3E **31**
Moorland Rd. *M20* 6F **125**
Moorland Rd. *Carr* 6G **89**
Moorland Rd. *Stoc* 1A **152**
  (in two parts)
Moorlands Av. *Urm* 4D **104**
Moorlands Cres. *Moss* 2F **89**
Moorlands Dri. *Moss* 6G **75**
Moorland St. *L'boro* 2G **17**
Moorland St. *Roch* 2G **27**
Moorland St. *Shaw* 6F **43**
Moorlands Vw. *Bolt* 5E **45**
Moorland Ter. *Roch* 2C **26**
Moor La. *M23* 1G **135**
Moor La. *Bolt* 1A **46**
Moor La. *Dob* 5C **60**
Moor La. *Roch* 1B **26**
Moor La. *Salf* 3E **81**
Moor La. *Urm* 4C **104**
Moor La. *Wilm* 4A **166**
Moor La. *Woodf* 4F **161**
Moor Lodge. *Stoc* 5D **126**
Moor Nook. *Sale* 6D **122**
Moor Pk. Av. *Roch* 3B **40**
Moor Pk. Rd. *M20* 3G **137**
Moor Platt. *Sale* 6C **122**
Moor Rd. *M23* 3E **135**
Moor Rd. *Holc* 1C **12**
  (in two parts)
Moor Rd. *L'boro* 6G **17**
Moorsbrook Gro.
  Wilm 6A **160**
Moorsholme Av. *M40* 4A **84**
Moorside. 4D **78**
  (Manchester)
Moorside. 3A **58**
  (Oldham)
Moorside. *L'boro* 3H **17**
Moorside. *Roch* 2F **41**
Moorside Av. *A'wth* 4D **34**
Moorside Av. *Bolt* 3E **31**
  (in two parts)
Moorside Av. *Droy* 2C **98**
Moorside Av. *Farn* 2D **62**
Moorside Av. *Oldh* 3B **58**
Moorside Ct. *Dent* 3F **113**
Moorside Ct. *Sale* 5B **122**
Moorside Cres. *Droy* 3C **98**
Moorside Ho. *Timp* 4C **134**
Moorside La. *Dent* 3G **113**
  (in three parts)
Moorside Leisure Cen.
  . . . . .4D **78**
Moorside Lodge. *Swin* 3D **78**
Moorside Rd. *M8* 2C **82**

Moorside Rd. *Moss* 2G **89**
Moorside Rd. *Salf* 3G **81**
Moorside Rd. *Stoc* 1C **138**
Moorside Rd. *Swin* 4C **78**
Moorside Rd. *T'ton* 5G **21**
Moorside Rd. *Urm* 4A **104**
Moorside St. *Droy* 3B **98**
Moorside Vw. *T'ton* 5H **21**
Moorsley Dri. *M9* 5H **69**
Moor St. *Bury* 2D **36**
Moor St. *Eccl* 4D **90**
Moor St. *Heyw* 3D **38**
  (in two parts)
Moor St. *Oldh* 2F **73**
Moor St. *Shaw* 1E **57**
Moor St. *Swin* 4F **79**
Moors Vw. *Rams* 3D **12**
Moorton Av. *M19* 2B **126**
Moorton Pk. *M19* 2B **126**
Moortop Clo. *M9* 4E **69**
Moor Top Pl. *Stoc* 6D **126**
Moor Vw. Clo. *Roch* 1B **26**
Moorville Rd. *Salf* 6A **80**
Moor Way. *Hawk* 1D **20**
Moorway. *Wilm* 4B **166**
Moorway Dri. *M9* 5A **70**
Moorwood Dri. *Oldh* 5G **73**
Moorwood Dri. *Sale* 6G **121**
Mora Av. *Chad* 6H **55**
Moran Clo. *Wilm* 5A **160**
Moran Wlk.
  M15 . . . . .1D **108** (6H **9**)
Morar Dri. *Bolt* 6A **34**
Morar Rd. *Duk* 6B **100**
Mora St. *M9* 3H **83**
Moravian Clo. *Duk* 4A **100**
Moravian Fld. *Droy* 5A **98**
Moray Clo. *Rams* 5C **12**
Moray Rd. *Chad* 5G **71**
Morbourne Clo. *M12* . . .1A **110**
Morden Av. *M11* 3E **97**
Morecombe Clo. *M40* . . .5B **84**
Morelands, The. *Bolt* 6E **31**
Moresby Dri. *M20* 3F **137**
Morestead Wlk.
  M40 . . . . . . .2G **95** (1F **7**)
Moreton Av. *Bram* 2G **161**
Moreton Av. *Sale* 6G **121**
Moreton Av. *Stret* 5D **106**
Moreton Av. *W'fld* 6D **50**
  (in two parts)
Moreton Clo. *Duk* 1B **114**
Moreton Dri. *Bury* 2H **35**
Moreton Dri. *Hand* 4A **160**
Moreton Dri. *Poy* 3F **163**
Moreton Ho. Alt 1D **144**
  (off Groby Rd.)
Moreton La. *Stoc* 4C **140**
Moreton St. *Chad* 1F **71**
Moreton Wlk. *Stoc* 4C **140**
Moreton Way. *Mot* 4B **116**
Morgan Pl. *Stoc* 5H **127**
Morgan St. *L'boro* 4F **17**
Morillon Rd. *Irlam* 3E **103**
Morland Rd. *M16* 3A **108**
Morley. 5A **158**
Morley Av. *M14* 6E **109**
Morley Av. *Swin* 5E **79**
Morley Green. 6B **158**
Morley Grn. Rd. *Wilm* . . .5A **158**
Morley Ho. Salf 2F **93**
  (off Sutton Dwellings)
Morley Rd. *Rad* 3D **48**
Morley St. *Bolt* 1H **45**
Morley St. *Bury* 5D **36**
Morley St. *Oldh* 6A **58**
Morley St. *Roch* 2B **28**
Morley St. *W'fld* 1D **66**
Morley Way. *G'fld* 4F **61**
Morna Wlk.
  M12 . . . . . .5H **95** (1H **11**)
Morningside Clo. *Droy* . . .5A **98**

Morningside Clo. *Roch* . . .5B **28**
Morningside Dri.
   M20 . . . . .3G **137**
Mornington Av. *Chea* . . .1H **149**
Mornington Ct. *Oldh* 1C **72**
Mornington Cres.
   M14 . . . . .1E **125**
Mornington Rd. *Bolt* 5F **31**
Mornington Rd. *Chea* . .1H **149**
Mornington Rd. *Roch* . . .3F **27**
Mornington Rd. *Sale* . . .4D **122**
Morpeth Clo. *M12* 2A **110**
Morpeth Clo. *Ash L* 1E **99**
Morpeth St. *Swin* 5E **79**
Morrell Rd. *M22* 3B **136**
Morris Green. 5G **45**
Morris Grn. *Bolt* 5G **45**
Morris Grn. Bus. Pk.
   Bolt 3G **45**
Morris Grn. La. *Bolt* 4G **45**
Morris Grn. St. *Bolt* 5G **45**
Morris Gro. *Urm* 1A **120**
Morris Hall. *M14* 3H **109**
Morrison St. *Bolt* 4A **46**
Morrison Wlk. *M40* 6A **84**
   (off Eldridge Dri.)
Morris St. *M20* 2F **125**
Morris St. *Bolt* 6C **32**
Morris St. *Oldh* 4E **73**
Morris St. *Rad* 2C **50**
Morrowfield Av. *M8* 4B **82**
Morrwell Rd. *M22* 3C **136**
Morse Rd. *M40* 6R **84**
Mortar St. *Oldh* 1G **73**
   (in two parts)
Mort Ct. *Bolt* 2G **31**
Mortfield Gdns. *Bolt* . . .5H **31**
Mortfield La. *Bolt* 5H **31**
   (Chorley Old Rd.)
Mortfield La. *Bolt* 4H **31**
   (Eskrick St.)
Mort Fold. *L Hul* 4C **62**
Mortimer Av. *M9* 5G **69**
Mortimer St. *Oldh* 0E **57**
Mortlake Clo. *Wors* 6D **62**
Mortlake Dri. *M40* 6B **84**
Mort La. *Tyl* 2A **76**
Morton St. *Fail* 4C **04**
Morton St. *Midd* 5A **54**
Morton St. *Rad* 5H **49**
Morton St. *Roch* 4A **28**
Morton St. *Stoc* 5G **127**
Morton Ter. *Dent* 6G **113**
   (off Adlington Way)
Morton Ter. *Woodl* 4H **129**
Mort St. *Farn* 1D **62**
Morven Av. *Haz G* 2F **153**
Morven Dri. *M23* 6G **136**
Morven Gro. *Bolt* 6H **33**
Morville Rd. *M21* 6B **108**
Morville St.
   M1 . . . . .5G **95** (1E **11**)
Moschatel Wlk. *Part* . . .6E **119**
Moscow Rd. *Stoc* 4F **139**
Moscow Rd. E. *Stoc* 4F **139**
Mosedale Clo. *M23* 5E **135**
Mosedale Rd. *Midd* 5F **53**
Moseldene Rd. *Stoc* 6D **140**
Moseley Ct. *M19* 6B **110**
Moseley Grange.
   Chea H 2B **150**
Moseley Rd.
   M14 & M19 . . . . .1A **126**
Moseley Rd. *Chea H* . . .2B **150**
Moseley St. *Stoc* 3G **139**
Moses Gate. 5E **47**
Moses Gate Country Pk.
   . . . . .5H **47**
Moses Ga. Workshops.
   Bolt 5E **47**
Mosley Arc. *M1* 6A **6**

Mosley Av. *Bury* 6F **23**
Mosley Av. *Rams* 1B **22**
Mosley Clo. *Timp* 4H **133**
Mosley Common. 4B **76**
Mosley Comn. Rd.
   Tyl & Wors 3A **76**
Mosley Rd. *Timp* 5B **134**
Mosley Rd. *Traf P* 3C **106**
   (in two parts)
Mosley St. *M2* . . .4E **95** (1H **9**)
Mosley St. *Rad* 3F **49**
Mossack Av. *M22* 4B **148**
Moss Av. *Roch* 5C **28**
Moss Bank. *M8* 3C **82**
Moss Bank. *Bram* 2E **161**
Moss Bank. *Shaw* 1F **57**
Moss Bank Av. *Droy* 3C **98**
Moss Bank Clo. *Bolt* 1H **31**
Moss Bank Ct. *Droy* 3C **98**
Moss Bank Gro. *Swin* . . .1D **78**
Moss Bank Rd. *Swin* 1D **78**
Moss Bank Trad. Est.
   Wors 5G **63**
Moss Bank Way. *Bolt* . . .4C **30**
Mossbray Av. *M19* 5H **125**
Moss Bri. Rd. *Roch* 5B **28**
Moss Brook Ct. M40 . . . .1G **95**
   (off Kentford Dri.)
Mossbrook Dri. *L Hul* . . .3A **62**
Moss Brook Rd. *M9* 4G **83**
Mossclough Ct. *M9* 4G **83**
Moss Colliery Rd. *Swin* . .6E **65**
Mosscot Clo.
   M13 . . . . . .6F **95** (3D **10**)
Moss Cft. Clo. *Urm* 4A **104**
Mossdale Av. *Bolt* 6B **30**
Mossdale Rd. *M23* 2F **135**
Mossdale Rd. *Sale* 2H **133**
Mossdown Rd. *Rytn* 4E **57**
Moss Farm Clo. *Midd* . . .3B **70**
Mossfield Clo. *Bury* 2G **37**
Mossfield Clo. *Stoc* 1D **138**
Mossfield Ct. *Bolt* 5A **32**
Mossfield Dri. *M9* 5A **70**
Mossfield Grn. *Eccl* 3G **103**
Mossfield Rd. *Farn* 1D **62**
Mossfield Rd. *Kear* 4H **63**
Mossfield Rd. *Swin* 1E **79**
Mossfield Rd. *Timp* 5D **134**
Moss Gate. 4D **42**
Moss Ga. Rd. *Shaw* 5D **42**
   (in two parts)
Moss Grange Av.
   M16 . . . . .3B **108**
Moss Grn. *C'ton* 3B **120**
Moss Grove. 1D **06**
Moss Gro. *Shaw* 4C **42**
Moss Gro. Ct. M15 . . . . .3C **108**
   (off Moss La. W.)
Mossgrove Rd. *Timp* . . .4H **133**
Mossgrove St. *Oldh* . . .1B **86**
Mosshall Clo.
   M15 . . . .1B **108** (6D **8**)
Moss Hall Rd. *Bury* 4H **37**
Moss Hey. 1G **57**
Moss Hey Dri. *M23* 2A **136**
Moss Hey St. *Shaw* 1F **57**
Moss Ho. La. *Wors* 6B **76**
   (in two parts)
Moss Ho. Ter. *M9* 2E **83**
Moss Ind. Est. *Roch* 6B **28**
Mossland Clo. *Heyw* 5F **39**
Mossland Gro. *Bolt* 5B **44**
Moss La. *Ald E* 5H **167**
Moss La. *Alt & Hale* 1F **145**
Moss La. *Ash L* 1D **98**
   (in three parts)
Moss La. *Bolt* 2E **31**
Moss La. *Bram* 2D **160**

Moss La. *Cad* 4B **118**
Moss La. *Kear* 4B **64**
Moss La. *Midd* 4H **69**
   (Manchester New Rd.)
Moss La. *Midd* 4A **70**
   (Mossway)
Moss La. *Part* 6D **118**
Moss La. *Roch* 5A **28**
Moss La. *Rytn* 4E **57**
Moss La. *Sale* 1E **133**
   (Firsway)
Moss La. *Sale* 6F **121**
   (Manor Av.)
Moss La. *Styal* 2B **158**
Moss La. *Swin* 1D **78**
Moss La. *Timp* 4H **133**
Moss La. *Urm* 2F **105**
Moss La. *W'fld* 1D **66**
Moss La. *Whitw* 2B **14**
Moss La. *Wors* 5G **63**
   (in two parts)
Moss La. E.
   M16 & M14 . . . . .3D **108**
Moss La. Ind. Est. *Rytn* . .4E **57**
Moss La. Ind. Est.
   W'fld 6D **50**
Moss La. Trad. Est.
   W'fld 6E **51**
Moss La. W. *M15* 3C **108**
Moss Lea. *Bolt* 1H **31**
Mosslee Av. *M8* 6B **68**
Mossley. 2G **89**
Mossley Brow. 2E **89**
Mossley Cross. 2D **88**
Mossley Rd. *Ash L* 2A **100**
Mossley Rd. *Grass* 5F **75**
Moss Lynn. *S'head* 2C **74**
Moss Mnr. *Sale* 6G **121**
Moss Mdw. Rd. *Salf* 1C **92**
Mossmere Rd.
   Chea H 1C **150**
Moss Mill St. *Roch* 6B **28**
Moss Nook. 6D **148**
Moss Nook Ind. Area.
   M22 . . . . .5D **148**
Moss Pk. Rd. *Stret* 5A **106**
Moss Pl. *Bury* 5C **36**
Moss Rd. *Ald E* 4H **167**
Moss Rd. *Cad* 6A **102**
Moss Rd. *Kear* 2G **63**
   (in two parts)
Moss Rd. *Sale* 5D **120**
Moss Rd. *Stret* 3C **106**
Moss Rose. *Ald E* 4H **167**
Moss Row. *Bury* 4D **36**
Moss Row. *Roch* 2H **25**
Moss Shaw Way. *Rad* . . .2D **48**
   (in two parts)
Moss Side. 3C **108**
Moss Side. *Bury* 6A **22**
Moss Side La. *Miln* 6C **28**
Moss Side Leisure Cen.
   . . . . .2D **108**
Moss Side Rd. *Cad* 3B **118**
Moss St. *Bury* 3C **36**
Moss St. *Dent* 4B **98**
Moss St. *Droy* 3B **98**
Moss St. *Farn* 6G **47**
Moss St. *Heyw* 3E **39**
Moss St. *Holl* 2F **117**
Moss St. *Oldh* 1A **74**
Moss St. *Roch* 5B **28**
Moss St. *Salf* 6H **81**
Moss St. *S'seat* 1D **22**
Moss St. E. *Ash L* 2H **99**
Moss St. W. *Ash L* 3F **99**
Moss Ter. *Ash L* 3G **99**
Moss Ter. *Roch* 5B **28**
Moss Ter. *Wilm* 6D **160**
Moss, The. *Midd* 3B **70**
Moss Va. Cres. *Stret* 3H **105**

Moss Va. Rd. *Stret* 4H **105**
Moss Va. Rd. *Urm* 5G **105**
Moss Vw. *M40* 1C **84**
Moss Vw. Rd. *Bolt* 5G **33**
Moss Vw. Rd. *Part* 6E **119**
Mossway. *Midd* 4H **69**
Moss Way. *Sale* 5G **121**
Mosswood Pk. *M20* 3F **137**
Mosswood Rd. *Wilm* . . .6A **160**
Moston. 3A **84**
Moston Bank Av. *M9* 4G **83**
Moston Fairway
   Nature Reserve. . . .3C **84**
Moston La. *M9 & M40* . . .3G **83**
Moston La. *M40* 1C **84**
Moston La. E. *M40* 1E **85**
Moston Rd. *Midd* 3D **70**
Moston St. *Salf* 4B **82**
Moston St. *Stoc* 2H **127**
Mostyn Av. *M14* 1A **126**
Mostyn Av. *Bury* 6F **23**
Mostyn Av. *Chea H* 4A **150**
Mostyn Rd. *Haz G* 4B **152**
Mostyn St. *Stal* 5D **100**
Motcombe Farm Rd.
   H Grn 4F **149**
Motcombe Gro.
   H Grn 2E **149**
Motcombe Rd. *H Grn* . . .3E **149**
Motherwell Av. *M19* 6C **110**
Motlow Wlk. *M23* 3D **134**
Mottershead Av. *L Lev* . . .3A **48**
Mottershead Rd. *M22* . . .1H **147**
Mottram Av. *M21* 4A **124**
Mottram Clo. *Chea* 6C **138**
Mottram Dri. *Timp* 6A **134**
Mottram Fold. *Mot* 4C **116**
Mottram Fold. *Stoc* 3H **139**
Mottram In Longdendale.
   . . . . .3C **116**
Mottram Moor. *Mot* 3C **116**
Mottram Old Rd.
   Hyde 1D **130**
Mottram Old Rd. *Stal* . . .4G **101**
Mottram Rd. *Ald E* 5H **167**
Mottram Rd. *B'btm* 6B **116**
Mottram Rd. *Hyde* 4C **114**
   (in two parts)
Mottram Rd. *Sale* 6E **123**
Mottram Rd. *Stal* 3F **101**
Mottram St. *Stoc* 3H **139**
   (Bamford St.)
Mottram St. *Stoc* 3H **139**
   (Millbrook St.)
Mottram Towers.
   Stoc 3H **139**
Mottram Way. Stoc 3H **139**
   (off Mottram Fold)
Mough La. *Chad* 2D **70**
Mouldsworth Av. *M20* . .2E **125**
Mouldsworth Av. *Stoc* . .3F **127**
Moulton St. *M8* 1C **94**
Moulton St. Precinct.
   M8 . . . . .1C **94**
Mountain Ash. *Roch* 6B **14**
Mountain Ash Clo.
   Roch 6B **14**
Mountain Ash Clo.
   Sale 4E **121**
Mountain Gro. *Wors* 5E **63**
Mountain St. *M40* 1F **97**
Mountain St. *Moss* 2E **89**
Mountain St. *Stoc* 1A **140**
Mountain St. *Wors* 5E **63**
Mount Av. *L'boro* 2E **17**
Mount Av. *Roch* 5C **16**
Mountbatten Av. *Duk* . . .1D **114**
Mountbatten Clo. *Bury* . .5F **51**
Mountbatten St. *M18* . . .2E **111**
Mt. Carmel Ct.
   Salf 6A **94** (3A **8**)
   (off Mt. Carmel Cres.)

Mt. Carmel Cres.
  Salf 6A **94** (3A **8**)
Mount Dri. Marp 6D **142**
Mount Dri. Urm 5H **105**
Mountfield. P'wich 5F **67**
Mountfield Rd. Bram . . .2G **161**
Mountfield Rd. Stoc 4E **139**
Mountfield Wlk. M11 . . . .4B **96**
  (off Hopedale Clo.)
Mountfield Wlk. Bolt 4A **32**
  (in two parts)
Mount Fold. Midd 2B **70**
Mountford Av. M8 . . . . . .1E **69**
Mount Gro. Gat 5D **136**
Mountheath Ind. Pk. P'wich2F **81**
Mount Pl. Roch 3G **27**
Mount Pleasant. Bolt 2E **47**
Mount Pleasant. Bury 6H **13**
Mount Pleasant.
  Haz G 2D **152**
Mount Pleasant. Midd 1E **69**
  (in two parts)
Mount Pleasant.
  P'wich 1A **68**
Mount Pleasant. Stoc . . .5G **141**
Mount Pleasant. Wilm . . .6F **159**
Mount Pleasant.
  Woodl 4H **129**
Mt. Pleasant Bus. Cen.
  Oldh 2F **73**
Mt. Pleasant Rd. Dent . . .5F **113**
Mt. Pleasant Rd. Farn . . .1B **62**
Mt. Pleasant.
  Ash L 1A **100**
  (in two parts)
Mt. Pleasant St. Aud 6F **99**
  (in two parts)
Mt. Pleasant St. Oldh 2F **73**
Mt. Pleasant Wlk. Rad . . .3G **49**
  (in two parts)
Mount Rd.
  M18 & M19 . . . . . .2E **111**
Mount Rd. Hyde 3E **131**
Mount Rd. Midd 2H **69**
Mount Rd. P'wich 2G **67**
Mount Rd. Stoc 1E **139**
Mt. Royal Clo.
  Hyde 2E **115**
Mt. St Joseph's Rd.
  Bolt 2F **45**
Mountside Clo. Roch . . .1H **27**
Mountside Cres.
  P'wich 5D **66**
Mt. Sion Rd. Rad 5D **48**
Mt. Skip La. L Hul 5C **62**
Mount St. M2 . . .5D **94** (1H **9**)
  (in two parts)
Mount St. Bolt 4A **32**
Mount St. Dent 6H **113**
Mount St. Eccl 5E **91**
Mount St. Heyw 4F **39**
Mount St. Hyde 5C **114**
Mount St. Rams 2D **12**
Mount St.
  Roch (OL11) 4C **40**
Mount St.
  Roch (OL12) 3G **27**
Mount St. Rytn 4C **56**
Mount St. Salf . . . 3B **94** (3D **4**)
  (in two parts)
Mount St. Shaw 6D **42**
Mount St. Swin 4F **79**
Mount Ter. Alt 1F **145**
  (off Central Way)
Mount Ter. Droy 2G **97**
Mount, The. Alt 6F **133**
Mount, The. Ash L 2B **100**
Mount, The. Haleb 5C **146**
Mount, The. Salf 3G **81**
Mount, The. Stoc 5C **128**
Mount Vw. Upperm 1F **61**

Mt. View Rd. Shaw 1G **57**
Mt. Zion Rd. Bury 2D **50**
Mousell St. M8 . . . . .1E **95**
Mouselow Clo. Had 4H **117**
Mowbray Av. P'wich 1G **81**
Mowbray Av. Sale 6C **122**
Mowbray St. Ash L 3G **99**
Mowbray St. Bolt 4F **31**
Mowbray St. Oldh 3D **72**
Mowbray St. Roch 2B **40**
Mowbray St. Stoc 3H **139**
Mowbray Wlk. Midd 5G **53**
Mow Halls La. Dob 6A **60**
Moxley Rd. M8 . . . . .2A **82**
Moyse Av. Wals 1F **35**
Mozart Clo. M4 . . .3G **95** (3F **7**)
Mudd. 5C 116
Mudhurst La. Dis 6H **165**
Muirfield Av. Bred 5G **129**
Muirfield Clo. M40 . . . . . .3C **84**
Muirfield Clo. Bolt 4D **44**
Muirfield Clo. Heyw 4F **39**
Muirfield Clo. P'wich 4F **67**
Muirfield Clo. Wilm 1G **167**
Muirhead Ct. Salf 6E **81**
Mulberry Av. Hey D 6B **38**
Mulberry Clo. H Grn . . .6G **149**
Mulberry Clo. Hey D 6B **38**
Mulberry Clo. Roch 6G **27**
Mulberry Ct. Salf 2G **93**
Mulberry Ct. Urm 5G **105**
Mulberry M. Stoc 1F **139**
Mulberry Mt. St. Stoc . . .3G **139**
Mulberry Rd. Salf 3C **93**
Mulberry St.
  M2 . . . . . . .4D **94** (6G **5**)
Mulberry St. Ash L 2A **100**
Mulberry Wlk. Droy 5G **97**
Mulberry Wlk. Sale 3F **121**
Mulberry Way. Hey D 6B **38**
Mule St. Bolt 5C **32**
Mulgrave Rd. Wors 3A **78**
Mulgrave St. Bolt 5G **45**
Mulgrave St. Swin 2D **78**
Mulgrove Wlk. M9 . . . . . .6G **69**
  (off Haverfield Rd.)
Mullacre Rd. M22 . . . . .5B **136**
Mull Av. M12 . . . . .2B **110**
Mulliner St. Bolt 4B **32**
Mullineux St. Wors 1F **77**
Mullion Clo. M19 . . . . . .5F **111**
Mullion Dri. Timp 4G **133**
Mullion Wlk. M8 . . . . . . .5D **82**
Mulmount Clo. Oldh 6A **72**
Mumps. 2E 73
Mumps. Oldh 2E **73**
Munday St. M4 . . .4H **95** (5G **7**)
Municipal Clo. Heyw 3F **39**
  (off Hartland St.)
Munn Rd. M9 . . . . .4D **68**
Munro Av. M22 . . . . . . .3D **148**
Munslow Wlk. M9 . . . . . .6H **69**
Munster St. M4 . . .2E **95** (2A **6**)
Muriel St. Heyw 3G **39**
Muriel St. Roch 6B **28**
Muriel St. Salf 6H **81**
Murieston Rd. Hale 3G **145**
Murrayfield. Roch 5A **26**
Murray Rd. Bury 3D **36**
Murray St. M4 . . . .3F **95** (4D **6**)
Murray St. Salf 5H **81**
Murrow Wlk. M9 . . . . . . .3F **83**
Murton Ter. Bolt 1A **32**
Musbury Av. Chea H 3D **150**
Muscari Wlk.
  M12 . . . . . .6G **95** (3E **11**)
Muscle & Fitness Gymnasium.
** 1F 79**
Musden Wlk. Stoc 2F **127**
Mus. of Science &
** Industry in Manchester.**
** . . . . .5C 94 (1E 9)**

Mus. of Transport. 5D 82
Museum St. M2 . . .5D **94** (1G **9**)
Musgrave Gdns. Bolt 5G **31**
Musgrave Rd. M22 . . . .2B **148**
Musgrave Rd. Bolt 5G **31**
Muslin St. Salf 4A **94** (6B **4**)
Muter Av. M22 . . . . .3D **148**
Mutual St. Heyw 2G **39**
Myerscroft Clo. M40 . . . . .2E **85**
Myrrh St. Bolt 2A **32**
Myrrh Wlk. Bolt 2A **32**
  (off Myrrh St.)
Myrtle Bank. P'wich 2E **81**
Myrtle Clo. Oldh 4C **72**
Myrtle Gdns. Bury 3F **37**
Myrtle Gro. Dent 4H **111**
Myrtle Gro. Droy 3C **98**
Myrtle Gro. P'wich 1F **81**
Myrtle Gro. W'fld 5B **50**
Myrtleleaf Gro. Salf 3D **92**
Myrtle Pl. Salf 1A **94**
Myrtle Rd. Midd 5C **54**
Myrtle Rd. Part 6B **118**
Myrtle St. M11 . . . . .5A **96**
Myrtle St. M16 . . . . .3A **108**
Myrtle St. Bolt 5H **31**
Myrtle St. Heyw 4G **39**
Myrtle St. Stoc 3D **138**
Myrtle St. N. Bury 3F **37**
Myrtle St. S. Bury 3F **37**
My St. Salf 4E **93**
Mytham Gdns. L Lev 5B **48**
Mytham Rd. L Lev 4B **48**
Mytholme Av. Cad 6A **118**
Mythorn Wlk. M40 . . . . . .5B **84**
  (off Harmer Clo.)
Mytton Rd. Bolt 1F **31**
Mytton St. M15 . . . . . . .2D **108**

N

Nabbs Fold. G'mnt 6B **12**
Nabbs Way. G'mnt 2A **22**
Nab La. Marp 4C **142**
Naburn Clo. Stoc 3C **128**
Naburn St. M13 . . . . . . .3H **109**
Nada Lodge. M8 . . . . . . .2B **82**
Nada Rd. M8 . . . . .2B **82**
Naden Wlk. W'fld 1E **67**
Nadine St. Salf 2E **93**
Nadin St. Oldh 6C **72**
Nailsworth Wlk. M13 . . . .2G **109**
  (off Plymouth Gro.)
Nairn Clo. M40 . . .2A **96** (2H **7**)
Nallgate. Roch 3A **42**
Nall St. M19 . . . . .2D **126**
Nall St. Miln 5E **29**
Nameplate Clo. Eccl 3D **90**
Nancy St. M15 . . . .1B **108** (5C **8**)
Nandywell. L Lev 4B **48**
Nangreave Rd. Stoc 5A **140**
Nangreave St.
  Salf 4A **94** (6C **4**)
Nan Nook Rd. M23 . . . . .2F **135**
Nansen Av. Eccl 2E **91**
Nansen Clo. Stret 3E **107**
Nansen Rd. Gat 1E **149**
Nansen St. M11 . . . . .5A **96**
Nansen St. Salf 3E **93**
Nansen St. Stret 4E **107**
Nansmoss Rd. Wilm 6B **158**
Nantes Ct. Bolt 3H **31**
Nantwich Av. Roch 6F **15**
Nantwich Clo. Chea 6C **138**
Nantwich Rd. M14 . . . . .6E **109**
Nantwich Wlk. Bolt 3A **46**
Nantwich Way. Hand 2A **160**
Napier Ct. M15 . . . .1A **108** (6B **8**)
Napier Ct. Hyde 6C **114**
Napier Ct. Stoc 5D **126**
Napier Grn. Salf 6H **93**

Napier Rd. M21 . . . . . . .1H **123**
Napier Rd. Eccl 2D **90**
Napier Rd. Stoc 6D **126**
Napier St. Haz G 2D **152**
Napier St. Hyde 6C **114**
Napier St. Shaw 5F **43**
Napier St. Swin 4D **78**
Napier St. E. Oldh 4B **72**
Napier St. W. Oldh 4A **72**
Naples Rd. Stoc 5D **138**
Naples St. M4 . . . .2E **95** (2B **6**)
Narbonne Av. Eccl 2A **92**
Narborough Wlk. M40 . . .5E **83**
Narburth Dri. M8 . . . . . . .4B **82**
Narcissus Wlk. Wors 6B **62**
Narrow Gate Brow. 6B 42
Narrow La. A'ton 6G **163**
Narrows, The. Alt 2E **145**
Narrow Wlk. Bow 3E **145**
Naseby Av. M9 . . . . .5H **69**
Naseby Ct. P'wich 4G **67**
Naseby Pl. P'wich 4G **67**
Naseby Rd. Stoc 1G **127**
Naseby Wlk. W'fld 1G **67**
Nash Rd. Traf P 5G **91**
Nash St. M15 . . . .1C **108** (6E **9**)
Nasmyth Av. Dent 3G **113**
Nasmyth Bus. Cen.
  Eccl 2F **91**
Nasmyth Rd. Eccl 5E **91**
Nasmyth St. M8 . . . . .6E **82**
Nathan Dri. Salf . . .3C **94** (3E **5**)
Nathans Rd. M22 . . . . .1A **148**
National Cycling Cen. . . .3C 96
National Ind. Salf 5H **93**
National Ind. Est. Ash L . . .3F **99**
National Squash Cen. . . .3B 96
National Trad. Est.
  Haz G 2C **152**
Naunton Rd. Midd 2B **70**
Naunton Wlk. M9 . . . . . . .3G **83**
Naval St. M4 . . . .3G **95** (3E **7**)
Nave Ct. Salf 1F **93**
Navenby Av. M16 . . . . . .3A **108**
Navigation Rd. Alt 4F **133**
Naylor Ct. M40 . . . .2G **95** (1F **7**)
Naylor St. M40 . . . .2H **95** (1G **7**)
Naylor St. Oldh 2C **72**
Nazeby Wlk. Oldh 4A **72**
Naze Ct. Oldh 1C **72**
Naze Wlk. Stoc 3C **128**
Neal Av. Ash L 2B **100**
Neal Av. H Grn 5E **149**
Neale Av. G'fld 4G **61**
Neale Rd. M21 . . . . . . .2G **123**
Near Barrowshaw. 6A 58
Near Birches Pde. Oldh . . .5A **74**
Nearbrook Rd. M22 . . . .1A **148**
Nearcroft Rd. M23 . . . . .4G **135**
Near Hey Clo. Rad 4E **49**
Nearmaker Av. M22 . . . .1A **148**
Nearmaker Rd. M22 . . . .1A **148**
Neary Way. Urm 2E **105**
Neasden Gro. Bolt 2G **45**
Neath Av. M22 . . . . .4B **136**
Neath Clo. Poy 2D **162**
Neath Clo. W'fld 2G **67**
Neath Fold. Bolt 4H **45**
Neath St. Oldh 2B **72**
Nebo St. Bolt 3H **45**
Nebraska St. Bolt 4A **32**
Neden Clo. M11 . . . . .5D **96**
Needham Av. M21 . . . .1H **123**
Needham Ct. W'fld 2D **66**
Needwood Clo. M40 . . . . .6F **83**
Needwood Rd. Woodl . . .4A **130**
Needwood St. M40 . . . . .5F **83**
Neenton Sq. M12 . . . . . . .6C **96**
Neild St. Oldh 5C **72**
Neild St. Salf 1C **94**
Neilson Clo. Midd 2C **70**
Neilson Ct. M23 . . . . . . .5G **135**

Neilston Av.—Newlands Rd.

Neilston Av. *M40* . . . 4B **84**
Neilston Ri. *Bolt* . . . 6B **30**
Nell Carrs. *Rams* . . . 1G **13**
Nellie St. *Heyw* . . . 3D **38**
Nell La. *M21 & M20* . . . 2A **124**
Nell St. *Bolt* . . . 1A **32**
Nelson Av. *Eccl* . . . 2F **91**
Nelson Av. *Poy* . . . 4G **163**
Nelson Bus. Cen.
Dent . . . 3F **113**
Nelson Clo. *M15* . . . 3C **108**
Nelson Clo. *Poy* . . . 4G **163**
Nelson Ct. *M40* . . . 1H **95**
Nelson Dri. *Cad* . . . 3C **118**
Nelson Dri. *Droy* . . . 3F **97**
Nelson Fold. *Swin* . . . 2G **79**
Nelson Mandela Ct.
M16 . . . *4C* ***108***
(off Range Rd.)
Nelson Rd. *M9* . . . 4F **69**
Nelson Sq. *Bolt* . . . 6B **32**
Nelson St. *M4* . . . 2E **95** (2B **6**)
Nelson St. *M13* . . . 2F **109**
Nelson St. *Aud* . . . 1F **113**
Nelson St. *Bolt* . . . 2C **46**
Nelson St. *Bury* . . . 5D **36**
(in two parts)
Nelson St. *Dent* . . . 3F **113**
(in two parts)
Nelson St. *Eccl* . . . 3F **91**
Nelson St. *Farn* . . . 1G **63**
Nelson St. *Haz G* . . . 1F **153**
Nelson St. *Heyw* . . . 4F **39**
Nelson St. *Hyde* . . . 5C **114**
Nelson St. *Lees* . . . 4A **74**
Nelson St. *L'boro* . . . 4F **17**
Nelson St. *L Lev* . . . 4B **48**
Nelson St. *Midd* . . . 2C **70**
(in two parts)
Nelson St.
Mile P . . . 1H **95** (1H **7**)
Nelson St. *Roch* . . . 4H **27**
Nelson St. *Salf* (M5) . . . 4E **93**
Nelson St. *Salf* (M7) . . . 6H **81**
Nelson St. *Stret* . . . 6D **106**
Nelson Way. *Chad* . . . 5H **71**
Nelstrop Cres. *Stoc* . . . 3F **127**
Nelstrop Rd. *Stoc* . . . 3F **127**
Nelstrop Rd. N.
Stoc & M19 . . . 2E **127**
Nelstrop Wlk. *Stoc* . . . 3E **127**
Nepaul Rd. *M9* . . . 2G **83**
Neptune Gdns. *Salf* . . . 6G **81**
Nero St. *Rams* . . . 2G **13**
Nesbit St. *Bolt* . . . 2D **32**
Nesfield Rd. *M23* . . . 1F **135**
Neston Av. *M20* . . . 3E **125**
Neston Av. *Bolt* . . . 6D **18**
Neston Av. *Sale* . . . 1E **135**
Neston Clo. *Shaw* . . . 6H **43**
Neston Gro. *Stoc* . . . 6F **139**
Neston Rd. *Roch* . . . 1A **42**
Neston Rd. *Wals* . . . 1F **35**
Neston St. *M11* . . . 6H **97**
Neston Way. *Hand* . . . 4H **159**
Neswick Wlk. *M23* . . . 1F **135**
Netherbury Clo. *M18* . . . 4E **111**
Nethercote Av. *M23* . . . 5H **135**
Nether Cft. *Roch* . . . 2A **26**
Nethercroft Ct. *Alt* . . . 6E **133**
Nethercroft Rd. *Timp* . . . 6C **134**
Netherfield Clo. *Oldh* . . . 5A **72**
Netherfield Rd. *Bolt* . . . 5H **45**
Netherfields. *Ald E* . . . 6G **167**
Netherhey La. *Rytn* . . . 5A **56**
Nether Hey St. *Oldh* . . . 4F **73**
(in two parts)
Nether Ho. Rd. *Shaw* . . . 6E **43**
Nether Lees. . . . **4H 73**
Netherlees. *Lees* . . . 4H **73**
Netherlow Ct. *Hyde* . . . 5C **114**
Nether St.
M12 . . . 5G **95** (2E **11**)
Nether St. *Hyde* . . . 1D **130**
Netherton Gro. *Farn* . . . 5D **46**
Netherton Rd. *M14* . . . 6E **109**
Nethervale Dri. *M9* . . . 4G **83**
Netherwood. *Fail* . . . 3H **85**
Netherwood Rd. *M22* . . . 4A **136**
Netley Av. *Roch* . . . 6F **15**
Netley Gdns. *Rad* . . . 3E **49**
Netley Rd. *M23* . . . 1G **147**
Nettlebarn Rd. *M22* . . . 6A **136**
Nettleford Rd. *M16* . . . 1C **124**
Nettleton Gro. *M9* . . . 2H **83**
Nevada St. *Bolt* . . . 4A **32**
Nevendon Dri. *M23* . . . 1F **147**
Nevern Clo. *Bolt* . . . 5D **30**
Nevile Ct. *Salf* . . . 3F **81**
Nevile Rd. *Salf* . . . 3F **81**
Neville Cardus Wlk.
M14 . . . *5G* ***109***
(off Taylor St.)
Neville Clo. *Bolt* . . . 5A **32**
Neville Dri. *Irlam* . . . 3E **103**
Neville St. *Chad* . . . 2A **72**
Neville St. *Haz G* . . . 2D **152**
Nevill Rd. *Bram* . . . 3G **151**
Nevin Av. *Chea H* . . . 4A **150**
Nevin Clo. *Bram* . . . 5A **152**
Nevin Clo. *Oldh* . . . 1H **85**
Nevin Rd. *M40* . . . 2D **84**
Nevis Gro. *Bolt* . . . 6B **18**
Nevis St. *Roch* . . . 3G **41**
New Allen St.
M40 . . . 2G **95** (2E **7**)
Newall Green. . . . **1G 147**
Newall Green Leisure Facility.
. . . **2F 147**
Newall Rd. *M23* . . . 2F **147**
Newall St. *L'boro* . . . 3F **17**
Newark Av. *M14* . . . 4F **109**
Newark Av. *Rad* . . . 2C **48**
Newark Pk. Way. *Rytn* . . . 6A **42**
Newark Rd. *Roch* . . . 6F **15**
Newark Rd. *Stoc* . . . 4H **127**
Newark Rd. *Swin* . . . 1H **79**
Newark Sq. *Roch* . . . 6F **15**
New Bailey St.
Salf . . . 4C **94** (4E **5**)
Newbank Chase. *Chad* . . . 1G **71**
New Bank St. *M12* . . . 1A **110**
New Bank St. *Had* . . . 2H **117**
Newbank Tower.
Salf . . . 2C **94** (1E **5**)
New Barn Clo. *Shaw* . . . 6E **43**
New Barn La. *Roch* . . . 6G **27**
New Barn Rd. *Oldh* . . . 1E **87**
New Barns Av. *M21* . . . 3A **124**
New Barn St. *Bolt* . . . 4F **31**
New Barn St. *Roch* . . . 6A **20**
Newbarn St. *Shaw* . . . 6E **43**
New Barton St. *Salf* . . . 6A **80**
Newbeck St. *M4* . . . 3E **95** (3B **6**)
New Beech Rd. *Stoc* . . . 1A **138**
(in two parts)
Newberry Gro. *Stoc* . . . 6F **139**
Newbold. . . . **4C 28**
Newbold Brow. . . . **3C 28**
Newbold Moss. *Roch* . . . 3B **28**
Newbold St. *Bury* . . . 3A **36**
Newbold St. *Roch* . . . 3C **28**
Newbold Wlk. *M15* . . . 5G **9**
Newboult Rd. *Chea* . . . 5A **138**
Newbourne Clo.
Haz G . . . 2D **152**
Newbreak Clo. *Oldh* . . . 1H **73**
Newbreak St. *Oldh* . . . 1H **73**
Newbridge Gdns. *Bolt* . . . 1G **33**
New Bri. La. *Stoc* . . . 2H **139**
New Bri. St.
Salf . . . 2D **94** (2C **5**)
Newbridge Vw. *Moss* . . . 3F **89**
New Briggs Fold. *Eger* . . . 1C **18**
New Brighton Cotts.
Whitw . . . *4G* ***15***
(off Ruth St.)
New Broad La. *Roch* . . . 2H **41**
Newbrook Av. *M21* . . . 5B **124**
New Bldgs. Pl. *Roch* . . . 3H **27**
Newburn Av. *M9* . . . 5H **69**
New Bury. . . . **2E 63**
Newbury Av. *Sale* . . . 5E **121**
Newbury Clo. *Chea H* . . . 1C **160**
Newbury Ct. *Timp* . . . 4H **133**
Newbury Dri. *Eccl* . . . 2D **90**
Newbury Dri. *Urm* . . . 2E **105**
Newbury Gro. *Heyw* . . . 5E **39**
Newbury Pl. *Salf* . . . 4H **81**
Newbury Rd. *H Grn* . . . 6G **149**
Newbury Rd. *L Lev* . . . 4H **47**
Newbury Wlk. M9 . . . *5F* ***83***
(off Ravelston Dri.)
Newbury Wlk. *Bolt* . . . 4A **32**
Newbury Wlk. Chad . . . *2A* ***72***
(off Kempton Way)
Newby Dri. *B'hth* . . . 5F **133**
Newby Dri. *Gat* . . . 5E **137**
Newby Dri. *Midd* . . . 4H **53**
Newby Dri. *Sale* . . . 6E **123**
Newby Rd. *Bolt* . . . 4G **33**
Newby Rd. *Haz G* . . . 3C **152**
Newby Rd. *Stoc* . . . 1E **139**
Newby Rd. Ind. Est.
Haz G . . . 3C **152**
Newcastle St.
M15 . . . 6D **94** (4H **9**)
(in two parts)
Newcastle Wlk. *Dent* . . . 6G **113**
New Cateaton St. *Bury* . . . 2D **36**
New Cathedral St.
M3 . . . 3D **94** (4H **5**)
New Century Ho.
Dent . . . 5C **112**
Newchurch. *Oldh* . . . 3E **87**
New Church Ct. *Rad* . . . 4H **49**
New Church Ct. W'fld . . . *2D* ***66***
(off Elizabeth St.)
New Church Rd. *Bolt* . . . 3D **30**
Newchurch St. *M11* . . . 5B **98**
New Church St. *Rad* . . . 4G **49**
Newchurch St. *Roch* . . . 4C **40**
New Church Wlk. *Rad* . . . 4H **49**
New City Rd. *Wors* . . . 3C **76**
Newcliffe Rd. *M9* . . . 5H **69**
New Coin St. *Rytn* . . . 4B **56**
Newcombe Clo. *M11* . . . 4B **96**
Newcombe Ct. *Sale* . . . 5H **121**
Newcombe Dri. *L Hul* . . . 3B **62**
Newcombe Rd. *Rams* . . . 2A **22**
Newcombe St.
M3 . . . 2D **94** (1H **5**)
New Ct. Dri. *Eger* . . . 1D **18**
Newcroft. *Fail* . . . 5H **85**
Newcroft Cres. *Urm* . . . 6H **105**
Newcroft Dri. *Stoc* . . . 5F **139**
Newcroft Dri. *Urm* . . . 6A **106**
Newcroft Rd. *Urm* . . . 6H **105**
New Cross. *M4* . . . 3F **95** (4C **6**)
New Cross St. *Rad* . . . 4H **49**
New Cross St. *Salf* . . . 3C **92**
New Cross St. *Swin* . . . 4G **79**
Newdale Rd. *M19* . . . 5D **110**
New Delph. . . . **4H 59**
New Earth. . . . **4G 73**
Newearth Rd. *Wors* . . . 3D **76**
New Earth St. *Moss* . . . 1F **89**
New Earth St. *Oldh* . . . 4G **73**
New Elizabeth St. *M8* . . . 6C **82**
New Ellesmere App.
Wors . . . 5E **63**
Newell Ter. *Roch* . . . 2G **27**
New Elm Rd.
M3 . . . 5D **94** (1D **8**)
Newfield Clo. *Rad* . . . 4E **49**
Newfield Clo. *Roch* . . . 3C **28**
Newfield Head La. *Miln* . . . 6H **29**
Newfield Vw. *Miln* . . . 5G **29**
(in three parts)
New Forest Rd. *M23* . . . 3C **134**
Newgate. . . . **2A 166**
Newgate. *Roch* . . . 4G **27**
Newgate Dri. *L Hul* . . . 3B **62**
Newgate Rd. *Sale* . . . 1E **133**
Newgate Rd. *Wilm* . . . 2A **166**
Newgate St. *M4* . . . 3E **95** (3B **6**)
New George St. *Bury* . . . 2A **36**
New Grn. *Bolt* . . . 5A **20**
Newhall Av. *Brad F* . . . 1B **48**
New Hall Av. *Eccl* . . . 6C **90**
New Hall Av. *H Grn* . . . 6F **149**
New Hall Av. *Salf* . . . 3H **81**
New Hall Clo. *Sale* . . . 5F **123**
New Hall Dri. *M23* . . . 1G **135**
New Hall La. *Bolt* . . . 4F **31**
New Hall M. *Bolt* . . . 4B **30**
Newhall Pl. *Bolt* . . . 5E **31**
New Hall Rd. *Bury* . . . 1A **38**
New Hall Rd. *Salf* . . . 3H **81**
Newhall Rd. *Stoc* . . . 5A **112**
Newham Av. *M11* . . . 3D **96**
Newham Dri. *Bury* . . . 4H **35**
Newhart Gro. *Wors* . . . 1E **77**
Newhaven Av. *M11* . . . 6H **97**
Newhaven Bus. Pk.
Eccl . . . 4G **91**
Newhaven Clo. *Bury* . . . 4C **22**
Newhaven Clo.
Chea H . . . 3E **151**
Newhaven Wlk. *Bolt* . . . 4D **32**
New Herbert St. *Salf* . . . 6A **80**
Newhey. . . . **1F 43**
Newhey Av. *M22* . . . 6B **136**
Newhey Rd. *M22* . . . 1B **148**
Newhey Rd. *Chea* . . . 5A **138**
Newhey Rd. *Miln* . . . 6G **29**
(in two parts)
New Heys Way. *Bolt* . . . 5H **19**
New Holder St. *Bolt* . . . 6A **32**
Newholme Ct. *Stret* . . . 5E **107**
Newholme Gdns. *Wors* . . . 6E **63**
Newholme Rd. *M20* . . . 4D **124**
Newhouse Clo. *Ward* . . . 3A **16**
Newhouse Cres. *Roch* . . . 3A **26**
Newhouse Rd. *Heyw* . . . 5F **39**
Newhouse St. *Ward* . . . 3A **16**
(in two parts)
Newick Wlk. M9 . . . *6G* ***69***
(off Leconfield Dri.)
Newington Av. *M8* . . . 6B **68**
Newington Ct. *Bow* . . . 2E **145**
Newington Dri. *Bolt* . . . 4B **32**
Newington Dri. *Bury* . . . 4G **35**
Newington Wlk. *Bolt* . . . 4B **32**
(in two parts)
New Inn Yd. *Roch* . . . 5C **16**
New Islington.
M4 . . . 3G **95** (4F **7**)
New Kings Head Yd.
Salf . . . *3D* ***94*** *(3G* ***5****)*
(off Chapel St.)
Newlands. *Fail* . . . 1G **97**
Newlands Av. *Bolt* . . . 4H **33**
Newlands Av. *Bram* . . . 5H **151**
Newlands Av. *Chea H* . . . 6C **150**
Newlands Av. *Eccl* . . . 6B **90**
Newlands Av. *Irlam* . . . 5D **102**
Newlands Av. *Roch* . . . 6F **15**
Newlands Av. *W'fld* . . . 6C **50**
Newlands Clo.
Chea H . . . 6C **150**
Newlands Clo. *Roch* . . . 6F **15**
Newlands Dri. *M20* . . . 3G **137**
Newlands Dri. *Had* . . . 3H **117**
Newlands Dri. *P'wich* . . . 4E **67**
Newlands Dri. *Swin* . . . 5A **80**
Newlands Dri. *Wilm* . . . 4B **166**
Newlands Rd. *M23* . . . 3E **135**

Newlands Rd. *Chea* 5H **137**
Newland St. *M8* 2D **82**
   (in two parts)
New La. *Bolt* 4F **33**
New La. *Eccl* 4D **90**
New La. *Midd* 6A **54**
New La. *Rytn* 3B **56**
New La. Ct. *Bolt* 3G **33**
New Lawns. *Stoc* 6A **112**
Newlea Clo. *Bolt* 3G **31**
New Lees St. *Ash L* 6H **87**
   (in two parts)
New Lester Way. *L Hul* . . .5A **62**
Newlyn Av. *Stal* 2H **101**
Newlyn Clo. *Haz G* 4D **152**
Newlyn Dri. *Bred* 6G **129**
Newlyn Dri. *Sale* 1C **134**
Newlyn St. *M14* 5F **109**
New Manchester. 2C 76
Newman St. *Ash L* 2G **99**
Newman St. *Hyde* 4C **114**
Newman St. *Roch* 6A **16**
New Market.
   M2 . . . . .4D **94** (5H **5**)
Newmarket Clo. *Sale* 1D **132**
Newmarket Gro. *Ash L* . . .6C **86**
New Mkt. La.
   M2 . . . . . . .4E **95** (5A **6**)
Newmarket M. *Salf* 5H **81**
Newmarket Rd. *Ash L* 6C **86**
Newmarket Rd. *L Lev* 5A **48**
New Mdw. *Los* 6A **30**
New Mill. *Roch* 1C **28**
New Mills. 6A 156
New Mill St. *L'boro* 4E **17**
Newmill Wlk. M8 . . . .*5B 82*
   (off Alderford Rd.)
New Moor La. *Haz G* 2D **152**
New Moss Rd. *Cad* 3B 118
New Moston. 2E 85
New Mount St.
   M4 . . . . . . .2E **95** (2B **6**)
Newnham St. *Bolt* 2A **32**
New Oak Clo. *Fail* 3A **86**
New Park Rd. *Salf* 6H **93**
Newpark Wlk. M8 . . . .*5C 82*
   (off Magnolia Dri.)
Newport Av. *Stoc* 2G **127**
Newport M. *Farn* 2F **63**
Newport Rd. *M21* 6G **107**
Newport Rd. *Bolt* 4C **46**
Newport Rd. *Dent* 1H **129**
Newport St. *M14* 4F **109**
Newport St. *Bolt* 6B **32**
   (BL1)
Newport St. *Bolt* 1B **46**
   (BL3)
Newport St. *Farn* 2F **63**
Newport St. *Midd* 6C **54**
Newport St. *Oldh* 4B **72**
Newport St. *Salf* 3E **93**
Newport St. *T'ton* 6A **22**
Newquay Av. *Bolt* 4D **34**
Newquay Av. *Stoc* 2G **127**
Newquay Dri. *Bram* 6H **151**
New Quay St.
   Salf 4C **94** (6E **5**)
New Radcliffe St. *Oldh* . . .2C **72**
New Ridd Ri. *Hyde* 1B **130**
New Riven Ct. *L Lev* 3A **48**
   (in two parts)
New Rd. *Oldh* 5C **72**
New Rd. *Rad* 5H **49**
New Rd. *Tin* 1H **117**
New Rd. *Whitw* 1B **14**
New Royd Av. *Lees* 1B **74**
Newry Rd. *Eccl* 5G **91**
Newry St. *Bolt* 2H **31**
Newry Wlk. *M9* 6D **68**
Newsham Clo. *Bolt* 2H **45**
Newsham Wlk. *M12* 4D **110**

Newshaw La. *Had* 4H **117**
Newsholme St. *M8* 4B **82**
New Smithfield Mkt.
   M11 . . . . .6E **97**
New Springs. *Bolt* 2F **31**
Newstead. Roch *3G 27*
   (off Spotland Rd.)
Newstead Av. *M20* 4H **125**
Newstead Av. *Ash L* 4G **87**
Newstead Clo. *Poy* 2D **162**
Newstead Dri. *Bolt* 5E **45**
Newstead Gro. *Bred* 6E **129**
Newstead Rd. *Urm* 4G **105**
Newstead Ter. *Timp* 4H **133**
New St. *M40* 1A **96**
New St. *Alt* 1E **145**
New St. *Bolt* 1A **46**
New St. *Droy* 5A **98**
New St. *Eccl* 4E **91**
New St. *Lees* 3A **74**
New St. *L'boro* 5D **16**
New St. *Miln* 6G **29**
New St. *Rad* 5H **49**
New St. *Roch* 1G **27**
New St. *Stal* 5E **101**
New St. *Swin* 2G **79**
New St. *T'ton* 5H **21**
New St. *Upperm* 1F **61**
New St. *Wilm* 4B **166**
New Tempest Rd. *Los* 3A **44**
New Ter. *Hyde* 2D **114**
   (Hamel St.)
New Ter. *Hyde* 6C **114**
   (Osborne Rd.)
New Ter. *Wilm* 1E **167**
New Thomas St. *Salf* 1G **93**
Newton. 3D 114
Newton Av. *Long* 3B **110**
Newton Av. *Wthtn* 3E **125**
Newton Bus. Pk.
   Hyde 2E **115**
Newton Cres. *Midd* 5F **53**
Newtondale Av. *Rytn* 3A **56**
Newton Dri. *G'mnt* 2A **22**
New Tong Fld. *Brom X* . . .4D **18**
Newton Grn. *Hyde* 2D **114**
Newton Hall Ct. *Hyde* . . .2A **114**
Newton Hall Rd. *Hyde* . . .2A **114**
Newton Heath. 6B 84
Newton Moor Ind. Est.
   Hyde 2C **114**
Newtonmore Wlk.
   Open 4D **96**
Newton Rd. *Alt* 4G **133**
Newton Rd. *Fail* 1G **97**
Newton Rd. *Midd* 2D **68**
Newton Rd. *Urm* 5E **105**
Newton Rd. *Wilm* 6E **159**
Newton St. *M1* 4F **95** (5C **6**)
Newton St. *M40* 5C **84**
Newton St. *Ash L* 2A **100**
Newton St. *Bolt* 3A **32**
Newton St. *Bury* 5F **23**
Newton St. *Droy* 2B **98**
Newton St. *Fail* 5C **84**
Newton St. *Hyde* 3B **114**
Newton St. *Roch* 6A **28**
Newton St. *Stal* 3D **100**
Newton St. *Stoc* 3G **139**
Newton St. *Stret* 6D **106**
Newton Ter. *Bolt* 3A **32**
Newton Ter. *Duk* 4H **99**
Newton Wlk. *Bolt* 3A **32**
Newton Wood. 1A 114
Newton Wood Rd.
   Duk 1H **113**
Newtown. 1F 95
   (Manchester)
New Town. 1F 57
   (Oldham)
Newtown. 4G 163
   (Stockport)

Newtown. 1E 79
   (Swinton)
Newtown Av. *Dent* 5F **113**
Newtown Clo. *M11* 5D **96**
Newtown Clo. *Swin* 1F **79**
Newtown Ct.
   M40 . . . . . . .1G **95** (1E **7**)
Newtown Ct. *P'wich* 5G **67**
Newtown M. *P'wich* 5G **67**
Newtown St. *P'wich* 5G **67**
Newtown St. *Shaw* 1F **57**
New Union St.
   M4 . . . . . . .3G **95** (4E **7**)
New Vernon St. *Bury* 1D **36**
New Viaduct St. *M11* 3A **96**
Newville Dri. *M20* 4H **125**
New Vine St.
   M15 . . . . . .1D **108** (5G **9**)
New Wakefield St.
   M1 . . . . . . .6E **95** (3A **10**)
New Way. *Whitw* 4G **15**
New Welcome St.
   M15 . . . . . .1D **108** (5G **9**)
New Windsor. . .3H 93 (5A 4)
New York. *Bolt* 2D **44**
New York St. *Heyw* 3D **38**
   (in two parts)
New Zealand Rd.
   Stoc 2A **140**
Neyland Clo. *Bolt* 6D **30**
Ney St. *Ash L* 5D **86**
Niagara St. *Stoc* 5A **140**
Nicholas Cft.
   M4 . . . . . . .3E **95** (4B **6**)
Nicholas Owen Clo.
   M11 . . . . .5E **97**
Nicholas Rd. *Oldh* 5C **72**
Nicholas St. *M1* . .4E **95** (6A **6**)
Nicholas St. *Bolt* 5C **32**
Nicholls St.
   M12 . . . . . .1H **109** (5G **11**)
Nicholls St. *Salf* 2H **93**
Nicholson Rd. *Hyde* 2A **114**
Nicholson Sq. *Duk* 5H **99**
Nicholson St. *Lees* 3A **74**
Nicholson St. *Roch* 6H **27**
Nicholson St. *Stoc* 1G **139**
Nicker Brow. *Dob* 5A **60**
   (in two parts)
Nickleby Rd. *Poy* 4D **162**
Nick Rd. La. *Ward* 2F **15**
Nico Ditch. *M18* 5E **111**
Nicolas Rd. *M21* 6G **107**
Nicola St. *Eger* 3C **18**
Nield Rd. *Dent* 4F **113**
Nields Brow. *Bow* 3E **145**
Nield St. *Moss* 1D **88**
Nields Way. *Rom* 6H **143**
Nigel Rd. *M9* 4H **83**
Nigher Moss Av. *Roch* . . .4C **28**
Nightingale Clo. *Wilm* . . .6F **159**
Nightingale Dri. *Aud* 3C **98**
Nightingale Gdns.
   M23 . . . . .2G **135**
Nightingale St.
   M3 . . . . . .2D **94** (2G **5**)
Nightingale Wlk. *Bolt* 4B **46**
Nile St. *Ash L* 5F **99**
Nile St. *Bolt* 2B **46**
Nile St. *Oldh* 1C **72**
Nile St. *Roch* 3A **28**
Nile Ter. *Salf* 6H **81**
Nimble Nook. 4G 71
Nimble Nook. *Chad* 4G **71**
Nina Dri. *M40* 6C **70**
Nine Acre Ct. *Salf* 6H **93**
Nine Acre Dri. *Salf* 6H **93**
Ninehouse La. *Bolt* 3B **46**
Ninfield Rd. *M23* 1H **147**
Ninian Ct. *Midd* 6H **53**
Ninian Gdns. *Wors* 6F **63**
Ninth Av. *Oldh* 2B **86**

Nipper La. *W'fld* 5C **50**
Nisbet Av. *M22* 2C **148**
Niven St. *M12* . . .6G **95** (3E **11**)
Nixon Rd. *Bolt* 4G **45**
Nixon Rd. S. *Bolt* 4G **45**
Nixon St. *Fail* 4E **85**
Nixon St. *Roch* 2B **40**
Nixon St. *Stoc* 3G **139**
Nob End. 5A 48
Noble Mdw. *Roch* 4B **16**
Noble St. *Bolt* 2A **46**
Noble St. *Oldh* 5D **72**
Noel Dri. *Sale* 5D **122**
Noel St. *Bolt* 6A **32**
Nolan St. *M9* 4G **83**
Nona St. *Salf* 3E **93**
Nook. 6H 43
Nook Cotts. *S'head* 1C **74**
Nook Farm Av. *Roch* 6F **15**
Nook Fields. *Bolt* 2G **33**
Nook La. *Ash L* 5H **87**
Nook Side. *Roch* 6F **15**
Nook Ter. *Roch* 6F **15**
Nook, The. *Bram* 2F **161**
Nook, The. *Bury* 4H **37**
Nook, The. *Eccl* 2C **90**
Nook, The. *G'fld* 5G **61**
Nook, The. *Urm* 6F **105**
Nook, The. *Wors* 3H **77**
Noon Sun Clo. *G'fld* 5E **61**
Noon Sun St. *Roch* 2H **27**
   (in two parts)
Norbet Wlk. *M9* 4G **83**
Norbreck Av. *M21* 2H **123**
Norbreck Av. *Chea* 5C **138**
Norbreck Gdns. *Bolt* 5E **33**
Norbreck St. *Bolt* 5E **33**
Norburn Rd. *M13* 5B **110**
Norbury Av. *Grass* 3E **75**
Norbury Av. *Hyde* 5B **114**
Norbury Av. *Marp* 5C **142**
Norbury Av. *Sale* 5H **121**
Norbury Av. *Salf* 6B **80**
Norbury Clo. *M40* 1A **96**
Norbury Cres. *Haz G* 3D **152**
Norbury Dri. *Marp* 5C **142**
Norbury Gro. *Bolt* 1C **32**
Norbury Gro. *Haz G* 3D **152**
Norbury Gro. *Swin* 2F **79**
Norbury Hollow Rd.
   Haz G 5H **153**
Norbury Ho. *Oldh* 4F **73**
Norbury La. *Oldh* 6H **73**
Norbury M. *Marp* 5C **142**
Norbury Moor. 5D 152
Norbury St. *Roch* 1H **41**
Norbury St. *Salf* 5A **82**
Norbury St. *Stoc* 2H **139**
Norbury Way. *Hand* 2A **160**
Norcliffe Wlk. *M18* 3D **110**
Norcot Wlk.
   M15 . . . . .1B **108** (5D **8**)
Norcross Clo. *Stoc* 6D **140**
Nordale Pk. *Roch* 1A **26**
Nordek Clo. *Rytn* 2B **56**
Nordek Dri. *Rytn* 2B **56**
Norden. 2H 25
Norden Av. *M20* 3E **125**
Norden Clo. *Roch* 1G **25**
Norden Ct. *Bolt* 3A **46**
Norden Rd. *Roch* 6H **25**
Nordens Dri. *Chad* 6F **55**
Nordens Rd. *Chad* 1F **71**
Nordens St. *Chad* 1G **71**
Norden Way. *Roch* 1G **25**
Noreen Av. *P'wich* 4G **67**
Norfield Clo. *Duk* 5A **100**
Norfolk Av. *M18* 3E **111**
Norfolk Av. *Dent* 4H **111**
Norfolk Av. *Droy* 2H **97**
Norfolk Av. *Heyw* 3C **38**
Norfolk Av. *Stoc* 3E **127**

Norfolk Av. *W'fld* 1E **67**
Norfolk Clo. *Cad* 4A **118**
Norfolk Clo. *L'boro* 6G **17**
Norfolk Clo. *L Lev* 3B **48**
Norfolk Clo. *Shaw* 6D **42**
Norfolk Cres. *Fail* 5E **85**
Norfolk Dri. *Farn* 6F **47**
Norfolk Gdns. *Urm* 4H **103**
Norfolk Ho. *Sale* 5D **122**
Norfolk Ho. *Salt* 2A **82**
Norfolk Rd. *M18* 3E **111**
Norfolk St. *M2* . . .4D **94** (5H **5**)
Norfolk St. *Hyde* 5B **114**
Norfolk St. *Oldh* 5H **71**
       (in two parts)
Norfolk St. *Roch* 5G **27**
Norfolk St. *Salf* 6E **81**
Norfolk St. *Wors* 3F **63**
Norfolk Way. *Rytn* 5B **56**
Norford Way. *Roch* 3A **26**
Norgate St. *M20* 6F **125**
Norlan Av. *Aud* 6E **99**
Norland Wlk. *M40* 6H **83**
Norleigh Rd. *M22* 3B **136**
Norley Av. *Stret* 4F **107**
Norley Clo. *Chad* 5H **55**
Norley Dri. *M19* 5E **111**
Norley Dri. *Sale* 5E **123**
Norman Av. *Haz G* 2C **152**
Normanby Chase. *Alt* . . .1D **144**
Normanby Gro. *Swin* 2E **79**
Normanby Rd. *Wors* 2E **77**
Normanby St. *M14* 3E **109**
Normanby St. *Bolt* 5F **45**
Normanby St. *Swin* 2E **79**
Norman Clo. *Midd* 6C **54**
Normandale Av. *Bolt* 4E **31**
Normandy Cres. *Rad* 4F **49**
Norman Gro. *M12* 3B **110**
Norman Gro. *Stoc* 2G **127**
Norman Rd. *M14* 5H **109**
Norman Rd. *Alt* 5E **133**
Norman Rd. *Ash L* 5G **87**
Norman Rd. *Hoch* 5F **27**
Norman Rd. *Sale* 5B **122**
Norman Rd. *Salf* 4A **82**
Norman Rd. *Stal* 3D **100**
Norman Rd. *Stoc* 6D **126**
Norman Rd. W. *M9* 4H **83**
Norman's Pl. *Alt* 1F **145**
Norman St. *M12* 2D **110**
Norman St. *Bolt* 3B **46**
Norman St. *Bury* 1F **37**
Norman St. *Fail* 2G **85**
Norman St. *Hyde* 5C **114**
Norman St. *Midd* 6B **54**
Norman St. *Oldh* 1B **72**
Norman St. Rad 3B **50**
      (off Sandford St.)
Normanton Av. *Salf* 2C **92**
Normanton Dri. *M9* 6G **69**
Normanton Rd. *Stoc* . . .4C **138**
Norman Weall Ct.
    Midd 5A **54**
Normington St. *Oldh* 2F **73**
Norreys Av. *Urm* 4A **104**
Norreys St. *Roch* 3A **28**
Norris Bank. 1D **138**
Norris Bank Ter. *Stoc* 2F **139**
Norris Hill. 1D **138**
Norris Hill Dri. *Stoc* 1E **139**
Norris Rd. *Sale* 1B **134**
Norris Rd. *W'houg* 6A **44**
Norris St. *Bolt* 2A **46**
Norris St. *Farn* 2E **63**
Norris St. *L Lev* 4A **48**
Norris Towers. Stoc 1G **139**
      (off Wilkinson Rd.)
Nortex Bus. Cen. *Bolt* . . .5G **31**
Northallerton Rd. *Salf* 5F **81**
Northampton Rd. *M40* . . .5H **83**

Northampton Way.
    Dent 6F **113**
North Av. *M19* 2B **126**
North Av. *Farn* 1C **62**
North Av. *G'fld* 4F **61**
North Av. *G'mnt* 2H **21**
North Av. *Stal* 2E **101**
North Av. *Uns* 3F **51**
Northavon Clo. Eccl 4A **92**
     (off Kearton Dri.)
N. Back Rd. Bury 3D **36**
     (off Rock, The)
N. Back Rd. Bury 3D **36**
     (off Tithebarn St.)
Northbank Gdns.
    M19 . . . . .3A **126**
Northbank Ho. *Wors* 6A **78**
Northbank Ind. Est.
    Cad 4C **118**
Northbank Ind. Pk.
    Irlam 3D **118**
     (Brinell Dri.)
Northbank Ind. Pk.
    Irlam 1E **119**
     (Fairhills Rd.)
Northbank Wlk. *M20* . . .6B **124**
N. Blackfield La. *Salf* 3C **81**
Northbourne St. *Salf* 3E **93**
Northbrook Av. *M8* 5B **68**
N. Brook Rd. *Had* 3G **117**
N. Broughton St.
    Salf 3C **94** (4E **5**)
North Circ. *W'fld* 3E **67**
N. Clifden La. *Salf* 5A **82**
Northcliffe Rd. *Stoc* 3C **140**
North Clo. *Tin* 1H **117**
Northcombe Rd. *Stoc* . . .6G **139**
Northcote Rd. *Bram* 6H **151**
North Cres. *M11* 2F **97**
N. Croft. *Oldh* 6E **73**
Northdale Rd. *M9* 4D **68**
N. Dean St. *Swin* 2G **79**
Northdene Dri. *Roch* 5B **26**
Northdown Av.
    M15 . . . . . .1B **108** (5C **8**)
Northdown Av. Woodl . . .4A **130**
N. Downs Rd. *Chea H* . . .2D **150**
N. Downs Rd. *Shaw* 5D **42**
North Dri. *Aud* 4C **98**
North Dri. *Swin* 4H **79**
Northenden. 2B **136**
Northenden Pde. *M22* . . .2B **136**
Northenden Rd. *Gat* 5E **137**
Northenden Rd. *Sale* 5C **122**
Northenden Vw. M20 . . .1F **137**
     (off South Rd.)
N. End Rd. *Stal* 3F **101**
Northen Gro. *M20* 5D **124**
Northerly Cres. *M40* 6D **70**
Northern Av. *Swin* 6A **66**
Northern Gro. *Bolt* 4G **31**
Northern Moor. 2F **135**
Northern Tennis Club.
    . . . . .5E **125**
Northfield Av. *M40* 1F **85**
Northfield Dri. Wilm 1G **167**
Northfield Rd. *M40* 1F **85**
Northfield Rd. *Bury* 5F **23**
Northfield St. *Bolt* 2G **45**
Northfleet Rd. Eccl 4R **90**
North Ga. *Oldh* 1C **86**
Northgate. *Whitw* 2C **14**
Northgate La. *Oldh* 3A **58**
Northgate Rd. *Stoc* 3E **139**
N. George St.
    Salf 2B **94** (2C **4**)
North Gro. *M13* 2H **109**
North Gro. *Urm* 6E **105**
North Gro. *Wors* 6E **63**
N. Harvey St. *Stoc* 2H **139**
N. Hill St. *Salf* 2B **94** (2D **4**)
Northland Rd. *M9* 6A **70**

Northland Rd. *Bolt* 5D **18**
Northlands. *Rad* 2E **49**
North La. *Roch* 3H **27**
Northleach Clo. *Bury* 2H **35**
Northleigh Dri. *P'wich* 6II **67**
Northleigh Ho. *M16* 5H **107**
Northleigh Rd. *M16* 4H **107**
N. Lonsdale St. *Stret* 4E **107**
N. Manchester Bus. Pk.
    M40 . . . . .5G **83**
North Meade. *M21* 2H **123**
North Moor. 2B **72**
Northmoor M. Oldh 1C **72**
Northmoor Rd. *M12* 3E **110**
North Nook. *Oldh* 1B **74**
Northolme Gdns.
    M19 . . . . .4A **126**
Northolt Ct. *M11* 3F **97**
Northolt Dri. *Bolt* 3B **46**
Northolt Fold. *Heyw* 6G **39**
Northolt Rd. *M23* 2F **135**
North Pde. *M3* . . .4D **94** (5G **5**)
North Pde. *Miln* 1G **43**
North Pde. *M3* 1D **134**
N. Park Rd. *Bram* 3F **151**
N. Phoebe St. *Salf* 5G **93**
North Pl. *Stoc* 2II **139**
North Reddish. 6G **111**
Northridge Rd. *M9* 3F **69**
North Ri. *G'fld* 4F **61**
North Rd. *M11* 3D **96**
North Rd. *Aud* 4C **98**
North Rd. *C'ton* 5H **119**
North Rd. *Hale* 5A **146**
North Rd. *P'wich* 4D **66**
North Rd. *Stal* 3F **101**
North Rd. *Stret* 3A **106**
Northside Av. *Urm* 6B **104**
North Stage. *Salf* 5B **93**
Northstead Av.
    Dent 5H **113**
North St. *M8* 6C **82**
North St. *Ash L* 3G **99**
North St. *Heyw* 3D **38**
North St. L'boro 4G **17**
     (off East St.)
North St. *Midd* 5A **54**
North St. *Rad* 3A **50**
North St. *Roch* 3A **20**
North St. *Rytn* 5B **56**
     (in two parts)
North St. *Whitw* 4G **15**
Northumberland Av.
    Ash L 1H **99**
Northumberland Clo.
    M16 . . . . .2A **108**
Northumberland Cres.
    M16 . . . . .2A **108**
Northumberland Rd.
    M16 . . . . . .3A **108** (6B **8**)
Northumberland Rd.
    Stoc 2B **128**
Northumberland St.
    Salf 4H **81**
Northumberland Way.
    M22 . . . . .5C **136**
Northumbria St. *Bolt* 2G **45**
Northurst Dri. *M8* 6B **68**
N. Vale Rd. *Timp* 5H **133**
North Vw. *Bury* 1B **22**
North Vw. *Moss* 2G **89**
North Vw. *W'fld* 5C **50**
North Vw. *Whitw* 4H **15**
N. View Clo. *Lyd* 4E **75**
Northward Rd. *Wilm* 3C **166**
Northway. *Alt* 5G **133**
North Way. *Bolt* 1D **32**
Northway. *Droy* 5A **98**
Northway. *Eccl* 3H **91**
North Way. *Hyde* 5C **114**
Northway. *Stoc* 3C **128**

N. Western St. *M1* &
    M12 . . . . . .5G **95** (2E **11**)
     (in two parts)
N. Western St. *Lev* 1C **126**
Northwold Dri. *M9* . . . . . .GB **70**
Northwold Dri. *Bolt* 5C **30**
Northwood. Bolt 1F **33**
Northwood Cres. *Bolt* 2G **45**
Northwood Gro. *Sale* 5B **122**
North Woodley. *Rad* 1A **66**
Norton Av. *M12* 4D **110**
Norton Av. *Dent* 4A **112**
Norton Av. *Sale* 3F **121**
Norton Av. *Urm* 3F **105**
Norton Grange. *P'wich* . .6H **67**
Norton Gro. *Stoc* 2D **138**
Norton Rd. *Roch* 6F **15**
Norton Rd. *Wors* 4A **76**
Norton St. *M1* 4G **95** (6F **7**)
Norton St. *Bolt* 2B **32**
Norton St. *Mile P* 1A **96**
Norton St. *Old T* 3A **108**
Norton St.
    Salf (M3) . . .3D **94** (3G **5**)
Norton St. *Salf* (M7) 4A **82**
Norview Dri. *M20* 4F **137**
Norville Av. *M40* 6D **70**
Norway Gro. *Stoc* 5H **127**
Norway St. *M11* 5A **96**
Norway St. *Bolt* 3H **31**
Norway St. *Salf* 3E **93**
Norway St. *Stret* 4E **107**
Norwell Rd. *M22* 6C **136**
Norwich Av. *Chad* 6G **55**
Norwich Av. *Dent* 6F **113**
Norwich Av. *Roch* 4C **26**
Norwich Clo. *Ash L* 4H **87**
Norwich Clo. *Duk* 6E **101**
Norwich Dri. Bury 2B **36**
Norwich Rd. *Stret* 4H **105**
Norwich St. *Roch* 6A **28**
Norwick Clo. *Bolt* 3C **44**
Norwood. *P'wich* 1F **81**
Norwood Av. *M20* 5H **125**
Norwood Av. *Bram* 2E **161**
Norwood Av. *Chea H* 2C **150**
Norwood Av. *H Lane* 0B **154**
Norwood Av. *Salf* 3F **81**
Norwood Clo. *Shaw* 5E **43**
Norwood Clo. *Wors* 3G **77**
Norwood Ct. *Stret* 6E **107**
Norwood Cres. *Rytn* 5C **56**
Norwood Dri. *Swin* 4C **78**
Norwood Dri. *Timp* 6D **134**
Norwood Gro. *Bolt* 5G **31**
Norwood Gro. *Rytn* 5C **56**
Norwood Lodge. *Salf* 3F **81**
Norwood Pk. *Alt* 6E **133**
Norwood Rd. *Gat* 5F **137**
Norwood Rd. *Stoc* 1D **152**
Norwood Rd. *Stret* 6E **107**
Nottingham Av. *Stoc* 3C **128**
Nottingham Clo. *Stoc* . . .4C **128**
Nottingham Dri. *Ash L* . . .4F **87**
Nottingham Dri. *Bolt* 4A **32**
Nottingham Dri. Fail 6G **85**
Nottingham Ter. *Stoc* 3C **128**
Nottingham Way.
    Dent 6G **113**
Nowell Ct. *Midd* 4A **54**
Nowell Ho. *Midd* 4A **54**
Nowell Rd. *Midd* 4A **54**
Nudger Clo. *Dob* 5H **59**
Nudger Grn. *Dob* 5H **59**
Nuffield Ho. *Bolt* 4F **31**
Nuffield Rd. *M22* 1C **148**
Nugent Rd. *Bolt* 4A **46**
     (in two parts)
Nugget St. *Oldh* 3F **73**
Nuneaton Dri.
    M40 . . . . . .2H **95** (1G **7**)
Nuneham Av. *M20* 2G **125**

Nunfield Clo. *M40* 1B **84**
Nunnery Rd. *Bolt* 3F **45**
Nunthorpe Dri. *M8* 3E **83**
Nursery Av. *Hale* 5G **145**
Nursery Brow. *Rad* 1H **65**
Nursery Clo. *Sale* 5D **122**
Nursery Clo. *Stoc* 4D **140**
Nursery Dri. *Poy* 3D **162**
Nursery Gdns. *Roch* 3C **28**
Nursery Gro. *Part* 5D **118**
Nursery La. *Stoc* 4C **138**
Nursery La. *Wilm* 3C **166**
Nursery Rd. *Chea H* 4B **150**
Nursery Rd. *Fail* 4G **85**
Nursery Rd. *P'wich* 3E **67**
Nursery Rd. *Stoc* 1E **139**
Nursery Rd. *Urm* 3C **104**
Nursery St. *M16* 4D **108**
Nursery St. *Salf* 2F **93**
Nuthatch Av. *Wors* 3F **77**
Nuthurst Rd. *M40* 2C **84**
Nutsford Vale. 3D **110**
Nutsford Va. *M18* 3D **110**
Nut St. *Bolt* 3H **31**
Nuttall. 5E **13**
Nuttall Av. *L Lev* 4C **48**
Nuttall Av. *W'fld* 1D **66**
Nuttall Clo. *Rams* 4E **13**
Nuttall Hall Cotts.
. . . *Rams* 4F **13**
Nuttall Hall Rd. *Rams* 5F **13**
Nuttall Lane. 4E **13**
Nuttall La. *Rams* 4D **12**
Nuttall M. *W'fld* 1D **66**
Nuttall Sq. *Bury* 2D **50**
Nuttall St. *M11* 6C **96**
Nuttall St. *M16* 2A **108**
Nuttall St. *Bury* 4E **37**
Nuttall St. *Cad* 3C **118**
Nuttall St. *Oldh* 5F **73**
Nutt La. *P'wich* 1A **68**

O

Oadby Clo. *M12* 2C **110**
Oak Av. *M21* 1H **123**
Oak Av. *Cad* 4B **118**
Oak Av. *Chea H* 3C **150**
Oak Av. *L Lev* 4B **48**
Oak Av. *Midd* 2A **70**
Oak Av. *Rams* 1A **22**
Oak Av. *Rom* 1A **142**
Oak Av. *Rytn* 1B **56**
Oak Av. *Stoc* 1D **138**
Oak Av. *W'fld* 2D **66**
Oak Av. *Wilm* 4C **166**
Oak Bank. 1E **67**
Oak Bank. *Carr* 4H **89**
Oak Bank. *P'wich* 2D **80**
Oak Bank Av. *M9* 2H **83**
Oakbank Av. *Chad* 1E **71**
Oak Bank Clo. *W'fld* 1F **67**
Oakbank Dri. *Bolt* 5B **18**
Oakbarton. *Los* 3A **44**
Oakcliffe Rd. *Roch* 5A **16**
Oak Clo. *Mot* 3C **116**
Oak Clo. *Whitw* 1H **15**
Oak Clo. *Wilm* 3C **166**
Oak Coppice. *Bolt* 6E **31**
Oak Cotts. *Styal* 3D **158**
Oak Ct. *Bred* 5G **129**
Oakcroft. *Stal* 6H **101**
Oakcroft Way. *M22* 5C **136**
Oakdale. *Bolt* 1F **33**
Oakdale Clo. *W'fld* 1B **66**
Oakdale Ct. *Alt* 6E **133**
Oakdale Ct. *Del* 4G **59**
Oakdale Dri. *M20* 2G **137**
Oakdale Dri. *H Grn* 3F **149**
Oakdean Ct. *Wilm* 6F **159**

Oakdene. *Swin* 5B **78**
Oakdene Av. *H Grn* 6F **149**
Oakdene Av. *Stoc* 4F **127**
Oakdene Cres. *Marp* 4D **142**
Oakdene Gdns. *Marp* 4D **142**
Oakdene Rd. *Marp* 4D **142**
Oakdene Rd. *Midd* 1C **70**
Oakdene Rd. *Timp* 3B **134**
Oakdene St. *M9* 3H **83**
Oak Dri. *M14* 6H **109**
Oak Dri. *Bram* 6E **151**
Oak Dri. *Dent* 3A **112**
Oak Dri. *Marp* 5B **142**
Oaken Bank Rd.
. . . . *Heyw & Midd* 2H **53**
Oaken Bottom. 6F **33**
Oakenbottom Rd. *Bolt* 6F **33**
Oaken Clough. *Ash L* 5D **86**
Oakenclough. *Oldh* 2C **72**
Oakenclough Clo.
. . . *Wilm* 5H **159**
Oaken Clough Dri.
. . . *Ash L* 5D **86**
Oakenclough Dri. *Bolt* 3D **30**
Oakenrod Hill. *Roch* 4E **27**
Oakenrod Vs. *Roch* 4F **27**
Oakenshaw Av. *Whitw* 3C **14**
Oakenshaw Vw. *Whitw* . . .3C **14**
Oaken St. *Ash L* 5E **87**
Oaker Av. *M20* 5C **124**
Oakes St. *Kear* 2H **63**
Oakfield. *Duk* 1C **114**
Oakfield. *P'wich* 6H **67**
Oakfield Av. *Carr* 5G **89**
Oakfield Av. *Chea* 5A **138**
Oakfield Av. *Droy* 4H **97**
Oakfield Av. *Firs* 4G **107**
Oakfield Av. *Whal R* 4B **108**
Oakfield Clo. *Ald E* 6E **167**
Oakfield Clo. *Bram* 3G **161**
Oakfield Ct. *Timp* 5H **133**
Oakfield Dri. *L Hul* 4A **62**
Oakfield Gro. *M18* 3F **111**
Oakfield Gro. *Farn* 3E **63**
Oakfield M. *Sale* 5A **122**
Oakfield M. *Stoc* 6H **139**
Oakfield Rd. *M20* 6E **125**
Oakfield Rd. *Ald E* 6E **167**
Oakfield Rd. *Alt* 6G **133**
Oakfield Rd. *Had* 4G **117**
Oakfield Rd. *Hyde* 2C **114**
Oakfield Rd. *Poy* 3F **163**
Oakfield Rd. *Stoc* 6H **139**
Oakfield St. *M8* 5C **82**
Oakfield St. *Alt* 6G **133**
Oakfield Ter. *Roch* 3E **27**
Oakfield Trad. Est. *Alt* 6G **133**
Oakfold Av. *Ash L* 5H **87**
Oakford Av.
. . . *M40* 2G **95** (2F **7**)
Oakford Wlk. *Bolt* 3G **45**
Oak Gates. *Eger* 2C **18**
Oak Gro. *Ash L* 5H **87**
Oak Gro. *Eccl* 4D **90**
Oak Gro. *Poy* 3D **162**
Oak Gro. *Urm* 5G **105**
Oakham Clo. *Bury* 6D **22**
Oakham M. *Salf* 2G **81**
Oakham Rd. *Dent* 6G **113**
Oak Hill. *L'boro* 4D **16**
Oakhill Clo. *Bolt* 6A **34**
Oakhill Ct. *Salf* 4B **82**
Oakhill Trad. Est.
. . . . *Wors* 4E **63**
Oakhill Way. *M8* 4B **82**
Oakhouse Dri. *M21* 2H **123**
Oakhurst Chase.
. . . . *Ald E* 4G **167**
Oakhurst Dri. *Stoc* 6D **138**
Oakington Av. *M14* 4F **109**

Oakland Av. *M16* 3G **107**
Oakland Av. *M19* 5A **126**
Oakland Av. *Salf* 1A **92**
Oakland Av. *Stoc* 5C **140**
Oakland Ct. *Poy* 3C **162**
Oakland Gro. *Bolt* 3E **31**
Oakland Ho. *M16* 3G **107**
Oaklands. *Bolt* 6D **30**
Oaklands. *Los* 5A **30**
Oaklands. *Wilm* 2G **167**
Oaklands Av. *Chea H* 3C **150**
Oaklands Av. *Marp B* 3G **143**
Oaklands Clo. *Wilm* 6A **160**
Oaklands Dene. *Hyde* 5E **115**
Oaklands Dri. *Haz G* 4E **153**
Oaklands Dri. *P'wich* 5F **67**
Oaklands Dri. *Sale* 4A **122**
Oaklands Ho. *M14* 6G **109**
Oaklands Pk. *Grass* 4G **75**
Oaklands Rd.
. . . . *G'fld & Oldh* 4H **75**
Oaklands Rd. *Hyde* 5E **115**
Oaklands Rd. *Rams* 3A **12**
Oaklands Rd. *Rytn* 5C **56**
Oaklands Rd. *Salf* 4E **81**
Oaklands Rd. *Swin* 5D **78**
Oaklands Ter. *Roch* 4C **40**
Oak La. *W'fld* 1F **67**
Oak La. *Wilm* 3C **166**
Oak Lea Av. *Wilm* 4D **166**
Oaklea Rd. *Sale* 4G **121**
Oakleigh. *Stoc* (SK3) 1H **151**
Oakleigh. *Stoc* (SK4) 6D **126**
Oakleigh Av. *M19* 2B **126**
Oakleigh Av. *Bolt* 5C **46**
Oakleigh Av. *Timp* 4A **134**
Oakleigh Clo. *Heyw* 6G **39**
Oakleigh Ct. *Timp* 4C **134**
Oakleigh Ho. *Sale* 6G **121**
Oakleigh M. *Sale* 6G **121**
Oakleigh Rd. *Chea H* 5A **150**
Oakley Clo. *M40* 6C **84**
Oakley Clo. *Rad* 1G **65**
Oakley Pk. *Bolt* 6D **30**
Oakley St. *L'boro* 5C **16**
Oakley St. *Salf* 4D **92**
Oakley Vs. *Stoc* 6D **126**
Oak Lodge. *Bram* 6H **151**
Oakmere Av. *Eccl* 1E **91**
Oakmere Clo. *M22* 1B **148**
Oakmere Rd. *Chea H* 1B **150**
Oakmere Rd. *Hand* 2H **159**
Oak M. *Wilm* 6G **159**
Oakmoor Dri. *Salf* 3E **81**
Oakmoor Rd. *M23* 5G **135**
Oakridge Wlk. *M9* 4F **83**
Oak Rd. *M20* 4F **125**
Oak Rd. *Chea* 5A **138**
Oak Rd. *Fail* 5F **85**
Oak Rd. *Hale* 2G **145**
Oak Rd. *Oldh* 1A **86**
Oak Rd. *Part* 6B **118**
Oak Rd. *Sale* 5D **122**
Oak Rd. *Salf* 5G **81**
Oaks Av. *Bolt* 6G **19**
Oaks Bus. Pk.,
. . . . The. *M23* 3E **135**
Oakshaw Dri. *Roch* 2C **26**
Oakside Clo. *Chea* 5H **137**
Oaks La. *Bolt* 6F **19**
Oaks, The. *M4* 3E **95** (4B **6**)
. . . . . (in two parts)
Oak St. *Aud* 1F **113**
Oak St. *Eccl* 4F **91**
Oak St. *Haz G* 2D **152**
Oak St. *Heyw* 2D **38**
Oak St. *Hyde* 3C **114**
Oak St. *L'boro* 4G **17**
Oak St. *Midd* 2D **70**
Oak St. *Miln* 2E **43**

Oak St. *Rad* 6A **50**
Oak St. *Rams* 4D **12**
Oak St. *Roch* 4H **27**
Oak St. *Shaw* 6G **43**
Oak St. *S'bri* 6D **16**
Oak St. *Stoc* 3D **138**
Oak St. *Swin* 2G **79**
Oak St. *Whitw* 1H **15**
Oak Ter. *L'boro* 5H **17**
Oak Tree Clo. *Hyde* 5E **115**
Oak Tree Clo. *Stoc* 3D **140**
Oak Tree Ct. *Chea* 6H **137**
Oak Tree Cres. *Stal* 5E **101**
Oak Tree Dri. *Duk* 6D **100**
Oak Vw. *Whitw* 1H **15**
Oak Vw. Rd. *G'fld* 4F **61**
Oakville Dri. *Salf* 1A **92**
Oakville Ter. *M40* 2H **83**
Oak Wlk. *Aud* 1E **113**
Oakway. *M20* 3G **137**
Oakway. *Midd* 3H **53**
Oakwell Dri. *Bury* 4F **51**
Oakwell Dri. *Salf* 2A **82**
Oakwell Mans. *Salf* 2A **82**
Oakwood. *Chad* 2E **71**
Oakwood. *Sale* 5E **121**
Oakwood Av. *M40* 2D **84**
Oakwood Av. *Aud* 6E **99**
Oakwood Av. *Gat* 6E **137**
Oakwood Av. *Swin* 5E **65**
Oakwood Av. *Wilm* 3B **166**
Oakwood Av. *Wors* 1H **77**
Oakwood Clo. *Bury* 2H **35**
Oakwood Ct. *Bow* 5D **144**
Oakwood Dri. *Bolt* 5D **30**
Oakwood Dri. *Salf* 6H **79**
Oakwood Dri. *Wors* 1H **77**
Oakwood Est. *Salf* 4D **92**
Oakwood Ho. *M21* 1A **124**
Oakwood La. *Bow* 4C **144**
Oakwood Rd. *Dis* 1H **165**
Oakwood Rd. *Rom* 1A **142**
Oakworth Cft. *Oldh* 3B **58**
Oakworth Dri. *Bolt* 6B **18**
Oakworth St. *M9* 1E **83**
Oatlands. *Ald E* 6H **167**
. . . . . (in two parts)
Oatlands Rd. *M22* 4A **148**
Oat St. *Stoc* 4A **140**
Oats Wlk. *M13* 3G **109**
Oban Av. *M40* 1D **96**
Oban Av. *Oldh* 6F **57**
Oban Cres. *Stoc* 1F **151**
Oban Dri. *Sale* 6E **123**
Oban Gro. *Bolt* 6C **18**
Oban St. *Bolt* 2H **31**
Oberlin St. *Oldh* 2H **73**
Oberlin St. *Roch* 6F **27**
Oberon Clo. *Eccl* 3F **91**
Occleston Clo. *Sale* 2E **135**
Occupiers La. *Haz G* 4G **153**
Ocean St. *Alt* 5D **132**
Ocean St. Trad. Est.
. . . . *B'hth* 4D **132**
Ocean Wlk.
. . . . *M15* 2D **108** (6H **9**)
Ockenden Dri. *M9* 4G **83**
Octagon Ct. *Bolt* 1B **46**
Octagon Theatre. 6B **32**
Octavia Dri. *M40* 1E **97**
Oddies Yd. *Roch* 1A **28**
Odell St. *M11* 6D **96**
Odessa Av. *Salf* 1B **92**
Odette St. *M18* 3E **111**
Off Duke St. *Moss* 2G **89**
Offerton. 5E **141**
Offerton Dri. *Stoc* 5D **140**
Offerton Fold. *Stoc* 4C **140**
Offerton Green. 5G **141**
Offerton Grn. *Stoc* 5F **141**
Offerton Ind. Est.
. . . . *Stoc* 3C **140**

Offerton La. *Stoc* 3B **140**
Offerton Rd.
    Haz G & Stoc 2G **153**
Offerton St. *Stoc* 1B **140**
Off Groom St. *Midd* 6B **54**
Off Grove Rd. *Mill* 1H **101**
Off Kershaw St. Shaw . . .6F *43*
   (off Kershaw St., in two parts)
Off Ridge Hill La. *Stal* . .3D **100**
Off Stamford St. *Mill* . . .1H **101**
Off Vaudrey La. *Dent* . .5G **113**
Off Vaudrey La. Hyde . .4H *113*
   (off Manchester Rd.)
Ogbourne Wlk.
   M13 . . . . . .1G *109* (6F *11*)
   (off Lauderdale Cres.)
Ogden Clo. *Heyw* 3C **38**
Ogden Clo. *W'fld* 6E **51**
Ogden Ct. *Hyde* 5C **114**
Ogden Gdns. *Duk* 5C **100**
Ogden Gro. *Gat* 1D **148**
Ogden La. *M11* 6F **97**
Ogden La. *Miln* 1H **43**
Ogden Rd. *Bram* 2E **161**
Ogden Rd. *Fail* 5F **85**
Ogden Sq. *Duk* 5H **99**
Ogden St. *M20* 6F **125**
Ogden St. *Chad* 1A **72**
Ogden St. *Midd* 1A **70**
Ogden St. *Oldh* 3H **73**
Ogden St. *P'wich* 5G **67**
Ogden St. *Roch* 3C **40**
Ogden St. *Swin* 4F **79**
Ogden Wlk. *W'fld* 1E **67**
Ogmore Wlk. *M40* 1G **84**
Ogwen Dri. *P'wich* 4F **67**
Ohio Av. *Salf* 5F **93**
O'Kane Ho. *Eccl* 4F **91**
Okehampton Clo. *Rad* . .2C **48**
Okehampton Cres.
   Sale 4F **121**
Okeover Rd. *Salf* 3H **81**
Olaf St. *Bolt* 4D **32**
Old Bank Clo. *Bred* 6G **129**
Old Bank St.
   M2 . . . . .4D **94** (5H **5**)
Old Bank Vw. *Oldh* 3G **57**
Old Barn Pl. *Brom X* . . .3E **19**
Old Barton Rd. *Urm* 6F **91**
   (in two parts)
Old Bedians Sports Cen.
   . . . . .3E **137**
Old Birley St.
   M15 . . . . . .2D **108** (6G **9**)
Old Birtle. 4C **24**
Old Broadway. *M20* 4F **125**
Old Brook Clo. *Shaw* . . .5H **43**
Oldbrook Fold. *Timp* . . .1B **146**
Old Brow. *Moss* 3E **89**
                (Park St.)
Old Brow. *Moss* 2E **89**
              (Seel St.)
Old Brow Ct. *Moss* 3E **89**
Old Brow La. *Roch* 6A **16**
Oldbury Clo.
   M40 . . . . . . .2H **95** (2G **7**)
Oldbury Clo. *Heyw* 6F **39**
Oldcastle Av. *M20* 1E **125**
Old Chapel St. *Stoc* 4F **139**
Old Church M. *Duk* 5C **100**
Old Church St. *M40* 5R **84**
Old Church St. *Oldh* 2D **72**
Old Clay Dri. *Roch* 5B **16**
Old Clough La. *Wors* . . .3H **77**
   (in two parts)
Oldcott Clo. *Wors* 6B **76**
Old Ct. Ho., The.
   Salf 3B **94** (4C **4**)
Old Ct. St. *Hyde* 5B **114**
Old Courtyard, The.
   M22 . . . . .6C **136**
Oldcroft. *S'head* 3C **74**

Old Cft. M. *Stoc* 4B **140**
Old Crofts Bank. *Urm* . . .3E **105**
Old Cross St. *Ash L* 2A **100**
Old Dairy M. *Hyde* 2A **114**
Old Delph Rd. *Roch* 2A **26**
Old Doctors St. *T'ton* . . .4H **21**
Old Eagley M. *Bolt* 5D **18**
Old Edge La.
   Rytn & Oldh 5C **56**
          (in two parts)
Old Elm St.
   M13 . . . . . .1G **109** (5F **11**)
Oldershaw Dri. *M9* 5F **83**
Old Farm Cres. *Droy* . . .5H **97**
Old Farm Dri. *Stoc* 5F **141**
Oldfield Brow. 5C **132**
Oldfield Dri. *Timp* 5H **133**
Oldfield Gro. *Sale* 4C **122**
Oldfield La. *Dun M* 1A **144**
Oldfield M. *Alt* 6E **133**
Oldfield Rd. *Alt* 6C **132**
Oldfield Rd. *P'wich* 2G **67**
Oldfield Rd. *Sale* 4C **122**
Oldfield Rd. *Salf* . . .5A **94** (3A **8**)
Oldfield St. *M11* 4D **96**
Old Fold. *Eccl* 1E **91**
Old Fold. *Haz G* 2D **152**
Old Gdns. St. *Stoc* 3H **139**
Old Garden, The.
   Timp 4B **134**
Oldgate Wlk.
   M15 . . . . . .1B **108** (6D **8**)
Old Grn. Bolt 5A **20**
Old Green. *G'mnt* 2H **21**
Old Ground St. *Rams* . . .3E **13**
Old Hall Clo. *Bury* 4B **22**
Old Hall Clo. *Mot* 2C **116**
Old Hall Clough. *Los* . . .6A **30**
          (in two parts)
Old Hall Ct. *Sale* 5E **123**
Old Hall Ct. *W'fld* 2A **66**
Old Hall Cres. *Hand* . . .4A **160**
Old Hall Dri. *M18* 3F **111**
Old Hall Dri. *Stoc* 5E **141**
Old Hall La.
   M14 & M13 . . . . . .6H **109**
Old Hall La. *Los* 4A **30**
Old Hall La. *Mell* 6F **143**
          (in two parts)
Old Hall La. *Mot* 2C **116**
Old Hall La. *P'wich & Midd*1B **68**
         (in four parts)
Old Hall La. *W'fld* 3A **66**
         (in two parts)
Old Hall La. *Woodf* 6F **161**
Old Hall La. *Wors* 4G **77**
Old Hall M. *Bolt* 4B **30**
Old Hall Rd. *Gat* 5E **137**
Old Hall Rd. *Sale* 5E **123**
Old Hall Rd. *Salf* 2H **81**
Old Hall Rd. *Stret* 3H **105**
Old Hall Rd. *W'fld* 2A **66**
Old Hall Sq. *Had* 2H **117**
Old Hall St. *M11* 6G **97**
Old Hall St. *Duk* 6G **99**
Old Hall St. *Kear* 2G **63**
Oldhall St. *Midd* 1H **69**
          (in two parts)
Old Hall St. N. *Bolt* 6B **32**
Oldham. 2D **72**
Oldham Art Gallery. 3D *72*
   (off Union St, Library)
Oldham Athletic Football Club.
   . . . . .5B **56**
        (Boundary Park)
Oldham Av. *Stoc* 2B **140**
Oldham B'way. Bus. Pk.
   Chad 5E **71**
Oldham Central Trad. Pk.
   Oldh 1E **73**

Oldham Ct. *M40* . . .2G **95** (2F **7**)
Oldham Crematorium.
   Oldh 2A **86**
Oldham Dri. *Bred* 5G **129**
Oldham Edge. 1D **72**
Oldham Ho. *Shaw* 2F **57**
Oldham Mus. 3D **72**
Oldham Rd.
   M4 & M40 . . .3F **95** (3D **6**)
Oldham Rd. *Ash L* 4E **87**
Oldham Rd. *Del* 1C **58**
Oldham Rd. *Fail* 5D **84**
Oldham Rd. *Lyd* 3E **75**
Oldham Rd. *Midd* 1A **70**
Oldham Rd. *Roch* 5A **28**
         (in two parts)
Oldham Rd. *Rytn* 3C **56**
Oldham Rd.
   Scout & Dob 1E **75**
Oldham Rd. *Shaw* 3F **57**
Oldham Rd. *S'head* 3B **74**
Oldham Rugby League
   Football Club. 5B **56**
Oldhams La. *Bolt* 6B **18**
         (in two parts)
Oldham Sports Cen. 2D **72**
Oldhams Ter. *Bolt* 1H **31**
Oldham St. *M1* . . .4E **95** (5B **6**)
Oldham St. *Dent* 5C **112**
Oldham St. *Droy* 3B **98**
Oldham St. *Hyde* 5B **114**
Oldham St. *Salf* . .4B **94** (6C **4**)
Oldham St. *Stoc* 2G **127**
Oldham Tourist Info. Cen.
   . . . . .3D **72**
Oldham Way. *Oldh* 1B **72**
Oldham Way. *Shaw* 3H **43**
           (Jubilee)
Oldham Way. *Shaw* 3E **43**
         (Moss Gate)
Old Heyes Rd. *Timp* 3B **134**
Old Ho. Ter. *Ash L* 6A **88**
Old Kiln La. *Bolt* 3A **30**
Old Kiln La. *G'ton* 5D **74**
Oldknow Rd. *Marp* 5E **143**
Old La. *M11* 5F **97**
Old La. *Aus* 1B **74**
Old La. *Bury* 3F **23**
Old La. *Chad* 5H **71**
Old La. *Dob* 5B **60**
Old La. *Grass* 3G **75**
Old La. *L Hul* 3B **62**
Old La. *Upperm* 6D **60**
Old Lansdowne Rd.
   M20 . . . . .5D **124**
Old Lees St. *Ash L* 6H **87**
Old Links Clo. *Bolt* 3C **30**
Old Mkt. Pl. *Alt* 6F **133**
Old Mkt. St. *M9* 1E **83**
Old Meadow Dri. *Dent* . .2F **113**
Old Meadow La. *Hale* . . .2B **146**
Old Medlock St.
   M3 . . . . .5B **94** (1D **8**)
Old Mill Clo. *Swin* 3B **79**
Old Mill Ho. *S'head* 4C **74**
Old Mill La. *G'ton* 4C **74**
Old Mill La. *Haz G* 5G **153**
Old Mills Hill. *Midd* 6D **54**
Old Mill St. *M4* . . .4G **95** (5E **7**)
Oldmill St. *Roch* 3H **27**
Old Moat La. *M20* 2E **125**
Oldmoor Rd. *Bred* 4E **129**
Old Mount St.
   M4 . . . . . . .2E **95** (2B **6**)
Old Nans La. *Bolt* 3H **33**
Old Nursery Fold. *Bolt* . .1G **33**
Old Oak Clo. *Bolt* 2B **48**
Old Oak Dri. *Dent* 4G **113**
Old Oake Clo. *Wors* 1G **77**
Old Oak St. *M20* 6F **125**
Old Orchard. *Wilm* 2D **166**

Old Orchard, The.
   Timp 3B **134**
Old Packhorse Rd. *Dig* . . .1B **60**
Old Pk. La. *Urm* 1E **105**
Old Parrin La. *Eccl* 2D **90**
Old Pasture Clo. *Stoc* . . .4E **141**
Old Quarry La. *Eger* 2D **18**
Old Rectory Gdns.
   Chea 6H **137**
Old River Clo. *Irlam* 5E **103**
Old Rd. *M9* 1F **83**
Old Rd. *Ash L* 6B **88**
Old Rd. *Bolt* 1A **32**
Old Rd. *Chea* 5B **138**
Old Rd. *Duk* 4A **100**
         (in two parts)
Old Rd. *Fail* 4E **85**
Old Rd. *Hand* 4H **159**
Old Rd. *Hyde* 2B **114**
Old Rd. *Mot* 2B **116**
Old Rd. *Stal* 5G **101**
Old Rd. *Stoc* 6G **127**
Old Rd. *Wilm* 1E **167**
Old School Cit. *M9* 1E **83**
Old School Ct. *Eccl* 1F **91**
Old School Dri. *M9* 1E **83**
Old School Ho., The.
   L'boro 3D *16*
        (off Shore Rd.)
Old School La.
   Chea H 5C **150**
         (in two parts)
Old School M. *Duk* 5C **100**
Old Shaw St. *Salf* 5H **93**
Old Sq. *Ash L* 2A **100**
Old Stables, The. *Aud* . . .1F **113**
Old Station St. *Eccl* 4E **91**
Oldstead Gro. *Bolt* 3D **44**
Oldstead Wlk. M9 . . . . . .5F *83*
     (off Kelvington Dri.)
Old St. *Ash L* 3G **99**
Old St. *Oldh* 4H **73**
Old St. *Stal* 3E **101**
Old Swan Clo. *Eger* 1C **18**
Old Swan Cotts. *Eger* . . .1C **18**
Old Tannery, The.
   Hyde 1D **130**
Old Thorn La. *G'fld* 3H **61**
Old Towns Clo. *T'ton* . . .4H **21**
Old Trafford. 2A **108**
Old Trafford Cricket Ground.
   . . . . .3G **107**
       (Lancashire C.C.C.)
Old Trafford Football Ground.
   . . . . .2F **107**
    (Manchester United F.C.)
Old Vicarage Gdns.
   Wors 6F **63**
Oldway Wlk. *M40* 6B **84**
Old Wellington Rd. *Eccl* . .3F **91**
Old Wells Clo. *L Hul* 3C **62**
Old Well Wlk. Sale 1E *133*
     (off Newgate Rd.)
Old Wood La. *Bolt* 5A **34**
         (in two parts)
Oldwood Rd. *M23* 3G **147**
Old Wool La. *Chea H* . . .1B **150**
       (Betleymere Rd.)
Old Wool La. *Chea H* . . .6B **138**
      (Pickmere Gdns.)
Old York St.
   M15 . . . . . .1C **108** (5E **9**)
Oleo Ter. *Irlam* 4G **103**
Olga St. *Bolt* 3H **31**
Olivant St. *Bury* 5C **36**
Olive Bank. *Bury* 1H **35**
Oliver Clo. *L'boro* 4D **16**
Olive Rd. *Timp* 3A **134**
Oliver St.
   M13 . . . . . .1E **109** (6B **10**)
Oliver St. *Oldh* 3D **72**
Oliver St. *Stoc* 3H **139**

Olive Shapley Av. *M20* 6F **125**
Olive St. *Bolt* 3H **45**
Olive St. *Bury* 3B **36**
Olive St. *Fail* 3E **85**
Olive St. *Heyw* 3G **39**
Olive St. *Rad* 4A **50**
Olive St. *Roch* 4D **40**
Olive Wlk. *Sale* 3E **121**
Olivia Ct. *Salf* 5A **94** (1B 8)
Olivia Gro. *M14* 4H **109**
Ollerbarrow Rd. *Hale* . .3G **145**
Ollerbrook Ct. *Bolt* 3B **32**
Ollerenshaw Hall.
    M14 . . . . .3H **109**
Ollerton. Roch *3G* **27**
            (off Sheriff St.)
Ollerton Av. *M16* 4A **108**
Ollerton Av. *Sale* 3F **121**
Ollerton Clo. *M22* 2C **136**
Ollerton Dri. *Fail* 5F **85**
Ollerton Rd. *Hand* 2H **159**
Ollerton St. *Bolt* 5D **18**
Ollerton Ter. Bolt *5D 18*
            (off Ollerton St.)
Ollier Av. *M12* 5C **110**
Olney. *Roch* 5G **27**
Olney Av. *M22* 5B **136**
Olney St. *M13* 3H **109**
Olsberg Clo. *Rad* 3A **50**
Olwen Av. *M12* 2C **110**
Olwen Cres. *Stoc* 1H **127**
Olympia Ct. *Irlam* 5E **103**
Olympia Trad. Est.
    M15 . . . . .6C **94** (3F 9)
Olympic Ct. *Salf* 5F **93**
Olympic Ho. *Man A* 6A **148**
Omega Dri. *Irlam* 3D **118**
Omer Av. *M13* 5B **110**
Omer Dri. *M19* 2A **126**
Onchan Av. *Oldh* 3F **73**
One Ash Clo. *Roch* 1H **27**
Oneoak Ct. *Bram* 3F **151**
One Oak La. *Wilm* 2H **167**
Ongar Wlk. *M9* 6D **68**
Onslow Av. *M40* 2E **85**
Onslow Clo. *Oldh* 1C **72**
Onslow Rd. *Stoc* 3E **139**
Onslow St. *Roch* 1C **40**
Ontario Ho. *Salf* 6G **93**
Onward St. *Hyde* 5B **114**
Oozewood. 1A **56**
Oozewood Rd. *Rytn* 2G **55**
Opal Ct. *M14* 1H **125**
Opal Gdns. *M14* 3H **109**
Opal St. *M19* 1D **126**
Openshaw. 5F **97**
Openshaw Ct. *Swin* 1G **79**
Openshaw Fold Rd.
    Bury 6B **36**
            (in two parts)
Openshaw La. *Cad* 3C **118**
Openshaw Pl. *Farn* 1D **62**
Openshaw St. *Bury* 4E **37**
Openshaw Wlk. *Open* . . .5E **97**
Opera House. 6F **5**
Oracle Ct. *Wors* 1E **77**
Orama Av. *Salf* 1A **92**
Orama Mill. *Whitw* 1C **14**
Oram St. *Bury* 1E **37**
            (in two parts)
Orange Hill Rd. *P'wich* . .4G **67**
Orbital Way. *Dent* 4D **112**
Orchard Av. *Bolt* 2B **32**
Orchard Av. *Part* 5D **118**
Orchard Av. *Wors* 4D **76**
Orchard Brow. *Shaw* 6D **42**
Orchard Clo. *Chea R* 6E **151**
Orchard Clo. *Poy* 4E **163**
Orchard Clo. *Wilm* 4C **166**
Orchard Ct. *Bury* 6C **36**
Orchard Ct. *Stoc* 5D **140**
Orchard Ct. *Timp* 4B **134**

Orchard Dri. *Glos* 6G **117**
Orchard Dri. *Hale* 2A **146**
Orchard Dri. *Hand* 4A **160**
Orchard Gdns. *Bolt* 2H **33**
Orchard Grn. *Ald E* 5H **167**
Orchard Gro. *M20* 4D **124**
Orchard Gro. *Shaw* 6E **43**
Orchard Ind. Est. *Salf* . . .6E **81**
Orchard Pl. *Poy* 3D **162**
Orchard Pl. *Sale* 4B **122**
Orchard Pl. *Timp* 4B **134**
Orchard Ri. *Hyde* 2D **130**
Orchard Rd. *Alt* 6G **133**
Orchard Rd. *Comp* 1F **143**
Orchard Rd. *Fail* 4F **85**
Orchard Rd. E. *M22* 1B **136**
Orchard Rd. W. *M22* 1B **136**
Orchards, The. Heyw *3G 39*
            (off Rochdale Rd. E.)
Orchards, The. *Shaw* 6D **42**
Orchards, The. *Stoc* 1H **151**
Orchard St. *M20* 4D **124**
Orchard St. *Heyw* 2G **39**
Orchard St. *Hyde* 5C **114**
Orchard St. *Kear* 2G **63**
Orchard St. *Salf* 6E **81**
            (in two parts)
Orchard St. *Stoc* 2H **139**
Orchard, The. *Ald E* 6H **167**
Orchard, The. *Oldh* 6G **73**
Orchard Trad. Est. *Salf* . .6D **80**
Orchard Va. *Stoc* 5E **139**
Orchard Wlk. G'mnt *2H 21*
            (off Lomax St.)
Orchid Av. *Farn* 6D **46**
Orchid Clo. *Irlam* 1C **118**
Orchid Clo. *Oldh* 6B **56**
Orchid Dri. *Bury* 6E **37**
Orchid St. *M9* 4F **83**
Orchid Way. *Roch* 6D **14**
Ordell Wlk. *M9* 6G **69**
Ordnance St. *Eccl* 3F **91**
Ordsall. 6H **93**
Ordsall Av. *L Hul* 5D **62**
Ordsall District Cen.
    Salf 5H **93**
Ordsall Dri. *Salf* 6H **93**
Ordsall Hall. 1H **107**
                (Museum)
Ordsall Recreation Cen.
    . . . . .6G **93**
Oregon Av. *Oldh* 6C **56**
Oregon Clo.
    M13 . . . . .1G **109** (5E 11)
Orford Av. *Dis* 1H **165**
Orford Clo. *H Lane* 6C **154**
Orford Rd. *M40* 6C **84**
Orford Rd. *P'wich* 4F **67**
Organ Way. *Holl* 2F **117**
Oriel Av. *Oldh* 6C **72**
Oriel Clo. *Chad* 4G **71**
Oriel Clo. *Stoc* 5B **140**
Oriel Ct. *Sale* 4B **122**
Oriel Rd. *M20* 5E **125**
Oriel St. *Bolt* 2G **45**
Oriel St. *Roch* 6H **27**
Orient Ho. *M1* 5E **95** (2B **10**)
Orient Rd. *Salf* 1A **92**
Orient Sq. M1 . . . .5E **95** (2B **10**)
            (off Granby Row)
Orient St. *Salf* 4B **82**
Orient, The. Urm 1F **105**
            (off Trafford Cen., The)
Oriole Clo. *Wors* 3D **76**
Orion Bus. Pk. *Stoc* 6D **138**
Orion Pl. *Salf* 1A **94**
Orion Trad. Est. *Traf P* . . .5A **92**
Orkney Clo. *M23* 1G **147**
Orkney Clo. *Rad* 3H **49**
Orkney Dri. *Urm* 2F **105**
Orlanda Av. *Salf* 1A **92**

Orlanda Dri. *Salf* 5B **82**
Orlando St. *Bolt* 2C **46**
            (in two parts)
Orleans Way. *Oldh* 2C **72**
Orley Wlk. *Oldh* 3H **57**
Orme Av. *Midd* 2A **70**
Orme Av. *Salf* 6H **79**
Orme Clo. *M11* 4A **96**
Orme Clo. *Urm* 5H **105**
Ormerod Av. *Rytn* 4C **56**
Ormerod Clo. *Rom* 2F **141**
Ormerod St. *M40* 2G **97**
Ormerod St. *Heyw* 4G **39**
Ormeston Lodge.
    Urm 6F **105**
Orme St. *M11* 4A **96**
Orme St. *Ald E* 5G **167**
Orme St. *Oldh* 4E **73**
Orme St. *Stoc* 1B **140**
Ormonde Av. *Salf* 1B **92**
Ormonde Ct. *Ash L* 1A **100**
Ormonde St. *Ash L* 1A **100**
Ormond St. *Bolt* 2F **47**
Ormond St. *Bury* 2E **37**
Ormrods, The. *Bury* 6D **24**
Ormrod St. *Bolt* 1A **46**
Ormrod St. *Brad* 1E **33**
Ormrod St. *Bury* 3E **37**
Ormrod St. *Farn* 1E **63**
Ormsby Av. *M18* 3D **110**
Ormsby Clo. *Stoc* 1G **151**
Ormsgill Clo.
    M15 . . . . .1D **108** (6G **9**)
Orms Gill Pl. *Stoc* 5E **141**
Ormskirk Av. *M20* 3D **124**
Ormskirk Clo. *Bury* 5G **35**
Ormskirk Rd. *Stoc* 3H **127**
Ornatus St. *Bolt* 6D **18**
Ornsay Wlk. *Open* 4E **97**
Oronsay Gro. *Salf* 4D **92**
Orphanage St. *Stoc* 6G **127**
Orpington Dri. *Bury* 4H **35**
Orpington Rd. *M9* 4G **83**
Orrell St. *M11* 5F **97**
Orrell St. *Bury* 2B **36**
Orrel St. *Salf* 3E **93**
Orrishmere Rd.
    Chea R 2B **150**
Orron St. *L'boro* 4E **17**
Orsett Clo. *M40* 2G **95** (1F **7**)
Orthes Gro. *Stoc* 4F **127**
Orton Av. *M23* 2G **135**
Orton Rd. *M23* 2G **135**
Orvietto Av. *Salf* 1A **92**
Orville Dri. *M19* 2B **126**
Orwell Av. *M22* 5B **136**
Orwell Av. *Dent* 4A **112**
Orwell Clo. *Bury* 1B **36**
Orwell Clo. *Wilm* 5H **159**
Orwell Rd. *Bolt* 3F **31**
Osborne Clo. *Bury* 5H **35**
Osborne Clo. *Wilm* 3G **167**
Osborne Dri. *Swin* 4A **80**
Osborne Gro. *Bolt* 4G **31**
Osborne Gro. *H Grn* 2E **149**
Osborne Ho. Eccl *3E 91*
            (off Police St.)
Osborne Ho. Rad *4F 49*
            (off Bolton Rd.)
Osborne Pl. *Had* 2H **117**
Osborne Rd. *M9* 4G **83**
Osborne Rd. *M19* 6B **110**
Osborne Rd. *Alt* 6G **133**
Osborne Rd. *Dent* 3F **113**
Osborne Rd. *Hyde* 6C **114**
Osborne Rd. *Oldh* 4B **72**
Osborne Rd. *Salf* 3A **92**
Osborne Rd. *Stoc* 4H **139**
Osborne St. *Bred* 6D **128**
Osborne St. *Col* 1G **95** (1E **7**)
Osborne St. *Did* 6E **125**
Osborne St. *Heyw* 4F **39**

Osborne St. *Oldh* 1A **72**
Osborne St. *Roch* 6G **27**
Osborne St. *Salf* 2F **93**
Osborne St. *Shaw* 1F **57**
Osborne Ter. *Ash L* 2A **100**
Osborne Ter. *Sale* 5B **122**
Osborne Trad. Est.
    Oldh 1A **72**
Osborne Wlk. *Rad* 3E **49**
Osbourne Clo. *Farn* 6F **47**
Osbourne Pl. *Alt* 1F **145**
Oscar St. *M40* 4A **84**
            (in two parts)
Oscar St. *Bolt* 3G **31**
Oscott Av. *L Hul* 3C **62**
Oscroft Clo. *M8* 5B **82**
Oscroft Wlk. M14 . . . . . .*2H 125*
            (off Lyth St.)
Osmond St. *Oldh* 2G **73**
Osmund Av. *Bolt* 6F **33**
Osprey Clo. *M15* 2C **108**
Osprey Clo. *Duk* 6C **100**
Osprey Ct. M15 . . . .*2C 108*
            (off Osprey Clo.)
Osprey Ct. *Salf* 5D **92**
Osprey Dri. *Droy* 2C **98**
Osprey Dri. *Irlam* 4E **103**
Osprey Dri. *Wilm* 1F **167**
Osprey Wlk.
    M13 . . . . . .1G **109** (6F **11**)
Ossington Wlk. *M23* 1G **135**
Ossory St. *M14* 4F **109**
Osterley Rd. *M9* 6H **69**
Ostlers Ga. *Droy* 3D **98**
Ostrich La. *P'wich* 6G **67**
Oswald Clo. *Salf* 6E **81**
Oswald La. *M21* 1H **107**
Oswald Rd. *Chor H* 6G **107**
Oswald St. *M4* 4H **95** (6G **7**)
            (Every St.)
Oswald St. *M4* 2E **95** (2A **6**)
            (Miller St.)
Oswald St. *Bolt* 3G **45**
            (in two parts)
Oswald St. *Roch* 3A **28**
Oswald St. *Shaw* 5G **43**
Oswald St. *Stoc* 4H **111**
Oswestry Clo. *G'mnt* 3G **21**
Otago St. *Oldh* 6G **57**
Othello Dri. *Eccl* 3F **91**
Otley Av. *Salf* 2C **92**
Otley Clo. *Chad* 3H **71**
Otley Gro. *Stoc* 1F **151**
Otmoor Way. *Rytn* 3E **57**
Otranto Av. *Salf* 1B **92**
Ottawa Clo. *M23* 1F **147**
Otterburn Ho. *Eccl* 2G **91**
Otterburn Pl. *Stoc* 5D **140**
Otterbury Clo. *Bury* 3F **35**
Otter Dri. *M8* 6A **82**
Otter Dri. *Bury* 3F **51**
Otterham Wlk. *M40* 6D **84**
Otterspool Rd. *Rom* 2H **141**
Oulder Hill. *Roch* 4D **26**
Oulder Hill Dri. *Roch* 4C **26**
Oulder Hill Recreation Cen.
    . . . . .3D **26**
Ouldfield Clo. *Roch* 5B **28**
Oulton Av. *Sale* 4E **123**
Oulton St. *Bolt* 6E **19**
Oulton Wlk.
    M40 . . . . . . .2H **95** (2H **7**)
Oundle Clo. *M14* 4G **109**
Ouse St. *Salf* 4C **92**
Outram Clo. *Marp* 1D **154**
Outram Ho. M1 . . . .4G **95** (6E **7**)
            (off Millbank St.)
Outram M. *Upperm* 6B **60**
Outram Rd. *Duk* 1H **113**
Outram Sq. *Droy* 5A **98**
Outrington Dri. *Open* 5C **96**
Outwood. 1F **65**

Outwood Av. Swin 5D 64
Outwood Dri. H Grn 5E 149
Outwood Gro. Bolt 6C 18
Outwood La. Man A 5A 148
Outwood Rd. Swin 5F 149
Outwood Rd. Rad 5G 49
Oval Dri. Duk . . . . .GH 99
Oval, The. H Grn 5F 149
Overbridge Rd.
    Salf 1C 94 (1F 5)
Overbrook Av. M40 . . . . . .6F 83
Overbrook Dri. P'wich 6F 67
Overcombe Wlk. M40 . . . . .5E 83
    (off Westmount Clo.)
Overdale. Alt 6D 132
Overdale. Marp 5D 142
    (off Hollins La.)
Overdale. Swin 5G 79
Overdale Clo. Oldh 6C 56
Overdale Crematorium.
    Bolt 1E 45
Overdale Cres. Urm 5B 104
Overdale Dri. Bolt 6F 31
Overdale Ho. Salf 1B 92
Overdale Rd. M22 . . . . . .6B 136
Overdale Rd. Rom 2F 141
Overdell Dri. Roch 6C 14
Overdene Clo. Los 1A 44
Overens St. Oldh 2F 73
Overfield Way. Roch 1H 27
Overgreen. Bolt 2G 33
Overhill Dri. Wilm 2H 167
Overhill La. Wilm 2H 167
Overhill Rd. Chad 1F 71
Overhill Rd. Wilm 2G 167
Overlea Dri. M19 . . . . . . .4A 126
Overlinks Dri. Salf 6H 79
Overstone Dri. M8 . . . . . . .4B 82
Overton Av. M22 . . . . . . .6B 136
Overton Cres. Haz G 1E 153
Overton Cres. Sale 1F 133
Overton La. Bolt 6B 30
Overton Rd. M22 . . . . . . .6B 136
Overton Way. Hand 2H 159
Over Town La. Roch 1G 25
    (in two parts)
Overt St. Roch 6H 27
Overwood Rd. M22 . . . . . .3B 136
Ovington Wlk. M40 . . . . . . .6E 83
Owen Fold. S'head 2B 74
Owenington Gro. L Hul 3C 62
Owens Clo. Chad 1E 71
Owens Farm Dri. Stoc 4E 141
Owens Pk. M14 . . . . .6H 109
Owen St. Eccl 4D 90
Owen St. M16 . . . . .4A 58
Owen St. Salf 6E 81
Owen St. Stoc 2F 139
Owler Barrow. 2G 35
Owlerbarrow Rd. Bury 2G 35
Owler La. Chad 6D 70
Owlwood Clo. L Hul 6A 62
Owlwood Dri. L Hul 6A 62
Oxbow Way. W'fld 1E 67
Oxbridge Clo. Sale 6F 121
Oxendale Dri. Midd 6F 53
Oxendon Av. M11 . . . . . . .2D 96
Oxenholme Wlk.
    M18 . . . . .1E 111
Oxenhurst Grn. Stoc 6E 141
Oxford Av. Droy 2H 97
Oxford Av. Roch 5C 26
Oxford Av. Sale 5F 121
Oxford Av. W'fld 1E 67
Oxford Clo. Farn 1B 62
Oxford Ct. M2 . . . . .5D 94 (1H 9)
Oxford Ct.
    M15 . . . . .1E 109 (5H 9)
Oxford Ct. Old T 2B 108
    (off Globe Clo.)
Oxford Dri. Midd 5C 54
Oxford Dri. Woodl 5A 130

Oxford Gro. Bolt 4G 31
    (in two parts)
Oxford Gro. Cad 3A 118
Oxford Ho. Oldh 3A 72
Oxford Pl. M14 . . . . .3G 109
Oxford Pl. Roch 6A 28
Oxford Rd.
    M1 & M13 . .6E 95 (3A 10)
    (in three parts)
Oxford Rd. Alt 2F 145
Oxford Rd. Duk 5B 100
Oxford Rd. Hyde 1C 130
Oxford Rd. L Lev 4H 47
Oxford Rd. Salf 1A 92
Oxford St. M1 . . . .5D 94 (1H 9)
Oxford St. M16 . . . . .2B 108
Oxford St. Bolt 6B 32
Oxford St. Bury 4E 37
Oxford St. Eccl 3G 91
Oxford St. Mill 1H 101
Oxford St. Oldh 4H 71
Oxford St. Shaw 1F 57
Oxford St. Stal 4G 101
Oxford St. E. Ash L 5F 99
Oxford St. W. Ash L 5F 99
Oxford Wlk. Dent 6G 113
Oxford Way. Roch 1G 27
Oxford Way. Stoc 6F 127
Ox Ga. Bolt 6H 19
Ox Hey Clo. Rams 2E 13
Oxhill Wlk. M40 . . . . .1D 84
Oxney Rd. M14 . . . . .3G 109
Ox St. Rams 4D 12
Oxted Wlk. M8 . . . . .5C 82
Oxton Av. M22 . . . . .1A 148
Oxton St. M11 . . . . .6H 97
Ozanam Ct. Salf 4H 81

P

Pacific Quays. 5D 92
Pacific Rd. B'hth 5C 132
Pacific Way. Salf 5C 92
Packer St. Bolt 3G 31
Packer Ct. Roch 4H 27
Packwood Chase. Chad . . .1F 71
Padbury Clo. Urm 4H 103
Padbury Ho. Salf 4F 93
    (off Cypress Clo.)
Padbury Wlk. M40 . . . . . . .6H 83
Padbury Way. Bolt 3F 33
Padden Brook. Rom 1H 141
Padden Brook M.
    Rom 1H 141
Paddington Av. M40 . . . . . .6B 84
Paddington Clo. Salf 3G 93
Paddison St. Swin 4E 79
Paddock Chase. Poy 1F 163
Paddock Ct. Fail 6F 85
Paddock Fld. Salf 5H 93
Paddock Head. L'boro 5C 16
Paddock La. Fail 6F 85
Paddock Rd. Hyde 1B 130
Paddocks, The. Stoc 6A 140
Paddock St.
    M12 . . . . . . .6G 95 (3E 11)
Paddock, The. Bram 4F 151
Paddock, The. Chea 6A 138
Paddock, The. G'fld 5H 75
Paddock, The. Had 2H 117
Paddock, The. Hand 3H 159
Paddock, The. Holl 2G 117
Paddock, The. Rams 2D 12
Paddock, The. Timp 1B 146
Paddock, The. W'fld 2A 66
Paddock, The. Wors 4G 77
Paderborn Ct. Bolt 1A 46
Padiham Clo. Bury 6B 36
Padstow Clo. Hyde 4H 115
Padstow Dri. Bram 6H 151
Padstow St. M40 . . . . .2A 96

Padstow Wlk. Hyde 4H 115
Padworth Wlk. M23 . . . . . .3D 134
Pagen St. Roch 3H 27
Paget St. M40 . . . . .6F 83
Paget St. Ash L 1A 100
Pagnall Ct. Chad 4H 71
Paignton Av. M19 . . . . . . .1B 126
Paignton Av. Hyde 5G 115
Paignton Dri. Sale 4F 121
Paignton Gro. Stoc 2G 127
Paignton Wlk. Hyde 5G 115
Pailin Dri. Droy 3C 98
Pailton Clo. Los 1B 44
Painswick Rd. M22 . . . . . .4H 147
Paisley Pk. Farn 6F 47
Paiton St. Bolt 1G 45
Palace Ct. Bolt 5B 32
Palace Gdns. Rytn 5B 56
Palace Rd. Ash L 6H 87
Palace Rd. Sale 4A 122
Palace St. Bolt 5B 32
Palace St. Bury 3E 37
Palace St. Stal 2A 72

Palace Theatre.
    . . . . .5E 95 (2A 10)
Palatine Av. M20 . . . . .3F 125
Palatine Av. Roch 3C 26
Palatine Clo. Irlam 6D 102
Palatine Cres. M20 . . . . . .4F 125
Palatine Dri. Bury 3F 23
Palatine Ho. Stoc 3G 139
    (off Old Chapel St.)
Palatine M. M20 . . . . .3F 125
Palatine Rd.
    M22 & M20 . . . . . .2A 136
Palatine Rd. Roch 3C 26
Palatine St. Bolt 6B 32
Palatine St. Dent 2E 113
Palatine St. Rams 3E 13
Palatine St. Roch 4C 28
Palatine Ter. Roch 3C 26
Paley St. Bolt 6B 32
Palfrey Pl.
    M12 . . . . . . .6G 95 (4F 11)
Palgrave Av. M40 . . . . .6F 83
Palin Wood Rd. Del 2H 59
Palladium, Tho. 4F 91
Pall Mall. M2 . . . .4D 94 (5H 5)
    (Marsden St.)
Pall Mall. M2 . . . .4D 94 (6H 6)
    (Tib La.)
Pall Mall Ct. M2 . . .4D 94 (5H 5)
Pallotine Wlk. Roch 6F 27
Palma Av. Man A 5G 147
Palm Bus. Cen. Chad 2H 71
Palm Clo. Sale 4E 121
Palmer Av. Chea 5B 138
Palmer Clo. M8 . . . . .1D 82
Palmer Clo. Oldh 5D 72
Palmerston Av. M16 . . . . . .5B 108
Palmerston Clo. Dent 4B 112
Palmerston Clo. Rams 5D 12
Palmerston Rd. Dent 4B 112
Palmerston Rd. Stoc 2A 152
Palmerston St.
    M12 . . . . . .5H 95 (1G 11)
Palmer St. Duk 4H 99
Palmer St. Sale 5A 122
Palmer St. Salf 6H 81
    (in two parts)
Palm Gro. Chad 1H 71
Palm St. M13 . . . . .4B 110
Palm St. Droy 3F 97
Palm St. Oldh 1G 73
Pandora St. M20 . . . . .4E 125
Panfield Rd. M22 . . . . . . .1A 148
Pangbourne Av. Urm 4G 105
Pangbourne Clo. Stoc 5E 139
Pankhurst Cen. 2F 109
    (Museum)
Pankhurst Wlk. M14 . . . . . .4F 109

Panmure St. Oldh 5D 72
Pansy Rd. Farn 1C 62
Paper Mill Rd. Brom X 4F 19
Parade Rd. Man A 6A 148
Parade, The. Ald E 5G 167
Parade, The. Rom 2G 141
Paradise St. Aud 6F 99
Paradise St. Had 2H 117
Paradise St. Rams 2E 13
Paradise Wharf.
    M1 . . . . .4F 95 (6E 7)
Parbold Av. M20 . . . . .3E 125
Parbrook Clo. M40 . . . . . . .6F 83
Pardoner's Ct. Salf 3B 92
Pares Land Wlk. Roch 5B 28
Parham Wlk. M9 . . . . .6G 69
Paris Av. Salf 6H 93
Parish Vw. Salf 5H 93
Paris St. Bolt 3F 45
Park Av. Bolt 1A 32
Park Av. Bram 2E 161
Park Av. Chad 6H 55
Park Av. Chea H 4B 150
Park Av. Fail 3D 84
Park Av. Hale 4H 145
Park Av. Hyde 3B 114
Park Av. Lev 6C 110
Park Av. Old T 2A 108
Park Av. Poy 3E 163
Park Av. P'wich 5F 67
Park Av. Rad 3B 50
Park Av. Rams 3F 13
Park Av. Rom 1A 142
Park Av. Sale 3A 122
Park Av. Salf 3B 82
Park Av. Stoc 4B 138
Park Av. Swin 4G 79
Park Av. Timp 3G 133
Park Av. Urm 5E 105
Park Av. W'fld 3B 66
Park Av. Wilm 1F 167
Park Bank. Salf 3D 92

Park Bridge. 1G 87
Pk. Bri. Heritage Cen.
    . . . . .2G 87
Pk. Dri. Rd. Ash L 2F 87
Pk. Bridge Rd.
    Oldh & Ash L 4E 87
Parkbridge Wlk.
    M13 . . . . . .1F 109 (6D 10)
Parkbrook Rd. M23 . . . . . .4H 135
Pk. Brow Clo. M21 . . . . . .1A 124
Park Bungalows.
    Marp 6D 142
Park Clo. Chad 6H 55
Park Clo. Stal 2D 100
Park Clo. Timp 3H 133
Park Clo. W'fld 3D 66
Park Cotts. Bolt 2G 31
Park Cotts. G'fld 1G 75
Park Cotts. Shaw 5D 42
Park Ct. M22 . . . . .2B 148
Park Ct. Roch 5G 27
    (Castle Av.)
Park Ct. Roch 5H 27
    (Suffolk St.)
Park Ct. Sale 4A 122
Park Ct. M. Chea 1A 150
Park Cres. M14 . . . . .4G 109
Park Cres. Ash L 3C 100
Park Cres. Chad 6F 55
Park Cres. Wilm 6F 159
Parkdale. Chad 6H 55
Parkdale Av. M18 . . . . . . .2E 111
Parkdale Av. Aud 6D 98
Parkdale Rd. Bolt 4E 33
Parkdene Clo. Bolt 1F 33
Park Dri. M16 . . . . .5A 108
Park Dri. Eccl 1F 91
Park Dri. Hale 3H 145
Park Dri. Hyde 3B 114
Park Dri. Stoc 1D 138

Park Dri. *Timp* 4A **134**
Parkend Rd. *M23* 6G **135**
Parker Arc. *M1* 6B **6**
Parker St. *M1* 4E **95** (6B **6**)
Parker St. *Bury* 3E **37**
Parkfield. *Chad* 6G **55**
Parkfield. *Eccl* 3G **103**
Parkfield. *Midd* 1H **69**
Parkfield. *Salf* 3D **92**
Parkfield Av. *M14* 4F **109**
Parkfield Av. *Farn* 2D **62**
Parkfield Av. *Marp* 5D **142**
Parkfield Av. *Oldh* 1H **85**
Parkfield Av. *P'wich* 6H **67**
Parkfield Av. *Urm* 6D **104**
Parkfield Ct. *Alt* 1E **145**
Parkfield Dri. *Midd* 1G **69**
Parkfield Est. *Swin* 5G **79**
Parkfield Ind. Est.
   Midd 1G **69**
Parkfield Rd. *Alt* 1E **145**
Parkfield Rd. *Bolt* 4B **46**
Parkfield Rd. *Chea H* . . .4B **150**
Parkfield Rd. N. *M40* 1E **85**
Parkfield Rd. S. *M20* 5E **125**
Parkfields. *Mill* 2H **101**
Parkfield St. *M14* 4F **109**
   (Claremont Rd.)
Parkfield St. *M14* 3F **109**
   (Moss La. E.)
Parkfield St. *Roch* 3H **41**
Parkgate. *Chad* 6H **55**
Parkgate. *Wals* 6G **21**
Park Ga. Av. *M20* 3F **125**
Parkgate Chase. *Roch* . . .3C **26**
Parkgate Clo. *Bolt* 4E **129**
Parkgate Dri. *Bolt* 6D **18**
Parkgate Dri. *Stoc* 1B **152**
Parkgate Dri. *Swin* 4G **79**
Pk. Gates Av. *Chea H* . . .4E **151**
Pk. Gates Dri. *Chea H* . . .4E **151**
Parkgate Way. *Hand* 3H **159**
Parkgate Way. *Shaw* 6A **43**
Park Gro. *M19* 5C **110**
Park Gro. *Rad* 3F **49**
Park Gro. *Stoc* 5D **126**
Park Gro. *Wors* 3F **77**
Park Hill. *P'wich* 2H **81**
Park Hill. *Roch* 2H **27**
Parkhill Av. *M8* 1D **82**
Pk. Hill Dri. *W'fld* 1C **66**
Pk. Hill Rd. *Hale* 4A **146**
Parkhills Rd. *Bury* 5C **36**
Pk. Hill St. *Bolt* 5H **31**
Park Ho. M23 . . . . .4C **134**
   (off Bridge Rd.)
Park Ho. *Droy* 5A **98**
Pk. House Bri. Est. *Salf* . .4D **80**
Pk. House Bri. Rd. *Salf* . .5D **80**
Parkhouse St. *M11* 5D **96**
Parkhouse St. Ind. Est.
   M11 . . . . .5D **96**
Parkhurst Av. *M40* 2E **85**
Parkin Clo. *Duk* 5A **100**
Parkinson St. *Bolt* 2G **45**
Parkinson St. *Bury* 6F **23**
Parkin St. *M12* 4C **110**
Pk. Lake Av. *Salf* 3A **82**
Parklands. *Poy* 3E **163**
Parklands. *Rytn* 6A **42**
Parklands. *Sale* 4C **122**
Parklands. *Shaw* 5H **43**
Parklands. *W'fld* 1C **66**
   (Higher La.)
Parklands. *W'fld* 5D **50**
   (Well La.)
Parklands. *Wilm* 2F **167**
Parklands Cres. *Hey D* . . .5C **38**
Parklands Dri. *Sale* 1F **133**
Parklands Ho. *Rytn* 1A **56**
Parklands Rd. *M23* 3F **135**

Parklands, The. *Rad* 2B **64**
Parklands, The. *Stoc* 5G **127**
Parklands Way. *Hey D* . . .5C **38**
Parklands Way. *Poy* 3E **163**
Park Lane. 2B **66**
Park La. *Duk* 5A **100**
Park La. *G'fld* 4G **61**
Park La. *Hale* 4A **146**
Park La. *Oldh* 1D **86**
Park La. *Poy* 3E **163**
Park La. *Roch* 2H **27**
Park La. *Rytn* 2B **56**
   (in three parts)
Park La. *Salf* (M6) 6A **80**
Park La. *Salf* (M7) 3H **81**
Park La. *Stoc* 3B **140**
Park La. *Swin* 4B **80**
Park La. *W'fld* 2B **66**
Park La. *Wors* 4A **76**
Park La. Ct. *Salf* 3H **81**
Park La. Ct. *W'fld* 2B **66**
Park La. W. *Swin* 4B **80**
Pk. Lea Ct. *Salf* 2A **82**
Parkleigh Dri. *M40* 1E **85**
Park Lodge. *M19* 6B **110**
Park Lodge. *Salf* 3H **81**
Pk. Lodge Clo. *Chea* 1A **150**
Park M. *M16* 5A **108**
Park M. *Rad* 3A **50**
Pk. Mill Ind. Est.
   Moss 6F **75**
Park Mt. *Gat* 6E **137**
Parkmount Rd. *M9* 2G **83**
Park Pde. *Ash L* 3G **99**
Park Pde. *Shaw* 4G **43**
Park Pde. Ind. Est.
   Ash L 3G **99**
Park Pl. *M4* 2E **95** (1A **6**)
Park Pl. *P'wich* 4G **67**
Park Pl. *Salf* 2A **92**
Park Pl. *Stoc* 1B **138**
Park Range. *M14* 4H **109**
Park Ri. *Rom* 6A **130**
Park Ri. *Stal* 2D **100**
Park Rd. *Aud* 5D **98**
Park Rd. *Bolt* 6G **31**
Park Rd. *Bow* 2C **144**
Park Rd. *Bury* 1C **36**
Park Rd. *Chea* 5A **138**
Park Rd. *Chea H* 4E **151**
Park Rd. *Dent* 4E **113**
Park Rd. *Dis* 1D **164**
Park Rd. *Duk* 4A **100**
Park Rd. *Eccl* 1F **91**
Park Rd. *Eccl & Salf* 1A **92**
Park Rd. *Gat* 5D **136**
Park Rd. *Hale* 4G **145**
Park Rd. *Hyde* 3B **114**
Park Rd. *L'boro* 3F **17**
Park Rd. *L Lev* 3H **47**
Park Rd. *Midd* 1H **69**
Park Rd. *Oldh* 3D **72**
Park Rd. *Part* 6E **119**
Park Rd. *P'wich* 6H **67**
Park Rd. *Rams* 6B **12**
Park Rd. *Roch* 1A **28**
   (in two parts)
Park Rd. *Rom* 6A **130**
Park Rd. *Sale* 3A **122**
Park Rd. *Stoc* 4D **126**
Park Rd. *Stret* 4C **106**
Park Rd. *Timp* 3G **133**
Park Rd. *W'houg* 6A **44**
Park Rd. *Wilm* 2D **166**
Park Rd. *Wors* 2E **77**
Park Rd. N. *Urm* 4E **105**
Park Rd. S. *Urm* 5E **105**
Park Row. *Bolt* 5D **18**
Park Row. *Stoc* 1A **138**
Park Seventeen. *W'fld* . . .6D **50**
Parkside. *Midd* 3G **69**
Parkside. *Whitw* 3H **15**

Parkside Av. *Eccl* 4E **91**
Parkside Av. *Fail* 6E **85**
Parkside Av. *Salf* 3A **82**
Parkside Av. *Shaw* 5G **43**
Parkside Av. *Wors* 2F **77**
Parkside Bowling &
   Tennis Club. 3A **122**
Parkside Clo. *H Lane* 5B **154**
Parkside Clo. *Rad* 3B **50**
Parkside Ho. *Rytn* 3C **56**
Parkside Ind. Est.
   Rytn 3C **56**
Parkside La. *Mell* 5G **143**
Parkside Rd. *M14* 5D **108**
Parkside Rd. *Sale* 6D **122**
Parkside St. *Bolt* 4E **33**
Parkside Wlk. *Bram* 2G **151**
Parkside Wlk. *Bury* 4D **36**
   (in two parts)
Park 66. *Bury* 1F **51**
Parks Nook. *Farn* 2E **63**
Park Sq. *M16* 5G **107**
Park Sq. *Ash L* 1C **100**
Parkstead Dri. *M9* 5F **83**
Parkstone Av. *M18* 1H **111**
Parkstone Av. *W'fld* 3B **66**
Parkstone Clo. *Bury* 3F **35**
Parkstone Ct. *L Lev* 4C **48**
Parkstone Dri. *Swin* 5H **79**
Parkstone La. *Wors* 1B **90**
Parkstone Rd. *Irlam* 4E **103**
Park St. *M3* 2D **94** (1H **5**)
   (Manchester)
Park St. *M3* 4B **94** (5C **4**)
   (Salford)
Park St. *Ash L* 3G **99**
   (Bentinck St.)
Park St. *Ash L* 4G **99**
   (William St.)
Park St. *Aud* 4D **112**
Park St. *Bolt* 5H **31**
Park St. *Bred* 6F **129**
Park St. *Droy* 3C **98**
Park St. *Farn* 6F **47**
Park St. *Heyw* 5G **39**
Park St. *Moss* 1B **90**
Park St. *Oldh* 4C **72**
   (in two parts)
Park St. *P'wich* 5G **67**
Park St. *Rad* 3A **50**
Park St. *Roch* 5H **27**
Park St. *Rytn* 3B **56**
Park St. *Salf* 3H **81**
Park St. *Shaw* 6F **43**
Park St. *Stal* 4F **101**
Park St. *Stoc* 1H **139**
Park St. *Swin* 4G **79**
Parksway. *M9* 4D **68**
Parksway. *P'wich* 1G **81**
Parksway. *Swin* 5A **80**
Parks Yd. *Bury* 3C **36**
Park Ter. *Bolt* 5D **18**
Park Ter. *Heyw* 2F **39**
Park Ter. *Moss* 3E **89**
Park Ter. *W'fld* 2B **66**
Park, The. *Grass* 4F **75**
Park, The. *G'fld* 4G **61**
Park Vw. *Aud* 5D **98**
Park Vw. *Bolt* 5D **18**
   (in two parts)
Park Vw. *Bred* 6C **128**
Park Vw. *Chad* 6G **55**
Park Vw. *Eger* 1C **18**
Park Vw. *Fall* 2A **126**
Park Vw. *Farn* 6F **47**
Park Vw. *Gat* 5E **137**
Park Vw. *Haz G* 5H **153**
Park Vw. *Kear* 3C **63**
Park Vw. *L'boro* 3F **17**
Park Vw. *Salf* 6H **93** (3A **8**)
Park Vw. *Shaw* 5C **42**

Park Vw. *Stoc* 4B **138**
   (Cheadle Heath)
Park Vw. *Stoc* 4B **140**
   (Stockport)
Pk. View Ct. *M32* 6F **107**
Pk. View Ct. *P'wich* 6E **67**
Pk. View Ct. *Rom* 1A **142**
Parkview Ct. *Stret* 6F **107**
Pk. View Rd. *Bolt* 3G **45**
Pk. View Rd. *P'wich* 6F **67**
Parkville Rd. *M20* 4G **125**
Parkville Rd. *P'wich* 2G **67**
Parkway. *Bram* 3G **151**
Parkway. *Chad* 5G **55**
Parkway. *Dent* 4C **112**
Park Way. *L Hul* 5A **62**
   (in two parts)
Parkway. *Roch* 3D **26**
Parkway. *Stoc* 4B **138**
Park Way.
   Urm & Traf P 3H **105**
Parkway. *Wilm* 3E **167**
Parkway Bus. Cen.
   M14 . . . . .5D **108**
Parkway Circ. *Traf P* 1A **106**
Parkway Four Ind. Est.
   Traf P 1A **106**
Parkway Gro. *L Hul* 5A **62**
Parkway Ind. Est.
   Traf P 1A **106**
Parkway Trad. Est.
   Stret 2A **106**
Parkwood. *Eger* 1B **18**
Parkwood Rd. *M23* 4A **136**
Parlane St. *M4* 2F **95** (1C **6**)
Parliament Pl. *Bury* 4C **36**
Parliament St. *Bury* 4C **36**
Parndon Dri. *Stoc* 4C **140**
Parnell Av. *M22* 3A **136**
Parnham Clo. *Rad* 2B **48**
Parrbrook Clo. *W'fld* 6E **51**
Parrbrook Wlk. *W'fld* 6F **51**
Parr Brow. 3A **76**
Parr Clo. *Farn* 1D **62**
Parrenthorn Rd.
   P'wich 1G **67**
Parrfield Rd. *Wors* 4A **78**
Parr Fold. 2F **77**
Parr Fold. *Bury* 5F **51**
Parr Fold Av. *Wors* 3E **77**
   (in two parts)
Parr Ho. *Oldh* 4D **72**
Parrin La. *Eccl* 2D **90**
Parr La. *Bury* 6E **51**
Parrot St. *M11* 4E **97**
Parrot St. *Bolt* 2A **46**
Parrs Ct. *Irlam* 5D **102**
Parrs Mt. M. *Stoc* 1B **138**
Parr St. *M11* 6G **97**
Parr St. *Eccl* 4F **91**
Parrs Wood Av. *M20* 1G **137**
Parrs Wood Ct. *M20* 2G **137**
Parrs Wood Entertainment
   Cen. 2H **137**
Parrs Wood La. *M20* 2G **137**
Parrs Wood Rd. *M20* 3F **137**
Parrs Wood Sports Cen.
   . . . . .2H **137**
Parry Mead. *Bred* 5G **129**
Parry Rd. *M12* 3C **110**
Parry Wlk. *Ash L* 1B **100**
Parslow Av. *M8* 3C **82**
Parsonage Clo. *Bury* 2E **37**
Parsonage Clo.
   Salf 5A **94** (2A **8**)
Parsonage Ct. *M20* 3F **125**
Parsonage Ct. *Stoc* 5D **126**
Parsonage Dri. *Wors* 1E **77**
Parsonage Gdns.
   M3 . . . . .4D **94** (5G **5**)
Parsonage Gdns. *Marp* . .1E **155**
Parsonage Grn. *Wilm* 2E **167**

Parsonage La.
　Salf 3D 94 (4G 5)
Parsonage Rd. M20 . . .3F 125
Parsonage Rd. Rad 2C 64
Parsonage Rd. Stoc . . .5D 126
Parsonage Rd. Urm 6A 104
　(in two parts)
Parsonage Rd. Wors 1E 77
Parsonage St. M8 . . . . .2B 82
Parsonage St. M15 . . . .2C 108
Parsonage St. Bury 2E 37
Parsonage St. Hyde 5B 114
Parsonage St. Rad 3G 49
Parsonage St. Stoc 1G 139
Parsonage Ter. Miln 4F 29
　(off Parsonage Wlk.)
Parsonage Wlk. Roch 4F 29
Parsonage Way. Chea . . .6D 138
Parson's Dri. Midd 5H 53
Parsons Fld. Salf 5E 81
Parsons La. Bury 3D 36
Parsons St. Oldh 3A 72
Parth St. Bury 4H 37
Partington. 6D 118
Partington Ct. Farn 6E 47
Partington La. Swin 4E 79
Partington Leisure Cen.
　. . . . . .6D 118
Partington Pk. Roch 5C 40
Partington Pl. Salf 4B 122
Partington Shop. Cen.
　Part 6D 118
Partington St. M40 . . . . .6H 83
Partington St. Bolt 5G 45
Partington St Fail 4F 85
Partington St. Heyw 3C 38
Partington St. Oldh 2E 73
Partington St. Roch 3B 40
Partington St Wors 4C 78
Partridge Av. M23 . . . . .5A 136
Partridge Clo. Irlam 3E 103
Partridge Clo. Roch 4B 26
Partridge Ct. Stoc 6B 140
Partridge Ri. Droy 2D 98
Partridge Rd. Fail 5A 86
Partridge Way. Stret 2F 107
Partridge Way. Chad 1D 70
Parvet Av. Droy 2H 97
Pascal St. M19 . . . . . . .1C 126
Passmonds. 2D 26
　Roch 3D 26
Passmonds Cres.
　Roch 3D 26
Passmonds Way.
　Roch 3D 26
Pass St. Oldh 3B 72
Pass, The. Roch 3A 28
Paston Rd. Shar I 4B 136
Pasture Clo. Heyw 4D 38
Pasturefield Clo. Sale . .6F 123
Pasture Rd. M22 . . .3D 148
Pasturegreen Way.
　Irlam 4F 103
Pastures La. Scout 1D 74
Patch Cft. Rd. M22 . . .4D 148
Patchett St. M12 . . . . . .1B 110
Patch La. Bram 2F 161
　(in two parts)
Patey St. M12 . . . . .4C 110
Pathfield Wlk. M9 . . . . . .3F 83
　(off Smallfield Dri.)
Patience St. Roch 2F 27
Patmos St. Rams 3F 13
Paton Av. Bolt 4C 46
Paton M. Bolt 4C 46
Paton St. M1 . . . .4F 95 (6C 6)
Paton St. Roch 6D 14
Patricia Dri. Wors 1G 77
Patrick Roddy Ct.
　M18 . . . . .2E 111
Patricroft. 4F 91
Patricroft Bri. Eccl 4E 91
Patricroft Rd. Eccl 3E 91

Patten St. M20 . . . . . . .3F 125
Patterdale. Chea 6G 137
Patterdale Av. Ash I 6D 86
Patterdale Av. Urm 3D 104
Patterdale Clo. Oldh 6E 57
Patterdale Clo. Roch 2B 40
Patterdale Clo. Stal 2E 101
Patterdale Dri. Bury 6C 36
Patterdale Dri. Midd 5G 53
Patterdale Rd. M22 . . . . .3C 136
Patterdale Rd. Ash L 6D 86
Patterdale Rd. Bolt 1H 33
Patterdale Rd. Part 6C 118
Patterdale Rd. Stoc 4B 140
Patterdale Rd. Wood! 5H 129
Patterdale Wlk. Timp 6D 134
Patterson Av. M21 . . . . .6G 107
Patterson St. Bolt 3E 45
Patterson St. Dent 3F 113
Patting Clo. Irlam 4G 103
Pattishall Clo.
　M4 . . . . . .4H 95 (6H 7)
Pattison Clo. Roch 6D 14
Patton Clo. Bury 5F 51
Patton Ct. Salf 1A 94
Paul Ct. Stoc 2A 140
Paulden Av. M23 . . . . . .5H 135
Paulden Av. Oldh 6A 58
Paulden Dri. Fail 4G 85
Paulette St. Bolt 3A 32
Paulhan Rd. M20 . . . . . .5H 125
Paulhan St. Bolt 4H 45
Paul Row. L'boro 6G 17
Pavilion Clo. Roch 1H 27
Pavilion Dri. Ash L 6H 87
Pavilion Lodge. M16 . . . .4G 107
Pavilions, The. M21 . . . .6A 108
Pavilions, The. Chea 1H 149
Pavilion Wlk. Rad 4F 49
Paxford Pl. Wilm 4D 166
Paxton Pl. Farn 1F 63
Paythorne Grn. Stoc 6E 141
Peabody St. Bolt 3A 46
Peacefield. Marp 6C 142
　(off Trafford Cen., The)
Peacehaven Av. M11 . . . .3E 97
Peace St. Bolt 2H 45
Peace St. Fail 2G 85
Peaceville Rd. M19 . . . . .6B 110
Peach Bank. Midd 1A 70
Peach Rd. Oldh 6H 57
　(in two parts)
Peach St. P'wich 4G 67
Peach Tree Clo. Salf 5B 82
Peach Tree Clo. Salf 3G 93
Peacock Av. Salf 6B 80
Peacock Clo. M18 . . . . .1E 111
Peacock Clo. Had 3G 117
Peacock Dri. H Grn 1F 159
Peacock Gro. M18 . . . . . .3F 111
Peacock Way. Hand 2H 159
Peak Clo. Oldh 3B 58
Peakdale Av. Crum 3D 82
Peakdale Av. H Grn 4F 149
Peakdale Rd. Droy 2G 97
Peakdale Rd. Glos 4G 117
Peakdale Rd. Marp 1E 155
Peaknaze Clo. Swin 3H 79
Peak St. M1 . . . . .4F 95 (6D 6)
Peak St. Bolt 3H 31
Peak St. Oldh 3A 72
Peak St. Stoc 2A 140
Peanock La. L'boro 1F 29
Pear Av. Bury 2G 37
Pear Clo. Midd 3B 70
Pear Av. Salf 2A 82
Pearl Mill Clo. Oldh 5F 73
Pearl St. Dent 4E 113
Pearl St. Haz G 1E 153
Pearl St. Roch 3E 27
Pearl Way. Mot 4C 116
Pearly Bank. Oldh 2H 57

Pear Mill Ind. Est.
　Bred 1C 140
Pearn Av. M19 . . . . . . .4B 126
Pearn Rd. M19 . . . . . . .4B 126
Pearson Clo. Miln 4F 29
Pearson Clo. Part 6E 119
Pearson Gro. Lees 3A 74
Pearson Ho. Eccl 5F 91
Pearson St. Bury 2F 37
Pearson St. Duk 1A 114
Pearson St. Roch 3C 28
Pearson St. Stoc 6H 127
Peart Av. Wood! 3A 130
Pear St. P'wich 4G 67
Pear Tree Clo. Had 3G 117
Pear Tree Clo. Marp B . . .3E 143
Pear Tree Clo. Salf 3G 93
Pear Tree Ct. Salf 3G 93
Pear Tree Dri. Stal 3F 101
Pear Tree Gro. Tyl 2A 76
Peartree Wlk. M22 . . . . .1H 147
Pear Tree Wlk. Sale 4E 121
Peart St. Dent 4E 113
Peary St. M4 . . . .2F 95 (1D 6)
Peaslake Clo. Rom 1B 142
Peatfield Av. Swin 1E 79
Peatfield Wlk. M15 . . . . .2D 108
Pebble Clo. Stal 1E 101
Pebworth Clo. Midd 4H 69
Peckford Dri. M40 . . . . . .6A 84
Peckforton Clo. Gat 6E 137
Peckforton Wlk. Wilm 6A 160
Peckmill Clo. Wilm 5A 160
Pedder St. Bolt 4G 31
Pedler Brow La.
　Roch & L'boro 3C 16
Pedley Wlk.
　M13 . . . . . .6F 95 (3D 10)
Peebles Dri. M40 . . . . . . .1F 97
Peel. 5B 62
Peel Av. Bow 3F 145
Peel Av. Rams 4C 12
Peel Av. Urm 1F 105
　(off Trafford Cen., The)
Peel Brow. 2F 13
Peel Brow. Rams 3E 13
Peel Cen., The. Stoc 1A 140
Peel Circ. Urm 1G 105
Peel Ct. Stoc 5H 139
Peel Cross Rd. Salf 4G 93
Peel Dri. L Hul 5B 62
Peel Dri. Sale 5E 123
Peelgate Dri. H Grn 3E 149
Peel Green. 5D 90
Peel Grn. Rd. Eccl 5D 90
Peel Grn. Trad. Est.
　Eccl 5D 90
Peel Gro. M12 . . . . .3C 110
Peel Gro. Wors 3G 77
Peel Hall 2D 148
Peel Hall Rd. M22 . . . . . .2C 148
Peel Hall Rd. S'seat 1B 22
Peel Ho. Eccl 3H 91
Peel Ind. Est. Bury 2C 36
Peel La. M8 . . . . .1E 95
Peel La. Heyw 2D 38
Peel La. Wors 6B 62
Peel Moat Ct. Stoc 4D 126
Peel Moat Rd. Stoc 4D 126
Peel Moat Sports Cen.
　. . . . . .4D 126
Peel Mt. Rams 5C 12
Peel Mt. Salf 2H 93 (1A 4)
Peel Pk. Cres.
　L Hul 5B 62
Peel Rd. Hale 2G 145
Peels Av. S'head 2C 74
Peel Sq. M18 . . . . .2F 111
Peel St. Ash L 2H 99
Peel St. Chad 3H 71
Peel St Dent 1E 113
　(Audenshaw)

Peel St. Dent 3E 113
　(Denton, in two parts)
Peel St. Droy 1H 97
Peel St. Duk 4A 100
Peel St. Eccl 3H 91
Peel St. Fail 5D 84
Peel St. Farn 1G 63
Peel St. Heyw 3D 38
Peel St. Hyde 6C 114
Peel St. L'boro 4F 17
Peel St. Rad 5H 49
Peel St. Roch 3G 27
Peel St. Shaw 6E 43
Peel St. Stal 4D 100
Peel St. Stoc 5H 139
Peel Ter. Duk 4H 99
　(off Hill St.)
Peel Vw. T'ton 5A 22
Peel Way. Bury 3C 36
Peelwood Av. L Hul 4C 62
Peerglow Pk. Est.
　Timp 3G 133
Peers Clo. Urm 3H 103
Peers Dri. T'ton 6H 21
Peers St. Bury 3A 36
Pegamoid St. Bolt 4D 32
Pegasus Cl. Bolt 5E 27
Pegasus Ct. Sale 4D 122
　(off Kingston Dri.)
Pegasus Sq.
　Salf 2A 94 (1B 4)
Pegwell Dri. Salf 6A 82
Pekin St. Ash L 1A 100
Pelham Pl. M8 . . . . .1D 82
Pelham St. Ash L 5E 99
Pelham St. Bolt 4G 45
Pelham St. Oldh 1D 86
Pellowe Rd. Oldh 6C 72
Pelton Av. Swin 1D 78
Pelton Wlk. M40 . . . . . . .6F 83
　(off Pitsford Rd.)
Pemberton Ho. Shaw 5F 43
　(off Napier St.)
Pemberton St. M16 . . . . .3A 108
Pemberton St. Bolt 1A 32
Pemberton St. L Hul 5D 62
Pemberton St. Roch 3C 40
Pemberton Way. Shaw . . .5F 43
Pembridge Fold. Midd 1C 70
Pembridge Rd. M9 . . . . . .5H 69
Pembroke Av. Eccl 3F 91
Pembroke Av. Sale 4H 121
Pembroke Clo.
　M13 . . . . .1H 109 (6G 11)
Pembroke Ct. Haz G 3E 153
Pembroke Ct. Roch 2H 27
Pembroke Ct. Rom 1F 141
Pembroke Dri. Bury 6C 36
Pembroke Dri. Oldh 3A 58
Pembroke Gro. Cad 3A 118
Pembroke Ho. Stoc 3G 139
　(off Bowden St.)
Pembroke St. Bolt 5H 31
Pembroke St. L'boro 3F 17
Pembroke St. Oldh 3B 72
Pembroke St. Salf 5A 82
　(Hightown)
Pembroke St. Salf 4E 93
　(Weaste)
Pembroke Way. Dent 6G 113
Pembry Clo. Stoc 4B 128
Pembury Clo. M22 . . . . .2A 148
Penarth Rd. M22 . . . . . .3B 136
Penarth Rd. Bolt 3F 45
Pencarrow Clo. M20 . . . .6D 124
Pencombe Clo. M12 . . . .2C 110
Pencroft Way. Man S 2E 109
Pendeen Clo. Wyth 4C 148
Pendennis. Roch 5G 27
Pendennis Av. Los 2B 44
Pendennis Clo. Rad 2C 48

Pendennis Rd. *Stoc* 6E **127**
Pender Wlk. *M18* 2F **111**
Pendle Av. *Bolt* 5C **18**
Pendlebury. 3H 79
Pendlebury Clo.
   P'wich 1D **80**
Pendlebury Ct. *Stoc* 6A **140**
Pendlebury Fold. *Bolt* . . .5B **44**
Pendlebury Ho. Swin . . .2G **79**
   (off Pendlebury Rd.)
Pendlebury Recreation Cen.
   . . . . .2E **79**
Pendlebury Rd. *Gat* 5E **137**
Pendlebury Rd. *Swin* . . .3F **79**
Pendlebury St. *Bolt* 2B **32**
Pendlebury St. *Rad* 4G **49**
Pendlebury Towers.
   Stoc 6H **127**
Pendle Clo. *Bury* 2H **35**
Pendle Clo. *Oldh* 4H **73**
Pendle Ct. *Bolt* 2H **31**
Pendlecroft Av. *Swin* . . .3A **80**
Pendlegreen Clo. *M11* . .5B **96**
Pendle Gro. *Rytn* 4A **56**
Pendle Ho. *Dent* 5F **113**
Pendle Rd. *Dent* 5F **113**
Pendleton. 2F 93
Pendleton Grn. Salf 2F **93**
   (off Nursery St.)
Pendleton Ho. Salf 1G **93**
   (off Broughton Rd.)
Pendleton Way. *Salf* 2F **93**
Pendle Wlk.
   M40 . . . . . .2H **95** (2G **7**)
Pendle Wlk. *Stoc* 4A **128**
Pendleway. *Swin* 2G **79**
Pendragon Pl. *Fail* 4G **85**
Pendrell Wlk. M9 . . . . . .6G **69**
   (off Sanderstead Rd.)
Penelope Rd. *Salf* 6B **80**
Penerley Dri. *M9* 5F **83**
Penfair Clo. *M11* 4C **96**
Penfield Clo.
   M1 . . . . .6F **95** (3C **10**)
Penfold Wlk. *M12* 1B **110**
Pengham Wlk. *M23* 2G **135**
Pengwern Av. *Bolt* 3F **45**
Penhale M. *Bram* 6H **151**
Penhall Wlk. *M40* 6H **83**
   (off Mansford Dri.)
Peninsula Building.
   Salf 4F **81**
Penistone Av. *M9* 6A **70**
Penistone Av. *Roch* 5C **28**
Penistone Av. *Salf* 2C **92**
Penketh Av. *M18* 3D **110**
Penmere Gro. *Sale* 2G **133**
Penmoor Chase.
   Haz G 4B **152**
Penmore Clo. *Shaw* 6G **43**
Pennant Dri. *P'wich* 4E **67**
Pennant St. *Oldh* 1F **73**
Pennell St. *M11* 4F **97**
Penn Grn. *Chea H* 4D **150**
Penn Ho. Clo. *Bram* 5G **151**
Pennine Av. *Chad* 4G **71**
Pennine Clo. *M9* 5H **69**
Pennine Clo. *Bury* 1G **35**
Pennine Clo. *Shaw* 6G **43**
Pennine Ct. *Oldh* 3E **73**
Pennine Ct. *Stal* 2H **101**
Pennine Ct. *Stoc* 5E **141**
   (in two parts)
Pennine Ct. *Swin* 2G **79**
Pennine Dri. *Alt* 6D **132**
Pennine Dri. *Ash L* 1C **100**
Pennine Dri. *Miln* 4G **29**
Pennine Dri. *Ward* 3A **16**
Pennine Gro. *Ash L* 5A **88**
Pennine Precinct.
   Miln 6F **29**
Pennine Rd. *Haz G* 4B **152**

Pennine Rd. *Woodl* 4A **130**
Pennine Ter. Duk 4A **100**
   (off Peel St.)
Pennine Va. *Shaw* 5G **43**
Pennine Vw. *Aud* 2E **113**
Pennine Vw. *H'rod* 1G **101**
Pennine Vw. *L'boro* 5H **17**
Pennine Vw. *Moss* 2F **89**
Pennine Vw. *Rytn* 3C **56**
Pennington Clo. *L Hul* . . .5A **62**
Pennington Rd. *Bolt* 4B **46**
Pennington St. *M12* 5C **110**
Pennington St. *Chad* 6H **71**
Pennington St. *Wals* 1E **35**
Pennington St. *Wors* 1G **77**
Pennistone Clo. *Irlam* . . .4F **103**
Penn St. *M40* 3H **83**
Penn St. *Farn* 1E **63**
Penn St. *Heyw* 4F **39**
Penn St. *Oldh* 4B **72**
Penn St. *Roch* 3H **27**
Penny Black Chambers.
   Wors 6H **77**
Penny Bri. La. *Urm* 6C **104**
   (in two parts)
Penny La. *Stoc* 1H **139**
   (in two parts)
Penny Mdw. *Ash L* 2A **100**
Pennymoor Dri. *Alt* 5D **132**
Penrhos Av. *Gat* 6D **136**
Penrhyn Av. *Chea H* 4A **150**
Penrhyn Av. *Midd* 2A **70**
Penrhyn Cres. *Haz G* 5C **152**
Penrhyn Dri. *P'wich* 5F **67**
Penrhyn Rd. *Stoc* 3D **138**
Penrice Clo. *Rad* 2D **48**
Penrice Fold. *Wors* 4D **76**
Penrith Av. *M11* 2D **96**
Penrith Av. *Ash L* 6D **86**
Penrith Av. *Bolt* 4E **31**
Penrith Av. *Oldh* 5A **72**
Penrith Av. *Sale* 1C **134**
Penrith Av. *Stoc* 6H **111**
Penrith Av. *W'fld* 2F **67**
Penrith Av. *Wors* 1H **77**
Penrith Clo. *Part* 5C **118**
Penrith St. *Roch* 6H **27**
Penrod Pl. *Salf* 1H **93**
Penrose Gdns. *Midd* 6B **54**
Penrose St. *Bolt* 6E **33**
Penrose Wlk. *Midd* 3A **54**
Penroy Av. *M20* 6B **124**
Penroyson Clo. *M12* 1B **110**
Penruddock Wlk.
   M13 . . . . .3B **110**
   (off Bates St.)
Penry Av. *Cad* 3C **118**
Penryn Av. *Rytn* 3D **56**
Penryn Av. *Sale* 2C **134**
Penryn Ct. *Salf* 2H **81**
Pensarn Av. *M14* 1A **126**
Pensarn Gro. *Stoc* 5H **127**
Pensby Clo. *Swin* 4A **80**
Pensby Wlk. *M40* 6F **83**
Pensford Ct. *Bolt* 5A **20**
Pensford Rd. *M23* 2F **147**
Penshurst Rd. *Stoc* 3B **128**
Penshurst Wlk. *Dent* 6G **113**
Penthorpe Dri. *Rytn* 4D **56**
Pentland Av. *M40* 1C **84**
Pentland Clo. *Haz G* 4B **152**
Pentlands Av. *Salf* 5H **81**
Pentlands Clo. *Shaw* 5D **42**
Pentland Ter. *Bolt* 4A **32**
Pentland Way. *Hyde* 1F **115**
Pentwyn Gro. *M23* 4H **135**
Penwell Fold. *Oldh* 6C **56**
Penzance St. *M40* 2A **96**
People's History Mus. . . .5E **5**

Peover Av. *Sale* 5E **123**
Peover Rd. *Hand* 2A **160**
Peover Wlk. *Chea* 6C **138**
Pepler Av. *M23* 1H **135**
Peploe Wlk. *M23* 2D **134**
Pepper Ct. *Wilm* 3D **166**
Pepperhill Rd. *M16* 3D **108**
Peppermint Clo. *Miln* 1G **43**
Pepper Rd. *Haz G* 3B **152**
Pepper St. *Mobb* 6A **156**
Perch Wlk. *M4* 5F **7**
Percival Clo. *M8* 5B **82**
Percival Rd. *Droy* 4B **98**
Percival Wlk. *Rytn* 4C **56**
Percy Dri. *Salf* 6H **93**
Percy Rd. *Dent* 5E **113**
Percy St. *M15* 1B **108** (6D **8**)
Percy St. *Bolt* 3B **32**
Percy St. *Bury* 2E **37**
Percy St. *Farn* 2G **63**
Percy St. *Oldh* 2G **73**
Percy St. *Rams* 4D **12**
Percy St. *Roch* 6B **28**
Percy St. *Stal* 4F **101**
Percy St. *Stoc* 1H **139**
Peregrine Cres. *Droy* 2C **98**
Peregrine Dri. *Irlam* 3E **103**
Peregrine Rd. *Stoc* 1F **153**
Peregrine St. *M15* 2D **108**
Perendale Ri. *Bolt* 1A **32**
Periton Wlk. M9 . . . . . . .6G **69**
   (off Leconfield Dri.)
Perivale Dri. *Oldh* 5F **73**
Perkins Av. *Salf* 6A **82**
Pernham St. *Oldh* 2G **73**
Perrin St. *Hyde* 5B **114**
Perry Av. *Hyde* 3E **115**
Perry Clo. *Roch* 6F **27**
Perrygate Av. *M20* 3E **125**
Perrymead. *P'wich* 3G **67**
Perry Rd. *Timp* 5B **134**
Pershore. *Roch* 3G **27**
   (off Spotland Rd.)
Pershore Rd. *Midd* 4A **54**
Perth. *Eccl* 3G **91**
   (off Monton La.)
Perth Av. *Chad* 5G **71**
Perth Clo. *Bram* 2G **161**
Perth Rd. *Roch* 3H **41**
Perth St. *Bolt* 4F **45**
   (in two parts)
Perth St. *Rytn* 3E **57**
Perth St. *Swin* 4D **78**
Peru St. *Salf* 3B **94** (3C **4**)
Peterborough Clo.
   Ash L 5F **87**
Peterborough Dri. *Bolt* . . .4B **32**
Peterborough St.
   M18 . . . . .1H **111**
Peterborough Wlk.
   Bolt 4A **32**
   (off Charnock Dri.)
Peterborough Wlk.
   Bolt 4B **32**
   (off Newington Wlk.)
Peterchurch Wlk. *Open* . .5E **97**
Peterhead Clo. *Bolt* 4H **31**
Peterhead Wlk. *Salf* 4G **93**
Peterhouse Gdns.
   Woodl 5A **130**
Peterloo Ct. Salf 3F **93**
   (off St Luke's Rd.)
Peterloo Ter. *Midd* 5A **54**
Peter Moss Way. *M19* . . .6E **111**
Petersburg Rd. *Stoc* 5E **139**
Peters Ct. Timp 6D **134**
   (off Norwood Dri.)
Petersfield Dri. *Bolt* 4D **134**
Petersfield Wlk. *Bolt* 4A **32**
Peter St. *M2* 5D **94** (1G **9**)
Peter St. *Alt* 2F **145**
Peter St. *Bury* 2D **36**

Peter St. *Dent* 4G **113**
Peter St. *Eccl* 4F **91**
Peter St. *Had* 1H **117**
Peter St. *Haz G* 2D **152**
Peter St. *Midd* 2E **69**
Peter St. *Oldh* 3D **72**
Peter St. *Stoc* 1A **140**
   (in two parts)
Peterswood Clo. *M22* . . .2H **147**
Peter Wood Gdns.
   Stret 6A **106**
Petheridge Dri. *M22* 4H **147**
Petre Bank. 3G 163
Petrel Av. *Poy* 3B **162**
Petrel Clo. *Droy* 2C **98**
Petrel Clo. *Roch* 4B **26**
Petrel Clo. *Stoc* 5F **139**
Petrie Ct. *Salf* 1H **93**
Petrie St. *Roch* 3H **27**
Petrock Wlk. *M40* 6C **84**
Petts Cres. *L'boro* 3E **17**
Petunia Wlk. Wors 6B **62**
   (off Madams Wood Rd.)
Petworth Clo. *M22* 5C **136**
Petworth Rd. *Chad* 3H **71**
Pevensey Ct. *M9* 1A **84**
Pevensey Rd. *Salf* 6C **80**
Pevensey Wlk. *Chad* 3H **71**
Peveril Clo. *W'fld* 2G **67**
Peveril Cres. *M21* 5G **107**
Peveril Dri. *Haz G* 5F **153**
Peveril Rd. *B'hth* 4E **133**
Peveril Rd. *Oldh* 6G **57**
Peveril Rd. *Salf* 3D **92**
Peveril St. *Bolt* 4F **45**
Peveril Ter. *Hyde* 1D **130**
Pewsey Rd. *M22* 2D **148**
Pexhill Ct. *Stoc* 1C **138**
Pexwood. *Chad* 6E **55**
Pheasant Clo. *Wors* 5D **76**
Pheasant Dri. *M21* 2B **124**
Pheasant Ri. *Bow* 4F **145**
Phelan Clo. *M40* 6E **83**
Phethean St. *Bolt* 6C **32**
Phethean St. *Farn* 6E **47**
Philip Av. *Dent* 2D **112**
Philip Dri. *Sale* 1B **134**
Philip Howard Ct. Farn . . .1E **63**
   (off Glynne St.)
Philips Av. *Farn* 2F **63**
Philips Dri. *W'fld* 3B **66**
Philips Park. 2C **96**
Philips Pk. Rd. *M11* 3A **96**
Philips Pk. Rd. E. *W'fld* . . .3D **66**
Philips Pk. Rd. W.
   W'fld 4A **66**
Philips Sports Cen. 1C **66**
Philip St. *Bolt* 2H **45**
Philip St. *Eccl* 4F **91**
Philip St. *Oldh* 1G **73**
Philip St. *Roch* 6H **27**
Phillimore St. *Lees* 4A **74**
Phillips Pl. *W'fld* 2D **66**
Phillip Way. *Hyde* 6A **116**
Phipps St. *Wors* 5E **63**
Phoebe St. *Bolt* 3G **45**
Phoebe St. *Salf* 5G **93**
Phoenix Cen., The.
   L Lev 4C **48**
Phoenix Clo. *Heyw* 4H **39**
Phoenix Ind. Est. *Fail* . . .3G **85**
Phoenix Pk. Ind. Est.
   Heyw 4H **39**
Phoenix Pl. S'head 3B **74**
Phoenix St. *M2* . . .4E **95** (5A **6**)
Phoenix St. *Bolt* 5C **32**
Phoenix St. *Bury* 3C **36**
Phoenix St. *Farn* 2F **63**
Phoenix St. *L'boro* 3F **17**
Phoenix St. *Oldh* 3D **72**
Phoenix St. *Roch* 2E **27**
Phoenix St. S'head 3B **74**

Phoenix Way—Plucksbridge Rd.

Phoenix Way. M15 . . . . . .2D 108 (6G 9)
Phoenix Way. Rad 5G 49
Phoenix Way. Urm 1G 105
Phyllis St. Midd 2C 70
Phyllis St. Roch 2D 26
Piccadilly. M1 . . . . .4E 95 (5B 6) (in two parts)
Piccadilly. Stoc 2H 139
Piccadilly Pl. M1 . . . . .5B 6
Piccadilly Plaza. M1 . . . . .4E 95 (6B 6)
Piccadilly Trad. Est. M1 . . . . .5G 95 (1F 11)
Piccadilly Village. 4G 95 (6D 6)
Piccard Clo. M40 . . . . . . .6F 83
Pickering Clo. Bury 6B 22
Pickering Clo. Rad 1A 64
Pickering Clo. Timp 4A 134
Pickering Clo. Urm 5D 104
Pickford Av. L Lev 4C 48
Pickford Ct. M15 . . . . . .2C 108
Pickford La. Duk 5A 100
Pickford M. Duk 5A 100
Pickford's Brow. Stoc . . .2H 139 (off High Bankside)
Pickford St. M4 . . .3F 95 (4D 6)
Pickford Wlk. Rytn 4C 56
Pickhill. Upperm 1F 61
Pickhill M. Upperm 1F 61
Pickmere Av. M20 . . . . . .1F 125
Pickmere Clo. Droy 4B 98
Pickmere Clo. Sale 1F 135
Pickmere Clo. Stoc 5E 139
Pickmere Ct. Hand 2H 159
Pickmere Gdns. Chea H 6B 138
Pickmere M. Upperm 1F 61
Pickmere Rd. Hand 2H 159
Pickmere Ter. Duk 4H 99
Pickup St. Roch 4A 28
Pickwick Rd. Poy 4D 162
Picton Clo. Salf . . .3C 94 (3E 5)
Picton Dri. Wilm 6A 160
Picton Sq. Oldh 3E 73
Picton St. Ash L 5E 87
Picton St. Salf 2B 94 (1D 4)
Picton Wlk. M16 . . . . . . .4D 108 (off Bedwell St.)
Pierce St. Oldh 6G 57
Piercy Av. Salf 1B 94
Piercy St. M4 . . . .4H 95 (5G 7)
Piercy St. Fail 4E 85
Piethorne Clo. Miln 1G 43
Pigeon St. M1 . . . .4F 95 (5D 6)
Piggott St. Farn 2E 63
Pike Av. Fail 5A 86
Pike Fold La. M9 . . . . .6E 69
Pike Mill Est. Bolt 3A 46
Pike Nook Workshops. Bolt 2H 45
Pike Rd. Bolt 3H 45
Pike St. Roch 6H 27
Pike Vw. Clo. Oldh 4F 73
Pilgrim Dri. M11 . . . . .4B 96
Pilkington Dri. W'fld 5F 51
Pilkington Rd. M9 . . . . . . .1A 84
Pilkington Rd. Kear 3H 63
Pilkington Rd. Rad 2F 49
Pilkington St. Bolt 2A 46
Pilkington St. Midd 6B 54
Pilkington St. Rams 4D 12
Pilkington Way. Rad 4G 49
Pilling Fld. Eger 2C 18
Pilling St. M40 . . . . .6H 83
Pilling St. Bury 2A 36
Pilling St. Dent 4F 113
Pilling St. Roch 3F 27
Pilling Wlk. Chad 3G 71
Pilning St. Bolt 3C 46
Pilot Ind. Est. Bolt 3D 46
Pilot St. Bury 4E 37
Pilsworth Ind. Est. Bury 6F 37
Pilsworth Rd. Bury . . . . . . .1E 51 (in two parts)
Pilsworth Rd. Heyw 3D 38
Pilsworth Rd. Ind. Est. Bury 1E 51
Pilsworth Way. Bury 1E 51
Pimblett St. M3 . . .2D 94 (1H 5)
Pimhole. 4E 37
Pimhole Fold. Bury 4E 37
Pimhole Rd. Bury 3E 37
Pimlico Clo. Salf 5H 81
Pimlott Gro. Hyde 2B 114
Pimlott Gro. P'wich 1D 80
Pimlott Rd. Bolt 2D 32
Pimmcroft Way. Sale 6F 123
Pincher Wlk. Open 4E 97
Pinder Wlk. M15 . . . . . .1D 108 (6H 9)
Pineapple St. Haz G 3E 153
Pine Av. W'fld 2D 66
Pine Clo. Aud 1E 113
Pine Clo. Marp 1C 154
Pine Ct. M20 . . . . .5E 125
Pine Ct. Bram 3F 151
Pine Gro. M14 . . . . .3A 110
Pine Gro. Dent 4G 113
Pine Gro. Duk 5D 100
Pine Gro. Eccl 1F 91
Pine Gro. Farn 1D 62
Pine Gro. P'wich 3E 67
Pine Gro. Rytn 1B 56
Pine Gro. Sale 3F 121
Pine Gro. Swin 4D 78
Pine Gro. Wors 3G 77
Pinehurst Rd. M40 . . . . . .6G 83
Pinelea. Alt 1H 145
Pine Lodge. Bram 6H 151
Pine Meadows. Rad 3C 64
Pine Rd. M20 . . . . .5E 125
Pine Rd. Bram 5H 151
Pine Rd. Poy 4F 163
Pine Rd. Stal 5C 100
Pine St. M1 . . . . . .4E 95 (6A 6)
Pine St. Ash L 1H 99
Pine St. Bolt 3B 32
Pine St. Bury 2F 37
Pine St. Chad 1G 71
Pine St. Heyw 3F 39
Pine St. Hyde 2B 114
Pine St. L'boro 3F 17
Pine St. Midd 2C 70
Pine St. Miln 2F 43
Pine St. Rad 3H 49
Pine St. Roch 4B 28
Pine St. Woodl 4H 129
Pine St. N. Bury . . . . .3F 37 (in two parts)
Pine St. S. Bury 3F 37
Pinetop Clo. M21 . . . . . .2B 124
Pine Tree Rd. Oldh 2B 86
Pine Trees. Mobb 6A 156
Pinetree St. M18 . . . . . . .2E 111
Pine Wlk. Part 6C 118
Pineway. Lees 3B 74
Pinewood. Bow 3C 144
Pinewood. Chad 2E 71
Pinewood. Sale 5F 121
Pinewood Clo. Bolt 3A 32
Pinewood Clo. Duk 4A 100
Pinewood Clo. Stoc 6C 126
Pinewood Ct. Halc 4G 145
Pinewood Ct. Sale 4D 122
Pinewood Ct. Wilm . . . . .6A 160 (off Pinewood Rd.)
Pinewood Cres. Rams . . .1B 22
Pinewood Rd. M21 . . . . .2G 123
Pinewood Rd. Wilm 1H 167
Pinewoods, The. Woodl 4H 129
Pinfield Ct. Stret . . . . . . .6C 106 (off Kingsway)
Pinfold. Had 3G 117
Pinfold. Roch 5G 27
Pinfold Av. M9 . . . . .1A 84
Pinfold Clo. Haleb 6D 146
Pinfold Ct. W'fld 1C 66
Pinfold Dri. Chea H 4C 150
Pinfold La. Rom 5B 130
Pinfold La. Timp . . . . . . .1F 157 (in two parts)
Pinfold La. W'fld 1C 66
Pinfold Rd. Wors 2E 77
Pingate Dri. Chea H 1C 160
Pingate La. Chea H 1C 160
Pingate La. S. Chea H . . .1C 160
Pingle La. Del 2G 59
Pingot. Shaw 4H 43
Pingot Av. M23 . . . . . . .1H 135
Pingot La. B'btm . . . . . . .6C 116 (in two parts)
Pingot, The. Irlam 4F 103
Pink Bank La. M12 . . . . .3C 110 (in two parts)
Pin Mill Brow. M12 . . . . . .5H 95 (1G 11)
Pinnacle Dri. Eger 1B 18
Pinner Pl. M19 . . . . .3C 126
Pinners Clo. Rams 2D 12
Pinnington La. Stret 6D 106
Pinnington Rd. M18 . . . .1F 111
Pintail Av. Stoc 5F 139
Pintail Clo. Roch 1D 26
Pioneer Ct. Ash L . . . . . . .4G 99 (off Benjamin St., in two parts)
Pioneer Rd. Swin 1B 80
Pioneer St. M11 . . . . .2D 96
Pioneer St. L'boro 4F 17
Pioneer St. Midd 2D 54
Pioneer St. Roch 5A 28
Pioneers Yd. Miln 6F 29
Piperhill Av. M22 . . . . . .1B 136
Pipers Clo. Roch 3H 25
Pipers Ct. Irlam 4G 103
Pipewell Av. M18 . . . . . .2E 111
Pipit Clo. Aud 3C 98
Pirie Wlk. M40 . . . . .5C 84
Pitcairn Ho. Eccl 4F 91
Pitchcombe Rd. M22 . . .3H 147
Pitcombe Clo. Bolt 4B 18
Pitfield Gdns. M23 . . . . .4F 135 (in two parts)
Pitfield La. Bolt 2H 33
Pitfield St. Bolt 6D 32
Pit La. Rytn . . . . .5A 42 (in two parts)
Pitman Clo. M11 . . . . . . .5C 96
Pitmore Wlk. M40 . . . . . .1D 84
Pitses. 5H 73
Pits Farm Av. Roch 4E 27
Pitsford Rd. M40 . . . . . . .6G 83
Pitshouse. Roch 1A 26
Pitshouse La. Roch 1A 26
Pit St. Chad 5H 71
Pittbrook St. M12 . . . . .6H 95 (3H 11)
Pitt St. Dent 4F 113
Pitt St. Heyw 3E 39
Pitt St. Hyde 4B 114
Pitt St. Oldh 3E 73
Pitt St. Rad 4E 49
Pitt St. Roch 3H 27
Pitt St. Stoc 3F 139
Pitt St. E. Oldh 4F 73
Pixmore Av. Bolt 1D 32
Place Rd. B'hth 5E 133
Plain Pitt St. Hyde . . . . .2A 114 (in two parts)
Plane Ct. Salf 3G 93
Plane Rd. Fail 6F 85
Plane St. Oldh 2G 73
Plane Tree Clo. Marp . . .6B 142
Planetree Rd. Hale 3A 146
Plane Tree Rd. Part 6B 118
Planet Way. Aud 2E 113
Plantagenet Wlk. M40 . . . .1F 97
Plantagenet St. Moss 6F 75
Plantation Av. Wors 5E 63
Plantation Gro. Uns 3G 51
Plantation Ind. Est. Ash L 3A 100
Plantation St. M18 . . . . .2G 111
Plantation St. Ash L 3B 100
Plantation Vw. Bury 6E 13
Plant Clo. Sale 4A 122
Plant Hill Rd. M9 . . . . . . .4E 69
Plantree Wlk. M23 . . . . . .3C 134
Plant St. M1 . . . . .4F 95 (6C 6)
Plasman Ind. Cen. M19 . . . . .6F 111
Plate St. Oldh 2D 72
Plato St. Oldh 2B 72
Platt Av. Ash L 5G 87
Plattbrook Clo. M14 . . . .6F 109
Platt Clo. Miln 6G 29
Platt Ct. M14 . . . . .5G 109
Platt Hall (Art Galley & Mus.) . . . . .5G 109 (Gallery of Costume)
Platt Hill Av. Bolt 3E 45
Platting Gro. Ash L 6D 86
Platting La. Roch 1G 41
Platting Rd. Scout & Lyd 1E 75
Platt La. M14 . . . . .6E 109
Platt La. Dob 5H 59
Platts Dri. Irlam 5E 103
Platt St. Chea 5A 138
Platt St. Duk 6G 99
Platt St. S'head 3B 74
Platt Wlk. Dent 6F 113
Plattwood Wlk. M15 . . . . . .1B 108 (6D 8)
Playfair Clo. Heyw 6G 39
Playfair St. M14 . . . . . . .3F 109
Play Fair St. Bolt 5D 18
Pleachway. Stoc 1B 138
Pleasant Ct. Roch 3C 40
Pleasant Gdns. Bolt 5A 32
Pleasant Rd. Eccl 4G 91
Pleasant St. M9 . . . . .4F 83
Pleasant St. Heyw 1E 39
Pleasant St. Roch 3C 40
Pleasant St. Wals 1F 35
Pleasant Ter. Duk . . . . . .4A 100 (off Astley St.)
Pleasant View. 3H 41
Pleasant Vw. M9 . . . . . . .5D 68
Pleasant Vw. Comp 6F 131
Pleasant Vw. Heyw 2D 38
Pleasant Vw. Lees 2B 74
Pleasant Vw. Rad 1H 65
Pleasant Vw. Shaw 1H 57
Pleasant Way. Chea H . . .1E 161
Pleasington Dri. M40 . . . .1C 84
Pleasington Dri. Bury 3E 35
Plevna St. Bolt 6C 32
Plodder La. Bolt & Farn . . . . 6E 45 & 1A 62
Ploughbank Dri. M21 . . .2B 124
Plough Clo. Urm 5G 103
Ploughfields. Wors 6C 76
Plough St. Duk 5B 100
Plover Clo. Roch 4B 26
Plover Dri. B'hth 3D 132
Plover Dri. Bury 1F 37
Plover Dri. Irlam 3E 103
Plover Ter. M21 . . . . .2B 124
Plover Way. Droy 2C 98
Plowden Clo. Bolt 4G 45
Plowden Rd. M22 . . . . . .3H 147
Plowley Clo. M20 . . . . . .1F 137
Plucksbridge Rd. Marp 2F 155

Plumbley Dri. *M16* 4A **108**
Plumbley St. *M11* 6G **97**
Plumley Clo. *Sale* 6F **123**
Plumley Rd. *Hand* 2H **159**
Plummer Av. *M21* 3H **123**
Plumpton Clo. *Rytn* 5C **56**
Plumpton Dri. *Bury* 5E **23**
Plumpton Rd. *Roch* 5A **44**
Plumpton Wlk. *M13* 3B **110**
Plum St. *Oldh* 4B **72**
Plumtree Clo. *Eccl* 3G **91**
Plum Tree Ct. *Salf* 3G **93**
Plunge Rd. *Rams* 2B **12**
Pluto Clo. *Salf* 1A **94**
Plymouth Av. *M13* 2A **110**
Plymouth Clo. *Ash L* 4F **87**
Plymouth Dri. *Bram* 6H **151**
Plymouth Dri. *Farn* 1B **62**
Plymouth Gro.
  M13 . . . . . .2G **109** (6E **11**)
Plymouth Gro. *Rad* 2D **48**
Plymouth Gro. *Stoc* 4D **138**
Plymouth Gro. W.
  M13 . . . . .2A **110**
Plymouth Rd. *Sale* 4F **121**
Plymouth St. *Oldh* 5D **72**
  (in two parts)
Plymouth Vw.
  M13 . . . . . .1G **109** (6E **11**)
Plymtree Clo. *M8* 1A **82**
Pobgreen. 6D **60**
Pobgreen La. *Upperm* . .6D **60**
Pochard Dri. *B'hth* 4D **132**
Pochard Dri. *Poy* 3A **162**
Pochin St. *M40* . . .2A **96** (1H **7**)
Pocket. 1G **45**
Pocket Nook. *Los* 4A **44**
Pocket Nook Rd. *Los* 4A **44**
Pocket Workshops, The.
  Bolt 1G **45**
Pocklington Dri. *M23* . . .4F **135**
Podsmead Rd. *M22* 3H **147**
Poise Brook Dri. *Stoc* . . .6F **141**
Poise Brook Rd. *Stoc* . . .6F **141**
Poise Clo. *Haz G* 2G **153**
Poland St. *M4* 3G **95** (3E **7**)
Poland St. *Aud* 5E **99**
  (in two parts)
Poland St. Ind. Est.
  M4 . . . . .3G **95** (3E **7**)
Polden Clo. *Oldh* 1C **86**
Polden Wlk. *M9* 2H **83**
Poleacre La. *Woodl* 3A **130**
Polebrook Av.
  M12 . . . . .1H **109** (6H **11**)
Pole Ct. *Bury* 4G **51**
Polefield App. *P'wich* 3F **67**
Polefield Circ. *P'wich* 3F **67**
Polefield Gdns. *P'wich* . . .3F **67**
Polefield Grange.
  P'wich 3F **67**
Polefield Gro. *P'wich* 3F **67**
Polefield Hall Rd.
  P'wich 3F **67**
  (in two parts)
Polefield Rd. *M9* 1F **83**
Polefield Rd. *P'wich* 3G **67**
Pole La. *Bury & P'wich* . .4G **51**
Pole La. *Fail* 3F **85**
Pole St. *Ash L* 1H **99**
Pole St. *Bolt* 4D **32**
Polesworth Clo. *M12* 1C **110**
Police St. *M2* 4D **94** (5G **5**)
Police St. *Alt* 6F **133**
Police St. *Eccl* 3E **91**
Pollard Ct. *Oldh* 1C **72**
Pollard Gro. *L'boro* 1G **17**
Pollard Ho. *Bolt* 5F **45**
Pollards La. *S'seat* 1C **22**
Pollard Sq. *Part* 6E **119**
Pollard St. *M4* 4G **95** (6F **7**)

Pollard St. E.
  M40 . . . . .3H **95** (4H **7**)
Pollen Clo. *Sale* 1D **134**
Pollen Rd. *B'hth* 5E **133**
Polletts Av. *Stoc* 3C **128**
Pollitt Av. *Ash L* 6G **87**
Pollitt Clo. *M12* 1B **110**
Pollitt Cft. *Rom* 2F **141**
Pollitts Clo. *Eccl* 3D **90**
Pollitt St. *Rad* 4A **50**
Polly Grn. *Roch* 6F **15**
Polonia St. *Oldh* 6A **72**
Polperro Clo. *Rytn* 3E **57**
Polperro Wlk. *Hyde* 4H **115**
Polruan Rd. *M21* 5G **107**
Polruan Wlk. *Hyde* 5A **116**
Polworth Rd. *M9* 2G **83**
Polygon Av.
  M13 . . . . . .1G **109** (5F **11**)
Polygon Rd. *M8* 2B **82**
Polygon St.
  M13 . . . . . .6G **95** (4F **11**)
Polygon, The. *Eccl* 3A **92**
Polygon, The. *Salf* 5G **81**
Pomfret St. *M12* 1C **110**
Pomfret St. *Salf* 6A **80**
Pomona Cres. *Salf* 6H **93**
  (in three parts)
Pomona Docks.
  M15 . . . . . .1A **108** (5A **8**)
Pomona Strand. *M16 & M15*
  . . . . .2G **107** (6A **8**)
  (in three parts)
Pomona St. *Roch* 6H **27**
Ponds Clo. *M21* 6H **107**
Pondwater Clo. *Wors* . . .6B **62**
Ponsford Av. *M9* 6A **70**
Ponsonby Rd. *Stret* 4D **106**
Pontefract Clo. *Swin* 4H **79**
Pool Bank St. *Midd* 2D **68**
  (in two parts)
Poolcroft. *Sale* 6F **123**
Poole Clo. *Bram* 4E **151**
Pooley Clo. *Midd* 6D **52**
Pool Fld. Clo. *Rad* 4D **48**
Pool Fold. *Fail* 5G **85**
Pool Fold Clo. *Bolt* 3E **31**
Pool Ho. Rd. *Poy* 2A **164**
Pool Pl. Bolt 3E **31**
  (off Church Rd.)
Pool St. Bolt 5A **32**
  (off Back La., in two parts)
Pool St. *Oldh* 5D **72**
Pool Ter. *Bolt* 3E **31**
Poolton Rd. *M9* 5D **68**
Pool Hall. *Roch* 5F **15**
Pope Way. *Dent* 1G **129**
Poplar Av. *M19* 1D **126**
Poplar Av. *Alt* 5G **133**
Poplar Av. *Bolt* 1B **32**
Poplar Av. *Brad* 5G **19**
Poplar Av. *Bury* 2F **37**
Poplar Av. *Lyd* 5E **75**
Poplar Av. *Oldh* 1B **86**
Poplar Av. *Roch* 2E **27**
Poplar Av. *Wilm* 4C **166**
Poplar Clo. *Gat* 6F **137**
Poplar Ct. *M14* 6H **109**
Poplar Ct. *Aud* 1F **113**
Poplar Dri. *P'wich* 1E **81**
Poplar Gro. *M18* 3F **111**
Poplar Gro. *Ash L* 6G **87**
Poplar Gro. *Cad* 3B **118**
Poplar Gro. *Rams* 2F **13**
Poplar Gro. *Sale* 6B **122**
Poplar Gro. *Stoc* 1C **152**
Poplar Gro. *Urm* 5G **105**
Poplar Rd. *M19* 6H **125**
Poplar Rd. *Duk* 6D **100**
Poplar Rd. *Eccl* 1G **91**
Poplar Rd. *Stret* 1B **122**
Poplar Rd. *Swin* 4D **78**

Poplar Rd. *Wors* 2G **77**
Poplars Rd. *Stal* 2H **101**
Poplars, The. *Alt* 1F **145**
Poplars, The. *Moss* 2G **89**
Poplar St. *M11* 5A **96**
Poplar St. *Aud* 1F **113**
Poplar St. *Fail* 5D **84**
Poplar St. *Midd* 2D **70**
Poplar St. *Stoc* 1A **138**
Poplar Wlk. Aud 1F **113**
  (off Poplar Ct.)
Poplar Wlk. *Chad* 1H **71**
Poplar Wlk. *Part* 6B **118**
Poplar Way. *H Lane* 6E **155**
Poplin Dri. *Salf* 2C **94**
Poppy Clo. *M23* 2E **135**
Poppy Clo. *Chad* 2E **71**
Poppyfield Vw. *Roch* 3A **26**
Poppythorn La. *P'wich* . . .4E **67**
  (in two parts)
Porchester Dri. *Rad* 2C **48**
Porchfield Sq.
  M3 . . . . .5C **94** (1F **9**)
Porlock Av. *Aud* 5C **98**
Porlock Av. *Hyde* 5G **115**
Porlock Clo. *Stoc* 3C **140**
Porlock Rd. *M23* 5H **135**
Porlock Rd. *Urm* 1C **120**
Porlock Wlk. *Hyde* 5G **115**
Porritt Clo. *Roch* 5A **26**
Porritt St. *Bury* 1E **37**
  (in two parts)
Porritt Way. *Rams* 2E **13**
Portal Ct. *Midd* 1C **70**
Portal Gro. *Dent* 6H **113**
Portal Wlk. M9 . . . . .3F **83**
  (off Alderside Rd.)
Porter Dri. *M40* 5F **83**
Porter St. *Bury* 1D **36**
Porter St. *Oldh* 4A **72**
Portfield Clo. *Bolt* 5D **30**
Portfield Wlk. M40 . . . . .5A **84**
  (off Harmer Clo.)
Portgate Wlk.
  M13 . . . . . .1H **109** (6G **11**)
Porthleven Dri. *M23* 5E **135**
Porthtowan Wlk.
  Hyde 5A **116**
Portico Library Gallery, The.
  . . . . .4E **95** (6A **6**)
Portinscale Clo. *Bury* 2H **35**
Portland Arc. *M1* 6B **6**
Portland Basin Mus. 4G **99**
Portland Clo. *Haz G* 4B **152**
Portland Ct. *M20* 6F **125**
Portland Cres. *M13* 2H **109**
Portland Gro. *Stoc* 5D **126**
Portland Ho. *Ash L* 3G **99**
Portland Ho. *Marp* 6C **142**
Portland Ho. *Salf* 2A **92**
Portland Ind. Est. Bury . . .1E **37**
  (off Portland St.)
Portland Pl. Ash L 3G **99**
Portland Pl. Roch 1G **41**
  (off Oldham Rd.)
Portland Pl. *Stal* 3F **101**
Portland Rd. *M13* 4B **110**
Portland Rd. *Bow* 2E **145**
Portland Rd. *Eccl* 2H **91**
Portland Rd. *Stret* 3E **107**
Portland Rd. *Swin* 4G **79**
Portland Rd. *Wors* 4E **63**
Portland St.
  M1 . . . . .5E **95** (1A **10**)
Portland St. *Ash L* 2G **99**
  (in two parts)
Portland St. *Bolt* 3A **32**
Portland St. *Bury* 1E **37**
Portland St. *Farn* 5F **47**
Portland St. S. *Ash L* 3G **99**
  (in two parts)
Portland Ter. *Ash L* 3G **99**

Portland, The. *M14* 1H **125**
Portloe Rd. *H Grn* 6F **149**
Portman Rd. *M16* 4C **108**
Portman St. *Moss* 2E **89**
Porton Wlk. *M22* 4H **147**
Portrea Clo. *Stoc* 6G **139**
Portree Clo. *Eccl* 3D **90**
Portree Ct. *Heyw* 4C **38**
Portrush Rd. *M22* 3C **148**
Portside Clo. *Wors* 5D **76**
Portslade Wlk. *M23* 6F **135**
Portsmouth Clo. *Salf* . . .6H **81**
Portsmouth St.
  M13 . . . . . .1F **109** (6D **10**)
  (in two parts)
Port Soderick Av. *Salf* . . .4G **93**
Portstone Clo. *M16* 3C **108**
Port St. *M1* 4F **95** (5C **6**)
Port St. *Oldh* 5D **72**
Port St. *Stoc* 2G **139**
Portugal Rd. *P'wich* 1F **81**
Portugal St. *M4* . . .3G **95** (3E **7**)
  (in two parts)
Portugal St. *Ash L* 4F **99**
Portugal St. *Bolt* 6D **32**
Portugal St. E.
  M1 . . . . .5G **95** (1E **11**)
Portville Rd. *M19* 5C **110**
Portway. *M22* 3H **147**
Portwood. 6B **128**
Portwood Ind. Est.
  Stoc 1A **140**
  (in two parts)
Portwood Pl. *Stoc* 1H **139**
Portwood Wlk. *M9* 4F **83**
Posnett St. *Stoc* 3E **139**
Postal St. *M1* 4F **95** (5C **6**)
Postbridge Clo.
  M13 . . . . . .1G **109** (6F **11**)
Post Office St. *Alt* 6F **133**
Potato Wharf.
  M3 . . . . .5B **94** (2D **8**)
Pot Green. 6B **12**
Pot Hill. *Ash L* 1A **100**
Pot Hill Sq. *Ash L* 1A **100**
Pot Ho. La. *Ward* 4F **15**
Pott St. *Alt* 1F **145**
Potter Ho. *Oldh* 4D **72**
Potter Rd. *Had* 4G **117**
Potter's La. *M9* 4G **83**
Potter St. *Bury* 2E **37**
Potter St. *Rad* 3B **50**
Pottery La.
  M12 & M11 . . . . . . .2B **110**
Pottery Row. *M11* 3A **96**
Pottery Wlk. *M40* 1D **84**
Pottinger St. *Ash L* 4F **99**
Pott St. *M40* 6D **84**
Pott St. *Swin* 1F **79**
Poulton Av. *Bolt* 6G **33**
Poulton St. *M11* 6G **97**
Poundswick La. *M22* . . .2A **148**
Powell Av. *Hyde* 4C **114**
Powell St. *Bury* 4H **35**
Powell St. *Clay* 3F **97**
Powell St. *Old T* 3A **108**
Powerleague Soccer Cen.
  . . . . .6H **95** (3G **11**)
  (Manchester)
Powerleague Soccer Cen.
  . . . . .2D **138**
  (Stockport)
Powicke Dri. *Rom* 2F **141**
Powis Rd. *Urm* 6G **103**
Pownall Av. *M20* 1E **125**
Pownall Av. *Bram* 1H **161**
Pownall Ct. *Wilm* 5G **166**
Pownall Green. 6G **151**
Pownall Park. 1C **166**
Pownall Rd. *Alt* 2F **145**
Pownall Rd. *Chea H* 4C **150**
Pownall Rd. *Wilm* 1C **166**

Pownall St. *Haz G* 2D **152**
Poynings Dri. *M22* 4A **148**
Poynt Chase. *Wors* 5D **76**
Poynter St. *M40* 2C **84**
Poynter Wlk. *Oldh* 3H **57**
Poynton. 3D **162**
Poynton Clo. *Bury* 4E **37**
Poynton Leisure Cen.
. . . . .5F **163**
Poynton St.
M15 . . . . . .1D **108** (6H **9**)
Poynton Tourist Info. Cen.
. . . . .3E **163**
Praed St. *Traf P* 2C **106**
Pratt Wlk. *M11* 4B **96**
(off Turnpike Wlk.)
Precinct Cen. *M13* 1E **109**
(5B **10**)
Precinct, The. *Chca H* . . .3D **150**
Precinct, The. *Holl* 2F **117**
Precinct, The. *Rams* 4E **12**
Precinct, The. *Stoc* 5D **140**
(Offerton)
Precinct, The. *Stoc* 4F **139**
(Stockport)
Preece Clo. *Hyde* 3E **115**
Preesall Av. *H Grn* 5F **149**
Preesall Clo. *Bury* 5F **35**
Premier Rd. *M8* 1D **94**
Premier St. *M16* 3B **108**
Prentice Wlk. *M11* 4C **96**
Prenton St. *Open* 5G **97**
Prenton Way. *Wals* 6H **21**
Presall St. *Bolt* 5E **33**
Prescot Clo. *Bury* 4E **37**
Prescot Rd. *M9* 4F **83**
Prescot Rd. *Hale* 3H **145**
Prescott Rd. *Wilm* 6F **159**
Prescott St. *Bolt* 3G **45**
Prescott St. *Roch* 1C **28**
Prescott St. *Wors* 6D **62**
Prescott Wlk. *Dent* 6H **113**
Press St. *M11* 6F **97**
Presswood Ct. *Salf* 5A **80**
Prestage St. *Long* 5D **110**
Prestage St. *Old T* 2A **108**
(in four parts)
Prestbury Av. *M14* 6D **108**
Prestbury Av. *Alt* 5G **133**
Prestbury Clo. *Bury* 4E **37**
Prestbury Clo. *Stoc* 1D **152**
Prestbury Dri. *Bred* 6E **129**
Prestbury Dri. *Oldh* 6B **56**
Prestbury Rd. *Bolt* 6E **19**
Prestbury St. *Stoc* 1D **152**
Prestfield Rd. *W'fld* 2E **67**
Presto Gdns. *Bolt* 3F **45**
Prestolee. 1A **64**
Prestolee Rd. *Bolt* 6A **48**
(in two parts)
Preston Av. *Eccl* 2A **92**
Preston Av. *Irlam* 2D **118**
Preston Clo. *Eccl* 2A **92**
Preston St. *M19* 1C **126**
Preston St. *M18* 1F **111**
Preston St. *Bolt* 3D **46**
Preston St. *Midd* 1A **70**
Preston St. *Oldh* 3E **73**
Preston St. *Roch* 3E **27**
Presto St. *Bolt* 3F **45**
Presto St. *Farn* 6G **47**
Prestwich. 4E **67**
Prestwich Clo. *Stoc* 4B **140**
Prestwich Hills. *P'wich* . . .6E **67**
Prestwich Park. 6E **67**
Prestwich Pk. Rd. S.
P'wich 6E **67**
Prestwich St. *Dent* 3E **113**
Prestwick Wlk. *M40* 1C **84**
Prestwood Clo. *Bolt* 4H **31**
Prestwood Dri. *Bolt* 4H **31**
Prestwood Rd. *Farn* 6C **46**

Prestwood Rd. *Salf* 1C **92**
Pretoria Rd. *Bolt* 6G **33**
Pretoria Rd. *Oldh* 6A **72**
Pretoria St. *Roch* 2E **27**
Prettywood. 3A **38**
Price St. *M4* 4H **95** (5H **7**)
Price St. *Bury* 4E **37**
Price St. *Duk* 5A **100**
Price St. *Farn* 6F **47**
Prickshaw La. *Whitw* 3A **14**
Pridmouth Rd. *M20* 3G **125**
Priest Av. *Gat* 1E **149**
Priest Hill St. *Oldh* 2C **72**
Priestley Rd. *Wors* 3C **78**
Priestley Way. *Shaw* 6H **43**
Priestnall Ct. *Stoc* 6B **126**
(off Priestnall Rd.)
Priestnall Recreation Cen.
. . . . .6B **126**
Priestnall Rd. *Stoc* 6B **126**
Priest St. *Stoc* 4H **139**
Priestwood Av. *Oldh* 3B **58**
Primary Clo. *Cad* 4B **118**
Primley Wlk. *M9* 3G **83**
(off Edward St.)
Primrose Av. *Farn* 6C **46**
Primrose Av. *Hyde* 2B **130**
Primrose Av. *Marp* 5C **142**
Primrose Av. *Upperm* 6C **60**
Primrose Av. *Urm* 5F **105**
Primrose Av. *Wors* 1D **76**
Primrose Bank. 4C **72**
Primrose Bank. *Bow* 4E **145**
Primrose Bank. *G'fld* 4F **61**
Primrose Bank. *Oldh* 4C **72**
Primrose Bank. *T'ton* 4G **21**
Primrose Bank. *Wors* 1D **76**
Primrose Clo. *Bolt* 1A **34**
Primrose Clo. *Salf* 3F **93**
Primrose Cotts. *Bow* 4E **145**
Primrose Cres. *Hyde* 1B **130**
Primrose Dri. *Bury* 1H **37**
Primrose Dri. *Droy* 2C **98**
Primrose Hill Cotts.
Heyw 1H **39**
Primrose Ho. *Oldh* 4C **72**
Primrose St. *M4* . .3F **95** (3D **6**)
Primrose St. *Bolt* 1B **32**
Primrose St. *Kear* 2G **63**
Primrose St. *Roch* 3F **27**
Primrose Ter. *Stal* 3F **101**
Primrose Wlk. *Marp* 5C **142**
Primrose Wlk. *Oldh* 4C **72**
Primula St. *Bolt* 1B **32**
Prince Albert Av. *M19* 5C **110**
Prince Charlie St. *Oldh* . . .1F **73**
Princedom St. *M9* 3G **83**
Prince Edward Av.
Dent 5F **113**
Prince Edward Av.
Oldh 2G **73**
Prince George St. *Oldh* . . .6G **57**
Prince of Wales Bus. Pk.
Oldh 1G **73**
Prince Rd. *Poy* 2A **164**
Princes Av. *M20* 5G **125**
Princes Av. *Bred* 6G **129**
Princes Av. *Irlam* 4G **103**
Princes Av. *L Lev* 3B **48**
Prince's Bri. *M3* . .5B **94** (1D **8**)
Princes Ct. *Eccl* 2F **91**
Princes Dri. *Marp* 4C **142**
Princes Dri. *Sale* 6D **122**
Prince's Incline. *Poy* 3E **163**
Princes Rd. *Bred* 6G **129**
Princes Rd. *B'hth* 5F **133**
Princes Rd. *Sale* 6C **122**
Princes Rd. *Stoc* 5C **126**
Princess Av. *Choa H* 2C **150**
Princess Av. *Dent* 4E **113**
Princess Av. *Kear* 3H **63**
Princess Av. *P'wich* 1G **81**

Princess Av. *Roch* 5A **16**
Princess Clo. *Duk* 5B **100**
Princess Clo. *Heyw* 4F **39**
Princess Clo. *Moss* 3G **89**
Princess Ct.
M15 . . . . . . .1B **108** (5C **8**)
Princess Ct. *P'wich* 6F **67**
Princess Dri. *Midd* 1G **69**
Princess Gro. *Farn* 1F **63**
(in two parts)
Princess Pde. *M14* 6D **108**
Princess Pde. *Bury* 3D **36**
Princess Parkway.
M23 . . . . .4A **136**
Princess Rd. *M15 & M14*
. . . . .1D **108** (5G **9**)
(in three parts)
Princess Rd.
M21 & M20 . . . . . . .6R **124**
Princess Rd. *Chad* 6E **71**
Princess Rd. *P'wich* 5G **67**
Princess Rd. *Roch* 4D **28**
Princess Rd. *Shaw* 1E **57**
Princess Rd. *Urm* 4D **104**
Princess Rd. *Wilm* 4C **166**
Princess St.
M2 & M1 . . .4D **94** (6H **5**)
Princess St.
M15 . . . . . . .1A **108** (5B **8**)
Princess St. *Ash L* 1B **100**
Princess St. *Bolt* 6B **32**
Princess St. *B'hth* 3E **133**
Princess St. *Chad* 4G **71**
Princess St. *Eccl* 3E **91**
Princess St. *Fail* 4C **85**
Princess St. *Hyde* 5C **114**
Princess St. *Lees* 3A **74**
Princess St. *Rad* 4E **49**
Princess St. *Roch* 3H **27**
Princess St. *Salf* 1G **93**
Princess St. *Swin* 4G **79**
Princess Wlk. *Bram* 6H **151**
Prince St. *Bolt* 5A **32**
Prince St. *Heyw* 3F **39**
Prince St. *Oldh* 2E **73**
Prince St. *Rams* 3E **13**
Prince St. *Roch* 6A **28**
Princes Wood Rd.
Poy 2A **164**
Princethorpe Clo. *Los* 1B **44**
Princeton Clo. *Salf* 2C **92**
Prince Way. *Rytn* 1A **56**
Prinknash Rd. *M22* 3B **148**
Printers Brow. *Holl* 2F **117**
Printers Fold. *Holl* 2F **117**
Printers La. *Bolt* 5G **19**
Printers Pk. *Holl* 2G **117**
Printer St. *M11* 5F **97**
Printer St. *Oldh* 3D **72**
Printon Av. *M9* 5D **68**
Printworks La. *M19* 6E **111**
Printworks Rd. *H'rod* 2B **101**
Printworks, The.
. . . . .3E **95** (3A **6**)
Prior St. *Oldh* 4F **73**
Priory Av. *M21* 1H **123**
Priory Av. *Salf* 5G **81**
Priory Clo. *Duk* 1B **114**
Priory Clo. *Oldh* 6D **72**
Priory Clo. *Sale* 3D **122**
Priory Ct. *Bow* 4E **145**
Priory Ct. *Eccl* 3G **91**
Priory Ct. *Stoc* 1G **127**
Priory Gdns. *M20* 5F **125**
Priory Gro. *Chad* 5G **71**
Priory Gro. *Salf* 5G **81**
Priory La. *Stoc* 1G **127**
Priory Pl. *Bolt* 3E **33**
Priory Pl. *Salf* 5G **81**
Priory Rd. *Bow* 5D **144**
Priory Rd. *Chea* 6C **138**

Priory Rd. *Sale* 4C **122**
Priory Rd. *Swin* 2E **79**
Priory Rd. *Wilm* 1B **166**
Priory St. *Bow* 5E **145**
Priory, The. *Salf* 5G **81**
Pritchard St.
M1 . . . . .5E **95** (2B **10**)
Pritchard St. *Stret* 5D **106**
Privet St. *Oldh* 6H **57**
Proctor St. *Bury* 4A **36**
Proctor Way. *Eccl* 6B **90**
(in two parts)
Progress Av. *Aud* 1F **113**
Progress St. *Ash L* 2G **99**
Progress St. *Bolt* 4B **32**
Progress St. *Roch* 4C **40**
Progress Way. *Dent* 5C **112**
Promenade St. *Heyw* 3G **39**
Propps Hall Dri. *Fail* 5D **84**
Prospect Av. *Bolt* 2H **33**
Prospect Av. *Cad* 3C **118**
Prospect Av. *Farn* 2F **63**
Prospect Ct. *T'ton* 4H **21**
Prospect Dri. *Fail* 6F **85**
Prospect Dri. *Haleb* 6D **146**
Prospect Ho. *M9* 4G **83**
(off Church La.)
Prospect Pl. *Ash L* 6H **87**
Prospect Pl. *Comp* 6F **131**
Prospect Pl. *Farn* 2E **63**
Prospect Pl. *Heyw* 2F **39**
Prospect Pl. *Swin* 4G **79**
Prospect Rd. *Ash L* 6A **88**
Prospect Rd. *Oldh* 2A **72**
Prospect St. *Bolt* 4B **32**
Prospect St. *Heyw* 4G **39**
Prospect St. *L'boro* 3F **17**
Prospect St. *Roch* 1E **41**
Prospect Ter. *Bury* 1B **36**
Prospect Ter. *Roch* 1G **25**
Prospect Va. *H Grn* 4F **149**
Prospect Vw. *Swin* 4G **79**
Prospect Vs. *M9* 2H **83**
Protector Way. *Irlam* 1D **118**
Prout St. *M12* 4C **110**
Providence St.
M4 . . . . .4H **95** (5G **7**)
Providence St. *Ash L* 1B **100**
Providence St. *Aud* 6F **99**
Providence St. *Bolt* 2B **46**
Provident Av. *M19* 6E **111**
Provident St. *Shaw* 6F **43**
Provident Way. *Timp* 4A **134**
Provis Rd. *M21* 2H **123**
Prubella Av. *Dent* 2E **113**
Pryce St. *Bolt* 4H **31**
Pryme St. *M15* 6C **94** (3E **9**)
Pudding La. *Hyde* 4G **115**
(in four parts)
Puffin Av. *Poy* 3B **162**
Puffingate Clo. *Carr* 4G **89**
Pugin Wlk. *M9* 5F **83**
(off Oldershaw Dri.)
Pulborough Clo. *Bury* 4B **22**
Pulford Av. *M21* 5B **124**
Pulford Rd. *Sale* 1C **134**
Pullman Clo. *M19* 1D **126**
Pullman Ct. *Bolt* 2C **46**
Pullman Dri. *Urm* 5H **105**
Pullman St. *Roch* 6H **27**
Pump St. *M40* . . .3A **96** (4H **7**)
Pump St. *Oldh* 1H **85**
Pump Yd. *M4* 3E **95** (3A **6**)
Punch La. *Bolt* 5B **44**
(in three parts)
Punch St. *Bolt* 1H **45**
Purbeck Clo. *M22* 4A **148**
Purbeck Dri. *Bury* 5C **22**
Purcell Clo. *Bolt* 4H **31**
Purcell St. *M12* 4C **110**

Purdon St.—Railway St.

Purdon St. Bury .5F 23
Purdy Ho. Oldh .4D 72
Puritan Wlk. M40 .6E 83
(off Ribblesdale Dri.)
Purley Av. M23 .2H 135
Purley Dri. Cad .4A 118
Purple St. Bolt .6B 32
Purslow Clo. M12 .4A 96
Purton Wlk. M9 .4G 83
(off Broadwell Dri.)
Putney Clo. Oldh .6C 56
Puzzletree Ct. Stoc .4C 140
Pymgate Dri. H Grn .3E 149
Pymgate La. H Grn .3E 149
Pym St. M40 .3H 83
Pym St. Eccl .3F 91
Pym St. Heyw .4F 39
Pyramid Ct. Salf .5H 81
Pyrus Clo. Eccl .5B 90
Pytha Fold Rd. M20 .4G 125

Q

Quadrant, The. M9 .6A 70
Quadrant, The. Droy .4H 97
Quadrant, The. Rom .1G 141
Quadrant, The. Stoc .2B 140
Quail Dri. Irlam .4E 103
Quail St. Oldh .4G 73
Quainton Ho. Salf .4F 93
(off Amersham St.)
Quakers Fld. T'ton .3H 21
Quantock Clo. Stoc .1G 139
Quantock Dri. Oldh .6D 72
Quantock St. M16 .3C 108
Quarlton Dri. Hawk .1D 20
Quarmby Rd. M18 .3H 111
Quarry Bank Mill (Museum). .5C 158
Quarry Bank Rd. Styal .4D 158
Quarry Clough. Stal .5H 101
Quarry Heights. Stal .5D 100
Quarry Hill. Roch .5E 15
Quarry Pond Rd. Wors .6B 62
Quarry Ri. Rom .6H 129
Quarry Ri. Stal .5D 100
Quarry Rd. Kear .2A 64
Quarry Rd. Rom .1H 141
Quarry St. Rad .4H 49
Quarry St. Rams .3F 13
(in two parts)
Quarry St. Roch .2G 27
Quarry St. Stal .4D 100
Quarry St. Woodl .4H 129
Quarry Vw. Roch .6E 15
Quarry Wlk. M11 .4B 96
(off Pilgrim Dri.)
Quayside Clo. Wors .6D 76
Quays, The. Salf .6F 93
Quay St. M3 .4C 94 (6E 5)
(Manchester)
Quay St. M3 .3C 94 (4F 5)
(Salford)
Quay St. Heyw .4G 39
Quayview. Salf .5G 93
Quay W. Traf P .1E 107
Quebec Pl. Bolt .2G 45
Quebec St. Bolt .2H 45
Quebec St. Dent .3E 113
Quebec St. Oldh .1A 72
Queen Alexandra Clo. Salf .5A 94 (2A 8)
Queen Ann Dri. Wors .4D 76
Queen Anne Clo. Uns .3G 51
Queenhill Dri. Hyde .2E 115
Queenhill Rd. M22 .2C 136
Queens Av. M18 .2D 110
Queens Av. Bred .6G 129
Queen's Av. Brom X .4E 19
Queen's Av. L Lev .3A 48
Queens Av. Roch .5A 16
Queensbrook. Bolt .6A 32
Queensbury Clo. Bolt .6B 18
Queensbury Clo. Wilm .1G 167
Queensbury Ct. M40 .2H 95 (2H 7)
Queensbury Pde. M40 .2A 96 (2H 7)
Queens Clo. Hyde .2C 130
Queens Clo. Stoc .1C 138
Queens Clo. Wors .4B 76
(Glendale Rd.)
Queen's Clo. Wors .5F 63
(Harriet St.)
Queen's Ct. M20 .5E 125
Queens Ct. M40 .6F 83
Queens Ct. Marp .5E 143
Queen's Ct. Stoc .1C 138
Queens Ct. Urm .5A 104
Queens Ct. Wilm .3D 166
Queenscroft. Eccl .2H 91
Queen's Dri. Chea H .3C 150
Queens Dri. Hyde .2D 130
Queen's Dri. P'wich .1G 81
Queens Dri. Roch .2E 41
Queen's Dri. Stoc .1C 138
Queensferry St. M40 .5C 84
Queens Gdns. Chea .5A 138
Queensgate. Bolt .5G 31
Queensgate. Bram .2G 161
Queensgate Dri. Rytn .1A 56
Queen's Gro. M12 .3C 110
Queensland Rd. M18 .2D 110
Queen's Pk. Rd. Heyw .1F 39
Queens Pk. St. Bolt .5H 31
Queens Pl. Bury .1C 22
Queen Sq. Ash L .1B 100
Queen's Rd. M8 & M9 .6C 82
Queen's Rd. M40 .5F 83
Queens Rd. Ash L .6H 87
Queens Rd. Bolt .3F 45
Queens Rd. Bred .6G 129
Queens Rd. Chad .2G 71
Queen's Rd. Chea H .1B 150
(in two parts)
Queen's Rd. Hale .2G 145
Queen's Rd. Haz G .2E 153
Queen's Rd. L'boro .4F 17
Queens Rd. Oldh .4E 73
Queens Rd. Sale .4H 121
Queen's Rd. Urm .6F 105
Queens Rd. Wilm .3D 166
Queen's Rd. Ter. L'boro .4F 17
(off Queen's Rd.)
Queens Ter. Duk .4H 99
Queens Ter. Hand .3H 159
Queenston Rd. M20 .5E 125
Queen St. M2 .4D 94 (6G 5)
Queen St. Ash L .3A 100
Queen St. Aud .3E 113
(Denton, in two parts)
Queen St. Aud .1F 113
(Audenshaw)
Queen St. Bolt .6A 32
Queen St. Bury .3E 37
Queen St. Chea .5B 138
Queen St. Duk .4H 99
Queen St. Fail .4E 85
Queen St. Farn .1F 63
Queen St. Had .3H 117
Queen St. Heyw .2F 39
Queen St. Hyde .5C 114
Queen St. L'boro .4F 17
Queen St. L Hul .6D 62
Queen St. Marp .5E 143
Queen St. Midd .1C 70
Queen St. Moss .2E 89
Queen St. Oldh .2D 72
Queen St. Rad .5A 50
Queen St. Rams .3D 12
Queen St. Roch .3H 27
Queen St. Rytn .1F 57
Queen St. Salf .6B 80
(Irlams o' th' Height)
Queen St. Salf .3C 94 (3F 5)
(Salford)
Queen St. Shaw .3B 56
Queen St. S'head .3B 74
Queen St. Stal .3E 101
Queen St. T'ton .6A 22
Queen St. W. M20 .2F 125
Queens Vw. L'boro .6E 17
Queen's Wlk. Droy .4A 98
Queensway. M19 .1H 137
Queensway. Duk .6D 100
Queensway. G'fld .3F 61
Queensway. H Grn .5F 149
Queensway. Irlam .5D 102
Queensway. Kear .4H 63
Queensway. Moss .3F 89
Queensway. Part .5D 118
Queensway. Poy .4D 162
Queensway. Roch .3C 40
Queensway. Swin .1G 79
Queensway. Urm .3G 105
Queensway. Wors .3D 76
Queensway Neighbourhood Cen. Roch .6A 28
Queen Victoria St. Eccl .3E 91
Queen Victoria St. Roch .1G 41
Quenby St. M15 .6B 94 (4D 8)
Quendon Av. Salf .1C 94
Quick. .5F 75
Quick Edge. .6E 75
Quick Edge La. G'ton .5D 74
Quickedge Rd. Moss & Lyd .1E 89
Quick Rd. Moss .5F 75
Quick Vw. Moss .6G 75
Quickwood. .1E 89
Quickwood. Dent .3G 113
(off Herbert S.)
Quickwood. Moss .1F 89
(off Roughtown Rd.)
Quill Ct. Irlam .3C 118
Quilter Gro. M9 .1E 83
Quinney Cres. M16 .3C 108
Quinn St. M11 .4C 96
Quinton. Roch .3G 27
(off Spotland Rd.)
Quinton Wlk. M13 .1F 109 (5D 10)
Quintrell Brow. Brom X .3E 19

R

Rabbit La. Mot .1C 116
Raby St. M14 .3D 108
Raby St. M16 .3C 108
Racecourse Pk. Wilm .3C 166
Racecourse Rd. Wilm .2B 166
Racecourse Wlk. Rad .3F 49
Racefield Hamlet. Chad .3H 55
Racefield Rd. Alt .1E 145
Race, The. Hand .5H 159
Rachel Rosing Wlk. M8 .3B 82
Rachel St. M12 .5G 95 (2F 11)
Rackhouse Rd. M23 .2H 135
Radbourne Clo. M12 .1C 110
Radbourne Gro. Bolt .3D 44
Radbourne Ho. Bolt .1D 46
Radcliffe. .4F 49
Radcliffe Moor Rd. Bolt & Rad .1B 48
Radcliffe New Rd. W'fld .5A 50
Radcliffe Pk. Cres. Salf .6A 80
Radcliffe Pk. Rd. Salf .6H 79
Radcliffe Rd. Bolt .6D 32
Radcliffe Rd. Bury .6B 36
Radcliffe Rd. Oldh .5H 57
Radcliffe St. Oldh .1D 72
(in two parts)
Radcliffe St. Rytn .3B 56
Radcliffe St. S'head .3C 74
Radcliffe Swimming Pool. .4G 49
Radcliffe Vw. Salf .6H 93
(off Ordsall Dri.)
Radclyffe St. Chad .1H 71
Radclyffe St. Midd .5A 54
Radclyffe Ter. Midd .5A 54
Radelan Gro. Rad .3D 48
Radford Clo. Stoc .4D 140
Radford Dri. M9 .3G 83
Radford Dri. Irlam .4E 103
Radford Ho. Stoc .4E 141
Radford St. Salf .3G 81
Radium St. M4 .3G 95 (3E 7)
Radlet Dri. Timp .3A 134
Radlett Wlk. M13 .2G 109
(off Plymouth Gro.)
Radley Clo. Bolt .4E 31
Radley Clo. Sale .6F 121
Radley St. M16 .4D 108
Radley St. Fail .5G 97
Radley Wlk. M16 .4D 108
(off Radley St.)
Radnor Av. Dent .4B 112
Radnor Ho. Stoc .3G 139
(off Moseley St.)
Radnormere Dri. Chea H .1B 150
Radnor St. Gort .3E 111
Radnor St. Hulme .2D 108
Radnor St. Oldh .4A 72
Radnor St. Stret .5D 106
Radstock Clo. M14 .6F 109
Radstock Clo. Bolt .4C 18
Radstock Rd. Stret .5C 106
Raeburn Dri. Marp B .3F 143
Rae St. Stoc .3E 139
Raglan Av. Swin .1H 79
Raglan Av. W'fld .2F 67
Raglan Clo. M11 .4B 96
Raglan Dri. Timp .3G 133
Raglan Rd. Sale .6H 121
Raglan Rd. Stret .4B 106
Raglan St. Bolt .3H 31
Raglan St. Hyde .5A 114
Raglan St. Roch .4C 40
Raglan Wlk. M15 .1D 108 (6H 9)
Ragley Clo. Poy .3F 163
Raikes Clough Ind. Est. Bolt .3E 47
Raikes La. Bolt .3D 46
(in two parts)
Raikes La. Ind. Est. Bolt .3D 46
Raikes Rd. Bolt .2F 47
Raikes Way. Bolt .2F 47
Railside Ter. Eccl .3H 91
Railton Av. M16 .4B 108
Railton Ter. M9 .4H 83
Railway App. Rad .4H 49
Railway App. Roch .3C 40
Railway Brow. Roch .4C 40
Railway Cotts. Bred .5F 129
Railway Rd. Chad .1G 85
Railway Rd. Marp .5B 142
Railway Rd. Oldh .3B 72
Railway Rd. Stoc .3G 139
Railway Rd. Stret .2E 107
Railway Rd. Urm .5F 105
Railway St. M18 .1E 111
Railway St. Alt .1F 145
Railway St. Bury .1C 22
Railway St. Duk .4H 99
Railway St. Farn .6G 47
Railway St. Heyw .4G 39

280 A-Z Manchester

Railway St. Hyde 5B 114
Railway St. L'boro 4F 17
Railway St. Miln 1F 43
Railway St. Rad 4G 49
Railway St. Rams 3E 13
Railway St. Roch 4A 28
Railway St. Stoc 1G 139
Railway St. Ind. Est.
   M18 . . . . .1E 111
Railway St. W. Bury 2H 37
Railway Ter. Bury 4A 36
Railway Ter. Dis 1H 165
Railway Ter. Heyw 4F 39
Railway Ter. S'seat 1C 22
   (off Miller St.)
Railway Vw. Hyde 6A 114
Railway Vw. Shaw 5G 43
Railway Vw. S'head 3D 30
Railway Vw. Stoc 5G 111
Raimond St. Bolt 2G 31
Rainbow Clo. M21 . . . . . .2H 123
Raincliff Av. M13 . . . . . .5B 110
Raines Crest. Miln 5G 29
Rainford Av. M20 . . . . . .1E 125
Rainford Av. Timp 5A 134
Rainford Ho. Bolt 5B 32
   (off Beta St.)
Rainford St. Bolt 5G 19
Rainforth St. M13 . . . . . .4B 110
Rainham Dri. M8 . . . . . .4C 82
Rainham Dri. Bolt 4A 32
Rainham Gro. Bolt 4B 32
   (off Rainham Dri.)
Rainham Way. Chad 3H 71
Rainham Way. Stoc 3B 128
Rainhill Wlk. M40 . . . . . .1F 97
Rainow Av. Droy 4G 97
Rainow Dri. Poy 5G 163
Rainow Rd. Stoc 6E 139
Rainow Way. Wilm 6H 159
Rainsdale Flats. Heyw 3E 39
   (off Meadow Clo.)
Rainshaw St. Bolt 1B 32
Rainshaw St. Oldh 1H 73
Rainshaw St. Rytn 3B 56
Rainsough. 2E 81
Rainsough Av. P'wich 2E 81
Rainsough Brow.
   P'wich 2D 80
Rainsough Clo. P'wich . . .2E 81
Rainsough Hill. P'wich . . .2D 80
Rainton Wlk. M40 . . . . . .1D 84
Rainwood. Chad 1E 71
Raja Clo. M8 . . . . .4D 82
Rake. Roch 4H 25
Rakehead Wlk. M15 . . . . .2E 109
   (off Botham Clo.)
Rake La. Swin 6G 65
Rake St. Bury 1D 36
Rake Ter. L'boro 3G 17
Rake, The. Rams 3D 12
Rake Top. Roch 2D 26
Rakewood. 2H 29
Rakewood Dri. Oldh 3A 58
Rakewood Rd. L'boro 6F 17
Raleigh Clo. M20 . . . . . .4E 125
Raleigh Clo. Oldh 1D 72
Raleigh Gdns. L'boro 6G 17
Raleigh St. Stoc 5G 127
Raleigh St. Stret 5D 106
Ralli Courts.
   Salf 4C 94 (5E 5)
Ralli Quays. Salf . . .4C 94 (5E 5)
Ralph Av. Hyde 2C 130
Ralph Grn. St. Chad 6H 71
Ralph Sherwin Ct.
   Roch 5B 16
Ralphs La. Duk 6A 100
Ralph St. M11 . . . . .4F 97
Ralph St. Bolt 3H 31
Ralph St. Roch 2A 28

Ralston Clo. M7 . . . . . . .3A 82
Ralstone Av. Oldh 5D 72
Ramage Wlk. M12 . . . . . .4A 96
Ramillies Av. Chea H 4D 150
Ramp Rd. E. Man A 6A 148
Ramp Rd. S. Man A 6A 148
   (off International App.)
Ramp Rd. W. Man A 6H 147
Ramsay Av. Farn 2C 62
Ramsay Pl. Roch 3A 28
Ramsay St. Bolt 1A 32
Ramsay St. Roch 3A 28
Ramsay Ter. Roch 3A 28
   (off Wardle Rd.)
Ramsbottom. 4D 12
Ramsbottom Heritage Cen.
   . . . . .2D 12
   (off Carr St.)
Ramsbottom La. Rams . . .2E 13
Ramsbottom Rd.
   Tur & Hawk 1B 20
Ramsbottom Row.
   P'wich 5E 67
Ramsbottom Swimming Pool.
   . . . . .2E 13
Ramsbury Dri. M40 . . . . .1D 84
Ramsdale Rd. Bram 5G 151
Ramsdale St. Chad 2G 71
Ramsden Clo. Oldh 2C 72
Ramsden Cres. Oldh 2C 72
Ramsden Fold. Swin 1F 79
Ramsden Rd. Ward 3A 16
   (off Wardle Rd.)
Ramsden Rd. Ward 2A 16
   (Wardle)
Ramsden Rd. Ward 1A 16
   (Watergrove Reservoir)
Ramsden St. Ash l 1H 99
Ramsden St. Bolt 2F 47
Ramsden St. Oldh 2C 72
Ramsey Av. M19 . . . . . .6F 111
Ramsey Gro. Bury 3H 35
Ramsey St. M40 . . . . . . .4B 84
Ramsey St. Chad 4H 71
Ramsey St. Oldh 1F 73
Ramsgate Rd. M40 . . . . .1C 97
Ramsgate Rd. Stoc 2H 127
Ramsgate St. Salf 6A 82
Ramsgill Clo. M23 . . . . . .2E 135
Ramsgreave Clo. Bury . . .6B 36
Ram St. L Hul 5B 62
Ramwell Gdns. Bolt 2H 45
Ramwells Brow.
   Brom X 3D 18
Ramwells Ct. Brom X 2F 19
Ramwells M. Brom X 3F 19
Ranby Av. M9 . . . . .5H 69
Randale Dri. Bury 4E 51
Randall Wlk. M11 . . . . . .4B 96
   (off Turnpike Wlk.)
Randal St. Bolt 3G 45
Randal St. Hyde 4C 114
Randerson St.
   M12 . . . . . . .6G 95 (3E 11)
Randlesham St. P'wich . . .5G 67
Randolph Pl. Stoc 4G 139
Randolph Rd. Kear 2H 63
Randolph St. M19 . . . . . .5D 110
Randolph St. Bolt 1G 45
Randolph St. Oldh 1A 86
Rands Clough Dri.
   Wors 5D 76
Rand St. Oldh 6H 57
Ranelagh Rd. Swin 4A 80
Ranelagh St. M11 . . . . . .3D 96
Raneley Gro. Roch 3G 41
Ranford Rd. M19 . . . . . .1C 126
Range Dri. Woodl 3A 130
Range Hall Ct. Stoc 2A 140
Rangemore Av. M22 . . . .3B 136
Range Rd. M16 . . . . . . .4C 108
Range Rd. Duk & Stal . . .6F 101
   (in two parts)

Range Rd. Stoc 4G 139
Range St. M11 . . . . .5E 97
Range St. Bolt 3H 45
Rankin Clo. M15 . . . . . . .2C 108
Rankine Ter. Bolt 1H 45
Ranmore Av. Open 5G 97
Rannoch Rd. Bolt 6H 33
Ransfield Rd. M21 . . . . . .5H 107
Ranulph Ct. Salf 6D 80
Ranworth Av. Stoc 1B 138
Ranworth Clo. M11 . . . . .5B 96
Ranworth Clo. Bolt 5E 19
Raper St. Oldh 1G 73
Raphael St. Bolt 3H 31
Rappax Rd. Hale 5A 146
Rasbottom St. Bolt 2A 46
Raspberry La. Irlam 3D 102
Rassbottom Brow.
   Stal 3D 100
Rassbottom Ind. Est.
   Stal 3C 100
Rassbottom St. Stal 3D 100
Rastell Wlk. M9 . . . . .6G 69
   (off Ravenswood Dri.)
Ratcliffe Av. Irlam 5E 103
Ratcliffe St. M19 . . . . . . .6D 110
Ratcliffe St. Stoc 3H 139
   (Middle Hillgate)
Ratcliffe St. Stoc 3H 139
   (Millbrook St.)
Ratcliffe Ter. Moss 3E 89
Ratcliffe Towers. Stoc . . .3H 139
Rathan Rd. Urm 3E 105
Rathbone St. Roch 4C 28
Rathbourne Av. M9 . . . . . .5F 69
Rathen Rd. M20 . . . . . . .4F 125
Rathmell Rd. M23 . . . . . .1F 135
Rathmore Av. M40 . . . . . .6G 83
Rathvale Dri. M22 . . . . . .5A 148
Rath Wlk. M40 . . . . .6C 84
Rathybank Clo. Bolt 4G 31
Rattenbury Ct. Salf 6A 80
Raveden Clo. Bolt 2G 31
Raveley Av. M14 . . . . . . .1H 125
Ravelston Dri. M9 . . . . . .5F 83
Raven Av. Chad 4G 71
Raven Clo. Droy 2C 98
Raven Ct. M15 . . . . .2C 108
Ravendale Clo. Roch 2C 26
Raven Dri. Irlam 4E 103
Ravenfield Gro. Bolt 5H 31
Ravenhead Clo. M14 . . . .1H 125
Ravenhead Sq. Carr 6G 89
Ravenhurst. Salf 2A 82
Ravenhurst Dri. Bolt 1B 44
Ravenna Av. M23 . . . . . .4D 134
Ravenoak Av. M19 . . . . . .1E 127
Ravenoak Dri. Fail 3G 85
Ravenoak Pk. Rd.
   Chea H 5D 150
Ravenoak Rd. Chea H . . .5D 150
Ravenoak Rd. Stoc 1A 152
Raven Rd. Bolt 3C 45
Raven Rd. Timp 2B 134
Ravensbury St. M11 . . . . .3D 96
Ravenscar Cres. M22 . . . .5B 148
Ravenscar Wlk. Farn 2F 63
Ravens Clo. P'wich 1A 82
Ravenscraig Rd. L Hul 3D 62
Ravensdale Gdns. Eccl 2G 91
Ravensdale Rd. Bolt 6B 30
Ravensdale St. M14 . . . . .4G 109
Ravensfield. Duk 6D 100
Ravensfield Ind. Est.
   Duk 4H 99
Ravens Holme. Bolt 6C 30
Ravenside Pk. Chad 4G 71
Ravenside Retail Pk.
   Bolt 1B 46
Ravens Pl. P'wich 1A 82
Ravenstonedale Dri.
   Rytn 2C 56

Ravenstone Dri. Sale 4E 123
Ravenstones Dri. Dig 4C 60
Raven St. M12 . . .5G 95 (2F 11)
Raven St. Bury 1D 36
Raven St. Roch 2A 26
Ravensway. P'wich 1H 81
Ravenswood. M20 . . . . . .6D 124
   (off Spath Rd.)
Ravens Wood. Bolt 6C 30
Ravenswood Av. Stoc . . .2C 138
Ravenswood Ct. Stoc 1H 151
Ravenswood Dri. M9 . . . . .6G 69
Ravenswood Dri. Bolt 5C 30
Ravenswood Dri.
   Chea H 5D 150
Ravenswood Rd.
   Stret 2F 107
Ravenswood Rd.
   Wilm 5D 166
Raven Ter. Duk 4A 100
   (off Peel St.)
Raven Way. Salf 2G 93
Ravenwood. Chad 2D 70
Ravenwood Dri. Aud 1E 113
Ravenwood Dri. Haleb . . .6D 146
Ravine Av. M9 . . . . .4G 83
Rawcliffe Av. Bolt 6H 33
Rawcliffe St. M14 . . . . . .4F 109
Rawdon Clo. M19 . . . . . .6D 110
Rawlyn Rd. Bolt 3E 31
Rawpool Gdns. M23 . . . .4G 135
Rawson Av. Farn 6G 47
Rawson Rd. Bolt 4G 31
Rawsons Rake. Rams 3C 12
Rawson St. Farn 6F 47
Rawsthorne Av. Rams 3A 12
Rawsthorne St. Bolt 3A 32
Rawstron St. Whitw 4G 15
Rayburn Way. M8 . . . . . .6C 82
Raycroft Av. M9 . . . . .1A 84
Raydon Av. M40 . . . . . . .6F 83
Rayleigh Av. Open 6H 97
Raymond Av. Bury 6F 23
Raymond Av. Chad 5H 71
Raymond Rd. M23 . . . . . .1H 135
Raymond St. Swin 2F 79
Rayner La. Ash L 4D 98
   (in two parts)
Rayners Clo. Stal 4D 100
Rayner St. Stoc 3B 140
Raynham Av. M20 . . . . . .6F 125
Raynham St. Ash L 2A 100
Raysonhill Dri. M9 . . . . . .1E 83
Reabrook Av. M12 . . . . . .1B 110
Reach, The. Wors 1G 77
Read Clo. Bury 6B 36
Reade Av. Urm 6A 104
Reade Ho. Urm 6B 104
Reading Clo. M11 . . . . . .5E 97
Reading Dri. Sale 5F 121
Reading St. Salf 6F 81
Reading Wlk. Dent 6F 113
Readitt Wlk. M11 . . . . . . .3D 96
Read St. Hyde 4A 114
Read St. W. Hyde 4A 114
Reaney Wlk. M12 . . . . . .1C 110
Rear Grn. Swin 1H 79
Reather Wlk.
   M40 . . . . . . .2G 95 (1F 7)
Rebecca St. M8 . . . . .3C 82
Recreation Rd. Fail 2H 85
Recreation St. Bolt 3A 46
Recreation St. Brad 6A 20
Recreation St. P'wich 5G 67
Rectory Av. M8 . . . . .2C 82
Rectory Av. P'wich 5F 67
Rectory Clo. Dent 5G 113
Rectory Clo. Rad 3B 50
Rectory Ct. Marp 6D 142
Rectory Fields. Stoc 2A 140
Rectory Gdns. P'wich 5F 67

Rectory Grn. *P'wich* 5E **67**
Rectory Grn. *Stoc* 2A **140**
Rectory Gro. *P'wich* 6F **67**
Rectory Hill. *Bury* 1H **37**
Rectory La. *Bury* 1H **37**
Rectory La. *P'wich* 4E **67**
Rectory La. *Rad* 4H **49**
Rectory Rd. *M8* 2B **82**
Rectory St. *Midd* 6H **53**
Redacre. *Poy* 1F **163**
Redacre Rd. *M18* 1G **111**
Red Bank.
 M4 & M8 . . . .2E **95** (1A **6**)
Redbank. *Bury* 5C **24**
Red Bank Rd. *Rad* 2F **49**
Redbarn Clo. *Bred* 5F **129**
Redbourne Dri. *Urm* 3B **104**
Redbrick Ct. *Ash L* 4G **99**
Red Bri. *Bolt* 4A **34**
Redbridge Gro. *M21* 1G **123**
Redbrook Av. *M40* 6G **83**
Redbrook Clo. *Farn* 6G **47**
Redbrook Gro. *Wilm* . . .6H **159**
Redbrook Rd. *Part* 6C **118**
Redbrook Rd. *Timp* 6D **134**
Red Brook St. *Roch* 4F **27**
Redburn Rd. *M23* 4H **135**
Redby St. *M11* 6D **96**
Redcar Av. *M20* 3F **125**
Redcar Av. *Urm* 3C **104**
Redcar Clo. *Haz G* 4F **153**
Redcar Clo. *Oldh* 6F **57**
Redcar Lodge. Swin 4A **80**
 (off Redcar Rd.)
Redcar Rd. *Bolt* 1F **31**
Redcar Rd. *L Lev* 4A **48**
Redcar Rd. *Swin* 4A **80**
Redcar St. *Roch* 3G **27**
Redcliffe Ct. *P'wich* 1F **81**
Redclyffe Av. *M14* 4G **109**
Redclyffe Circ. *Urm* 1E **105**
Redclyffe Rd. *M20* 4E **125**
Redclyffe Rd. *Urm* 5F **91**
Redcot Ct. *W'fld* 2A **66**
Redcote St. *M40* 3A **84**
Redcourt Av. *M20* 5F **125**
Redcroft Gdns. *M19* 5A **126**
Redcroft Rd. *Sale* 3G **121**
Redcross St. *Roch* 3H **27**
Redcross St. N. *Roch* 2G **27**
Reddaway Clo. *Salf* 6E **81**
Reddish. 2H **127**
Reddish Clo. *Bolt* 5A **20**
Reddish Green. 2F **127**
Reddish La. *M18* 3G **111**
Reddish Rd. *Stoc* 2H **127**
Reddish Sports Cen. . . .2G **127**
Reddish Swimming Pool.
 . . . . .1H **127**
Reddish Vale. 2A **128**
Reddish Vale Country Nature
 Reserve. 1B **128**
Reddish Vale Country Pk.
 . . . . .2C **128**
Reddish Va. Rd. *Stoc* . .2H **127**
Reddish Vale Sports Cen.
 . . . . .2A **128**
Reddish Vale Vis. Cen.
 . . . . .2A **128**
Reddyshore Brow.
 L'boro 1G **17**
Redesmere Clo. *Droy* 4B **98**
Redesmere Clo. *Timp* . . .5D **134**
Redesmere Dri. *Ald E* . . .5F **167**
Redesmere Dri.
 Chea H 1B **150**
Redesmere Pk. *Urm* 1D **120**
Redesmere Rd. *Hand* . . .2H **159**
Redfearn Wood. *Roch* . . .1D **26**
Redfern Av. *Sale* 6E **123**
Redfern Cotts. *Roch* 2H **25**
Redfern Ho. *Rom* 1G **141**

Redfern St. *M4* . . .3E **95** (3A **6**)
Redfern Way. *Roch* 2H **25**
Redfield Clo. *M11* 4B **96**
Redford Dri. *Bram* 3A **152**
Redford Rd. *M8* 5B **68**
Redford St. *Bury* 2A **36**
 (in two parts)
Red Gables. *Ash L* 1G **99**
Redgate. *Hyde* 1B **130**
Redgate La. *M12* 1B **110**
 (in two parts)
Redgates Wlk. M21 . . . .6H **107**
 (off Manchester Rd.)
Redgate Way. *Farn* 6B **46**
Redgrave Pl. *Oldh* 1H **73**
Redgrave St. *Oldh* 1G **73**
Redgrave Wlk. *M19* 6E **111**
Red Hall St. *Oldh* 3G **73**
Redhill Dri. *Bred* 6D **128**
Redhill Gro. *Bolt* 4A **32**
Redhouse La. *Bred* 5F **129**
Redhouse La. *Dis* 1H **165**
Redington Clo. *Wors* 5C **76**
Redisher Clo. *Rams* 6B **12**
Redisher Cft. *Holc* 6B **12**
Redisher La. *Hawk* 5A **12**
Redland Av. *Stoc* 4H **127**
Redland Clo. *L'boro* 3F **17**
Redland Cres. *M21* 3H **123**
Red La. *Bolt* 4F **33**
 (in two parts)
Red La. *Dig* 1C **60**
Red La. *Dis* 2F **165**
Red La. *Roch* 1B **28**
Red Lion St. *M4* . . .3E **95** (4B **6**)
Red Lodge. *Dis* 1E **165**
Redlynch Wlk. *M8* 4C **82**
Redmere Gro. *M14* 1G **125**
Redmire M. *Duk* 6D **100**
Redmires Ct. *Salf* 4G **93**
Redmond Clo. *Aud* 6E **99**
Redmoor Sq.
 M13 . . . . . .6F **95** (3D **10**)
Red Pike Wlk. *Oldh* 1E **73**
Redpoll Clo. *Wors* 4D **76**
Red Rock La. *Rad* 3D **64**
Redrose Cres. *M19* 2E **127**
Red Rose Gdns. *Sale* 3B **122**
Red Rose Gdns. *Wors* 5C **62**
Red Rose Retail Cen.
 Salf 4H **93** (1A **8**)
Red Row. *Haz G* 5H **153**
Redruth St. *M14* 5F **109**
Redscar Wlk. *Midd* 6F **53**
Redshaw Av. *Bolt* 5F **19**
Redshaw Clo. *M14* 6H **109**
Redstart Gro. *Wors* 3F **77**
Redstone Rd. *M19* 6H **125**
Redthorn Av. *M19* 2B **126**
Redvale Dri. *Salf* 5A **82**
Redvales. 1C **50**
Redvales Rd. *Bury* 6C **36**
Redvale Wlk. *Salf* 5A **82**
Redvers St. *M11* 5A **96**
Redvers St. *Oldh* 1B **72**
Redwater Clo. *Wors* 5C **76**
Redwing Cen. *Traf P* 1C **106**
Redwing Rd. *G'mnt* 1H **21**
Redwood. *Chad* 2D **70**
Redwood. *Sale* 5E **121**
Redwood Clo. *Roch* 6B **14**
Redwood Dri. *M8* 6D **82**
Redwood Dri. *Aud* 1E **113**
Redwood Dri. *Bred* 6F **129**
Redwood Ho. *M22* 2C **136**
Redwood La. *Lees* 2A **74**
Redwood Pk. Gro. *Fir* 4D **28**
Redwood Rd. *Upperm* 2G **61**
Redwood St. *Salf* 1G **93**
Reece Ct. *Duk* 5B **100**
Reedbank. *Rad* 1G **65**

Reed Ct. *Oldh* 1C **72**
Reedham Clo. *Bolt* 5G **31**
Reedham Wlk. M40 . . . . .1A **96**
 (off Lifton Av.)
Reedham Wlk. *Oldh* 5A **72**
Reed Hill. *Roch* 3H **27**
Reedley Dri. *Wors* 3E **77**
Reedmace Clo. *Wors* 2G **77**
Reedshaw Bank. *Stoc* . . .6D **140**
Reedshaw Rd. *M9* 5E **83**
Reed St. *M18* 1F **111**
Reed St. *Oldh* 2D **72**
Reeman Clo. *Bred* 5G **129**
Reeman Ct. *Wilm* 5F **159**
Reeve Clo. *Stoc* 6F **141**
Reeve's Ct. *Salf* 3A **92**
Reeves Rd. *M21* 2H **123**
Reevey Av. *Haz G* 3C **152**
Reform St. *Roch* 3H **27**
Reform Wlk. *Open* 5D **96**
Refuge St. *Shaw* 1F **57**
Regal Clo. *W'fld* 1F **67**
Regal Ind. Est. *M12* 6C **96**
Regal Wlk. *M40* 5C **84**
Regan Av. *M21* 2B **124**
Regan St. *Bolt* 2H **31**
Regan St. *Rad* 5H **49**
Regatta Clo. *Chad* 6G **71**
Regatta St. *Salf* 5D **80**
Regency Clo. *M40* 6F **83**
Regency Clo. *Oldh* 5B **72**
Regency Ct. *Chea H* 3C **150**
Regency Ct. *Roch* 4B **26**
Regency Gdns.
 Chea H 5A **150**
Regency Lodge.
 P'wich 5E **67**
Regent Av. *M14* 5E **109**
Regent Av. *L Hul* 5E **63**
Regent Bank. *Wilm* 4C **166**
Regent Clo. *Bram* 3E **151**
Regent Clo. *Chea H* 1E **151**
Regent Clo. *Heyw* 4D **38**
Regent Clo. *Wilm* 4C **166**
Regent Ct. *Alt* 1F **145**
Regent Ct. *Haleb* 5C **146**
Regent Ct. *Salf* 2H **81**
Regent Ct. *Stoc* 4E **127**
Regent Cres. *Fail* 5E **85**
Regent Cres. *Rytn* 5B **56**
Regent Dri. *Dent* 6D **112**
Regent Dri. *Los* 6A **30**
Regent Dri. *Moss* 3E **89**
Regent Ho. *M14* 4H **109**
Regent Pl. *M14* 3G **109**
Regent Rd. *Alt* 1E **145**
Regent Rd. *Los* 6A **30**
Regent Rd. *Salf* . . .5H **93** (2A **8**)
Regent Rd. *Stoc* 5A **140**
Regent Rd. Ind. Area.
 Salf 5B **94** (2C **8**)
Regents Ct. *M15* 6E **9**
Regents Cres. Urm 1F **105**
 (off Trafford Cen., The)
Regents Pk. Ct. *Wilm* . . .4C **166**
Regent Sq. *Salf* . . .5H **93** (2A **8**)
 (in two parts)
Regents Retail Pk.
 Salf 5A **94** (1C **8**)
Regent St. *M40* 6D **84**
Regent St. *Bury* 1D **36**
Regent St. *Eccl* 3H **91**
Regent St. *Heyw* 4D **38**
Regent St. *Midd* 5H **53**
Regent St. *Oldh* 2E **73**
Regent St. *Rams* 4C **12**
Regent St. *Shaw* 6F **43**
Regent Trad. Est.
 Salf 4B **94** (5C **4**)

Regent Wlk. *Farn* 1F **63**
 (in two parts)
Regina Av. *Stal* 3E **101**
Regina Ct. *Salf* 2A **92**
Reginald Latham Ct.
 M40 . . . . . . .2H **95** (1H **7**)
Reginald St. *Bolt* 5E **45**
Reginald St. *Eccl* 5C **90**
Reginald St. *Open* 6H **97**
Reginald St. *Swin* 2D **78**
Reid Clo. *Dent* 1G **129**
Reigate Clo. *Bury* 4H **35**
Reigate Rd. *Urm* 1A **120**
Reilly St. *M15* 1D **108** (5G **9**)
Reins Lea Av. *Oldh* 1E **87**
Reins Lee Rd. *Ash L* 5E **87**
Reliance St. *M40* 4C **84**
Reliance St. Enterprise Pk.
 M40 . . . . .5B **84**
Reliance Trad. Est.
 M40 . . . . .5C **84**
Rembrandt Wlk. *Oldh* . . .3G **57**
Rena Clo. *Stoc* 6F **127**
Rena Ct. *Stoc* 6F **127**
Rendel Clo. *Stret* 5D **106**
Renfrew Clo. *Bolt* 4D **44**
Renfrew Dri. *Bolt* 4D **44**
Rennell St. *Roch* 4A **28**
Rennie Clo. *Stret* 5E **107**
Renshaw Av. *Eccl* 4F **91**
Renshaw Dri. *Bury* 2G **37**
Renshaw Sq. *Eccl* 4E **91**
Renshaw St. *Alt* 6G **133**
Renshaw St. *Eccl* 4F **91**
Renton Rd. *M22* 1B **148**
Renton Rd. *Bolt* 4F **45**
Renton St. *Stret* 5E **107**
Renwick Gro. *Bolt* 4G **45**
Repton Av. *M40* 2E **85**
Repton Av. *Dent* 4A **112**
Repton Av. *Droy* 2F **97**
Repton Av. *Hyde* 4C **114**
Repton Av. *Oldh* 6B **72**
Repton Av. *Urm* 5H **103**
Repton Clo. *Sale* 6F **121**
Reservoir Rd. *Stoc* 4F **139**
Reservoir St. *Roch* 3C **28**
Reservoir St. *Salf* 3F **93**
 (Pendleton)
Reservoir St.
 Salf 2C **94** (2F **5**)
 (Salford)
Retford Av. *Roch* 2H **41**
Retford Clo. *Bury* 6D **22**
Retford St. *Oldh* 4F **73**
Retiro St. *Oldh* 2D **72**
Retreat, The. *Rom* 2A **142**
Retreat, The. *Wors* 3H **77**
Reuben St. *Stoc* 5G **127**
Revers St. *Bury* 2B **36**
Reveton Grn. *Bram* 3A **152**
Rex Bldgs. *Wilm* 2E **167**
Rex Ct. *G'ton* 3D **74**
Reynard Av. *M13* 3A **110**
Reynard Rd. *M21* 2H **123**
Reynard St. *Hyde* 4B **114**
Reynell Rd. *M13* 5B **110**
Reyner St. *M1* 5E **95** (1A **10**)
Reyner St. *Ash L* 3C **100**
Reynolds Dri. *M18* 1F **111**
Reynolds Dri. *Marp B* . . .3F **143**
Reynolds M. *Wilm* 1H **167**
Reynolds Rd. *M16* 3A **108**
Reynold St. *Hyde* 5B **114**
Rhine Clo. *T'ton* 4H **21**
Rhine Dri. *M8* 6A **82**
Rhiwlas Dri. *Bury* 5D **36**
Rhodehouses. *Marp* 2D **154**
Rhodes. 2E **69**
Rhodes Av. *Lees* 4B **74**
Rhodes Av. *Upperm* 6C **60**
Rhodes Bank. 3D **72**

Rhodes Bank. *Oldh* 3D 72
Rhodes Cres. *Roch* 2F 41
Rhodes Drl. *Bury* 5E 51
Rhodes Green. 1D 68
Rhodes Hill. *Lees* 4B 74
Rhodes St. *Hyde* 4A 114
Rhodes St. *Oldh* 2E 73
Rhodes St. *Roch* 6H 15
Rhodes St. *Shaw* 4E 57
Rhodes St. *S'head* 2B 74
Rhodes St. N. *Hyde* 4A 114
Rhode St. *T'ton* 5H 21
Rhos Av. *M14* 1A 126
Rhos Av. *Chea H* 4B 150
Rhos Dri. *Midd* 2A 70
Rhos Dri. *Haz G* 4D 152
Rhosleigh Av. *Bolt* 1H 31
Rial Pl. *M15* 1E 109 (6A 10)
Rialto Gdns. *Salf* 5A 82
Ribble Av. *Bolt* 6G 33
Ribble Av. *Chad* 6E 55
Ribble Av. *L'boro* 3D 16
Ribble Drl. *Bury* 3F 23
Ribble Dri. *Kear* 4A 64
Ribble Dri. *W'fld* 6E 51
Ribble Dri. *Wors* 5B 76
Ribble Gro. *Heyw* 2C 38
Ribble Rd. *Oldh* 6A 72
Ribblesdale Clo. *Heyw* . . .6G 39
Ribblesdale Dri. *M40* 6E 83
Ribblesdale Rd. *Bolt* 3H 45
Ribble St. *Roch* 1D 40
Ribbleton Clo. *Bury* 4F 35
Ribble Wlk. *Droy* 5A 98
Ribchester Dri. *Bury* 0B 30
Ribchester Gro. *Bolt* 4G 33
Riber Bank. *Glos* 6G 117
(in two parts)
Riber Clo. Glos 6G 117
(off Riber Bank)
Riber Fold. Glos 6G 117
(off Riber Bank)
Riber Grn. Glos 6G 117
(off Riber Bank)
Ribston St.
M15 . . . . . .1C 108 (6E 9)
Rice St. *M3* 5C 94 (1E 9)
Richard Burch St. *Bury* . . .2D 36
Richard Reynolds Ct.
Irlam 3C 118
Richards Clo. *Aud* 1E 113
Richardson Clo. *W'fld* 6D 50
Richardson Rd. *Eccl* 3G 91
Richardson St. *M11* 4A 96
Richardson St. *Stoc* 4A 140
Richard St. *Fail* 4F 85
Richard St. *Rad* 4F 49
Richard St. *Rams* 2G 13
Richard St. *Roch* 5H 27
Richard St. *Shaw* 2E 57
Richard St. *Stoc* 1H 139
(in two parts)
Richbell Clo. *Irlam* 2C 118
Richborough Clo. *Salf* 6A 82
Richelieu St. *Bolt* 3C 46
Richmal Ter. *Rams* 2D 12
Richmond Av. *Chad* 5G 71
Richmond Av. *Hand* 2H 159
Richmond Av. *P'wich* 2G 81
Richmond Av. *Rytn* 3B 56
Richmond Av. *Urm* 5G 105
Richmond Clo. *Duk* 1B 114
Richmond Clo. *Moss* 3G 89
Richmond Clo. *Roch* 2A 42
Richmond Clo. *Sale* 6F 123
Richmond Clo. *Shaw* 2F 57
Richmond Clo. *Stal* 4E 101
Richmond Clo. *T'ton* 5H 21
Richmond Clo. *W'fld* 2B 66
Richmond Ct. M9 . . . . . . .4C 68
(off Deanswood Dri.)
Richmond Ct. *M13* 3H 109

Richmond Ct. *Aud* 1E 113
Richmond Ct. *Bow* 3D 144
Richmond Ct. *Chea* 6G 137
Richmond Ct. *Stoc* 6D 140
Richmond Cres. *Moss* 3G 89
Richmond Dri. *Wors* 3C 78
Richmond Gdns. *Bolt* 4D 46
Richmond Grn. *Bow* 3D 144
Richmond Gro. *M12* 2A 110
Richmond Gro. *M13* 3H 109
Richmond Gro.
Chea H 3B 150
Richmond Gro. Eccl 2G 91
Richmond Gro. *Farn* 6C 46
Richmond Hill. *Bow* 3D 144
Richmond Hill. *Hyde* 6D 114
(in three parts)
Richmond Hill Rd.
Chea 6G 137
Richmond Ho. *Stal* 4E 101
Richmond Ho. Swin 1F 79
(off Berry St.)
Richmond Rd. *M14* 1H 125
Richmond Rd. *Alt* 6F 133
Richmond Rd. *Bow* 3D 144
Richmond Rd. *Dent* 4A 112
Richmond Rd. *Duk* 1B 114
Richmond Rd. *Fail* 3G 85
Richmond Rd. Rom 6A 130
(off Guywood La.)
Richmond Rd. *Rom* 6A 130
(High Meadows)
Richmond Rd. *Stoc* 1B 138
Richmond Rd. *Traf P* 6A 92
Richmond Rd. Wors 4A 76
Richmond St.
M1 . . . . .5E 95 (1B 10)
Richmond St. *Ash L* 1F 99
Richmond St. Aud 1E 113
Richmond St. *Bury* 5C 36
Richmond St. *Droy* 3C 98
Richmond St. *Hyde* 5C 114
Richmond St.
Salf 2C 94 (2E 5)
Richmond St. *Stal* 3F 101
Richmond Ter. *Ald E* 5G 167
Richmond Ter. *H Lane* . . .4F 155
Richmond Vw. Ash L 2H 99
(off Union St)
Richmond Vw. Moss 2G 89
(off Mansfield Rd.)
Richmond Wlk. *Oldh* 3B 72
Richmond Wlk. *Rad* 1F 49
Ricroft Rd. *Comp* 6F 131
Ridd Cotts. *Roch* 3G 25
Riddell Ct. *Salf* 3C 92
Ridding Av. *M22* 3C 148
Ridding Clo. *Stoc* 5D 140
Riddings St. *Timp* 3H 133
Riddings Rd. *Hale* 4H 145
Riddings Rd. *Timp* 3H 133
Riders Ga. *Bury* 1B 38
Ridge Av. *Haleb* 1D 156
Ridge Av. *Marp* 1E 155
Ridge Clo. *Had* 3G 117
Ridge Clo. *Rom* 1C 142
Ridge Cres. *Marp* 2D 154
Ridge Cres. *W'fld* 1F 67
Ridgecroft. *Ash L* 5F 87
Ridgedale Cen. *Marp* 5D 142
Ridge End Fold. Marp 3E 155
Ridgefield. *M2* 4D 94 (6G 5)
Ridgefield St. *Fail* 4D 84
(in two parts)
Ridgegreen. *Wors* 6C 76
Ridge Gro. *W'fld* 1F 67
Ridge Hill. 2D 100
Ridge Hill La. *Stal* 3D 100
(in two parts)
Ridge La. *Dig* 2D 60
Ridge Leisure Cen. 6D 142
Ridgemont Av. *Stoc* 1D 138

Ridgemont Wlk. *M23* . . .1F 135
Ridge Pk. *Bram* 1F 161
Ridge Rd. *Marp* 1E 155
Ridge, The. *Marp* 2E 155
Ridge Wlk. *M9* 6F 69
Ridgeway. *Swin* 1H 79
Ridgeway. *Wilm* 2H 167
Ridgeway Ga. *Bolt* 6B 32
Ridgewood Av. *M40* 6F 83
Ridgewood Av. Chad 1E 71
Ridgway Rd. *Timp* 6C 134
Ridgway, The. *Dis* 6G 155
Ridgway St.
M40 . . . . .3H 95 (3G 7)
Ridgway St. E.
M4 . . . . .3H 95 (4G 7)
Ridgway, Thc. *Rom* 2G 141
Riding Fold. *Droy* 2D 98
Ridingfold La. *Wors* 6A 78
Riding Ga. *Bolt* 5A 20
Riding Ga. M. *Bolt* 5A 20
Riding Head La. *Rams* 1H 13
Ridings Ct. *Dob* 5A 60
Ridings Rd. *Had* 2H 117
Ridings St. *M11* 5D 96
Ridings St. *M40* 6H 83
Ridings, The. *Wilm* 5A 166
Riding St. *Salf* 3C 94 (4E 5)
Ridings Way. *Chad* 3H 71
Ridley Dri. *Timp* 2G 133
Ridley Gro. *Sale* 6F 123
Ridley St. *Oldh* 3E 73
Ridley Wlk. M15 . . . . .2E 109
(off Wellhead Clo.)
Ridling La. *Hyde* 5C 114
Ridsdale Av. *M20* 3E 125
Ridsdale Wlk. Salf 6E 81
Ridyard St. *L Hul* 5D 62
Ridyard St. *M40* 6H 83
Riefield. *Bolt* 2F 31
Rifle Rd. *Sale* 4F 123
Rifle St. *Oldh* 1D 72
Riga Rd. *M14* 6G 109
Riga St. *M4* 3E 95 (3B 6)
Rigby Av. *Rad* 2A 50
Rigby Ct. *Bolt* 3B 46
(in two parts)
Rigby Ct. *Roch* 2A 26
Rigby St. *Salf* 4H 81
Rigby Gro. *L Hul* 5A 62
Rigby La. *Bolt* 5G 19
(in two parts)
Rigby St. *Bolt* 3B 46
Rigby St. *Bow* 2F 145
Rigby St. *Salf* 4H 81
(in two parts)
Rigby Wlk. *Salf* 5A 82
Rigel Pl. *Salf* 2A 94 (1B 4)
Rigel St. *M4* 2G 95 (2F 7)
Righton Gallery. 5B 10
Rigi Mt. *Rytn* 1B 56
Rigton Clo. *M12* 2C 110
Riley Clo. *Sale* 2D 132
Riley Ct. *Bolt* 4B 32
Riley Ct. *Bury* 3A 36
Riley St. *Bolt* 4B 32
Riley Wood Clo. *Rom* 2F 141
Rilldene Wlk. *Roch* 3H 25
Rimington Clo. *Midd* 4F 53
Rimmer Clo. *M11* 4A 96
Rimmington Clo. *M9* 1A 84
Rimsdale Clo. *Gat* 2E 149
Rimsdale Wlk. *Bolt* 2C 44
(in two parts)
Rimworth Dri.
M40 . . . . . . .1G 95 (1F 7)
Ringcroft Gdns. *M40* 2B 84
Ringford Wlk. *M40* 6G 83
Ringley. 2C 64
Ringley Chase. *W'fld* 1B 66
Ringley Clo. *W'fld* 1B 66

Ringley Dri. *W'fld* 1B 66
Ringley Gro. *Bolt* 6C 18
Ringley Hey. *W'fld* 1B 66
Ringley Meadows. *Rad* 2C 64
Ringley M. *Rad* 1H 65
Ringley Old Brow. *Rad* 2C 64
Ringley Pk. *W'fld* 1B 66
Ringley Rd. *Rad* 1B 64
(in three parts)
Ringley Rd. *W'fld* 1A 66
Ringley Rd. W. *Rad* 1E 65
Ringley St. *M9* 3F 83
Ringlow Av. *Swin* 4C 78
Ringlow Pk. Rd. *Swin* 5C 78
Ring Lows La. *Roch* 5F 15
Ringmer Dri. *M22* 4A 148
Ringmere Ct. *Oldh* 1C 72
Ringmore Rd. *Bram* 3A 152
Ring O Bells La. *Dis* 1H 165
Rings Clo. *Fail* 5F 85
Ringstead Clo. *Wilm* 6H 159
Ringstead Dri.
M40 . . . . .1G 95 (1E 7)
Ringstead Dri. *Wilm* 6H 159
Ringstone Clo. *P'wich* 6E 67
Ringway. 1F 157
Ringway Gro. *Sale* 1E 135
Ringway M. *M22* 6C 136
Ringway Rd.
Man A & M22 . . . . .6A 148
Ringway Rd. W.
Man A & M22 . . . . .5A 148
Ringway Trad. Est.
M22 . . . . .5C 148
Ringwood Av. *M12* 5D 110
Ringwood Av. *Aud* 4C 98
Ringwood Av. *Haz G* 4B 152
Ringwood Av. *Hyde* 6E 115
Ringwood Av. *Rad* 6H 49
Ringwood Av. *Rams* 5C 12
Ringwood Way. *Chad* 1A 72
Rink St. *M14* 2H 125
Ripley Av. *Choa H* 2D 160
Ripley Av. *Stoc* 1B 152
Ripley Clo. *M4* 5H 95 (1G 11)
Ripley Clo. *Haz G* 5E 153
Ripley Cres. *Urm* 2B 104
Ripley St. *Bolt* 1D 32
Ripley Way. *Dent* 1F 129
Ripon Av. *Bolt* 4D 30
Ripon Av. *Bury* 5D 50
Ripon Clo. *Chad* 3H 71
Ripon Clo. *Hale* 4C 146
Ripon Clo. *L Lev* 4H 47
Ripon Clo. *Rad* 2B 50
Ripon Clo. *Stoc* 3H 139
Ripon Clo. *W'fld* 5D 50
Ripon Cres. *Stret* 4H 105
Ripon Dri. *Bolt* 4D 30
Ripon Gro. *Sale* 3H 121
Ripon Hall Av. *Rams* 5D 12
Ripon Rd. *Stret* 4H 105
Ripon St. *M15* 2E 109
Ripon St. *Ash L* 2A 100
Ripon St. *Oldh* 1B 72
Ripon Wlk. *Rom* 2G 141
Rippenden Av. *M21* 5G 107
Rippingham Rd. *M20* 2F 125
Rippleton Rd. *M22* 1C 148
Rippondcn Rd. *Oldh* 1G 73
Rippondcn St. *Oldh* 6G 57
Ripton Wlk. M9 . . . . .5D 68
(off Selston Rd.)
Risbury Wlk. *M40* 5C 84
Rises, The. *Had* 2H 117
Rise, The. *S'head* 2B 74
Rishton Av. *Bolt* 4B 46
Rishton La. *Bolt* 3B 46
Rishworth Clo. *Stoc* 6D 140
Rishworth Dri. *M40* 3E 85
Rishworth Ri. *Shaw* 4D 42
Rising La. *Oldh* 1C 86

Rising La. Clo. Oldh 1C 86
Risley Av. M9 ....3F 83
Risley St. Oldh 1D 72
Rissington Av. M23 ...5H 135
Rita Av. M14 ....4F 109
Ritson Clo. M18 ......1D 110
Riva Rd. M19 ....1H 137
Riverbank. Dob 6H 59
Riverbank Dri. Bury ...1B 36
Riverbank Lawns.
   Salf 2C 94 (1E 5)
Riverbanks. Bolt 2E 47
River Bank, The. Rad ...1A 64
Riverbank Tower.
   Salf 2C 94 (2E 5)
Riverbank Wlk. M20 ...5B 124
Riverdale Ct. M9 ......6D 68
Riverdale Rd. M9 .....6C 68
River La. Dent 4H 113
Riverdale Rd. Part 5D 118
Rivermead. Miln 2F 43
Rivermead Av. Haleb ...1C 156
Rivermead Clo. Dent ...2G 129
Rivermead Rd. Dent ...1G 129
Rivermead Way. W'fld ...1E 67
Riverpark Rd. M40 ....2C 96
River Pl. M15 ...6C 94 (3F 9)
River Pl. Miln 5F 29
Riversdale Ct. P'wich ...5E 67
   (in two parts)
Riversdale Dri. Oldh ...2E 87
Riversdale Rd. Chea ...5G 137
Riversdale Vw. Woodl ...4G 129
Rivershill. Sale 3A 122
Rivershill Dri. Heyw ...4D 38
Rivershill Gdns.
   Haleb 1D 156
Riverside. Bolt 3B 32
Riverside. Chad 6E 55
River Side. Duk 3A 100
Riverside. Salf ...2A 94 (2B 4)
Riverside Av. M21 ....5A 124
Riverside Av. Irlam ...6F 103
Riverside Bus. Pk.
   Wilm 2E 167
Riverside Clo. Rad 3B 50
Riverside Ct. M20 ....6D 124
Riverside Ct. Marp B ...3E 143
Riverside Ct. Whitw ...1H 15
Riverside Dri. Rad 1B 64
Riverside Dri. Roch ...1B 28
Riverside Dri. S'seat ...1B 22
Riverside Dri. Urm 1D 120
   M22 ....2C 136
Riverside Rd. Rad 3B 50
Riverside Works.
   Wilm 1E 167
Rivers La. Urm 2D 104
Riversleigh Clo. Bolt ...2D 30
Riversmeade. Brom X ...4G 19
Riverstone Bri. L'boro ...4E 17
Riverstone Dri. M23 ...4D 134
River St. M12 ...5G 95 (2F 11)
River St. M15 ...6D 94 (4G 9)
River St. Bolt 6C 32
River St. Heyw 1F 39
River St. Rad 4H 49
River St. Rams 3E 13
River St. Roch 4H 27
River St. Stoc 6B 128
River St. Wilm 1E 167
Riversvale Arboretum.
   ....4D 86
River Tame Path.
   Carr & Stal 5E 89
River Tame Path.
   Dent 1C 128
   (off Stockport Rd.)
River Tame Path.
   Dent 2G 113
   (off Broomstair Rd.)

River Tame Path.
   Dent 5H 113
   (off Fairlea, in two parts)
River Tame Path.
   Duk & Ash L ...3H 99
River Tame Path.
   Moss 2F 89
River Tame Path.
   Stoc 3B 128
   (Northumberland Rd.)
River Tame Path.
   Stoc 6H 127
   (Tiviot Way, in two parts)
Riverton Rd. M20 .....3F 137
River Vw. Stoc 2A 128
River Vw. Clo. P'wich ...1D 80
River Vw. Ct. Salf 3G 81
Riverview Wlk. Bolt ...1H 45
   (off Bridgewater St.)
Riviera Ct. Roch 1G 25
Rivington. Salf 1C 92
Rivington Av. Swin ...3A 80
Rivington Ct. W'fld ...2A 66
Rivington Cres. Swin ...3A 80
Rivington Dri. Bury ...4G 35
Rivington Dri. Shaw ...6H 43
Rivington Gro. Aud ...5C 98
Rivington Gro. Cad ...3B 118
Rivington Hall Clo.
   Rams 5E 13
Rivington Rd. Hale ...3H 145
Rivington Rd. Salf 1C 92
Rivington Rd. S'head ...2C 74
Rivington St. Oldh 6D 56
Rivington St. Roch 2H 27
Rivington Wlk. M12 ...2B 110
Rixson St. Oldh 6H 57
Rix St. Bolt 3A 32
Rixton Ct. M16 ....4H 107
Roach Bank Ind. Est.
   Bury 6F 37
Roach Bank Rd. Bury ...6F 37
Roach Ct. M40 ....1G 95
   (off Hamerton Rd.)
Roaches. 6G 75
Roaches Ind. Est.
   Moss 5G 75
Roaches M. Moss 6F 75
Roaches Way. Moss ...6G 75
Roachill Clo. Alt 6D 132
Roach Pl. Roch 3A 28
Roach St. Bury 3D 50
   (Manchester Rd.)
Roach St. Bury 3G 37
   (Waterfold La.)
Roach Va. Roch 1C 28
Roachwood Clo. Chad ...2E 71
Road End. 4F 61
Roading Brook Rd.
   Bolt 2A 34
Road La. Roch 5D 14
Roads Ford Av. Miln ...4F 29
Roan Way. Ald E 6H 167
Roaring Ga. La. Hale ...2E 147
Robert Hall St.
   Salf 5H 93 (2A 8)
Robert Lawrence Ct.
   Urm 6C 104
Robert Malcolm Clo.
   M40 ....6F 83
Robert Owen Gdns.
   M22 ....3B 136
Robert Owen St. Droy ...3C 98
Robert Salt Ct. Alt 5G 133
Roberts Av. M14 .....3F 109
Robert Saville Ct.
   Roch 5D 26
   (off Half Acre M.)
Robertscroft Clo.
   M22 ....1A 148
Robertshaw Av.
   M21 ....3H 123

Robert Sheldon Way.
   Ash L 4D 98
   (in two parts)
Robertson Clo. M18 ...2E 111
Robertson St. Rad 3G 49
Roberts Pas. L'boro ...5H 17
Roberts Pl. L'boro 6D 16
Roberts St. Eccl 4F 91
Robert St. M3 ...2D 94 (1H 5)
Robert St. M40 ......6H 83
Robert St. Bolt 6A 20
Robert St. Bury 2A 36
Robert St. Duk 5H 99
Robert St. Fail 2G 85
Robert St. Farn 1G 63
Robert St. Heyw 5G 39
Robert St. Hyde 4A 114
Robert St. Oldh 6H 71
Robert St. Platt B 4A 12
Robert St. P'wich 5G 67
Robert St. Rad 3G 49
Robert St. Rams 4A 12
Robert St. Roch 3A 28
Robert St. Sale 5E 123
Robeson Way. M22 ...5D 136
Robe Wlk. M18 ......1F 111
Robin Clo. Farn 2B 62
Robin Cft. Bred 6D 128
Robin Dri. Irlam 4E 103
Robin Hood St. M8 ...3B 82
Robinia Clo. Eccl 5B 90
Robin La. W'fld 2D 66
   (Bury New Rd.)
Robin La. W'fld 2D 66
   (Higher La.)
Robin Rd. Bury 6D 12
Robinsbay Rd. M22 ...5C 148
Robins Clo. Bram 6G 151
Robins Clo. Droy 2C 98
Robins La. Bram 6F 151
Robinson Pl. S'head ...2D 74
Robinsons Fold.
   S'head 2D 74
Robinson St. Hyde ...4D 114
Robinson St. Stoc 4F 139
Robin St. Oldh 1C 72
Robins Way. Bow 4E 145
Robinswood Rd. M22 ...3B 148
Robinwood Lodge.
   Glos 6G 117
   (off Bleaklow La.)
Robson Av. Urm 6G 91
Robson St. Oldh 3D 72
Roby Rd. Eccl 5E 91
Roby St. M1 ...4F 95 (6C 6)
Roch Av. Heyw 3C 38
Rochbury Clo. Roch ...5B 26
Roch Clo. W'fld 6F 51
Roch Cres. W'fld 5F 51
Rochdale. 3H 27
Rochdale Art Gallery & Mus.
   ....4G 27
Rochdale Central Leisure Cen.
   ....4A 28
Rochdale Crematorium.
   Roch 4E 27
Rochdale Exchange Shop. Cen.
   Roch 4G 27
Rochdale Football Club.
   ....3E 27
   (Spotland)
Rochdale Hornets
Rugby League Football Club.
   ....3E 27
Rochdale Ind. Cen. Roch ...5F 27
Rochdale La. Heyw ...3F 39
Rochdale La. Rytn 2B 56
Rochdale Old Rd. Bury ...2G 37
Rochdale Pioneers Mus.
   ....3H 27
Rochdale Rd.
   M4 & M40 ...3F 95 (3C 6)

Rochdale Rd. M9 ....3F 83
Rochdale Rd. Bury 3E 37
Rochdale Rd.
   Fir & Miln 4D 28
Rochdale Rd. Heyw ...3F 39
Rochdale Rd. Midd ...5A 54
Rochdale Rd.
   Rams & Roch ...2B 12
Rochdale Rd. Rytn 6A 42
Rochdale Rd.
   Rytn & Oldh ...6C 56
Rochdale Rd. Shaw ...4C 42
Rochdale Rd. Sower B ...1H 13
Rochdale Rd. E. Heyw ...3G 39
Rochdale Tourist Info. Cen.
   ....4H 27
Rochdale Town Hall. ...4H 27
Roche Gdns. Chea H ...1D 160
Roche Rd. Del 2G 59
Rochester Av. Bolt ...4G 33
Rochester Av. P'wich ...1G 81
Rochester Av. Wors ...2E 77
Rochester Clo. Ash L ...4G 87
Rochester Clo. Duk ...6E 101
Rochester Dri. Timp ...2G 133
Rochester Gro. Haz G ...2E 153
Rochester Rd. Urm ...3F 105
Rochester Way. Chad ...3H 71
Rochford Av. W'fld ...2B 66
Rochford Clo. W'fld ...2B 66
Rochford Ho. Aud 1E 113
Rochford Pl. Heyw ...6H 39
Rochford Rd. Eccl 5B 90
Roch Mills Cres. Roch ...6E 27
Roch Mills Gdns. Roch ...6E 27
Roch St. Roch 2B 28
Roch Valley Way. Roch ...5E 27
Roch Wlk. W'fld 6F 51
Roch Way. W'fld 6F 51
Rockall Wlk. M11 ....4B 96
Rock Av. Bolt 3G 31
Rock Bank. Moss 2E 89
Rockdove Av.
   M15 ....6D 94 (3G 4)
Rocket St. Salf ...4B 94 (5D 4)
Rockfield Dri. M9 ....3G 83
Rock Fold. Eger 2D 18
Rock Gdns. Hyde 2C 130
Rock Hall (Vis. Cen.) ...5G 47
Rockhampton St.
   M18 ....2F 111
Rockhouse Clo. Eccl ...5E 91
Rockingham Clo.
   M12 ...1H 109 (6H 11)
Rockingham Clo.
   Shaw 5C 42
Rockland Wlk. M40 ...1C 84
Rockley Gdns. Salf ...1H 93
Rocklyn Av. M40 .....1C 84
Rocklynes. Rom 1H 141
Rockmead Dri. M9 ...6G 69
Rock Nook. L'boro ...6H 17
Rock Rd. Urm 5H 105
Rock St. M11 ....5G 97
Rock St. Ash L 6E 87
   (in two parts)
Rock St. Heyw 4G 39
Rock St. Hyde 2C 130
Rock St. Oldh 2D 72
   (in two parts)
Rock St. Rams 2G 13
Rock St. Salf 5H 81
Rock Ter. Duk 4A 100
Rock Ter. Eger 2D 18
Rock Ter. Moss 5E 89
   (Manchester Rd.)
Rock Ter. Moss 6F 75
   (Stockport Rd.)
Rock, The. Bury 3C 36
   (in three parts)
Rocky La. Eccl 6D 78
Roda St. M9 ....4H 83

Rodborough Gdns.
  M23 . . . . .2F 147
Rodborough Rd. M23 . . . .2F 147
Rodcheath Clo. Wilm . . .2Q 167
Rodenhurst Dri. M40 . . . .4A 84
Rodepool Clo. Wilm 5H 159
Rodgers Ho. Ash L 5B 88
Rodmell Av. M40 . . . . . .6F 83
Rodmell Clo. Brom X . . .4D 18
Rodmill Ct. M14 . . . . . .6G 109
Rodmill Dri. Gat 2E 149
Rodney Ct. M4 . . .2G 95 (2E 7)
Rodney Dri. Bred 4G 129
Rodney St. M4 . . .3G 95 (3F 7)
Rodney St. Ash L 1B 100
Rodney St. Roch 3B 40
Rodney St. Salf . . .4B 94 (5D 4)
Roeacre St. Heyw 3G 39
Roebuck Clo. Sale 5A 122
Roebuck La. Oldh 4C 58
Roebuck La. Sale 5A 122
Roebuck Low. Oldh 4C 58
Roebuck M. Sale 5B 122
Roeburn Wlk. W'fld 1G 67
Roe Cross. 1B 116
Roe Cross Grn. Mot 2B 116
Roe Cross Ind. Pk.
  Mot 2C 116
Roe Cross Rd. Mot 1B 116
Roedean Gdns. Urm 5G 103
Roefield. Roch 3F 27
Roefield Ter. Roch 3E 27
Roe Green. 3A 78
Roe Grn. Wors 3H 77
Roe Grn. Av. Wors 3A 78
Roe La. Oldh 4H 73
Roe St. M4 . . . . .2G 95 (2E 7)
Roe St. Roch 2E 27
Rogate Dri. M23 . . . . . .6G 135
Roger Byrne Clo.
  M40 . . . . .6B 84
Roger Clo. Rom 2F 141
Roger Hey. Chea H 2D 150
Rogerson Clo. Timp 4C 134
Rogerstead. Bolt 1G 45
Roger Ct. M4 . . . .2C 95 (1D 6)
Rokeby Av. Strat 6D 106
Roker Av. M13 . . . . .5B 110
Roker Ind. Est. Oldh 1F 73
Roker Pk. Av. Aud 6D 98
Roland Ct. Bolt 3G 45
Roland Rd. Stoc 2H 127
Role Row. P'wich 2F 81
Rolla St. Salf . . .3C 94 (3F 5)
Rollesby Clo. Bury 6D 22
Rolleston Av.
  M40 . . . . .3H 95 (3G 7)
Rollins La. Rom 2E 143
Rolls Cres.
  M15 . . . . . . .1C 108 (6E 9)
Rollswood Dri. M40 . . . . .5A 84
Roman Amphitheatre. . . .1G 9
Roman Ct. Salf 6H 81
Roman Rd. Fail & Oldh . .3G 85
Roman Rd. P'wich 2E 81
Roman Rd. Stoc 1G 139
Roman St. M4 . . .3E 95 (4B 6)
Roman St. Moss 6F 75
Roman St. Rad 4E 49
Romer Av. M40 . . . . .2E 85
Rome Rd. M40 . . .2G 95 (2E 7)
Romer St. Bolt 6E 33
Romford Av. Dent 3G 113
Romford Clo. Oldh 4C 72
Romford Rd. Sale 3G 121
Romford Wlk. M9 . . . . . .6C 68
Romiley. 1A 142
Romiley Cres. Bolt 5F 33
Romiley Dri. Bolt 5F 33
Romiley Marina Pool &
  Gymnasium. 1H 141

Romiley Precinct.
  Rom 1A 142
Romiley St. Salf 6B 80
Romiley Ct. Otoc 1D 140
Romley Rd. Urm 3F 105
Romney Av. Roch 3F 41
Romney Chase. Bolt 1A 32
Romney Rd. Bolt 3C 30
Romney St. M40 . . . . . . .3A 84
Romney St. Ash L 2A 100
Romney St. Salf 6F 81
Romney Towers. Stoc . . .3B 128
Romney Wlk. Chad 3H 71
Romney Way. Stoc 4B 128
Romsdal Vs. Rom 1H 141
Romsey. Roch 3G 27
  (off Spotland Rd.)
Romsey Av. Midd 4H 53
Romsey Dri. Chea H 1D 160
Romsey Gdns. M23 . . . . .5F 135
Romsley Clo. M12 . . . . . .1C 110
Romsley Dri. Bolt 4G 45
Ronaldsay Gdns. Salf 4E 93
Ronald St. M11 . . . . .4F 97
Ronald St. Oldh 2G 73
Ronald St. Roch 4C 40
Rona Wlk. M12 . . . . .2B 110
Rondin Rd.
  M12 & M11 . . . . .5A 96
Ronnis Mt. Ash L 4E 87
Ronton Wlk. M8 . . . . .3E 83
Roocroft Ct. Bolt 4H 31
Rooden Ct. P'wich 5G 67
Roods La. Roch 2G 25
Rookery Av. M18 . . . . . . .1H 111
Rookery Clo. Stal 6H 101
Rookerypool Clo.
  Wilm 5H 159
Rooke St. Eccl 5C 90
Rookfield. Sale 4C 122
Rookfield Av. Sale 4C 122
Rookley Wlk. M14 . . . . . .4G 109
Rook St. M15 . . . . .2C 108
Ruuk St. Oldh 4G 73
Rook St. Rams 3E 13
Rookwood Dri. Rooh 2B 40
Rookway. Midd 2H 69
Rookwood. Chad 6E 55
Rookwood Av. M23 . . . . .4F 135
Rookwood Hill. Bram 4G 151
Rooley Moor Rd. Roch . . .4A 14
  (Rooley Moor)
Rooley Moor Rd. Roch . . .1D 26
  (Stocks Ga.)
Rooley St. Roch 2E 27
Rooley Ter. Roch 3E 27
Roosevelt Rd. Kear 2H 63
Rooth St. Stoc 1F 139
Ropefield Way. Roch 6E 15
Rope St. Roch 3G 27
Ropewalk. Salf . . .2C 94 (2F 5)
Ropley Wlk. M9 . . . . .2H 83
  (off Oak Bank Av.)
Rosa Gro. Salf 5H 81
Rosalind Ct.
  Salf 5A 94 (2B 8)
Rosamond Dri.
  Salf 3B 94 (4D 4)
Rosamond St. Bolt 3G 45
Rosamond St. W.
  M15 . . . . . . .1E 109 (5A 10)
Rosary Clo. Oldh 2D 86
Rosary Rd. Oldh 2E 87
Roscoe Pk. Est. Alt 3G 133
Roscoe Rd. Irlam 6C 102
Roscoe St. Oldh 3D 72
  (in two parts)
Roscoe St. Stoc 3F 139
Roscow Av. Bolt 5G 33
Roscow Fold. 5F 33
Roscow Rd. Kear 2A 64
Rose Acre. Wors 4D 76

Roseacre Clo. Bolt 5E 33
Roseacre Cres. Heyw 3F 39
Roseacre Dri. H Grn 4G 149
Rose Av. Fam 6C 47
Rose Av. Irlam 6D 102
Rose Av. Roch 1H 25
Rose Bank. Los 6A 30
Rosebank Clo. A'wth 4C 34
Rosebank Clo. Holl 2F 117
Rose Bank Rd. M40 . . . . .1D 96
Rosebank Rd. Cad 6A 118
Roseberry Av. Oldh 6F 57
Roseberry Clo. Rams 6E 13
Roseberry St. Bolt 3G 45
Roseberry St. Oldh 3B 72
Rosebery St. M14 . . . . . . .4D 108
Rosebery St. Stoc 1D 152
Rose Cottage Rd. M14 . . .1F 125
Rose Cotts. M14 . . . . . . .1H 125
  (off Ladybarn La.)
Rose Cres. Irlam 6D 102
Rosecroft Clo. Stoc 1G 151
Rosedale Av. Bolt 6C 18
Rosedale Clo. Oldh 6F 57
Rosedale Ct. Dent 4E 113
Rosedale Rd. M14 . . . . . .5E 109
Rosedale Rd. Stoc 4F 127
Rosedale Way. Duk 1B 114
Rosefield Clo. Stoc 6G 139
Rosefield Cres. Roch 4C 28
Rosegarth Av. M20 . . . . . .5B 124
Rose Gro. Bury 3G 35
Rose Gro. Kear 2H 63
Rosehay Av. Dent 5F 113
Rose Hey La. Fail 1G 97
Rosehill. 3E 145
  (Altrincham)
Rose Hill. 2C 46
  (Bolton)
Rose Hill. Bolt 2C 46
Rose Hill. Del 4H 59
Rose Hill. Dent 4D 112
Rose Hill. Rams 3D 12
Rose Hill. Stal 6E 101
Rose Hill Av. M40 . . . . . . .1D 96
Rose Hill Clo. Ash L 6A 88
Rose Hill Clo. Brom X 4E 19
Rosehill Clo. Salf 3F 93
Rose Hill Ct. Oldh 1A 74
Rusehill Ct. Salf 3F 93
Rose Hill Cres. Ash L 6B 88
Rose Hill Dri. Brom X 4E 19
Rosehill M. Swin 1F 79
Rose Hill Rd. Ash L 6B 88
Rosehill Rd. Swin 1F 79
  (in two parts)
Rose Hill St. Heyw 3D 38
Roseland Av. M20 . . . . . . .5F 125
Roseland Dri. P'wich 3G 67
Roselands Av. Sale 1H 133
Rose La. Marp 5C 142
Rose Lea. Bolt 1G 33
Roseleigh Av. M19 . . . . . .2B 126
Rosemary Dri. Hyde 2B 130
Rosemary Dri. L'boro 3D 16
Rosemary Gro. Salf 6G 81
Rosemary La. Stoc 2A 140
Rosemary Rd. Chad 1E 71
Rosemary Wlk. Part 6D 118
  (off Erskine Rd.)
Rosemead Ct. Stoc 3H 127
Rosemount. Hyde 2B 114
Rosemount. Midd 5H 53
Rosemount Cres.
  Hyde 2A 114
Roseneath. Bram 4F 151
Roseneath Av. M19 . . . . . .6E 111
Roseneath Gro. Bolt 5H 45
Roseneath Rd. Bolt 4H 45
Roseneath Rd. Urm 4E 105

Rosen Sq. Chad 2H 71
Rose St. Bolt 2C 46
Rose St. Chad 6G 71
Rose St. Midd 1C 70
Rose St. Stoc 6H 127
Rose Ter. Stal 4E 101
Rosethorns Clo. Midd 3H 53
Rosette Wlk. Swin 4F 79
Rose Va. H Grn 4F 149
Rosevale Av. M19 . . . . . . .4A 126
Rose Wlk. Marp 5C 142
Rose Wlk. Part 6C 118
Roseway. Bram 3H 151
Rosewell Clo. M40 . . . . . . .1H 95
Rosewood. Dent 4D 112
Rosewood. Roch 2A 26
Rosewood Av. Droy 3B 98
Rosewood Av. Stoc 2C 138
Rosewood Av. T'ton 6A 22
Rosewood Clo. Duk 1B 114
Rosewood Cres. Chad 6H 55
Rosewood Gdns. Gat 5D 136
Rosewood Gdns. Sale 6F 123
  (off Maizefield Clo.)
Rosewood Wlk. M23 . . . . .3C 134
Rosford Av. M14 . . . . .5F 109
Rosgill Clo. Stoc 1A 138
Rosgill Wlk. M18 . . . . .2E 111
Rosina St. M11 . . . . .6H 97
Roslin Gdns. Bolt 2G 31
Roslin St. M11 . . . . .3F 97
Roslyn Av. Urm 1A 120
Roslyn Rd. Stoc 6G 139
Rossall Av. Rad 6A 50
Rossall Av. Stret 4C 106
Rossall Clo. Bolt 5E 33
Rossall Dri. Bram 1G 161
Rossall Rd. Bolt 5E 33
  (in two parts)
Rossall Rd. Roch 1A 28
Rossall St. Bolt 5E 33
Rossall Way. Salf 2G 93
Russ Av. M19 . . . . .6B 110
Ross Av. Chad 6F 71
Ross Av. Stoc 6G 139
Ross Av. W'fld 3D 66
Ross Dri. Swin 5E 65
Rossenclough Clo.
  Wilm 6H 159
Rossendale Av. M9 . . . . . . .2H 83
Rossendale Clo. Shaw 6H 43
Rossendale Rd.
  H Grn 5G 149
Rossendale Way. Shaw . . .5F 43
Rossett Av. M22 . . . . .5B 148
Rossett Av. Timp 3A 134
Rossett Dri. Urm 3B 104
Rossetti Wlk. Dent 2G 129
Ross Gro. Urm 5F 105
Rosshill Wlk.
  M15 . . . . . . .1B 108 (5D 8)
Rossington St. M40 . . . . . .6D 84
Rossini St. Bolt 2H 31
Rosslare Rd. M22 . . . . . . .3C 148
Ross Lave La. Dent 1B 128
Rosslave Wlk. Stoc 2C 128
Rosslyn Gro. Timp 5A 134
Rosslyn Rd. H Grn 4H 149
Rosslyn Rd. Most 2A 84
Rosslyn Rd. Old T 5G 107
Rossmere Av. Roch 5E 27
Rossmill La. Haleb 6B 146
Ross St. Bolt 4A 32
Ross St. Oldh 4B 72
Rostherne. Wilm 5D 166
Rostherne Av. Fall 6E 109
Rostherne Av. H Lane 5C 154
Rostherne Av. Old T 4A 108
Rostherne Ct. Bow 2F 145
Rostherne Gdns. Bolt 3F 45
Rostherne Rd. Sale 6F 123

Rostherne Rd. *Stoc* 6G **139**
Rostherne Rd. *Wilm* 4C **166**
Rostherne St. *Alt* 2F **145**
(in two parts)
Rostherne St. *Salf* 3E **93**
Rosthernmere Rd.
  Chea H 1B **150**
Rosthwaite Clo. *Midd* 6E **53**
Roston Ct. *Salf* 3A **82**
Roston Rd. *Salf* 3A **82**
Rostrevor Rd. *Stoc* 6G **139**
(in two parts)
Rostron Av. *M12* 1A **110**
Rostron Brow. *Stoc* 2H **139**
(off Churchgate)
Rostron Rd. *Rams* 3D **12**
Rostron St. *M19* 6D **110**
Rostron St. *Rad* 3G **49**
Rothay Clo. *Bolt* 4H **33**
Rothay Dri. *Midd* 4G **53**
Rothay Dri. *Stoc* 1H **127**
Rothbury Av. *Ash L* 1E **99**
Rothbury Clo. *Bury* 3F **35**
Rothbury Ct. *Bolt* 4F **45**
Rotherby Rd. *M22* 6C **136**
Rotherdale Av. *Timp* 6D **134**
Rothermere Wlk. *M23* 4E **135**
Rotherwood Av. *Stret* 4E **107**
Rotherwood Rd.
  Wilm 3A **166**
(in two parts)
Rothesay Av. *Duk* 6A **100**
Rothesay Cres. *Sale* 1E **133**
Rothesay Rd. *M8* 1A **82**
Rothesay Rd. *Bolt* 4F **45**
Rothesay Rd. *Oldh* 6G **57**
Rothesay Rd. *Swin* 4A **80**
Rothesay Ter. *Roch* 1A **42**
Rothiemay Rd. *Urm* 6A **104**
Rothley Av. *M22* 6B **136**
Rothman Clo. *M40* 5C **84**
Rothwell Cres. *L Hul* 3A **62**
Rothwell La. *L Hul* 4A **62**
Rothwell St. *M40* 5C **84**
Rothwell St. *Bolt* 2A **46**
(in two parts)
Rothwell St. *Fail* 4F **85**
Rothwell St. *Rams* 3D **12**
Rothwell St. *Roch* 2A **28**
Rothwell St. *Rytn* 4A **56**
Rothwell St. *Wors* 6H **63**
Rottingdene Dri. *M22* 4A **148**
Rough Bank. *Whitw* 4C **14**
Roughey Gdns. *M22* 1A **148**
Rough Hey Wlk. *Roch* 5B **28**
Rough Hill La. *Bury* 1H **37**
Roughlee Av. *Swin* 3D **78**
Roughtown 1F **89**
Roughtown Ct. *Moss* 6F **75**
Roughtown Rd. *Moss* 1F **89**
Roundcroft. *Rom* 6C **130**
Roundham Wlk. *M9* 3G **83**
Roundhey. *H Grn* 5F **149**
Round Hill Clo. *Had* 4H **117**
Round Hill Way. *Bolt* 5B **32**
Roundhill Way. *Oldh* 6A **58**
Roundthorn 5E **135**
(Manchester)
Roundthorn 4G **73**
(Oldham)
Roundthorn Ct. *M23* 4F **135**
Roundthorn Ind. Est.
  M23 . . . . .5E **135**
Roundthorn Rd. *M23* 5F **135**
Roundthorn Rd. *Midd* 2B **70**
Roundthorn Rd. *Oldh* 3F **73**
Roundway. *Bram* 1F **161**
Roundwood Rd. *M22* 4B **136**
Rousden Clo. *M40* 6F **83**
Rouse St. *Roch* 1C **40**
Routledge Wlk. *M9* 3G **83**

Rowan Av. *M16* 4B **108**
Rowan Av. *Sale* 1C **134**
Rowan Av. *Urm* 4F **105**
Rowan Clo. *Fail* 5F **85**
Rowan Clo. *Roch* 6A **14**
Rowan Ct. *M14* 2H **125**
Rowan Ct. Hyde 6C **114**
(off Ashley Gdns.)
Rowan Cres. *Duk* 6D **100**
Rowan Dri. *Chea H* 5E **151**
Rowanlea. *P'wich* 5G **67**
Rowan Lodge. *Bram* 6H **151**
Rowan Pl. *P'wich* 6F **67**
Rowans Clo. *Stal* 2G **101**
Rowanside Dri. *Wilm* 1H **167**
Rowans St. *Bury* 1A **36**
Rowans, The. *Bolt* 6C **30**
Rowans, The. *Moss* 2F **89**
Rowans, The. *Wors* 4A **76**
Rowan St. *Hyde* 6D **114**
Rowanswood Dri.
  Hyde 4E **115**
Rowan Tree Dri. *Sale* 2B **134**
Rowan Tree Rd. *Oldh* 2B **86**
Rowan Wlk. *Had* 3G **117**
Rowan Wlk. *Part* 6C **118**
Rowanwood. *Chad* 2E **71**
Rowany Clo. *P'wich* 1E **81**
Rowarth Av. *Dent* 1G **129**
Rowarth Av. *Glos* 5F **117**
(off Eyam La.)
Rowarth Bank. Glos 5F **117**
(off Grassmoor Cres.)
Rowarth Clo. Glos 5F **117**
(off Eyam La.)
Rowarth Fold. Glos 5F **117**
(off Eyam La.)
Rowarth Rd. *M23* 3F **147**
Rowarth Way. Glos 5F **117**
(off Eyam La.)
Rowbotham St. *Hyde* 1C **130**
Rowbottom Wlk. *Oldh* 4C **72**
Rowcon Clo. *Aud* 2E **113**
Rowdell Wlk. *M23* 1H **135**
Rowden Rd. *Oldh* 5A **74**
Rowe Grn. *Dent* 4F **113**
Rowena St. *Bolt* 5E **47**
Rowendale St.
  M1 . . . . .5D **94** (2G **9**)
Rowfield Dri. *M23* 2F **147**
Rowland Av. *Urm* 4G **105**
Rowland Ct. *Roch* 5B **28**
Rowland Ho. *Shaw* 3D **56**
Rowlands. 1D **22**
Rowlands Rd. *Bury* 1C **22**
Rowlands St. *Roch* 5B **28**
Rowland St. *Salf* 5G **93**
Rowlands Way. *M22* 3B **148**
Rowland Way. *Lees* 2A **74**
Rowley Dri. *Haz G* 5E **153**
Rowley St. *Ash L* 5H **87**
Row-of-Trees. 6A **166**
Rowood Av. *M8* 5D **82**
Rowood Av. *Stoc* 5H **111**
Rowrah Cres. *Midd* 6D **52**
Rowsley Av. *M20* 5C **124**
Rowsley Av. *Bolt* 4E **31**
Rowsley Clo. *Glos* 5G **117**
Rowsley Grn. Glos 5G **117**
(off Rowsley Clo.)
Rowsley Gro. Glos 5G **117**
(off Rowsley Clo.)
Rowsley Gro. *Stoc* 2G **127**
Rowsley M. *Glos* 5G **117**
Rowsley Rd. *Eccl* 5E **91**
Rowsley Rd. *Stret* 4A **106**
Rowsley St. *M11* 3A **96**
Rowsley St. *Salf* 6F **81**
Rowsley Wlk. Glos 5G **117**
(off Rowsley Clo.)
Rowson Ct. *Sale* 5D **122**
Rowson Dri. *Cad* 3B **118**

Rowton St. *Bolt* 2D **32**
Roxalina St. *Bolt* 3A **46**
Roxburgh St. *M18* 2F **111**
Roxbury. 4G **73**
Roxbury Av. *Oldh* 4H **73**
Roxby Clo. *Wors* 6D **62**
Roxby Wlk. *M40* 1D **84**
Roxholme Wlk. *M22* 5A **148**
Roxton Rd. *Stoc* 3E **127**
Roxwell Wlk. M9 . . . .*3F 83*
(off Alderside Rd.)
Royal Av. *M21* 1G **123**
Royal Av. *Bury* 6F **23**
Royal Av. *Droy* 3B **98**
Royal Av. *Heyw* 4F **39**
Royal Av. *Urm* 5F **105**
Royal Ct. Dri. *Bolt* 5H **31**
Royal Cres. *Chea* 3G **149**
Royal Exchange.
  M2 . . . . .4D **94** (5H **5**)
Royal Exchange Arc. *M2* . .5H **5**
Royal Exchange Theatre.
  . . . . .5H **5**
Royal Gdns. *Bow* 3B **144**
Royal George Cotts.
  G'fld 4G **75**
(off Armit Rd.)
Royal George St.
  Stoc 3G **139**
(in two parts)
Royal Ho. *Rams* 3H **31**
Royal Oak Ind. Est.
  Stoc 4H **139**
(off Longshut La.)
Royal Oak Rd. *M23* 4F **135**
(in two parts)
Royal Oak Yd. *Stoc* 2D **40**
Royal Pennine Trad. Est.
  Roch 2D **40**
Royal Rd. *Dis* 2H **165**
Royal St. *Roch* 6A **16**
Royalthorn Av. *M22* 5B **136**
Royalthorn Dri. *M22* 5A **136**
Royalthorn Rd. *M22* 5A **136**
Royce Av. *Alt* 6G **133**
Royce Clo. *Oldh* 6D **72**
Royce Ct. *M15* 6D **8**
Royce Pl. *M15* 1C **108** (6E **9**)
Royce Rd.
  M15 . . . . . . .1C **108** (5D **8**)
Royce Trad. Est. *Traf P* . .6G **91**
Roydale St. *M40* 2A **96**
Royden Av. *M9* 4F **69**
Royden Av. *Irlam* 1D **118**
Roydes St. *Midd* 5B **54**
Royds Clo. *M13* 2H **109**
Royds Clo. *T'ton* 6A **22**
Royds Pl. *Roch* 6A **28**
Royds St. *L'boro* 4G **17**
Royds St. *Miln* 6G **29**
Royds St. *Roch* 6B **28**
Royds St. *T'ton* 4H **21**
Royds St. W. *Roch* 6A **28**
Royd St. *Bury* 1H **37**
Royd St. *Oldh* 5A **72**
Roy Grainger Ct. *M16* 4C **108**
Royland Av. *Bolt* 4C **46**
Royland Ct. *Bolt* 4B **46**
Royle Barn Rd. *Roch* 3C **40**
Royle Clo. *Stoc* 6A **140**
Royle Grn. Rd. *M22* 3C **136**
Royle-Higginson Ct.
  Urm 6E **105**
Roylelands Bungalows.
  Roch 2C **40**
Royle Rd. *Roch* 2C **40**
Royles Cotts. *Sale* 6B **122**
Royle St. *M14* 2H **125**
Royle St. *Dent* 2F **113**
Royle St. *Salf* 4F **93**
Royle St. *Stoc* 4H **139**
Royle St. *Wors* 1F **77**

Royley. 4A **56**
Royley. *Rytn* 4A **56**
Royley Carr Flats.
  Bred 6F **129**
(off Field St.)
Royley Clough. *Rytn* 3A **56**
Royley Cres. *Rytn* 4A **56**
Royley Ho. *Rytn* 4A **56**
Royley Rd. *Oldh* 5C **72**
Royley Way. *Rytn* 4A **56**
Royon Dri. *Stoc* 4D **138**
Royston Av. *M16* 4B **108**
Royston Av. *Bolt* 5D **32**
Royston Av. *Dent* 4A **112**
Royston Clo. *G'mnt* 2H **21**
Royston Ct. *M16* 4B **108**
Royston Rd. *M16* 4H **107**
Royston Rd. *Urm* 4G **105**
Roy St. *Bolt* 3F **45**
Roy St. *Rytn* 3B **56**
Royton. 3B **56**
Royton Av. *Sale* 1D **134**
Royton Hall Pk. *Rytn* 3C **56**
Royton Hall Wlk. *Rytn* 3C **56**
Royton Ho. *Shaw* 2F **57**
Royton Sports Cen. 3C **56**
Rozel Sq. *M3* 5C **94** (1F **9**)
Ruabon Rd. *M20* 1G **137**
Rubens Clo. *Marp B* 3F **143**
Ruby St. *M15* . . .1E **109** (6A **10**)
Ruby St. *Bolt* 2B **32**
Ruby St. *Bury* 6E **13**
Ruby St. *Dent* 5E **113**
Ruby St. Pas. *Roch* 5G **27**
Rudcroft Clo.
  M13 . . . . .1F **109** (5D **10**)
Rudding St. *Rytn* 5E **57**
Ruddpark Rd. *M22* 4B **148**
Rudd St. *M40* 4A **84**
Rudford Gdns. *Bolt* 3B **46**
Rudgwick Dri. *Bury* 4C **22**
Rudheath Av. *M20* 2E **125**
Rudman Dri.
  Salf 5A **94** (2A **8**)
Rudman St. *Ash L* 4G **99**
Rudman St. *Roch* 1G **27**
Rudolph St. *Bolt* 4B **46**
Rudston Av. *M40* 1B **84**
Rudyard Gro. *Roch* 3F **41**
Rudyard Gro. *Sale* 1G **133**
Rudyard Gro. *Stoc* 3F **127**
Rudyard Rd. *Midd* 4C **54**
Rudyard Rd. *Salf* 6A **80**
Rudyard St. *Salf* 5H **81**
Rufford Av. *Hyde* 5D **114**
Rufford Av. *Roch* 1D **40**
Rufford Clo. *Ash L* 4G **87**
Rufford Clo. *Shaw* 6D **42**
Rufford Clo. *W'fld* 5E **51**
Rufford Dri. *Bolt* 5H **45**
Rufford Dri. *W'fld* 5D **50**
Rufford Gro. *Bolt* 5H **45**
Rufford Pl. *M18* 3H **111**
Rufford Rd. *M16* 4B **108**
Rufus St. *M14* 2A **126**
Rugby Dri. *Sale* 1A **134**
Rugby Rd. *Roch* 2A **28**
Rugby Rd. *Salf* 2A **92**
Rugby Rd. Ind. Est.
  Roch 2A **28**
Rugby St. *Salf* 1C **94**
Rugeley St. *Salf* 6F **81**
Ruins. 1G **33**
Ruins La. *Bolt* 1G **33**
Ruislip Av. *M40* 6G **83**
Ruislip Clo. *Oldh* 5F **73**
Rumbles La. *Del* 3H **59**
Rumbold St. *M18* 1G **111**
Rumworth Rd. *Los* 1A **44**
Rumworth St. *Bolt* 3H **45**
Runcorn St.
  M15 . . . . .6A **94** (4B **8**)

Runger La. *Timp* 6F **147**
Runhall Clo. *M12* 1C **110**
Running Hill Ga.
  Upperm 6D **60**
           (in two parts)
Running Hill La. *Dob* 5D **60**
Runnymead Ct. *Rytn* 3C **56**
Runnymeade.
  Swin & Salf 5G **79**
Runnymede Clo. *Stoc* . . .5E **139**
Runnymede Ct. *Bolt* 2H **45**
Runnymede Ct. *Stoc* 5E **139**
Rupert St. *M40* 1G **97**
Rupert St. *Bolt* 3B **46**
Rupert St. *Rad* 6H **49**
Rupert St. *Roch* 2E **27**
Rupert St. *Stoc* 2G **127**
           (in two parts)
Rupert Ter. *Stoc* 2G **127**
Ruscombe Fold. *Midd* 4F **53**
Rush Acre Clo. *Rad* 4E **49**
Rushall Wlk. *M23* 3F **147**
Rush Bank. *Shaw* 5D **42**
Rushbrooke Av. *M11* 2E **97**
Rushbury Dri. *Rytn* 3D **56**
Rushcroft Ct. *M9* 1A **84**
Rushcroft Rd. *Shaw* 5D **42**
Rushden Rd. *M19* 5D **110**
Rushen St. *M11* 4E **97**
Rushes, The. *Had* 3H **117**
Rushey Av. *M22* 5A **136**
Rushey Clo. *Haleb* 6D **146**
Rushey Fld. *Brom X* 3D **18**
Rushey Fold Ct. *Bolt* 3H **31**
Rushey Fold La. *Bolt* 3H **31**
Rusheylea Clo. *Bolt* 3G **31**
Rushey Rd. *M22* 6A **136**
Rushfield Dri. *M13* 4B **110**
Rushfield Rd. *Chea H* . . .1C **160**
Rushford Av. *M19* 5C **110**
Rushford Clo. *M19* 5C **110**
        (off Rushford Av.)
Rushford Gro. *Bolt* 1B **32**
Rushford Park. 5C **110**
Rushford St. *M12* 3C **110**
Rush Gro. *Upperm* 2F **61**
Rush Hill Rd. *Upperm* 2F **61**
Rush Hill Ter. *Upperm* 2F **61**
Rushlake Dri. *Bolt* 4A **32**
Rushlake Gdns. *Rosh* 3A **26**
Rushley Av. *Salf* 5F **81**
Rushmere. *Ash L* 5A **88**
Rushmere Av. *Lev* 6D **110**
Rushmere Dri. *Bury* 6C **22**
Rushmere Wlk. *Old T* . . .2B **108**
Rushmoor Clo. *Irlam* 5E **103**
Rush Mt. *Shaw* 5D **42**
Rusholme. 4G **109**
Rusholme Gdns. M14 . . .5G **109**
      (off Wilmslow Rd.)
Rusholme Gro. *M14* 4G **109**
Rusholme Gro. W.
  M14 . . . . .4G **109**
Rusholme Pl. *M14* 3G **109**
Rushside Rd. *Chea H* . . .1B **160**
Rush St. *Duk* 5D **100**
Rushton Clo. *Marp* 6E **143**
Rushton Dri. *Bram* 3F **151**
Rushton Dri. *Marp* 6D **142**
Rushton Dri. *Rom* 6A **130**
Rushton Gdns. *Bram* 2F **151**
Rushton Gro. *Oldh* 4A **58**
Rushton Gro. *Open* 6G **97**
Rushton Rd. *Bolt* 4F **31**
Rushton Rd. *Chea H* 1C **160**
Rushton Rd. *Stoc* 4D **138**
Rushton St. *M20* 1F **137**
Rushton St. *Wors* 1F **77**
Rushwick Av. *M40* 6G **83**
Rushworth Ct. *Stoc* 4E **127**
Rushycroft. *Mot* 3C **116**
Rushyfield Cres. *Rom* . . .6B **130**

Rushy Hill Vw. *Roch* 2E **27**
Ruskin Av. *M14* 3F **109**
Ruskin Av. *Aud* 6C **98**
Ruskin Av. *Chad* 0F **71**
Ruskin Av. *Dent* 6D **112**
Ruskin Av. *Kear* 2H **63**
Ruskin Cres. *P'wich* 6D **66**
Ruskin Dri. *Sale* 4E **121**
Ruskin Gdns. *Bred* 6G **129**
Ruskin Gro. *Bred* 6G **129**
Ruskington Dri. *M9* 4F **83**
Ruskin Rd. *M16* 4A **108**
Ruskin Rd. *Drov* 3A **98**
Ruskin Rd. *L Lev* 3B **48**
Ruskin Rd. *P'wich* 6D **66**
Ruskin Rd. *Roch* 3E **41**
Ruskin Rd. *Stoc* 6G **111**
Ruskin St. *Oldh* 1B **72**
Ruskin St. *Rad* 3A **50**
Rusland Ct. *M9* 6A **70**
Rusland Ct. *Sale* 4A **122**
Rusland Dri. *Bolt* 3G **33**
Rusland Wlk. *M22* 3A **148**
Russell Av. *M16* 5B **108**
Russell Av. *H Lane* 6C **154**
Russell Av. *Sale* 4D **122**
Russell Clo. *Bolt* 5G **31**
Russell Ct. *Farn* 2G **63**
Russell Ct. *L Hul* 6E **63**
Russell Dri. *Irlam* 5E **103**
Russell Fox Ct. *Stoc* 2G **127**
Russell Gdns. *Stoc* 2D **138**
Russell Rd. *M16* 4B **108**
Russell Rd. *Part* 6E **119**
Russell Rd. *Salf* 6H **79**
Russell St. *M8* 1C **94**
Russell St. *M16* 4D **108**
Russell St. *Ash L* 1B **100**
Russell St. *Bolt* 5H **31**
Russell St. *Bury* 1D **36**
Russell St. *Chad* 2H **71**
Russell St. *Comp* 6F **131**
Russell St. *Dent* 4F **113**
Russell St. *Duk* 5A **100**
Russell St. *Eccl* 3H **91**
Russell St. *Farn* 2G **63**
Russell St. *Heyw* 3G **39**
Russell St. *Hyde* 5B **114**
Russell St. *L Hul* 6E **63**
Russell St. *Moss* 2E **89**
Russell St. *P'wich* 5F **67**
Russell St. *Stoc* 5A **140**
Russet Rd. *M9* 2F **83**
Russet Wlk. *Bolt* 1A **32**
Rustons Wlk. *M40* 2E **85**
Ruth Av. *M40* 2E **85**
Ruthen La. *M16* 3H **107**
Rutherford Av. *M14* 4F **109**
Rutherford Clo. *Hyde* . . .5B **114**
Rutherford Way.
  Hyde 5A **114**
        (Birchfield M.)
Rutherford Way.
  Hyde 5A **114**
        (Mall, The)
Rutherglade Clo. *M40* . . .5E **83**
Rutherglen Dri. *Bolt* 1D **44**
Rutherglen Wlk. *M40* . . .6G **83**
Ruthin Av. *M9* 4E **69**
Ruthin Av. *Chea H* 3A **150**
Ruthin Av. *Midd* 2A **70**
Ruthin Clo. *Oldh* 1H **85**
Ruthin Clo. *Salf* 3G **93**
Ruth St. *M18* 4F **111**
Ruth St. *Bolt* 5A **32**
Ruth St. *Bury* 1D **36**
Ruth St. *Oldh* 1D **72**
Ruth St. *Rams* 3A **12**
Ruth St. *Whitw* 4G **15**
Rutland. *Roch* 5G **27**
Rutland Av. *Dent* 5G **113**

Rutland Av. *Firs* 4G **107**
Rutland Av. *Swin* 1F **79**
Rutland Av. *Urm* 5G **105**
Rutland Av. *Wthtn* 3E **125**
Rutland Clo. *Ash L* 3B **100**
Rutland Clo. *Gat* 5F **137**
Rutland Clo. *L Lev* 3B **48**
Rutland Ct. *M20* 4F **125**
Rutland Ct. *Stoc* 6A **140**
Rutland Cres. *Stoc* 4D **128**
Rutland Dri. *Bury* 5E **37**
Rutland Dri. *Salf* 3G **81**
Rutland Gro. *Bolt* 4G **31**
Rutland Gro. *Farn* 2E **63**
Rutland La. *Sale* 5F **123**
        (in three parts)
Rutland Rd. *B'hth* 5F **133**
Rutland Rd. *Cad* 4B **118**
Rutland Rd. *Droy* 3G **97**
Rutland Rd. *Eccl* 1H **91**
Rutland Rd. *Haz G* 5E **153**
Rutland Rd. *Wors* 2E **77**
Rutland St. *M18* 1G **111**
Rutland St. *Ash L* 3B **100**
Rutland St. *Bolt* 3H **45**
Rutland St. *Droy* 5B **98**
Rutland St. *Fail* 3F **85**
Rutland St. *Heyw* 2F **39**
Rutland St. *Hyde* 2B **114**
Rutland St. *Oldh* 4A **72**
Rutland St. *Swin* 2E **79**
Rutland Way. *Shaw* 5G **43**
Rutter's La. *Haz G* 3C **152**
Ryall Av. *Salf* 5H **93**
Ryall Av. S. *Salf* 5H **93**
Ryan St. *Open* 6G **97**
Ryburn Flats. *Heyw* 3E **39**
      (off Meadow Clo.)
Ryburn Sq. *Roch* 5A **26**
Rydal Av. *Chad* 6E **55**
Rydal Av. *Droy* 4G **97**
Rydal Av. *Eccl* 1D **90**
Rydal Av. *Haz G* 2C **152**
Rydal Av. *H Lane* 5C **154**
Rydal Av. *Hyde* 2A **114**
Rydal Av. *Midd* 3H **69**
Rydal Av. *Rytn* 5A **42**
Rydal Av. *Sale* 3H **121**
Rydal Av. *Urm* 1C **120**
Rydal Clo. *Bury* 6C **36**
Rydal Clo. *Dent* 5B **112**
Rydal Clo. *Gat* 2F **149**
Rydal Ct. *Bolt* 4D **30**
Rydal Cres. *Swin* 5F **79**
Rydal Cres. *Wors* 2G **77**
Rydal Dri. *Haleb* 5D **146**
Rydale Av. *M40* 6G **83**
Rydal Gro. *Ash L* 1G **99**
Rydal Gro. *Farn* 2B **62**
Rydal Gro. *Heyw* 5F **39**
Rydal Gro. *W'fld* 1E **67**
Rydal Mt. *Ald E* 6B **166**
Rydal Mt. *Stoc* 5H **111**
Rydal Rd. *Bolt* 4E **31**
Rydal Rd. *L Lev* 4A **48**
Rydal Rd. *Oldh* 2G **73**
Rydal Rd. *Stret* 4D **106**
Rydal Wlk. *Oldh* 2H **73**
Rydal Wlk. *Stal* 2E **101**
Ryde Av. *Dent* 1H **129**
Ryde Av. *Stoc* 1D **138**
Ryder Av. *Alt* 4G **133**
Ryder Brow. 4F **111**
Ryder Brow. *M18* 3F **111**
Ryderbrow Rd.
  M18 . . . . .3F **111**
Ryder St. *M40* 1G **95**
Ryder St. *Bolt* 3G **31**
Ryder St. *Heyw* 3F **39**
Ryder St. *Rad* 4B **50**
Ryde St. *Bolt* 3F **45**
Rydings Rd. *Roch* 5H **15**

Rydley St. *Bolt* 1D **46**
Ryebank Gro. *Ash L* 6H **87**
Ryebank M. *Chor H* 6F **107**
Ryebank Rd. *Chor H* 6F **107**
Rye Bank Rd. *Firs* 5G **107**
Ryeburn Av. *M22* 2B **148**
Ryeburn Dri. *Bolt* 6F **19**
Ryeburne St. *Oldh* 2G **73**
Ryeburn Wlk. *Urm* 3B **104**
Rye Clift. *W'fld* 2A **66**
Ryecroft Av. *Heyw* 3G **39**
Ryecroft Av. *Salf* 2C **92**
Ryecroft Av. *T'ton* 5H **21**
Ryecroft Bus. Cen.
  Ash L 4F **99**
      (off Ryecroft St.)
Ryecroft Clo. *Chad* 6F **71**
        (in two parts)
Ryecroft Gro. *M23* 4G **135**
Ryecroft Ho. Ash L 4G **99**
      (off Park St.)
Ryecroft La. *Aud* 6E **99**
Ryecroft La. *Wors* 1B **90**
Ryecroft Leisure Cen.
  . . . . .4B **150**
Ryecroft Rd. *Stret* 6C **106**
Ryecroft St. *Ash L* 4F **99**
Ryecroft Vw. *Aud* 5C **98**
Ryedale Clo. *Stoc* 6D **126**
Ryefield. *Ash L* 4F **99**
Ryefield. *Salf* 5B **80**
Ryefield Clo. *Timp* 6C **134**
Ryefield Rd. *Sale* 1E **133**
Ryefields. *Roch* 5B **16**
Ryefields Dri. *Upperm* 6B **60**
Ryefield St. *Bolt* 4C **32**
Ryelands Clo. *Roch* 1H **41**
Rye St. *Heyw* 2G **39**
Rye Top La. *Upperm* 2H **61**
Rye Wlk. *M13* 2G **109**
Rye Wlk. *Chad* 3G **71**
Rygate Wlk. *M8* 5B **82**
Ryhope Wlk. *Salf* 6A **82**
Ryland Clo. *Stoc* 6H **111**
Rylands Ct.
  M15 . . . . .1B **108** (6C **8**)
Rylands St. *M18* 1G **111**
Rylane Wlk. *M40* 6F **83**
Rylatt Ct. *Sale* 4A **122**
Ryley Av. *Bolt* 2F **45**
Ryleys La. *Ald E* 5F **167**
Ryley St. *Bolt* 1G **45**
Rylstone Av. *M21* 6B **124**
Ryther Gro. *M9* 4D **68**
Ryton Av. *M18* 4C **111**

S

Sabden Clo. *M40* 2A **96**
Sabden Clo. *Bury* 4F **23**
Sabden Clo. *Heyw* 3C **38**
Sabden Rd. *Bolt* 3C **30**
Sabrina St. *M8* 6A **82**
Sack St. *Hyde* 2D **114**
Sackville Clo. *Shaw* 4E **43**
Sackville St.
  M1 . . . . . . .5E **95** (1B **10**)
        (in two parts)
Sackville St. *Ash L* 2H **99**
Sackville St. *Bolt* 6E **33**
Sackville St. *Bury* 2D **36**
Sackville St. *Roch* 4C **40**
Sackville St.
  Salf 3C **94** (4E **5**)
Saddleback Clo. *Wors* 5D **76**
Saddlecote. *Wors* 1C **90**
Saddle Gro. *Droy* 2D **98**
Saddle St. *Bolt* 3D **32**
Saddlewood Av. *M19* 1H **137**
Saddleworth. 1F **61**

Saddleworth Bus. Pk.
Del 3H 59
Saddleworth Fold.
Upperm 6C 60
Saddleworth Mus. &
Art Gallery. 1F 61
Saddleworth Swimming Pool.
. . . . .2F 61
Saddleworth Tourist Info. Cen.
. . . . .1F 61
Sadie Av. Stret 3A 106
Sadler Clo. M14 . . . . .4E 109
Sadler Ct. M15 . . .2C 108 (6E 9)
Sadler St. Bolt 3C 46
Sadler St. Midd 6H 53
Saffron Dri. Oldh 5H 57
Saffron Wlk. M22 . . . .4B 148
Saffron Wlk. Part 6D 118
Sagars Rd. Hand 3F 159
(in two parts)
Sagar St. M8 . . . . .1D 94
St Agnes Rd. M13 . . . .5B 110
St Agnes St. Stoc 4H 111
St Aidans Clo. Rad 6G 49
St Aidan's Gro. Salf 5F 81
St Albans Av. M40 . . . .6B 84
St Albans Av. Ash L 5F 87
St Alban's Av. Stoc 4E 127
St Albans Clo. Oldh 5D 72
St Albans Ct. Roch 5G 27
St Alban's Cres.
W Timp 3E 133
St Albans Ho. Roch 5G 27
(off St Albans St.)
St Albans St. Roch 5G 27
St Alban's Ter. M8 . . . .6A 82
St Alban's Ter. Roch 5G 27
St Aldates. Rom 1F 141
St Aldwyn's Rd. M20 . . .4F 125
St Ambrose Gdns. Salf . .3F 93
St Ambrose Rd. Oldh . . .6G 57
St Andrew's Av. Droy . . .4G 97
St Andrews Av. Eccl 4G 91
St Andrew's Av. Timp . .4G 133
St Andrews Clo. L'boro . .4C 16
St Andrews Clo. Rams . . .4E 13
St Andrew's Clo.
Rom 2H 141
St Andrews Clo. Sale . . .2E 133
St Andrews Clo. Stoc . . .5D 126
St Andrew's Ct. Bolt . . .6B 32
(off Chancery La.)
St Andrews Ct. Hale . . .2H 145
St Andrews Ct. Stoc 2A 140
St Andrew's Dri. Heyw . . .4F 39
St Andrew's Rd.
H Grn 4G 149
St Andrews Rd. Rad 1F 49
St Andrews Rd. Stoc . . .5D 126
St Andrews Rd. Stret . .5B 106
St Andrew's Sq.
M1 . . . . . . .5G 95 (1F 11)
St Andrew's St.
M1 . . . . . . .5G 95 (1E 11)
St Andrews St. Rad 1F 49
St Andrews Vw. Rad . . .1F 49
St Anne's Av. Rytn 4B 56
St Anne's Av. Salf 2E 93
St Anne's Ct. Aud 1E 113
St Annes Ct. Sale 5C 122
St Annes Ct. Salf 1F 93
St Anne's Cres. Grass . .4E 75
St Anne's Dri. Dent 3G 113
St Annes Gdns. Heyw . . .3H 39
St Annes M. W. T'ton . . .4H 21
St Annes Rd. M21 . . . .2H 123
St Anne's Rd. Aud 2F 113
St Annes Sq. Del 3H 59
St Annes's Rd. Aud 1F 113
St Anne's St. M40 . . . . .6H 83

St Anne's St. Bury 1D 36
St Ann's All. M2 . . .4D 94 (5G 5)
(off St Ann's Pl.)
St Ann's Arc. M2 . . . . . .5H 5
St Ann's Chyd. M2 . . . . .5H 5
St Anns Clo. P'wich 6E 67
St Anns Pde. Wilm 2E 167
(off Alderley Rd.)
St Ann's Pl. M2 . . .4D 94 (5H 5)
St Anns Rd. Haz G 4C 152
St Ann's Rd. P'wich 6D 66
St Ann's Rd. Roch 3C 28
St Ann's Rd. N. H Grn . . .4G 149
St Ann's Rd. S. H Grn . . .5G 149
St Ann's Sq.
M2 . . . . . . .4D 94 (5H 5)
St Ann's Sq. H Grn 5G 149
St Ann's St. Sale 6F 123
St Ann's St. Swin 3E 79
St Ann St. M2 . . . .4D 94 (5G 5)
St Ann St. Bolt 4A 32
St Anthony's Dri. Moss . . .1F 89
St Asaph's Dri. M7 . . . . .3B 82
St Asaph's Dri. Ash L 5F 87
St Aubin's Rd. Bolt 1D 46
St Augustine's Ct.
Bolt 4D 32
St Augustine's Rd.
Stoc 3D 138
St Augustine St. M40 . . . .6F 83
St Augustine St. Bolt 3H 31
St Austell Dri. G'mnt . . .1H 21
St Austell Dri. H Grn 5F 149
St Austell Rd. M16 . . . .6C 108
St Austells Dri. P'wich . . .4F 67
St Austell's Dri. Swin 4A 80
St Barnabas Dri. L'boro . .3E 17
St Barnabas Sq. M11 . . .5D 96
St Bartholomew's Dri.
Salf 5A 94 (1A 8)
St Bartholomew St.
Bolt 3C 46
St Bede's Av. Bolt 5F 45
St Bees Clo. M14 . . . . .3E 109
St Bees Clo. Gat 2F 149
St Bees Rd. Bolt 3E 33
St Bees Wlk. Midd 5G 53
St Benedict's Av. M12 . . .1B 110
St Bernards Clo. Salf 6G 81
(in two parts)
St Bernard's Clo. Salf 6F 81
St Bernard's Dri. Salf 6G 81
St Boniface Rd. Salf 1A 94
St Brannock's Rd.
M21 . . . . .6A 108
St Brannocks Rd.
Chea H 6D 150
St Brelades Dri. Salf 3B 82
St Brendan's Rd. M20 . . .2F 125
St Brendan's Rd. N.
M20 . . . . .2F 125
St Bride St. M16 . . . . . .2B 108
St Brides Way. M16 . . . .2B 108
St Catherines Dri. Farn . . .1B 62
St Catherine's Rd.
M20 . . . . .2F 125
St Chads Av. Rom 1A 142
St Chads Clo. Roch 4H 27
(off School La.)
St Chads Cres. Oldh 2B 86
St Chads Cres.
Upperm 1G 61
St Chads Gro. Rom 1A 142
St Chads Rd. M20 . . . . .2H 125
St Chad's St.
M8 . . . . . . .1E 95 (1A 6)
St Charles Clo. Had 2H 117
St Christopher's Av.
Ash L 5A 88
St Christophers Clo.
M20 . . . . .3D 124

St Christopher's Dri.
Rom 1G 141
St Christopher's Rd.
Ash L 5H 87
St Clair Rd. G'mnt 6B 12
St Clements Ct. Irlam . . .4F 103
St Clements Ct. Oldh 4C 72
St Clement's Ct. P'wich . . .5G 67
St Clements Ct. Roch 3E 27
St Clement's Dri. Salf 6H 93
(4A 8)
St Clements Fold. Urm . .5G 105
St Clement's Rd. M21 . . .1G 123
St Cuthbert's Fold.
Oldh 2E 87
St Davids Av. Rom 1H 141
St David's Clo. Ash L 4H 87
St Davids Clo. Sale 6A 122
St Davids Ct. M8 . . . . . .6C 82
St David's Rd. Chea 6B 138
St Davids Rd. Haz G 4C 152
St David's Wlk. Stret . . .5A 106
St Domingo St. Oldh 2C 72
St Dominic's M. Bolt 4G 45
St Dominics Way.
Midd 2A 70
St Dunstan Wlk. M40 . . . .5A 84
(off Rollswood Dri.)
St Edmund Hall Clo.
Rams 5E 13
St Edmund's Rd. M40 . . .5G 83
St Edmund St. Bolt 6A 32
St Edmund's Wlk.
L Hul 5D 62
St Elizabeth Pk. Dent . . .4D 112
St Elizabeth's Way.
Stoc 2G 127
St Elmo Av. Stoc 4D 140
St Elmo Pk. Poy 3A 164
St Ethelbert's Av. Bolt . . .2F 45
St Gabriels Clo. Roch 4D 40
St Gabriel's Ct. Roch 3C 40
(off Atkinson St.)
St Georges. 1B 108 (5D 8)
St George's Av.
M15 . . . . . . .6B 94 (4C 8)
St George's Av. Timp . . .4A 134
St Georges Cen. Salf 1H 93
St Georges Ct.
M15 . . . . . .1C 108 (6E 9)
(Mallow St.)
St George's Ct. Aud 1F 113
(off Richmond St.)
St George's Ct. Bolt 5B 32
(Bridge St.)
St George's Ct. Bolt 5A 32
(Vernon St.)
St George's Ct. Bury 4G 51
St Georges Ct. Eccl 4H 91
St George's Ct. Hyde . . .5C 114
St George's Ct. Stret . . .6C 106
St George's Cres. Salf . . .2A 92
St George's Cres.
Timp 3A 134
St George's Cres. Wors . .1F 77
St George's Dri. M40 . . . .4B 84
St George's Dri. Hyde . . .6B 114
St George's Gdns.
Dent 6G 113
St Georges Ho. Stal 3E 101
St Georges Pl. Salf 6E 81
St George's Rd. M14 . . .2A 126
St George's Rd. Bolt 5A 32
St George's Rd. Bury 3G 51
St George's Rd. C'ton . . .3H 119
St George's Rd. Droy 2H 97
St Georges Rd. Roch 3B 26
St Georges Rd. Stret . . .5C 106

St Georges Sq. Bolt 5B 32
St George's Sq. Chad 6E 71
St George's St. Bolt 5B 32
St George's St. Stal 2D 100
St Georges Way. Salf 6E 81
(in two parts)
St Germain St. Farn 1E 63
St Giles Dri. Hyde 5D 114
St Gregorys Clo. Farn 2E 63
St Gregory's Rd.
M12 . . . . . . .6G 95 (3F 11)
St Helena Rd. Bolt 6A 32
(in two parts)
St Helens Rd. Bolt 6E 45
St Helier's Dri. Salf 3B 82
St Helier Sq. M19 . . . . .4B 126
St Helier St. Bolt 3H 45
St Herberts Ct. Chad 2H 71
St Higher Bri. St. Bolt 5B 32
St Hilda's Clo. M22 . . . .2C 136
St Hilda's Dri. Oldh 1B 72
St Hilda's Rd. Aud 1E 113
St Hilda's Rd. N'den 2B 136
St Hilda's Rd. Old T 2A 108
St Hilda's Vw. Aud 2E 113
St Hugh's Clo. Timp 3G 133
St Ignatius Wlk.
Salf 5H 93 (1A 8)
St Ives Av. Chea 5B 138
St Ives Cres. Sale 2A 134
St Ives Rd. M14 . . . . . .5F 109
St James Av. Bolt 5G 33
St James Av. Bury 1H 35
St James Clo. Roch 5A 42
St James Clo. Salf 2B 92
St James' Ct.
M15 . . . . . . .1C 108 (5F 9)
(off Old York St.)
St James Ct. M20 . . . . . .3F 137
(Millgate La.)
St James' Ct. M20 . . . . . .6F 125
(Moorland Rd.)
St James Ct. Alt 1G 145
St James Ct. Chea H 1C 160
St James Ct. Oldh 1G 73
St James Ct. Salf 2B 92
St James Dri. Sale 6A 122
St James Dri. Wilm 3D 166
St James Gro. Heyw 3E 39
St James Gro. Timp 2H 133
St James Ho. Stoc 6F 127
St James Lodge. Stoc . . .1A 152
(off Crescent, The)
St James Rd. Stoc 4D 126
St James's Rd. Salf 5A 82
St James's Sq.
M2 . . . . . . .4D 94 (6H 5)
St James St.
M1 . . . . .5E 95 (1H 9)
St James St. Ash L 3B 100
St James St. Eccl 3G 91
St James St. Farn 2D 62
St James St. Heyw 3E 39
St James St. Miln 5F 29
St James St. Oldh 2F 73
St James St. Shaw 6F 43
St James Ter. Heyw 3E 39
St James Way.
Chea H 1B 160
St Johns Av. Droy 3B 98
St Johns Clo. Duk 5C 100
St Johns Clo. Rom 1H 141
St John's Ct. Bow 2F 145
St John's Ct. Hyde 4D 114
St John's Ct. Lees 2B 74
St John's Ct. Rad 5A 50
St John's Ct. Roch 5B 28
St John's Ct. Salf 3F 93
(off Milford St., M6)
St John's Ct.
Salf (M7) 5G 81
St Johns Dri. Hyde 4D 114

St John's Dri. *Roch* 5B **28**
St John's Gdns. *Moss* 1F **89**
St John's Ind. Est.
  Lees 3A **74**
St John's Pas.
  M3 . . . . .4C **94** (1F **9**)
St John's Pl. *Stoc* 1A **138**
St John's Rd. *Alt* 2E **145**
St John's Rd. *Dent* 2F **113**
St Johns Rd. *Haz G* . . .4B **152**
St John's Rd. *Long* 3B **110**
St John's Rd. *Old T* 3A **108**
St John's Rd. *Stoc* 1A **138**
St John's Rd.
  W'houg & Los 3A **44**
St John's Rd. *Wilm* 6B **166**
St John's Rd. *Wors* 4A **76**
St John's St. *Chad* 4A **72**
St John's St. *Farn* 1G **63**
St John St. *Rad* 5H **49**
St John's St. *Salf* 5H **81**
St John St. *M3* 5C **94** (1F **9**)
St John St. *Droy* 5H **97**
St John St. *Duk* 5C **100**
    (in two parts)
St John St. *Eccl* 4F **91**
St John St. *Irlam* 5E **103**
St John St. *Lees* 3A **74**
St John's St. *Swin* 5B **80**
St John St. *Wors* 5E **63**
St John's Wlk. *Oldh* 3A **72**
St Johns Wlk. *Stoc* 3D **138**
    (off Oak St.)
St Johns Wood. *Los* 3A **44**
St Joseph's Av. *W'fld* 2F **67**
St Joseph's Clo. *Shaw* . . .5G **43**
St Joseph's Dri. *Roch* . . .1H **41**
St Joseph's Dri. *Salf* 5H **93**
St Joseph St. *Bolt* 3H **31**
St Kilda Av. *Kear* 3H **63**
St Kilda's Av. *Droy* 2H **97**
St Kilda's Dri. *Salf* 3B **82**
St Lawrence Ct. *Dent* . . .5F **113**
St Lawrence Quay. *Salf* . . .6F **93**
St Lawrence Rd. *Dent* . . .4F **113**
St Leonard's Ct. *Dale* . . .5H **121**
St Leonards Dri.
  Timp 5H **133**
St Leonards Rd. *Stoc* . . .4F **127**
St Leonards Sq. *Midd* 6A **54**
    (off High St.)
St Leonards St. *Midd* 6A **54**
St Lesmo Ct. *Stoc* 4E **139**
St Lesmo Rd. *Stoc* 3D **138**
St Lukes Ct. *Bolt* 5G **31**
St Lukes Ct. *Chad* 2G **71**
St Lukes Ct. *Roch* 6H **27**
St Lukes Cres. *Duk* 5A **100**
St Luke's Rd. *Salf* 3D **92**
St Luke St. *Roch* 6H **27**
St Lukes Wlk. *M40* 5A **84**
St Margaret's Av.
  M19 . . . . .3B **126**
St Margarets Clo. *Alt* 1E **145**
St Margarets Clo. *Bolt* . . .5F **31**
St Margarets Clo.
  P'wich 3G **67**
St Margaret's Gdns.
  Oldh 6A **72**
St Margaret's Rd. *M40* . .6D **70**
St Margaret's Rd. *Alt* . . .2F **145**
St Margaret's Rd. *Bolt* . . .5F **31**
St Margaret's Rd.
  Chea 5C **138**
St Margaret's Rd.
  P'wich 4G **67**
St Mark's Av. *Alt* 6C **132**
St Marks Av. *Rytn* 3E **57**
St Marks Clo. *Roch* 3E **57**
St Marks Ct. M22 . . . . .4A **148**
    (off Stoneacre Rd.)
St Mark's Ct. *Chad* 1H **71**

St Marks Cres. *Wors* 2F **77**
St Mark's La. *M8* 4B **82**
St Marks Sq. *Bury* 1D **36**
St Mark's St. *M19* 5E **111**
St Mark's St. *Bolt* 2B **46**
St Mark's St. *Bred* 5G **129**
St Mark St. *Duk* 4II **99**
St Mark's Vw. *Bolt* 2B **46**
St Mark's Wlk. *Bolt* 3A **46**
St Martin's Av. *Stoc* 1E **139**
St Martin's Clo. *Droy* 2H **97**
St Martin's Clo. *Hyde* . . .5D **114**
St Martin's Dri. *Salf* 3B **82**
St Martin's Rd. *Marp* 5E **143**
St Martin's Rd. *Oldh* 1E **87**
St Martins Rd. *Sale* 3F **121**
St Martins St. *Roch* 4D **40**
St Mary's Av. *Bolt* 2F **45**
St Mary's Av. *Dent* 1G **129**
St Mary's Clo. *P'wich* 5E **67**
St Mary's Clo. *Roch* 1H **41**
St Marys' Clo. *Stoc* 2A **140**
St Mary's Ct. *M8* 2B **82**
St Mary's Ct. *M40* 3B **84**
St Marys Ct. *Oldh* 2C **72**
St Mary's Ct. *P'wich* 5E **67**
St Mary's Crest. *G'fld* 4G **61**
St Mary's Dri. *Chea* 5B **138**
St Mary's Dri. *G'fld* 4G **61**
St Mary's Dri. *Stoc* 3H **127**
St Mary's Ga.
  M1 . . . . .3D **94** (4H **5**)
St Mary's Ga. *Roch* 4G **27**
St Marys Ga. *Shaw* 6F **43**
St Mary's Ga. *Stoc* 2H **139**
St Mary's Ga. *Upperm* 1F **61**
St Mary's Hall Rd. *M8* 2B **82**
St Mary's Parsonage.
  M3 . . . . .4C **94** (5F **5**)
St Mary's Pl. *Bury* 3C **36**
St Mary's Rd. *M40* 4B **84**
St Mary's Rd. *Bow* 3D **144**
    (in two parts)
St Marys Rd. *Dis* 2H **165**
St Marys Rd. *Eccl* 3H **91**
St Mary's Rd. *Hyde* 2O **114**
St Mary's Rd. *Sale* 4H **121**
St Mary's Rd. *Wors* 4E **63**
St Mary's St.
  M3 . . . . .4D **94** (5G **5**)
St Mary's St. *Hulme* 2C **108**
St Mary's St. *Oldh* 1D **72**
St Mary St. *Salf* . . .3B **94** (4D **4**)
St Mary's Way. *Oldh* 2C **72**
St Mary's Way. *Stoc* 1A **140**
St Matthews Ct. *Rad* 2C **48**
St Matthew's Av. *Bram* . . .6G **151**
St Matthews Dri. *Chad* . . .5G **55**
St Matthews Grange.
  Bolt 4A **32**
St Matthew's Rd. *Stoc* . . .3F **139**
St Matthews Ter. Bolt 4A **32**
    (off St Matthews Wlk.)
St Matthew's Ter. *Stoc* . . .3F **139**
St Matthews Wlk. *Bolt* . . .4A **32**
    (in two parts)
St Mawes Ct. *Rad* 2C **48**
St Michael's Av. *Bolt* 5D **46**
St Michael's Av. *Bram* . . .6G **151**
St Michael's Clo. *Bury* 5G **35**
St Michael's Ct. *Eccl* 5C **90**
St Michaels Ct. *Sale* 3G **121**
St Michaels Gdns.
  W'fld 6F **51**
St Michael's Pl.
  M4 . . . . . .2F **95** (2B **6**)
    (off Aspin La.)
St Michaels Rd. *Hyde* . . .5D **114**
St Michael's Sq.
  M4 . . . . . . .2E **95** (2B **6**)
St Michael's Sq.
  Ash L 2A **100**

St Modwen Rd.
  Stret 2H **105**
St Nicholas Rd.
  M15 . . . . . . .6C **94** (4E **9**)
St Osmund's Dri. *Bolt* . . .6G **33**
St Osmund's Gro. *Bolt* . . .6G **33**
St Oswalds Rd. *Lev* 5D **110**
St Ouen Cen. *Wors* 6F **63**
St Pauls Clo. *Ash L* 3F **99**
St Pauls Clo. *Rad* 6G **49**
St Paul's Clo. *Stal* 3G **101**
St Pauls Ct. *Bury* 2E **37**
St Pauls Ct. *Oldh* 5D **72**
St Paul's Ct. *Salf* 2G **81**
St Paul's Ct. *Wors* 1F **77**
St Paul's Hill Rd.
  Hyde 5D **114**
St Paul's M. Stoc 6B **128**
    (off St Paul's St.)
St Paul's Pl. *Bolt* 2G **31**
St Paul's Rd. *M20* 3G **125**
St Paul's Rd. *Salf* 2G **81**
St Paul's Rd. *Stoc* 5D **126**
St Paul's Rd. *Wors* 1G **77**
St Paul's St. *Bury* 2E **37**
St Paul's St. *Hyde* 4C **114**
St Paul's St. *Rams* 2E **13**
St Paul's St. *Stal* 3G **101**
St Paul's St. *Stoc* 6A **128**
St Pauls Trad. Est.
  Stal 3G **101**
St Paul's Vs. *Bury* 2E **37**
St Peter Quay. *Salf* 6G **93**
St Peter's Av. *Bolt* 3E **31**
St Peter's Ct. *Stret* 4E **107**
St Peter's Dri. *Hyde* 5D **114**
St Petersgate. *Stoc* 2G **139**
St Peter's Rd. *Bury* 6C **36**
St Peter's Rd. *Swin* 4E **79**
St Peter's Sq.
  M2 . . . . . . .5D **94** (1H **9**)
St Peter's Sq. *Stoc* 2G **139**
St Peters St. *Ash L* 3G **99**
St Peter's St. *Roch* 5B **28**
St Peter's Ter. *Farn* 2F **63**
St Peter's Way.
  Bolt (BL1,BL2) 4B **32**
St Peter's Way.
  Bolt (BL3) 2D **46**
St Philip's Av. *Bolt* 3H **45**
St Philip's Pl.
  Salf 3B **94** (4C **4**)
St Philip's Rd. *M18* 3H **111**
St Philip's Sq.
  Salf 3B **94** (4C **4**)
    (off Bank St.)
St Phillip's Dri. *Rytn* 6C **56**
St Saviour's Rd. *Stoc* . . .6C **140**
Saintsbridge Rd. *M22* . . .3A **148**
St Simons Clo. *Stoc* . . .3C **140**
St Simon St.
  Salf 2B **94** (1D **4**)
St Stephen's Av. *Aud* 5E **99**
St Stephens Clo.
  M13 . . . . .2H **109** (6H **11**)
St Stephens Clo. *Bolt* 2E **47**
St Stephens Ct. M9 . . . . .4F **83**
    (off Shieldborn Dri.)
St Stephens Gdns.
  Kear 3A **64**
St Stephen's Gdns.
  Midd 5A **54**
St Stephen's St. *Kear* 3A **64**
St Stephens St. *Oldh* 1E **73**
St Stephen St.
  Salf 3B **94** (4D **4**)
St Stephens Vw. *Droy* . . .3A **98**
St Teresa's Rd. *M16* . . .4G **107**
St Thomas Circ. *Oldh* 4B **72**
St Thomas Clo. *Rad* 4G **49**
St Thomas Ct. *Bury* 3F **37**
St Thomas's Pl. *M8* 1E **95**

St Thomas's Pl. *Stoc* . . .3H **139**
St Thomas St. *Bolt* 3H **31**
St Thomas St. N. *Oldh* . . .4B **72**
St Thomas St. S. *Oldh* . . .4B **72**
St Vincent St.
  M4 . . . . .3G **95** (4F **7**)
St Werburgh's Rd.
  M21 . . . . .6A **108**
St Wilfred's Dri. *Roch* . . .6D **14**
St Wilfrid's St.
  M15 . . . . . .1C **108** (5E **9**)
St Williams Av. *Bolt* 4A **46**
St Winifred's Pl. *Stal* 3D **100**
Salcombe Av. *Bolt* 4D **34**
Salcombe Clo. *Sale* 4G **121**
Salcombe Gro. *Bolt* 1A **48**
Salcombe Rd. *M11* 5F **97**
Salcombe Rd. *Stoc* 3C **140**
Salcot Wlk. *M40* . . .2G **95** (1F **7**)
Sale. **4B 122**
Sale Circ. *M23* 1H **135**
Sale Heys Rd. *Sale* 6H **121**
Sale La. *Tyl* 2A **76**
Sale Leisure Cen. **4C 122**
Salem. **4H 73**
Salem Gro. *Oldh* 3H **73**
Sale Rd. *M23* 1G **135**
Sale Sharks Rugby Union
  Football Club. **6B 122**
Sale's La. *Bury* 2G **23**
Sale St. *L'boro* 3F **17**
Sale Water Pk. **3E 123**
Salford. . . . .**5H 93 (6A 4)**
Salford App.
  Salf 3D **94** (4G **5**)
Salford City Reds Rugby
  League Club. **3D 92**
Salford Enterprise Cen.
  Salf 4C **92**
Salford Foyer. *Salf* 2F **93**
Salford Leisure Cen. **2A 4**
Salford Mus. & Art Gallery.
  . . . .**3A 94 (3A 4)**
Salford Quays. **6F 93**
Salford R.C. Cathedral.
  . . . .**3B 94 (4D 4)**
Salford Shop. City. *Salf* . .2G **93**
Salford St. *Bury* 1E **37**
Salford St. *Oldh* 4G **73**
Salford Tourist Info. Cen.
  . . . .**6G 93**
Salford University Bus. Pk.
  Salf 2H **93** (1A **4**)
Salik Gdns. *Roch* 6H **27**
Salisbury Av. *Heyw* 5E **39**
Salisbury Cotts. *Had* 2H **117**
Salisbury Cres. *Ash L* 4H **87**
Salisbury Dri. *Duk* 6E **101**
Salisbury Dri. *P'wich* 1G **81**
Salisbury Ho. *M1* 2B **10**
Salisbury Ho. *Salf* 3E **5**
Salisbury Rd. *M21* 6H **107**
Salisbury Rd. *Alt* 4F **133**
Salisbury Rd. *Eccl* 1H **91**
Salisbury Rd. *Oldh* 3F **73**
Salisbury Rd. *Rad* 2E **49**
Salisbury Rd. *Swin* 4E **79**
Salisbury Rd. *Urm* 3F **105**
Salisbury St. *M14* 3E **109**
Salisbury St. *Bolt* 1H **45**
Salisbury St. *Midd* 6B **54**
Salisbury St. *Shaw* 5D **42**
Salisbury St. *Stoc* 1H **127**
Salisbury Ter. *L Lev* 4B **48**
Salix Cl. *Salf* 2G **93**
Salkeld St. *Roch* 6H **27**
Salley St. *L'boro* 5G **17**
Salmesbury Hall Clo.
  Rams 4D **12**
Salmon Fields. *Rytn* 4C **56**
Salmon St. *M4* 3E **95** (4B **6**)

Salop St.—Saxon Dri.

Salop St. *Bolt* 1C **46**
Salop St. *Salf* 1G **93**
Saltash Clo. *M22* 4B **148**
Saltburn Wlk. M9 . . . . . . .3G 83
(off Naunton Wlk.)
Saltdene Rd. *M22* 4A **148**
Saltergate Clo. *Bolt* 3C **44**
Saltergate M. *Salf* 3G **93**
Saltersbrook Gro.
Wilm 6A **160**
Salterton Dri. *Bolt* 5D **44**
Salterton Wlk. *M40* 4A **84**
Salteye Rd. *Eccl* 4C **90**
Saltford Av. *M4* . . .3H **95** (4F **7**)
(in two parts)
Saltford Ct. *M4* . . .3H **95** (4G **7**)
Salthill Av. *Heyw* 6G **39**
Salthill Dri. *M22* 3C **148**
Salthouse Clo. *Bury* 5C **22**
Saltire Gdns. *Salf* 3A **82**
Saltney Av. *M20* 2D **124**
Saltram Clo. *Rad* 2C **48**
Saltrush Rd. *M22* 3B **148**
Salts Dri. *L'boro* 3E **17**
Salts St. *Shaw* 6E **43**
Saltwood Gro. *Bolt* 4B **32**
Salutation St.
M15 . . . . .1D **108** (5H **9**)
Salvin Wlk. *M9* 6G **69**
Sam Cowan Clo. *M14* . . .4E **109**
Samian Gdns. *Salf* 6G **81**
Samlesbury Clo. *M20* . . .6D **124**
Samlesbury Clo. *Shaw* . . .6D **42**
Sammy Cookson Clo.
M14 . . . . .4E **109**
(in two parts)
Samouth Clo.
M40 . . . . . . .2H **95** (2G **7**)
Sampson Sq. *M14* 3E **109**
Sam Rd. *Dig* 2C **60**
Samson St. *Roch* 3C **28**
Sam Swire St. *M15* 2D **108**
Samuel La. *Shaw* 5C **42**
Samuel Ogden St.
M1 . . . . .5E **95** (2B **10**)
Samuel St. *M19* 1D **126**
Samuel St. *Bury* 2E **37**
Samuel St. *Fail* 3F **85**
Samuel St. *Holl* 3E **117**
Samuel St. *Midd* 5A **54**
Samuel St. *Roch* 3C **40**
Samuel St. *Stoc* 6F **127**
Sanby Av. *M18* 3E **111**
Sanby Rd. *M18* 3E **111**
Sanctuary Clo. *M15* 2F **109**
Sanctuary, The.
M15 . . . . . . .1C **108** (6F **9**)
Sandacre Rd. *M23* 4H **135**
Sandal Ct. *M40* 2A **96**
Sandal St. *M40* 2A **96**
Sandbach Av. *M14* 1D **124**
Sandbach Rd. *Sale* 6F **123**
Sandbach Rd. *Stoc* 5G **111**
Sandbach Wlk. *Chea* 1C **150**
Sandbank Gdns.
Whitw 3G **15**
Sand Banks. *Bolt* 5D **18**
Sandbed. **1D 88**
Sandbed La. *Del* 2A **60**
Sandbed La. *Moss* 1E **89**
Sandbrook Pk. *Roch* 1E **41**
Sandbrook Way. *Dent* . . .2F **113**
Sandbrook Way. *Roch* . . .1E **41**
Sandby Dri. *Marp B* 3F **143**
Sanderling Rd. *Stoc* 6G **141**
Sanderson Clo. *Wors* 4A **78**
Sanderson Ct. *M40* 6G **83**
Sanderson St. *M40* 6G **83**
Sanderson St. *Bury* 2E **37**
Sanderstead Dri. *M9* 6G **69**
Sandfield Dri. *Los* 1A **44**
Sandfield Rd. *Roch* 6B **28**
Sandfold. *Stoc* 5G **111**
Sandfold La. *M19* 5E **111**
(in two parts)
Sandford Av. *M18* 1F **111**
Sandford Clo. *Bolt* 1G **33**
Sandford Rd. *Sale* 6F **123**
Sandford St. *Rad* 3B **50**
Sandford St.
Salf 2C **94** (1E **5**)
Sandgate Av. *M11* 3F **97**
Sandgate Av. *Rad* 2B **64**
Sandgate Dri. *Urm* 3E **105**
Sandgate Rd. *Chad* 3H **71**
Sandgate Rd. *W'fld* 2F **67**
Sandham St. *Bolt* 3B **46**
Sandham Wlk. *Bolt* 3B **46**
Sandheys. *Dent* 2F **113**
Sandheys Gro. *M18* 3G **111**
Sandhill Clo. *Bolt* 3B **46**
Sandhill La.
Marp B & Chis 1H **143**
Sandhill St. *Hyde* 4D **114**
Sandhill Wlk. *M22* 3H **147**
Sand Hole La. *Roch* 6A **26**
(Bury Rd.)
Sand Hole La. *Roch* 4F **41**
(Hill Top Dri.)
Sand Hole Rd. *Kear* 3A **64**
Sandhurst Av. *M20* 3E **125**
Sandhurst Clo. *Bury* 2H **35**
Sandhurst Ct. *Bolt* 1G **47**
Sandhurst Dri. *Bolt* 1G **47**
Sandhurst Dri. *Wilm* 6G **159**
Sandhurst Rd. *M20* 1F **137**
(in two parts)
Sandhurst Rd. *Stoc* 6B **140**
Sandhutton St. *M9* 2F **83**
Sandilands Rd. *M23* 3D **134**
Sandilea Ct. Salf 2F 81
(off Kellbrook Cres.)
Sandileigh Av. *M20* 4F **125**
Sandileigh Av. *Chea* 5C **138**
Sandileigh Av. *Hale* 2H **145**
Sandileigh Av. *Stoc* 5B **128**
Sandileigh Dri. *Hale* 2H **145**
Sandimoss Ct. *Sale* 5H **121**
Sandiway. *Bram* 3G **151**
Sandiway. *Bred* 6F **129**
Sandiway. *Heyw* 3G **39**
Sandiway. *Irlam* 5E **103**
Sandi Way. *P'wich* 6E **67**
Sandiway Clo. *Marp* 3D **142**
Sandiway Dri. *M20* 6E **125**
Sandiway Pl. *Alt* 6F **133**
Sandiway Rd. *Alt* 5F **133**
Sandiway Rd. *Hand* 2H **159**
Sandiway Rd. *Sale* 5H **121**
Sandmere Wlk. *M9* 6G **69**
Sandon St. *Bolt* 3H **45**
Sandown Av. *Salf* 3E **93**
Sandown Clo. *Oldh* 6E **57**
Sandown Clo. *Wilm* 1G **167**
Sandown Cres. *M18* 4F **111**
Sandown Cres. *L Lev* 5A **48**
Sandown Dri. *Dent* 1H **129**
Sandown Dri. *Haleb* 1D **156**
Sandown Dri. *Sale* 6G **121**
Sandown Gdns. *Urm* . . .5C **104**
Sandown Rd. *Bolt* 2G **33**
Sandown Rd. *Bury* 4E **51**
Sandown Rd. *Haz G* 3F **153**
Sandown Rd. *Stoc* 3D **138**
Sandown St. *M18* 1G **111**
Sandpiper Clo. *Duk* 6C **100**
Sandpiper Clo. *Farn* 2B **62**
Sandpiper Clo. *Roch* 4B **26**
Sandpiper Dri. *Stoc* 5F **139**
Sandpits. *Heyw* 5H **39**
Sandray Clo. *Bolt* 2D **44**
Sandray Gro. *Salf* 4E **93**
Sandridge Clo. *Kear* 1G **63**
Sandridge Wlk. *M12* 1A **110**
Sandringham Av. *Aud* . . .1D **112**
Sandringham Av.
Dent 4A **112**
Sandringham Av. *Stal* . . .2E **101**
Sandringham Clo.
Bow 3B **144**
Sandringham Ct. M9 . . . .4C 68
(off Deanswood Dri.)
Sandringham Ct. *Sale* . . .3C **134**
Sandringham Ct.
Wilm 3D **166**
Sandringham Dri.
Duk 6D **100**
Sandringham Dri.
G'mnt 2A **22**
Sandringham Dri. *Miln* . . .5G **29**
Sandringham Dri.
Poy 4D **162**
Sandringham Dri.
Stoc 2C **138**
Sandringham Grange.
P'wich 6A **68**
Sandringham Rd.
Bred 6C **128**
Sandringham Rd.
Chea H 2C **150**
Sandringham Rd.
Haz G 3F **153**
Sandringham Rd.
Hyde 2C **130**
Sandringham Rd.
Wors 5C **76**
Sandringham St. *M18* . . .3E **111**
Sandringham Way.
Rytn 1A **56**
Sandringham Way.
Wilm 3D **166**
Sands Av. *Chad* 6D **54**
Sands Clo. *Hyde* 6H **115**
Sandsend Clo. *M8* 6A **82**
Sandsend Rd. *Urm* 4E **105**
Sandstone Rd. *Miln* 4F **29**
Sandstone Way. *M21* . . .2B **124**
Sand St. *M40* 1G **95**
Sand St. *Stal* 5D **100**
Sands Wlk. *Hyde* 6H **115**
Sandwell Dri. *Sale* 3B **122**
Sandwich Rd. *Eccl* 2H **91**
Sandwich St. *Wors* 1F **77**
Sandwick Cres. *Bolt* 2H **45**
Sandwood Av. *Bolt* 2C **44**
Sandy Acre. *Moss* 3E **89**
Sandy Bank. *Shaw* 5D **42**
Sandy Bank Av. *Hyde* . . .6H **115**
Sandybank Clo. *Had* 3G **117**
Sandy Bank Ct. *Hyde* . . .6H **115**
Sandy Bank Rd. *M8* 3B **82**
Sandy Bank Wlk.
Hyde 6H **115**
Sandybrook Clo. *T'ton* . . .5H **21**
Sandy Brow. *M9* 1F **83**
Sandy Clo. *Bury* 3D **50**
Sandy Ga. Clo. *Swin* 4E **79**
Sandy Gro. *Duk* 4B **100**
Sandy Gro. *Salf* 2E **93**
Sandy Gro. *Swin* 3F **79**
Sandy Haven Clo.
Hyde 6H **115**
Sandy Haven Wlk.
Hyde 6H **115**
Sandyhill Ct. *M9* 6C **68**
Sandyhill Rd. *M9* 6C **68**
Sandyhills. *Bolt* 3A **46**
Sandylands Dri. *P'wich* . . .2E **81**
Sandy La. *M21* 1H **123**
Sandy La. *M23* 4D **134**
Sandy La. *Dob* 5A **60**
Sandy La. *Droy* 2C **98**
Sandy La. *Duk* 5B **100**
Sandy La. *Irlam* 4E **103**
Sandy La. *Midd* 1B **70**
Sandy La. *P'wich* 6D **66**
Sandy La. *Roch* 4E **27**
Sandy La. *Rom* 1A **142**
Sandy La. *Rytn* 3B **56**
Sandy La. *Salf* 2E **93**
Sandy La. *Stoc* 6G **127**
Sandy La. *Stret* 6B **106**
Sandy La. *Wilm* 1A **166**
Sandy Meade. *P'wich* 6D **66**
Sandys Av. *Oldh* 6B **72**
Sandyshot Wlk. *M22* . . .2D **148**
Sandy Va. *Duk* 4C **100**
Sandy Wlk. *Rytn* 3B **56**
Sandywell Clo. *M11* 6F **97**
Sandywell St. *M11* 5F **97**
Sandywood. *Salf* 2E **93**
Sangster Ct. *Salf* 5G **93**
Sankey Gro. *M9* 6D **68**
Sankey St. *Bury* 3B **36**
Santiago St. *M14* 4F **109**
Santley St. *M12* 4C **110**
Santon Av. *M14* 1A **126**
Sapling Gro. *Sale* 1F **133**
Sapling Rd. *Bolt* 5F **45**
Sapling Rd. *Swin* 6D **78**
Sarah Butterworth Ct.
Roch 4B **28**
Sarah Butterworth St.
Roch 5B **28**
Sarah Jane St. *Miln* 5F **29**
Sarah Moor. **6D 56**
Sarah St. *M11* 5B **96**
Sarah St. *Eccl* 4D **90**
Sarah St. *Midd* 1H **69**
Sarah St. *Oldh* 1B **86**
Sarah St. *Rams* 2B **12**
Sarah St. *Roch* 5A **28**
Sarah St. *Shaw* 2E **57**
Sardina Ct. *Salf* 4H **81**
Sargent Dri. *M16* 3C **108**
Sargent Rd. *Bred* 1D **140**
Sark Rd. *M21* 5G **107**
Sarn Av. *M22* 1B **148**
Sarnesfield Clo. *M12* . . .3C **110**
Satinwood Wlk. *Salf* 2E **5**
Saturn Gro. *Salf* 1A **94**
Saunton Av. *Bolt* 2H **33**
Saunton Rd. *Open* 5F **97**
Sautridge Clo. *Midd* 6D **40**
Savernake Rd. *Woodl* . . .4A **130**
Savick Av. *Bolt* 6G **33**
Saville Rd. *Gat* 5F **137**
Saville Rd. *Rad* 6F **35**
Saville St. *Bolt* 6C **32**
Saville St. *Midd* 2D **70**
Saviours Ter. *Bolt* 2G **45**
Savio Way. *Midd* 2A **70**
Savoy Ct. *W'fld* 5C **50**
Savoy Dri. *Rytn* 5B **56**
Savoy St. *Oldh* 4F **73**
Savoy St. *Roch* 3E **27**
Sawley Av. *L'boro* 2E **17**
Sawley Av. *Oldh* 5H **73**
Sawley Av. *W'fld* 5D **50**
Sawley Dri. *Chea H* 1D **160**
Sawley Rd.
M40 . . . . . . .1H **95** (1H **7**)
Saw Mill Way. *L'boro* 4D **16**
Sawston Wlk. *M40* 6C **70**
Saw St. *Bolt* 3A **32**
Sawyer Brow. *Hyde* 3D **114**
Sawyer St. *Bury* 1H **35**
Sawyer St. *Roch* 2H **27**
Saxbrook Wlk. *M22* 2D **148**
Saxby Av. *Brom X* 3D **18**
Saxby St. *Salf* 6A **80**
Saxelby Dri. *M8* 4D **82**
Saxfield Dri. *M23* 5A **136**
Saxholme Wlk. *M22* 3A **148**
Saxon Av. *M8* 2C **82**
Saxon Av. *Duk* 5A **100**
Saxon Clo. *Bury* 3H **35**
Saxon Dri. *Aud* 6E **99**

Saxon Dri. Chad 1E 71
Saxon Dri. Droy 3B 98
　　　　(in two parts)
Saxonholme Rd. Roch 6C 40
Saxon Ho. M16 . . . . .4B 108
Saxon Ho. L'boro 4G 17
Saxonside. Midd 4G 53
Saxon St. M40 . . . . .2A 96
Saxon St. Dent 4F 113
Saxon St. Droy 3B 98
Saxon St. Midd 1B 70
Saxon St. Moss 6F 75
Saxon St. Oldh 2G 73
Saxon St. Rad 4F 49
Saxon St. Roch 4F 27
Saxthorpe Clo. Sale 4F 121
Saxthorpe Wlk. M12 . . . . .2A 110
Saxwood Av. M9 . . . . .2F 83
Saxwood Clo. Roch 2B 26
Scafell Av. Ash L 1F 99
Scafell Clo. H Lane 5C 154
Scafell Clo. Oldh 6D 56
　　　　(in two parts)
Scalby Wlk. M22 . . . . . . .4B 148
Scale St. Salf 4G 93
Scant Row. Hor 2A 30
Scarborough St. M40 . . . .3A 84
Scarcroft Rd. M12 . . . . . .2C 110
Scarfield Dri. Roch 2A 26
Scargill Clo. M14 . . . . . . .1G 125
Scargill Rd. Bolt 3E 45
Scarisbrick Av. M20 . . . . .6H 125
Scarisbrick Rd. M19 . . . . .1B 126
Scarr Av. Rad 5A 50
Scarr Dri. Roch 6F 15
Scarr La. Shaw 6G 43
Scarr Ter. Whitw 3H 15
Scarr Wheel. Salf 5G 81
Scarsdale Av. Bolt 4E 31
Scarsdale Rd. M14 . . . . . .3A 110
Scarsdale St. Salf 2H 93
Scarthwood Clo. Bolt 6A 20
Scawfell Av. Bolt 3D 32
Scawton Wlk. M9 . . . . . . .4U 68
Schofield Pl. L'boro 5H 17
Ochofield Rd. Droy 4D 90
Sohofield St. Eool 4C 90
Schofield St. M11 . . . . . . .4E 97
Schofield St. Fail 3F 85
Eohofield Ct. Hayw 3F 39
Schofield St. L'boro 3G 17
Schofield St. Miln 6G 29
Schofield St. Oldh 6C 72
Schofield St. Rad 3H 49
Schofield St. Roch 1G 41
Schofield St. Rytn 2B 56
Schofield St. Summ 5H 17
Scholars Dri. M20 . . . . . .2E 125
Scholar's Way. Midd 6H 53
Scholes Clo. Salf 3B 82
Scholes Dri. M40 . . . . . . .1E 85
Scholes La. P'wich 6F 67
Scholes St. Bury 2A 36
Scholes St. Chad 5G 71
Scholes St. Fail 2G 85
Scholes St. Oldh 2E 73
Scholes St. Roch 4C 40
Scholes St. Swin 3G 79
Scholes Wlk. P'wich 6G 67
Scholey St. Bolt 2C 46
Scholfield Av. Urm 6H 105
School Av. Ash L 5H 87
School Av. Stret 4F 107
School Brow. Bury 3D 36
School Brow. Rom 1G 141
School Brow. Wors 5H 77
School Clo. Poy 3F 163
School Ct. M4 . . . . .3G 95 (4E 7)
School Ct. Eger 1C 18
　　　(off Bk. Water St.)
School Ct. Rams 3A 12
School Ct. Stoc 5H 139

School Cres. Stal 2D 100
School Dri. Duk 1C 114
School Gro. P'wich 1F 81
School Gro. W. M20 . . . . .3G 125
School Gro. Wlk. Oldh 1H 85
School La. M9 . . . . .1E 83
School La.
　　　M20 & M19 . . . . . .6F 125
School La. A'wrth 3G 25
School La. Bury 3E 23
School La. Cad 4B 118
School La. Chea H 5B 150
　　　　(in two parts)
School La. Comp 6F 131
School La. Dun M 4A 132
School La. Hyde 2C 130
School La. Irlam 5D 102
School La. Poy 4E 163
　　　　(in two parts)
School La. Roch 4H 27
School La. Stoc 4E 127
School M. Bram 6G 151
School Rd. Eccl 5E 91
School Rd. Fail 4F 85
School Rd. Hale 2H 145
School Rd. Hand 3H 159
School Rd. Oldh 1H 85
School Rd. Sale 4B 122
　　　　(in two parts)
School Rd. Stret 5C 106
Schools Hill. Chea 2H 149
Schoolside La. Midd 2D 68
Schools Rd. M18 . . . . . . .2G 111
School St. M4 . . . .2F 95 (2B 6)
School St. Brom X 4D 18
School St. Bury 4F 37
School St. Eccl 2D 90
School St. Haz G 3E 153
School St. Heyw 3E 39
School St. L'boro 4C 16
School St. L Lev 4D 40
School St. Oldh 4B 72
School St. Rad 4F 49
School St. Rams 4D 12
Cchool Ct. Roch 6H 27
School St. Salf 1C 94
School St. S'head 3C 74
School St. Upperm 1F 61
School St. Ind. Est.
　　　Haz G 3E 153
School Ter. Midd 5A 54
　　　(off Rochdale Rd.)
School Ter. Whitw 4G 15
　　　　(off Lloyd St.)
School Wlk. M16 . . . . . . .2B 108
School Yd. Stoc 2A 138
Schwabe St. Midd 1E 69
Scobell St. T'ton 6H 21
Scoltock Way. Oldh 2D 72
Scope o' th' La. Bolt 1E 33
Scopton St. Bolt 5G 31
Score St. M11 . . . . .4C 96
Scorton Av. Bolt 6H 33
Scorton Wlk. M40 . . . . . .1D 84
Scotforth Clo.
　　　M15 . . . . .6C 94 (4F 9)
Scotland. M4 . . . .2E 95 (2A 6)
Scotland Hall Rd. M40 . . .6B 84
Scotland La. Bury 3A 24
Scotland Pl. Rams 3E 13
Scotland St. M40 . . . . . . .6C 84
Scotland St. Ash L 2A 100
Scotta Rd. Eccl 5D 90
Scott Av. M21 . . . . .5H 107
Scott Av. Bury 1D 50
Scott Av. Eccl 2E 91
Scott Clo. Stoc 5H 127

Scott Dri. Alt 1H 145
Scott Dri. Marp B 3F 143
Scottfield. Oldh 4C 72
Scottfield Rd. Oldh 4D 72
Scott Ga. Aud 6E 99
Scott Rd. Dent 6E 113
Scott Rd. Droy 3A 98
Scott Rd. P'wich 6D 66
Scotts Ind. Pk. Roch 5A 28
Scott St. Miln 1D 42
Scott St. Oldh 4D 72
Scott St. Rad 2D 64
Scott St. Salf 1A 94
Scout Dri. M23 . . . . .1F 147
Southead. 1D 74
Scout Vw. T'ton 5A 22
Scovell St. Salf 5H 81
Scowcroft La. Shaw 2E 57
Scowcroft St. Bolt 4D 32
Scribe Pl. Irlam 3C 118
Scroggins La. Part 5C 118
　　　　(in two parts)
Scropton St. M40 . . . . . . .5F 83
Seabright Wlk. M11 . . . . .4B 96
Seabrook Cres. Urm 3E 105
Seabrook Rd. M40 . . . . . .1E 97
Seacombe Av. M14 . . . . .6E 109
Seacombe Gro. Stoc 3D 138
Seaford Rd. Bolt 5A 20
Seaford Rd. Salf 6F 81
Seaford Wlk. M9 . . . . .6E 69
Seaford Wlk. Chad 3H 71
Seaforth Rd. Bolt 6C 18
Seaham Dri. Bury 6C 22
Seaham Wlk. M14 . . . . . .4F 109
Sealand Clo. Sale 1E 135
Sealand Dri. Eccl 5C 90
Sealand Ho. P'wich 4G 67
Sealand Rd. M23 . . . . . . .1F 135
Sealand Way. Hand 3H 159
Seale Av. Aud 6D 98
Sealey Wlk. M40 . . . . .1A 96
　　　　(off Filby Wlk.)
Seal Rd. Bram 5H 151
Seamons Dri. Alt 6D 132
Seamons Rd. Alt 5C 132
Seamons Wlk. Alt 6D 132
Searby Rd. M18 . . . . .3D 110
Searness Rd. Midd 5E 53
Seascale Av. M11 . . . . . . .2D 96
Seascale Wlk. Midd 5G 53
Seathwaite Rd. Farn 2B 62
Seathwaite Wlk. M18 . . . .2E 111
Seatoller Ct. Rytn 3C 56
　　　　(off Shaw St.)
Seatoller Dri. Midd 6E 53
Seaton Clo. Haz G 4D 152
Seaton M. Ash L 1E 99
Seaton Rd. Bolt 3G 31
Seaton Way. M14 . . . . . . .3E 109
Sebastopol Wlk.
　　　M4 . . . . .3G 95 (4E 7)
Second Av. M11 . . . . .3E 97
Second Av. Bolt 6F 31
Second Av. Bury 1H 37
Second Av. Carr 6G 89
Second Av. L Lev 3H 47
Second Av. Oldh 1A 86
Second Av. Poy 6D 162
Second Av. Swin 6D 78
Second Av. Traf P 2D 106
Second St. Bolt 1D 30
Section St. Bolt 1B 46
　　　　(off Soho St.)
Sedan Clo. Salf 4G 93
Sedburgh Clo. Sale 6F 121
Sedbury Clo. M23 . . . . . .2F 135
　　　　(in two parts)
Seddon Av. M18 . . . . . . .1F 111
Seddon Av. Rad 2B 50
Seddon Clo. Rad 3G 49
Seddon Gdns. Rad 1A 64

Seddon La. Rad 1A 64
Seddon Rd. Hale 3F 145
Seddons Av. Bury 5G 35
Seddon St. M12 . . . . .5D 110
Seddon St. L Hul 4B 62
Seddon St. L Lev 4B 48
Seddon St. Rad 4G 49
Sedgeborough Rd.
　　　M16 . . . . .3C 108
Sedge Clo. Stoc 1A 128
Sedgefield Clo. Salf 3G 93
Sedgefield Dri. Bolt 2F 31
Sedgefield Pk. Oldh 3H 73
Sedgefield Rd. Rad 1F 65
Sedgeford Wlk. M23 . . . . .1F 135
Sedgeford Clo. Wilm 6G 159
Sedgeford Rd. M40 . . . . . .6F 83
Sedgemoor Clo.
　　　Chea H 3D 150
Sedgemoor Va. Bolt 3H 33
Sedgemoor Way. Oldh . . .2C 72
Sedgley Av. P'wich 1G 81
Sedgley Av. Roch 1H 41
Sedgley Bldgs. Droy 5A 98
Sedgley Clo. Midd 2C 70
Sedgley Ct. Midd 2C 70
Sedgley Park. 1G 81
Sedgley Pk. Rd. P'wich . . .1G 81
Sedgley Pk. Trad. Est.
　　　P'wich 2F 81
Sedgley Rd. M8 . . . . .3C 82
Sedgley St. Midd 2C 70
Seedfield. 6E 23
Seedfield Rd. Bury 6F 23
Seedley. 2F 93
Seedley Av. L Hul 5D 62
Seedley Pk. Rd. Salf 3E 93
Seedley St. M14 . . . . .4F 109
Seedley Ter. 2E 93
Seedley Vw. Rd. Salf 2E 93
Seed St. Bolt 6G 31
Seel St. Moss 2D 88
Sefton Clo.
　　　M13 . . . .1F 109 (5D 10)
Sefton Clo. Midd 1G 69
Sefton Clo. Oldh 3C 57
Sefton Ct. Bolt 5A 32
　　　　(off School Hill)
Sefton Ct. Bury 5F 23
Sefton Cres. Sale 3B 122
Sefton Dri. Bury 5G 23
Sefton Dri. Swin 5D 78
Sefton Dri. Wilm 5G 159
Sefton Dri. Wors 6A 78
Sefton Rd. M21 . . . . .1H 123
Sefton Rd. Bolt 3F 31
Sefton Rd. Midd 1G 69
Sefton Rd. Rad 6E 35
Sefton Rd. Sale 4B 122
Sefton Rd. Swin 2F 79
Sefton St. M8 . . . . .3C 82
Sefton St. Bury 5F 23
Sefton St. Heyw 4G 39
Sefton St. Oldh 1H 85
Sefton St. Rad 6A 50
Sefton St. W'fld 2D 66
Segal Clo. Salf 4H 81
Selborne Rd. M21 . . . . . .6H 107
Selbourne Clo. Stoc 5G 111
Selbourne St. Oldh 2E 87
Selby Av. Chad 5G 55
Selby Av. W'fld 5D 50
Selby Clo. Miln 5E 29
Selby Clo. Poy 2D 162
Selby Clo. Rad 2B 50
Selby Clo. Stret 4A 106
Selby Dri. Salf 2B 92
Selby Dri. Urm 2B 104
Selby Gdns. Chea H 1D 160
Selby Rd. Midd 4H 53
Selby Rd. Stret 4A 106

Selby St. *M11* 5C **96**
Selby St. *Roch* 3B **28**
Selby St. *Stoc* 5F **127**
Selby Wlk. *Bury* 3F **35**
Selden St. *Oldh* 4B **72**
Selham Wlk.
   M13 . . . . . .6G **95** (4E **11**)
Selhurst Av. *M11* 3E **97**
Selkirk Av. *Oldh* 5B **72**
Selkirk Dri. *M9* 6H **69**
Selkirk Pl. *Heyw* 4C **38**
Selkirk Rd. *Bolt* 6B **18**
Selkirk Rd. *Chad* 5F **71**
Sellars Sq. *Droy* 5A **98**
Sellers Way. *Chad* 6G **71**
Selsby Av. *Eccl* 3D **90**
Selsey Av. *Sale* 6H **121**
Selsey Av. *Stoc* 4B **138**
Selsey Dri. *M20* 3G **137**
Selside Wlk. *M14* 1G **125**
Selstead Rd. *M22* 4H **147**
Selston Rd. *M9* 5D **68**
Selwood Wlk. M9 . . . . . .*4F 83*
   (off Carisbrook St.)
Selworth Av. *Sale* 5E **123**
Selworth Clo. *Timp* 5G **133**
Selworthy Rd. *M16* 3C **108**
Selwyn Av. *M9* 3F **83**
Selwyn Clo. *Oldh* 4C **72**
Selwyn Dri. *Chea H* 6E **151**
Selwyn St. *Bolt* 1C **46**
Selwyn St. *Oldh* 4C **72**
Senior Av. *M14* 2A **126**
Senior Rd. *Eccl* 5C **90**
Senior St. *Salf* 2C **94** (2F **5**)
Sepal Clo. *Stoc* 6A **112**
Sepia Gro. *Midd* 6H **53**
Sequoia St. *M9* 3G **83**
Sergeants La. *W'fld* 2A **66**
Serin Clo. *Stoc* 6F **141**
Service St. *Stoc* 3D **138**
Sesame Gdns. *Irlam* 4G **103**
Set St. *Stal* 4D **100**
Settle Clo. *Bury* 3F **35**
Settle St. *Bolt* 4H **45**
Settle St. *L Lev* 4C **48**
Settstones La. *Upperm* . . .6D **60**
Sevenacres. *Del* 2H **59**
Seven Acres Country Pk.
   . . . . .4F **33**
Seven Acres La. *Roch* 1A **26**
Sevenoaks Av. *Stoc* 5C **126**
Sevenoaks Av. *Urm* 3F **105**
Sevenoaks Dri. *Bolt* 4A **46**
Sevenoaks Dri. *Swin* 5G **79**
Sevenoaks Rd. *Chea* 5F **137**
Sevenoaks Wlk.
   M13 . . . . . .2G **109** (6F **11**)
   (off Lauderdale Cres.)
Seven Stiles Dri.
   Marp 4C **142**
Seventh Av. *Oldh* 2A **86**
Severn Clo. *Alt* 5E **133**
Severn Clo. *Bury* 4F **23**
Severn Dri. *Bram* 1E **161**
Severn Dri. *Miln* 5G **29**
Severn Rd. *Chad* 1F **71**
Severn Rd. *Heyw* 2C **38**
Severn Rd. *Oldh* 2H **85**
   (in two parts)
Severnside Trad. Est.
   Traf P 2B **106**
Severn Way. *Kear* 3B **64**
Severn Way. *Stoc* 4H **127**
Sevilles Bldgs. *Moss* 1E **89**
Seville St. *Rytn* 5C **56**
Seville St. *Shaw* 2E **57**
Sewell Way. *L Hul* 6B **62**
Sewerby St. *M16* 3D **108**
Sexa St. *M11* 5F **97**
Sexton St. *Heyw* 3E **39**
Seymour Av. *M11* 3F **97**

Seymour Clo. *M16* 2A **108**
Seymour Ct. Rad *4H 49*
   (in two parts)
Seymour Ct. *Salf* 3B **82**
Seymour Ct. *Stoc* 1A **138**
Seymour Dri. *Bolt* 5G **19**
Seymour Gro. *M16* 2H **107**
Seymour Gro. *Farn* 6C **46**
Seymour Gro. *Marp* 5C **142**
Seymour Gro. *Roch* 2H **41**
Seymour Gro. *Sale* 5B **122**
Seymour Gro. *Timp* 6A **134**
Seymour Pl. *M16* 2H **107**
Seymour Rd. *M8* 2B **82**
Seymour Rd. *Bolt* 2A **32**
Seymour Rd. *Chea H* . . .5C **150**
Seymour Rd. *Stoc* 6B **140**
Seymour Rd. S. *M11* 3F **97**
Seymour St. *M18* 1F **111**
Seymour St. *Bolt* 5G **19**
Seymour St. *Dent* 4D **112**
   (in two parts)
Seymour St. *Heyw* 4E **39**
   (in two parts)
Seymour St. *Rad* 4H **49**
   (Church St. W.)
Seymour St. *Rad* 4H **49**
   (Darbyshire St.)
Seymour Wlk. Rad *4H 49*
   (off Haworth Wlk.)
Shackleton Ct. *M40* 1E **97**
Shackleton Gro. *Bolt* 3C **30**
Shackleton St. *Eccl* 2E **91**
   (in two parts)
Shackliffe Rd. *M40* 1B **84**
Shaddock Av. *Roch* 2B **26**
Shade Av. *S'head* 4B **74**
Shade St. *Haz G* 3E **153**
Shade Ter. *H Lane* 6D **154**
Shadow Brook Av.
   M23 . . . . .1G **147**
Shadowbrook Clo.
   Oldh 6C **56**
Shadow Moss Rd.
   M22 . . . . .6C **148**
Shadows La. *Moss* 5G **75**
Shadows M. *Moss* 5G **75**
Shadwell St. E. *Heyw* 2G **39**
Shadwell St. W. *Heyw* 2F **39**
Shadworth Clo. *Moss* 5G **75**
Shadworth La. *G'fld* 6H **75**
Shady La. *M23* 4D **134**
Shady La. *Brom X* 5F **19**
Shady Oak Rd. *Stoc* 5F **141**
Shaftesbury Av.
   Chea H 4E **151**
Shaftesbury Av. *Eccl* 5E **91**
Shaftesbury Av. *L'boro* . . .6D **16**
Shaftesbury Av. *Timp* . . .6B **134**
Shaftesbury Clo. *Bolt* 4A **32**
Shaftesbury Dri. *Heyw* . . .5E **39**
Shaftesbury Dri. *Ward* 3B **16**
Shaftesbury Gdns.
   Urm 5G **103**
Shaftesbury Rd. *M8* 4C **82**
Shaftesbury Rd. *Stoc* . . .5C **138**
Shaftesbury Rd. *Swin* 4F **79**
Shafton Wlk. *M40* 1D **84**
Shakespeare Av. *Bury* . . .1D **50**
Shakespeare Av. *Dent* . . .1F **129**
Shakespeare Av. *Mill* 1H **101**
Shakespeare Av. *Rad* 3E **49**
Shakespeare Clo.
   L'boro 6G **17**
Shakespeare Cres.
   Droy 3A **98**
Shakespeare Cres. *Eccl* . . .3F **91**
Shakespeare Dri.
   Chea 5B **138**
   (in two parts)
Shakespeare Rd. *Bred* . . .6E **129**
Shakespeare Rd. *Droy* . . .3A **98**

Shakespeare Rd.
   Oldh 5F **57**
Shakespeare Rd.
   P'wich 6D **66**
Shakespeare Rd. *Swin* . . .3D **78**
Shakespeare Wlk.
   M13 . . . . . .1G **109** (6F **11**)
Shakleton Av. *M9* 6A **70**
Shalbourne Rd. *Wors* 6E **63**
Shaldon Dri. *M40* 1G **97**
Shalfleet Clo. *Bolt* 6A **20**
Shamrock Ct. *Wors* 6D **62**
Shandon Av. *M22* 2A **136**
Shanklin Clo. *M21* 6G **107**
Shanklin Clo. *Dent* 1H **129**
Shanklin Ho. *M21* 6G **107**
Shanklin Wlk. *Bolt* 2E **47**
Shanklyn Av. *Urm* 5E **105**
Shanley Ct. *Chad* 1H **71**
Shannon Clo. *Heyw* 2C **38**
Shannon Rd. *M22* 1C **148**
Shap Av. *Timp* 6D **134**
Shap Cres. *Wors* 2H **77**
Shap Dri. *Wors* 1H **77**
Shapwick Clo. *M9* 4F **83**
Sharcott Clo. *M16* 3D **108**
Shardlow Clo.
   M40 . . . . . . .1H **95** (1G **7**)
Shargate Clo. *Wilm* 6G **159**
Sharman St. *Bolt* 2D **46**
Sharnbrook Wlk. *M8* 1A **82**
Sharnbrook Wlk. *Bolt* 4D **32**
Sharnford Clo. *Bolt* 1D **46**
Sharnford Sq. *M12* 1C **110**
Sharon. 4G **75**
Sharon Av. *Grass* 4G **75**
Sharon Clo. *Ash L* 4E **99**
Sharples. 1H **31**
Sharples Av. *Bolt* 5C **18**
Sharples Dri. *Bury* 1F **35**
Sharples Hall. *Bolt* 5D **18**
Sharples Hall Dri. *Bolt* . . .5D **18**
Sharples Hall Fold.
   Bolt 6D **18**
Sharples Hall M. *Bolt* 5D **18**
Sharples Hall St. *Oldh* . . .6H **57**
Sharples Leisure Cen.
   . . . . .6D **18**
Sharples Pk. *Bolt* 1H **31**
Sharples St. *Stoc* 6G **127**
Sharples Va. *Bolt* 2A **32**
Sharples Va. Cotts.
   Bolt 2A **32**
Sharp St. *M4* 2F **95** (2C **6**)
Sharp St. *Midd* 1A **70**
Sharp St. *P'wich* 5E **67**
Sharp St. *Wors* 6G **63**
Sharrington Dri. *M23* . . .5E **135**
Sharrow Wlk. M9 . . . . . .*4G 83*
   (off Broadwell Dri.)
Sharston. 4B **136**
Sharston Grn. Bus. Pk.
   M22 . . . . .5D **136**
Sharston Ind. Area.
   M22 . . . . .4C **136**
Sharston Rd. *Shar I* 5B **136**
Shaving La. *Wors* 2F **77**
Shaw. 1F **57**
Shaw Av. *Hyde* 1D **130**
Shawbrook Av. *Wors* 3D **76**
Shawbrook Rd. *M19* 3B **126**
Shawbury Gro. *Sale* 1H **133**
Shawbury Rd. *M23* 1H **147**
Shawbury St. *Midd* 2C **70**
Shawclough. 1G **27**
Shawclough Clo. *Roch* . . .6D **14**
Shawclough Dri. *Roch* . . .6C **14**
Shawclough Ri. Roch *1F 27*
   (off Shawclough Rd.)
Shawclough Rd. *Roch* . . .5C **14**
Shawclough Trad. Est.
   Roch 6D **14**

Shawclough Way.
   Roch 6C **14**
Shawcroft Clo. *Shaw* 2E **57**
Shawcross Fold. *Stoc* . . .1H **139**
Shawcross La. *M22* 3C **136**
Shawcross St. *Hyde* 1D **130**
Shawcross St. *Salf* 4F **93**
Shawcross St. *Stoc* 3A **140**
Shawdene Rd. *M22* 3A **136**
Shaw Edge. 3F **57**
Shawe Hall Av. *Urm* 1C **120**
Shawe Hall Cres. *Urm* . .1C **120**
Shawe Rd. *Urm* 5C **104**
Shawe Vw. *Urm* 5C **104**
Shawfield. 1B **26**
Shawfield Clo. *M14* 1E **125**
Shawfield Ct. *Stoc* 6D **140**
Shawfield Gro. *Roch* 1B **26**
Shawfield La. *Roch* 2A **26**
   (in two parts)
Shawfield Rd. *Had* 4H **117**
Shawfields. *Stal* 2H **101**
Shawfold. *Shaw* 6F **43**
Shawford Cres. *M40* 1C **84**
Shawford Rd. *M40* 1C **84**
Shaw Ga. *Upperm* 2H **61**
Shawgreen Clo.
   M15 . . . . . . .1B **108** (6D **8**)
Shawhall. 2F **115**
   (Hyde)
Shaw Hall. 3H **75**
   (Oldham)
Shaw Hall. *M14* 3H **109**
Shaw Hall Av. *Hyde* 2F **115**
Shaw Hall Bank. 4H **75**
Shaw Hall Bank Rd.
   G'fld 4H **75**
Shaw Hall Clo. *G'fld* 4H **75**
Shawhead Dri. *Fail* 5F **85**
Shaw Heath. 4G **139**
Shaw Heath. *Stoc* 3G **139**
Shawheath Clo.
   M15 . . . . . . .1B **108** (6D **8**)
Shawhill Wlk. *M40* 3A **96**
Shaw Ho. Farn *2F 63*
   (off Moorfield Chase)
Shaw Ho. *Shaw* 2F **57**
Shaw La. *Glos* 5G **117**
   (in two parts)
Shaw La. *Roch* 2G **29**
Shawlea Av. *M19* 3A **126**
Shaw Lee. *Dig* 3D **60**
Shaw Moor Av. *Stal* 4G **101**
Shaw Rd. *Miln* 2F **43**
Shaw Rd. *Oldh* 6E **57**
Shaw Rd. *Roch* 4H **41**
Shaw Rd. *Rytn* 4C **56**
Shaw Rd. *Stoc* 4D **126**
Shaw Rd. S. *Stoc* 5G **139**
   (in two parts)
Shaws. *Upperm* 2G **61**
Shaws Fold. *S'head* 3D **74**
Shaws Fold. *Styal* 3D **158**
Shaw Side. 2F **57**
Shaws La. *Upperm* 1G **61**
Shaw's Rd. *Alt* 1F **145**
Shaw St. *M3* 2D **94** (2B **5**)
Shaw St. *Ash L* 2B **100**
Shaw St. *Bolt* 2A **46**
Shaw St. *Bury* 4C **36**
Shaw St. *G'fld* 3E **61**
Shaw St. *Mot* 3C **116**
Shaw St. *Oldh* 1D **72**
Shaw St. *Roch* 1B **28**
Shaw St. *Rytn* 3C **56**
Shaw St. *S'head* 3C **74**
Shaw Ter. *Duk* 4A **100**
Shay Av. *Hale* 4E **147**
Shayfield Av. *M22* 6B **136**
Shayfield Av. *Chad* 2E **71**
Shayfield Dri. *M22* 5B **136**

Shayfield Rd. *M22* 6B **136**
Shay La. *Haleh* 4C **146**
Sheader Dri. *Salf* 3C **92**
Sheaf Fld. Wlk. *Rad* 3G **49**
Sheard Av. *Ash L* 5H **87**
Sheardhall Av. *Dis* 2H **165**
Shearer Way. *Swin* 4B **80**
Shearing Av. *Roch* 2B **26**
Shearsby Clo.
   M15 . . . . .2C **108** (6F **9**)
Shearwater Dri. *Wors* . . .6E **63**
Shearwater Gdns. *Eccl* . . .5C **90**
Shearwater Rd. *Stoc* . . .6F **141**
Sheddings, The. *Bolt* . . .3C **46**
Shed St. *Whitw* 4H **15**
Sheepfoot La. *Oldh* 6B **56**
Sheepfoot La. *P'wich* . . .6H **67**
Sheep Gap. *Roch* 2D **26**
Sheep Ga. Dri. *I'ton* 6G **21**
Sheep Hey. *Rams* 4A **12**
Sheep La. *Wors* 3B **76**
Sheerness St *M18* 2F **111**
Sheffield Rd. *Hyde* 3D **114**
   (in two parts)
Sheffield St.
   M1 . . . . . . .5F **95** (1D **10**)
Sheffield St. *Stoc* 6G **127**
Shefford Clo. *M11* 5B **96**
Sheiling Ct. *Alt* 1E **145**
Shelbourne Av. *Bolt* 4F **31**
Shelden Clo. Glos 6F **117**
   (off Brassington Cres.)
Shelden Fold. Glos 6F **117**
   (off Brassington Cres.)
Shelden M. Glos 6F **117**
Shelden Pl. Glos 6F **117**
   (off Brassington Cres.)
Shelderslow. 3C **74**
Shelderton Clo. *M40* 4A **84**
Sheldon Av. *Urm* 5D **104**
Sheldon Clo. *Farn* 5D **46**
Sheldon Clo. *Part* 6D **118**
Sheldon Ct. *Ash L* 4A **8**
Sheldon Rd. *Haz G* 6E **153**
Sheldon Rd. *Poy* 5A **164**
Sholdon St. *M11* 3D **96**
Sheldrake Clo. *Duk* 6C **100**
Sheldrake Rd. *B'hth* 3D **132**
Sholfield. *Roch* 3B **26**
Sholfield Clo. *Roch* 3B **26**
Shelfield La. *Roch* 2A **26**
Shelford Av. *M18* 3D **110**
Shellbrook Gro. *Wilm* . . .6H **159**
Shelley Av. *Midd* 4B **54**
Shelley Ct. *Chea H* 4C **150**
Shelley Gro. *Droy* 3A **98**
Shelley Gro. *Hyde* 2B **114**
Shelley Ri. *Duk* 6F **101**
Shelley Rd. *Chad* 6F **71**
Shelley Rd. *L Hul* 4C **62**
Shelley Rd. *Oldh* 6G **57**
Shelley Rd. *P'wich* 6D **66**
Shelley Rd. *Stoc* 6F **111**
Shelley Rd. *Swin* 3D **78**
Shelley St. *M40* 3C **84**
Shelley Wlk. *Bolt* 4H **31**
Shelley Way. *Dent* 1F **129**
Shelmerdine Clo. *Mot* . . .5B **116**
Shelmerdine Gdns.
   Salf 1C **92**
Shelton Av. *Sale* 5F **121**
Shenfield Wlk.
   M40 . . . . . .2H **95** (1G **7**)
Shenhurst Clo. *Wilm* 4B **166**
Shentonfield Rd.
   Shar I 5C **136**
Shenton Pk. Av. *Sale* . . .1E **133**
Shenton St. *Hyde* 3A **114**
Shepherd Ct. *Roch* 5B **28**
Shepherd Cross St.
   Bolt 4G **31**

Shepherd Cross St. Ind. Est.
   Bolt 3H **31**
   (off Shepherd Cross St.)
Shepherds Brow.
   Bow 2C **144**
Shepherds Clo. *G'mnt* . .2H **21**
Shepherds Grn. *G'fld* . . .4H **61**
Shepherd St. *M9* 2G **83**
Shepherd St. *Bury* 4D **36**
Shepherd St. *G'mnt* 3H **21**
Shepherd St. *Heyw* 3E **39**
Shepherd St.
   Roch (OL11) 2H **25**
Shepherd St.
   Roch (OL12) 3H **27**
Shepherd St. *Rytn* 3C **56**
   (in two parts)
Shepherds Way. *Miln* . . .6F **29**
Shepherd Wlk. *Dent* . . .1F **129**
Shepley Av. *Bolt* 2G **45**
Shepley Clo. *Duk* 5B **100**
Shepley Clo. *Haz G* 5D **152**
Shepley Dri. *Haz G* 4D **152**
Shepley Ho. *Haz G* 4E **153**
Shepley Ind. Est. N.
   Aud 6F **99**
Shepley Ind. Est. S.
   Aud 1G **113**
Shepley La. *Marp* 2D **154**
Shepley La. Ind. Est.
   Marp 2D **154**
Shepley Rd. *Aud* 1F **113**
Shepley St. *M1* . . .5F **95** (1C **10**)
Shepley St. *Aud* 6F **99**
Shepley St. *Fail* 2G **85**
Shepley St. *Glos* 4G **117**
Shepley St. *Hyde* 5C **114**
Shepley St. *Lees* 3A **74**
Shepley St. *Stal* 3E **101**
Shepton Clo. *Bolt* 4B **18**
Shepton Dri. *M23* 3G **147**
Shepway Ct. *Eccl* 3D **90**
Sheraton Rd. *Oldh* 5C **72**
Sherborne Clo. *Rad* 2D **48**
Sherborne Ho. *Midd* 4A **54**
Sherborne Rd. *Midd* 1H **53**
Sherborne Rd. *Stoc* 4C **138**
Sherborne St.
   M3 & M8 . . . .1C **94** (1F **5**)
   (in two parts)
Sherborne St. Trad. Est.
   M8 . . . . .6C **82**
   (1F **5**)
Sherborne St. W. *Salf* . . .2C **94**
   (1F **5**)
Sherbourne Clo. *Chea H* .1D **160**
Sherbourne Clo. *Oldh* . . .5G **73**
Sherbourne Ct. *P'wich* . . .5E **67**
Sherbourne Dri. *Heyw* . . .2C **38**
Sherbourne Rd. *Bolt* 4E **31**
Sherbourne Rd. *Urm* 4G **105**
Sherbourne St. *P'wich* . . .5E **67**
Sherbrooke Av.
   Upperm 6C **60**
Sherbrooke Clo. *Sale* . . .5H **121**
Sherbrooke Rd. *Dis* 1H **165**
Sherbrook Ri. *Wilm* 3F **167**
Sherdley Ct. *M8* 2C **82**
Sherdley Rd. *M8* 2C **82**
Sherford Clo. *Haz G* 3A **152**
Sheridan Ct. *M40* 6G **83**
Sheridan Way. *Chad* 1E **71**
Sheridan Way. *Dent* 1F **129**
Sheriffs Dri. *Tyl* 2A **76**
Sheriff St. *Bolt* 4D **32**
Sheriff St. *Miln* 6G **29**
Sheriff St. *Roch* 2G **27**
   (in two parts)
Sheringham Dri. *Bury* . . .6D **22**
Sheringham Dri. *Hyde* . . .4E **115**
Sheringham Dri. *Swin* . . .5F **79**
Sheringham Pl. *Bolt* 2H **45**
Sheringham Rd. *M14* . . .2H **125**

Sherlock St. *M14* 2H **125**
Sherratt St. *M4* . . .3F **95** (3D **6**)
Sherrington St. *M12* 4C **110**
Sherway Dri. *Timp* 5C **134**
Sherwell Rd. *M9* 6D **68**
Sherwin Way. *Roch* 4D **40**
Sherwood Av. *M14* 1G **125**
Sherwood Av. *Chea H* . . .3B **150**
Sherwood Av. *Droy* 3C **98**
Sherwood Av. *Rad* 5F **35**
Sherwood Av. *Sale* 4C **122**
Sherwood Av. *Salf* 4F **81**
Sherwood Av. *Stoc* 2C **138**
Sherwood Bus. Pk.
   Roch 3D **40**
Sherwood Clo. *Ash L* 4G **87**
Sherwood Clo. *Marp* 1D **154**
Sherwood Clo. *Salf* 2D **92**
Sherwood Clo. *I'ton* 4H **21**
Sherwood Dri. *Swin* 4H **79**
Sherwood Ind. Pk.
   Roch 3D **40**
Sherwood M. Ash L 1B **100**
   (off King's Rd.)
Sherwood Rd. *Dent* 4B **112**
Sherwood Rd. *Woodl* . . .4H **129**
Sherwood Rd. *M14* 1G **125**
Sherwood St. *Bolt* 2B **32**
Sherwood St. *Oldh* 6B **56**
Sherwood St. Roch 3D **40**
   (off Queensway)
Sherwood Way. *Shaw* . . .5C **42**
Shetland Circ. *Urm* 2E **105**
Shetland Rd.
   M40 . . . . . .1H **95** (1G **7**)
Shetland Way. *Rad* 2G **49**
Shetland Way. *Urm* 2E **105**
Shevington Gdns.
   M23 . . . . .2H **135**
Shieldborn Dri. *M9* 4F **83**
Shield Clo. *Oldh* 3C **72**
Shield Dri. *Wors* 3C **78**
Shield St. *Stoc* 3G **139**
Shields Vw. *Salf* 4A **8**
Shiel St. *Wors* 6F **63**
Shierc Dri. *Chea* 1A **150**
Shiffnall St. *Bolt* 1C **46**
Shilford Dri. *M4* . . .2G **95** (2D **6**)
Shillingford Rd. *Farn* 1E **62**
Shillingstone Clo. *Bolt* . . .2H **33**
Shillington Clo. *Wors* 6B **62**
Shiloh La. *S'head* 5C **58**
Shilton Gdns. *Bolt* 2A **46**
Shilton St. *Rams* 4D **12**
Shilton Wlk. *M40* 1D **84**
Shipla Clo. *Oldh* 2C **72**
Ship La. *Del* 2C **58**
Shipley Av. *Salf* 2C **92**
Shipley Vw. *Urm* 2B **104**
Shipper Bottom La.
   Rams 4F **13**
   (in two parts)
Shippey St. *M14* 2H **125**
Shipston Clo. *Bury* 2H **35**
Shipton St. *Bolt* 4F **31**
Shirburn. *Roch* 5G **27**
Shireburn Av. *Bolt* 5E **33**
Shiredale Clo. *Chea H* . . .1D **150**
Shiredale Dri. *M9* 4F **83**
Shire Gdns. *Rad* 3F **49**
Shiregreen Av. *M40* 6E **83**
Shirehills. *P'wich* 6E **67**
Shireoak Rd. *M20* 2H **125**
Shires, The. *Droy* 2D **98**
Shires, The. *Rad* 2G **49**
Shirley Av. *Aud* 5C **98**
Shirley Av. *Chad* 1E **85**
Shirley Av. *Dent* 4H **111**
Shirley Av. *Eccl* 5F **91**
Shirley Av. *H Grn* 6G **149**
Shirley Av. *Hyde* 2B **114**

Shirley Av. *Marp* 5C **142**
Shirley Av. *Salf* 3E **81**
Shirley Av. *Stret* 4F **107**
Shirley Av. *Swin* 4A **80**
Shirley Clo. *Haz G* 3C **152**
Shirley Ct. *Sale* 5C **122**
Shirley Gro. *Stoc* 5G **139**
Shirley Rd. *M8* 4C **82**
Shirley St. *Roch* 3C **40**
Shoecroft Av. *Dent* 5E **113**
Sholver. 3H **57**
Sholver Hey La. *Oldh* 3H **57**
Sholver Hill Clo. *Oldh* 3A **58**
Sholver La. *Oldh* 3H **57**
Shone Av. *M22* 3D **148**
Shore. 3D **16**
Shore Av. *Shaw* 4G **43**
Shoreditch Clo. *Stoc* 4D **126**
Shorefield Clo. *Miln* 4F **29**
Shorefield Mt. *Eger* 3C **18**
Shore Fold. *L'boro* 3D **16**
Shoreham Clo. *M16* 3C **108**
Shoreham Wlk. *Chad* 3G **71**
Shore Hill. *L'boro* 3G **17**
Shore La. *L'boro* 4G **17**
Shore Lea. *L'boro* 3D **16**
Shore Mt. *L'boro* 3D **16**
Shore Rd. *L'boro* 3D **16**
Shore St. *Miln* 5F **29**
Shore St. *Oldh* 2E **73**
Shoreswood. *Bolt* 6B **18**
Shorland St. *Swin* 4C **78**
Shorrocks St. *Bury* 2F **35**
Short Av. *Droy* 5H **97**
Shortland Cres. *M19* 6H **125**
Shortlands Av. *Bury* 4D **36**
Short St. *M4* 4E **95** (5B **6**)
Short St. *Ash L* 2H **99**
Short St. *Haz G* 2D **152**
Short St. *Heyw* 4D **38**
Short St. *Salf* 2C **94** (1E **5**)
   (in two parts)
Short St. *Stoc* 6F **127**
   (in two parts)
Short St. E. *Stoc* 6G **127**
Shortwood Clo. *M40* 5A **84**
Shottery Walks. *Bred* 6F **129**
Shotton Wlk. *M14* 4G **109**
Shottwood Fold.
   L'boro 1G **17**
Shrewsbury Gdns.
   Chea H 1E **161**
Shrewsbury Rd. *Bolt* 5F **31**
Shrewsbury Rd. *Droy* 3A **98**
Shrewsbury Rd. *P'wich* . . .6E **67**
Shrewsbury Rd. *Sale* 1A **134**
Shrewsbury St. *M16* 2A **108**
Shrewsbury St. *Oldh* 1G **73**
Shrewsbury Way.
   Dent 6G **113**
Shrigley Clo. *Wilm* 6H **159**
Shrigley Rd.
   Poy & Boll 5A **164**
Shrigley Rd. N. *Poy* 4A **164**
Shrigley Rd. S. *Poy* 4A **164**
Shrivenham Wlk. *M23* . . .4F **135**
Shropshire Av. *Stoc* 3C **128**
Shropshire Rd. *Fail* 5G **85**
Shropshire Sq. *M12* 1B **110**
Shrowbridge Wlk.
   M12 . . . . .1C **110**
Shrub St. *Bolt* 5G **45**
Shude Hill. *M4* . . .3E **95** (4A **6**)
Shudehill Rd. *Wors* 2C **76**
Shurmer St. *Bolt* 3G **45**
Shutt La. *Dob* 5H **59**
Shuttle St. *Eccl* 3H **91**
Shuttle St. *Had* 6A **50**
Shuttleworth 1G **13**
Shuttleworth Clo.
   M16 . . . . .1C **124**

Shutts La. *Stal* 5H **101**
Siam St. *M11* 5B **96**
Sibley Rd. *Stoc* 6D **126**
Sibley St. *M18* 2F **111**
Siblies Wlk. *M22* 4H **147**
Sibson Ct. *M21* 6G **107**
Sibson Rd. *M21* 6G **107**
Sibson Rd. *Sale* 4E **95** (5A 6)
Sickle St. *M2* 4E **95** (5A 6)
Sickle St. *Oldh* 4E **73**
Sidbury Rd. *M21* 1A **124**
Sidcup Rd. *Round I.* . . .6F **135**
Siddall St. *M12* 5C **110**
Siddall St. *Dent* 4F **113**
Siddall St. *Heyw* 5G **39**
Siddall St. *Oldh* 1D **72**
Siddall St. *Rad* 3G **49**
Siddall St. *Shaw* 6F **43**
Siddal Moor. 6F **39**
Siddington Av. *M20* . . .2E **125**
Siddington Av. *Stoc* . . .5E **139**
Siddington Rd. *Hand* . .2H **159**
Siddington Rd. *Poy* . . .5F **163**
Side Av. *Bow* 4E **145**
Sidebothom St. *Bred* . .5F **129**
Sidebottom St. *Droy* . . .4H **97**
Sidebottom St. *Oldh* . . .1A **74**
Sidebottom St. *Stal* . . .3E **101**
Side of the Moor. 5B **20**
Side St. *M11* 4D **96**
Side St. *Oldh* 1A **86**
Sidford Clo. *Bolt* 2F **47**
Sidings, The. *Wors* 6A **78**
Sidlaw Clo. *Oldh* 1D **86**
Sidley Av. *M9* 5H **69**
Sidley Pl. *Hyde* 4D **114**
Sidley St. *Hyde* 4D **114**
Sidmouth Av. *Urm* 4A **104**
Sidmouth Dri. *M9* 1F **83**
Sidmouth Gro.
   Chea H 6B **150**
Sidmouth Rd. *Sale* 4F **121**
Sidmouth St. *Aud* 6C **98**
   (in two parts)
Sidmouth St. *Oldh* 4A **72**
Sidney Rd. *M9* 2F **83**
Sidney St. *M1* . . .6E **95** (4B 10)
Sidney St. *Bolt* 2B **46**
Sidney St. *Oldh* 6E **57**
Sidwell Wlk.
   M4 . . . . . . .4H **95** (5H 7)
Siebers Bank. *Roch* 1F **27**
Siemens Rd. *M20* 4C **124**
Siemens Rd. *Irlam* 4C **118**
Sienna Clo. *Irlam* 3C **118**
Sighthill Wlk. *M9* 3F **83**
Signal Clo. *Eccl* 3D **90**
Signal Ct. *M40* 5F **83**
Signet Wlk. *M8* 6D **82**
Silas St. *Ash L* 6H **87**
Silburn Way. *Midd* 2E **69**
Silbury Wlk. *M8* *6B 82*
   (off Steeple Clo.)
Silchester Dri. *M40* 5F **83**
Silchester Wlk. *Oldh* . . .2D **72**
Silchester Way. *Bolt* . . .4G **33**
Silfield Clo. *M11* 4A **96**
Silkhey Gro. *Wors* 2F **77**
Silkin Clo. *M13* . . .6F **95** (4C 10)
Silkin Ct. *M13* 4D **10**
Silk Mill. *Poy* 3B **162**
Silk St. *M4* 3G **95** (3D 6)
Silk St. *M40* 5C **84**
Silk St. *Midd* 1H **69**
Silk St. *Roch* 1C **40**
Silk St. *Salf* 2B **94** (2C 4)
Sillavan Way.
   Salf 3C **94** (4E 5)
Silsden Av. *M9* 4D **68**
Silsden Wlk. *Salf* 3D **80**
Silton St. *M9* 4H **83**
Silverbirch Clo. *Sale* . . .1F **133**

Silver Birches. *Dent* 6H **113**
Silver Birch Gro. *Swin* . . .5H **79**
Silver Birch Rd. *Duk* 6C **100**
Silverbirch Way. *Fail* 4F **85**
Silver Clo. *Duk* 6H **99**
Silver Ct. *W'fld* 6C **50**
Silvercroft St.
   M15 . . . . . .6C **94** (3E **9**)
Silverdale. *Alt* 1E **145**
Silverdale. *Swin* 1G **79**
Silverdale Av. *Chad* 3G **71**
Silverdale Av. *Dent* 5G **113**
Silverdale Av. *Irlam* 3F **103**
Silverdale Av. *L Hul* 4C **62**
Silverdale Av. *P'wich* 1A **82**
Silverdale Clo. *H Lane* . . .5C **154**
Silverdale Dri. *Lees* 3B **74**
Silverdale Dri. *Wilm* 5D **166**
Silverdale Rd. *M21* 6A **108**
Silverdale Rd. *Bolt* 6G **31**
Silverdale Rd. *Farn* 6C **46**
Silverdale Rd. *Gat* 1F **149**
Silverdale Rd. *Stoc* 5E **127**
Silverdale St. *M11* 6H **97**
Silver Hill. *Miln* 4F **29**
Silver Hill Rd. *Hyde* 6C **114**
Silver Jubilee Wlk. *M4* . . .4C **6**
Silverlea Dri. *M9* 1E **83**
Silvermere. *Ash L* 5A **88**
Silver Springs. *Hyde* 1D **130**
Silverstone Dri. *M40* 1F **97**
Silver St. *M1* 5E **95** (1A **10**)
   (Abingdon St.)
Silver St. *M1* 4E **95** (6B **6**)
   (Chorlton St., in two parts)
Silver St. *Bury* 3C **36**
Silver St. *Irlam* 3F **103**
Silver St. *Oldh* 3C **72**
Silver St. *Rams* 3E **13**
Silver St. *W'fld* 6C **50**
Silverthorne Clo. *Stal* . . .4E **101**
Silverton Clo. *Hyde* 5A **116**
   (in two parts)
Silverton Gro. *Bolt* 1B **32**
Silverton Gro. *Midd* 4F **53**
Silverton Ho. *Salf* *2A 92*
   (off Devon Clo.)
Silverwell La. *Bolt* 6B **32**
Silverwell St. *M40* 6D **84**
Silverwell St. *Bolt* 6B **32**
Silver Wings Sports Club.
   . . . . .1C **146**
Silverwood. *Chad* 2E **71**
Silverwood Av. *M21* 1H **123**
Silvine Wlk. *M40* *1A 96*
   (off Bednal Av.)
Simeon St. *M4* . . .2F **95** (2C **6**)
Simeon St. *Miln* 5F **29**
Simister. 1A **68**
Simister Dri. *Bury* 5E **51**
Simister Grn. *P'wich* 6A **52**
Simister La.
   P'wich & Midd 1H **67**
Simister Rd. *Fail* 4F **85**
Simister St. *M9* 3G **83**
Simkin Way. *Oldh* 2D **86**
Simmondley La. *Glos* 6H **117**
Simms Clo. *Salf* . . .3B **94** (4C **4**)
Simonbury Clo. *Bury* 3F **35**
Simon Freeman Clo.
   M19 . . . . .2E **127**
Simon Ho. *Stoc* 3E **127**
Simon La. *Midd* 5C **52**
Simons Clo. *Sale* 6A **122**
Simonsway. *M22* 2H **147**
Simonsway Ind. Est.
   M22 . . . . .4C **148**
Simpson Av. *Swin* 1A **80**
Simpson Clough. 6G **25**
Simpson Gro. *Wors* 5C **76**
Simpson Hill Clo.
   Heyw 2H **39**

Simpson Rd. *Wors* 5C **76**
Simpsons Pl. *Roch* 2H **27**
Simpson Sq. *Chad* 6A **72**
Simpson St. *M4* . . .2E **95** (2B **6**)
Simpson St. *Chad* 5H **71**
Simpson St. *Hyde* 4B **114**
Simpson St. *Wilm* 3C **166**
Sinclair Av. *M8* 2B **82**
Sinclair St. *Roch* 2D **40**
Sinderland La. *Dun M* 2A **132**
Sinderland Rd. *B'hth* 2C **132**
Sinderland Rd. *Part* 5G **119**
Sindsley Ct. Swin *2D 78*
   (off Moss La.)
Sindsley Gro. *Bolt* 4A **46**
Sindsley Rd. *Swin* 1D **78**
Singapore Av. *Man A* 5G **147**
Singleton Clo. *Salf* 2G **81**
Singleton Lodge. *Salf* 2H **81**
Singleton Rd. *Salf* 2G **81**
Singleton Rd. *Stoc* 5D **126**
Singleton St. *Rad* 3D **48**
Sion St. *Rad* 5F **49**
Sir Charles Groves Hall.
   M15 . . . . .5A **10**
Sirdar St. *M11* 5H **97**
Sirius Pl. *Salf* 2B **94** (1C **4**)
Sir Matt Busby Way.
   M16 . . . . .2F **107**
Sir Robert Thomas Ct.
   M9 . . . .*3F 83*
   (off Coningsby Dri.)
Siskin Rd. *Stoc* 6F **141**
Sisley Clo. *Salf* 3F **81**
Sisson St. *Fail* 4F **85**
Sisters St. *Droy* 5A **98**
Sixpools Gro. *Wors* 3E **77**
Sixth Av. *Bolt* 6F **31**
Sixth Av. *Bury* 1H **37**
Sixth Av. *L Lev* 3H **47**
Sixth Av. *Oldh* 2A **86**
Sixth St. *Traf P* 2D **106**
Size St. *Whitw* 4G **15**
Skagen Ct. *Bolt* 4A **32**
   (in two parts)
Skaife Rd. *Sale* 5E **123**
Skarratt Clo. *M12* 1B **110**
Skegness Clo. *Bury* 6D **22**
Skelton Gro. *M13* 5B **110**
Skelton Gro. *Bolt* 5H **33**
Skelton Rd. *Stret* 4D **106**
Skelton Rd. *Timp* 4G **133**
Skelwith Av. *Bolt* 5B **46**
Skelwith Clo. *Urm* 3C **104**
Skerry Clo.
   M13 . . . . . .6F **95** (4D **10**)
Skerton Rd. *M16* 3H **107**
Skilgate Wlk. *M40* 5C **84**
Skip Pl. *M3* 2E **95** (1A **6**)
Skipton Av. *M40* 2D **84**
Skipton Av. *Chad* 6F **55**
Skipton Clo. *Bury* 3F **35**
Skipton Clo. *Haz G* 5C **152**
Skipton Dri. *Urm* 2B **104**
Skipton St. *Bolt* 6E **33**
Skipton St. *Oldh* 5F **73**
Skipton Wlk. *Bolt* 6E **33**
Skrigge Clo. *M7* 5B **82**
Skye Clo. *Heyw* 4B **38**
Skye Rd. *Urm* 2F **105**
Skye Wlk. *M23* 1G **147**
Slackey Brow. *Kear* 3C **64**
Slack Fold La.
   Farn & Bolt 5G **45**
Slack Ga. *Whitw* 1E **15**
Slack Hall. *Aus* 1B **74**
Slack La. *Bolt* 4H **19**
Slack La. *Del* 1E **59**
Slack La. *Swin* 2G **79**
Slack Rd. *M9* 2E **83**

Slack St. *Hyde* 3D **114**
Slack St. *Roch* 4H **27**
Slade Gro. *M13* 4B **110**
Slade Hall. 5C **110**
Slade Hall Rd. *M12* 5C **110**
Slade La. *M19 & M13* . . .1B **126**
Slade Mt. *M19* 1B **126**
Sladen St. *Roch* 2H **27**
Sladen Ter. *L'boro* 1H **17**
Slade St. *L Lev* 4A **48**
Slades Vw. Clo. *Dig* 2C **60**
Slaidburn Av. *Bolt* 1H **47**
Slaidburn Clo. *Miln* 6F **29**
Slaidburn Dri. *Bury* 2E **35**
Slaithwaite Dri. *M11* 3E **97**
Slateacre Rd. *Hyde* 2D **130**
Slate Av. *M4* 4G **95** (5F **7**)
Slate La. *Ash L* 1C **99**
   (in three parts)
Slate La. *Aud* 5C **98**
Slaterfield. *Bolt* 2A **46**
Slater La. *Bolt* 5C **32**
Slater St. *Bolt* 5B **32**
Slater St. *Eccl* 3D **90**
Slater St. *Fail* 2F **85**
Slater St. *Farn* 1F **63**
Slater St. *Oldh* 3C **72**
Slater Way. *Mot* 5B **116**
Slate Wharf.
   M15 . . . . . . .5B **94** (3D **8**)
Slattocks. 1D **54**
Slattocks Link Rd.
   Midd 2D **54**
Slaunt Bank. *Roch* 1H **25**
Slawson Way. *Heyw* 2H **39**
Sleaford Clo.
   M40 . . . . . . .2H **95** (1G **7**)
Sleaford Clo. *Bury* 6D **22**
Sleddale Clo. *Stoc* 6D **140**
Sledmere Clo. *M11* 4C **96**
Sledmere Clo. *Bolt* 3B **32**
Sledmoor Rd. *M23* 2F **135**
Slimbridge Clo. *Bolt* 4A **34**
Sloane Av. *Lees* 1B **74**
Sloane St. *Ash L* 2A **100**
Sloane St. *Bolt* 4F **45**
Slough Ind. Est.
   Salf 5A **94** (2B **8**)
Smallbridge. 6A **16**
Smallbridge Clo. *Wors* 3E **77**
Smallbrook. *Shaw* 5G **43**
Small Brook Rd. *Shaw* 3G **43**
Smalldale Av. *M16* 4D **108**
Smalley St. *Roch* 3C **40**
Smallfield Dri. *M9* 3F **83**
Small La. *Mobb* 6A **156**
Smallridge Clo.
   M40 . . . . . . .2H **95** (2G **7**)
Smallshaw. 5G **87**
Smallshaw Fold. *Ash L* 6F **87**
Smallshaw La. *Ash L* 6F **87**
Smallshaw Rd. *Roch* 5A **14**
Smallwood St. *M40* 5C **84**
Smart St. *M12* 4C **110**
Smeaton Clo. *Stret* 5E **107**
Smeaton St. *M8* 5E **83**
Smedley. 5D **82**
Smedley Av. *M8* 5D **82**
Smedley Av. *Bolt* 4C **46**
Smedley La. *M8* 5D **82**
   (in two parts)
Smedley Rd.
   M8 & M40 . . . . . . .5D **82**
Smedley St. *M8* 5C **82**
Smethurst Ct. Bolt *5F 45*
   (off Smethurst La.)
Smethurst La. *Bolt* 5F **45**
Smethurst Rd. *Bury* 1A **38**
Smethurst St. *M9* 2F **83**
Smethurst St. *Bury* 1H **35**
Smethurst St. *Heyw* 3D **38**

Smethurst St. *Midd* 2D **70**
Smithalls Cft. Rd. *Bolt* . . .2E **31**
Smith Farm Clo. *Oldh* 1B **74**
Smithfold La. *Wors* 6C **62**
Smith Hill. *Miln* 5F **29**
Smithies Av. *Midd* 5A **54**
Smithies St. *Heyw* 3G **39**
Smithills. 1F **31**
Smithills Dean Rd. *Bolt* . . .1E **31**
Smithills Dri. *Bolt* 3D **30**
Smithills Hall Clo.
   Rams 4E **13**
Smithills Hall Country Pk.
   . . . . .1F **31**
Smithills Hall Mus. . . .1F **31**
Smith La. *Eger* 3D **18**
Smiths Lawn. *Wilm* 4D **166**
Smith's Rd. *Bolt* 4F **47**
Smith St. *M16* 1A **108** (5A **8**)
Smith St. *Ash L* 4F **99**
Smith St. *Bury* 2E **37**
Smith St. *Chea* 5B **138**
Smith St. *Dent* 5F **113**
Smith St. *Duk* 5G **99**
Smith St. *Heyw* 3F **39**
Smith St. *Hyde* 2B **114**
Smith St. *Lees* 1A **74**
Smith St. *L'boro* 4F **17**
Smith St. *Moss* 1D **88**
Smith St. *Rams* 4D **12**
Smith St. *Roch* 4H **27**
Smith St. *Wors* 6F **63**
Smithy Bridge. 6D **16**
Smithy Bri. Rd.
   Roch & L'boro 5C **16**
Smithy Cft. *Brom X* 3D **18**
Smithy Fld. *L'boro* 3E **17**
Smithy Fold. *Roch* 2E **27**
Smithy Fold Rd. *Hyde* . .6C **114**
Smithy Green. 6C **150**
Smithy Grn. *Chea H* 5C **150**
   (in two parts)
Smithy Grn. *Woodl* 4H **129**
Smithy Gro. *Ash L* 1A **100**
Smithy Hill. *Bolt* 3E **45**
Smithy La. *M3* 4D **94** (5G **5**)
Smithy La. *Alt* 2A **144**
Smithy La. *Hyde* 6C **114**
Smithy La. *Part* 6D **118**
Smithy La. *Upperm* 1F **61**
Smithy Nook. *L'boro* 6G **17**
Smithy St. *Haz G* 2D **152**
Smithy St. *Rams* 3E **13**
Smithy Yd. *Upperm* 1F **61**
   (off Smithy La.)
Smyrna St. *Heyw* 4E **39**
Smyrna St. *Oldh* 3G **73**
Smyrna St. *Rad* 3F **49**
Smyrna St. *Salf* 4E **93**
Smyrna Wlk. Rad 3F **49**
   (off Smyrna St.)
Snapebrook Gro. *Wilm* . .6A **160**
Snape St. *Rad* 1F **49**
   (in two parts)
Snell St. *M4* 4H **95** (6G **7**)
Snipe Av. *Roch* 4B **26**
Snipe Clo. *Poy* 3A **162**
Snipe Retail Pk. *Ash L* . . .4E **99**
   (in two parts)
Snipe Rd. *Oldh* 1F **87**
Snipe St. *Bolt* 2B **46**
Snipe Way. *Aud* 5D **98**
Snowberry Wlk. *Part* 6C **118**
Snowden Av. *Urm* 1D **120**
Snowden St. *Bolt* 5A **32**
Snowden St. *Heyw* 5G **39**
Snowden St. *Oldh* 5D **72**
Snowden Wlk. *M40* 1C **84**
Snowdon Rd. *Eccl* 2A **92**
Snowdon St. *Roch* 3G **41**
Snowdrop Wlk. *Salf* 5H **81**
Snow Hill Rd. *Bolt* 2F **47**

Snow Hill Ter. *P'wich* 5G **67**
Snydale Way. *Bolt* 6A **44**
Soapstone Way. *Irlam* . . .1E **119**
Soap St. *M4* 3E **95** (4B **6**)
Society St. *Shaw* 6F **43**
Sofa St. *Bolt* 4F **31**
Soho St. *Bolt* 1B **46**
Soho St. *Oldh* 2F **73**
Solent Av. *M8* 1C **82**
Solent Dri. *Bolt* 2F **47**
Solness St. *Bury* 5F **23**
Solway Clo. *Bolt* 4H **45**
Solway Clo. *Oldh* 4C **72**
Solway Clo. *Swin* 5E **65**
Solway Rd. *M22* 1C **148**
Somerby Dri. *M22* 4A **148**
Somerdale Av. *Bolt* 5E **31**
Somerfield Rd. *M9* 2F **83**
Somerford Av. *M20* 1E **125**
Somerford Rd. *Stoc* 5H **111**
Somerford Way.
   Hand 2H **159**
Somersby Ct. *Bram* 4G **151**
Somersby Dri. *Brom X* . . .3D **18**
Somersby Wlk. Bolt 2B **46**
   (off Hallington Clo.)
Somerset Av. *Shaw* 6D **42**
Somerset Clo. *Cad* 3B **118**
Somerset Clo. *Stoc* 5C **128**
Somerset Dri. *Bury* 5D **36**
Somerset Gro. *Roch* 3C **26**
Somerset Pl. *Sale* 3B **122**
Somerset Rd. *Bolt* 5F **31**
Somerset Rd. *B'hth* 5F **133**
Somerset Rd. *Droy* 2H **97**
Somerset Rd. *Eccl* 1A **92**
Somerset Rd. *Fail* 5E **85**
Somerset St. *Oldh* 3G **73**
Somers Rd. *Stoc* 6H **111**
Somers Wlk. *M9* 6D **68**
Somerton Av. *M22* 2A **148**
Somerton Av. *Sale* 6C **122**
Somerton Ct. *M9* 6A **70**
Somerton Rd. *Bolt* 1H **47**
Somerville Gdns.
   Timp 4H **133**
Somerville Sq. *Bolt* 2G **31**
Somerville St. *Bolt* 2G **31**
Somerville Wlk.
   M12 . . . . .1B **110**
Sommerville Ct. *Salf* 3H **81**
Sonning Dri. *Bolt* 5E **45**
Sonning Wlk. *M8* 5D **82**
Sopwith Dri. *M14* 6E **109**
Sorby Rd. *Irlam* 2E **119**
Sorrel Bank. *Salf* 1F **93**
Sorrel Dri. *L'boro* 3D **16**
Sorrell Bank. *Stoc* 6A **112**
Sorrel St. *M15* 1C **108** (5E **9**)
Sorrel Way. *Oldh* 5A **58**
Sorton St. *M1* 6E **95** (3B **10**)
Soudan Rd. *Stoc* 5A **140**
Soudan St. *Midd* 6C **54**
Souracre. 2F **101**
Sour Acre Fold. *H'rod* . . .2F **101**
Southacre Dri. *Hand* 4H **159**
Southall St. *M3* . . .2D **94** (1G **5**)
Southampton Clo.
   Salf 6H **81**
Southam St. *M7* 4R **82**
South Av. *M19* 2B **126**
South Av. *G'fld* 3F **61**
South Av. *Heyw* 3D **38**
South Av. *Kear* 3H **63**
South Av. *Swin* 6D **78**
South Av. *W'fld* 6C **50**
South Bk. Rock. Bury 3D **36**
   (off Butcher La.)
S. Bank Clo. *Ald E* 4H **167**
Southbank Rd. *M19* 4H **125**
S. Bank Rd. *Bury* 4C **36**
Southbourne Av. *Urm* . . .5H **105**

Southbourne St. *Salf* 3E **93**
Southbrook Av. *M8* 6B **68**
Southbrook Clo. *Had* . . .3G **117**
Southbrook Gro. *Bolt* 4B **46**
Southchurch Pde. *M40* . .1G **95**
Southcliffe Rd. *Stoc* 3H **127**
S. Cliffe St. *M11* 6H **97**
South Clo. *Bury* 4E **51**
South Clo. *Tin* 1H **117**
South Clo. *Wilm* 3C **166**
Southcombe Wlk.
   M15 . . . . .2D **108**
South Ct. *Roch* 3A **28**
South Cres. *M11* 3F **97**
South Cft. *Oldh* 6F **73**
Southcross Rd. *M18* 4F **111**
S. Cross St. *Bury* 3D **36**
   (in two parts)
S. Croston St. *M16* 3B **108**
Southdene Av. *M20* 5C **124**
Southdown Clo. *Roch* 1C **40**
Southdown Clo. *Stoc* 1F **139**
Southdown Cres.
   Chea H 5B **150**
Southdown Dri. *Wors* 5B **76**
S. Downs Clo. *Shaw* 5D **42**
S. Downs Dri. *Hale* 5F **145**
S. Downs Rd.
   Bow & Hale 4E **145**
South Dri. *M21* 2G **123**
South Dri. *Bolt* 2G **33**
South Dri. *Gat* 1E **149**
South Dri. *Timp* 4A **134**
South Dri. *Urm* 2B **104**
South Dri. *Wilm* 3C **166**
Southend Av.
   M15 . . . . . .1B **108** (5C **8**)
Southend St. *Bolt* 4G **45**
Southerly Cres. *M40* 6D **70**
Southern App. *Swin* 1A **80**
Southernby Clo. *M13* . . .3B **110**
Southern Clo. Bram 4H **151**
Southern Clo. *Dent* 1F **129**
Southern Cres. Dram . . .3H **161**
Southern Ho. Bolt 4H **31**
   (off Kirk Hope Dri.)
Southern Rd. *Sale* 3A **122**
Southern St. *M3* . . .5C **94** (2F **9**)
Southern St. *Salf* 3E **93**
Southern St. *Wors* 4F **63**
Southey Clo. *L'boro* 6D **16**
Southey St. *Dent* 1G **129**
Southey Wlk. *Dent* 2G **129**
Southfield Av. *Bury* 5F **23**
Southfield Clo. *Duk* 1B **114**
Southfield Clo. *Hand* 4G **159**
South Field Ind. Est.
   Traf P 1C **106**
Southfield Rd. *Rams* 1A **22**
Southfields. *Bow* 3E **145**
Southfields. *M11* 3E **97**
Southfields Dri. *Timp* 4B **134**
Southfield St. *Bolt* 3D **46**
Southgarth Rd. *Salf* 2E **93**
Southgate. *M3* 4D **94** (5G **5**)
Southgate. *Chor H* 2H **123**
Southgate. *Dob* 5A **60**
Southgate. *Har* 1G **33**
Southgate. *Stoc* 4E **127**
Southgate. *Urm* 1D **120**
Southgate. *Whitw* 2B **14**
Southgate Av. *M40* 1C **96**
Southgate Ct. *Sale* 4C **122**
Southgate Ho. Oldh 3D **72**
   (off Southgate St.)
Southgate Ind. Est.
   Heyw 4G **39**
Southgate M. *Stoc* 4E **127**
Southgate Rd. *Bury* 4D **50**
Southgate Rd. *Chad* 6E **71**
Southgate St. *Oldh* 3D **72**

Southgate Way. *Ash L* 4F **99**
South Gro. *M13* 2H **109**
South Gro. *Ald E* 5G **167**
South Gro. *Sale* 6B **122**
South Gro. *Wors* 1E **77**
Southgrove Av. *Bolt* 5C **18**
S. Hall St. *Salf* 5A **94** (2B **8**)
South Hill. *S'head* 4B **74**
S. Hill St. *Oldh* 3E **73**
S. King St. *M2* 4D **94** (5G **5**)
S. King St. *Eccl* 3D **90**
Southlands. *Bolt* 5G **33**
Southlands Av. *Eccl* 5B **90**
S. Langworthy Rd. *Salf* . . .5E **93**
Southlea Rd.
   M20 & M19 . . . . .4H **125**
Southleigh Dri. *Bolt* 1A **48**
Southlink. *Oldh* 3E **73**
Southlink Bus. Pk.
   Oldh 3E **73**
Southlink Bus. Pk. Workshops.
   Oldh 3E **73**
   (off Southlink)
Southlink Ind. Pk. *Oldh* . .2F **73**
S. Lonsdale St. *Stret* 4E **107**
South Manchester Gymnastics
   Cen. 6C **136**
South Mead. *Poy* 2B **162**
South Meade. *M21* 2H **123**
South Meade. *P'wich* 1H **81**
South Meade. *Swin* 5E **79**
South Meade. *Timp* 4A **134**
South Meadway.
   H Lane 6D **154**
Southmere Clo. *M40* 6C **70**
S. Mesnefield Rd. *Salf* . . .3E **81**
   (in two parts)
Southmill St.
   M2 . . . . . . .5D **94** (1G **9**)
   (in two parts)
Southmoor Bus. Pk.
   M23 . . . . .4E **135**
Southmoor Ind. Est.
   M23 . . . . .5F **135**
Southmoor Rd.
   Round I 4F **135**
Southmoor Wlk. Bolt 2A **46**
   (off Parrot St.)
S. Oak La. *Wilm* 3C **166**
Southolme Gdns.
   M19 . . . . .5A **126**
South Pde. *Bram* 3H **151**
South Pde. *Roch* 4H **27**
S. Park Dri. *Poy* 3E **163**
S. Park Rd. *Gat* 5F **137**
South Pl. *Roch* 3A **28**
Southpool Clo. *Bram* 3A **152**
S. Pump St.
   M1 . . . . .5F **95** (1C **10**)
S. Radford St. *Salf* 4E **81**
South Reddish. 4H **127**
South Ridge. *Dent* 2F **113**
South Rd. *M20* 1F **137**
South Rd. *Bow* 3E **145**
   (in two parts)
South Rd. *Hale* 5F **145**
South Rd. *Stret* 3A **106**
South Rd. *Swin* 1B **80**
South Row. *P'wich* 2D **80**
S. Royd St. *T'ton* 4H **21**
Southsea St. *M11* 6F **97**
Southside. *Bred* 3E **129**
South Side. *Hyde* 1D **130**
South Stage. *Salf* 5F **93**
South St. *Ald E* 5G **167**
South St. *Ash L* 5E **99**
South St. *Bolt* 4A **46**
South St. *Heyw* 3D **38**
South St. *Long* 2A **110**
South St. *Oldh* 1H **85**
South St. *Open* 5D **96**
   (in two parts)

South St. *Rams* 3F **13**
    (Derby St.)
South St. *Rams* 3F **13**
    (Peel Brow)
South Ter. *Ald E* 6G **167**
South Ter. *Bury* 6B **36**
South Ter. *Roch* 2B **26**
S. Terrace Ct. *Roch* 6A **28**
S. Vale Cres. *Timp* 6H **133**
South Vw. *M14* 5G **109**
South Vw. *Carr* 5H **89**
South Vw. *Duk* 4A **100**
South Vw. *Roch* 5A **26**
South Vw. *Stoc* 4H **111**
South Vw. *Woodl* 3A **130**
South Vw. Gdns.
    Chea 2G **149**
Southview Rd. *Roch* 5C **16**
S. View St. *Bolt* 6E **33**
S. View Ter. *Roch* 5C **16**
Southview Wlk. *Oldh* 6A **58**
South Wlk. *Stal* 4E **101**
Southwark Dri. *Duk* 1B **114**
Southway. *M40* 1F **85**
Southway. *Alt* 5G **133**
Southway. *Ash L* 5F **87**
Southway. *Droy* 5A **98**
Southway. *Eccl* 3H **91**
South Way. *Oldh* 1C **86**
Southwell Clo. *Bolt* 5H **31**
Southwell Clo. *Rom* 2G **141**
Southwell Ct. *Stret* 6C **106**
Southwell Gdns. *Ash L* . . .4F **87**
Southwell St. *M9* 4G **83**
Southwick Rd. *M23* 1G **135**
S. William St.
    Salf 4B **94** (5C **4**)
Southwold Clo. *M19* 6E **111**
Southwood Clo. *Bolt* 4B **46**
Southwood Dri. *M9* 4C **68**
Southwood Rd. *Stoc* 1B **152**
Southworth Ct.
    Salf 3B **94** (4C **4**)
Southyard St. *M19* 1C **126**
Sovereign Enterprise Pk.
    Salf 6G **93**
Sovereign Hall Cvn. Pk.
    Moss 2D **88**
Sovereign Ho. *Chea* 5B **138**
Sovereign St. *Salf* 1G **93**
Sowerby Clo. *Bury* 3F **35**
Sowerby Wlk. M9 . . . . . .5D **68**
    (off Chapel La.)
Spa Clo. *Stoc* 1G **127**
Spa Cres. *L Hul* 3B **62**
Spa Gro. *L Hul* 3C **62**
Spa La. *L Hul* 3C **62**
Spa La. *Oldh* 4H **73**
Spalding Dri. *M23* 3G **147**
Sparkford Av. *M23* 2D **134**
Sparkle St. *M1* 4F **95** (6D **6**)
Spark Rd. *M23* 4F **135**
Spa Rd. *Bolt* 1H **45**
Sparrow Clo. *Stoc* 5G **111**
Sparrowfield Clo. *Carr* . . .4G **89**
Sparrow Hill. *Roch* 4G **27**
Sparrow St. *Rytn* 5C **56**
Sparta Av. *Wors* 1E **77**
Sparta Wlk. *Open* 5C **96**
Sparth Bottoms Rd.
    Roch 5F **27**
Sparth Ct. *Stoc* 6F **127**
Sparthfield Av. *Roch* 6G **27**
Sparthfield Rd. *Stoc* 6F **127**
Sparth Hall. *Stoc* 6F **127**
Sparth La. *Stoc* 6F **127**
Sparth Rd. *M40* 6D **84**
Spa St. *M15* 2F **109**
Spathfield Ct. *Stoc* 6F **127**
Spath Holme. *M20* 6E **125**
Spath La. *Chea H* 2B **160**
    (in two parts)

Spath La. *Hand* 2H **159**
Spath La. E. *Chea H* 2D **160**
Spath Rd. *M20* 5D **124**
Spath Wlk. *Chea H* 2D **160**
Spaw St. *Salf* 3C **94** (4E **5**)
    (in two parts)
Spean Wlk. *M11* 4E **97**
Spear St. *M1* 4E **95** (5B **6**)
Spectator St.
    M4 . . . . .3H **95** (4H **7**)
Specton Wlk. *M12* 4D **110**
Speedwell. *Tin* 1H **117**
Speedwell Clo. *Tin* 1H **117**
Speke Wlk. *Dent* 6E **113**
Spencer Av. *M16* 5A **108**
Spencer Av. *Hyde* 2B **114**
Spencer Av. *L Lev* 4C **48**
Spencer Av. *W'fld* 5C **50**
Spencer La. *Roch* 6A **26**
Spencer St. *Bury* 2A **36**
Spencer St. *Chad* 5H **71**
Spencer St. *Duk* 5A **100**
Spencer St. *Eccl* 4E **91**
Spencer St. *L'boro* 3G **17**
Spencer St. *Moss* 2D **88**
Spencer St. *Oldh* 2E **73**
Spencer St. *Rad* 3A **50**
Spencer St. *Rams* 4D **12**
Spencer St. *Stoc* 1H **127**
Spender Av. *M8* 5C **82**
Spen Fold. *Bury* 5G **35**
Spen Fold. *L'boro* 5E **17**
Spenlow Clo. *Poy* 6E **163**
Spennithorne Rd.
    Urm 5D **104**
Spenser Av. *Dent* 1G **129**
Spenser Av. *Rad* 3E **49**
Spenwood Rd. *L'boro* 4D **16**
Spey Clo. *Alt* 5E **133**
Spey Ho. *Stoc* 5H **111**
Speyside Clo. *W'fld* 1E **67**
Spindle Av. *Stal* 2G **101**
Spindle Ct. Rytn 3C **56**
    (off High Barn St.)
Spindle Cft. *Farn* 1F **63**
Spindlepoint Dri. *Wors* . . .3E **77**
Spindles, The. *Moss* 3F **89**
Spindles, The. *Oldh* 2D **72**
Spindlewood Clo.
    Stal 3H **101**
Spinks St. *Oldh* 4F **73**
Spinners Gdns. *Ward* . . .5A **16**
Spinners Grn. *Roch* 1H **27**
Spinners La. *Poy* 3C **162**
Spinners M. *Bolt* 5A **32**
Spinners Way. *Oldh* 3A **58**
Spinney Clo. *Hand* 4G **159**
Spinney Dri. *Bury* 5E **23**
Spinney Dri. *Sale* 6F **121**
Spinney Gro. *Dent* 2F **113**
Spinney Nook. *Bolt* 3F **33**
Spinney Rd. *M23* 4H **135**
Spinney, The. *Bolt* 6F **31**
Spinney, The. *Chea* 2A **150**
Spinney, The. *Roch* 6D **14**
Spinney, The. *Scout* 1C **74**
Spinney, The. *Tur* 1G **19**
Spinney, The. *Urm* 5C **104**
Spinney, The. *W'fld* 2A **66**
Spinningdale. *L Hul* 3A **62**
Spinningfield.
    M3 . . . . .4D **94** (6G **5**)
Spinningfields. *Bolt* 5H **31**
Spinningfield Way.
    Heyw 6F **39**
Spinning Jenny Wlk.
    M4 . . . . .4G **95** (4F **7**)
Spinning Meadows.
    Bolt 5H **31**
Spinnings, The. *S'seat* 6E **13**
Spire Wlk.
    M12 . . . . . .5A **96** (1H **11**)

Spirewood Gdns.
    Rom 2G **141**
Spodden Cotts. *Whitw* . . .3H **15**
Spodden Fold. *Whitw* 1C **14**
Spodden St. *Roch* 3F **27**
Spodden Wlk. *W'fld* 6G **51**
Spod Rd. *Roch* 2E **27**
    (in two parts)
Spokeshave Way. *Roch* . . .1C **28**
Spooner Rd. *Eccl* 4E **91**
Sporting Club, The. 5B **6**
Sportside Av. *Wors* 6G **63**
Sportside Clo. *Wors* 6F **63**
Sportside Gro. *Wors* 5F **63**
Sportsmans Dri. *Oldh* 6E **73**
Spotland Bridge. 3F **27**
Spotland Fold. 2E **27**
Spotland Rd. *Roch* 3F **27**
Spotland Tops. *Roch* 2D **26**
Spout Brook Rd. *Stal* 6D **88**
Spreadbury St. *M40* 4A **84**
Spring Av. *Hyde* 1D **130**
Spring Av. *W'fld* 5C **50**
Spring Bank. *Bow* 2F **145**
Springbank. *Chad* 2G **71**
Springbank. *Had* 2H **117**
Springbank. *Heal* 5D **14**
Spring Bank. *Salf* 2E **93**
Spring Bank. *Stal* 5F **101**
Springbank. *Upperm* 1F **61**
Spring Bank. *Whitw* 4H **15**
Spring Bank Av. *Ash L* . . .6F **87**
Spring Bank Av. *Aud* 6D **98**
Spring Bank Clo.
    Woodl 3A **130**
Springbank Ct. *M8* 1B **82**
Springbank Ct. *Woodl* . . .4H **129**
Spring Bank La. *Carr* 6E **89**
Spring Bank La. *Roch* 3A **26**
    (in two parts)
Springbank Pl. *Stoc* 3G **139**
Spring Bank Rd.
    Woodl 3A **130**
Spring Bank St. *Oldh* 5A **72**
Spring Bank St. *Stal* 4F **101**
Spring Bank Ter. *Aud* 6C **98**
Springburn Clo. *Wors* 5C **76**
Spring Clo. *Rams* 3D **12**
Spring Clo. *T'ton* 5G **21**
Spring Clough. *Swin* 6B **78**
Spring Clough Av.
    Wors 1H **77**
Springclough Dri. *Oldh* . . .5F **73**
Spring Clough Dri.
    Wors 1H **77**
Spring Cotts. Aud 1F **113**
    (off Guide La.)
Spring Cotts. Moss 1E **89**
    (off Bk. Mill La.)
Spring Ct. *Roch* 2H **27**
Spring Ct. M. *Holl* 2E **117**
Springdale Gdns.
    M20 . . . . .6E **125**
Springfield. 1C **46**
Springfield. *Bolt* 1C **46**
Springfield. *Rad* 3C **64**
Springfield. *Urm* 5E **105**
Springfield Av. *Haz G* . . .2D **152**
Springfield Av. *L'boro* 2E **17**
Springfield Av. *Marp* 5D **142**
Springfield Av. *Stoc* 2G **127**
Springfield Clo. *Fail* 3E **85**
Springfield Clo. *Had* 3G **117**
Springfield Clo. *Heyw* 4G **39**
Springfield Dri. *Wilm* 4A **166**
Springfield Gdns. *Kear* . . .3A **64**
Springfield Ind. Est.
    Fail 3E **85**
Springfield La. *Irlam* 5D **102**
Springfield La. *Roch* 6B **16**

Springfield La. *Rytn* 6A **42**
Springfield La.
    Salf 2C **94** (1F **5**)
Springfield Rd. *Alt* 6F **133**
Springfield Rd. *Bolt* 4C **18**
Springfield Rd. *Droy* 3H **97**
Springfield Rd. *Farn* 6C **46**
Springfield Rd. *Gat* 1F **149**
Springfield Rd. *Kear* 3G **63**
Springfield Rd. *Midd* 6H **53**
Springfield Rd. *Rams* 1A **22**
Springfield Rd. *Sale* 5B **122**
Springfield St. *Ash L* 6A **88**
Springfield St. *Aud* 1F **113**
Springfield St. *Bolt* 3C **46**
Springfield St. *Heyw* 3C **38**
Springfield Trad. Est.
    Traf P 1D **106**
Spring Gdns.
    M2 . . . . .4E **95** (5A **6**)
Spring Gdns. *Bolt* 1G **33**
Spring Gdns. *Had* 2H **117**
Spring Gdns. *Haz G* 2D **152**
Spring Gdns. *Hyde* 3B **114**
Spring Gdns. *Midd* 5A **54**
Spring Gdns. *Roch* 4G **27**
Spring Gdns. *Rytn* 3B **56**
Spring Gdns. *Salf* 2F **93**
Spring Gdns. *Stoc* 2A **140**
Spring Gdns. *Timp* 6C **134**
Spring Garden St. *Rytn* . . .3B **56**
    (in two parts)
Spring Gro. *G'fld* 4F **61**
Spring Gro. *W'fld* 5C **50**
Spring Hall Ri. *Oldh* 3B **58**
Springhead. 3C **74**
Springhead Av. *M20* 2E **125**
Springhead Av. *S'head* . . .4B **74**
Spring Hill. 6H **57**
Spring Hill. *Roch* 2H **41**
Springhill. *Rytn* 3B **56**
Spring Hill Ct. *Oldh* 1H **73**
Spring La. *Lees* 4A **74**
Spring La. *Rad* 4G **49**
Springlawns. *Bolt* 5D **30**
Spring Lees Ct.
    S'head 3B **74**
Spring Mdw. La.
    Upperm 1G **61**
Spring Mill Clo. *Bolt* 3A **46**
Spring Mill Wlk. *Roch* 6A **16**
Spring Pl. *Whitw* 3H **15**
Spring Ri. *Shaw* 4E **43**
Spring Ri. *Stal* 2D **100**
    (in two parts)
Spring Rd. *Hale* 3F **145**
Spring Rd. *Poy* 5F **163**
Springside. *Heat C* 2F **127**
Spring Side. *Roch* 1H **15**
Springside Av. *Wors* 6G **63**
Springside Clo. *Wors* 6G **63**
Springside Gro. *Wors* 6G **63**
Springside Rd. *Bury* 3D **22**
    (in two parts)
Springside Vw. *Bury* 4B **22**
Springside Vw. Cotts.
    Bury 4C **22**
Springside Wlk.
    M15 . . . . . .1B **108** (6D **8**)
Springs La. *Stal* 1D **100**
Springs Rd. *Midd* 3E **71**
Springs, The. *Bow* 3D **144**
    (in two parts)
Springs, The. *Roch* 4A **26**
Spring St. *M12* 5C **110**
Spring St. *Bolt* 2B **46**
Spring St. *Bury* 3D **36**
Spring St. *Farn* 6F **47**
Spring St. *Holl* 2E **117**
Spring St. *Moss* 1E **89**
Spring St. *Oldh* 1G **73**

Spring St. *Rams* 3D **12**
(Bolton St.)
Spring St. *Rams* 2F **13**
(Henry St.)
Spring St. *S'head* 3C **74**
Spring St. *Stal* 3E **101**
Spring St. *T'ton* 4G **21**
Spring St. *Upperm* 1F **61**
Spring St. *Wals* 1F **35**
Spring St. *Wilm* 2D **166**
Spring Ter. *Chad* 2G **71**
Spring Ter. *Miln* 2F **43**
Spring Ter. *Roch* 3C **28**
Spring Ter. T'ton 4G **21**
(off Spring St.)
Spring Va. *Haz G* 3E **153**
Spring Va. *Midd* 1A **70**
Spring Va. *P'wich* 1E **81**
Springvale Clo. *Ash L* . . .6D **86**
Spring Va. Cl. *Midd* 6B **54**
Springvale Dri. *T'ton* 4G **21**
Spring Va. St. *T'ton* 5G **21**
Spring Va. Ter. *L'boro* 4F **17**
(off Church St.)
Spring Va. Way. *Rytn* . . .2E **57**
Spring Vw. *Kear* 3A **64**
Spring Vw. *L Lev* 4B **48**
Springville Av. *M9* 4H **83**
Springwater Av. *Rams* . . .6C **12**
Springwater Av. *Swin* . . .5H **79**
Springwater Clo. *Bolt* . . .2G **33**
Spring Water Dri.
Had 4G **117**
Springwater La. *W'fld* . . .5C **50**
Springwell Clo. *Salf* 3E **93**
Springwell Gdns.
Hyde 6A **116**
Springwell Way. *Hyde* . .6A **116**
Springwood. *Del* 2G **59**
Springwood Av. *Chad* . . .8E **55**
Springwood Av. *Swin* . . .5H **79**
Springwood Cres.
Rom 1C **142**
Springwood Hall Rd.
Oldh 1E **87**
Springwood La. *Rom* . . .1D **142**
Springwood Way.
Ash L 5E **87**
Spruce Av. *Bury* 3F **37**
Spruce Ct. *Salf* 3H **93**
Spruce Cres. *Bury* 4F **23**
Spruce Lodge. *Chea* 5H **137**
Spruce St.
M15 . . . . . .1C **108** (6E **9**)
Spruce St. *Rams* 5C **12**
Spruce St. *Roch* 5B **28**
Spruce Wlk. *Sale* 3E **121**
Sprucewood. *Chad* 1D **70**
Spurn La. *Dig* 4B **60**
Spurstow M. *Chea H* . . .5D **150**
Spur, The. *Oldh* 6E **73**
Spur Wlk. *M8* 4B **82**
Square Fold. *Droy* 3B **98**
Square, The. *Bolt* 4D **44**
Square, The. *Bury* 3D **36**
Square, The. *Dob* 5A **60**
(Dobcross)
Square, The. *Dob* 1F **61**
(Uppermill)
Square, The. *Haleb* 5C **146**
Square, The. *Hyde* 5B **114**
Square, The. *Stoc* 6E **127**
(Norris Bank)
Square, The. *Stoc* 2G **139**
(Stockport)
Square, The. *Swin* 6E **79**
Square, The. *W'fld* 1B **66**
Squire Rd. *M8* 4B **82**
Squire's Ct. *Salf* 3A **92**
Squirrel Dri. *B'hth* 3E **133**
Squirrels Jump. *Ald E* . . .5H **167**

Stablefold. *Moss* 3E **89**
Stable Fold. *Rad* 3G **49**
Stable Fold. *Wors* 6A **78**
Stablefold Av. *Eccl* 1E **91**
Stables, The. *Droy* 2D **98**
Stables, The. *P'wich* 6G **67**
Stable St. *Chad* 1G **85**
Stable St. *Oldh* 1F **73**
Stablings, The. *Wilm* 4D **166**
Stafford Ct. *Roch* 5C **16**
Stafford Rd. *Eccl* 2G **91**
Stafford Rd. *Fail* 0G **85**
Stafford Rd. *Swin* 3F **79**
Stafford Rd. *Wors* 2E **77**
Stafford St. *Bury* 1B **36**
Stafford St. *Oldh* 5A **72**
Stafford Vw.
Salf 6H **93** (4A **8**)
Stafford Wlk. *Dent* 6G **113**
Stag Ind. Est. *B'hth* 5D **132**
Stag Pasture Rd. *Oldh* . . .2B **86**
Stainburne Rd. *Stoc* 5C **140**
Stainburn Rd. *M11* 5D **96**
Staindale. *Oldh* 3H **73**
Stainer St. *M12* 4C **110**
Stainforth Clo. *Bury* 2F **35**
Stainforth St. *M11* 5B **96**
Stainmoor Ct. *Stoc* 5D **140**
Stainmore Av. *Ash L* 4G **87**
Stainsbury St. *Bolt* 3G **45**
Stainton Av. *M18* 3G **111**
Stainton Clo. *Rad* 2F **49**
Stainton Dri. *Midd* 4F **53**
Stainton Rd. *Rad* 2E **49**
Staithes Rd. *M22* 5B **148**
Stakeford Dri. *M8* 3E **83**
Stake Hill. 3D **54**
Stakehill Ind. Est. *Midd* . .3D **54**
Stakehill La. *Midd* 1D **54**
Staley Clo. *Stal* 3G **101**
Staley Hall Cres. *Stal* . . .2G **101**
Staley Hall Rd. *Stal* 2G **101**
Staley Rd. *Moss* 3F **89**
(in two parts)
Staley St. *Oldh* 3F **73**
Staley St. *S'head* 3B **74**
Stalham Clo.
M40 . . . . . . .2H **95** (1H **7**)
Stalham Wlk.
M40 . . . . . . .2H **95** (1G **7**)
Stalmine Av. *H Grn* 5F **149**
Stalybridge. 4E **101**
Stalybridge Celtic
Football Club. . . .5G **101**
Stalybridge Rd. *Mot* 3C **116**
Stalyhill Dri. *Stal* 6H **101**
(in two parts)
Staly Ind. Est. *Stal* 3F **101**
Stambourne Dri. *Bolt* 1B **32**
Stamford Arc. *Ash L* 2A **100**
Stamford Av. *Alt* 6C **132**
Stamford Av. *Stal* 3C **100**
Stamford Clo. *Stal* 3C **100**
Stamford Ct. *Ash L* 3B **100**
Stamford Dri. *Fail* 5H **85**
Stamford Dri. *Stal* 3C **100**
Stamford Grange. *Alt* 1E **145**
Stamford Gro. *Stal* 3D **100**
Stamford New Rd. *Alt* 1F **145**
Stamford Pk. 2C **100**
Stamford Pk. Rd.
Alt & Hale 2G **145**
Stamford Pl. *Sale* 5C **122**
Stamford Pl. *Wilm* 2E **167**
Stamford Rd. *M13* 4A **110**
Stamford Rd. *Ald E* 5H **167**
Stamford Rd. *Aud* 6D **98**
Stamford Rd. *Bow* 3E **145**
Stamford Rd. *C'ton* 3H **119**
Stamford Rd. *Lees* 1B **74**
Stamford Rd. *Moss* 1E **89**

Stamford Rd. *Salf* 5F **81**
Stamford Rd. *Urm* 5D **104**
Stamford Rd. *Wilm* 6E **159**
Stamford St. *Stal* 3C **100**
Stamford Sq. *Alt* 6F **133**
Stamford Sq. *Ash L* 3C **100**
Stamford St. *M16* 2A **108**
(in two parts)
Stamford St. *Alt* 6F **133**
Stamford St. *Ash L* 2A **100**
(in two parts)
Stamford St. *Heyw* 4G **39**
Stamford St. *Lees* 3A **74**
Stamford St. *Mill* 1H **101**
Stamford St. *Moss* 3D **88**
Stamford St. *Roch* 5B **28**
Stamford St. *Sale* 3A **122**
Stamford St. *Stal* 3C **100**
(in two parts)
Stamford St. *Swin* 2G **79**
Stamford St. Central.
Ash L 3H **99**
Stamford St. W. *Ash L* . . .3G **99**
Stamford Way. *Alt* 6F **133**
Stampstone St. *Oldh* 1F **73**
Stanage Av. *M9* 5H **69**
Stanbank St. *Stoc* 5G **127**
Stanbridge Ct. *Stoc* 1G **139**
Stanbrook St. *M19* 6E **111**
Stanbury Clo. *Bury* 4H **37**
Stanbury Dri. *Duk* 5B **100**
Stanbury Wlk.
M40 . . . . . .2H **95** (1H **7**)
(off Berkshire Rd.)
Stancliffe Rd. *M22* . . . . .GC **136**
Stancross Rd. *M23* 2C **134**
Stand. 2A **66**
Standall Wlk. *M9* 2G **83**
Stand Av. *W'fld* 6C **50**
Stand Clo. *W'fld* 1A **66**
Standedge Rd. *Dig* 4B **60**
Standedge Tunnel. 2D **60**
Standedge Wlk.
Ash L 2A **100**
(off Westbury St.)
Standedge Wlk. *Carr* 5G **89**
(off Crowswood Dri.)
Standfield Cen. *Wors* 5C **76**
(off Simpson Rd.)
Standfield Dri. *Wors* 4C **76**
Standish Rd. *M14* 1H **125**
Standish Wlk. *Dent* 6E **113**
Stand La. *Rad & W'fld* 5H **49**
Standmoor Ct. *W'fld* 2B **66**
Standmoor Rd. *W'fld* 2B **66**
Standon Wlk. *M40* 1D **84**
Standring Av. *Bury* 5G **35**
Stand Ri. *Rad* 1H **65**
Stanedge Clo. *Rams* 6E **13**
Stanford Clo. *Rad* 2C **64**
Stanford Hall Cres.
Rams 5D **12**
Stangate Wlk. *M11* 5B **96**
Stanhope Av. *Aud* 2E **113**
Stanhope Av. *P'wich* 4E **67**
Stanhope Clo. *Dent* 2E **113**
Stanhope Clo. *Wilm* 1G **167**
Stanhope Ct. *P'wich* 4E **67**
Stanhope Rd. *Bow* 3C **144**
Stanhope Rd. *Salf* 6C **80**
Stanhope St. *M19* 6D **110**
Stanhope St. *Ash L* 1B **100**
Stanhope St. *Aud* 2E **113**
Stanhope St. *Moss* 3E **89**
Stanhope St. *Roch* 6H **27**
Stanhope St. *Stoc* 2G **127**
Stanhope Way. *Fail* 3E **85**
Stanhorne Av. *M8* 1C **82**
Stanhurst. *Eccl* 2G **91**
Stanier Av. *Eccl* 2F **91**
Stanier St. *M9* 3G **83**

Stanion Gro. *Duk* 5B **100**
Stan Jolly Wlk. *M11* 5E **97**
Stanlaw Ho. *Eccl* 4G **91**
Stanley Av. *M14* 4G **109**
Stanley Av. *Haz G* 2D **152**
Stanley Av. *Hyde* 3C **114**
Stanley Av. *Marp* 4B **142**
Stanley Av. N. *P'wich* 3E **67**
Stanley Av. S. *P'wich* 3E **67**
Stanley Clo. *M16* 2A **108**
Stanley Clo. *W'fld* 6D **50**
Stanley Ct. *Bury* 2D **36**
Stanley Dri. *Hand* 1H **159**
Stanley Dri. *Timp* 6A **134**
Stanley Dri. *W'fld* 3D **66**
Stanley Green. 1A **160**
Stanley Grn. Ind. Est.
Chea H 1A **160**
(in three parts)
Stanley Grn. Retail Pk.
Chea H 1B **160**
Stanley Gro.
M12 & M18 . . . . . . .3B **110**
Stanley Gro. *Chor H* 1G **123**
Stanley Gro. *Stoc* 5D **126**
Stanley Gro. *Urm* 5F **105**
Stanley Hall La. *Dis* 1G **165**
Stanley M. *Bolt* 6F **33**
Stanley Mt. *Sale* 6A **122**
Stanley Pk. Wlk. *Bolt* 6E **33**
Stanley Pl. *Roch* 3G **27**
Stanley Rd. *Bolt* 4F **31**
Stanley Rd. *Chad* 5H **71**
Stanley Rd. *Chea H* 1H **159**
Stanley Rd. *Dent* 3B **112**
Stanley Rd. *Eccl* 4F **91**
Stanley Rd. *Farn* 1A **62**
Stanley Rd. *Old T* 2H **107**
Stanley Rd. *Rad* 1E **49**
Stanley Rd. *Salf* 3A **82**
Stanley Rd. *Stoc* 5D **126**
Stanley Rd. *Swin* 3G **79**
Stanley Rd. *Whal R* 5C **108**
Stanley Rd. *W'fld* 6D **50**
Stanley Rd. *Wors* 1F **77**
Stanley Sq. *Stal* 4D **100**
Stanley St. *M8* 1E **95** (1B **6**)
Stanley St. *M40* 6H **83**
Stanley St. *Chad* 2H **71**
Stanley St. *Heyw* 4F **39**
Stanley St. *Lees* 4A **74**
Stanley St. *Open* 6G **97**
Stanley St. *P'wich* 5G **67**
Stanley St. *Rams* 4D **12**
Stanley St. *Roch* 2G **27**
Stanley St. *Salf* 4C **94** (6E **5**)
(in two parts)
Stanley St. *S'head* 3C **74**
Stanley St. *Stal* 4D **100**
Stanley St. *Stoc* 1A **140**
Stanley St. *W'fld* 6D **50**
Stanley St. S. *Bolt* 1A **46**
Stanlo Ho. *M1* 2B **10**
Stanmere Ct. *Hawk* 1D **20**
Stanmore Av. *Stret* 5B **106**
Stanmore Dri. *Bolt* 2G **45**
Stanmore Ho. *Aud* 5C **98**
Stannard Rd. *Eccl* 4B **90**
Stanneybrook Clo.
Roch 3D **20**
Stanney Clo. *Miln* 6E **29**
Stanneylands Clo.
Wilm 5G **159**
Stanneylands Dri.
Wilm 5F **159**
Stanneylands Rd.
Styal & Wilm 3F **159**
(in two parts)
Stanney Rd. *Roch* 3B **28**
Stannybrook Rd. *Fail* 4B **86**
Stanrose Clo. *Eger* 2C **18**
Stanrose Vs. *Eger* 1C **18**

Stansbury Pl.—Stockwood Wlk.

Stansbury Pl. Stoc 5E 141
Stansby Gdns.
M12 . . . . .1A 110 (6H 11)
Stansfield Clo. Bolt 5D 32
Stansfield Dri. Roch 2A 26
Stansfield Hall. L'boro 6G 17
Stansfield Rd. Fail 3G 85
Stansfield Rd. Hyde 3C 114
Stansfield St. M11 . . . . . .5F 97
Stansfield St. M40 . . . . . .1F 97
Stansfield St. Chad 4H 71
Stansfield St. Oldh 1C 72
Stansted Wlk. M23 . . . . .2D 134
Stanthorne Av. M20 . . . .1E 125
Stanton Av. M20 . . . . . . .5C 124
Stanton Av. Salf 5F 81
Stanton Ct. Stret 3D 106
Stanton Gdns. Stoc 2D 138
Stanton St. M11 . . . . .3E 97
Stanton St. Chad 6H 71
Stanton St. Stret 3D 106
Stanway Av. Bolt 1H 45
Stanway Clo. Bolt 1H 45
Stanway Clo. Midd 3B 70
Stanway Dri. Hale 2H 145
Stanway Rd. W'fld 1F 67
Stanway St. M9 . . . . .3G 83
Stanway St. Stret 4D 106
Stanwell Rd. M40 . . . . . . .2C 84
Stanwell Rd. Swin 4E 79
Stanwick Av. M9 . . . . .5C 68
Stanworth Av. Bolt 6G 33
Stanworth Clo. M16 . . . .4C 108
Stanyard Ct. Salf 5G 93
Stanycliffe. 4B 54
Stanycliffe La. Midd 4B 54
Stanyforth St. Had 3H 117
Stapleford Clo. M23 . . . .1F 147
Stapleford Clo. Bury 3G 35
Stapleford Clo. Sale 4E 123
Stapleford Wlk. Dent 6E 113
Staplehurst Rd. M40 . . . . .1C 96
Staplers Wlk. M14 . . . . .4G 109
Stapleton Av. Bolt 4C 30
Stapleton St. Salf 6A 80
Starbeck Clo. Bury 3F 35
Starcliffe St. Bolt 5F 47
Starcross Wlk. M40 . . . . . .5B 84
Starfield Av. L'boro 1F 29
Star Gro. Salf 5A 82
Star Ind. Est. Oldh 4D 72
Starkey St. Heyw 2F 39
(in two parts)
Starkie Rd. Bolt 6D 32
(Bury Rd.)
Starkie Rd. Bolt 4D 32
(Tonge Moor Rd.)
Starkies. Bury 6C 36
Starkie St. Wors 3A 78
Starling. 4F 35
Starling Clo. Droy 2D 98
Starling Dri. Farn 2B 62
Starling Rd.
Rad & Bury 5E 35
Starmoor Dri. M8 . . . . . . .5C 82
Starmoor Wlk. M8 . . . . . .5C 82
Starmount Clo. Brad F . . .1A 48
Starring Gro. L'boro 4D 16
(off Starring Rd.)
Starring La. L'boro 4C 16
Starring Rd. L'boro 3C 16
(in two parts)
Starring Way. L'boro 4D 16
Starry Wlk. Salf . . .1A 94 (1B 4)
Stash Gro. M23 . . . . . . .4H 135
Statham Clo. Dent 4G 113
Statham Fold. Hyde 3E 115
Statham St. Salf 2H 93
Statham Wlk.
M13 . . . . . . .6F 95 (3D 10)
Station App. M1 . . .4F 95 (6C 6)
(Oxford Rd. Station)
Station App.
M1 . . . . .5E 95 (2A 10)
(Piccadilly Station)
Station App. Alt 1G 145
Station App. H Grn 5E 149
Station App. Bus. Cen.
Roch 5H 27
(off Station Rd.)
Station Bri. Urm 5F 105
Station Clo. Hyde 5A 114
Station Cotts. B'hth 3F 133
Station Cotts. Chea H . . .3D 150
Station Cotts. Dig 2D 60
(off Lee Side)
Station Cotts. Part 5E 119
Stationers Entry. Roch . . .4H 27
(off Butts, The)
Station La. G'fld 4E 61
Station La. G'ton 4C 74
Station Rd. M8 . . . . .2C 82
Station Rd. Chea H 3C 150
Station Rd. Eccl 4F 91
Station Rd. G'mnt 2H 21
Station Rd. G'ton 4C 74
Station Rd. Had 2H 117
Station Rd. Hand 4H 159
Station Rd. Heat M 2A 138
Station Rd. Hyde 5E 115
Station Rd. Irlam 2C 118
Station Rd. Kear 2H 63
Station Rd. L'boro 4F 17
Station Rd. Marp 5D 142
Station Rd. Miln 6F 29
Station Rd. Moss 2F 89
Station Rd. N Mills 4G 155
Station Rd. Oldh 5E 57
Station Rd. Redd 5G 111
Station Rd. Roch 5H 27
Station Rd. Stret 4D 106
Station Rd. Styal 4E 159
Station Rd. Swin 3F 79
Station Rd. Upperm 2D 60
(Diggle)
Station Rd. Upperm 1F 61
(Uppermill)
Station Rd. Urm 5F 105
Station Rd. Whitw 2H 15
(Hoyle St.)
Station Rd. Whitw 4B 14
(Market St.)
Station Rd. Wilm 2E 167
Station Rd. Woodl 4H 129
Station Sq. Moss 2E 89
Station St. Bolt 1B 46
Station St. Duk 4H 99
Station St. Haz G 3D 152
Station St. S'head 3B 74
Station Vw. M19 . . . . . . .6C 110
Station Vw. Droy 6A 98
Staton Av. Bolt 5E 33
Staton St. M11 . . . . .5E 97
Statter St. Bury 3E 51
Staveleigh Mall. Ash L . . .2H 99
Staveley Av. Bolt 5C 18
Staveley Av. Stal 2E 101
Staveley Clo. Midd 5G 53
Staveley Clo. Shaw 1H 57
Stavely Wlk. Rytn 3C 56
(off Shaw St.)
Staverton Clo.
M13 . . . . . . .6G 95 (4E 11)
Staveton Clo. Bram 2A 152
Stavordale. Roch 3G 27
(off Spotland Rd.)
Staycott St. M16 . . . . . .3D 108
Stayley Dri. Stal 3G 101
Stead St. Rams 3E 13
Steadway. G'fld 4G 61
Stedman Clo. M11 . . . . . .4A 96
Steele Gdns. Bolt 2G 47
Steeles Av. Hyde 4C 114
Steeple Clo. M8 . . . . .6B 82
Steeple Dri. Salf 5G 93
Steeple Vw. Rytn 3B 56
Stelfox Av. M14 . . . . . . .6E 109
Stelfox Av. Timp 3C 134
Stelfox La. Aud 6E 99
Stelfox St. Eccl 5D 90
Stella St. M9 . . . . .5D 68
Stelling St. M18 . . . . . . .2F 111
Stenbury Clo. M14 . . . . .4G 109
Stenner La. M20 . . . . . . .1E 137
Stenson Sq. Open 6F 97
Stephen Clo. Bury 3A 36
(off Stephen St.)
Stephen Lowry Wlk.
M9 . . . . .4A 84
Stephenson Av. Droy 4A 98
Stephenson Rd. Stret . . .5E 107
Stephenson St. Fail 2G 85
Stephenson St. Oldh 1H 73
Stephens Rd. M20 . . . . .4G 125
Stephens Rd. Stal 1D 100
Stephens St. Bolt 6F 33
Stephens Ter. M20 . . . . .6F 125
Stephen St. M3 . . .1D 94 (1H 5)
Stephen St. Bury 3A 36
Stephen St. Stoc 3B 140
Stephen St. Urm 5G 105
Stephen St. S. Bury 4A 36
Stephen Wlk. Stoc 3B 140
Stepping Hill. 1C 152
Steps Mdw. Roch 5A 16
Stern Av. Salf 5G 93
Sterndale Rd. Rom 2H 141
Sterndale Rd. Stoc 6G 139
Sterndale Rd. Wors 5B 76
Sterratt St. Bolt 6H 31
Stetchworth Dri. Wors . . .4D 76
Stevenson Ct. Kear 2G 63
Stevenson Dri. Oldh 3A 58
Stevenson Pl.
M1 . . . . .4F 95 (5C 6)
Stevenson Rd. Swin 3E 79
Stevenson Sq.
M1 . . . . .4F 95 (5C 6)
Stevenson Sq. Roch 6A 16
Stevenson St.
Salf 4B 94 (5C 4)
Stevenson St. Wors 6D 62
Stevens St. Ald E 5G 167
Stewart Av. Farn 2D 62
Stewart St. Ash L 3F 99
Stewart St. Bolt 4A 32
Stewart St. Bury 2H 35
(in two parts)
Stewart St. Miln 2F 43
Steynton Clo. Bolt 5D 30
Stile Clo. Urm 5G 103
Stiles Av. Marp 4C 142
Stiles Clo. Had 2G 117
Stilton Dri. M11 . . . . .5C 96
Stirling. Eccl 3H 91
(off Monton La.)
Stirling Av. M20 . . . . . . .1D 124
Stirling Av. Haz G 4D 152
Stirling Av. Marp 6D 142
Stirling Clo. Stoc 5E 139
Stirling Ct. Stoc 4E 127
Stirling Dri. Stal 2E 101
Stirling Gro. W'fld 1E 67
Stirling Pl. Heyw 4B 38
Stirling Rd. Bolt 6C 18
Stirling Rd. Chad 5F 71
Stirling St. Oldh 2A 72
Stirrup Brook Gro.
Wors 6B 76
Stirrup Ga. Wors 6A 78
Stitch La. Stoc 6F 127
Stitch Mi La. Bolt 3G 33
Stiups La. Roch 1H 41
Stobart Av. P'wich 1G 81
Stock Brook. 2H 71
Stockburn Dri. Fail 4A 86
Stockbury Clo. Bolt 4B 32
(off Lindbury Dri.)
Stock Clo. Roch 1G 27
Stockdale Av. Stoc 6H 139
Stockdale Gro. Bolt 4H 33
Stockdale Rd. M9 . . . . . . .5G 69
Stockfield Mt. Chad 3H 71
Stockfield Rd. Chad 2H 71
Stock Gro. Miln 4F 29
Stockholm Rd. Stoc 5F 139
Stockholm St. M11 . . . . .3D 96
Stockland Clo.
M13 . . . . . . .6F 95 (4C 10)
Stock La. Chad 2H 71
Stockley Av. Bolt 3G 33
Stockley Wlk.
M15 . . . . . .1B 108 (6D 8)
Stockport. 2H 139
Stockport Art Gallery.
. . . . .3H 139
Stockport County
Football Club. . . .4G 139
(Edgeley Park)
Stockport Crematorium.
Stoc 4A 140
Stockport Great Moor.
. . . . .6C 140
Stockport Little Moor.
. . . . .3C 140
Stockport Megabowl.
. . . . .3G 139
Stockport Mus. 1B 140
Stockport Rd. M12 &
M13 . . . . . .1G 109 (5F 11)
Stockport Rd. Ash L 5F 99
Stockport Rd.
Chea & Stoc 5H 137
Stockport Rd. Dent 4F 113
Stockport Rd. Hyde 6A 116
(Hattersley)
Stockport Rd. Hyde 6C 114
(Hyde)
Stockport Rd. Lyd 4E 75
Stockport Rd. Marp 5H 141
Stockport Rd. Moss 1E 89
Stockport Rd. Rom 1H 141
Stockport Rd. Timp 6G 133
Stockport Rd. E.
Bred 5F 129
Stockport Rd. W.
Bred 6C 128
Stockport Tourist Info. Cen.
. . . . .2G 139
Stockport Town Hall.
. . . . .3H 139
Stockport Trad. Est.
Stoc 2E 139
Stockport Viaduct. 2G 139
Stockport Village.
Stoc 2G 139
Stock Rd. Roch 1A 28
Stocksfield Dri. M9 . . . . . .6G 69
Stocksfield Dri. L Hul 4B 62
Stocks Gdns. Stal 4G 101
Stocks Ga. Roch 1D 26
Stocks Ind. Est. Eccl 3E 91
Stocks La. Stal 4F 101
Stocks St. M8 . . . .2E 95 (1A 6)
Stocks St. Roch 3B 40
Stocks St. E.
M8 . . . . .2E 95 (1A 6)
Stock St. Bury 6E 23
Stockton Av. Stoc 3D 138
Stockton Dri. Bury 6B 22
Stockton Pk. Oldh 3H 73
Stockton Rd. M21 . . . . .1G 123
Stockton Rd. Farn 5E 47
Stockton Rd. Wilm 5C 166
Stockton St. M16 . . . . . .3C 108
Stockton St. L'boro 4E 17
Stockton St. Swin 3E 79
Stockwood Wlk. M9 . . . . .4F 83

Stoke Abbot Clo.
    Bram 6G 151
Stoke Abbot Lodge.
    Bram 6G 151
Stokesay Clo. Bury 2D 50
Stokesay Clo. Shaw . . .3E 57
Stokesay Dri. Haz G . . .4C 152
Stokesay Rd. Sale 4G 121
Stokesby Gdns. Los 5A 30
Stokesley Wlk. Bolt 3A 46
    (in two parts)
Stokes St. M11 . . . . . . .3F 97
Stoke St. Roch 5B 28
Stokoe Av. Alt 6C 132
Stolford Wlk. M8 . . . . .5B 82
    (off Ermington Dri.)
Stonall Av.
    M15 . . . . . .1B 108 (5D 8)
Stoneacre Ct. Swin 3F 79
Stoneacre Rd. M22 . . . .3A 148
Stonebeck Ct. W'houg . .6D 44
Stonebeck Rd. M23 . . . .6F 135
Stone Breaks. 3D 74
Stone Breaks. S'head . . .2C 74
Stone Breaks Rd.
    S'head 3C 74
Stonebridge Clo. Los . . .1A 44
Stonechat Clo. Droy 2C 98
Stonechat Clo. Wors 3D 76
Stonechurch. Bolt 2H 45
Stonecliffe Av. Stal 3E 101
Stonecliffe Ter. Stal 2E 101
Stone Clo. Rams 5C 12
Stoneclough. 2B 64
Stoneclough Rd.
    Kear & Rad 2H 63
Stonecroft. Oldh 2C 72
Stonedelph Clo. A'wth . .4D 34
Stonefield Dri. M8 . . . . .6A 82
Stonefield St. Miln 6F 29
Stoneflat Ct. Roch 3F 27
Stonehaven. Bolt 4D 44
Stonehead St. M9 . . . . .4H 83
Stonehewer St. Rad 5H 49
Stonehill Croc. Roch . . .6A 14
Stonehill Dri. Roch 6A 14
Stone Hill Ind Est. Farn . .3F 63
Stone Hill La. Roch 6A 14
Stone Hill Rd. Farn 3F 63
Stonehill Rd. Roch 6A 14
Stonehouse. Brom X 4F 19
Stonehouse Wlk. M23 . .4E 135
    (off Sandy La.)
Stonehurst. Marp 6C 142
Stonehurst Clo. M12 . . . .1C 110
Stonelands Way. G'ton . .5C 74
Stoneleigh Av. Sale 4F 121
Stoneleigh Dri. Rad 2B 64
Stoneleigh Rd. S'head . . .2C 74
Stoneleigh St. Oldh 6F 57
Stonelow Clo.
    M15 . . . . . .1D 108 (5H 9)
Stonemead. Rom 6C 130
Stone Mead Av. Haleb . .6C 146
Stonemead Clo. Bolt 3B 46
Stonemill Ter. Stoc 6H 127
Stonepail Clo. Gat 6D 136
Stonepail Rd. Gat 6E 137
Stone Pale. W'fld 2D 66
Stone Pits. Rams 2B 12
Stone Pl. M14 . . . . . . .4G 109
Stoneridge. Had 2H 167
Stone Row. Marp 5E 143
    (in two parts)
Stonesby Clo. M16 . . . .3B 108
Stonesdale Clo. Rytn . . .2C 56
Stones Mdw. Cvn. Pk.
    Urm 2A 120
Stonesteads Dri.
    Brom X 3E 19
Stonesteads Way.
    Brom X 3E 19

Stone St. M3 . . . .5C 94 (2F 9)
Stone St. Bolt 4D 32
Stone St. Miln 6F 29
Stoneswood Dri. Moss . .1F 89
Stoneswood Rd. Del 4G 59
Stoneyhank. Had 2C 64
Stoneyfield. 1F 41
Stoneyfield. Stal 1E 101
Stoneyfield Clo. M16 . . .5D 108
Stoneygate Wlk. Open . . .6F 97
Stoney Knoll. Salf 5H 81
Stoney La. Wilm 4C 166
Stoneyroyd. Whitw 4H 15
Stoneyside Av. Wors . . .5G 63
Stoneyside Gro. Wors . . .5G 63
Stoney St. M3 . . .4D 94 (6G 5)
Stoneyvale Ct. Roch 1F 41
Stonie Heys Av. Roch . . .1B 28
Stonyford Rd. Sale 5D 122
Stony Head. L'boro 5G 17
    (off Higher Calderbrook Rd.)
Stonyhurst Av. Bolt 6C 18
Stopes Rd.
    L Lev & Rad 4C 48
Stopford Av. L'boro 5C 16
Stopford St. M11 . . . . . .6G 97
Stopford St. Stoc 3F 139
Stopford Wlk. Dent 4F 113
Stopley Wlk. Open 5C 96
Store Pas. L'boro 4E 17
Stores Cotts. Grass 3G 75
Stores Rd. Man A 1G 157
Stores St. P'wich 5G 67
Store St. M1 . . . .5F 95 (1D 10)
Store St. Ash L 5E 87
Store St. Open 6D 96
Store St. Roch 2A 26
Store St. Shaw 5G 43
Store St. Stoc 1C 152
Storeton Clo. M22 . . . . .3C 148
Stormer Hill Fold.
    T'ton 3H 21
Stortford Dri. M23 . . . . .1H 135
Stothard Rd. Stret 6B 106
Stott Dri. Urm 6H 103
Stottfield. Rytn 4H 55
Stott Ho. Oldh 4C 72
Stott La. Bolt 4D 32
Stott La. Midd 2H 53
Stott La. Salf 2B 92
Stott Milne St. Chad 4H 71
Stott Rd. Chad 6E 71
Stott Rd. Swin 5D 78
Stott's La. M40 . . . . . . .5D 84
Stott St. Fail 5D 84
Stott St. Roch (OL12) . . .2H 27
Stott St. Roch (OL16) . . .6B 16
Stourbridge Av. L Hul . . .3C 62
Stour Clo. Alt 5E 133
Stourport Clo. Rom 2G 141
Stourport St. Oldh 6E 57
Stovell Av. Long 5C 110
Stovell Rd. M40 . . . . . .3A 84
Stow Clo. Bury 6D 22
Stowell Ct. Bolt 4A 32
Stowell St. Bolt 4A 32
Stowell St. Salf 4E 93
Stowfield Clo. M9 . . . . .5D 68
Stow Gdns. M20 . . . . . .3E 125
Stracey St. M40 . . . . . .2A 96
    (in two parts)
Stradbroke Clo. M18 . . .2D 110
Strain Av. M9 . . . . .5F 69
Strand Ct. Stret 1C 122
Strand, The. Roch 3F 41
Strand Way. Rytn 5B 56
Strangeways. 1D 94
Strangford St. Rad 3D 48
Strang St. Rams 3E 13
Stranton Dri. Wors 3C 78
Stratfield Av. M23 . . . . .2D 134
Stratford Av. M20 . . . . .4D 124

Stratford Av. Bolt 4E 31
Stratford Av. Bury 3E 23
Stratford Av. Eccl 5E 91
Stratford Av. Oldh 6C 72
Stratford Av. Roch 6G 27
Stratford Clo. Farn 6B 46
Stratford Gdns. Bred 6F 129
Stratford Rd. Midd 4B 70
Stratford Sq. H Grn 6G 149
Strathaven Pl. Heyw 4B 38
Strathblane Clo. M20 . . .2F 125
Strathblane St. Salf 5H 137
    (off Achfield Rd.)
Strathfield Dri. M11 . . . . .3E 97
Strathmere Av. Stret 4D 106
Strathmore Av. M16 . . . .5H 107
Strathmore Av. Dent 5H 113
Strathmore Clo. Rams . . .5E 13
Strathmore Rd. Bolt 4G 33
Stratton Rd. M16 . . . . . .5H 107
Stratton Rd. Stoc 3C 140
Stratton Rd. Swin 2F 79
Strawberry Bank. Salf . . .2H 93
Strawberry Clo. B'hth . . .4D 132
Strawberry Hill.
    Salf 2H 93 (1A 4)
Strawberry Hill Rd.
    Bolt 2D 46
Strawberry La. Moss 5E 75
Strawberry La. Wilm 3B 166
Strawberry Rd. Salf 2G 93
Stray St. M11 . . . . .5G 97
Stray, The. Bolt 1D 32
Streamside Clo. Timp . . .1B 146
Stream Ter. Stoc 2B 140
Street Bridge. 4G 55
Street Bri. Rd. Oldh 5G 55
Street End. 3G 85
Streetgate. L Hul 4B 62
Streethouse La. Dob 6H 59
St James' Ct. Hyde 5H 115
Street La. Rad 5E 35
Street Lodge. Roch 4B 40
Street, The. Shaw 6H 43
Stretford. 6D 106
Stretford Ho. Stret 6C 106
Stretford Leisure Cen.
    . . . . .3F 107
Stretford Motorway Est.
    Stret 2A 100
Stretford Pl. Roch 6E 15
Stretford Rd. M16 &
    M15 . . . . . .2A 108 (6C 8)
Stretford Rd. Urm 6F 105
Stretton Av. M20 . . . . . .6G 125
Stretton Av. Sale 5G 121
Stretton Av. Stret 4A 106
Stretton Clo. M40 . . . . . .6F 83
Stretton Rd. Bolt 3F 45
Stretton Rd.
    Rams & G'mnt 1A 22
Stretton Way. Hand 2H 159
Striding Edge Wlk.
    Oldh 6E 57
Strine Dale. 3B 58
Strines. 4G 155
Strines Ct. Hyde 3C 114
Strines Rd. Marp 5E 143
Stringer Av. Mot 5B 116
Stringer Clo. Mot 5B 116
Stringer Av. Stoc 1A 140
Stringer Way. Mot 5B 116
Stroma Gdns. Urm 2E 105
Stromness Gro. Heyw . . .4B 38
Strong St. Salf 1C 94
Strongstry. 3A 12
Strontian Wlk. Open 4E 97
Stroud Av. Eccl 2D 90
Stroud Clo. Midd 4A 70
Struan Ct. Alt 6E 133
Stuart Av. Irlam 5D 102
Stuart Av. Marp 4B 142

Stuart Hampson Ct.
    Part 6D 118
Stuart Ho. Droy 5A 98
Stuart Rd. Bred 3D 128
Stuart Rd. B'hth 4D 132
Stuart Rd. Stret 4D 106
Stuart St. M11 . . . . .3C 96
    (in two parts)
Stuart St. Midd 1C 70
Stuart St. Oldh 4C 72
Stuart St. Roch 5A 28
    (in two parts)
Stuart St F. M11 . . . . . . .3C 96
Stuart Wlk. Midd 2H 69
Stubbins. 1E 13
Stubbins Clo. M23 . . . . .2E 135
Stubbins La. Rams 2E 13
Stubbins St. Rams 1E 13
Stubbins Va. Rd. Rams . .1E 13
Stubbins Va. Ter.
    Rams 1D 12
Stubbs Clo. Salf 3F 81
Stubley. 4D 16
Stubley Gdns. L'boro . . .4E 17
Stubley La. L'boro 4D 16
Stubley Mill Rd. L'boro . .5C 16
    (in four parts)
Studforth Wlk. M15 . . . .2E 109
    (off Botham Clo.)
Studland Rd. M22 . . . . .1D 148
Studley Clo. Rytn 3E 57
Styal. 4D 158
Styal Av. Stoc 3H 127
Styal Av. Stret 4A 106
Styal Country Pk. 5C 158
Styalgate. Gat 6D 136
Styal Gro. Gat 2E 149
Styal Rd.
    M22 & H Grn 1D 158
Styal Rd.
    Styal & Wilm 4E 159
Styal St. Bolt 5F 31
Styal Vw. Wilm 5F 159
Styhead Dri. Midd 4F 53
Style St. M4 . . . .2E 95 (2B 6)
Styperson Way. Poy 4C 163
Sudbury Clo. M16 . . . . .2A 108
Sudbury Dri. H Grn 5G 149
Sudbury Dri. Los 1A 44
Sudbury Rd. Haz G 5E 153
Sudden. 1C 40
Sudden St. Roch 1C 40
Sudell St.
    M4 & M40 . . .2F 95 (2D 6)
Sudell St. Ind. Est. M4 . .2D 6
Sudley Rd. Roch 6E 27
Sudlow St. Roch 1B 28
Sudren St. Bury 2F 35
Sue Patterson Wlk.
    M40 . . . . .6F 83
Suffield St. Midd 1H 69
Suffield Wlk. M22 . . . . . .4B 148
Suffolk Av. Droy 2A 98
Suffolk Clo. L Lev 2B 48
Suffolk Dri. Stoc 3C 128
Suffolk Pl. Wilm 6G 159
Suffolk Rd. Alt 1D 144
Suffolk St. Oldh 4H 71
Suffolk St. Roch 5H 27
Suffolk St. Salf 6E 81
Sugar La. Dob 5A 60
Sugden Sports Cen.
    . . . . .6E 95 (4B 10)
Sugden St. Ash L 2B 100
Sulby Av. Stret 5E 107
Sulby St. M40 . . . . .3A 84
Sulby St. Rad 2B 64
Sulgrave Av. Poy 3F 163
Sullivan St. M12 . . . . . .4C 110
Sultan St. Bury 5D 36
Sulway Clo. Swin 4G 79
Sumac St. M11 . . . . . . .3F 97

Sumbland Ho. *Swin* 1H 79
Summer Av. *Urm* 5G 105
Summer Castle. *Roch* . . .4H 27
Summercroft. *Chad* 6H 71
Summerdale Dri.
   Rams 1B 22
Summerfield Av. *Droy* . . .2G 97
Summerfield Ct. *M32* . . .6F 107
Summerfield Dri. *Midd* . . .5C 54
Summerfield Dri.
   P'wich 2E 81
Summerfield Pl.
   Wilm 4D 166
Summerfield Rd.
   M22 . . . . .3A 148
Summerfield Rd. *Bolt* . . .3B 46
Summerfield Rd. *Wors* . . .4A 78
Summerfields Village Cen.
   Wilm 6H 159
Summerfield Vw. *Oldh* . . .6G 73
Summer Hill. Dent 4E 113
   (off Duke St.)
Summer Hill. Moss 1F 89
   (off Greenhill Cotts.)
Summer Hill Clo. *Bolt* . . .5B 18
Summerhill Ct. *Gat* 6F 137
Summerlea. *Chea H* 5D 150
Summer Pl. *M14* 5G 109
Summers Av. *Stal* 3G 101
Summerseat. 1C 22
Summerseat Clo. *Salf* . . .5G 93
Summerseat Clo.
   S'head 2C 74
Summerseat La. *Rams* . .6C 12
   (in three parts)
Summersgill Clo.
   Heyw 4G 39
Summershades La.
   Grass 3F 75
Summershades Ri.
   Oldh 3F 75
Summers St. *Chad* 2A 72
Summer St. *Roch* 4A 28
Summerton Ho. Salf 4G 93
   (off Buckingham St.)
Summerville Av. *M9* 4H 83
Summerville Rd. *Salf* . . .6C 80
Summit. 3C 38
   (Heywood)
Summit. 5H 17
   (Littleborough)
Summit. 5A 42
   (Oldham)
Summit Clo. *Bury* 1B 38
Summit St. *Heyw* 3B 38
Sumner Av. *Bolt* 4D 34
Sumner Rd. *Salf* 6B 80
Sumner St. *Bolt* 5F 45
Sumner St. *Shaw* 2F 57
Sumner Way. *Urm* 5E 105
Sunadale Clo. *Bolt* 2F 45
Sunbank Clo. *Roch* 1F 27
Sunbank La. *Ring* 2D 156
Sunbeam Wlk. M11 . . . . .4B 96
   (off Hopedale Clo.)
Sunbury Clo. *Duk* 5D 100
Sunbury Clo. *Wilm* 5A 160
Sunbury Dri. *M40* 1F 97
Sundance Ct. *Salf* 5E 93
Sunderland Av. *Ash L* . . .1A 100
Sunderton Wlk. *M12* 1A 110
Sundew Pl. *Midd* 2D 70
Sundial Clo. *Hyde* 4H 115
Sundial Rd. *Stoc* 4D 140
Sundial Wlk. *Hyde* 4H 115
Sundridge Clo. *Bolt* 4E 45
Sunfield. *Rom* 6H 129
Sunfield Av. *Oldh* 3A 58
Sunfield Cres. *Rytn* 4C 56
Sunfield Dri. *Rytn* 4D 56
Sunfield Est. *Dig* 3C 60
Sunfield La. *Dig* 3C 60

Sunfield Rd. *Oldh* 1C 72
Sunfield Way. *Lees* 2A 74
Sunflower Mdw. *Irlam* . . .5F 103
Sun Ga. *L'boro* 2F 29
Sun Hill. 2A 74
Sunhill Clo. *Roch* 3H 41
Sunk La. *Midd* 1A 70
   (in two parts)
Sunlight Rd. *Bolt* 6G 31
Sunningdale Av. *M11* . . .3D 96
Sunningdale Av. *Rad* . . .2D 48
Sunningdale Av. *Sale* . . .6E 123
Sunningdale Av. *W'fld* . . .2A 66
Sunningdale Clo. *Bury* . .5G 35
Sunningdale Clo.
   Hyde 2D 114
Sunningdale Ct. *Dent* . . .4B 112
Sunningdale Dri.
   Bram 6H 151
Sunningdale Dri. *Heyw* . . .5F 39
Sunningdale Dri.
   Irlam 4D 102
Sunningdale Dri.
   P'wich 4F 67
Sunningdale Dri. *Salf* . . .6G 79
Sunningdale Ho. *Sale* . . .6E 123
Sunningdale Rd.
   Chea H 6C 150
Sunningdale Rd. *Dent* . . .6G 113
Sunningdale Rd. *Urm* . . .6D 104
Sunningdale Wlk. *Bolt* . . .2H 45
Sunninghey Ct. *Ald E* . . .4F 167
Sunning Hill St. *Bolt* 3H 45
Sunny Av. *Bury* 6F 23
Sunny Bank. 4E 51
Sunny Bank. *Lees* 4A 74
Sunny Bank. *Rad* 1A 64
Sunnybank. *Wilm* 3D 166
Sunny Bank Av. *Droy* . . .4H 97
Sunnybank Av. *Eccl* 2H 91
Sunny Bank Av. *Stoc* 5B 126
Sunnybank Dri. *Wilm* . . .5A 166
Sunnybank Rd. *Bolt* 3G 31
Sunny Bank Rd. *Bow* . . .4E 145
Sunny Bank Rd. *Bury* . . .4D 50
Sunnybank Rd. *Droy* 4H 97
Sunny Bower St. *T'ton* . . .5G 21
Sunny Brow Rd. *M18* 2E 111
Sunny Brow Rd. *Midd* . . .1G 69
Sunny Dri. *P'wich* 5D 66
Sunnyfield Rd. *P'wich* . . .2G 67
Sunnyfield Rd. *Stoc* 6B 126
Sunnylea Av. *M19* 4A 126
Sunny Lea M. *Wilm* 3D 166
Sunnymead Av. *Bolt* 1B 32
Sunnymede Va. *Rams* . . .6C 12
Sunnyside. *Ash L* 6D 86
Sunnyside. *Droy* 2H 97
Sunnyside Av. *Droy* 1H 97
Sunny Side Cotts.
   Roch 1F 25
Sunny Side Cotts.
   Stret 5F 107
Sunnyside Ct. *M20* 6G 125
Sunnyside Ct. *Droy* 2H 97
Sunnyside Cres.
   Ash L 3B 100
Sunnyside Gro. *Ash L* . . .3B 100
Sunnyside Rd. *Bolt* 3G 31
Sunnyside Rd. *Droy* 2H 97
Sunnywood Dri. *T'ton* . . .5A 22
Sunny Wood La. *T'ton* . . .5A 22
Sunrise Vw. *L'boro* 6H 17
Sunset Av. *M22* 1B 136
Sun St. *Moss* 2E 89
Sun St. *Rams* 2D 12
Sunwell Ter. *Marp* 1D 154
Surbiton Rd. *M40* 1D 96
Surma Clo. *Oldh* 2B 72
Surma Clo. *Roch* 6B 28

Surrey Av. *Droy* 2H 97
Surrey Av. *Shaw* 6D 42
Surrey Clo. *L Lev* 3B 48
Surrey Dri. *Bury* 5D 36
Surrey Pk. Clo. *Shaw* 5F 43
Surrey Rd. *M9* 1F 83
Surrey St. *M9* 1E 83
Surrey St. *Ash L* 6H 87
Surrey St. *Chad* 4A 72
Surrey Way. *Stoc* 5C 128
Surtees Rd. *M23* 1G 135
Sussex Av. *M20* 5F 125
Sussex Av. *Bury* 4A 38
Sussex Clo. *Chad* 3H 71
Sussex Clo. *Swin* 1F 79
Sussex Dri. *Bury* 5D 36
Sussex Dri. *Droy* 2A 98
Sussex Pl. *Hyde* 2D 114
Sussex Rd. *Cad* 3A 118
Sussex Rd. *Part* 6C 118
Sussex Rd. *Stoc* 3D 138
Sussex St. *M2* 4D 94 (5H 5)
Sussex St. *Roch* 5H 27
Sussex St. *Salf* . . .2B 94 (1C 4)
Sutcliffe Av. *M12* 5D 110
Sutcliffe St. *Ash L* 4F 99
Sutcliffe St. *Bolt* 3A 32
Sutcliffe St. *L'boro* 3F 17
Sutcliffe St. *Midd* 1C 70
Sutcliffe St. *Oldh* 4C 72
Sutcliffe St. *Rytn* 4E 57
Sutherland Clo. *Oldh* 2D 86
Sutherland Flats. Heyw . . .3E 39
   (off Meadow Clo.)
Sutherland Gro. *Farn* 1E 63
Sutherland Rd. *M16* 4G 107
Sutherland Rd. *Bolt* 4E 31
Sutherland Rd. *Heyw* 4A 38
Sutherland St. *Ash L* 2C 100
Sutherland St. *Eccl* 2D 90
Sutherland St. *Farn* 1E 63
Sutherland St. *Swin* 3E 79
Suthers St. *Oldh* 3A 72
Suthers St. *Rad* 6A 50
Sutton Clo. *Bury* 5H 35
Sutton Dri. *Droy* 2G 97
Sutton Ho. Salf 2F 93
   (off Sutton Dwellings)
Sutton Mnr. *M21* 6G 107
Sutton Rd. *M18* 4E 111
Sutton Rd. *Ald E* 4F 167
Sutton Rd. *Bolt* 3D 44
Sutton Rd. *Poy* 5F 163
Sutton Rd. *Stoc* 6E 127
Suttons La. *Marp* 6E 143
Sutton Way. *Hand* 2A 160
Sutton Way. *Salf* 2G 93
Swailes St. *Oldh* 3F 73
Swaine St. *Stoc* 2G 139
Swainsthorpe Dri. *M9* . . .3G 83
Swain St. *Roch* 2G 27
Swalecliff Av. *M23* 2D 134
Swale Clo. *Wilm* 5A 160
Swaledale Clo. *Rytn* 2C 56
Swale Dri. *Alt* 5E 133
Swallow Bank Dri.
   Roch 2B 40
Swallow Clo. *Carr* 4H 89
Swallow Dri. *Bury* 1F 37
Swallow Dri. *Irlam* 4E 103
Swallow Dri. *Roch* 4B 26
Swallow Fold. *Glos* 6H 117
Swallow La. *Carr* 4H 89
   (in two parts)
Swallow St. *M11* 4B 96
Swallow St. *M12* 5C 110
Swallow St. *Oldh* 1B 86
Swallow St. *Stoc* 4H 139
Swanage Av. *M23* 3D 134
Swanage Av. *Stoc* 5D 140
Swanage Clo. *Bury* 5C 22
Swanage Rd. *Eccl* 2D 90

Swanbourne Gdns.
   Stoc 5E 139
Swan Clo. *Poy* 3B 162
Swan Ct. *Shaw* 1F 57
Swanhill Clo. *M18* 1H 111
Swan La. *Bolt* 3H 45
Swanley Av. *M40* 6G 83
Swann Ct. *Chea H* 4D 150
Swann Gro. *Chea H* 4D 150
Swan La. *Chea H* 4C 150
Swan Rd. *G'mnt* 1H 21
Swan Rd. *Timp* 2A 134
Swan St. *M4* . . .3E 95 (3B 6)
Swan St. *Ash L* 2A 100
Swan St. *Rad* 5H 49
Swan St. *Wilm* 2E 167
Swan Ter. *Eccl* 5E 91
Swanton Wlk. M8 . . . . . .5B 82
   (off Kenford Wlk.)
Swan Wlk. *M22* 3B 148
Swarbrick Dri. *P'wich* . . .1D 80
Swayfield Av. *M13* 4B 110
Swaylands Dri. *Sale* 2B 134
Sweet Briar Clo. *Roch* . . .1G 27
Sweetbriar Clo. *Shaw* . . .6F 43
Sweet Briar La. *Roch* 1G 27
Sweetlove's Gro. *Bolt* . . .6C 18
Sweetlove's La. *Bolt* 6C 18
Sweetnam Dri. *M11* 3D 96
Swettenham Rd.
   Hand 2H 159
Swift Bank. *Glos* 6H 117
Swift Clo. *Woodl* 4A 130
Swift Rd. *Oldh* 3A 58
Swift Rd. *Roch* 4B 26
Swift St. *Ash L* 6H 87
Swiftsure Av.
   Salf 4B 94 (5C 4)
Swift Wlk. *M40* 5C 84
Swinbourne Gro.
   M20 . . . . .2G 125
Swinburne Av. *Droy* 2A 98
Swinburne Grn. *Stoc* . . .6F 111
Swinburne Way. *Dent* . . .2G 129
Swinburn St. *M9* 2H 83
Swindell's St. *M11* 6G 97
Swindells St. *Hyde* 2C 114
Swindon Clo. *M18* 2F 111
Swinfield Av. *M21* 1F 123
Swinford Gro. *Rytn* 2E 57
Swinford Wlk. *M9* 6G 69
Swinley Chase. *Wilm* . . .6B 160
Swinside Clo. *Midd* 5E 53
Swinside Rd. *Bolt* 5H 33
Swinstead Av. *M40* 6G 83
Swinton. 3F 79
Swinton Ct. Swin 4G 79
   (off Park St.)
Swinton Cres. *Bury* 6E 51
Swinton Gro. *M13* 2G 109
Swinton Hall Rd. *Swin* . . .3F 79
Swinton Ind. Est. *Swin* . . .3G 79
Swinton Leisure Cen. . . .3F 79
Swinton Library Art Gallery.
   . . . . .3F 79
Swinton Lions Rugby League
   Football Club. 6D 36
Swinton Park. 5G 79
Swinton Pk. Rd. *Salf* 6H 79
Swinton Shop. Cen.
   Swin 3F 79
Swinton St. *Bolt* 6G 33
Swinton St. *Oldh* 4G 73
Swiss Hill. *Ald E* 5H 167
Swithin Rd. *M22* 5C 148
Swithun Wells Ct.
   L Hul 4C 62
Swythamley Clo. *Stoc* . . .3C 138
Swythamley Rd. *Stoc* . . .3C 138
Sybil St. *L'boro* 3E 17
Sycamore Av. *Alt* 6C 132

Sycamore Av. *Chad* 5F **71**
Sycamore Av. *Dent* 5F **113**
Sycamore Av. *Heyw* 5G **39**
Sycamore Av. *Miln* 2E **43**
Sycamore Av. *Oldh* 1H **73**
Sycamore Av. *Rad* 1F **65**
Sycamore Clo. *M20* 2G **125**
Sycamore Clo.
  Duk (OL6) 3C **100**
Sycamore Clo.
  Duk (SK16) 5D **100**
Sycamore Clo. *L'boro* 4D **16**
Sycamore Clo. *Wilm* 6F **159**
Sycamore Ct. *M16* 4B **108**
Sycamore Ct. *M40* 2A **96**
Sycamore Ct. *Salf* 2G **93**
Sycamore Cres. *Ash L* . . .6G **87**
Sycamore Dri. *Bury* 5F **23**
Sycamore Dri. *Rad* 2G **49**
Sycamore Gro. *Fail* 4H **85**
Sycamore Lodge.
  Bram 6H **151**
Sycamore Pl. *W'fld* 3D **66**
Sycamore Rd. *Bred* 5G **129**
Sycamore Rd. *Eccl* 1C **90**
Sycamore Rd. *Part* 6B **118**
Sycamore Rd. *T'ton* 6H **21**
Sycamores, The. *Alt* 1D **144**
Sycamores, The. *Had* . . .4H **117**
Sycamores, The. *Lees* 1A **74**
Sycamores, The. *Moss* . . .2G **89**
Sycamores, The. *Rad* 3B **64**
Sycamores, The. *Sale* . . .6C **122**
Sycamores, The. *Stal* 5F **101**
Sycamore St. *Sale* 5E **123**
Sycamore St. *Stal* 4D **100**
Sycamore St. *Stoc* 3D **138**
Sycamore Wlk. *Chea* 5H **137**
Syddal Clo. *Bram* 2F **161**
Syddal Cres. *Bram* 3F **161**
Syddal Grn. *Bram* 2F **161**
Syddall Av. *H Grn* 5H **149**
Syddall St. *Hyde* 6D **114**
Syddal Rd. *Bram* 2F **161**
Cydonham St. *Oldh* 6E **57**
    (in two parts)
Sydenham Ter. *Roch* 6D **14**
Sydney Av. *Eccl* 3F **91**
Sydney Av. *Man A* 5G **147**
Sydney Gdns. *L'boro* 6G **17**
Sydney Jones Ct. *M40* . . .2C **84**
Sydney Rd. *Bram* 2H **161**
Sydney St. *Fail* 4E **85**
Sydney St. *Moss* 3F **89**
Sydney St.
  Salf (M3) 4B **94** (4D **4**)
Sydney St. *Salf* (M6) 3E **93**
Sydney St. *Stoc* 4C **140**
Sydney St. *Stret* 5D **106**
Sydney St. *Swin* 4D **78**
Syke. 5F **15**
Syke Cft. *Rom* 6B **130**
Syke La. *Roch* 5F **15**
Syke Rd. *L'boro* 1H **29**
Syke Rd. *Roch* 5F **15**
Sykes Av. *Bury* 3F **51**
Sykes Clo. *G'fld* 4F **61**
Sykes Ct. *Roch* 5B **28**
Sykes Mdw. *Stoc* 4F **139**
Sykes St. *Bury* 2E **37**
Sykes St. *Hyde* 6D **114**
Sykes St. *Miln* 1E **43**
Sykes St. *Roch* 5B **28**
Sykes St. *Stoc* 1H **127**
Sykes Wlk. *Stoc* 1H **127**
    (off Sykes St.)
Sylvan Av. *M16* 4B **108**
Sylvan Av. *Fail* 6E **85**
Sylvan Av. *Sale* 6C **122**
Sylvan Av. *Timp* 3H **133**
Sylvan Av. *Urm* 4F **105**
Sylvan Av. *Wilm* 4C **166**

Sylvan Clo. *Midd* 5F **53**
Sylvandale Av. *M19* 6C **110**
Sylvan Gro. *Alt* 6F **133**
Sylvan St. *Oldh* 2A **72**
Sylvester Av. *Stoc* 5B **140**
Sylvester Clo. *Hyde* 5A **116**
Sylvester Way. *Dent* 2G **129**
Sylvester Way. *Hyde* 5A **116**
Sylvia Gro. *Stoc* 2G **127**
Symms St. *Salf* 1H **93**
Symond Rd. *M9* 4G **69**
Symons Rd. *Sale* 4B **122**
Symons St. *Salf* 4A **82**
Syndall Av.
  M12 . . . . .1H **109** (5G **11**)
Syndall St.
  M12 . . . . .1H **109** (5G **11**)

T

Tabley Av. *M14* 5F **109**
Tabley Ct. *Alt* 6F **133**
    (off Victoria St.)
Tabley Gdns. *Droy* 4B **98**
Tabley Gdns. *Marp* 1E **155**
Tabley Gro. *M13* 5B **110**
Tabley Gro. *Stoc* 2G **127**
Tabley Gro. *Timp* 2H **133**
Tableymere Gdns.
  Chea H 2B **150**
Tabley M. *Alt* 6F **133**
Tabley Rd. *Bolt* 3F **45**
Tabley Rd. *Hand* 2H **159**
Tabley Rd. *Sale* 1E **135**
Tabley St. *Duk* 5C **100**
Tabley St. *Moss* 3F **89**
Tabley St. *Salf* 6F **81**
Tabor St. *Midd* 5H **53**
Tackler Clo. *Swin* 4F **79**
Tadcaster Wlk. *Oldh* 2D **72**
Taddington Pl. *Glos* 6G **117**
    (off Castleton Cres.)
Tadlow Wlk.
  M40 . . . . .2G **95** (1F **7**)
Tadman Gro. *Alt* 5C **132**
Tadmor Clo. *L Hul* 5B **62**
Tagge La. *Swin* 5C **80**
Tagore Clo. *M13* 3A **110**
Tahir Clo. *M8* 4D **82**
Tait M. *Heat M* 1B **138**
Talavera St. *Salf* 6H **81**
Talbenny Clo. *Bolt* 5D **30**
Talbot Av. *L Lev* 3A **48**
Talbot Clo. *Oldh* 1G **73**
Talbot Ct. *Bolt* 1B **32**
Talbot Ct. *Stret* 4E **107**
Talbot Gro. *Bury* 5G **23**
Talbot Pl. *M16* 2H **107**
Talbot Rd. *Ald E* 5H **167**
Talbot Rd. *Bow* 3D **144**
    (in two parts)
Talbot Rd. *Fall* 2A **126**
Talbot Rd. *Hyde* 2C **114**
Talbot Rd. *Sale* 5E **123**
Talbot Rd.
  Stret & M16 . . . . .4E **107**
Talbot St. *Ash L* 2G **99**
Talbot St. *Eccl* 4G **91**
Talbot St. *Haz G* 1D **152**
Talbot St. *Midd* 5A **54**
Talbot St. *Roch* 5H **27**
Talford Gro. *M20* 4E **125**
Talgarth Rd. *M40* 1G **95**
Talkin Dri. *Midd* 4G **53**
Talland Wlk. *M13* 2H **109**
Tallarn Clo. *M20* 2G **125**
Tallis St. *M12* 4C **110**
Tallow Way. *Irlam* 1E **119**
Tall Trees. *Salf* 2H **81**
Tall Trees Clo. *Rytn* 3A **56**
Tall Trees Pl. *Stoc* 5C **140**

Tallyman Way. *Swin* 4C **80**
Talmine Av. *M40* 6G **83**
Tamar Clo. *Kear* 4B **64**
Tamar Clo. *W'fld* 1E **67**
Tamar Ct. *M15* . . .1B **108** (6C **8**)
Tamar Dri. *M23* 1G **135**
Tamarin Clo. *Swin* 2C **78**
Tamar Way. *Heyw* 2C **38**
Tame Bank. *Moss* 6F **75**
Tame Barn Clo. *Miln* 5G **29**
Tame Clo. *Stal* 2G **101**
Tame Ct. *Stal* 3F **101**
Tame La. *Del* 1E **60**
Tamerton Dri. *M8* 5C **82**
Tameside Bus. Development
  Cen. *Dent* 4D **112**
Tameside Ct. *Duk* 6H **99**
Tameside Ct. *Hyde* 5A **116**
Tameside Leisure Pool.
  . . . . .5D **114**
Tameside Pk. Ind. Est.
  Duk 5H **99**
Tameside Work Cen.
  Ash L 4F **99**
Tame St. *M4* 4H **95** (6G **7**)
Tame St. *Aud* 2E **113**
    (Audenshaw)
Tame St. *Aud* 2E **113**
    (Denton)
Tame St. *Moss* 6G **75**
Tame St. *Stal* 4C **100**
Tame St. *Upperm* 1F **61**
Tame Valley. 4B **100**
Tame Valley Clo. *Moss* . . .6G **75**
Tame Vw. *Moss* 1E **89**
Tame Wlk. *Wilm* 5A **160**
Tame Water. 6H **59**
Tamewater Vs. Dob 6H **59**
    (off Brook La.)
Tamworth Av. *Salf* 5H **93**
Tamworth Av. *W'fld* 2E **67**
Tamworth Av. W. *Salf* . . .5G **93**
Tamworth Clo. *M15* 2C **108**
Tamworth Clo. *Haz G* . . .5C **152**
Tamworth Ct. *M15* 2C **108**
Tamworth St. *Chad* 4A **72**
Tamworth Dri. *Bury* 6C **22**
Tamworth Grn. *Stoc* 1B **140**
Tamworth St. *M15* 3C **108**
Tamworth St. *Oldh* 4A **72**
Tamworth St. *Stoc* 1B **140**
Tamworth Wlk. *Salf* 5H **93**
Tandis Ct. *Salf* 1A **92**
Tandle Hill Countryside Cen.
  . . . . .1G **55**
Tandle Hill Countryside Pk.
  . . . . .1G **55**
Tandle Hill Rd. *Rytn* 1H **55**
Tandle Hill Ter. *Roch* 5H **41**
Tandlewood M. M40 . . . .8C **84**
Tandle Wood Pk. *Rytn* . . .1H **55**
Tanfield Dri. *Rad* 2B **64**
Tanfield Rd. *M20* 4F **137**
Tang. 1H **141**
Tangmere Av. *Heyw* 6G **39**
Tangmere Clo. *M40* 6C **70**
Tangmere Ct. *M16* 4B **108**
Tangshutts La. *Rom* 1B **142**
Tang, The. *Rom* 1H **141**
Tanhill Clo. *Stoc* 5E **141**
Tanhill La. *Oldh* 1C **87**
Tanhouse Rd. *Urm* 4H **103**
Tanner Brook Clo. *Bolt* . . .3A **46**
Tanners. 3D **12**
Tanners Cft. *Rams* 3D **12**
Tannersfield Lodge.
  Fail 5E **85**
Tanners Fold. *Oldh* 1E **87**
Tanners Grn. Salf 2F **93**
    (off Nursery St.)
Tanners St. *M18* 2G **111**
Tanners St. *Rams* 3D **12**

Tanner St. *Hyde* 4B **114**
Tannery Way. *Timp* 4G **133**
Tannock Ct. *Haz G* 4F **153**
Tannock Rd. *Haz G* 4F **153**
Tan Pit Cotts. *Heyw* 1F **39**
Tanpits Rd. *Bury* 2C **36**
Tanpit Wlk. *M22* 3A **148**
Tansey Gro. *Salf* 4B **82**
Tansley Rd. *M8* 1D **82**
Tanworth Wlk. *Bolt* 3A **32**
Tan Yd. *Brow*. *M18* 3G **111**
Tanyard Dri. *Haleb* 1C **156**
Tanyard Grn. *Stoc* 4H **127**
Tanyard La. *Timp* 2A **156**
Taper St. *Rams* 3D **12**
Taper St. *Rams* 3D **12**
Tapley Av. *Poy* 5E **163**
Taplin Dri. *M18* 2E **111**
Taplow Gro. *Chea H* 3B **150**
Taplow Wlk. *M14* 4A **110**
Tara Sports & Leisure Cen.
  . . . . .6G **43**
Tarbet Dri. *Bolt* 6H **33**
Tarbet Rd. *Duk* 6A **100**
Tarbet Wlk. *M8* 5B **82**
Tarbolton Cres. *Hale* 2C **146**
Tarden. 6H **143**
Target Fitness Cen. 4B **152**
    (Hazel Grove)
Target Fitness Cen. 4D **126**
    (Peel Moat)
Tariff St. *M1* 4F **95** (5C **6**)
Tarland Wlk. *Open* 4E **97**
Tarleton Clo. *Bury* 4F **35**
Tarleton Ho. *Salf* 1C **92**
Tarleton Pl. *Bolt* 4E **45**
Tarleton Wlk.
  M13 . . . . .1H **109** (6G **11**)
Tarnbrook Clo. *W'fld* 1G **67**
    (in two parts)
Tarnbrook Wlk. *M15* 2E **109**
    (off Wellhead Clo.)
Tarn Dri. *Bury* 1C **50**
Tarn Gro. *Wors* 2H **77**
Tarnside Clo. *Roch* 6A **16**
Tarnside Clo. Stoc 5F **141**
Tarnside Ho. *M8* 1D **82**
Tarns, The. *Gat* 2F **149**
Tarporley Av. *M14* 1E **125**
Tarporley Wlk. *Wilm* 5A **160**
Tarran Gro. *Dent* 6H **113**
Tarran Pl. *Alt* 5G **133**
Tarrington Clo. *M12* 2C **110**
Tartan St. *M11* 3D **96**
Tarves Wlk. *Open* 4D **96**
Tarvin Av. *M20* 2E **125**
Tarvin Av. *Stoc* 2F **127**
Tarvin Dri. *Bred* 5E **129**
Tarvington Clo. *M40* 5E **83**
Tarvin Rd. *Chea* 6C **138**
Tarvin Wlk. *Bolt* 3A **32**
Tarvin Way. *Hand* 2H **159**
Tasle All. *M2* 4D **94** (6H **5**)
Tatchbury Rd. *Fail* 4G **85**
Tate St. *Oldh* 5F **73**
Tatham Clo. *M13* 4B **110**
Tatham St. *Roch* 4A **28**
Tatland Dri. *M22* 2D **148**
Tattenhall Wlk. *M14* 1H **125**
Tattersall Av. *Bolt* 3C **30**
Tattersall St. *Oldh* 3B **72**
Tatton Bldgs. *Gat* 5F **137**
Tatton Clo. *Chea* 1C **150**
Tatton Clo. *Haz G* 1F **153**
Tatton Ct. *M14* 1H **125**
Tatton Ct. *Hand* 2A **160**
Tatton Ct. *Stoc* 5E **127**
Tatton Gdns. *Woodl* 4B **130**
Tatton Gro. *M20* 3F **125**
Tatton Ho. *Bolt* 6G **31**
Tatton Mere Dri. *Droy* . . .4B **98**

Tattonmere Gdns.
  Chea H 1C **150**
Tatton Pl. *M13* 3A **110**
Tatton Pl. *Sale* 4B **122**
Tatton Rd. *Dent* 6G **113**
Tatton Rd. *Hand* 2A **160**
Tatton Rd. *Sale* 4B **122**
Tatton Rd. N. *Stoc* . . .4E **127**
Tatton Rd. S. *Stoc* 5E **127**
Tatton St. *M15* . .1B **108** (5C **8**)
Tatton St. *Hyde* 2C **130**
Tatton St. *Salf* 5H **93**
Tatton St. *Stal* 3F **101**
  (in two parts)
Tatton St. *Stoc* 2H **139**
Tatton Ter. *Duk* 4H **99**
Tatton Vw. *M20* 3F **125**
Taunton. 6C **86**
Taunton Av. *Ash L* 1G **99**
Taunton Av. *Eccl* 2D **90**
Taunton Av. *Roch* 4D **26**
Taunton Av. *Stoc* 4C **128**
Taunton Av. *Urm* 1D **120**
Taunton Brook La.
  Ash L 6C **86**
Taunton Clo. *Ash L* 4G **31**
Taunton Clo. *Haz G* . . .3G **153**
Taunton Dri. *Farn* 6B **46**
Taunton Grn. *Ash L* 6D **86**
Taunton Gro. *W'fld* 3E **67**
Taunton Hall Clo.
  Ash L 6D **86**
Taunton Lawns. *Ash L* . . .6E **87**
Taunton Pl. *Ash L* 6D **86**
Taunton Platting.
  Ash L 5D **86**
Taunton Rd. *Ash L* 1G **99**
Taunton Rd. *Chad* 5G **55**
Taunton Rd. *Sale* 5F **121**
Taunton St. *M4* . . .4H **95** (5H **7**)
Taunton Wlk. *Dent* 6G **113**
Taurus St. *Oldh* 1G **73**
Tavern Ct. *Fail* 4H **85**
Tavern Ct. Av. *Fail* 4G **85**
Tavern Rd. *Had* 4G **117**
Tavery Clo. *M4* 3H **95** (4F **7**)
Tavistock Clo. *Hyde* . . .5A **116**
Tavistock Dri. *Chad* . . .6F **55**
Tavistock Rd. *Bolt* 1H **45**
Tavistock Rd. *Roch* 2F **41**
Tavistock Rd. *Sale* 4F **121**
Tavistock Sq. *M9* 4F **83**
  (off Grangewood Dri.)
Tawton Av. *Hyde* 4A **116**
Taxi Rd. *M90* 6H **147**
Tay Clo. *Oldh* 4C **72**
Tayfield Rd. *M22* 3A **148**
Taylor Av. *Roch* 3B **26**
Taylor Bldgs. *Kear* 3B **64**
Taylor Grn. Way. *Lees* . . .2B **74**
Taylor Ho. *Bury* 6C **22**
Taylor La. *Dent* 3D **112**
Taylor Rd. *Alt* 6C **132**
Taylor Rd. *Urm* 6G **91**
Taylor's La. *M40* 6C **84**
Taylor's La. *Bolt* 6A **34**
  (in two parts)
Taylorson St. *Salf* 1H **107**
  (in two parts)
Taylorson St. S. *Salf* 1G **107**
Taylor's Pl. *Oldh* 3E **73**
Taylors Pl. *Roch* 2H **27**
Taylor's Rd. *Stret* 3D **106**
Taylor St. *M14* 5G **109**
Taylor St. *M18* 1E **111**
Taylor St. *Bolt* 1B **46**
Taylor St. *Bury* 1D **36**
Taylor St. *Chad* 2G **71**
Taylor St. *Dent* 3F **113**
Taylor St. *Droy* 4H **97**
Taylor St. *Heyw* 3E **39**
Taylor St. *Holl* 2F **117**

Taylor St. *Hyde* 4D **114**
Taylor St. *Lees* 3A **74**
Taylor St. *Midd* 1A **70**
  (in two parts)
Taylor St. *Oldh* 1G **73**
Taylor St. *P'wich* 5G **67**
Taylor St. *Rad* 4G **49**
Taylor St. *Roch* 2H **27**
Taylor St. *Rytn* 2B **56**
Taylor St. *Stal* 4F **101**
Taylor St. *Whitw* 1D **14**
Taylor Ter. *Duk* 4H **99**
  (off Hill St.)
Taylor Ter. *L'boro* 4G **17**
  (off Ealees Rd.)
Taywood Rd. *Bolt* 5B **44**
Teak Dri. *Kear* 5D **64**
Teak St. *Bury* 3F **37**
Teal Av. *Poy* 3A **162**
Tealby Av. *M16* 3A **108**
Tealby Cl. *M21* 1A **124**
Tealby Rd. *M18* 3D **110**
Teal Clo. *B'hth* 3D **132**
Teal Clo. *Stoc* 6F **141**
Teal Ct. *Roch* 4B **26**
Teal St. *Bolt* 3B **46**
Teasdale Clo. *Chad* 6E **71**
Tebbutt St. *M4* . . .2F **95** (2D **6**)
Tedburn Wlk. *M40* 1D **84**
Tedder Clo. *Bury* 5F **51**
Tedder Dri. *M22* 6D **148**
Teddington Rd. *M40* . . .2C **84**
Ted Jackson Wlk. *M11* . . .5B **96**
  (off Newchurch St.)
Teer St. *M40* 3H **95** (4H **7**)
Teesdale Av. *Urm* 3C **104**
Teesdale Clo. *Stoc* 5E **141**
Teesdale Wlk. *M9* 6G **69**
Tees St. *Roch* 5B **28**
Tees Wlk. *Oldh* 4C **72**
Teignmouth Av. *M40* . . .1G **95**
Telegraphic Ho. *Salf* . . .6G **93**
Telegraph Rd. *Traf P* . . .1A **106**
Telfer Av. *M13* 5A **110**
Telfer Rd. *M13* 5A **110**
Telford Clo. *Aud* 6E **99**
Telford M. *Upperm* 6B **60**
Telford Rd. *Marp* 1E **155**
Telford St. *M8* 6E **83**
Telford Wlk. *M16* 3B **108**
Telford Way. *Roch* 3G **41**
Telham Wlk. *M23* 6G **135**
Tellson Clo. *Salf* 5B **80**
Tellson Cres. *Salf* 5B **80**
Tell St. *Roch* 4F **27**
Telryn Wlk. *M8* 3E **83**
  (off Stakeford Dri.)
Temperance Sq. *Mot* 3C **116**
Temperance St.
  M12 . . . . . .5G **95** (2E **11**)
Temperance St. *Bolt* . . .2A **46**
Temperance Ter.
  Marp 5D **142**
Tempest Chase. *Los* . . .3A **44**
Tempest Rd. *Ald E* . . .5H **167**
Tempest St. *Los* 4A **44**
Tempest St. *Bolt* 3F **45**
Temple Clo. *Lees* 1A **74**
Templecombe Dri. *Bolt* . . .5B **18**
Temple Dri. *Bolt* 2G **31**
  (in two parts)
Temple Dri. *Swin* 4H **79**
Temple La. *L'boro* 6G **17**
Temple Rd. *Bolt* 2G **31**
  (in two parts)
Temple Rd. *Sale* 5D **122**
Temple Sq. *M8* 5D **82**
Temple St. *Heyw* 3F **39**
Temple St. *Midd* 6B **54**
Temple St. *Oldh* 2F **73**
Templeton Dri. *Alt* . . .5D **132**
Temsbury Wlk. *M40* . . .6G **83**

Ten Acre Ct. *W'fld* 2A **66**
Ten Acre Dri. *W'fld* 2B **66**
Ten Acres La. *M40* 6A **84**
Ten Acres Recreation Cen.
  . . . . .6A **84**
Tenax Circ. *Traf P* 5B **92**
Tenax Rd. *Traf P* 6B **92**
Tenbury Clo. *Salf* 2F **93**
Tenbury Dri. *Midd* 4A **70**
Tenby Av. *M20* 3F **125**
Tenby Av. *Bolt* 4E **31**
Tenby Av. *Stret* 3F **107**
Tenby Ct. *M15* . . .1A **108** (6B **8**)
Tenby Dri. *Chea H* 4D **150**
Tenby Dri. *Salf* 6B **80**
Tenby Gro. *Roch* 2E **27**
Tenby Rd. *Oldh* 1H **85**
Tenby Rd. *Stoc* 4D **138**
Tenby St. *Roch* 2E **27**
Tenement La. *Bram* 2E **151**
  (in two parts)
Teneriffe St. *Salf* 6H **81**
Tenham Wlk. *M9* 6G **69**
  (off Ravenswood Dri.)
Ten Houses. *Oldh* 1G **87**
Tennis St. *M16* 3H **107**
Tennis St. *Bolt* 2H **31**
Tennyson Av. *Bury* 1D **50**
Tennyson Av. *Dent* 2G **129**
  (in two parts)
Tennyson Av. *Duk* 6E **101**
Tennyson Av. *Rad* 3E **49**
Tennyson Clo. *Stoc* 1C **138**
Tennyson Gdns.
  P'wich 6D **66**
Tennyson Rd. *Chea* 5B **138**
Tennyson Rd. *Droy* 3A **98**
Tennyson Rd. *Farn* 3D **62**
Tennyson Rd. *Midd* 5B **54**
Tennyson Rd. *Stoc* 6F **111**
Tennyson St. *M13* 3G **109**
Tennyson St. *Bolt* 4H **31**
Tennyson St. *Oldh* 6G **57**
Tennyson St. *Roch* 6A **28**
Tennyson St. *Salf* 1A **94**
Tennyson Wlk. *Bolt* 3A **32**
Tensing Av. *Ash L* 6F **87**
Tensing St. *Oldh* 3E **87**
Tenter Brow. *Stal* 3D **100**
Tentercroft. *Oldh* 2C **72**
Tentercroft. *Roch* 4G **27**
Tenterden St. *Bury* 3B **36**
Tenterhill La. *Roch* 1H **25**
Tentersfield. 3B **36**
Tenterden St. *Bury* 3B **36**
Tenth St. *Traf P* 1D **106**
Terence St. *M40* 6D **84**
Terminal Rd. E.
  Man A 6H **147**
Terminal Rd. N. *Man A* . .6H **147**
Terminal Rd. S.
  Man A 6H **147**
Tern Av. *Farn* 1B **62**
Tern Clo. *B'hth* 3D **132**
Tern Clo. *Duk* 6C **100**
Tern Clo. *Roch* 4B **26**
Tern Dri. *Poy* 3B **162**
Ternhill Ct. *Farn* 1F **63**
Terrace, The. *P'wich* 6F **67**
Terrington Clo. *M21* 2C **124**
Tetbury Dri. *Bolt* 4H **33**
Tetbury Rd. *M22* 4H **147**
Tetlow Gro. *Eccl* 4E **91**
Tetlow La. *Salf* 3A **82**
Tetlow St. *M40* 6C **84**
Tetlow St. *Hyde* 2C **114**
Tetlow St. *Midd* 1A **70**
Tetlow St. *Oldh* 3B **72**

Tetlows Yd. *L'boro* 5H **17**
Tetsworth Wlk. *M40* 1D **84**
Teviot St. *M13* 3A **110**
Tewkesbury Av. *Ash L* 4G **87**
Tewkesbury Av. *Chad* . . .5G **55**
Tewkesbury Av. *Droy* . . .2A **98**
Tewkesbury Av. *Hale* 2C **146**
Tewkesbury Av. *Midd* . . .4H **53**
Tewkesbury Av. *Urm* . . .3F **105**
Tewkesbury Clo.
  Chea H 1D **160**
Tewkesbury Clo. *Poy* . . .2D **162**
Tewkesbury Dri.
  P'wich 1G **81**
Tewkesbury Rd.
  M40 . . . . . . .2H **95** (2H **7**)
Tewkesbury Rd. *Stoc* . . .5D **138**
Texas St. *Ash L* 3A **100**
Textile St. *M12* 6C **96**
Textilose Rd. *Traf P* 2B **106**
Teynham Wlk. *M22* 4A **148**
Thackeray Clo. *M8* 5C **82**
Thackeray Gro. *Droy* . . .3A **98**
Thackeray Rd. *Oldh* . . .6G **57**
Thames Clo. *M11* 5D **96**
Thames Clo. *Bury* 3F **23**
Thames Ct.
  M15 . . . . . . .1B **108** (6C **8**)
Thames Ind. Est.
  M12 . . . . . .6H **95** (3G **11**)
Thames Rd. *Miln* 5H **29**
Thames St. *Oldh* 1E **73**
Thames St. *Roch* 5B **28**
Thames Trad. Cen.
  Irlam 2D **118**
Thanet Clo. *Salf* 6A **82**
Thankerton Av. *Aud* . . .4D **98**
Thatcher Clo. *Bow* 5E **145**
Thatcher St. *Oldh* 5E **73**
Thatch Leach. 4F **71**
Thatch Leach. *Chad* . . .4F **71**
Thatch Leach La. *W'fld* . . .2E **67**
Thaxmead Dri. *M40* . . .1F **97**
Thaxted Dri. *Stoc* 6G **141**
Thaxted Pl. *Bolt* 5G **31**
Thaxted Wlk. *M22* 5A **148**
Theatre St. *Oldh* 2D **72**
Theatre, The. 4D **150**
Thekla St. *Oldh* 1B **72**
Thelma St. *Rams* 3D **12**
Thelwall Av. *M14* 1D **124**
Thelwall Av. *Bolt* 5F **33**
Thelwall Rd. *Sale* 6E **123**
Thelwell Clo. *Timp* . . .5G **133**
Theobald Rd. *Bow* 4F **145**
Theta Clo. *M11* 3D **96**
Thetford. *Roch* 3G **27**
  (off Spotland Rd.)
Thetford Clo. *Bury* 6D **22**
Thetford Dri. *M8* 4C **82**
Thicketford Brow. 4E **33**
Thicketford Brow. *Bolt* . . .4F **33**
Thicketford Clo. *Bolt* . . .3E **33**
Thicketford Rd. *Bolt* . . .4D **32**
Thimble Clo. *Roch* 5B **16**
Thimbles, The. *Roch* . . .5B **16**
Third Av. *Bolt* 6F **31**
Third Av. *Bury* 1H **37**
Third Av. *Carr* 5G **89**
Third Av. *Clay* 2E **97**
Third Av. L *Lev* 3H **47**
Third Av. *Oldh* 1A **86**
Third Av. *Poy* 6D **162**
Third Av. *Swin* 6E **79**
Third Av. *Traf P* 2D **106**
  (in three parts)
Third St. *Bolt* 1D **30**
Thirkhill Pl. *Eccl* 3H **91**
Thirlby Dri. *M22* 4B **148**
Thirlmere Av. *Ash L* . . .1F **99**
Thirlmere Av. *Stret* . . .4C **106**
Thirlmere Av. *Swin* . . .4G **79**

Thirlmere Clo. *Ald E* 5F **167**
Thirlmere Clo. *Stal* 1E **101**
Thirlmere Dri. *Bury* 6C **36**
Thirlmere Dri. *L Hul* 4C **62**
Thirlmere Dri. *Midd* 5G **53**
Thirlmere Gro. *Farn* 1A **62**
Thirlmere Gro. *Rytn* 1B **56**
Thirlmere Rd. *M22* 3H **147**
Thirlmere Rd. *Part* 5C **118**
Thirlmere Rd. *Roch* 1B **40**
Thirlmere Rd. *Urm* 4A **104**
Thirlmere Rd. *Stoc* 4B **140**
Thirlspot Clo. *Bolt* 5C **18**
Thirlstone Av. *Oldh* 3B **58**
Thirsfield Dri. *M11* 3E **97**
Thirsk Av. *Chad* 6F **55**
Thirsk Av. *Sale* 6E **121**
Thirsk M. *Salf* 5H **81**
Thirsk Rd. *L Lev* 4A **48**
Thirsk St. *M12* . .1G **95** (3E 11)
Thistle Bank Clo. *M9* 2E **83**
Thistle Clo.
 Stal . . . . .6H **101** & 1A **116**
Thistledown Clo. *Eccl* 5E **91**
Thistle Grn. *Miln* 4E **29**
Thistle Sq. *Part* 6C **118**
Thistleton Rd. *Bolt* 4D **44**
Thistle Wlk. *Part* 6C **118**
Thistle Way. *Oldh* 5H **57**
Thistlewood Dri.
 Wilm 2G **167**
Thistleyfield. *Miln* 4E **29**
Thistley Fields. *Hyde* 1A **130**
Thomas Clo. *Dent* 3G **113**
Thomas Ct. *M15* 4D **8**
Thomas Ct. *Brom X* 4F **19**
 (off Toppings Grn.)
Thomas Dri. *Bolt* 2H **45**
Thomas Garnet Ct.
 Farn 1E **63**
 (off Glynne St.)
Thomas Gibbon Clo.
 Stret 6C **100**
Thomas Henshaw Ct.
 Roch 1C **40**
Thomas Holden St.
 Bolt 5H **31**
Thomas Ho. Rytn 3C **56**
 (off Royton Hall Wlk.)
Thomas Johnson Clo.
 Eccl 4E **91**
Thomas More Clo.
 Kear 3H **63**
Thomas Regan Ct.
 M18 . . . . .1F **111**
Thomasson Clo. *Bolt* 4A **32**
Thomas St. *M4* . .3E **95** (4B 6)
Thomas St. *M8* 3B **82**
Thomas St. *Alt* 1G **145**
Thomas St. *Bolt* 2H **45**
Thomas St. *Bred* 6F **129**
Thomas St. *Comp* 1F **143**
Thomas St. *Farn* 1G **63**
Thomas St. *Hyde* 5C **114**
Thomas St. *Kear* 2G **63**
Thomas St. *Lees* 4A **74**
Thomas St. *L'boro* 5C **16**
Thomas St. *Rad* 4H **49**
Thomas St. *Roch* 3A **28**
Thomas St. *Rytn* 4D **56**
Thomas St. *Shaw* 1G **57**
Thomas St. *Stoc* 4H **139**
Thomas St. *Stret* 4D **106**
Thomas St. *Whitw* 3H **15**
Thomas St. W. *Stoc* 4H **139**
Thomas Telford Basin.
 M1 . . . . . .4C **95** (6E 7)
Thompson Av. *Bolt* 4D **34**
Thompson Av. *W'fld* 2E **67**
Thompson Clo. *Dent* 4B **112**

Thompson Ct. *Dent* 4B **112**
Thompson Ct. Stal 3D **100**
 (off Thompson Fold)
Thompson Dri. *Bury* 2G **37**
Thompson Fold. *Stal* 3D **100**
Thompson La. *Chad* 5G **71**
Thompson Rd. *Bolt* 4F **31**
Thompson Rd. *Dent* 4B **112**
Thompson Rd. *Traf P* . . .5G **91**
Thompson St.
 M3 . . . . .2D **94** (1G 5)
Thompson St.
 M4 . . . . . . .2F **95** (2C 6)
Thompson St. *M40* 6H **83**
Thompson St. *Bolt* 2B **46**
Thomson Rd. *M18* 3E **111**
Thomson St.
 M13 . . . . . .1G **109** (6F 11)
Thomson St. *Stoc* 3G **139**
Thoralby Clo. *M12* 2C **110**
Thorburn Dri. *Whitw* 2B 14
Thoresby Clo. *Rad* 2C **48**
Thoresway Rd. *M13* 4A **110**
Thoresway Rd. *Wilm* 4C **166**
Thorgill Wlk. *M40* 4A **84**
Thor Gro. *Salf* 5A **94** (2B **8**)
Thorley Clo. *Chad* 1F **85**
Thorley Dri. *Timp* 6B **134**
Thorley Dri. *Urm* 5F **105**
Thorley La.
 Hale & Man A 4F **147**
Thorley La. *Timp* 5B **134**
Thorley M. *Bram* 6H **151**
Thorley St. *Fail* 3F **85**
Thornaby Wlk. M9 . . . . . .5F **83**
 (off Lathbury Rd.)
Thornage Dri.
 M40 . . . . . . .1G **95** (1F 7)
Thorn Av. *Fail* 5E **85**
Thorn Bank. *Carr* 4H **89**
Thornbank. *Eccl* 2G **91**
Thornbank Clo. *Heyw* 6G **39**
Thornbank E. Bolt 2G **45**
 (off Deane Rd.)
Thornbank Est. *Bolt* 1G **45**
Thorn Bank Lodge.
 Stoc 5D **126**
Thornbeck Dri. *Bolt* 4D **30**
Thornbeck Rd. *Bolt* 4D **30**
Thornbridge Av. *M21* . . .1H **123**
Thornbury. *Roch* 5G **27**
Thornbury Av. *Hyde* 5A **116**
Thornbury Clo. *Bolt* 5A **32**
Thornbury Clo.
 Chea H 4E **151**
Thornbury Rd. *Stret* 3E **107**
Thornbury Way. *M18* . . .2E **111**
Thornbush Way. *Roch* . . .3C **28**
Thornby Wlk. *M23* 6G **135**
Thorncliff Av. *Oldh* 6C **72**
Thorncliffe Av. *Duk* 6A **100**
Thorncliffe Gro. *M19* 6E **111**
Thorncliffe Pk. *Rytn* 1A **56**
Thorncliffe Rd. *Bolt* 6C **18**
Thorncliffe Rd. *Had* 3H **117**
Thorncliffe Wood.
 Holl 2F **117**
Thorn Clo. *Heyw* 2D **38**
Thorncombe Rd. *M16* . . .3C **108**
Thorn Ct. *Salf* 3H **93**
Thorncross Clo.
 M15 . . . . . . .6A **94** (4B **8**)
Thorndale Clo. *Rytn* 2D **56**
Thorndale Ct. *Timp* 6A **134**
Thorndale Gro. *Timp* 6A **134**
Thornden Rd. *M40* 1H **95**
Thorn Dri. *M22* 5E **149**
Thorndyke Av. *Bolt* 6C **18**
Thorndyke Wlk. *P'wich* . . .6F **67**
Thorne Av. *Urm* 4C **104**

Thorne Ho. *M14* 5H **109**
Thorneside. *Dent* 2F **113**
 (in two parts)
Thorne St. *Farn* 6E **47**
Thorneycroft Av. M21 . . .4H **123**
Thorneycroft Clo.
 Timp 6B **134**
Thorneycroft Rd.
 Timp 6B **134**
Thorney Dri. *Bram* 1E **161**
Thorney Hill Clo. *Oldh* . . .3E **73**
Thorneyholme Clo. Los . . .1A **44**
Thorneylea. *Whitw* 4H **15**
Thornfield Ct. Stoc 6C **126**
 (off Thornfield Rd.)
Thornfield Cres. *L Hul* . . .4B **62**
Thornfield Dri. *Swin* 4E **79**
Thornfield Gro. *Ash L* . . .2C **100**
Thornfield Gro.
 Chea H 3C **150**
Thornfield Gro. *L Hul* 4B **62**
Thornfield Hey. *Wilm* 1H **167**
Thornfield Rd. *M19* 4A **126**
Thornfield Rd. *Stoc* 6C **126**
Thornfield St. *Salf* 4D **92**
Thornfield Ter. *Ash L* 3A **100**
Thornford Wlk. *M40* 1D **84**
Thorngate Rd. *M8* 6C **82**
Thorn Gro. *M14* 1H **125**
Thorn Gro. *Chea H* 1C **160**
Thorn Gro. *Hale* 2G **145**
Thorn Gro. *Sale* 5B **122**
Thorngrove Av. *M23* 4D **134**
Thorngrove Dri. *Wilm* . . .3F **167**
Thorngrove Hill. *Wilm* . . .3F **167**
Thorngrove Ho. *M23* 4D **134**
Thorngrove Rd. *Wilm* . . .3F **167**
Thornham Clo. *Bury* 5C **22**
Thornham Ct. *Roch* 5A **42**
Thornham Dri. *Bolt* 5D **18**
Thornham Fold. 6F **41**
Thornham La. *Midd* 1D **54**
Thornham La. *Rytn* 5A **42**
Thornham New Rd.
 Roch 5D **40**
Thornham Old Rd.
 Rytn 6G **41**
Thornham Rd. Sale 1G **133**
Thornham Rd. *Shaw* 6B **42**
Thornhill Clo. *Bolt* 2G **31**
Thornhill Clo. *Dent* 5A **112**
Thornhill Dri. *Wors* 3G **77**
Thornhill Rd. *Droy* 3B **98**
Thornhill Rd. *Rams* 2A **22**
Thornhill Rd. *Stoc* 1B **138**
Thornholme Clo. *M18* . . .4D **110**
Thornholme Rd. *Marp* . . .1D **154**
Thornlea.
 M4 . . . . .3E **95** (4A **6**)
Thornlea. *M9* 1A **84**
Thornlea. *Alt* 1H **145**
Thorn Lea. *Bolt* 1F **33**
Thornlea. *Droy* 4G **97**
Thornlea Av. *Oldh* 2A **86**
Thornlea Av. *Swin* 5D **78**
Thorn Lea Clo. *Bolt* 6D **30**
Thornlea Dri. *Roch* 1D **26**
Thornlea Ct. G'ton 4D **74**
Thornleigh Rd. M14 . . . .6E **109**
Thornley Av. *Bolt* 3G **31**
Thornley Clo. *G'ton* 4C **74**
Thornley Cres. *Bred* 5G **129**
Thornley Cres. *G'ton* 4C **74**
Thornley La. G'ton 4C **74**
Thornley La. N. *Stoc* . . .4H **111**
Thornley La. S.
 Stoc & Dent 5H **111**
Thornley Pk. Rd. *G'ton* . . .4C **74**
Thornley Rd. *P'wich* 2G **67**
Thornleys Rd. *Dent* 3G **113**
Thornley St. *Hyde* 6C **114**

Thornley St. *Midd* 6B **54**
Thornley St. *Rad* 5H **49**
Thornmere Clo. Swin 1C **78**
Thorn Pl. *Salf* 3H **93**
Thorn Rd. *Bram* 2F **161**
Thorn Rd. *Oldh* 6G **73**
Thorn Rd. *Swin* 5E **79**
Thorns Av. *Bolt* 2H **31**
Thorns Clo. *Bolt* 2H **31**
Thorns Clough. *Dig* 2C **60**
Thornsett Clo. *M9* 3G **83**
Thorns Green. 2C **156**
Thorns Rd. *Bolt* 2H **31**
Thorns, The. *M21* 2H **123**
Thorn St. *Bolt* 3B **32**
Thorn St. *S'seat* 6E **13**
Thorns Villa Gdns.
 Wors 6C **76**
Thornton Av. *Aud* 5C **98**
Thornton Av. *Bolt* 4D **30**
Thornton Av. *Urm* 5C **104**
Thornton Clo. *M16* 2A **108**
Thornton Clo. *Farn* 2D **62**
Thornton Clo. *L Lev* 4C **48**
Thornton Clo. *Wors* 4A **76**
Thornton Cres. *P'wich* . . .4D **66**
Thornton Dri. *Hand* 4H **159**
Thornton Ga. *Gat* 5E **137**
Thornton Pl. *Stoc* 5D **126**
Thornton Rd. *M14* 5E **109**
Thornton Rd. *H Grn* 4G **149**
Thornton Rd. *Wors* 4A **76**
Thornton St. *M40* 1G **95**
Thornton St. *Oldh* 4D **72**
Thornton St. *Roch* 6H **27**
Thornton St. N. *M40* 1G **95**
Thorntree Clo. *M9* 4G **83**
Thorntree Pl. *Roch* 3G **27**
Thorn Vw. *Bury* 2G **37**
Thorn Wlk. *Part* 6C **118**
Thornway. *Bram* 5E **151**
Thornway. *H Lane* 6D **154**
Thornway. Wors 3C **76**
Thornwood Av. *M18* 3G **111**
Thorold Gro. *Sale* 5E **123**
Thorp. 2A **56**
Thorpe Av. Rad 2B **50**
Thorpe Av. *Swin* 2E **79**
Thorpebrook Rd. *M40* . . .5A **84**
Thorpe Clo. *Aus* 1C **74**
Thorpe Clo. *Dent* 3F **113**
Thorpe Clo. *Timp* 4C **134**
Thorpe Gro. *Stoc* 3F **127**
Thorpe Hall Gro.
 Hyde 1D **114**
Thorpe Hill. *Oldh* 3C **72**
Thorpe La. Aud 2F **113**
Thorpe La.
 Aus & Scout 1B **74**
Thorpeness Sq. *M18* 1F **111**
Thorpe St. *M16* 3A **108**
Thorpe St. *Bolt* 3H **31**
Thorpe St. *Midd* 2E **69**
Thorpe St. *Rams* 4D **12**
Thorpe St. *Wors* 5F **63**
Thorpe Vw. Salf . .6A **94** (3A **8**)
 (off Ordsall Dri.)
Thorp Rd. *M40* 5A **84**
Thorp Rd. *Rytn* 3B **56**
Thorp St. *Eccl* 5D **90**
Thorp St. *W'fld* 5C **50**
Thorp Vw. *Rytn* 1A **56**
Thorsby Av. *Hyde* 5D **114**
Thorsby Clo. *M18* 2G **111**
Thorsby Clo. *Brom X* 3D **18**
Thorsby Rd. *Timp* 6G **133**
Thorsby Way. *Dent* 1G **129**
Thorverton Sq. *M40* 3B **84**
Thrapston Av. *Aud* 4D **98**

Threadfold Way.
 Brom X 4D **18**
Threaphurst La.
 Haz G 4A **154**
Threapwood Rd. M22 . . .4C **148**
Three Acre Av. Rytn 3E **57**
Three Acres Dri. Stoc . . .4G **127**
Three Lane Ends (Junct.)
 Dent 5F **113**
 (off Two Trees La.)
Three Owls Bird Sanctuary.
 . . . . .2H **25**
Three Owls Bird Sanctuary
 Vis. Cen. 2G **25**
Three Pits. Midd 2C **54**
Threlkeld Clo. Midd 6E **53**
Threlkeld Ct. Midd 6E **53**
Threlkeld Rd. Bolt 5B **18**
 (in two parts)
Threlkeld Rd. Midd 6E **53**
Thresher Clo. Sale 6F **123**
Threshfield Clo. Bury . . .4F **23**
Threshfield Dri. Timp . .4B **134**
Throstle Bank St.
 Hyde 3A **114**
Throstle Ct. Rytn 4B **56**
Throstle Gro. Bury 6C **22**
Throstle Gro. Marp 6B **142**
Throstle Hall Ct. Midd . . .6H **53**
Throstles Clo. Droy 2C **98**
Thrum Fold. Roch 6D **14**
Thrum Hall La. Roch 6E **15**
 (Daffodil Clo.)
Thrum Hall La. Roch 6D **14**
 (Gt. Lee)
Thrush Av. Farn 1B **62**
Thrush Dri. Bury 1F **37**
Thrush St. Roch 2E **27**
Thruxton Clo. M16 . . . . .4C **108**
Thurland Rd. Oldh 3G **73**
Thurland St. Chad 1E **71**
Thurlby Av. M9 . . . . . . .4G **69**
Thurlby St. M13 . . . . . .3H **109**
Thurleigh Rd. M20 . . . .5F **125**
Thurlestone Av. Bolt 4D **34**
Thurlestone Dri.
 Haz G 2A **152**
Thurlestone Dri. Urm . . .4E **105**
Thurlestone Rd. Alt 6D **132**
Thurloe St. M14 . . . . . .4G **109**
Thurlow St. Salf 5F **93**
 (in three parts)
Thurlston Cres. M8 . . . .4D **82**
Thurlwood Av. M20 . . . .2E **125**
Thurnham St. Bolt 4G **45**
Thurnley Wlk. M8 . . . . .6B **82**
Thursby Av. M20 . . . . . .3E **125**
Thursby Wlk. Midd 5E **53**
Thursfield St. Salf 6F **81**
Thurstane St. Bolt 3G **31**
Thurston Clo. Bury 5E **51**
Thurston Clough Rd.
 Scout & Dob 6E **59**
Thurston Grn. Ald E 5G **167**
Thyme Clo. M21 . . . . . .5B **124**
Thynne St. Bolt 1B **46**
Thynne St. Farn 6E **47**
Tiber Av. Oldh 2A **86**
Tib La. M2 . . . . . .4D **94** (6H **5**)
Tib St. M4 . . . . .4E **95** (5B **6**)
Tib St. Dent 5F **113**
Tib St. Rams 4D **12**
Tideswell Av.
 M40 . . . . . . .2H **95** (2G **7**)
Tideswell Bank. Glos . . .6G **117**
Tideswell Clo. H Grn . . .6H **149**
Tideswell Rd. Droy 2G **97**
Tideswell Rd. Haz G 5E **153**
Tideswell Wlk. Glos . . .6G **117**
 (off Riber Bank)
Tideswell Way. Dent . . .1G **129**
Tideway Clo. Salf 3D **80**

Tidworth Av.
 M4 . . . . . . .3H **95** (4G **7**)
Tiefield Wlk. M21 . . . . .2C **124**
Tiflis St. Roch 3G **27**
Tig Fold Rd. Farn 1A **62**
Tilbury St. Oldh 1C **72**
Tilbury Wlk.
 M40 . . . . . . .2H **95** (1G **7**)
Tilby Clo. Urm 5A **104**
Tildsley St. Bolt 3A **46**
Tilehurst Ct. Salf 4F **81**
Tile St. Bury 2D **36**
Tilgate Wlk. M9 . . . . . . .6G **69**
 (off Haverfield Rd.)
Tillard Av. Stoc 3D **138**
Tillhey Rd. M22 . . . . . .3B **148**
Tillington Clo. Bolt 2A **32**
Tilney Av. Stret 6E **107**
Tilshead Wlk.
 M13 . . . . .1G **109** (6F **11**)
 (off Dilston Clo.)
Tilside Gro. Los 6A **30**
Tilson Rd. Round I 1E **135**
Tilstock Wlk. M23 . . . . .3D **134**
Tilston Wlk. Wilm 5A **160**
Tilton St. Oldh 6G **57**
Timberbottom. Bolt 1E **33**
Timbercliffe. 6H **17**
Timbercliffe. L'boro 6H **17**
Timberhurst. Bury 3H **37**
Timbersbrook Gro.
 Wilm 5H **159**
Timber Wharf.
 M15 . . . . . . .6B **94** (3C **8**)
Times Retail Pk. Heyw . . .3E **39**
Times St. Midd 1B **70**
Timothy Clo. Salf 2B **92**
Timperley. 5B **134**
Timperley Clo. Oldh 1F **87**
Timperley Cricket, Hockey,
 Tennis & Lacrosse Club.
 . . . . .6H **133**
Timperley Fold. Ash L . . .5G **87**
Timperley Rd. Ash L 5G **87**
Timperley St. M11 . . . . .5E **97**
Timperley St. Oldh 2C **72**
Timpson Rd. Round I . . .4E **135**
Timsbury Clo. Bolt 2H **47**
Timson St. Fail 4F **85**
Tim's Ter. Miln 5F **29**
Tindall St. Eccl 5D **90**
Tindall St. Stoc 4H **111**
Tindle St. Wors 6H **63**
Tinker's Pas. Hyde 5C **114**
Tinker St. Hyde 4B **114**
Tinline St. Bury 3E **37**
Tinningham Clo. M11 . . . .6G **97**
Tinsdale Wlk. Midd 6E **53**
Tinshill Clo. M12 . . . . .2C **110**
Tinsley Clo.
 M40 . . . . . .3A **96** (3H **7**)
Tinsley Gro. Bolt 5D **32**
Tin St. Bolt 2A **46**
Tintagel Ct. Rad 2C **48**
Tintagel Ct. Stal 3D **100**
Tintagel Wlk. Hyde 4A **116**
Tintern Av. M20 . . . . . .4D **124**
Tintern Av. Bolt 3D **32**
Tintern Av. Heyw 1E **39**
Tintern Av. L'boro 2E **17**
Tintern Av. Roch 6E **15**
Tintern Av. Urm 1C **120**
Tintern Av. W'fld 6D **50**
Tintern Clo. Poy 2D **162**
Tintern Dri. Hale 3C **146**
Tintern Gro. Stoc 2B **140**
Tintern Pl. Heyw 1E **39**
Tintern Rd. Chea H 1D **160**
Tintern Rd. Midd 4H **53**
Tintern St. M14 . . . . . . .5F **109**
Tipperary St. Carr 6G **89**
Tipping St. Alt 2F **145**

Tipton Clo. Chea H 1D **150**
Tipton Clo. Rad 2D **48**
Tipton Dri. M23 . . . . . . .1H **135**
Tiptree Wlk. M9 . . . . . . .3G **83**
Tiree Clo. Haz G 4F **153**
Tirza Av. M19 . . . . .1B **126**
Tissington Bank. Glos . .6F **117**
 (off Youlgreave Cres.)
Tissington Grn. Glos . . .6F **117**
 (off Youlgreave Cres.)
Tissington Ter. Glos 6F **117**
 (off Youlgreave Cres.)
Titchfield Rd. Oldh 5G **73**
Tithe Barn Clo. Roch 5B **16**
Tithe Barn Ct. Stoc 5B **126**
Tithe Barn Cres. Bolt . . .1D **32**
Tithebarn Rd. Haleb 5C **146**
Tithe Barn Rd. Stoc 5B **126**
Tithebarn St. Bury 3D **36**
Tithebarn St. Rad 3B **50**
Titian Ri. Oldh 2H **57**
 (in two parts)
Titterington Av. M21 . . .5H **107**
Tiverton Av. Sale 6H **121**
Tiverton Clo. Rad 2C **48**
Tiverton Dri. Sale 6H **121**
Tiverton Dri. Wilm 6H **159**
Tiverton Ho. Salf 2A **92**
Tiverton Pl. Ash L 6E **87**
Tiverton Rd. Urm 3G **105**
Tiverton Wlk. Bolt 4G **31**
Tiviot Dale. Stoc 1H **139**
Tiviot Way. Stoc 6H **127**
Tivol St. M3 . . . .4C **94** (6F **5**)
Tixall Wlk. M8 . . . . .1A **82**
Toad La. Roch 3H **27**
 (in two parts)
Toad Pond Clo. Swin 5C **78**
Tobermory Clo. M11 . . . .4F **97**
Tobermory Rd. H Grn . .4G **149**
Todd's Pl. M8 . . . . .2E **83**
Todd St. M3 . . . .3E **95** (3A **6**)
Todd St. Bury 1C **36**
Todd St. Heyw 3C **38**
Todd St. Roch 4A **28**
Todd St. Salf 5H **81**
Toft Rd. M18 . . . . .3E **111**
Toft Way. Hand 3A **160**
Toledo St. M11 . . . . . . .4F **97**
Tolland La. Hale 5H **145**
Tollard Av. M40 . . . . . . .6F **83**
Tollard Clo. Chea H 1D **160**
Toll Bar St. M12 . . . . . .1A **110**
Tollbar St. Stoc 3H **139**
Tollemache Clo. Mot . . .2C **116**
Tollemache Rd. Mot 2C **116**
Tollesbury Clo. M40 . . . .1H **95**
Toll Ga. Clo. M13 . . . . .3A **110**
Tollgate Way. Roch 3C **28**
Toll St. Rad 3D **48**
Tolmount Way. Chad . . .1F **71**
Tolworth Dri. M8 . . . . . .4D **82**
Tomcroft La. Dent 5D **112**
Tom La. Alt 6A **144**
Tomlinson Clo. Oldh 4C **72**
Tomlinson St.
 M15 . . . . . .1C **108** (6F **9**)
Tomlinson St. M40 . . . . .6C **70**
Tomlinson St. Roch 1C **40**
Tomlin Sq. Bolt 6E **33**
Tom Lomas Wlk. M11 . . .3D **96**
Tommy Browell Clo.
 M14 . . . . .4E **109**
Tommy Johnson Wlk.
 M14 . . . . .4E **109**
Tommy La. Bolt 4C **34**
Tommy Taylor Clo.
 M40 . . . . .6C **84**
Tom Pendry Sq. Stal . . .4E **101**
 (off Dean St.)
Tom Shepley St. Hyde . .5C **114**
Tonacliffe. 3C **14**

Tonacliffe Rd. Whitw 4C **14**
Tonacliffe Ter. Whitw . . .2C **14**
Tonacliffe Way. Whitw . . .3C **14**
Tonbridge Clo. Bury 4C **22**
Tonbridge Pl. Bolt 4D **32**
Tonbridge Rd. M19 . . . .1D **126**
Tonbridge Rd. Stoc 1H **127**
Tong Clough. Brom X . . .3D **18**
 (in two parts)
Tonge Bri. Ind. Est.
 Bolt 5D **32**
Tonge Bri. Way Ind. Est.
 Bolt 6D **32**
 (off Tonge Bri. Way)
Tonge Clo. W'fld 6F **51**
Tonge Ct. Midd 1B **70**
Tonge Fold. 6E **33**
Tonge Fold Rd. Bolt 6D **32**
Tonge Grn. Mat 1A **116**
Tonge Hall Clo. Midd . . .1B **70**
Tonge Moor. 3D **32**
Tonge Moor Rd. Bolt . . .4D **32**
Tong End. Whitw 3G **15**
Tonge Old Rd. Bolt 6E **33**
Tonge Pk. Av. Bolt 4E **33**
Tonge Roughs. Midd . . .1D **70**
Tonge St. M12 . . .6H **95** (3H **11**)
Tonge St. Heyw 3F **39**
Tonge St. Midd 3E **71**
Tonge St. Roch 5A **28**
Tong Fields. Eger 3D **18**
Tong Head Av. Bolt 1D **32**
Tong La. Whitw 4G **15**
Tongley Wlk. M40 . . . . .1D **84**
Tong Rd. L Lev 3A **48**
Tong St. Kear 4C **64**
Tonman St. M3 . . .5C **94** (1F **9**)
Tontin St. Salf 3H **93**
Tooley Ho. Eccl 5F **91**
Toon Cres. Bury 5C **22**
Tootal Dri. Salf & M5 . . .2C **92**
Tootal Gro. Salf 3C **92**
Tootal Rd. Salf 3C **92**
Topcroft Clo. M22 . . . .3C **136**
Topfield Rd. M22 . . . . . .2A **148**
Topfields. Salf 4H **81**
Topham St. Bury 5E **37**
 (in two parts)
Top of Heap. 4B **38**
Top of Heap. Heyw 3B **38**
Top of Hebers. 4B **54**
Top of Moor. 1H **73**
Top o' th' Brow. 3F **33**
Top o' th' Brow. Bolt . . .5A **20**
Top o' th' Fields. W'fld . .2D **66**
 (in two parts)
Top o' th' Gorses. Bolt . .2E **47**
Top o' th' Grn. Chad . . .5A **72**
Top o' th' La. Bolt 2F **47**
Top o' th' Meadows. 6C **58**
Top o' th' Meadows La.
 W'head 6C **58**
Top o' th' Wood. 6F **25**
Topphome Ct. Farn 2G **63**
Topping Fold Rd. Bury . .2G **37**
Toppings. 4F **19**
Toppings Grn. Brom X . . .4E **19**
Toppings, The. Bred . . .6G **129**
Topping St. Bolt 4A **32**
Topping St. Bury 2D **36**
Topp St. Farn 2G **63**
Topp Way. Bolt 5A **32**
Top Schwabe St. Midd . .1E **69**
Topsham Wlk. M40 . . . .6D **84**
Top St. Midd 6H **53**
Top St. Oldh 1H **73**
Torah St. M8 . . . . .1E **95**
Tor Av. G'mnt 2H **21**
Torbay Clo. Bolt 1G **45**
Torbay Dri. Stoc 4B **140**

Torbay Rd. *M21* 1A **124**
Torbay Rd. *Urm* 6G **105**
Turbrook Gro. *Wilm* 0H **169**
Torcross Rd. *M9* 4D **68**
Tor Hey M. *G'mnt* 1H **21**
Torkington 3F **153**
Torkington Av. *Swin* 2F **79**
Torkington Ho. *Haz G* . .3F **153**
Torkington La.
  Haz G & Marp 2B **154**
Torkington Rd. *Gat* . . .6F **137**
Torkington Rd. *Haz G* . .3E **153**
Torkington Rd. *Wilm* . . .3F **187**
Torkington St. *Stoc* 4F **139**
Torksey Wlk. *M9* 4D **68**
Torness Wlk. *Open* 4D **96**
Toronto Av. *Man A* 6H **147**
Toronto Rd. *Stoc* 5A **140**
Toronto St. *Bolt* 5G **33**
Torpoint Wlk. *M40* 2C **84**
Torquay Clo.
  M13 . . . . . .1H **109** (6F **11**)
Torquay Gro. *Stoc* 1B **152**
Torra Barn Clo. *Eger* . . .1C **18**
Torrax Clo. *Salf* 5H **79**
Torre Clo. *Midd* 4A **54**
Torrens St. *Salf* 6B **80**
Torridon Rd. *Bolt* 6H **33**
Torridon Wlk. *M22* 5A **148**
Torrin Clo. *Stoc* 6H **139**
Torrington Av. *M9* 1A **84**
Torrington Av. *Bolt* 3A **32**
Torrington Dri. *Hyde* 5H **115**
  (in two parts)
Torrington Rd. *Swin* 5H **79**
Torrington St. *Heyw* 5G **39**
Torrisdale Clo. *Bolt* 2F **45**
Torside Way. *Swin* 1F **79**
Torver Dri. *Bolt* 5H **33**
Torver Dri. *Midd* 5F **53**
Torver Wlk. *M22* 4H **147**
Torwood Rd. *Chad* 6E **55**
Total Fitness. 3C **160**
Totland Clo. *M12* 4D **110**
Totley Av. *Glos* 6F **117**
  (off Totley Dri.)
Totley Clo. *Glos* 6F **117**
  (off Totley M.)
Totley Gdns. *Glos* 6F **117**
  (off Totley M.)
Totley Grn. *Glos* 6F **117**
Totley Lanes. *Glos* 6F **117**
  (off Totley M.)
Totley M. *Glos* 6F **117**
Totley Pl. *Glos* 6F **117**
  (off Totley M.)
Totnes Av. *Bram* 3A **152**
Totnes Av. *Chad* 6F **55**
Totnes Rd. *M21* 1A **124**
Totnes Rd. *Sale* 4F **121**
Totridge Clo. *Stoc* 6D **140**
Tottenham Dri. *M23* 4D **134**
Tottington. 5H **21**
Tottington Av. *S'head* . . .2B **74**
Tottington Fold. *Bolt* 6A **20**
Tottington La. *P'wich* 4C **66**
Tottington Rd. *Bolt* 6A **20**
Tottington Rd. *Bury* 6B **22**
Tottington Rd.
  Tur & Hawk 1B **20**
Tottington St. *M11* 3E **97**
Totton Rd. *Fail* 4F **85**
Touchet Hall Rd.
  Midd 3D **54**
Tours Av. *M23* 1G **135**
Towcester Clo.
  M4 . . . . .4H **95** (5H **7**)
Tower Av. *Rams* 4C **12**
Tower Ct. *G'mnt* 3H **21**
Tower Dri. *Tur* 1G **19**
Tower Grange. *Salf* 3H **81**
Towers Av. *Bolt* 3E **45**

Towers Bus. Pk., The.
  M20 . . . . .2F **137**
Towers Clo. *Poy* 2F **163**
Tower Sq.
  M13 . . . . .1G **109** (5E **11**)
Towers Rd. *Poy* 6F **153**
Towers St. *Oldh* 6H **57**
Tower St. *Duk* 4B **100**
Tower St. *Heyw* 4D **38**
Tower St. *Hyde* 6B **114**
Tower St. *Rad* 3B **50**
Tower Ter. *G'mnt* 3H **21**
Tuwey Clo. *M18* 1F **111**
Towncliffe Wlk.
  M15 . . . . .1B **108** (6D **8**)
Towncroft. *Dent* 3F **113**
Towncroft Av. *Midd* 5H **53**
Towncroft La. *Bolt* 5C **30**
Townend St. *Hyde* 5C **114**
Townfield. *Urm* 6D **104**
Townfield Gdns. *Alt* 6F **133**
Townfield Rd. *Alt* 6F **133**
Townfields Clo. *Bury* 4D **36**
Townfield St. *Oldh* 2F **73**
Townfield Wlk.
  M15 . . . . .1B **108** (5D **8**)
Town Fold. *Marp B* 4F **143**
Towngate Bus. Cen.
  L Hul 4A **62**
Town Ga. Dri. *Urm* 5G **103**
Towngreen Ct. *M8* 1B **82**
Town Hall La. *M2* 5H **5**
Town Hall Sq. *Roch* 4H **27**
  (off Packer St.)
Town Head. 3G **27**
Town Ho. Rd. *L'boro* 3F **17**
  (in four parts)
Town La. *Dent* 6D **112**
Town La. *Duk* 5A **100**
Townley Fold. *Hyde* 1F **115**
Townley Pk. Ind. Est.
  Midd 6A **54**
Townley Rd. *Miln* 5F **29**
Townley St. *M8* 6B **82**
Townley St. *M11* 5B **96**
Townley St. *Midd* 6A **54**
Townley Ter. *Marp* 5E **143**
  (off Canal St.)
Town Meadows. *Roch* . . .4G **27**
  (off Esplanade, The)
Town Mill Brow. *Roch* . . .4G **27**
Townrow St. *Heyw* 3F **39**
Townscliffe La.
  Marp B 4F **143**
Towns Cft. Lodge.
  Sale 3G **121**
Townsend Rd. *Swin* 2F **79**
Towns Gate. 5G **103**
Townside Row. *Bury* 4D **36**
Townsley Gro. *Ash L* 6A **88**
Town Sq. *Sale* 5B **122**
Town Sq. Shop. Cen.
  Oldh 3D **72**
Town St. *Marp B* 4F **143**
Towns Yd. *Rytn* 3C **56**
  (off Park St.)
Towton St. *M9* 3G **83**
Towyn Av. *Salf* 3G **93**
Toxteth St. *M11* 6G **97**
Tracey St. *M8* 2C **82**
Traders Av. *Urm* 1G **105**
Trafalgar Av. *Aud* 6C **98**
Trafalgar Av. *Poy* 4G **163**
Trafalgar Bus. Pk. *M8* . . .1C **94**
Trafalgar Clo. *Poy* 4G **163**
Trafalgar Ct. *M16* 5C **108**
Trafalgar Gro. *Salf* 6H **81**
Trafalgar Ho. *Alt* 5F **133**
Trafalgar Ho. *Aud* 6C **98**
  (off Trafalgar Av.)
Trafalgar Pl. *M20* 5E **125**
Trafalgar Rd. *Sale* 3C **122**

Trafalgar Rd. *Salf* 2A **92**
Trafalgar Sq. *Ash L* 4F **99**
Trafalgar Sq. *Moss* 2D **88**
Trafalgar Sq. *Roch* 3A **28**
Trafalgar St. *Ash L* 5E **99**
Trafalgar St. *Oldh* 1C **72**
Trafalgar St. *Roch* 3A **28**
Trafalgar St. *Salf* 6A **82**
Trafalgar Wlk. *Hulme* . . .2C **108**
Trafalgar Wlk. *Open* 5C **96**
Trafford Athletic Stadium.
  . . . . .6F **107**
Trafford Av. *Urm* 4G **105**
Trafford Bank Rd.
  M16 . . . . .2A **108** (6A **8**)
Trafford Boulevard.
  Urm 1E **105**
Trafford Cen., The.
  Urm 1F **105**
Trafford Ct.
  M15 . . . . .1B **108** (6C **8**)
Trafford Dri. *L Hul* 4D **62**
Trafford Dri. *Timp* 3D **134**
Trafford Ecology Pk. . .6C **92**
Trafford Enterprise Cen.
  Traf P 2D **106**
Trafford Gro. *Farn* 6G **47**
Trafford Gro. *Stret* 6D **106**
Trafford Ho. *Stret* 2F **107**
Trafford Mans. *M16* 5H **107**
Trafford Park. 2C **106**
Trafford Pk. Heritage Cen.
  . . . . .1C **106**
Trafford Pk. Rd. *Traf P* . . .5B **92**
Trafford Pl.
  M15 . . . . .1B **108** (6C **8**)
Trafford Pl. *Wilm* 3G **167**
Trafford Retail Pk.
  Urm 2E **105**
Trafford Rd. *Ald E* 5G **167**
Trafford Rd. *Eccl* 5F **91**
Trafford Rd. *Salf* 1G **107**
Trafford Rd. *Wilm* 6F **159**
Trafford St. *M3* . . .5C **94** (2F **9**)
Trafford St. *Farn* 6F **47**
Trafford St. *Oldh* 4C **72**
Trafford St. *Roch* 6G **27**
Trafford Water Sports Cen.
  . . . . .3E **123**
Trafford Way. *Urm* 6E **91**
Trafford Wharf Rd.
  Traf P 6D **92**
Tragan Clo. *Stoc* 5D **140**
Tragan Dri. *Stoc* 5D **140**
Trail St. *Salf* 3E **93**
Trajan Ho. *Oldh* 2D **72**
Tramore Wlk. *M22* 3B **148**
Tram St. *M11* 5E **97**
Tramway Rd. *Irlam* 2D **118**
Tranby Clo. *M22* 1D **148**
Tranmere Clo. *M18* 1D **110**
Tranmere Dri. *Hand* 4A **160**
Tranmere Rd. *Stoc* 3C **138**
Trans Pennine Trad. Est.
  Roch 2D **40**
Transvaal St. *M11* 4F **97**
Travis Brow. *Stoc* 2F **139**
Travis Ct. *Rytn* 3C **56**
Travis St. *M1* 5F **95** (2D **10**)
Travis St. *Hyde* 6C **114**
Travis St. *Miln* 1F **43**
Travis St. *Shaw* 6F **43**
Trawden Av. *Bolt* 3G **31**
Trawden Dri. *Bury* 3F **23**
Trawden Grn. *Stoc* 1D **152**
Traylen Way. *Roch* 2C **26**
Treacle Brow. *Hyde* 1D **130**
Tree Av. *Droy* 2A **98**
Tree Ho. Av. *Ash L* 5D **86**
Treelands Wlk. *Salf* 1H **107**
Trees St. *M8* 3B **82**
Tree Tops. *Brom X* 5G **19**

Treetops Av. *Rams* 6C **12**
Treetops Clo. *Dob* 5H **59**
Tretail St. *Salf* 6C **106**
Trefoil Way. *L'boro* 3D **16**
Tregaer Fold. *Midd* 1C **70**
Tremain Wlk. *M9* 4F **83**
  (off Stockwood Wlk.)
Trenam Pl. *Salf* 3H **93**
Trenant Rd. *Salf* 6B **80**
Trenchard Ct. *M11* 3F **97**
Trenchard Dri. *M22* 6D **148**
Trencherbone. *Rad* 2E **49**
Trengrove St. *Roch* 2F **27**
Trent Av. *Chad* 1E **71**
Trent Av. *Heyw* 2C **38**
Trent Av. *Miln* 5G **29**
Trent Bri. Wlk. *M16* 4G **107**
Trent Clo. *Bram* 1E **161**
Trent Clo. *Stoc* 4C **128**
Trent Ct. *M15* 1B **108** (6C **8**)
Trent Ct. *Stoc* 4G **139**
Trent Dri. *Bury* 3F **23**
Trent Dri. *Wors* 1D **76**
Trentham Av. *Farn* 6E **47**
Trentham Av. *Stoc* 6B **126**
Trentham Clo. *Farn* 6E **47**
Trentham Gro. *M40* 2A **84**
Trentham Lawns. *Salf* . . .1H **93**
Trentham Rd. *M16* 4G **107**
Trentham St.
  M15 . . . . .6A **94** (4B **8**)
Trentham St. *Farn* 6E **47**
Trentham St. *Swin* 2E **79**
Trent Rd. *Shaw* 5E **43**
Trent St. *Roch* 5B **28**
Trent Wlk. *Droy* 4B **98**
Trent Way. *Kear* 4B **64**
  (in two parts)
Tresco Av. *Stret* 6F **107**
Trevarrick Ct. *Oldh* 1G **73**
Trevelyan St. *Eccl* 3A **92**
Trevor Av. *Bolt* 5H **45**
Trevor Av. *Sale* 1H **133**
Trevor Dri. *M40* 1E **85**
Trevor Gro. *Stoc* 3A **140**
Trevor Rd. *Eccl* 2D **90**
Trevor Rd. *Swin* 5D **70**
Trevor Rd. *Urm* 4B **104**
Trevor St. *Open* 6G **97**
Trevor St. *Roch* 2D **40**
Triangle, The.
  M4 . . . . . . .3D **94** (4H **5**)
Triangle, The. *Timp* 4B **134**
Tribune Av. *B'hth* 4D **132**
Trident Rd. *Eccl* 6B **90**
Trillo Av. *Bolt* 1D **46**
Trimdon Clo. *M11* 3D **96**
Trimingham Dri. *Bury* 6C **22**
Trimley Av. *M40* 6F **83**
Tring Wlk. *M9* 6D **68**
Trinity Av. *Sale* 5D **122**
Trinity Bldgs. Dent 4E **113**
  (off Victoria St.)
Trinity Bldgs. Moss 1F **89**
  (off Roughtown Rd.)
Trinity Clo. *Duk* 5C **100**
Trinity Ct. *Salf* 3B **94** (4D **4**)
Trinity Cres. *Wors* 1G **77**
Trinity Gdns.
  Salf 3B **94** (3D **4**)
Trinity Gdns. *Stoc* 2H **151**
Trinity Grn. *Rams* 1B **22**
Trinity Ho. *Oldh* 1C **72**
Trinity Retail Pk. *Bolt* 1C **46**
Trinity Rd. *Sale* 5C **122**
Trinity Sports Cen.
  . . . . .2E **109** (6A **10**)
Trinity St. *Bolt* 1A **46**
Trinity St. *Bury* 4D **36**
Trinity St. *Marp* 5D **142**
Trinity St. *Midd* 1H **69**
Trinity St. *Oldh* 1C **72**

Trinity St. *Roch* 1A **26**
Trinity St. *Stal* 3E **101**
(in two parts)
Trinity Ter. *Marp* 5E **143**
Trinity Wlk. *M14* 4F **109**
Trinity Way. *Salf* . .4B **94** (5D **4**)
Trippier Rd. *Eccl* 5B **90**
Tripps M. *M20* 5D **124**
Triscombe Way. *M16* 4C **108**
Tristam Clo.
M13 . . . . . .1G **109** (5E **11**)
Trojan Gdns. *Salf* 6G **81**
Trongate Wlk. *M9* 4G **83**
Troon Clo. *Bolt* 4D **44**
Troon Clo. *Bram* 6A **152**
Troon Dri. *H Grn* 4G **149**
Troon Rd. *M23* 5F **135**
Troughgate. *Oldh* 1B **86**
Troutbeck Av.
M4 . . . . . . .3G **95** (4F **7**)
Troutbeck Clo. *Hawk* 1D **20**
Troutbeck Dri. *Rams* 1E **13**
Troutbeck Rd. *Gat* 2F **149**
Troutbeck Rd. *Timp* 6D **134**
Troutbeck Wlk. *Rytn* *3C 56*
(off Shaw St.)
Troutbeck Way. *Roch* 1B **40**
Trowbridge Dri. *M40* 2C **84**
Trowbridge Rd. *Dent* 6G **113**
Trows La. *Roch* 4D **40**
(in two parts)
Trowtree Av. *M12* 1A **110**
Troydale Dri. *M40* 5A **84**
Troy Wlk. *Salf* 6H **93**
Trub. 5D **40**
Trumpet St. *M1* . . .5D **94** (2G **9**)
Truro Av. *Ash L* 4H **87**
Truro Av. *Stoc* 4C **128**
Truro Av. *Stret* 5E **107**
Truro Clo. *Bram* 6H **151**
Truro Clo. *Bury* 2B **36**
Truro Dri. *Sale* 5F **121**
Truro Rd. *Chad* 6G **55**
Truro Wlk. *Dent* 6F **113**
Trust Rd. *M18* 4E **111**
Tudbury Way.
Salf 2B **94** (3D **4**)
Tudor Av. *M9* 2G **83**
Tudor Av. *Bolt* 6F **31**
Tudor Av. *Chad* 6D **70**
Tudor Av. *Farn* 2D **62**
Tudor Av. *Stal* 2H **101**
Tudor Clo. *Moss* 2G **89**
Tudor Clo. *Stoc* 2G **127**
Tudor Ct. M16 . . . .*2A 108*
(off Stanley Rd.)
Tudor Ct. *Bolt* 5A **32**
Tudor Ct. *Heyw* 4E **39**
Tudor Ct. *P'wich* 6G **67**
Tudor Ct. *Roch* 2B **28**
Tudor Ct. *Wors* 3H **77**
Tudor Grn. *Wilm* 6A **160**
Tudor Gro. *Midd* 4F **53**
Tudor Hall St. *Roch* 3C **40**
Tudor Ind. Est. *Duk* 1G **113**
Tudor Rd. *B'hth* 4D **132**
Tudor Rd. *Wilm* 6A **160**
Tudors. *Bram* 1F **161**
Tudor St. *Bolt* 3G **45**
Tudor St. *Midd* 1B **70**
Tudor St. *Oldh* 4B **72**
(in two parts)
Tudor St. *Shaw* 6F **43**
Tuer St. *M13* 1E **109** (6B **10**)
Tuffley Rd. *M23* 2G **147**
Tufton Wlk. *M9* 4F **83**
Tugford Clo. *M16* 3C **108**
Tuley St. *M11* 6B **96**
Tulip Av. *Farn* 6C **46**
Tulip Av. *Kear* 4H **63**
Tulip Clo. *Chad* 2E **71**
Tulip Clo. *Sale* 5E **121**

Tulip Clo. *Stoc* 6F **139**
Tulip Dri. *Timp* 5H **133**
Tulip Gro. *Roch* 6E **15**
Tulip Rd. *Part* 6C **118**
Tulip Wlk. *Salf* 1B **94** (1C **4**)
Tulketh St. Ind. Est.
M40 . . . . .3H **83**
Tulle Ct. *P'wich* 5E **67**
Tully St. *Salf* 4A **82**
Tully St. S. *Salf* 5A **82**
Tulpen Sq. *Chad* 2H **71**
Tulworth Rd. *Poy* 3D **162**
Tumblewood Dri.
Chea 1H **149**
Tumbling Bank. *M9* 6F **69**
Tumbling Bank Ter.
Lees 4B **74**
Tunbridge Sq. *Salf* 3G **93**
Tunshill Gro. *Miln* 5G **29**
Tunshill La. *Miln* 4H **29**
Tunshill Rd. *M23* 2E **135**
Tuns Rd. *Oldh* 1F **87**
Tunstall Rd. *Oldh* 3G **73**
Tunstall St. *M11* 6G **97**
Tunstall St. *Stoc* 1G **139**
Tunstead. 3G **61**
Tunstead Av. *M20* 3D **124**
Tunstead La. *G'fld* 3G **61**
Turbary Wlk. *Miln* 5D **28**
Turf Clo. *Rytn* 4C **56**
Turf Hill. 1H **41**
Turf Hill Rd. *Roch* 6B **28**
Turf Ho. Clo. *L'boro* 2D **16**
Turfland Av. *Rytn* 4C **56**
Turf La. *Chad* 6F **71**
Turf La. *Rytn* 4C **56**
(in two parts)
Turf Lea. 4F **155**
Turf Lea Rd. *Marp* 3E **155**
Turfnell Way. *Wors* 6A **78**
Turf Pk. Rd. *Rytn* 4C **56**
Turf Pit La. *Oldh* 4A **58**
Turf Pits. *Oldh* 4A **58**
Turf St. *Rad* 4F **49**
Turf Ter. *L'boro* 3E **17**
Turfton Rd. *Rytn* 4D **56**
Turks Rd. *Rad* 2D **48**
Turk St. *Bolt* 5G **31**
Turley St. *M8* 5D **82**
Turnberry. *Bolt* 4D **44**
Turnberry Dri. *Wilm* 1F **167**
Turnberry Rd. *H Grn* 4G **149**
Turnberry Wlk. *M8* 3E **83**
Turnbull Av. *P'wich* 2G **67**
Turnbull Rd. *Gort* 3H **111**
Turnbull Rd. *Long* 5B **110**
Turnbury Clo. *Sale* 3B **122**
Turnbury Rd. *M22* 6C **136**
Turncliffe Cres. *Marp* 4B **142**
Turncroft La. *Stoc* 2A **140**
Turncroft Way. *Wors* 4B **76**
Turner Av. *Fail* 5E **85**
Turner Av. *Irlam* 4E **103**
Turner Bri. Rd. *Bolt* 5E **33**
Turner Dri. *Urm* 5H **105**
Turnerford Clo. *Eger* 2C **18**
Turner Gdns. *Hyde* 3C **114**
Turner La. *Ash L* 1H **99**
Turner La. *Hyde* 3D **114**
Turner La. *Rom* 2F **129**
Turner Rd. *Marp* 5D **142**
Turners Pl. *Roch* 6E **15**
Turner St. *M4* 3E **95** (4B **6**)
Turner St. *M11* 4E **97**
Turner St. *M16* . . .1A **108** (5B **8**)
Turner St. *Ash L* 1H **99**
Turner St. *Bolt* 5C **32**
Turner St. *Dent* 2E **113**
Turner St. *Duk* 6G **99**
Turner St. *Gort* 2F **111**
Turner St. *Lees* 1A **74**
Turner St. *Roch* 2G **27**

Turner St. *Salf* 4A **82**
Turner St. *Stoc* 1H **139**
Turnfield Clo. *Roch* 6B **16**
Turnfield Rd. *Chea* 2G **149**
Turnhill Rd. *Roch* 2H **41**
Turn Moss Rd. *Stret* 1F **123**
Turnough Rd. *Miln* 4F **29**
Turnpike Clo. *Dig* 2C **60**
Turnpike Ct. *M16* 4B **108**
Turnpike Grn. Salf *2F 93*
(off Nursery St.)
Turnpike, The. *Marp* 4B **142**
Turnpike Wlk. *M11* 4B **96**
Turnstone Av. *Bolt* 1G **13**
Turnstone Rd. *Bolt* 1C **46**
Turnstone Rd. *Stoc* 6G **141**
Turn St. *Ash L* 1B **100**
Turton Av. *L Lev* 3A **48**
Turton Clo. *Bury* 5G **35**
Turton Clo. *Heyw* 3C **38**
Turton Heights. *Bolt* 5F **19**
Turton La. *P'wich* 4D **66**
Turton Leisure Cen. 4F **19**
Turton Rd. *Bolt* 5F **19**
Turton Rd. *Tur* 1C **20**
Turton St. *Bolt* 5B **32**
Turton St. *Open* 6F **97**
Turves Rd. *Chea H* 4A **150**
Tuscan Rd. *M20* 3E **137**
Tuscany Vw. *Salf* 3F **81**
Tutbury St. *M4* . . .4H **95** (6H **7**)
Tuxford Wlk. M40 . . . .*6F 83*
(off Monsall St.)
Tweedale Av. *M9* 4E **69**
Tweedale St. *Roch* 5G **27**
Tweedale Way. *Oldh* 1F **85**
Tweed Clo. *Alt* 5E **133**
Tweed Clo. *Oldh* 4C **72**
Tweedle Hill Rd. *M9* 5D **68**
Tweedsdale Clo. *W'fld* 6F **51**
Tweenbrook Av. *M23* 2G **147**
Twelve Yards Rd. *Irlam &*
Eccl . . . . . . .3B **102** & 6A **90**
(in three parts)
Twigworth Rd. *M22* 3A **148**
Twillbrook Dri.
Salf 2C **94** (2F **5**)
Twinegate. *Roch* 6E **15**
Twining Brook Rd.
Chea H 2D **150**
Twining Rd. *Traf P* 5G **91**
Twinnies Ct. *Wilm* 6F **159**
Twinnies Rd. *Wilm* 6F **159**
Twin St. *Heyw* 4G **39**
Twirl Hill Rd. *Ash L* 2A **88**
Twisse Rd. *Bolt* 6H **33**
Twoacre Av. *M22* 6A **136**
Two Acre Dri. *Shaw* 5D **42**
Two Acre La. *S'head* 5C **58**
Two Bridges Rd. *Miln* 2F **43**
Two Brooks La. *Hawk* 1D **20**
Two Trees La. *Dent* 5F **113**
Twyford Clo. *M20* 6D **124**
Tybyrne Clo. *Wors* 4B **76**
Tydden St. *Oldh* 6D **72**
Tydeman Wlk. *Miln* 6G **29**
Tyersall Clo. *Eccl* 1G **91**
Tyldesley St. *M14* 4E **109**
Tyler St. *Ald E* 5G **167**
Tymm St. *M40* 3C **84**
Tyndall Av. *M40* 2A **84**
Tyndall St. *Oldh* 3G **73**
Tyne Ct. *Wors* 6E **63**
Tynedale Clo. *Stoc* 4G **127**
Tynesbank. *Wors* 1E **77**
Tyne St. *Oldh* 2G **73**
Tynwald St. *Oldh* 2G **73**
Tynwell Wlk. *M40* 6E **83**
Tyrol Wlk. *M11* 5B **96**
Tyrone Clo. *M23* 3D **134**
Tyrone Dri. *Roch* 6A **26**
Tyrrell Gro. *Hyde* 6E **115**

Tyrrell Rd. *Stoc* 6H **111**
Tysoe Gdns.
Salf 3B **94** (3D **4**)
Tyson St. *M8* 3B **82**
Tytherington Dri. *M19* 6F **111**
Tywald Mt. *Rytn* 4C **56**

U

Uganda St. *Bolt* 5G **45**
Ukraine Rd. *Salf* 5F **81**
Uldale Dri. *Midd* 6G **53**
Ullesthorpe. *Roch* *3G 27*
(off Sheriff St.)
Ullswater Clo. *L Lev* 4H **47**
Ullswater St. *Bolt* 3B **32**
Ullock Wlk. *Midd* 5F **53**
Ullswater Av. *Ash L* 1G **99**
Ullswater Av. *Roch* 2E **27**
Ullswater Av. *Rytn* 1B **56**
Ullswater Dri. *Bury* 6C **36**
Ullswater Dri. *Farn* 2A **62**
Ullswater Dri. *Midd* 4H **53**
Ullswater Gro. *Heyw* 5F **39**
Ullswater Rd. *M22* 3H **147**
Ullswater Rd. *Hand* 3G **159**
Ullswater Rd. *Stoc* 4B **140**
Ullswater Rd. *Urm* 3A **104**
Ullswater Ter. *Stal* 1E **101**
Ullswater Wlk. M9 . . . .*6G 69*
(off Rockmead Dri.)
Ulster Av. *Roch* 6G **27**
Ulundi St. *Rad* 4G **49**
Ulverston Av. *M20* 2D **124**
Ulverston Av. *Chad* 3G **71**
UMIST Hardy Farm
Sports Ground. 3G **123**
Una Rd. *Moss* 6G **75**
Uncouth Rd. *Roch* 4E **29**
Underhill. *Rom* 1H **141**
Underhill Rd. *Oldh* 6C **56**
Underhill Wlk. *M40* 1D **96**
Under La. *Chad* 6H **71**
Under La. *G'ton* 5D **74**
Under St. *Chad* 6H **71**
Underwood. *Roch* 4G **27**
Underwood Clo. *M18* 1H **111**
Underwood Rd. *Ald E* 5H **167**
Underwood Rd. *Hyde* 5G **115**
Underwood St. *Duk* 5H **99**
Underwood Vs. L'boro *5C 16*
(off Oakley St.)
Underwood Wlk.
Hyde 5H **115**
Underwood Way.
Shaw 5H **43**
Undsworth Ct. *Heyw* 3F **39**
Unicorn St. *Eccl* 5D **90**
Unicorn St. *Rad* 4E **49**
Union Arc. *Bury* 3D **36**
Union Bldgs. *Bolt* 1B **46**
Union Ct. *Bolt* 3C **32**
Union Rd. *Ash L* 1A **100**
Union Rd. *Bolt* 3C **32**
Union Rd. *Marp* 5D **142**
Union Rd. *Roch* 5C **16**
Union St. *M4* 3E **95** (4B **6**)
Union St. *M14* 4F **109**
Union St. *Abb H* 1G **113**
Union St. *Ard* 6G **95** (3F **11**)
Union St. *Ash L* 2H **99**
Union St. *Bury* 3D **36**
Union St. *Chad* 5H **71**
Union St. *Eger* 1B **18**
Union St. *Hyde* 5C **114**
Union St. *Lees* 3A **74**
Union St. *Midd* 6A **54**
Union St. *Oldh* 3C **72**
Union St. *Rams* 3E **13**
Union St. *Roch* 3H **27**
(in two parts)

Union St. *Rytn* 3B 56
Union St. *Salf* 1G 93
Union St. *Stoc* 3H 139
Union St. *Swin* 3E 79
(Chorley Rd.)
Union St. *Swin* 3G 79
(Hilton Sq.)
Union St. *Whitw* 1C 14
Union St. W. *Oldh* 3C 72
(in two parts)
Union Ter. *Salf* 3B 82
Union Yd. *Oldh* 3F 73
United Trad. Est. *M16* . . .2E 107
Unity Clo. *Heyw* 4D 38
Unity Cres. *Heyw* 4D 38
Unity Dri. *Salf* 5A 82
Unity St. *Heyw* 4D 38
Unity Way. *Stoc* 3H 139
Universities. 1E 109
University of Manchester
. . . . .1F 109
University of Manchester
Institute of Science &
Technology, The.
. . . . .5F 95 (2C 10)
University of Salford
. . . . .3B 94 (3C 4)
(Adelphi Campus)
University of Salford . . .2H 93
(Frederick Rd. Campus)
University of Salford
. . . . .3A 94 (3A 4)
(Cockcroft Rd.)
University of Salford
. . . . .2A 94 (2B 4)
(Meadow Rd.)
University Rd.
Salf 2H 93 (1A 4)
University Rd. W. *Salf* . . .3H 93
Unsworth. 4F 51
Unsworth St. *Rad* 3F 49
Unsworth Way. *Oldh* 1C 72
Unwin Av. *M18* 3F 111
Unwin Ct. *Salf* 3F 93
Upavon Ct. *M7* 5B 82
Upavon Rd. *M22* 2D 148
Upcast La. *Ald E* 6A 166
Upland Dri. *L Hul* 3B 62
Upland Rd. *Oldh* 5C 72
Uplands. *Midd* 2A 70
Uplands Av. *Rad* 5A 50
Uplands Rd. *Hyde* 3E 131
Uplands Rd. *Urm* 1A 120
Uplands, The. *Moss* 2F 89
Up. Brook St. *M13* &
M14 . . . . . .6F 95 (4C 10)
Up. Brook St. *Stoc* 2H 139
Up. Camp St. *Salf* 6H 81
Up. Chorlton Rd. *M16* . . .5A 108
Up. Cliff Hill. *Shaw* 4G 43
Up. Conran St. *M9* 3G 83
Up. Cyrus St. *M40* 3A 96
Up. Downs. *Bow* 2E 145
Up. George St. *Roch* 2H 27
Up. Gloucester St. *Salf* . .2G 93
Up. Hayes Clo. *Roch* 3C 28
Up. Helena St.
M40 . . . . . .3A 96 (3H 7)
Up. Hibbert La. *Marp* . . .1D 154
Up. Kent Rd. *M14* 4H 109
Up. Kirby St.
M4 . . . . . .4G 95 (5F 7)
Up. Lloyd St. *M14* 4E 109
Up. Mead. *Eger* 2D 18
Up. Medlock St.
M15 . . . . . .1D 108 (5H 9)
Uppermill. 6B 60
Uppermill Dri. *M19* 6H 125
Up. Monsall St. *M40* 5G 83
Up. Moss La.
M15 . . . . . .1C 108 (6E 9)
Up. Park Rd. *M14* 3G 109

Up. Park Rd. *Salf* 2H 81
Up. Passmonds Gro.
Roch 3D 26
Up. Stone Dri. *Miln* 5D 28
Up. West Gro. *M13* 2H 109
Up. Wharf St.
Salf 4A 94 (5B 4)
Up. Wilton St. *P'wich* 5G 67
Uppingham Dri. *Rams* . . .2D 12
Upton. *Roch* 5G 27
Upton Av. *Chea H* 5C 150
Upton Av. *Stoc* 5A 126
Upton Clo. *Midd* 4A 70
Upton Dri. *Timp* 3G 133
Upton St. *M1* 4F 95 (1C 10)
Upton Wlk. *Ash L* 4G 99
Upton Way. *Hand* 2H 159
Upton Way. *Wals* 6H 21
Upwood Wlk. *M9* 6G 69
Urban Av. *Alt* 1G 145
Urban Av. *Alt* 1G 145
Urban Rd. *Alt* 1G 145
Urban Rd. *Sale* 5A 122
Urbis. 3E 95 (3A 6)
(Museum)
Urmson St. *Oldh* 6D 72
Urmston. 5F 105
Urmston La. *Stret* 6A 106
Urmston Leisure Cen.
. . . . .5C 104
Urmston Pk. *Urm* 5G 105
Urwick Rd. *Rom* 1H 141
Usk Clo. *W'fld* 2G 67
Utley Fld. Vw. *Hale* 2G 145
Uttley St. *Bolt* 3H 31
Uttley St. *Roch* 1C 40
Uvedale Ho. *Eccl* 4F 91
(off Adelaide St.)
Uxbridge Av. *M11* 3E 97
Uxbridge St. *Ash L* 2G 99

V

Vaal St. *Oldh* 6A 72
Valance Clo. *M12* 1C 110
Valdene Clo. *Farn* 2F 63
Valdene Dri. *Farn* 2F 63
Valdene Dri. *Wors* 3F 77
Vale Av. *Bury* 6B 36
Vale Av. *Hyde* 4E 115
Vale Av. *Rad* 2C 64
Vale Av. *Sale* 4E 123
Vale Av. *Swin* 2G 79
Vale Av. *Urm* 6A 104
Vale Clo. *Haz G* 1E 153
Vale Clo. *Rom* 1D 142
Vale Clo. *Stoc* 1B 138
Vale Coppice. *Rams* 6E 13
Vale Cotts. *L'boro* 4E 17
Vale Ct. *Bow* 4D 144
Vale Ct. *Midd* 1B 70
Vale Cres. *Chea H* 3B 150
Vale Dri. *Oldh* 3B 72
Vale Dri. *P'wich* 1E 81
Vale Edge. *Rad* 2G 49
Vale Head. *Hand* 5H 159
Vale Ho. *Stoc* 2A 138
Vale Ho. Dri. *Had* 1H 117
Vale La. *Fail* 1A 98
Vale Mt. *Had* 2H 117
Valencia Rd. *Salf* 5F 81
Valentia Rd. *M9* 5F 69
Valentine St. *Fail* 4E 85
Valentine St. *Oldh* 3G 73
Vale Pk. Ind. Est. *M8* 4E 83
Valerie Wlk.
M15 . . . . . .6D 94 (4H 9)
(off Loxford St.)
Vale Rd. *Bow* 4D 144
Vale Rd. *Carr* 5G 89
Vale Rd. *Droy* 2B 98

Vale Rd. *Rom* 2H 141
Vale Rd. *Shaw* 1H 57
Vale Rd. *Stoc* 2B 138
Vale Rd. *Timp* 6B 134
Vale Rd. *Wilm* 1C 166
Vale Side. *Moss* 3E 89
Vale St. *M11* 3E 97
Vale St. *Ash L* 5E 87
Vale St. *Bolt* 6A 34
Vale St. *Heyw* 3G 39
(in two parts)
Vale St. *Midd* 1B 70
Vale, The. *Moss* 2D 88
Valetta Clo. *M14* 1F 125
Vale Vw. *Bow* 4E 145
Vale Vw. *Brom X* 4D 18
Valewood Av. *Stoc* 2C 138
Valiant Wlk. *M40* 2E 85
Valletts La. *Bolt* 4G 31
Valletts S. Bldgs. *Bolt* 4G 31
Valley Av. *Bury* 1H 35
Valley Clo. *Chea* 2A 150
Valley Clo. *Moss* 1D 88
Valley Cotts. *Moss* 1F 89
Valley Dri. *Hand* 4G 159
Valley Gdns. *Hyde* 6A 116
Valley Gro. *Dent* 5H 113
Valley New Rd. *Rytn* 4C 56
Valley Pk. Rd. *P'wich* 4D 66
Valley Ri. *Shaw* 4E 43
Valley Rd. *Bram* 4H 151
Valley Rd. *Bred* 5D 128
Valley Rd. *Chea* 1A 150
Valley Rd. *Glos* 6H 117
Valley Rd. *Hyde* 6A 116
Valley Rd. *Midd* 5B 54
Valley Rd. *Rytn* 4C 56
Valley Rd. *Stoc* 2B 138
Valley Rd. *Urm* 4H 103
(in two parts)
Valley Rd. S. *Urm* 5G 103
Valley Vw. *Brom X* 4E 19
Valley Vw. *Hyde* 3E 115
Valley Vw. *Whitw* 1H 15
Valley Wlk. *M11* 4B 96
Valley Way. *Stal* 4G 101
Valpy Av. *Bolt* 2D 32
Vancouver Quay. *Salf* 6F 93
Vandyke Av. *Salf* 2B 92
Vandyke St. *Roch* 2B 26
Vane St. *Eccl* 3F 91
(in two parts)
Vanguard Clo. *Eccl* 6B 90
Vantomme St. *Bolt* 1A 32
Varden Gro. *Stoc* 6F 139
Vardon Rd. *Poy* 4B 163
Vardon Rd. *Wilm* 3G 167
Varey St. *M18* 2F 111
Varley Rd. *Bolt* 3E 45
Varley St. *M40* 1H 95 (1H 7)
Varna St. *M11* 6F 97
Vauban Drl. *Salf* 2B 92
Vaudrey Dri. *Chea H* 2C 150
Vaudrey Dri. *Haz G* 3E 153
Vaudrey Dri. *Timp* 3A 134
Vaudrey La. *Dent* 5G 113
Vaudrey Rd. *Woodl* 4G 129
Vaudrey St. *Stal* 4E 101
Vaughan Av. *M40* 3A 84
Vaughan Gro. *Lees* 3B 74
Vaughan Ind. Est.
M12 . . . . .6B 96
Vaughan Rd. *M21* 1B 124
Vaughan Rd. *Stoc* 6F 127
Vaughan St. *M12* 6B 96
Vaughan St. *Eccl* 2D 90
Vaughan St. *Rytn* 4C 56
Vauxhall St. *M40* 1G 95
(off Hamerton Rd.)

Vauxhall Ind. Est.
Stoc 3G 127
Vauxhall St. *M40* 1F 95
Vavasour Ct. *Roch* 5B 28
Vavasour St. *Roch* 5B 28
(in two parts)
Vawdrey Dri. *M23* 1F 135
Vaynor. *Roch* 3G 27
(off Spotland Rd.)
Vega St. *M8* 1C 94
Vela Wlk. *Salf* 2A 94 (2B 4)
Velmere Av. *M9* 4C 68
Velour Clo. *Salf* 2B 94 (1C 4)
Velvet Ct. *M1* 5E 95 (2B 10)
(off Granby Row)
Velvet Sq. *M1* 5E 95 (2B 10)
(off Bombay St.)
Vendale Av. *Swin* 5D 78
Venesta Av. *Salf* 1B 92
Venetia St. *M40* 6C 84
Venice Ct. *M1* 5E 95 (2B 10)
(off Samuel Ogden St.)
Venice Sq. *M1* 5E 95 (2B 10)
Venice St. *M1* 5E 95 (2B 10)
Venice St. *Bolt* 3G 45
Venlo Gdns. *Chea H* 4D 150
Ventnor Av. *M19* 1D 126
Ventnor Av. *Bolt* 2B 32
Ventnor Av. *Bury* 4D 50
Ventnor Av. *Sale* 3B 122
Ventnor Clo. *Dent* 1H 129
Ventnor Rd. *M20* 6G 125
Ventnor Rd. *Stoc* 1C 138
Ventnor St. *M9* 3F 83
Ventnor St. *Roch* 6H 27
Ventnor St. *Salf* 6F 81
Ventura Clo. *M14* 6E 109
Venture Scout. *M8* 6B 82
Venture Way. *Poy* 4F 163
Venwood Ct. *P'wich* 1D 80
Venwood Rd. *P'wich* 1D 80
Verbena Av. *Farn* 6C 46
Verbena Clo. *Part* 6D 118
Verdant La. *Eccl* 5B 90
Verdant Way. *Roch* 2A 42
Verdon St. *M4* 2E 96 (2A 6)
Verdun Av. *Salf* 2B 92
Verdun Cres. *Roch* 3E 27
Verdun Rd. *Eccl* 1D 90
Verdure Av. *Bolt* 5C 30
Verdure Av. *Sale* 2C 134
Verdure Clo. *Fail* 4H 85
Vere St. *Salf* 4F 93
Verity Clo. *M20* 3F 125
Verity Clo. *Rytn* 5B 56
Verity Wlk. *M9* 6D 68
Vermont St. *Bolt* 5H 31
Verna St. *Rams* 3E 13
Verne Av. *Swin* 3E 79
Verne Dri. *Oldh* 2A 58
Verney Rd. *Rytn* 5C 56
Vernham Wlk. *Bolt* 3A 46
Vernon Av. *Eccl* 3H 91
Vernon Av. *Stoc* 1B 140
Vernon Clo. *Chea H* 4A 150
Vernon Clo. *Poy* 5D 162
Vernon Ct. *Salf* 2G 81
Vernon Dri. *Marp* 4B 142
Vernon Dri. *P'wich* 1F 81
Vernon Gro. *Sale* 5E 123
Vernon Ho. *Stoc* 2B 140
Vernon Lodge. *Poy* 5D 162
Vernon Pk. 1B 140
Vernon Pk. *Timp* 4A 134
Vernon Rd. *Bred* 1E 141
(in two parts)
Vernon Rd. *Droy* 3G 97
Vernon Rd. *G'mnt* 2H 21
Vernon Rd. *Poy* 5D 162
Vernon Rd. *Salf* 2G 81
Vernon St. *Ash L* 1A 100

Vernon St.—Wade St.

Vernon St. *Bolt* 5A **32**
Vernon St. *Bury* 1D **36**
Vernon St. *Farn* 1G **63**
Vernon St. *Harp* 4G **83**
Vernon St. *Haz G* 2D **152**
Vernon St. *Hyde* 5C **114**
Vernon St. *Moss* 1E **89**
Vernon St. *Old T* 2B **108**
Vernon St. *Salf* 6H **81**
Vernon St. *Stoc* 1H **139**
Vernon Ter. *M12* 2B **110**
Vernon Vw. *Bred* 6F **129**
Vernon Wlk. *Bolt* 5A **32**
Vernon Wlk. *Stoc* 2G **139**
Verona Dri. *M40* 1E **97**
Veronica Rd. *M20* 6G **125**
Verrill Av. *M23* 2A **136**
Verwood Wlk. *M23* 6G **135**
Vesper St. *Fail* 3G **85**
Vesta St. *M4* 4G **95** (5F **7**)
Vesta St. *Rams* 3D **12**
Vestris Dri. *Salf* 2B **92**
Viaduct Rd. *B'hth* 4F **133**
Viaduct St. *M12* 4A **96** (6H **7**)
Viaduct St. *Salf* 3C **94** (3F **5**)
Viaduct St. *Stoc* 2G **139**
Vicarage Av. *Chea H* 5D **150**
Vicarage Clo. *Bury* 3E **23**
Vicarage Clo. *Duk* 5C **100**
Vicarage Clo. *Salf* 2B **92**
Vicarage Clo. *S'head* 2B **74**
Vicarage Cres. *Ash L* 6H **87**
Vicarage Dri. *Duk* 5B **100**
Vicarage Dri. *Roch* 6A **16**
Vicarage Gdns. *Hyde* 5C **114**
Vicarage Gro. *Eccl* 3H **91**
Vicarage La. *Bolt* 2G **31**
Vicarage La. *Bow* 4E **145**
Vicarage La. *Midd* 2D **70**
Vicarage La. *Poy* 2D **162**
Vicarage Rd. *Ash L* 6F **87**
Vicarage Rd. *Irlam* 5E **103**
Vicarage Rd. *Stoc* 5G **139**
Vicarage Rd. *Swin* 3E **79**
Vicarage Rd. *Urm* 3D **104**
Vicarage Rd. *Wors* 5E **63**
Vicarage Rd. N. *Roch* 4C **40**
Vicarage Rd. S. *Roch* 4C **40**
Vicarage St. *Bolt* 2H **45**
Vicarage St. *Oldh* 6A **72**
Vicarage St. *Rad* 4G **49**
Vicarage St. *Shaw* 6F **43**
Vicarage Vw. *Roch* 4D **40**
Vicarage Way. *Shaw* 1E **57**
Vicars Dri. *Roch* 5H **27**
Vicars Ga. *Roch* 4H **27**
Vicars Hall Gdns. *Wors* 5B **76**
Vicars Hall La. *Wors* 6B **76**
(in two parts)
Vicars Rd. *M21* 1G **123**
Vicars St. *Eccl* 2H **91**
Viceroy Ct. *M20* 1F **137**
Vicker Clo. *Swin* 1F **79**
Vicker Gro. *M20* 4D **124**
Vickerman St. *Bolt* 3H **31**
Vickers St. *M40* 2A **96** (1H **7**)
Vickers St. *Bolt* 2H **45**
Victor Av. *Bury* 1C **36**
Victoria Av. *M9* 4C **68**
Victoria Av. *Bred* 6F **129**
Victoria Av. *Chea H* 3C **150**
Victoria Av. *Did* 6E **125**
Victoria Av. *Eccl* 2H **91**
Victoria Av. *Haz G* 2E **153**
Victoria Av. *Lev* 1C **126**
Victoria Av. *Swin* 3G **79**
Victoria Av. *Timp* 4G **133**
Victoria Av. *W'fld* 1E **67**
Victoria Av. E.
M9 & M40 5G **69**
Victoria Bri. St.
Salf 3D **94** (4G **5**)
Victoria Building, The.
Salf 5F **93**
Victoria Clo. *Bram* 1F **161**
Victoria Clo. *Stoc* 4G **139**
Victoria Clo. *Wors* 5C **76**
Victoria Ct. *Ash L* 4G **99**
Victoria Ct. *Farn* 5E **47**
Victoria Ct. *Stret* 5C **106**
Victoria Cres. *Eccl* 2H **91**
Victoria Dri. *Sale* 6D **122**
Victoria Gdns. *Hyde* 3D **114**
Victoria Gdns. *Shaw* 6F **43**
Victoria Gro. *M14* 2G **125**
Victoria Gro. *Bolt* 4G **31**
Victoria Gro. *Stoc* 4E **127**
Victoria Hall. *M15* 5A **10**
Victoria Ho. *Eccl* 3H **91**
Victoria Ho. *Open* 5E **97**
Victoria Ho. *Salf* 1A **92**
Victoria Ind. Est.
M4 4H **95** (5G **7**)
Victoria La. *Swin* 3D **78**
Victoria La. *W'fld* 2D **66**
Victoria Lodge. *Salf* 6G **81**
Victoria M. *Bury* 5F **51**
Victoria M. *Duk* 1A **114**
Victorian Lanterns.
Bury 1C **22**
Victoria Pde. *Urm* 5F **105**
Victoria Park. 3H **109**
Victoria Pk. *M14* 3A **110**
Victoria Pk. *Stoc* 3B **140**
Victoria Pl. *Dent* 1G **129**
Victoria Pl. *Traf P* 2F **107**
Victoria Rd. *Bolt* 6B **30**
Victoria Rd. *Duk* 1A **114**
Victoria Rd. *Eccl* 2G **91**
Victoria Rd. *Fall* 1F **125**
Victoria Rd. *Hale* 2F **145**
Victoria Rd. *Irlam* 6D **102**
Victoria Rd. *Kear* 3A **64**
Victoria Rd. *Lev* 6B **110**
Victoria Rd. *N'den* 3B **136**
Victoria Rd. *Sale* 6D **122**
Victoria Rd. *Salf* 1A **92**
Victoria Rd. *Stoc* 2B **140**
Victoria Rd. *Stret* 5D **106**
Victoria Rd. *Timp* 5A **134**
Victoria Rd. *Urm* 5D **104**
Victoria Rd. *Whal R* 5B **108**
Victoria Rd. *Wilm* 3D **166**
Victoria Row. *Bury* 3B **36**
Victoria Sq. *M4* 3F **95** (3D **6**)
Victoria Sq. *Bolt* 6B **32**
(in three parts)
Victoria Sq. *W'fld* 2D **66**
Victoria Sq. *Wors* 6F **63**
Victoria Sta. App.
M3 3E **95** (3H **5**)
Victoria St. *M3* 3D **94** (4H **5**)
Victoria St. *A'wth* 4C **34**
Victoria St. *Alt* 6F **133**
Victoria St. *Ash L* 4G **99**
Victoria St. *Bar* 3D **86**
Victoria St. *Bury* 3B **36**
(in two parts)
Victoria St. *Chad* 2H **71**
Victoria St. *Dent* 4E **113**
(in two parts)
Victoria St. *Duk* 5B **100**
Victoria St. *Fail* 5D **84**
Victoria St. *Farn* 5D **46**
Victoria St. *Heyw* 4G **39**
Victoria St. *Hyde* 3C **114**
Victoria St. *Lees* 3A **74**
Victoria St. *L'boro* 4F **17**
Victoria St. *Midd* 1A **70**
Victoria St. *Mill* 1H **101**
Victoria St. *Oldh* 3E **73**
Victoria St. *Open* 5E **97**
Victoria St. *Rad* 4G **49**
Victoria St. *Rams* 3D **12**
Victoria St. *Roch* 2H **27**
Victoria St. *Shaw* 1F **57**
Victoria St. *Stal* 3D **100**
Victoria St. *T'ton* 4G **21**
Victoria St. *Whitw* 1C **14**
Victoria St. *Wors* 5C **76**
Victoria St. E. *Ash L* 3G **99**
Victoria Ter. *M12* 3B **110**
Victoria Ter. *Heyw* 1E **39**
Victoria Ter. *Miln* 6G **29**
Victoria Trad. Est.
Chad 6H **71**
Victoria Wlk. *Chad* 6A **56**
Victoria Way. *Bram* 1F **161**
Victoria Way. *Rytn* 1A **56**
Victor Mann St. *M11* 6A **98**
Victor St. *M40* 1G **95**
Victor St. *Heyw* 5G **39**
Victor St. *Oldh* 2H **85**
Victor St. *Salf* 3B **94** (4D **4**)
Victory. 5G **31**
Victory Gro. *Aud* 6C **98**
Victory Rd. *Cad* 5A **118**
Victory Rd. *L Lev* 3A **48**
Victory St. *M14* 4G **109**
Victory St. *Bolt* 5G **31**
(in two parts)
Victory Trad. Est. *Bolt* 2C **46**
Vienna Rd. *Stoc* 5F **139**
Vienna Rd. E. *Stoc* 5F **139**
Viewfield Wlk. M9 4G **83**
(off Nethervale Dri.)
Viewlands Dri. *Hand* 5H **159**
View St. *Bolt* 2H **45**
Vigo Av. *Bolt* 4F **45**
Vigo St. *Heyw* 4G **39**
Vigo St. *Oldh* 4H **73**
Viking Clo. *M11* 4B **96**
Viking St. *Bolt* 3C **46**
Viking St. *Roch* 3E **27**
Village Circ. *Traf P* 1D **106**
Village Ct. *Traf P* 1C **106**
Village Ct. Whitw 4G **15**
(off North St.)
Village Ct. *Wilm* 6H **159**
Village Grn. Upperm 1F **61**
(off New St.)
Village St. *Salf* 6G **81**
Village, The. *Chea* 1A **150**
Village, The. *Urm* 1B **120**
Village Wlk. *Open* 4E **97**
Village Way. *M4* 3E **95** (3B **6**)
Village Way. *Traf P* 1B **106**
Village Way. *Wilm* 6H **159**
Villa Rd. *Oldh* 5D **72**
Villdale Av. *Stoc* 4C **140**
Villemoble Sq. *Droy* 4A **98**
Villiers Ct. *W'fld* 3E **67**
Villiers Dri. *Oldh* 4C **72**
Villiers St. *Ash L* 3B **100**
Villiers St. *Bury* 2E **37**
Villiers St. *Hyde* 5D **114**
Villiers St. *Salf* 1F **93**
Vinca Gro. *Salf* 5H **81**
Vincent Av. *M21* 6G **107**
Vincent Av. *Eccl* 1F **91**
Vincent Av. *Oldh* 1G **73**
Vincent Ct. *Bolt* 4A **46**
Vincent St. *M11* 5E **97**
Vincent St. *Bolt* 1H **45**
Vincent St. *Hyde* 6D **114**
Vincent St. *L'boro* 3E **17**
Vincent St. *Midd* 5A **54**
Vincent St. *Roch* 6A **28**
Vincent St. *Salf* 4H **81**
Vine Av. *Swin* 3H **79**
Vine Clo. *Sale* 4E **121**
Vine Clo. *Shaw* 6F **43**
Vine Ct. *Roch* 4B **28**
Vine Ct. *Stret* 6D **106**
Vine Fold. *M40* 2F **85**
Vine Gro. *Stoc* 5C **140**
Vine Pl. *Roch* 6H **27**
Vinery Gro. *Dent* 4E **113**
Vine St. *M11 & M18* 6G **97**
Vine St. *Chad* 6H **71**
Vine St. *Eccl* 4E **91**
Vine St. *Haz G* 2D **152**
Vine St. *P'wich* 4G **67**
Vine St. *Rams* 5C **12**
(in two parts)
Vine St. *Salf* 3F **81**
Vineyard Clo. *Ward* 2A **16**
Vineyard Cotts. *Roch* 2A **16**
Vineyard Ho. Roch 2A **16**
(off Knowl Syke St.)
Vineyard St. *Oldh* 3F **73**
Viola St. *M11* 3F **97**
Viola St. *Bolt* 2A **32**
Violet Av. *Farn* 6C **46**
Violet Ct. *M22* 2B **148**
Violet Hill Ct. *Oldh* 1A **74**
Violet St. *M18* 1H **111**
Violet St. *Stoc* 5H **139**
Violet Way. *Midd* 2D **70**
V.I.P. Centre Ind. Est.
Oldh 6G **57**
Virgil St. *M15* 1A **108** (5B **8**)
Virgina Ho. *M11* 6D **96**
Virginia Chase.
Chea H 5B **150**
Virginia Clo. *M23* 4D **134**
Virginia Ho. *Farn* 2F **63**
Virginia St. *Bolt* 3F **45**
Virginia St. *Roch* 1E **41**
Viscount Dri. *H Grn* 6H **149**
Viscount Dri. *Timp* 6F **147**
Viscount St. *M14* 4G **109**
Vista, The. *Cad* 5A **118**
Vivian Pl. *M14* 3A **110**
Vivian St. *Roch* 6G **27**
Vixen Clo. *M21* 2B **124**
Voewood Ho. *Stoc* 3B **140**
Voltaire Av. *Salf* 2B **92**
Vorlich Dri. *Chad* 1F **71**
Vulcan St. *Oldh* 6F **57**
Vulcan Ter. L'boro 4D **16**
(off Spenwood Rd.)
Vulcan Works.
M4 4H **95** (6G **7**)
Vyner Gro. *Sale* 3H **121**

W

Wadcroft Wlk. *M9* 3G **83**
Waddicor Av. *Ash L* 5A **88**
Waddington Clo. *Bury* 3E **35**
Waddington Fold.
Roch 3A **42**
Waddington Rd. *Bolt* 4E **31**
Waddington St. *Oldh* 1A **72**
Wadebridge Av. *M23* 4D **134**
Wadebridge Clo. *Bolt* 4C **32**
Wadebridge Dri. *Bury* 3F **35**
Wadebrook Gro.
Wilm 6A **160**
Wade Clo. *Eccl* 4F **91**
Wadeford Clo.
M4 2G **95** (2E **7**)
(in two parts)
Wade Hill La. *Dob* 1G **75**
Wade Ho. Eccl 4F **91**
(off Wade Clo.)
Wade Row. *Upperm* 1F **61**
Wade Row Top.
Upperm 1F **61**
(off Wade Row)
Wadesmill Wlk.
M13 6F **95** (4C **10**)
Wadeson Rd.
M13 6F **95** (3D **10**)
Wade St. *Bolt* 4B **46**
Wade St. *Midd* 3D **70**

Wade Wlk. *Open* 5C **96**
Wadham Gdns.
   Woodl 4A **130**
Wadham Way. *Hale* . . .4H **145**
Wadhurst Wlk. *M13* . . .2G **109**
Wadlow Clo.
   Salf 2B **94** (2E **5**)
Wadsley St. *Bolt* 5A **32**
Wadsworth Clo. *Hand* . .4A **160**
Wadsworth Ind. Pk.
   Bolt 3A **46**
Wadsworth M. *Droy* 4H **97**
Wagg Fold. *L'boro* 2D **16**
Waggoners Ct. *Swin* 4F **79**
Waggon Rd. *Bolt* 4F **33**
Waggon Rd. *Moss* 3E **89**
Wagner St. *Bolt* 2H **31**
Wagstaff Dri. *Fail* 4F **85**
Wagstaffe St. *Midd* 6A **54**
Wagstaff St. *Stal* 4C **100**
Wagtail Clo. *Wors* 3F **77**
Waincliffe Av. *M21* 5B **124**
Wain Clo. *Eccl* 3D **90**
Waingap Cres. *Whitw* . . .1D **14**
Waingap Ri. *Roch* 5E **15**
Waingap Vw. *Whitw* 2D **14**
Wainman St. *Salf* 6F **81**
Wain Stones Grn. *Stoc* . .6E **141**
Wainwright Av. *Dent* 4H **111**
Wainwright Clo. *S'head* . .2C **74**
Wainwright Clo. *Stoc* . . .4A **140**
Wainwright Rd. *Alt* 6D **132**
Wainwright St. *Duk* 4B **100**
Wainwright St. *Oldh* 4C **72**
Waithlands Rd. *Roch* 5B **28**
Wakefield Cres. *Rom* 2G **141**
Wakefield Dri. *Chad* 6A **56**
Wakefield Dri. *Swin* 4D **64**
Wakefield Fold.
   Brom X 4D **18**
Wakefield M. *Brom X* . . .4D **18**
Wakefield Rd. *Stal* 3E **101**
Wakefield St.
   M1 . . . . .6E **95** (3A **10**)
Wakefield St. *Chad* 6A **56**
Wakefield Wlk. *Dent* . . .6G **113**
Wakeling Rd. *Dent* 1E **129**
Walcott Clo. *M13* 2H **109**
Wald Av. *M14* 2A **126**
Waldeck St. *Bolt* 5G **31**
Waldeck Wlk. *M9* 6G **69**
   (off Ravenswood Dri.)
Walden Av. *Oldh* 5H **57**
Walden Clo. *M14* 1E **125**
Walden Cres. *Haz G* 2C **152**
Walden Flats. *Heyw* 3E **39**
   (off Brunswick St.)
Walderton Av. *M40* 4A **84**
Waldon Av. *Chea* 6H **137**
Waldon Clo. *Bolt* 3G **45**
Wales St. *Oldh* 6G **57**
Walford St. *M16* 3C **108**
Walkden. 6F **63**
Walkdene Av. *Wors* 6D **62**
Walkden Gdns. 6C **122**
Walkden Mkt. Pl. *Wors* . .6E **63**
Walkden Recreation Cen.
   . . . . .2G **77**
Walkden Rd. *Wors* 1F **77**
Walkden St. *Roch* 2H **27**
Walker Av. *Bolt* 4B **46**
Walker Av. *Fail* 5H **85**
Walker Av. *Stal* 3G **101**
Walker Av. *W'fld* 3E **67**
Walker Clo. *Hyde* 5D **114**
Walker Clo. *Kear* 4A **64**
Walker Fold. *Hyde* 5D **114**
Walker Fold Rd. *Bolt* 2A **30**
Walker Grn. *Eccl* 6B **78**
Walker Ho. *Eccl* 4F **91**
Walker La. *Hyde* 5C **114**
Walker Rd. *M9* 5G **69**

Walker Rd. *Chad* 1F **85**
Walker Rd. *Eccl* 1C **90**
Walker Rd. *Irlam* 6D **102**
Walkers. 3B **74**
Walkers Bldgs. *M1* 6D **6**
Walkers Ct. *Farn* 1F **63**
Walkers Ct. *S'head* 3C **74**
Walker's Cft.
   Salf 3D **94** (3H **5**)
Walker's La. *S'head* 3C **74**
Walker's Rd. *Oldh* 1A **86**
Walker St. *Oldh* 3B **72**
Walker St. *Rad* 6A **50**
Walker St. *Roch* 4A **28**
Walker St. *Stoc* 2G **139**
Walkers Vw. *S'head* 2C **74**
Walkerwood Dri. *Stal* . . .2H **101**
Walkmill. *Dob* 6H **59**
Walk Mill Clo. *Roch* 5B **16**
Walk, The. *Roch* 4H **27**
Walkway, The. *Bolt* 2D **44**
   (in two parts)
Wallace Av. *M14* 4H **109**
Wallace St. *Oldh* 5D **72**
Wallasey Av. *M14* 6F **109**
Wallbank. 2B **14**
Wallbank Dri. *Whitw* 2B **14**
Wall Bank La. *Whitw* 2B **14**
Wallbank Rd. *Bram* 4A **152**
Wallbank St. *T'ton* 4H **21**
Wallbrook Cres. *L Hul* 3C **62**
Wallbrook Gro. *Farn* 5D **46**
Walled Garden, The.
   Swin 5D **78**
Waller Av. *M14* 1G **125**
Walley St. *Bolt* 2A **32**
Wallhead Rd. *Roch* 4D **28**
Wall Hill. 6G **59**
Wall Hill Rd. *Dob* 6G **59**
Wallingford Rd. *Hand* 2G **159**
Wallingford Rd. *Urm* 4G **105**
Wallis St. *M40* 6C **84**
Wallis St. *Chad* 5G **71**
Wallis St. *P'wich* 4E **67**
Wallness. 2H **93** (2A **4**)
Wallness La.
   Salf 1H **93** (1A **4**)
Wallshaw Pl. *Oldh* 2E **73**
Wallshaw St. *Oldh* 2E **73**
   (in two parts)
Wall St. *Oldh* 4D **72**
Wall St. *Salf* 3F **93**
Wall Way. *M18* 3G **111**
Wallwork Clo. *Roch* 2A **26**
Wallwork St. *Open* 5G **97**
Wallwork St. *Rad* 3G **49**
Wallwork St. *Stoc* 5H **111**
Wallworth Av. *M18* 2F **111**
Wallworth Ter. *Wilm* . . .1B **166**
Wally Sq. *Salf* 5A **82**
Walmer Dri. *Bram* 4H **151**
Walmersley. 3F **23**
Walmersley Old Rd.
   Bury 3F **23**
Walmersley Rd. *M40* 1E **85**
Walmersley Rd. *Bury* 1E **23**
Walmer St. *Abb H* 1G **111**
Walmer St. *Rush* 4F **109**
Walmer St. E. *Rush* 4G **109**
Walmley Gro. *Bolt* 4G **45**
Walmsley Av. *L'boro* 6D **16**

Walmsley Gro. *Urm* 5F **105**
Walmsley St. *Bury* 1H **35**
Walmsley St. *Stal* 5E **101**
Walmsley St. *Stoc* 6E **127**
Walney Rd. *M22* 1B **148**
Walnut Av. *Bury* 2F **37**
Walnut Av. *Oldh* 1H **73**
Walnut Clo. *Hyde* 5E **115**
Walnut Clo. *Swin* 5D **64**
Walnut Clo. *Wilm* 1H **167**
Walnut Gro. *Sale* 4A **122**
   (Ashlands)
Walnut Gro. *Sale* 5A **122**
   (Oakfield)
Walnut Rd. *Eccl* 1C **90**
Walnut Rd. *Part* 6B **118**
Walnut St. *M18* 1F **111**
Walnut St. *Bolt* 2B **32**
Walnut Tree Rd. *Stoc* . . .3C **138**
Walnut Wlk. *Stret* 6C **106**
Walpole St. *Roch* 4A **28**
Walsall St. *Salf* 6E **81**
Walsden St. *M11* 3F **97**
Walsh Av. *M9* 1F **83**
Walshaw. 1F **35**
Walshaw Brook Clo.
   Bury 1F **35**
Walshaw Dri. *Swin* 4F **79**
Walshaw La. *Bury* 1F **35**
Walshaw Rd. *Bury* 1F **35**
Walshaw Wlk. *T'ton* 6H **21**
Walshaw Way. *T'ton* 6H **21**
Walshe St. *Bury* 3B **36**
Walsh Fold. *Brom X* 1H **19**
Walsh St. *Chad* 3H **71**
Walsingham Av. *M20* 5D **124**
Walsingham Av. *Midd* 4A **70**
Walter Greenwood Ct.
   Salf 2G **93**
   (off Belvedere Rd.)
Walter La. *Bury* 6E **51**
Walter Scott St. *Oldh* 1F **73**
Walters Dri. *Oldh* 6E **73**
Walter St. *M9* 3F **83**
Walter St. *Abb H* 1G **111**
Walter St. *Oldh* 3D **72**
Walter St. *Old T* 3A **108**
Walter St. *P'wich* 5D **66**
Walter St. *Rad* 6F **35**
Walter Ct. *Wors* 1F **77**
Waltham Dri. *Chea H* . . .1D **160**
Waltham Gdns. *Rad* 3E **49**
Waltham Rd. *M16* 6C **108**
Waltham St. *Oldh* 5G **73**
Walton Clo. *Heyw* 5F **39**
   (in two parts)
Walton Clo. *Midd* 6E **53**
Walton Ct. *Bolt* 3B **46**
Walton Dri. *Bury* 3E **23**
Walton Dri. *Marp* 4B **142**
Walton Hall Dri. *M19* 6F **111**
Walton Ho. *Fail* 3F **85**
Walton Pl. *Kear* 2G **63**
Walton Rd. *M9* 4F **69**
Walton Rd. *Alt* 6D **132**
Walton Rd. *Sale* 2H **133**
Walton Sports Cen. 1A **134**
Walton St. *Ash L* 6E **87**
Walton St. *Heyw* 5F **39**
Walton St. *Midd* 5A **54**
Walton St. *Stoc* 4H **139**
Walton Way. *Dent* 6H **113**
Walworth Clo. *Rad* 2C **64**
Walworth St. *Bolt* 3G **45**
Walwyn Clo. *Stret* 6E **107**
Wandsworth Av. *M11* 3F **97**
Wanley Wlk. *M9* 6G **69**
Wansbeck Clo. *Stret* 6E **107**
Wansbeck Lodge.
   Stret 6E **107**

Wansfell Wlk.
   M4 . . . . .3H **95** (4H **7**)
Wansford St. *M14* 4E **109**
Wanstead Av. *M9* 6B **70**
Wapping St. *Bolt* 3H **31**
Warbeck Clo. *Stoc* 5A **112**
Warbeck Rd. *M40* 1D **84**
Warbreck Clo. *Bolt* 6H **33**
Warbreck Gro. *Sale* 6D **122**
Warbrick Dri. *Urm* 6D **104**
Warburton Clo. *Haleb* . . .1D **156**
Warburton Clo. *Rom* 2G **141**
Warburton Dri. *Haleb* . . .1D **156**
Warburton La. *Lymm* 6C **118**
Warburton Rd. *Hand* 3H **159**
Warburton St. *M20* 6F **125**
Warburton St. *Bolt* 3B **32**
Warburton St. *Eccl* 4G **91**
Warburton St. *Salf* 1H **107**
Warburton Way. *Timp* . . .4C **134**
Warcock Rd. *Oldh* 2G **73**
Wardale Ct. *Sale* 5C **122**
Ward Ct. *Dig* 3C **60**
Wardend Clo. *L Hul* 3C **62**
Warden La. *M40* 5B **84**
Warden St. *M40* 5B **84**
Warde St. *M15* . . .1C **108** (6E **9**)
Ward La. *Dig* 3C **60**
Wardle. 3A **16**
Wardle Brook Av.
   Hyde 4G **115**
Wardle Brook Wlk.
   Hyde 4H **115**
Wardle Clo. *Rad* 2E **49**
Wardle Clo. *Stret* 5E **107**
Wardle Edge. *Roch* 6H **15**
Wardle Fold. 2A **16**
Wardle Fold. *Ward* 2A **16**
Wardle Gdns. *Roch* 6A **16**
Wardle Rd. *Roch* 6A **16**
Wardle Rd. *Sale* 6B **122**
Wardle St. *M40* 2A **96** (2H **7**)
Wardle St. *Bolt* 2D **46**
Wardle St. *L'boro* 3E **17**
Wardley. 1C **78**
Wardley Av. *M16* 6C **108**
Wardley Av. *Wors* 6D **62**
Wardley Gro. *Bolt* 6F **31**
Wardley Hall La. *Wors* 3A **78**
   (in two parts)
Wardley Hall Rd.
   Wors & Swin 2B **78**
Wardley Ho. *Salf* 1C **92**
Wardley Ind. Est. *Wors* . . .2C **78**
Wardley St. *Swin* 3F **79**
Wardlow Av. *Glos* 6F **117**
   (off Wardlow M.)
Wardlow Fold. *Glos* 6F **117**
   (off Wardlow M.)
Wardlow Gdns. *Glos* 6F **117**
   (off Wardlow M.)
Wardlow Gro. *Glos* 6F **117**
   (off Wardlow M.)
Wardlow M. *Glos* 8F **117**
Wardlow St. *Bolt* 3F **45**
Wardlow Wlk. *Glos* 6F **117**
   (off Wardlow M.)
Ward Rd. *Droy* 4B **98**
Wardsend. 6F **163**
Wardsend Wlk.
   M15 . . . . .1B **108** (5D **8**)
Ward St. *M9* 1E **83**
Ward St. *Bred* 6F **129**
Ward St. *Chad* 2A **72**
Ward St. *Did* 6F **125**
Ward St. *Fail* 3E **85**
Ward St. *Hyde* 5C **114**
Ward St. *Most* 3H **83**
Ward St. *Oldh* 1B **72**
Ward St. *Stoc* 4A **140**
Wareham Gro. *Eccl* 2F **91**
Wareham St. *M8* 2D **82**

Wareham St.—Watson Gdns.

Wareham St. Wilm 2E 167
Wareings Yd. Roch 1G 41
Wareing Way. Bolt 1A 46
Warfield Wlk. M9 6G 69
Warford Av. Poy 5G 163
Warford St. M4 1F 95 (1C 6)
Warhill. 4C 116
Warhurst Fold. Had 2H 117
Warke, The. Wors 5H 77
Warley Clo. Chea 5A 138
Warley Gro. Duk 5A 100
Warley Rd. M16 4G 107
Warley St. L'boro 3F 17
Warlingham Clo. Bury 4H 35
Warlow Crest. G'fld 5E 61
Warlow Dri. G'fld 5E 61 (in two parts)
Warmco Ind. Pk. Moss 1F 89
Warmington Dri. M12 1A 110 (6H 11)
Warmley Rd. M23 3D 134
Warne Av. Droy 3C 98
Warner Wlk. M11 4B 96 (off Hopedale Clo.)
Warnford Clo. M40 1F 97
War Office Rd. Roch 5A 26
Warp Wlk. M4 3G 95 (4E 7) (off Jackroom Dri.)
Warren Av. Chea 6H 137
Warren Bank. M9 6F 69
Warren Bruce Rd. Traf P 1D 106
Warren Clo. Bram 3F 151
Warren Clo. Dent 5D 112
Warren Clo. Poy 3B 162
Warren Dri. Haleb 6D 146
Warren Dri. Swin 6D 78
Warrener St. Sale 5D 122
Warren Hey. Wilm 1H 167
Warren La. Oldh 5F 73
Warren Lea. Comp 1F 143
Warren Lea. Poy 2E 163
Warren Rd. Chea H 3D 150
Warren Rd. Stoc 5G 139
Warren Rd. Traf P 1B 106
Warren Rd. Wors 6G 63
Warren St. M9 1E 83
Warren St. Bury 4H 35
Warren St. Salf 3B 82
Warren St. Stoc 1H 139 (in two parts)
Warre St. Ash L 2H 99
Warrington Rd. M9 5E 69
Warrington St. Ash L 2H 99
Warrington St. Lees 4A 74
Warrington St. Stal 4F 101
Warsall Rd. Shar I 4C 136
Warslow Dri. Sale 2E 135
Warsop Av. M22 6C 136
Warstead Wlk. M13 2G 109 (off Plymouth Gro.)
Warth Cotts. Dig 3C 60
Warth Fold. 6B 36
Warth Fold Rd. Rad 1A 50 (in two parts)
Warth Rd. Bury 6B 36
Warton Clo. Bram 6A 152
Warton Clo. Bury 4F 35
Warton Dri. M23 6G 135
Warwick Av. M20 5D 124
Warwick Av. Dent 6F 113
Warwick Av. Swin 1D 78
Warwick Av. W'fld 2F 67
Warwick Clo. Bury 1H 35
Warwick Clo. Chea H 1C 150
Warwick Clo. Duk 1A 114
Warwick Clo. G'mnt 2A 22
Warwick Clo. Midd 3A 70
Warwick Clo. Shaw 6D 42
Warwick Clo. Stoc 5F 127
Warwick Clo. W'fld 2E 67
Warwick Ct. M16 4G 107
Warwick Ct. Midd 1A 70
Warwick Ct. Stoc 5F 127
Warwick Dri. Hale 4G 145
Warwick Dri. Haz G 4D 152
Warwick Dri. Sale 5D 122
Warwick Dri. Urm 3D 104
Warwick Gdns. Bolt 5F 45
Warwick Gro. Aud 5C 98
Warwick Ho. M19 5C 110
Warwick Ho. Sale 5D 122
Warwick Mall. Chea 5H 137
Warwick Rd. Ash L 6G 87
Warwick Rd. Cad 4B 118
Warwick Rd. Chor H 6H 107
Warwick Rd. Fail 6F 85
Warwick Rd. Hale 4G 145
Warwick Rd. Midd 3B 70
Warwick Rd. Old T 2F 107
Warwick Rd. Rad 1F 49
Warwick Rd. Rom 1G 141
Warwick Rd. Stoc 6E 127
Warwick Rd. Wors 2E 77
Warwick Rd. S. M16 4G 107
Warwick St. M1 3F 95 (4C 6)
Warwick St. M15 2D 108 (6G 9)
Warwick St. Bolt 1A 32
Warwick St. Oldh 5A 72 (in two parts)
Warwick St. P'wich 5E 67 (in two parts)
Warwick St. Roch 1B 28
Warwick St. Swin 2F 79
Warwick Ter. Duk 4H 99 (off Hill St.)
Wasdale Av. Bolt 4H 33
Wasdale Av. Urm 4D 104
Wasdale Dri. Gat 2F 149
Wasdale Dri. Midd 5G 53
Wasdale St. Roch 4D 40
Wasdale Ter. Stal 1E 101
Wasdale Wlk. Oldh 1E 73
Wash Brook. Chad 5H 71
Washbrook Av. Wors 2D 76
Washbrook Ct. Chad 5H 71
Washbrook Dri. Stret 5B 106
Wash Brow. Bury 6B 22
Wash Fold. Bury 6B 22
Washford Dri. M23 3D 134
Washington Clo. Chea H 5B 150
Washington Ct. Bury 2D 36
Washington St. Bolt 1G 45
Washington St. Oldh 2A 72
Wash La. Bury 2E 37
Wash La. Ter. Bury 3F 37
Wash Ter. Bury 6B 22
Washway Rd. Sale 2G 133
Washwood Clo. L Hul 3D 62
Wasnidge Wlk. M15 2D 108 (6H 9)
Wasp Av. Roch 2G 41
Wastdale Av. Bury 4E 51
Wastdale Rd. M23 1F 147
Wast Water St. Oldh 6E 57
Watchgate Clo. Midd 4F 53
Waterbridge. Wors 6H 77
Watercroft. Roch 2H 25
Waterdale Clo. Wors 5D 76
Waterdale Dri. W'fld 1E 67
Waterfield Clo. Bury 4F 23
Waterfield Way. Fail 5G 85
Waterfold. Bury 4F 37
Waterfold La. Bury 4G 37
Waterfold Pk. Bury 3F 37
Waterfoot Cotts. Mot 3C 116
Waterford Av. M20 6B 124
Waterford Av. Rom 1D 142
Waterford Pl. H Grn 5F 149
Waterfront Ho. Eccl 2E 91
Waterfront Quay. Salf 6F 93
Watergate. Aud 5C 98 (in two parts)
Water Ga. Upperm 1F 61
Watergate La. Bolt 6G 45
Watergate Milne Ct. Oldh 1H 73
Watergrove Rd. Duk 6D 100
Waterhead. 1A 74
Waterhead. Oldh 1A 74
Waterhouse Clo. Ward 4A 16
Waterhouse Rd. M18 3G 111
Waterhouse St. Roch 3H 27
Water La. Droy 4G 97 (in two parts)
Water La. Holl 2F 117
Water La. Kear 2G 63
Water La. Miln 6G 29
Water La. Rad 4F 49
Water La. Rams 3A 12
Water La. Wilm 2D 166
Water La. St. Rad 4F 49 (in two parts)
Waterloo. 6E 87
Waterloo Ct. M20 4E 125 (off Lapwing La.)
Waterloo Ct. Bury 5C 36
Waterloo Est. M8 5C 82
Waterloo Gdns. Ash L 6A 88
Waterloo Ind. Pk. Bolt 4C 32
Waterloo Pde. M8 1D 94
Waterloo Pk. Ind. Est. Stoc 2A 140
Waterloo Pl. Stoc 2H 139 (off Watson Sq.)
Waterloo Rd. M8 6B 82
Waterloo Rd. Ash L 6F 87
Waterloo Rd. Bram 4H 151
Waterloo Rd. Poy 5G 163
Waterloo Rd. Rom 1C 142
Waterloo Rd. Stal 3E 101
Waterloo Rd. Stoc 2H 139
Waterloo St. M1 5E 95 (1A 10)
Waterloo St. M8 & M9 3E 83
Waterloo St. Ash L 1B 100
Waterloo St. Bolt 4B 32
Waterloo St. Bury 3B 36
Waterloo St. Oldh 2D 72
Watermans Clo. M9 3H 83
Waterman Vw. Roch 3C 28
Watermead. Sale 2A 134
Watermead Clo. Stoc 1G 151
Water Mead Works. Bolt 4B 32
Watermeetings La. Rom 1C 142
Watermill Clo. Roch 5D 28
Water Mill Clough. Rytn 5A 56
Watermill Ct. Ash L 6E 87
Watermillock Gdns. Bolt 1B 32
Water Palace, The. 1B 46
Waterpark Hall. Salf 2A 82
Waterpark Rd. Salf 3A 82
Water Rd. Stal 3D 100
Waters Edge. Farn 5C 46
Waters Edge. G'fld 4E 61
Waters Edge. Marp B 3E 143
Watersedge. Wors 1H 77
Waters Edge Bus. Pk. Salf 1H 107
Watersedge Clo. Chea H 2D 150
Waters Edge Fold. Oldh 3G 57
Watersfield Clo. Chea H 5B 150
Watersheddings. 6G 57
Watersheddings St. Oldh 6H 57
Watersheddings Way. Oldh 6H 57
Waterside. Bolt 2E 47
Waterside. G'fld 5G 61
Waterside. Had 1H 117
Waterside. Hyde 5H 115
Waterside. Marp 1D 154
Waterside. Traf P 1F 107
Waterside Av. Marp 6D 142
Waterside Bus. Pk. Had 1H 117
Waterside Clo. M21 5B 124
Waterside Clo. Hyde 5H 115
Waterside Clo. Oldh 3G 57
Waterside Clo. Rad 3B 50
Waterside Ct. Urm 5H 103
Waterside Ho. Wors 6A 78
Waterside Ind. Pk. Bolt 4F 47
Waterside La. Roch 3B 28
Waterside Rd. Bury 1B 22
Waterside Rd. Dis & N Mills 6H 155
Waterside Wlk. Hyde 5G 115
Waterslea. Eccl 3E 91
Waterslea Dri. Bolt 5D 30
Watersmead Clo. Bolt 3B 32
Watersmead St. Bolt 3B 32
Watersmeet. Stret 3D 106
Waters Meeting Rd. Bolt 2B 32
Waterson Av. M40 4A 84
Waters Reach. H Lane 6C 154
Waters Reach. Poy 2F 163
Waters Reach. Traf P 1F 107
Water St. M3 5B 94 (2C 8) (in three parts)
Water St. M9 3F 83
Water St. M12 5G 95 (2F 11)
Water St. Ash L 2H 99
Water St. Aud 6E 99 (Audenshaw)
Water St. Aud 3C 112 (Denton)
Water St. Bolt 6B 32
Water St. Eger 1B 18
Water St. Hyde 4B 114
Water St. Midd 1H 69 (in two parts)
Water St. Miln 5F 29
Water St. Oldh 2C 72
Water St. Rad 4F 49
Water St. Rams 4D 12
Water St. Roch 4H 27
Water St. Rytn 3E 57
Water St. Stal 3E 101 (in two parts)
Water St. Stoc 6H 127
Water St. Whitw 1C 14
Waterton Av. Moss 1D 88
Waterton La. Moss 1D 88
Waterview Clo. Miln 2F 43
Waterway Enterprise Pk. Traf P 1F 107
Waterworks Rd. Oldh 6A 58
Watfield Wlk. M9 4F 83 (off Foleshill Av.)
Watford Av. M14 5F 109
Watford Clo. Bolt 3A 32 (off Chesham Av.)
Watford Rd. M19 3C 126
Watkin Av. Had 3G 117
Watkin Clo. M13 1G 109 (6D 10)
Watkins Dri. P'wich 6A 68
Watkin St. Hyde 2E 115
Watkin St. Roch 1G 41
Watkin St. Salf 2B 94 (1D 4)
Watling St. Aff 1B 20
Watling St. Bury 4F 35
Watlington Clo. Oldh 4H 57
Watson Gdns. Roch 1F 27

Watson Rd. Farn 1B 62
Watson Sq. Stoc 2H 139
Watson St. M3 . .5D 94 (2G 9)
(in two parts)
Watson St. Dent 4H 113
Watson St. Eccl 3E 91
Watson St. Oldh 1G 73
Watson St. Rad 3G 49
Watson Clo. Swin 2F 79
Watton Clo. Swin 1F 79
Watts St. M19 . . . . .1D 126
Watts St. Chad 2H 71
Watts St. Oldh 1B 86
Watts St. Roch 3A 28
Waugh Av. Fail 5F 85
Wavell Av. M22 . . . . . .2B 148
Waveney Dri. Alt 5E 133
Waveney Dri. Wilm 5H 159
Waveney Flats. Heyw 3E 39
(off Fox St.)
Waveney Rd. M22 . . . . .1C 148
Waveney Rd. Shaw 5E 43
Waverley. Roch 3G 27
(off Sheriff St.)
Waverley Av. Kear 3H 63
Waverley Av. Stret 4E 107
Waverley Ct. M9 . . . . . . .4C 68
Waverley Cres. Droy 2A 98
Waverley Dri. Chea H . .1D 160
Waverley Pl. Rad 4G 49
Waverley Rd. M9 . . . . . . .4H 83
Waverley Rd. Bolt 2A 32
Waverley Rd. Hyde 1B 130
Waverley Rd. Midd 4A 54
Waverley Rd. Sale 3C 122
Waverley Rd. Stoc 4E 139
Waverley Rd. Swin 4A 80
Waverley Rd. Wors 2D 76
Waverley Rd. W. M9 . . . .4H 83
Waverley Sq. Farn 3E 63
Waverley St. Oldh 1F 73
Waverley St. Roch 4C 40
Waverton Av. Stoc 2F 127
Waverton Rd. M14 . . . . .6E 109
Wavertree Ct. Bolt 5A 32
(off School Hill)
Wavertree Rd. M9 . . . . . .5E 69
Waybridge Ind. Est.
Salf 5D 92
Wayfarers Way. Swin 4E 79
Wayford St. M9 . . . . .4E 83
(off Hendham Va.)
Wayland Rd. M18 . . . . . .3F 111
Wayland Rd. S. M18 . . . .4F 111
Wayne Clo. Droy 1C 98
Wayne St. Open 5G 97
Wayside Dri. Poy 3C 162
Wayside Gdns. Haz G . . .3G 153
Wayside Gro. Wors 5G 63
Weald Clo.
M13 . . . . . .1G 109 (5E 11)
Wealdstone Gro. Bolt . . .3D 32
Weardale Rd. M9 . . . . . . .4D 68
Wearhead Row. Salf 4F 93
Weaste. 3D 92
Weaste Av. L Hul 5D 62
Weaste Dri. Salf 2D 92
Weaste La. Salf & M5 . . .2C 92
(in two parts)
Weaste Rd. Salf 3D 92
Weaste Trad. Est. Salf . . .3D 92
Weatherall St. N. Salf 4B 82
(in two parts)
Weatherley Dri. Marp . . .5B 142
Weatherly Clo. Oldh 2D 86
Weaver Av. Wors 1C 76
Weaver Clo. Bow 4E 145
Weaver Ct.
M15 . . . . . . .1B 108 (6C 8)
Weaver Dri. Bury 3F 23
Weaverham Clo. M13 . . . .4B 110

Weaverham Wlk. Sale . . .6E 123
Weaverham Way.
Hand 3A 160
Weaver Ho. Salf 6G 81
Weavers Ct. Bolt 2A 46
Weavers Ct. Midd 6H 53
Weavers Ct. Mot 3C 116
Weavers Grn. Farn 1F 63
Weavers La. Bram 1F 161
Weavers Rd. Midd 6H 53
Weaver Wlk. Open 6F 97
Webb Gro. Hyde 6A 116
Webb La. Stoc 2A 140
(in two parts)
Webb St. Bury 2B 36
Webb Wlk. Hyde 6B 116
Webdale Dri. M40 . . . . . .4A 84
Weber Dri. Bolt 2H 45
Webster Gro. P'wich 1D 80
Webster St. Bolt 2D 46
Webster St. Moss 1E 89
Webster St. Oldh 4D 72
Webster St. Roch 2G 27
Wedgewood St. M40 . . . .1B 96
Wedgwood Rd. Swin 1A 80
Wedhurst St. Oldh 2G 73
Wedneshough. Holl 2E 117
Weedall Av. Salf 1G 107
Weeder Sq. Shaw 5H 43
Weedon St. Roch 3B 28
Weedon Av. Bolt 6H 33
Weft Wlk. M4 . . . .4G 95 (5F 7)
Weighbridge Ct. Irlam . . .4G 103
Weir Rd. Miln 4E 29
Weir St. M15 . . . . .2C 108
Weir St. Fail 4E 85
Weir St. Roch 4H 27
Welbeck Av. Chad 6D 70
Welbeck Av. L'boro 3E 17
Welbeck Av. Urm 4G 105
Welbeck Clo. Miln 5E 29
Welbeck Clo. W'fld 5D 50
Welbeck Gro. Salf 4A 82
Welbeck Ho. Ash L 3G 99
Welbeck Rd. Bolt 5E 31
Welbeck Rd. Eccl 1G 91
Welbeck Rd. Hyde 5D 114
Welbeck Rd. Roch 1H 41
Welbeck Rd. Stoc 6H 111
Welbeck Rd. Wors 5B 78
Welbeck St. M18 . . . . . . .1F 111
Welbeck St. N. Ash L 3G 99
Welbeck St. S. Ash L 3G 99
(in two parts)
Welbeck Ter. Ash L 3G 99
Welburn Av. M22 . . . . . .2C 148
Welburn St. Roch 6H 27
Welbury Rd. M23 . . . . . . .2F 135
Welby St. M13 . . . . .3H 109
Welch Rd. Hyde 3D 114
Welcomb Clo. Bred 5F 129
Welcomb St. M11 . . . . . .6D 96
Welcomb Wlk. W'fld 2D 66
Welcome Pde. Oldh 6G 73
Welcroft St. Stoc 3H 139
Weldon Av. Bolt 5E 45
Weldon Cres. Stoc 1G 151
Weldon Dri. M9 . . . . .4F 69
Weldon Rd. B'hth 5E 133
Weld Rd. M20 . . . . .2H 125
Welford Clo. Wilm 1H 167
Welford Grn. Stoc 4H 127
Welford Rd. M8 . . . . .6B 68
Welford St. Salf 1H 93
Welkin Rd. Bred 6C 128
Welkin Rd. Ind. Est.
Bred 6B 128
Wellacre Av. Urm 5H 103
Welland Av. Heyw 2C 38
Welland Clo.
M15 . . . . . . .1B 108 (6C 8)

Welland Rd. Shaw 5E 43
Welland Rd. Wilm 5H 159
Welland St. Upen 5F 97
Welland St. Stoc 6H 111
Wellbank. P'wich 6D 66
Wellbank Stal 5H 101
Wellbank Av. Ash L 5A 88
Wellbank Clo. Oldh 5F 73
Wellbank St. T'ton 5H 21
Wellbank Vw. Roch 2B 26
Wellbridge Rd. Duk 1H 113
Well Brow. Del 3H 59
Well Brow Ter. Roch 1G 27
Wellbrow Wlk. M9 . . . . . .6G 69
Wellburn Clo. Bolt 5D 44
Wellens Way. Midd 2E 69
Weller Av. M21 . . . . .2B 124
Weller Av. Poy 5D 162
Weller Clo. Poy 5D 162
Weller Gdns. M21 . . . . . .2B 124
Wellesbourne Dri.
M23 . . . . .4F 135
Wellesley Av. M18 . . . . . .1F 111
Wellfield. Rom 5A 130
Wellfield Clo. Bury 1C 50
Wellfield Gdns. Hale 2C 146
Wellfield La. Hale 1C 146
Wellfield Pl. Roch 6A 28
Wellfield Rd. Bag 4G 135
Wellfield Rd. Bolt 2G 45
Wellfield Rd. Crum 3C 82
Wellfield Rd. Stoc 5C 140
Wellfield St. Roch 6A 28
Wellgate Av. M19 . . . . . .1D 126
Well Green. 2C 146
Well Grn. L'boro 4F 17
Wellgreen Clo. Hale 2C 146
Wellgreen Lodge.
Hale 2C 146
Well Gro. W'fld 5C 50
Wellhead Clo. M15 . . . . . .2E 109
Wellhouse Dri. M40 . . . . .6C 70
Well-i-Hole Rd. G'fld 5G 75
Welling Rd. M40 . . . . .3E 85
Welling St. Bolt 4D 32
Wellington Av. M16 . . . .5B 108
Wellington Bri.
Salf 2D 94 (2G 5)
(off Trinity Way)
Wellington Bldgs. Oldh . . .3D 72
Wellington Cen.
Ash L 3B 100
Wellington Clough.
Ash L 5E 87
Wellington Ct. Bury 4H 35
Wellington Ct. Oldh 5B 72
Wellington Ct. T'ton 5H 21
Wellington Cres. M16 . . .4A 108
Wellington Dri. Tyl 2A 76
Wellington Gdns. Bury . . .3H 36
Wellington Gro.
M15 . . . . . .1B 108 (6D 8)
Wellington Gro. Stoc 4H 139
Wellington Ho. Bury 4H 35
(off Haig Rd.)
Wellington Ho. Stret 6C 106
Wellington Lodge.
L'boro 3F 17
(off Lodge St.)
Wellington Pde. Duk 4H 99
(off Hill St.)
Wellington Pl.
M3 . . . . .5C 94 (1E 9)
Wellington Pl. Alt 1F 145
Wellington Pl. Hoch 3A 28
Wellington Rd.
M20 & M14 . . . . . . .2G 125
Wellington Rd. Ash L 2G 99
Wellington Rd. Bury 5C 36
Wellington Rd. Crum 3D 82
Wellington Rd. Eccl 3G 91

Wellington Rd. G'fld 3E 61
Wellington Rd. Haz G . . .5H 153
Wellington Rd. Oldh 5B 72
(Hampton St.)
Wellington Rd. Oldh 5A 72
(Heron St.)
Wellington Rd. Swin 3F 79
Wellington Rd. Timp 5G 133
Wellington Rd.
Whal R 5C 108
Wellington Rd. N.
Stoc 2D 126
Wellington Rd. S.
Stoc 2G 139
Wellington Sq. Bury 4H 35
Wellington St. M18 . . . . .2F 111
Wellington St. Ash L 3H 99
Wellington St. Aud 1F 113
Wellington St. Bolt 1H 45
Wellington St. Bury 4A 36
Wellington St. Chad 1H 71
Wellington St. Fail 2G 85
Wellington St. Farn 1F 63
Wellington St. Haz G 2F 153
Wellington St. Hyde 4A 114
Wellington St. Miln 5G 29
Wellington St. Oldh 3D 72
Wellington St. Rad 3A 50
(in two parts)
Wellington St. Roch 2H 27
(in two parts)
Wellington St.
Salf 3B 94 (3D 4)
Wellington St. Stoc 2G 139
Wellington St. Stret 6C 106
Wellington St. E. Salf 4H 81
Wellington St. W. Salf 5H 81
Wellington Ter. Duk 4H 99
(off Queen St.)
Wellington Ter. Salf 3D 92
Wellington Vs. Bury 4A 36
Wellington Wlk. Bolt 1H 45
Wellington Wlk. Bury 4H 35
Well i' th' La. Roch 6A 28
Well La. W'fld 5D 50
Well Mead. Bred 6E 129
Wellmead Clo. M8 . . . . . .6B 82
Well Mdw. Hyde 3B 114
Well Mdw. La. Upperm . . .1G 61
Wellock St. M40 . . . . .5H 83
Wellpark Wlk. M40 . . . . . .6C 84
Well Row. Hyde 2F 115
Wells Av. Chad 6G 55
Wells Av. P'wich 1G 81
Wells Clo. Fail 5H 97
Wells Clo. H Grn 6G 149
Wells Clo. Midd 2E 69
Wells St. Duk 1A 114
Wells Dri. Duk 1A 114
Wells Dri. Stoc 1H 137
Wellside Wlk. M8 . . . . . . .5C 82
Wellsprings. Bolt 6B 32
(off Victoria Sq.)
Wells Rd. Oldh 3A 58
Wells St. Bury 4C 36
Wellstock La. L Hul 3B 62
Well St. M4 . . . . .3E 95 (4A 6)
Well St. A'wth 4C 34
Well St. Bolt 6C 32
Well St. Heyw 4G 39
Well St. Roch 6A 28
Well St. N. Rams 3A 12
Well St. W. Rams 4D 12
(off Holt St. W.)
Wellwood Dri. M40 . . . . . .4A 84
Wellyhole St. Oldh 3H 73
Welman Way. Alt 1H 145
Welney Rd. M16 . . . . .4H 107
Welshpool Clo. M23 . . . .1H 135
Welshpool Way. Dent 6G 113
Welton Av. M20 . . . . .1G 137
Welton Clo. Wilm 5C 166

Welton Dri. *Wilm* 5B **166**
Welton Gro. *Wilm* 5B **166**
Welwyn Clo. *Urm* 2D **104**
Welwyn Dri. *Salf* 6G **79**
Welwyn Wlk.
   M40 . . . . .3H **95** (3G **7**)
Wembley Gro. *M14* 1G **125**
Wembley Rd. *M18* 4E **111**
Wembury St. *M9* 3G **83**
Wembury St. N. *M9* 3G **83**
Wembury Wlk. *Hyde* 5A **116**
Wemsley Gro. *Bolt* 4D **32**
Wem St. *Chad* 5G **71**
Wemyss Av. *Stoc* 6H **111**
Wenderholme Lodge.
   Bolt 5C **30**
Wendlebury Grn. *Rytn* . . .2E **57**
Wendon Rd. *M23* 6H **135**
Wendover Dri. *Bolt* 2C **44**
Wendover Ho. *Salf* 4G **93**
Wendover Rd. *M23* 2D **134**
Wendover Rd. *Urm* 5E **105**
Wendy's Memory La. . . .3H **99**
   (Museum)
Wenfield Dri. *M9* 6B **70**
Wenlock Av. *Ash L* 6F **87**
Wenlock Clo. *Stoc* 5F **141**
Wenlock Ct. M12 . . . . . . *1B* **110**
   (off Wenlock Way)
Wenlock Rd. *Sale* 1A **134**
Wenlock St. *Swin* 3D **78**
Wenlock Way. *M12* 1B **110**
Wenning Clo. *W'fld* 6G **51**
Wensley Ct. *Salf* 2E **81**
Wensleydale Av. *Chea* . . .5G **137**
Wensleydale Clo. *M23* . . .2F **147**
Wensleydale Clo. *Bury* 4E **51**
Wensleydale Clo. *Rytn* . . .2A **56**
Wensley Dri. *M20* 4F **125**
Wensley Dri. *Haz G* 6D **152**
Wensley Rd. *Chea* 5G **137**
Wensley Rd. *Salf* 3E **81**
Wensley Rd. *Stoc* 5H **127**
Wensley Way. *Roch* 5B **28**
Wentbridge Rd. *Bolt* 5H **31**
Wentworth Av. *M18* 1G **111**
Wentworth Av. *Bury* 1H **35**
Wentworth Av. *Farn* 2E **63**
Wentworth Av. *Heyw* 5F **39**
Wentworth Av. *Irlam* 4E **103**
Wentworth Av. *Salf* 2C **92**
Wentworth Av. *Timp* 5A **134**
Wentworth Av. *Urm* 6D **104**
Wentworth Av. *W'fld* 2B **66**
Wentworth Clo. *Marp* 3D **142**
Wentworth Clo. *Midd* 1G **69**
Wentworth Clo. *Rad* 3D **48**
Wentworth Ct. *Fail* 5F **85**
Wentworth Dri. *Bram* 6A **152**
Wentworth Dri. *Sale* 4H **121**
Wentworth Rd. *Eccl* 1H **91**
Wentworth Rd. *Stoc* 6H **111**
Wentworth Rd. *Swin* 4D **78**
Wentworth Wlk. *Hyde* 2D **114**
Werneth. 5A **72**
Werneth Av. *M14* 5F **109**
Werneth Av. *Hyde* 1D **130**
Werneth Clo. *Dent* 5F **113**
Werneth Clo. *Haz G* 1E **153**
Werneth Ct. *Hyde* 6C **114**
Werneth Cres. *Oldh* 5A **72**
Werneth Hall Rd. *Oldh* . . .4B **72**
Werneth Hollow.
   Woodl 4H **129**
Werneth Low Country Pk.
   . . . . .2F **131**
Werneth Low Rd.
   Rom & Hyde 5B **130**
Werneth Recreation Cen.
   . . . . .1F **141**
Werneth Ri. *Hyde* 2D **130**
Werneth Rd. *Hyde* 5D **114**

Werneth Rd. *Woodl* 4A **130**
Werneth St. *Aud* 2F **113**
Werneth St. *Stoc* 1B **140**
Werneth Vw. *Haz G* 5A **154**
Werneth Wlk. *Dent* 5F **113**
Wesley Clo. *Roch* 6H **15**
Wesley Ct. *Stoc* 1B **138**
Wesley Ct. *T'ton* 4G **21**
Wesley Dri. *Wors* 5F **63**
Wesley Dri. *Ash L* 5H **87**
Wesley Dri. *Wors* 3H **77**
Wesley Grn. *Salf* 5H **93**
Wesley Ho. *T'ton* 4G **21**
Wesley M. *Bolt* 6C **32**
Wesley Mt. Stoc *1G* **139**
   (off Dodge Hill)
Wesley Sq. *Urm* 5C **104**
Wesleys, The. *Farn* 1B **62**
Wesley St. *M11* 5C **96**
Wesley St. *Bolt* 2A **46**
Wesley St. *Brom X* 3E **19**
Wesley St. *Eccl* 3E **91**
Wesley St. *Fail* 2G **85**
   (in two parts)
Wesley St. *Farn* 2G **63**
Wesley St. *Haz G* 2E **153**
Wesley St. *Heyw* 3E **39**
Wesley St. *Miln* 5E **29**
Wesley St. Roch *6H* **15**
   (off Wesley Clo.)
Wesley St. *Rytn* 4C **56**
Wesley St. *Stoc* 2H **139**
Wesley St. *Stret* 4E **107**
Wesley St. *Swin* 3F **79**
Wesley St. *T'ton* 4G **21**
Wessenden Bank E.
   Stoc 6D **140**
Wessenden Bank W.
   Stoc 6D **140**
Wessex Pk. Clo. *Shaw* 5F **43**
Wessington Bank.
   Glos *5G* **117**
   (off Wessington M.)
Wessington Fold.
   Glos *5G* **117**
   (off Wessington M.)
Wessington Grn. Glos *5G* **117**
   (off Wessington M.)
Wessington M. *Glos* 5G **117**
Westage Gdns. *M23* 4G **135**
W. Ashton St. *Salf* 4F **93**
West Av. *Abb H* 2A **112**
West Av. *Alt* 6C **132**
West Av. *Burn* 2B **126**
West Av. *Farn* 1D **62**
West Av. *H Grn* 4G **149**
West Av. *New M* 3D **84**
West Av. *Roch* 6A **16**
West Av. *Stal* 3E **101**
West Av. *W'fld* 5C **50**
West Av. *Wors* 6E **63**
West Bank. *Ald E* 6H **167**
West Bank. *G'fld* 4H **75**
West Bank. *Open* 6A **98**
Westbank Rd. *M20* 4H **125**
Westbank Rd. *Los* 1A **44**
W. Bank St. *Salf* . . .5A **94** (1A **8**)
Westbourne Av. *Bolt* 4C **46**
Westbourne Av. *Swin* 4D **64**
Westbourne Av. *W'fld* 6B **50**
Westbourne Av. *Ash L* 1G **99**
Westbourne Dri.
   Wilm 6H **159**
Westbourne Gro. *M9* 3F **83**
Westbourne Gro. *Sale* 5A **122**
Westbourne Gro.
   Stoc 1H **127**
Westbourne Gro.
   Wthtn 3E **125**
Westbourne Pk. *Urm* 4F **105**
Westbourne Range.
   M18 . . . . .3H **111**

Westbourne Rd. *M14* 1H **125**
Westbourne Rd. *Dent* 5E **113**
Westbourne Rd. *Eccl* 2D **90**
Westbourne Rd. *Urm* 5F **105**
Westbourne St. *Oldh* 2B **72**
Westbrook Clo. *Roch* 5D **40**
Westbrook Ct. *M18* 4G **111**
Westbrook Ct. *Bolt* 1C **46**
Westbrook Rd. *Swin* 4E **79**
Westbrook Rd. *Traf P* 6C **92**
Westbrook Sq. *M12* 1D **110**
Westbrook St. *Bolt* 1C **46**
   (in two parts)
Westbrook Trad. Est.
   Traf P 6D **92**
Westbrook Wlk. *M20* 1E **125**
Westbury Av. *Sale* 2E **133**
Westbury Clo. *Bury* 4G **35**
Westbury Dri. *Marp* 5C **142**
Westbury Rd. *M8* 2D **82**
Westbury St. *Ash L* 2A **100**
Westbury St. *Hyde* 2A **114**
Westbury St. ind. Est.
   Hyde 2A **114**
Westbury Way. *Rytn* 5B **56**
Westby Clo. *Bram* 5A **152**
Westby Gro. *Bolt* 5E **33**
W. Central Dri. *Swin* 4H **79**
W. Charles St.
   Salf 4H **93** (5A **4**)
V.l. Church St. *Heyw* 3E **39**
Westcliffe Ho. *Roch* 5B **16**
Westcliffe Rd. *Bolt* 5D **18**
Westcombe Dri. *Bury* 1A **36**
West Cotts. *G'fld* 4H **75**
Westcott Av. *M20* 3E **125**
Westcott Clo. *Bolt* 6A **20**
Westcott Gro. *Rytn* 2E **57**
Westcourt Rd. *Bolt* 4H **45**
Westcourt Rd. *Sale* 3H **121**
W. Craig Av. *M40* 6C **70**
W. Craven St. *Salf* 6H **93**
West Cres. *Midd* 2H **69**
W. Croft Ind. Est. *Midd* 2F **69**
Westcroft Rd.
   M20 & M19 . . . . . .5H **125**
W. Crown Av. *Salf* 5H **93**
Westdale Gdns. *M19* 4C **126**
Westdean Cres. *M19* 4B **126**
W. Dean St. *Salf* . . .4A **94** (6B **4**)
West Didsbury. 4D **124**
Westdown Gdns. *Shaw* 5D **42**
W. Downs Rd.
   Chea H 2B **150**
West Dri. *Bury* 6E **23**
   (in three parts)
West Dri. *Droy* 4H **97**
West Dri. *Gat* 1E **149**
West Dri. *Salf* 5C **80**
West Dri. *Swin* 4H **79**
West Dri. *Tin* 1C **117**
W. Duke St. *Salf* . . .4B **94** (6C **4**)
W. Egerton St. *Salf* 4H **93**
West End. *B'btm* 6B **116**
W. End Av. *Gat* 5E **137**
Westend St. *Farn* 1D **62**
W. End St. *Oldh* 2B **72**
W. End Trad. Est. *Swin* 2E **79**
Westerdale. *Oldh* 3G **73**
   (in two parts)
Westerdale Dri. *Bolt* 2E **45**
Westerdale Dri. *Rytn* 2A **56**
Westerham Av. *Salf* 4G **93**
Westerham Clo. *Bury* 4C **22**
Wester Hill Rd. *Oldh* 2E **87**
Westerling Way. *M16* 4C **108**
Western Av. *Swin* 1B **80**
Western Circ. *M19* 3B **126**
Western Pk. *Salf* 5E **93**
Western Rd. *Urm* 6A **104**
Western St. *M18* 1G **111**
Western St. *Salf* 2E **93**

Westerton Ct. *Bolt* 2H **45**
Westfield. *Bow* 2E **145**
Westfield. *Salf* 1E **93**
Westfield Av. *Midd* 2A **70**
Westfield Clo. *Roch* 2B **26**
Westfield Dri. *Grass* 4G **75**
Westfield Dri. *Woodl* 4A **130**
Westfield Gro. *Aud* 2E **113**
Westfield Lodge. Alt *3G* **133**
   (off Park Rd.)
Westfield Rd. *M21* 6H **107**
Westfield Rd. *Bolt* 5F **45**
Westfield Rd. *Chea H* 5B **150**
Westfield Rd. *Droy* 3G **97**
Westfields. *Hale* 5H **145**
Westfield St. *Chad* 1A **72**
Westfield St. *Salf* 2H **81**
Westford Villa. *Chea* 6G **137**
Westgate. *Hale* 3G **145**
Westgate. *Sale* 5A **122**
Westgate. *Urm* 6D **104**
Westgate. *Whitw* 2B **14**
Westgate. *Wilm* 4D **166**
Westgate Av. *M9* 1E **83**
Westgate Av. *Bolt* 6G **31**
Westgate Av. *Bury* 4C **36**
Westgate Av. *Rams* 1A **22**
Westgate Clo. *Whitw* 2B **14**
Westgate Dri. *Swin* 5F **79**
Westgate Rd. *Salf* 1C **92**
Westgate St. *Ash L* 4G **99**
West Gorton. 1B **110**
West Grn. *Midd* 2D **68**
West Gro. *M13* 2H **109**
West Gro. *Moss* 2E **89**
West Gro. *Sale* 6B **122**
Westgrove Av. *Bolt* 5C **18**
Westhide Wlk. *M9* 2H **83**
W. High St. *Salf* 3G **93**
West Hill. *Roch* 5G **27**
West Hill Clo. *Stal* 3D **100**
Westholm Av. *Stoc* 2D **126**
Westholme Ct. *Ald E* 4G **167**
Westholme Rd. *M20* 4F **125**
Westholme Rd. *P'wich* 2G **67**
W. Hope St.
   Salf 4H **93** (5A **4**)
Westhorne Fold. *M8* 1A **82**
West Hulme. 6B **56**
Westhulme Av. *Oldh* 1B **72**
Westhulme St. *Oldh* 6B **56**
Westhulme Way. *Oldh* 6A **56**
Westinghouse Rd.
   Traf P 1B **106**
W. King St. *Salf* . . .3C **94** (3E **5**)
Westland Av. *Bolt* 4E **31**
Westland Av. *Farn* 3E **63**
Westland Av. *Stoc* 2B **140**
Westland Dri. *M9* 5F **69**
Westlands. *W'fld* 3D **66**
Westlands, The. *Swin* 5H **79**
West Lea. *Dent* 4G **113**
Westlea Dri. *M18* 4F **111**
Westleigh. *Stoc* 5C **126**
Westleigh Dri. *P'wich* 6H **67**
Westleigh St. *M9* 2G **83**
W. Malling Clo. *Heyw* 6H **39**
Westmarsh Clo. *Bolt* 4A **32**
W. Marwood St. *Salf* 5A **82**
Westmead Dri. *Timp* 4B **134**
West Meade. *M21* 2G **123**
West Meade. *Bolt* 5A **46**
West Meade. *P'wich* 1H **81**
West Meade. *Swin* 5E **79**
Westmeade Rd. *Wors* 4E **63**
West Mdw. *Stoc* 6A **112**
Westmere Dri. *M9* 5E **83**
Westminster Av. *M16* 5A **108**
Westminster Av. *Ash L* 4H **87**
Westminster Av. *Farn* 1E **63**
Westminster Av. *Rad* 3D **48**

Westminster Av. *Rytn* . . .1A **56**
Westminster Av. *Stoc* . . .2G **127**
Westminster Av. *W'fld* . . .1D **66**
Westminster Clo.
  Marp 4B **142**
Westminster Clo. *Sale* . .6F **121**
Westminster Clo. *Shaw* . .5F **43**
Westminster Dri.
  Chea H 1D **160**
Westminster Dri.
  Wilm 5D **166**
Westminster Ho. *Salf* 2F **5**
Westminster Rd. *Bolt* . . .6C **18**
Westminster Rd. *Eccl* . . .2G **91**
Westminster Rd. *Fail* 3H **85**
Westminster Rd. *Hale* . . .2A **146**
Westminster Rd. *Urm* . . .3F **105**
Westminster Rd. *Wors* . . .1F **77**
Westminster St.
  M15 . . . . . .6A **94** (4B **8**)
Westminster St. *Bury* . . .4C **36**
Westminster St. *Farn* . . .1E **63**
Westminster St. *Lev* 6D **110**
Westminster St. *Oldh* . . .1F **73**
Westminster St. *Roch* . . .6F **27**
Westminster St. *Swin* . . .2D **78**
Westminster Wlk. *Farn* . . .1E **63**
Westminster Way.
  Duk 1A **114**
Westmoor Gables.
  Stoc 5C **126**
Westmorland Av.
  Ash L 1H **99**
Westmorland Av. *Duk* . . .5C **100**
Westmorland Clo.
  Bow 5C **144**
Westmorland Clo. *Bury* . .1C **50**
Westmorland Clo.
  Stoc 3C **128**
Westmorland Dri.
  Stoc 3B **128**
Westmorland Dri.
  Ward 3B **16**
Westmorland Rd.
  M20 . . . . .1E **137**
Westmorland Rd. *Eccl* . . .GG **79**
Westmorland Rd.
  Sale 1C **134**
Westmorland Rd.
  Urm 6C **105**
Westmorland Wlk.
  Rytn 3C **56**
W. Mosley St.
  M2 . . . . . . .5D **94** (1H **9**)
  (in four parts)
Westmount Clo. *M40* . . .5E **83**
W. Oak Pl. *Chea H* 4B **150**
Weston Av. *M40* 2E **85**
Weston Av. *Roch* 1H **41**
Weston Av. *Swin* 5F **65**
Weston Av. *Urm* 6D **104**
Weston Ct. *M14* 5H **109**
Weston Dri. *Chea H* 1F **151**
Weston Dri. *Dent* 4G **113**
W. One Retail Pk.
  Salf 4A **92**
Weston Gro. *M22* 3C **136**
Weston Gro. *Stoc* 3E **127**
Weston Rd. *Irlam* 5F **103**
Weston Rd. *Rad* 1E **49**
Weston Rd. *Wilm* 3H **167**
Weston St. *Bolt* 3B **46**
Weston St. *Miln* 5E **29**
  (in two parts)
Weston St. *Stoc* 5G **127**
West Over. *Rom* 3G **141**
Westover Rd. *Urm* 4E **105**
Westover St. *Swin* 2F **79**
West Pde. *Sale* 6E **121**
West Park. *Bolt* 6G **31**
West Pk. *Hyde* 2C **130**
West Pk. Av. *Dent* 5H **113**

W. Park Av. *Poy* 3A **162**
W. Park Rd. *Bram* 3F **151**
W. Park Rd. *Stoc* 1B **140**
W. Park St. *Salf* . .6H **93** (3A **8**)
West Pl. *M19* 2B **126**
West Point. *M16* 2A **108**
W. Point Enterprise Pk.
  Traf P 6H **91**
W. Point Lodge. *M19* . . .1B **126**
Westray Cres. *Salf* 4E **93**
Westray Rd. *M13* 5A **110**
West Rd. *Bow* 3E **145**
West Rd. *P'wich* 4D **66**
West Rd. *Stret* 3A **106**
West Rd. *Urm* 6G **91**
W. Starkey St. *Heyw* 2E **39**
West St. *M9* 6C **68**
West St. *M11* 3D **96**
West St. *Ald E* 5G **167**
West St. *Ash L* 2H **99**
West St. *Bolt* 6G **31**
West St. *Droy* 3F **97**
West St. *Duk* 4H **99**
West St. *Fail* 4F **85**
West St. *Farn* 6G **47**
West St. *Heyw* 3F **39**
West St. *Hyde* 2B **114**
West St. *Lees* 4A **74**
West St. *L'boro* 4G **17**
West St. *Midd* 5A **54**
West St. *Oldh* 3B **72**
  (Arkwright St.)
West St. *Oldh* 2C **72**
  (King St.)
West St. *Rad* 4G **49**
West St. *Rams* 4D **12**
West St. *Roch* 3A **28**
  (Buckley St.)
West St. *Roch* 4D **28**
  (Larchway)
West St. *Stal* 3D **100**
West St. *Stoc* 2F **139**
West St. *Tin* 1H **117**
W. Towers St. *Salf* 1F **93**
West Va. *Rad* 2G **49**
W. Vale Rd. *Timp* 5H **133**
West Vw. *Aud* 6E **99**
West Vw. *Dol* 1E **59**
West Vw. *L'boro* 4G **17**
Westview Gro. *W'fld* 6B **50**
W. View Rd. *M22* 3C **136**
Westville Gdns. *M19* 4A **126**
West Wlk. *Eger* 1B **18**
Westward Ho. *Miln* 5F **29**
Westward Rd. *Wilm* 3C **166**
Westway. *M9* 3D **68**
West Way. *Bolt* 2D **32**
Westway. *Droy* 6A **98**
Westway. *Lees* 4A **74**
West Way. *L Hul* 4C **62**
Westway. *Shaw* 1F **57**
Westwell Gdns. *Bolt* 4B **32**
  (off Halliwell Rd.)
Westwick Ter. *Bolt* 3A **32**
Westwood. 2A **72**
Westwood. *Alt* 1D **144**
Westwood Av. *M40* 2E **85**
Westwood Av. *Hyde* 4F **115**
Westwood Av. *Salf* 3A **82**
Westwood Av. *Timp* 4H **133**
Westwood Av. *Urm* 6H **105**
Westwood Av. *Wors* 6C **62**
Westwood Bus. Cen.
  Oldh 3B **72**
Westwood Clo. *Farn* 1F **63**
Westwood Cres. *Eccl* 1C **90**
Westwood Dri. *Oldh* 2B **72**
Westwood Dri. *Sale* 1B **134**
Westwood Dri. *Swin* 5A **80**
Westwood Ho. *Farn* 1F **63**
  (off Hesketh Wlk.)

Westwood Ind. Est.
  Oldh 2A **72**
Westwood Park. 1D **90**
Westwood Rd. *Bolt* 5G **31**
Westwood Rd. *H Grn* . . .5F **149**
Westwood Rd. *Stoc* 1B **152**
Westwood Rd. *Stret* 5B **106**
Westwood St. *M14* 3D **108**
Westworth Clo. *Bolt* 5H **31**
Wetheral Dri. *Bolt* 4A **46**
Wetherall St. *Lev* 6D **110**
Wetherby Dri. *Haz G* . . .3G **153**
Wetherby St. *M11* 6G **97**
Wetherby Dri. *Rytn* 2A **56**
Wexford Wlk. *M22* 3C **148**
Weybourne Av. 1A **84**
Weybourne Dri. *Bred* . . .5F **129**
Weybourne Gro. *Bolt* . . .1D **32**
Weybridge Clo. *Bolt* 5A **32**
Weybridge Rd.
  M4 . . . . . . .3G **95** (4F **7**)
Weybrook Rd. *Stoc* 2D **126**
Weycroft Clo. *Bolt* 1A **48**
Wey Gates Dri. *Haleb* . . .6C **146**
Weyhill Rd. *M23* 6G **135**
Weylands Gro. *Salf* 6H **79**
Weymouth Rd. *Ash L* . . .5A **88**
Weymouth Rd. *Eccl* 2D **90**
Weymouth St. *Bolt* 3A **32**
Weythorne Dri. *Bolt* 1B **32**
Weythorne Dri. *Bury* 6D **24**
Whalley Av. *Bolt* 2D **30**
Whalley Av. *Chor H* 2A **124**
Whalley Av. *Lev* 5D **110**
Whalley Av. *L'boro* 3E **17**
Whalley Av. *Sale* 4C **122**
Whalley Av. *Urm* 4G **105**
Whalley Av. *Whal R* 4B **108**
Whalley Clo. *Miln* 5E **29**
Whalley Clo. *Timp* 3H **133**
Whalley Clo. *W'fld* 6D **50**
Whalley Dri. *Bury* 3F **35**
Whalley Gdns. *Roch* 2D **26**
Whalley Gro. *M16* 5B **108**
Whalley Gro. *Ash L* 4G **87**
Whalley Range. 4B **108**
Whalley Rd. *M16* 4A **108**
Whalley Rd. *Hale* 3A **146**
Whalley Rd. *Heyw* 3C **38**
Whalley Rd. *Midd* 4H **53**
Whalley Rd. *Rams* 4B **12**
Whalley Rd. *Roch* 2D **26**
Whalley Rd. *Stoc* 4C **140**
Whalley Rd. *W'fld* 6D **50**
Wham Bar Dri. *Heyw* . . .3D **38**
Wham Bottom La.
  Roch 5D **14**
Wham St. *Heyw* 3D **38**
Wharf Circ. *Traf P* 6C **92**
Wharf Clo. *M1* . . .4F **95** (6D **6**)
Wharf Clo. *Alt* 4F **133**
Wharf Cotts. *Moss* 2F **89**
Wharfdale Av. *M40* 2A **84**
Wharfedale Rd. *Stoc* 1G **127**
Wharf End. *Traf P* 1G **107**
Wharf Rd. *Alt* 4F **133**
Wharf Rd. *Sale* 4C **122**
Wharfside Av. *Eccl* 5F **91**
Wharfside Bus. Cen.
  Traf P 1F **107**
Wharfside Way. *Traf P* . . .1E **107**
Wharf St. *Chad* 6H **71**
Wharf St. *Duk* 4H **99**
Wharf St. *Stoc* 6G **127**
Wharmton Ris. *Grass* 3F **75**
Wharmton Vw. *G'fld* 4E **61**
Wharmton Vw. *Moss* 6G **75**
Wharncliffe Clo. *Had* 3G **117**
Wharton Av. *M21* 2B **124**
Wharton La. *L Hul* 4A **62**

Wharton Lodge. *Eccl* 2G **91**
Wheat Clo. *M13* 2G **109**
  (in two parts)
Wheatcroft. *Had* 3G **117**
Wheat Cft. *Stoc* 6H **139**
Wheater's Cres. *Salf* 1A **94**
Wheater's St. *Salf* 1B **94**
Wheater's Ter. *Salf* 1B **94**
Wheatsheaf Cen., The.
  Stal 6H **101**
Wheatfield Clo. *Bred* 5G **129**
Wheatfield Clo. *Bury* 4F **23**
Wheatfield Cres. *Rytn* . . .4A **56**
Wheatfield St. *Bolt* 2D **46**
Wheathill St. *Roch* 1G **41**
Wheatley Rd. *Swin* 1D **78**
Wheatley Wlk. *M12* 1B **110**
Wheatsheaf Cen., The.
  Roch 3H **27**
Wheatsheaf Ind. Est. *Swin* 2H **79**
Wheeldale. *Oldh* 3H **73**
Wheeldale Clo. *Bolt* 3A **32**
Wheeldon St. *M14* 4E **109**
Wheelock Clo. *Wllm* 6H **159**
Wheelton Clo. *Bury* 4G **35**
Wheelwright Clo.
  Marp 3D **142**
Wheelwright Clo. *Roch* . . .1B **40**
Wheelwright Dri. *Roch* . . .6A **16**
Whelan Av. *Bury* 6C **36**
Whelan Clo. *Bury* 6C **36**
Wheler St. *M11* 5F **97**
Whelmar Est. *Chea H* . . .2D **150**
Whernside Av. *M40* 2A **84**
Whernside Av. *Ash L* 4G **87**
Whernside Clo. *Stoc* . . . .GG **127**
Whetstone Hill Clo.
  Oldh 5F **57**
Whetstone Hill La.
  Oldh 6G **57**
  (in two parts)
Whetstone Hill Rd.
  Oldh 5F **57**
Whewell Av. *Rad* 2B **50**
Whickham Clo. *M14* 4F **109**
Whiley St. *M13* 3B **110**
Whimberry Clo.
  Salf 6H **93** (3A **8**)
Whimberry Dri. *Carr* 6F **89**
Whimberry Way. *M20* . . .3H **125**
Whimbrel Rd. *Stoc* 6G **141**
Whinberry Rd. *B'hth* 4D **132**
Whinberry Way. *Oldh* . . .3A **58**
Whinchat Clo. *Stoc* 1G **153**
Whinfell Dri. *Midd* 4E **53**
Whingroves Wlk. *M40* . . .4A **84**
Whinmoor Wlk. *M40* 4B **84**
Whins Av. *Farn* 1A **62**
Whins Crest. *Los* 6A **30**
Whinslee Ct. *Los* 6A **30**
Whinslee Dri. *Los* 6A **30**
Whinstone Way. *Chad* . . .6E **55**
Whipney La. *G'mnt* 1F **21**
Whipp St. *Heyw* 2D **38**
Whirley Clo. *Stoc* 4F **127**
Whiston Dri. *Bolt* 1E **47**
Whiston Rd. *M8* 3D **82**
Whitbrook Way. *Midd* . . .2D **54**
Whitburn Av. *M13* 5A **110**
Whitburn Clo. *Bolt* 3C **44**
Whitburn Dri. *Bury* 6C **22**
Whitburn Rd. *M23* 1G **147**
Whitby Av. *Fall* 1A **126**
Whitby Av. *Heyw* 2E **39**
Whitby Av. *Salf* 2C **92**
Whitby Av. *Urm* 5G **105**
Whitby Av. *Whal R* 4B **108**
Whitby Clo. *Bury* 3F **35**
Whitby Clo. *Poy* 3C **162**
Whitby Clo. *Chea* 5G **137**
Whitby Clo. *Poy* 3C **162**
Whitby Rd. *M14* 1H **125**
Whitby Rd. *Oldh* 6G **73**
Whitby St. *Midd* 6C **54**

Whitby St. *Roch* 6A **28**
Whitchurch Dri. *M16* 2B **108**
Whitchurch Gdns. *Bolt* *3A 32*
(off Gladstone St.)
Whitchurch Rd. *M20* 2D **124**
Whitchurch St.
Salf 2C **94** (1F **5**)
Whiteacre Rd. *Ash L* . . .2A **100**
Whiteacres. *Swin* 4C **78**
Whiteacre Wlk. *M15* *2C 108*
(off Shearsby Clo.)
White Ash. *Bury* 6C **24**
White Ash Ter. *Bury* 6C **24**
Whitebank Av. *Stoc* 5C **128**
White Bank Rd. *Oldh* 1B **86**
Whitebarn Rd. *Ald E* 6H **167**
Whitebeam Clo. *Miln* 2E **43**
Whitebeam Clo. *Salf* 2G **93**
Whitebeam Clo. *Timp* 6E **135**
Whitebeam Ct. *Salf* 2G **93**
Whitebeam Wlk. *Sale* 4F **121**
Whitebeck Ct. *M9* 5A **70**
White Birk Clo. *G'mnt* 1H **21**
White Brook La.
Upperm 3H **61**
(Greenfield)
White Brook La.
Upperm 1G **61**
(Uppermill)
Whitebrook Rd. *M14* 6F **109**
White Brow. 2D **50**
White Brow. *Bury* 2D **50**
Whitecar Av. *M40* 2E **85**
White Carr La. *Bury* 2G **23**
Whitecarr La.
Hale & M23 . . . . . .2D **146**
Whitechapel Clo. *Bolt* 6G **33**
Whitechapel St. *M20* 6F **125**
Whitechapel St.
M17 & M16 . . . . .2G **107**
White City Circ.
M17 & M16 . . . . .2G **107**
White City Retail Pk.
M16 . . . . .2G **107**
White City Way. *M16* 2G **107**
Whitecliff Clo. *M14* 4G **109**
White Ct. *Swin* 4C **78**
White Cft. *Bolt* 5A **32**
Whitecroft Av. *Shaw* 6H **43**
Whitecroft Dri. *Bury* 2F **35**
Whitecroft Gdns.
M19 . . . . .5A **126**
Whitecroft Rd. *Bolt* 4D **30**
Whitecroft Rd. *Strin* 4G **155**
Whitecroft St. *Oldh* 6G **57**
Whitefield. 2C **66**
Whitefield. *Salf* 5B **80**
Whitefield. *Stoc* 6F **127**
Whitefield Av. *Roch* 3B **26**
Whitefield Cen. *W'fld* 1F **67**
Whitefield Rd. *Bred* 5E **129**
Whitefield Rd. *Bury* 6B **36**
(in two parts)
Whitefield Rd. *Sale* 4A **122**
White Friar Ct.
Salf 2C **94** (2E **5**)
Whitefriars Wlk. *M22* 5B **148**
White Gate. 6G **71**
Whitegate. *Bolt* 5A **44**
Whitegate. *L'boro* 5C **16**
Whitegate Av. *Chad* 5F **71**
Whitegate Clo. *M40* 2E **85**
Whitegate Dri. *Bolt* 6D **18**
Whitegate Dri. *Salf* 2D **92**
Whitegate Dri. *Swin* 1H **79**
White Gate End. 6E **71**
Whitegate La. *Chad* 5F **71**
(in two parts)
Whitegate M. *Eger* 6C **13**
Whitegate Pk. *Urm* 5A **104**
Whitegate Rd. *Chad* 6D **70**
Whitegates. *Chea* 6H **137**
Whitegates. *S'head* 5D **58**
Whitegates Clo. *Timp* 6B **134**

Whitegates La. *S'head* . . .5C **58**
Whitegates Rd. *Chea* 6H **137**
Whitegates Rd. *Midd* 3C **54**
Whitehall. *Oldh* 3B **58**
Whitehall Clo. *Wilm* 4D **166**
Whitehall La. *Oldh* 3B **58**
Whitehall Rd. *M20* 6G **125**
Whitehall Rd. *Sale* 1B **134**
Whitehall St. *Oldh* 1D **72**
Whitehall St. *Roch* 2H **27**
(in two parts)
White Hart Mdw. *Midd* . . .5A **54**
White Hart St. *Hyde* 3B **114**
Whitehaven Gdns.
M20 . . . . .1E **137**
Whitehaven Pl. *Hyde* 2A **114**
Whitehaven Rd. *Bram* . . .2E **161**
Whitehead Cres. *Bury* 6C **22**
Whitehead Cres. *Rad* 2C **64**
Whitehead Rd. *M21* 1F **123**
Whitehead Rd. *Swin* 1H **79**
Whiteheads Pl. *S'head* 2B **74**
Whitehead St. *Aud* 6E **99**
Whitehead St. *Midd* 6C **54**
Whitehead St. *Miln* 1H **43**
(Bethany La.)
Whitehead St. *Miln* 5E **29**
(Rochdale Rd.)
Whitehead St. *Shaw* 5D **42**
Whitehead St. *Wors* 5F **63**
White Hill Clo. *Roch* 5D **14**
Whitehill Cotts. *Bolt* 5B **18**
Whitehill Dri. *M40* 4A **84**
Whitehill Ind. Est.
Stoc 4G **127**
Whitehill La. *Bolt* 5B **18**
Whitehill St. *Stoc* 5G **127**
(in two parts)
Whitehill St. W. *Stoc* 5F **127**
Whiteholme Av. *M21* 5B **124**
White Horse Gdns.
Swin 5C **78**
White Horse Meadows.
B'edge 3A **42**
White Ho. Av. *M8* 6A **68**
Whitehouse Av. *Oldh* 3G **73**
Whitehouse Clo. *Heyw* 6F **39**
Whitehouse Dri. *M23* 6G **135**
Whitehouse Dri. *Hale* 5B **146**
Whitehouse La.
Dun M 4A **132**
Whitehouse Ter. *M9* 2H **83**
Whitehurst Rd. *Stoc* 5B **126**
Whitekirk Clo. *M13* 1F **109**
(5D **10**)
White Lady Clo. *Wors* 6B **62**
Whitelake Av. *Urm* 5B **104**
Whitelake Vw. *Urm* 4B **104**
Whiteland Av. *Bolt* 2G **45**
Whitelands. *Ash L* 3A **100**
Whitelands Ind. Est.
Stal 3C **100**
Whitelands Rd. *Ash L* 3A **100**
Whitelands Ter. *Ash L* 3A **100**
Whitelea Dri. *Stoc* 6F **139**
Whitelees M. *L'boro* 4E **17**
Whitelees Rd. *L'boro* 4E **17**
Whitelegge St. *Bury* 1H **35**
Whiteley Dri. *Midd* 2C **70**
Whiteley Pl. *Alt* 5F **133**
Whiteleys Pl. *Roch* 3G **27**
Whiteley St. *M11* 3L **96**
Whiteley St. *Chad* 5H **71**
White Lion Brow. *Bolt* 6A **32**
Whitelow Rd. *M21* 1G **123**
Whitelow Rd. *Bury* 3G **13**
Whitelow Rd. *Stoc* 6C **126**
White Meadows. *Swin* 4F **79**
White Moss. *Roch* 1D **26**
White Moss Av. *M21* 1A **124**
White Moss Gdns. *M9* 1A **84**
White Moss Rd. *M9* 6G **69**

White Moss Rd. E.
M9 . . . . .5H **69**
Whiteoak Clo. *Marp* 4C **142**
Whiteoak Ct. *M14* 1G **125**
Whiteoak Rd. *M14* 1G **125**
Whiteoak Vw. *Bolt* 2F **47**
Whites Cft. *Swin* 3F **79**
Whiteside Clo. *Salf* 3D **92**
Whiteside Fold. *Roch* 2C **26**
Whitesmead Clo. *Dis* . . .2H **165**
Whitestone Clo. *Los* 1B **44**
Whitestone Wlk. *M13* . . .2H **109**
White St. *M15* 1B **108** (6C **8**)
White St. *Bury* 4A **36**
White St. *Salf* 4E **93**
White Swallows Rd.
Swin 5G **79**
White Swan Ind. Est.
Oldh *1G 73*
(off Derker St.)
Whitethorn Av. *Burn* 2B **126**
Whitethorn Av.
Whal R 4B **108**
Whitethorn Clo. *Marp* . . .4C **142**
Whitewater Dri. *Salf* 4D **80**
Whiteway St. *M9* 4G **83**
Whitewell Clo. *Bury* 6B **36**
Whitewell Clo. *Roch* 3C **28**
Whitewillow Clo. *Fail* 5G **85**
Whitfield Bottoms.
Miln 2F **43**
Whitfield Brow. *L'boro* . . .2G **17**
Whitfield Cres. *Miln* 2F **43**
Whitfield Dri. *Miln* 6E **29**
Whitfield Ri. *Shaw* 4H **43**
Whitfield St. *M3* . . .2E **95** (1A **6**)
Whitfield Wlk.
M40 . . . . .2H **95** (1G **7**)
Whiting Gro. *Bolt* 1C **44**
Whitland Av. *Bolt* 5D **30**
Whitland Dri. *Oldh* 1H **85**
Whit La. *Salf* 5D **80**
(in two parts)
Whitley Gdns. *Timp* 3B **134**
Whitley Pl. *Timp* 4B **134**
Whitley Rd. *M40* 1G **95**
Whitley Rd. *Stoc* 6D **126**
Whitley St. *Bolt* 5F **47**
Whitley Wlk. *Glos* 6H **117**
Whitlow Av. *B'hth* 3D **132**
Whitman St. *M9* 3H **83**
Whitmore Rd. *M14* 6F **109**
Whitnall St. *M16* 4C **108**
Whitnall St. *Hyde* 2B **114**
Whitsand Rd. *M22* 6C **136**
Whitsbury Av. *M18* 4F **111**
Whitstable Clo. *Chad* 3H **71**
Whitstable Rd. *M40* 2C **84**
Whitsters Hollow. *Bolt* 2F **31**
Whitswood Clo. *M16* 4C **108**
Whittaker Clo. *P'wich* 5G **67**
Whittaker Dri. *L'boro* 1F **29**
Whittaker Ho. *Rad* 3G **49**
Whittaker La. *P'wich* 5G **67**
Whittaker La. *Roch* 2H **25**
Whittaker St. *M40* 3H **83**
Whittaker St. *Ash L* 6H **87**
Whittaker St. *Midd* 1H **69**
Whittaker St. *Rad* 3H **49**
Whittaker St. *Roch* 2A **26**
Whittaker St. *Rytn* 3B **56**
Whittingham Dri.
Rams 5E **13**
Whittingham Gro. *Oldh* . . .1B **72**
Whittington St. *Ash L* 4G **99**
Whittle Brook. 1H **77**
Whittle Brook Clo. *Uns* . . .2F **51**
Whittlebrook Gro.
Heyw 6G **39**
Whittle Dri. *Shaw* 5H **43**
Whittle Dri. *Wors* 4E **63**

Whittle Gro. *Bolt* 4F **31**
(in two parts)
Whittle Gro. *Wors* 6G **63**
Whittle Hill. *Eger* 1C **18**
Whittle La. *Heyw* 2C **52**
Whittles Av. *Dent* 4G **113**
Whittle's Cft.
M1 . . . . .4F **95** (6D **6**)
Whittles St. *Roch* 1H **15**
Whittles Ter. *Miln* 1H **43**
Whittle St. *M4* 3F **95** (4C **6**)
Whittle St. *Bury* 2A **36**
Whittle St. *L'boro* 4D **16**
Whittle St. *Swin* 4E **79**
Whittle St. *Wors* 6F **63**
Whittles Wlk. *Dent* 5G **113**
Whitwell Bank. *Glos* 5F **117**
(off Whitwell Clo.)
Whitwell Clo. *Glos* 5F **117**
Whitwell Fold. *Glos* 5F **117**
(off Whitwell Clo.)
Whitwell Grn. *Glos* 5G **117**
(off Whitwell Clo.)
Whitwell Lea. *Glos* 5F **117**
(off Whitwell Clo.)
Whitwell Wlk. *M13* 3A **110**
Whitwell Way. *M18* 2E **111**
Whitworth. 4G **15**
Whitworth Art Gallery, The.
. . . . .3F **109**
Whitworth Clo. *Ash L* . . .1A **100**
Whitworth La. *M14* 6H **109**
Whitworth Mus. 4G **15**
Whitworth Pk. Mans.
M14 . . . . .3E **109**
Whitworth Rake.
Whitw 1D **14**
Whitworth Rd. *Roch* 5D **14**
Whitworth Sq. *Whitw* 1D **14**
Whitworth St.
M1 . . . . .5E **95** (2A **10**)
Whitworth St. *Miln* 5F **29**
Whitworth St. Open 6C **96**
(in two parts)
Whitworth St. E. *M11* 6E **97**
Whitworth St. W.
M1 . . . . .5D **94** (2F **9**)
Whitworth Swimming Pool.
. . . . .3H **15**
Whixhall Av. *M12* 1A **110**
Whoolden St. *Farn* 6E **47**
Whowell Fold. *Bolt* 2G **31**
Whowell St. *Bolt* 1A **46**
Wibbersley Pk. *Urm* 5B **104**
Wichbrook Rd. *Wors* 6B **62**
Wicheaves Cres. *Wors* 6B **62**
Wicheries, The. *Wors* 6B **62**
Wicken Bank. *Heyw* 6G **39**
Wickenby Dri. *Sale* 5A **122**
Wicken St. *Stoc* 4C **140**
Wickentree Holt. *Roch* 2C **26**
Wickentree La. *Fail* 2F **85**
Wicker La. *Haleb* 5B **146**
Wicket Gro. *Swin* 5E **65**
Wickham Ter. *Midd* 6A **54**
Wickliffe Pl. *Roch* 5H **27**
Wickliffe St. *Bolt* 5A **32**
Wicklow Av. *Stoc* 4D **138**
Wicklow Dri. *M22* 3C **148**
Wicklow Gro. *Oldh* 6C **72**
Widcombe Dri. *Bolt* 2H **47**
Widdop St. *Oldh* 2B **72**
Widecombe Clo. *Urm* 3D **104**
Widgeon Clo. *M14* 1F **125**
Widgeon Clo. *Poy* 3B **162**
Widgeon Rd. *B'hth* 3D **132**
Wigan Rd. *Bolt* 5B **44**
Wiggins Teape Rd.
Bury 1F **51**
Wiggins Wlk. *M14* 4G **109**
Wighurst Wlk. *M22* 4B **148**

Wigley St. M12 . . . . .6A **96**
Wigmore Rd. M8 . . . . . . .4D **82**
Wigmore St. Ash L 1B **100**
Wigsby Av. M40 . . . . . . .1C **84**
Wigwam Clo. Poy 3C **162**
Wike St. Bury 2B **36**
Wilberforce Clo. M15 . . .2C **108**
Wilbraham Rd.
    M16 & M14 . . . . . .6D **108**
Wilbraham Rd. M21 . . . .6G **107**
Wilbraham Rd. Wors 6E **75**
Wilburn St. Salf . . .5B **94** (1C **8**)
    (in two parts)
Wilby Av. L Lev 2A **48**
Wilby Clo. Bury 6D **22**
Wilby St. M8 . . . . .5D **82**
Wilcockson Ho. Farn 1F **63**
    (off Hesketh Wlk.)
Wilcock St. M16 . . . . .3C **108**
Wilcott Dri. Sale 4G **121**
Wilcott Dri. Wilm 5C **166**
Wilcott Rd. Gat 6E **137**
Wildbank Chase. Stal . . .1A **116**
Wildbrook Clo. L Hul 6A **62**
Wildbrook Cres. Oldh 6E **73**
    (in two parts)
Wildbrook Gro. L Hul 6A **62**
Wildbrook Rd. L Hul 5A **62**
Wildbrook Ter. Oldh 1E **87**
Wild Clough. Hyde 6D **114**
Wildcroft Av. M40 . . . . . .2A **84**
Wilders Moor Clo.
    Wors 3E **77**
Wilderswood Clo.
    M20 . . . . .4G **125**
Wildhouse Ct. Miln 3F **29**
Wild Ho. La. Miln 3F **29**
Wildman La. Farn 1B **62**
Wildmoor Av. Oldh 5A **74**
Wildmoor Wood Clo.
    Carr 6F **89**
Wilds Bldgs. Roch 4D **28**
Wild's Pas. L'boro 5H **17**
    (Chapel St.)
Wild's Pas. L'boro 5C **16**
    (New Rd.)
Wilds Pl. Rams 4D **12**
Wilds Sq. Moss 1E **89**
Wild St. Bred 1F **141**
Wild St. Dent 4F **113**
Wild St. Duk 5B **100**
Wild St. Haz G 3D **152**
Wild St. Heyw 3G **39**
Wild St. Lees 3A **74**
Wild St. Oldh 2E **73**
Wild St. Rad 3B **50**
Wild St. Shaw 1G **57**
Wild St. Stoc 5A **140**
Wildwood Clo. Rams 5C **12**
Wileman Cft. Salf 3C **92**
Wilford Av. Sale 1A **134**
Wilfred Dri. Bury 1F **37**
    (off Huntley Mt. Rd.)
Wilfred Geere Ho., The.
    Farn 1A **62**
Wilfred Rd. Eccl 5C **90**
Wilfred Rd. Wors 1F **77**
Wilfred St. M40 . . . . .3A **84**
Wilfred St. Drom X 4E **19**
Wilfred St. Salf . . .1C **94** (1F **5**)
Wilfred St. Swin 3F **79**
Wilham Av. Eccl 4F **91**
Wilkes St. Oldh 3H **57**
Wilkin Cft. Chea H 4A **150**
Wilkins La. Wilm 2C **158**
Wilkinson Av. L Lev 2A **48**
Wilkinson Rd. Bolt 6B **18**
Wilkinson Rd. Stoc 1G **139**
    (in two parts)
Wilkinson St. Ash L 3G **99**
Wilkinson St. Midd 6H **53**

Wilkinson St. Sale 5D **122**
Wilks Av. M22 . . . . .3D **148**
Willand Clo. Bolt 1A **48**
Willand Dri. Bolt 2A **48**
Willan Enterprise Cen.
    Traf P 1C **106**
Willan Ind. Est. Salt 4F **93**
Willan Rd. M9 . . . . .5E **69**
Willan Rd. Eccl 3G **91**
Willard St. Haz G 2D **152**
Willaston Clo. M21 . . . . .2G **123**
Willaston Way. Hand 2H **159**
Willbutts La. Roch 3E **27**
Willdale Clo. M11 . . . . . . .3C **96**
Willdor Gro. Stoc 5D **138**
Willenhall Rd. M23 . . . . .1A **136**
Willerby Rd. M8 . . . . . . .6A **82**
Willert St. M40 . . . . .6F **83**
Willesden Av. M13 . . . . .4A **110**
Will Griffith Wlk. M11 . . . .5A **96**
William Chadwick Clo.
    M40 . . . . .2G **95** (1F **7**)
William Clo. Urm 6E **105**
William Coates Ct.
    M16 . . . . .4B **108**
William Ford Ho. Mot 3C **116**
William Greenwood Clo.
    Heyw 3E **39**
William Henry St.
    Roch 1G **41**
William Jessop Ct.
    M1 . . . . .4G **95** (6E **7**)
William Kay Clo. M16 . . .3C **108**
William Lister Clo. M40 . . .1F **97**
William Murray Ct.
    M4 . . . . .3G **95** (4F **7**)
    (off Winder Dri.)
Williams Cres. Chad 6F **71**
Williamson Av. Bred 5G **129**
Williamson Av. Rad 1F **49**
Williamson La. Droy 5B **98**
Williamson St.
    M4 . . . . .2F **95** (1C **6**)
Williamson St. Ash L 3H **99**
Williamson St. Stoc 2H **127**
Williamson's Yd. Oldh . . .2F **73**
Williams Rd. Gort 2E **111**
Williams Rd. Most 4B **84**
Williams St. M18 . . . . . .2E **111**
William St.
    M12 . . . . .5H **95** (2G **11**)
William St. M20 . . . . . . .6F **125**
William St. Ash L 3F **99**
William St. Fail 2G **85**
William St. Hurs 5B **16**
William St. L'boro 4E **17**
William St. L Lev 4B **48**
William St. Midd 1B **70**
William St. Rad 3H **49**
William St. Rams 1E **13**
William St. Roch 5H **27**
William St. Salf . . .3C **94** (4E **5**)
William St. Whitw 4G **15**
William Wlk. Alt 2F **145**
Willingdon Clo. Bury 4C **22**
Willingdon Dri. P'wich 4F **67**
Willis Rd. Oldh 3E **87**
Willis Rd. Stoc 5G **139**
Willis St. Bolt 3G **45**
Williton Wlk. M22 . . . . . .2D **148**
Willock St. Salf 5B **82**
Willoughby Av. M20 . . . .5G **125**
Willoughby Clo. Sale 4A **122**
Willow Av. Chea H 3B **150**
Willow Av. Midd 2C **70**
Willow Av. Stoc 5H **127**
Willow Av. Urm 5G **105**
Willow Bank. M9 . . . . . . .3G **83**
    (off Church La.)
Willow Bank. M14 . . . . . .1G **125**
Willow Bank. Chea H 1C **160**
Willowbank. Lees 1A **74**

Willowbank. Rad 1F **65**
Willowbank. Swin 1G **79**
Willow Bank. Timp 5A **134**
Willowbank Av. Bolt 1D **46**
Willow Bank Ct. M20 . . .3F **137**
Willowbrook Av. M40 . . . .4A **84**
Willow Clo. Bolt 3F **45**
Willow Clo. Duk 6D **100**
Willow Clo. Poy 4E **163**
Willow Ct. M14 . . . . .6H **109**
    (Mosley Rd.)
Willow Ct. M14 . . . . .1G **125**
    (Willow Bank)
Willow Ct. Gat 5E **137**
Willow Ct. Marp 6C **142**
Willow Ct. Sale 4E **123**
Willowdale Av. H Grn 3F **149**
Willowdene Clo. M40 . . . .6E **83**
Willowdene Clo.
    Brom X 3D **18**
Willow Dri. Hand 4H **159**
Willow Dri. Sale 1G **133**
Willowfield Rd. Oldh 5H **57**
Willow Fold. Droy 5B **98**
Willow Gro. M18 . . . . . .3G **111**
Willow Gro. Chad 1H **71**
Willow Gro. Dent 4E **113**
Willow Gro. Marp 6D **142**
Willow Hey. Brom X 4G **19**
Willow Hill Rd. M8 . . . . . .1C **82**
Willow Lawn. Chea H 2C **150**
Willowmead Way.
    Roch 1C **26**
Willowmoss Clo.
    Wors 2G **77**
Willow Pk. M14 . . . . .1G **125**
Willow Ri. L'boro 6D **16**
Willow Rd. Eccl 1C **90**
Willow Rd. H Lane 6D **154**
Willow Rd. Part 6C **118**
Willow Rd. P'wich 3E **67**
Willow Rd. Upperm 2G **61**
Willows. 2G **45**
Willows Cotts. Miln 4E **29**
Willows Dri. Fail 1H **97**
Willows End. Stal 2H **101**
Willows La. Bolt 3F **45**
Willows La. Roch 5D **28**
Willows Rd. Salf 3D **92**
Willows, The. M21 . . . . . .2C **120**
Willows, The. Brad F 2A **48**
Willows, The. Lees 4A **74**
Willows, The. Moss 2G **89**
Willows, The. Part 6D **118**
Willows, The. Whitw 4C **14**
    (off Tonacliffe Rd.)
Willow St. M11 . . . . .4C **96**
Willow St. Bury 3F **37**
    (in two parts)
Willow St. Fail 4D **84**
Willow St. Heyw 3F **39**
Willow St. Oldh 2E **73**
Willow St. Salf 1C **94**
Willow St. Swin 6D **78**
Willow St. Wors 4C **78**
Willow Tree Clo. Eccl 4E **91**
Willow Tree Ct. Sale 6B **122**
Willow Tree M. H Grn 4F **149**
Willowtree Rd. Hale 3F **145**
Willow Wlk. Droy 3C **98**
Willow Way. M20 . . . . . .6G **125**
    (in two parts)
Willow Way. Bram 6E **151**
Willow Wood Clo.
    Ash L 2C **100**
Wilma Av. M9 . . . . .5E **69**
Wilmcote Clo. Los 1B **44**
Wilmcote Gdns. Bred 6F **129**
Wilmcote Rd. M40 . . . . . .1H **95**
Wilmers. L'boro 5G **17**
Wilmington Rd. Strct 5B **106**
Wilmot St. Bolt 2G **31**

Wilmott St.
    M15 . . . . .6D **94** (4H **9**)
    (Hulme St.)
Wilmott St.
    M15 . . . . . .1E **109** (5A **10**)
    (Knowles Pl.)
Wilmslow. 2E **167**
Wilmslow Av. Bolt 6C **18**
Wilmslow By-Pass.
    Wilm 5D **166**
Wilmslow Leisure Cen.
    . . . . .2E **167**
Wilmslow Old Rd.
    Ring 1F **157**
Wilmslow Park. 1H **167**
Wilmslow Pk. N.
    Wilm 2F **167**
Wilmslow Pk. Rd.
    Wilm 2F **167**
Wilmslow Pk. S.
    Wilm 2F **167**
Wilmslow Rd. M14 . . . . .3G **109**
Wilmslow Rd. M20 . . . . .3F **125**
Wilmslow Rd. Ald E 4G **167**
Wilmslow Rd. Chea 6H **137**
    (in three parts)
Wilmslow Rd. Hand 2H **159**
Wilmslow Rd. Ring 1F **157**
Wilmslow Rd. Woodf 6D **160**
Wilmslow Tourist Info. Cen.
    . . . . .3E **167**
Wilmur Av. Salf 5A **82**
Wilmur Av. W'fld 2E **67**
Wilpshire Av. M12 . . . . . .4D **110**
Wilshaw Gro. Ash L 5E **87**
Wilshaw La. Ash L 6E **87**
Wilshaw Pl. Ash L 6E **87**
Wilson Av. Heyw 3C **38**
Wilson Av. Swin 1H **79**
Wilson Cres. Ash L 1C **100**
Wilson Pk. M40 . . . . .6G **83**
Wilson Rd. M9 . . . . .2F **83**
Wilson Rd. Stoc 5D **126**
Wilsons Brow. Farn 6H **47**
Wilson St. M11 . . . . .5C **96**
Wilson St.
    M13 . . . . .1G **109** (6F **11**)
Wilson St. M40 . . . . .1A **96**
Wilson St. Bolt 1B **46**
Wilson St. Bury 4E **37**
Wilson St. Farn 1G **63**
Wilson St. G'fld 4F **61**
Wilson St. Hyde 5C **114**
Wilson St. Oldh 5C **72**
Wilson St. Rad 3F **49**
Wilson St. Roch 3H **27**
Wilson St. Sale 4B **122**
Wilson St. Stret 3E **107**
Wilson Way. Oldh 1D **72**
Wilthorpe Clo. M19 . . . . .3E **127**
Wilton Av. M16 . . . . .4G **107**
Wilton Av. H Grn 6G **149**
Wilton Av. P'wich 1H **81**
Wilton Av. Swin 4A **80**
Wilton Ct. M9 . . . . .6C **68**
Wilton Ct. Dent 3A **112**
Wilton Ct. P'wich 1A **68**
Wilton Cres. Ald E 4F **167**
Wilton Dri. Bury 2E **51**
Wilton Dri. Haleb 5C **146**
Wilton Gdns. Rad 2A **50**
Wilton Gro. Dent 3A **112**
Wilton Gro. Heyw 4F **39**
Wilton Paddock. Dent 3A **112**
Wilton Pl. Salf 3B **94** (4C **4**)
Wilton Polygon. M8 . . . . .2B **82**
Wilton Rd. Bolt 6C **18**
Wilton Rd. Chor H 1H **123**
Wilton Rd. Crum 1B **82**
Wilton Rd. Salf 1B **92**
Wilton St.
    M13 . . . . .1F **109** (6C **10**)

Wilton St. *Bolt* 2B **32**
Wilton St. *Chad* 6H **71**
Wilton St. *Dent* 3E **113**
Wilton St. *Heyw* 3D **38**
Wilton St. *Midd* 2D **68**
Wilton St. *P'wich* 5G **67**
Wilton St. *Stoc* 5H **111**
Wilton Ter. *W'fld* 2D **66**
Wilton Ter. *Roch* 3G **27**
Wiltshire Clo. *Bury* 5C **128**
Wiltshire Clo. *Bury* 5E **37**
Wiltshire Rd. *Chad* 4H **71**
Wiltshire Rd. *Fail* 5G **85**
Wiltshire Rd. *Part* 6C **118**
Wiltshire Rd. *Sale* 6B **122**
(off Crescent Ct.)
Wiltshire St. *Salf* 5A **82**
Wimbledon Dri. *Roch* . . .6F **27**
Wimbledon Rd. *Stoc* 4E **139**
Wimbledon Rd. *Fail* 3H **85**
Wimbledon Ter. *M40* 1D **96**
Wimborne Av. *Urm* 3F **105**
Wimborne Clo.
Chea H 1E **151**
Wimborne Wlk. *Salf* 3G **93**
Wimbourne Av. *Chad* 6G **55**
Wimpenny Ho. *Oldh* 4C **72**
Wimpole St. *Ash L* 2A **100**
(in three parts)
Wimpole St. *Oldh* 6E **57**
Wimpory St. *M11* 6F **97**
Winbolt St. *Stoc* 1C **152**
Winby St. *Roch* 1G **41**
Wincanton Av. *M23* 3D **134**
Wincanton Dri. *Bolt* 4B **18**
Wincanton Pk. *Oldh* 3H **73**
Wincebrook. *Midd* 1A **70**
Wince Clo. *Midd* 3C **70**
Wincham Clo.
M15 . . . . . .1B **108** (6D **8**)
Wincham Rd. *Sale* 1G **133**
Winchester Av. *Ash L* . . .3H **87**
Winchester Av. *Chad* 6F **55**
Winchester Av. *Dent* 6F **113**
Winchester Av. *Heyw* 5E **39**
Winchester Av. *P'wich* 1G **81**
Winchester Clo. *Bury* 4C **22**
Winchester Clo. *Roch* 4C **26**
Winchester Clo. *Wilm* . . .4B **166**
Winchester Dri. *Sale* 5F **121**
Winchester Dri. *Stoc* 1D **138**
Winchester Pk. *M20* 6D **124**
Winchester Rd. *Duk* 6E **101**
Winchester Rd. *Eccl* 6G **79**
Winchester Rd. *Hale* 4C **146**
Winchester Rd. *Rad* 2D **48**
Winchester Rd. *Salf* 1C **92**
Winchester Rd.
Urm & Stret 4F **105**
Winchester Way.
Bolt 4F **33**
Wincle Av. *Poy* 5F **163**
Wincombe St. *M14* 5F **109**
Windale. *Wors* 6D **62**
Windcroft Clo. *M11* 5B **96**
Winder Dri. *M4* . . .3G **95** (5F **7**)
Windermere Av. *Dent* . . .5A **112**
Windermere Av. *L Lev* . . .3A **48**
Windermere Av. *Swin* 4G **79**
Windermere Clo. *Open* . . .5C **96**
Windermere Clo.
P'wich 4D **66**
Windermere Clo.
Stret 4C **106**
Windermere Cres.
Ash L 1F **99**
Windermere Dri. *Ald E* . . .5F **167**
Windermere Dri. *Bury* 6C **36**
Windermere Dri. *Rams* . . .2E **13**
Windermere M. *Midd* . . .4G **53**
Windermere Rd. *Farn* 1A **62**

Windermere Rd.
Hand 3G **159**
Windermere Rd.
H Lane 5C **154**
Windermere Rd.
Hyde 2A **114**
Windermere Rd. *Midd* 5E **53**
Windermere Rd. *Rytn* 6B **42**
Windermere Rd. *Stal* 2E **101**
Windermere Rd. *Stoc* 4B **140**
Windermere Rd. *Urm* 6E **105**
Windermere St. *Bolt* 2B **32**
Windermere Wlk. *Oldh* . .1G **73**
(in two parts)
Winder St. *Bolt* 5B **32**
Winders Way. *Salf* 1H **93**
Windfields Clo.
Chea H 2D **150**
Windgate Ri. *Stal* 6F **89**
Windgate St. *Roch* 6A **16**
Windle Av. *M8* 6B **68**
Windle Ct. *Stoc* 6E **141**
Windlehurst. 4C **154**
Windlehurst Ct.
H Lane 6B **154**
Windlehurst Dri. *Wors* . . .4D **76**
Windlehurst Hall.
H Lane 4C **154**
Windlehurst Old Rd.
Marp 3D **154**
Windlehurst Rd.
H Lane & Marp 5B **154**
Windley St. *Bolt* 5C **32**
Windmill Av.
Salf 6H **93** (3A **8**)
Windmill Clo. *Dent* 5B **112**
Windmill Clo. *Wors* 4E **63**
Windmill Ct. *Roch* 5B **28**
Windmill La. *Stoc* 6H **111**
Windmill La. Ind. Est.
Dent 4C **112**
Windmill Rd. *Sale* 6F **123**
Windmill Rd. *Wors* 4E **63**
Windmill St.
M2 . . . . . . .5D **94** (1G **9**)
Windmill St. *Roch* 5B **28**
Windover St. *Bolt* 3E **45**
Windrush Av. *Rams* 1A **22**
Windrush Dri. *M9* 4F **83**
Windrush, The. *Roch* 5C **14**
Windsor Av. *Chad* 5G **71**
Windsor Av. *Fail* 3H **85**
Windsor Av. *Gat* 6D **136**
Windsor Av. *Heyw* 3D **38**
Windsor Av. *Irlam* 4F **103**
Windsor Av. *L Hul* 4D **62**
Windsor Av. *L Lev* 4A **48**
Windsor Av. *Sale* 3B **122**
Windsor Av. *Stoc* 6C **126**
Windsor Av. *Swin* 1G **79**
Windsor Av. *Urm* 5B **104**
Windsor Av. *W'fld* 2E **67**
Windsor Av. *Wilm* 2C **166**
Windsor Clo. *G'mnt* 2A **22**
Windsor Clo. *Poy* 3D **162**
Windsor Ct. *M8* 4B **68**
Windsor Ct. *Sale* 4H **121**
Windsor Ct. *Shaw* 5F **43**
Windsor Cres. *P'wich* 6A **68**
Windsor Dri. *Ash L* 1F **99**
Windsor Dri. *Aud* 4D **98**
Windsor Dri. *Bow* 4B **144**
Windsor Dri. *Bred* 6C **128**
Windsor Dri. *Bury* 5H **35**
Windsor Dri. *Duk* 6D **100**
Windsor Dri. *Marp* 6C **142**
Windsor Dri. *Stal* 2E **101**
Windsor Dri. *Timp* 3H **133**
Windsor Gro. *Ash L* 4G **87**
Windsor Gro. *Bolt* 4G **31**
Windsor Gro. *Chea H* 5B **150**

Windsor Gro. *Rad* 2B **64**
Windsor Gro. *Rom* 1C **142**
Windsor Ho. *Dent* 4A **112**
Windsor Rd. *Brom X* 4E **19**
Windsor Rd. *Dent* 3A **112**
Windsor Rd. *Droy* 3F **97**
Windsor Rd. *Harp* 4G **83**
Windsor Rd. *Haz G* 3F **153**
Windsor Rd. *Hyde* 2B **130**
Windsor Rd. *Lev* 6C **110**
Windsor Rd. *Newt H* 1G **97**
Windsor Rd. *Oldh* 4B **72**
(in two parts)
Windsor Rd. *P'wich* 1A **82**
(in two parts)
Windsor St. *Fail* 3G **85**
Windsor St. *Gort* 3E **111**
Windsor St. *Newt H* 1G **97**
Windsor St. *Oldh* 6E **57**
Windsor St. *Roch* 6A **28**
Windsor St. *Salf* 4H **93**
Windsor St. *Stoc* 5A **140**
Windsor Ter. *Miln* 5E **29**
Windsor Ter. *Roch* 4C **28**
Windsor Ter. *Stoc* 5A **140**
(off Russell St.)
Windybank. *M9* 4E **69**
Windycroft. *Brom X* 3F **19**
Windy Harbour La.
Brom X 3F **19**
(in two parts)
Windyhill Dri. *Bolt* 4E **45**
Winfell Dri.
M40 . . . . . .2H **95** (2H **7**)
Winfield Av. *M20* 3H **125**
Winfield Dri. *M18* 1F **111**
Winfield Gro. *Marp B* . . .2F **143**
Winfield St. *Hyde* 5D **114**
Winford Rd. *Midd* 3C **70**
Winford St. *M9* 3G **83**
Wingate Av. *Bury* 3H **35**
Wingate Dri. *M20* 1G **137**
Wingate Dri. *Timp* 6B **134**
Wingate Dri. *W'fld* 6C **50**
Wingate I. *L Hul* 5D **62**
Wingate St. *Stoc* 5E **127**
Wingate St. *Roch* 2A **26**
Wingfield Av. *Wilm* 3B **166**
Wingfield Dri. *Swin* 5G **79**
Wingfield Dri. *Wilm* 3B **166**
Wingfield St. *Stret* 3D **106**
Wingfield Vs. *L'boro* 2G **17**
Wingrave Ho. *Salf* 4G **93**
Wings Gro. *Heyw* 6F **39**
Winifred Av. *Bury* 1B **38**
Winifred Rd. *M20* 6F **125**
Winifred Rd. *M40* 4B **84**
Winifred Rd. *Farn* 6C **46**
Winifred Rd. *Stoc* 6A **140**
Winifred Rd. *Urm* 5F **105**
Winifred St. *Eccl* 4D **90**
Winifred St. *Hyde* 2C **130**
Winifred St. *Rams* 4D **12**
Winifred St. *Roch* 2D **26**
Winmarith Dri. *Haleb* . . .6D **146**
Winmarleigh Clo. *Bury* . . .4F **35**
Winnall Wlk. *M40* 5C **84**
Winnie St. *M40* 3A **84**
Winning Hill Clo. *M18* . . .3F **111**
Winning Grn. *Stoc* 6D **140**
Winnington Rd. *Marp* . . .3D **142**
Winnipeg Quay. *Salf* 6F **93**
Winnows, The. *Dent* 4D **112**
Winscombe Dri. *M40* . . .1G **95**
Winser St. *M1* . . .5E **95** (2A **10**)
Winsfield Dri. *Haz G* 5D **152**
Winsford Dri. *Roch* 6B **26**
Winsford Gro. *Bolt* 2D **44**
Winsford Rd. *M14* 6E **109**
Winsford Wlk. *Sale* 6E **123**

Winskill Rd. *Irlam* 1E **119**
Winslade Clo. *Haz G* 3A **152**
Winslade Clo. *Oldh* 6H **57**
Winslade M. *Farn* 6F **47**
Winsley Rd. *M23* 1F **135**
Winslow Av. *Mot* 5B **116**
Winslow Pl. *M19* 3B **126**
Winslow Rd. *Bolt* 5A **44**
Winslow St. *M11* 5C **96**
Winson Clo. *Bolt* 3A **46**
Winstanley Clo. *Salf* 6B **80**
Winstanley Rd.
M40 . . . . . .2H **95** (1G **7**)
Winstanley Rd. *Sale* 4C **122**
Winster Av. *M20* 5C **124**
Winster Av. *Salf* 5F **81**
Winster Av. *Stret* 4A **106**
Winster Clo. *Bolt* 4H **33**
Winster Clo. *W'fld* 1F **67**
Winster Dri. *Bolt* 4G **33**
Winster Dri. *Midd* 5G **53**
Winster Grn. *Eccl* 5D **90**
Winster Gro. *Stoc* 5A **140**
Winster Ho. *Urm* 4B **104**
Winster M. Glos 5G **117**
(off Melandra Castle Rd.)
Winster Rd. *Eccl* 5D **90**
Winston Av. *L Lev* 4C **48**
Winston Av. *Roch* 5A **26**
Winston Clo. *Marp* 4B **142**
Winston Clo. *Rad* 2E **49**
Winston Clo. *Sale* 4H **121**
Winston Rd. *M9* 2H **83**
Winston St. *M9* 3H **83**
Winswell Clo. *M11* 3D **96**
Winterbottom Gro.
Mot 5B **116**
Winterbottom St. *Oldh* . . .3B **72**
Winterbottom Wlk.
Mot 5B **116**
Winterburn Av. *M21* 5A **124**
Winterburn Av. *Bolt* 5F **19**
Winterdyne St. *M9* 4G **83**
Winterfield Dri. *Bolt* 4E **45**
Winterford Av.
M13 . . . . .2H **109** (6H **11**)
Winterford La. *Moss* 1F **89**
Winterford Rd. *Moss* 1F **89**
Winterford Rd. *Salf* 4B **82**
Wintergreen Wlk.
Part 6D **118**
Wintermans Rd. *M21* . . .2B **124**
Winterslow Av. *M23* 2D **134**
Winter St. *Bolt* 2H **31**
Winterton Rd. *Stoc* 6A **112**
Winthrop Av. *M40* 6F **83**
Winton. 3D **90**
Winton Av. *M40* 2D **84**
Winton Av. *Aud* 6D **98**
Winton Clo. *Bram* 4E **151**
Winton Ct. *Bow* 3E **145**
Winton Gro. *Bolt* 3C **44**
Winton Rd. *Bow* 3E **145**
Winton Rd. *Salf* 5B **80**
Winton St. *Ash L* 2H **99**
Winton St. *L'boro* 4F **17**
Winton St. *Stal* 4F **101**
Winward St. *Bolt* 3E **45**
Winwood Dri. *Midd* 6B **54**
Winwood Fold. *Midd* 3H **53**
Winwood Rd. *M20* 3G **137**
Wirral Clo. *Swin* 1G **79**
Wirral Cres. *Stoc* 3C **138**
Wisbech Dri. *M23* 2F **135**
Wisbeck Rd. *Bolt* 5E **33**
Wiseley St. *M11* 5A **96**
Wiseman Ter. *P'wich* 5G **67**
Wishaw Sq. *M21* 2C **124**
Wisley Clo. *Stoc* 1H **127**
Wistaria Rd. *M18* 2F **111**
Witham Av. *M22* 6C **136**

Witham Clo. *Heyw* 2C **38**
Witham St. *Ash L* 1C **100**
Withenfield Rd. *M23* 3F **135**
Withens Grn. *Stoc* 5E **141**
Withern Flats. Heyw *3E 39*
 (off Hill St.)
Withies, The. *Eccl* 3D **90**
Withington. 3E **125**
Withington Grn. *Midd* 3A **54**
Withington Pool Fitness Cen.
 . . . . .3F **125**
Withington Rd
 M21 & M16 . . . .1B **124**
Withington St. *Heyw* 5G **39**
Withington St. *Salf* 2H **93**
Withins Av. *Rad* 2A **50**
Withins Clo. *Bolt* 5G **33**
Withins Dri. *Bolt* 5G **33**
Withins Gro. *Bolt* 5G **33**
Withins La. *Bolt* 5G **33**
Withins La. *Rad* 2A **50**
Withins Leisure Cen. . . .3G **33**
Withins Rd. *Oldh* 1H **85**
Withins St. *Rad* 3A **50**
Withnell Dri. *Bury* 4G **35**
Withnell Rd. *M19* 6H **125**
Withycombe Pl. *Salf* 6E **81**
Withy Gro. *M4* 3E **95** (4A **6**)
Withypool Dri. *Stoc* 6D **140**
Withytree Gro. *Dent* 5G **113**
Witley Dri. *Sale* 3F **121**
Witley Rd. *Roch* 4B **28**
Witney Clo. *Bolt* 3A **32**
Wittenborg Rd. *Stoc* 1D **138**
Witterage Clo. *M12* 1B **110**
Witton Wlk. *M8* 5B **82**
Woburn Abbey.
 Upperm 6A **60**
Woburn Av. *Bolt* 2E **33**
Woburn Clo. *Miln* 5E **29**
Woburn Ct. *Poy* 4F **163**
Woburn Dri. *Bury* 2D **50**
Woburn Dri. *Hale* 3B **146**
Woburn Rd. *M16* 4G **107**
Woburn St. *M18* 4D **100**
Woden's Av.
 Salf 5A **94** (2A **8**)
Woden St. *Salf* . . .6A **94** (3B **8**)
Woking Gdns. *Bolt* 4A **32**
Woking Rd. *Chea H* 1B **160**
Woking Ter. Bolt *4A 32*
 (off Bk. Woking Gdns.)
Wolfenden St. *Bolt* 3A **32**
Wolfenden Ter. *Bolt* 3A **32**
Wollaton Wlk. *Dent* 6E **113**
Wolseley Ho. *Sale* 3C **122**
Wolseley Pl. *M20* 4F **125**
Wolseley Rd. *Sale* 3B **122**
Wolseley St. *Bury* 4H **35**
Wolseley St. *Miln* 1F **43**
Wolsey Clo. *Rad* 4G **49**
Wolsey Dri. *Bow* 4C **144**
Wolsey St. *Heyw* 4E **39**
Wolsey St. *Rad* 4G **49**
Wolstenholme. 2G **25**
Wolstenholme Av. *Bury* . . .5F **23**
Wolstenholme Coalpit La.
 Roch 1F **25**
Wolstenholme La.
 Roch 1G **25**
 (in two parts)
Wolstenvale Clo. *Midd* . . .6B **54**
Wolver Clo. *L Hul* 3D **62**
Wolverton Av. *Oldh* 6B **72**
Wolverton Dri. *Wilm* . . .6G **159**
Wolverton St. *M11* 6B **96**
Wolvesey. *Roch* 5G **27**
Woodacre. *M16* 6C **108**
Woodacre Clo. *Sale* 1A **134**
Woodacres Ct. *Wilm* 3C **166**
Woodall Clo. *Sale* 5D **122**

Woodark Clo. *S'head* 4B **74**
Woodbank. *Bolt* 3F **33**
Woodbank Av. *Bred* 6E **129**
Woodbank Av. *Stoc* 3C **140**
Woodbank Ct. *Urm* 4D **104**
Woodbank Dri. *Bury* 1A **36**
Woodbank Rd. *L'boro* 6E **17**
Woodbank Ter. *Moss* 1F **89**
Woodbank Works Ind. Est.
 Stoc 2B **140**
Woodbine Cres.
 Stoc 4H **139**
Woodbine Pas.
 L'boro *4E 17*
 (off William St.)
Woodbine Rd. *Bolt* 4G **45**
 (in two parts)
Woodbine St. *M14* 3E **109**
Woodbine St. *Roch* 6A **28**
 (in two parts)
Woodbine St. E. *Roch* 6B **28**
Woodbine Ter. *Irlam* 5F **103**
Woodbourne Ct. *Sale* 1B **134**
Woodbourne Rd. *Sale* . . .1A **134**
Woodbourne Rd. *Stoc* 3E **127**
Woodbray Av. *M19* 4A **126**
Woodbridge Av. *Aud* 6D **98**
Woodbridge Dri. *Bolt* 4D **32**
Woodbridge Gdns.
 Roch 1E **27**
Woodbridge Gro. *M23* . . .2G **135**
Woodbridge Rd. *Urm* 4H **103**
Woodbrook Av.
 S'head 2C **74**
Woodbrooke Av.
 Hyde 5D **114**
Wood Brook La.
 S'head 2D **74**
Woodbrook Rd.
 Ald E 5H **167**
Wood Brook Rd.
 S'head 2C **74**
Woodburn Dri. *Bolt* 2F **31**
Woodburn Rd. *M22* 3B **136**
Woodbury Cres. *Duk* 6H **99**
Woodbury Rd. *Stoc* 4D **138**
Woodchurch Clo. *Bolt* 4A **32**
Woodchurch Wlk.
 Chad 3H **71**
Woodchurch Wlk.
 Sale 6F **123**
Woodcliffe Lodge.
 P'wich 1F **81**
Woodcock Clo. *Droy* 2C **98**
Woodcock Clo. *Roch* 4B **26**
Woodcote Av. *Bram* 3E **151**
Woodcote Rd.
 Dun M & M31 . . . .2C **132**
Woodcote Rd.
 W Timp 2F **133**
Woodcote Vw. *Wilm* 6B **160**
Woodcote Wlk. M8 . . . . .*3E 83*
 (off Crescent Rd.)
Wood Cottage Clo.
 Wors 6B **62**
Wood Cotts. *Woodl* 3G **129**
Woodcott Bank. *Bolt* 1A **32**
Woodcott Gro. *Wilm* 6A **160**
Woodcroft. *Stoc* 5D **140**
Woodcroft Av. *M19* 5A **126**
Woodeaton Clo. *Rytn* 3E **57**
Wooded Clo. *Bury* 6F **23**
Wood Edge Clo. *Bolt* 5E **47**
Woodend. 1F **89**
 (Ashton-under-Lyne)
Woodend. 6G **157**
 (Knutsford)
Wood End. 5F **43**
 (Oldham)

Woodend. 5H **155**
 (Stockport)
Woodend. 3E **159**
 (Wilmslow)
Wood End. *Bram* 3F **151**
Woodend. *Shaw* 5G **43**
Woodend Cen. Ind. Pk.
 Moss 1F **89**
Woodend Ct. *Hyde* 6B **114**
Woodend Dri. *Stal* 1H **115**
Woodend Fold. *Strin* 5H **155**
Woodend La. *Hyde* 6B **114**
Woodend La. *Mobb* 6E **157**
Woodend La. *Stal* 6H **101**
Woodend La. *Ward* 3B **16**
Woodend Rd. *M22* 1B **148**
Woodend Rd. *Stoc* 1H **151**
Woodend St. *Oldh* 6C **56**
Woodend St. *S'head* 4B **74**
Woodend Vw. *Moss* 1F **89**
Woodfield. *M22* 2B **148**
Woodfield Av. *Bred* 5G **129**
Woodfield Av. *Hyde* 1B **130**
Woodfield Av. *Roch* 1G **27**
Woodfield Clo. *Had* 3H **117**
Woodfield Clo. *Oldh* 5A **72**
Woodfield Ct. *Stoc* 1A **152**
Woodfield Cres. *Rom* 1F **141**
Woodfield Dri. *Wors* 5D **76**
Woodfield Gro. *Eccl* 4E **91**
Woodfield Gro. *Farn* 3E **63**
Woodfield Gro. *Sale* 3A **122**
Woodfield M. *Hyde* 1B **130**
Woodfield Rd. *M8* 2C **82**
Woodfield Rd. *Alt* 5E **133**
Woodfield Rd.
 Chea H 6D **150**
Woodfield Rd. *Midd* 3G **69**
Woodfield Rd. *Salt* 1U **92**
Wood Fields. 2D **36**
Woodfields Retail Pk.
 Bury 2C **36**
Woodfield St. *Bolt* 4C **46**
Woodfield Ter. *Heyw* 2G **39**
Wood Fold. *Brom X* 5G **19**
Woodfold Av. *M19* 5C **110**
Woodford. 5G **161**
Woodford Aerodrome.
 . . . . .6H **161**
Woodford Av. *Dent* 3G **113**
Woodford Av. *Eccl* 3D **90**
Woodford Av. *Shaw* 6H **43**
Woodford Ct. Droy *5B 98*
 (off Williamson La.)
Woodford Dri. *Swin* 1E **79**
Woodford Gdns. *M20* . . .1E **137**
Woodford Gro. *Bolt* 3G **45**
Woodford Rd. *Bram* 2G **161**
Woodford Rd. *Fail* 3G **85**
Woodford Rd. *Poy* 3A **162**
Wood Gdns. *Ald E* 4H **167**
Woodgarth Av. *M40* 6D **84**
Woodgarth Dri. *Swin* 5E **79**
Woodgarth La. *Wors* 6H **77**
Woodgate Av. *Bury* 1H **37**
Woodgate Av. *Roch* 5C **26**
Woodgate Clo. *Bred* 6F **129**
Woodgate Dri. *P'wich* 3G **67**
Woodgate Hill. 1H **37**
Woodgate Hill Rd.
 Bury 2G **37**
 (Fern Grove, in two parts)
Woodgate Hill Rd.
 Bury 1H **37**
 (Woodgate Hill)
Woodgate Rd. *M16* 6C **108**
Woodgate St. *Bolt* 4C **46**
Woodgrange Clo. *Salf* 3E **93**
Woodgreen Dri. *Rad* 1G **65**
Wood Gro. *Dent* 3F **113**
Wood Gro. *W'fld* 4C **50**
Wood Gro. *Woodl* 4G **129**

Woodhall Av. *M20* 2E **125**
Woodhall Av. *W'fld* 3B **66**
Woodhall Clo. *Bolt* 2E **33**
Woodhall Clo. *Bury* 6D **22**
Woodhall Clo. *Woodl* 4G **161**
Woodhall Cres. *Stoc* 5A **128**
Woodhall Rd. *Stoc* 5H **127**
Woodhall St. *Fail* 3F **85**
Woodhall St. *M8* 3C **82**
Woodham Rd. *M23* 2F **135**
Woodham Wlk. *Bolt* 2H **45**
Woodhead Clo. *Lees* 2A **74**
Woodhead Clo. *Rams* 5E **13**
Woodhead Dri. *Hale* 4H **145**
Woodhead Rd. *Hale* 4H **145**
Woodhead St. *M16* 3C **108**
Woodhey. 6C **12**
Wood Hey Clo. *Rad* 4D **48**
Wood Hey Ct. *Sale* 2G **133**
Wood Hey Gro. *Dent* 5G **113**
Wood Hey Gro. *Roch* 5E **15**
Woodheys. *Stoc* 6B **126**
Woodheys Dri. *Sale* 2F **133**
Woodheys Rd. *L'boro* 1G **29**
Woodheys St. *Salf* 4F **93**
Woodhill. 2A **36**
Wood Hill. *Midd* 5H **53**
Woodhill Clo. *M12* 3D **110**
Woodhill Clo. *Midd* 5H **53**
Woodhill Dri. *P'wich* 6F **67**
Woodhill Fold. 2B **36**
Woodhill Fold. *Bury* 2B **36**
 (in two parts)
Woodhill Gro. *P'wich* 6F **67**
Woodhill Rd. *Bury* 2B **36**
 (in two parts)
Woodhill St. *Bury* 1B **36**
Woodhouse Ct. *Urm* 3C **104**
Woodhouse Farm Cotts.
 Roch 1H **25**
Woodhouse Green. 4A **86**
Woodhouse Knowl.
 Del 3G **59**
Woodhouse La.
 Dun M 1A **144**
 (in two parts)
Woodhouse La.
 Man A 6B **148**
Woodhouse La. *Roch* 1H **25**
Woodhouse La. *Sale* 2D **132**
 (in three parts)
Woodhouse La. E.
 Timp 2A **134**
Woodhouse La. N.
 M22 . . . . .5B **148**
Woodhouse Park. 4H **147**
Woodhouse Rd. *M22* 5B **148**
Woodhouse Rd. *Shaw* 4G **43**
Woodhouse Rd. *Urm* 3B **104**
Woodhouses. 5A **86**
 (Manchester)
Woodhouses. 1E **133**
 (Sale)
Woodhouse St. *M18* 2G **111**
Woodhouse St. *M40* 6H **83**
Woodhouse St. *Oldh* 4D **72**
Wooding Clo. *Part* 5E **119**
Woodlake Av. *M21* 5A **124**
Woodland Av. *M18* 3G **111**
Woodland Av. *Bolt* 5D **46**
Woodland Av. *Haz G* 4D **152**
Woodland Cres. *P'wich* 1F **81**
Woodland Gro. *Eger* 1B **18**
Woodland Pk. *Rytn* 1H **55**
Woodland Rd. *Burn* 1C **126**
Woodland Rd. *Gort* 3G **111**
Woodland Rd. *Heyw* 2G **39**
Woodland Rd. *Roch* 1E **27**
Woodlands. 6H **103**
 (Manchester)

Woodlands. 6H 101
(Stalybridge)
Woodlands. *Fail* 1G 97
Woodlands. *P'wich* 2D 80
Woodlands. *Roch* 6A 16
Woodlands. *Stal* 6G 101
Woodlands. *Urm* 4E 105
Woodlands Av.
Chea H 3C 150
Woodlands Av. *Eccl* 5C 90
Woodlands Av. *Irlam* 4E 103
Woodlands Av. *Roch* 5C 26
Woodlands Av. *Stret* 5D 106
Woodlands Av. *Swin* 5C 78
Woodlands Av. *Urm* 5G 103
Woodlands Av. *W'fld* 6C 50
Woodlands Av.
Woodl 4G 129
Woodlands Clo.
B'btm 6B 116
Woodlands Clo.
Chea H 5C 150
Woodlands Clo. *Stal* 6H 101
Woodlands Clo. *Tin* 1H 117
Woodlands Clo. *Wors* 4G 77
Woodlands Ct. *Stoc* 3E 141
Woodlands Ct. *Timp* 6H 133
Woodlands Dri. *Sale* 2C 134
Woodlands Dri. *Stoc* 3C 140
Woodlands Dri.
Woodl 4G 129
Woodlands Gro.
B'btm 6B 116
Woodlands Gro. *Bury* 2H 35
Woodlands La. *Timp* 6G 133
Woodlands Pk. Rd.
Stoc 3D 140
Woodlands Parkway.
Timp 6G 133
Woodlands Rd. *M8* 3C 82
Woodlands Rd. *Alt* 6F 133
Woodlands Rd. *Ash L* . . .4H 87
Woodlands Rd. *Dis* 1E 165
Woodlands Rd. *Hand* 4A 160
Woodlands Rd. *Miln* 6E 29
Woodlands Rd. *Rams* 3A 12
Woodlands Rd. *Sale* 4C 122
Woodlands Rd. *Stal* 6G 101
Woodlands Rd. *Stoc* 1H 137
Woodlands Rd.
Whal R 6C 108
Woodlands Rd. *Wilm* . . .6D 158
Woodlands Rd. *Wors* 4G 77
Woodlands St. *M8* 3C 82
Woodlands, The. *Bury* . . .6D 22
Woodlands, The. *Droy* . . .2G 97
Woodlands, The. *Heyw* . . .5G 39
Woodlands, The. *Los* 5A 30
Woodlands, The. *Swin* . . .4H 79
Woodland St. *M12* 2D 110
Woodland St. *Heyw* 4G 39
Woodland St. *Roch* 1A 28
Woodland St. *Salf* 6A 82
Woodlands Vw. *Rams* 3E 13
Woodlands Vw. *Roch* 3C 28
Woodlands Way. *Midd* . . .3H 69
Woodland Ter. *Part* 6C 118
Woodland Ter. *Salf* 6H 81
Woodland Vw. *Brom X* . . .3F 19
Wood La. *Ash L* 6F 87
Wood La. *Marp* 6B 142
Wood La. *Midd* 2B 70
Wood La. *Mobb* 6A 156
Wood La. *Part* 6B 118
Wood La. *Rams* 3A 12
Wood La. *Timp* 6A 134
Wood Lane End. 6H 163
Wood La. N. *A'ton* 6H 163
Wood La. W. *A'ton* 6F 163
Woodlark Clo.
Salf 4B **94** (5D **4**)
Woodlawn Ct. *M16* 4A **108**

Woodlea. *Alt* 1H **145**
Woodlea. *Chad* 2D **70**
Woodlea. *Eccl* 1E **91**
Woodlea. *Wors* 3G **77**
Woodlea Av. *M19* 3A **126**
Woodleigh. *Alt* 6C **132**
Woodleigh Ct. *Ald E* 4G **167**
Woodleigh Dri. *Droy* 1C **98**
Woodleigh Rd.
S'head 2C **74**
Woodleigh St. *M9* 2H **83**
Woodley. 4G **129**
Woodley Av. *Rad* 6H **49**
Woodley Clo. *Stoc* 4D **140**
Woodley Precinct.
Woodl 4G **129**
Woodley St. *Bury* 5D **36**
Woodliffe St. *M16* 2A **108**
Woodlinn Wlk. *M9* 4F **83**
Woodman Dri. *Bury* 5E **23**
Woodman St. *Stoc* 1G **139**
Woodmeadow Ct.
Moss 1E **89**
Woodmere Dri. *M9* 6G **69**
Wood Mt. *Timp* 6B **134**
Woodmount Clo.
Rom 1C **142**
Wood Newton Clo.
M18 . . . . .3E **111**
Wood Park. 3C **86**
Woodpark Clo. *Oldh* 6E **73**
Woodpecker Pl. *Wors* . . .3F **77**
Woodridings. *Bow* 2D **144**
Wood Road. 2C **22**
Wood Rd. *M16* 4A **108**
Wood Rd.
Timp & Sale 2B **134**
Wood Rd. La. *Bury* 1C **22**
Wood Rd. N. *M16* 4A **108**
Woodrow Wlk. *M12* 1B **110**
Woodrow Way. *Irlam* 2D **118**
Woodroyd Clo. *Bram* 4F **151**
Woodroyd Dri. *Bury* 2G **37**
Woodruffe Gdns.
Rom 3G **141**
Woodruff Wlk. *Part* 6D **118**
Wood's Ct. *Bolt* 6B **32**
Woods Ct. Midd 2E **69**
(off Broad St.)
Woods End. 4H **103**
Woodsend Circ. *Urm* 4H **103**
(in two parts)
Woodsend Cres. *Urm* 5H **103**
Woodsend Grn. *Urm* 4H **103**
Woodsend Rd. *Urm* 3H **103**
Woodsend Rd. S.
Urm 5A **104**
(in two parts)
Woods Gro. *Chea H* 6D **150**
Woodshaw Gro. *Wors* . . .3E **77**
Woodside. *Miln* 1G **43**
Woodside. *Poy* 3F **163**
Woodside. *Shaw* 5H **43**
Woodside. *Stoc* 2B **138**
Woodside Av. *M19* 4B **126**
Woodside Av. *Wors* 1H **77**
Woodside Clo. *Lees* 3A **74**
Woodside Dri. *H Lane* . . .6C **154**
Woodside Dri. *Hyde* 6C **114**
Woodside Dri. *Rams* 4C **12**
Woodside Dri. *Salf* 2C **92**
Woodside Gdns. *Part* 5D **118**
Woodside La. *Poy* 3E **163**
Woodside M. *Bram* 3E **151**
Woodside Pl. *Bolt* 2E **47**
Woodside Rd. *M16* 5H **107**
Woodside Sq. *Bolt* 2E **47**
Woodside St. *Carr* 5G **89**
Woods La. *Chea H* 6D **150**
Woods La. *Dob* 6A **60**
Woods Lea. *Bolt* 6D **30**

Woodsleigh Coppice.
Bolt 6D **30**
Woodsley Rd. *Bolt* 3D **30**
Woods Moor. 1B **152**
Woodsmoor. *Stoc* 1A **152**
Woodsmoor Rd. *Swin* . . .4D **78**
Woods Pas. *L'boro* 4D **16**
Wood Sq. *Droy* 5A **98**
Wood Sq. *G'fld* 3F **61**
Woods Rd. *Irlam* 1D **118**
Woods, The. *Alt* 5G **133**
Woods, The. *G'ton* 3D **74**
Woods, The. *Roch* 1C **40**
Woodstock Av.
Chea H 6C **150**
Woodstock Av. *Stoc* 4H **127**
Woodstock Clo. *Heyw* . . .3G **39**
Woodstock Cres.
Woodl 4G **129**
Woodstock Dri. *Bolt* 4E **31**
Woodstock Dri. *Swin* 5G **79**
Woodstock Dri. *T'ton* 4F **21**
Woodstock Dri. *Wors* 6A **78**
Woodstock Grn. *Oldh* 6E **73**
Woodstock Grn. *Stoc* 3A **128**
Woodstock Rd. *B'hth* 3E **133**
Woodstock Rd. *Most* 2C **84**
Woodstock Rd. *Old T* 4H **107**
Woodstock Rd.
Woodl 4G **129**
Woodstock St. *Oldh* 4D **72**
Woodstock St. *Roch* 2E **27**
Wood St. *M3* 4C **94** (6F **5**)
(Manchester)
Wood St. *M3* 3C **94** (4F **5**)
(Salford)
Wood St. *Alt* 1F **145**
Wood St. *Ash L* 3H **99**
Wood St. *Bolt* 6B **32**
Wood St. *Bury* 2A **36**
Wood St. *Chea* 5H **137**
Wood St. *Dent* 3F **113**
Wood St. *Duk* 1A **114**
Wood St. *Eccl* 4H **91**
Wood St. *Farn* 5F **47**
Wood St. *Heyw* 3F **39**
Wood St. *Holl* 2F **117**
Wood St. *Hyde* 5C **114**
Wood St. *L'boro* 4E **17**
Wood St. *Midd* 5F **53**
Wood St. *Oldh* 1F **73**
Wood St. *Open* 5D **96**
Wood St. *Rad* 1E **65**
Wood St. *Rams* 4G **13**
Wood St. *Roch* 1G **43**
(Huddersfield Rd.)
Wood St. *Roch* 5A **28**
(Oldham Rd.)
Wood St. *Shaw* 5C **42**
Wood St. *Stal* 3E **101**
Wood St. *Stoc* 3F **139**
Wood Ter. *A'wth* 4D **34**
Woodthorpe Ct.
P'wich 1H **81**
Woodthorpe Dri.
Chea 2C **150**
Woodthorpe Grange.
P'wich 1H **81**
Wood Top Av. *Roch* 6B **26**
Wood Top Clo. *Stoc* 4E **141**
Woodvale. *Bow* 3E **145**
Woodvale. *Midd* 3A **54**
Woodvale Av. *Bolt* 5H **45**
Woodvale Dri. *Bolt* 5H **45**
Woodvale Gdns. *Bolt* 5H **45**
Woodvale Gro. *Bolt* 5H **45**
Woodvale Wlk. M11 . . . .4B **96**
(off Redfield Clo.)
Wood Vw. *M22* 2B **136**
Woodview Av. *M19* 4B **126**
Woodville Dri. *Marp* 6B **142**

Woodville Dri. *Sale* 4A **122**
Woodville Dri. *Stal* 2H **101**
Woodville Gro. *Stoc* 3H **127**
Woodville Rd. *Alt* 1E **145**
Woodville Rd. *Sale* 4A **122**
Woodville Ter. *M40* 2H **83**
Woodward Clo. *Bury* 6F **23**
Woodward Ct.
M4 . . . . .3H **95** (3G **7**)
Woodward Pl.
M4 . . . . .3G **95** (4F **7**)
Woodward Rd. *P'wich* . . .1D **80**
Woodward St.
M4 . . . . .3G **95** (4F **7**)
Woodwise La. *M23* 2E **135**
Wood Yd. *Roch* 4B **42**
Woolden Rd. *Cad* 1A **118**
Woolden St. *Eccl* 2D **90**
Woolden St. *Swin* 1E **79**
Woolfall Clo. *M12* 1B **110**
Woolfold. 1H **35**
Woolfold Trad. Est.
Bury 1A **36**
Woollacot St. *Oldh* 2D **72**
Woollam Pl. *M3* . . .5B **94** (1D **8**)
Woolley Av. *Poy* 5D **162**
Woolley Bridge. 3F **117**
Woolley Bri. *Had* 3F **117**
Woolley Bri. Rd. *Had* 3G **117**
Woolley Clo. *Holl* 3F **117**
Woolley La. *Holl* 3E **117**
(Market St.)
Woolley La. *Holl* 1F **117**
(Woolley Mill La.)
Woolley Mill La. *Tin* 1G **117**
Woolley St. *M8* 1D **94**
Woolley St. *Ash L* 5A **88**
Woolley Ter. *Duk* 4H **99**
Woolmore Av. *Oldh* 6C **56**
Woolpack Grn. *Salf* 2F **93**
Wool Rd. *Dob* 6B **60**
Woolston Ho. *Salf* 1C **92**
Woolton Clo. *M40* 1C **84**
Wootton St. *Hyde* 3B **114**
(in two parts)
Worcester Av. *Dent* 6G **113**
Worcester Av. *Stoc* 5C **128**
Worcester Clo. *Ash L* 3H **87**
Worcester Clo. *Bury* 5E **37**
Worcester Clo. *Rom* 2G **141**
Worcester Clo. *Salf* 1C **92**
Worcester Rd.
Chea H 1C **150**
Worcester Rd. *L Lev* 4H **47**
Worcester Rd. *Midd* 4H **69**
Worcester Rd. *Sale* 6F **121**
Worcester Rd. *Salf* 1C **92**
Worcester Rd. *Swin* 1D **78**
Worcester St. *Bolt* 4A **32**
Worcester St. *Bury* 1B **36**
Worcester St. *Oldh* 4H **71**
Worcester St. *Roch* 1E **41**
Wordsworth Av. *M8* 5C **82**
Wordsworth Av. *Bury* 1D **50**
Wordsworth Av. *Droy* 3A **98**
Wordsworth Av. *Farn* 2D **62**
Wordsworth Av. *Rad* 3E **49**
Wordsworth Clo. *Duk* 6E **101**
Wordsworth Cres.
Ash L 6C **86**
Wordsworth Cres.
L'boro 1F **29**
Wordsworth Gdns.
P'wich 6D **66**
Wordsworth Ind. Est.
Bolt 3H **31**
Wordsworth Rd. *M16* . . .4H **107**
Wordsworth Rd. *Dent* . . .2G **129**
Wordsworth Rd. *L Hul* . . .4D **62**
Wordsworth Rd. *Midd* . . .5B **54**
Wordsworth Rd. *Oldh* 6F **57**
Wordsworth Rd. *Stoc* 6F **111**

Wordsworth Rd. *Swin* 2D **78**
Wordsworth St. *Bolt* 4H **31**
Wordsworth St. *Salf* 1A **94**
Wordsworth Way.
   Roch 5A **26**
Workesleigh St. *M40* 6C **84**
World Trade Cen. *Salf* . . .1G **107**
World Way. *Man A* 5H **147**
Worrall St. *M40* 5A **84**
Worrall St. *Roch* 1F **27**
Worrall St. *Salf* . . .6A **94** (3A **8**)
Worrall St. *Stoc* 4G **139**
      (In two parts)
Worrell Clo. *Rad* 3F **49**
Worsbrough Av. *Wors* 1E **77**
Worsefold St. *M40* 3A **84**
Worsel St. *Bolt* 3G **45**
Worsley. 4G **77**
Worsley Av. *M40* 2H **83**
Worsley Av. *Wors* 6C **62**
Worsley Brow. *Wors* 5H **77**
Worsley Bus. Pk. *Wors* . .3B **76**
Worsley Ct. *M14* 5G **109**
Worsley Cres. *Stoc* 4B **140**
Worsley Gro. *M19* 6C **110**
Worsley Gro. *Wors* 1C **76**
Worsley Pl. *Roch* 4B **28**
Worsley Pl. *Shaw* 1E **57**
Worsley Rd. *Bolt* 3E **45**
Worsley Rd. *Eccl* 1C **90**
Worsley Rd. *Farn* 3F **63**
Worsley Rd.
   Wors & Swin 6H **77**
Worsley Rd. N. *Wors* 4F **63**
Worsley St. *M3* . . .5C **94** (2B **9**)
      (Manchester)
Worsley St. *M3* . . .4C **94** (4F **5**)
      (Salford)
Worsley St.
   M15 . . . . .6B **94** (3C **8**)
Worsley St. *Bolt* 2A **46**
Worsley St. *Oldh* 4F **73**
Worsley St. *Rad* 4D **20**
Worsley St. *Swin* 1F **79**
      (Devon St.)
Worsley St. *Swin* 4G **79**
      (Victoria Av.)
Worsley St. *T'ton* 4G **21**
Worsley Swimming Pool.
   . . . . .1E **77**
Worsley Trad. Est.
   L Hul 4A **62**
Worston Av. *Bolt* 2D **30**
Worthenbury Wlk.
   M13 . . . . .4A **110**
Worthing Clo. *Stoc* 5D **140**
Worthing St. *M14* 5F **109**
Worthington Av. *Heyw* . . .6G **39**
Worthington Av. *Part* 6D **118**
Worthington Clo. *Ash L* . .6E **87**
Worthington Clo.
   Hyde 5A **116**
Worthington Ct. *Sale* 5F **123**
Worthington Dri. *Salf* 2H **81**
Worthington Rd. *Dent* . . .6H **113**
Worthington Rd. *Sale* 5E **123**
Worthington St. *M40* 3C **84**
Worthington St. *Ash L* 6E **87**
Worthington St. *Bolt* 4G **45**
Worthington St. *Old T* . . .3A **108**
Worthington St. *Stal* 4D **100**
Worth's La. *Dent* 2G **129**
Wortley Av. *Salf* 2C **92**
Wortley Gro. *M40* 1B **84**
Wragby Clo. *Bury* 6D **22**
Wrath Clo. *Bolt* 6F **19**
Wray Pl. *Roch* 5C **28**
Wraysbury Wlk. *M40* 4A **84**
      (off Hugo St.)
Wrayton Lodge. *Sale* . . .1B **134**

Wrekin Av. *M23* 2G **147**
Wren Av. *Swin* 6H **65**
Wrenbury Av. *M20* 2D **124**
Wrenbury Cres. *Stoc* 5E **139**
Wrenbury Dri. *Bolt* 5D **18**
Wrenbury Dri. *Chea* 5A **138**
Wrenbury Dri. *Roch* 2A **42**
Wrenbury Wlk. *Sale* 6E **123**
Wren Clo. *Aud* 4C **98**
Wren Clo. *Farn* 1B **62**
Wren Clo. *Stoc* 6F **141**
Wren Dri. *Bury* 1F **37**
Wren Dri. *Irlam* 3E **103**
Wren Gdns. *Midd* 6H **53**
Wren Grn. *Roch* 5B **28**
Wrens Nest Av. *Shaw* . . .5G **43**
Wren St. *Chad* 1H **71**
Wren St. *Oldh* 3G **73**
Wrenswood Dri. *Wors* . . .3E **77**
Wrexham Clo. *Oldh* 1H **85**
Wrigglesworth Clo.
   Bury 2F **35**
Wright Robinson Clo.
   M11 . . . . .5A **96**
Wrights Bank N. *Stoc* . . .6D **140**
Wrights Bank S. *Stoc* . . .6E **141**
Wright St. *M16* . . .1A **108** (6A **8**)
Wright St. *Ash L* 1B **100**
Wright St. *Aud* 5E **99**
Wright St. *Chad* 4H **71**
Wright St. *Fail* 3F **85**
Wright St. *Oldh* 2E **73**
Wright St. *Rad* 4F **49**
Wright Tree Vs. *Cad* 4B **118**
Wrigley Cres. *Fail* 4F **85**
Wrigley Fold. *Midd* 4F **53**
Wrigley Head. *Fail* 3F **85**
Wrigley Head Cres. *Fail* . .3F **85**
Wrigley Pl. *L'boro* 6D **16**
Wrigley's Pl. *Oldh* 6C **72**
Wrigley Sq. *Lees* 3B **74**
Wrigley's Sq. *Roch* 3H **27**
Wrigley St. *Ash L* 1H **99**
Wrigley St. *Lees* 3A **74**
Wrigley St. *Oldh* 2F **73**
Wrigley St. *Scout* 1D **74**
Wroe St. *Salf* 4B **94** (5C **4**)
Wroe St. *S'head* 3B **74**
Wroe St. *Swin* 6F **65**
Wroe Ter. *Swin* 6F **65**
Wrotham Clo. *Salf* 4G **93**
Wroxeter Wlk. *M12* 1B **110**
      (off Wenlock Way)
Wroxham Av. *Dent* 4A **112**
Wroxham Av. *Urm* 4D **104**
Wroxham Clo. *Bury* 6D **22**
Wroxham Rd. *M9* 6D **68**
Wuerdle. 5C **16**
Wuerdle Clo. *Roch* 5C **16**
Wuerdle Farm Way.
   Roch 5C **16**
Wuerdle Pl. *Roch* 5C **16**
Wuerdle St. *Roch* 5C **16**
Wyatt Av. *Salf* 6H **93** (3A **8**)
Wyatt St. *Duk* 5A **100**
Wyatt St. *Stoc* 1G **139**
Wybersley Rd. *H Lane* . . .5E **155**
Wychbury St. *Salf* 3E **93**
Wychelm Rd. *Part* 6D **118**
Wycherley Rd. *Roch* 1D **26**
Wych Fold. *Hyde* 2C **130**
      (in two parts)
Wych St. *Ash L* 3H **99**
Wychwood. *Bow* 4D **144**
Wychwood Clo. *Midd* 2B **70**
Wycliffe Av. *Wilm* 2D **166**
Wycliffe Ct. *Urm* 5E **105**
Wycliffe Rd. *Urm* 5E **105**
Wycliffe St. *Eccl* 3E **91**
Wycliffe St. *Stoc* 1F **139**
Wycombe Av. *M18* 1G **111**
Wycombe Clo. *Urm* 2E **105**

Wye Av. *Fail* 4F **85**
Wyecroft Clo. *Woodl* 4H **129**
Wye St. *Oldh* 4B **72**
Wykeham Gro. *Roch* 2D **26**
Wykeham M. *Bolt* 6E **31**
Wykeham St. *M14* 4E **109**
Wyke Pk. *Oldh* 3H **73**
Wylam Wlk. *M12* 4D **110**
Wylde, The. *Bury* 3C **36**
Wynchgate Rd. *Haz G* . . .2G **153**
Wyndale Dri. *Fail* 6F **85**
Wyndale Rd. *Oldh* 6D **72**
Wyndcliffe Dri. *Urm* 6A **104**
      (in two parts)
Wyndham Av. *Bolt* 5E **45**
Wyndham Av. *Swin* 6F **65**
Wyndham Clo. *Bram* 6H **151**
Wyne Clo. *Haz G* 2G **153**
Wynfield Av. *M22* 6D **148**
Wynford Sq. *Salf* 4F **93**
Wyngate Rd. *Chea H* 4B **150**
Wyngate Rd. *Hale* 5H **145**
Wynne Av. *Swin* 6F **65**
Wynne Clo. *M11* 5B **96**
Wynne Clo. *Dent* 6F **113**
Wynne Gro. *Dent* 6E **113**
Wynne St. *Bolt* 3A **32**
Wynne St. *L Hul* 5C **62**
Wynne St. *Salf* 1H **93** (1A **4**)
Wynnstay Gro. *M14* 1G **125**
Wynnstay Rd. *Sale* 4B **122**
Wynn St. *M40* 2E **85**
Wynt, The. *Part* 5D **118**
Wynyard Clo. *Sale* 1D **134**
Wynyard Rd. *M22* 2A **148**
Wyre Clo. *W'fld* 6F **51**
Wyre Dri. *Wors* 4D **76**
Wyresdale Rd. *Bolt* 5G **31**
Wyre St. *M1* 5F **95** (2D **10**)
Wyre St. *Moss* 2D **88**
Wythall Av. *L Hul* 3D **62**
Wythburn Av. *M8* 5E **83**
Wythburn Av. *Bolt* 4E **31**
Wythburn Av. *Urm* 4D **104**
Wythburn Rd. *Midd* 4G **53**
Wythburn Rd. *Stoc* 4B **140**
Wythburn St. *Salf* 3E **93**
Wythenshawe. 2B **148**
**Wythenshawe Community
   Farm.** 3G **135**
Wythenshawe Forum Cen.
   . . . . .2A **148**
Wythenshawe Hall. 3H **135**
     (Art Gallery & Mus.)
Wythenshawe Rd.
   M23 . . . . .3E **135**
Wythenshawe Rd.
   Sale 5E **123**
Wythenshawe Theatre.
   . . . . .2A **148**
Wythens Rd. *H Grn* 5F **149**
Wythop Gdns. *Salf* 4G **93**
Wyvern Av. *Stoc* 4G **127**
Wyverne Rd. *M21* 6B **108**
Wyville Clo. *Haz G* 2G **153**
Wyville Dri. *M9* 3D **68**
Wyville Dri. *Salf* 2F **93**
Wyville Dri. *Swin* 5E **79**
Wyvis Clo. *Chad* 6G **55**

X

Xs Superbowl. 3C **78**

Y

Yarburgh St. *M16* 4C **108**
Yardley Av. *Stret* 5A **106**
Yardley Clo. *Stret* 5A **106**
Yarmouth Dri. *M23* 2H **135**

Yarnton Clo. *Rytn* 2E **57**
Yarn Wlk. *M4* 4G **95** (5F **7**)
Yarrow Clo. *Roch* 6H **27**
Yarrow Pl. *Bolt* 4H **31**
Yarrow Wlk. *W'fld* 6G **51**
Yarwell. *Roch* 3G **27**
      (off Falinge Rd.)
Yarwood Av. *M23* 4F **135**
Yarwood Clo. *Heyw* 2G **39**
Yarwoodheath La.
   Rost 5A **144**
Yarwood St. *Bow* 2F **145**
Yarwood St. *Bury* 3E **37**
Yasmin Gdns. *Oldh* 1B **72**
Yates Dri. *Wors* 6C **62**
Yates St. *Bolt* 4C **32**
Yates St. *Midd* 2E **69**
Yates St. *Oldh* 1E **73**
Yates St. *Stoc* 6B **128**
Yates Ter. *Bury* 6F **23**
Yattendon Av. *M23* 3D **134**
Yeadon Rd. *M18* 4F **111**
Yealand Av. *Stoc* 6F **127**
Yealand Clo. *Roch* 5D **26**
Yeardsley Clo. *Bram* 2G **151**
Yeargate Ind. Est. *Bury* . .3H **37**
Yelverton Wlk.
   M13 . . . . . .1G **109** (6E **11**)
      (off Copeman Clo.)
Yeotord Dri. *Alt* 5D **132**
Yeoman Clo. *Haz G* 2D **152**
Yeomanry Ct. *M16* 4B **108**
Yeoman's Clo. *Miln* 4F **29**
Yeoman Wlk. *M11* 4B **96**
Yeovil St. *M16* 4D **108**
Yewbarrow Rd. *Oldh* 1E **73**
Yew Clo. *Bolt* 3F **45**
Yew Ct. *Roch* 1B **28**
Yewdale. *Swin* 1H **79**
Yewdale Av. *Bolt* 3H **33**
Yew Dale Dri. *Fail* 3A **86**
Yewdale Dri. *Midd* 6G **53**
Yewdale Gdns. *Bolt* 3H **33**
Yewdale Gdns. *Roch* 1B **40**
Yewdale Rd. *Stoc* 4B **140**
Yewlands Av. *M9* 4F **69**
Yew St. *M15* 2C **108** (6E **9**)
Yew St. *Aud* 2F **113**
Yew St. *Bury* 2G **37**
Yew St. *Heyw* 3D **38**
Yew St. *Salf* 5G **81**
Yew St. *Stoc* 3D **138**
Yew Tree. 6D **100**
Yew Tree Av. *Fall* 5E **109**
Yew Tree Av. *Haz G* 4F **153**
Yew Tree Av. *Lev* 6C **110**
Yew Tree Av. *N'den* 2B **136**
Yew Tree Clo. *Ash L* 5E **87**
Yew Tree Clo. *Marp* 0C **142**
Yew Tree Clo. *Wilm* 2G **167**
Yew Tree Cotts. *Comp* . . .6F **131**
Yew Tree Cotts. *Dig* 1C **60**
Yew Tree Cres. *M14* 6F **109**
Yew Tree Dri. *M22* 2B **136**
Yew Tree Dri. *Bred* 6D **128**
Yew Tree Dri. *Chad* 2D **70**
Yew Tree Dri. *Los* 1A **44**
Yew Tree Dri. *P'wich* 5F **67**
Yew Tree Dri. *Salc* 5E **123**
Yew Tree Dri. *Urm* 3B **104**
Yewtree Gro. *H Grn* 2E **149**
Yew Tree La. *M23* 1H **135**
      (in two parts)
Yew Tree La. *Bolt* 6E **19**
Yew Tree La. *Duk* 6C **100**
      (in two parts)
Yewtree La. *Poy* 5E **163**
Yew Tree Pk. Rd.
   Chea H 1D **160**
Yew Tree Rd. *M14* 4F **109**
Yew Tree Rd. *A'ton* 6H **163**

Yew Tree Rd. *Dent* 6E **113**
Yew Tree Rd. *Stoc* 2H **151**
Yew Wlk. *Part* 6C **118**
York Arc. *M1* 6B **6**
York Av. *M16* 5A **108**
York Av. *L Lev* 4A **48**
York Av. *Oldh* 5B **72**
York Av. *P'wich* 1H **81**
York Av. *Roch* 5C **26**
York Av. *Sale* 4B **122**
York Av. *Swin* 1D **78**
York Av. *Urm* 4G **105**
York Clo. *Chea* 6C **138**
York Clo. *Dent* 3F **113**
York Cres. *Wilm* 2F **167**
Yorkdale. *Oldh* 2H **73**
York Dri. *Bow* 4F **145**
York Dri. *Haz G* 3F **153**
York Dri. *Rams* 5C **12**
York Dri. *Timp* 6F **147**
York Ho. *Sale* 4B **122**
York Pl. *Ash L* 3G **99**

York Rd. *M21* 1H **123**
York Rd. *Bow* 4E **145**
York Rd. *Cad* 4B **118**
York Rd. *Chad* 1F **71**
York Rd. *Dent* 3E **113**
York Rd. *Droy* 2H **97**
York Rd. *Hyde* 1C **130**
York Rd. *Sale* 4A **122**
York Rd. *Stoc* 4D **126**
York Rd. E. *Midd* 4C **70**
York Rd. W. *Midd* 4C **70**
Yorkshire St. *Ash L* 1H **99**
(in two parts)
Yorkshire St. *Oldh* 2D **72**
Yorkshire St. *Roch* 4H **27**
(in three parts)
Yorkshire St.
Salf 3C **94** (4F **5**)
York Sq. *Rytn* 3B **56**
York St. *M1* 5E **95** (2A **10**)
(in two parts)
York St. *M2* 4E **95** (5A **6**)

York St. *M9* 3G **83**
(in two parts)
York St. *M13* 6E **95** (4B **10**)
York St. *M20* 6F **125**
York St. *Alt* 2F **145**
York St. *Aud* 5E **99**
York St. *Bury* 3E **37**
York St. *Farn* 1G **63**
York St. *Heyw* 3F **39**
York St. *Lev* 1C **126**
York St. *Oldh* 3C **72**
York St. *Roch* 5B **28**
York St. *Rad* 2B **50**
York St. *Stoc* 3G **139**
York St. *W'fld* 1D **66**
York Ter. *Bolt* 3A **32**
York Ter. *Sale* 3A **122**
Youlgreave Cres. *Glos* . . .6F **117**
Young St. *M3* 4C **94** (6F **5**)
Young St. *Farn* 2G **63**
Young St. *Rad* 2F **49**
Young St. *Rams* 3D **12**

Yulan Dri. *Sale* 5E **121**
Yule St. *Stoc* 3F **139**

Z

Zama St. *Rams* 5C **12**
Zealand St. *Oldh* 1G **73**
Zebra St. *Salf* 4B **82**
Zedburgh. *Roch* 3G **27**
(off Spotland Rd.)
Zeta St. *M9* 4H **83**
Zetland Av. *Bolt* 5F **45**
Zetland Av. N. *Bolt* 5F **45**
Zetland Pl. *Roch* 3B **28**
Zetland Rd. *M21* 1H **123**
Zetland St. *Duk* 4A **100**
Zinnia Dri. *Irlam* 1C **118**
Zion Ter. *Roch* 2A **26**
Zulu St. *Bolt* 6D **32**
Zurich Gdns. *Bram* 2G **151**
Zyburn Ct. *Salf* 2A **92**

HOSPITALS and HOSPICES
covered by this atlas
with their map square reference

N.B. Where Hospitals and Hospices are not named on the map,
the reference given is for the road in which they are situated.

ALEXANDRA BMI HOSPITAL (VICTORIA PARK) —3H **109**
110-112 Daisy Bank Rd.
MANCHESTER
M14 5QH
Tel: 0161 2572233

ALEXANDRA HOSPITAL (CHEADLE), THE —5H **137**
Mill La., CHEADLE
Cheshire
SK8 2PX
Tel: 0161 4283656

ALTRINCHAM GENERAL HOSPITAL —1F **145**
Market St., ALTRINCHAM
Cheshire
WA14 1PE
Tel: 0161 9286111

ALTRINCHAM PRIORY HOSPITAL —5A **146**
Rappax Rd., Hale
ALTRINCHAM
Cheshire
WA15 0NX
Tel: 0161 9040050

BEALEY COMMUNITY HOSPITAL —3B **50**
Dumers La., Radcliffe
MANCHESTER
M26 2QD
Tel: 0161 7232371

BEAUMONT BMI HOSPITAL, THE   6A **30**
Old Hall Clough, Chorley New Rd.
Lostock
BOLTON
BL6 4LA
Tel: 01204 404404

BEECHWOOD CANCER CARE CENTRE —5F **139**
Chelford Gro.
STOCKPORT
Cheshire
SK3 8LS
Tel: 0161 4760384

BIRCH HILL HOSPITAL —4B **16**
Union Rd., ROCHDALE
Lancashire
OL12 9QB
Tel: 01706 377777

BOLTON HOSPICE —6H **31**
Queens Pk. St.
BOLTON
BL1 4QT
Tel. 01204 364375

BOOTH HALL CHILDREN'S HOSPITAL —6H **69**
Charlestown Rd.
MANCHESTER
M9 7AA
Tel: 0161 7957000

BURY GENERAL HOSPITAL —6F **23**
Walmersley Rd., BURY
Lancashire
BL9 6PG
Tel: 0161 7646081

BURY HOSPICE —3B **50**
Dumers La., Radcliffe
MANCHESTER
M26 2QD
Tel. 0161 7259800

CHEADLE ROYAL HEALTHCARE —3G **149**
100 Wilmslow Rd., Heald Green
CHEADLE
Cheshire
SK8 3DG
Tel: 0161 4289511

CHERRY TREE HOSPITAL —6C **140**
Cherry Tree La.
STOCKPORT
Cheshire
SK2 7PZ
Tel: 0161 4831010

CHRISTIE HOSPITAL —3F **125**
550 Wilmslow Rd.
MANCHESTER
M20 4BX
Tel: 0161 4463000

DR. KERSHAW'S HOSPICE —4D **56**
Turf La., Royton
OLDHAM
OL2 6EU
Tel. 0161 0242727

FAIRFIELD GENERAL HOSPITAL —1A **38**
Rochdale Old Rd.
BURY
Lancashire
BL9 7TD
Tel: 0161 7646081

FRANCIS HOUSE CHILDREN'S HOSPICE —1G **137**
390 Parrswood Rd.
MANCHESTER
M20 5NA
Tel: 0161 4344118

HIGHFIELD BMI HOSPITAL, THE —6G **27**
Manchester Rd.
ROCHDALE
Lancashire
OL11 4LZ
Tel: 01706 655121

HOPE HOSPITAL —2B **92**
Stott La., SALFORD
M6 8HD
Tel. 0161 7897373

HULTON HOSPITAL —4F **45**
Hulton La., BOLTON
BL3 4JZ
Tel: 01204 390390

HYDE HOSPITAL —6D **114**
Grange Rd. S.
HYDE
Cheshire
SK14 5NY
Tel: 0161 3668833

MANCHESTER BUPA HOSPITAL —4B **108**
Russell Rd., MANCHESTER
M16 8AJ
Tel: 0161 2260112

MANCHESTER CHILDRENS HOSPITAL —4A **80**
Hospital Rd., Pendlebury
Swinton
MANCHESTER
M27 4HA
Tel: 0161 7944696

MANCHESTER ROYAL EYE HOSPITAL —2F **109**
Nelson St., MANCHESTER
M13 9WH
Tel: 0161 2765526

MANCHESTER ROYAL INFIRMARY —2G **109**
Oxford Rd., MANCHESTER
M13 9WL
Tel: 0161 2761234

MEADOWS HOSPITAL, THE —4E **141**
Owens Farm Dri., STOCKPORT
Cheshire
SK2 5EQ
Tel: 0161 4196000

MENTAL HEALTH SERVICES FOR SALFORD —4D **66**
Bury New Rd., Prestwich
MANCHESTER
M25 3BL
Tel: 0161 7739121

NEIL CLIFFE CANCER CARE CENTRE —1F **147**
Wythenshaw Hospital, Southmoor Rd.
MANCHESTER
M23 9LT
Tel: 0161 2912913

NORTH MANCHESTER GENERAL HOSPITAL —2D **82**
Delaunays Rd., MANCHESTER
M8 5RB
Tel: 0161 7954567

OAKLANDS HOSPITAL —2B **92**
19 Lancaster Rd., SALFORD
M6 8AQ
Tel: 0161 7877700

ORCHARD HOUSE DAY HOSPITAL —3C **56**
Milton St., Royton
OLDHAM
OL2 6QX
Tel: 0161 6336219

RAMSBOTTOM COTTAGE HOSPITAL —4D **12**
Nuttall La., Ramsbottom
BURY
Lancashire
BL0 9JZ
Tel: 01706 823123

ROCHDALE INFIRMARY —2G **27**
Whitehall St., ROCHDALE
Lancashire
OL12 0NB
Tel: 01706 377777

ROYAL BOLTON HOSPITAL —6B **46**
Minerva Rd., Farnworth
BOLTON
BL4 0JR
Tel: 01204 390390

ROYAL OLDHAM HOSPITAL, THE —6B **56**
Rochdale Rd., OLDHAM
OL1 2JH
Tel: 0161 6240420

ST ANN'S HOSPICE —5C **62**
Peel La., Worsley
MANCHESTER
M28 0FE
Tel: 0161 7028181

ST ANN'S HOSPICE —3G **149**
St Ann's Rd. N., Heald Green
CHEADLE
Cheshire
SK8 3SZ
Tel: 0161 4378136

ST ANNES HOSPITAL —2E **145**
Woodville Rd., ALTRINCHAM
Cheshire
WA14 2AQ
Tel: 0161 9285851

ST MARY'S HOSPITAL FOR WOMEN & CHILDREN —3G **109**
Hathersage Rd., MANCHESTER
M13 0JH
Tel: 0161 2761234

ST THOMAS' HOSPITAL —4G **139**
Shaw Heath, STOCKPORT
Cheshire
SK3 8BL
Tel: 0161 4831010

SPRINGHILL HOSPICE —2H **41**
Broad La., ROCHDALE
Lancashire
OL16 4PZ
Tel: 01706 649920

STEPPING HILL HOSPITAL —1C **152**
Poplar Gro., STOCKPORT
Cheshire
SK2 7JE
Tel: 0161 4831010

STRETFORD MEMORIAL HOSPITAL —4H **107**
226 Seymour Gro., MANCHESTER
M16 0DU
Tel: 0161 8815353

TAMESIDE GENERAL HOSPITAL —1C **100**
Fountain St., ASHTON-UNDER-LYNE
Lancashire
OL6 9RW
Tel: 0161 3316000

TRAFFORD GENERAL HOSPITAL —4C **104**
Moorside Rd., Urmston
MANCHESTER
M41 5SL
Tel: 0161 7484022

UNIVERSITY DENTAL HOSPITAL —1E **109** (6B **10**)
Higher Cambridge St., MANCHESTER
M15 6FH
Tel: 0161 2756666

WILLOW WOOD HOSPICE —2C **100**
Willow Wood Clo.
ASHTON-UNDER-LYNE
Lancashire
OL6 6SL
Tel: 0161 3301100

WITHINGTON HOSPITAL —3D **124**
Nell La., MANCHESTER
M20 2LR
Tel: 0161 4458111

WOODLANDS —5B **62**
Peel La., Worsley
MANCHESTER
M28 0FE
Tel: 0161 7904222

WYTHENSHAWE HOSPITAL —1F **147**
Southmoor Rd., MANCHESTER
M23 9LT
Tel: 0161 9987070

RAIL, METROLINK & EAST LANCASHIRE RAILWAY STATIONS

with their map square reference

Alderley Edge Station. Rail —4G **167**
Altrincham Station. Rail & Met —1G **145**
Anchorage Station. Met —5G **93**
Ardwick Station. Rail —6H **95**
Ashburys Station. Rail —6C **96**
Ashton-under-Lyne Station. Rail —2H **99**

Belle Vue Station. Rail —2E **111**
Besses o' th' Barn Station. Met —2E **67**
Bolton Station. Rail —1B **46**
Bowker Vale Station. Met —6B **68**
Bramhall Station. Rail —1G **161**
Bredbury Station. Rail —5F **129**
Brinnington Station. Rail —3C **128**
Broadway Station. Met —5F **93**
Bromley Cross Station. Rail —4F **19**
Brooklands Station. Met —6A **122**
Burnage Station. Rail —5H **125**
Bury Station. Met —3C **36**
Bury Bolton Street Station. ELR —3C **36**

Castleton Station. Rail —3C **40**
Chassen Road Station. Rail —6D **104**
Cheadle Hulme Station. Rail —3D **150**
Clifton Station. Rail —1A **80**
Cornbrook Station. Met —6A **94** (4B **8**)
Crumpsall Station. Met —2C **82**

Dane Road Station. Met —3C **122**
Davenport Station. Rail —6H **139**
Dean Lane Station. Rail —5B **84**
Deansgate Station. Rail —5C **94** (2F **9**)
Denton Station. Rail —3C **112**
Derker Station. Rail —1E **73**
Dinting Station. Rail —5H **117**
Disley Station. Rail —1G **165**

East Didsbury Station. Rail —2G **137**
Eccles Station. Met —3H **91**
Eccles Station. Rail —3H **91**
Exchange Quay Station. Met —1G **107**
Failsworth Station. Rail —3C **05**

Fairfield Station. Rail —6A **98**
Farnworth Station. Rail —6G **47**
Flixton Station. Rail —6B **104**
Flowery Field Station. Rail —2B **114**

Gatley Station. Rail —5F **137**
G Mex Station. Met —5C **94** (2F **9**)
Godley Station. Rail —4C **115**
Gorton Station. Rail —1F **111**
Greenfield Station. Rail —3E **61**
Guide Bridge Station. Rail —5F **99**

Hale Station. Rail —3F **145**
Hall i' th' Wood Station. Rail —2D **32**
Handforth Station. Rail —4H **159**
Harbour City Station. Met —5F **93**
Hattersley Station. Rail —6G **115**
Hazel Grove Station. Rail —3D **152**

Heald Green Station. Rail —5E **149**
Heaton Chapel Station. Rail —4E **127**
Heaton Park Station. Met —5G **67**
Hollinwood Station. Rail —1G **85**
Humphrey Park Station. Rail —4A **106**
Hyde Central Station. Rail —5A **114**
Hyde North Station. Rail —2A **114**

Irlam Station. Rail —2C **118**

Kearsley Station. Rail —2A **64**

Ladywell Station. Met —3A **92**
Langworthy Station. Met —4E **93**
Levenshulme Station. Rail —6C **110**
Littleborough Station. Rail —4F **17**
Lostock Station. Rail —1A **44**

Manchester Airport Station. Rail —6H **147**
Market Street Station. Met —4E **95** (4B **6**)
Marple Station. Rail —4E **143**
Mauldeth Road Station. Rail —3A **126**
Middlewood Station. Rail —1B **164**
Mills Hill Station. Rail —6D **54**
Milnrow Station. Rail —6F **29**
Moorside Station. Rail —2D **78**
Moses Gate Station. Rail —5E **47**
Mosley Street Station. Met —4E **95** (5A **6**)
Mossley Station. Rail —2E **89**
Moston Station. Rail —1D **84**

Navigation Road Station. Rail & Met —5G **133**
Newhey Station. Rail —1F **43**
Newton For Hyde Station. Rail —3D **114**

Oldham Mumps Station. Rail —3E **73**
Oldham Werneth Station. Rail —3B **72**
Old Trafford Station. Met —3G **107**
Oxford Road Station. Rail —6D **94** (2A **10**)

Patricroft Station. Rail —3E **91**
Piccadilly Station. Rail & Met —5F **95** (1D **10**)
Piccadilly Gardens Station. Met —4E **95** (6B **6**)
Pomona Station. Met —1H **107**
Poynton Station. Rail —3C **162**
Prestwich Station. Met —4E **67**

Radcliffe Station. Met —4H **49**
Ramsbottom Station. ELR —3E **13**
Reddish North Station. Rail —5H **111**
Reddish South Station. Rail —2H **127**
Rochdale Station. Rail —5H **27**
Romiley Station. Rail —1A **142**
Rose Hill Marple Station. Rail —5C **142**
Ryder Brow Station. Rail —3F **111**

St Peter's Square Station. Met —5D **94** (1H **9**)
Sale Station. Met —5B **122**
Salford Central Station. Rail —4C **94** (5E **5**)